loc	locative	местный падеж	*pron,*	pronoun(s)	местоимени|е, -я
m	masculine	мужской род			
math	mathematics	математика			
med	medicine	медицина			
meteorol	meteorology	метеорология			
mil	military	военный термин			
mus	music(al)	музыка			
n	noun	существительное			
naut	nautical	морской термин			
neg	negative	отрицательный	*sb*	somebody	кто-нибудь, тельное
neut	neuter	средний род			
nn	nouns	имена существительные	*sg*	singular	единственное число
nom	nominative (case)	именительный падеж	*sl*	slang	сленг
o.s.	oneself	себя	*s.o.*	someone	кто-нибудь
			sth	something	что-нибудь
parl	parliamentary	парламентский термин	*superl*	superlative	превосходная степень
part	participle	причастие	*tech*	technical	техника
partl	particle	частица	*tel*	telephony	телефония
pers	person	лицо	*theat*	theatre	театр, театральный термин
pf	perfective	совершенный вид			
philos	philosophy	философия	*theol*	theology	богословие
phon	phonetics	фонетика	*trans*	transitive	переходный глагол
phot	photography	фотография	*univ*	university	университетский жаргон
phys	physics	физика			
pl	plural	множественное число	*usu*	usually	обычно
			v	verb	глагол
polit	political	политический термин	*v aux*	auxiliary verb	вспомогательный глагол
poss	possessive	притяжательное	*vbl*	verbal	отглагольное
predic	predicate; predicative	сказуемое; предикативный	*vi*	intransitive verb	непереходный глагол
pref	prefix	префикс	*voc*	vocative (case)	звательный падеж
prep	preposition; prepositional (case).	предлог; предложный падеж	*vt*	transitive verb	переходный глагол
			vulg	vulgar(ism)	грубое
			vv	verbs	глаголы
pres	present (tense)	настоящее время	*zool*	zoology	зоология

Oxford
Russian
Minidictionary

Edited by
Della Thompson

OXFORD
UNIVERSITY PRESS

OXFORD

UNIVERSITY PRESS

Great Clarendon Street, Oxford OX2 6DP

Oxford University Press is a department of the University of Oxford.
It furthers the University's objective of excellence in research, scholarship,
and education by publishing worldwide in

Oxford New York

Auckland Cape Town Dar es Salaam Hong Kong Karachi
Kuala Lumpur Madrid Melbourne Mexico City Nairobi
New Delhi Shanghai Taipei Toronto

With offices in
Argentina Austria Brazil Chile Czech Republic France Greece
Guatemala Hungary Italy Japan Poland Portugal Singapore
South Korea Switzerland Thailand Turkey Ukraine Vietnam

Oxford is a registered trade mark of Oxford University Press
in the UK and in certain other countries

Published in the United States
by Oxford University Press Inc., New York

British Library Cataloguing in Publication Data

Data available

Library of Congress Cataloging in Publication Data

Data available

ISBN 0-19-861457-8   978-019-861457-9 (OUP main edition)
ISBN 0-19-920375-X   978-019-920375-8 (Special edition)
ISBN 0-19-920374-1   978-019-920374-1 (Special edition)
ISBN 0-19-920373-3   978-019-920373-4 (Special edition)

10 9 8 7 6 5 4 3 2 1

Typeset in Arial, Argo, and Times by Interactive Sciences Ltd, Gloucester
Printed and bound in Italy by Legoprint S.P.A.

Contents

Preface

The *Oxford Russian Minidictionary* is a handy yet extremely comprehensive reference work, designed for students of both Russian and English, as well as for tourists and business people. This new edition has been updated to include the latest familiar terms in areas such as computing and business.

The student of Russian is aided by the provision of inflected forms where these cause difficulty, and the indication of the stressed syllable of every Russian word as well as changes in stress. The student of English is helped by the provision of phonetic transcriptions of English entries and a table of English irregular verbs at the back of the book.

A completely new feature of this edition is the **Phrasefinder**, located in the centre of the dictionary and providing essential words and phrases for everyday use, grouped together according to topic and covering subjects such as travel, food and drink, shopping, using the telephone, and finding overnight accommodation. Thanks are due to Lucy Popova for help in compiling this section.

D.J.T.

Introduction

In order to save space, related words are often grouped together in paragraphs, as are cross-references and compound entries.

The swung dash (~) and the hyphen are also used to save space. The swung dash represents the headword preceding it in bold, or the preceding Russian word, e.g. **Georgian** *n* грузи́н, ~ка. The hyphen is mainly used in giving grammatical forms, to stand for part of the preceding, or (less often) following, Russian word, e.g. **приходи́ть**, (-ожу́, -о́дишь).

Russian headwords are followed by inflexional information where considered necessary. So-called regular inflexions for the purpose of this dictionary are listed in the Appendices.

Where a noun ending is given but not labelled in the singular, it is the genitive ending; other cases are named; in the plural, where cases are identifiable by their endings, they are not labelled, e.g. **сестра́** (*pl* сёстры, сестёр, сёстрам). The gender of Russian nouns can usually be deduced from their endings and it is indicated only in exceptional cases (e.g. for masculine nouns in **-а**, **-я**, and **-ь**, neuter nouns in **-мя**, and all indeclinable nouns).

Verbs are labelled *impf* or *pf* to show their aspect. Where a perfective verb is formed by the addition of a prefix to the imperfective, this is shown at the headword by a light vertical stroke, e.g. **про|лепета́ть**. When a verb requires

....

the use of a case other than the accusative, this is indicated, e.g. **маха́ть** *impf*, **махну́ть** *pf* + *instr* wave, brandish.

Both the comma and the ampersand (&) are used to show alternatives, e.g. **хоте́ть** + *gen*, *acc* means that the Russian verb may govern either the genitive or accusative; **сирота́** *m* & *f* orphan means that the Russian noun is treated as masculine or feminine according to the sex of the person denoted; **Cossack** *n* каза́к, -а́чка represents the masculine and feminine translations of Cossack; **dilate** *vt* & *i* расширя́ть(ся) means that the Russian verb forms cover both the transitive and intransitive English verbs.

Stress

The stress of Russian words is shown by an acute accent over the vowel of the stressed syllable. The vowel **ё** has no stress mark since it is almost always stressed. The presence of two stress marks indicates that either of the marked syllables may be stressed.

Changes of stress in inflexion are shown, e.g.

i) **предложи́ть** (-жу́, -жишь)

The absence of a stress mark on the second person singular indicates that the stress is on the preceding syllable and that the rest of the conjugation is stressed in this way.

ii) **нача́ть** (..............; на́чал, -а́, -о)

The final form, на́чало, takes the stress of the first of the two preceding forms when these differ from each other. Forms that are not shown, here на́чали, are stressed like the last form given.

iii) **дождь** (-дя́)

The single form given in brackets is the genitive singular and all other forms have the same stressed syllable.

iv) **душа́** (*acc* -у; *pl* -и)

If only one case-labelled form is given in the singular, it is an exception to the regular paradigm. If only one plural form is given (the nominative), the rest follow this. In other words, in this example, the accusative singular and all the plural forms have initial stress.

v) **скоба́** (*pl* -ы, -а́м)

In the plural, forms that are not shown (here instrumental and prepositional) are stressed like the last form given.

Символы фонетической транскрипции, используемые в Словаре

Согласные

b	*but*	s	*sit*
d	*dog*	t	*top*
f	*few*	v	*voice*
g	*get*	w	*we*
h	*he*	z	*zoo*
j	*yes*	ʃ	*she*
k	*cat*	ʒ	deci*si*on
l	*leg*	θ	*thin*
m	*man*	ð	*this*
n	*no*	ŋ	ri*ng*
p	*pen*	tʃ	*ch*ip
r	*red*	ʤ	*jar*

Гласные

æ	*cat*	aɪ	*my*
ɑ:	*arm*	aʊ	*how*
e	*bed*	eɪ	*day*
ə:	*her*	əʊ	*no*
ɪ	*sit*	eə	*hair*
i:	*see*	ɪə	*near*
ɒ	*hot*	ɔɪ	*boy*
ɔ:	*saw*	ʊə	*poor*
ʌ	*run*	aɪə	*fire*
ʊ	*put*	aʊə	*sour*
u:	*too*		
ə	*ago*		

(ə) обозначает безударный беглый гласный, который слышится в таких словах, как gar*d*en, car*n*al и rhyth*m*.

(r) в конце слова обозначает согласный r, который произносится в случае, если следующее слово начинается с гласного звука, как, например, в clutter up и an acre of land.

Тильда ˜ обозначает носовой гласный звук, как в некоторых заимствованиях из французского языка, например ã в n*uance* /ˈnjuːɑ̃s/.

Основное ударение в слове отмечается знаком ˈ перед ударным слогом.

Вторичное ударение в многосложном слове отмечается знаком ˌ перед соответствующим слогом.

A

a[1] *conj* and, but; **a (не) то** or else, otherwise.

a[2] *int* oh, ah.

абажу́р lampshade.

абба́тство abbey.

аббревиату́ра abbreviation.

абза́ц indention; paragraph.

абонеме́нт subscription, season ticket. **абоне́нт** subscriber.

абориге́н aborigine.

або́рт abortion; **де́лать** *impf*, **с~** *pf* ~ have an abortion.

абрико́с apricot.

абсолю́тно *adv* absolutely. **абсолю́тный** absolute.

абстра́ктный abstract.

абсу́рд absurdity; the absurd. **абсу́рдный** absurd.

абсце́сс abscess.

аванга́рд advanced guard; vanguard; avant-garde. **аванга́рдный** avant-garde. **аванпо́ст** outpost; forward position.

ава́нс advance (*of money*); *pl* advances, overtures. **ава́нсом** *adv* in advance, on account.

авансце́на proscenium.

авантю́ра (*derog*) adventure; venture; escapade; shady enterprise. **авантюри́ст** (*derog*) adventurer. **авантюри́стка** (*derog*) adventuress. **авантю́рный** adventurous; adventure.

авари́йный breakdown; emergency. **ава́рия** accident; crash; breakdown.

а́вгуст August. **а́вгустовский** August.

а́виа *abbr* (*of* авиапо́чтой) by airmail.

авиа- *abbr in comb* (*of* авиацио́нный) air-, aero-; aircraft; aviation. **авиакомпа́ния** airline. **~ли́ния** air-route, airway. **~но́сец (-сца)** aircraft carrier. **~по́чта** airmail.

авиацио́нный aviation; flying; aircraft. **авиа́ция** aviation; aircraft.

авока́до *neut indecl* avocado (pear).

аво́сь *adv* perhaps; **на~** at random, on the off-chance.

австрали́ец (-и́йца), австрали́йка Australian. **австрали́йский** Australian. **Австра́лия** Australia.

австри́ец (-и́йца), австри́йка Austrian. **австри́йский** Austrian. **А́встрия** Austria.

авто- *in comb* self-; auto-; automatic; motor-. **автоба́за** motor-transport depot. **~биографи́ческий** autobiographical. **~биогра́фия** autobiography; curriculum vitae. **авто́бус** bus. **~вокза́л** bus-station. **авто́граф** autograph. **~запра́вочная ста́нция** petrol station. **~кра́т** autocrat. **~крати́ческий** autocratic. **~кра́тия** autocracy. **~магистра́ль** motorway. **~маши́на** motor vehicle. **~моби́ль** *m* car. **~но́мия** au-

tonomy. ∼но́мный autonomous; self-contained. ∼пило́т automatic pilot. ∼портре́т self-portrait. ∼ру́чка fountain-pen. ∼ста́нция bus-station. ∼стра́да motorway.

автома́т slot-machine; automatic device, weapon, etc.; sub-machine gun; robot; (телефо́н-)∼ public call-box. **автоматиза́ция** automation. **автоматизи́ровать** *impf & pf* automate; make automatic. **автомати́ческий** automatic.

а́втор author; composer; inventor; (*fig*) architect.

авторизо́ванный authorized.

авторите́т authority. **авторите́тный** authoritative.

а́вторск|ий author's; ∼ий гонора́р royalty; ∼ое пра́во copyright. **а́вторство** authorship.

ага́ *int* aha; yes.

аге́нт agent. **аге́нтство** agency. **агенту́ра** (network of) agents.

агита́тор agitator, propagandist; canvasser. **агитацио́нный** propaganda. **агита́ция** propaganda, agitation; campaign. **агити́ровать** *impf (pf* с∼) agitate, campaign; (try to) persuade, win over. **агитпу́нкт** *abbr* agitation centre.

аго́ния agony.

агра́рный agrarian.

агрега́т aggregate; unit.

агресси́вный aggressive. **агре́ссия** aggression. **агре́ссор** aggressor.

агроно́м agronomist. **агроно́мия** agriculture.

ад (*loc* -ý) hell.

ада́птер adapter; (*mus*) pick-up.

адвока́т lawyer. **адвокату́ра** legal profession; lawyers.

администрати́вный administrative. **администра́тор** administrator; manager. **администра́ция** administration; management.

адмира́л admiral.

а́дрес (*pl* -á) address. **адреса́т** addressee. **а́дресный** address; ∼ая кни́га directory. **адресова́ть** *impf & pf* address, send.

а́дский infernal, hellish.

адъюта́нт aide-de-camp; ста́рший ∼ adjutant.

ажу́рный delicate, lacy; ∼ая рабо́та openwork; tracery.

аза́рт heat; excitement; fervour, ardour, passion. **аза́ртный** venturesome; heated; ∼ая игра́ game of chance.

а́збука alphabet; ABC.

Азербайджа́н Azerbaijan. **азербайджа́нец** (-нца), **азербайджа́нка** Azerbaijani. **азербайджа́нский** Azerbaijani.

азиа́т, ∼ка Asian. **азиа́тский** Asian, Asiatic. **А́зия** Asia.

азо́т nitrogen.

аи́ст stork.

ай *int* ah; oo.

а́йсберг iceberg.

акаде́мик academician. **академи́ческий** academic. **акаде́мия** academy.

аквала́нг aqualung.

акваре́ль water-colour.

аква́риум aquarium.

акведу́к aqueduct.

акклиматизи́ровать *impf & pf* acclimatize; ∼ся become acclimatized.

аккомпанеме́нт accompaniment; под ∼+*gen* to the accompaniment of. **аккомпаниа́тор** accompanist. **аккомпани́ровать** *impf* +*dat* accompany.

акко́рд chord.

аккордео́н accordion.

акко́рдн|ый by agreement; **~ая рабо́та** piece-work.

аккредити́в letter of credit. **аккредитова́ть** *impf* & *pf* accredit.

аккумуля́тор accumulator.

аккура́тный neat, careful; punctual; exact, thorough.

акри́л acrylic. **акри́ловый** acrylic.

акроба́т acrobat.

аксессуа́р accessory; (stage) props.

аксио́ма axiom.

акт act; deed, document; **обвини́тельный ~** indictment.

актёр actor.

акти́в (*comm*) asset(s).

активиза́ция stirring up, making (more) active. **активизи́ровать** *impf* & *pf* make (more) active, stir up. **акти́вный** active.

акти́ровать *impf* & *pf* register, record.

а́ктовый зал assembly hall.

актри́са actress.

актуа́льный topical, urgent.

аку́ла shark.

аку́стика acoustics. **акусти́ческий** acoustic.

акушёр obstetrician. **акушёрка** midwife.

акце́нт accent, stress. **акценти́ровать** *impf* & *pf* accent; accentuate.

акционе́р shareholder. **акционе́рный** joint-stock. **а́кция¹** share; *pl* stock. **а́кция²** action.

а́лгебра algebra.

а́либи *neut indecl* alibi.

алиме́нты (*pl*; *gen* -ов) (*law*) maintenance.

алкоголи́зм alcoholism. **алко-**

го́лик alcoholic. **алкого́ль** *m* alcohol. **алкого́льный** alcoholic.

аллего́рия allegory.

аллерги́я allergy.

алле́я avenue; path, walk.

аллига́тор alligator.

алло́ hello! (*on telephone*).

алма́з diamond.

алта́рь (-я́) *m* altar; chancel; sanctuary.

алфави́т alphabet. **алфави́тный** alphabetical.

а́лчный greedy, grasping.

а́лый scarlet.

альбо́м album; sketch-book.

альмана́х literary miscellany; almanac.

альпи́йский Alpine. **альпини́зм** mountaineering. **альпини́ст**, **альпини́стка** (mountain-)climber.

альт (-а́; *pl* -ы́) alto; viola.

альтернати́ва alternative. **альтернати́вный** alternative.

альтруисти́ческий altruistic.

алюми́ний aluminium.

амазо́нка Amazon; horse-woman; riding-habit.

амба́р barn; storehouse, ware-house.

амби́ция pride; arrogance.

амбулато́рия out-patients' department; surgery. **амбулато́рный больно́й** *sb* outpatient.

Аме́рика America. **америка́нец** (-нца), **америка́нка** American. **америка́нский** American; US.

аминокислота́ amino acid.

ами́нь *m* amen.

аммиа́к ammonia.

амни́стия amnesty.

амора́льный amoral; im-moral.

амортиза́тор shock-absorber. **амортиза́ция** depreciation; shock-absorption.

ампе́р (*gen pl* ампе́р) ampere.

ампута́ция amputation. **ампути́ровать** *impf & pf* amputate.

амфетами́н amphetamine.

амфи́бия amphibian.

амфитеа́тр amphitheatre; circle.

ана́лиз analysis; ~ кро́ви blood test. **анализи́ровать** *impf & pf* analyse. **анали́тик** analyst. **аналити́ческий** analytic(al).

анана́с pineapple.

анархи́ст, ~ка anarchist. **анархи́ческий** anarchic. **ана́рхия** anarchy.

анатоми́ческий anatomical. **анато́мия** anatomy.

анахрони́зм anachronism. **анахрони́ческий** anachronistic.

анга́р hangar.

а́нгел angel. **а́нгельский** angelic.

анги́на sore throat.

англи́йск|ий English; ~ая була́вка safety-pin. **англича́нин** (*pl* -ча́не, -ча́н) Englishman. **англича́нка** Englishwoman. **А́нглия** England, Britain.

анекдо́т anecdote, story; funny thing.

анеми́я anaemia.

анестезио́лог anaesthetist. **анестези́ровать** *impf & pf* anaesthetize. **анестези́рующее сре́дство** anaesthetic. **анестези́я** anaesthesia.

анке́та questionnaire, form.

аннекси́ровать *impf & pf* annex. **анне́ксия** annexation.

аннули́ровать *impf & pf* annul; cancel, abolish.

анома́лия anomaly. **анома́льный** anomalous.

аноними́я anonymous letter. **анони́мный** anonymous.

анонси́ровать *impf & pf* announce.

анорекси́я anorexia.

анса́мбль *m* ensemble; company, troupe.

антагони́зм antagonism.

Анта́рктика the Antarctic.

анте́нна antenna; aerial.

антибио́тик antibiotic(s).

антидепресса́нт antidepressant.

антиква́р antiquary; antique-dealer. **антиквариа́т** antique-shop. **антиква́рный** antiquarian; antique.

антило́па antelope.

антипа́тия antipathy.

антисемити́зм anti-Semitism. **антисеми́тский** anti-Semitic.

антисе́птик antiseptic. **антисепти́ческий** antiseptic.

антите́зис (*philos*) antithesis.

антите́ло (*pl* -а́) antibody.

антифри́з antifreeze.

анти́чность antiquity. **анти́чный** ancient, classical.

антоло́гия anthology.

антра́кт interval.

антраци́т anthracite.

антреко́т entrecôte, steak.

антрепренёр impresario.

антресо́ли (*pl; gen* -е́й) mezzanine; shelf.

антропо́лог anthropologist. **антропологи́ческий** anthropological. **антрополо́гия** anthropology.

анфила́да suite (of rooms).

анчо́ус anchovy.

аншла́г 'house full' notice.

апарте́ид apartheid.

апати́чный apathetic. апа́тия apathy.

апелли́ровать *impf* & *pf* appeal. апелляцио́нный суд Court of Appeal. апелля́ция appeal.

апельси́н orange; orange-tree. апельси́нный, апельси́новый orange.

аплоди́ровать *impf* +*dat* applaud. аплодисме́нты *m pl* applause.

апло́мб aplomb.

Апока́липсис Revelation. апокалипти́ческий apocalyptic.

апо́стол apostle.

апостро́ф apostrophe.

аппара́т apparatus; machinery, organs. аппарату́ра apparatus, gear; (*comput*) hardware. аппара́тчик operator; apparatchik.

аппе́ндикс appendix. аппендици́т appendicitis.

аппети́т appetite; прия́тного ~а! bon appétit! аппети́тный appetizing.

апре́ль *m* April. апре́льский April.

апте́ка chemist's. апте́карь *m* chemist. апте́чка medicine chest; first-aid kit.

ара́б, ара́бка Arab. ара́бский Arab, Arabic.

арави́йский Arabian.

аранжи́ровать *impf* & *pf* (*mus*) arrange. аранжиро́вка (*mus*) arrangement.

ара́хис peanut.

арби́тр arbitrator. арбитра́ж arbitration.

арбу́з water-melon.

аргуме́нт argument. аргумен-

та́ция reasoning; arguments. аргументи́ровать *impf* & *pf* argue, (try to) prove.

аре́на arena, ring.

аре́нда lease. аренда́тор tenant. аре́ндная пла́та rent. аре́ндовать *impf* & *pf* rent.

аре́ст arrest. арестова́ть *pf*, аре́стовывать *impf* arrest; seize, sequestrate.

аристокра́т, ~ка aristocrat. аристократи́ческий aristocratic. аристокра́тия aristocracy.

арифме́тика arithmetic. арифмети́ческий arithmetical.

а́рия aria.

а́рка arch.

А́рктика the Arctic. аркти́ческий arctic.

армату́ра fittings; reinforcement; armature. армату́рщик fitter.

арме́йский army.

Арме́ния Armenia.

а́рмия army.

армяни́н (*pl* -я́не, -я́н), армя́нка Armenian. армя́нский Armenian.

арома́т scent, aroma. ароматера́пия aromatherapy. арома́тный aromatic, fragrant.

арсена́л arsenal.

арте́рия artery.

арти́куль *m* (*gram*) article.

артилле́рия artillery.

арти́ст, ~ка artiste, artist; expert. артисти́ческий artistic.

артри́т arthritis.

а́рфа harp.

арха́йческий archaic.

арха́нгел archangel.

архео́лог archaeologist. археологи́ческий archaeological. археоло́гия archaeology.

архи́в archives. **архиви́ст** archivist. **архи́вный** archive, archival.

архиепи́скоп archbishop. **архиере́й** bishop.

архипела́г archipelago.

архите́ктор architect. **архитекту́ра** architecture. **архитекту́рный** architectural.

арши́н arshin *(71 cm.)*.

асбе́ст asbestos.

асимметри́чный asymmetrical. **асимметри́я** asymmetry.

аске́т ascetic. **аскети́зм** asceticism. **аскети́ческий** ascetic.

асоциа́льный antisocial.

аспира́нт, **∼ка** post-graduate student. **аспиранту́ра** post-graduate course.

аспири́н aspirin.

ассамбле́я assembly.

ассигна́ция banknote.

ассимиля́ция assimilation.

ассисте́нт assistant; junior lecturer, research assistant.

ассортиме́нт assortment.

ассоциа́ция association. **ассоции́ровать** *impf & pf* associate.

а́стма asthma. **астмати́ческий** asthmatic.

астро́лог astrologer. **астроло́гия** astrology.

астрона́вт astronaut. **астроно́м** astronomer. **астрономи́ческий** astronomical. **астроно́мия** astronomy.

асфа́льт asphalt.

ата́ка attack. **атакова́ть** *impf & pf* attack.

атама́н ataman *(Cossack chieftain)*; (gang-)leader.

атеи́зм atheism. **атеи́ст** atheist.

ателье́ *neut indecl* studio; atelier.

а́тлас¹ atlas.

атла́с² satin. **атла́сный** satin.

атле́т athlete; strong man. **атле́тика** athletics. **атлети́ческий** athletic.

атмосфе́ра atmosphere. **атмосфе́рный** atmospheric.

а́том atom. **а́томный** atomic.

атташе́ *m indecl* attaché.

аттеста́т testimonial; certificate; pedigree. **аттестова́ть** *impf & pf* attest; recommend.

аттракцио́н attraction; sideshow; star turn.

ау́ *int* hi, cooee.

аудито́рия auditorium, lecture-room.

аукцио́н auction.

ауто́псия autopsy.

афе́ра speculation, trickery. **афери́ст** speculator, trickster.

афи́ша placard, poster.

афори́зм aphorism.

А́фрика Africa. **африка́нец** (**-нца**), **африка́нка** African. **африка́нский** African.

аффе́кт fit of passion; temporary insanity.

ах *int* ah, oh. **а́хать** *impf (pf* **а́хнуть)** sigh; exclaim; gasp.

аэро|вокза́л air terminal. **∼дина́мика** aerodynamics. **∼дро́м** aerodrome, air-field. **∼зо́ль** *m* aerosol. **∼по́рт** *(loc* -ý**)** airport.

Б

б *partl: see* **бы**

ба́ба *(coll)* (old) woman; **снѐжная ∼** snowman.

ба́бочка butterfly.

ба́бушка grandmother; grandma.

бага́ж (**-á**) luggage. **бага́жник** carrier; luggage-rack; boot. **ба-**

га́жный ваго́н luggage-van.

баго́р (-гра́) boat-hook.

багро́вый crimson, purple.

бадминто́н badminton.

ба́за base; depot; basis; ~ да́нных database.

база́р market; din.

ба́зис base; basis.

байда́рка canoe.

ба́йка flannelette.

бак¹ tank, cistern.

бак² forecastle.

бакала́вр (*univ*) bachelor.

бакале́йный grocery. **бакале́я** groceries.

ба́кен buoy.

бакенба́рды (*pl*; *gen* -ба́рд) side-whiskers.

баклажа́н (*gen pl* -ов *or* -жа́н) aubergine.

бакте́рия bacterium.

бал (*loc* -у́; *pl* -ы́) dance, ball.

балага́н farce.

балала́йка balalaika.

бала́нс (*econ*) balance.

баланси́ровать *impf* (*pf* с~) balance; keep one's balance.

балбе́с booby.

балдахи́н canopy.

балери́на ballerina. **бале́т** ballet.

ба́лка¹ beam, girder.

ба́лка² gully.

балко́н balcony.

балл mark (*in school*); degree; force; **ве́тер в пять ~ов** wind force 5.

балла́да ballad.

балла́ст ballast.

балло́н container, carboy, cylinder; balloon tyre.

баллоти́ровать *impf* vote; put to the vote; **~ся** stand, be a candidate (**в** *or* **на**+*acc* for).

балова́ть *impf* (*pf* из~) spoil, pamper; **~ся** play about, get up to tricks; amuse o.s. **баловство́** spoiling; mischief.

Балти́йское мо́ре Baltic (Sea).

бальза́м balsam; balm.

балюстра́да balustrade.

бамбу́к bamboo.

ба́мпер bumper.

бана́льность banality; platitude. **бана́льный** banal.

бана́н banana.

ба́нда band, gang.

банда́ж (-а́) truss; belt, band.

бандеро́ль wrapper; printed matter, book-post.

ба́нджо *neut indecl* banjo.

банди́т bandit; gangster.

банк bank.

ба́нка jar; tin.

банке́т banquet.

банки́р banker. **банкно́та** banknote. **банкро́т** bankrupt. **банкро́тство** bankruptcy.

банкома́т cash machine.

бант bow.

ба́ня bath; bath-house.

бар bar; snack-bar.

бараба́н drum. **бараба́нить** *impf* drum, thump. **бараба́нная перепо́нка** ear-drum. **бараба́нщик** drummer.

бара́к wooden barrack, hut.

бара́н ram; sheep. **бара́нина** mutton; lamb.

бара́нка ring-shaped roll; (steering-)wheel.

барахло́ old clothes, jumble; odds and ends. **барахо́лка** flea market.

бара́шек (-шка) young ram; lamb; wing nut; catkin. **бара́шковый** lambskin.

баржа́ (*gen pl* барж(е́й)) barge.

ба́рин (*pl* -ре *or* -ры, бар) landowner; sir.

барито́н baritone.

ба́рка barge.

ба́рмен barman.

баро́кко *neut indecl* baroque.

баро́метр barometer.

баро́н baron. **бароне́сса** baroness.

баро́чный baroque.

баррика́да barricade.

барс snow-leopard.

ба́рский lordly; grand.

барсу́к (-а́) badger.

барха́н dune.

ба́рхат (-у) velvet. **ба́рхатный** velvet.

ба́рыня landowner's wife; madam.

бары́ш (-а́) profit. **бары́шник** dealer; (ticket) speculator.

бары́шня (*gen pl* -шень) young lady; miss.

барье́р barrier; hurdle.

бас (*pl* -ы́) bass.

баскетбо́л basket-ball.

басносло́вный mythical, legendary; fabulous. **ба́сня** (*gen pl* -сен) fable; fabrication.

басо́вый bass.

бассе́йн (*geog*) basin; pool; reservoir.

бастова́ть *impf* be on strike.

баталья́н battalion.

батаре́йка (-), **батаре́я** battery; radiator.

бато́н long loaf; stick, bar.

ба́тька *m*, **ба́тюшка** *m* father; priest. **ба́тюшки** *int* good gracious!

бах *int* bang!

бахва́льство bragging.

бахрома́ fringe.

бац *int* bang! crack!

баци́лла bacillus. **бациллоноси́тель** *m* carrier.

бачо́к (-чка́) cistern.

башка́ head.

башлы́к (-а́) hood.

башма́к (-а́) shoe; **под ~о́м у+***gen* under the thumb of.

ба́шня (*gen pl* -шен) tower; turret.

баю́кать *impf* (*pf* у~) sing lullabies (to). **ба́юшки-баю́** *int* hushaby!

бая́н accordion.

бде́ние vigil. **бди́тельность** vigilance. **бди́тельный** vigilant.

бег (*loc* -у́; *pl* -а́) run, running; race. **бе́гать** *indet* (*det* **бежа́ть**) *impf* run.

бегемо́т hippopotamus.

бегле́ц (-а́), **бегля́нка** fugitive. **бе́глость** speed, fluency, dexterity. **бе́глый** rapid, fluent; fleeting, cursory; *sb* fugitive, runaway. **бегово́й** running; race. **бего́м** *adv* running, at the double. **беготня́** running about; bustle. **бе́гство** flight; escape. **бегу́н** (-а́), **бегу́нья** (*gen pl* -ний) runner.

беда́ (*pl* -ы) misfortune; disaster; trouble; **~ в том, что** the trouble is (that). **бедне́ть** *impf* (*pf* о~) grow poor. **бе́дность** poverty; the poor. **бе́дный** (-ден, -дна́, -дно) poor. **бедня́га** *m*, **бедня́жка** *m & f* poor thing. **бедня́к** (-а́), **бедня́чка** poor peasant; poor man, poor woman.

бедро́ (*pl* бёдра, -дер) thigh; hip.

бе́дственный disastrous. **бе́дствие** disaster. **бе́дствовать** *impf* live in poverty.

бежа́ть (бегу́ *det*; *indet* бе́гать) *impf* (*pf* по~) run; flow; fly; boil over; *impf & pf* escape. **бе́женец** (-нца), **бе́женка** refugee.

без *prep+gen* without; ~ пяти́ (мину́т) три five (minutes) to three; ~ че́тверти a quarter to.

без-, безъ-, бес- *in comb* in-, un-; non-; -less. **без**\алкого́льный non-alcoholic. ~апелляцио́нный peremptory, categorical. ~бо́жие atheism. ~бо́жный godless; shameless, outrageous. ~боле́зненный painless. ~бра́чный celibate. ~бре́жный boundless. ~ве́стный unknown; obscure. ~вку́сие lack of taste, bad taste. ~вку́сный tasteless. ~вла́стие anarchy. ~во́дный arid. ~возвра́тный irrevocable; irrecoverable. ~возме́здный free, gratis. ~во́лие lack of will. ~во́льный weak-willed. ~вре́дный harmless. ~вре́менный untimely. ~вы́ходный hopeless, desperate; uninterrupted. ~гла́зый one-eyed; eyeless. ~гра́мотный illiterate. ~грани́чный boundless, infinite. ~да́рный untalented. ~де́йственный inactive. ~де́йствие inertia, idleness; negligence. ~де́йствовать *impf* be idle, be inactive; stand idle.

безде́лица trifle. **безде́лушка** knick-knack. **безде́льник** idler; ne'er-do-well. **безде́льничать** *impf* idle, loaf.

бе́здна abyss, chasm; a huge number, a multitude.

без-. **бездоказа́тельный** unsubstantiated. ~до́мный homeless. ~до́нный bottomless; fathomless. ~доро́жье lack of (good) roads; season when roads are impassable. ~ду́мный unthinking. ~ду́шный heartless; inanimate; life-

less. ~жа́лостный pitiless, ruthless. ~жи́зненный lifeless. ~забо́тный carefree; careless. ~заве́тный selfless, wholehearted. ~зако́ние lawlessness; unlawful act. ~зако́нный illegal; lawless. ~засте́нчивый shameless, barefaced. ~защи́тный defenceless. ~зву́чный silent. ~зло́бный good-natured. ~ли́чный characterless; impersonal. ~лю́дный uninhabited; sparsely populated; lonely.

безме́н steelyard.

безме-. безме́рный immense; excessive. ~мо́лвие silence. ~мо́лвный silent, mute. ~мяте́жный serene, placid. ~наде́жный hopeless. ~надзо́рный neglected. ~нака́занно *adv* with impunity. ~нака́занный unpunished. ~но́гий legless; one-legged. ~нра́вственный immoral.

безо *prep+gen* = **без** (*used before* весь *and* вся́кий).

безобра́зие ugliness; disgrace, scandal. **безобра́зничать** *impf* make a nuisance of o.s. **безобра́зный** ugly; disgraceful.

без-. безогово́рочный unconditional. ~опа́сность safety; security. ~опа́сный safe; secure. ~ору́жный unarmed. ~основа́тельный groundless. ~остано́вочный unceasing; non-stop. ~отве́тный unanswering; dumb. ~отве́тственный irresponsible. ~отка́зно *adv* without a hitch. ~отка́зный trouble-free, smooth-(running). ~отлага́тельный urgent. ~относи́тельно *adv+к+dat* irrespective of. ~отчётный unaccountable. ~оши́бочный unerring.

correct. **~рабо́тица** unemployment. **~рабо́тный** unemployed. **~разли́чие** indifference. **~разли́чно** adv indifferently; it is all the same. **~разли́чный** indifferent. **~рассу́дный** reckless, imprudent. **~ро́дный** alone in the world; without relatives. **~ро́потный** uncomplaining; meek. **~рука́вка** sleeveless pullover. **~ру́кий** armless; one-armed. **~уда́рный** unstressed. **~уде́ржный** unrestrained; impetuous. **~укори́зненный** irreproachable.

безу́мец (-мца) madman. **безу́мие** madness. **безу́мный** mad. **безу́мство** madness.

без-. **безупре́чный** irreproachable, faultless. **~усло́вно** adv unconditionally; of course, undoubtedly. **~усло́вный** unconditional, absolute; indisputable. **~успе́шный** unsuccessful. **~уста́нный** tireless. **~уте́шный** inconsolable. **~уча́стие** indifference, apathy. **~уча́стный** indifferent, apathetic. **~ымя́нный** nameless, anonymous; **~ымя́нный па́лец** ring-finger. **~ыску́сный** artless, ingenuous. **~ысхо́дный** irreparable; interminable.

бейсбо́л baseball.

бека́р (mus) natural.

бека́с snipe.

беко́н bacon.

Белару́сь Belarus.

беле́ть impf (pf по**~**) turn white; show white.

белизна́ whiteness. **бели́ла** (pl; gen -и́л) whitewash; Tippex (propr). **бели́ть** (бе́лишь) impf (pf вы́**~**, на**~**, по**~**) whitewash; whiten; bleach.

бе́лка squirrel.

беллетри́ст writer of fiction. **беллетри́стика** fiction.

бело- in comb white-, leuco-. **белогварде́ец** (-е́йца) White Guard. **~кро́вие** leukaemia. **~ку́рый** fair, blonde. **~ру́с**, **~ру́ска**, **~ру́сский** Belorussian. **~сне́жный** snow-white.

белови́к (-а́) fair copy. **белово́й** clean, fair.

бело́к (-лка́) white (of egg, eye); protein.

белоше́йка seamstress. **белошве́йный** linen.

белу́га white sturgeon. **белу́ха** white whale.

бе́лый (бел, -а́, бе́ло́) white; clean, blank; sb white person; **~ая берёза** silver birch; **~ое кале́ние** white heat; **~ый медве́дь** polar bear; **~ые но́чи** white nights, midnight sun.

бельги́ец, **-ги́йка** Belgian. **бельги́йский** Belgian. **Бе́льгия** Belgium.

бельё linen; bedclothes; underclothes; washing.

бельмо́ (pl -а) cataract.

бельэта́ж first floor; dress circle.

бемо́ль m (mus) flat.

бенефи́с benefit (performance).

бензи́н petrol.

бензо- in comb petrol. **бензоба́к** petrol-tank. **~во́з** petrol tanker. **~запра́вочная** sb filling-station. **~коло́нка** petrol pump. **~прово́д** petrol pipe, fuel line.

бе́рег etc.: see **бере́чь**

бе́рег (loc -у́; pl -а́) bank, shore; coast; **на ~у́ мо́ря** at the seaside. **берегово́й** coast; coastal.

бережёшь etc.: see **бере́чь. бе-**

режли́вый thrifty. **бе́режный** careful.

берёза birch. **Берёзка** hard-currency shop.

бере́менеть *impf* (*pf* за∼) be(come) pregnant. **бере́менная** pregnant (+*instr* with). **бере́менность** pregnancy; gestation.

берéт beret.

берéчь (-регу́, -режёшь; -рёг, -ла́) *impf* take care of; keep; cherish; husband; be sparing of; ∼ся take care; beware (+*gen* of).

берло́га den, lair.

беру́ *etc.*: *see* **брать**

бес devil, demon.

бес-: *see* **без-**

бесéда talk, conversation. **бесéдка** summer-house. **бесéдовать** *impf* talk, converse.

беси́ть (бешу́, бéсишь) *impf* (*pf* вз∼) enrage; ∼ся go mad; be furious.

бесо́вский devilish.

бес-. **беспáмятство** unconsciousness. **беспартийный** non-party **бесперспективный** without prospects; hopeless. **∼пéчность** carelessness, unconcern. **∼плáтно** *adv* free. **∼плáтный** free. **∼плóдие** sterility, barrenness. **∼плóдность** futility. **∼плóдный** sterile, barren; futile. **∼поворóтный** irrevocable. **∼позвонóчный** invertebrate.

беспокóить *impf* (*pf* о∼, по∼) disturb, bother; trouble; ∼ся worry; trouble. **беспокóйный** anxious; troubled, fidgety. **бес-**

покóйство anxiety.

бес-. **бесполéзный** useless. **∼пóмощный** helpless; feeble. **∼порóдный** mongrel, not thoroughbred. **∼поря́док** (-дка) disorder; untidy state. **∼поря́дочный** disorderly; untidy. **∼посáдочный** non-stop. **∼пóчвенный** groundless. **∼пóшлинный** duty-free. **∼пощáдный** merciless. **∼прáвный** without rights. **∼предéльный** boundless. **∼предмéтный** aimless; abstract. **∼препя́тственный** unhindered; unimpeded. **∼преры́вный** continuous. **∼престáнный** continual.

беспризóрник, -ница waif, homeless child. **беспризóрный** neglected; homeless; *sb* waif, homeless child.

бес-. **беспримéрный** unparalleled. **∼принципный** unscrupulous. **∼пристрáстие** impartiality. **∼пристрáстный** impartial. **∼просвéтный** pitch-dark; hopeless; unrelieved. **∼пу́тный** dissolute. **∼свя́зный** incoherent. **∼сердéчный** heartless. **∼си́лие** impotence; feebleness. **∼си́льный** impotent, powerless. **∼слáвный** inglorious. **∼слéдно** *adv* without trace. **∼словéсный** dumb; silent, meek; (*theat*) walk-on. **∼смéнный** permanent, continuous. **∼смéртие** immortality. **∼смéртный** immortal. **∼смы́сленный** senseless; foolish; meaningless. **∼смы́слица** nonsense. **∼со́вестный** unscrupulous; shameless. **∼сознáтельный** unconscious; involuntary. **∼со́нница** insomnia. **∼спóрный** indisputable. **∼срóчный** indefinite; without a time limit. **∼страстный** im-

passive. **~стра́шный** fearless. **~сты́дный** shameless. **~та́ктный** tactless.

бестолко́вщина confusion, disorder. **бестолко́вый** muddle-headed, stupid; incoherent.

бес-. бесфо́рменный shapeless. **~хара́ктерный** weak, spineless. **~хи́тростный** artless; unsophisticated. **~хозя́йственный** improvident. **~цве́тный** colourless. **~це́льный** aimless; pointless. **~це́нный** priceless. **за ~це́нок** very cheap, for a song. **~церемо́нный** unceremonious. **~челове́чный** inhuman. **~че́стить (-е́щу)** *impf* (*pf* **о~че́стить**) dishonour. **~че́стный** dishonourable. **~чи́сленный** innumerable, countless.

бесчу́вственный insensible; insensitive. **бесчу́вствие** insensibility; insensitivity.

бес-. бесшу́мный noiseless.

бето́н concrete. **бето́нный** concrete. **бетономеша́лка** concrete-mixer. **бето́нщик** concrete-worker.

бечева́ tow-rope; rope. **бечёвка** cord, string.

бе́шенство rabies; rage. **бе́шеный** rabid; furious.

бешу́ *etc.*: *see* **беси́ть**

библе́йский biblical. **библиографи́ческий** bibliographical. **библиогра́фия** bibliography. **библиоте́ка** library. **библиоте́карь** *m*, **~те́карша** librarian. **би́блия** bible.

бива́к bivouac, camp.

би́вень (-вня) *m* tusk.

бигуди́ *pl indecl* curlers.

бидо́н can; churn.

бие́ние beating; beat.

бижуте́рия costume jewellery.

би́знес business. **бизнесме́н** businessman.

биле́т ticket; card; pass. **биле́тный** ticket.

биллио́н billion.

билья́рд billiards.

бино́кль *m* binoculars.

бинт (-а́) bandage. **бинтова́ть** *impf* (*pf* **за~**) bandage. **бинто́вка** bandaging.

био́граф biographer. **биографи́ческий** biographical. **биогра́фия** biography. **био́лог** biologist. **биологи́ческий** biological. **биоло́гия** biology. **биохи́мия** biochemistry.

би́ржа exchange.

би́рка name-plate; label.

бирюза́ turquoise.

бис *int* encore.

би́сер (*no pl*) beads.

бискви́т sponge cake.

бита́ bat.

би́тва battle.

битко́м *adv*: **~ наби́т** packed.

биту́м bitumen.

бить (бью, бьёшь) *impf* (*pf* **за~, по~, про~, ударя́ть**) beat; hit; defeat; sound; thump, bang; smash; **~ в цель** hit the target; **~ на**+*acc* strive for; **~ отбо́й** beat a retreat; **~ по**+*dat* damage, wound; **~ся** fight; beat; struggle; break; +*instr* knock, hit, strike; **+над**+*instr* struggle with, rack one's brains over.

бифште́кс beefsteak.

бич (-а́) whip, lash; scourge; homeless person. **бичева́ть** (**-чу́ю**) *impf* flog; castigate.

бла́го good; blessing.

бла́го- *in comb* well-, good-. **Благове́щение** Annunciation. **~ви́дный** plausible. **~во-**

ле́ние goodwill. ~**воспи́тан-ный** well-brought-up.

благодари́ть (-рю́) *impf* (*pf* по~) thank; **не сто́ит благода́рности** don't mention it. **благода́р-ный** grateful. **благодаря́** *prep+dat* thanks to, owing to.

благо-. благоде́тель *m* bene-factor. ~**де́тельница** benefac-tress. ~**де́тельный** beneficial. ~**ду́шный** placid; good-humoured. ~**жела́тель** *m* well-wisher. ~**жела́тельный** well-disposed; benevolent. ~**зву́ч-ный** melodious, harmonious. ~**надёжный** reliable. ~**наме́-ренный** well-intentioned. ~**по-лу́чие** well-being; happiness. ~**получно** *adv* all right, well; happily; safely. ~**получный** happy, successful; safe. ~**при-я́тный** favourable. ~**прия́т-ствовать** *impf +dat* favour. ~**разу́мие** sense; prudence. ~**разу́мный** sensible. ~**роди́е: ва́ше** ~**ро́дие** Your Honour. ~**ро́дный** noble. ~**ро́дство** nobility. ~**скло́нность** favour, good graces. ~**скло́нный** fa-vourable; gracious. ~**слови́ть** *pf*, **благословля́ть** *impf* bless. ~**состоя́ние** prosperity. ~**тво-ри́тель** *m*, -**ница** philanthrop-ist. ~**твори́тельный** charit-able, charity. ~**творный** salu-tary; beneficial; wholesome. ~**устро́енный** well-equipped, well-planned; with all amen-ities.

блаже́нный blissful; simple-minded. **блаже́нство** bliss.

бланк form.

блат (*sl*) string-pulling; pull, in-fluence. **блатно́й** criminal.

бледне́ть (-е́ю) *impf* (*pf* по~)

(grow) pale. **бле́дность** pale-ness, pallor. **бле́дный** (-ден, -дна́, -о) pale.

блеск brightness, brilliance, lustre; magnificence.

блесну́ть (-ну́, -нёшь) *pf* flash, gleam; shine. **блесте́ть** (-ещу́, -сти́шь *or* бле́щешь) *impf* shine; glitter. **блёстка** sparkle; sequin.

блестя́щий shining, bright; brilliant.

бле́ять (-е́ет) *impf* bleat.

ближа́йший nearest, closest; next. **бли́же** *comp of* бли́зкий. **бли́зко. бли́жний** near, close; neighbouring; *sb* neighbour.

близ *prep+gen* near, by. **бли́з-кий** (-зок, -зка́, -о) near; close; imminent; ~**кие** *sb pl* one's nearest and dearest, close rela-tives. **бли́зко** *adv* near (or+gen to). **близне́ц** (-а́) twin; *pl* Gem-ini. **близору́кий** short-sighted. **бли́зость** closeness, proximity.

блик patch of light; highlight.

блин (-а́) pancake.

блинда́ж (-а́) dug-out.

блиста́ть *impf* shine; sparkle.

блог (*comput.*) blog, weblog. **бло́ггер** (*comput.*) blogger, weblogger.

блок block, pulley, sheave.

блока́да blockade. **блоки́ро-вать** *impf & pf* blockade; ~**ся** form a bloc. **блокно́т** writing-pad, note-book.

блонди́н, блонди́нка blond(e).

блоха́ (*pl* -и, -а́м) flea.

блуд lechery. **блудни́ца** whore.

блужда́ть *impf* roam, wander.

блу́за, блу́зка blouse.

блю́дечко saucer; small dish. **блю́до** dish; course. **блю́дце** saucer.

боб (-а́) bean. **бобо́вый** bean.

бобр (-á) beaver.

Бог (*voc* Бóже) God; дай ~ God grant; ~ егó знáет who knows? не дай ~ God forbid; Бóже (мой)! my God! good God!; рáди ~a for God's sake; слáва ~y thank God.

богатéть *impf* (*pf* раз~) grow rich. **богáтство** wealth. **богáтый** rich, wealthy; *sb* rich man. **богáч** (-á) rich man.

богатыірь (-яí) *m* hero; strong man.

богиіня goddess. **Богомáтерь** Mother of God. **богомóлец** (-льца) **богомóлка** devout person; pilgrim. **богомóлье** pilgrimage. **богомóльный** religious, devout. **Богорóдица** the Virgin Mary. **богослóв** theologian. **богослóвие** theology. **богослужéние** divine service. **боготворíть** *impf* idolize; deify. **богохýльство** blasphemy.

бодрíть *impf* stimulate, invigorate; ~ся try to keep up one's spirits. **бóдрость** cheerfulness, courage. **бóдрствовать** be awake; stay awake; keep vigil. **бóдрый** (бодр, -á, -о) cheerful, bright.

боевíк (-á) smash hit. **боевóй** fighting, battle. **боегóловка** warhead. **боеприпáсы** (*pl*; *gen* -ов) ammunition. **боеспосóбный** battle-worthy. **боéц** (бойцá) soldier; fighter, warrior.

Бóже: *see* **Бог. бóжеский** divine; just. **божéственный** divine. **божествó** deity; divinity. **бóжий** God's; ~ья корóвка ladybird. **божóк** (-жкá) idol.

бой (*loc* -ю́; *pl* -и́, -ёв) battle, action; fight; fighting; slaughtering; striking; breakage(s).

бóйкий (бóек, бойкá, -о) smart,

sharp; glib; lively.

бойкóт boycott.

бóйня (*gen pl* бóен) slaughterhouse; butchery.

бок (*loc* -у́; *pl* -á) side; flank; ~ó ~ side by side; нá ~ to the side; на ~у́ on one side; пóд ~ом near by; с ~y from the side, from the flank; с ~y нá бок from side to side.

бокáл glass; goblet.

боковóй lateral. **бóком** *adv* sideways.

бокс boxing. **боксёр** boxer.

болвáн blockhead. **болвáнка** pig (*of iron etc.*).

болгáрин (*pl* -гáры), **болгáрка** Bulgarian. **болгáрский** Bulgarian. **Болгáрия** Bulgaria.

бóлее *adv* more; ~ всегó most of all; тем ~, что especially as.

болéзненный sickly; unhealthy; painful. **болéзнь** illness, disease; abnormality.

болéльщик, -щица fan, supporter. **болéть¹** (-éю) *impf* be ill, suffer. **болéть²** (-лúт) *impf* ache, hurt.

болóтистый marshy. **болóто** marsh, bog.

болтáть¹ *impf* stir; shake; dangle; ~ся dangle; swing; hang about.

болтáть² *impf* chat, natter. **болтлíвый** talkative; indiscreet. **болтнý** talk; chatter; gossip. **болтýн** (-á) **болтýнья** chatterbox.

боль *f* pain; ache. **больнíца** hospital. **больнíчный** hospital; ~ листóк medical certificate. **бóльно¹** *adv* painfully, badly; *predic*+*dat* it hurts. **бóльно²** *adv* very, terribly. **больнóй** (-лен, -льнá) ill, sick; diseased;

sore; *sb* patient, invalid.

бóльше *comp of* **большóй**, **мнóго**; bigger, larger; greater; more; ~ не any more, no longer; ~ тогó and what is more; *adv* for the most part.

большевик Bolshevik. **бóльший** greater, larger; ~ей чáстью for the most part. **большинствó** majority. **большóй** big, great; grown-up; ~áя бýква capital letter; ~óй пáлец thumb; big toe; ~ие *sb pl* grown-ups.

бóмба bomb. **бомбардирóвать** *impf* bombard; bomb. **бомбардирóвка** bombardment, bombing. **бомбардирóвщик** bomber. **бомбёжка** bombing. **бомбить** (-блю) bomb. **бомбоубéжище** bomb shelter.

бор (*loc* -ý; *pl* -ы́) coniferous forest.

бордóвый wine-red.

бордюр border.

борéц (-рцá) fighter; wrestler.

бóрзый swift.

бормашина (dentist's) drill.

бормотáть (-очý, -óчешь) *impf* (*pf* про~) mutter, mumble.

бородá (*acc* бóроду; *pl* бóроды, -рóд, -áм) beard. **бородáвка** wart. **бородáтый** bearded.

бороздá (*pl* бóрозды, -óзд, -áм) furrow. **бороздить** (-зжý) *impf* (*pf* вз~) furrow.

боронá (*acc* бóрону; *pl* бóроны, -рóн, -áм) harrow. **боронить** *impf* (*pf* вз~) harrow.

борóться (-рю́сь, бóрешься) *impf* wrestle; struggle, fight.

борт (*loc* -ý; *pl* -á), ship's side; front; за ~, за ~ом overboard; на ~, на ~ý on board. **бортпроводник** (-á) air stew

ard. **бортпроводница** air hostess.

борщ (-á) borsch (*beetroot soup*).

борьбá wrestling; struggle, fight.

босикóм *adv* barefoot.

боснец (-ийца), **боснийка** Bosnian. **боснийский** Bosnian. **Бóсния** Bosnia.

босóй (бос, -á, -о) barefooted. **босонóжка** sandal.

бот, бóтик small boat.

ботáник botanist. **ботáника** botany. **ботанический** botanical.

ботинок (-нка; *gen pl* -нок) (*ankle-high*) boot.

бóцман boatswain.

бóчка barrel. **бочóнок** (-нка) keg, small barrel.

боязливый timid, timorous. **боязнь** fear, dread.

боя́рин boyar. **боя́рский** boyar.

боя́рышник hawthorn.

боя́ться (боюсь) *impf* +*gen* be afraid of, fear; dislike.

брак¹ marriage.

брак² defective goods; flaw. **браковáть** *impf* (*pf* за~) reject.

браконьéр poacher.

бракоразвóдный divorce. **бракосочетáние** wedding.

бранить *impf* (*pf* вы́~) scold; abuse, curse; ~ся (*pf* по~) swear, curse; quarrel. **брáнный** abusive; ~ое слóво swearword.

брань bad language; abuse.

браслéт bracelet.

брасс breast stroke.

брат (*pl* -ья, -тьев) brother; comrade; mate; lay brother, monk. **братáться** *impf* (*pf* по~) fraternize. **братоубий

ство fratricide. **бра́тский** brotherly, fraternal. **бра́тство** brotherhood, fraternity.

брать (беру́, -рёшь; брал, -а́, -о) *impf* (*pf* взять) take; obtain; hire; seize; demand, require; surmount, clear; work; +*instr* succeed by means of; ~ся +за+*acc* touch; seize; get down to; +за+*acc or inf* undertake; appear, come.

бра́чный marriage; mating.

бреве́нчатый log. **бревно́** (*pl* брёвна, -вен) log, beam.

бред (*loc* -ý) delirium; raving(s). **бре́дить** (-éжу) *impf* be delirious, rave; +*instr* rave about, be infatuated with. **бредо́вый** delirious; fantastic, nonsensical.

бреду́ etc.: *see* **брести́**. **бре́жу** etc.: *see* **бре́дить**.

бре́згать *impf* (*pf* по~) +*inf* or *instr* be squeamish about. **брезгли́вый** squeamish.

брезе́нт tarpaulin.

бре́зжить(ся *impf* dawn; gleam faintly, glimmer.

брёл etc.: *see* **брести́**.

брело́к charm, pendant.

бременить *impf* (*pf* о~) burden. **бре́мя** (-мени) *neut* burden; load.

бренча́ть (-чý) *impf* strum; jingle.

брести́ (-едý, -едёшь; брёл, -á) *impf* stroll; drag o.s. along.

брете́ль, брете́лька shoulder strap.

брешь breach; gap.

бре́ю etc.: *see* **брить**.

брига́да brigade; crew; team. **бригади́р** brigadier; team-leader; foreman.

бриллиа́нт, брилья́нт diamond.

брита́нец (-нца), **брита́нка**

Briton. **брита́нский** British; Б~ие острова́ the British Isles.

бри́тва razor. **бри́твенный** shaving. **бри́тый** shaved; clean-shaven. **брить** (бре́ю) *impf* (*pf* по~) shave (o.s.).

бровь (*pl* -и, -éй) (eye)brow.

брод ford.

броди́ть (-ожу́, -о́дишь) *impf* wander, roam, stroll; ferment. **бродя́га** *m & f* tramp, vagrant. **бродя́жничество** vagrancy. **бродя́чий** vagrant; wandering. **броже́ние** ferment, fermentation.

бро́кер broker.

броне- *in comb* armoured, armour. **броневи́к** (-á) armoured car. ~**во́й** armoured. ~**но́сец** (-сца) battleship; armadillo.

бро́нза bronze; bronzes. **бро́нзовый** bronze; tanned.

бронирóванный armoured.

брони́ровать *impf & pf* (*pf also* за~) reserve, book.

бронхи́т bronchitis.

броня́[1] reservation; commandeering.

броня́[2] armour.

броса́ть *impf*, **бро́сить** (-о́шу) *pf* throw down; leave, desert; give up, leave off; ~**ся** throw o.s., rush; +*inf* begin; +*instr* squander; pelt one another with; ~**ся в глаза́** be striking. **бро́ский** striking; garish, glaring. **бросо́к** (-ска́) throw; bound, spurt.

бро́шка, брошь brooch.

брошю́ра pamphlet, brochure.

брус (*pl* -сья, -сьев) squared beam, joist; (**паралле́льные**) ~**ья** parallel bars.

брусни́ка red whortleberry; red whortleberries.

брусо́к (-ска́) bar; ingot.

брýтто *indecl adj* gross.

бры́згать (-зжу *or* -гаю) *impf*, **бры́знуть** (-ну) *pf* splash; sprinkle. **бры́зги** (брызг) *pl* spray, splashes; fragments.

брыка́ть *impf*, **брыкну́ть** (-ну́, -нёшь) *pf* kick.

брюзга́ *m & f* grumbler. **брюзгли́вый** grumbling, peevish. **брюзжа́ть** (-жу́) *impf* grumble.

брю́ква swede.

брю́ки (*pl; gen* брюк) trousers.

брюне́т dark-haired man. **брюне́тка** brunette.

брю́хо (*pl* -́и) belly; stomach.

брюшно́й abdominal; ~ тиф typhoid.

бряца́ть *impf* rattle; clank, clang.

бубен (-бна) tambourine. **бубене́ц** (-нца́) small bell.

бубны́ (*pl; gen* -бён, *dat* -бна́м) (*cards*) diamonds. **бубно́вый** diamond.

буго́р (-гра́) mound, hillock; bump, lump.

будди́зм Buddhism. **будди́йский** Buddhist. **будди́ст** Buddhist.

бу́дет that will do.

буди́льник alarm-clock. **буди́ть** (бужу́, бу́дишь) *impf* (*pf* про~, раз~) wake; arouse.

бу́дка box, booth; hut; stall.

бу́дни (*pl; gen* -ней) weekdays; working days; humdrum existence. **бу́дний, бу́дничный** weekday; everyday; humdrum.

бу́дто *conj* as if, as though; ~ (бы), (как) ~ apparently, ostensibly.

бу́ду *etc.: see* быть. **бу́дучи** being. **бу́дущий** future; next; ~ее *sb* future. **бу́дущность** future. **бу́дь(те):** *see* быть

бужу́: *see* буди́ть

бузина́ (*bot*) elder.

буй (*pl* -и́, -ёв) buoy.

бу́йвол buffalo.

бу́йный (буен, буйна́, -о) violent, turbulent; luxuriant, lush. **бу́йство** unruly behaviour. **бу́йствовать** *impf* create an uproar, behave violently.

бук beech.

бука́шка small insect.

бу́ква (*gen pl* букв) letter; ~ в бу́кву literally. **буква́льно** *adv* literally. **буква́льный** literal. **буква́рь** (-я́) *m* ABC. **буквое́д** pedant.

буке́т bouquet; aroma.

букини́ст second-hand bookseller.

бу́кля curl, ringlet.

бу́ковый beech.

букси́р tug-boat; tow-rope. **букси́ровать** *impf* tow.

буксова́ть *impf* spin, slip.

була́вка pin.

бу́лка roll; white loaf. **бу́лочка** roll, bun. **бу́лочная** *sb* baker's. **бу́лочник** baker.

булы́жник cobble-stone, cobble.

бульва́р avenue; boulevard.

бульдо́г bulldog.

бульдо́зер bulldozer.

бу́лькать *impf* gurgle.

бульо́н broth.

бум (*sport*) beam.

бума́га cotton; paper; document. **бума́жка** piece of paper; (bank)note. **бума́жник** wallet; paper-maker. **бума́жный** cotton; paper.

бу́нкер bunker.

бунт (*pl* -ы́) rebellion; riot; mutiny. **бунта́рь** (-я́) *m* rebel; insurgent. **бунтова́ть(ся** *impf* (*pf*

вз~) rebel; riot. **бунтовщи́к** (-á), **-щи́ца** rebel, insurgent.

бур auger.

бура́в (-á; *pl* -á) auger; gimlet. **бура́вить** (-влю) *impf* (*pf* про~) bore, drill.

бура́н snowstorm.

буреве́стник stormy petrel.

буре́ние boring, drilling.

буржуа́ *m indecl* bourgeois. **буржуази́я** bourgeoisie. **буржуа́зный** bourgeois.

бури́льщик borer, driller. **бури́ть** *impf* (*pf* про~) bore, drill.

бурли́ть *impf* seethe.

бу́рный (-рен, -рна́, -о) stormy; rapid; energetic.

бурово́й boring; ~**áя вы́шка** derrick; ~**áя** (**сква́жина**) borehole; ~**óй стано́к** drilling rig.

бу́рый (бур, -á, -о) brown.

бурья́н tall weeds.

бу́ря storm.

буси́на bead. **бу́сы** (*pl*; *gen* бус) beads.

бутафо́рия (*theat*) props.

бутербро́д open sandwich.

буто́н bud.

бу́тсы (*pl*; *gen* -ов) *pl* football boots.

буты́лка bottle. **буты́ль** large bottle; carboy.

буфе́т snack bar; sideboard; counter. **буфе́тчик** barman. **буфе́тчица** barmaid.

бух *int* bang, plonk. **бу́хать** *impf* (*pf* **бу́хнуть**) thump, bang; bang down; thunder, thud; blurt out.

буха́нка loaf.

бухга́лтер accountant. **бухгалте́рия** accountancy; accounts department.

бу́хнуть (-ну) *impf* swell.

бу́хта bay.

бушева́ть (-шу́ю) *impf* rage, storm.

буя́н rowdy. **буя́нить** *impf* create an uproar.

бы, б *partl* I. +*past tense or inf* indicates the conditional or subjunctive. II. (+**ни**) forms indef *prons and conjs.*

быва́лый experienced; former; habitual, familiar. **быва́ть** *impf* be; happen; be inclined to be; **как ни в чём не быва́ло** as if nothing had happened; **быва́ло** *partl* used to, would; **мать быва́ло ча́сто пе́ла э́ту пе́сню** my mother would often sing this song. **бы́вший** former, ex-.

бык (-á) bull, ox; pier.

были́на ancient Russian epic.

бы́ло *partl* nearly, on the point of; (only) just. **был|о́й** past, bygone; ~**óе** *sb* the past. **быль** true story; fact.

быстрота́ speed. **бы́стрый** (быстр, -á, -о) fast, quick.

быт (*loc* -ý) way of life. **бытие́** being, existence; objective reality; **кни́га Бытия́** Genesis. **бытово́й** everyday; social.

быть (*pres 3rd sg* есть, *pl* суть; *fut* бу́ду; *past* был, -á, -о; *imper* бу́дь(те)) *impf* be; be situated; happen. **бытьё** way of life.

бычо́к (-чка́) steer.

бью *etc.: see* **бить**

бюдже́т budget.

бюллете́нь *m* bulletin; ballot-paper; doctor's certificate.

бюро́ *neut indecl* bureau; office; writing-desk. **бюрокра́т** bureaucrat. **бюрократи́зм** bureaucracy. **бюрократи́ческий** bureaucratic. **бюрокра́тия** bureaucracy; bureaucrats.

бюст bust. **бюстга́льтер** bra-

В

в, во *prep* **I.** +*acc* into; to; on; at; within; through; **быть в** take after; **в два ра́за бо́льше** twice as big; **в на́ши дни** in our day; **войти́ в дом** go into the house; **в понеде́льник** on Monday; **в тече́ние**+*gen* during; **в четы́ре часа́** at four o'clock **высото́й в три ме́тра** threemetres high; **игра́ть в ша́хматы** play chess; **пое́хать в Москву́** go to Moscow; **сесть в ваго́н** get into the carriage; **смотре́ть в окно́** look out of the window. **II.** +*prep* in; at; **в двадца́том ве́ке** in the twentieth century; **в теа́тре** at the theatre; **в трёх киломе́трах от го́рода** three kilometres from the town; **в э́том году́** this year; **в январе́** in January.

ваго́н carriage, coach; **~-рестора́н** restaurant car. **ваго́нетка** truck, trolley. **вагоновожа́тый** *sb* tram-driver.

ва́жничать *impf* give o.s. airs; +*instr* plume o.s., pride o.s., on. **ва́жность** importance; pomposity. **ва́жный** (-жен, -жна́, -о) important; weighty; pompous.

ва́за vase, bowl.

вазели́н Vaseline (*propr*).

вака́нсия vacancy. **вака́нтный** vacant.

ва́кса (shoe-)polish.

ва́куум vacuum.

вакци́на vaccine.

вал¹ (*loc* -у́; *pl* -ы́) bank; rampart; billow, roller; barrage.

вал² (*loc* -у́; *pl* -ы́) shaft.

ва́ленок (-нка; *gen pl* -нок) felt boot.

вале́т knave, Jack.

ва́лик roller, cylinder.

вали́ть¹ *impf* flock, throng.

вали́ть² (-лю́, -лишь) *impf* (*pf* по~, с~) throw down, bring down; pile up; **~ся** fall, collapse.

валли́ец (-и́йца) Welshman. **валли́йка** Welshwoman.

валово́й gross; wholesale.

валто́рна French horn.

валу́н (-а́) boulder.

вальс waltz. **вальси́ровать** *impf* waltz.

валю́та currency; foreign currency.

валя́ть *impf* (*pf* на~, с~) drag; roll; shape; bungle; **~ дурака́** play the fool; **~ся** lie, lie about; roll, wallow.

вам, ва́ми: *see* **вы**

вампи́р vampire.

ванда́л vandal. **вандали́зм** vandalism.

вани́ль vanilla.

ва́нна bath. **ва́нная** *sb* bathroom.

ва́рвар barbarian. **ва́рварский** barbaric. **ва́рварство** barbarity; vandalism.

ва́режка mitten.

варёный boiled. **варе́нье** jam.

вари́ть (-рю́, -ришь) *impf* (*pf* с~) boil; cook; **~ся** boil; cook.

вариа́нт version; option; scenario.

вас: *see* **вы**

василёк (-лька́) cornflower.

ва́та cotton wool; wadding.

ватерли́ния water-line. **ватерпа́с** (spirit-)level.

вати́н (sheet) wadding. **ва́тник** quilted jacket. **ва́тный** quilted, wadded.

ватру́шка cheese-cake.

ватт (*gen pl* ватт) watt.

ва́учер coupon (*exchangeable*

for government-issued share.

вáфля (*gen pl* -фель) wafer; waffle.

вáхта (*naut*) watch. **вахтёр** janitor, porter.

ваш (-его) *m*, **вáша** (-ей) *f*, **вáше** (-его) *neut*, **вáши** (-их) *pl*, *pron* your, yours.

вбегáть *impf*, **вбежáть** (вбегу) *pf* run in.

вберу *etc.: see* вобрáть

вбивáть *impf of* вбить

вбирáть *impf of* вобрáть

вбить (вобью, -бьёшь) *pf* (*impf* вбивáть) drive in, hammer in.

вблизи *adv* (+от+*gen*) close (to), near by.

вбок *adv* sideways, to one side.

вброд *adv*: переходить ~ ford, wade.

ввáливать *impf*, **ввалить** (-лю, -лишь) *pf* throw heavily, heave, bundle; ~ся fall heavily; sink, become sunken; burst in.

введéние introduction. **введу** *etc.: see* ввести

ввезти (-зу́, -зёшь; ввёз, -ла́) *pf* (*impf* ввозить) import; bring in.

ввéрить *pf* (*impf* вверя́ть) entrust, confide; ~ся +*dat* trust in, put one's faith in.

ввернуть (-ну́, -нёшь) *pf*, **ввёртывать** *impf* screw in; insert.

вверх *adv* up, upward(s); ~дном upside down; ~ (по лéстнице) upstairs. **вверху́** *adv* above, overhead.

вверя́ть(ся) *impf of* ввéрить(ся)

ввести (-еду́, -едёшь; ввёл, -а́) *pf* (*impf* вводить) bring in; introduce.

ввиду́ *prep*+*gen* in view of.

ввинтить (-нчу́) *pf*, **ввинчивать** *impf* screw in.

ввод lead-in. **вводить** (-ожу́, -óдишь) *impf of* ввести. **вводный** introductory; parenthetic.

ввожу *see* вводить, ввозить

ввоз importation; import(s). **ввозить** (-ожу́, -óзишь) *impf of* ввезти.

вво́лю *adv* to one's heart's content.

ввысь *adv* up, upward(s).

ввяза́ть (-яжу́, -я́жешь) *pf*, **ввя́зывать** *impf* knit in; involve; ~ся meddle, get or be mixed up (in).

вглубь *adv & prep*+*gen* deep (into), into the depths.

вгляде́ться (-яжу́сь) *pf*, **вгля́дываться** *impf* peer, look closely (в+*acc* at).

вгоня́ть *impf of* вогна́ть. **вдава́ться** (вдаю́сь, -ёшься) *impf of* вда́ться

вдави́ть (-авлю́, -а́вишь) *pf*, **вда́вливать** *impf* press in.

вдалеке́, вдали́ *adv* in the distance, far away. **вдаль** *adv* into the distance.

вда́ться (-а́мся, -а́шься, -а́стся -ади́мся; -а́лся, -ла́сь) *pf* (*impf* вдава́ться) jut out; penetrate, go in; (*fig*) get immersed.

вдво́е *adv* twice; double; ~ бо́льше twice as big, as much, as many. **вдвоём** *adv* (the) two together, both. **вдвойне́** *adv* twice, double; doubly.

вдева́ть *impf of* вдеть

вде́лать *pf*, **вде́лывать** *impf* set in, fit in.

вдёргивать *impf*, **вдёрнуть** (-ну) *pf* в+*acc* thread through.

вдеть (-е́ну) *pf* (*impf* вдева́ть) put in, thread.

вдоба́вок *adv* in addition; besides.

вдова́ widow. **вдове́ц** (-вца́) widower.

вдо́воль *adv* enough; in abundance.

вдого́нку *adv* (за+*instr*) after, in pursuit (of).

вдоль *adv* lengthwise; ∼ и поперёк far and wide; in detail; *prep*+*gen* or по+*dat* along.

вдох breath. **вдохнове́ние** inspiration, **вдохнове́нный** inspired. **вдохнови́ть** (-влю́) *pf*, **вдохновля́ть** *impf* inspire. **вдохну́ть** (-ну́, -нёшь) *pf* (*impf* **вдыха́ть**) breathe in.

вдре́безги *adv* to smithereens.

вдруг *adv* suddenly.

вду́маться *pf*, **вду́мываться** *impf* ponder, meditate; +в+*acc* think over. **вду́мчивый** thoughtful.

вдыха́ние inhalation. **вдыха́ть** *impf of* **вдохну́ть**

веб-са́йт (*comput*) website. **веб-страни́ца** (*comput*) web page.

вегетариа́нец (-нца), **-нка** vegetarian. **вегетариа́нский** vegetarian.

ве́дать *impf* know; +*instr* manage, handle. **ве́дение**[1] authority, jurisdiction.

веде́ние[2] conducting, conduct; ∼ книг book-keeping.

ве́домость (*gen pl* -е́й) list, register. **ве́домственный** departmental. **ве́домство** department.

ведро́ (*pl* вёдра, -дер) bucket; vedro (*approx* 12 litres).

веду́ *etc.: see* **вести́**. **веду́щий** leading.

ведь *partl* & *conj* you see, you know; isn't it? is it?

ве́дьма witch.

ве́ер (*pl* -á) fan.

ве́жливость politeness. **ве́жливый** polite.

везде́ *adv* everywhere.

везе́ние luck. **везу́чий** lucky. **везти́** (-зу́, -зёшь; вёз, -ла́) *impf* (*pf* **по**-) convey; bring, take; *impers*+*dat* be lucky; ему́ не везло́ he had no luck.

век (*loc* -ý; *pl* -á) century; age; life(time). **век** *adv* for ages.

ве́ко (*pl* -и, век) eyelid.

веково́й ancient, age-old.

ве́ксель (*pl* -я́, -е́й) *m* promissory note, bill of (exchange).

вёл *etc.: see* **вести́**

веле́ть (-лю́) *impf* & *pf* order; не ∼ forbid.

велика́н giant. **вели́кий** (вели́к, -а *or* -á) great; big, large; too big; ∼ пост Lent.

велико- in comb great. **Великобрита́ния** Great Britain. **великоду́шие** magnanimity. **∼ду́шный** magnanimous. **∼ле́пие** splendour. **∼ле́пный** splendid.

велича́вый stately, majestic. **велича́йший** greatest, supreme. **вели́чественный** majestic, grand. **вели́чество** Majesty. **вели́чие** greatness, grandeur. **величина́** (*pl* -и́ны, -áм) size; quantity, magnitude; value; great figure.

велосипе́д bicycle. **велосипеди́ст** cyclist.

вельве́т velveteen; ∼ в ру́бчик corduroy.

вельмо́жа *m* grandee.

ве́на vein.

венге́рец (-рца), **венге́рка** Hungarian. **венге́рский** Hungarian. **Ве́нгрия** Hungary.

венде́тта vendetta.

венери́ческий venereal.

вене́ц (-нца́) crown; wreath.

ве́ник besom; birch twigs.

вено́к (-нка́) wreath, garland.

ве́нтиль *m* valve.

вентиля́тор ventilator; extractor (fan). **вентиля́ция** ventilation.

венча́ние wedding; coronation. **венча́ть** *impf* (*pf* об~, по~, у~) crown; marry; ~ся be married, marry. **ве́нчик** halo; corolla; rim; ring, bolt.

ве́ра faith, belief.

вера́нда veranda.

ве́рба willow; willow branch. **ве́рбный**; ~ое воскресе́нье Palm Sunday.

верблю́д camel.

вербова́ть *impf* (*pf* за~) recruit; win over. **вербо́вка** recruitment.

верёвка rope; string; cord. **верёвочный** rope.

верени́ца row, file, line, string.

веретено́ (*pl* -тёна) spindle.

вереща́ть (-щу́) *impf* squeal; chirp.

ве́рить *impf* (*pf* по~) believe, have faith; +*dat* or в+*acc* trust (in), believe in.

вермише́ль vermicelli.

верне́е *adv* rather. **ве́рно** *partl* probably, I suppose. **ве́рность** faithfulness, loyalty.

верну́ть (-ну́, -нёшь) *pf* (*impf* возвраща́ть) give back, return; ~ся return.

ве́рный (-рен, -рна́, -о) faithful, loyal; true; correct; reliable.

ве́рование belief. **ве́ровать** *impf* believe. **вероиспове́дание** religion; denomination. **вероло́мный** treacherous, perfidious. **вероотсту́пник**

apostate. **веротерпи́мость** (religious) toleration. **вероя́тно** *adv* probably. **вероя́тность** probability. **вероя́тный** probable.

ве́рсия version.

верста́ (*pl* вёрсты) verst (*1.06 km.*).

верста́к (-а́) work-bench.

ве́ртел (*pl* -á -и́) spit, skewer. **верте́ть** (-чу́, -тишь) *impf* turn (round); twirl; ~ся turn (round); spin. **вертля́вый** fidgety; flighty.

вертика́ль vertical line. **вертика́льный** vertical.

вертолёт helicopter.

верту́шка flirt.

ве́рующий *sb* believer.

верфь shipyard.

верх (*loc* -ý; *pl* -и́) top; summit; height; *pl* upper crust, top brass; high notes. **ве́рхний** upper; top. **верхо́вный** supreme. **верхово́й** riding; *sb* rider. **верхо́вье** (*gen pl* -ьев) upper reaches. **верхола́з** steeple-jack. **верхо́м** *adv* on horseback; astride. **верху́шка** top, summit; apex; top brass.

верчу́ *etc.*: *see* верте́ть

верши́на top, summit; peak; apex. **верши́ть** *impf* +*instr* manage, control.

вершо́к vershok (*4.4 cm.*); smattering.

вес (*loc* -ý; *pl* -á) weight.

весели́ть *impf* (*pf* раз~) cheer, gladden; ~ся enjoy o.s.; amuse o.s. **ве́село** *adv* merrily. **весёлый** (ве́сел, -á, -о) merry; cheerful. **весе́лье** merriment.

весе́нний spring.

ве́сить (ве́шу) *impf* weigh. **ве́ский** weighty, solid.

весло́ (*pl* вёсла, -сел) oar.

весна́ (*pl* вёсны, -сен) spring. весно́й *adv* in (the) spring. весну́шка freckle.

вест (*naut*) west; west wind.

вести́ (веду́, -дёшь; вёл, -а́) *impf* (*pf* по~) lead; take; conduct; drive; run; keep; ~себя́ behave, conduct o.s.; ~сь be the custom.

вестибю́ль *m* (entrance) hall, lobby.

ве́стник herald; bulletin. весть¹ (*gen pl* -е́й) news; без вести without trace. весть²: Бог ~ God knows.

весы́ (*pl*, *gen* -о́в) scales, balance; Libra.

весь (всего́ *m*, вся, всей *f*, все, всего́ *neut*, все, всех *pl*) *pron* all, the whole of; всего́ хоро́шего! all the best!; всё everything; без всего́ without anything; все everybody.

весьма́ *adv* very, highly.

ветвь (*gen pl* -е́й) branch; bough.

ве́тер (-тра, *loc* -у́) wind. ветеро́к (-рка́) breeze.

ветера́н veteran.

ветерина́р vet.

ве́тка branch; twig.

ве́то *neut indecl* veto.

ве́тошь old clothes, rags.

ве́треный windy; frivolous. ветров|о́й wind; ~о́е стекло́ windscreen. ветря́к (-а́) wind turbine; windmill.

ве́тхий (ветх, -а́, -о) old; dilapidated; В~ заве́т Old Testament.

ветчина́ ham.

ветша́ть *impf* (*pf* об~) decay; become dilapidated.

ве́ха landmark.

ве́чер (*pl* -а́) evening; party. вече́ринка party. вече́рний even-

ing. вече́рня (*gen pl* -рен) vespers. ве́чером *adv* in the evening.

ве́чно *adv* for ever, eternally. вечнозелёный evergreen. ве́чность eternity; ages. ве́чный eternal.

ве́шалка peg, rack; tab, hanger. ве́шать *impf* (*pf* взве́сить, пове́сить, све́шать) hang; weigh (out); ~ся hang o.s.; weigh o.s.

ве́шу *etc.*: *see* ве́сить

веща́ние broadcasting. веща́ть *impf* broadcast.

вещево́й clothing; ~ мешо́к hold-all, kit-bag. веще́ственный substantial, material, real. вещество́ substance; matter. вещь (*gen pl* -е́й) thing.

ве́ялка winnowing-machine. ве́яние winnowing; blowing; trend. ве́ять (ве́ю) *impf* (*pf* про~) winnow; blow; flutter.

взад *adv* backwards; ~ и вперёд back and forth.

взаи́мность reciprocity. взаи́мный mutual, reciprocal. взаимо- *in comb* inter-. взаимоде́йствие interaction; co-operation. ~де́йствовать *impf* interact; cooperate. ~отноше́ние interrelation; *pl* relations. ~по́мощь mutual aid. ~понима́ние mutual understanding. ~связь interdependence, correlation.

взаймы́ *adv*: взять ~ borrow; дать ~ lend.

взаме́н *prep*+*gen* instead of; in return for.

взаперти́ *adv* under lock and key; in seclusion.

взба́лмошный unbalanced, eccentric.

взбега́ть *impf*, взбежа́ть (-егу́) *pf* run up.

взберу́сь *etc.*: *see* **взобра́ться**.

взбе́сить (-ешу́(сь), -е́сишь(ся) *pf.* **взбива́ть** *impf of* взбить. **взбира́ться** *impf of* взобра́ться

взби́тый whipped, beaten. **взбить** (взобью́, -бьёшь) *pf* (*impf* **взбива́ть**) beat (up), whip; shake up.

вз|**борозди́ть** (-зжу́) *pf.* **вз**|**бунтова́ть**ся *pf.*

взбуха́ть *impf*, **взбу́хнуть** (-нет; -ух) *pf* swell (out).

взва́ливать *impf*, **взвали́ть** (-лю́, -лишь) *pf* load; +**на**+*acc* saddle with.

взве́сить (-е́шу) *pf* (*impf* **ве́**-**шать**, **взве́шивать**) weigh.

взвести́ (-еду́, -едёшь; -ёл, -а́) *pf* (*impf* **взводи́ть**) lead up; raise; cock; +**на**+*acc* impute to.

взве́шивать *impf of* взве́сить **взви́ва**ть(ся *impf of* взви́ть(ся

взвизг scream; yelp. **взви́зги**вать *impf*, **взви́згнуть** (-ну) *pf* scream; yelp.

взвинти́ть (-нчу́) *pf*, **взви́нчи**вать *impf* excite, work up; inflate. **взви́нченный** worked up; nervy; inflated.

взвить (взовью́, -ёшь; -ил, -ила́, -о) *pf* (*impf* **взвива́ть**) raise; ~**ся** rise, be hoisted; soar.

взвод[1] platoon, troop. **взвод**[2] notch. **взводи́ть** (-ожу́, -о́дишь) *impf of* взвести́

взволно́ванный agitated; worried. **взволнова́ть**(ся (-ну́ю(сь) *pf.*

взгляд look; glance; opinion. **взгля́дыва**ть *impf*, **взгляну́ть** (-яну́, -я́нешь) *pf* look, glance.

взго́рье hillock.

вздёргивать *impf*, **вздёрнуть** (-ну) *pf* hitch up; jerk up; turn up.

вздор nonsense. **вздо́рный** cantankerous; foolish.

вздорожа́ние rise in price. **вз**|**дорожа́ть** *pf.*

вздох sigh. **вздохну́ть** (-ну́, -нёшь) *pf* (*impf* **вздыха́ть**) sigh.

вздра́гивать *impf* (*pf* **вздро́г**-**нуть**) shudder, quiver.

вздремну́ть *pf* have a nap, doze.

вздро́гнуть (-ну) *pf* (*impf* **вздра́гивать**) start; wince.

вздува́ть(ся *impf of* вздуть[1](ся

вздумать *pf* take it into one's head; **не вздумай(те)!** don't you dare!

вздутие swelling. **вздутый** swollen. **вздуть**[1] *pf* (*impf* **взду**-**ва́ть**) inflate; ~**ся** swell.

вздуть[2] *pf* thrash.

вздыха́ть *impf* (*pf* **вздохну́ть**) breathe; sigh.

взима́ть *impf* levy, collect.

взла́мывать *impf of* взлома́ть. **вз**|**леле́ять** *pf.*

взлёт flight; take-off. **взлета́ть** *impf*, **взлете́ть** (-лечу́) *pf* fly (up); take off. **взлётный** take-off; **взлётно-поса́дочная полоса́** runway.

взлом breaking open, breaking in. **взлома́ть** *pf* (*impf* **взла́мы**-**вать**) break open; break up. **взло́мщик** burglar.

взлохма́ченный dishevelled.

взмах stroke, wave, flap. **взма́**-**хива**ть *impf*, **взмахну́ть** (-ну́, -нёшь) *pf* +*instr* wave, flap.

взмо́рье seaside; coastal waters.

взму́тить (-учу́, -у́тишь) *pf.*

взнос payment; fee, dues.

взнузда́ть *pf*, **взну́здыва**ть *impf* bridle.

взобра́ться (взберу́сь, -е́шься; -а́лся, -ла́сь, -ло́сь) *pf* (*impf* **взбира́ться**) climb (up).

взобью́ *etc.: see* **взбить**. **взовью́** *etc.: see* **взвить**

взойти́ (-йду́, -йдёшь; -ошёл, -шла́) *pf* (*impf* **вос-, всходи́ть**) rise, go up; **на**+*acc* mount.

взор look, glance.

взорва́ть (-ву́, -вёшь; -а́л, -а́, -о) *pf* (*impf* **взрыва́ть**) blow up; exasperate; **~ся** burst, explode.

взро́слый *adj & sb* adult.

взрыв explosion; outburst. **взрыва́тель** *m* fuse. **взрыва́ть** *impf*, **взрыть** (-ро́ю) *pf* (*pf also* **взорва́ть**) blow up; **~ся** explode. **взрывно́й** explosive; blasting. **взрывча́тка** explosive. **взры́вчатый** explosive.

взъеро́шенный tousled, dishevelled. **взъеро́шивать** *impf*, **взъеро́шить** (-шу) *pf* tousle, rumple.

взыва́ть *impf of* **воззва́ть**

взыска́ние penalty; exaction. **взыска́тельный** exacting. **взыска́ть** (-ыщу́, -ы́щешь) *pf*, **взы́скивать** *impf* exact, recover; call to account.

взя́тие taking, capture. **взя́тка** bribe. **взя́точничество** bribery. **взя́ть(ся** (возьму́(сь, -мёшь(ся; -я́л(ся, -а́с(ь, -о(сь) *pf of* **брать(ся**

вибра́ция vibration. **вибри́ровать** *impf* vibrate.

вивисе́кция vivisection.

вид[1] (*loc* -у́) look; appearance; shape, form; condition; view; prospect; sight; aspect; **де́лать вид** pretend; **име́ть в ~у́** intend; mean; bear in mind.

вид[2] kind; species.

вида́ть *impf* (*pf* **по~**) meet. **ви́дение**[1] sight, vision. **виде́-**

-ние[2] vision, apparition.

ви́део *neut indecl* video (cassette) recorder; video film; video cassette. **видеоигра́** video game. **видеока́мера** video camera. **видеокассе́та** video cassette. **видеомагнитофо́н** video (cassette) recorder.

ви́деть (ви́жу) *impf* (*pf* **у~**) see; **~ во сне** dream (of); **~ся** see one another; appear. **ви́димо** *adv* evidently. **ви́димость** visibility; appearance. **ви́димый** visible; apparent, evident. **ви́дный** (-ден, -дна́, -о) visible; distinguished.

видоизмене́ние modification. **видоизмени́ть** *pf*, **видоизменя́ть** *impf* modify.

видоиска́тель *m* view-finder.

ви́жу *see* **ви́деть**

ви́за visa.

визг squeal; yelp. **визжа́ть** (-жу́) *impf* squeal, yelp, squeak.

визи́т visit. **визи́тка** business card.

викто́рина quiz.

ви́лка fork; plug. **ви́лы** (*pl; gen* вил) pitchfork.

вильну́ть (-ну́, -нёшь) *pf*, **виля́ть** *impf* twist and turn; prevaricate; +*instr* wag.

вина́ (*pl* ви́ны) fault, guilt; blame.

винегре́т Russian salad; medley.

вини́тельный accusative. **вини́ть** *impf* accuse; **~ся** (*pf* **по~**) confess.

ви́нный wine; winy. **вино́** (*pl* -а) wine.

винова́тый guilty. **вино́вник** initiator; culprit. **вино́вный** guilty.

виногра́д vine; grapes. **виногра́дина** grape. **виногра́дник**

vineyard. **виногра́дный** grape; wine. **винику́ренный заво́д** distillery.

винт (-á) screw. **винти́ть** (-нчу́) *impf* screw up. **винто́вка** rifle. **винтово́й** screw; spiral.

виолонче́ль cello.

вира́ж (-á) turn; bend.

виртуа́льный (*comput*) virtual.

виртуо́з virtuoso. **виртуо́зный** masterly.

ви́рус virus. **ви́русный** virus.

ви́селица gallows. **висе́ть** (вишу́) *impf* hang. **ви́снуть** (-ну; вис(нул)) *impf* hang; droop.

ви́ски *neut indecl* whisky.

висо́к (-ска́) (*anat*) temple.

високо́сный год leap-year.

вист whist.

вися́чий hanging; ~ замо́к padlock; ~ мост suspension bridge.

витами́н vitamin.

витиева́тый flowery, ornate. **вито́й** twisted, spiral. **вито́к** (-тка́) turn, coil.

витра́ж (-á) stained-glass window. **витри́на** shop-window; showcase.

вить (вью, вьёшь; вил, -á, -о) *impf* (*pf* с~) twist, wind, weave; ~ся wind, twine; curl; twist; whirl.

вихо́р (-хра́) tuft. **вихра́стый** shaggy.

вихрь *m* whirlwind; vortex; сне́жный ~ blizzard.

ви́це- *pref* vice-. **вице-адмира́л** vice-admiral. **~президе́нт** vice-president.

ВИЧ (*abbr of* ви́рус иммунодефици́та челове́ка) HIV.

вишнёвый cherry. **ви́шня** (*gen pl* -шен) cherry, cherries; cherry-tree.

вишу́: *see* висе́ть

вишь *partl* look, just look!

вка́лывать *impf* (*sl*) work hard; *impf of* вколо́ть

вка́пывать *impf of* вкопа́ть

вка́тывать (-áчу, -áтишь) *pf*, **вка́тывать** *impf* roll in; administer.

вклад deposit; contribution. **вкла́дка, вкладно́й лист** loose leaf, insert. **вкла́дчик** depositor.

вкла́дывать *impf of* вложи́ть

вкле́иваться *impf*, **вкле́ить** *pf* stick in.

вкли́ниваться *impf*, **вкли́ниться** *pf* edge one's way in.

включа́тель *m* switch. **включа́ть** *impf*, **включи́ть** (-чу́) *pf* include; switch on; plug in; ~ся в+*acc* join in, enter into. **включа́я** including. **включе́ние** inclusion, insertion; switching on. **включи́тельно** *adv* inclusive.

вкола́чивать *impf*, **вколоти́ть** (-очу́, -о́тишь) *pf* hammer in, knock in.

вколо́ть (-олю́, -о́лешь) *pf* (*impf* вка́лывать) stick (in).

вкопа́ть *pf* (*impf* вка́пывать) dig in.

вкось *adv* obliquely.

вкра́дчивый ingratiating. **вкра́дываться** *impf*, **вкра́сться** (-аду́сь, -адёшься) *pf* creep in; insinuate o.s.

вкра́тце *adv* briefly, succinctly.

вкривь *adv* aslant; wrongly, perversely.

вкруг = вокру́г

вкруту́ю *adv* hard(-boiled).

вкус taste. **вкуси́ть** (-ушу́, -у́сишь) *pf*, **вкуша́ть** *impf* taste; partake of. **вку́сный** (-сен, -сна́, -о) tasty, nice.

вла́га moisture.

влага́лище vagina.

владе́лец (-льца), **-лица** owner. **владе́ние** ownership; possession; property. **владе́тель** *m*, **-ница** possessor; sovereign. **владе́ть** (-е́ю) *impf* +*instr* own, possess; control.

влады́ка *m* master, sovereign. **влады́чество** dominion, sway.

вла́жность humidity; moisture. **вла́жный** (-жен, -жна́, -о) damp, moist, humid.

вла́мываться *impf of* **вломи́ться**

вла́ствовать *impf* +(над)+ *instr* rule, hold sway over. **власте́лин** ruler; master. **вла́стный** imperious, commanding, empowered, competent. **власть** (*gen pl* -е́й) power; authority.

вле́во *adv* to the left (от+*gen* of).

влеза́ть *impf*, **влезть** (-зу; влез) *pf* climb in; get in; fit in.

влёк *etc.: see* **влечь**

влета́ть *impf*, **влете́ть** (-ечу́) *pf* fly in; rush in.

влече́ние attraction; inclination. **влечь** (-еку́, -ечёшь; влёк, -ла́) *impf* draw; attract; ~ за собо́й involve, entail.

влива́ть *impf*, **влить** (волью́, -ёшь; влил, -а́, -о) *pf* pour in; instil.

влия́ние influence. **влия́тельный** influential. **влия́ть** *impf* (*pf* по~) на+*acc* influence, affect.

вложе́ние enclosure; investment. **вложи́ть** (-ожу́, -о́жишь) *pf* (*impf* **вкла́дывать**) put in, insert; enclose; invest.

вломи́ться (-млю́сь, -мишься) *pf* (*impf* **вла́мываться**) break in.

влюби́ть (-блю́ -бишь) *pf*, влю-

бля́ть *impf* make fall in love (в+*acc* with); ~ся fall in love. **влюблённый** (-лён, -á) in love; *sb* lover.

вма́зать (-а́жу) *pf*, **вма́зывать** *impf* cement, putty in.

вмени́ть *pf*, **вменя́ть** *impf* impute; impose. **вменя́емый** (*law*) responsible; sane.

вме́сте *adv* together; ~ с тем at the same time, also.

вмести́лище receptacle. **вмести́мость** capacity; tonnage. **вмести́тельный** capacious. **вмести́ть** (-ещу́) *pf* (*impf* **вмеща́ть**) hold, accommodate; put; ~ся go in.

вме́сто *prep*+*gen* instead of.

вмеша́тельство interference; intervention. **вмеша́ть** *pf*, **вме́шивать** *impf* mix in; implicate; ~ся interfere, intervene.

вмеща́ть(ся *impf of* **вмести́ть(ся**

вмиг *adv* in an instant.

вмина́ть *impf*, **вмять** (вомну́, -нёшь) *pf* press in, dent. **вмя́тина** dent.

внаём, внаймы́ *adv* to let; for hire.

внача́ле *adv* at first.

вне *prep*+*gen* outside; ~ себя́ beside o.s.

вне- *pref* extra-; outside; -less. **внебра́чный** extra-marital; illegitimate. **~вре́менный** timeless. **~кла́ссный** extra-curricular. **~очередно́й** out of turn; extraordinary. **~шта́тный** freelance, casual.

внедре́ние introduction; inculcation. **внедри́ть** *pf*, **внедря́ть** *impf* inculcate; introduce; ~ся take root.

внеза́пно *adv* suddenly. **вне-**

за́п난 sudden.

вне́млю etc.: see **внима́ть**

внесе́ние bringing in; deposit.

внести́ (-су́, -сёшь; внёс, -ла́) pf (impf **вноси́ть**) bring in; introduce; deposit; insert.

вне́шне adv outwardly. **вне́шний** outer; external; outside; foreign. **вне́шность** exterior; appearance.

вниз adv down(wards). **~ по**+dat down. **внизу́** adv below; downstairs.

вника́ть impf, **вни́кнуть** (-ну; вник) pf **в**+acc go carefully into, investigate thoroughly.

внима́ние attention. **внима́тельный** attentive. **внима́ть** impf (pf **внять**) listen to; heed.

вничью́ adv: **око́нчиться** ~ end in a draw; **сыгра́ть** ~ draw.

вновь adv anew, again.

вноси́ть (-ошу́, -о́сишь) impf of **внести́**

внук grandson; pl grandchildren, descendants.

вну́тренний inner; internal. **вну́тренность** interior; pl entrails; internal organs. **внутри́** adv & prep+gen inside, in; within. **внутрь** adv & prep+gen inside, in; inwards.

внуча́та (pl; gen -ча́т) grandchildren. **внуча́тый** second, great-; ~ **брат** second cousin; ~ **племя́нник** great-nephew. **вну́чка** grand-daughter.

внуша́ть impf, **внуши́ть** (-шу́) pf instil; +dat inspire with. **внуше́ние** suggestion; reproof. **внуши́тельный** inspiring; imposing.

вня́тный distinct. **внять** (no fut; -ял, -а́, -о) pf of **внима́ть**

во: see **в**

вобра́ть (вберу́, -рёшь; -а́л, -а́, -о) pf (impf **вбира́ть**) absorb; inhale.

вобью́ etc.: see **вбить**

вовлека́ть impf, **вовле́чь** (-еку́, -ечёшь; -ёк, -екла́) pf draw in, involve.

во́время adv in time; on time.

во́все adv quite; ~ **не** not at all.

во-вторы́х adv secondly.

вогна́ть (вгоню́, -о́нишь; -гна́л, -а, -о) pf (impf **вгоня́ть**) drive in. **во́гнутый** concave. **вогну́ть** (-ну́, -нёшь) pf (impf **вгиба́ть**) ~ press inwards.

вода́ (acc во́ду, gen -ы́; pl -ы) water; pl the waters; spa.

водвори́ть pf, **водворя́ть** impf settle, install; establish.

води́ть m driver. **води́ть** (вожу́, во́дишь) impf lead; conduct; take; drive; **~ся** be found; associate (with); be the custom.

во́дка vodka. **во́дный** water; **~ые лы́жи** water-skiing; waterskis.

водо- in comb water, water-; hydraulic; hydro-. **водобоя́знь** hydrophobia. **~воро́т** whirlpool; maelstrom. **~ём** reservoir. **~измеще́ние** displacement. **~ка́чка** water-tower, pumping station. **~ла́з** diver. **~ле́й** Aquarius. **~непроница́емый** waterproof. **~отво́дный** drainage. **~па́д** waterfall. **~по́й** watering-place. **~прово́д** water-pipe, water-main; water supply. **~прово́дчик** plumber. **~разде́л** watershed. **~ро́д** hydrogen. **во́доросль** waterplant; seaweed. **~снабже́ние** water supply. **~сто́к** drain, gutter. **~храни́лище** reservoir.

водружа́ть impf, **водрузи́ть**

(-ужу́) *pf* hoist; erect.

водяни́стый watery. **водяно́й** water.

воева́ть (вою́ю) *impf* wage war. **воево́да** *m* voivode; commander.

воеди́но *adv* together.

военко́м military commissar.

военно- *in comb* military; war. **вое́нно-возду́шный** air-, air-force. **вое́нно-морско́й** naval. **∼пле́нный** *sb* prisoner of war. **вое́нно-полево́й суд** court-martial. **∼слу́жащий** *sb* serviceman.

вое́нный military; war; *sb* serviceman. **∼ое положе́ние** martial law; **∼ый суд** court-martial.

вожа́к (-á) guide; leader. **вожа́тый** *sb* guide; tram-driver.

вожделе́ние desire, lust.

вождь (-á) *m* leader, chief.

вожжа́ (*pl* -и, -éй) rein.

вожу́ *etc.*: *see* **води́ть, вози́ть**

воз (*loc* -ý; *pl* -ы́) cart; cart-load.

возбуди́мый excitable. **возбуди́тель** *m* agent; instigator. **возбуди́ть** (-ужу́) *pf*, **возбужда́ть** *impf* excite, arouse; incite. **возбужда́ющий: ∼ее сре́дство** stimulant. **возбужде́ние** excitement. **возбуждённый** excited.

возвести́ (-еду́, -дёшь, -вёл, -лá) *pf* (*impf* **возводи́ть**) elevate; erect; level; +к+*dat* trace to.

возвести́ть (-ещу́) *pf*, **возвеща́ть** *impf* proclaim.

возводи́ть (-ожу́, -о́дишь) *impf of* **возвести́**

возвра́т return; repayment. **возврати́ть** (-ащу́) *pf*, **возвраща́ть** *impf* (*pf also* **верну́ть**) return; give back; **∼ся** return; go

back, come back. **возвра́тный** return; reflexive. **возвраще́ние** return.

возвы́сить *pf*, **возвыша́ть** *impf* raise; ennoble; **∼ся** rise. **возвыше́ние** rise; raised place. **возвы́шенность** height; loftiness. **возвы́шенный** high; elevated.

возгла́вить (-влю) *pf*, **возглавля́ть** *impf* head.

во́зглас exclamation. **возгласи́ть** (-ашу́) *pf*, **возглаша́ть** *impf* proclaim.

возгора́емый inflammable. **возгора́ться** *impf*, **возгоре́ться** (-рю́сь) *pf* flare up; be seized (with).

воздава́ть (-даю́, -даёшь) *impf*, **возда́ть** (-áм, -áшь, -áст, -ади́м; -áл, -á, -о) *pf* render.

воздвига́ть *impf*, **воздви́гнуть** (-ну; -двиг) *pf* raise.

возде́йствие influence. **возде́йствовать** *impf* & *pf* +на+*acc* influence.

возде́лать *pf*, **возде́лывать** *impf* cultivate, till.

воздержа́ние abstinence; abstention. **возде́ржанный** abstemious. **воздержа́ться** (-жу́сь, -жишься) *pf*, **возде́рживаться** *impf* refrain; abstain.

во́здух air. **воздухонепроница́емый** air-tight. **возду́шный** air, aerial; airy; flimsy; **∼ый змей** kite; **∼ый шар** balloon.

воззва́ние appeal. **воззва́ть** (-зову́, -вёшь) *pf* (*impf* **взыва́ть**) appeal (o+*prep* for).

воззре́ние opinion, outlook.

вози́ть (вожу́, во́зишь) *impf* convey; carry; bring; take; **∼ся** romp, play noisily; busy o.s.; potter about.

возлага́ть *impf of* **возложи́ть**

во́зле *adv & prep+gen* by, near; near by; past.

возлага́ть (-жу́, -жи́шь) *pf* (*impf* **возлага́ть**) lay; place.

возлага́ть *impf of* **возложи́ть**

возлю́бленный beloved; *sb* sweetheart.

возме́здие retribution.

возмести́ть (-ещу́) *pf*, **возмеща́ть** *impf* compensate for; refund. **возмеще́ние** compensation; refund.

возмо́жно *adv* possibly; +*comp* as ... as possible. **возмо́жность** possibility; opportunity. **возмо́жный** possible.

возмужа́лый mature; grown up. **возмужа́ть** *pf* grow up; gain strength.

возмути́тельный disgraceful. **возмути́ть** (-ущу́) *pf*, **возмуща́ть** *impf* disturb; stir up; rouse to indignation; ~ся be indignant. **возмуще́ние** indignation. **возмущённый** (-щён, -щена́) indignant.

вознагради́ть (-ажу́) *pf*, **вознагражда́ть** *impf* reward. **вознагражде́ние** reward; fee.

возненави́деть (-и́жу) *pf* conceive a hatred for.

вознесе́ние Ascension. **вознести́** (-несу́, -несёшь; -нёс, -ла́) *pf* (*impf* **возноси́ть**) raise, lift up; ~сь rise; ascend.

возника́ть *impf*, **возни́кнуть** (-нет, -ник) *pf* arise, spring up. **возникнове́ние** rise, beginning, origin.

возни́ца *m* coachman.

возноси́ть(ся (-ошу́(сь, -о́сишь(ся) *impf of* **вознести́(сь. возноше́ние** raising, elevation.

возня́ row, noise; bother.

возобнови́ть (-влю́) *pf*, **возобновля́ть** *impf* renew; restore; ~ся begin again. **возобновле́-**

ние renewal; revival.

возража́ть *impf*, **возрази́ть** (-ажу́) *pf* object. **возраже́ние** objection.

во́зраст age. **возраста́ние** growth, increase. **возраста́ть** *impf*, **возрасти́** (-тёт, -ро́с, -ла́) *pf* grow, increase.

возроди́ть (-ожу́) *pf*, **возрожда́ть** *impf* revive; ~ся revive. **возрожде́ние** revival; Renaissance.

возро́с *etc.*: *see* **возрасти́. возро́сший** increased.

во́зчик carter, carrier.

возьму́ *etc.*: *see* **взять**

во́ин warrior; soldier. **во́инский** military; ~ая повинность conscription. **во́инственный** warlike. **во́инствующий** militant.

вой howl(ing); wail(ing).

войду́ *etc.*: *see* **войти́**

во́йлок felt. **во́йлочный** felt.

война́ (*pl* -ы) war.

во́йско (-а́) army; *pl* troops, forces. **войсково́й** military.

войти́ (-йду́, -йдёшь; вошёл, -шла́) *pf* (*impf* **входи́ть**) go in, come in, enter; get in(to); ~ в систе́му (*comput*) log on.

вокза́л (railway) station.

во́кмен Walkman (*propr*), personal stereo.

вокру́г *adv & prep+gen* round, around.

вол (-а́) ox, bullock.

вола́н flounce; shuttlecock.

волды́рь (-я́) *m* blister; bump.

волево́й strong-willed.

волейбо́л volleyball.

во́лей-нево́лей *adv* willy-nilly.

волк (*pl* -и, -о́в) wolf. **волкода́в** wolf-hound.

волна́ (*pl* -ы, во́лнам) wave. **вол-**

не́ние choppiness; agitation; emotion. **волни́стый** wavy. **волнова́ть** *impf* (*pf* вз~) disturb; agitate; excite; ~ся be disturbed; worry, be nervous. **волноло́м**, **волноре́з** breakwater. **волну́ющий** disturbing; exciting.

волоки́та red tape; rigmarole.

волокни́стый fibrous, stringy. **волокно́** (*pl* -а) fibre.

волоку́ *etc.: see* **воло́чь**

во́лос (*pl* -ы, -о́с, -а́м) *pl* hair. **волоса́тый** hairy. **волосно́й** capillary.

во́лость (*pl* -и, -е́й) volost (*administrative division*).

волочи́ть (-очу́, -о́чишь) *impf* drag; drag, trail; ~ся+instr run after, court. **воло́чь** (-оку́, -о́чешь; -о́к, -ла́) *impf* drag.

во́лчий wolf's; wolfish. **волчи́ха**, **волчи́ца** she-wolf.

волчо́к (-чка́) top; gyroscope.

волчо́нок (-нка; *pl* -ча́та, -ча́т) wolf cub.

волше́бник magician; wizard. **волше́бница** enchantress. **волше́бный** magic, magical; enchanting. **волшебство́** magic, enchantment.

вольнонаёмный civilian. **во́льность** liberty; license. **во́льный** (-лен, -льна́, -о, во́льны́) free; free-style.

вольт[1] (*gen pl* вольт) volt.

вольт[2] (*loc* -у́) vault.

вольфра́м tungsten.

во́ля will; liberty.

вомну́ *etc.: see* **вмять**

вон *adv* out; off, away.

вон *partl* there, there.

вонза́ть *impf*, **вонзи́ть** (-нжу́) *pf* plunge, thrust.

вонь stench. **воню́чий** stinking. **воня́ть** stink.

вообража́емый imaginary. **вообража́ть** *impf*, **вообрази́ть** (-ажу́) *pf* imagine. **воображе́ние** imagination. **вообрази́мый** imaginable.

вообще́ *adv* in general; generally.

воодушеви́ть (-влю́) *pf*, **воодушевля́ть** *impf* inspire. **воодушевле́ние** inspiration; fervour.

вооружа́ть *impf*, **вооружи́ть** (-жу́) *pf* arm, equip; ~ся arm o.s.; take up arms. **вооруже́ние** arming; arms; equipment. **вооружённый** (-жён, -а́) armed; equipped.

воо́чию *adv* with one's own eyes.

во-пе́рвых *adv* first, first of all.

вопи́ть (-плю́) *impf* yell, howl. **вопию́щий** crying; scandalous.

воплоти́ть (-ощу́) *pf*, **воплоща́ть** *impf* embody. **воплоще́ние** embodiment.

вопль *m* cry, wail; howling.

вопреки́ *prep+dat* in spite of.

вопро́с question; problem. **вопроси́тельный** interrogative; questioning; ~ знак question-mark.

вор (*pl* -ы, -о́в) thief; criminal.

ворва́ться (-ву́сь, -вёшься; -а́лся, -ла́сь, -а́ло́сь) *pf* (*impf* **врыва́ться**) burst in.

воркотня́ grumbling.

воробе́й sparrow.

ворова́тый thievish; furtive. **ворова́ть** *impf* (*pf* с~) steal. **воро́вка** woman thief. **воровски́** *adv* furtively. **воровско́й** thieves'. **воровство́** stealing; theft.

во́рон raven. **воро́на** crow.

воро́нка funnel; crater.

вороно́й black.

во́рот[1] collar; neckband.

во́рот[2] winch; windlass.

воро́та (*pl*; *gen* -ро́т) gate(s); gateway; goal.

вороти́ть (-очу́, -о́тишь) *pf* bring back, get back; turn back; ~ся return.

воротни́к (-а́) collar.

во́рох (*pl* -а́) heap, pile; heaps.

воро́чать *impf* turn; move; +*instr* have control of; ~ся move, turn.

вороча́ю(сь *etc.*: *see* вороти́ть(ся

вороши́ть (-шу́) *impf* stir up; turn (over).

ворс nap, pile.

ворча́ть (-чу́) *impf* grumble; growl. **ворчли́вый** peevish; grumpy.

восвоя́си *adv* home.

восемна́дцатый eighteenth. **восемна́дцать** eighteen. **во́семь** (-сьми́, *instr* -семью́ *or* -семью́) eight. **во́семьдесят** (-сьми́десяти, -семью́десятью) eighty. **восемьсо́т** (-сьмисо́т, -ста́ми) eight hundred. **во́семью** *adv* eight times.

воск wax, beeswax.

восклики́нуть (-ну) *pf*, **восклица́ть** *impf* exclaim. **восклица́ние** exclamation. **восклица́тельный** exclamatory; ~ знак exclamation mark.

восково́й wax; waxy; waxed.

воскреса́ть *impf*, **воскре́снуть** (-ну; -ес) *pf* rise from the dead; revive. **воскресе́ние** resurrection. **воскресе́нье** Sunday. **воскреси́ть** (-ешу́) *pf*, **воскреша́ть** *impf* resurrect; revive. **воскреше́ние** resurrection; revival.

воспале́ние inflammation.

воспалённый (-лён, -а́) inflamed. **воспали́ть** *pf*, **воспаля́ть** *impf* inflame; ~ся become inflamed.

воспита́ние upbringing, education. **воспи́танник**, **-ница** pupil. **воспи́танный** well-brought-up. **воспита́тель** *m* tutor; educator. **воспита́тельный** educational. **воспита́ть** *pf*, **воспи́тывать** *impf* bring up; foster; educate.

воспламени́ть *pf*, **воспламеня́ть** *pf* ignite; fire; ~ся ignite; flare up. **воспламеня́емый** inflammable.

вос|**по́льзоваться** *pf*.

воспомина́ние recollection, memory; *pl* memoirs; reminiscences.

вос|**препя́тствовать** *pf*.

воспрети́ть (-ещу́) *pf*, **воспреща́ть** *impf* forbid. **воспреще́ние** prohibition. **воспрещённый** (-щён, -а́) prohibited.

восприи́мчивый impressionable; susceptible. **воспринима́ть** *impf*, **восприня́ть** (-иму́, -и́мешь; -и́нял, -а́, -о) *pf* perceive; grasp. **восприя́тие** perception.

воспроизведе́ние reproduction. **воспроизвести́** (-еду́, -едёшь; -вёл, -а́) *pf*, **воспроизводи́ть** (-ожу́, -о́дишь) *impf* reproduce. **воспроизводи́тельный** reproductive.

вос|**проти́виться** (-влюсь) *pf*.

воссоедине́ние reunification. **воссоедини́ть** *pf*, **воссоединя́ть** *impf* reunite.

восстава́ть (-таю́, -таёшь) *impf of* восста́ть.

восста́ние insurrection, uprising.

восстанови́ть (-влю́, -вишь) *pf*

(*impf* восстана́вливать) restore; reinstate; recall; ~ про́тив+*gen* set against. восстановле́ние restoration.

восста́ть (-а́ну) *pf* (*impf* восстава́ть) rise (up).

восто́к east.

восто́рг delight, rapture. восторга́ться+*instr* be delighted with, go into raptures over. восто́рженный enthusiastic.

восто́чный east, eastern; easterly; oriental.

востре́бование: до востре́бования to be called for, poste restante.

восхвали́ть (-лю́, -лишь) *pf*, восхваля́ть *impf* praise, extol.

восхити́тельный entrancing; delightful. восхити́ть (-хищу́) *pf*, восхища́ть *impf* enrapture; ~ся +*instr* be enraptured by. восхище́ние delight; admiration.

восхо́д rising. восходи́ть (-ожу́, -о́дишь) *impf of* взойти́; ~ к+*dat* go back to, date from. восхожде́ние ascent. восходя́щий rising.

восше́ствие accession.

восьма́я *sb* eighth; octave. восьмёрка eight; figure eight; No. 8; figure of eight.

восьми- *in comb* eight-; octo-; восьмигра́нник octahedron. ~деся́тый eightieth. ~ле́тний eight-year; eight-year-old. ~со́тый eight-hundredth. ~уго́льник octagon. ~уго́льный octagonal.

восьмо́й eighth.

вот *partl* here (is), there (is) this (is); ~ и всё and that's all; ~ как! no! really? ~ та́к! that's right!; ~ что! no! not really?

вот-во́т *adv* just, on the point

of; *partl* that's right!

воткну́ть (-ну́, -нёшь) *pf* (*impf* втыка́ть) stick in, drive in.

вотру́ *etc.*: *see* втере́ть

воцари́ться *pf*, воцаря́ться *impf* come to the throne; set in.

вошёл *etc.*: *see* войти́

вошь (вши; *gen pl* вше́й) louse.

вошью́ *etc.*: *see* вшить

во́ю *etc.*: *see* выть

вою́ю *etc.*: *see* воева́ть

впада́ть *impf*, впасть (-аду́) *pf* flow; lapse; fall in; ~в+*acc* verge on, approximate to. впаде́ние confluence, (river) mouth. впа́дина cavity, hollow; socket. впа́лый sunken.

впервы́е *adv* for the first time.

вперёд *adv* forward(s), ahead; in future; in advance; идти́ ~ (*of clock*) be fast. впереди́ *adv* in front, ahead; in (the) future; *prep*+*gen* in front of, before.

впечатле́ние impression. впечатли́тельный impressionable.

вписа́ть (-ишу́, -и́шешь) *pf*, впи́сывать *impf* enter, insert; ~ся be enrolled, join.

впита́ть *pf*, впи́тывать *impf* absorb, take in; ~ся soak.

впи́хивать *impf*, впихну́ть (-ну́, -нёшь) *pf* cram in; shove.

вплавь *adv* (by) swimming.

вплести́ (-ету́ -етёшь; -ёл, -а́) *pf*, вплета́ть *impf* plait in, intertwine; involve.

вплотну́ю *adv* close; in earnest.

вплоть *adv*; ~ до+*gen* (right) up to.

вполго́лоса *adv* under one's breath.

вполне́ *adv* fully, entirely; quite.

впопыха́х *adv* hastily; in one's haste.

впóру *adv* at the right time; just right, exactly.

впослéдствии *adv* subsequently.

впотьмáх *adv* in the dark.

вправе *adv*: **быть** ~ have a right.

вправо *adv* to the right (**от**+*gen* of).

впредь *adv* in (the) future; ~ **до**+*gen* until.

вприголодь *adv* half starving.

впрочем *conj* however, but; though.

впрыскивание injection. **впрыскивать** *impf*, **впрыснуть** (-ну) *pf* inject.

впрягáть *impf* **впрячь** (-ягý, -яжёшь; -яг, -лá) *pf* harness.

впуск admittance. **впускáть** *impf*, **впустить** (-ущý, -ýстишь) *pf* admit, let in.

впустую *adv* to no purpose, in vain.

впущý *etc.*: *see* **впустить**

враг (-á) enemy. **враждá** enmity. **враждéбный** hostile. **враждовáть** be at enmity. **врáжеский** enemy.

вразбрóд *adv* separately, disunitedly.

вразрéз *adv*: **идти** ~ **с**+*instr* go against.

вразумительный intelligible, clear; persuasive.

врасплóх *adv* unawares.

врастáть *impf*, **врасти** (-тёт; врос, -лá) *pf* grow in; take root.

вратáрь (-я́) *m* goalkeeper.

врать (вру, врёшь; -ал, -á, -о) *impf* (*pf* **на**~, **со**~) lie, tell lies; talk nonsense.

врач (-á) doctor. **врачéбный** medical.

вращáть *impf* rotate, revolve;

~**ся** revolve, rotate. **вращéние** rotation, revolution.

вред (-á) harm; damage. **вредитель** *m* pest; wrecker; *pl* vermin. **вредительство** wrecking, (act of) sabotage. **вредить** (-ежý) *impf* (*pf* **по**~) +*dat* harm; damage. **вредный** (-ден, -днá, -о) harmful.

врéзать (-éжу) *pf*, **врезáть** *impf* cut in; set in; (*sl*) +*dat* hit; ~**ся** cut (into); run (into); be engraved; fall in love.

временáми *adv* at times. **врéменно** *adv* temporarily. **временнóй** temporal. **врéменный** temporary; provisional. **врéмя** (-мени; *pl* -менá, -мён, -áм) *neut* time; tense; ~ **гóда** season; ~ **от врéмени** at times, from time to time; **на** ~ for a time; **скóлько врéмени?** what is the time?; **тем врéменем** meanwhile.

врóвень *adv* level, on a level.

врóде *prep*+*gen* like; *partl* such as, like; apparently.

врождённый (-дён, -á) innate.

врознь, врозь *adv* separately, apart.

врос *etc.*: *see* **врасти**. **врý** *etc.*: *see* **врать**

врун (-á), **врýнья** liar.

вручáть *impf*, **вручить** (-чý) *pf* hand, deliver; entrust.

вручную *adv* by hand.

врывáть(ся *impf of* **ворвáться**

вряд (ли) *adv* it's not likely; hardly, scarcely.

всадить (-ажý, -áдишь) *pf*, **всáживать** *impf* thrust in; sink in. **всáдник** rider, horseman. **всáдница** rider, horsewoman.

всáсывать *impf of* **всосáть**

всё, все *pron*: *see* **весь**. **всё** *adv* always, all the time; ~ **(ещё)** still; *conj* however, nevertheless;

~ же all the same.

все- in comb all-, omni-. **все-возмо́жный** of every kind; all possible. **~дозво́ленность** permissiveness. **~ме́рный** of every kind. **~ми́рный** world, world-wide; Всеми́рная паути́на the (world-wide) Web; **~мо́гущий** omnipotent. **~наро́дно** adv publicly. **~наро́дный** national; nation-wide. **~объе́млющий** comprehensive, all-embracing. **~росси́йский** All-Russian. **~си́льный** omnipotent. **~сторо́нний** all-round; comprehensive.

всегда́ always.

всего́ adv in all, all told; only.

вселе́нная sb universe.

всели́ть pf, **вселя́ть** impf install, lodge; inspire; **~ся** move in, install o.s.; be implanted.

всено́щная sb night service.

всео́бщий general, universal.

всерьёз adv seriously, in earnest.

всё-таки conj & partl all the same, still. **всеце́ло** adv completely.

вска́кивать impf of вскочи́ть

вскачь adv at a gallop.

вскипа́ть impf, **вс|кипе́ть** (-плю́) pf boil up; flare up.

вс|кипяти́ть(ся (-ячу́(сь) pf

всколыхну́ть (-ну́, -нёшь) pf stir; stir up.

вско́льзь adv slightly; in passing.

вско́ре adv soon, shortly after.

вскочи́ть (-очу́, -о́чишь) pf (impf вска́кивать) jump up.

вскри́кивать impf, **вскри́кнуть** (-ну) pf shriek, scream.

вскрича́ть (-чу́) pf exclaim.

вскрыва́ть impf, **вскрыть**

(-ро́ю) pf open; reveal; dissect. **вскры́тие** opening; revelation; post-mortem.

вслед adv & prep+dat after; ~ за+instr after, following. **всле́дствие** prep+gen in consequence of.

вслепу́ю adv blindly; blind-fold.

вслух adv aloud.

вслу́шаться pf, **вслу́шиваться** impf listen attentively.

всма́триваться impf, **всмотре́ться** (-рю́сь, -ришься) pf look closely.

всмя́тку adv soft(-boiled).

всо́вывать impf of всу́нуть

всоса́ть (-су́, -сёшь) pf (impf вса́сывать) suck in; absorb; imbibe.

вс|паха́ть (-ашу́, -а́шешь) pf, **вспа́хивать** impf plough up. **вспа́шка** ploughing.

вс|пе́ниться pf

всплеск splash. **всплёскивать** impf, **всплесну́ть** (-ну́, -нёшь) pf splash; ~ рука́ми throw up one's hands.

всплыва́ть impf, **всплыть** (-ыву́, -ывёшь; -ы́л, -а́, -о) pf rise to the surface; come to light.

вспомина́ть impf, **вспо́мнить** pf remember; **~ся** impers +dat: мне вспо́мнилось I remembered.

вспомога́тельный auxiliary.

вс|поте́ть pf

вспры́гивать impf, **вспры́гнуть** (-ну) pf jump up.

вспуха́ть impf, **вс|пу́хнуть** (-нет; -ух) pf swell up.

вспыли́ть pf flare up. **вспы́льчивый** hot-tempered.

вспы́хивать impf, **вспыхну́ть** (-ну) pf blaze up; flare up.

вспышка flash; outburst; outbreak.

вставать (-таю́, -таёшь) *impf of* встать

вста́вить (-влю) *pf*, **вставля́ть** *impf* put in, insert. **вста́вка** insertion; framing, inset. **вставно́й** inserted; set in; ~ы́е зу́бы false teeth.

встать (-а́ну) *pf* (*impf* встава́ть) get up; stand up.

встрево́женный *adj* anxious. **встрево́жить(ся** (-жу) *pf*.

встрепену́ться (-ну́сь, -нёшься) *pf* rouse o.s.; start (up); beat faster.

встре́тить (-е́чу) *pf*, **встреча́ть** *impf* meet (with); ~ся *vi* meet; be found. **встре́ча** meeting. **встре́чный** coming to meet; contrary, head; counter; *sb* person met with; **пе́рвый** ~ the first person you meet, anybody.

встря́ска shaking; shock. **встря́хивать** *impf*, **встряхну́ть** (-ну́, -нёшь) *pf* shake (up); rouse; ~ся shake o.s.; rouse o.s.

вступа́ть *impf*, **вступи́ть** (-плю́, -пишь) *pf* +в+*acc* enter (into); join (in); +на+*acc* go up, mount; ~ся intervene; +за+*acc* stand up for. **вступи́тельный** introductory; entrance. **вступле́ние** entry, joining; introduction.

всу́нуть (-ну) *pf* (*impf* всо́вывать) put in, stick in.

всхли́пнуть (-ну) *pf*, **всхли́пывать** *impf* sob.

всходи́ть (-ожу́, -о́дишь) *impf of* взойти́. **всхо́ды** *pl*; *gen* -ов (corn-)shoots.

всю: *see* весь

всю́ду *adv* everywhere.

вся: *see* весь

вся́к|ий any; every, all kinds of;

~ом слу́чае in any case; **на** ~ий слу́чай just in case; *pron* anyone. **вся́чески** *adv* in every possible way.

вта́йне *adv* secretly.

вта́лкивать *impf of* втолкну́ть. **вта́птывать** *impf of* втопта́ть. **вта́скивать** *impf*, **вта́щить** (-щу́, -щишь) *pf* drag in.

втере́ть (вотру́, вотрёшь; втёр) *pf* (*impf* втира́ть) rub in; ~ся insinuate o.s., worm in.

втира́ть(ся *impf of* втере́ть(ся

вти́скивать *impf*, **вти́снуть** (-ну) *pf* squeeze in; ~ся squeeze (o.s.) in.

втихомо́лку *adv* surreptitiously.

втолкну́ть (-ну́, -нёшь) *pf* (*impf* вта́лкивать) push in.

втопта́ть (-пчу́, -пчешь) *pf* (*impf* вта́птывать) trample (in).

вторга́ться *impf*, **вто́ргнуться** (-нусь; вто́ргся, -лась) *pf* invade; intrude. **вторже́ние** invasion; intrusion.

втори́ть *impf* play or sing second part; +*dat* repeat, echo. **втори́чный** second, secondary. **вто́рник** Tuesday. **второ́й** second; ~о́е *sb* second course. **второстепе́нный** secondary, minor.

второпя́х *adv* in haste.

в-тре́тьих *adv* thirdly. **втро́е** *adv* three times. **втроём** *adv* three (together). **втро́йне** *adv* three times as much.

вту́лка plug.

втыка́ть *impf of* воткну́ть.

втя́гивать *impf*, **втяну́ть** (-ну́, -нешь) *pf* draw in; ~ся +в+*acc* enter; get used to.

вуа́ль veil.

вуз *abbr* (*of* вы́сшее уче́бное заведе́ние) higher educational es-

tablishment; college.

вулка́н volcano.

вульга́рный vulgar.

вундерки́нд infant prodigy.

вход entrance; entry. **входи́ть** (-ожу́, -о́дишь) *impf of* **войти́**. **входно́й** entrance.

вхолосту́ю *adv* idle, free.

вцепи́ться (-плюсь, -пишься) *pf*, **вцепля́ться** *impf* +в+*acc* clutch, catch hold of.

вчера́ *adv* yesterday. **вчера́шний** yesterday's.

вчерне́ in rough.

вче́тверо *adv* four times. **вчетверо́м** *adv* four (together).

вши *etc.: see* **вошь**

вшива́ть *impf of* **вшить**

вши́вый lousy.

вширь *adv* in breadth; widely.

вшить (вошью́, -ёшь) *pf* (*impf* **вшива́ть**) sew in.

въе́дливый corrosive; caustic.

въезд entry; entrance. **въезжа́ть** *impf*, **въе́хать** (-е́ду, -е́дешь) *pf* (+в+*acc*) ride in(to); drive in(to); crash into.

вы (вас, вам, ва́ми, вас) *pron* you.

выбега́ть *impf*, **вы́бежать** (-егу, -ежишь) *pf* run out.

вы|белить *pf*.

вы́беру *etc.: see* **вы́брать**. **выбива́ть(ся** *impf of* **вы́бить(ся**. **выбира́ть(ся** *impf of* **вы́брать(ся**

вы́бить (-бью) *pf* (*impf* **выбива́ть**) knock out; dislodge; ∼**ся** break loose; come out; ∼**ся** из сил exhaust o.s.

вы́бор choice; selection; *pl* election(s). **вы́борный** elective; electoral. **вы́борочный** selective.

вы|бранить *pf*. **выбра́сы-**

вать(ся *impf of* **вы́бросить(ся**

вы́брать (-беру) *pf* (*impf* **выбира́ть**) choose; elect; take out. ∼**ся** get out.

выбрива́ть *impf*, **вы́брить** (-рею) *pf* shave.

вы́бросить (-ошу) *pf* (*impf* **выбра́сывать**) throw out; throw away; ∼**ся** throw o.s. out, leap out.

выбыва́ть *impf*, **вы́быть** (-буду) *pf* из+*gen* leave, quit.

выва́ливать *impf*, **вы́валить** *pf* throw out; pour out; ∼**ся** tumble out.

вы́везти (-зу; -ез) *pf* (*impf* **вывози́ть**) take, bring, out; export; rescue.

вы́верить *pf* (*impf* **выверя́ть**) adjust, regulate.

вы́вернуть (-ну) *pf*, **вывёртывать** *impf* turn inside out; unscrew; wrench.

выверя́ть *impf of* **вы́верить**

вы́весить (-ешу) *pf* (*impf* **выве́шивать**) weigh; hang out. **вы́веска** sign; pretext.

вы́вести (-еду; -ел) *pf* (*impf* **выводи́ть**) lead, bring, take, out; drive out; remove; exterminate; deduce; hatch; grow, breed; erect; depict; draw; ∼**сь** go out of use; become extinct; come out; hatch out.

выве́тривание airing.

выве́шивать *impf of* **вы́весить**

вы́вих dislocation. **вывихивать** *impf*, **вы́вихнуть** (-ну) *pf* dislocate.

вы́вод conclusion; withdrawal. **выводи́ть(ся** (-ожу́(сь, -о́дишь(ся) *impf of* **вы́вести(сь**. **вы́водок** (-дка) brood; litter.

вывожу́ *see* **выводи́ть**, **вывози́ть**

вывоз export; removal. **вывозить** (-ожу, -озишь) *impf of* **вывезти. вывозной** export.

выгадать *pf,* **выгадывать** *impf* gain, save.

выгиб curve. **выгибать** *impf of* **выгнуть**

выгладить (-ажу) *pf.*

выглядеть (-яжу) *impf* look, look like. **выглядывать** *impf,* **выглянуть** (-ну) *pf* look out; peep out.

выгнать (-гоню) *pf (impf* **выгонять)** drive out; distil.

выгнутый curved, convex. **выгнуть** (-ну) *pf (impf* **выгибать)** bend, arch.

выговаривать *impf,* **выговорить** *pf* pronounce, speak; +*dat* reprimand; **~ся** speak out. **выговор** pronunciation; reprimand.

выгода advantage; gain. **выгодный** advantageous; profitable.

выгон pasture; common. **выгонять** *impf of* **выгнать**

выгорать *impf,* **выгореть** (-рит) *pf* burn down; fade.

выгравировать *pf.*

выгружать *impf,* **выгрузить** (-ужу) *pf* unload; disembark. **выгрузка** unloading; disembarkation.

выдавать (-даю, -даёшь) *impf,* **выдать** (-ам, -ашь, -аст, -адим) *pf* give (out), issue; betray; extradite; +**за**+*acc* pass off as; **~ся** protrude; stand out; present itself. **выдача** issue; payment; extradition. **выдающийся** prominent.

выдвигать *impf,* **выдвинуть** (-ну) *pf* move out; pull out; put forward, nominate; **~ся** move forward, move out; come out;

get on (in the world). **выдвижение** nomination; promotion.

выделение secretion; excretion; isolation; apportionment. **выделить** *pf,* **выделять** *impf* pick out; detach; allot; secrete; excrete; isolate; **~ курсивом** italicize; **~ся** stand out, be noted (+*instr* for).

выдёргивать *impf of* **выдернуть**

выдержанный consistent; self-possessed; firm; matured, seasoned. **выдержать** (-жу) *pf,* **выдерживать** *impf* bear; endure; contain o.s.; pass (*exam*); sustain. **выдержка**[1] endurance; self-possession; exposure.

выдержка[2] excerpt.

выдернуть *pf (impf* **выдёргивать)** pull out.

выдохнуть (-ну) *pf (impf* **выдыхать)** breathe out; **~ся** have lost fragrance or smell; be past one's best.

выдра otter.

выдрать (-деру) *pf.* **выдрессировать** *pf.*

выдувать *impf of* **выдуть**

выдуманный made-up, fabricated. **выдумать** *pf,* **выдумывать** *impf* invent; fabricate. **выдумка** invention; device; inventiveness.

выдуть *pf (impf* **выдувать)** blow; blow out.

выдыхание exhalation. **выдыхать(ся** *impf of* **выдохнуть(ся**

выезд departure; exit. **выездной** exit; **~ая сессия суда** assizes. **выезжать** *impf of* **выехать**

выемка taking out; excavation; hollow.

выехать (-еду) *pf (impf* **выезжать)**

жа́ть) go out, depart; drive out, ride out; move (house).

вы́жать (-жму, -жмешь) *pf* (*impf* **выжима́ть**) squeeze out; wring out.

вы́жечь (-жгу) *pf* (*impf* **выжига́ть**) burn out; cauterize.

выжива́ние survival. **выжива́ть** *impf of* **вы́жить**

выжига́ть *impf of* **вы́жечь**

выжида́тельный waiting; temporizing.

выжима́ть *impf of* **вы́жать**

вы́жить (-иву) *pf* (*impf* **выжива́ть**) survive; hound out; ~ из ума́ become senile.

вы́звать (-зову) *pf* (*impf* **вызыва́ть**) call (out); send for; challenge; provoke; ~ся volunteer.

выздора́вливать *impf*, **вы́здороветь** (-ею) *pf* recover. **выздоровле́ние** recovery; convalescence.

вы́зов call; summons; challenge.

вы́золоченный gilt.

вызу́бривать *impf*, **вы́зубрить** *pf* learn by heart.

вызыва́ть(ся *impf of* **вы́звать(ся. вызыва́ющий** defiant; provocative.

вы́играть *pf*, **выи́грывать** *impf* win; gain. **вы́игрыш** win; gain; prize. **вы́игрышный** winning; advantageous.

вы́йти (-йду; -шел, -шла) *pf* (*impf* **выходи́ть**) go out; come out; get out; appear; turn out; be used up; have expired; ~ в свет appear; ~ за́муж (за+*acc*) marry; ~ из себя́ lose one's temper; ~ из систе́му (*comput*) log off.

выка́лывать *impf of* **вы́колоть. выка́пывать** *impf of* **вы́копать**

выка́рмливать *impf of* **вы́кормить**

вы́качать *pf*, **выка́чивать** *impf* pump out.

выки́дывать *impf*, **вы́кинуть** *pf* throw out, reject; put out; miscarry, abort; ~ флаг hoist a flag. **вы́кидыш** miscarriage, abortion.

вы́кладка laying out; lay-out; facing; kit; computation, calculation. **выкла́дывать** *impf of* **вы́ложить**

выключа́тель *m* switch. **выключа́ть** *impf*, **вы́ключить** (-чу) *pf* turn off, switch off; remove, exclude.

выкола́чивать *impf*, **вы́колотить** (-лочу) *pf* knock out, beat out; beat; extort, wring out. **вы́колоть** (-лю) *pf* (*impf* **выка́лывать**) put out; gouge out; tattoo.

вы́копать *pf* (*impf also* **выка́пывать**) dig; dig up, dig out; exhume; unearth.

вы́кормить (-млю) *pf* (*impf* **выка́рмливать**) rear, bring up.

вы́корчевать (-чую) *pf*, **выкорчёвывать** *impf* uproot, root out; eradicate.

выкра́ивать *impf of* **вы́кроить**

вы́красить (-ашу) *pf*, **выкра́шивать** *impf* paint; dye.

выкри́кивать *impf*, **вы́крикнуть** (-ну) *pf* cry out; yell.

вы́кроить *pf* (*impf* **выкра́ивать**) cut out; find (*time etc.*). **вы́кройка** pattern.

вы́крутить (-учу) *pf*, **выкру́чивать** *impf* unscrew; twist; ~ся extricate o.s.

вы́куп ransom; redemption. **вы́купать¹(ся** *pf.* **выкупа́ть²** *impf*, **вы́купить**

(-плю) *pf* ransom, redeem.

вы́лазка sally, sortie; excursion.

вылама́ывать *impf of* **вы́ломать**

вылеза́ть *impf,* **вы́лезти** (-зу; -лез) *pf* climb out; come out.

вы́лепить (-плю) *pf*

вы́лет flight; take-off. **вылета́ть** *impf,* **вы́лететь** (-ечу) *pf* fly out; take off.

выле́чивать *impf,* **вы́лечить** (-чу) *pf* cure; **~ся** recover, be cured.

выпива́ть(ся *pf of* **вы́лить(ся**

вы́|линять *pf*

вы́лить (-лью) *pf* (*impf* **вылива́ть**) pour out; cast, found; **~ся** flow (out); be expressed.

вы́ложить (-жу) *pf* (*impf* **выкла́дывать**) lay out.

вы́ломать *pf,* **вы́ломить** (-млю) *pf* (*impf* **выла́мывать**) break open.

вы́лупиться (-плюсь) *pf,* **вылупля́ться** *impf* hatch (out).

вы́лью *etc.: see* **вы́лить**

вы́|мазать (-мажу) *pf,* **вима́зывать** *impf* smear, dirty.

выма́ивать *impf,* **вы́манить** *pf* entice, lure.

вы́мереть (-мрет; -мер) *pf* (*impf* **вымира́ть**) die out; become extinct. **вы́мерший** extinct.

вы́мести (-ету) *pf,* **вымета́ть** *impf* sweep (out).

вымога́тельство blackmail, extortion. **вымога́ть** *impf* extort.

вымока́ть *impf,* **вы́мокнуть** (-ну; -ок) *pf* be drenched; soak; rot.

вы́молвить (-влю) *pf* say, utter.

вы́|мостить (-ощу) *pf.* **вы́мою**

etc.: see **вы́мыть**

вы́мпел pennant.

вы́мреть *see* **вы́мереть. вымыва́ть** (-аю) *pf of* **вы́мыть(ся**

вы́мысел (-сла) invention, fabrication; fantasy.

вы́мыть (-мою) *pf* (*impf also* **вымыва́ть**) wash; wash out, off; wash away; **~ся** wash o.s.

вы́мышленный fictitious.

вы́мя (-мени) *neut* udder.

вына́шивать *impf of* **вы́носить²**

вы́нести (-су; -нес) *pf* (*impf* **выноси́ть¹**) carry out, take out; carry away; endure.

вынима́ть *impf of* **вы́нуть**

вы́нос carrying out. **выноси́ть¹** (-ошу, -о́сишь) *impf of* **вы́нести**. **вы́носить²** *pf* (*impf* **вына́шивать**) bear; nurture. **вы́носка** carrying out; removal; footnote. **вы́носливость** endurance; hardiness.

вы́нудить (-ужу) *pf,* **вынужда́ть** *impf* force, compel. **вы́нужденный** forced.

вы́нуть (-ну) *pf* (*impf* **вынима́ть**) take out.

вы́пад attack; lunge. **выпада́ть** *impf of* **вы́пасть**

выпа́лывать *impf,* **вы́полоть**

выпа́ривать *impf,* **вы́парить** evaporate; steam.

выпа́рывать *impf of* **вы́пороть²**

вы́пасть (-аду; -ал) *pf* (*impf* **выпада́ть**) fall out; fall; occur, turn out; lunge.

выпека́ть *impf,* **вы́печь** (-еку; -ек) *pf* bake.

выпива́ть *impf of* **вы́пить**; enjoy a drink. **вы́пивка** drinking bout; drinks.

выпи́ливать *impf*, **вы́пилить** *pf* saw, cut out.

вы́писать (-ишу) *pf*, **выпи́сывать** *impf* copy out; write out; order; subscribe to; send for; discharge, release; **~ся** be discharged; check out. **вы́писка** writing out; extract; ordering, subscription; discharge.

вы́пить (-пью) *pf* (*impf also* **выпива́ть**) drink; drink up.

вы́плавить (-влю) *pf*, **выпла́вля́ть** *impf* smelt. **вы́плавка** smelting; smelted metal.

вы́плата payment. **вы́платить** (-ачу) *pf*, **выпла́чивать** *impf* pay (out); pay off.

выплёвывать *impf of* **вы́плюнуть**

выплыва́ть *impf*, **вы́плыть** (-ыву) *pf* swim out, sail out; emerge; crop up.

вы́плюнуть (-ну) *pf* (*impf* **выплёвывать**) spit out.

выполза́ть *impf*, **вы́ползти** (-зу; -олз) *pf* crawl out.

выполне́ние execution, carrying out; fulfilment. **вы́полнить** *pf*, **выполня́ть** *impf* execute, carry out; fulfil.

вы́полоскать (-ощу) *pf*

вы́полоть (-лю) *pf* (*impf also* **выпа́лывать**) weed out; weed.

вы́пороть[2] (-рю) *pf* (*impf* **выпа́рывать**) rip out, rip up.

вы́потрошить (-шу) *pf*

вы́правка bearing; correction. **выпра́шивать** *impf of* **вы́просить**; solicit.

выпрова́живать *impf*, **вы́проводить** (-ожу) *pf* send packing.

вы́просить (-ошу) *pf*, **выпра́шивать** *impf* (ask for and) get.

выпряга́ть *impf of* **вы́прячь**

вы́прямить (-млю) *pf*, **выпрямля́ть** *impf* straighten (out); rectify; **~ся** become straight; draw o.s. up.

вы́прячь (-ягу; -яг) *pf* (*impf* **выпряга́ть**) unharness.

вы́пуклый protuberant; bulging; convex.

вы́пуск output; issue; discharge; part, instalment; final-year students; omission. **выпуска́ть** *impf*, **вы́пустить** (-ущу) *pf* let out; issue; produce; omit. **выпускни́к** (-а́), **-и́ца** final-year student. **выпускно́й** discharge; exhaust; final-year. **~о́й экза́мен** finals, final examination.

вы́путать *pf*, **выпу́тывать** *impf* disentangle; **~ся** extricate o.s.

вы́пью *etc.*: *see* **вы́пить**

выраба́тывать *impf*, **вы́работать** *pf* work out; work up; draw up; produce; make; earn. **вы́работка** manufacture; production; working out; drawing up; output; make.

выра́внивать(ся *impf of* **вы́ровнять(ся**

выража́ть *impf*, **вы́разить** (-ажу) *pf* express; **~ся** express o.s. **выраже́ние** expression. **вырази́тельный** expressive.

выраста́ть *impf*, **вы́расти** (-ту; -рос) *pf* grow, grow up. **вы́растить** (-ащу) *pf*, **выра́щивать** *impf* bring up; breed; cultivate.

вы́рвать[1] *pf* (*impf* **вырыва́ть**[2]) pull out, tear out; extort; **~ся** break loose, break free; escape; shoot.

вы́рвать[2] (-ву) *pf*.

вы́рез cut; décolletage. **вы́резать** (-ежу) *pf*, **выреза́ть** *impf*, **вырезы́вать** *impf* cut (out); engrave. **вы́резка** cutting out, ex-

cision; cutting; fillet.

вы́ровнять pf (impf **выра́внивать**) level; straighten (out); draw up; ~ся become level; equalize; catch up.

вы́родиться pf, **вырожда́ться** impf degenerate. **вы́родок** (-дка) degenerate; black sheep. **вырожде́ние** degeneration.

вы́ронить pf drop.

вы́рос etc.: see **вы́расти**

вы́рою etc.: see **вы́рыть**

выруба́ть impf, **вы́рубить** (-блю) pf cut down; cut (out); carve (out). **вы́рубка** cutting down; hewing out.

вы́ругать(ся pf.

выру́ливать impf, **вы́рулить** pf taxi.

выруча́ть impf, **вы́ручить** (-чу) pf rescue; help out; gain; make. **вы́ручка** rescue; gain; proceeds; earnings.

вырыва́ть[1] impf, **вы́рыть** (-рою) pf dig up, unearth.

вырыва́ть[2](**ся** impf of **вы́рвать(ся**

вы́садить (-ажу) pf, **выса́живать** impf set down; put ashore; transplant; smash; ~ся alight; disembark. **вы́садка** disembarkation; landing; transplanting.

выса́сывать impf of **вы́сосать**

вы́свободить (-божу) pf, **высвобожда́ть** impf free; release.

высека́ть impf of **вы́сечь**[2]

выселе́ние eviction. **вы́селить** pf, **выселя́ть** impf evict; evacuate, move; ~ся move, remove.

вы́сечь[1] (-еку; -сек) pf. **вы́сечь**[2] (-еку; -сек) (impf **высека́ть**) cut down; carve.

вы́сидеть (-ижу) pf, **выси́живать** impf sit out; stay; hatch.

вы́ситься impf rise, tower.

выска́бливать impf of **вы́скоблить**

вы́сказать (-кажу) pf, **выска́зывать** impf express; state; ~ся speak out. **выска́зывание** utterance; pronouncement.

выска́кивать impf of **вы́скочить**

вы́скоблить pf (impf **выска́бливать**) scrape out; erase; remove.

вы́скочить (-чу) pf (impf **выска́кивать**) jump out; spring out; ~ c+instr come out with. **вы́скочка** upstart.

вы́слать (вы́шлю) pf (impf **высыла́ть**) send (out); exile; deport.

вы́следить (-ежу) pf, **высле́живать** impf trace; shadow.

выслу́живать impf, **вы́служить** (-жу) pf qualify for; serve (out); ~ся gain promotion; curry favour.

вы́слушать pf, **выслу́шивать** impf hear out; sound; listen to.

высме́ивать impf, **вы́смеять** (-ею) pf ridicule.

вы́|сморкать(ся pf. **высо́вывать(ся** impf of **вы́сунуть(ся**

высо́кий (-о́к, -а́, -о́ко) high; tall; lofty; elevated.

высоко- in comb high-, highly. **высокоблагоро́дие** (your) Honour, Worship. ~**во́льтный** high-tension. ~**го́рный** mountain. ~**ка́чественный** high-quality. ~**квалифици́рованный** highly qualified. ~**ме́рие** haughtiness. ~**ме́рный** haughty. ~**па́рный** high-flown; bombastic. ~**часто́тный** high-frequency.

вы́сосать (-осу) pf (impf **выса́сывать**) suck out.

высота́ (*pl* -ы) height, altitude. высо́тный high-altitude; highrise.

вы́сохнуть (-ну; -ох) *pf* (*impf also* высыха́ть) dry (out); dry up; wither (away).

вы́спаться (-плюсь, -пишься) *pf* (*impf* высыпа́ться²) have a good sleep.

вы́ставить (-влю) *pf*, выставля́ть *impf* display, exhibit; post; put forward; set down; take out; +*instr* represent as; ~ся show off. вы́ставка exhibition.

выста́ивать *impf of* вы́стоять.

вы|стегать *pf*. вы|стирать *pf*.

вы́стоять (-ою) *pf* (*impf* вы́ста́ивать) stand; stand one's ground.

вы́страдать *pf* suffer; gain through suffering.

выстра́ивать(ся *impf of* вы́строить(ся

вы́стрел shot; report. вы́стрелить *pf* shoot, fire.

вы|строгать *pf*.

вы́строить *pf* (*impf* выстра́ивать) build; draw up, order, arrange; form up. ~ся form up.

вы́ступ protuberance, projection. выступа́ть *impf*, вы́ступить (-плю) *pf* come forward; come out; perform; speak; +из+*gen* go beyond. выступле́ние appearance, performance; speech; setting out.

вы́сунуть (-ну) *pf* (*impf* высо́вывать) put out, thrust out; ~ся show o.s., thrust o.s. forward.

вы́сушить(ся (-шу(сь) *pf*.

вы́сший highest; high; higher.

высыла́ть *impf of* вы́слать. вы́сылка sending, dispatch; expulsion, exile.

вы́сыпать (-плю) *pf*, высыпа́ть *impf* pour out; spill; ~ся¹ pour out; spill.

высыпа́ться² *impf of* вы́спаться

высыха́ть *impf of* вы́сохнуть

высь height; summit.

выта́лкивать *impf of* вы́толкать, вы́толкнуть. выта́скивать *impf of* вы́тащить. выта́чивать *impf of* вы́точить

вы́тащить (-щу) *pf* (*impf also* выта́скивать) drag out; pull out.

вы|твердить (-ржу) *pf*.

вытека́ть *impf* (*pf* вы́течь); ~ из+*gen* flow from, out of; result from.

вы́тереть (-тру, -тер) *pf* (*impf* вытира́ть) wipe (up); dry; wear out.

вы́терпеть (-плю) *pf* endure.

вы́тертый threadbare.

вытесня́ть, вы́теснять *impf* force out; oust; displace.

вы́течь (-чет; -ек) *pf* (*impf* вытека́ть) flow out, run out.

вытира́ть *impf of* вы́тереть

вы́толкать *pf*, вы́толкнуть (-ну) *pf* (*impf* выта́лкивать) throw out; push out.

вы́точенный turned. вы́точить (-чу) *pf* (*impf also* выта́чивать) turn; sharpen; gnaw through.

вы́травить (-влю) *pf*, вытра́вливать, вытравля́ть *impf* exterminate, destroy; remove; etch; trample down, damage.

вытрезви́тель *m* detoxification centre. вытрезви́ть(ся (-влю(сь) *pf*, вытрезвля́ть(ся *impf* sober up.

вы́тру *etc.: see* вы́тереть

вы́|трясти (-су; -яс) *pf* shake out.

вытря́хивать *impf*, **вы́тряхнуть** (-ну) *pf* shake out.

выть (вою) *impf* howl; wail.

выта́гивать *impf*, **вы́тянуть** (-ну) *pf* stretch (out); extend; extract; endure; ~ся stretch, stretch out, stretch o.s.; stretch up; draw o. s. up. **вы́тяжка** drawing out, extraction; extract.

вы́|утюжить (-жу) *pf*.

выу́чивать *impf*, **вы́учить** (-чу) *pf* learn; teach; ~ся +*dat or inf* learn.

выха́живать *impf of* вы́ходить[2]

вы́хватить (-ачу) *pf*, **выхва́тывать** *impf* snatch out, up, away; pull out.

вы́хлоп exhaust. **выхлопно́й** exhaust, discharge.

вы́ход going out; departure; way out, exit; vent; appearance; yield; ~ за́муж marriage. **вы́ходец** (-дца) emigrant; immigrant.

выходи́ть[1] (-ожу, -о́дишь) *impf of* вы́йти; ~ на+*acc* look out on.

вы́ходить[2] (-ожу) *pf* (*impf* выха́живать) nurse; rear, bring up.

вы́ходка trick; prank.

выходно́й exit; going-out, outgoing; discharge; ~о́й день day off; ~о́й *sb* person off duty; day off. **выхожу́** *etc.: see* выходи́ть[1]. **вы́хожу** *etc.: see* вы́ходить[2]

вы́цвести (-ветет) *pf*, **выцвета́ть** *impf* fade. **вы́цветший** faded.

вычёркивать *impf*, **вы́черкнуть** (-ну) *pf* cross out.

вы́черпать *pf*, **выче́рпывать** *impf* bale out.

вы́честь (-чту, -чел, -чла) *pf* (*impf* **вычита́ть**) subtract. **вы́чет** deduction.

вычисле́ние calculation. **вычисли́тель** *m* calculator. **вычисли́тельный** calculating, computing; ~ая маши́на computer; ~ая те́хника computers; **вы́числить** *pf*, **вычисля́ть** *impf* calculate, compute.

вы́чистить (-ищу) *pf* (*impf also* вычища́ть) clean, clean up.

вычита́ние subtraction. **вычита́ть** *impf of* вы́честь

вычища́ть *impf of* вы́чистить. **вы́чту** *etc.: see* вы́честь

вы́швырнуть (-ну) *pf*, **вышвы́ривать** *impf* chuck out.

вы́ше higher, taller; *prep*+*gen* beyond; over; *adv* above.

вы́ше- *in comb* above-, afore-. **вышеизло́женный** foregoing. **~на́званный** afore-named. **~ска́занный**, **~ука́занный** aforesaid. **~упомя́нутый** afore-mentioned.

вы́шел *etc.: see* вы́йти

вышиба́ла *m* chucker-out. **вышиба́ть** *impf*, **вы́шибить** (-бу; -иб) *pf* knock out; chuck out.

вышива́ние embroidery, needlework. **вышива́ть** *impf of* вы́шить. **вы́шивка** embroidery.

вышина́ height.

вы́шить (-шью) *pf* (*impf* вышива́ть) embroider. **вы́шитый** embroidered.

вы́шка tower; (бурова́я) ~ derrick.

вы́шлю *etc.: see* вы́слать. **вы́шью** *etc.: see* вы́шить

вы́явить (-влю) *pf*, **выявля́ть** *impf* reveal; make known; expose; ~ся come to light, be revealed.

выясне́ние elucidation; ex-

planation. **вы́яснить** *pf*, **выясня́ть** *impf* elucidate; explain; **~ся** become clear; turn out.

Вьетна́м Vietnam. **вьетна́мец, -мка** Vietnamese. **вьетна́мский** Vietnamese.

вью *etc.: see* вить

вью́га snow-storm, blizzard.

вьюно́к (-нка́) bindweed.

вью́чный pack; **~ое живо́тное** beast of burden.

вью́щийся climbing; curly.

вяжу́ *etc.: see* вяза́ть. **вя́жущий** binding; astringent.

вяз elm.

вяза́ние knitting, crocheting; binding, tying. **вя́занка¹** knitted garment. **вяза́нка²** bundle. **вя́заный** knitted, crocheted. **вяза́нье** knitting; crochet(-work). **вяза́ть** (вяжу́, вя́жешь) *impf* (*pf* с**~**) tie, bind; knit, crochet; be astringent; **~ся** accord; tally. **вя́зка** tying; knitting, crocheting; bunch.

вя́зкий (-зок, -зка́, -о) viscous; sticky; boggy. **вя́знуть** (-ну; вяз(-нул), -зла) *impf* (*pf* за**~**, у**~**) stick, get stuck.

вя́зовый elm.

вязь ligature; arabesque.

вя́леный dried; sun-cured.

вя́лый limp; sluggish; slack. **вя́нуть** (-ну; вял) *impf* (*pf* за**~**, у**~**) fade, wither; flag.

Г

г. *abbr* (*of* год) year; (*of* го́род) city; (*of* господи́н) Mr.

г *abbr* (*of* грамм) gram.

га *abbr* (*of* гекта́р) hectare.

га́вань harbour.

гага́чий пух eiderdown.

гад reptile; repulsive person; *pl* vermin.

гада́лка fortune-teller. **гада́ние** fortune-telling; guess-work. **гада́ть** *impf* (*pf* по**~**) tell fortunes; guess.

га́дина reptile; repulsive person; *pl* vermin. **га́дить** (га́жу) *impf* (*pf* на**~**) +в+*prep*, на+*acc*, *prep* foul, dirty, defile. **га́дкий** (-док, -дка́, -о) nasty, vile repulsive. **га́дость** filth, muck; dirty trick; *pl* filthy expressions. **гадю́ка** adder, viper; repulsive person.

га́ечный ключ spanner, wrench.

газ¹ gauze.

газ² gas; wind; **дать ~** step on the gas; **сба́вить ~** reduce speed.

газе́та newspaper. **газе́тчик** journalist; newspaper-seller.

газиро́ванный aerated. **га́зовый** gas.

газо́н lawn. **газонокоси́лка** lawn-mower.

газопрово́д gas pipeline; gas-main.

га́йка nut; female screw.

гала́ктика galaxy.

галантере́йный магази́н haberdasher's. **галантере́я** haberdashery. **гала́нтный** gallant.

галере́я gallery. **галёрка** gallery, gods.

галифе́ *indecl pl* riding-breeches.

га́лка jackdaw.

галлюцина́ция hallucination.

гало́п gallop.

га́лочка tick.

га́лстук tie; neckerchief.

галу́шка dumpling.

га́лька pebble; pebbles, shingle.

гам din, uproar.

гама́к (-á) hammock.

га́мма scale; gamut; range.

гангре́на gangrene.

га́нгстер gangster.

ганте́ль f dumb-bell.

гара́ж (-á) garage.

гаранти́ровать impf & pf guarantee. **гара́нтия** guarantee.

гардеро́б wardrobe; cloakroom. **гардеро́бщик, -щица** cloakroom attendant.

гарди́на curtain.

гармонизи́ровать impf & pf harmonize.

гармо́ника accordion, concertina. **гармони́ческий, гармони́чный** harmonious. **гармо́ния** harmony; concord. **гармо́нь** accordion, concertina.

гарнизо́н garrison.

гарни́р garnish; vegetables.

гарниту́р set; suite.

гарь burning; cinders.

гаси́тель m extinguisher; suppressor. **гаси́ть** (гашу́, га́сишь) impf (pf за~, по~) extinguish; suppress. **га́снуть** (-ну; гас) impf (pf за~, по~, у~) be extinguished, go out; grow feeble.

гастро́ли f pl tour; guest-appearance, performance. **гастроли́ровать** impf (be on) tour.

гастроно́м gourmet; provision shop. **гастрономи́ческий** gastronomic; provision. **гастроно́мия** gastronomy; provisions; delicatessen.

гауптва́хта guardroom.

гаши́ш hashish.

гварде́ец (-е́йца) guardsman. **гварде́йский** guards'. **гва́рдия** Guards.

гво́здик tack. **гвозди́ка**

pink(s), carnation(s); cloves. **гво́здики** (-ов) pl stilettos. **гвоздь** (-я́; pl -и, -е́й) m nail; tack; crux; highlight, item.

гг. abbr (of го́ды) years.

где adv where; ~ бы ни wherever. **где́-либо** adv anywhere. **где́-нибудь** adv somewhere; anywhere. **где́-то** adv somewhere.

гекта́р hectare.

ге́лий helium.

гемоглоби́н haemoglobin.

геморро́й haemorrhoids. **гемофили́я** haemophilia.

ген gene.

ге́незис origin, genesis.

генера́л general. **генера́льный** general; ~ая репети́ция dress rehearsal.

генера́тор generator.

гене́тик geneticist. **гене́тика** genetics. **генети́ческий** genetic.

гениа́льный brilliant. **ге́ний** genius.

ге́ном genome.

гео- in comb geo-. **геогра́ф** geographer. ~графи́ческий geographical. ~гра́фия geography. **гео́лог** geologist. ~логи́ческий geological. ~ло́гия geology. ~метри́ческий geometric. ~ме́трия geometry.

георги́н dahlia.

геофи́зика geophysics.

гепа́рд cheetah.

гепати́т hepatitis.

гера́нь f geranium.

герб arms, coat of arms. **ге́рбовый** heraldic; ~ая печа́ть official stamp.

геркуле́с Hercules; rolled oats.

герма́нец (-нца) ancient German. **Герма́ния** Germany. **гер-**

ма́нский Germanic.

гермафроди́т hermaphrodite.

метри́чный hermetic; hermetically sealed; air-tight.

геро́изм heroism. **геро́иня** heroine. **герои́ческий** heroic. **геро́й** hero. **геро́йский** heroic.

герц (*gen pl* герц) hertz.

ге́рцог duke. **герцоги́ня** duchess.

г-жа *abbr* (*of* госпожа́) Mrs.; Miss.

гиаци́нт hyacinth.

ги́бель death; destruction, ruin; loss; wreck; downfall. **ги́бельный** disastrous, fatal.

ги́бкий (-бок, -бка́, -бко) flexible, adaptable, versatile; supple. **ги́бкость** flexibility; suppleness.

ги́бнуть (-ну; гиб(нул)) *impf* (*pf* по∼) perish.

гибри́д hybrid.

гига́нт giant. **гига́нтский** gigantic.

гигие́на hygiene. **гигиени́ческий**, **-и́чный** hygienic, sanitary.

гид guide.

гидравли́ческий hydraulic.

гидро- *pref* hydro-. ∼**электроста́нция** hydro-electric power-station.

гие́на hyena.

ги́льза cartridge-case; sleeve; (cigarette-)wrapper.

гимн hymn.

гимна́зия grammar school, high school.

гимна́ст gymnast. **гимна́стика** gymnastics. **гимнасти́ческий** gymnastic.

гинеко́лог gynaecologist. **гинеколо́гия** gynaecology.

гипе́рбола hyperbole.

гипно́з hypnosis. **гипнотизёр**

hypnotist. **гипнотизи́ровать** *impf* (*pf* за∼) hypnotize. **гипноти́ческий** hypnotic.

гипо́теза hypothesis. **гипотети́ческий** hypothetical.

гиппопота́м hippopotamus.

гипс gypsum, plaster (of Paris); plaster cast. **ги́псовый** plaster.

гирля́нда garland.

ги́ря weight.

гистерэктоми́я hysterectomy.

гита́ра guitar.

гл. *abbr* (*of* глава́) chapter.

глав- *abbr in comb* head, chief, main.

глава́ (*pl* -вы) head; chief; chapter; cupola. **глава́рь** (-я́) *m* leader, ring-leader. **главк** central directorate. **главнокома́ндующий** *sb* commander-in-chief. **гла́вный** chief, main; ∼ым о́бразом chiefly, mainly, for the most part; ∼ое *sb* the main thing; the essentials.

глаго́л verb.

гла́дить (-а́жу) *impf* (*pf* вы́∼, по∼) stroke; iron. **гла́дкий** smooth; plain. **гла́дко** *adv* smoothly; plain. **гладь** smooth surface.

глаз (*loc* -ý; *pl* -а́, глаз) eye; в ∼а́ to one's face; за ∼а́+*gen* behind the back of; смотре́ть во все ∼а́ be all eyes.

глазиро́ванный glazed; glossy; iced; glacé.

глазни́ца eye-socket. **глазно́й** eye; optic; ∼ врач oculist. **глазо́к** (-зка́) peephole.

глазу́нья fried eggs.

глазу́рь glaze; syrup; icing.

гла́нды (гланд) *pl* tonsils.

гла́сность publicity; glasnost, openness. **гла́сный** public; vowel; *sb* vowel.

гли́на clay. **гли́нистый** clayey.

гли́няный clay; clayey.
гли́ссер speed-boat.
глист (*intestinal*) worm.
глицери́н glycerine.
глоба́льный global; extensive.
гло́бус globe.
глота́ть *impf* swallow. **гло́тка** gullet; throat. **глото́к** (-тка́) gulp; mouthful.
гло́хнуть (-ну; глох) *impf* (*pf* за~, о~) become deaf; die away, subside; grow wild.
глубина́ (*pl* -ы) depth; heart, interior. **глубо́кий** (-о́к, -а́, -о́ко) deep; profound; late, advanced, extreme. **глубокомы́слие** profundity. **глубокоуважа́емый** (*in formal letters*) dear.
глуми́ться *impf* mock, jeer (над+*instr* at). **глумле́ние** mockery.
глупе́ть (-е́ю) *impf* (*pf* по~) grow stupid. **глупе́ц** (-пца́) fool. **глу́пость** stupidity. **глу́пый** (глуп, -а́, -о) stupid.
глуха́рь *m* capercaillie. **глухо́й** (глух, -а́, -о) deaf; muffled; obscure, vague; dense; wild; remote; deserted; sealed; blank; ~о́й, ~а́я *sb* deaf man, woman. **глухонемо́й** deaf and dumb; *sb* deaf mute. **глухота́** deafness. **глуши́тель** *m* silencer. **глуши́ть** (-шу́) *impf* (*pf* за~, о~) stun; muffle; dull; jam; extinguish; stifle; oppress. **глушь** backwoods.
глы́ба clod; lump, block.
глюко́за glucose.
гляде́ть (-яжу́) *impf* (*pf* по~, гля́нуть) look, gaze, peer; ~ в о́ба be on one's guard; (того́ и) гляди́ it's here; I'm afraid; гля́дя по+*dat* depending on.
гля́нец (-нца) gloss, lustre; polish.

гля́нуть (-ну) *pf* (*impf* гляде́ть) glance.
гм *int* hm!
г-н *abbr* (*of* господи́н) Mr.
гнать (гоню́, го́нишь; гнал, -а́, -о) *impf* drive; urge (on); hunt, chase; persecute; distil; ~ся за+*instr* pursue.
гнев anger, rage. **гне́ваться** *impf* (*pf* раз~) be angry. **гне́вный** angry.
гнедо́й bay.
гнездо́ (*pl* гнёзда) nest.
гнёт weight; oppression. **гнету́щий** oppressive.
гни́да nit.
гние́ние decay, putrefaction, rot. **гнило́й** (-ил, -а́, -о) rotten; muggy. **гнить** (-ию́, -иёшь; -ил, -а́, -о) *impf* (*pf* с~) rot. **гное́ние** suppuration. **гнои́ться** *impf* (*pf* с~) suppurate, discharge matter. **гной** pus. **гно́йник** abscess; ulcer. **гно́йный** purulent.
гну́сный (-сен, -сна́, -о) vile.
гнуть (гну, гнёшь) *impf* (*pf* со~) bend; aim at; ~ся bend; stoop.
гнуша́ться *impf* (*pf* по~) disdain; +*gen or instr* shun; abhor.
гобеле́н tapestry.
гобо́й oboe.
гове́ть (-е́ю) *impf* fast.
говно́ (*vulg*) shit.
говори́ть *impf* (*pf* по~, сказа́ть) speak, talk; say; tell; ~ся: как говори́тся as they say.
говя́дина beef. **говя́жий** beef.
го́гот cackle; loud laughter. **гогота́ть** (-очу́, -о́чешь) *impf* cackle; roar with laughter.
год (*loc* -у́; *pl* -ы *or* -а́, *gen* -о́в *or* лет) year. **года́ми** *adv* for years (on end).
годи́ться (-жу́сь) *impf* be fit, suitable; serve.

годи́чный a year's; annual.

го́дный (-ден, -дна́, -о, -ы *or* -ы́) fit, suitable; valid.

годова́лый one-year-old. **годово́й** annual. **годовщи́на** anniversary.

гожу́сь *etc.*: *see* **годи́ться**

гол goal.

голени́ще (boot-)top. **го́лень** shin.

голла́ндец (-дца) Dutchman. **Голла́ндия** Holland. **голла́ндка** Dutchwoman; tiled stove. **голла́ндский** Dutch.

голова́ (*acc* го́лову; *pl* го́ловы, -о́в, -а́м) head. **голова́стик** tadpole. **голо́вка** head; cap, nose, tip. **головн|о́й** head; leading; ~ая боль headache; ~о́й мозг brain, cerebrum; ~о́й убо́р headgear, headdress. **головокруже́ние** dizziness. **головоло́мка** puzzle. **головоре́з** cutthroat; rascal.

го́лод hunger; famine; acute shortage. **голода́ние** starvation; fasting. **голода́ть** *impf* go hungry, starve; fast. **голо́дный** (го́лоден, -дна́, -о, -ы *or* -ы́) hungry. **голодо́вка** hungerstrike.

гололёд, гололе́дица (period of) black ice.

го́лос (*pl* -а́) voice; part; vote. **голоси́ть** (-ошу́) *impf* sing loudly; wail.

голосло́вный unsubstantiated, unfounded.

голосова́ние voting; poll. **голосова́ть** *impf* (*pf* про~) vote; vote on.

голосов|о́й vocal; ~ая по́чта voice mail.

голу́бка pigeon; (my) dear, darling. **голубо́й** light blue. **голу́бчик** my dear (fellow); darling.

го́лубь *m* pigeon, dove. **голубя́тня** (*gen pl* -тен) dovecot, pigeon-loft.

го́лый (гол, -ла́, -ло) naked, bare.

гольф golf.

го́мон hubbub.

гомосексуали́ст homosexual. **гомосексуа́льный** homosexual.

гондо́ла gondola.

гоне́ние persecution. **го́нка** race; dashing; haste.

гонора́р fee.

го́ночный racing.

гонча́р (-а́) potter.

го́нщик racing driver *or* cyclist.

гоню́ *etc.*: *see* **гнать. гоня́ть** *impf* drive; send on errands; ~ся +за+*instr* chase, hunt.

гора́ (*acc* го́ру; *pl* го́ры, -а́м) mountain; hill; в го́ру uphill; под го́ру downhill.

гора́здо *adv* much, far, by far.

горб (-а́, *loc* -у́) hump; bulge. **горба́тый** hunchbacked. **горби́ть** (-блю) *impf* (*pf* с~) arch, hunch; ~ся stoop. **горбу́н** (-а́) *m*, **горбу́нья** (*gen pl* -ний) hunchback. **горбу́шка** (*gen pl* -шек) crust (*of loaf*).

горди́ться (-ржу́сь) *impf* put on airs; +*instr* be proud of. **го́рдость** pride. **го́рдый** (горд, -а́, -о, го́рды) proud. **горды́ня** arrogance.

го́ре grief, sorrow; trouble. **горева́ть** (-рю́ю) *impf* grieve.

горе́лка burner. **горе́лый** burnt. **горе́ние** burning, combustion; enthusiasm.

го́рестный sad; mournful. **го́ресть** sorrow; *pl* misfortunes.

горе́ть (-рю́) *impf* burn; be on fire.

го́рец (-рца) mountain-dweller.

го́речь bitterness; bitter taste.

горизо́нт horizon. **горизонта́ль** horizontal. **горизонта́льный** horizontal.

гори́стый mountainous, hilly. **го́рка** hill; hillock; steep climb.

го́рло throat; neck. **горлово́й** throat; guttural; raucous. **го́рлышко** neck.

гормо́н hormone.

горн¹ furnace, forge.

горн² bugle.

го́рничная sb maid, chambermaid.

горнорабо́чий sb miner.

горноста́й ermine.

го́рный mountain; mountainous; mineral; mining. **горня́к** (-á) miner.

го́род (pl -á) town; city. **городо́к** (-дка́) small town. **городско́й** urban; city; municipal. **горожа́нин** (pl -а́не, -а́н) m, **-жа́нка** town-dweller.

гороско́п horoscope.

горо́х pea, peas. **горо́шек** (-шка) spots, spotted pattern; души́стый ~ sweet peas; зелёный ~ green peas. **горо́шина** pea.

горсове́т abbr (of городско́й сове́т) city soviet, town soviet.

горсть (gen pl -е́й) handful.

горта́нный guttural. **горта́нь** larynx.

горчи́ца mustard. **горчи́чник** mustard plaster.

горшо́к (-шка́) flowerpot; pot; potty; chamber-pot.

го́рький (-рек, -рька́, -о) bitter.

горю́чий combustible; ~ее sb fuel. **горя́чий** (-ря́ч, -а́) hot; passionate; ardent.

горя́чи́ться (-чу́сь) impf (pf раз~) get excited. **горя́чка** fever; feverish haste. **горя́чность** zeal.

гос- abbr in comb (of госуда́рственный) state.

го́спиталь m (military) hospital.

го́споди int good heavens! **господи́н** (pl -ода́, -о́д, -а́м) master; gentleman; Mr; pl ladies and gentlemen. **госпо́дство** supremacy. **госпо́дствовать** impf hold sway; prevail. **Госпо́дь** (Го́спода, voc Го́споди) m God, the Lord. **госпожа́** lady; Mrs.

гостеприи́мный hospitable. **гостеприи́мство** hospitality. **гости́ная** sb sitting-room, living-room, drawing-room. **гости́ница** hotel. **гости́ть** (гощу́) impf be on a visit. **гость** (gen pl -е́й) m, **го́стья** (gen pl -ий) guest, visitor.

госуда́рственный State, public. **госуда́рство** State. **госуда́рыня**, **госуда́рь** m sovereign; Your Majesty.

готи́ческий Gothic.

гото́вить (-влю) impf (pf с~) prepare; ~ся prepare (o.s.); be at hand. **гото́вность** readiness. **гото́вый** ready.

гофриро́ванный corrugated; waved; pleated.

грабёж robbery; pillage. **граби́тель** m robber. **граби́тельский** predatory; exorbitant. **гра́бить** (-блю) impf (pf o~) rob, pillage.

гра́бли (-бель or -блей) pl rake.

гравёр, **гравиро́вщик** engraver.

гра́вий gravel. **гравирова́ть** impf (pf вы́~) engrave; etch. **гравиро́вка** engraving.

гравитацио́нный gravitational.

гравю́ра engraving, print; etching.

град¹ city, town.

град² hail; volley. **гра́дина** hailstone.

гра́дус degree. **гра́дусник** thermometer.

граждани́н (pl гра́ждане, -дан), **гражда́нка** citizen. **гражда́нский** civil; civic; civilian. **гражда́нство** citizenship.

грамза́пись (gramophone) recording.

грамм gram.

грамма́тика grammar. **граммати́ческий** grammatical.

гра́мота reading and writing; official document; deed. **гра́мотность** literacy. **гра́мотный** literate; competent.

грампласти́нка (gramophone) record.

грана́т pomegranate; garnet. **грана́та** shell, grenade.

грандио́зный grandiose.

гранёный cut, faceted; cut-glass.

грани́т granite.

грани́ца border; boundary; limit; **за грани́цей**, **за грани́цу** abroad. **грани́чить** impf border.

грант grant.

грань border, verge; side, facet.

граф count; earl.

графа́ column. **гра́фик** graph; chart; schedule; graphic artist. **гра́фика** drawing; graphics; script.

графи́н carafe; decanter.

графи́ня countess.

графи́т graphite.

графи́ческий graphic.

графлёный ruled.

гра́фство county.

грацио́зный graceful. **гра́ция** grace.

грач (-á) rook.

гребёнка comb. **гре́бень** (-бня)

m comb; crest. **гребе́ц** (-бца́) rower, oarsman. **гребно́й** rowing. **гребу́** etc.: see **грести́**

грёза day-dream, dream. **гре́зить** (-éжу) impf dream.

грек Greek.

гре́лка hot-water bottle.

греме́ть impf (pf про~) thunder, roar; rattle; resound. **грему́чая змея́** rattlesnake.

грести́ (-бу́, -бёшь; грёб, -бла́) impf row; rake.

греть (-е́ю) impf warm, heat; ~ся warm o.s., bask.

грех (-á) sin. **грехо́вный** sinful. **грехопаде́ние** the Fall; fall.

Гре́ция Greece. **гре́цкий оре́х** walnut. **греча́нка** Greek. **гре́ческий** Greek, Grecian.

гречи́ха buckwheat. **гре́чневый** buckwheat.

греши́ть (-шу́) impf (pf по~, со~) sin. **гре́шник**, **-ница** sinner. **гре́шный** (-шен, -шна́, -о) sinful.

гриб (-á) mushroom. **грибно́й** mushroom.

гри́ва mane.

гри́венник ten-copeck piece.

грим make-up; grease-paint. **гримирова́ть** impf (pf за~) make up; +instr make up as.

грипп flu.

гриф neck (of violin etc.).

гри́фель m pencil lead.

гроб (loc -у́; pl -ы́ or -á) coffin; grave. **гробни́ца** tomb. **гробово́й** coffin; deathly. **гробовщи́к** (-á) coffin-maker; undertaker.

гроза́ (pl -ы) (thunder-)storm.

гроздь (pl -ди or -дья, -де́й or -дьев) cluster, bunch.

грози́ть(ся (-ожу́(сь) impf (pf по~, при~) threaten. **гро́зный** (-зен, -зна́, -о) menacing; terrible; severe.

гром (*pl* -ы, -óв) thunder.

громáда mass; bulk, pile. **громáдный** huge, colossal.

громи́ть (-млю́) *impf* destroy; smash, rout.

гро́мкий (-мок, -мка́, -о) loud; famous; notorious; fine-sounding. **гро́мко** *adv* loud(ly); aloud. **громкоговори́тель** m loud-speaker. **громово́й** thunder; thunderous; crushing. **громогла́сный** loud; public.

громозди́ть (-зжу́) *impf* (*pf* на~) pile up; ~**ся** tower; clamber up. **гро́здкий** cumbersome.

гро́мче *comp of* **гро́мкий, гро́мко**

гроссмéйстер grand master.

гроте́скный grotesque.

гро́хот crash, din.

грохотáть (-очу́ -о́чешь) *impf* (*pf* про~) crash; rumble; roar.

грош (-á) half-copeck piece; farthing. **грошо́вый** cheap; trifling.

грубéть (-éю) *impf* (*pf* за~, о~, по~) grow coarse. **груби́ть** (-блю́) *impf* (*pf* на~) be rude. **грубия́н** boor. **гру́бость** rudeness; coarseness; rude remark. **гру́бый** (груб, -á, -о) coarse; rude.

гру́да heap, pile.

груди́на breastbone. **груди́нка** brisket; breast. **грудно́й** breast, chest; pectoral. **грудь** (-й *or* -и, *instr* -ю, *loc* -и́; *pl* -и, -éй) breast, chest.

груз load; burden.

грузи́н (*gen pl* -и́н), **грузи́нка** Georgian. **грузи́нский** Georgian.

грузи́ть (-ужу́, -у́зишь) *impf* (*pf* за~, на~, по~) load; ~**ся** load, take on cargo.

Гру́зия Georgia.

грузны́й (-зен, -зна́, -о) weighty; bulky. **грузови́к** (*gen* -á) truck. **грузово́й** goods, cargo. **гру́зчик** stevedore; loader.

грунт ground, soil; priming. **грунтовáть** *impf* (*pf* за~) prime. **грунтово́й** soil, earth; priming.

гру́ппа group. **группировáть** *impf* (*pf* с~) group; ~**ся** group, form groups. **группиро́вка** grouping. **группово́й** group; team.

грусти́ть (-ущу́) *impf* grieve, mourn; +*no*+*dat* pine for. **гру́стный** (-тен, -тна́, -о) sad. **грусть** sadness.

гру́ша pear.

гры́жа hernia, rupture.

грызть (-зу́, -зёшь; грыз) *impf* (*pf* раз~) gnaw; nag; ~**ся** fight; squabble. **грызу́н** (-á) rodent.

гряда́ (*pl* -ы, -áм) ridge; bed; row, series; bank. **гря́дка** (flower)-bed.

гряду́щий approaching; future.

грязни́ть (-зня́-о) *impf* muddy; dirty. **грязь** (*loc* -и́) mud; dirt, filth; *pl* mud-cure.

гря́нуть (-ну) *pf* ring out, crash out; strike up.

губá (*pl* -ы, -áм) lip; *pl* pincers.

губернáтор governor. **губéрния** province. **губéрнский** provincial.

губи́тельный ruinous; pernicious. **губи́ть** (-блю́, -бишь) *impf* (*pf* по~) ruin; spoil.

гу́бка sponge.

губнáя помáда lipstick.

гу́бчатый porous, spongy.

гувернáнтка governess. **гувернёр** tutor.

гудéть (гужу́) *impf* (*pf* про~) hum; drone; buzz; hoot. **гудо́к**

(-*дка*) hooter, siren, horn, whistle; hoot.

гудро́н tar. **гудро́нный** tar, tarred.

гул rumble. **гу́лкий** (-лок, -лка, -о) resonant; booming.

гуля́нье (*gen pl* -ний) walk; fête; outdoor party. **гуля́ть** *impf* (*pf* по~) stroll; go for a walk; have a good time.

гуманита́рный of the humanities; humane. **гума́нный** humane.

гумно́ (*pl* -а, -мен *or* -мён, -ам) threshing-floor; barn.

гурт (-а́) herd; flock. **гуртовщи́к** (-а́) herdsman. **гурто́м** *adv* wholesale; en masse.

гуса́к (-а́) gander.

гу́сеница caterpillar; (caterpillar) track. **гу́сеничный** caterpillar.

гусёнок (-нка; *pl* -ся́та, -ся́т) gosling. **гуси́ный** goose; **~ая ко́жа** goose-flesh.

густе́ть (-е́ет) *impf* (*pf* за~) thicken. **густо́й** (густ, -а́, -о) thick, dense; rich. **густота́** thickness, density; richness.

гусы́ня goose. **гусь** (*pl* -и, -е́й) *m* goose. **гусько́м** *adv* in single file.

гутали́н shoe-polish.

гу́ща grounds, sediment; thicket; thick. **гу́ще** *comp of* густо́й.

ГЭС *abbr* (*of* гидроэлектроста́нция) hydro-electric power station.

Д

д. *abbr* (*of* дере́вня) village; (*of* дом) house.

да *conj* and; but.

да *partl* yes; really! well; +*3rd pers of v*, may, let; **да здра́вствует...!** long live ...!

дава́ть (даю́, -ёшь) *impf of* дать; **дава́й(те)** let us, let's; come on; ~ся yield; come easy.

дави́ть (-влю́, -вишь) *impf* (*pf* за~, по~, раз~, у~) press; squeeze; crush; oppress; ~ся choke; hang o.s. **да́вка** crushing; crush. **давле́ние** pressure.

да́вний ancient; of long standing. **давно́** *adv* long ago; for a long time. **да́вность** antiquity; remoteness; long standing. **давны́м-давно́** *adv* long long ago.

дади́м *etc*.: *see* дать. **даю́** *etc*.: *see* дава́ть

да́же *adv* even.

дале́е *adv* further; **и так ~** and so on, etc. **далёкий** (-ёк, -а, -ёко́) distant, remote; (-away). **далеко́** *adv* far; far off; by a long way; **~ за** long after; **~ не** far from. **даль** (*loc* -и́) distance. **дальне́йший** further. **да́льний** distant, remote; long; **~ Восто́к** the Far East. **дальнозо́ркий** long-sighted. **да́льность** distance; range. **да́льше** *adv* further; then; next; longer.

дам *etc*.: *see* дать.

да́ма lady; partner; queen.

да́мба dyke; dam.

да́мский ladies'.

Да́ния Denmark.

да́нные *sb pl* data; facts. **да́нный** given, present. **дань** tribute; debt.

данти́ст dentist.

дар (*pl* -ы́) gift. **дари́ть** (-рю́, -ришь) *impf* (*pf* по~) +*dat* give, make a present.

дарова́ние talent. **дарова́ть** *impf* & *pf* grant, confer. **даро-**

ви́тый gifted. **дарово́й** free (of charge). **да́ром** *adv* free, gratis; in vain.

да́та date.

да́тельный dative.

дати́ровать *impf & pf* date.

да́тский Danish. **датча́нин** (*pl* -а́не, -а́н), **датча́нка** Dane.

дать (дам, дашь, даст, дади́м; дал, -а́, да́ло) *pf* (*impf* **дава́ть**) give; grant; let; **~ взаймы́** lend; **~ся** *pf of* **дава́ться**

да́ча dacha; **на да́че** in the country. **да́чник** (holiday) visitor.

два *m & neut*, **две** *f* (двух, -ум, -умя́, -ух) two. **двадцатиле́тний** twenty-year; twenty-year-old. **двадца́тый** twentieth; **~ые го́ды** the twenties. **два́дцать** (-и́, *instr* -ью́) twenty. **два́жды** *adv* twice; double. **двена́дцатый** twelfth. **двена́дцать** twelve.

дверь (*loc* -и́; *pl* -и, -е́й, *instr* -я́ми *or* -ьми́) door.

две́сти (двухсо́т, -умста́м, -умяста́ми, -ухста́х) two hundred.

дви́гатель *m* engine, motor; motive force. **дви́гать** (-аю *or* -и́жу) *impf*, **дви́нуть** (-ну) *pf* move; set in motion; advance; **~ся** move; advance; get started. **движе́ние** movement; motion; exercise; traffic. **дви́жимость** chattels; personal property. **дви́жимый** movable; moved. **дви́жущий** motive.

дво́е (-и́х) two; two pairs.

двое- *in comb* two-; double(-). **двоебо́рье** biathlon. **~же́нец** (-нца) bigamist. **~же́нство** bigamy. **~то́чие** colon.

двои́ться *impf* divide in two; appear double; **у него́ двои́лось в глаза́х** he saw double. **двойч-**

ный binary. **дво́йка** two; figure 2; No. 2. **двойни́к** (-а́) double. **двойно́й** double, twofold; binary. **дво́йня** (*gen pl* -о́ен) twins. **дво́йственный** two-faced; dual.

двор (-а́) yard; courtyard; homestead; court. **дворе́ц** (-рца́) palace. **дво́рник** caretaker; windscreen-wiper. **дворня́** servants. **дворо́вый** yard, courtyard; *sb* house-serf. **дворяни́н** (*pl* -я́не, -я́н), **дворя́нка** member of the nobility or gentry. **дворя́нство** nobility, gentry.

двою́родн|ый; **~ый брат**, **~ая сестра́** first cousin; **~ый дя́дя**, **~ая тётка** first cousin once removed. **двоя́кий** double; twofold.

дву-, двух- *in comb* two-; bi-; double. **двубо́ртный** double-breasted. **~ли́чный** two-faced. **~но́гий** two-legged. **~ру́чный** two-handed; two-handled. **~ру́шник** double-dealer. **~смы́сленный** ambiguous. **~(х)спа́льный** double. **~сторо́нний** double-sided; two-way; bilateral. **~хго́дичный** two-year. **~хле́тний** two-year; two-year-old; biennial. **~хме́стный** two-seater; two-berth. **~хмото́рный** twin-engined. **~хсотле́тие** bicentenary. **~хсо́тый** two-hundredth. **~хта́ктный** two-stroke. **~хэта́жный** two-storey. **~язы́чный** bilingual.

деба́ты (-ов) *pl* debate.

дебе́т debit. **дебетова́ть** *impf & pf* debit.

дебит yield, output.

де́бри (-ей) *pl* jungle; thickets; the wilds.

дебю́т début.

дéва maid; maiden; Virgo.

девальвáция devaluation.

девáться impf of **дéться**

девúз motto; device.

девúца spinster. **девúчий** girlish, maidenly; **~ья фамúлия** maiden name. **дéвка** wench, lass; tart. **дéвочка** (little) girl.

дéвственник, -ица virgin. **дéвственный** virgin; innocent. **дéвушка** girl. **девчóнка** girl.

девянóсто ninety. **девянóстый** ninetieth. **дéвять** nine; figure 9; No. 9. **девятнáдцатый** nineteenth. **девятнáдцать** nineteen. **девя́тый** ninth. **дéвять** (-ú, -ью́) nine. **девятьсóт** (-тисóт, -тистáм, -тьюстáми, -тистáх) nine hundred.

дегенерúровать impf & pf degenerate.

дéготь (-гтя) tar.

дегустáция tasting.

дед grandfather; grandad. **дéдушка** grandfather; grandad.

деепричáстие adverbial participle.

дежýрить impf be on duty. **дежýрный** duty; on duty; sb person on duty. **дежýрство** (being on) duty.

дезертúр deserter. **дезертúровать** impf & pf desert.

дезинфéкция disinfection. **дезинфицúровать** impf & pf disinfect.

дезодорáнт deodorant; airfreshener.

дезориентáция disorientation. **дезориентúровать** impf & pf disorient; **~ся** lose one's bearings.

дéйственный efficacious; effective. **дéйствие** action; operation; effect; act. **действú-**

тельно adv really; indeed. **действúтельность** reality; validity; efficacy. **действúтельный** actual; valid; efficacious; active. **дéйствовать** impf (pf по~) affect; have an effect; act; work. **дéйствующий** active; in force; working; **~ее лицó** character; **~ие лúца** cast.

декабрúст Decembrist. **декáбрь** (-я́) m December. **декáбрьский** December.

декáда ten-day period or festival.

декáн dean. **деканáт** office of dean.

деклáмация recitation, declamation. **деклáмúровать** impf (pf про~) recite, declaim.

декларáция declaration.

декоратúвный decorative. **декорáтор** scene-painter. **декорáция** scenery.

декрéт decree; maternity leave. **декрéтный óтпуск** maternity leave.

дéланный artificial, affected. **дéлать** impf (pf с~) make; do; **~ вид** pretend; **~ся** become; happen.

делегáт delegate. **делегáция** delegation; group.

делёж (-á), **делёжка** sharing; partition. **делéние** division; point (on a scale).

делéц (-льцá) smart operator.

деликáтный delicate.

делúмое sb dividend. **делúмость** divisibility. **делúтель** m divisor. **делúть** (-лю́, -лишь) impf (pf по~, раз~) divide; share; **~ шесть нá три** divide six by three; **~ся** divide; be divisible; +instr share.

дéло (pl -á) business; affair; matter; deed; thing; case;

в са́мом де́ле really, indeed; ~ в том the point is; как (ва́ши) дела́? how are things?; на са́мом де́ле in actual fact; по де́лу, по дела́м on business. делови́тый business-like, efficient. делово́й business; business-like. де́льный efficient; sensible.

де́льта delta.

дельфи́н dolphin.

демаго́г demagogue.

демобилиза́ция demobilization. демобилизова́ть impf & pf demobilize.

демокра́т democrat. демократиза́ция democratization. демократизи́ровать impf & pf democratize. демократи́ческий democratic. демокра́тия democracy.

де́мон demon.

демонстра́ция demonstration. демонстри́ровать impf & pf demonstrate.

де́нежный monetary; money; ~ перево́д money order.

де́нусь etc.: see де́ться

день (дня) m day; afternoon; днём in the afternoon; на днях the other day; one of these days; че́рез ~ every other day.

де́ньги (-нег, -ьга́м) pl money.

депа́ртамент department.

депо́ neut indecl depot.

депорта́ция deportation. депорти́ровать impf & pf deport.

депута́т (parl) deputy; delegate.

дёргать impf (pf дёрнуть) pull, tug; pester; ~ся twitch; jerk.

дереве́нский village; rural. дере́вня (pl -и, -ве́нь, -вня́м) village; the country. де́рево (pl -е́вья, -ьев) tree; wood. дере-

вя́нный wood; wooden.

держа́ва power. держа́ть (-жу́, -жишь) impf hold; support; keep; ~ пари́ bet; ~ себя́ behave; ~ся hold on to; be held up; hold o.s.; hold out; +gen keep to.

дерза́ние daring. дерза́ть impf, дерзну́ть (-ну́, -нёшь) pf dare. де́рзкий impudent; daring. де́рзость impertinence; daring.

дёрн turf.

дёрнуть(ся (-ну(сь) pf of дёргать(ся

деру́ etc.: see драть

деса́нт landing; landing force.

десе́рт dessert.

де́скать partl indicating reported speech.

десна́ (pl дёсны, -сен) gum.

де́спот despot.

десятиле́тие decade; tenth anniversary. десятиле́тка ten-year (secondary) school. десятиле́тний ten-year; ten-year-old. десяти́чный decimal. деся́тка ten; figure 10; No. 10; tenner (10-rouble note). деся́ток (-тка) ten. деся́тый tenth. де́сять (-и, instr -ью) ten.

дета́ль detail; part, component. дета́льный detailed; minute.

детдо́м (pl -а́) children's home.

детекти́в detective story.

детёныш young animal; pl young. де́ти (-те́й, -тям, -тьми, -тях) pl children. детса́д (pl -ы́) kindergarten.

де́тская sb nursery. де́тский children's; childish. де́тство childhood.

де́ться (де́нусь) pf (impf дева́ться) get to, disappear to.

дефе́кт defect.

дефи́с hyphen.

дефици́т deficit; shortage. дефици́тный scarce.

дешеве́ть (-е́ет) *impf* (*pf* по~) fall in price. деше́вле *comp of* деше́во, деше́вый. деше́во *adv* cheap, cheaply. деше́вый (дёшев, -а́, -о) cheap.

де́ятель *m*: госуда́рственный ~ statesman; обще́ственный ~ public figure. де́ятельность activity; work. де́ятельный active, energetic.

джаз jazz.

дже́мпер pullover.

джентльме́н gentleman.

джинсо́вый denim. джи́нсы (-ов) *pl* jeans.

джо́йстик joystick.

джу́нгли (-ей) *pl* jungle.

диабе́т diabetes. диабе́тик diabetic.

диа́гноз diagnosis.

диагона́ль diagonal.

диагра́мма diagram.

диале́кт dialect. диале́ктика dialectics.

диало́г dialogue.

диа́метр diameter.

диапазо́н range; band.

диапозити́в slide.

диафра́гма diaphragm.

дива́н sofa; divan.

диверса́нт saboteur. диве́рсия sabotage.

диви́зия division.

ди́вный marvellous. ди́во wonder, marvel.

дида́ктика didactics.

дие́з (*mus*) sharp.

дие́та diet. диети́ческий dietetic.

диза́йн design. диза́йнер designer.

ди́зель *m* diesel; diesel engine. ди́зельный diesel.

дизентери́я dysentery.

дика́рь (-я́) *m*, дика́рка savage. ди́кий wild; savage; queer; posterous. дикобра́з porcupine. дикорасту́щий wild. ди́кость wildness, savagery; absurdity.

дикта́нт dictation. дикта́тор dictator. диктату́ра dictatorship.

диктова́ть *impf* (*pf* про~) dictate. ди́ктор announcer. ди́кция diction.

диле́мма dilemma.

дилета́нт dilettante.

дина́мика dynamics.

динами́т dynamite.

динами́ческий dynamic.

дина́стия dynasty.

диноза́вр dinosaur.

дипло́м diploma; degree; degree work. диплома́т diplomat. дипломати́ческий diplomatic.

директи́ва instructions; directives. дире́ктор (*pl* ~а́) director; principal. дире́кция management.

дирижа́бль *m* airship, dirigible.

дирижёр conductor. дирижи́ровать *impf* +*instr* conduct.

диск disc, disk; dial; discus.

ди́скант treble.

дисково́д disk drive.

дискоте́ка discotheque.

дискре́тный discrete.

дискримина́ция discrimination.

дискуссия discussion, debate.

диспансе́р clinic.

диспе́тчер controller.

ди́спут public debate.

диссерта́ция dissertation, thesis.

дистанцио́нный distance, dis-

tant, remote; remote-control. **диста́нция** distance; range; region.

дисципли́на discipline.

дитя́ (дитя́ти; pl де́ти, -е́й) neut child; baby.

дифтери́я diphtheria.

дифто́нг diphthong.

диффама́ция libel.

дичь game.

длина́ length. **дли́нный** (-нен, -нна́, -о) long. **дли́тельность** duration. **дли́тельный** long, protracted. **дли́ться** impf (pf про~) last.

для prep+gen for; for the sake of; ~ того́, что́бы... in order to.

дне́вальный sb (mil) orderly. **дневни́к** (-а́) diary, journal. **дневно́й** adj; daily. **днём** adv in the day time; in the afternoon. **дни** etc.: see день

дни́ще bottom.

ДНК abbr (of **дезоксирибону-клеи́новая кислота́**) DNA.

дно (dna; pl до́нья, -ьев) bottom.

до prep+gen (up) to; as far as; until; before; to the point of; **до на́шей э́ры** BC; **до сих пор** till now; **до тех пор** till then, before; **до того́, как** before; **до того́, что** to such an extent that, until; **мне не до** I'm not in the mood for.

доба́вить (-влю) pf, **добавля́ть** impf (+acc or gen) add. **доба́вка** addition; second helping. **добавле́ние** addition; supplement; extra. **доба́вочный** additional.

добега́ть impf, **добежа́ть** (-егу́) pf +до+gen run to, as far as; reach.

добива́ть impf, **доби́ть** (-бью́, -бьёшь) pf finish (off); ~ся +gen

get, obtain; ~ся своего́ get one's way.

добира́ться impf of **добра́ться**

до́блесть valour.

добра́ться (-беру́сь, -ёшься; -а́лся, -ла́сь, -а́ло́сь) pf (impf **добира́ться**) +до+gen get to, reach.

добро́ good; ~ пожа́ловать! welcome!; э́то не к добру́ it is a bad sign.

добро- in comb good-, well-. **доброво́лец** (-льца) volunteer. **~во́льно** adv voluntarily. **~во́льный** voluntary. **~де́тель** virtue. **~де́тельный** virtuous. **~ду́шие** good nature. **~ду́шный** good-natured. **~жела́тельный** benevolent. **~ка́чественный** of good quality; benign. **~со́вестный** conscientious.

доброта́ goodness, kindness. **добро́тный** of good quality. **до́брый** (добр, -а́, -о, до́бры́) good; kind; бу́дьте добры́ +imper please; would you be kind enough to.

добыва́ть impf, **добы́ть** (-бу́ду; до́бы́л, -а́, -о) pf get, obtain, procure; mine. **добы́ча** output; mining; booty.

добью́ etc.: see **доби́ть**. **доведу́** etc.: see **довести́**

довезти́ (-зу́, -зёшь; -вёз, -ла́) pf (impf **довози́ть**) take (to), carry (to), drive (to).

дове́ренность warrant; power of attorney. **дове́ренный** trusted; sb agent, proxy. **дове́рие** trust, confidence. **дове́рить** (pf (impf **доверя́ть**) entrust; ~ся +dat trust in; confide in.

до́верху adv to the top.

дове́рчивый trustful, credu-

lous. **доверя́ть** *impf* of **дове́-
рить**; (+*dat*) to trust.

дове́сок (-ска) makeweight.

довести́ (-еду́, -едёшь; -вёл, -а́)
pf, **доводи́ть** (-ожу́, -о́дишь)
impf lead, take (to); bring, drive
(to). **до́вод** argument, reason.

довое́нный pre-war.

довози́ть (-ожу́, -о́зишь) *impf* of
довезти́

дово́льно *adv* enough; quite,
fairly. **дово́льный** satisfied;
pleased. **дово́льство** content-
ment. **дово́льствоваться** *impf*
(*pf* y~) be content.

догада́ться *pf*, **дога́дываться**
impf guess; suspect. **дога́дка**
surmise, conjecture. **дога́дли-
вый** quick-witted.

до́гма dogma.

догна́ть (-гоню́, -го́нишь; -гна́л,
-а́, -о) *pf* (*impf* **догоня́ть**) catch
up (with).

догова́риваться *impf*, **догово-
ри́ться** *pf* come to an agreement; arrange. **до́говор** (*pl* -ы
or -а́, -о́в) agreement; contract;
treaty. **догово́рный** contract-
ual; agreed.

догоня́ть *impf* of **догна́ть**

догора́ть *impf*, **догоре́ть** (-ри́т)
pf burn out, burn down.

дойду́ *etc.: see* **дойти́. доез-
жа́ть** *impf* of **дое́хать**

дое́хать (-е́ду) *pf* (*impf* **доез-
жа́ть**) +**до**+*gen* reach, arrive at.

дожда́ться (-ду́сь, -дёшься;
-а́лся, -ла́сь, -а́ло́сь) *pf* wait
for, wait until.

дождеви́к (-а́) raincoat. **дожде-
во́й** rain(y). **дожди́вый** rainy.
дождь (-я́) *m* rain; ~ идёт it is
raining.

дожива́ть *impf*, **дожи́ть** (-иву́,
-ивёшь; до́жил, -а́, -о) *pf* live out;
spend.

дожида́ться *impf* +*gen* wait
for.

до́за dose.

дозво́лить *pf*, **дозволя́ть** *impf*
permit.

дозвони́ться *pf* get through,
reach by telephone.

дозо́р patrol.

дозрева́ть *impf*, **дозре́ть** (-е́ет)
pf ripen.

доистори́ческий prehistoric.

дои́ть *impf* (*pf* по~) milk.

дойти́ (дойду́, -дёшь; дошёл,
-шла́) *pf* (*impf* **доходи́ть**)
+**до**+*gen* reach; get through to.

док dock.

доказа́тельный conclusive.
доказа́тельство proof, evidence. **доказа́ть** (-ажу́, -а́жешь)
pf, **дока́зывать** *impf* demonstrate, prove.

докати́ться (-ачу́сь, -а́тишься)
pf, **дока́тываться** *impf* roll;
boom; +**до**+*gen* sink into.

докла́д report; lecture. **докла́д-
ная (запи́ска)** report; memo.
докла́дчик speaker, lecturer.
докла́дывать *impf* of **доло-
жи́ть**

до́красна́ *adv* to red heat; to
redness.

до́ктор (*pl* -а́) doctor. **до́ктор-
ский** doctoral. **до́кторша**
woman doctor; doctor's wife.

доктри́на doctrine.

докуме́нт document; deed. **до-
кумента́льный** documentary.
документа́ция documentation;
documents.

долби́ть (-блю́) *impf* hollow;
chisel; repeat; swot up.

долг (*loc* -у́; *pl* -и́) duty; debt;
взять в ~ borrow; дать в ~
lend.

до́лгий (до́лог, -лга́, -о) long.

до́лго adv long, (for) a long time. **долгове́чный** lasting; durable. **долгожда́нный** long-awaited. **долгоигра́ющая пласти́нка** LP.

долголе́тие longevity. **долголе́тний** of many years; longstanding. **долгосро́чный** long-term.

долгота́ (pl -ы) length; longitude.

долево́й lengthwise. **до́лее** adv longer.

должа́ть impf (pf за∼) borrow.

до́лжен (-жна́) predic+dat in debt to; +inf obliged; bound; likely; must, have to, ought to; **должно́ быть** probably. **должни́к** (-а́), **-ни́ца** debtor. **до́лжное** sb due. **должностно́й** official. **до́лжность** (gen pl -е́й) post, office; duties. **до́лжный** due, fitting.

доли́на valley.

до́ллар dollar.

доложи́ть¹ (-ожу́, -о́жишь) pf (impf докла́дывать) add.

доложи́ть² (-ожу́, -о́жишь) pf (impf докла́дывать) +acc or o+prep report; announce.

доло́й adv away, off; +acc down with!

долото́ (pl -а) chisel.

до́лька segment; clove.

до́льше adv longer.

до́ля (gen pl -е́й) portion; share; lot, fate.

дом (pl -а́) house; home. **до́ма** adv at home. **дома́шний** house; home; domestic; home-made; ∼яя **хозя́йка** housewife.

до́менный blast-furnace; ∼ая **печь** blast-furnace.

домини́ровать impf dominate, predominate.

домкра́т jack.

до́мна blast-furnace.

домовладе́лец (-льца), **-лица** house-owner; landlord. **домово́дство** housekeeping; domestic science. **домо́вый** house; household; housing.

домога́тельство solicitation; bid. **домога́ться** impf +gen solicit, bid for.

домо́й adv home, homewards.

домохозя́йка housewife. **домрабо́тница** domestic servant, maid.

домофо́н entryphone (propr).

доне́льзя adv in the extreme.

донесе́ние dispatch, report. **донести́** (-су́, -сёшь; -нёс, -сла́) pf (impf доноси́ть) report, announce; +dat inform; +на+acc inform against; ∼сь be heard; +до+gen reach.

до́низу adv to the bottom; све́рху ∼ from top to bottom.

до́нор donor.

доно́с denunciation, information. **доноси́ть(ся** (-ношу́(сь, -но́сишь(ся impf of донести́(ся

доно́счик informer.

донско́й Don.

доны́не adv hitherto.

до́нья etc.: see дно

до на́шей э́ры abbr (до на́шей э́ры) BC.

допла́та additional payment, excess fare. **доплати́ть** (-ачу́, -а́тишь) pf, **допла́чивать** impf pay in addition; pay the rest.

допо́длинно adv for certain. **допо́длинный** authentic, genuine.

дополне́ние supplement, addition; (gram) object. **дополни́тельно** adv in addition. **дополни́тельный** supplementary, additional. **допо́лнить** pf, **дополня́ть** impf supplement.

допрáшивать impf, **допросúть** (-ошý, -óсишь) pf interrogate. **допрóс** interrogation.

дóпуск right of entry, admittance. **допускáть** impf, **допустúть** (-ущý, -ýстишь) pf admit; permit; tolerate; suppose. **допустúмый** permissible, acceptable. **допущéние** assumption.

дореволюциóнный pre-revolutionary.

дорóга road; way; journey; route; **по дорóге** on the way.

дóрого adv dear, dearly. **дороговúзна** high prices. **дорогóй** (дóрог, -á, -о) dear.

дорóдный portly.

дорожáть impf (pf вз~, по~) rise in price, go up. **дорóже** comp of **дóрого, дорогóй. дорожúть** (-жý) impf +instr value.

дорóжка path; track; lane; runway; strip, runner, stair-carpet. **дорóжный** road; highway; travelling.

досáда annoyance. **досадúть** (-ажý) pf, **досаждáть** impf +dat annoy. **досáдный** annoying. **досáдовать** be annoyed (**на**+acc with).

доскá (acc дóску; pl -и, -сóк, -скáм) board; slab; plaque.

дослóвный literal; word-for-word.

досмóтр inspection.

доспéхи pl armour.

досрóчный ahead of time, early.

доставáть(ся (-таю́(сь, -ёшь(ся impf pf **достáть(ся**

доставúть (-влю) pf, **доставлять** impf deliver; supply; cause, give. **достáвка** delivery.

достаю́ etc.: see **достáть**
достáток (-тка) sufficiency; prosperity. **достáточно** adv

enough, sufficiently. **достáточный** sufficient; adequate.

достáть (-áну) pf (impf **доставáть**) take (out); get, obtain; +gen or до+gen touch; reach; impers suffice; ~**ся** +dat be inherited by; fall to the lot of; **емý достáнется** he'll catch it.

достигáть impf, **достúгнуть, достúчь** (-úгну; -стúг) pf +gen reach, achieve; +gen or до+gen reach. **достижéние** achievement.

достовéрный reliable, trustworthy; authentic.

достóинство dignity; merit; value. **достóйный** deserved; suitable; worthy; +gen worthy of.

достопримечáтельность sight, notable place.

достоя́ние property.

дóступ access. **достýпный** accessible; approachable; reasonable; available.

досýг leisure, (spare) time. **досýжий** leisure; idle.

дóсыта adv to satiety.

досьé neut indecl dossier.

досягáемый attainable.

дотáция grant, subsidy.

дотлá utterly; to the ground.

дотрáгиваться impf, **дотрóнуться** (-нусь) pf +до+gen touch.

дотя́гивать impf, **дотяну́ть** (-яну́, -я́нешь) pf draw, drag, stretch out; hold out; live; put off; ~**ся** stretch; reach; drag on.

дóхлый dead; sickly. **дóхнуть¹** (-нет; дох) (pf из~, по~, с~) die; kick the bucket.

дохнýть² (-нý, -нёшь) pf draw a breath.

дохóд income; revenue. **дохо-**

дои́ть (-ою́, -ои́шь) *impf of* **подои́ть**. **дохо́дный** profitable. **дохо́дчивый** intelligible.

доце́нт reader, senior lecturer.

до́чиста *adv* clean; completely.

до́чка daughter. **дочь** (-чери, *instr* -черью; *pl* -чери, -черей, *instr* -черьми́) daughter.

дошёл *etc.: see* **дойти́**

дошко́льник, -ница child under school age. **дошко́льный** pre-school.

доща́тый plank, board. **до́щечка** small plank, board; plaque.

доя́рка milkmaid.

драгоце́нность jewel; treasure; *pl* jewellery; valuables. **драгоце́нный** precious.

дразни́ть (-ню́, -нишь) *impf* tease.

дра́ка fight.

драко́н dragon.

дра́ма drama. **драмати́ческий** dramatic. **драмату́рг** playwright. **драматурги́я** dramatic art; plays.

драп thick woollen cloth.

драпиро́вка draping; curtain; hangings. **драпиро́вщик** upholsterer.

драть (деру́, -рёшь; драл, -а́, -о) *impf* (*pf* вы́~, за~, со~) tear (up); irritate; make off; flog; ~ся fight.

дре́безги *pl*; в ~ to smithereens. **дребезжа́ть** (-жи́т) *impf* jingle, tinkle.

древеси́на wood; timber. **древе́сный** wood; ~ у́голь charcoal.

дре́вко (*pl* -и, -ов) pole, staff; shaft.

древнегре́ческий ancient Greek. **древнееврейский** Hebrew. **древнеру́сский** Old Russian. **дре́вний** ancient; aged. **дре́вность** antiquity.

дрейф drift; leeway. **дрейфова́ть** *impf* drift.

дрема́ть (-млю́, -млешь) *impf* doze; slumber. **дремо́та** drowsiness.

дрему́чий dense.

дрессиро́ванный trained; performing. **дрессирова́ть** *impf* (*pf* вы́~) train; school. **дрессиро́вка** training. **дрессиро́вщик** trainer.

дроби́ть (-блю́) *impf* (*pf* раз~) break up, smash; crush; ~ся break to pieces, smash. **дробови́к** (-а́) shot-gun. **дробь** (small) shot; drumming; fraction. **дро́бный** fractional.

дрова́ (дров) *pl* firewood.

дро́гнуть (-ну) *pf*, **дрожа́ть** (-жу́) *impf* tremble; shiver; quiver.

дро́жжи (-ей) *pl* yeast.

дрожь shivering, trembling.

дрозд (-а́) thrush; чёрный ~ blackbird.

дро́ссель *m* throttle, choke.

дро́тик javelin, dart.

друг[1] (*pl* -узья́, -зей) friend; boyfriend. **друг**[2]; ~ дру́га (дру́гу) each other, one another. **друго́й** other, another; different; на ~ день (the) next day. **дру́жба** friendship. **дружелюбный, дру́жеский, дру́жественный** friendly. **дружи́ть** (-жу́, -у́жи́шь) *impf* be friends. **дру́жный** (-жен, -жна́, -о) friendly; harmonious; simultaneous, general; concerted.

дря́блый (-бл, -а́, -о) flabby.

дря́зги (-зг) *pl* squabbles.

дрянно́й worthless; good-for-nothing. **дрянь** rubbish.

дряхле́ть (-е́ю) *impf* (*pf* о∼) become decrepit. **дря́хлый** (-хл, -на́, -о) decrepit, senile.

дуб (*pl* -ы́) oak; blockhead. **дуби́на** club, cudgel; blockhead. **дуби́нка** truncheon, baton.

дублёнка sheepskin coat.

дублёр understudy. **дублика́т** duplicate. **дубли́ровать** duplicate; understudy; dub.

дубо́вый oak; coarse; clumsy.

дуга́ (*pl* -и) arc; arch.

ду́дка pipe, fife.

ду́ло muzzle; barrel.

ду́ма thought; Duma (*lower house of Russian parliament*). **ду́мать** *impf* (*pf* по∼) think; +*inf* think of, intend. **ду́маться** *impf* (*impers* +*dat*) seem.

дунове́ние puff, breath.

дупло́ (*pl* -а, *gen pl* -пел) hollow; hole; cavity.

ду́ра, дура́к (-а́) fool. **дура́чить** (-чу) *impf* (*pf* о∼) fool, dupe; ∼ся play the fool.

дуре́ть (-е́ю) *impf* (*pf* о∼) grow stupid.

дурма́н narcotic; intoxicant. **дурма́нить** *impf* (*pf* о∼) stupefy.

дурно́й (-рен, -рна́, -о) bad, evil; ugly; мне ду́рно I feel faint, sick. **дурнота́** faintness; nausea.

ду́тый hollow; inflated. **ду́ть** (ду́ю) *impf* (*pf* по∼) blow; ду́ет there is a draught. **ду́ться** (ду́юсь) *impf* pout; sulk.

дух spirit; spirits; heart; mind; breath; ghost; smell; в хоро́шем ду́хе in a good mood; не в мо́ём ∼е not to my taste; ни слу́ху ни ∼у no news; not a word. **духи́** (-о́в) *pl* scent, perfume. **Ду́хов день** Whit Monday. **духове́нство** clergy. **духови́дец** (-дца) clairvoyant; medium. **духо́вка** oven.

духо́вный spiritual; ecclesiastical. **духово́й** wind. **духота́** stuffiness, closeness.

душ shower(-bath).

душа́ (*acc* -у; *pl* -и) soul; heart; feeling; spirit; inspiration; в душе́ inwardly; at heart; от всей души́ with all one's heart.

душева́я *sb* shower-room.

душевнобольно́й mentally ill, insane; *sb* mental patient; lunatic. **душе́вный** mental; sincere, cordial.

души́стый fragrant; ∼ горо́шек sweet pea(s).

души́ть (-шу́, -шишь) *impf* (*pf* за∼) strangle; stifle, smother.

души́ться (-шу́сь, -шишься) *impf* (*pf* на∼) use, put on, perfume.

ду́шный (-шен, -шна́, -о) stuffy, close.

дуэ́ль duel.

дуэ́т duet.

ды́бом *adv* on end; у меня́ во́лосы вста́ли ∼ my hair stood on end. **дыбы́**: станови́ться на ∼ rear; resist.

дым (*loc* -у́; *pl* -ы́) smoke. **дыми́ть** (-млю́) *impf* (*pf* на∼) smoke; ∼ся smoke; billow. **ды́мка** haze. **ды́мный** smoky. **дымово́й**: ∼а́я труба́ flue, chimney. **дымо́к** (-мка́) puff of smoke. **дымохо́д** flue.

ды́ня melon.

дыра́ (*pl* -ы), **ды́рка** (*gen pl* -рок) hole; gap.

дыха́ние breathing; breath. **дыха́тельный** respiratory; breathing; ∼ое го́рло windpipe. **дыша́ть** (-шу́, -шишь) *impf* breathe.

дья́вол devil. **дья́вольский** devilish, diabolical.

дья́кон (*pl* -а́) deacon.

дю́жина dozen.

дюйм inch.

дю́на dune.

дя́дя (gen pl -ей) m uncle.

дя́тел (-тла) woodpecker.

Е

ева́нгелие gospel; the Gospels. **евангели́ческий** evangelical.

евре́й, евре́йка Jew; Hebrew. **евре́йский** Jewish.

е́вро indecl euro

Евро́па Europe. **европе́ец** (-е́йца) European. **европе́йский** European.

Еги́пет Egypt. **еги́петский** Egyptian. **египтя́нин** (pl -я́не, -я́н), **египтя́нка** Egyptian.

его́ see он, оно́; pron his; its.

еда́ food; meal.

едва́ adv & conj hardly; just; scarcely; ~ (ли) не almost, all but.

еди́м etc.: see есть¹

едине́ние unity. **едини́ца** (figure) one; unity; unit; individual. **едини́чный** single; individual.

едино- in comb mono-, uni-; one; co-. **единобра́чие** monogamy. **~вла́стие** autocracy. **~вре́менно** adv only once; simultaneously. **~гла́сие**, **~ду́шие** unanimity. **~гла́сный**, **~ду́шный** unanimous. **~кро́вный брат** half-brother. **~мы́слие** like-mindedness; agreement. **~мы́шленник** like-minded person. **~утро́бный брат** half-brother.

еди́нственно adv only, solely. **еди́нственный** only, sole. **еди́нство** unity. **еди́ный** one; single; united.

е́дкий (е́док, едка́, -о) caustic; pungent.

едо́к (-á) mouth, head; eater.

е́ду etc.: see е́хать

её see она́; pron her, hers; its.

ёж (ежа́) hedgehog.

еже- in comb every; -ly. **ежего́дник** annual, year-book. **~го́дный** annual. **~дне́вный** daily. **~ме́сячник**, **~ме́сячный** monthly. **~неде́льник**, **~неде́льный** weekly.

ежеви́ка (no pl; usu collect) blackberry; blackberries; blackberry bush.

е́жели conj if.

ёжиться (ёжусь) impf (pf съ~) huddle up; shrink away.

езда́ ride, riding; drive, driving; journey. **е́здить** (е́зжу) impf go; ride, drive; ~ верхо́м ride. **ездо́к** (-á) rider.

ей see она́

ей-бо́гу int really! truly!

ел etc.: see есть¹

е́ле adv scarcely; only just. **е́ле-е́ле** emphatic variant of е́ле

ёлка fir-tree, spruce; Christmas tree. **ёлочка** herring-bone pattern. **ёлочный** Christmas-tree. **ель** fir-tree; spruce.

ем etc.: see есть¹

ёмкий capacious. **ёмкость** capacity.

ему́ see он, оно́

епи́скоп bishop.

е́ресь heresy. **ерети́к** (-á) heretic. **ерети́ческий** heretical.

ёрзать impf fidget.

еро́шить (-шу) impf (pf взъ~) ruffle, rumple.

ерунда́ nonsense.

е́сли conj if; ~ бы if only; ~ бы не but for, if it were not for; ~ не unless.

ест *see* **есть**[1]

есте́ственно *adv* naturally. **есте́ственный** natural. **есте́ство** nature; essence. **естествозна́ние** (natural) science.

есть[1] (ем, ешь, ест, еди́м; ел) *impf* (*pf* съ~) eat; corrode, eat away.

есть[2] *see* **быть**; is, are; there is, there are; ~ у меня́ I have.

ефре́йтор lance-corporal.

е́хать (е́ду) *impf* (*pf* по~) go; ride, drive; travel; ~ верхо́м ride.

ехи́дный malicious, spiteful.

ешь *see* **есть**[1]

ещё *adv* still; yet; (some) more; any more; yet, further; again; +*comp* still, even; всё ~ still; ~ бы! of course! and how!; ~ нет ~ not yet; ~ раз once more; кто ~? who else? пока́ ~ for the time being. что ~? what else?

е́ю *see* **она́**

Ж

ж *conj*: *see* **же**

жа́ба toad.

жа́бра (*gen pl* -бр) gill.

жа́воронок (-нка) lark.

жа́дничать *impf* be greedy; be mean. **жа́дность** greed; meanness. **жа́дный** (-ден, -дна́, -о) greedy; avid; mean.

жа́жда thirst; +*gen* thirst, craving for. **жа́ждать** (-ду) *impf* thirst, yearn.

жаке́т, **жаке́тка** jacket.

жале́ть (-е́ю) *impf* (*pf* по~) pity, feel sorry for; regret; +*acc or gen* grudge.

жа́лить *impf* (*pf* у~) sting, bite.

жа́лкий (-лок, -лка́, -о) pitiful.

жа́лко *predic: see* **жаль**

жа́ло sting.

жа́лоба complaint. **жа́лобный** plaintive.

жа́лованье salary. **жа́ловать** *impf* (*pf* по~) +*acc* or *gen* of person, *instr* or *acc* of thing grant, bestow on; ~ся complain (на+*acc* of, about).

жа́лостливый compassionate. **жа́лостный** piteous; compassionate. **жа́лость** pity. **жаль**, **жа́лко** *predic, impers* (it is) a pity; +*dat* it grieves; +*gen* grudge; как ~ what a pity; мне ~ его́ I'm sorry for him.

жалюзи́ *neut indecl* Venetian blind.

жанр genre.

жар (*loc* -у́) heat; heat of the day; fever; (high) temperature; ardour. **жара́** heat; hot weather.

жарго́н slang.

жа́реный roast; grilled; fried. **жа́рить** *impf* (*pf* за~, из~) roast; grill; fry; scorch; burn; ~ся roast, fry. **жа́ркий** (-рок, -рка́, -о) hot; passionate; -ое roast (meat). **жаро́вня** (*gen pl* -вен) brazier. **жар-пти́ца** Firebird. **жа́рче** *comp of* **жа́ркий**

жа́тва harvest. **жать**[1] (жну, жнёшь) *impf* (*pf* с~) reap, cut.

жать[2] (жму, жмёшь) *impf* press, squeeze; pinch; oppress.

жва́чка chewing, rumination; cud; chewing-gum. **жва́чный** ruminant; -ое *sb* ruminant.

жгу *etc.: see* **жечь**

жгут (-а́) plait; tourniquet.

жгу́чий burning. **жёг** *etc.: see* **жечь**

ждать (жду, ждёшь; -ал, -а́, -о) *impf* +*gen* wait (for); expect.

же, **ж** *conj* but; and; however; also; *partl* giving emphasis or

expressing identity; **мне же ка́-
жется** it seems to me, however;
сего́дня же this very day; **что же
ты де́лаешь?** what on earth are
you doing?

жева́тельная рези́нка
chewing-gum. **жева́ть** (жую́,
жуёшь) *impf* chew; ruminate.

жезл (-á) rod; staff.

жела́ние wish, desire. **жела́н-
ный** longed-for; beloved. **жела́-
тельный** desirable; advisable. **жела́-
ть** *impf* (*pf* по~) +*gen*
wish for, desire; want.

желе́ *neut indecl* jelly.

железа́ (*pl* же́лезы, -лёз, -за́м)
gland; *pl* tonsils.

железнодоро́жник railwayman. **железнодоро́жный** railway. **желе́зный** iron; **~ая до-
ро́га** railway. **желе́зо** iron.

железобето́н reinforced concrete.

жёлоб (*pl* -á) gutter. **желобо́к**
(-бка́) groove, channel, flute.

желте́ть (-е́ю) *impf* (*pf* по~)
turn yellow; be yellow. **желто́к**
(-тка́) yolk. **желту́ха** jaundice.
жёлтый (жёлт, -á, жёлто)
yellow.

желу́док (-дка) stomach. **желу́-
дочный** stomach; gastric.

жёлудь (*gen pl* -е́й) *m* acorn.

жёлчный bilious; gall; irritable.
жёлчь bile, gall.

жема́ниться *impf* mince, put
on airs. **жема́нный** mincing, affected. **жема́нство**
affectedness.

же́мчуг (*pl* -á) pearl(s). **жемчу́-
жина** pearl. **жемчу́жный**
pearl(y).

жена́ (*pl* жёны) wife. **жена́тый**
married.

жени́ть (-ню́, -нишь) *impf & pf*
(*pf also* по~) marry. **жени́тьба**

marriage. **жени́ться** (-ню́сь,
-нишься) *impf & pf* (+**на**+*prep*)
marry, get married (to). **жени́х**
(-á) fiancé; bridegroom. **жéн-
ский** woman's; feminine; female. **жéнственный** womanly,
feminine. **жéнщина** woman.

жердь (*gen pl* -е́й) pole; stake.

жеребёнок (-нка; *pl* -бя́та, -бя́т)
foal. **жеребе́ц** (-бца́) stallion.

жеребьёвка casting of lots.

жерло́ (*pl* -а́) muzzle; crater.

жёрнов (*pl* -á, -о́в) millstone.

же́ртва sacrifice; victim. **же́рт-
венный** sacrificial. **же́ртво-
вать** *impf* (*pf* по~) present,
make a donation (of); +*instr*
sacrifice.

жест gesture. **жестикули́ро-
вать** *impf* gesticulate.

жёсткий (-ток, -тка́, -о) hard,
tough; rigid, strict; **~ диск**
(*comput*) hard disk.

жесто́кий (-то́к, -á, -о) cruel; severe. **жесто́кость** cruelty.

жесть tin(-plate). **жестяно́й**
tin.

жето́н medal; counter; token.

жечь (жгу, жжёшь; жёг, жгла) *impf*
(*pf* с~) burn; **~ся** burn, sting;
burn o.s.

живи́тельный invigorating.
жи́вность poultry, fowl.
живо́й (жив, -á, -о) living, alive;
lively; vivid; brisk; animated;
bright; **на ~ую ни́тку** hastily,
anyhow; **ши́ть на ~ую ни́тку**
tack. **живопи́сец** (-сца) painter.
живопи́сный picturesque. **жи́-
вопись** painting. **жи́вость** liveliness.

живо́т (-á) abdomen; stomach.
животново́дство animal hus-
bandry. **живо́тное** *sb* animal.
живо́тный animal.

живу́ *etc.*: *see* жить. **живу́чий**

hardy. **живём** adv alive.

жи́дкий (-док, -дка́, -о) liquid; watery; weak; sparse; ~**ий криста́лл** liquid crystal. **жи́дкость** liquid, fluid; wateriness, weakness. **жи́жа** sludge; slush; liquid. **жи́же** comp of **жи́дкий**

жи́зненный life, of life; vital; living; ~ **у́ровень** standard of living. **жизнеописа́ние** biography. **жизнера́достный** cheerful. **жизнеспосо́бный** capable of living; viable. **жизнь** life.

жи́ла vein; tendon, sinew.

жиле́т, жиле́тка waistcoat.

жиле́ц (-льца́), **жили́ца** lodger; tenant; inhabitant.

жили́ще dwelling, abode. **жили́щный** housing; living.

жи́лка vein; fibre; streak.

жило́й dwelling; habitable; ~**о́й дом** dwelling house; block of flats; ~**а́я пло́щадь, жилпло́щадь** floor-space; housing; accommodation. **жильё** habitation; dwelling.

жир (loc -у́; pl -ы́) fat; grease. **жире́ть** (-е́ю) impf (pf о~, раз~) grow fat. **жи́рный** (-рен, -рна́, -о) fatty; greasy; rich. **жирово́й** fatty; fat.

жира́ф giraffe.

жите́йский worldly; everyday. **жи́тель** m inhabitant; dweller. **жи́тельство** residence. **жи́тница** granary. **жи́то** corn, cereal. **жить** (живу́, -вёшь; жил, -á, -о) impf live. **житьё** life; existence; habitation.

жму etc.: see **жать²**

жму́риться impf (pf за~) screw up one's eyes, frown.

жнивьё (pl -ья, -ьев) stubble (-field). **жну** etc.: see **жать¹**

жоке́й jockey.

жонглёр juggler.

жрать (жру, жрёшь; -ал, -á, -о) guzzle.

жре́бий lot; fate, destiny; ~ **бро́шен** the die is cast.

жрец priest. **жри́ца** priestess.

жужжа́ть (-жу́) hum, buzz, drone; whiz(z).

жук (-á) beetle.

жу́лик petty thief; cheat. **жу́льничать** impf (pf с~) cheat.

жура́вль (-я́) m crane.

жури́ть impf reprove.

журна́л magazine, periodical. **журнали́ст** journalist. **журнали́стика** journalism.

журча́ние babble; murmur. **журча́ть** (-чи́т) impf babble, murmur.

жу́ткий (-ток, -тка́, -о) uncanny; terrible, terrifying. **жу́тко** adv terrifyingly; terribly, awfully.

жую́ etc.: see **жева́ть**

жюри́ neut indecl judges.

З

за prep I. +acc (indicating motion or action) or instr (indicating rest or state) behind; beyond; across, the other side of; at; to; **за́ город, за́ городом** out of town; **за рубежо́м** abroad; **сесть за роя́ль** sit down at the piano; **сиде́ть за роя́лем** be at the piano; **за́ угол, за угло́м** round the corner. II. +acc after; over; during, in the space of; by; for; to; **за ва́ше здоро́вье!** your health!; **вести́ за́ руку** lead by the hand; **далеко́ за́ полночь** long after midnight; **за два дня до+gen** two days before; **за три киломе́тра от дере́вни** three kilometres from the village; **пла-**

тúть за билéт pay for a ticket; **за послéднее врéмя** lately. **III.** +*instr* after; for; because of; at, during; **год за гóдом** year after year; **идтú за молокóм** go for milk; **за обéдом** at dinner.

забáва amusement; game; fun. **забавля́ть** *impf* amuse; **~ся** amuse o.s. **забáвный** amusing, funny.

забастовáть *pf* strike; go on strike. **забастóвка** strike. **забастóвщик** striker.

забвéние oblivion.

забéг heat, race. **забегáть** *impf*, **забежáть** (-eгý) *pf* run up; **+к**+*dat* drop in on; **~ вперёд** run ahead; anticipate.

за|берéменеть (-ею) *pf* become pregnant.

заберý etc.: see **забрáть**

забивáние jamming. **забивáть(ся** *impf* of **забúть(ся**[1]

забинтовáть *pf*, **забинтóвывать** *impf* bandage.

забирáть(ся *impf* of **забрáть(ся**

забúтый downtrodden. **забúть**[1] (-бью, -бьёшь) *pf* (*impf* **забивáть**) drive in, hammer in; score; seal, block up; obstruct; choke; jam; cram; beat up; beat; **~ся** hide, take refuge; become cluttered or clogged; **+в**+*acc* get into, penetrate. **забúть(ся**[2] *pf* begin to beat. **забия́ка** *m & f* squabbler; bully.

заблаговрéменно *adv* in good time; well in advance. **заблаговрéменный** timely.

заблестéть (-ещý, -éстишь or -éщешь) *pf* begin to shine, glitter, glow.

заблудúться (-ужýсь, -ýдишься) *pf* get lost. **заблýдший** lost, stray. **заблуждáться** *impf* be

mistaken. **заблуждéние** error; delusion.

забóй (pit-)face.

заболевáемость sickness rate. **заболевáние** sickness, illness; falling ill. **заболевáть**[1] *impf*, **заболéть**[1](-éю) *pf* fall ill; +*instr* go down with. **заболевáть**[2] *impf*, **заболéть**[2] (-лúт) *pf* (begin to) ache, hurt.

забóр[1] fence.

забóр[2] taking away; obtaining on credit.

забóта concern; care; trouble(s). **забóтить** (-óчу) *impf* (*pf* **о~**) trouble, worry; **~ся** *impf* (*pf* **по~**) worry; take care (**о**+*prep* of); take trouble; care. **забóтливый** solicitous, thoughtful.

за|бракóвать *pf*.

забрáсывать *impf* of **забросáть**, **забрóсить**

забрáть (-берý, -берёшь; -áл, -á, -о) *pf* (*impf* **забирáть**) take; take away; seize; appropriate; **~ся** climb; get to, into.

забредáть *impf*, **забрестú** (-едý, -едёшь; -ёл, -á) *pf* stray, wander; drop in.

за|бронúровать *pf*.

забросáть *pf* (*impf* **забрáсывать**) fill up; bespatter, deluge. **забрóсить** (-óшу) *pf* (*impf* **забрáсывать**) throw; abandon; neglect. **забрóшенный** neglected; deserted.

забры́згать *pf*, **забры́згивать** *impf* splash, bespatter.

забывáть *impf*, **забы́ть** (-бýду) *pf* forget; **~ся** doze off; lose consciousness; forget o.s. **забы́вчивый** forgetful. **забытьé** oblivion; drowsiness.

забью́ etc.: see **забúть**

завáливать *impf*, **завалúть**

(-лю́, -лишь) *pf* block up; pile; cram; overload; knock down; make a mess of; ~ся fall; collapse; tip up.

завáривать *impf*, **завари́ть** (-арю́, -а́ришь) *pf* make; brew; weld. **завáрка** brewing; brew; welding.

заведéние establishment. **завéдовать** *impf* +*instr* manage.

завéдомо *adv* wittingly. **завéдомый** notorious, undoubted.

заведу́ *etc.*: *see* **завести́**

завéдующий *sb* (+*instr*) manager; head.

завезти́ (-зу́, -зёшь; -ёз, -ла́) *pf* (*impf* **завози́ть**) convey, deliver.

за|вербовáть *pf*.

завери́тель *m* witness. **завéрить** *pf* (*impf* **заверя́ть**) assure; certify; witness.

заверну́ть (-ну́, -нёшь) *pf* (*impf* **завёртывать**, **завора́чивать**) wrap, wrap up; roll up; screw tight, screw up; turn (off); drop in, call in.

заверте́ться (-рчу́сь, -ртишься) *pf* begin to turn *or* spin; lose one's head.

завёртывать *impf of* **заверну́ть**

заверша́ть *impf*, **заверши́ть** (-шу́) *pf* complete, conclude. **завершéние** completion; end.

заверя́ть *impf of* **завéрить**

завéса veil, screen. **завéсить** (-éшу) *pf* (*impf* **завéшивать**) curtain (off).

завести́ (-еду́, -ёшь; -вёл, -á) *pf* (*impf* **заводи́ть**) take, bring; drop off; start up; acquire; introduce; wind (up), crank; ~сь be; appear; be established; start.

завéт behest, bidding, ordinance; Testament. **завéтный**

cherished; secret.

завéшивать *impf of* **завéсить**

завещáние will, testament. **завещáть** bequeath.

завзя́тый inveterate.

завивáть(ся *impf of* **зави́ть(ся**. **зави́вка** waving; wave.

зави́дно *impers+dat*: мне ~ I feel envious. **зави́дный** enviable. **зави́довать** *impf* (*pf* по~) +*dat* envy.

завинти́ть (-нчу́) *pf*, **зави́нчивать** *impf* screw up.

зави́сеть *impf*, **зави́снуть** (-нет, -вис(нул)) *pf* (*comput*) crash.

зави́сеть (-и́шу) *impf* +от+*gen* depend on. **зави́симость** dependence; в зави́симости от depending on, subject to. **зави́симый** dependent.

зави́стливый envious. **зáвисть** envy.

завито́й (зáвит, -á, -о) curled, waved. **завито́к** (-тка́) curl, lock; flourish. **зави́ть** (-вью́, -вьёшь; -и́л, -á, -о) *pf* (*impf* **завивáть**) curl, wave; ~ся curl, wave, twine; have one's hair curled.

завладевáть *impf*, **завладéть** (-éю) *pf* +*instr* take possession of; seize.

завлекáтельный alluring; fascinating. **завлекáть** *impf*, **завлéчь** (-еку́, -ечёшь; -лёк, -ла́) *pf* lure; fascinate.

завóд[1] factory; works; studfarm.

завóд[2] winding mechanism. **заводи́ть(ся** (-ожу́(сь, -óдишь(ся) *impf of* **завести́(сь**. **заводнóй** clockwork; winding, cranking.

заводскóй factory; *sb* factory worker. **завóдчик** factory owner.

зáводь backwater.

завоева́ние winning; conquest; achievement. **завоева́тель** *m* conqueror. **завоева́ть** (-ою́ю) *pf*, **завоёвывать** *impf* conquer; win, gain; try to get.

завожу́ *etc.*: *see* **заводи́ть**, **завози́ть**

заво́з delivery; carriage. **завози́ть** (-ожу́, -о́зишь) *impf of* **завезти́**

завора́чивать *impf of* **заверну́ть**. **заворо́т** turn, turning; sharp bend.

завою́ *etc.*: *see* **завы́ть**

завсегда́ *adv* always. **завсегда́тай** habitué, frequenter.

за́втра tomorrow. **за́втрак** breakfast; lunch. **за́втракать** *impf* (*pf* **по~**) have breakfast; have lunch. **за́втрашний** tomorrow's; ~ **день** tomorrow.

завыва́ть *impf*, **завы́ть** (-во́ю) *pf* (begin to) howl.

завяза́ть (-яжу́, -я́жешь) *pf* (*impf* **завя́зывать**), tie, tie up; start; ~**ся** start; arise; (*of fruit*) set. **завя́зка** string, lace; start; opening.

завя́знуть (-ну, -я́з) *pf*. **завя́зывать(ся** *impf of* **завяза́ть(ся**

завя́нуть (-ну; -я́л) *impf*.

загада́ть *pf*, **зага́дывать** *impf* think of; plan ahead; guess at the future; ~ **зага́дку** ask a riddle. **зага́дка** riddle; enigma. **зага́дочный** enigmatic, mysterious.

зага́р sunburn, tan.

загаси́ть (-ашу́, -а́сишь) *pf*. **зага́снуть** (-ну) *pf*.

загво́здка snag; difficulty.

заги́б fold; exaggeration. **загиба́ть** *impf of* **загну́ть**

загипнотизи́ровать *pf*.

загла́вие title; heading. за-

гла́вн|ый title; ~**ая бу́ква** capital letter.

загла́дить (-а́жу) *pf*, **загла́живать** *impf* iron, iron out; make up for; expiate; ~**ся** iron out, become smooth; fade.

загло́хнуть (-ну; -о́х) *pf*.

заглуша́ть *impf*, **заглуши́ть** (-шу́) *pf* drown, muffle; jam; suppress, stifle; alleviate.

загляде́нье lovely sight. **загляде́ться** (-яжу́сь) *pf*, **загля́дываться** *impf* на+*acc* stare at; be lost in admiration of. **загля́дывать** *impf*, **загляну́ть** (-ну́, -нешь) *pf* peep; drop in.

загна́ть (-гоню́, -го́нишь; -а́л, -а́, -о) *pf* (*impf* **загоня́ть**) drive in, drive home; drive; exhaust.

загнива́ние decay; suppuration. **загнива́ть** *impf*, **загни́ть** (-ию́, -ии́шь; -и́л, -а́, -о) *pf* rot; decay; fester.

загну́ть (-ну́, -нёшь) *pf* (*impf* **загиба́ть**) turn up, turn down; bend.

загова́ривать *impf*, **заговори́ть** *pf* begin to speak; tire out with talk; cast a spell over; protect with a charm (**от**+*gen* against). **загово́р** plot; spell. **загово́рщик** conspirator.

заголо́вок (-вка) title; heading; headline.

заго́н enclosure, pen; driving in. **загоня́ть**[1] *impf of* **загна́ть**. **загоня́ть**[2] *pf* tire out; work to death.

загора́живать *impf of* **загороди́ть**

загора́ть *impf*, **загоре́ть** (-рю́) *pf* become sunburnt; ~**ся** catch fire; blaze; *impers*+*dat* want very much. **загоре́лый** sunburnt.

загороди́ть (-рожу́, -ро́ди́шь) *pf*

(*impf* загора́живать) enclose, fence in; obstruct. **загоро́дка** fence, enclosure.

за́городный suburban; country.

загота́вливать *impf*, **заготовля́ть** *impf*, **загото́вить** (-влю) *pf* lay in (a stock of); store; prepare. **загото́вка** (State) procurement.

загради́ть (-ажу́) *pf*, **загражда́ть** *impf* block, obstruct; bar. **загражде́ние** obstruction; barrier.

заграни́ца abroad, foreign parts. **заграни́чный** foreign.

загреба́ть *impf*, **загрести́** (-ебу́, -ебёшь; -ёб, -ла́) *pf* rake up; gather; rake in.

загри́вок (-вка) withers; nape (of the neck).

загримирова́ть *pf*.

загроможда́ть *impf*, **загромозди́ть** (-зжу́) *pf* block up, encumber; cram.

загружа́ть *impf*, **загрузи́ть** (-ужу́, -у́зишь) *pf* load; feed; (*comput*) boot; load; download; ∼ся +*instr* load up with, take on. **загру́зка** loading, feeding, charge, load, capacity.

загрунтова́ть *pf*.

загрусти́ть (-ущу́) *pf* grow sad.

загрязне́ние pollution. **за-гря́зни́ть** *pf*, **загрязня́ть** *impf* soil; pollute; ∼ся become dirty.

загс *abbr* of (отде́л) за́писи а́ктов гражда́нского состоя́ния) registry office.

загуби́ть (-блю́, -бишь) *pf* ruin; squander, waste.

загуля́ть, **загу́ливать** *impf* take to drink.

загусте́ть *pf*.

зад (*loc* -ý; *pl* -ы́) back; hindquarters; buttocks; ∼ом на-

перёд back to front.

задава́ть(ся (-даю́(сь) *impf* of **зада́ть(ся**

задави́ть (-влю́, -вишь) *pf* crush; run over.

задади́м *etc*., **зада́м** *etc*.: *see* **зада́ть**

зада́ние task, job.

зада́тки (-тков) *pl* abilities, promise.

зада́ток (-тка) deposit, advance.

зада́ть (-а́м, -а́шь, -а́ст, -ади́м; за́дал, -а́, -о) *pf* (*impf* **задава́ть**) set; give; ∼ вопро́с ask a question; ∼ся мы́слью, це́лью make up one's mind. **зада́ча** problem; task.

задвига́ть *impf*, **задви́нуть** (-ну) *pf* bolt; bar; push; ∼ся shut; slide. **задви́жка** bolt; catch.

задво́рки (-рок) *pl* back yard; backwoods.

задева́ть *impf of* **заде́ть**

заде́лать *pf*, **заде́лывать** *impf* do up; block up, close up.

заде́ну *etc*.: *see* **заде́ть**. **заде́рживать** *impf* of **задёрнуть**

задержа́ние detention. **задержа́ть** (-жу́, -жишь) *pf*, **заде́рживать** *impf* delay; withhold; arrest; ∼ся stay too long; be delayed. **заде́ржка** delay.

задёрнуть (-ну) *pf* (*impf* **задёргивать**) pull; draw.

задеру́ *etc*.: *see* **задра́ть**

заде́ть (-е́ну) *pf* (*impf* **задева́ть**) brush (against); graze; offend; catch (against).

задира́ *m* & *f* bully; troublemaker. **задира́ть** *impf* of **задра́ть**

за́дний back, rear; дать ∼ий ход reverse; ∼яя мысль ulterior

motive; ~ий план background; ~ий прохо́д anus. за́дник back; backdrop.

задо́лго adv +до+gen long before.

задолжа́ть pf. задо́лженность debts.

задо́р fervour. **задо́рный** provocative; fervent.

задохну́ться (-ну́сь, -нёшься, -о́хся or -у́лся) pf (impf задыха́ться) suffocate; choke; pant.

заздра́ть (-деру́, -дерёшь, -а́л, -а́, -о) pf (impf also задира́ть) tear to pieces, kill; lift up; break; provoke, insult.

задрема́ть (-млю́, -млешь) pf doze off.

задрожа́ть (-жу́) pf begin to tremble.

задува́ть impf of заду́ть

заду́мать pf, заду́мывать impf plan; intend; think of; ~ся become thoughtful; meditate. заду́мчивость reverie. заду́мчивый pensive.

заду́ть (-у́ю) pf (impf задува́ть) blow out; begin to blow.

заду́шевный sincere; intimate.

задуши́ть (-ушу́, -у́шишь) pf

задыха́ться impf of задохну́ться

заеда́ть impf of зае́сть

зае́зд calling in; lap, heat. зае́здить (-зжу) pf override; wear out. заезжа́ть impf of зае́хать. зае́зженный hackneyed; worn out. зае́зжий visiting.

заём (за́йма) loan.

зае́сть (-е́м, -е́шь, -е́ст, -еди́м) pf (impf заеда́ть) torment; jam; entangle.

зае́хать (-е́ду) pf (impf заезжа́ть) call in; enter, ride in, drive in; reach; +за+acc go past; +за+instr call for, fetch.

зажа́рить(ся pf.

зажа́ть (-жму́, -жмёшь) pf (impf зажима́ть) squeeze; grip; suppress.

заже́чь (-жгу́, -жжёшь, -жёг, -жгла́) pf (impf зажига́ть) set fire to; kindle; light; ~ся catch fire.

зажива́ть impf of зажи́ть. заживи́ть (-влю́) pf, заживля́ть impf heal. **за́живо** adv alive.

зажига́лка lighter. зажига́ние ignition. зажига́тельный inflammatory; incendiary. зажига́ть(ся impf of заже́чь(ся

зажи́м clamp; terminal; suppression. зажима́ть impf of зажа́ть. зажи́мный tight-fisted.

зажи́точный prosperous. зажи́ть (-иву́, -ивёшь; -ил, -а́, -о) pf (impf зажива́ть) heal; begin to live.

зажму́ etc.: see зажа́ть. за|жму́риться pf.

звенеть (-и́т) pf begin to ring.

зазелене́ть (-е́ет) pf turn green.

землпе́ние earthing; earth. землми́ть pf, землля́ть impf earth.

зазнава́ться (-наю́сь, -наёшься impf, зазна́ться pf give o.s. airs.

зазу́брина notch.

за|зубри́ть (-рю́, -у́бри́шь) pf

заи́грывать impf flirt.

за́ика m & f stammerer. заика́ние stammer. заика́ться impf, заикну́ться (-ну́сь, -нёшься) pf stammer, stutter; +о+prep mention.

займствование borrowing. займствовать impf & pf (pf also по~) borrow.

заинтересо́ванный interested. заинтересова́ть pf, за-

интересо́вывать *impf* interest; ~ся +*instr* become interested in.

зайскивать *impf* ingratiate o.s.

зайду́ *etc.: see* зайти́. **займу́** *etc.: see* заня́ть

зайти́ (-йду́, -йдёшь; зашёл, -шла́) *pf* (*impf* заходи́ть) call; drop in; set; +в+*acc* reach; +за+*acc* go behind, turn; +за +*instr* call for, fetch.

за́йчик little hare (*esp. as endearment*); reflection of sunlight. **за́йчиха** doe hare.

закабали́ть, закабаля́ть *impf* enslave.

закады́чный intimate, bosom.

зака́з order; на ~ to order. заказа́ть (-ажу́, -а́жешь) *pf*, зака́зывать *impf* order; book. зака́з-н|о́й made to order; ~о́е (письмо́) registered letter. зака́зчик customer, client.

зака́л temper; cast. закаля́ть *impf*, закали́ть (-лю́) *pf* (*impf also* зака́ливать) temper; harden. зака́лка tempering, hardening.

зака́лывать *impf of* заколо́ть. зака́пать *impf of* закапи́ть. зака́нчивать(ся *impf of* зако́нчить(ся

зака́пать *pf*, зака́пывать¹ *impf* begin to drip; rain; spot.

зака́пывать² *impf of* закопа́ть.

зака́т sunset. закати́ть *pf*, зака́тывать¹ *impf* begin to roll; roll up; roll out. закати́ть (-ачу́, -а́тишь) *pf*, зака́тывать² *impf* roll; wrap; set.

заква́ска ferment; leaven.

закида́ть *pf*, заки́дывать¹ *impf* shower; bespatter.

заки́дывать² *impf*, заки́нуть (-ну) *pf* throw (out, away).

закипа́ть *impf*, закипе́ть (-пи́т) *pf* begin to boil.

закиса́ть *impf*, заки́снуть (-ну; -и́с, -ла) *pf* turn sour; become apathetic. за́кись oxide.

закла́д pawn; pledge; bet; би́ться об ~ to bet. в ~е in pawn.

закла́дка laying; bookmark.

закладно́й pawn. закла́дывать *impf of* заложи́ть

закле́ивать *impf*, закле́ить *pf* glue up.

заклейми́ть (-млю́) *pf*.

заклепа́ть *pf*, заклёпывать *impf* rivet. заклёпка rivet; riveting.

заклина́ние incantation; spell. заклина́ть *impf* invoke; entreat.

заключа́ть *impf*, заключи́ть (-чу́) *pf* conclude; enter into; confine. заключа́ться consist; lie; be enclosed. заключе́ние conclusion; decision; confinement. заключённый *sb* prisoner. заключи́тельный final, concluding.

закля́тие pledge. закля́тый sworn.

закова́ть (-кую́, -куёшь) *pf*, зако́вывать *impf* chain; shackle.

закола́чивать *impf of* заколоти́ть

заколдо́ванный bewitched; ~ круг vicious circle. заколдова́ть *pf* bewitch; lay a spell on.

зако́лка hair-grip; hair-slide.

заколоти́ть (-лочу́, -ло́тишь) *pf* (*impf* зака́лачивать) board up; knock in; knock insensible.

заколо́ть (-олю́, -о́лешь) *pf* (*impf also* зака́лывать) stab; pin up; (*impers*) у меня́ заколо́ло в боку́ I have a stitch.

зако́н law. законнорождённый legitimate. зако́нность legality. зако́нный legal; legitimate.

зако́но- *in comb* law, legal. зако́-

нове́дение law, jurisprudence. **~дательный** legislative. **~да́тельство** legislation. **~ме́рность** regularity, normality. **~ме́рный** regular, natural. **~прое́кт** bill.

за|консерви́ровать pf. за|**консперти́ровать** pf.

зако́нченность completeness. **зако́нченный** finished; accomplished. **зако́нчить** (**-чу**) pf (impf зака́нчивать) end, finish; **~ся** end, finish.

закопа́ть pf (impf зака́пывать²) begin to dig; bury.

закопте́лый sooty, smutty. **за|копте́ть** (**-ти́т**) pf. **за|копти́ть** (**-нчу́**) pf.

закоренéлый deep-rooted; inveterate.

закосне́лый incorrigible.

закоу́лок (**-лка**) alley; nook.

закоченéлый numb with cold. **за|коченéть** (**-éю**) pf.

закра́дываться impf of закра́сться

закра́сить (**-а́шу**) pf (impf зака́рашивать) paint over.

закра́сться (**-аду́сь, -адёшься**) pf (impf закра́дываться) steal in, creep in.

закра́шивать impf of закра́сить

закрепи́тель m fixative. **закрепи́ть** (**-плю́**) pf, **закрепля́ть** impf fasten; fix; consolidate; +за+instr assign to; **~ за собо́й** secure.

закрепости́ть (**-ощу́**) pf, **закрепоща́ть** impf enslave. **закрепоще́ние** enslavement; slavery, serfdom.

закрича́ть (**-чу́**) pf cry out; begin to shout.

закро́йщик cutter.

закро́ю etc.: see **закры́ть**

закругле́ние rounding; curve. **закругли́ть** (**-лю́**) pf, **закругля́ть** impf make round; round off; **~ся** become round; round off.

закружи́ться (**-ужу́сь, -у́жи́шься**) pf begin to whirl or go round.

закрути́ть (**-учу́, -у́тишь**) pf, **закру́чивать** impf twist, twirl; wind round; turn; screw in; turn the head of; **~ся** twist, twirl, whirl; wind round.

закрыва́ть impf, **закры́ть** (**-ро́ю**) pf close, shut; turn off; close down; cover; **~ся** close, shut; end; close down; cover o.s.; shelter. **закры́тие** closing; shutting; closing down; shelter. **закры́тый** closed, shut; private.

закули́сный behind the scenes; backstage.

закупа́ть impf, **закупи́ть** (**-плю́, -пишь**) pf buy up; stock up with. **заку́пка** purchase.

закупо́ривать impf, **закупо́рить** pf cork; stop up; coop up. **заку́порка** corking; thrombosis.

заку́почный purchase. **заку́пщик** buyer.

заку́ривать impf, **закури́ть** (**-рю́, -ришь**) pf light up; begin to smoke.

закуси́ть (**-ушу́, -у́сишь**) pf, **заку́сывать** impf have a snack; **~** grab hold of. **заку́ска** hors d'oeuvre; snack. **заку́сочная** sb snack-bar.

за|ку́тать pf, **заку́тывать** impf wrap up; **~ся** wrap o.s. up.

зал hall; **~ ожида́ния** waiting-room.

залега́ть impf of залéчь

за|ледене́ть (**-éю**) pf.

залежа́лый stale, long unused. **залежа́ться** (**-жу́сь**) pf, залёжи-

ваться *impf* lie too long; find no market; become stale. **за́лежь** deposit, seam; stale goods.

залеза́ть *impf*, **зале́зть** (-зу; -ез) *pf* climb, climb up; get in; creep in.

за|лепи́ть (-плю́, -пишь) *pf*, **ле́плять** *impf* paste over; glue up.

залета́ть *impf*, **залете́ть** (-ечу́) *pf* fly; +**в**+*acc* fly into.

зале́чивать *impf*, **залечи́ть** (-чу́, -чишь) *pf* heal, cure; ~**ся** heal (up).

зале́чь (-ля́гу, -ля́жешь; -лёг, -ла́) *pf* (*impf* **залега́ть**) lie down; lie low; lie, be deposited.

зали́в bay; gulf. **залива́ть** *impf*, **зали́ть** (-лью́, -льёшь; за́лил, -а́, -о) *pf* flood, inundate; spill on; extinguish; spread; ~**ся** be flooded; pour, spill +*instr* break into.

зало́г deposit; pledge; security; mortgage; token; voice. **зало-жи́ть** (-жу́, -жишь) *pf* (*impf* **закла́дывать**) lay; put; mislay; pile up; pawn, mortgage; harness; lay in. **зало́жник** hostage.

залп volley, salvo; ~**ом** without pausing for breath.

залью́ *etc.*: *see* **зали́ть**. **заля́гу** *etc.*: *see* **зале́чь**

зам *abbr* (*of* **замести́тель**) assist-ant, deputy. **зам-** *abbr in comb* (*of* **замести́тель**) assistant, deputy, vice-.

за|ма́зать (-а́жу) *pf*, **зама́зы-вать** *impf* paint over; putty; smear; soil; get dirty. **за-ма́зка** putty; puttying.

зама́лчивать *impf* *of* **замол-ча́ть**

зама́нивать *impf*, **замани́ть** (-ню́, -нишь) *pf* entice; decoy. **за-**

ма́нчивый tempting.

за|маринова́ть *pf*

за|маскирова́ть *pf*, **замаски-ро́вывать** *impf* mask; disguise; ~**ся** disguise o.s.

зама́хиваться *impf*, **замах-ну́ться** (-ну́сь, -нёшься) *pf* +*instr* raise threateningly.

зама́чивать *impf* *of* **замочи́ть**

замедле́ние slowing down, de-celeration; delay. **заме́длить** *pf*, **замедля́ть** *impf* slow down; slacken; delay; ~**ся** slow down.

замёл *etc.*: *see* **замести́**

заме́на substitution; substitute. **заменя́мый** replaceable. **заме-ни́тель** *m* (+*gen*) substitute (for). **замени́ть** (-ню́, -нишь) *pf*, **заменя́ть** *impf* replace; be a substitute for.

замере́ть (-мру́, -мрёшь; за́мер, -ла́, -о) *pf* (*impf* **замира́ть**) stand still; freeze; die away.

замерза́ние freezing. **замер-за́ть** *impf*, **замёрзнуть** (-ну; замёрз) *pf* freeze (up); freeze to death.

заме́рить *pf* (*impf* **замеря́ть**) measure, gauge.

замеси́ть (-ешу́, -е́сишь) *pf* (*impf* **заме́шивать²**) knead.

замести́ (-ету́, -етёшь; -мёл, -а́) *pf* (*impf* **замета́ть**) sweep up; cover.

замести́тель *m* substitute; as-sistant, deputy, vice-. **заме-сти́ть** (-ещу́) *pf* (*impf* **замеща́ть**) replace; deputize for.

замета́ть *impf* *of* **замести́**

заме́тить (-е́чу) *pf* (*impf* **замеча́ть**) notice; note; remark. **заме́тка** mark; note. **заме́тный** noticeable; outstanding.

замеча́ние remark; reprimand. **замеча́тельный** remarkable;

splendid. **замеча́ть** impf of за**ме́тить**

замеша́тельство confusion; embarrassment. **заме́шать** pf, **заме́шивать**[1] impf mix up, entangle. **заме́шивать**[2] impf of **замеси́ть**

замеща́ть impf of **замести́ть**. **замеще́ние** substitution; filling.

зами́нка hitch; hesitation.

замира́ть impf of **замере́ть**

за́мкнутый reserved; closed, exclusive. **замкну́ть** (-ну́, -нёшь) pf (impf **замыка́ть**) lock; close; ∼**ся** close; shut o.s. up; become reserved.

за́мок[1] (-мка) castle.

замо́к[2] (-мка́) lock; padlock; clasp.

замолка́ть impf, **замо́лкнуть** (-ну; -мо́лк) pf fall silent; stop.

замолча́ть (-чу́) pf (impf **зама́лчивать**) fall silent; cease corresponding; hush up.

замора́живать impf, **заморо́зить** (-о́жу) pf freeze. **заморо́женный** frozen; iced. **за́морозки** (-ов) pl (slight) frosts.

замо́рский overseas.

за|мочи́ть (-чу́, -чишь) pf (impf also **зама́чивать**) wet; soak; ret.

замо́чная сква́жина keyhole.

замру́ etc.: see **замере́ть**

за́муж: вы́йти ∼ (за+acc) marry. **за́мужем** adv married (за+instr to).

за|му́чить (-чу) pf torment; wear out; bore to tears. **за|му́читься** (-чусь) pf.

за́мша suede.

замыка́ние locking; short circuit. **замыка́ть(ся** impf of за**мкну́ть(ся**

за́мысел (-сла) project, plan.

замы́слить pf, **замышля́ть** impf plan; contemplate.

за́навес, занаве́ска curtain.

занести́ (-су́, -сёшь; -ёс, -ла́) pf (impf **заноси́ть**) bring; note down; (impers) cover with snow etc.; (impers) skid.

занима́ть impf (pf **заня́ть**) occupy; interest; engage; borrow; ∼**ся** +instr be occupied with; work at; study.

зано́за splinter. **занози́ть** (-ожу́) pf get a splinter in.

зано́с snow-drift; skid. **заноси́ть** (-ошу́, -о́сишь) impf of зане**сти́**. **зано́счивый** arrogant.

заня́тие occupation, pl studies. **заня́той** busy. **за́нятый** (-нят, -á, -о) occupied; taken; engaged. **заня́ть(ся** (займу́(сь, -мёшь(ся; за́нял(ся, -á(сь, -о(сь) pf of зани**ма́ть(ся**

заодно́ adv in concert; at one; at the same time.

заостри́ть pf, **заостря́ть** impf sharpen; emphasize.

зао́чник, -ница student taking correspondence course; external student. **зао́чно** adv in one's absence; by correspondence course. **зао́чный курс** correspondence course.

за́пад west. **за́падный** west, western; westerly.

западня́ (gen pl -не́й) trap; pitfall, snare.

запакова́ть pf, **запако́вывать** impf pack; wrap up.

запа́л ignition; fuse. **запа́льная свеча́** (spark-)plug.

запа́с reserve; supply; hem. **запаса́ть** impf, **запасти́** (-су́, -сёшь; -ás, -ла́) pf provide o.s. of; ∼**ся** +instr stock up with. **запасно́й, запа́сный** spare; reserve; ∼ **вы́ход** emergency exit.

за́пах smell.

запа́хивать *impf*, **запахну́ть²** (-ну́, -нёшь) *pf* wrap up.

запахну́ть¹ (-ну; -а́х) *pf* begin to smell.

за|па́чкать *pf*.

запева́ть *impf of* **запе́ть**; lead the singing.

запека́ть(ся *impf of* **запе́чь(ся. запеку́** *etc.: see* **запе́чь**

за|пелена́ть *pf*.

запере́ть (-пру́, -прёшь; за́пер, -ла́, -ло) *pf* (*impf* **запира́ть**) lock; lock in; bar; **∼ся** lock o.s. in.

запе́ть (-пою́, -поёшь) *pf* (*impf* **запева́ть**) begin to sing.

запеча́тать, **запеча́тывать** *impf* seal. **запечатлева́ть** *impf*, **запечатле́ть** (-е́ю) *pf* imprint, engrave.

запе́чь (-еку́, -ечёшь; -нёк, -ла́) *pf* (*impf* **запека́ть**) bake; **∼ся** bake; become parched; clot, coagulate.

запива́ть *impf of* **запи́ть**

запина́ться *impf of* **запну́ться. запи́нка** hesitation.

запира́ть(ся *impf of* **запере́ть(ся**

записа́ть (-ишу́, -и́шешь) *pf*, **запи́сывать** *impf* note; take down; record; enter; enrol; **∼ся** register, enrol (**в**+*acc* at). **запи́ска** note. **записно́й** note; inveterate; **∼а́я кни́жка** notebook. **за́пись** recording; registration; record.

запи́ть (-пью́, -пьёшь; за́пил, -а́, -о) *pf* (*impf* **запива́ть**) begin drinking; wash down (with).

запиха́ть *pf*, **запи́хивать** *impf*, **запихну́ть** (-ну́, -нёшь) *pf* push in, cram in.

запишу́ *etc.: see* **записа́ть**

запла́кать (-а́чу) *pf* begin to cry.

за|плани́ровать *pf*.

запла́та patch.

за|плати́ть (-ачу́, -а́тишь) *pf* pay (**за**+*acc* for).

заплачу́ *etc.: see* **запла́кать. запла́чу** *see* **заплати́ть**

заплести́ (-ету́, -етёшь; -ёл, -а́) *pf*, **заплета́ть** *impf* plait.

за|пломбирова́ть *pf*.

заплы́ть heat, round. **заплыва́ть** *impf*, **заплы́ть** (-ыву́, -ывёшь; -ы́л, -а́, -о) *pf* swim in, sail in; swim out, sail out; be bloated.

запну́ться (-ну́сь, -нёшься) *pf* (*impf* **запина́ться**) hesitate, stumble.

запове́дник reserve; preserve; **госуда́рственный ∼** national park. **запове́дный** prohibited. **за́поведь** precept; commandment.

заподо́зривать *impf*, **заподо́зрить** *pf* suspect (**в**+*prep* of).

запозда́лый belated; delayed. **запозда́ть** *pf* (*impf* **запа́здывать**) be late.

запо́й hard drinking.

заползать *impf*, **заползти́** *pf* (-зу́, -зёшь; -о́лз, -зла́) creep, crawl.

заполни́ть, **заполня́ть** *impf* fill (in, up).

запомина́ть *impf*, **запо́мнить** *pf* remember; memorize; **∼ся** stay in one's mind.

за́понка cuff-link; stud.

запо́р bolt; lock; constipation.

за|поте́ть (-е́ет) *pf* mist over.

запою́ *etc.: see* **запе́ть**

запра́вить (-влю) *pf*, **заправля́ть** *impf* tuck in; insert; refuel; season, dress; mix in; **∼ся** refuel. **запра́вка** refuelling; seasoning; dressing.

запра́шивать *impf of* **запроси́ть**

запре́т prohibition, ban. **запрети́ть** (-ещу́) *pf,* **запреща́ть** *impf* prohibit, ban. **запре́тный** forbidden. **запреще́ние** prohibition.

за|программи́ровать *pf.*

запро́с inquiry; overcharging; *pl* needs. **запроси́ть** (-ошу́, -о́сишь) *pf* (*impf* **запра́шивать**) inquire.

за́просто *adv* without ceremony.

запрошу́ *etc.: see* **запроси́ть**.

запру́ *etc.: see* **запере́ть**

запру́да dam, weir; mill-pond.

запряга́ть *impf,* **запря́чь** (-ягу́, -яжёшь; -я́г, -ла́) *pf* harness; yoke.

запуга́ть *pf,* **запу́гивать** *impf* cow, intimidate.

за́пуск launching. **запуска́ть** *impf,* **запусти́ть** (-ущу́, -у́стишь) *pf* thrust (in); start; launch; (+*acc or instr*) fling; neglect. **запусте́лый** neglected; desolate. **запусте́ние** neglect; desolation.

за|пу́тать *pf,* **запу́тывать** *impf* tangle; confuse; **∼ся** get tangled; get involved.

запущу́ *etc.: see* **запусти́ть**

запча́сть (*gen pl* -е́й) *abbr* (*of* **запасна́я часть**) spare part.

запыха́ться *pf* be out of breath.

запью́ *etc.: see* **запи́ть**.

запя́стье wrist.

запята́я *sb* comma.

за|пятна́ть *pf.*

зараба́тывать *impf,* **зарабо́тать** *pf* earn; start (up). **зарабо́тный:** **∼ая пла́та** wages; pay. **за́работок** (-тка) earnings.

заража́ть *impf,* **зарази́ть** (-ажу́)

pf infect; **∼ся** +*instr* be infected with, catch. **зара́за** infection. **зарази́тельный** infectious. **зара́зный** infectious.

зара́нее *adv* in good time; in advance.

зараста́ть *impf,* **зарасти́** (-ту́, -тёшь; -ро́с, -ла́) *pf* be overgrown; heal.

за́рево glow.

за|регистри́ровать(ся *pf.*

за|ре́зать (-е́жу) *pf* kill, knife; slaughter.

зарека́ться *impf of* **заре́чься**

зарекомендова́ть *pf:* **∼ себя́** +*instr* show o.s. to be.

заре́чься (-еку́сь, -ечёшься; -ёкся, -екла́сь) *pf* (*impf* **зарека́ться**) +*inf* renounce.

за|ржаве́ть (-е́ет) *pf.*

зарисо́вка sketching; sketch.

зароди́ть (-ожу́) *pf,* **зарожда́ть** *impf* generate; **∼ся** be born; arise. **заро́дыш** foetus; embryo. **зарожде́ние** conception; origin.

заро́к vow, pledge.

заро́с *etc.: see* **зарасти́**

зарою́ *etc.: see* **зары́ть**

зарпла́та *abbr* (*of* **за́работная пла́та**) wages; pay.

заруба́ть *impf of* **заруби́ть**

зарубе́жный foreign.

зарубе́жье foreign countries.

заруби́ть (-блю́, -бишь) *pf* (*impf* **заруба́ть**) kill, cut down; notch. **зару́бка** notch.

заруча́ться *impf,* **заручи́ться** (-учу́сь) *pf* +*instr* secure.

зарыва́ть *impf,* **зары́ть** (-ро́ю) *pf* bury.

заря́ (*pl* зо́ри, зорь) dawn.

заря́д charge; supply. **заряди́ть** (-яжу́, -я́дишь) *pf,* **заряжа́ть** *impf* load; charge; stoke; **∼ся**

loaded; be charged. **заря́дка** loading; charging; exercises.

заса́да ambush. **засади́ть** (-ажу́, -а́дишь) *pf*, **заса́живать** *impf* plant; drive; set (за+*acc* to); ~ (в тюрьму́) put in prison.

заса́ливать *impf of* **засоли́ть**

засвети́ть (-ечу́, -е́тишь) *pf* light; ~ся light up.

за|свиде́тельствовать *pf*.

засе́в sowing; seed; sown area. **засева́ть** *impf of* **засе́ять**

заседа́ние meeting; session. **заседа́ть** *impf* sit, be in session.

засе́ивать *impf of* **засе́ять**. **засе́к** *etc.: see* **засе́чь**. **засека́ть** *impf of* **засе́чь**

засекре́тить (-е́чу) *pf*, **засекре́чивать** *impf* classify as secret; clear, give access to secret material.

засеку́ *etc.: see* **засе́чь**. **засе́л** *etc.: see* **засе́сть**

заселе́ние settlement. **засели́ть** *pf*, **заселя́ть** *impf* settle; colonize; populate.

засе́сть (-ся́ду; -се́л) *pf* (*impf* **заса́живаться**) sit down; set tight; settle; lodge in.

засе́чь (-еку́, -ечёшь; -ёк, -ла́) *pf* (*impf* **засека́ть**) flog to death; notch.

засе́ять (-е́ю) *pf* (*impf* **засева́ть**, **засе́ивать**) sow.

заси́лье dominance, sway.

заслони́ть *pf*, **заслоня́ть** *impf* cover, screen; push into the background. **засло́нка** (*furnace, oven*) door.

заслу́га merit, desert; service. **заслу́женный** deserved, merited; Honoured; time-honoured. **заслу́живать** *impf*, **заслужи́ть** (-ужу́, -у́жишь) *pf* deserve; earn; +*gen* be worthy of.

засмея́ться (-ею́сь, -еёшься) begin to laugh.

заснима́ть *impf of* **засня́ть**

засну́ть (-ну́, -нёшь) *pf* (*impf* **засыпа́ть**) fall asleep.

засня́ть (-ниму́, -и́мешь; -я́л, -а́, -о) *pf* (*impf* **заснима́ть**) photograph.

засо́в bolt, bar.

засо́вывать *impf of* **засу́нуть**

засо́л salting, pickling. **засоли́ть** (-олю́, -о́лишь) *pf* (*impf* **заса́ливать**) salt, pickle.

засоре́ние littering; contamination; obstruction. **засори́ть** *pf*, **засоря́ть** *impf* litter; get dirt into; clog.

за|со́хнуть (-ну; -со́х) *pf* (*impf also* **засыха́ть**) dry (up); wither.

заста́ва gate; outpost.

застава́ть (-таю́, -таёшь) *impf of* **заста́ть**

заста́вить (-влю) *pf*, **заставля́ть** *impf* make; compel.

заста́иваться *impf of* **застоя́ться**. **заста́ну** *etc.: see* **заста́ть**

заста́ть (-а́ну) *pf* (*impf* **застава́ть**) find; catch.

застёгивать *impf*, **застегну́ть** (-ну́, -нёшь) *pf* fasten, do up. **застёжка** fastening; clasp, buckle; ~-мо́лния zip.

застекли́ть *pf*, **застекля́ть** *impf* glaze.

засте́нок (-нка) torture chamber.

засте́нчивый shy.

застига́ть *impf*, **засти́гнуть**, **засти́чь** (-и́гну; -сти́г) *pf* catch; take unawares.

засти́чь *see* **засти́гнуть**

засто́й stagnation. **засто́йный** stagnant.

за|стопо́риться *pf*.

застоя́ться (-и́тся) *pf* (*impf* застоя́ваться) stagnate; stand too long.

застра́ивать *impf of* застро́ить

застрахо́ванный insured. за|страхова́ть *pf*, застрахо́вывать *impf* insure.

застрева́ть *impf of* застря́ть

застрели́ть (-елю́, -е́лишь) *pf* shoot (dead); ~ся shoot o.s.

застро́ить (-о́ю) *pf* (*impf* застра́ивать) build over, on, up. застро́йка building.

застря́ть (-я́ну) *pf* (*impf* застрева́ть) stick; get stuck.

за́ступ spade.

заступа́ть *impf*, **заступи́ться** (-плю́сь, -пишься) *pf* +за+*acc* stand up for. засту́пник defender. засту́пничество protection; intercession.

застыва́ть *impf*, **засты́ть** (-ы́ну) *pf* harden, set; become stiff; freeze; be petrified.

засу́нуть (-ну) *pf* (*impf* засо́вывать) thrust in, push in.

за́суха drought.

засыпа́ть[1] (-плю) *pf*, **засыпа́ть** *impf* fill up; strew.

засыпа́ть[2] *impf of* засну́ть

засыха́ть *impf of* засо́хнуть. **зася́ду** *etc.*: *see* засе́сть

затаённый (-ён, -ена́) secret; repressed. **зата́ивать** *impf*, **затаи́ть** *pf* suppress; conceal; harbour; ~ дыха́ние hold one's breath.

зата́пливать *impf of* затопи́ть **зата́птывать** *impf of* затопта́ть

зата́скивать *impf*, **затащи́ть** (-щу́, -щишь) *pf* drag in; drag off; drag away.

затвердева́ть *impf*, **за|тверде́ть** (-е́ет) *pf* become hard; set.

затверде́ние hardening; callus.

затво́р bolt; lock; shutter; flood-gate. **затвори́ть** (-рю́, -ришь) *pf*, **затворя́ть** *impf* shut, close; ~ся shut up, lock o.s. in. **затво́рник** hermit, recluse.

затева́ть *impf of* зате́ять

зате́к *etc.*: *see* зате́чь. **затека́ть** *impf of* зате́чь

зате́м *adv* then, next; ~ что because.

затемне́ние darkening, obscuring; blacking out; black-out. затемни́ть *pf*, **затемня́ть** *impf* darken, obscure; black out.

зате́ривать *impf*, **затеря́ть** *pf* lose, mislay; ~ся be lost; be mislaid; be overlooked.

зате́чь (-ечёт, -еку́т; -тёк, -кла́) *pf* (*impf* затека́ть) pour, flow; swell up; become numb.

зате́я undertaking, venture; escapade; joke. **зате́ять** *pf* (*impf* затева́ть) undertake, venture.

затиха́ть *impf*, **зати́хнуть** (-ну; -тих) *pf* die down, abate; fade. **зати́шье** calm; lull.

заткну́ть (-ну́, -нёшь) *pf* (*impf* затыка́ть) stop up; stick, thrust.

затмева́ть *impf*, **затми́ть** (-ми́шь) *pf* darken; eclipse; overshadow. **затме́ние** eclipse.

зато́ *conj* but then, but on the other hand.

затону́ть (-о́нет) *pf* sink, be submerged.

затопи́ть[1] (-плю́, -пишь) *pf* (*impf* зата́пливать) light; turn on the heating.

затопи́ть[2] (-плю́, -пишь) *pf*, **затопля́ть** *impf* flood, submerge; sink.

затопта́ть (-пчу́, -пчешь) *pf* (*impf* зата́птывать) trample (down).

зато́р obstruction, jam; congestion.

за|тормози́ть (-ожу́) *pf.*

заточа́ть *impf*, **заточи́ть** (-чу́) *pf* incarcerate. **заточе́ние** incarceration.

затра́гивать *impf of* **затро́нуть**

затра́та expense; outlay. **затра́тить** (-а́чу) *pf*, **затра́чивать** *impf* spend.

затре́бовать *pf* request, require; ask for.

затро́нуть (-ну) *pf* (*impf* **затра́гивать**) affect; touch (on).

затрудне́ние difficulty. **затрудни́тельный** difficult. **затрудни́ть** (-ню́) *pf*, **затрудня́ть** *impf* trouble; make difficult; hamper; ~ся +*inf* or *instr* find difficulty in.

за|тупи́ться (-пится) *pf.*

за|туши́ть (-шу́, -шишь) *pf* extinguish; suppress.

затыка́ть *impf of* **заткну́ть**

заты́лок (-лка) back of the head; scrag-end.

затя́гивать *impf*, **затяну́ть** (-ну́, -нешь) *pf* tighten; cover; close, heal; spin out; ~ся be covered; close; be delayed; drag on; inhale. **затя́жка** inhaling; prolongation; delaying, putting off; lagging. **затяжно́й** long-drawn-out.

заура́дный ordinary; mediocre.

заутреня morning service.

зау́чивать *impf*, **заучи́ть** (-чу́, -чишь) *pf* learn by heart.

за|фарширова́ть *pf.* **за|фикси́ровать** *pf.* **за|фрахтова́ть** *pf.*

захва́т seizure, capture. **захвати́ть** (-ачу́, -а́тишь) *pf*, **захва́тывать** *impf* take; seize; thrill. **за-**

хва́тнический aggressive. **захва́тчик** aggressor. **захва́тывающий** gripping.

захлебну́ться (-ну́сь, -нёшься) *pf*, **захлёбываться** *impf* choke (от+*gen* with).

захлестну́ть (-ну́, -нёшь) *pf*, **захлёстывать** *impf* flow over, swamp, overwhelm.

захло́пнуть (-ну) *pf*, **захло́пывать** *impf* slam, bang; ~ся slam (to).

захо́д sunset; calling in. **заходи́ть** (-ожу́, -о́дишь) *impf of* **зайти́**

захолу́стный remote, provincial. **захолу́стье** backwoods.

за|хорони́ть (-ню, -нишь) *pf.* **за|хоте́ть(ся** (-очу́(сь, -о́чешь(ся, -отим(ся) *pf.*

зацвести́ (-ете́т; -вёл, -а́) *pf*, **зацвета́ть** *impf* come into bloom.

зацепи́ть (-плю́, -пишь) *pf*, **зацепля́ть** *impf* hook; engage; sting; catch (за+*acc* on); ~ся за+*acc* catch on; catch hold of.

зачасту́ю *adv* often.

зача́тие conception. **зача́ток** (-тка) embryo; rudiment; germ. **зача́точный** rudimentary. **зача́ть** (-чну́, -чнёшь; -ча́л, -а́, -о) *pf* (*impf* **зачина́ть**) conceive.

зачёл *etc.: see* **заче́сть**

заче́м *adv* why; what for. **заче́м-то** *adv* for some reason.

зачёркивать *impf*, **зачеркну́ть** (-ну́, -нёшь) *pf* cross out.

зачерпну́ть (-ну́, -нёшь) *pf*, **заче́рпывать** *impf* scoop up; draw up.

за|черстве́ть (-е́ет) *pf.*

заче́сть (-чту́, -чтёшь; -чёл, -чла́) *pf* (*impf* **зачи́тывать**) take into account, reckon as credit. **зачёт**

test; **получи́ть**, **сдать** ~ **по**+*dat* pass a test in; **поста́вить** ~ **по**+*dat* pass in. **зачётная кни́жка** (student's) record book.

зачина́ть *impf of* **зача́ть**. **зачи́нщик** instigator.

зачи́слить *pf*, **зачисля́ть** *impf* include; enter; enlist; ~**ся** join, enter.

зачи́тывать *impf of* **заче́сть**. **зачту́** *etc.: see* **заче́сть**. **зашёл** *etc.: see* **зайти́**

зашива́ть *impf*, **заши́ть** (-шью, -шьёшь) *pf* sew up.

за|шифрова́ть *pf*, **зашифро́вывать** *impf* encipher, encode.

за|шнурова́ть *pf*, **зашнуро́вывать** *impf* lace up.

за|шпаклева́ть (-люю) *pf*. **за|штопать** *pf*. **за|штрихова́ть** *pf*. **зашью́** *etc.: see* **заши́ть**

защи́та defence; protection. **защити́ть** (-ищу́) *pf*, **защища́ть** *impf* defend, protect. **защи́тник** defender. **защи́тный** protective.

заяви́ть (-влю́, -вишь) *pf*, **заявля́ть** *impf* announce, declare; ~**ся** turn up. **зая́вка** claim; demand. **заявле́ние** statement; application.

за́яц (за́йца) hare; stowaway; **е́хать за́йцем** travel without a ticket.

зва́ние rank; title. **зва́ный** invited; ~ **обе́д** banquet, dinner. **зва́тельный** vocative. **звать** (зову́, -вёшь; звал, -а́, -о) *impf* (*pf* **по**~) call; ask, invite; **как вас зову́т?** what is your name?; ~**ся** be called.

звезда́ (*pl* звёзды) star. **звёздный** *adj* starry; starlit; stellar. **звёздочка** little star; asterisk.

звене́ть (-ню́) *impf* ring; +*instr* jingle, clink.

звено́ (*pl* зве́нья, -ьев) link; team, section; unit; component. **звероводство** *sb* section breeding.

зве́ринец (-нца) menagerie. **зверово́дство** fur farming. **зве́рский** brutal; terrific. **зве́рство** atrocity. **зве́рствовать** *impf* commit atrocities. **зверь** (*pl* -и, -е́й) *m* wild animal.

звон ringing (sound); peal, chink, clink. **звони́ть** *impf* (*pf* **по**~) ring; ring up; ~ **кому́-нибудь** (**по телефо́ну**) ring s.o. up. **зво́нкий** (-нок, -нка́, -о) ringing, clear. **звоно́к** (-нка́) bell; (*telephone*) call.

звук sound. **зву́ко**- *in comb* sound. **звукоза́пись** (sound) recording. ~**изоля́ция** sound-proofing. ~**непроница́емый** sound-proof. ~**сни́матель** *m* pick-up. **звуково́й** sound; audio; acoustic. **звуча́ние** sound(ing); vibration. **звуча́ть** (-чит) *impf* (*pf* **про**~) be heard; sound. **зву́чный** (-чен, -чна́, -о) sonorous.

зда́ние building.

здесь *adv* here. **зде́шний** local; **не** ~ a stranger here.

здоро́ваться *impf* (*pf* **по**~) exchange greetings. **здо́рово** *adv* splendidly; very (much); well done!; great! **здоро́вый** healthy, strong; well; wholesome, sound. **здоро́вье** health; **за ва́ше** ~? your health! **как ва́ше** ~? how are you? **здра́вница** sanatorium. **здравомы́слящий** sensible, judicious. **здравоохране́ние** public health.

здра́вствовать *impf* be healthy; prosper. **здрав-**

ствуй(те) how do you do?; hello! **да здра́вствует!** long live! **здра́вый** sensible; ~ **смысл** common sense.

зе́бра zebra.

зева́ть impf, **зевну́ть** (-ну́, -нёшь) pf yawn; gape; (pf also **про~**) miss, let slip, lose. **зево́к** (-вка́), **зевота́** yawn.

зелене́ть (-е́ет) impf (pf **по~**) turn green; show green. **зелёный** (зе́лен, -а́, -о) green; ~ **лук** spring onions. **зе́лень** green; greenery; greens.

земе́льный land.

земле- in comb land; earth. **земле-**
~владе́лец (-льца) landowner.
~де́лец (-льца) farmer.
~де́лие farming, agriculture.
~де́льческий agricultural.
~ко́п navvy. **~ро́йный** excavating. **~трясе́ние** earthquake.

земля́ (acc -ю; pl -и, земе́ль, -ям) earth; ground; land; soil. **земля́к** (-а́) fellow-countryman. **земляни́ка** (no pl; usu collect) wild strawberry; wild strawberries. **земля́нка** dug-out; mud hut. **земляно́й** earthen; earth. **земля́чка** countrywoman. **земно́й** earthly; terrestrial; ground; mundane; ~ **шар** the globe.

зени́т zenith. **зени́тный** zenith; anti-aircraft.

зе́ркало (pl -á) mirror. **зер-**
ка́льный mirror; smooth; plate-glass.

зерни́стый grainy. **зерно́** (pl зёрна, зёрен) grain; seed; kernel; core; **ко́фе в зёрнах** coffee beans. **зерново́й** grain. **зерно-**
вы́е sb pl cereals. **зернохрани́-**
лище granary.

зигза́г zigzag.

зима́ (acc -у; pl -ы) winter. **зим-**

ний winter, wintry. **зимова́ть** impf (pf **пере~**, **про~**) spend the winter; hibernate. **зимо́вка** wintering; hibernation. **зи́-**
мовье winter quarters. **зимо́й** adv in winter.

зия́ть impf gape, yawn.

злак grass; cereal.

злить (злю) impf (pf **обо~**, **о~**, **разо~**) anger; irritate; ~**ся** be angry, be in a bad temper; rage. **зло** (gen pl зол) evil; harm; misfortune; malice.

зло- in comb evil, harm, malice. **злове́щий** ominous. **~во́ние** stink. **~во́нный** stinking. **~ка́-**
чественный malignant; pernicious. **~па́мятный** rancorous, unforgiving. **~ра́дный** malevolent, gloating. **~сло́вие** malicious gossip. **~умы́шленник** malefactor; plotter. **~язы́чный** slanderous.

зло́ба spite; anger; ~ **дня** topic of the day, latest news. **зло́б-**
ный malicious. **злободне́вный** topical. **злоде́й** villain. **зло-**
де́йский villainous. **злоде́й-**
ство villainy; crime, evil deed. **злодея́ние** crime, evil deed. **злой** (зол, зла) evil; wicked; malicious; vicious; bad-tempered; severe. **зло́стный** malicious; intentional. **злость** malice; fury.

злоупотреби́ть (-блю́) pf, **злоупотребля́ть** impf + instr abuse. **злоупотребле́ние** + instr abuse of.

змеи́ный snake; cunning. **змей** snake; dragon; kite. **змея́** (pl -и) snake.

знак sign; mark; symbol.

знако́мить (-млю) impf (pf **о~**, **по~**) acquaint; introduce; ~**ся** become acquainted; get to know; + **с** + instr meet, make the

acquaintance of. **знакомство** acquaintance; (circle of) acquaintances. **знакомый** familiar; **быть ~ым с+**instr be acquainted with, know; **~ый, ~ая** sb acquaintance.

знаменатель m denominator. **знаменательный** significant. **знамение** sign. **знаменитость** celebrity. **знаменитый** celebrated, famous. **знамя** (-мени; pl -мёна) neut banner; flag.

знание knowledge.

знатный (-тен, -тна, -о) distinguished; aristocratic; splendid. **знаток** (-а) expert; connoisseur. **знать** impf know; **дать** ~ inform, let know.

значение meaning; significance; importance. **значит** so then; that means. **значительный** considerable; important; significant. **значить** (-чу) impf mean; signify; be of importance; **~ся** be; be mentioned, appear. **значок** (-чка) badge; mark.

знающий expert; learned.

знобить impf, impers+acc: **меня,** etc., **знобит** I feel shivery. **зной** intense heat. **знойный** hot; burning.

зов call, summons. **зову** etc.: see **звать**

зодчество architecture. **зодчий** sb architect.

зол see **зло, злой**

зола ashes, cinders.

золовка sister-in-law (husband's sister).

золотистый golden. **золото** gold. **золотой** gold; golden. **золочёный** gilt, gilded.

зона zone; region.

зонд probe. **зондировать** impf sound, probe.

зонт (-а), **зонтик** umbrella.

зоолог zoologist. **зоологический** zoological. **зоология** zoology. **зоопарк** zoo. **зоотехник** livestock specialist.

зори etc.: see **заря**

зоркий (-рок, -рка, -о) sharp-sighted; perspicacious.

зрачок (-чка) pupil (of the eye).

зрелище sight; spectacle.

зрелость ripeness; maturity; **аттестат зрелости** school-leaving certificate. **зрелый** (зрел, -а, -о) ripe, mature.

зрение (eye)sight, vision; **точка зрения** point of view.

зреть (-ею) impf (pf со~) ripen; mature.

зримый visible.

зритель m spectator, observer; pl audience. **зрительный** visual; optic; ~ **зал** hall, auditorium.

зря adv in vain.

зуб (pl -ы or -бья, -ов or -бьев) tooth; cog. **зубило** chisel. **зубной** dental; tooth; ~ **врач** dentist. **зубоврачебный** dentists'; dental; ~ **кабинет** dental surgery. **зубочистка** toothpick.

зубр (European) bison; die-hard.

зубрить (-рю, зубришь) impf (pf вы~, за~) cram.

зубчатый toothed; serrated.

зуд itch. **зудеть** (-ит) itch.

зыбкий (-бок, -бка, -о) unsteady, shaky; vacillating. **зыбь** (gen pl -ей) ripple, rippling.

зюйд (naut) south; south wind.

зяблик chaffinch.

зябнуть (-ну; зяб) impf suffer from cold, feel the cold.

зябь land ploughed in autumn for spring sowing.

зять (*pl* -тья́, -тьёв) son-in-law; brother-in-law (*sister's husband or husband's sister's husband*).

И, Й

и *conj* and; even; too; (*with neg*) either; **и... и** both ... and.

и́бо *conj* for.

и́ва willow.

игла́ (*pl* -ы) needle; thorn; spine; quill. **иглоука́лывание** acupuncture.

игнори́ровать *impf & pf* ignore.

и́го yoke.

иго́лка needle.

иго́рный gaming, gambling. **игра́** (*pl* -ы) play, playing; game; hand; turn; **~ слов** pun. **игра́льный** playing; **~ые ко́сти** dice. **игра́ть** *impf* (*pf* сыгра́ть) play; act; **~ в**+*acc* play (*game*); **~ на**+*prep* play (*an instrument*). **игри́вый** playful. **игро́к** (-а́) player; gambler. **игру́шка** toy.

идеа́л ideal. **идеали́зм** idealism. **идеа́льный** ideal.

иде́йный high-principled; acting on principle; ideological.

идеологи́ческий ideological. **идеоло́гия** ideology.

идёт *etc*.: *see* идти́

иде́я idea; concept.

иди́ллия idyll.

идио́т idiot.

и́дол idol.

идти́ (иду́, идёшь; шёл, шла) *impf* (*pf* пойти́) go; come; run, work; pass; go on, be in progress; be on; fall; **+**(к+)*dat* suit.

иере́й priest.

иждиве́нец (-нца), **-ве́нка** *pl* dependant. **иждиве́ние** mainten-

ance; **на иждиве́нии** at the expense of.

из, изо *prep*+*gen* from, out of, of.

изба́ (*pl* -ы) izba (*hut*).

изба́вить (-влю) *pf*, **избавля́ть** *impf* save, deliver; **~ся** be saved, escape; **~ся от** get rid of; get out of.

избало́ванный spoilt. **из|бало́вать**.

избега́ть *impf*, **избе́гнуть** (-ну; -бе́г(нул)) *pf*, **избежа́ть** (-егу́) *pf* +*gen* or *inf* avoid; escape.

изберу́ *etc*.: *see* избра́ть

избива́ть *impf* or **изби́ть**. **изби́ение** slaughter, massacre; beating, beating-up.

избира́тель *m*, **~ница** elector, voter. **избира́тельный** electoral; election. **избира́ть** *impf* or **избра́ть**.

изби́тый trite, hackneyed. **изби́ть** (изобью́, -бьёшь) *pf* (*impf* избива́ть) beat unmercifully, beat up; massacre.

и́збранный selected; select; **~ые** *sb pl* the élite. **избра́ть** (-беру́, -берёшь; -а́л, -а́, -о) *pf* (*impf* избира́ть) elect; choose.

избы́ток (-тка) surplus; abundance. **избы́точный** surplus; abundant.

изве́рг monster. **изверже́ние** eruption; expulsion; excretion.

изверну́ться (-ну́сь, -нёшься) *pf* (*impf* извора́чиваться) dodge, be evasive.

изве́стие news; information; *pl* proceedings. **извести́ть** (-ещу́) *pf* (*impf* извеща́ть) inform, notify.

изве́стка lime.

изве́стно it is (well) known; of course, certainly. **изве́стность** fame, reputation. **изве́стный**

known; well-known, famous; notorious; certain.

известня́к (-á) limestone. **и́з-весть** lime.

извеща́ть *impf of* **извести́ть**. **извеще́ние** notification; advice.

извива́ться *impf* coil; writhe; twist, wind; meander. **изви́-лина** bend, twist. **изви́листый** winding; meandering.

извине́ние excuse; apology. **из-вини́ть** *pf*, **извиня́ть** *impf* excuse; **извини́те (меня́)** excuse me, (I'm) sorry; **~ся** apologize; excuse o.s.

изви́ться (изовью́сь, -вьёшься; -и́лся, -а́сь, -о́сь) *pf* coil; writhe.

извлека́ть *impf*, **извле́чь** (-еку́, -ечёшь; -ёк, -ла́) *pf* extract; derive, elicit.

извне́ *adv* from outside.

изво́зчик cabman; carrier.

извора́чиваться *impf of* **из-верну́ться**. **изворо́т** bend, twist; *pl* tricks, wiles. **изворо́т-ливый** resourceful; shrewd.

изврати́ть (-ащу́) *pf*, **извра-ща́ть** *impf* distort; pervert. **из-враще́ние** perversion; distortion. **извращённый** perverted, unnatural.

изги́б bend, twist. **изгиба́ть(ся** *impf of* **изогну́ть(ся**

изгна́ние banishment; exile. **из-гна́нник** exile. **изгна́ть** (-гоню́, -го́нишь; -а́л, -а́, -о) *pf* (*impf* **изго-ня́ть**) banish; exile.

изголо́вье bed-head.

изголода́ться be famished, starve; **+no+**dat yearn for.

изгоню́ *etc.: see* **изгна́ть**. **изго-ня́ть** *impf of* **изгна́ть**

и́згородь fence, hedge.

изгота́вливать *impf*, **изгото́-вить** (-влю) *pf*, **изготовля́ть**

impf make, manufacture; **~ся** get ready. **изготовле́ние** making, manufacture.

издава́ть (-даю́, -даёшь) *impf of* **изда́ть**

и́здавна *adv* from time immemorial; for a very long time.

издади́м *etc.: see* **изда́ть**

издалека́, и́здали *advs* from afar.

изда́ние publication; edition; promulgation. **изда́тель** *m* publisher. **изда́тельство** publishing house. **изда́ть** (-а́м, -а́шь, -а́ст, -ади́м; -а́л, -а́, -о) *pf* (*impf* **издава́ть**) publish; promulgate; produce; emit; **~ся** be published.

издева́тельство mockery; taunt. **издева́ться** *impf* (**+над +**instr) mock (at).

изде́лие work; make; article; *pl* wares.

изде́ржки (-жек) *pl* expenses; costs; cost.

издо́хнуть (-ну) *pf*.

изжа́рить(ся *pf*.

изжо́га heartburn.

из-за *prep+*gen from behind; because of.

излага́ть *impf of* **изложи́ть**

излече́ние treatment; recovery; cure. **излечи́ть** (-чу́, -чишь) cure; **~ся** be cured; **+от+**gen rid o.s. of.

изли́шек (-шка) surplus; excess. **изли́шество** excess; over-indulgence. **изли́шний** (-шен, -шня) superfluous.

изложе́ние exposition; account. **изложи́ть** (-жу́, -жишь) *pf* (*impf* **излага́ть**) expound; set forth; word.

изло́м break, fracture; sharp bend. **излома́ть** *pf* break; smash; wear out; warp.

излуча́ть *impf* radiate, emit. **излуче́ние** radiation; emanation.

из|ма́зать (-а́жу) *pf* dirty, smear all over; use up; ~**ся** get dirty, smear o.s. all over.

изме́на betrayal; treason; infidelity.

измене́ние change, alteration; inflection. **измени́ть**[1] (-ню́, -нишь) *pf* (*impf* **изменя́ть**[1]) change, alter; ~**ся** change.

измени́ть[2] (-ню́, -нишь) *impf* **изменя́ть**[2]) +*dat* betray; be unfaithful to. **изме́нник, -ица** traitor.

изменя́емый variable. **изменя́ть**[1,2]**ся** *impf of* **измени́ть**[1,2]**ся**

измере́ние measurement, measuring. **изме́рить** (-рю) *pf*, **измеря́ть** *impf* measure, gauge.

измождённый (-ён, -а́) worn out.

из|му́чить (-чу) *pf* torment; tire out, exhaust; ~**ся** be exhausted. **изму́ченный** worn out.

измышле́ние fabrication, invention.

измя́тый crumpled, creased; haggard, jaded. **из|мя́ть(ся** (изомну́(сь, -нёшь(ся) *pf*

изна́нка wrong side; seamy side.

из|наси́ловать *pf* rape, assault.

изна́шивание wear (and tear). **изна́шивать(ся** *impf of* **износи́ть(ся**

изне́женный pampered; delicate; effeminate.

изнемога́ть *impf*, **изнемо́чь** (-огу́, -о́жешь; -о́г, -ла́) *pf* be exhausted. **изнеможе́ние** exhaustion.

изно́с wear; wear and tear; deterioration. **износи́ть** (-ошу́, -о́сишь) *pf* (*impf* **изна́шивать**) wear out; ~**ся** wear out; be used up. **изно́шенный** worn out; threadbare.

изнуре́ние exhaustion. **изнурённый** (-ён, -ена́) exhausted, worn out; jaded. **изнури́тельный** exhausting.

изнутри́ *adv* from inside, from within.

изо *see* **из**

изоби́лие abundance, plenty. **изоби́ловать** *impf* +*instr* abound in, be rich in. **изоби́льный** abundant.

изоблича́ть *impf*, **изобличи́ть** (-чу́) *pf* expose; show. **изобличе́ние** exposure; conviction.

изобража́ть *impf*, **изобрази́ть** (-ажу́) *pf* represent, depict, portray (+*instr* as); ~ **из себя́** +*acc* make o.s. out to be. **изображе́ние** image; representation; portrayal. **изобрази́тельный** graphic; decorative; ~**ые иску́с-ства fine arts.

изобрести́ (-ету́, -етёшь; -ёл, -а́) *pf*, **изобрета́ть** (*impf* изобре́тать) invent; devise. **изобрета́тель** *m* inventor. **изобрета́тельный** inventive. **изобрете́ние** invention.

изобью́ *etc.: see* **изби́ть**. **изовью́сь** *etc.: see* **изви́ться**

изо́гнутый bent, curved; winding. **изогну́ть(ся** (-ну́(сь, -нёшь(ся) *pf* (*impf* **изгиба́ть(ся**) bend, curve.

изоли́ровать *impf* & *pf* isolate; insulate. **изоля́тор** insulator; isolation ward; solitary confinement cell. **изоля́ция** isolation; quarantine; insulation.

изомну́(сь *etc.: see* **измя́ть**

изо́рванный tattered, torn. **изорва́ть** (-ву́, -вёшь; -а́л, -а́, -о)

pf tear, tear to pieces; **~ся** be in tatters.

изощрённый (-рён, -á) refined; keen. **изощри́ться** *pf*, **изощря́ться** *impf* acquire refinement; excel.

из-под *prep+gen* from under.

Изра́иль *m* Israel. **изра́ильский** Israeli.

изразхо́довать(ся *pf*.

и́зредка *adv* now and then.

изре́зать (-éжу) *pf* cut up.

изрече́ние dictum, saying.

изры́ть (-ро́ю) *pf* dig up, plough up. **изры́тый** pitted.

изря́дно *adv* fairly, pretty. **изря́дный** fair, handsome; fairly large.

изуве́чить (-чу) *pf* maim, mutilate.

изуми́тельный amazing. **изуми́ть** (-млю) *pf*, **изумля́ть** *impf* amaze; **~ся** be amazed. **изумле́ние** amazement.

изумру́д emerald.

изуро́дованный maimed; disfigured. **изуро́довать** *pf*.

изуча́ть *impf*, **изучи́ть** (-чу́, -чишь) *pf* learn, study. **изуче́ние** study.

изъе́здить (-зжу) *pf* travel all over; wear out.

изъявля́ть (-влю, -вишь) *pf*, **изъявля́ть** *impf* express.

изъя́н defect, flaw.

изъя́тие withdrawal; removal; exception. **изъя́ть** (изыму́, -мешь) *pf* **изыма́ть** *impf* withdraw.

изыска́ние investigation, research; prospecting; survey. **изы́сканный** refined. **изыска́ть** (-ыщу́, -ыщешь) *pf*, **изы́скивать** *impf* search out; (try to) find.

изю́м raisins.

изя́щество elegance, grace. **изя́щный** elegant, graceful.

ика́ть *impf*, **икну́ть** (-ну́, -нёшь) *pf* hiccup.

ико́на icon.

ико́та hiccup, hiccups.

икра́¹ (hard) roe; caviare.

икра́² (*pl* -ы) calf (*of leg*).

ил silt; sludge.

и́ли *conj* or; **~... ~** either ... or.

и́листый muddy, silty.

иллюзиони́ст conjurer. **иллю́зия** illusion.

иллюмина́тор porthole. **иллюмина́ция** illumination.

иллюстра́ция illustration. **иллюстри́ровать** *impf* & *pf* illustrate.

им *see* он, они́, оно́

им. *abbr* (*of* и́мени) named after.

и́мени *etc.: see* и́мя

имени́ны (-и́н) *pl* name-day (party). **имени́тельный** nominative. **и́менно** *adv* namely; exactly, precisely; **вот ~!** exactly!

име́ть (-е́ю) *impf* have; **~ де́ло с+*instr*** have dealings with; **~ ме́сто** take place; **~ся** be; be available.

и́ми *see* они́

имита́ция imitation. **имити́ровать** *impf* imitate.

иммигра́нт, **~ка** immigrant. **иммигра́ция** immigration.

импера́тор emperor. **импера́торский** imperial. **императри́ца** empress. **империали́зм** imperialism. **империали́ст** imperialist. **империалисти́ческий** imperialist(ic). **импе́рия** empire.

и́мпорт import. **импорти́ро-**

вать *impf & pf* import. **и́мпортный** import(ed).

импровиза́ция improvisation. **импровизи́ровать** *impf & pf* improvise.

и́мпульс impulse.

иму́щество property.

и́мя (и́мени; *pl* имена́, -ён) *neut* name; first name; noun; ~ прилага́тельное adjective; ~ существи́тельное noun; ~ числи́тельное numeral.

и́на́че *adv* differently, otherwise; так и́ли ~ in any event; *conj* otherwise, or else.

инвали́д disabled person; invalid. **инвали́дность** disablement, disability.

инвента́рь (-я́) *m* stock; equipment; inventory.

инде́ец (-е́йца) (American) Indian. **инде́йка** (*gen pl* -е́ек) turkey(-hen). **инде́йский** (American) Indian.

и́ндекс index; code.

индиа́нка Indian; American Indian. **инде́ец** (-и́йца) Indian.

индивидуали́зм individualism. **индивидуа́льность** individuality. **индивидуа́льный** individual. **индиви́дуум** individual.

инди́йский Indian. **И́ндия** India. **инду́с, инду́ска** Hindu.

индустриализа́ция industrialization. **индустриализи́ровать** *impf & pf* industrialize. **индустриа́льный** industrial. **инду́стрия** industry.

индю́к, индю́шка turkey.

и́ней hoar-frost.

ине́ртность inertia; sluggishness. **ине́рция** inertia.

инжене́р engineer; ~-меха́ник mechanical engineer; ~-строи́тель *m* civil engineer.

инжи́р fig.

инициа́л initial.

инициати́ва initiative. **инициа́тор** initiator.

инквизи́ция inquisition.

инкруста́ция inlaid work, inlay.

инкуба́тор incubator.

ино- *in comb* other, different; hetero-. **иногоро́дний** of, from, another town. **~ро́дный** foreign. **~сказа́тельный** allegorical. **~стра́нец** (-нца) **~стра́нка** (*gen pl* -нок) foreigner. **~стра́нный** foreign. **~язы́чный** foreign.

иногда́ *adv* sometimes.

ино́й different; other; some; ~ раз sometimes.

и́нок monk. **и́нокиня** nun.

инотде́л foreign department.

инсектици́д insecticide.

инспе́ктор inspector. **инспе́кция** inspection; inspectorate.

инста́нция instance.

инсти́нкт instinct. **инстинкти́вный** instinctive.

институ́т institute.

инстру́ктор instructor. **инстру́кция** instructions.

инструме́нт instrument; tool.

инсули́н insulin.

инсцениро́вка dramatization, adaptation; pretence.

интегра́ция integration.

интелле́кт intellect. **интеллектуа́льный** intellectual.

интеллиге́нт intellectual. **интеллиге́нтный** cultured, educated. **интеллиге́нция** intelligentsia.

интенси́вность intensity. **интенси́вный** intensive.

интеракти́вный interactive.

интерва́л interval.

интервéнция intervention.

интервью́ *neut indecl* interview.

интерéс interest. **интерéсный** interesting. **интересовáть** *impf* interest; ~**ся** be interested (+*instr*).

интернáт boarding-school.

интернациональный international.

Интернéт the Internet; **в ~е** on the Internet.

интернировать *impf & pf* intern.

интерпретáция interpretation. **интерпретировать** *impf & pf* interpret.

интерьéр interior.

интимный intimate.

интонáция intonation.

интрига intrigue; plot. **интриговáть** *impf*, (*pf* за~) intrigue.

интуи́ция intuition.

инфáркт infarct; coronary (thrombosis), heart attack.

инфекционный infectious. **инфéкция** infection.

инфля́ция inflation.

информáтика IT.

информáция information.

инфракрáсный infra-red.

йод *etc.*: see **йод**

ио́н ion.

ипохо́ндрик hypochondriac. **ипохо́ндрия** hypochondria.

ипподро́м racecourse.

Ирáк Iraq. **ирáкец** (-кца) Iraqi. **ирáкский** Iraqi.

Ирáн Iran. **ирáнец** (-нца) Iranian. **ирáнка** Iranian. **ирáнский** Iranian.

ирлáндец (-дца) Irishman. **Ирлáндия** Ireland. **ирлáндка** Irishwoman. **ирлáндский** Irish.

ирони́ческий ironic. **иро́ния** irony.

ирригáция irrigation.

иск suit, action.

искажáть *impf*, **искази́ть** (-ажу́) *pf* distort, pervert; misrepresent. **искажéние** distortion, perversion.

искалéченный crippled, maimed. **искалéчить** (-чу) *pf* cripple, maim; break.

искáть (ищу́, и́щешь) *impf* (+*acc or gen*) seek, look for.

исключáть *impf*, **исключи́ть** (-чу́) *pf* exclude; eliminate; expel. **исключáя** *prep*+*gen* except. **исключéние** exception; exclusion; expulsion; elimination; **за исключéнием** +*gen* with the exception of. **исключи́тельно** *adv* exceptionally; exclusively. **исключи́тельный** exceptional; exclusive.

иско́нный primordial.

ископáемое *sb* mineral; fossil. **ископáемый** fossilized, fossil.

искорени́ть *pf*, **искореня́ть** *impf* eradicate.

и́скоса *adv* askance; sidelong.

и́скра spark.

и́скренний sincere. **и́скренность** sincerity.

искривлéние bend; distortion, warping.

ис|купáть¹(ся *pf.*

искупáть² *impf*, **искупи́ть** (-плю́, -пишь) *pf* atone for; make up for. **искуплéние** redemption, atonement.

искуси́ть (-ушу́) *pf* of **искушáть**

искýсный skilful; expert. **искýсственный** artificial; feigned. **искýсство** art; skill. **искусствовéд** art historian.

искушáть *impf* (*pf* **искуси́ть**) tempt; seduce. **искушéние** temptation, seduction.

испа́нец (-нца) Spaniard. **Испа́- ния** Spain. **испа́нка** Spanish woman. **испа́нский** Spanish.

испаре́ние evaporation; *pl* fumes. **испари́ться** *pf*, **испа- ря́ться** *impf* evaporate.

испа́чкать *pf*. see **пе́чь** (-еку́, -ечёшь) *pf*.

испове́дать *impf* & *pf* con- fess; profess; **~ся** confess; make one's confession; +в+*prep* un- burden o.s. of. **и́споведь** con- fession.

исподти́шка *adv* in an under- hand way; on the quiet.

исполи́н giant. **исполи́нский** gigantic.

исполко́м *abbr* (*of* **исполни́- тельный комите́т**) executive committee.

исполне́ние fulfilment, execu- tion. **исполни́тель** *m*, **~ница** executor; performer. **исполни́- тельный** executive. **испо́лнить** *pf*, **исполня́ть** *impf* carry out, execute; fulfil; perform; **~ся** be fulfilled.

испо́льзование utilization. **испо́льзовать** *impf* & *pf* make (good) use of, utilize.

испо́ртить(ся) *pf*, see **по́ртить(ся)**. **испо́рченный** depraved; spoiled; rotten.

исправи́тельный correc- tional; corrective. **испра́вить** (-влю) *pf*, **исправля́ть** *impf* rectify, correct; mend; reform; **~ся** improve, reform. **исправ- ле́ние** repairing; improvement; correction. **испра́вленный** im- proved, corrected; revised; re- formed. **испра́вный** in good order; punctual; meticulous.

испро́бовать *pf*.

испу́г fright. **испуга́ть(ся)** *pf*.

испуска́ть *impf*, **испусти́ть**

(-ущу́, -у́стишь) *pf* emit, let out.

испыта́ние test, trial; ordeal. **испыта́ть** *pf*, **испы́тывать** *impf* test; try; experience.

иссле́дование investigation; research. **иссле́дователь** *m* re- searcher; investigator. **иссле́- довательский** research. **иссле́- довать** *impf* & *pf* investi- gate, examine; research into.

истаска́ться *pf*, **иста́ски- ваться** *impf* wear out; be worn out.

истека́ть *impf* of **исте́чь**. **исте́к- ший** past.

исте́рика hysterics. **истери́че- ский** hysterical. **истери́я** hys- teria.

истече́ние outflow; expiry. **ис- те́чь** (-ечёт; -тёк, -ла́) *pf* (*impf* **истека́ть**) elapse; expire.

и́стина truth. **и́стинный** true.

истлева́ть *impf*, **истле́ть** (-е́ю) *pf* rot, decay; be reduced to ashes.

исто́к source.

истолкова́ть *pf*, **истолко́вы- вать** *impf* interpret; com- ment on.

ис|толо́чь (-лку́ -лчёшь; -ло́к, -лкла́) *pf*.

исто́ма languor.

исторга́ть *impf*, **исто́ргнуть** (-ну; -о́рг) *pf* throw out.

исто́рик historian. **истори́че- ский** historical; historic. **исто́- рия** history; story; incident.

исто́чник spring; source.

истоща́ть *impf*, **истощи́ть** (-щу́) *pf* exhaust; emaciate. **ис- тоще́ние** emaciation; exhaus- tion.

ис|тра́тить (-а́чу) *pf*.

истреби́тель *m* destroyer; fighter. **истреби́ть** (-блю́) *pf*,

истребля́ть *impf* destroy; exterminate.

ис|тупи́ться (-пится) *pf.*

истяза́ние torture. истяза́ть *impf* torture.

исхо́д outcome; end; Exodus. исходи́ть (-ожу́, -о́дишь) *impf* (+из *or* от+gen) issue (from), come (from); proceed (from). исхо́дный initial; departure.

исхуда́лый undernourished, emaciated.

исцеле́ние healing; recovery. исцели́ть *pf*, исцеля́ть *impf* heal, cure.

исчеза́ть *impf*, исче́знуть (-ну; -е́з) *pf* disappear, vanish. исчезнове́ние disappearance.

исче́рпать *pf*, исче́рпывать *impf* exhaust; conclude. исче́рпывающий exhaustive.

исчисле́ние calculation; calculus.

ита́к *conj* thus; so then.

Ита́лия Italy. италья́нец (-нца) италья́нка Italian. италья́нский Italian.

ИТАР-ТА́СС *abbr* (*of* Информацио́нное телегра́фное аге́нтство Росси́и; *see* ТАСС) ITAR-Tass.

и т.д. *abbr* (*of* и так да́лее) etc., and so on.

ито́г sum; total; result. итого́ *adv* in all, altogether.

и т.п. *abbr* (*of* и тому́ подо́бное) etc., and so on.

иуде́й, иуде́йка Jew. иуде́йский Judaic.

их their, theirs; *see* они́.

иша́к (-а́) donkey.

ище́йка bloodhound; police dog.

ищу́ *etc.*: *see* иска́ть.

ию́ль *m* July. ию́льский July.

ию́нь *m* June. ию́ньский June.

йо́га yoga.

йод iodine.

йо́та iota.

К

к, ко *prep+dat* to, towards; by; for; on; on the occasion of; к пе́рвому января́ by the first of January; к тому́ вре́мени by then; к тому́ же besides, moreover; к чему́? what for?

-ка *partl* modifying force of *imper* or expressing decision or intention; да́йте-ка пройти́ let me pass, please; скажи́-ка мне do tell me.

каба́к (-а́) tavern.

кабала́ servitude.

каба́н (-а́) wild boar.

кабаре́ *neut indecl* cabaret.

кабачо́к (-чка́) marrow.

ка́бель *m* cable. ка́бельтов cable, hawser.

каби́на cabin; booth; cockpit; cubicle; cab. кабине́т study; surgery; room; office; Cabinet.

каблу́к (-а́) heel.

кабота́ж coastal shipping. кабота́жный coastal.

кабы́ if.

кавале́р knight; partner, gentleman. кавалери́йский cavalry. кавалери́ст cavalryman. кавале́рия cavalry.

каве́рзный tricky.

Кавка́з the Caucasus. кавка́зец (-зца), кавка́зка Caucasian. кавка́зский Caucasian.

кавы́чки (-чек) *pl* inverted commas, quotation marks.

каде́т cadet. каде́тский ко́рпус military school.

ка́дка tub, vat.

кадр frame, still; close-up; cadre; *pl* establishment; staff; personnel; specialists. **кáдро́вый** (*mil*) regular; skilled; trained.

кады́к (-á) Adam's apple.

каждодне́вный daily, everyday. **кáждый** each, every; *sb* everybody.

кáжется *etc*.: *see* казáться

казáк (-á; *pl* -áки́, -áко́в), **казáчка** Cossack.

казáрма barracks.

казáться (кажу́сь, кáжешься) *impf* (*pf* по~) seem, appear; *impers* кáжется, казáлось apparently; казáлось бы it would seem; +*dat*: мне кáжется I think.

Казахстáн Kazakhstan. **казáчий** Cossack.

каземáт casemate.

казённый State; government; fiscal; public; formal; banal, conventional. **казнá** Exchequer, Treasury; public purse; the State. **казначе́й** treasurer, bursar; paymaster.

казино́ *neut indecl* casino.

казни́ть *impf & pf* execute; punish; castigate. **казнь** execution.

кайма́ (*gen pl* каём) border, edging.

как *adv* how; what; вот ~! you don't say!; ~ вы дýмаете? what do you think?; ~ его́ зовýт? what is his name?; ~ же naturally, of course; ~ же так? how is that?; ~ ни however. **как** *conj* as; like; when; since; +*neg* but, except, than; в то вре́мя ~ while, whereas; ~ мо́жно, ~ нельзя́+*comp* as ... as possible; ~ мо́жно скоре́е as soon as possible; ~ нельзя́ лýчше as well as possible; ~ то́лько as soon as,

when; ме́жду тем, ~ while, whereas. **как бýдто** *conj* as if; *partl* apparently. **как бы** how; as if; как бы... ~ however, supposing; как бы... ни however. **кáк-либо** *adv* somehow; anyhow. **кáк-нибудь** *adv* somehow; anyhow. **как раз** *adv* just, exactly. **кáк-то** *adv* somehow; once.

какáо *neut indecl* cocoa.

каково́ (-á, -ó, -ы́) *pron* what, what sort (of); ~ он? what is he like?; ~ он собо́й? what does he look like?; погóда-то какова́! what weather! **каково́** *adv* how. **какóй** *pron* what; (such) as; which; ~... ни whatever, whichever. **какóй-либо**, **какóй-нибудь** *prons* some; any; only. **какóй-то** *pron* some; a kind of.

как раз, кáк-то *see* как

кáктус cactus.

кал faeces, excrement.

каламбýр pun.

кале́ка *m & f* cripple.

календáрь (-я́) *m* calendar.

кале́ние incandescence.

кале́чить (-чу) *impf* (*pf* ис~, по~) cripple, maim; ~ся become a cripple.

кали́бр calibre; bore; gauge.

кáлий potassium.

кали́тка (wicket-)gate.

каллигрáфия calligraphy.

кало́рия calorie.

калóша galosh.

кáлька tracing-paper; tracing.

калькуля́ция calculation.

кальсо́ны (-н) *pl* long johns.

кáльций calcium.

кáмбала flat-fish; plaice; flounder.

камени́стый stony, rocky. **ка́-менноугóльный** coal; ~ бас-

сейн coal-field. **ка́менный** stone; rock; stony; hard, immovable; ~ **век** Stone Age; ~ **у́голь** coal. **каменоло́мня** (*gen pl* -мен) quarry. **ка́менщик** (stone)mason; bricklayer. **ка́мень** (-мня; *pl* -мни, -мней) *m* stone.

ка́мера chamber; cell; camera; inner tube, (football) bladder; ~ **хране́ния** cloak-room, left-luggage office. **ка́мерный** chamber. **камерто́н** tuning-fork.

ками́н fireplace; fire.

камко́рдер camcorder.

камо́рка closet, very small room.

кампа́ния campaign; cruise.

камы́ш (-á) reed, rush; cane.

кана́ва ditch; gutter.

Кана́да Canada. **кана́дец** (-дца), **кана́дка** Canadian. **кана́дский** Canadian.

кана́л canal; channel. **канализа́ция** sewerage (system).

канаре́йка canary.

кана́т rope; cable.

канва́ canvas; groundwork; outline, design.

кандалы́ (-о́в) *pl* shackles.

кандида́т candidate; ~ **нау́к** person with higher degree. **кандидату́ра** candidature.

кани́кулы (-ул) *pl* vacation; holidays.

кани́стра can, canister.

канони́ческий canon(ical).

кано́э *neut indecl* canoe.

кант edging; mount. **кантова́ть** *impf*; **«не ~»** 'this way up'.

кану́н eve.

ка́нуть (-ну) *pf* drop, sink; как **в во́ду ~** vanish into thin air.

канцеля́рия office. **канцеля́р-**

ский office; clerical. **канцеля́р-щина** red-tape.

ка́нцлер chancellor.

ка́пать (-аю *or* -плю) *impf* (*pf* **ка́пнуть, на~**) drip, drop; trickle; +*instr* spill.

капе́лла chapel; choir.

ка́пелька small drop; a little; ~ **росы́** dew-drop.

капельме́йстер conductor; bandmaster.

капилля́р capillary.

капита́л capital. **капитали́зм** capitalism. **капитали́ст** capitalist. **капиталисти́ческий** capitalist. **капита́льный** capital; main, fundamental; major.

капита́н captain; skipper.

капитули́ровать *impf & pf* capitulate. **капитуля́ция** capitulation.

капка́н trap.

ка́пля (*gen pl* -пель) drop; bit, scrap. **ка́пнуть** (-ну) *pf of* **ка́пать**

капо́т hood, cowl, cowling; bonnet; house-coat.

капри́з caprice. **капри́зничать** *impf* play up. **капри́зный** capricious.

капу́ста cabbage.

капюшо́н hood.

ка́ра punishment.

кара́бкаться *impf* (*pf* **вс~**) clamber.

карава́н caravan; convoy.

кара́кули *f pl* scribble.

караме́ль caramel; caramels.

каранда́ш (-á) pencil.

каранти́н quarantine.

кара́т carat.

кара́тельный punitive. **кара́ть** *impf* (*pf* **по~**) punish.

карау́л guard; watch; ~**!** help! **карау́лить** *impf* guard; lie in

wait for. **карау́льный** guard; *sb* sentry, sentinel, guard.

карбюра́тор carburettor.

каре́та carriage, coach.

ка́рий brown; hazel.

карикату́ра caricature; cartoon.

карка́с frame; framework.

ка́ркать *impf*, **ка́ркнуть** (-ну) *pf* caw, croak.

ка́рлик, **ка́рлица** dwarf; pygmy. **ка́рликовый** dwarf; pygmy.

карма́н pocket. **карма́нник** pickpocket. **карма́нный** *adj* pocket.

карни́з cornice; ledge.

карп carp.

ка́рта map; (playing-)card.

карта́вить (-влю) *impf* burr.

картёжник gambler.

карте́чь case-shot, grape-shot.

карти́на picture; scene. **карти́нка** picture; illustration. **карти́нный** picturesque; picture.

карто́н cardboard. **карто́нка** cardboard box.

картоте́ка card-index.

карто́фель *m* potatoes; potato(-plant). **карто́фельный** potato; ~ое пюре́ mashed potatoes.

ка́рточка card; season ticket; photo. **ка́рточный** card.

карто́шка potatoes; potato.

ка́ртридж cartridge.

карусе́ль merry-go-round.

ка́рцер cell, lock-up.

карье́р¹ full gallop.

карье́р² quarry; sand-pit.

карье́ра career. **карьери́ст** careerist.

каса́ние contact. **каса́тельная** *sb* tangent. **каса́ться** *impf* (*pf* **косну́ться**) +*gen* or до+*gen*

touch; touch on; concern; что каса́ется as regards.

ка́ска helmet.

каска́д cascade.

каспи́йский Caspian.

ка́сса till; cash-box; booking-office; box-office; cash-desk; cash.

кассе́та cassette. **кассе́тный магнитофо́н** cassette recorder.

касси́р, **касси́рша** cashier.

кастра́т eunuch. **кастра́ция** castration. **кастри́ровать** *impf* & *pf* castrate, geld.

кастрю́ля saucepan.

катало́г catalogue.

ката́ние rolling; driving; ~ верхо́м riding; ~ на конька́х skating.

катапу́льта catapult. **катапульти́ровать(ся** *impf* & *pf* catapult.

ката́р catarrh.

катара́кта cataract.

катастро́фа catastrophe. **катастрофи́ческий** catastrophic.

ката́ть *impf* roll; (take for a) drive; ~ся (*pf* **по**~) roll, roll about; go for a drive; ~ся верхо́м ride, go riding; ~ся на конька́х skate, go skating.

категори́ческий categorical. **катего́рия** category.

ка́тер (*pl* -а́) cutter; launch.

кати́ть (-ачу́, -а́тишь) *impf* bowl along, rip, tear; ~ся rush, tear; flow, stream, roll; кати́сь, кати́тесь get out! clear off! **като́к** (-тка́) skating-rink; roller.

като́лик, **католи́чка** Catholic. **католи́ческий** Catholic.

ка́торга penal servitude, hard labour. **ка́торжник** convict. **ка́торжный** penal; ~ые рабо́ты hard labour; drudgery.

катýшка reel, bobbin; spool; coil.

каучýк rubber.

кафé *neut indecl* café.

кáфедра pulpit; rostrum; chair; department.

кáфель *m* Dutch tile.

качáлка rocking-chair. **качáние** rocking, swinging; pumping. **качáть** *impf* (*pf* качнýть) +*acc or instr* rock, swing; shake; ∼ся rock, swing; roll; reel. **качéли** (-ей) *pl* swing.

кáчественный qualitative; high-quality. **кáчество** quality; в кáчестве+*gen* as, in the capacity of.

кáчка rocking; tossing.

качнýть(ся (-нý(сь, -нёшь(ся) *pf of* качáть(ся. качý *etc.: see* катить

кáша gruel, porridge; **заварить кáшу** stir up trouble.

кáшель (-шля) cough. **кáшлянуть** (-ну) *pf*, **кáшлять** *impf* (have a) cough.

каштáн chestnut. **каштáновый** chestnut.

каю́та cabin, stateroom.

кáющийся penitent. **кáяться** (кáюсь) *impf* (*pf* по∼, рас∼) repent; confess; кáюсь I (must) confess.

кв. *abbr* (*of* квадрáтный) square; (*of* квартúра) flat.

квадрáт square; quad; в квадрáте squared; возвести́ в ∼ square. **квадрáтный** square; quadratic.

квáкать *impf*, **квáкнуть** (-ну) *pf* croak.

квалификáция qualification. **квалифици́рованный** qualified, skilled.

квант, **квáнта** quantum. **квáнтовый** quantum.

квартáл block; quarter. **квартáльный** quarterly.

квартéт quartet.

квартúра flat; apartment(s); quarters. **квартирáнт, -рáнтка** lodger; tenant. **квартúрная плáта, квартплáта** rent.

кварц quartz.

квас (*pl* -ы́) kvass. **квáсить** (-áшу) *impf* sour; pickle. **квáшеная капýста** sauerkraut.

квéрху *adv* up, upwards.

квит, квúты quits.

квитáнция receipt. **квитóк** (-ткá) ticket, check.

КГБ *abbr* (*of* Комитéт госудáрственной безопáсности) KGB.

кéгля skittle.

кедр cedar.

кéды (-ов) *pl* trainers.

кекс (fruit-)cake.

кéлья (*gen pl* -лий) cell.

кем *see* кто

кéмпинг campsite.

кенгурý *m indecl* kangaroo.

кéпка cloth cap.

керáмика ceramics.

керогáз stove. **кероси́н** paraffin. **кероси́нка** paraffin stove.

кéта Siberian salmon. **кéтовый**: ∼ая икрá red caviare.

кефи́р kefir, yoghurt.

кибернéтика cybernetics.

кивáть *impf*, **кивнýть** (-нý, -нёшь) *pf* (головóй) nod (one's head); (+на+*acc*) motion (to). **кивóк** (-вкá) nod.

кидáть *impf* (*pf* ки́нуть) throw, fling; ∼ся fling o.s.; rush; +*instr* throw.

кий (-я́; *pl* -и́, -ёв) (billiard) cue.

килевóй keel. ∼áя кáчка pitching.

кило́ *neut indecl* kilo. **киловáтт**

kilowatt. **килогра́мм** kilogram. **киломе́тр** kilometre.

киль m keel; fin. **кильва́тер** wake.

ки́лька sprat.

кинжа́л dagger.

кино́ neut indecl cinema.

кино- in comb film-, cine-. **киноаппара́т** cinecamera. **~арти́ст**, **~арти́стка** film actor, actress. **~журна́л** news-reel. **~за́л** cinema; auditorium. **~звезда́** film-star. **~зри́тель** m film-goer. **~карти́на** film. **~опера́тор** camera-man. **~плёнка** film. **~режиссёр** film director. **~теа́тр** cinema. **~хро́ника** news-reel.

ки́нуть(ся) (-ну(сь) pf of кида́ть(ся)

кио́ск kiosk, stall.

ки́па pile, stack; bale.

кипари́с cypress.

кипе́ние boiling. **кипе́ть** (-плю́) impf (pf вс~) boil, seethe.

кипу́чий boiling, seething; ebullient. **кипяти́льник** kettle, boiler. **кипяти́ть** (-ячу́) impf (pf вс~) boil; **~ся** boil; get excited. **кипято́к** (-тка́) boiling water. **кипячёный** boiled.

Кирги́зия Kirghizia.

кирка́ pick(axe).

кирпи́ч (-а́) brick; bricks. **кирпи́чный** brick-red.

кисе́ль m kissel, blancmange.

кисе́т tobacco-pouch.

кисея́ muslin.

кислоро́д oxygen. **кислота́** (pl -ы) acid; acidity. **кисло́тный** acid. **ки́слый** sour; acid. **ки́снуть** (-ну; кис) impf (pf про~) turn sour.

ки́сточка brush; tassel; kiss. **кисть** (gen pl -éй) cluster, bunch;

brush; tassel; hand.

кит (-á) whale.

кита́ец (-а́йца; pl -цы, -цев) Chinese. **Кита́й** China. **кита́йский** Chinese. **китая́нка** Chinese (woman).

китобо́й whaler. **кито́вый** whale.

кичи́ться (-чу́сь) impf plume o.s.; strut. **кичли́вость** conceit. **кичли́вый** conceited.

кише́ть (-ши́т) impf swarm, teem.

кише́чник bowels, intestines. **кише́чный** intestinal. **кишка́** gut, intestine; hose.

клавеси́н harpsichord. **клавиату́ра** keyboard. **кла́виша** key. **кла́вишный**: **~ инструме́нт** keyboard instrument.

клад treasure.

кла́дбище cemetery, graveyard. **кла́дка** laying; masonry. **кладова́я** sb pantry; store-room. **кладови́к** (-á) storeman. **кладу́** etc.: see **класть**

кла́няться impf (pf поклони́ться) +dat bow to; greet.

кла́пан valve; vent.

кларне́т clarinet.

класс class; class-room. **кла́ссик** classic. **кла́ссика** the classics. **классифици́ровать** impf & pf classify. **класси́ческий** classical. **кла́ссный** class; first-class. **кла́ссовый** class.

класть (-аду́, -адёшь; -ал) impf (pf положи́ть, сложи́ть) lay; put.

клева́ть (клюю́, клюёшь) impf (pf клю́нуть) peck; bite.

клёвер (pl -á) clover.

клевета́ slander; libel. **клевета́ть** (-ещу́, -е́щешь) impf (pf на~) +на+acc slander; libel.

клеветни́к (-á), **-ница** slan-

derer. **клеветни́ческий** slanderous; libellous.
клеёнка oilcloth. **кле́ить** *impf* (*pf* c∼) glue; stick; ∼ся stick; become sticky. **клей** (*loc* -ю́; *pl* -и́) glue, adhesive. **кле́йкий** sticky.
клейми́ть (-млю́) *impf* (*pf* за∼) brand; stamp; stigmatize. **клеймо́** (*pl* -а) brand; stamp; mark.
кле́йстер paste.
клён maple.
клепа́ть *impf* rivet.
кле́тка cage; check; cell. **кле́точка** cellule. **кле́точный** cellular. **клетча́тка** cellulose. **кле́тчатый** checked.
клёш flare.
клешня́ (*gen pl* -е́й) claw.
кле́щи (-е́й) *pl* pincers, tongs.
клие́нт client. **клиенту́ра** clientèle.
кли́зма enema.
клик cry, call. **кли́кать** (-и́чу) *impf*, **кли́кнуть** (-ну) *pf* call.
кли́макс menopause.
кли́мат climate. **климати́ческий** climatic.
клин (*pl* -нья, -ньев) wedge. **клино́к** (-нка́) blade.
кли́ника clinic. **клини́ческий** clinical.
клипс clip-on ear-ring.
клич call. **кли́чка** name; nickname. **кли́чу** *etc.*: *see* **кли́кать**
клок (-а́; *pl* -о́чья, -ьев *or* -и́, -о́в) rag, shred; tuft.
клоко́т bubbling; gurgling. **клокота́ть** (-о́чет) *impf* bubble; gurgle; boil up.
клони́ть (-ню́, -нишь) *impf* bend; incline; +к+*dat* drive at; ∼ся bow, bend; +к+*dat* near, approach.

клон clone.
клоп (-а́) bug.
кло́ун clown.
клочо́к (-чка́) scrap, shred. **кло́чья** *etc.*: *see* **клок**
клуб[1] club.
клуб[2] (*pl* -ы́) puff; cloud.
клу́бень (-бня) *m* tuber.
клуби́ться *impf* swirl; curl.
клубни́ка (*no pl*; *usu collect*) strawberry; strawberries.
клубо́к (-бка́) ball; tangle.
клу́мба (flower-)bed.
клык (-а́) fang; tusk; canine (tooth).
клюв beak.
клю́ква cranberry; cranberries.
клю́нуть (-ну) *pf of* **клева́ть**
ключ[1] (-а́) key; clue; keystone; clef; wrench, spanner.
ключ[2] (-а́) spring; source.
ключево́й key. **ключи́ца** collarbone.
клю́шка (hockey) stick; (golf-) club.
клюю́ *etc.*: *see* **клева́ть**
кля́кса blot, smudge.
кляну́ *etc.*: *see* **клясть**
клянчить (-чу) *impf* (*pf* вы́∼) beg.
кляп gag.
клясть (-яну́, -янёшь; -ял, -а́, -о) *impf* curse; ∼ся (*pf* по∼ся) swear, vow. **кля́тва** oath, vow. **кля́твенный** on oath.
кни́га book.
книго- *in comb* book, biblio-. **книгове́дение**[1] bibliography. ∼**ве́дение**[2] book-keeping. ∼**изда́тель** *m* publisher. ∼**лю́б** bibliophile. ∼**храни́лище** library; book-stack.
кни́жечка booklet. **кни́жка** book; note-book; bank-book. **кни́жный** book; bookish.

кни́зу *adv* downwards.

кно́пка drawing-pin; press-stud; (push-)button, knob.

кнут (-а́) whip.

княги́ня princess. **кня́жество** principality. **княжна́** (*gen pl* -жо́н) princess. **князь** (*pl* -зья́, -зе́й) *m* prince.

ко *see* **к** *prep.*

коали́ция coalition.

кобура́ holster.

кобы́ла mare; (vaulting-)horse.

ко́ваный forged; wrought; terse.

кова́рный insidious, crafty; perfidious. **кова́рство** insidiousness, craftiness; perfidy.

кова́ть (кую́, -ёшь) *impf* (*pf* под~) forge; hammer; shoe.

ковёр (-вра́) carpet; rug; mat.

коверка́ть *impf* (*pf* ис~) distort, mangle, ruin.

ко́вка forging; shoeing.

коври́жка honeycake, gingerbread.

ко́врик rug; mat.

ковче́г ark.

ковш (-а́) scoop, ladle.

ковы́ль *m* feather-grass.

ковыля́ть *impf* hobble.

ковыря́ть (-ну́, -нёшь) *pf*, **ковыря́ть** *impf* dig into; tinker; +в+*prep* pick (at); ~ся rummage; tinker.

когда́ *adv* when; ~ (бы) ни whenever; *conj* when; while; as; if. **когда́-либо**, **когда́-нибудь** *advs* some time; ever. **когда́-то** *adv* once; formerly; some time.

кого́ *see* **кто**

ко́готь (-гтя; *pl* -гти, -гте́й) *m* claw; talon.

код code.

кодеи́н codeine.

ко́декс code.

ко́е-где́ *adv* here and there. **ко́е-ка́к** *adv* anyhow; somehow (or other). **ко́е-како́й** *pron* some. **ко́е-кто́** *pron* somebody; some people. **ко́е-что́** (-чего́) *pron* something; a little.

ко́жа skin; leather; peel. **ко́жанка** leather jacket. **ко́жаный** leather. **коже́венный** leather; tanning. **ко́жный** skin. **кожура́** rind, peel, skin.

коза́ (*pl* -ы) goat, nanny-goat. **козёл** (-зла́) billy-goat. **козеро́г** ibex; Capricorn. **ко́зий** goat; ~ **пух** angora. **козлёнок** (-нка; *pl* -ля́та, -ля́т) kid.

ко́злы (-зел) *pl* coach driver's seat; trestle(s); saw-horse.

ко́зни (-ей) *pl* machinations.

козырёк (-рька́) peak.

козырно́й trump. **козырну́ть** (-ну́, -нёшь) *pf*, **козыря́ть** *impf* lead trumps; trump; play one's trump card; salute. **ко́зырь** (*pl* -и, -е́й) *m* trump.

ко́йка (*gen pl* ко́ек) berth, bunk; bed.

кока́ин cocaine.

ко́ка-ко́ла Coca-Cola (*propr*).

коке́тка coquette. **коке́тство** coquetry.

коклю́ш whooping-cough.

ко́кон cocoon.

коко́с coconut.

кокс coke.

кокте́йль *m* cocktail.

кол (-а́; *pl* -лья, -ьев) stake, picket.

ко́лба retort.

колбаса́ (*pl* -ы) sausage.

колго́тки (-ток) *pl* tights.

колдова́ть *impf* practise witchcraft. **колдовство́** sorcery. **колду́н** (-а́) sorcerer, wizard. **колду́нья** (*gen pl* -ний) witch, sorceress.

колеба́ние oscillation; variation; hesitation. **колеба́ть** (-е́блю) *impf* (*pf* по~) shake; ~ся oscillate; fluctuate; hesitate.

коле́но (*pl* -и, -ей, -ям) knee; (*in pl*) lap. **коле́нчатый** crank, cranked; bent; ~ вал crankshaft.

колесни́ца chariot. **колесо́** (*pl* -ёса) wheel.

коле́я rut; track, gauge.

ко́лика (*usu pl*) colic; stitch.

коли́чественный quantitative; ~ое числи́тельное cardinal number. **коли́чество** quantity; number.

колле́га *m & f* colleague. **колле́гия** board; college.

коллекти́в collective. **коллективиза́ция** collectivization. **коллекти́вный** collective. **коллекционе́р** collector. **колле́кция** collection.

колли́зия clash, conflict.

коло́да block; pack (*of cards*).

коло́дец (-дца) well.

ко́локол (*pl* -а́, -о́в) bell. **колоко́льный** bell. **колоко́льня** bell-tower. **колоко́льчик** small bell; bluebell.

колониали́зм colonialism. **колониа́льный** colonial. **колониза́тор** colonizer. **колониза́ция** colonization. **колонизова́ть** *impf & pf* colonize. **коло́ния** colony.

коло́нка geyser; (*street*) water fountain; stand-pipe; column; бензи́новая ~ petrol pump. **коло́нна** column.

колори́т colouring, colour. **колори́тный** colourful, graphic.

ко́лос (-о́сья, -ьев) ear. **коло́ситься** *impf* form ears.

колосса́льный huge; terrific.

колоти́ть (-очу́, -о́тишь) *impf* (*pf* по~) beat; pound; thrash; smash; ~ся pound, thump.

коло́ть[1] (-лю́, -лешь) *impf* (*pf* рас~) break, chop.

коло́ть[2] (-лю́, -лешь) *impf* (*pf* за~, кольну́ть) prick; stab; sting; slaughter; ~ся prick.

колпа́к (-а́) cap; hood, cowl.

колхо́з *abbr* (*of* коллекти́вное хозя́йство) kolkhoz, collective farm. **колхо́зник**, **-ица** kolkhoz member. **колхо́зный** kolkhoz.

колыбе́ль cradle.

колыха́ть (-ы́шу) *impf*, **колыхну́ть** (-ну́, -нёшь) *pf* sway, rock; ~ся sway; flutter.

кольну́ть (-ну́, -нёшь) *pf of* коло́ть

кольцо́ (*pl* -а, -ле́ц, -льцам) ring.

колю́чий prickly; sharp; ~ая про́волока barbed wire. **колю́чка** prickle; thorn.

коля́ска carriage; pram; side-car.

ком (*pl* -мья, -мьев) lump; ball.

ком *see* кто

кома́нда command; order; detachment; crew; team. **команди́р** commander. **командирова́ть** *impf & pf* post, send on a mission. **командиро́вка** posting; mission, business trip. **командиро́вочные** *sb pl* travelling expenses. **кома́ндование** command. **кома́ндовать** *impf* (*pf* с~) give orders; be in command; +*instr* command. **кома́ндующий** *sb* commander.

кома́р (-а́) mosquito.

комба́йн combine harvester.

комбина́т industrial complex. **комбина́ция** combination.

manoeuvre; slip. **комбинезо́н** overalls, boiler suit; dungarees. **комбини́ровать** *impf* (*pf* с~) combine.

коме́дия comedy.

коменда́нт commandant; manager; warden. **комендату́ра** commandant's office.

коме́та comet.

ко́мик comic actor; comedian. **ко́микс** comic, comic strip.

комисса́р commissar.

комиссионе́р (commission-)agent, broker. **комиссио́нный** commission; ~ый магази́н second-hand shop; ~ые *sb pl* commission. **коми́ссия** commission; committee.

комите́т committee.

коми́ческий comic; comical. **коми́чный** comical, funny.

ко́мкать *impf* (*pf* с~) crumple.

коммента́рий commentary; *pl* comment. **коммента́тор** commentator. **комменти́ровать** *impf* & *pf* comment (on).

коммерса́нт merchant; businessman. **комме́рция** commerce. **комме́рческий** commercial.

коммивояжёр commercial traveller.

комму́на commune. **коммуна́льный** communal; municipal. **коммуни́зм** communism.

коммуника́ция communication.

коммуни́ст, ~ка communist. **коммунисти́ческий** communist.

коммута́тор switchboard.

коммюнике́ *neut indecl* communiqué.

ко́мната room. **ко́мнатный** room; indoor.

комо́д chest of drawers.

комо́к (-мка́) lump.

компа́кт-ди́ск compact disc. **компа́ктный** compact.

компа́ния company. **компаньо́н**, ~ка a companion; partner.

компа́ртия Communist Party.

ко́мпас compass.

компенса́ция compensation. **компенси́ровать** *impf* & *pf* compensate.

ко́мплекс complex. **ко́мплексный** complex, compound, composite; combined. **компле́кт** (complete) set; complement; kit. **комплектова́ть** *impf* (*pf* с~, у~) complete; bring up to strength. **комплéкция** build; constitution.

комплиме́нт compliment.

компози́тор composer. **компози́ция** composition.

компоне́нт component.

компо́ст compost.

компо́стер punch. **компости́ровать** *impf* (*pf* про~) punch.

компо́т stewed fruit.

компре́ссор compressor.

компромети́ровать *impf* (*pf* с~) compromise. **компроми́сс** compromise.

компью́тер computer.

комсомо́л Komsomol. **комсомо́лец** (-льца), **-лка** Komsomol member. **комсомо́льский** Komsomol.

кому́ *see* **кто**

комфо́рт comfort.

конве́йер conveyor.

конве́рт envelope; sleeve.

конво́ир escort. **конвои́ровать** *impf* escort. **конво́й** escort, convoy.

конгре́сс congress.

конденса́тор condenser.

конди́терская *sb* confectioner's, cake shop.

кондиционе́р air-conditioner. **кондицио́нный** air-conditioning.

конду́ктор (*pl* -á), -торша conductor; guard.

конево́дство horse-breeding. **конёк** (-нька́) *dim of* **конь**; hobby(-horse).

коне́ц (-нца́) end; **в конце́ концо́в** in the end, after all. **коне́чно** *adv* of course. **коне́чность** extremity. **коне́чный** final, last; ultimate; finite.

кони́ческий conic, conical.

конкре́тный concrete.

конкуре́нт competitor. **конкуре́нция** competition. **конкури́ровать** *impf* compete. **ко́нкурс** competition; contest.

ко́нница cavalry. **ко́нный** horse; mounted; equestrian; ~ **заво́д** stud.

конопля́ hemp.

консервати́вный conservative. **консерва́тор** Conservative.

консервато́рия conservatoire.

консерви́ровать *impf & pf* (*pf also* за~) preserve; can, bottle. **консе́рвный** preserving; ~ая **ба́нка** tin; ~ый **нож** tin-opener. **консе́рвооткрыва́тель** *m* tin-opener. **консе́рвы** (-ов) *pl* tinned goods.

конси́лиум consultation.

конспе́кт synopsis, summary. **конспекти́ровать** *impf* (*pf* за~, про~) make an abstract of.

конспирати́вный secret, clandestine. **конспира́ция** security.

констата́ция ascertaining; establishment. **констати́ровать** *impf & pf* ascertain; establish.

конституцио́нный constitutional. **конститу́ция** constitution.

конструи́ровать *impf & pf* (*pf also* с~) construct; design. **констру́ктивный** structural; constructional; constructive. **констру́ктор** designer, constructor. **констру́кция** construction; design.

ко́нсул consul. **ко́нсульство** consulate.

консульта́ция consultation; advice; clinic; tutorial. **консульти́ровать** *impf* (*pf* про~) advise; +**с**+*instr* consult; ~ся obtain advice; +**с**+*instr* consult.

конта́кт contact. **конта́ктные ли́нзы** *f pl* contact lenses.

конте́йнер container.

конте́кст context.

контине́нт continent.

конто́ра office. **конто́рский** office.

контраба́нда contraband. **контрабанди́ст** smuggler.

контраба́с double-bass.

контра́кт contract.

контра́льто *neut*/*fem indecl* contralto (*voice*/*person*).

контрама́рка complimentary ticket.

контрапу́нкт counterpoint.

контра́ст contrast.

контрибу́ция indemnity.

контрнаступле́ние counter-offensive.

контролёр inspector; ticket-collector. **контроли́ровать** *impf* (*pf* про~) check; inspect. **контро́ль** *m* control; check; inspection. **контро́льный** control; ~ая **рабо́та** test.

контрразве́дка counter-

intelligence; security service. **контрреволюция** counter-revolution.

контузия bruising; shell-shock.

контур contour, outline; circuit.

конура kennel.

конус cone.

конфедерация confederation.

конференция conference.

конфета sweet.

конфисковать impf & pf confiscate.

конфликт conflict.

конфорка ring (on stove).

конфуз discomfort, embarrassment. **конфузить** (-ужу) impf (pf c~) confuse, embarrass; ~ся feel embarrassed.

концентрат concentrate. **концентрационный** concentration. **концентрация** concentration. **концентрировать(ся** impf (pf c~) concentrate.

концепция conception.

концерт concert; concerto. **концертмейстер** leader. **концертный** concert.

концлагерь abbr (of **концентрационный лагерь**) concentration camp.

кончать impf, **кончить** pf finish; end +inf stop; ~ся end, finish; expire. **кончик** tip. **кончина** decease.

конь (-я; pl -и, -ей) m horse; knight. **коньки** (-ов) pl skates; ~ на роликах roller skates. **конькобежец** (-жца) skater.

коньяк (-а) cognac.

конюх groom, stable-boy. **конюшня** (gen pl -шен) stable.

кооператив cooperative. **кооперативный** cooperative. **кооперация** cooperation.

координата coordinate. **коор-**

динация coordination.

копать impf (pf копнуть, вы~) dig; dig up, dig out; ~ся rummage.

копейка copeck.

копи (-ей) pl mines.

копилка money-box.

копирка carbon paper. **копировальный** copying. **копировать** impf (pf c~) copy; imitate.

копить (-плю, -пишь) impf (pf на~) save (up); accumulate; ~ся accumulate.

копия copy.

копна (pl -ы, -пён) shock, stook.

копнуть (-ну, -нёшь) pf of **копать**

копоть soot.

коптеть (-пчу) impf swot; vegetate. **коптить** (-пчу) impf (pf за~, на~) smoke, cure; blacken with smoke. **копчение** smoking; smoked foods. **копчёный** smoked.

копыто hoof.

копьё (pl -я, -пий) spear, lance.

кора bark; cortex; crust.

корабельный ship; naval. **кораблевождение** navigation. **кораблекрушение** shipwreck. **кораблестроение** ship-building. **корабль** (-я) m ship, vessel; nave.

коралл coral.

корейский Korean. **Корея** Korea.

коренастый thickset. **корениться** impf be rooted. **коренной** radical, fundamental; native. **корень** (-рня; pl -и, -ей) m root. **корешок** (-шка) root(let); spine; counterfoil.

корзина, корзинка basket.

коридо́р corridor.

кори́ца cinnamon.

кори́чневый brown.

ко́рка crust; rind, peel.

корм (*loc* -ý; *pl* -á) fodder.

кормá stern.

корми́|лец (-льца) bread-winner. корми́ть (-млю́, -мишь) *impf* (*pf* на~, по~, про~) feed; ~ся feed; +*instr* live on, make a living by. кормле́ние feeding. кормово́й¹ fodder.

кормово́й² stern.

корнево́й root; radical. корне-плóды (-ов) root-crops.

коро́бить (-блю) *impf* (*pf* по~) warp; jar upon; ~ся (*pf also* с~ся) warp.

коро́бка box.

коро́ва cow.

короле́ва queen. короле́вский royal. короле́вство kingdom. коро́ль (-я́) *m* king.

коромы́сло yoke; beam; rock-ing shaft.

коро́на crown.

коронаротромбо́з coronary (thrombosis).

коро́нка crown. коронова́ть *impf & pf* crown.

коро́ткий (коро́ток, -ткá, коро́тко, коро́тки) short; intimate. ко́ротко *adv* briefly; intimately. коротково́лновый short-wave. коро́че *comp* of коро́ткий, ко́ротко

корпора́ция corporation.

ко́рпус (*pl* -ы, -ов *or* -á, -óв) corps; services; building; hull; housing, case; body.

корректи́ровать *impf* (*pf* про~, с~) correct, edit. коррéктный correct, proper. коррéктор (*pl* -á) proof-reader. корректу́ра proof-reading; proof.

корреспонде́нт correspond-ent. корреспонде́нция corres-pondence.

корро́зия corrosion.

корру́пция corruption.

корт (tennis-)court.

корте́ж cortège; motorcade.

ко́ртик dirk.

ко́рточки (-чек) *pl*: сиде́ть на ко́рточках squat.

корчева́ть (-чу́ю) *impf* root out.

ко́рчить (-чу) *impf* (*pf* с~) con-tort; *impers* convulse; ~ из себя́ pose as; ~ся writhe.

ко́ршун kite.

коры́стный mercenary. ко-ры́сть avarice; profit.

коры́то trough; wash-tub.

корь measles.

косá¹ (*acc* -у; *pl* -ы) plait, tress.

косá² (*acc* ко́су; *pl* -ы) spit.

косá³ (*acc* ко́су; *pl* -ы) scythe.

ко́свенный indirect.

коси́лка mowing-machine; mower. коси́ть¹ (кошý, ко́сишь) *impf* (*pf* с~) cut; mow (down).

коси́ть² (кошý) *impf* (*pf* по~, с~) squint; be crooked; ~ся slant; look sideways; look askance.

косме́тика cosmetics, make-up.

косми́ческий cosmic; space. космодро́м spacecraft launching-site. космона́вт, -на́втка cosmonaut, astronaut. ко́смос cosmos; (outer) space.

косноязы́чный tongue-tied.

косну́ться (-ну́сь, -нёшься) *pf of* каса́ться

косогла́зие squint. косо́й (кос, -á, -о) slanting; oblique; side-long; squinting, cross-eyed.

костёр (-трá) bonfire; camp-fire.

костля́вый bony. ко́стный

bone. **косточка** (small) bone; stone.

костыль (-я́) *m* crutch.

кость (*loc* и́; *pl* -и, -е́й) bone; die.

костюм clothes; suit. **костюми́рованный** fancy-dress.

костяно́й bone; ivory.

косы́нка (*triangular*) headscarf, shawl.

кот (-а́) tom-cat.

котёл (-тла́) boiler; copper, cauldron. **котело́к** (-лка́) pot; messtin; bowler (hat). **коте́льная** *sb* boiler-room, -house.

котёнок (-нка; *pl* -тя́та, -тя́т) kitten. **ко́тик** fur-seal; sealskin.

котле́та rissole; burger; **отбивна́я** ~ chop.

котлова́н foundation pit, trench.

кото́мка knapsack.

кото́рый *pron* which, what; who; that; ~ час? what time is it?

котя́та *etc.: see* **котёнок**

ко́фе *m indecl* coffee. **кофева́рка** percolator. **кофе́йн** caffeine.

ко́фта, ко́фточка blouse, top.

коча́н (-а́ *or* -чна́) (cabbage-) head.

кочева́ть (-чу́ю) *impf* be a nomad; wander; migrate. **коче́вник** nomad. **кочево́й** nomadic.

кочега́р stoker, fireman. **кочега́рка** stokehold, stokehole.

кочене́ть *impf* (*pf* за-, о-) grow numb.

кочерга́ (*gen pl* -рёг) poker.

ко́чка hummock.

кошелёк (-лька́) purse.

ко́шка cat.

кошма́р nightmare. **кошма́р-**

ный nightmarish.

кошу́ *etc.: see* **коси́ть**

кощу́нство blasphemy.

коэффицие́нт coefficient.

КП *abbr* (*of* Коммунисти́ческая па́ртия) Communist Party. **КПСС** *abbr* (*of* Коммунисти́ческая па́ртия Сове́тского Сою́за) Communist Party of the Soviet Union, CPSU.

краб crab.

кра́деный stolen. **краду́** *etc.: see* **красть**

кра́жа theft; ~ со взло́мом burglary.

край (*loc* -ю́; *pl* -я́, -ёв) edge; brink; land; region. **кра́йне** *adv* extremely; **кра́йний** extreme; last; outside, wing; **по кра́йней ме́ре** at least. **кра́йность** extreme; extremity.

крал *etc.: see* **красть**

кран tap; crane.

крапи́ва nettle.

краса́вец (-вца) handsome man. **краса́вица** beauty. **краси́вый** handsome; beautiful.

краси́тель *m* dye. **кра́сить** (-а́шу) *impf* (*pf* вы́-, о-, по-) paint; colour; dye; stain; ~ся (*pf* на-) make-up. **кра́ска** paint, dye; colour.

красне́ть (-е́ю) *impf* (*pf* по-) blush; redden; show red.

красноарме́ец (-е́йца) Red Army man. **красноарме́йский** Red Army. **красноречи́вый** eloquent.

краснота́ redness. **красну́ха** German measles. **кра́сный** (-сен, -сна́, -о) red; beautiful; fine; ~ое де́рево mahogany; ~ая сморо́дина (*no pl*; *usu collect*) redcurrant; redcurrants; ~ая строка́ (first line of) new paragraph.

красова́ться *impf* impress by one's beauty; show off. красота́ (*pl* -ы) beauty. красо́чный paint; ink; colourful.

красть (-аду́, -адёшь; крал) *impf* (*pf* y~) steal; ~ся creep.

кра́тер crater.

кра́ткий (-ток, -тка́, -о) short; brief. кратковре́менный brief; transitory. краткосро́чный short-term.

кра́тное *sb* multiple. кратча́йший *superl of* кра́ткий. кра́тче *comp of* кра́ткий, кра́тко

крах crash; failure.

крахма́л starch. крахма́лить *impf* (*pf* на~) starch.

кра́ше *comp of* краси́вый, краси́во

кра́шеный painted; coloured; dyed; made up. кра́шу *etc.: see* кра́сить.

креве́тка shrimp; prawn.

креди́т credit. креди́тный credit. кредито́р creditor. кредитоспосо́бный solvent.

кре́йсер (*pl* -а́, -ов) cruiser.

крем cream.

кремато́рий crematorium.

креме́нь (-мня́) *m* flint.

кремль (-я́) *m* citadel; Kremlin.

кре́мний silicon.

кре́мовый cream.

крен list, heel; bank. крени́ться *impf* (*pf* на~) heel over, list; bank.

крепи́ть (-плю́) *impf* strengthen; support; make fast; constipate. ~ся hold out. кре́п|кий (-пок, -пка́, -о) strong; firm; ~ие напи́тки spirits. крепле́ние strengthening; fastening.

кре́пнуть (-ну; -еп) *impf* (*pf* o~) get stronger.

крепостни́чество serfdom.

крепостн|о́й serf; ~о́е пра́во serfdom; ~о́й *sb* serf.

кре́пость fortress; strength. кре́пче *comp of* кре́пкий. кре́пко

кре́сло (*gen pl* -сел) arm-chair; stall.

крест (-а́) cross. крести́ны (-и́н) *pl* christening. крести́ть (крещу́, -ести́шь) *impf & pf also* o~, пере~) christen; make sign of the cross over; ~ся cross o.s.; be christened. крест-на́крест *adv* crosswise. кре́стник, кре́стница god-child. крёстн|ый; ~ая (мать) godmother; ~ый оте́ц godfather. кресто́вый похо́д crusade. крестоно́сец (-сца) crusader.

крестья́нин (*pl* -я́не, -я́н), крестья́нка peasant. крестья́нский peasant. крестья́нство peasantry.

креще́ние christening; Epiphany. крещён|ый (-ён, -ена́) baptized; *sb* Christian. крещу́ *etc.: see* крести́ть

крива́я *sb* curve. кривизна́ crookedness; curvature. криви́ть (-влю́) *impf* (*pf* по~, с~) bend, distort; ~ душо́й go against one's conscience; ~ся become crooked or bent; make a wry face. кривля́ться *impf* give o.s. airs.

криво́й (крив, -а́, -о) crooked; curved; one-eyed.

кри́зис crisis.

крик cry, shout.

кри́кет cricket.

кри́кнуть (-ну) *pf of* крича́ть

кримина́льный criminal.

криста́лл crystal. кристалли́ческий crystal.

крите́рий criterion.

кри́тик critic. кри́тика criticism.

critique. **критикова́ть** *impf* criticize. **крити́ческий** critical.

крича́ть (-чу́) *impf* (*pf* **кри́кнуть**) cry, shout.

кров roof; shelter.

крова́вый bloody.

крова́тка, крова́ть bed.

кровено́сный blood-; circulatory.

кро́вля (*gen pl* -вель) roof.

кро́вный blood; thoroughbred; vital, intimate.

крово- *in comb* blood. **кровожа́дный** bloodthirsty. ~**излия́ние** haemorrhage. ~**обраще́ние** circulation. ~**проли́тие** bloodshed. ~**проли́тный** bloody. ~**смеше́ние** incest. ~**тече́ние** bleeding; haemorrhage. ~**точи́ть** (-чи́т) *impf* bleed.

кровь (*loc* -и́) blood. **кровяно́й** blood.

крои́ть (крою́) *impf* (*pf* **с**~) cut (out). **кро́йка** cutting out.

крокоди́л crocodile.

кро́лик rabbit.

кроль *m* crawl(-stroke).

кро́льчиха she-rabbit, doe.

кро́ме *prep+gen* except; besides; ~ **того́** besides, moreover.

кро́мка edge.

кро́на crown; top.

кроншта́йн bracket; corbel.

кропотли́вый painstaking; laborious.

кросс cross-country race.

кроссво́рд crossword (puzzle).

крот (-а́) mole.

кро́ткий (-ток, -тка́, -тко) meek, gentle. **кро́тость** gentleness; mildness.

кро́хотный, кро́шечный tiny. **кро́шка** crumb; a bit.

круг (*loc* -у́; *pl* -и́) circle; circuit;

sphere. **круглосу́точный** round-the-clock. **кру́глый** (кругл, -а́, -о) round; complete; ~ **год** all the year round. **кругово́й** circular; all-round. **кругозо́р** prospect; outlook. **круго́м** *adv* around; *prep+gen* round. **кругосве́тный** round-the-world.

кружевно́й lace; lacy. **кру́жево** (*pl* -а́, -ев, -а́м) lace.

кружи́ть (-ужу́, -у́жи́шь) *impf* whirl, spin round; ~**ся** whirl, spin round.

кру́жка mug.

кружо́к (-жка́) circle, group.

круи́з cruise.

крупа́ (*pl* -ы) groats; sleet. **крупи́ца** grain.

кру́пный large, big; great; coarse; ~**ый план** close-up.

крутизна́ steepness.

крути́ть (-учу́, -у́тишь) *impf* (*pf* **за**~, **с**~) twist, twirl; roll; turn, wind; ~**ся** turn, spin; whirl.

круто́й (крут, -а́, -о) steep; sudden; sharp; severe; drastic. **кру́ча** steep slope. **кру́че** *comp of* **круто́й**, **кру́то**.

кручу́ *etc.*: *see* **крути́ть**

круше́ние crash; ruin; collapse.

крыжо́вник gooseberries; gooseberry bush.

крыла́тый winged. **крыло́** (*pl* -лья, -льев) wing; vane; mudguard.

крыльцо́ (*pl* -а́, -ле́ц, -ца́м) porch; (front, back) steps.

Крым the Crimea. **кры́мский** Crimean.

кры́са rat.

крыть (кро́ю) *impf* cover; roof; trump; ~**ся** be, lie; be concealed. **кры́ша** roof. **кры́шка** lid.

крюк (-á; pl -ки, -кóв or -ючья, -чьев) hook; detour. **крючóк** (-чкá) hook.

кряду adv in succession.

кряж ridge.

крякать impf, **крякнуть** (-ну) pf quack.

кряхтéть (-хчý) impf groan.

кстáти adv to the point; opportunely; at the same time; by the way.

кто (когó, комý, кем, ком) pron who; anyone; ~ (бы) ни whoever. **кто́-либо**, **кто́-нибудь** prons anyone; someone. **кто́-то** pron someone.

куб (pl -ы́) cube; boiler; в ~е cubed.

кýбик cube, block.

кубúнский Cuban.

кубúческий cubic; cube.

кýбок (-бка) goblet; cup.

кубомéтр cubic metre.

кувшúн jug; pitcher. **кувшúнка** water-lily.

кувыркáться impf, **кувыркнýться** (-нýсь) pf turn somersaults. **кувырко́м** adv head over heels; topsy-turvy.

кудá adv where (to); what for; +comp much, far; ~ (бы) ни wherever. **кудá-либо**, **кудá-нибудь** adv anywhere, somewhere. **кудá-то** adv somewhere.

кýдри (-éй) pl curls. **кудря́вый** curly; florid.

кузнéц (-á) blacksmith. **кузнéчик** grasshopper. **кýзница** forge, smithy.

кýзов (pl -á) basket; body.

кýкла doll; puppet. **кýколка** dolly; chrysalis. **кýкольный** doll's; puppet.

кукурýза maize.

кукýшка cuckoo.

кулáк (-á) fist; kulak. **кулáцкий** kulak. **кулáчный** fist.

кулёк (-лькá) bag.

кулúк (-á) sandpiper.

кулинáрия cookery. **кулинáрный** culinary.

кулúсы (-úс) wings; за кулúсами behind the scenes.

кулúч (-á) Easter cake.

кулуáры (-ов) pl lobby.

кульминáция culmination.

культ cult. **культивúровать** impf cultivate.

культýра culture; standard; cultivation. **культурúзм** body-building. **культýрно** adv in a civilized manner. **культýрный** cultured; cultivated; cultural.

кумúр idol.

кумы́с koumiss (fermented mare's milk).

кунúца marten.

купáльный bathing. **купáльня** bathing-place. **купáть** impf (pf вы́~, ис~) bathe; bath; ~ся bathe; take a bath.

купé neut indecl compartment.

купéц (-пцá) merchant. **купéческий** merchant. **купúть** (-плю́, -пишь) pf (impf покупáть) buy.

кýпол (pl -á) cupola, dome.

купóн coupon.

купчúха merchant's wife; female merchant.

курáнты (-ов) pl chiming clock; chimes.

кургáн barrow; tumulus.

курéние smoking. **курúльщик**, **-щица** smoker.

курúный hen's; chicken's.

курúть (-рю́, -ришь) impf (pf по~) smoke; ~ся burn; smoke.

курúца (pl кýры, кур) hen, chicken.

курóк (-ркá) cocking-piece; взве-

стй ~ cock a gun; спусти́ть ~ pull the trigger.

куропа́тка partridge.

куро́рт health-resort; spa.

курс course; policy; year; exchange rate. **курса́нт** student.

курси́в italics.

курси́ровать *impf* ply.

курсо́р (*comput*) cursor.

ку́ртка jacket.

курча́вый curly(-headed).

ку́ры *etc.*: *see* **ку́рица**

курьёз a funny thing. **курьёзный** curious.

курье́р messenger; courier. **курье́рский** express.

куря́тник hen-house.

куря́щий *sb* smoker.

куса́ть *impf* bite; sting; ~ся bite.

кусо́к (-ска́) piece; lump. **кусо́чек** (-чка) piece.

куст (-а́) bush, shrub. **куста́рник** bush(es), shrub(s).

куста́рн|**ый** hand-made; handicrafts; primitive; ~ая промы́шленность cottage industry. **куста́рь** (-я́) *m* craftsman.

ку́тать *impf* (*pf* за~) wrap up; ~ся muffle o.s. up.

кути́ть (кучу́, ку́тишь) *impf*, **кутну́ть** (-ну́, -нёшь) *pf* carouse; go on a binge.

куха́рка cook. **ку́хня** (*gen pl* -хонь) kitchen; cuisine. **ку́хонный** kitchen.

ку́ча heap; heaps.

ку́чер (*pl* -а́) coachman.

ку́чка small heap *or* group.

кучу́ *see* **кути́ть**

куша́к (-а́) sash; girdle.

ку́шанье food; dish. **ку́шать** *impf* (*pf* по~, с~) eat.

куше́тка couch.

кую́ *etc.*: *see* **кова́ть**

Л

лабора́нт, -а́нтка laboratory assistant. **лаборато́рия** laboratory.

ла́ва lava.

лави́на avalanche.

ла́вка bench; shop. **ла́вочка** small shop.

лавр bay tree, laurel.

ла́герный camp. **ла́герь** (*pl* -я́ *or* -и, -ей *or* -ей) *m* camp; campsite.

лад (*loc* -у́; *pl* -ы́, -о́в) harmony; manner, way; stop, fret.

ла́дан incense.

ла́дить (ла́жу) *impf* get on, be on good terms. **ла́дно** *adv* all right; very well! **ла́дный** fine, excellent; harmonious.

ладо́нь palm.

ладья́ rook, castle; boat.

ла́жу *etc.*: *see* **ла́дить, ла́зить**

лазаре́т field hospital; sick-bay.

ла́зать *see* **ла́зить. лазе́йка** hole; loop-hole.

ла́зер laser.

ла́зить (ла́жу), **ла́зать** *impf* climb, clamber.

лазу́рный sky-blue, azure. **лазу́рь** azure.

лазу́тчик scout; spy.

лай bark, barking. **ла́йка**[1] (Siberian) husky, laika.

ла́йка[2] kid. **ла́йковый** kid; kidskin.

ла́йнер liner; airliner.

лак varnish, lacquer.

лака́ть *impf* (*pf* вы́~) lap.

лаке́й footman, man-servant; lackey.

лакирова́ть *impf* (*pf* от~) varnish; lacquer.

ла́кмус litmus.

ла́ковый varnished, lacquered.

ла́комиться (-млюсь) *impf* (*pf* по~) +*instr* treat o.s. to. ла́комка *m* & *f* gourmand. ла́комство delicacy. ла́комый dainty, tasty; +до fond of.

лакони́чный laconic.

ла́мпа lamp; valve, tube. лампа́да icon-lamp. ла́мпочка lamp; bulb.

ландша́фт landscape.

ла́ндыш lily of the valley.

лань fallow deer; doe.

ла́па paw; foot. ла́поть (-птя; *pl* -и, -е́й) *m* bast shoe. ла́почка pet, sweetie.

лапша́ noodles; noodle soup.

ларёк (-рька́) stall. ларь (-я́) *m* chest; bin.

ла́ска¹ caress.

ла́ска² weasel.

ласка́ть *impf* caress, fondle; ~ся +к+*dat* make up to; fawn upon. ла́сковый affectionate, tender.

ла́сточка swallow.

латви́ец (-и́йца), -и́йка Latvian. латви́йский Latvian. Ла́твия Latvia.

лати́нский Latin.

лату́нь brass.

ла́ты (лат) *pl* armour.

латы́нь Latin.

латы́ш, латы́шка Latvian, Lett. латы́шский Latvian, Lettish.

лауреа́т prize-winner.

ла́цкан lapel.

лачу́га hovel, shack.

ла́ять (ла́ю) *impf* bark.

лба *etc.*: *see* лоб

лгать (лгу, лжёшь; лгал, -а́, -о) *impf* (*pf* на~, со~) lie; tell lies; +на+*acc* slander. лгун (-а́) liar. лгу́нья liar.

лебеди́ный swan. лебёдка swan, pen; winch. ле́бедь (*pl* -и, -е́й) *m* swan, cob.

лев (льва) lion.

левобере́жный left-bank. левша́ (*gen pl* -е́й) *m* & *f* left-hander. ле́вый *adj* left; left-hand; left-wing.

лёг *etc.*: *see* лечь

лега́льный legal.

леге́нда legend. легенда́рный legendary.

лёгк|ий (-гок, -гка́, лёгки́) light; easy; slight, mild; ~ая атле́тика field and track events. легко́ *adv* easily, lightly, slightly.

легко- *in comb* light; easy, easily. легкове́рный credulous. ~ве́с light-weight. ~мы́сленный thoughtless; flippant, frivolous, superficial. ~мы́слие flippancy, frivolity.

легков|о́й: ~а́я маши́на (private) car. лёгкое *sb* lung. лёгкость lightness; easiness. ле́гче *comp of* лёгкий, легко́.

лёд (льда, *loc* -у́) ice. ледене́ть (-е́ю) *impf* (*pf* за~, о~) freeze; grow numb with cold. ледене́ц (-нца́) fruit-drop. леденя́щий chilling, icy.

ле́ди *f indecl* lady.

ле́дник ice-box; refrigerator van. ледни́к² (-а́) glacier. леднико́вый glacial; ~ пери́од Ice Age. ледо́вый icy. ледоко́л ice-breaker. ледяно́й icy.

лежа́ть (-жу́) *impf* lie; be, be situated. лежа́чий lying (down).

ле́звие (cutting) edge; razor-blade.

лезть (-зу; лез) *impf* (*pf* по~) climb; clamber, crawl; get, go; fall out.

лейбори́ст Labourite.

ле́йка watering-can.

лейтена́нт lieutenant.

лека́рство medicine.

ле́ксика vocabulary. **лексико́н** lexicon; vocabulary.

ле́ктор lecturer. **ле́кция** lecture.

леле́ять (-е́ю) *impf* (*pf* вз~) cherish, foster.

лён (льна) flax.

лени́вый lazy.

ленингра́дский (of) Leningrad. **ле́нинский** (of) Lenin; Leninist.

лени́ться (-ню́сь, -ни́шься) *impf* (*pf* по~) be lazy; +*inf* be too lazy to.

ле́нта ribbon; band; tape.

лентя́й, -я́йка lazy-bones. **лень** laziness.

лепесто́к (-тка́) petal.

ле́пет babble; prattle. **лепета́ть** (-ечу́, -е́чешь) *impf* (*pf* про~) babble, prattle.

лепёшка scone; tablet, pastille.

лепи́ть (-плю́, -пишь) *impf* (*pf* вы́~, за~, с~) model, fashion; mould; ~ся cling; crawl. **ле́пка** modelling. **лепно́й** modelled, moulded.

лес (*loc* -у́; *pl* -а́) forest, wood; *pl* scaffolding.

леса́ (*pl* лёсы) fishing-line.

лесни́к (-а́) forester. **лесни́чий** *sb* forestry officer; forest warden. **лесно́й** forest.

лесо- in *comb* forest, forestry; timber wood. **лесово́дство** forestry. **~загото́вка** logging. **~пи́лка, ~пи́льня** (*gen pl* -лен) sawmill. **~ру́б** woodcutter.

ле́стница stairs, staircase; ladder.

ле́стный flattering. **лесть** flattery.

лёт (*loc* -у́) flight, flying.

лета́ (лет) *pl* years; age; ско́лько вам лет? how old are you?

лета́тельный flying. **лета́ть** *impf*, **лете́ть** (лечу́) *impf* (*pf* по-лете́ть) fly; rush; fall.

ле́тний summer.

лётный flying, flight.

ле́то (*pl* -а́) summer; *pl* years. **ле́том** *adv* in summer.

ле́топись chronicle.

летосчисле́ние chronology.

летучий flying; passing; brief; volatile; ~ая мышь bat. **лётчик, -чица** pilot.

лече́бница clinic. **лече́бный** medical; medicinal. **лече́ние** (medical) treatment. **лечи́ть** (-чу́, -чишь) *impf* treat (for); ~ся be given, have treatment (от for).

лечу́ *etc.: see* лете́ть, лечи́ть

лечь (ля́гу, ля́жешь; лёг, -ла́) *pf* (*impf* ложи́ться) lie, lie down; go to bed.

лещ (-а́) bream.

лжесвиде́тельство false witness.

лжец (-а́) liar. **лжи́вый** lying; deceitful.

ли, ль *interrog partl* & *conj* whether, if; ли,... не whether ... or; ра́но ли, по́здно ли sooner or later.

либера́л liberal. **либера́льный** liberal.

ли́бо *conj* or; ~... ~ either ... or.

ли́вень (-вня) *m* heavy shower, downpour.

ливре́я livery.

ли́га league.

ли́дер leader. **лиди́ровать** *impf* & *pf* be in the lead.

лиза́ть (лижу́, -ешь) *impf*, **лизну́ть** (-ну́, -нёшь) *pf* lick.

ликвида́ция liquidation; aboli-

tion. **ликвиди́ровать** *impf* & *pf* liquidate; abolish.

ликёр liqueur.

ликова́ние rejoicing. **ликова́ть** *impf* rejoice.

ли́лия lily.

лило́вый lilac, violet.

лима́н estuary.

лими́т limit.

лимо́н lemon. **лимона́д** lemonade; squash. **лимо́нный** lemon.

ли́мфа lymph.

лингви́ст linguist. **лингви́стика** linguistics. **лингвисти́ческий** linguistic.

лине́йка ruler; line. **лине́йный** linear; **~ кора́бль** battleship.

ли́нза lens.

ли́ния line.

лино́леум lino(leum).

линя́ть *impf* (*pf* вы́~, по~, с~) fade; moult.

ли́па lime tree.

ли́пкий (-пок, -пка́, -о) sticky. **ли́пнуть** (-ну; лип) *impf* stick.

ли́повый lime.

ли́ра lyre. **ли́рик** lyric poet. **ли́рика** lyric poetry. **лири́ческий** lyric; lyrical.

лиса́ (*pl* -ы), **-си́ца** fox.

лист (-а́; *pl* -ы́ *or* -ья, -о́в *or* -ьев) leaf; sheet; page; form; **игра́ть с ~а́** play at sight. **листа́ть** *impf* leaf through. **листва́** foliage. **ли́ственница** larch **ли́ственный** deciduous. **листо́вка** leaflet. **листово́й** sheet, plate; leaf. **листо́к** (-тка́) *dim of* **лист**; leaflet; form, pro-forma.

Литва́ Lithuania.

лите́йный founding, casting. **литера́тор** man of letters. **литерату́ра** literature. **литерату́рный** literary.

лито́вец (-вца), **лито́вка** Lithuanian. **лито́вский** Lithuanian.

лито́й cast.

литр litre.

лить (лью, льёшь; лил, -а́, -о) *impf* (*pf* ли́ть) pour; shed; cast, mould. **литьё** founding, casting; moulding; castings, mouldings. **ли́ться** (льётся; ли́лся, -ась, ли́лось) *impf* flow; pour.

лиф bodice. **ли́фчик** bra.

лифт lift.

лихо́й[1] (лих, -á, -о) dashing, spirited.

лихо́й[2] (лих, -á, -о, ли́хи́) evil.

лихора́дка fever. **лихора́дочный** feverish.

лицево́й facial; exterior; front.

лицеме́р hypocrite. **лицеме́рие** hypocrisy. **лицеме́рный** hypocritical.

лицо́ (*pl* -а) face; exterior; right side; person; **быть к лицу́** +*dat* suit, befit. **личи́нка** larva, grub; maggot. **ли́чно** *adv* personally, in person. **ли́чность** personality; person. **ли́чный** personal; private; **~ соста́в** staff, personnel.

лиша́й lichen; herpes; shingles. **лиша́йник** lichen.

лиша́ть(ся *impf of* **лиши́ть(ся**

лише́ние deprivation; privation. **лишённый** (-ён, -ена́) +*gen* lacking in, devoid of. **лиши́ть** (-шу́) *pf* (*impf* **лиша́ть**) +*gen* deprive of; **~ся** +*gen* lose, be deprived of. **ли́шний** superfluous; unnecessary; spare; **~ раз** once more; **с ~им** odd, and more.

лишь *adv* only; *conj* as soon as; **~ бы** if only, provided that.

лоб (лба, *loc* лбу) forehead.

ло́бзик fret-saw.

лови́ть (-влю́, -вишь) *impf* (*pf*

поймать) catch, try to catch.

ловкий (-вок, -вка, -о) adroit; cunning. ловкость adroitness; cunning.

ловля (gen pl -вель) catching, hunting; fishing-ground. ловушка trap.

ловче comp of ловкий

логарифм logarithm.

логика logic. логический, логичный logical.

логовище, логово den, lair.

лодка boat.

лодырничать impf loaf, idle about. лодырь m loafer, idler.

ложбина hollow.

ложе couch; bed.

ложиться (-жусь) impf of лечь

ложка spoon.

ложный false. ложь (лжи) lie, falsehood.

лоза (pl -ы) vine.

лозунг slogan, catchword.

локатор radar or sonar apparatus.

локомотив locomotive.

локон lock, curl.

локоть (-ктя; pl -и, -ей) m elbow.

лом (pl -ы, -ов) crowbar; scrap, waste. ломаный broken. ломать impf (pf по~, с~) break; cause to ache; ~ся break; crack; put on airs; be obstinate.

ломбард pawnshop.

ломберный стол card-table.

ломить (ломит) impf break; break through, rush; impers cause to ache; ~ся be (near to) breaking. ломка breaking; pl quarry. ломкий (-мок, -мка, -о) fragile, brittle.

ломоть (-мтя; pl -мти) m large slice; hunk; chunk. ломтик slice.

лоно bosom, lap.

лопасть (pl -и, -ей) blade; fan, vane; paddle.

лопата spade; shovel. лопатка shoulder-blade; shovel; trowel.

лопаться impf, лопнуть (-ну) pf burst; split; break; fail; crash.

лопух (-á) burdock.

лорд lord.

лосина elk-skin, chamois leather; elk-meat.

лоск lustre, shine.

лоскут (-á; pl -ы or -ья, -ов or -ьев) rag, shred, scrap.

лосниться impf be glossy, shine.

лосось m salmon.

лось (pl -и, -ей) m elk.

лосьон lotion; aftershave; cream.

лот lead, plummet.

лотерея lottery, raffle.

лоток (-тка) hawker's stand or tray; chute; gutter; trough.

лохматый shaggy; dishevelled.

лохмотья (-ьев) pl rags.

лоцман pilot.

лошадиный horse; equine. лошадь (pl -и, -ей, instr -дьми or -дями) horse.

лощёный glossy, polished.

лощина hollow, depression.

лояльный fair, honest; loyal.

лубок (-бка) splint; popular print.

луг (loc -ý; pl -á) meadow.

лужа puddle.

лужайка lawn, glade.

лужёный tin-plated.

лук¹ onions.

лук² bow.

лукавить (-влю) impf (pf с~) be cunning. лукавство craftiness. лукавый crafty, cunning.

луковица onion; bulb

луна́ (*pl* -ы) moon. **луна́тик** sleep-walker.

лу́нка hole; socket.

лу́нный moon; lunar.

лу́па magnifying-glass.

лупи́ть (-плю́, -пишь) *impf* (*pf* от~) peel.

луч (-а́) ray; beam. **лучево́й** ray, beam; radial; radiation. **луче-за́рный** radiant.

лучи́на splinter.

лу́чше better; ~ всего́, ~ всех best of all. **лу́чший** better; best; в ~ем слу́чае at best; всего́ ~его! all the best!

лы́жа ski. **лы́жник** skier. **лы́ж-ный спорт** skiing. **лыжня́** ski-track.

лы́ко bast.

лысе́ть (-е́ю) *impf* (*pf* об~, по~) grow bald. **лы́сина** bald spot; blaze. **лы́сый** (лыс, -а́, -о) bald.

ль *see* **ли**

льва *etc.*: *see* **лев. льви́ный** lion, lion's. **льви́ца** lioness.

льго́та privilege; advantage. **льго́тный** privileged; favour-able.

льда *etc.*: *see* **лёд. льди́на** block of ice; ice-floe.

льна *etc.*: *see* **лён. льново́д-ство** flax-growing.

льнуть (-ну, -нёшь) *impf* (*pf* при~) +к+*dat* cling to; have a weakness for; make up to.

льняно́й flax, flaxen; linen; lin-seed.

льстец (-а́) flatterer. **льсти́вый** flattering; smooth-tongued. **льстить** (льщу) *impf* (*pf* по~) +*dat* flatter.

лью *etc.*: *see* **лить**

любе́зность courtesy; kind-ness; compliment. **любе́зный** courteous; obliging; kind;

бу́дьте ~ы be so kind (as to).

люби́мец (-мца) -**мица** pet, fa-vourite. **люби́мый** beloved; fa-vourite. **люби́тель** *m*, -**ница** lover; amateur. **люби́тель-ский** amateur. **люби́ть** (-блю́, -бишь) *impf* love; like.

любова́ться *impf* (*pf* по~) +*instr* or на+*acc* admire.

любо́вник lover. **любо́вница** mistress. **любо́вный** love-; lov-ing. **любо́вь** (-бви́, *instr* -бо́вью) love.

любозна́тельный inquisitive.

любо́й any; either; *sb* anyone.

любопы́тный curious; inquisi-tive. **любопы́тство** curiosity.

любя́щий loving.

лю́ди (-е́й, -ям, -дьми́, -ях) *pl* people. **лю́дный** populous; crowded. **людое́д** cannibal; ogre. **людско́й** human.

люк hatch(way); trap; manhole.

лю́лька cradle.

люминесце́нтный lumines-cent. **люминесце́нция** lumi-nescence.

лю́стра chandelier.

лю́тня (*gen pl* -тен) lute.

лю́тый (лют, -а́, -о) ferocious.

ляга́ть *impf*, **лягну́ть** (-ну́, -нёшь) *pf* kick; ~ся kick.

ля́гу *etc.*: *see* **лечь**

лягу́шка frog.

ля́жка thigh, haunch.

ля́згать *impf* clank; +*instr* rattle.

ля́мка strap; тяну́ть ля́мку toil.

M

мавзоле́й mausoleum.

мавр, маврита́нка Moor. **маврита́нский** Moorish.

магази́н shop.

маги́стр (holder of) master's degree.

магистра́ль main; main line, main road.

маги́ческий magic(al). **ма́гия** magic.

магнети́зм magnetism.

ма́гний magnesium.

магни́т magnet. **магни́тный** magnetic. **магнитофо́н** tape-recorder.

мада́м *f indecl* madam, madame.

мажо́р major (key); cheerful mood. **мажо́рный** major; cheerful.

ма́зать (ма́жу) *impf* (*pf* вы́-, за́-, из-, на-, по-, про-) oil, grease; smear, spread; soil; **~ся** get dirty; make up. **мазо́к** (-зка́) touch, dab; smear. **мазу́т** fuel oil. **мазь** ointment; grease.

маи́с maize.

май May. **ма́йский** May.

ма́йка T-shirt.

майо́р major.

мак poppy, poppy-seeds.

макаро́ны (-н) *pl* macaroni.

мака́ть *impf* (*pf* макну́ть) dip.

маке́т model; dummy.

макну́ть (-ну́, -нёшь) *pf of* мака́ть

макре́ль mackerel.

максима́льный maximum. **ма́ксимум** maximum; at most.

макулату́ра waste paper; pulp literature.

маку́шка top; crown.

мал *etc.: see* ма́лый

малахи́т malachite.

мале́йший least, slightest. **ма́ленький** little; small.

мали́на (*no pl; usu collect*) raspberry; raspberries; raspberry

bush. **мали́новый** raspberry.

ма́ло *adv* little, few; not enough; **~ того́** moreover; **~ того́ что...** not only ....

мало- *in comb* (too) little. **малова́жный** of little importance. **~вероя́тный** unlikely. **~гра́мотный** semi-literate; crude. **~ду́шный** faint-hearted. **~иму́щий** needy. **~кро́вие** anaemia. **~ле́тний** young; juvenile; minor. **~о́пытный** inexperienced. **~чи́сленный** small (in number), few.

мало-ма́льски *adv* in the slightest degree; at all. **мало-пома́лу** *adv* little by little.

ма́лый (мал, -а́) little, (too) small; **са́мое ~ое** at the least; *sb* fellow; lad. **малы́ш** (-а́) kiddy; little boy. **ма́льчик** boy. **мальчи́шка** *m* urchin, boy. **мальчуга́н** little boy. **малю́тка** *m & f* baby.

маля́р (-а́) painter, decorator.

маля́рия malaria.

ма́ма mother, mummy. **мама́ша** mummy. **ма́мин** mother's.

ма́монт mammoth.

мандари́н mandarin, tangerine.

манда́т warrant; mandate.

манёвр manoeuvre; shunting. **маневри́ровать** *impf* (*pf* с~) manoeuvre; shunt; +*instr* make good use of.

мане́ж riding-school.

манеке́н dummy; mannequin. **манеке́нщик, -щица** model.

мане́ра manner; style. **мане́рный** affected.

манже́та cuff.

маникю́р manicure.

манипули́ровать *impf* manipulate. **манипуля́ция** manipulation; machination.

мани́ть (-ню́, -нишь) *impf* (*pf* по~) beckon; attract; lure.

манифе́ст manifesto. **манифеста́ция** demonstration.

мани́шка (false) shirt-front.

ма́ния mania; ~ вели́чия megalomania.

ма́нная ка́ша semolina.

мано́метр pressure-gauge.

ма́нтия cloak; robe, gown.

мануфакту́ра manufacture; textiles.

манья́к maniac.

марафо́нский бег marathon.

ма́рганец (-нца) manganese.

маргари́н margarine.

маргари́тка daisy.

марино́ванный pickled. **маринова́ть** *impf* (*pf* за~) pickle; put off.

марионе́тка puppet.

ма́рка stamp; counter; brand; trade-mark; grade; reputation.

ма́ркетинг marketing.

ма́ркий easily soiled.

маркси́зм Marxism. **маркси́ст** Marxist. **маркси́стский** Marxist.

ма́рлевый gauze. **ма́рля** gauze; cheesecloth.

мармела́д fruit jellies.

ма́рочный high-quality.

Марс Mars.

март March. **ма́ртовский** March.

марты́шка marmoset; monkey.

марш march.

ма́ршал marshal.

марширова́ть *impf* march.

маршру́т route, itinerary.

ма́ска mask. **маскара́д** masked ball; masquerade. **маскирова́ть** *impf* (*pf* за~) disguise; camouflage. **маскиро́вка** disguise; camouflage.

Ма́сленица Shrovetide. **масле́нка** butter-dish; oil-can. **масли́на** olive. **ма́сло** (*pl* -á, -сел, -слам) butter; oil; oil paints. **масло́бойка** churn. **маслозаво́д** dairy. **масляни́стый** oily. **ма́сляный** oil.

ма́сса mass; a lot, lots.

масса́ж massage. **масси́ровать** *impf* & *pf* massage.

масси́в massif; expanse, tract. **масси́вный** massive.

ма́ссовый mass.

ма́стер (*pl* -á), **мастери́ца** foreman, forewoman; (master) craftsman; expert. **мастери́ть** *impf* (*pf* с~) make, build. **мастерска́я** *sb* workshop. **мастерско́й** masterly. **мастерство́** craft; skill.

масти́ка mastic; putty; floor-polish.

масти́тый venerable.

масть (*pl* -и, -е́й) colour; suit.

масшта́б scale.

мат¹ checkmate.

мат² mat.

мат³ foul language.

матема́тик mathematician. **матема́тика** mathematics. **математи́ческий** mathematical.

материа́л material. **материали́зм** materialism. **материали́стический** materialist. **материа́льный** material.

матери́к (-á) continent; mainland. **материко́вый** continental.

матери́нский maternal, motherly. **матери́нство** maternity.

мате́рия material; pus; topic.

ма́тка womb; female.

ма́товый matt; frosted;

матра́с, матра́ц mattress.

матрёшка Russian doll.

ма́трица matrix; die, mould.

матро́с sailor, seaman.

матч match.

мать (ма́тери, *instr* -рью; *pl* -тери, -рей) mother.

ма́фия Mafia.

мах swing, stroke. маха́ть (машу́, ма́шешь) *impf*, махну́ть (-ну́, -нёшь) *pf* +*instr* wave; brandish; wag; flap; go; rush.

махина́ция machinations.

махови́к (-а́) fly-wheel.

махро́вый dyed-in-the-wool; terry.

ма́чеха stepmother.

ма́чта mast.

маши́на machine; car. маши-на́льный mechanical. машини́ст operator; engine-driver; scene-shifter. маши́нистка typist; ~-стенографи́стка shorthand-typist. маши́нка machine; typewriter; sewing-machine. машинопи́сный typewritten. маши́нопись typing; typescript. машиностро-е́ние mechanical engineering.

мая́к (-а́) lighthouse; beacon.

ма́ятник pendulum. ма́яться *impf* toil; suffer; languish.

мгла haze; gloom.

мгнове́ние instant, moment. мгнове́нный instantaneous, momentary.

ме́бель furniture. меблиро́-ванный furnished. меблиро́вка furnishing; furniture.

мегава́тт (*gen pl* -а́тт) megawatt. мего́м megohm. мега-то́нна megaton.

мёд (*loc* -у́; *pl* -ы́) honey.

меда́ль medal. медальо́н medallion.

медве́дица she-bear. медве́дь *m* bear. медве́жий bear('s). медвежо́нок (-нка; *pl* -жа́та, -жа́т) bear cub.

ме́дик medical student; doctor. медикаме́нты (-ов) *pl* medicines.

медици́на medicine. медици́нский medical.

ме́дленный slow. медли́тель-ный sluggish; slow. ме́длить *impf* linger; be slow.

ме́дный copper; brass.

медо́вый honey; ~ ме́сяц honeymoon.

медосмо́тр medical examination, check-up. медпу́нкт first aid post. медсестра́ (*pl* -сёстры, -сестёр, -сёстрам) nurse.

меду́за jellyfish.

медь copper.

меж *prep*+*instr* between.

меж- *in comb* inter-.

межа́ (*pl* -и, меж, -а́м) boundary.

междоме́тие interjection.

ме́жду *prep*+*instr* between; among; ~ про́чим incidentally, by the way; ~ тем meanwhile; ~ тем, как while.

между- *in comb* inter-. между-горо́дный inter-city. ~наро́д-ный international.

межконтинента́льный inter-continental. межплане́тный interplanetary.

мезони́н attic (storey); mezzanine (floor).

Ме́ксика Mexico.

мел (*loc* -у́) chalk.

мёл *etc.*: *see* мести́

меланхо́лия melancholy.

меле́ть (-е́ет) *impf* (*pf* об~) grow shallow.

мелиора́ция land improvement.

ме́лкий (-лок, -лка́, -о) small; shallow; fine; petty. **ме́лко** adv fine, small. **мелкобуржуа́зный** petty bourgeois. **мелково́дный** shallow.

мелоди́чный melodious, melodic. **мело́дия** melody.

ме́лочный petty. **ме́лочь** (pl -и, -е́й) small items; (small) change; pl trifles, trivialities.

мель (loc -и́) shoal; bank; на мели́ aground.

мелька́ть impf, **мелькну́ть** (-ну́, -нёшь) pf be glimpsed fleetingly. **ме́льком** adv in passing; fleetingly.

ме́льник miller. **ме́льница** mill.

мельча́йший superl of ме́лкий. **ме́льче** comp of ме́лкий, ме́лко. **мелюзга́** small fry.

мелю́ etc.: see мели́ть

мембра́на membrane; diaphragm.

мемора́ндум memorandum. **мемуа́ры** (-ов) pl memoirs.

ме́на exchange, barter.

ме́неджер manager.

ме́нее adv less; тем не ∼ none the less.

мензу́рка measuring-glass.

мeново́й exchange; barter.

менуэ́т minuet.

ме́ньше smaller; less. **меньшеви́к** (-а́) Menshevik. **ме́ньший** lesser, smaller; younger. **меньшинство́** minority.

меню́ neut indecl menu.

меня́ see я pron

меня́ть impf (pf об∼, по∼) change; exchange; ∼ся change; +instr exchange.

ме́ра measure.

мере́щиться (-щусь) impf (pf по∼) seem, appear.

мерза́вец (-вца) swine, bastard. **ме́рзкий** (-зок, -зка́, -о) disgusting.

мерзлота́: ве́чная ∼ permafrost. **мёрзнуть** (-ну) impf (pf за∼) freeze.

ме́рзость vileness; abomination.

меридиа́н meridian.

ме́рило standard, criterion.

ме́рин gelding.

ме́рить impf (pf по∼, с∼) measure; try on. **ме́рка** measure.

ме́рный measured; rhythmical. **мероприя́тие** measure.

мертве́ть (-е́ю) impf (pf о∼, по∼) grow numb; be benumbed. **мертве́ц** (-а́) corpse, dead man. **мёртвый** (мёртв, -а́, мёртво) dead.

мерца́ть impf twinkle; flicker.

меси́ть (мешу́, ме́сишь) impf (pf с∼) knead.

ме́сса Mass.

места́ми adv here and there, in places. **месте́чко** (pl -и, -чек) small town.

мести́ (мету́, -тёшь; мёл, -а́) impf sweep; whirl.

ме́стность terrain; locality; area. **ме́стный** local; locative. -**ме́стный** in comb -berth, -seater. **ме́сто** (pl -а́) place; site; seat; room; job. **местожи́тельство** (place of) residence. **местоиме́ние** pronoun. **местонахожде́ние** location, whereabouts. **месторожде́ние** deposit; layer.

месть vengeance, revenge.

ме́сяц month; moon. **ме́сячный** monthly; sb pl period.

мета́лл metal. **металли́ческий** metal, metallic. **металлу́ргия** metallurgy.

метáн methane.

метáние throwing, flinging. метáть[1] (мечу́, мéчешь) *impf* (*pf* метну́ть) throw; fling; ~ся rush about; toss (and turn).

метáть[2] *impf* (*pf* на~, с~) tack.

метафи́зика metaphysics.

метáфора metaphor.

метёлка panicle.

метéль snow-storm.

метеóр meteor. метеори́т meteorite. метеоро́лог meteorologist. метеорологи́ческий meteorological. метеороло́гия meteorology.

метеосво́дка weather report. метеостáнция weather-station.

мéтить[1] (мéчу) *impf* (*pf* на~, по~) mark.

мéтить[2] (мéчу) *impf* (*pf* на~) aim; mean.

мéтка marking, mark.

мéткий (-ток, -ткá, -о) well-aimed, accurate.

метлá (*pl* мётлы, -тел) broom.

метну́ть (-ну́, -нёшь) *pf* of метáть[1]

мéтод method. методика method(s); methodology. методи́чный methodical. методоло́гия methodology.

метр metre.

мéтрика birth certificate. метри́ческий[1]: ~ое свидéтельство birth certificate.

метри́ческий[2] metric; metrical.

метро́ *neut indecl*, метрополитéн Metro; underground.

мету́ *etc.*: *see* мести́

мех[1] (*loc* -ý; *pl* -á) fur.

мех[2] (*pl* -и́) wine-skin, water-skin; *pl* bellows.

механизáция mechanization. механи́зм mechanism; gear(ing). механик mechanic. механика mechanics; trick; knack. механи́ческий mechanical; mechanistic.

меховóй fur.

меч (-á) sword.

мéченый marked.

мечéть mosque.

мечтá (day-)dream. мечтáтельный dreamy. мечтáть *impf* dream.

мéчу *etc.*: *see* мéтить. мечу́ *etc.*: *see* метáть

мешáлка mixer.

мешáть[1] *impf* (*pf* по~) +*dat* hinder; prevent; disturb.

мешáть[2] *impf* (*pf* по~, с~) stir; mix up; ~ся (в+*acc*) interfere (in), meddle (with).

мешóк (-шкá) bag; sack. мешкови́на sacking, hessian.

мещани́н (*pl* -áне, -áн) petty bourgeois; Philistine. мещáнский bourgeois, narrow-minded; Philistine. мещáнство petty bourgeoisie; philistinism, narrow-mindedness.

миг moment, instant.

мигáть *impf*, мигну́ть (-ну́, -нёшь) *pf* blink; wink, twinkle.

мигом *adv* in a flash.

мигрáция migration.

мигрéнь migraine.

мизантрóп misanthrope.

мизи́нец (-нца) little finger; little toe.

микрóб microbe.

микроволнóвая печь microwave oven.

микрóн micron.

микрооргани́зм microorganism.

микроскóп microscope. ми-

кроскопи́ческий microscopic.
микросхе́ма microchip.
микрофо́н (*gen pl* -**н**) microphone.
ми́ксер (*cul*) mixer, blender.
миксту́ра medicine, mixture.
ми́ленький pretty; sweet; dear.
милитари́зм militarism.
милиционе́р militiaman, policeman. **мили́ция** militia, police force.
милли́ард billion, a thousand million. **миллиме́тр** millimetre. **миллио́н** million. **миллионе́р** millionaire.
милосе́рдие mercy, charity. **милосе́рдный** merciful, charitable.
ми́лостивый gracious, kind. **ми́лостыня** alms. **ми́лость** favour, grace. **ми́лый** (мил, -а́, -о) nice; kind; sweet; dear.
ми́ля mile.
ми́мика (facial) expression; mimicry.
ми́мо *adv & prep* +*gen* by, past. **мимолётный** fleeting. **мимохо́дом** *adv* in passing.
ми́на[1] mine; bomb.
ми́на[2] expression, mien.
минда́ль (-я́) *m* almond(-tree); almonds.
минера́л mineral. **минерало́гия** mineralogy. **минера́льный** mineral.
миниатю́ра miniature. **миниатю́рный** miniature; tiny.
минима́льный minimum. **ми́нимум** minimum.
министе́рство ministry. **мини́стр** minister.
минова́ть *impf & pf* pass; *impers* +*dat* escape.
миномёт mortar. **миноно́сец** (-сца) torpedo-boat.

мино́р minor (key); melancholy.
мину́вший past; ~ее *sb* the past.
ми́нус minus.
мину́та minute. **мину́тный** minute; momentary.
мину́ть (-нешь; ми́нул) *pf* pass.
мир[1] (*pl* -ы́) world.
мир[2] peace.
мира́ж mirage.
мири́ть *impf* (*pf* по~, при~) reconcile; ~ся be reconciled. **ми́рный** peace; peaceful.
мировоззре́ние (world-)outlook; philosophy. **мирово́й** world. **мирозда́ние** universe.
миролюби́вый peace-loving.
ми́ска basin, bowl.
мисс *f indecl* Miss.
миссионе́р missionary.
ми́ссис *f indecl* Mrs.
ми́ссия mission.
ми́стер Mr.
ми́стика mysticism. **мистифика́ция** hoax.
ми́тинг mass meeting; rally.
митрополи́т metropolitan.
миф myth. **мифи́ческий** mythical. **мифологи́ческий** mythological. **мифоло́гия** mythology.
ми́чман warrant officer.
мише́нь target.
ми́шка (Teddy) bear.
младе́нец (-нца) baby; infant. **мла́дший** younger; youngest; junior.
млекопита́ющие *sb pl* mammals. **Мле́чный Путь** Milky Way.
мне *see* **я** *pron*
мне́ние opinion.
мни́мый imaginary; sham. **мни́тельный** hypochondriac;

mistrustful. **мнить** (мню) *impf* think.

мно́гие *sb pl* many (people); **~ое** *sb* much, a great deal. **мно́го** *adv+gen* much; many; **на ~** by far.

много- *in comb* many-, poly-, multi-, multiple-. **многобо́рье** combined event. **~гра́нный** polyhedral; many-sided. **~де́тный** having many children. **~жёнство** polygamy. **~значи́тельный** significant. **~кра́тный** repeated; frequentative. **~ле́тний** lasting, living, many years; of many years' standing; perennial. **~лю́дный** crowded. **~национа́льный** multinational. **~обеща́ющий** promising. **~обра́зие** diversity. **~сло́вный** verbose. **~сторо́нний** multi-lateral; many-sided; versatile. **~то́чие** dots, omission points. **~уважа́емый** respected; Dear. **~уго́льный** polygonal. **~цве́тный** multicoloured; multiflorous. **~чи́сленный** numerous. **~эта́жный** many-storeyed. **~язы́чный** polyglot.

мно́жественный plural. **мно́жество** great number. **мно́жить** (-жу) *impf* (*pf* **у~**) multiply; increase.

мной *etc.: see* **я** *pron.* **мну** *etc.: see* **мять**

мобилиза́ция mobilization. **мобилизова́ть** *impf & pf* mobilize.

мог *etc.: see* **мочь**

моги́ла grave. **моги́льный** (of the) grave; sepulchral.

могу́ *etc.: see* **мочь. могу́чий** mighty. **могу́щественный** powerful. **могу́щество** power, might.

мо́да fashion.

модели́ровать *impf & pf* design. **моде́ль** model; pattern. **моделье́р** fashion designer. **моде́льный** model; fashionable.

модернизи́ровать *impf & pf* modernize.

моде́м (*comput*) modem. **моди́стка** milliner.

модифика́ция modification. **модифици́ровать** *impf & pf* modify.

мо́дный (-ден, -дна́, -о) fashionable; fashion.

мо́жет *see* **мочь**

можжеве́льник juniper.

мо́жно one may, one can; it is permissible; it is possible; **как ~+comp** as … as possible; **как ~ скоре́е** as soon as possible.

мозаи́ка mosaic; jigsaw.

мозг (*loc* -ý; *pl* -и́) brain; marrow. **мозгово́й** cerebral.

мозо́ль (*f*) corn; callus.

мой (моего́) *m*, **моя́** (мое́й) *f*, **моё** (моего́) *neut*, **мои́** (-и́х) *pl pron* my; mine; **по-мо́ему** in my opinion; in my way.

мо́йка washing.

мо́кнуть (-ну; мок) *impf* get wet; soak. **мокро́та** phlegm. **мо́крый** wet, damp.

мол (*loc* -ý) mole, pier.

молва́ rumour, talk.

моле́бен (-бна) church service.

моле́кула molecule. **молекуля́рный** molecular.

моли́тва prayer. **моли́ть** (-лю́, -лишь) *impf* pray; beg; **~ся** (*pf* по**~ся**) pray.

моллю́ск mollusc.

молниено́сный lightning. **мо́лния** lightning; zip(fastener).

молодёжь youth, young people. **молодеть** (-éю) *impf* (*pf* по~) get younger, look younger. **молодец** (-дцá) fine fellow or girl; ~! well done! **новобрачные** молодожёны (-ов) *pl* newly-weds. **молодой** (мóлод, -á, -о) young. **молодость** youth. **моложе** *comp of* молодой

молоко milk.

молот hammer. **молотить** (-очý, -óтишь) *impf* (*pf* с~) thresh; hammer. **молоток** (-ткá) hammer. **молотый** ground. **молоть** (мелю, мéлешь) *impf* (*pf* с~) grind, mill.

молочная *sb* dairy. **молочный** milk; dairy; milky.

молча *adv* silently, in silence. **молчаливый** silent, taciturn; tacit. **молчание** silence. **молчать** (-чý) *impf* be or keep silent.

моль moth.

мольба entreaty.

мольберт easel.

момент moment; feature. **моментально** *adv* instantly. **моментальный** instantaneous.

монарх monarch. **монархист** monarchist.

монастырь (-я) *m* monastery; convent. **монах** monk. **монахиня** nun.

монгол, ~ка Mongol.

монета coin.

монография monograph.

монолитный monolithic.

монолог monologue.

монополия monopoly.

монотонный monotonous.

монтаж (-á) assembling, mounting; editing. **монтажник** rigger, fitter. **монтёр** fitter, mechanic. **монтировать** *impf* (*pf* с~) mount; install, fit; edit.

монумент monument. **монументальный** monumental.

мораль moral; morals, ethics. **моральный** moral; ethical.

морг morgue.

моргать *impf*, **моргнуть** (-нý, -нёшь) *pf* blink; wink.

морда snout, muzzle; (ugly) mug.

море (*pl* -я, -ей) sea.

мореплавание navigation. **мореплаватель** *m* seafarer. **мореходный** nautical.

морж (-á), **моржиха** walrus.

Морзе *indecl* Morse; **азбука** ~ Morse code.

морить *impf* (*pf* у~) exhaust; ~ голодом starve.

морковка carrot. **морковь** carrot, carrots.

мороженое *sb* ice-cream. **мороженый** frozen, chilled. **мороз** frost; *pl* intensely cold weather. **морозилка** freezer compartment; freezer. **морозильник** deep-freeze. **морозить** (-óжу) freeze. **морозный** frosty.

моросить *impf* drizzle.

морской sea; maritime; marine, nautical; ~ая свинка guinea-pig; ~ой флот navy, fleet.

морфий morphine.

морщина wrinkle; crease. **морщить** (-щу) *impf* (*pf* на~, по~, с~) wrinkle; pucker; ~ся knit one's brow; wince; crease, wrinkle.

моряк (-á) sailor, seaman.

москвич (-á), ~ка Muscovite. **московский** (of) Moscow.

мост (мостá, *loc* -ý; *pl* -ы́) bridge. **мостик** bridge. **мостить** (-ощý) *impf* (*pf* вы~) pave. **мостки** (-óв) *pl* planked footway. **мо-**

стова́я sb roadway; pavement. **мостово́й** bridge.

мота́ть¹ impf (pf мотну́ть, на~) wind, reel.

мота́ть² impf (pf про~) squander.

мота́ться impf dangle; wander; rush about.

моти́в motive; reason; tune; motif. **мотиви́ровать** impf & pf give reasons for, justify. **мотиви́ровка** reason(s); justification.

мотну́ть (-ну́, -нёшь) pf of мота́ть

мото- in comb motor-, engine-. **мотого́нки** (-нок) pl motor-cycle races. **~пе́д** moped. **~пехо́та** motorized infantry. **~ро́ллер** (motor-)scooter. **~ци́кл** motor cycle.

мото́к (-тка́) skein, hank.

мото́р motor, engine. **мотори́ст** motor-mechanic. **мото́рный** motor; engine.

моты́га hoe, mattock.

мотылёк (-лька́) butterfly, moth.

мох (мха or мо́ха, loc мху; pl мхи, мхов) moss. **мохна́тый** hairy, shaggy.

моча́ urine.

моча́лка loofah.

мочево́й пузы́рь bladder. **мочи́ть** (-чу́, -чишь) impf (pf за~, на~) wet, moisten; soak; **~ся** (pf по~ся) urinate.

мо́чка ear lobe.

мочь (могу́, мо́жешь; мог, -ла́) impf (pf с~) be able; **мо́жет (быть)** perhaps.

моше́нник rogue. **моше́нничать** (-аю) impf (pf с~) cheat, swindle. **моше́ннический** rascally.

мо́шка midge. **мошкара́** (swarm of) midges.

мо́щность power; capacity. **мо́щный** (-щен, -щна́, -о) powerful.

мощу́ etc.: see мости́ть

мощь power.

мо́ю etc.: see мыть. **мо́ющий** washing; detergent.

мрак darkness, gloom. **мракобе́с** obscurantist.

мра́мор marble. **мра́морный** marble.

мра́чный dark; gloomy.

мсти́тельный vindictive. **мстить** (мщу) impf (pf ото~) take vengeance on; **+за+acc** avenge.

мудре́ц (-а́) sage, wise man. **му́дрость** wisdom. **му́дрый** (-др, -á, -о) wise, sage.

муж (pl -жья́ or -и́) husband. **мужа́ть** impf grow up; mature; **~ся** take courage. **мужеподо́бный** mannish; masculine. **му́жественный** manly, steadfast. **му́жество** courage.

мужи́к (-а́) peasant; fellow.

мужско́й masculine; male. **мужчи́на** m man.

му́за muse.

музе́й museum.

му́зыка music. **музыка́льный** musical. **музыка́нт** musician.

му́ка¹ torment.

мука́² flour.

мультиплика́ция, **мультфи́льм** cartoon film.

му́мия mummy.

мунди́р (full-dress) uniform. **мундшту́к** (-а́) mouthpiece; cigarette-holder.

муниципа́льный municipal.

мураве́й (-вья́) ant. **мураве́йник** ant-hill.

мурлы́кать (-ы́чу or -каю) impf purr.

муска́т nutmeg.

му́скул muscle. **му́скульный** muscular.

му́сор refuse; rubbish. **му́сорный я́щик** dustbin.

мусульма́нин (*pl* -ма́не, -ма́н), **-а́нка** Muslim.

мути́ть (мучу́, му́тишь) *impf* (*pf* вз~) make muddy; stir up, upset. **му́тный** (-тен, -тна́, -о) turbid, troubled; dull. **муть** sediment; murk.

му́ха fly.

муче́ние torment, torture. **му́ченик, му́ченица** martyr. **мучи́тельный** agonizing. **му́чить** (-чу) *impf* (*pf* за~, из~) torment; harass; **~ся** torment o.s.; suffer agonies.

мучно́й flour, meal; starchy.

мха *etc.*: *see* мох

мчать (мчу) *impf* rush along, whirl along; **~ся** rush.

мщу *etc.*: *see* мстить

мы (нас, нам, на́ми, нас) *pron* we; **мы с ва́ми** you and I.

мы́лить (*pf* на~) soap; **~ся** wash o.s. **мы́ло** (*pl* -а́) soap. **мы́льница** soap-dish. **мы́льный** soap, soapy.

мыс cape, promontory.

мы́сленный mental. **мы́слимый** conceivable. **мысли́тель** *m* thinker. **мы́слить** *impf* think; conceive. **мысль** thought; idea. **мы́слящий** thinking.

мыть (мо́ю) *impf* (*pf* вы́~, по~) wash; **~ся** wash (o.s.).

мыча́ть (-чу́) *impf* (*pf* про~) low, moo; bellow; mumble.

мышело́вка mousetrap.

мы́шечный muscular.

мышле́ние thinking, thought.

мы́шца muscle.

мышь (*gen pl* -е́й) mouse.

мэр mayor. **мэ́рия** town hall.

мя́гкий (-гок, -гка́, -о) soft; mild; **~ знак** soft sign, the letter ь.

мя́гче *comp of* мя́гкий, мя́гко.

мя́коть fleshy part, flesh; pulp.

мяси́стый fleshy; meaty. **мясни́к** (-а́) butcher. **мясно́й** meat. **мя́со** meat; flesh. **мясору́бка** mincer.

мя́та mint; peppermint.

мяте́ж (-а́) mutiny, revolt. **мяте́жник** mutineer, rebel. **мяте́жный** rebellious; restless.

мя́тный mint, peppermint.

мять (мну, мнёшь) *impf* (*pf* из~, раз~, с~) work up; knead; crumple; **~ся** become crumpled; crush (easily).

мя́укать *impf* miaow.

мяч (-а́), **мя́чик** ball.

Н

на[1] *prep* **I.** +*acc* on; on to, to, into; at; till, until; for; by. **II.** +*prep* on; in; at.

на[2] *partl* here; here you are.

наба́вить (-влю) *pf*, **набавля́ть** *impf* add (to), increase.

наба́т alarm-bell.

набе́г raid, foray.

набекре́нь *adv* aslant.

набели́ть (-е́лишь) *pf*. **на́бело** *adv* without corrections.

на́бережная *sb* embankment, quay.

наберу́ *etc.*: *see* набра́ть

набива́ть(ся *impf of* наби́ть(ся. **наби́вка** stuffing, padding; (textile) printing.

набира́ть(ся *impf of* набра́ть(ся

наби́тый packed, stuffed; crowded. **наби́ть** (-бью́, -бьёшь

pf (*impf* **набива́ть**) stuff, pack, fill; smash; print; hammer, drive; **~ся** crowd in.

наблюда́тель *m* observer. **наблюда́тельный** observant; observation. **наблюда́ть** *impf* observe, watch; **+за**+*instr* look after; supervise. **наблюде́ние** observation; supervision.

на́божный devout, pious.

на́бок *adv* on one side, crooked.

наболе́вший sore, painful.

набо́р recruiting; collection; set; type-setting.

набра́сывать(ся *impf of* **наброса́ть, набро́сить(ся**

набра́ть (-беру́, -берёшь; -а́л, -а, -о) *pf* (*impf* **набира́ть**) gather; enlist; compose, set up; **~ но́мер** dial a number; **~ся** assemble, collect; +*gen* find, acquire, pick up; **~ся сме́лости** pluck up courage.

набрести́ (-еду́, -едёшь; -ёл, -ела́) *pf* **+на**+*acc* come across.

наброса́ть *pf* (*impf* **набра́сывать**) throw (down); sketch; jot down. **набро́сить** (-о́шу) *pf* (*impf* **набра́сывать**) throw; **~ся** throw o.s.; **~ся на** attack. **набро́сок** (-ска) sketch, draft.

набуха́ть *impf*, **набу́хнуть** (-нет, -ух) *pf* swell.

набы́ть *etc.: see* **наби́ть**

наважде́ние delusion.

нава́ливать *impf*, **навали́ть** (-лю́, -лишь) *pf* heap, pile up; load; **~ся** lean; **+на**+*acc* fall (up)on.

наведе́ние laying (on); placing.

наведу́ *etc.: see* **навести́**

наве́к, наве́ки *adv* for ever.

навёл *etc.: see* **навести́**

наве́рно, наве́рное *adv* prob-

ably. **наверняка́** *adv* certainly, for sure.

наверста́ть *pf*, **навёрстывать** *impf* make up for.

наве́рх *adv* up(wards); upstairs. **наверху́** *adv* above; upstairs.

наве́с awning.

наве́сить (-е́шу) *pf* (*impf* **наве́шивать**) hang (up). **навесно́й** hanging.

навести́ (-еду́, -едёшь; -вёл, -а́) *pf* (*impf* **наводи́ть**) direct; aim; cover (with), spread; introduce, bring; make.

навести́ть (-ещу́) *pf* (*impf* **навеща́ть**) visit.

навеша́ть *pf*, **наве́шивать**[1] *impf* hang (out); weigh out.

наве́шивать[2] *impf of* **наве́сить. навеща́ть** *impf of* **навести́ть**

на́взничь *adv* backwards, on one's back.

навзры́д *adv*: **пла́кать ~** sob.

навига́ция navigation.

нависа́ть *impf*, **нави́снуть** (-нет; -вис) *pf* overhang, hang (over); threaten. **нави́сший** beetling.

навлека́ть *impf*, **навле́чь** (-еку́, -ечёшь; -ёк, -ла́) *pf* bring, draw; incur.

наводи́ть (-ожу́, -о́дишь) *impf of* **навести́; наводя́щий вопро́с** leading question. **наво́дка** aiming; applying.

наводне́ние flood. **наводни́ть** *pf*, **наводня́ть** *impf* flood; inundate.

наво́з dung, manure.

на́волочка pillowcase.

навра́ть (-ру́, -рёшь; -а́л, -а́, -о) *pf* tell lies, romance; talk nonsense; **+в**+*prep* make mistake(s) in.

навреди́ть (-ежу́) pf +dat harm.

навсегда́ adv for ever.

навстре́чу adv to meet; идти́ ~ go to meet; meet halfway.

на́выворот adv inside out; back to front.

на́вык experience, skill.

на́вынос adv to take away.

на́выпуск adv worn outside.

навью́чивать impf, **навью́чить** (-чу) pf load.

навяза́ть (-яжу́, -я́жешь) pf, **навя́зывать** impf tie, fasten; thrust, foist; **~ся** thrust o.s. **навя́зчивый** importunate; obsessive.

нага́дить (-а́жу) pf.

нага́н revolver.

нагиба́ть(ся impf of **нагну́ть(ся**

нагишо́м adv stark naked.

нагле́ц (-а́) impudent fellow. **на́глость** impudence. **на́глый** (нагл, -а́, -о) impudent.

нагля́дный clear, graphic; visual.

нагна́ть (-гоню́, -го́нишь; -а́л, -а́, -о) pf (impf **нагоня́ть**) overtake, catch up (with); inspire, arouse.

нагнести́ (-ету́, -етёшь) pf **нагнета́ть** impf compress; supercharge.

нагное́ние suppuration. **нагно́иться** pf suppurate.

нагну́ть (-ну́, -нёшь) pf (impf **нагиба́ть**) bend; **~ся** bend, stoop.

нагова́ривать impf, **наговори́ть** (-рю́) pf slander; talk a lot (of); record.

наго́й (наг, -а́, -о) naked, bare. **на́голо** naked, bare.

нагоня́ть impf of **нагна́ть**

нагора́ть (-ну́, -нёшь), **нагоре́ть** (-ри́т) pf be consumed; impers+dat be scolded.

наго́рный upland, mountain; mountainous.

нагота́ nakedness, nudity.

награ́бить (-блю) pf amass by dishonest means.

награ́да reward; decoration; prize. **награди́ть** (-ажу́) pf, **награжда́ть** impf reward; decorate; award prize to.

нагрева́тельный heating. **нагрева́ть** impf, **нагре́ть** (-е́ю) pf warm, heat; **~ся** get hot, warm up.

нагроможда́ть impf, **нагромозди́ть** (-зжу́) pf heap up, pile up. **нагроможде́ние** heaping up; conglomeration.

нагруби́ть (-блю́) pf.

нагружа́ть impf, **нагрузи́ть** (-ужу́, -у́зишь) pf load; **~ся** load o.s. **нагру́зка** loading; load; work; commitments.

нагря́нуть (-ну) pf appear unexpectedly.

над, надо prep+instr over, above; on, at.

надави́ть (-влю́, -вишь) pf, **нада́вливать** impf press; squeeze out; crush.

надба́вка addition, increase.

надвига́ть impf, **надви́нуть** (-ну) pf move, pull, push; **~ся** approach.

на́двое adv in two.

надгро́бие epitaph. **надгро́бный** (on or over a) grave.

надева́ть impf of **наде́ть**

наде́жда hope. **наде́жность** reliability. **наде́жный** reliable.

наде́л allotment.

наде́лать pf make; cause; do.

надели́ть (-лю́, -ли́шь) pf, **наделя́ть** impf endow, provide.

наде́ть (-е́ну) pf (impf **надева́ть**) put on.

надея́ться (-е́юсь) *impf* (*pf* по~) hope; rely.

надзира́тель *m* overseer, supervisor. **надзира́ть** *impf* +за+*instr* supervise, oversee. **надзо́р** supervision; surveillance.

надла́мывать(ся *impf of* надломи́ть(ся

надлежа́щий fitting, proper, appropriate. **надлежи́т** (-жа́ло) *impers* (+*dat*) it is necessary, is required.

надло́м break; crack; breakdown. **надломи́ть** (-млю́, -мишь) *pf* (*impf* надла́мывать) break; crack; breakdown; ~ся break, crack, breakdown. **надло́мленный** broken.

надме́нный haughty, arrogant.

на́до¹ (+*dat*) it is necessary, I (*etc.*) must, ought to; I (*etc.*) need. **на́добность** necessity, need.

на́до²: *see* над.

надоеда́ть *impf*, **надое́сть** (-е́м, -е́шь, -е́ст, -еди́м) *pf* +*dat* bore, pester. **надое́дливый** boring, tiresome.

надо́лго *adv* for a long time.

надорва́ть (-ву́, -вёшь; -а́л, -а́, -о) *pf* (*impf* надрыва́ть) tear; strain; ~ся tear; overstrain o.s.

на́дпись inscription.

надре́з cut, incision. **надре́зать** (-е́жу) *pf*, **надреза́ть** (-а́ю), **надре́зывать** *impf* make an incision in.

надруга́тельство outrage. **надруга́ться** *pf* +над+*instr* outrage, insult.

надры́в tear; strain; breakdown; outburst. **надрыва́ть(ся** *impf of* надорва́ть(ся. **надры́вный** hysterical; heartrending.

надста́вить (-влю) *pf*, **надстав-**ля́ть *impf* lengthen.

надстра́ивать *impf*, **надстро́ить** (-о́ю) *pf* build on top; extend upwards. **надстро́йка** building upwards; superstructure.

надува́тельство swindle. **надува́ть(ся** *impf. of* наду́ть(ся. **надувно́й** pneumatic, inflatable.

наду́манный far-fetched.

наду́тый swollen; haughty; sulky. **наду́ть** (-у́ю) *pf* (*impf* надува́ть) inflate; swindle; ~ся swell out; sulk.

наду́шить(ся (-шу́(сь, -шишь(ся) *pf*

наеда́ться *impf of* нае́сться

наедине́ *adv* privately, alone.

нае́зд flying visit; raid. **нае́здник, -ица** rider. **наезжа́ть** *impf of* нае́здить, нае́хать; pay occasional visits.

наём (на́йма) hire; renting; **взять в ~** rent; **сдать в ~** let. **наёмник** hireling; mercenary. **наёмный** hired, rented.

нае́сться (-е́мся, -е́шься, -е́стся, -еди́мся) *pf* (*impf* наеда́ться) eat one's fill; stuff o.s.

нае́хать (-е́ду) *pf* (*impf* наезжа́ть) arrive unexpectedly; +на+*acc* run into, collide with.

нажа́ть (-жму́, -жмёшь) *pf* (*impf* нажима́ть) press; put pressure (on).

нажда́к (-а́) emery. **нажда́чная бума́га** emery paper.

нажи́ва profit, gain.

нажива́ть(ся *impf of* нажи́ть(ся

нажи́м pressure; clamp. **нажима́ть** *impf of* нажа́ть.

нажи́ть (-иву́, -ивёшь; на́жил, -а́, -о) *pf* (*impf* нажива́ть) acquire;

contract; incur; ~ся (-жи́лся, -а́сь) get rich.

нажму́ *etc.: see* нажа́ть

наза́втра *adv* (the) next day.

наза́д *adv* back(wards); (тому́) ~ ago.

назва́ние name; title. **назва́ть** (-зову́, -зовёшь; -а́л, -а́, -о) *pf* (*impf* называ́ть) call, name; ~ся be called.

назе́мный ground, surface.

назло́ *adv* out of spite; to spite.

назнача́ть *impf*, **назна́чить** (-чу) *pf* appoint; fix, set; prescribe. **назначе́ние** appointment; fixing, setting; prescription.

назову́ *etc.: see* назва́ть

назо́йливый importunate.

назрева́ть *impf*, **назре́ть** (-е́ет) *pf* ripen, mature; become imminent.

называ́емый: так ~ so-called. **называ́ть(ся** *impf of* назва́ть(ся.

наибо́лее *adv* (the) most. **наибо́льший** greatest, biggest.

наи́вный naive.

наивы́сший highest.

наигра́ть *impf*, **наи́грывать** *impf* win; play, pick out.

наизна́нку *adv* inside out.

наизу́сть *adv* by heart.

наилу́чший best.

наименова́ние name; title.

на́искось *adv* obliquely.

найму́ *etc.: see* наня́ть

найти́ (-йду́, -йдёшь; нашёл, -шла́, -шло́) *pf* (*impf* находи́ть) find; ~сь be found; be situated.

наказа́ние punishment. **наказа́ть** (-ажу́, -а́жешь) *pf*, **нака́зывать** *impf* punish.

нака́л incandescence. **нака́ливать** *impf*, **накали́ть** *pf*, **нака-**

-ля́ть *impf* heat; make red-hot; strain, make tense; ~ся become incandescent; become strained.

нака́пливать(ся *impf of* накопи́ть(ся

накану́не *adv* the day before.

нака́пливать(ся *impf of* накопи́ть(ся

нака́чать *pf*, **нака́чивать** *impf* pump (up).

наки́дка cloak, cape; extra charge. **наки́нуть** (-ну) *pf*, **наки́дывать** *impf* throw; throw on; ~ся throw o.s.; ~ся на attack.

на́кипь scum; scale.

накладна́я *sb* invoice. **накладно́й** laid on; false; ~ые расхо́ды overheads. **накла́дывать** *impf of* наложи́ть

наклевета́ть (-ещу́, -е́щешь) *pf*

накле́ивать *impf*, **накле́ить** *pf* stick on. **накле́йка** sticking (on, up); label.

накло́н slope, incline. **наклоне́ние** inclination; mood. **наклони́ть** (-ню́, -нишь) *pf*, **наклоня́ть** *impf* incline, bend; ~ся incline, bend. **накло́нный** inclined, sloping.

нако́лка pinning; (pinned-on) ornament for hair; tattoo. **наколо́ть**[1] (-лю́, -лешь) *pf* (*impf* нака́лывать) prick; pin; ~ся prick o.s.

наколо́ть[2] (-лю́, -лешь) *pf* (*impf* нака́лывать) chop.

наконе́ц *adv* at last. **наконе́чник** tip, point.

накопля́ть (-плю́, -пишь) *pf*, **накопля́ть** *impf* (*impf also* нака́пливать) accumulate; ~ся accumulate. **накопле́ние** accumulation.

на|копти́ть (-пчу́) *pf.* **на|кор-**

ми́ть (-млю́, -мишь) *pf.*

накра́сить (-а́шу) *pf* paint; make up. **на**|**кра́ситься** (-а́шусь) *pf.*

на|**крахма́лить** *pf.* **накрени́ться** (-ни́тся) *pf,* **накреня́ться** *impf* tilt; list.

накрича́ть (-чу́) *pf* (+**на**+*acc*) shout (at).

накро́ю *etc.: see* накры́ть

накрыва́ть *impf,* **накры́ть** (-ро́ю) *pf* cover; catch; ~ на стол lay the table; ~ся cover o.s.

накури́ть (-рю́, -ришь) *pf* fill with smoke.

налага́ть *impf of* наложи́ть

нала́дить (-а́жу) *pf,* **нала́живать** *impf* regulate, repair; organize; ~ся come right; get going.

на|**лга́ть** (-лгу́, -лжёшь; -а́л, -а́, -о) *pf*

нале́во *adv* to the left.

налёг *etc.: see* нале́чь. **налега́ть** *impf of* нале́чь

налегке́ *adv* lightly dressed; without luggage.

налёт raid; flight; thin coating. **налета́ть¹** *pf* have flown. **налета́ть²** *impf,* **налете́ть** (-лечу́) *pf* swoop down; come flying; spring up.

нале́чь (-ля́гу, -ля́жешь; -нёг, -гла́) *pf* (*impf* налега́ть) lean, apply one's weight; lie; apply o.s.

налжёшь *etc.: see* налга́ть

налива́ть(ся *impf of* на|ли́ть(ся. **нали́вка** fruit liqueur.

нали́ть (-лью́, -льёшь; на́ли́л, -а́, -о) *pf* (*impf* налива́ть) pour (out), fill; ~ся (-и́лся, -а́сь, -и́лось) pour in; ripen.

налицо́ *adv* present; available.

нали́чие presence. **нали́чный** on hand; cash; ~ые (де́ньги) ready money.

нало́г tax. **налогоплате́льщик** taxpayer. **нало́женн**|**ый**: ~ым платежо́м C.O.D. **наложи́ть** (-жу́, -жишь) *pf* (*impf* накла́дывать, налага́ть) lay (in, on), put (in, on); apply; impose.

налью́ *etc.: see* нали́ть

наля́гу *etc.: see* нале́чь

нам *etc.: see* мы

на|**ма́зать** (-а́жу) *pf,* **нама́зывать** *impf* oil, grease; smear, spread.

нама́тывать *impf of* намота́ть

нама́чивать *impf of* намочи́ть

намёк hint. **намека́ть** *impf,* **намекну́ть** (-ну́, -нёшь) *pf* hint.

намерева́ться *impf* +*inf* intend to. **наме́рен** *predic*: я ~(а)+*inf* I intend to. **наме́рение** intention. **наме́ренный** intentional.

на|**мета́ть** *pf.* **на**|**мети́ть¹** (-е́чу) *pf.*

наме́тить² (-е́чу) *pf* (*impf* намеча́ть) plan; outline; nominate; ~ся be outlined, take shape.

намно́го *adv* much, far.

намока́ть *impf,* **намо́кнуть** (-ну) *pf* get wet.

намо́рдник muzzle.

на|**мо́рщить(ся** (-щу(сь) *pf.*

на|**мота́ть** *pf* (*impf also* нама́тывать) wind, reel.

на|**мочи́ть** (-очу́, -о́чишь) *pf* (*impf also* нама́чивать) wet; soak; splash, spill.

намы́ливать *impf,* **на**|**мы́лить** *pf* soap.

нанести́ (-су́, -сёшь; -ёс, -ла́) *pf* (*impf* наноси́ть) carry, bring; draw, plot; inflict.

на|**низа́ть** (-ижу́, -и́жешь) *pf,* **на-**

низывать *impf* string, thread.

наниматель *m* tenant; employer. **нанимать(ся** *impf of* **нанять(ся**

наносить (-ошу, -осишь) *impf of* **нанести**

нанять (найму, -мёшь; нанял, -а, -о) *pf* (*impf* **нанимать**) hire; rent; **~ся** get a job.

наоборот *adv* on the contrary; back to front; the other, the wrong, way (round); vice versa.

наотмашь *adv* violently.

наотрез *adv* flatly, point-blank.

нападать *impf of* **напасть**. **нападающий** *sb* forward. **нападение** attack; forwards.

напарник co-driver, (work-)mate.

напасть (-аду, -адёшь; -ал) *pf* (*impf* **нападать**) **на**+*acc* attack; descend on; seize; come upon. **напасть** misfortune.

напев tune. **напевать** *impf of* **напеть**

наперебой *adv* interrupting, vying with, one another.

наперёд *adv* in advance.

наперекор *adv*+*dat* in defiance of, counter to.

напёрсток (-тка) thimble.

напеть (-пою, -поёшь) *pf* (*impf* **напевать**) sing; hum, croon.

напечатать(ся *pf*. **напиваться** *impf of* **напиться**

напильник file.

написать (-ишу, -ишешь) *pf*.

напиться (-пьюсь, -пьёшься; -ился, -ась, -илось) *pf* (*impf* **напиваться**) quench one's thirst, drink; get drunk.

напихать *pf*, **напихивать** *impf* cram, stuff.

наплевать (-люю, -люёшь) *pf*;

~! to hell with it! who cares?

наплыв influx; accumulation; canker.

наплюю *etc.*: *see* **наплевать**

наповал *adv* outright.

наподобие *prep*+*gen* like, not unlike.

на|**поить** (-ою, -оишь) *pf*.

напоказ *adv* for show.

наполнитель *m* filler. **наполнить(ся** *pf*, **наполнять(ся** *impf* fill.

наполовину *adv* half.

напоминание reminder. **напоминать** *impf*, **напомнить** *pf* (+*dat*) remind.

напор pressure, pushing. **напористый** energetic, pushing.

напоследок *adv* in the end; after all.

напою *etc.*: *see* **напеть, напоить**

напр. *abbr* (*of* **например**) e.g., for example.

направить (-влю) *pf*, **направлять** *impf* direct; send; sharpen; **~ся** make (for), go (towards). **направление** direction; trend; warrant; order. **направленный** purposeful.

направо *adv* to the right.

напрасно *adv* in vain, for nothing; unjustly, mistakenly.

напрашиваться *impf of* **напроситься**

например for example.

на|**проказничать** *pf*.

напрокат *adv* for, on, hire.

напролёт *adv* through, without a break.

напролом *adv* straight, regardless of obstacles.

напроситься (-ошусь, -осишься) *pf* (*impf* **напрашиваться**) thrust o.s.; suggest itself; **~ на** ask for, invite.

напро́тив *adv* opposite; on the contrary. **напро́тив** *prep+gen* opposite.

напряга́ть(ся *impf of* **напря́чь(ся. напряже́ние** tension; exertion; voltage. **напряжённый** tense; intense; intensive.

напрями́к *adv* straight (out).

напря́чь (-ягу́, -яжёшь; -яг, -ла́) *pf* (*impf* **напряга́ть**) strain; ~ся strain o.s.

на|пуга́ть(ся *pf.* **на|пу́дриться** *pf.*

напуска́ть *impf*, **напусти́ть** (-ущу́, -у́стишь) *pf* let in; let loose; ~ся +на+*acc* fly at, go for.

напу́тать *pf* +в+*prep* make a mess of.

на|пыли́ть *pf.*

напью́сь *etc.: see* **напи́ться**

наравне́ *adv* level; equally.

нараспа́шку *adv* unbuttoned.

нараста́ние growth, accumulation. **нараста́ть** *impf*, **нарасти́** (-тёт; -ро́с, -ла́) *pf* grow; increase.

нарасхва́т *adv* very quickly, like hot cakes.

нарва́ть[1] (-рву́, -рвёшь; -а́л, -а́, -о) *pf* (*impf* **нарыва́ть**) pick; tear up.

нарва́ть[2] (-вёт; -а́л, -а́, -о) *pf* (*impf* **нарыва́ть**) gather.

нарва́ться (-ву́сь, -вёшься; -а́лся, -ала́сь, -а́лось) *pf* (*impf* **нарыва́ться**) +на+*acc* run into, run up against.

наре́зать (-е́жу) *pf*, **нареза́ть** *impf* cut (up), slice, carve; thread, rifle.

наре́чие[1] dialect.

наре́чие[2] adverb.

на|рисова́ть *pf.*

нарко́з narcosis. **наркома́н, -ма́нка** drug addict. **наркома́ния** drug addiction. **нарко́тик** narcotic.

наро́д people. **наро́дность** nationality; national character. **наро́дный** national; folk; popular; people's.

наро́с *etc.: see* **нарасти́**

наро́чно *adv* on purpose, deliberately. **наро́чный** *sb* courier.

нару́жность exterior. **нару́жный** external, outward. **нару́жу** *adv* outside.

нару́чник handcuff. **нару́чный** wrist.

наруше́ние breach; infringement. **наруши́тель** *m* transgressor. **нару́шить** (-шу) *pf*, **наруша́ть** *impf* break; disturb, infringe, violate.

нарци́сс narcissus; daffodil.

на́ры (нар) *pl* plank-bed.

нары́в abscess, boil. **нарыва́ть(ся** *impf of* **нарва́ть(ся**

наря́д[1] order, warrant.

наря́д[2] attire; dress. **наряди́ть** (-яжу́) *pf* (*impf* **наряжа́ть**) dress (up); ~ся dress up. **наря́дный** well-dressed.

наряду́ *adv* alike, equally; side by side.

наряжа́ть(ся *impf of* **наряди́ть(ся. нас** *see* **мы**

насади́ть (-ажу́, -а́дишь) *pf*, **насажда́ть** *impf* (*impf also* **наса́живать**) plant; propagate; implant. **наса́дка** setting, fixing. **насажде́ние** planting; plantation; propagation. **наса́живать** *impf of* **насади́ть**

насеко́мое *sb* insect.

населе́ние population. **населённость** density of population. **населённый** populated; ~ пункт settlement; built-up

area. **населить** *pf*, **населять** *impf* settle, people.

насилие violence, force. **насиловать** *impf* (*pf* из~) coerce; rape. **насилу** *adv* with difficulty. **насильник** aggressor; rapist; violator. **насильно** *adv* by force. **насильственный** violent, forcible.

наскакивать *impf of* **наскочить**

насквозь *adv* through, throughout.

насколько *adv* how much?, how far?; as far as.

наскоро *adv* hastily.

наскочить (-очу́, -о́чишь) *pf* (*impf* **наскакивать**) +на+*acc* run into; collide with; fly at.

наскучить (-чу) *pf* bore.

насладиться (-ажусь) *pf*, **наслаждаться** *impf* (+*instr*) enjoy, take pleasure. **наслаждение** pleasure, enjoyment.

наследие legacy; heritage. **на|следить** (-ежу) *pf*. **наследник** heir; successor. **наследница** heiress. **наследный** next in succession. **наследовать** *impf* & *pf* (*pf also* y~) inherit, succeed to. **наследственность** heredity. **наследственный** hereditary, inherited. **наследство** inheritance; heritage.

насмерть *adv* to (the) death.

на|смешить (-шу) *pf* **насмешка** mockery; gibe. **насмешливый** mocking.

насморк runny nose; cold.

на|сорить *pf*.

насос pump.

наспех *adv* hastily.

на|сплетничать *pf*. **наставать** (-таёт) *impf of* **настать**

наставление exhortation; directions, manual.

наставник tutor, mentor.

наставать[1] *impf of* **настать**[1].

наставлять[2](ся *impf of* настоять[2](ся

настежь *adv* (open).

настелю *etc.: see* **настлать**

настигать *impf*, **настигнуть**, **настичь** (-и́гну; -и́г) *pf* catch up with, overtake.

настил flooring, planking. **настилать** *impf of* **настлать**

настичь *see* настигать

настлать (-телю́, -те́лешь) *pf* (*impf* **настилать**) lay, spread.

настойка liqueur, cordial.

настойчивый persistent; urgent.

настолько *adv* so, so much.

настольный table, desk; reference.

настораживать *impf*, **насторожить** (-жу́) *pf* set; prick up; ~ся prick up one's ears. **насторо́женный** (-ен, -енна) guarded; alert.

настоятельный insistent; urgent. **настоять**[1] (-ою́) *pf* (*impf* **настаивать**[1]) insist.

настоять[2] (-ою́) *pf* (*impf* **настаивать**[2]) brew; ~ся draw, stand.

настоящее *sb* the present. **настоящий** (the) present, this; real, genuine.

настраивать(ся *impf of* **настроить(ся**

настричь (-игу́, -ижёшь; -иг) *pf* shear, clip.

настроение mood. **настроить** (-ою) *pf* (*impf* **настраивать**) tune (in); dispose; ~ся dispose of. **настройка** tuning. **настройщик** tuner.

настрочи́ть (-чу́) *pf.*

наступа́тельный offensive.

наступа́ть[1] *impf of* наступи́ть[1].

наступа́ть[2] *impf of* наступи́ть[2]. **наступа́ющий**[1] coming.

наступа́ющий[2] *sb* attacker.

наступи́ть[1] (-плю́, -пишь) *pf* (*impf* наступа́ть[1]) tread; attack; advance.

наступи́ть[2] (-у́пит) *pf* (*impf* наступа́ть[2]) come, set in. **наступле́ние**[1] offensive.

наступле́ние[2] offensive, attack.

насу́питься (-плюсь) *pf,* насу́пливаться *impf* frown.

на́сухо *adv* dry. насуши́ть (-шу́, -шишь) *pf* dry.

насу́щный urgent, vital; хлеб ~ daily bread.

насчёт *prep+gen* about, concerning; as regards. насчита́ть *pf,* насчи́тывать *impf* count; hold; ~ся +*gen* number.

насыпа́ть (-плю) *pf,* насыпа́ть *impf* pour in, on; fill; spread; heap up. на́сыпь embankment.

насы́тить (-ы́щу) *pf,* насыща́ть *impf* satiate; saturate; ~ся be full; be saturated.

ната́лкивать(ся *impf of* натолкну́ть(ся. ната́лпливать *impf of* натопи́ть

натаска́ть *pf,* ната́скивать *impf* train; coach; cram; bring in, lay in.

натвори́ть *pf* do, get up to.

натере́ть (-тру́, -трёшь, -тёр) *pf* (*impf* натира́ть) rub on, in; polish; chafe; grate; ~ся rub o.s.

на́тиск onslaught.

наткну́ться (-ну́сь, -нёшься) *pf* (*impf* натыка́ться) +на+*acc* run into; strike, stumble on.

натолкну́ть (-ну́, -нёшь) *pf* (*impf*

ната́лкивать) push; lead; ~ся run against, across.

натопи́ть (-плю́, -пишь) *pf* (*impf* ната́пливать) heat (up); stoke up; melt.

наточи́ть (-чу́, -чишь) *pf.*

натоща́к *adv* on an empty stomach.

натра́вить (-влю́, -вишь) *pf,* натра́вливать *impf,* натравля́ть *impf* set (on); stir up.

натренирова́ть(ся *pf.*

на́трий sodium.

нату́ра nature. натура́льный natural; genuine. нату́рщик, -щица artist's model.

натыка́ть(ся *impf of* наткну́ть(ся

натюрмо́рт still life.

натя́гивать *impf,* натяну́ть (-ну́, -нешь) *pf* stretch; draw; pull (on); ~ся stretch. натя́нутость tension. натя́нутый tight; strained.

науга́д *adv* at random.

нау́ка science; learning.

нау́тро *adv* (the) next morning.

научи́ть(ся (-чу́(сь, -чишь(ся *pf.*

нау́чный scientific; ~ая фанта́стика science fiction.

нау́шник ear-flap; ear-phone.

нафтали́н naphthalene.

наха́л, -ха́лка impudent creature. наха́льный impudent. наха́льство impudence.

нахвата́ть(ся *pf,* нахва́тывать *impf* pick up, get hold of; ~ся +*gen* pick up.

нахле́бник hanger-on.

нахлы́нуть (-нет) *pf* well up; surge; gush.

нахму́рить(ся *pf.*

находи́ть(ся (-ожу́(сь, -о́дишь(ся) *impf of* найти́(сь. на-

хо́дка find. **нахо́дчивый** resourceful, quick-witted.

наце́ливать impf, **наце́лить** pf aim; **~ся** (take) aim.

наце́нка surcharge, mark-up.

наци́зм Nazism. **национализа́ция** nationalization. **национализи́ровать** impf & pf nationalize. **национали́зм** nationalism. **националисти́ческий** nationalist(ic). **национа́льность** nationality; ethnic group. **национа́льный** national. **наци́ст, -и́стка** Nazi. **наци́стский** Nazi. **на́ция** nation. **нацме́н, -ме́нка** abbr member of national minority.

нача́ло beginning; origin; principle, basis. **нача́льник** head, chief; boss. **нача́льный** initial; primary. **нача́льство** the authorities; command. **нача́ть** (-чну́, -чнёшь; на́чал, -а́, -о) pf (impf **начина́ть**) begin; **~ся** begin.

начерта́ть pf trace, inscribe. **начерти́ть** (-рчу́, -ртишь) pf.

начина́ние undertaking. **начина́ть(ся** impf of **нача́ть(ся**. **начина́ющий** sb beginner.

начини́ть impf, **начини́ть** impf stuff, fill. **начи́нка** stuffing, filling.

начи́стить (-и́щу) pf (impf **начища́ть**) clean. **на́чисто** adv clean; flatly, decidedly; openly, frankly. **начистоту́** adv openly, frankly.

начи́танность learning; wide reading. **начи́танный** well-read.

начища́ть impf of **начи́стить**

наш (-его) m, **на́ша** (-ей) f, **на́ше** (-его) neut, **на́ши** (-их) pl, pron our, ours.

нашаты́рный спирт ammonia. **нашаты́рь** (-я́) m sal-

ammoniac; ammonia.

нашёл etc.: see **найти́**

наше́ствие invasion.

нашива́ть impf, **наши́ть** (-шью, -шьёшь) pf sew on. **наши́вка** stripe, chevron; tab.

нашлёпать impf slap.

нашуме́ть (-млю) pf make a din; cause a sensation.

нашью etc.: see **наши́ть**

нащу́пать pf, **нащу́пывать** impf grope for.

наэлектризова́ть pf.

наяву́ adv awake; in reality.

не- pref un-, in-, non-, mis-, dis-; -less; not. **неаккура́тный** careless; untidy; unpunctual. **небезразли́чный** not indifferent. **небезызве́стный** not unknown; notorious; well-known.

небеса́ etc.: see **не́бо²**. **небе́сный** heavenly; celestial.

не-. неблагода́рный ungrateful; thankless. **неблагонадёжный** unreliable. **неблагополу́чный** unsuccessful, bad, unfavourable. **неблагоприя́тный** unfavourable. **неблагоразу́мный** imprudent. **неблагоро́дный** ignoble, base.

нёбо¹ palate.

не́бо² (pl -беса́, -бе́с) sky; heaven.

не-. небога́тый of modest means, modest. **небольшо́й** small, not great; **с небольши́м** a little over.

небосво́д firmament. **небоскло́н** horizon. **небоскрёб** skyscraper.

небо́сь adv I dare say; probably.

не-. небре́жный careless. **небыва́лый** unprecedented; fan-

tastic. **небыли́ца** fable, cock-and-bull story. **небытие́** non-existence. **небью́щийся** unbreakable. **нева́жно** adv not too well, indifferently. **нева́жный** unimportant; indifferent. **невдалеке́** adv not far away. **неве́дение** ignorance. **неве́домый** unknown; mysterious. **неве́жа** m & f boor, lout. **неве́жда** m & f ignoramus. **неве́жественный** ignorant. **неве́жество** ignorance. **неве́жливый** rude. **невели́кий** (-и́к, -а́, -и́ко́) small. **неве́рие** unbelief, atheism; scepticism. **неве́рный** (-рен, -рна́, -о) incorrect, wrong; inaccurate, unsteady; unfaithful. **невероя́тный** improbable; incredible. **неве́рующий** unbelieving; sb atheist. **невесёлый** joyless, sad. **невесо́мый** weightless; imponderable. **неве́ста** fiancée; bride. **неве́стка** daughter-in-law; brother's wife, sister-in-law.

не-. невзго́да adversity. **невзира́я на** prep+acc regardless of. **невзнача́й** adv by chance. **невзра́чный** unattractive, plain. **неви́данный** unprecedented, unheard-of. **неви́димый** invisible. **неви́нность** innocence. **неви́нный, невино́вный** innocent. **невмеша́тельство** non-intervention; non-interference. **невмоготу́, невмочь** advs unbearable, too much (for). **невнима́тельный** inattentive, thoughtless.

не́вод seine(-net).

не-. невозврати́мый, невозвра́тный irrevocable, irrecoverable. **невозмо́жный** impossible. **невозмути́мый** imperturbable.

нево́льник, -ница slave. **нево́льный** involuntary; unintentional; forced. **нево́ля** captivity; necessity.

не-. невообрази́мый unimaginable, inconceivable. **невооружённый** unarmed; ~ным гла́зом with the naked eye. **невоспи́танный** ill-bred, bad-mannered. **невоспламеня́ющийся** non-flammable. **невосприи́мчивый** unreceptive; immune.

невралги́я neuralgia. **невреди́мый** safe, unharmed. **невро́з** neurosis. **неврологи́ческий** neurological. **невроти́ческий** neurotic.

не-. невы́годный disadvantageous; unprofitable. **невы́держанный** lacking self-control; unmatured. **невыноси́мый** unbearable. **невыполни́мый** impracticable. **невысо́кий** (-со́к, -а́, -о́ко́) low; short.

не́га luxury; bliss.

негати́вный negative.

не́где adv (there is) nowhere.

не-. неги́бкий (-бок, -бка́, -о) inflexible, stiff. **негла́сный** secret. **неглубо́кий** (-о́к, -а́, -о) shallow. **неглу́пый** (-у́п, -а́, -о) sensible, quite intelligent. **него́дный** (-ден, -дна́, -о) unfit, unsuitable; worthless. **негодова́ние** indignation. **негодова́ть** impf be indignant. **негодя́й** scoundrel. **негостеприи́мный** inhospitable.

негр Negro, black man.

негра́мотность illiteracy. **негра́мотный** illiterate.

негритя́нка Negress, black woman. **негритя́нский** Negro.

не-. негро́мкий (-мок, -мка́, -о) quiet. **неда́вний** recent. **не-**

да́вно adv recently. **недале́кий** (-ёк, -а́, -ёко́) near; short; not bright, dull-witted. **недалеко́** adv not far, near. **неда́ром** adv not for nothing, not without reason. **недви́жимость** real estate. **недви́жимый** immovable. **недвусмы́сленный** unequivocal. **недействи́тельный** ineffective; invalid. **недели́мый** indivisible.

неде́льный of a week, week's. **неде́ля** week.

не-. **недёшево** adv dear(ly). **недоброжела́тель** m illwisher. **недоброжела́тельность** hostility. **недоброка́чественный** of poor quality. **недобросо́вестный** unscrupulous; careless. **недо́брый** (-бр, -бра́, -о) unkind; bad. **недове́рие** distrust. **недове́рчивый** distrustful. **недово́льный** dissatisfied. **недово́льство** dissatisfaction. **недоеда́ние** malnutrition. **недоеда́ть** impf be undernourished.

не-. **недо́лгий** (-лог, -лга́, -о) short, brief. **недо́лго** adv not long. **недолгове́чный** shortlived. **недомога́ние** indisposition. **недомога́ть** impf be unwell. **недомы́слие** thoughtlessness. **недоно́шенный** premature. **недооце́нивать** impf, **недооцени́ть** (-ню́, -нишь) pf underestimate; underrate. **недооце́нка** underestimation. **недопусти́мый** inadmissible, intolerable. **недоразуме́ние** misunderstanding. **недорого́й** (-дорог, -а́, -о) inexpensive. **недосмотре́ть** (-рю́,-ришь) pf overlook. **недоспа́ть** (-плю́, -ал, -а́, -о) pf (impf **недосыпа́ть**) not have enough sleep.

недостава́ть (-таёт) impf, **недоста́ть** (-а́нет) pf impers be missing, be lacking. **недоста́ток** (-тка) shortage, deficiency; insufficient, inadequate. **недоста́ча** lack, shortage.

не-. **недостижи́мый** unattainable. **недосто́йный** unworthy, **недосту́пный** inaccessible. **недосчита́ться** pf, **недосчи́тываться** impf miss, find missing, be short (of). **недосыпа́ть** impf of **недоспа́ть**. **недосяга́емый** unattainable.

недоумева́ть impf be at a loss, be bewildered. **недоуме́ние** bewilderment.

не-. **недоу́чка** m & f halfeducated person. **недочёт** deficit; defect.

не́дра (недр) pl depths, heart, bowels. **не́друг** enemy. **недружелю́бный** unfriendly.

неду́г illness, disease.

недурно́й not bad; not badlooking.

не-. **неесте́ственный** unnatural. **нежда́нный** unexpected. **нежела́ние** unwillingness. **нежела́тельный** undesirable. **не́жели** than.

нежена́тый unmarried.

не́женка m & f mollycoddle.

нежило́й uninhabited; uninhabitable.

не́житься (-жусь) impf luxuriate, bask. **не́жность** tenderness; pl endearments. **не́жный** tender; affectionate.

не-. **незабве́нный** unforgettable. **незабу́дка** forget-me-not. **незабыва́емый** unforgettable. **незави́симость** independence. **незави́симый** independent.

незадо́лго *adv* not long. неза-конноро́жденный illegitimate. незако́нный illegal; illicit; illegitimate. незако́нченный unfinished. незамени́мый irreplaceable. незамерза́ющий ice-free; anti-freeze. незаме́тный imperceptible. незаму́жняя unmarried. незапа́мятный immemorial. незаслу́женный unmerited. незауря́дный uncommon, outstanding.

не́зачем *adv* there is no need.
не-. незащищённый unprotected. незва́ный uninvited. нездоро́виться *impf*, *impers* +*dat* нездоро́вится I don't feel well. нездоро́вый unhealthy. нездоро́вье ill health. незнако́мец (-мца), незнако́мка stranger. незнако́мый unknown, unfamiliar. незна́ние ignorance. незначи́тельный insignificant. незре́лый unripe, immature. незри́мый invisible. незы́блемый unshakable, firm. неизбе́жность inevitability. неизбе́жный inevitable. неизве́данный unknown.

неизве́стность uncertainty; ignorance; obscurity. неизве́стный unknown; *sb* stranger.
не-. неизлечи́мый incurable. неизме́нный unchanged, unchanging; devoted. неизме́нный unalterable. неизмери́мый immeasurable, immense. неизу́ченный unstudied; unexplored. неиму́щий poor. неинтере́сный uninteresting. нейскренний insincere. нейску́шенный inexperienced, unsophisticated. неиспо́лнимый impracticable. неиспра́вимый incorrigible; irrep-

arable. неиспра́вный out of order, defective; careless. неис-сле́дованный unexplored. неисся́каемый inexhaustible. не́йстовство fury, frenzy; atrocity. не́йстовый furious, frenzied, uncontrolled. неисто-щи́мый, неисчерпа́емый inexhaustible. неисчисли́мый innumerable.

нейло́н, нейло́новый nylon. нейро́н neuron.
нейтрализа́ция neutralization. нейтрализова́ть *impf* & *pf* neutralize. нейтралите́т neutrality. нейтра́льный neutral. нейтро́н neutron.
неквалифици́рованный unskilled.

не́кий *pron* a certain, some.
не́когда[1] *adv* once, formerly.
не́когда[2] *adv* there is no time; мне ~ I have no time.
не́кого (не́кому, не́кем, не́ о ком) *pron* there is nobody.
некомпете́нтный not competent, unqualified.
не́который *pron* some; ~ые *sb pl* some (people).
некраси́вый plain, ugly; not nice.
некроло́г obituary.
некста́ти *adv* at the wrong time, out of place.
не́кто *pron* somebody; a certain.
не́куда *adv* there is nowhere.
не-. некульту́рный uncivilized, uncultured. некуря́щий *sb* non-smoker. нела́дный wrong. нелега́льный illegal. нелёгкий not easy; heavy. неле́пость absurdity, nonsense. неле́пый absurd. нело́вкий awkward. нело́вкость awkwardness.

нельзя *adv* it is impossible; it is not allowed.

не-. нелюбимый unloved. **нелюди́мый** unsociable. **нема́ло** *adv* quite a lot (of). **нема́лый** considerable. **неме́дленно** *adv* immediately. **неме́дленный** immediate.

неме́ть (-е́ю) *impf* (*pf* о~) become dumb. **не́мец** (-мца) German. **неме́цкий** German.

неминуемый inevitable.

не́мка German woman.

немно́гие *sb pl* (a) few. **немно́го** *adv* a little; some; a few. **немно́жко** *adv* a little.

немо́й (нем, -а́, -о) dumb, mute, silent. **немота́** dumbness.

не́мощный feeble.

немы́слимый unthinkable.

ненави́деть (-и́жу) *impf* hate. **ненави́стный** hated; hateful. **не́нависть** hatred.

не-. ненагля́дный beloved. **ненадёжный** unreliable. **ненадо́лго** *adv* for a short time. **нена́стье** bad weather. **ненасы́тный** insatiable. **ненорма́льный** abnormal. **нену́жный** unnecessary, unneeded. **необду́манный** thoughtless, hasty. **необеспе́ченный** without means, unprovided for. **необита́емый** uninhabited. **необозри́мый** boundless, immense. **необосно́ванный** unfounded, groundless. **необрабо́танный** uncultivated; crude; unpolished. **необразо́ванный** uneducated.

необходи́мость necessity. **необходи́мый** necessary.

не-. необъясни́мый inexplicable. **необъя́тный** immense. **необыкнове́нный** unusual. **необыча́йный** extraordinary.

необы́чный unusual. **необяза́тельный** optional. **неограни́ченный** unlimited. **неоднокра́тный** repeated. **неодобри́тельный** disapproving. **неодушевлённый** inanimate.

неожи́данность unexpectedness. **неожи́данный** unexpected, sudden.

не-. неоко́нченный unfinished. **неопла́ченный** unpaid. **неопра́вданный** unjustified. **неопределённый** indefinite; infinitive; vague. **неопровержи́мый** irrefutable. **неопублико́ванный** unpublished. **нео́пытный** inexperienced. **неоргани́ческий** inorganic. **неоспори́мый** incontestable. **неосторо́жный** careless. **неосуществи́мый** impracticable. **неотврати́мый** inevitable.

нео́ткуда *adv* there is nowhere.

не-. неотло́жный urgent. **неотрази́мый** irresistible. **неотсту́пный** persistent. **неотъе́млемый** inalienable. **неофициа́льный** unofficial. **неохо́та** reluctance. **неохо́тно** *adv* reluctantly. **неоцени́мый** inestimable, invaluable. **непарти́йный** non-party; unbefitting a member of the (Communist) Party. **непереводи́мый** untranslatable. **непереходя́щий** intransitive. **неплатёжеспосо́бный** insolvent.

не-. непло́хо *adv* not badly, quite well. **непло́хой** not bad, quite good. **непобеди́мый** invincible. **неповинове́ние** insubordination. **неповоро́тливый** clumsy. **неповтори́мый** inimitable, unique. **непого́да** bad weather. **непогреши́мый**

infallible. **неподалёку** adv not far (away). **неподвижный** motionless, immovable; fixed. **неподдельный** genuine; sincere. **неподкупный** incorruptible. **неподражаемый** inimitable. **неподходящий** unsuitable, inappropriate. **неколебимый** unshakable, steadfast. **непокорный** recalcitrant, unruly.

не-. неполадки (-док) pl defects. **неполноценность; комплекс неполноценности** inferiority complex. **неполноценный** defective; inadequate. **неполный** incomplete; not (a) full. **непомерный** excessive. **непонимание** incomprehension, lack of understanding. **непонятный** incomprehensible. **непоправимый** irreparable. **непорядок** (-дка) disorder. **непорядочный** dishonourable. **непоседа** m & f fidget. **непосильный** beyond one's strength. **непоследовательный** inconsistent. **непослушание** disobedience. **непослушный** disobedient. **непосредственный** immediate; spontaneous. **непостижимый** incomprehensible. **непостоянный** inconstant, changeable. **непохожий** unlike; different.

не-. неправда untruth. **неправдоподобный** improbable. **неправильно** adv wrong. **неправильный** irregular; wrong. **неправый** wrong. **непрактичный** unpractical. **непревзойдённый** unsurpassed. **непредвиденный** unforeseen. **непредубеждённый** unprejudiced. **непредусмотренный** unforeseen. **непредусмотрительный** short-sighted. **непреклонный** inflexible; adamant.

непреложный immutable. **не-. непременно** adv without fail. **непременный** indispensable. **непреодолимый** insuperable. **непререкаемый** unquestionable. **непрерывно** adv continuously. **непрерывный** continuous. **непрестанный** incessant. **неприветливый** unfriendly; bleak. **непривлекательный** unattractive. **непривычный** unaccustomed. **непригодный** unattractive. **непригодный** unfit, useless. **неприемлемый** unacceptable. **неприкосновенность** inviolability, immunity. **неприкосновенный** inviolable; reserve. **неприличный** indecent. **непримиримый** irreconcilable. **непринуждённый** unconstrained; relaxed. **неприспособленный** unadapted; maladjusted. **непристойный** obscene. **неприступный** inaccessible. **непритязательный, неприхотливый** unpretentious, simple. **неприязненный** hostile, inimical. **неприязнь** hostility. **неприятель** m enemy. **неприятельский** enemy. **неприятность** unpleasantness; trouble. **неприятный** unpleasant.

не-. непроверенный unverified. **непроглядный** pitch-dark. **непроезжий** impassable. **непрозрачный** opaque. **непроизводительный** unproductive. **непроизвольный** involuntary. **непромокаемый** waterproof. **непроницаемый** impenetrable. **непростительный** unforgivable. **непроходимый** impassable. **непрочный** (-чен, -чна, -о) fragile, flimsy.

не прочь predic not averse.

не-. **непрóшеный** uninvited, unsolicited. **неработоспосóбный** disabled. **нерабóчий:** ~ **день** day off. **неравéнство** inequality. **неравномéрный** uneven. **нерáвный** unequal. **нерадúвый** lackadaisical. **неразберúха** muddle. **неразбóрчивый** not fastidious; illegible. **неразвитóй** (-рáзвит, -á, -о) undeveloped; backward. **неразговóрчивый** taciturn. **неразделённый:** ~**ая любóвь** unrequited love. **неразличúмый** indistinguishable. **неразлучный** inseparable. **неразрешённый** unsolved; forbidden. **неразрешúмый** insoluble. **неразрывный** indissoluble. **неразумный** unwise; unreasonable. **нераствори́мый** insoluble.

нерв nerve. **нéрвничать** impf fret, be nervous. **нервнобольнóй** sb neurotic. **нéрвный** (-вен, -внá, -о) nervous; nerve; irritable. **нервóзный** nervy, irritable.

не-. **нереáльный** unreal; unrealistic. **нерéдкий** (-док, -дкá, -о) not infrequent, not uncommon. **нерешúтельность** indecision. **нерешúтельный** indecisive, irresolute. **нержавéющая сталь** stainless steel. **нерóвный** (-вен, -внá, -о) uneven, rough; irregular. **нерушúмый** inviolable.

нерйха m & f sloven. **неряшлúвый** slovenly.

не-. **несбытóчный** unrealizable. **несварéние желудка** indigestion. **несвéжий** (-éж, -á) not fresh; tainted; weary. **несвоеврéменный** ill-timed; overdue. **несвóйственный** not

characteristic. **несгорáемый** fireproof. **несерьёзный** not serious.

несессéр case.

несимметрúчный asymmetrical.

несклáдный incoherent; awkward.

несклоняемый indeclinable.

нéсколько (-их) pron some, several; adv several.

не-. **несконча́емый** interminable. **нескрóмный** (-мен, -мнá, -о) immodest; indiscreet. **несло́жный** simple. **неслы́ханный** unprecedented. **неслы́шный** inaudible. **несме́тный** countless, incalculable. **несмолка́емый** ceaseless.

несмотря́ на prep+acc in spite of.

не-. **несно́сный** intolerable. **несоблюде́ние** non-observance. **несовершенноле́тний** under-age; sb minor. **несоверше́нный** imperfect, incomplete; imperfective. **несоверше́нство** imperfection. **несовмести́мый** incompatible. **несогла́сие** disagreement. **несогласо́ванный** uncoordinated. **несозна́тельный** irresponsible. **несоизмери́мый** incommensurable. **несокруши́мый** indestructible. **несомне́нный** undoubted, unquestionable. **несообра́зный** incongruous. **несоотве́тствие** disparity. **несостоя́тельный** insolvent; of modest means; untenable. **неспе́лый** unripe. **неспоко́йный** restless; uneasy. **неспосо́бный** not bright; incapable. **несправедли́вость** injustice. **несправедли́вый** unjust, unfair; incorrect.

сравне́нный (-ёнон, -е́нна) incomparable. **несравни́мый** incomparable. **нестерпи́мый** unbearable.

нести́ (-су́, -сёшь; нёс, -ла́) *impf* (*pf* по~, с~) carry; bear; bring, take; suffer; incur; lay; ~**сь** rush, fly; float, be carried.

не-. нестойкий unstable. **несуще́ственный** immaterial, inessential.

несу́ *etc.*: *see* **нести́**

несхо́дный unlike, dissimilar.

несчастли́вый unfortunate, unlucky; unhappy. **несча́стный** unhappy, unfortunate; ~ **слу́чай** accident. **несча́стье** misfortune; **к несча́стью** unfortunately.

несчётный innumerable.

нет *partl* no, not; nothing. **нет, не́ту** there is not, there are not.

не-. нетакти́чный tactless. **нетвёрдый** (-ёрд, -а́, -о) unsteady, shaky. **нетерпели́вый** impatient. **нетерпе́ние** impatience. **нетерпи́мый** intolerable, intolerant. **неторопли́вый** leisurely. **нето́чный** (-чен, -чна́, -о) inaccurate, inexact. **нетре́звый** drunk. **нетро́нутый** untouched; chaste, virginal. **нетрудово́й дохо́д** unearned income. **нетрудоспосо́бность** disability.

не́тто *indecl adj & adv* net(t).

не́ту *see* **нет**

не-. неубеди́тельный unconvincing. **неуваже́ние** disrespect. **неуве́ренность** uncertainty. **неуве́ренный** uncertain. **неувяда́емый, неувяда́ющий** unfading. **неугомо́нный** indefatigable. **неуда́ча** failure. **неуда́чливый** unlucky. **неуда́чник, -ница** un-

lucky person, failure. **неуда́чный** unsuccessful, unfortunate. **неудержи́мый** irrepressible. **неудо́бный** uncomfortable, inconvenient; embarrassing. **неудо́бство** discomfort; inconvenience; embarrassment. **неудовлетворе́ние** dissatisfaction. **неудовлетворённый** dissatisfied. **неудовлетвори́тельный** unsatisfactory. **неудово́льствие** displeasure.

неуже́ли? *partl* really?

не-. неузнава́емый unrecognizable. **неукло́нный** steady; undeviating. **неуклю́жий** clumsy. **неулови́мый** elusive; subtle. **неуме́лый** inept; clumsy. **неуме́ренный** immoderate. **неуме́стный** inappropriate; irrelevant. **неумоли́мый** implacable, inexorable. **неумы́шленный** unintentional.

не-. неупла́та non-payment. **неуравнове́шенный** unbalanced. **неурожа́й** bad harvest. **неуро́чный** untimely, inopportune. **неуря́дица** disorder, mess. **неуспева́емость** poor progress. **неусто́йка** forfeit. **неусто́йчивый** unstable; unsteady. **неуступчивый** unyielding. **неуте́шный** inconsolable. **неутоли́мый** unquenchable. **неутоми́мый** tireless. **неу́ч** ignoramus. **неучти́вый** discourteous. **неуязви́мый** invulnerable.

нефри́т jade.

нефте- *in comb* oil, petroleum. **нефтено́сный** oil-bearing. ~**перего́нный заво́д** oil refinery. ~**прово́д** (oil) pipeline. ~**проду́кты** (-ов) *pl* petroleum products.

нефть oil, petroleum. **нефтяно́й** oil, petroleum.

не-. **нехва́тка** shortage. **нехорошо́** adv badly. **нехоро́ший** (-о́ш, -а́) bad; ~**о́** it is bad, it is wrong. **нехотя** adv unwillingly; unintentionally; **нецелесообра́зный** inexpedient; pointless. **нецензу́рный** unprintable. **неча́янный** unexpected; accidental.

не́чего (не́чему, -чем, не́ о чём) pron (with separable pref) (there is) nothing.

нечелове́ческий inhuman, superhuman.

нече́стный dishonest, unfair.

нечётный odd.

нечистопло́тный dirty; slovenly; unscrupulous. **нечистота́** (pl -о́ты, -о́т) dirtiness, filth; pl sewage. **нечи́стый** (-и́ст, -а́, -о) dirty, unclean; impure; unclear. **не́чисть** evil spirits; scum.

нечленоразде́льный inarticulate.

не́что pron something.

не-. **неэконо́мичный** uneconomical. **неэффекти́вный** ineffective; inefficient. **нея́вка** failure to appear. **нея́ркий** dim, faint, dull, subdued. **нея́сный** (-сен, -сна́, -о) not clear; vague.

ни partl not a; **ни оди́н** (одна́, одно́) not a single; (with prons and pronominal advs) -ever; **кто́... ни** whoever. **ни** conj: **ни... ни** neither ...; nor; **ни то ни сё** neither one thing nor the other.

ни́ва cornfield, field.

нивели́р level.

нигде́ adv nowhere.

нидерла́ндец (-дца; gen pl -дцев) Dutchman. **нидерла́ндка** Dutchwoman. **нидерла́ндский** Dutch. **Нидер-**

ла́нды (-ов) pl the Netherlands.

ни́же adj lower, humbler; adv below; prep+gen below, beneath. **нижесле́дующий** following. **ни́жний** lower, under-; ~**ее бельё** underclothes; ~**ий эта́ж** ground floor. **низ** (loc -у́; pl -ы́) bottom; pl lower classes; low notes.

низа́ть (нижу́, ни́жешь) impf (pf на~) string, thread.

низверга́ть impf, **низве́ргнуть** (-ну; -е́рг) pf throw down, overthrow; ~**ся** crash down; be overthrown. **низверже́ние** overthrow.

низи́на low-lying place. **ни́зкий** (-зок, -зка́, -о) low; base. **низкопокло́нство** servility. **низкопро́бный** low-grade. **низкоро́слый** undersized. **низкосо́ртный** low-grade.

ни́зменность lowland; baseness. **ни́зменный** low-lying; base.

низо́вье (gen pl -ьев) the lower reaches. **ни́зость** baseness, meanness. **ни́зший** lower, lowest; ~**ее образова́ние** primary education.

никако́й adv in no way. **никако́й** pron no; no ... whatever

ни́кель m nickel.

нике́м see **никто́**. **никогда́** adv never. **никто́** (-кого́, -кому́, -ке́м, ни о ко́м) pron (with separable pref) nobody, no one. **никуда́** adv nowhere. **никчёмный** useless. **нима́ло** adv not in the least.

нимб halo, nimbus.

ни́мфа nymph; pupa.

ниотку́да adv from nowhere.

нипочём adv it is nothing; dirt cheap; in no circumstances.

ниско́лько adv not at all.

ниспроверга́ть *impf*, **ниспрове́ргнуть** (-ну; -ёрг) *pf* overthrow. **ниспроверже́ние** overthrow.

нисходя́щий descending.

ни́тка thread; string; **до ни́тки** to the skin; **на живу́ю ни́тку** hastily, anyhow. **ни́точка** thread. **нить** thread; filament.

ничего́ *etc.*: *see* **ничто́**. **ничего́** *adv* all right; it doesn't matter, never mind; *as indecl adj* not bad, pretty good. **ниче́й** (-чья́, -чьё) *pron* nobody's; **ничья́ земля́** no man's land. **ничья́** *sb* draw; tie.

ничко́м *adv* face down, prone.

ничто́ (-чего́, -чему́, -чём, ни о чём) *pron* (*with separable pref*) nothing. **ничто́жество** nonentity, nobody. **ничто́жный** insignificant; worthless.

ничу́ть *adv* not a bit.

ничье́, ничья́: *see* **ниче́й**

ни́ша niche, recess.

ни́щенка beggar-woman. **ни́щенский** beggarly. **нищета́** poverty. **ни́щий** (нищ, -á, -е) destitute, poor; *sb* beggar.

но *conj* but; still.

нова́тор innovator. **нова́торский** innovative. **нова́торство** innovation.

Но́вая Зела́ндия New Zealand.

нове́йший newest, latest.

нове́лла short story.

нове́нький brand-new.

новизна́ novelty; newness. **нови́нка** novelty. **новичо́к** (-чка́) novice.

ново- *in comb* new(ly). **новобра́нец** (-нца) new recruit. **~бра́чный** *sb* newly-wed. **~введе́ние** innovation. **~го́дний** new year's. **~зела́ндец**

(-дца; *gen pl* -дцев), **~зела́ндка** New-Zealander. **~зела́ндский** New Zealand. **~лу́ние** new moon. **~прибы́вший** newly-arrived; *sb* newcomer. **~рождённый** newborn. **~сёл** new settler. **~селье** new home; house-warming. **новостро́йка** new building.

но́вость (*gen pl* -éй) news; novelty. **но́вшество** innovation, novelty. **но́вый** (нов, -á, -о) new; modern; **~ год** New Year.

нога́ (*acc* но́гу; *pl* но́ги, ног, нога́м) foot, leg.

но́готь (-гтя; *gen pl* -тéй) *m* finger-nail, toe-nail.

нож (-á) knife.

но́жка small foot or leg; leg; stem, stalk.

но́жницы (-иц) *pl* scissors, shears.

но́жны (-жен) *pl* sheath, scabbard.

ножо́вка saw, hacksaw.

ноздря́ (*pl* -и, -éй) nostril.

нока́ут knock-out. **нокаути́ровать** *impf* & *pf* knock out.

нолево́й, нулево́й zero. **ноль** (-я́), **нуль** (-я́) *m* nought, zero, nil.

номенклату́ра nomenclature; top positions in government.

но́мер (*pl* -á) number; size; (hotel-)room; item; trick. **номеро́к** (-рка́) tag; label, ticket.

номина́л face value. **номина́льный** nominal.

нора́ (*pl* -ы) burrow, hole.

Норве́гия Norway. **норве́жец** (-жца), **норве́жка** Norwegian. **норве́жский** Norwegian.

норд (*naut*) north; north wind.

но́рка mink.

но́рма standard, norm; rate.

нормализа́ция standardization. **норма́льно** all right, OK. **норма́льный** normal; standard. **нормирова́ние**, **нормиро́вка** regulation; rate-fixing; rationing. **норми́ровать** *impf & pf* regulate, standardize; ration.

нос (*loc* -ý; *pl* -ы́) nose; beak; bow, prow. **но́сик** (*small*) nose; spout.

носи́лки (-лок) *pl* stretcher; litter. **носи́льщик** porter. **носи́тель** *m*, **~ница** (*fig*) bearer; (*med*) carrier. **носи́ть** (-ошу́, -о́сишь) *impf* carry, bear; wear; **~ся** rush, tear along, fly; float, be carried; wear. **носка́** carrying, wearing. **но́ский** hard-wearing.

носово́й nose; nasal; **~ плато́к** (pocket) handkerchief. **носо́к** (-ска́) little nose; toe; sock. **носоро́г** rhinoceros.

но́та note; *pl* music. **нота́ция** notation; lecture, reprimand.

нота́риус notary.

ночева́ть (-чу́ю) *impf* (*pf* пере~) spend the night. **ночёвка** spending the night. **ночле́г** place to spend the night; passing the night. **ночле́жка** doss-house. **ночни́к** (-á) night-light. **ночно́й** night, nocturnal; **~áя руба́шка** nightdress; **~óй горшо́к** potty; chamber-pot. **ночь** (*loc* -и́; *gen pl* -éй) night. **но́чью** *adv* at night.

но́ша burden. **но́шеный** worn; second-hand.

но́ю *etc.*: *see* **ныть**

ноя́брь (-я́) *m* November. **ноя́брьский** November.

нрав disposition; temper; *pl* customs, ways. **нра́виться** (-влюсь) *impf* (*pf* по~) +*dat* please; мне

нра́вится I like. **нра́вственность** morality, morals. **нра́вственный** moral.

ну *int & partl* well, well then.

ну́дный tedious.

нужда́ (*pl* -ы) need. **нужда́ться** *impf* be in need; +*в*+*prep* need, require. **ну́жный** (-жен, -жна́, -о, ну́жны) necessary; **~о** it is necessary; +*dat* I, *etc.*, must, ought to.

нулево́й, нуль *see* **нолево́й, ноль**

нумера́ция numeration; numbering. **нумерова́ть** *impf* (*pf* про~) number.

нутро́ inside, interior; instinct(s).

ны́не *adv* now; today. **ны́нешний** present; today's. **ны́нче** *adv* today; now.

нырну́ть (-ну́, -нёшь) *pf*, **ныря́ть** *impf* dive.

ныть (но́ю) *impf* ache; whine. **нытьё** whining.

н.э. *abbr* (*of* на́шей э́ры) AD.

нюх scent; flair. **ню́хать** *impf* (*pf* по~) smell, sniff.

ня́нчить (-чу) *impf* nurse, look after; **~ся** *c*+*instr* nurse; fuss over. **ня́нька** nanny. **ня́ня** (*children's*) nurse, nanny.

О

о, об, обо *prep* I. +*prep* of, about, concerning. II. +*acc* against; on, upon.

о *int* oh!

оа́зис oasis.

об *see* **о** *prep.*

о́ба (обо́их) *m & neut*, **о́бе** (обе́их) *f* both.

обалдева́ть *impf*, **обалде́ть**

(-ею) *pf* go crazy; become stunned.

обанкро́титься (-о́чусь) *pf* go bankrupt.

обая́ние fascination, charm. **обая́тельный** fascinating, charming.

обва́л fall(ing); crumbling; collapse; caving-in; landslide; (сне́жный) ~ avalanche. **обвали́ть** (-лю́, -лишь) *pf* (*impf* обва́ливать) cause to fall or collapse; crumble; heap round; ~ся collapse, cave in; crumble.

обва́ливать *impf*, **обвари́ть** (-рю́, -ришь) *pf* pour boiling water over; scald; ~ся scald o.s.

обведу́ *etc.*: see обвести́. **обвёл** *etc.*: see обвести́. **обве́нча́ть(ся** *pf.*

обверну́ть (-ну́, -нёшь) *pf*, **обвёртывать** *impf* wrap, wrap up.

обве́с short weight. **обве́сить** (-е́шу) *pf* (*impf* обве́шивать) cheat in weighing.

обвести́ (-еду́, -едёшь, -ёл, -ела́) *pf* (*impf* обводи́ть) lead round, take round; encircle; surround; outline; dodge.

обве́тренный weather-beaten. **обветша́лый** decrepit. **об|ветша́ть** *pf.*

обве́шивать *impf* of обве́сить. **обвива́ть(ся** *impf* of обви́ть(ся

обвине́ние charge, accusation; prosecution. **обвини́тель** *m* accuser; prosecutor. **обвини́тельный** accusatory; ~ акт indictment; ~ пригово́р verdict of guilty. **обвини́ть** *pf*, **обвиня́ть** *impf* prosecute, indict; +в+*prep*

accuse of, charge with. **обвиня́емый** *sb* the accused; defendant.

обви́ть (обовью́, обовьёшь; обви́л, -а́, -о) *pf* (*impf* обвива́ть) wind round; ~ся wind round.

обвожу́ (-ожу́, -о́дишь) *impf* of обвести́

обвора́живать *impf*, **обворожи́ть** (-жу́) *pf* charm, enchant. **обворожи́тельный** charming, enchanting.

обвяза́ть (-яжу́, -я́жешь) *pf*, **об-вя́зывать** *impf* tie round; ~ся +*instr* tie round o.s.

обго́н passing. **обгоня́ть** *impf* of обогна́ть

обгора́ть *impf*, **обгоре́ть** (-рю́) *pf* be burnt, be scorched. **обгоре́лый** burnt, charred, scorched.

обде́лать *pf* (*impf* обде́лывать) finish; polish; set; manage, arrange.

обдели́ть (-лю́, -лишь) *pf* (*impf* обделя́ть) +*instr* do out of one's (fair) share of.

обде́лывать *impf* of обде́лать.

обделя́ть *impf* of обдели́ть.

обдеру́ *etc.*: see ободра́ть. **обдира́ть** *impf* of ободра́ть

обду́манный deliberate, well-considered. **обду́мать** *pf*, **обду́мывать** *impf* consider, think over.

обе́ see о́ба. **обега́ть** *pf* of обежа́ть. **обегу́** *etc.*: see обе-жа́ть

обе́д dinner, lunch. **обе́дать** *impf* (*pf* по~) have dinner, have lunch, dine. **обе́денный** dinner.

обедне́вший impoverished. **обедне́ние** impoverishment. **о|бедне́ть** (-е́ю) *pf.*

обе́дня (*gen pl* -ден) Mass.

обежа́ть (-егу́) *pf* (*impf* обега́ть) run round; run past.

обезбо́ливание anaesthetization. **обезбо́ливать** *impf*, **обезбо́лить** *pf* anaesthetize.

обезвре́дить (-е́жу) *pf*, **обезвре́живать** *impf* render harmless.

обездо́ленный unfortunate, hapless.

обеззара́живающий disinfectant.

обезли́ченный depersonalized; robbed of individuality.

обезобра́живать *impf*, o**безобра́зить** (-а́жу) *pf* disfigure.

обезопа́сить (-а́шу) *pf* secure.

обезору́живать *impf*, **обезору́жить** (-жу) *pf* disarm.

обезу́меть (-ею) *pf* lose one's senses, lose one's head.

обезья́на monkey; ape.

обели́ть *pf*, **обеля́ть** *impf* vindicate; clear of blame.

оберега́ть *impf*, **обере́чь** (-егу́, -ежёшь; -рёг, -ла́) *pf* guard; protect.

оберну́ть (-ну́, -нёшь) *pf*, **обёртывать** *impf* (*impf also* обора́чивать) twist; wrap up; turn; ~ся turn (round); turn out; +*instr* or **в**+*acc* turn into. **обёртка** wrapper; (dust-) jacket, cover. *see* **обёрточный** wrapping.

оберу́ *etc.: see* **обобра́ть**

обескура́живать *impf*, **обескура́жить** (-жу) *pf* discourage; dishearten.

обескро́вить (-влю) *pf*, **обескро́вливать** *impf* drain of blood, bleed white; render lifeless.

обеспе́чение securing, guaranteeing; ensuring; provision; guarantee; security. **обеспе́-** ченность security; +*instr* provision of. **обеспе́ченный** wellto-do; well provided for. **обеспе́чивать** *impf*, **обеспе́чить** (-чу) *pf* provide for; secure; ensure; protect; +*instr* provide with.

o**беспоко́ить(ся** *pf*.

обесси́леть (-ею) *pf* grow weak, lose one's strength. **обесси́ливать** *impf*, **обесси́лить** *pf* weaken.

o**бессла́вить** (-влю) *pf*.

обессме́ртить (-рчу) *pf* immortalize.

обесцене́ние depreciation. **обесце́нивать** *impf*, **обесце́нить** *pf* depreciate; cheapen; ~ся depreciate.

o**бесче́стить** (-е́щу) *pf*.

обе́т vow, promise. **обетова́нный** promised. **обеща́ние** promise. **обеща́ть** *impf & pf* (*pf also* по~) promise.

обжа́лование appeal. **обжа́ловать** *pf* appeal against.

обже́чь (обожгу́, обожжёшь; обжёг, обожгла́) *pf*, **обжига́ть** *impf* burn; scorch; bake; ~ся burn o.s.; burn one's fingers.

обжо́ра *m & f* glutton. **обжо́рство** gluttony.

обзавести́сь (-еду́сь, -едёшься; -вёлся, -ла́сь) *pf*, **обзаводи́ться** (-ожу́сь, -о́дишься) *impf* +*instr* provide o.s. with; acquire.

обзову́ *etc.: see* **обозва́ть**

обзо́р survey, review.

обзыва́ть *impf of* **обозва́ть**

обива́ть *impf of* **оби́ть**. **оби́вка** upholstering; upholstery.

оби́да offence, insult; nuisance. **оби́деть** (-и́жу), **обижа́ть** *impf* offend; hurt, wound; ~ся take offence; feel hurt. **оби́дный** offensive; annoying. **оби́д-**

чи́вый touchy. **оби́женный** offended.

оби́лие abundance. **оби́льный** abundant.

обира́ть *impf of* **обобра́ть**

обита́емый inhabited. **обита́тель** *m* inhabitant. **обита́ть** *impf* live.

оби́ть (обобью́, -ьёшь) *pf* (*impf* **обива́ть**) upholster; knock off.

обихо́д custom, (general) use, practice. **обихо́дный** everyday.

обкла́дывать(ся *impf of* **обложи́ть(ся**

обкра́дывать *impf of* **обокра́сть**

обла́ва raid; cordon, cordoning off.

облага́емый taxable. **облага́ть(ся** *impf of* **обложи́ть(ся: ~ся нало́гом** be liable to tax.

облада́ние possession. **облада́тель** *m* possessor. **облада́ть** *impf* +*instr* possess.

о́блако (*pl* -а́, -о́в) cloud.

обла́мывать(ся *impf of* **обломма́ть(ся, обломи́ться**

облага́емый taxable. **облага́ть(ся** *impf of* **обложи́ть(ся: ~ся нало́гом** be liable to tax.

областно́й regional. **о́бласть** (*gen pl* -е́й) region; field, sphere.

о́блачность cloudiness. **о́блачный** cloudy.

облёг etc.: see **обле́чь. облега́ть** *impf of* **обле́чь**¹

облегча́ть *impf*, **облегчи́ть** (-чу́) *pf* lighten; relieve; alleviate; facilitate. **облегче́ние** relief.

обледене́лый ice-covered. **обледене́ние** icing over. **обледене́ть** (-е́ет) *pf* become covered with ice.

обле́злый shabby; mangy.

облека́ть(ся *impf of* **обле́чь**¹**(ся. облеку́** etc.: see **обле́чь**²

облепи́ть (-плю́, -пишь) *pf*, **облепля́ть** *impf* stick to, cling to; throng round; plaster.

облета́ть *impf*, **облете́ть** (-лечу́) fly (round); spread (all over); fall.

обле́чь¹ (-ля́жет; -лёг, -ла́) *pf* (*impf* **облега́ть**) cover, envelop; fit tightly.

обле́чь² (-еку́, -ечёшь; -ёк, -кла́) *pf* (*impf* **облека́ть**) clothe, invest; **~ся** clothe o.s.; +*gen* take the form of.

облива́ть(ся *impf of* **обли́ть(ся**

облига́ция bond.

облиза́ть (-ижу́, -и́жешь) *pf*, **обли́зывать** *impf* lick (all over); **~ся** smack one's lips.

о́блик look, appearance.

обли́тый (о́бли́т, -а́, -о) covered, enveloped. **обли́ть** (оболью́, -льёшь; о́бли́л, -ила́, -о) *pf* (*impf* **облива́ть**) pour, sluice, spill; **~ся** sponge down, take a shower; pour over o.s.

облицева́ть (-цу́ю) *pf*, **облицо́вывать** *impf* face. **облицо́вка** facing; lining.

облича́ть *impf*, **обличи́ть** (-чу́) *pf* expose; point to. **обличе́ние** exposure, denunciation. **обличи́тельный** denunciatory.

обложе́ние taxation; assessment. **обложи́ть** (-жу́, -жишь) *pf* (*impf* **обкла́дывать, облага́ть**) edge; face; cover; surround; assess; **круго́м обложи́ло (не́бо)** the sky is completely overcast; **~ нало́гом** tax; **~ся** +*instr* surround o.s. with. **обло́жка** (dust-)cover; folder.

облока́чиваться *impf*, **облокоти́ться** (-очу́сь, -о́тишься) *pf* **на**+*acc* lean one's elbows on.

обломáть (*impf* **облáмывать**) break off; **~ся** break off. **обломи́ться** (-мится) *pf* (*impf* **облáмываться**) break off. **обло́мок** (-мка) fragment.

облу́пленный chipped.

облучи́ть (-чý) *pf*, **облучáть** *impf* irradiate. **облучéние** irradiation.

об|лысéть (-éю) *pf*.

обля́жет *etc.*: *see* **облéчь**[1]

обмáзать (-áжу) *pf*, **обмáзывать** *impf* coat; putty; besmear; **~ся** +*instr* get covered with.

обмáкивать *impf*, **обмакну́ть** (-нý, -нёшь) *pf* dip.

обмáн deceit; illusion; **~ зрéния** optical illusion. **обмáнный** deceitful. **обману́ть** (-нý, -нешь) *pf*, **обмáнывать** *impf* deceive; cheat; **~ся** be deceived. **обмáнчивый** deceptive. **обмáнщик** deceiver; fraud.

обмáтывать(ся *impf of* **обмотáть(ся**

обмáхивать *impf*, **обмахну́ть** (-нý, -нёшь) *pf* brush off; fan; **~ся** fan o.s.

обмёл *etc.*: *see* **обмести́**

обмелéние shallowing. **об|мелéть** (-éет) *pf* become shallow.

обмéн exchange; barter; **~ за+***acc* in exchange for; **~ вещéств** metabolism. **обмéнивать** *impf*, **обмени́ть** (-ню́, -нишь) *pf*, **об|меня́ть** *pf* exchange; **~ся** +*instr* exchange. **обмéнный** exchange.

обмéр measurement; false measure.

обмерéть (обомру́, -рёшь; о́бмер, -лá, -о) *pf* (*impf* **обмирáть**) faint; **~ от у́жаса** be horror-struck.

обмéривать *impf*, **обмéрить**

обмести́ (-етý, -етёшь; -мёл, -á) *pf*, **обметáть**[1] *impf* sweep off, dust.

обметáть[2] (-ечý *or* -áю, -éчешь *or* -áешь) *pf* (*impf* **обмётывать**) oversew.

обметý *etc.*: *see* **обмести́**. **обмётывать** *impf of* **обметáть**. **обмирáть** *impf of* **обмерéть**

обмо́лвиться (-влюсь) *pf* make a slip of the tongue; **~** +*instr* say, utter. **обмо́лвка** slip of the tongue.

обморо́женный frost-bitten.

о́бморок fainting-fit, swoon.

обмотáть *pf* (*impf* **обмáтывать**) wind round; **~ся** +*instr* wrap o.s. in. **обмо́тка** winding; *pl* puttees.

обмо́ю *etc.*: *see* **обмы́ть**

обмундировáние fitting out (with uniform); uniform. **обмундировáть(ся** *pf*, **обмундиро́вывать** *impf* fit out (with uniform).

обмывáть *impf*, **обмы́ть** (-мо́ю) *pf* bathe, wash; **~ся** bathe, wash.

обмяка́ть *impf*, **обмя́кнуть** (-ну; -мя́к) *pf* become soft *or* flabby.

обнадёживать *impf*, **обнадёжить** (-жу) *pf* reassure.

обнажáть *impf*, **обнажи́ть** (-жу́) *pf* bare, uncover; reveal. **обнажённый** (-ён, -енá) naked, bare; nude.

обнаро́довать *impf* & *pf* promulgate.

обнарýжéние revealing; discovery; detection. **обнарýживать** *impf*, **обнарýжить** (-жу) *pf* display; reveal; discover; **~ся** come to light.

обнести́ (-су́, -сёшь; -нёс, -ла́) pf (impf **обносить**) enclose; +instr serve round; pass over, leave out.

обнима́ть(ся impf of **обня́ть(ся. обниму́** etc.: see **обня́ть**

обнища́ние impoverishment.

обнови́ть (-влю) pf, **обновля́ть** impf renovate; renew. **обно́вка** new acquisition; new garment. **обновле́ние** renovation, renewal.

обноси́ть (-ошу́, -о́сишь) impf of **обнести́**; **~ся** have worn out one's clothes.

обня́ть (-ниму́, -ни́мешь; о́бнял, -á, -о) pf (impf **обнима́ть**) embrace; clasp; **~ся** embrace; hug one another.

обо prep.

обобра́ть (оберу́, -рёшь; обра́л, -á, -о) pf (impf **обира́ть**) rob; pick.

обобща́ть impf, **обобщи́ть** (-щу́) pf generalize. **обобществи́ть** (-влю́) pf, **обобществля́ть** impf socialize; collectivize. **обобществле́ние** socialization; collectivization.

обобью́ etc.: see **обби́ть. обо́вью** etc.: see **обви́ть**

обогати́ть (-ащу́) pf, **обогаща́ть** impf enrich; **~ся** become rich; enrich o.s. **обогаще́ние** enrichment.

обогна́ть (обгоню́, -о́нишь; обогна́л, -á, -о) pf (impf **обгоня́ть**) pass; outstrip.

обогну́ть (-ну́, -нёшь) pf (impf **огиба́ть**) round, skirt; bend round.

обогрева́тель m heater. **обогрева́ть** impf, **обогре́ть** (-е́ю) pf heat, warm; **~ся** warm up.

о́бод (pl -о́дья, -ьев) rim. **ободо́к** (-дка́) thin rim, narrow border.

обо́дранный ragged. **ободра́ть** (обдеру́, -рёшь; -ал, -á, -о) pf (impf **обдира́ть**) skin, flay; peel; fleece.

ободре́ние encouragement, reassurance. **ободри́тельный** encouraging, reassuring. **ободри́ть** pf, **ободря́ть** impf encourage, reassure; **~ся** cheer up, take heart.

обожа́ть impf adore.

обожгу́ etc.: see **обже́чь**

обожестви́ть (-влю́) pf, **обожествля́ть** impf deify.

обожжённый (-ён, -ена́) burnt, scorched.

обо́з string of vehicles; transport.

обозва́ть (обзову́, -вёшь; -ал, -á, -о) pf (impf **обзыва́ть**) call; call names.

обозлённый (-ён, -á) angered, embittered. **обозли́ть** pf, **озли́ть** pf anger; embitter; **~ся** get angry.

обозна́ться pf mistake s.o. for s.o. else.

обознача́ть impf, **обозна́чить** (-чу) pf mean; mark; **~ся** appear, reveal o.s. **обозначе́ние** sign, symbol.

обозрева́тель m reviewer; columnist. **обозрева́ть** impf, **обозре́ть** (-рю́) pf survey. **обозре́ние** survey; review; revue. **обозри́мый** visible.

обо́и (-ев) pl wallpaper.

обо́йма (gen pl -о́йм) cartridge clip.

обойти́ (-йду́, -йдёшь; -ошёл, -ошла́) pf (impf **обходи́ть**) go round; pass; avoid; pass over;

~сь manage, make do; **+с+**instr treat.

обокра́сть (обкраду́, -дёшь) pf (impf **обкра́дывать**) rob.

оболо́чка casing; membrane; cover, envelope, jacket; shell.

обольсти́тель m seducer. **обольсти́тельный** seductive. **обольсти́ть** (-льщу́) pf, обольща́ть impf seduce. **обольще́ние** seduction; delusion.

оболью́ etc.: see **обли́ть**

обомру́ etc.: see **обмере́ть**

обоня́ние (sense of) smell. **обоня́тельный** olfactory.

обопру́ etc.: see **опере́ть**

обора́чивать(ся impf of **оберну́ть(ся, обороти́ть(ся**

обо́рванный torn, ragged. **оборва́ть** (-ву́, -вёшь; -а́л, -а́, -о) pf (impf **обрыва́ть**) tear off; break; snap; cut short; **~ся** break; snap; fall; stop suddenly.

обо́рка frill, flounce.

оборо́на defence. **оборони́тельный** defensive. **обороня́ть** pf, **обороня́ть** impf defend; **~ся** defend o.s. **оборо́нный** defensive, defensive.

оборо́т turn; revolution; circulation; turnover; back; **~ ре́чи** (turn of) phrase; **смотри́ на ~е** P.T.O. **обороти́ть** (-рочу́, -ро́тишь) pf (impf **обора́чивать**) turn; **~ся** turn (round); +instr or в+acc turn into. **оборо́тный** circulating; reverse; **~ капита́л** working capital.

обору́дование equipping; equipment. **обору́довать** impf & pf equip.

обоснова́ние basing; basis; ground. **обосно́ванный** well-founded. **обоснова́ть** (-ну́ю) pf, **обосно́вывать** impf ground, base; substantiate. **~ся** settle down.

обосо́бленный isolated, solitary.

обостре́ние aggravation. **обострённый** keen; strained; sharp, pointed. **обостри́ть** pf, **обостря́ть** impf sharpen; strain; aggravate; **~ся** become strained; be aggravated; become acute.

оботру́ etc.: see **отере́ть**

обо́чина verge; shoulder, edge.

обошёл etc.: see **обойти́**. **обошью́** etc.: see **обши́ть**

обою́дный mutual, reciprocal.

обраба́тывать impf, **обрабо́тать** pf cultivate; work, work up; treat, process. **обрабо́тка** working (up); processing; cultivation.

об|ра́довать(ся pf.

о́браз shape, form; image; manner; way; icon; **гла́вным ~ом** mainly; **таки́м ~ом** thus. **образе́ц** (-зца́) model; pattern; sample. **о́бразный** graphic; figurative. **образова́ние** formation; education. **образо́ванный** educated. **образова́тельный** educational. **образова́ть** impf & pf, **образо́вывать** impf form; **~ся** form; arise; turn out well.

образу́мить (-млю) pf bring to reason; **~ся** see reason.

образцо́вый model. **обра́зчик** specimen, sample.

обра́мить (-млю) pf, **обрамля́ть** impf frame.

обраста́ть impf, **обрасти́** (-ту́, -тёшь; -ро́с, -ла́) pf be overgrown.

обрати́мый reversible, convertible. **обраща́ть** (-ащу́) pf, **обраща́ть** impf turn; convert; **~ внима́ние на+**acc pay or draw attention to; **~ся** turn; appeal;

apply; address; **+в**+*acc* turn into; **+с**+*instr* treat; handle. **обра́тно** *adv* back; backwards; conversely; **~ пропорциона́льный** inversely proportional. **обра́тный** reverse; return; opposite; inverse. **обраще́ние** appeal, address; conversion; (**+с**+*instr*) treatment (of); handling (of); use (of).

обре́з edge; sawn-off gun; **в ~**+*gen* only just enough. **обре́зать** (-е́жу) *pf*, **обреза́ть** *impf* cut (off); clip, trim; pare; prune; circumcise; **~ся** cut o.s. **обре́зок** (-зка) scrap; *pl* ends; clippings.

обрека́ть *impf of* **обре́чь**. **обреку́** *etc.: see* **обре́чь**. **обрёк** *etc.: see* **обрести́**

обремени́тельный onerous. **обремени́ть** *pf*, **обременя́ть** *impf* burden.

обрести́ (-ету́, -етёшь; -рёл, -а́) *pf*, **обрета́ть** *impf* find.

обрече́ние doom. **обречённый** doomed. **обре́чь** (-еку́, -ечёшь; -ёк, -ла́) *pf* (*impf* **обрека́ть**) doom.

обрисова́ть *pf*, **обрисо́вывать** *impf* outline, depict; **~ся** appear (in outline).

оброни́ть (-ню́, -нишь) *pf* drop; let drop.

обро́с *etc.: see* **обрасти́**

обруба́ть *impf*, **обруби́ть** (-блю́, -бишь) *pf* chop off; cut off. **обру́бок** (-бка) stump.

обруга́ть *pf*.

о́бруч (*pl* -и, -е́й) hoop. **обруча́льный** engagement; **~ое кольцо́** betrothal ring, wedding ring. **обручи́ть** (-чу́) betroth; **~ся** +с+*instr* become engaged to. **обруче́ние** engagement.

обру́шивать *impf*, **обру́шить** (-шу) *pf* bring down; **~ся** come down, collapse.

обры́в precipice. **обрыва́ть(ся** *impf of* **оборва́ть(ся. обры́вок** (-вка) scrap; snatch.

обры́згать *pf*, **обры́згивать** *impf* splash; sprinkle.

обрю́зглый flabby.

обря́д rite, ceremony.

обсервато́рия observatory.

обслу́живание service; maintenance. **обслу́живать** *impf*, **обслужи́ть** (-жу́, -жишь) *pf* serve; operate.

обсле́дование inspection. **обсле́дователь** *m* inspector. **обсле́довать** *impf & pf* inspect.

обсо́хнуть (-ну; -ох) *pf* (*impf* **обсыха́ть**) dry (out).

обста́вить (-влю) *pf*, **обставля́ть** *impf* surround; furnish; arrange. **обстано́вка** furniture; situation, conditions; set.

обстоя́тельный thorough, reliable; detailed. **обстоя́тельство** circumstance. **обстоя́ть** (-ои́т) *impf* be; go; **как обстои́т де́ло?** how is it going?

обстре́л firing, fire; **под ~ом** under fire. **обстре́ливать** *impf*, **обстреля́ть** *pf* fire at; bombard.

обступа́ть *impf*, **обступи́ть** (-у́пит) *pf* surround.

обсуди́ть (-ужу́, -у́дишь) *pf*, **обсужда́ть** *impf* discuss. **обсужде́ние** discussion.

обсчита́ть *pf*, **обсчи́тывать** *impf* shortchange; **~ся** miscount, miscalculate.

обсы́пать (-плю) *pf*, **обсыпа́ть** *impf* sprinkle.

обсыха́ть *impf of* **обсо́хнуть**. **обта́чивать** *impf of* **обточи́ть**. **обтека́емый** streamlined.

обтере́ть (оботру́, -трёшь; обтёр) *pf* (*impf* **обтира́ть**) wipe; rub; **~ся** dry o.s.; sponge down.

о(б)теса́ть (-ешу́, -е́шешь), **о(б)тёсывать** *impf* rough-hew; teach good manners to; trim.

обтира́ть(ся *pf of* **обтере́ть(ся**

обточи́ть (-чу́, -чишь) *pf* (*impf* **обта́чивать**) grind; machine.

обтрёпанный frayed; shabby.

обтяга́ть *impf*, **обтяну́ть** (-ну́, -нешь) *pf* cover; fit close. **обтя́жка** cover; skin; **в обтя́жку** close-fitting.

обува́ть(ся *impf of* **обу́ть(ся**. **о́бувь** footwear; boots, shoes.

обу́гливать *impf*, **обу́глить** *pf* char; carbonize; **~ся** char, become charred.

обу́за burden.

обузда́ть *pf*, **обу́здывать** *impf* bridle, curb.

обурева́ть *impf* grip; possess.

обусло́вить (-влю) *pf*, **обусло́вливать** *impf* cause; **+instr** make conditional on; **~ся +instr** be conditional on; depend on.

обу́тый shod. **обу́ть** (-у́ю) *pf* (*impf* **обува́ть**) put shoes on; **~ся** put on one's shoes.

о́бух butt, back.

обуча́ть *impf*, **об|учи́ть** (-чу́, -чишь) *pf* teach; train; **~ся +dat** *or in* learn. **обуче́ние** teaching; training.

обхва́т girth; **в ~е** in circumference. **обхвати́ть** (-ачу́, -а́тишь) *pf*, **обхва́тывать** *impf* embrace; clasp.

обхо́д round(s); roundabout way; bypass. **обходи́тельный** courteous; pleasant. **обходи́ть(ся** (-ожу́(сь, -о́дишь(ся)

impf of **обойти́(сь. обхо́дный** roundabout.

обша́ривать *impf*, **обша́рить** *pf* rummage through, ransack.

обшива́ть *impf of* **обши́ть. обши́вка** edging; trimming; boarding, panelling; plating. **обши́рный** extensive; vast.

обши́ть (обошью́, -шьёшь) *pf* (*impf* **обшива́ть**) edge; trim; make outfit(s) for; plank.

обшла́г (-а́; *pl* -а́, -о́в) cuff.

обща́ться *impf* associate.

обще- *in comb* common(ly), general(ly). **общедосту́пный** moderate in price; popular. **~жи́тие** hostel. **~изве́стный** generally known. **~наро́дный** national, public. **~образова́тельный** of general education. **~при́нятый** generally accepted. **~сою́зный** *hist* All-Union. **~челове́ческий** common to all mankind; universal.

обще́ние contact; social intercourse. **обще́ственность** public; public opinion; community. **обще́ственный** social, public; voluntary. **о́бщество** society; company.

о́бщий general; common; **в ~ем** on the whole, in general. **общи́на** community; commune.

об|щипа́ть (-плю́, -плешь) *pf*.

общи́тельный sociable. **о́бщность** community.

объеда́ть(ся *impf of* **объ|е́сть(ся**

объедине́ние unification; merger; union, association. **объединённый** (-ён, -а́) united. **объедини́тельный** unifying. **объедини́ть** *pf*, **объединя́ть** *impf* unite; join; combine; **~ся** unite.

объе́дки (-ов) pl leftovers, scraps.

объе́зд riding round; detour.

объе́здить (-зжу, -здишь) pf (impf **объезжа́ть**) travel over; break in.

объезжа́ть impf of **объе́здить**, **объе́хать**

объе́кт object; objective; establishment, works. **объекти́в** lens. **объекти́вность** objectivity. **объекти́вный** objective.

объём volume; scope. **объёмный** by volume, volumetric.

объе́сть (-ем, -ешь, -е́ст, -еди́м) pf (impf **объеда́ть**) gnaw (round), nibble; ~ся overeat.

объе́хать (-е́ду) pf (impf **объезжа́ть**) drive or go round; go past; travel over.

объяви́ть (-влю́, -вишь) pf, **объявля́ть** impf declare, announce; ~ся turn up; +instr declare o.s. **объявле́ние** declaration, announcement; advertisement.

объясне́ние explanation. **объясни́мый** explainable. **объясни́ть** pf, **объясня́ть** impf explain; ~ся be explained; make o.s. understood; +c+instr have it out with.

объя́тие embrace.

обыва́тель m Philistine. **обыва́тельский** narrow-minded.

обыгра́ть pf, **обы́грывать** impf beat (in a game).

обы́денный ordinary; everyday.

обыкнове́ние habit. **обыкнове́нно** adv usually. **обыкнове́нный** usual; ordinary.

обы́ск search. **обыска́ть** (-ыщу́, -ы́щешь) pf, **обы́скивать** impf search.

обы́чай custom; usage. **обы́чно** adv usually. **обы́чный** usual.

обя́занность duty; responsibility. **обя́занный** (+inf) obliged; +dat indebted to (+instr for).

обяза́тельно adv without fail. **обяза́тельный** obligatory. **обяза́тельство** obligation; commitment. **обяза́ть** (-яжу́, -я́жешь) pf, **обя́зывать** impf bind; commit; oblige; ~ся pledge o.s., undertake.

ова́л oval. **ова́льный** oval.

ова́ция ovation.

овдове́ть (-е́ю) pf become a widow, widower.

овёс (овса́) oats.

ове́чка dim of овца́; harmless person.

овладева́ть impf, **овладе́ть** (-е́ю) pf +instr seize; capture; master.

о́вод (pl -ы or -á) gadfly.

о́вощ (pl -и, -е́й) vegetable. **овощно́й** vegetable.

овра́г ravine, gully.

овся́нка oatmeal; porridge. **овся́ный** oat, oatmeal.

овца́ (pl -ы, ове́ц, о́вцам) sheep; ewe. **овча́рка** sheep-dog. **овчи́на** sheepskin.

ога́рок (-рка) candle-end.

огиба́ть impf of **обогну́ть**

оглавле́ние table of contents.

огласи́ть (-ашу́) pf, **оглаша́ть** impf announce; fill (with sound); ~ся resound. **огла́ска** publicity. **оглаше́ние** publication.

огло́бля (gen pl -бель) shaft.

о|гло́хнуть (-ну; -о́х) pf of **гло́хнуть**

оглуша́ть impf, **оглуши́ть** (-шу́) pf deafen; stun. **оглуши́тельный** deafening.

огляде́ть (-яжу́) pf, **огля́ды-**

вать *impf*, **огляну́ть** (-ну́, -нешь) *pf* look round; look over; **~ся** look round; look back. **огля́дка** looking back.

огнево́й fire; fiery. **о́гненный** fiery. **огнеопа́сный** inflammable. **огнеприпа́сы** (-ов) *pl* ammunition. **огнесто́йкий** fireproof. **огнестре́льный**: **~ое ору́жие** firearm(s). **огнетуши́тель** *m* fire-extinguisher. **огнеупо́рный** fire-resistant.

ого́ *int* oho!

огова́ривать *impf*, **оговори́ть** *pf* slander; stipulate (for); **~ся** make a proviso; make a slip (of the tongue). **огово́р** slander. **огово́рка** reservation, proviso; slip of the tongue.

оголённый bare, nude. **оголи́ть** *pf* (*impf* **оголя́ть**) bare; strip; **~ся** strip o.s.; become exposed.

оголя́ть(ся *impf of* **оголи́ть(ся**

огонёк (-нька́) (*small*) light; zest. **ого́нь** (огня́) *m* fire; light.

огора́живать *impf*, **огороди́ть** (-рожу́, -ро́ди́шь) *pf* fence in, enclose; **~ся** fence o.s. in. **огоро́д** kitchen-garden. **огоро́дный** kitchen-garden.

огорча́ть *impf*, **огорчи́ть** (-чу́) *pf* grieve, pain; **~ся** grieve, be distressed. **огорче́ние** grief; chagrin.

о|**гра́бить** (-блю) *pf*. **ограбле́ние** robbery; burglary. **огра́да** fence. **огради́ть** (-ажу́) *pf*, **огражда́ть** *impf* guard, protect.

ограниче́ние limitation, restriction. **ограни́ченный** limited. **ограни́чивать** *impf*, **ограни́чить** (-чу) *pf* limit, restrict; **~ся** +*instr* limit *or* confine o.s. to; be limited to.

огро́мный huge; enormous.

о|**грубе́ть** (-ею) *pf*.

огры́зок (-зка) bit, end; stub.

огуре́ц (-рца́) cucumber.

ода́лживать *impf of* **одолжи́ть**

одарённый gifted. **ода́ривать** *impf*, **одари́ть** *pf*, **одаря́ть** *pf* give presents (to); +*instr* endow (with).

одева́ть(ся *impf of* **оде́ть(ся**

оде́жда clothes; clothing.

одеколо́н eau-de-Cologne.

одели́ть *pf*, **оделя́ть** *impf* (+*instr*) present (with); endow (with).

оде́ну *etc.: see* **оде́ть. одёргивать** *impf of* **одёрнуть**

о|**деревене́ть** (-ею) *pf*.

одержа́ть (-жу́, -жишь) *pf*, **оде́рживать** *impf* gain. **одержи́мый** possessed.

одёрнуть (-ну) *pf* (*impf* **одёргивать**) pull down, straighten.

оде́тый dressed; clothed. **оде́ть** (-е́ну) *pf* (*impf* **одева́ть**) dress; clothe; **~ся** dress o.s. **одея́ло** blanket. **одея́ние** garb, attire.

оди́н (одного́), **одна́** (одно́й), **одно́** (одного́); *pl* **одни́** (одни́х) one; a, an; a certain; alone; only; nothing but; same; **оди́н и тот же** the same thing; **оди́н на оди́н** in private; **оди́н раз** once; **одни́м сло́вом** in a word; **по одному́** one by one.

одина́ковый identical, the same, equal.

одиннадцатый eleventh. **одиннадцать** eleven.

одино́кий solitary; lonely; single. **одино́чество** solitude; loneliness. **одино́чка** *m & f* (one) person alone. **одино́чный** individual; one-man; single; **~ое заключе́ние** solitary confinement.

одича́лый wild.

одна́жды adv once; one day; once upon a time.

одна́ко conj however.

одно- in comb single, one; uni-, mono-, homo-. **однобо́кий** one-sided. **~вре́менно** adv simultaneously, at the same time. **~вре́менный** simultaneous. **~зву́чный** monotonous. **~зна́чащий** synonymous. **~зна́чный** synonymous; one-digit. **~и́менный** of the same name. **~кла́ссник** classmate. **~кле́точный** unicellular. **~кра́тный** single. **~ле́тний** one-year; annual. **~ме́стный** single-seater. **~обра́зие**, **~обра́зность** monotony. **~обра́зный** monotonous. **~ро́дность** homogeneity, uniformity. **~ро́дный** homogeneous; similar. **~сторо́нний** one-sided; unilateral; one-way. **~фами́лец** (-льца) person of the same name. **~цве́тный** one-colour; monochrome. **~эта́жный** one-storeyed.

одобре́ние approval. **одобри́тельный** approving. **одо́брить** pf, **одобря́ть** impf approve (of).

одолева́ть impf, **одоле́ть** (-е́ю) pf overcome.

одолжа́ть impf, **одолжи́ть** (-жу́) pf lend; **+у**+gen borrow from. **одолже́ние** favour.

о|дряхле́ть (-е́ю) pf.

одува́нчик dandelion.

оду́маться pf, **оду́мываться** impf change one's mind.

одуре́лый stupid. **о|дуре́ть** (-е́ю) pf.

одурма́нивать impf, **о|дурма́нить** pf stupefy. **одуря́ть** impf stupefy.

одухотворённый inspired; spiritual. **одухотвори́ть** pf, **одухотворя́ть** impf inspire.

одушеви́ть (-влю́) pf, **одушевля́ть** impf animate. **одушевле́ние** animation.

оды́шка shortness of breath.

ожере́лье necklace.

ожесточа́ть impf, **ожесточи́ть** (-чу́) pf embitter, harden. **ожесточе́ние** bitterness. **ожесточённый** bitter; hard.

ожива́ть impf of **ожи́ть**

оживи́ть (-влю́) pf, **оживля́ть** impf revive; enliven; **~ся** become animated. **оживле́ние** animation; reviving; enlivening. **оживлённый** animated, lively.

ожида́ние expectation; waiting. **ожида́ть** impf +gen or acc wait for; expect.

ожире́ние obesity. **о|жире́ть** (-е́ю) pf.

ожи́ть (-иву́, -ивёшь; о́жил, -а́, -о) pf (impf **ожива́ть**) come to life, revive.

ожо́г burn, scald.

озабо́ченность preoccupation; anxiety. **озабо́ченный** preoccupied; anxious.

озагла́вить (-влю) pf, **озагла́вливать** impf entitle; head.

озада́чивать impf, **озада́чить** (-чу) pf perplex, puzzle.

озари́ть pf, **озаря́ть** impf light up, illuminate; **~ся** light up.

оздорови́тельный бег jogging. **оздоровле́ние** sanitation.

озелени́ть pf, **озеленя́ть** impf plant (with trees etc.).

о́зеро (pl озёра) lake.

ози́мые sb winter crops. **ози́мый** winter. **о́зимь** winter crop.

озира́ться *impf* look round; look back.

озли́ть(ся: *see* обозли́ть(ся

о|зло́бить (-блю), озлобля́ть *impf* embitter; ~ся grow bitter. озлобле́ние bitterness, animosity. озло́бленный embittered.

о|знако́мить (-млю), ознакомля́ть *impf* c+*instr* acquaint with; ~ся c+*instr* familiarize o.s. with.

ознаменова́ть *pf*, ознаменовывать *impf* mark; celebrate. означа́ть *impf* mean, signify.

озно́б shivering, chill.

озо́н ozone.

озо́рник (-á) mischief-maker. озо́рный naughty, mischievous. озо́рство mischief.

озя́бнуть (-ну; озя́б) *pf* be cold, be freezing.

ой *int* oh.

оказа́ть (-ажу́, -а́жешь) *pf* (*impf* ока́зывать) render, provide, show; ~ся turn out, prove; find o.s., be found.

ока́зия unexpected event, funny thing.

ока́зывать(ся *impf of* оказа́ть(ся

окамене́лость fossil. окамене́лый fossilized; petrified. о|камене́ть (-е́ю) *pf*.

оканто́вка mount.

ока́нчивать(ся *impf of* око́нчить(ся. ока́пывать(ся *impf of* окопа́ть(ся

окая́нный damned, cursed.

океа́н ocean. океа́нский ocean; oceanic.

окида́ть *impf*, оки́нуть (-ну) *pf*; ~ взгля́дом take in at a glance, glance over.

о́кисел (-сла) oxide. окисле́ние oxidation. о́кись oxide.

оккупа́нт invader. оккупа́ция occupation. оккупи́ровать *impf & pf* occupy.

окла́д salary scale; (basic) pay.

оклевета́ть (-ещу́, -е́щешь) *pf* slander.

окле́ивать *impf*, окле́ить *pf* cover; paste over; ~ обо́ями paper.

окно́ (*pl* о́кна) window.

о́ко (*pl* о́чи, оче́й) eye.

око́вы (око́в) *pl* fetters.

околдова́ть *pf*, околдо́вывать *impf* bewitch.

о́коло *adv & prep+gen* by; close (to); near; around; about.

око́льный roundabout.

око́нный window.

оконча́ние end; conclusion, termination; ending. оконча́тельный final. око́нчить (-чу) *pf* (*impf* ока́нчивать) finish, end; ~ся finish, end.

око́п trench. окопа́ть *pf* (*impf* ока́пывать) dig round; ~ся entrench o.s., dig in. око́пный trench.

око́рок (*pl* -á, -о́в) ham, gammon.

окочене́лый stiff with cold. о|кочене́ть (-е́ю) *pf*.

око́шечко, око́шко (*small*) window.

окра́ина outskirts, outlying districts.

о|кра́сить (-а́шу) *pf*, окра́шивать *impf* paint, colour; dye. окра́ска painting; colouring; dyeing; colouration.

о|кре́пнуть (-ну) *pf*. о|крести́ть(ся (-ещу́(сь, -е́стишь(ся) *pf*.

окре́стность environs. окре́стный neighbouring.

óкрик hail; shout. **окри́кивать** *impf*, **окри́кнуть** (-ну) *pf* hail, call, shout to.

окровáвленный blood-stained.

óкруг (*pl* -á) district. **окру́га** neighbourhood. **округли́ть**, **округля́ть** *impf* round; round off. **окру́глый** rounded. **окружа́ть** *impf*, **окружи́ть** (-жу́) *pf* surround; encircle. **окружáю-щий** surrounding; ~ee *sb* environment; ~ие *sb* associates. **окруже́ние** encirclement; environment. **окружнóй** district. **окру́жность** circumference.

окрыли́ть, **окрыля́ть** *impf* inspire, encourage.

октáва octave.

октáн octane.

октя́брь (-я́) *m* October. **октя́брьский** October.

окули́ст oculist.

окунáть *impf*, **окуну́ть** (-ну́, -нёшь) *pf* dip; ~ся dip; plunge; become absorbed.

óкунь (*pl* -и, -éй) *m* perch.

окупáть *impf*, **окупи́ть** (-плю́, -пишь) *pf* compensate, repay; ~ся be repaid, pay for itself.

окýрок (-рка) cigarette-end.

окýтать *pf*, **окýтывать** *impf* wrap up; shroud, cloak.

окýчивать *impf*, **окýчить** (-чу) *pf* earth up.

олáдья (*gen pl* -ий) fritter; drop-scone.

оледене́лый frozen. **о**|**ледене́ть** (-éю) *pf*.

оле́ний deer, deer's; **оле́нина** venison. **олéнь** *m* deer; reindeer.

оли́ва olive. **оли́вковый** olive; olive-coloured.

олигáрхия oligarchy.

олимпиáда olympiad; Olym-

pics. **олимпи́йский** Olympic; Olympian; ~ие и́гры Olympic games.

оли́фа drying oil (*e.g. linseed oil*).

олицетворе́ние personification; embodiment. **олицетвори́ть** *pf*, **олицетворя́ть** *impf* personify, embody.

óлово tin. **оловя́нный** tin.

ом ohm.

омáр lobster.

омерзе́ние loathing. **омерзи́тельный** loathsome.

омертве́лый stiff, numb; necrotic. **о**|**мертве́ть** (-éю) *pf*.

омле́т omelette.

омоложе́ние rejuvenation.

омóним homonym.

омóю *etc.*: *see* **омы́ть**

омрачáть *impf*, **омрачи́ть** (-чу́) *pf* darken, cloud.

óмут whirlpool; maelstrom.

омывáть *impf*, **омы́ть** (омóю) *pf* wash; ~ся be washed.

он (егó, ему́, им, о нём) *pron* he. **онá** (её, ей, ей (éю), о ней) *pron* she.

ондáтра musk-rat.

онеме́лый numb. **о**|**неме́ть** (-éю) *pf*.

они́ (их, им, и́ми, о них) *pron* they. **онó** (егó, ему́, им, о нём) *pron* it; this, that.

опадáть *impf* of **опáсть**.

опáздывать *impf* of **опоздáть**

опáла disgrace.

о|**пали́ть** *pf*.

опáловый opal.

опáлубка casing.

опасáться *impf* +*gen* fear; avoid, keep off. **опасéние** fear; apprehension.

опáсность danger; peril. **опáсный** dangerous.

опа́сть (-адёт) *pf* (*impf* **опада́ть**) fall, fall off; subside.

опе́ка guardianship; trusteeship. **опека́емый** *sb* ward. **опека́ть** *impf* be guardian of; take care of. **опеку́н** (-а́), **-у́нша** guardian; tutor; trustee.

о́пера opera.

операти́вный efficient; operative, surgical; operation(s), operational. **опера́тор** operator; cameraman. **операцио́нный** operating; ~**ая** *sb* operating theatre. **опера́ция** operation.

опереди́ть (-режу́) *pf*, **опережа́ть** *impf* outstrip, leave behind.

опере́ние plumage.

опере́тта, **-е́тка** operetta.

опере́ть (обопру́, -рёшь; опёр, -ла́) *pf* (*impf* **опира́ть**) +*o*+*acc* lean against; ~**ся** на *or* *o*+*acc* lean on, lean against.

опери́ровать *impf* & *pf* operate on; operate, act; +*instr* use.

о́перный opera; operatic.

о|печа́лить(ся *pf*.

опеча́тать *pf* (*impf* **опеча́тывать**) seal up.

опеча́тка misprint.

опеча́тывать *impf* *of* **опеча́тать**

опе́шить (-шу) *pf* be taken aback.

опи́лки (-лок) *pf* sawdust; filings.

опира́ть(ся *impf* *of* **опере́ть(ся**

описа́ние description. **описа́тельный** descriptive. **описа́ть** (-ишу́, -и́шешь) *pf*, **опи́сывать** *impf* describe; ~**ся** make a slip of the pen. **опи́ска** slip of the pen. **о́пись** inventory.

о́пиум opium.

опла́кать *impf* *of* **опла́кивать**

опла́кивать *impf* mourn for; bewail.

опла́та payment. **оплати́ть** (-ачу́, -а́тишь) *pf*, **опла́чивать** *impf* pay (for).

оплачу́ *etc.: see* **опла́кать**. **оплачу́** *etc.: see* **оплати́ть**.

оплеу́ха slap in the face.

оплодотвори́ть *pf*, **оплодотворя́ть** *impf* impregnate; fertilize.

о|пломбирова́ть *pf*.

опло́т stronghold, bulwark.

опло́шность blunder, mistake.

оповести́ть (-ещу́) *pf*, **оповеща́ть** *impf* notify. **оповеще́ние** notification.

опозда́вший *sb* late-comer. **опозда́ние** lateness; delay. **опозда́ть** (*impf* **опа́здывать**) be late; +**на**+*acc* miss.

опознава́тельный distinguishing; ~ **знак** landmark. **опознава́ть** (-наю́, -наёшь) *impf*, **опозна́ть** *pf* identify. **опозна́ние** identification.

о|позо́рить(ся *pf*.

оползать *impf*, **оползти́** (-зёт; -о́лз, -ла́) *pf* slip, slide. **о́ползень** (-зня) *m* landslide.

ополче́ние militia.

опо́мниться *pf* come to one's senses.

опо́р: во весь ~ at full speed.

опо́ра support; pier; **то́чка опо́ры** fulcrum, foothold.

опора́жнивать *impf* *of* **опоро́жни́ть**

опо́рный support, supporting; supported; bearing.

опоро́жни́ть *pf*, **опорожня́ть** *impf* (*impf* *also* **опора́жнивать**) empty.

о|поро́чить (-чу) *pf*.

опохмели́ться *pf*, **опохмеля́ться** *impf* take a hair of the

dog that bit you.

опо́шлить (-шлю́), **опошля́ть** *impf* vulgarize, debase.

опоя́сать (-я́шу) *pf*, **опоя́сывать** *impf* gird; girdle.

оппозицио́нный opposition. **оппози́ция** *n* opposition.

оппортуни́зм opportunism.

опра́ва setting, mounting; spectacle frames.

оправда́ние justification; excuse; acquittal. **оправда́тельный пригово́р** verdict of not guilty. **оправда́ть** *pf*, **опра́вдывать** *impf* justify; excuse; acquit; ~**ся** justify o.s.; be justified.

опра́вить (-влю) *pf*, **оправля́ть** *impf* set right, adjust; mount; ~**ся** put one's dress in order; recover; +**от**+*gen* get over.

опра́шивать *impf of* **опроси́ть**

определе́ние definition; determination; decision. **определённый** definite; certain. **определи́мый** definable. **определи́ть** *pf*, **определя́ть** *impf* define; determine; appoint; ~**ся** be formed; be determined; find one's position.

опрове́рга́ть *impf*, **опрове́ргнуть** (-ну; -вéрг) *pf* refute, disprove. **опроверже́ние** refutation; denial.

опроки́дывать *impf*, **опроки́нуть** (-ну) *pf* overturn; topple; ~**ся** overturn; capsize.

опроме́тчивый rash, hasty.

опро́с (cross-)examination; (opinion) poll. **опроси́ть** (-ошу́, -о́сишь) *pf* (*impf* **опра́шивать**) question; (cross-)examine. **опро́сный лист** questionnaire.

опры́скать *pf*, **опры́скивать** *impf* sprinkle; spray.

опря́тный neat, tidy.

о́птик optician. **о́птика** optics. **опти́ческий** optic, optical.

оптима́льный optimal. **оптими́зм** optimism. **оптими́ст** optimist. **оптимисти́ческий** optimistic.

опто́вый wholesale. **о́птом** *adv* wholesale.

опубликова́ние publication; promulgation. **о|публикова́ть** *pf*, **опублико́вывать** *impf* publish; promulgate.

опуска́ть(ся *impf of* **опусти́ть(ся**

опусте́лый deserted. **о|пусте́ть** (-е́ет) *pf*.

опусти́ть (-ущу́, -у́стишь) *pf* (*impf* **опуска́ть**) lower; let down; turn down; omit; post; ~**ся** lower o.s.; sink; fall; go down; go to pieces.

опустоша́ть *impf*, **опустоши́ть** (-шу́) *pf* devastate. **опустоше́ние** devastation. **опустоши́тельный** devastating.

опу́тать *pf*, **опу́тывать** *impf* entangle; ensnare.

опуха́ть *impf*, **о|пу́хнуть** (-ну; опу́х) *pf* swell, swell up. **о́пухоль** swelling; tumour.

опу́шка edge of a forest; trimming.

опущу́ *etc.: see* **опусти́ть**

опыле́ние pollination. **опыли́ть** *pf*, **опыля́ть** *impf* pollinate.

о́пыт experience; experiment. **о́пытный** experienced; experimental.

опьяне́ние intoxication. **о|пьяне́ть** (-е́ю) *pf*, **о|пьяни́ть** *pf*, **опьяня́ть** *impf* intoxicate, make drunk.

опя́ть *adv* again.

ора́ва crowd, horde.

ора́кул oracle.

орангута́нг orangutan.

ора́нжевый orange. **оранже-ре́я** greenhouse, conservatory.

ора́тор orator. **орато́рия** oratorio.

ора́ть (ору́, орёшь) *impf* yell.

орби́та orbit; (eye-)socket.

о́рган[1] organ; body. **орга́н**[2] (*mus*) organ. **организа́тор** organizer. **организацио́нный** organization(al). **организа́ция** organization. **органи́зм** organism. **организо́ванный** organized. **организова́ть** *impf & pf* (*pf also* c∼) organize; ∼ся be organized; organize. **органи́ческий** organic.

о́ргия orgy.

орда́ (*pl* -ы) horde.

о́рден (*pl* -а́) order.

о́рдер (*pl* -а́) order; warrant; writ.

ордина́та ordinate.

ордина́тор house-surgeon.

орёл (орла́) eagle; ∼ и́ли ре́шка? heads or tails?

орео́л halo.

оре́х nut, nuts; walnut. **оре́ховый** nut; walnut. **оре́шник** hazel; hazel-thicket.

оригина́л original; eccentric. **оригина́льный** original.

ориента́ция orientation. **ориенти́р** landmark; reference point. **ориенти́роваться** *impf & pf* orient o.s.; +на+*acc* head for; aim at. **ориентиро́вка** orientation. **ориентиро́вочный** reference; tentative; approximate.

орке́стр orchestra.

орли́ный eagle; aquiline.

орна́мент ornament; ornamental design.

о|**робе́ть** (-е́ю) *pf*.

ороси́тельный irrigation.

ороси́ть (-ошу́) *pf*, **ороша́ть** *impf* irrigate. **ороше́ние** irrigation; **поля́ ороше́ния** sewage farm.

ору́ *etc.*: *see* **ора́ть**

ору́дие instrument; tool; gun. **оруди́йный** gun. **ору́довать** *impf* +*instr* handle; run. **ору́жейный** arms; gun. **ору́жие** arm, arms; weapons.

орфографи́ческий orthographic(al). **орфогра́фия** orthography, spelling.

оса́ (*pl* -ы) wasp.

оса́да siege. **осади́ть**[1] (-ажу́) *pf* (*impf* **осажда́ть**) besiege.

осади́ть[2] (-ажу́, -а́дишь) *pf* (*impf* **оса́живать**) check; force back; rein in; take down a peg.

оса́дный siege.

оса́док (-дка) sediment; fall-out; after-taste; *pl* precipitation, fall-out. **оса́дочный** sedimentary.

осажда́ть *impf* of **осади́ть**[1]

оса́живать *impf* of **осади́ть**[2]. **осажу́** *see* **осади́ть**[1,2]

оса́нка carriage, bearing.

осва́ивать(ся *impf* of **осво́ить(ся**

осведоми́тельный informative; information. **осве́домить** (-млю) *pf*, **осведомля́ть** *impf* inform; ∼ся о+*prep* inquire about, ask after. **осведомле́ние** notification. **осведомлённый** well-informed, knowledgeable.

освежа́ть *impf*, **освежи́ть** (-жу́) *pf* refresh; air. **освежи́тельный** refreshing.

освети́тельный illuminating. **освети́ть** (-ещу́) *pf*, **освеща́ть** *pf* light up; illuminate; throw light on; ∼ся light up. **освеще́-**

ние lighting, illumination.
освещённый (-ён, -á) lit.

о|свиде́тельствовать pf.

освиста́ть (-ищу́, -и́щешь), **освисты́вать** impf hiss (off); boo.

освободи́тель m liberator. **освободи́тельный** liberation, emancipation. **освободи́ть** (-ожу́) pf, **освобожда́ть** impf liberate; emancipate; dismiss; vacate; empty; **~ся** free o.s.; become free. **освобожде́ние** liberation; release; emancipation; vacation. **освобождённый** (-ён, -á) freed, free; exempt.

освое́ние mastery; opening up. **осво́ить** pf (impf осва́ивать) master; become familiar with; **~ся** familiarize o.s.

освяще́нный (-ён, -ена́) consecrated; sanctified; **~ века́ми** time-honoured.

оседа́ть impf of осе́сть

о|седла́ть pf, **осёдлывать** impf saddle.

осе́длый settled.

осека́ться impf of осе́чься

осёл (-сла́) donkey; ass.

осело́к (-лка́) touchstone; whetstone.

осени́ть pf (impf осеня́ть) overshadow; dawn upon.

осе́нний autumn(al). **о́сень** autumn. **о́сенью** adv in autumn.

осеня́ть impf of осени́ть

осе́сть (ося́ду; осе́л) pf (impf оседа́ть) settle; subside.

осётр (-á) sturgeon. **осетри́на** sturgeon.

осе́чка misfire. **осе́чься** (-еку́сь, -ечёшься; -ёкся, -екла́сь) pf (impf осека́ться) stop short.

оси́ливать impf, **оси́лить** pf overpower; master.

оси́на aspen.

о|си́пнуть (-ну; оси́п) get hoarse.

осироте́лый orphaned. **осироте́ть** (-е́ю) pf be orphaned.

оска́ливать impf, **о|ска́лить** pf; **~ зу́бы**, **~ся** bare one's teeth.

о|сканда́лить(ся pf.

оскверни́ть pf, **оскверня́ть** impf profane; defile.

оско́лок (-лка) splinter; fragment.

оско́мина bitter taste (in the mouth); **наби́ть оско́мину** set the teeth on edge.

оскорби́тельный insulting, abusive. **оскорби́ть** (-блю́) pf, **оскорбля́ть** impf insult; offend; **~ся** take offence. **оскорбле́ние** insult. **оскорблённый** (-ён, -á) insulted.

ослабева́ть impf, **о|слабе́ть** (-е́ю) pf weaken; slacken. **осла́бить** (-блю) pf, **ослабля́ть** impf weaken; slacken. **ослабле́ние** weakening; slackening; relaxation.

ослепи́тельный blinding, dazzling. **ослепи́ть** (-плю́) pf, **ослепля́ть** impf blind, dazzle. **ослепле́ние** blinding, dazzling; blindness. **о|сле́пнуть** (-ну; -е́п) pf.

осли́ный donkey; asinine. **осли́ца** she-ass.

осложне́ние complication. **осложни́ть** pf, **осложня́ть** impf complicate; **~ся** become complicated.

ослы́шаться (-шусь) pf mishear.

осма́тривать(ся impf of осмотре́ть(ся. **осме́ивать** impf of осмея́ть

о|смеле́ть (-е́ю). pf. **осмели́-**

ваться *impf*, **осме́литься** *pf* dare; venture.

осме́ять (-е́ю, -е́ешь) *pf* (*impf* **осме́ивать**) ridicule.

осмо́тр examination, inspection. **осмотре́ть** (-рю́, -ришь) *pf* (*impf* **осма́тривать**) examine, inspect; look round; **~ся** look round. **осмотри́тельный** circumspect.

осмы́сленный sensible, intelligent. **осмы́сливать** *impf*, **осмы́слить** *pf*, **осмысля́ть** *impf* interpret; comprehend.

оснасти́ть (-ащу́) *pf*, **оснаща́ть** *impf* fit out, equip. **осна́стка** rigging. **оснаще́ние** fitting out; equipment.

осно́ва base, basis, foundation; *pl* fundamentals; stem (*of a word*). **основа́ние** founding, foundation; base; basis; reason; **на како́м основа́нии?** on what grounds? **основа́тель** *m* founder. **основа́тельный** well-founded; solid; thorough. **основа́ть** (-ную́, -нуёшь) *pf*, **осно́вывать** *impf* found; base; **~ся** settle; be founded; be based. **основно́й** fundamental, basic; main; **в основно́м** in the main, on the whole. **основополо́жник** founder.

осо́ба person. **осо́бенно** *adv* especially. **осо́бенность** peculiarity; **в осо́бенности** in particular. **осо́бенный** special, particular, peculiar. **особня́к** (-а́) private residence; detached house. **особняко́м** *adv* by o.s. **осо́бо** *adv* apart; especially. **осо́бый** special; particular.

осознава́ть (-наю́, -наёшь) *impf*, **осозна́ть** *pf* realize.

осо́ка sedge.

о́спа smallpox; pock-marks.

оспа́ривать *impf*, **оспо́рить** *pf* dispute; contest.

о|**срами́ть(ся** -млю́(сь) *pf*. **оста-ва́ться** (-таю́сь, -таёшься) *impf of* **оста́ться**

ост (*naut*) east; east wind.

оста́вить (-влю) *pf*, **оставля́ть** *impf* leave; abandon; reserve.

остально́й the rest of; **~о́е** *sb* the rest; **~ы́е** *sb pl* the others.

остана́вливать(ся *impf of* **останови́ть(ся**

оста́нки (-ов) *pl* remains.

останови́ть (-влю́, -вишь) *pf* (*impf* **остана́вливать**) stop; restrain; **~ся** stop, halt; stay; +**на**+*prep* dwell on; settle on. **остано́вка** stop.

оста́ток (-тка) remainder; rest; residue; *pl* remains; leftovers. **оста́ться** (-а́нусь) *pf* (*impf* **оставáться**) remain; stay; *impers* it remains, it is necessary; **нам не оста́ётся ничего́ друго́го** we have no choice but.

остекли́ть *pf*, **остекля́ть** *impf* glaze.

остервене́ть *pf* become enraged.

остерега́ть *impf*, **остере́чь** (-регу́, -режёшь; -рёг, -ла́) *pf* warn; **~ся** (+*gen*) beware (of).

о́стов frame, framework; skeleton.

о|**столбене́ть** (-е́ю) *pf*

осторо́жно *adv* carefully; **~!** look out! **осторо́жность** care, caution. **осторо́жный** careful, cautious.

острига́ть(ся *impf of* **остри́чь(ся**

острие́ point; spike; (cutting) edge. **остри́ть**[1] *impf* sharpen. **остри́ть**[2] *impf* (*pf* **c~**) be witty.

о|**стри́чь** (-игу́, -ижёшь; -и́г) *pf*

(*impf also* остригáть) cut, clip; ∼ся have one's hair cut.

óстров (*pl* -á) island. **островóк** (-вкá) islet; ∼ **безопáсности** (traffic) island.

острóта[1] witticism. **острота**[2] sharpness; keenness; pungency.

остроýмие wit. **остроýмный** witty.

óстрый (остр, -á, -о) sharp; pointed; acute; keen. **остря́** (-á) wit.

о|студи́ть (-ужý, -ýдишь) *pf*, **остужáть** *impf* cool.

оступáть *impf of* **оступи́ться**

оступáться *impf*, **оступи́ться** (-плю́сь, -пишься) *pf* stumble.

остывáть *impf of* **осты́ть** (-ы́ну) *pf* get cold; cool down.

осуди́ть (-ужý, -ýдишь) *pf*, **осуждáть** *impf* condemn; convict. **осуждéние** condemnation; conviction. **осуждённый** (-ён, -á) condemned, convicted, *sb* convict.

осýнуться (-нусь) *pf* grow thin, become drawn.

осушáть *impf*, **осуши́ть** (-шý, -шишь) *pf* drain; dry. **осушéние** drainage.

осуществи́мый feasible. **осуществи́ть** (-влю́) *pf*, **осуществля́ть** *impf* realize; bring about; accomplish; ∼ся be fulfilled, come true. **осуществлéние** realization; accomplishment.

осчастли́вить (-влю) *pf*, **осчастли́вливать** *impf* make happy.

осы́пать (-плю) *pf*, **осыпáть** *impf* strew; shower; ∼ся crumble; fall. **óсыпь** scree.

ось (*gen pl* -éй) axis; axle.

осьминóг octopus.

осты́ду *etc.*: *see* **осéсть**

осязáемый tangible. **осязáние** touch. **осязáтельный** tactile; tangible. **осязáть** *impf* feel.

от, **ото** *prep+gen* from; of; against.

отáпливать *impf of* **отопи́ть**

отáра flock (*of sheep*).

отбáвить (-влю) *pf*, **отбавля́ть** *impf* pour off; **хоть отбавля́й** more than enough.

отбегáть *impf*, **отбежáть** (-егý) *pf* run off.

отберý *etc.*: *see* **отобрáть**

отбивáть(ся *impf of* **отби́ть(ся**

отбивнáя котлéта cutlet, chop.

отбирáть *impf of* **отобрáть**

отби́ть (отобью́, -ёшь) *pf* (*impf* **отбивáть**) beat (off), repel; win over; break off; ∼ся break off; drop behind; +**от**+*gen* defend o.s. against.

óтблеск reflection.

отбóй repelling; retreat; ringing off; **бить** ∼ beat a retreat; **дать** ∼ ring off.

отбóйный молотóк (-ткá) pneumatic drill.

отбóр selection. **отбóрный** choice, select(ed).

отбрáсывать *impf*, **отбрóсить** (-óшу) *pf* throw off or away; hurl back; reject; ∼ **тень** cast a shadow. **отбрóсы** (-ов) *pl* garbage.

отбывáть *impf*, **отбы́ть** (-бýду; óтбыл, -á, -о) *pf* depart; serve (*a sentence*).

отвáга courage, bravery.

отвáживаться *impf*, **отвá-житься** (-жусь) *pf* dare. **отвáж-ный** courageous.

отвáл dump, slag-heap; casting off; **до** ∼а to satiety. **отвáли-вать** *impf*, **отвали́ть** (-лю́,

-лишь) *pf* push aside; cast off; fork out.

отвáр broth; decoction. **отвá-ривать** *impf*, **отвари́ть** (-рю́, -ришь) *pf* boil. **отварно́й** boiled.

отвéдать *pf* (*impf* отвéдывать) taste, try.

отведу́ *etc*. *see* отвести́

отвéдывать *impf of* отвéдать

отвезти́ (-зу́, -зёшь; -вёз, -ла́) *pf* (*impf* отвози́ть) take *or* cart away.

отвёл *etc*. *see* отвести́

отверга́ть *impf*, **отвéргнуть** (-ну; -вéрг) *pf* reject; repudiate. **отвéрженный** outcast.

отверну́ть (-ну́, -нёшь) *pf* (*impf* **отвёртывать**, **отвора́чивать**) turn aside; turn down; turn on; unscrew; screw off; ~ся turn away; come unscrewed.

отвéрстие opening; hole.

отвертéть (-рчу́, -ртишь) *pf* (*impf* **отвёртывать**) unscrew; twist off; ~ся come unscrewed; get off. **отвёртка** screwdriver.

отвёртывать(ся *impf of* отверну́ть(ся, отвертéть(ся

отвéс plumb; vertical slope. **отвéсить** (-éшу) *pf* (*impf* **отвéши-вать**) weigh out. **отвéсный** perpendicular, sheer.

отвести́ (-еду́, -едёшь; -вёл, -á) *pf* (*impf* **отводи́ть**) lead, take; draw *or* take aside; deflect; draw off; reject; allot.

отвéт answer.

ответви́ться *pf*, **ответ-вля́ться** *impf* branch off. **ответ-вле́ние** branch, offshoot.

отвéтить (-éчу) *pf*, **отвечáть** *impf* answer; +на+*acc* answer; +за+*acc* answer for. **отвéтный** in reply, return. **отвéтствен-ность** responsibility. **отвéтст-**

ственный responsible. **отвéт-чик** defendant.

отвéшивать *impf of* отвéсить. **отвéшу** *etc*. *see* отвéсить

отвинти́ть (-нчу́) *pf*, **отви́нчи-вать** *impf* unscrew.

отвисáть *impf*, **отви́снуть** (-нет; -и́с) *pf* hang down, sag. **от-ви́слый** hanging, baggy.

отвлекáть *impf*, **отвлéчь** (-еку́, -ечёшь; -влёк, -ла́) *pf* distract, divert; ~ся be distracted. **от-влечённый** abstract.

отво́д taking aside; diversion; leading, taking; rejection; allotment. **отводи́ть** (-ожу́, -о́дишь) *impf of* отвести́.

отвоевáть (-ою́ю) *pf*, **отвоёвы-вать** *impf* win back; spend in fighting.

отвози́ть (-ожу́, -о́зишь) *impf of* отвезти́. **отворáчивать(ся** *impf of* отверну́ть(ся

отвори́ть (-рю́, -ришь) *pf* (*impf* отворя́ть) open; ~ся open.

отвори́ть(ся *etc*. *see* отво-ри́ть(ся. отвою́ю *etc*. *see* отво-евáть

отврати́тельный disgusting. **отвраще́ние** disgust, repugnance.

отвыкáть *impf*, **отвы́кнуть** (-ну; -вык) *pf* +от *or* inf lose the habit of; grow out of.

отвя́зывать *impf* (-жу́, -я́жешь) *pf*, **отвя́зывать** *impf* untie, unfasten; ~ся come untied, come loose; +от+*gen* get rid of; leave alone.

отгадáть *pf*, **отгáдывать** *impf* guess. **отгáдка** answer.

отгибáть(ся *impf of* ото-гну́ть(ся

отглади́ть (-áжу) *pf*, **отглáжи-вать** *impf* iron (out).

отговáривать *impf*, **отгово-ри́ть** *pf* dissuade; ~ся +*instr*

plead. **отгово́рка** excuse, pretext.

отголо́сок (-ска) echo.

отгоня́ть *impf of* **отогна́ть**

отгора́живать *impf*, **отгороди́ть** (-ожу́, -о́дишь) *pf* fence off; partition off; **~ся** shut o.s. off.

отдава́ть¹(ся (-даю́(сь) *impf of* **отда́ть**(ся. **отдава́ть²** (-аёт) *impf impers+instr* taste of; smell of; smack of; **от него́ отдаёт во́дкой** he reeks of vodka.

отдале́ние removal; distance. **отдалённый** remote. **отдали́ть** *pf*, **отдаля́ть** *impf* remove; estrange; postpone; **~ся** move away; digress.

отда́ть (-а́м, -а́шь, -а́ст, -ади́м; о́тдал, -а́, -о) *pf* (*impf* **отдава́ть¹**) give back, return; give up; give away; recoil; cast off; **~ся** give o.s. (up); resound. **отда́ча** return; payment; casting off; efficiency; output; recoil.

отде́л department; section.

отде́лать *pf* (*impf* **отде́лывать**) finish, put the finishing touches to; trim; **~ся +от+gen** get rid of; **+instr** get off with.

отделе́ние separation; department; compartment; section. **отдели́ть** (-елю́, -е́лишь) *pf* (*impf* **отделя́ть**) separate; detach; **~ся** separate; detach o.s.; get detached.

отде́лка finishing; finish, decoration. **отде́лывать(ся** *impf of* **отде́лать(ся**

отде́льно separately; apart. **отде́льный** separate. **отделя́ть(ся** *impf of* **отдели́ть(ся**

отдёргивать *impf*, **отдёрнуть** (-ну) *pf* draw or pull aside or back.

отдеру́ *etc.: see* **отодра́ть**. **отдира́ть** *impf of* **отодра́ть**

отдохну́ть (-ну́, -нёшь) *pf* (*impf* **отдыха́ть**) rest.

отду́шина air-hole, vent.

о́тдых rest. **отдыха́ть** *impf* (*pf* **отдохну́ть**) rest; be on holiday. **отдыша́ться** (-шу́сь, -шишься) *pf* recover one's breath.

отека́ть *impf of* **оте́чь**. **оте́литься** (-е́лится) *pf*

оте́ль *m* hotel.

отеса́ть *etc.: see* **обтеса́ть**

оте́ц (отца́) father. **оте́ческий** fatherly, paternal. **оте́чественный** home, native. **оте́чество** native land, fatherland.

оте́чь (-еку́, -ечёшь; отёк, -ла́) *pf* (*impf* **отека́ть**) swell (up).

отжива́ть *impf*, **отжи́ть** (-иву́, -ивёшь; о́тжил, -а́, -о) *pf* become obsolete or outmoded. **отжи́вший** obsolete; outmoded.

о́тзвук echo.

отзы́в¹ opinion; reference; review; response. **отзы́в²** recall. **отзыва́ть(ся** *impf of* **отозва́ть(ся. отзы́вчивый** responsive.

отка́з refusal; repudiation; failure; natural. **отказа́ть** (-ажу́, -а́жешь) *pf*, **отка́зывать** *impf* break down; deny (+*dat* в+*prep*) refuse, deny (*s.o. sth*); **~ся** (+*от+gen or +inf*) refuse; turn down; renounce, give up.

отка́лывать(ся *impf of* **отколо́ть(ся. отка́пывать** *impf of* **откопа́ть. отка́рмливать** *impf of* **откорми́ть**

откати́ть (-ачу́, -а́тишь) *pf*, **отка́тывать** *impf* roll away; **~ся** roll away or back; be forced back.

откача́ть *pf*, **отка́чивать** *impf* pump out; give artificial respiration to.

отка́шливаться *impf*, **отка́шляться** *pf* clear one's throat.

откидно́й folding, collapsible. **отки́дывать** *impf*, **отки́нуть** (-ну) *pf* fold back; throw aside.

откла́дывать *impf of* отложи́ть

откле́ивать *impf*, **откле́ить** (-е́ю) *pf* unstick; ∼ся come unstuck.

о́тклик response; comment; echo. **откли́ка́ться** *impf*, **откли́кнуться** (-нусь) *pf* answer, respond.

отклоне́ние deviation; declining, refusal; deflection. **отклони́ть** (-ню́, -нишь) *pf*, **отклоня́ть** *impf* deflect; decline; ∼ся deviate; diverge.

отключа́ть *impf*, **отключи́ть** (-чу́) *pf* cut off, disconnect.

отколоти́ть (-очу́, -о́тишь) *pf* knock off; beat up.

отколо́ть (-лю́, -лешь) *pf* (*impf* **отка́лывать**) break off; chop off; unpin; ∼ся break off; come unpinned; break away.

откопа́ть *pf* (*impf* **отка́пывать**) dig up; exhume.

откорми́ть (-млю́, -мишь) *pf* (*impf* **отка́рмливать**) fatten.

отко́с slope.

открепи́ть (-плю́) *pf*, **открепля́ть** *impf* unfasten; ∼ся become unfastened.

открове́ние revelation. **открове́нный** frank; outspoken; unconcealed. **откро́ю** *etc.: see* **откры́ть**

открути́ть (-учу́, -у́тишь) *pf*, **откру́чивать** *impf* untwist, unscrew.

открыва́ть *impf*, **откры́ть** (-ро́ю) *pf* open; reveal; discover; turn on; ∼ся open; come to light, be revealed. **откры́тие** discovery; revelation; opening. **откры́тка** postcard; card. **кры́то** openly. **откры́тый** open.

отку́да *adv* from where; from which; how; ∼ ни возьми́сь from out of nowhere. **отку́да-либо**, **-нибудь** from somewhere or other. **отку́да-то** from somewhere.

отку́поривать *impf*, **отку́порить** *pf* uncork.

откуси́ть (-ушу́, -у́сишь) *pf*, **отку́сывать** *impf* bite off.

отлага́тельство delay. **отлага́ть** *impf of* **отложи́ть**

от|**лакирова́ть** *pf*. **отла́мывать** *impf of* отлома́ть, отломи́ть

отлепи́ть (-плю́, -пишь) *pf* unstick, take off; ∼ся come unstuck, come off.

отлёт flying away; departure. **отлета́ть** *impf*, **отлете́ть** (-лечу́) *pf*, fly, fly away, fly off; rebound.

отли́в ebb, ebb-tide; tint; play of colours. **отлива́ть** *impf*, **отли́ть** (отолью́; о́тлил, -а́, -о) *pf* pour off; pump out; cast, found; (*no pf*) +*instr* be shot with. **отли́вка** casting; moulding.

отлича́ть *impf*, **отличи́ть** (-чу́) *pf* distinguish; ∼ся distinguish o.s.; differ; +*instr* be notable for. **отли́чие** difference; distinction; знак отли́чия order, decoration; с отли́чием with honours. **отли́чник** outstanding student, worker; *etc.* **отличи́тельный** distinctive; distinguishing. **отли́чный** different; excellent.

отло́гий sloping.

отложе́ние sediment; deposit. **отложи́ть** (-ожу́, -о́жишь) *pf* (*impf* **откла́дывать**, **отлага́ть**) put aside; postpone; deposit.

отлома́ть, **отломи́ть** (-млю,

-мишь) *pf* (*impf* **отла́мывать**) break off.

отлупи́ть *pf*.

отлуча́ть *impf*, **отлучи́ть** (-чу́) *pf* (**от це́ркви**) excommunicate; **~ся** absent o.s. **отлу́чка** absence.

отлы́нивать *impf* +**от**+*gen* shirk.

отма́хиваться *impf*, **отмахну́ться** (-ну́сь, -нёшься) *pf* **от**+*gen* brush off; brush aside.

отмежёвываться (-жу́юсь), от**межева́ться** *impf* **от**+*gen* dissociate o.s. from.

о́тмель (sand-)bank.

отме́на abolition; cancellation. **отмени́ть** (-ню́, -нишь) *pf*, **отменя́ть** *impf* repeal; abolish; cancel.

отмере́ть (отомрёт; о́тмер, -ла́, -ло) *pf* (*impf* **отмира́ть**) die off; die out.

отме́ривать *impf*, **отме́рить** *pf*, **отмеря́ть** *impf* measure off.

отмести́ (-ету́, -етёшь; -ёл, -а́) *pf* (*impf* **отмета́ть**) sweep aside.

отмета́ть *impf of* **отмести́**

отме́тить (-е́чу) *pf*, **отмеча́ть** *impf* mark, note; celebrate; **~ся** sign one's name; sign out. **отме́тка** note; mark.

отмира́ть *impf of* **отмере́ть**

отмора́живать *impf*, **отморо́зить** (-о́жу) *pf* injure by frost-bite. **отморо́жение** frost-bite. **отморо́женный** frost-bitten.

отмо́ю *etc.*: *see* **отмы́ть**

отмыва́ть *impf*, **отмы́ть** (-мо́ю) *pf* wash clean; wash off; **~ся** wash o.s. clean; come out.

отмы́чка master key.

отнести́ (-су́, -сёшь; -нёс, -ла́) *pf* (*impf* **относи́ть**) take; carry

away; ascribe, attribute; **~сь** **к**+*dat* treat; regard; apply to; concern, have to do with.

отнима́ть(ся *impf of* **отня́ть(ся**

относи́тельно *adv* relatively; *prep*+*gen* concerning. **относи́тельность** relativity. **относи́тельный** relative. **относи́ть(ся** (-ошу́(сь, -о́сишь(ся) *impf of* **отнести́(сь**. **отноше́ние** attitude; relation; respect; ratio; в отноше́нии+*gen*, по отноше́нию к+*dat* with regard to; в прямо́м (обра́тном) отноше́нии in direct (inverse) ratio.

отны́не *adv* henceforth.

отню́дь not at all.

отня́тие taking away; amputation. **отня́ть** (-ниму́, -ни́мешь; о́тнял, -а́, -о) *pf* (*impf* **отнима́ть**) take (away); amputate; **~ от груди́** wean; **~ся** be paralysed.

ото: *see* **от**

отобража́ть *impf*, **отобрази́ть** (-ажу́) *pf* reflect; represent. **отображе́ние** reflection; representation.

отобра́ть (отберу́, -рёшь; отобра́л, -а́, -о) *pf* (*impf* **отбира́ть**) take (away); select.

отобью́ *etc.*: *see* **отби́ть**

отовсю́ду *adv* from everywhere.

отогна́ть (отгоню́, -о́нишь; отогна́л, -а́, -о) *pf* (*impf* **отгоня́ть**) drive away, off.

отогну́ть (-ну́, -нёшь) *pf* (*impf* **отгиба́ть**) bend back; **~ся** bend.

отогрева́ть *impf*, **отогре́ть** (-е́ю) *pf* warm.

отодвига́ть *impf*, **отодви́нуть** (-ну) *pf* move aside; put off.

отодра́ть (отдеру́, -рёшь; отодра́л, -а́, -о) *pf* (*impf* **отдира́ть**) tear off, rip off.

отож(д)еств́ить (-влю́) *pf*, от-ож(д)еств́лять *impf* identify.

отозва́ть (отзову́, -вёшь; ото-зва́л, -а́, -о) *pf* (*impf* отзыва́ть) take aside; recall; ~ся на+*acc* answer; на+*acc or prep* tell on; have an affect on.

отойти́ (-йду́, -йдёшь; отошёл, -шла́) *pf* (*impf* отходи́ть) move away; depart; withdraw; digress; come out; recover.

отолью́ *etc.: see* **отли́ть**. **ото-мрёт** *etc.: see* **отмере́ть**. **ото|мсти́ть** (-мщу́) *pf.*

отомкну́ть (-ну́, -нёшь) *pf* (*impf* отмыка́ть) unlock, unbolt.

отопи́тельный heating. **от-опи́ть** (-плю́, -пишь) *pf* (*impf* отáпливать) heat. **отопле́ние** heating. •

отопру́ *etc.: see* **отпере́ть**. **от-опью́** *etc.: see* **отпи́ть**.

ото́рванный cut off, isolated. **оторва́ть** (-ву́, -вёшь) *pf* (*impf* отрыва́ть) tear off; tear away; ~ся come off, be torn off; be cut off, lose touch; break away; tear o.s. away; ~ся от земли́ take off.

оторопе́ть (-ею) *pf* be struck dumb.

отосла́ть (-ошлю́, -ошлёшь) *pf* (*impf* отсыла́ть) send (off); send back; +к+*dat* refer to.

отоспа́ться (-сплю́сь, -а́лся, -ала́сь, -а́лось) *pf* (*impf* отсы-па́ться) catch up on one's sleep.

отошёл *etc.: see* **отойти́**. **ото-шлю́** *etc.: see* **отосла́ть**

отпада́ть *impf of* **отпа́сть**

от|пари́ровать *pf.* **отпа́ры-вать** *impf of* **отпоро́ть**

отпа́сть (-адёт) *pf* (*impf* отпа-да́ть) fall off; fall away; pass.

отпева́ние funeral service. **отпере́ть** (отопру́, -прёшь; о́тпер,

-ла́, -ло) *pf* (*impf* отпира́ть) un-lock; ~ся open; +от+*gen* deny; disown.

от|печа́тать, отпеча́тывать *impf* print (off); type (out); im-print. **отпеча́ток** (-тка) imprint, print.

отпива́ть *impf of* **отпи́ть**

отпи́ливать, **отпили́ть** (-лю́, -лишь) *pf* saw off.

от|пира́тельство denial. **от-пира́ть(ся** *impf of* **отпере́ть(ся**

отпи́ть (отопью́, -пьёшь; о́тпил, -а́, -о) *pf* (*impf* отпива́ть) take a sip of.

отпи́хивать *impf*, **отпихну́ть** (-ну́, -нёшь) *pf* push off; shove aside.

отплати́ть (-ачу́, -а́тишь) *pf*, **от-пла́чивать** *impf* +*dat* pay back.

отплыва́ть *impf*, **отплы́ть** (-ыву́, -ывёшь; -ы́л, -а́, -о) *pf* (*sal*) sail; swim (off). **отплы́тие** sail-ing, departure.

отпове́дь rebuke.

отполза́ть *impf*, **отползти́** (-зу́, -зёшь; -о́лз, -ла́) *pf* crawl away.

от|полирова́ть *pf.* **от|поло-ска́ть** (-ощу́) *pf.*

отпо́р repulse; rebuff.

отпоро́ть (-рю́, -решь) *pf* (*impf* отпа́рывать) rip off.

отправи́тель *m* sender. **отпра́-вить** (-влю) *pf*, **отправля́ть** *impf* send, dispatch; ~ся set off, start. **отпра́вка** dispatch. **от-правле́ние** sending; departure; performance. **отправн|о́й**: ~о́й пункт, ~а́я то́чка starting-point.

от|пра́здновать *pf.*

отпра́шиваться *impf*, **отпро-си́ться** (-ошу́сь, -о́сишься) *pf* ask for leave, get leave.

отпры́гивать *impf*, **отпры́г-**

нуть (-ну) *pf* jump *or* spring back *or* aside.

о́тпрыск offshoot, scion.

отпряга́ть *impf of* **отпря́чь**

отпря́нуть (-ну) *pf* recoil, start back.

отпря́чь (-ягу́, -яжёшь; -я́г, -ла́) *pf* (*impf* **отпряга́ть**) unharness.

отпуга́ть *impf*, **отпугну́ть** (-ну́, -нёшь) *pf* frighten off.

о́тпуск (*pl* -а́) leave, holiday(s). **отпуска́ть** *impf*, **отпусти́ть** (-ущу́, -у́стишь) *pf* let go, let off; set free; release; slacken; (let) grow; allot; remit. **отпускни́к** (-а́) person on leave. **отпускно́й** holiday; leave. **отпуще́ние** remission; козёл отпуще́ния scapegoat.

отраба́тывать *impf*, **отрабо́тать** *pf* work off; master. **отрабо́танный** worked out; waste, spent, exhaust.

отра́ва poison. **отрави́ть** (-влю́, -вишь) *pf*, **отравля́ть** *impf* poison.

отра́да joy, delight. **отра́дный** gratifying, pleasing.

отража́тель *m* reflector; scanner. **отража́ть** *impf*, **отрази́ть** (-ажу́) *pf* reflect; repulse; **~ся** be reflected; +на+*prep* affect. **отраже́ние** reflection; repulse.

о́трасль branch.

отраста́ть *impf*, **отрасти́** (-тёт; отро́с, -ла́) *pf* grow. **отрасти́ть** (-ащу́) *pf*, **отра́щивать** *impf* (let) grow.

от|реаги́ровать *pf.* **от|регули́ровать** *pf.* **от|редакти́ровать** *pf.*

отре́з cut; length. **отре́зать** (-е́жу) *pf*, **отреза́ть** *impf* cut off; snap.

о|трезве́ть (-е́ю) *pf.* **отрезви́ть** (-влю́, -вишь) *pf*, **отрезвля́ть**

impf sober; **~ся** sober up.

отре́зок (-зка) piece; section; segment.

отрека́ться *impf of* **отре́чься**

от|рекомендова́ть(ся *pf.* **отрёкся** *etc.*: *see* **отре́чься**. **от|ремонти́ровать** *pf.* **от|репети́ровать** *pf.*

отре́пье, отре́пья (-ьев) *pl* rags.

от|реставри́ровать *pf.*

отрече́ние renunciation; ~ от престо́ла abdication. **отре́чься** (-еку́сь, -ечёшься) *pf* (*impf* **отрека́ться**) renounce.

отреша́ться *impf*, **отреши́ться** (-шу́сь) *pf* renounce; get rid of.

отрица́ние denial; negation. **отрица́тельный** negative. **отрица́ть** *impf* deny.

отро́с *etc.*: *see* **отрасти́**. **отро́сток** (-тка) shoot, sprout; appendix.

о́трочество adolescence.

отруба́ть *impf of* **отруби́ть**

о́труби (-е́й) *pl* bran.

отруби́ть (-блю́, -бишь) *pf* (*impf* **отруба́ть**) chop off; snap back.

от|руга́ть *pf.*

отры́в tearing off; alienation; isolation; в ~е от+*gen* out of touch with; ~ (от земли́) take-off. **отрыва́ть(ся** *impf of* **оторва́ть(ся**. **отры́вистый** staccato; disjointed. **отрывно́й** tear-off. **отры́вок** (-вка) fragment, excerpt. **отры́вочный** fragmentary, scrappy.

отры́жка belch; throw-back.

от|ры́ть (-ро́ю) *pf.*

отря́д detachment; order.

отря́хивать *impf*, **отряхну́ть** (-ну́, -нёшь) *pf* shake down *or* off.

от|салютова́ть *pf.*

отса́сывание suction. **отса́-**

сыва́ть *impf of* отсоса́ть

отсвéчивать *impf* be reflected; +*instr* shine with.

отсéв sifting, selection; dropping out. отсéивать(ся, отсéивать(ся *impf of* отсéять(ся

отсéк compartment. отсека́ть *impf*, отсéчь (-еку́, -ечёшь; -сёк, -ла́) *pf* chop off.

отсéять (-éю) *pf* (*impf* отсева́ть, отсéивать) sift, screen; eliminate; ~ся drop out.

отсидéть (-ижу́) *pf*, отси́живать *impf* make numb by sitting; sit through; serve out.

отска́кивать *impf*, отскочи́ть (-чу́, -чишь) *pf* jump aside or away; rebound; come off.

отслу́живать *impf*, отслужи́ть (-жу́, -жишь) *pf* serve one's time; be worn out.

отсоса́ть (-осу́, -осёшь) *pf* (*impf* отса́сывать) suck off, draw off.

отсо́хнуть (-ну) *pf* (*impf* отсыха́ть) wither.

отсро́чивать *impf*, отсро́чить *pf* postpone, defer. отсро́чка postponement, deferment.

отстава́ние lag, lagging behind. отстава́ть (-таю́, -аёшь) *impf of* отста́ть

отста́вить (-влю) *pf*, отставля́ть *impf* set or put aside. отста́вка resignation; retirement; в отста́вке retired; вы́йти в отста́вку resign, retire. отставно́й retired.

отста́ивать(ся *impf of* отстоя́ть(ся

отста́лость backwardness. отста́лый backward. отста́ть (-а́ну) *pf* (*impf* отстава́ть) fall behind; lag behind; become detached; lose touch; break (off); be slow. отстаю́щий *sb* backward pupil.

от|стега́ть *pf*.

отстёгивать *impf*, отстегну́ть (-ну́, -нёшь) *pf* unfasten, undo; ~ся come unfastened *or* undone.

отстоя́ть[1] (-ою́) *pf* (*impf* отста́ивать) defend; stand up for. отстоя́ть[2] (-ои́т) *impf* на+*acc* ... distant (от+*gen* from). отстоя́ться (*pf* (*impf* отста́иваться) settle; become stabilized.

отстра́ивать(ся *impf of* отстро́ить(ся

отстранéние pushing aside; dismissal. отстрани́ть *pf*, отстраня́ть *impf* push aside; remove; suspend; ~ся move away; keep aloof; ~ся от dodge.

отстрéливаться *impf*, отстрели́ться *pf* fire back.

отстрига́ть *impf*, отстри́чь (-игу́, -ижёшь; -риг) *pf* cut off.

отстро́ить *pf* (*impf* отстра́ивать) finish building; build up.

отступа́ть *impf*, отступи́ть (-плю́, -пишь) *pf* step back; recede; retreat; back down; ~ от+*gen* give up; deviate from; ~ся от give up; go back on. отступлéние retreat; deviation; digression. отступно́й: ~ые дéньги, ~óе *sb* indemnity, compensation. отступя́ *adv* (farther) off, away (от+*gen* from).

отсу́тствие absence; lack. отсу́тствовать *impf* be absent. отсу́тствующий absent; *sb* absentee.

отсчита́ть *pf*, отсчи́тывать *impf* count off.

отсыла́ть *impf of* отосла́ть

отсы́пать (-плю) *pf*, отсы́па́ть *impf* pour out; measure off.

отсыпа́ться *impf of* отосыпа́ться

отсыре́лый damp. от|сыре́ть (-е́ет) *pf.*

отсыха́ть *impf of* отсо́хнуть

отсю́да *adv* from here; hence.

отта́ивать *impf of* отта́ять

отта́лкивать *impf of* оттолкну́ть. отта́лкивающий repulsive, repellent.

отта́чивать *impf of* отточи́ть

отта́ять (-а́ю) *pf (impf* отта́ивать) thaw out.

отте́нок (-нка) shade, nuance; tint.

о́ттепель thaw.

оттесни́ть *pf*, оттесня́ть *impf* drive back; push aside.

о́ттиск impression; off-print, reprint.

оттого́ *adv* that is why; ~, что because.

оттолкну́ть (-ну́, -нёшь) *pf (impf* отта́лкивать) push away; antagonize; ~ся push off.

оттопы́ренный protruding. оттопы́ривать *impf*, оттопы́рить *pf* stick out; ~ся protrude; bulge.

отточи́ть (-чу́, -чишь) *pf (impf* отта́чивать) sharpen.

отту́да *adv* from there.

оття́гивать *impf*, оттяну́ть (-ну́, -нешь) *pf* draw out; draw off; delay. оття́жка delay.

отупе́ние stupefaction. о|тупе́ть (-е́ю) *pf* sink into torpor.

от|утю́жить (-жу) *pf.*

отуча́ть *impf*, отучи́ть (-чу́, -чишь) *pf* break (of); ~ся break o.s. (of).

отха́ркать *pf*, отха́ркивать *impf* expectorate.

отхвати́ть (-чу́, -тишь) *pf*, отхва́тывать *impf* snip or chop off.

отхлебну́ть (-ну́, -нёшь) *pf*, отхлёбывать *impf* sip, take a sip of.

отхлы́нуть (-нет) *pf* flood *or* rush back.

отхо́д departure; withdrawal. отходи́ть (-ожу́, -о́дишь) *impf of* отойти́. отхо́ды (-ов) *pl* waste.

отцвести́ (-ету́, -ете́шь; -ёл, -а́) *pf*, отцвета́ть *impf* finish blossoming, fade.

отцепи́ть (-плю́, -пишь) *pf*, отцепля́ть *impf* unhook; uncouple.

отцо́вский father's; paternal.

отча́иваться *impf of* отча́яться

отча́ливать *impf*, отча́лить *pf* cast off.

отча́сти *adv* partly.

отча́яние despair. отча́янный desperate. отча́яться (-а́юсь) *pf (impf* отча́иваться) despair.

отчего́ *adv* why. отчего́-либо, -нибудь *adv* for some reason or other. отчего́-то *adv* for some reason.

от|чека́нить *pf.*

о́тчество patronymic.

отчёт account; отда́ть себе́ ~ в+*prep* be aware of, realize. отчётливый distinct; clear. отчётность book-keeping; accounts. отчётный *adj*: ~ год financial year, current year; ~ докла́д report for the year.

отчи́зна native land. о́тчий paternal. о́тчим step-father.

отчисле́ние deduction; dismissal. отчи́слить *pf*, отчисля́ть *impf* deduct; dismiss.

отчита́ть *pf*, отчи́тывать *impf* tell off; ~ся report back.

отчужде́ние alienation; estrangement.

отшатну́ться (-ну́сь, -нёшься) *pf*, отша́тываться *impf* start

back, recoil; +от+gen give up, forsake.

отшвы́ривать impf, **отшвырну́ть** (-ну́, -нёшь) pf fling away; throw off.

отше́льник hermit; recluse.

отшлёпать pf spank.

от|**шлифова́ть** pf. **от**|**штукату́рить** pf.

отщепе́нец (-нца) renegade.

отъе́зд departure. **отъезжа́ть** impf, **отъе́хать** (-е́ду) pf drive off, go off.

отъя́вленный inveterate.

отыгра́ть pf, **оты́грывать** impf win back; ~ся win back what one has lost.

отыска́ть (-ыщу́, -ы́щешь) pf, **оты́скивать** impf find; look for; ~ся turn up, appear.

отяготи́ть (-ощу́) pf, **отягоща́ть** impf burden.

офице́р officer. **офице́рский** officer's, officers'.

официа́льный official.

официа́нт waiter. **официа́нтка** waitress.

официо́з semi-official organ. **официо́зный** semi-official.

оформи́тель m designer; stage-painter. **офо́рмить** (-млю) pf, **оформля́ть** impf design; put into shape; make official; process; ~ся take shape, go through the formalities. **оформле́ние** design; mounting, staging; processing.

ох int oh! ah!

оха́пка armful.

о|**характеризова́ть** pf.

о́хать impf (pf **о́хнуть**) moan, sigh.

охва́т scope; inclusion; outflanking. **охвати́ть** (-ачу́, -а́тишь) pf, **охва́тывать** impf

envelop; seize; comprehend.

охладева́ть impf, **охладе́ть** (-е́ю) pf grow cold. **охлади́ть** (-ажу́) pf, **охлажда́ть** impf cool; ~ся become cool, cool down. **охлажде́ние** cooling; coolness.

о|**хмеле́ть** (-е́ю) pf. **о́хнуть** (-ну) pf of **о́хать**

охо́та[1] hunt, hunting; chase. **охо́та**[2] wish, desire.

охо́титься (-о́чусь) impf hunt. **охо́тник**[1] hunter.

охо́тник[2] volunteer; enthusiast. **охо́тничий** hunting.

охо́тно adv willingly, gladly.

о́хра ochre.

охра́на guarding; protection; guard. **охрани́ть** pf, **охраня́ть** impf guard, protect.

охри́плый, охри́пший hoarse. **о**|**хри́пнуть** (-ну; охри́п) pf become hoarse.

о|**цара́пать(ся** pf.

оце́нивать impf, **оцени́ть** (-ню́, -нишь) pf estimate; appraise. **оце́нка** estimation; appraisal; estimate. **оце́нщик** valuer.

о|**цепене́ть** (-е́ю) pf.

оцепи́ть (-плю́, -пишь) pf, **оцепля́ть** impf surround; cordon off.

оча́г hearth; centre; breeding ground; hotbed.

очарова́ние charm, fascination. **очарова́тельный** charming. **очарова́ть** pf, **очаро́вывать** impf charm, fascinate.

очеви́дец (-дца) eye-witness. **очеви́дно** adv obviously, evidently. **очеви́дный** obvious.

о́чень adv very; very much.

очередно́й next in turn; usual, regular; routine. **о́чередь** (gen pl -е́й) turn; queue.

о́черк essay, sketch.

оче́рнить pf.

очерстве́ть (-е́ю) pf.

очерта́ние outline(s), contour(s). **очерти́ть** (-рчу́, -ртишь) pf, **оче́рчивать** impf outline.

о́чи etc.: see **о́ко**

очисти́тельный cleansing. **очи́стить** (-и́щу) pf, **очища́ть** impf clean; refine; clear; peel; ~ся clear o.s.; become clear (**от**+gen of). **очи́стка** cleaning, purification; clearance. **очи́стки** (-ов) pl peelings. **очище́ние** cleansing; purification.

очки́ (-о́в) pl spectacles. **очко́** (gen pl -о́в) pip; point. **очко́вая змея́** cobra.

очну́ться (-ну́сь, -нёшься) pf wake up; regain consciousness.

о́чный: ~ое обуче́ние classroom instruction; ~ая ста́вка confrontation.

очути́ться (-у́тишься) pf find o.s.

оше́йник collar.

ошеломи́тельный stunning. **ошеломи́ть** (-млю́) pf, **ошеломля́ть** impf stun.

ошиба́ться impf, **ошиби́ться** (-бу́сь, -бёшься, -и́бся) pf be mistaken, make a mistake; be wrong. **оши́бка** mistake; error. **оши́бочный** erroneous.

ошпа́ривать impf, **о|шпа́рить** pf scald.

о|штрафова́ть pf. **о|штукату́рить** pf.

ощети́ниваться impf, **о|щети́ниться** pf bristle (up).

ощипа́ть (-плю́, -плешь) pf, **ощи́пывать** impf pluck.

ощу́пать pf, **ощу́пывать** impf feel; grope about. **о́щупь: на** ~ to the touch; by touch. **о́щупью** adv gropingly; by touch.

ощути́мый, ощути́тельный perceptible; appreciable. **ощути́ть** (-ущу́) pf, **ощуща́ть** impf feel, sense. **ощуще́ние** sensation; feeling.

П

па neut indecl dance step.

павильо́н pavilion; film studio.

павли́н peacock.

па́водок (-дка) (sudden) flood.

па́вший fallen.

па́губный pernicious, ruinous.

па́даль carrion.

па́дать impf (pf пасть, упа́сть) fall; ~ ду́хом lose heart. **паде́ж** (-á) case. **паде́ние** fall; degradation; incidence. **па́дкий на**+acc or **до**+gen having a weakness for.

па́дчерица step-daughter.

паёк (пайка́) ration.

па́зуха bosom; sinus; axil.

пай (pl -и́, -ёв) share. **па́йщик** shareholder.

паке́т package; packet; paper bag.

Пакиста́н Pakistan. **пакиста́нец** (-нца), **-а́нка** Pakistani. **пакиста́нский** Pakistani.

па́кля tow; oakum.

пакова́ть impf (pf за~, у~) pack.

па́костный dirty, mean. **па́кость** dirty trick; obscenity.

пакт pact.

пала́та chamber, house. **пала́тка** tent; stall, booth.

пала́ч (-á) executioner.

па́лец (-льца) finger; toe.

палиса́дник (small) front garden.

палиса́ндр rosewood.

пали́тра palette.

пали́ть[1] *impf* (*pf* о∼, с∼) burn; scorch.

пали́ть[2] *impf* (*pf* вы́∼, пальну́ть) fire, shoot.

па́лка stick; walking-stick.

пало́мник pilgrim. **пало́мничество** pilgrimage.

па́лочка stick; bacillus; wand; baton.

па́луба deck.

пальба́ fire.

па́льма palm(-tree). **па́льмовый** palm.

пальну́ть (-ну́, -нёшь) *pf of* пали́ть

пальто́ *neut indecl* (over)coat.

паля́щий burning, scorching.

па́мятник monument; memorial. **па́мятный** memorable; memorial. **па́мять** memory; consciousness; **на** ∼ as a keepsake.

панаце́я panacea.

пане́ль footpath; panel(ling); wainscot(ing). **пане́льный** panelling.

па́ника panic. **паникёр** alarmist.

панихи́да requiem.

пани́ческий panic; panicky.

панно́ *neut indecl* panel.

панора́ма panorama.

пансио́н boarding-house; board and lodging. **пансиона́т** holiday hotel. **пансионе́р** boarder; guest.

пантало́ны (-о́н) *pl* knickers.

панте́ра panther.

пантоми́ма mime.

па́нцирь *m* armour, coat of mail.

па́па[1] *m* pope.

па́па[2] *m*, **папа́ша** *m* daddy.

папа́ха tall fur cap.

папиро́са (*Russian*) cigarette.

па́пка file; folder.

па́поротник fern.

пар[1] (*loc* -ý; *pl* -ы́) steam.

пар[2] (*loc* -ý; *pl* -ы́) fallow.

па́ра pair; couple; (two-piece) suit.

пара́граф paragraph.

пара́д parade; review. **пара́дный** parade; gala; main, front; ∼ая фо́рма full dress (uniform).

парадо́кс paradox. **парадокса́льный** paradoxical.

парази́т parasite.

парализова́ть *impf & pf* paralyse. **парали́ч** (-á) paralysis.

паралле́ль parallel. **паралле́льный** parallel.

пара́метр parameter.

парано́йя paranoia.

парашю́т parachute.

паре́ние soaring.

па́рень (-рня; *gen pl* -рне́й) *m* lad; fellow.

пари́ *neut indecl* bet; держа́ть ∼ bet, lay a bet.

пари́к (-á) wig. **парикма́хер** hairdresser. **парикма́херская** *sb* hairdresser's.

пари́ровать *impf & pf* (*pf also* от∼) parry, counter.

парите́т parity.

пари́ть[1] *impf* soar, hover.

па́рить[2] *impf* steam; stew; *impers* па́рит it is sultry; ∼ся (*pf* по∼ся) steam, sweat; stew.

парк park; depot; stock.

парке́т parquet.

парла́мент parliament. **парламента́рный** parliamentarian. **парламентёр** envoy; bearer of flag of truce. **парла́ментский** parliamentary; ∼ зако́н Act of Parliament.

парни́к (-á) hotbed; seed-bed.

парнико́вый adj: ~ые расте́ния hothouse plants.

парни́шка m boy, lad.

парно́й fresh; steamy.

па́рный (forming a) pair; twin.

паро- in comb steam-. **парово́з** (steam-)engine, locomotive. ~обра́зный vaporous. ~хо́д steamer; steamship. ~хо́дство steamship-line.

парово́й steam; steamed.

паро́дия parody.

паро́ль m password.

паро́м ferry(-boat).

парт- abbr in comb Party. **партбиле́т** Party (membership) card. ~ко́м Party committee. ~организа́ция Party organization.

па́рта (school) desk.

партёр stalls; pit.

партиза́н (gen pl -а́н) partisan; guerilla. **партиза́нский** partisan, guerilla; unplanned.

парти́йный party; Party; sb Party member.

партиту́ра (mus) score.

па́ртия party; group; batch; game, set; part.

партнёр partner.

па́рус (pl -а́, -о́в) sail. **паруси́на** canvas. **па́русник** sailing vessel. **па́русный** sail; ~ спорт sailing.

парфюме́рия perfumes.

парча́ (gen pl -е́й) brocade.

па́сека apiary, beehive.

пасётся see **пасти́сь**

па́сквиль m lampoon; libel.

па́смурный overcast; gloomy.

па́спорт (pl -а́) passport.

пасса́ж passage; arcade.

пассажи́р passenger.

пасси́вный passive.

па́ста paste.

па́стбище pasture.

па́ства flock.

пасте́ль pastel.

пастерна́к parsnip.

пасти́ (-су́, -сёшь; пас, -ла́) impf graze; tend.

пасти́сь (-сётся; па́сся, -ла́сь) impf graze. **пасту́х** (-а́) shepherd. **па́стырь** m pastor.

пасть¹ mouth; jaws.

пасть² (паду́, -дёшь; пал) pf of **па́дать**

Па́сха Easter; Passover.

па́сынок (-нка) stepson, stepchild.

пат stalemate.

пате́нт patent.

патети́ческий passionate.

па́тока treacle; syrup.

патоло́гия pathology.

патриа́рх patriarch.

патрио́т (-а) patriot. **патриоти́зм** patriotism. **патриоти́ческий** patriotic.

патро́н cartridge; chuck; lamp-socket.

патру́ль (-я́) m patrol.

па́уза pause; (also mus) rest.

пау́к (-а́) spider. **паути́на** cobweb; gossamer; web.

па́фос zeal, enthusiasm.

пах (loc -у́) groin.

па́харь m ploughman. **паха́ть** (пашу́, па́шешь) impf (pf вс~) plough.

па́хнуть¹ (-ну; пах) impf smell (+instr of).

пахну́ть² (-нёт) pf puff, blow.

па́хота ploughing. **па́хотный** arable.

паху́чий odorous, strong-smelling.

пацие́нт, ~ка patient.

пацифи́зм pacifism. **пацифи́ст** pacifist.

па́чка bundle; packet; pack; tutu.

па́чкать *impf* (*pf* за~, ис~) dirty, soil, stain.

пашу́ *etc*.: see **паха́ть**. **па́шня** (*gen pl* -шен) ploughed field.

паште́т pâté.

пая́льная ла́мпа blow-lamp. **пая́льник** soldering iron. **пая́ть** (-я́ю) *impf* solder.

пая́ц clown, buffoon.

певе́ц (-вца́), **певи́ца** singer. **пе-ву́чий** melodious. **пе́вчий** singing; *sb* chorister.

пе́гий piebald.

педаго́г teacher; pedagogue. **педаго́гика** pedagogy. **педагоги́ческий** pedagogical; educational; ~ **институ́т** (teachers') training college.

педа́ль pedal.

педиа́тр paediatrician. **педиатри́ческий** paediatric.

педикю́р chiropody.

пейза́ж landscape; scenery.

пёк see **печь**. **пека́рный** baking. **пека́рня** (*gen pl* -рен) bakery. **пе́карь** (*pl* -я́, -е́й) *m* baker. **пе́кло** scorching heat; hell-fire. **пеку́** *etc*.: see **печь**

пелена́ (*gen pl* -лён) shroud. **пелена́ть** (*pf* за~) swaddle; put a nappy on.

пе́ленг bearing. **пеленгова́ть** *impf* & *pf* take the bearings of. **пелёнка** nappy.

пельме́нь *m* meat dumpling.

пе́на foam; scum; froth.

пена́л pencil-case.

пе́ние singing.

пе́нистый foamy; frothy. **пе́ниться** *impf* (*pf* вс~) foam.

пе́нка skin. **пенопла́ст** plastic foam.

пеницилли́н penicillin.

пенсионе́р, **пенсионе́рка** pensioner. **пенсио́нный** pensionable. **пе́нсия** pension.

пень (пня) *m* stump, stub.

пе́пел (-пла) ash, ashes. **пе́пельница** ashtray.

перве́йший the first; first-class. **пе́рвенец** (-нца) first-born. **пе́рвенство** first place; championship. **пе́рвенствовать** *impf* take first place; take priority. **перви́чный** primary.

перво- *in comb* first; prime. **перво-бы́тный** primitive; primeval. ~**исто́чник** source; origin. ~**кла́ссный** first-class. ~**ку́рсник** first-year student. ~**нача́льный** original; primary. ~**со́ртный** best-quality; first-class. ~**степе́нный** paramount.

пе́рвое *sb* first course. **пе́рвый** first; former.

перга́мент parchment.

перебега́ть *impf*, **перебежа́ть** (-бегу́) *pf* cross, run across; desert. **перебе́жчик** deserter; turncoat.

переберу́ *etc*.: see **перебра́ть**

перебива́ть(ся *impf of* **переби́ть(ся**

перебира́ть(ся *impf of* **перебра́ть(ся**

переби́ть (-бью́, -бьёшь) *pf* (*impf* **перебива́ть**) interrupt; slaughter; beat; break; re-upholster; ~**ся** break; make ends meet. **перебо́й** interruption; stoppage; irregularity.

перебо́рка sorting out; partition; bulkhead.

переборо́ть (-рю́, -решь) *pf* overcome.

переборщи́ть (-щу́) *pf* go too far; overdo it.

перебра́сывать(ся *impf of* **переброси́ть(ся**

перебра́ть (-беру́, -берёшь; -ал, -а́, -о) *pf* (*impf* **перебира́ть**) sort out; look through; turn over in one's mind; finger; ~ся get over, cross; mess.

переброси́ть (-о́шу) *pf* (*impf* **перебра́сывать**) throw over; transfer; ~ся fling o.s.; spread. **перебро́ска** transfer.

перебью́ *etc.: see* **перебить**

перева́л crossing; pass. **перева́ливать** *impf*, **перевали́ть** (-лю́, -лишь) *pf* transfer; shift; cross, pass.

перева́ривать *impf*, **перевари́ть** (-рю́, -ришь) *pf* reheat; overcook; digest; tolerate.

переведу́ *etc.: see* **перевести́**

перевезти́ (-зу́, -зёшь; -вёз, -ла́) *pf* (*impf* **перевози́ть**) take across; transport; (re)move.

переверну́ть (-ну́, -нёшь) *pf*, **перевёртывать** *impf* (*impf also* **перевора́чивать**) turn (over); upset; turn inside out; ~ся turn (over).

переве́с preponderance; advantage. **переве́сить** (-е́шу) *pf* (*impf* **переве́шивать**) re-weigh; outweigh; tip the scales; hang elsewhere.

перевести́ (-веду́, -ведёшь; -вёл, -а́) *pf* (*impf* **переводи́ть**) take across; transfer, move, shift; translate; convert; ~сь be transferred; run out; become extinct.

переве́шивать *impf of* **переве́сить. перевира́ть** *impf of* **переврать**

перево́д transfer, move, shift; translation; conversion; waste. **переводи́ть(ся** (-ожу́(сь, -о́дишь(ся) *impf of* **переве-**

сти́(сь. **переводн|о́й** ~а́я бума́га carbon paper; ~а́я карти́нка transfer. **перево́дный** transfer; translated. **перево́дчик, ~ица** translator; interpreter.

перево́з transporting; ferry. **перевози́ть** (-ожу́, -о́зишь) *impf of* **перевезти́. перево́зка** conveyance. **перево́зчик** ferryman; removal man.

перевооружа́ть *impf*, **перевооружи́ть** (-жу́) *pf* rearm; ~ся rearm. **перевооруже́ние** rearmament.

перевоплоти́ть (-лощу́) *pf*, **перевоплоща́ть** *impf* reincarnate; ~ся be reincarnated. **перевоплоще́ние** reincarnation.

перевора́чивать(ся *impf of* **переверну́ть(ся. переворо́т** revolution; overturn; cataclysm; **госуда́рственный** ~ coup d'état.

перевоспита́ние re-education. **перевоспита́ть** *pf*, **перевоспи́тывать** *impf* re-educate.

перевра́ть (-ру́, -рёшь; -ал, -а́, -о) *pf* (*impf* **перевира́ть**) garble; misquote.

перевыполне́ние overfulfilment. **перевы́полнить** *pf*, **перевыполня́ть** *impf* overfulfil.

перевяза́ть (-яжу́, -я́жешь) *pf*, **перевя́зывать** *impf* bandage; tie up; re-tie. **перевя́зка** dressing; bandage.

переги́б bend; excess, extreme. **перегиба́ть(ся** *impf of* **перегну́ть(ся**

перегля́дываться *impf*, **перегляну́ться** (-ну́сь, -нешься) *pf* exchange glances.

перегна́ть (-гоню́, -го́нишь; -ал,

-á, -о) *pf* (*impf* **перегоня́ть**) out-distance; surpass; drive; distil.

перегно́й humus.

перегну́ть (-ну́, -нёшь) *pf* (*impf* **перегиба́ть**) bend; ~ **па́лку** go too far; ~**ся** bend; lean over.

перегова́ривать *impf*, **перегово́рить** *pf* talk; out-talk; ~**ся** (c+*instr*) exchange remarks (with). **перегово́ры** (-ов) *pl* negotiations, parley. **перегово́рный** *adj*: ~ **пункт** public call-boxes; trunk-call office.

перего́н driving; stage. **перего́нка** distillation. **перего́нный** distilling, distillation. **перегоню́** *etc.*: *see* **перегна́ть**. **перегоня́ть** *impf of* **перегна́ть**

перегора́живать *impf of* **перегороди́ть**

перегора́ть *impf*, **перегоре́ть** (-ри́т) *pf* burn out, fuse.

перегороди́ть (-рожу́, -ро́дишь) *pf* (*impf* **перегора́живать**) partition off; block. **перегоро́дка** partition.

перегре́в overheating. **перегрева́ть** *impf*, **перегре́ть** (-е́ю) *pf* overheat; ~**ся** overheat.

перегружа́ть *impf*, **перегрузи́ть** (-ужу́, -у́зишь) *pf* overload; transfer. **перегру́зка** overload; transfer.

перегрыза́ть *impf*, **перегры́зть** (-зу́, -зёшь; -гры́з) *pf* gnaw through.

пе́ред, пе́редо, пред, пре́до *prep*+*instr* before; in front of; compared to. **перёд** (пе́реда; *pl* -á) front, forepart.

передава́ть (-даю́, -даёшь) *impf*, **переда́ть** (-áм, -а́шь, -áст, -ади́м; пе́редал, -á, -о) *pf* pass, hand, hand over; transfer; hand down; make over; tell; communicate; convey; give too much;

~**ся** pass; be transmitted; be communicated; be inherited. **переда́тчик** transmitter. **переда́ча** passing; transmission; communication; transfer; broadcast; drive; gear, gearing.

передвига́ть *impf*, **передви́нуть** (-ну) *pf* move, shift; ~**ся** move, shift. **передвиже́ние** movement; transportation. **передви́жка** movement; *in comb* travelling; itinerant. **передвижно́й** movable, mobile.

переде́лать *pf*, **переде́лывать** *impf* alter; refashion. **переде́лка** alteration.

передёргивать(ся *impf of* **передёрнуть(ся**

передержа́ть (-жу́, -жишь) *pf*, **переде́рживать** *impf* overdo; overcook; overexpose.

передёрнуть (-ну) *pf* (*impf* **передёргивать**) pull aside *or* across; cheat; distort; ~**ся** wince.

пере́дний front; ~ **план** foreground. **пере́дник** apron. **пере́дняя** *sb* (entrance) hall, lobby. **пере́до**: *see* **пе́ред**. **передови́к** (-á) exemplary worker. **передови́ца** leading article. **передово́й** advanced; foremost; leading.

передохну́ть (-ну́, -нёшь) *pf* pause for breath.

передра́знивать *impf*, **передразни́ть** (-ню́, -нишь) *pf* mimic.

переду́мать *pf*, **переду́мывать** *impf* change one's mind.

переды́шка respite.

перее́зд crossing; move. **перееж́ать** *impf*, **перее́хать** *pf* cross; run over, knock down; move (house).

пережа́ривать *impf*, **пережа́-**

рить pf overdo, overcook.

переждáть (-жду́, -ждёшь; -ал, -á, -о) pf (impf **пережида́ть**) wait for the end of.

пережёвывать impf chew; repeat over and over again.

пережива́ние experience.

пережива́ть impf of **пережи́ть**

пережида́ть impf of **переждáть**

пережито́е sb the past. **пережи́ток** (-тка) survival; vestige. **пережи́ть** (-иву́, -ивёшь; пе́режи́л, -á, -о) pf (impf **пережива́ть**) experience; go through; endure; outlive.

перезаряди́ть (-яжу́, -яди́шь) pf, **перезаряжа́ть** impf recharge, reload.

перезва́нивать impf, **перезвони́ть** pf +dat ring back.

пере|зимова́ть etc.: see **зимова́ть**

перезре́лый overripe.

переигра́ть pf, **переи́грывать** impf play again; overact.

переизбира́ть impf, **переизбра́ть** (-беру́, -берёшь; -бра́л, -á, -о) pf re-elect. **переизбра́ние** re-election.

переиздава́ть (-даю́, -даёшь) impf, **переизда́ть** (-а́м, -а́шь, -а́ст, -ади́м; -а́л, -á, -о) pf republish, reprint. **переизда́ние** republication; new edition.

переименова́ть pf, **переимено́вывать** impf rename.

перейму́ etc.: see **переня́ть**

перейти́ (-йду́, -йдёшь; перешёл, -шла́) pf (impf **переходи́ть**) cross; go, walk, pass; move, change, switch; turn (**в**+acc into).

перека́пывать impf of **перекопа́ть**

перекати́ть (-чу́, -тишь) pf,

перека́тывать impf roll; ~ся roll.

перекача́ть pf, **перека́чивать** impf pump (across).

переквалифици́роваться impf & pf retrain.

переки́дывать impf, **переки́нуть** (-ну) pf throw over; ~ся leap.

пе́рекись peroxide.

перекла́дина cross-beam; joist; horizontal bar.

перекла́дывать impf of **переложи́ть**

перекли́чка roll-call.

переключа́тель m switch. **переключа́ть** impf, **переключи́ть** (-чу́) pf switch (over); ~ся switch (over) (**на**+acc to).

перекова́ть (-кую́, -куёшь) pf, **переко́вывать** impf re-shoe; re-forge.

перекопа́ть pf (impf **перека́пывать**) dig (all of); dig again.

перекоси́ть (-ошу́, -о́сишь) pf warp; distort; ~ся warp; become distorted.

перекочева́ть (-чу́ю) pf, **перекочёвывать** impf migrate.

переко́шенный distorted, twisted.

перекра́ивать impf of **перекрои́ть**

перекра́сить (-а́шу) pf, **перекра́шивать** impf (re-)paint; (re-)dye; ~ся change colour; turn one's coat.

пере|крести́ть (-ещу́, -е́стишь) pf, **перекре́щивать** impf cross; ~ся cross, intersect; cross o.s. **перекрёстный** cross; **~ый допро́с** cross-examination; **~ый огонь** cross-fire; **~ая ссылка** cross-reference. **перекрёсток** (-тка) cross-roads, crossing.

перекри́кивать impf, **пере-**

крича́ть (-чу́) *pf* shout down.

перекрои́ть (-ою́) *pf* (*impf* перекра́ивать) cut out again; reshape.

перекрыва́ть *impf*, перекры́ть (-ро́ю) *pf* re-cover; exceed. перекры́тие ceiling.

перекую́ *etc.*: *see* перекова́ть

перекупа́ть *impf*, перекупи́ть (-плю́, -пишь) *pf* buy up; buy by outbidding s.o. перекупщик second-hand dealer.

перекуси́ть (-ушу́, -у́сишь) *pf*, переку́сывать *impf* bite through; have a snack.

перелага́ть *impf of* переложи́ть

перела́мывать *impf of* переломи́ть

перелеза́ть *impf*, переле́зть (-зу; -ез) *pf* climb over.

переле́сок (-ска) copse.

перелёт migration; flight. перелета́ть *impf*, перелете́ть (-лечу́) *pf* fly over. перелётный migratory.

перелива́ние decanting; transfusion. перелива́ть *impf of* перели́ть. перелива́ться *impf of* перели́ться; gleam; modulate.

перелиста́ть *pf*, перели́стывать *impf* leaf through.

перели́ть (-лью́, -льёшь; -и́л, -а́, -о) *pf* (*impf* перелива́ть) pour; decant; let overflow; transfuse. перели́ться (-льётся; -ли́лся, -лила́сь, -ли́ло́сь) *pf* (*impf* перелива́ться) flow; overflow.

перелицева́ть (-цу́ю) *pf*, перелицо́вывать *impf* turn; have turned.

переложе́ние arrangement. переложи́ть (-жу́, -жишь) *pf* (*impf* перекла́дывать, перелага́ть) put elsewhere; shift; transfer; interlay; put in too much.

set; arrange; transpose.

перело́м breaking; fracture; turning-point, crisis; sudden change. перелома́ть *pf* break. ∼ся break, be broken. переломи́ть (-млю́, -мишь) *pf* (*impf* перела́мывать) break in two; master. перело́мный critical.

перелью́ *etc.*: *see* перели́ть

перема́нивать *impf*, перемани́ть (-ню́, -нишь) *pf* win over; entice.

перемежа́ться *impf* alternate.

переме́на change; break. перемени́ть (-ню́, -нишь) *pf*, переменя́ть *impf* change; ∼ся change. переме́нный variable; ∼ ток alternating current. переме́нчивый changeable.

перемести́ть (-мещу́) *pf* (*impf* перемеща́ть) move; transfer; ∼ся move.

перемеша́ть *pf*, переме́шивать *impf* mix; mix up; shuffle; ∼ся get mixed up.

перемеща́ть(ся *impf of* перемести́ть(ся. перемеще́ние transference; displacement. перемещённый displaced; ∼ые ли́ца displaced persons.

переми́рие armistice, truce.

перемыва́ть *impf*, перемы́ть (-мо́ю) *pf* wash (up) again.

перенапряга́ть *impf*, перенапря́чь (-ягу́, -яжёшь: -я́г, -ла́) *pf* overstrain.

перенаселе́ние overpopulation. перенаселённый (-лён, -á) overpopulated; overcrowded.

перенести́ (-су́, -сёшь; -нёс, -ла́) *pf* (*impf* переноси́ть) carry, move, take; transfer; take over; postpone; endure, bear; ∼сь be carried; be carried away.

перенима́ть *impf of* переня́ть

перено́с transfer; word division; знак ~а end-of-line hyphen. **переноси́мый** endurable. **переноси́ть(ся** (-ошу́(сь, -о́сишь(ся) *impf of* перенести́(сь

перено́сица bridge (*of the nose*).

перено́ска carrying over; transporting; carriage. **перено́сный** portable; figurative. **перено́счик** carrier.

пере|ночева́ть (-чу́ю) *pf.* **переношу́** *etc.: see* переноси́ть

переня́ть (-ейму́, -еймёшь; пе́ренял, -á, -о) *pf* (*impf* перенима́ть) imitate; adopt.

переобору́довать *impf & pf* re-equip.

переобува́ться *impf*, **переобу́ться** (-у́юсь, -у́ешься) *pf* change one's shoes.

переодева́ться *impf*, **переоде́ться** (-е́нусь) *pf* change (one's clothes).

переосвиде́тельствовать *impf & pf* re-examine.

переоце́нивать *impf*, **переоцени́ть** (-ню́, -нишь) *pf* overestimate; revalue. **переоце́нка** overestimation; revaluation.

перепа́чкать *pf* make dirty; ~ся get dirty.

пе́репел (*pl* -á) quail.

перепелена́ть *pf* change (*a baby*).

перепеча́тать *pf*, **перепеча́тывать** *impf* reprint. **перепеча́тка** reprint.

перепи́ливать *impf*, **перепили́ть** (-лю́, -лишь) *pf* saw in two.

переписа́ть (-ишу́, -и́шешь) *pf*, **перепи́сывать** *impf* copy; re-write; make a list of. **перепи́ска** copying; correspondence. **перепи́сываться** *impf* correspond. **пе́репись** census.

переплави́ть (-влю) *pf*, **переплавля́ть** *impf* smelt.

переплати́ть (-ачу́, -а́тишь) *pf*, **перепла́чивать** *impf* overpay.

переплести́ (-лету́, -летёшь; -лёл, -á) *pf*, **переплета́ть** *impf* bind; interlace, intertwine; re-plait; ~ся interlace, interweave; get mixed up. **переплёт** binding. **переплётчик** bookbinder.

переплыва́ть *impf*, **переплы́ть** (-ыву́, -ывёшь; -ы́л, -á, -о) *pf* swim *or* sail across.

переподгото́вка further training; refresher course.

переполза́ть *impf*, **переползти́** (-зу́, -зёшь; -о́лз, -ла́) *pf* crawl *or* creep across.

переполне́ние overfilling; overcrowding. **переполне́нный** overcrowded; too full. **переполни́ть** *pf*, **переполня́ть** *impf* overfill; overcrowd.

переполо́х commotion.

перепо́нка membrane; web.

перепра́ва crossing; ford.

переправля́ть (-влю) *pf*, **переправля́ть** *impf* convey; take across; forward; ~ся cross, get across.

перепродава́ть (-даю́, -даёшь) *impf*, **перепрода́ть** (-áм, -áшь, -áст, -ади́м; -про́дал, -á, -о) *pf* re-sell. **перепрода́жа** re-sale.

перепроизво́дство overproduction.

перепры́гивать *impf*, **перепры́гнуть** (-ну) *pf* jump (over).

перепуга́ть *pf* frighten; scare; ~ся get a fright.

пере|пу́тать *pf*, **перепу́тывать** *impf* tangle; confuse, mix up. **перепу́тье** cross-roads.

перераба́тывать *impf*, **перерабо́тать** *pf* convert; treat;

re-make; re-cast; process; work overtime; overwork; ∼ся overwork. **перерабо́тка** processing; reworking; overtime work.

перераспределе́ние redistribution. **перераспредели́ть** pf, **перераспределя́ть** impf redistribute.

перераста́ние outgrowing; escalation; development (into). **перераста́ть** impf, **перерасти́** (-ту́, -тёшь; -ро́с, -ла́) pf outgrow; develop.

перерасхо́д over-expenditure; overdraft. **перерасхо́довать** impf and pf expend too much of.

перерасчёт recalculation.

перерва́ть (-ву́, -вёшь; -а́л, -а́, -о) pf (impf **перерыва́ть**) break, tear asunder; ∼ся break, come apart.

перере́зать (-е́жу) pf, **перере́за́ть** impf, **перере́зывать** impf cut; cut off; kill.

перероди́ть (-ожу́) pf, **перерожда́ть** impf regenerate; ∼ся be reborn; be regenerated; degenerate. **перерожде́ние** regeneration; degeneration.

переро́с etc.: see **перерасти́**. **переро́ю** etc.: see **перерыть**

переруба́ть impf, **переруби́ть** (-блю́, -бишь) pf chop in two.

переры́в break; interruption; interval.

перерыва́ть¹(ся impf of **перерва́ть(ся**

перерыва́ть² impf, **переры́ть** (-ро́ю) pf dig up; rummage through.

пересади́ть (-ажу́, -а́дишь) pf, **переса́живать** impf transplant; graft; seat somewhere else. **переса́дка** transplantation; grafting; change.

переса́живаться impf of пере-

се́сть. переса́ливать impf of пересоли́ть

пересдава́ть (-даю́сь) impf, **переcда́ть** (-а́м, -а́шь, -а́ст, -ади́м; -да́л, -а́, -о) pf sublet; re-sit.

переска́ть(ся impf of пересе́чь(ся

пересе́ленец (-нца) settler; immigrant. **переселе́ние** migration; immigration, resettlement; moving. **пересели́ть** pf, **переселя́ть** impf move; ∼ся move; migrate.

пересе́сть (-ся́ду) pf (impf **переса́живаться**) change one's seat; change (trains etc.).

пересече́ние crossing, intersection. **пересе́чь** (-секу́, -сечёшь; -сёк, -ла́) pf (impf **пересека́ть**) cross; intersect; ∼ся cross, intersect.

переси́ливать impf, **переси́лить** pf overpower.

переска́з (re)telling; exposition. **пересказа́ть** (-ажу́, -а́жешь) pf, **переска́зывать** impf retell.

переска́кивать impf, **перескочи́ть** (-чу́, -чишь) pf jump or skip (over).

пересла́ть (-ешлю́, -шлёшь) pf (impf **пересыла́ть**) send; forward.

пересма́тривать impf, **пересмотре́ть** (-трю́, -тришь) pf look over; reconsider. **пересмо́тр** revision; reconsideration; review.

пересоли́ть (-олю́, -о́лишь) pf (impf **переса́ливать**) over-salt; overdo it.

пересо́хнуть (-нет; -о́х) pf (impf **пересыха́ть**) dry up, become parched.

переспа́ть (-плю́; -а́л, -а́, -о) pf oversleep; spend the night.

переспе́лый overripe.

переспра́шивать impf, пере-

спроси́ть (-ошу́, -о́сишь) *pf* ask again.

переставáть (-таю́, -таёшь) *impf of* перестáть

перестáвить (-влю) *pf*, переставля́ть *impf* move; re-arrange; transpose. перестанóвка rearrangement; transposition.

перестáть (-áну) *pf* (*impf* переставáть) stop, cease.

перестрадáть *pf* have suffered.

перестрáивать(ся *impf of* перестрóить(ся

перестрахóвка re-insurance; overcautiousness.

перестрéлка exchange of fire. перестреля́ть *pf* shoot (down).

перестрóить *pf* (*impf* перестрáивать) rebuild; reorganize; retune; ~ся re-form; reorganize o.s.; switch over (на+*acc* to). перестрóйка reconstruction; reorganization; retuning; perestroika.

переступáть *impf*, переступи́ть (-плю́, -пишь) *pf* step over; cross; overstep.

пересчитáть *pf*, пересчи́тывать *impf* (*pf also* перечéсть) re-count; count.

пересылáть *impf of* пересла́ть. пересы́лка sending, forwarding.

пересыпáть *impf*, пересы́пать (-плю, -плешь) *pf* pour; sprinkle; pour too much.

пересыхáть *impf of* пересóхнуть. пересу́ду *etc.: see* пересéсть. перетáпливать *impf of* перетопи́ть

перетáскивать *impf*, перетащи́ть (-щу́, -щишь) *pf* drag (over, through); move.

перетерéть (-тру́, -трёшь; -тёр) *pf*, перетирáть *impf* wear out, wear down; grind; wipe; ~ся wear out *or* through.

перетопи́ть (-плю́, -пишь) *pf* (*impf* перетáпливать) melt.

перетру́ *etc.: see* перетерéть

перетéть (пру, прёшь; пёр, -ла) *impf* go; make *or* force one's way; haul; come out.

перетя́гивать *impf*, перетяну́ть (-ну́, -нешь) *pf* pull, draw; win over; outweigh.

переубеди́ть *etc.: see* переубежда́ть *impf* make change one's mind.

переу́лок (-лка) side street, alley, lane.

переустрóйство reconstruction, reorganization.

переутоми́ть (-млю́) *pf*, переутомля́ть *impf* overtire; ~ся overtire o.s. переутомлéние overwork.

переучёт stock-taking.

переу́чивать *impf*, переучи́ть (-чу́, -чишь) *pf* teach again.

перефрази́ровать *impf & pf* paraphrase.

перехвати́ть (-ачу́, -áтишь) *pf*, перехвáтывать *impf* intercept; snatch a bite (of); borrow.

перехитри́ть *pf* outwit.

перехóд transition; crossing; conversion. переходи́ть (-ожу́, -óдишь) *impf of* перейти́. перехóдный transitional; transitive. переходя́щий transient; intermittent; brought forward.

пéрец (-рца) pepper.

перечéл *etc.: see* перечéсть

пéречень (-чня) *m* list, enumeration.

перечёркивать *impf*, перечеркну́ть (-ну́, -нёшь) *pf* cross out, cancel.

перече́сть (-чту́, -чтёшь; -чёл, -чла́) *pf: see* **пересчита́ть, перечита́ть**

перечисле́ние enumeration; transfer. **перечи́слить** *pf*, **перечисля́ть** *impf* enumerate; transfer.

перечита́ть *pf*, **перечи́тывать** *impf* (*pf also* **перече́сть**) re-read.

пере́чить (-чу) *impf* contradict; cross, go against.

пе́речница pepper-pot.

перечту́ *etc.: see* **перече́сть**. **перечу́** *etc.: see* **пере́чить**

переша́гивать *impf*, **перешагну́ть** (-ну́, -нёшь) *pf* step over.

переше́ек (-е́йка) isthmus, neck.

перешёл *etc.: see* **перейти́**

перешива́ть *impf*, **переши́ть** (-шью, -шьёшь) *pf* alter; have altered.

перешлю́ *etc.: see* **пересла́ть**

переэкзамено́вывать *pf*, **переэкзамено́вывать** *impf* re-examine; ~ся retake an exam.

пери́ла (-и́л) *pl* railing(s); banisters.

пери́на feather-bed.

пери́од period. **периоди́ка** periodicals. **периоди́ческий** periodical; recurring.

пе́ристый feathery; cirrus.

перифери́я periphery.

перламу́тр mother-of-pearl. **перламу́тровый** mother-of-pearl. **перло́вый**: ~ая крупа́ pearl barley.

перма́нент perm. **перма́нентный** permanent.

перна́тый feathered. **перна́тые** *sb pl* birds. **перо́** (*pl* пе́рья, -ьев) feather; nib. **перочи́нный нож,**

но́жик penknife.

перпендикуля́рный perpendicular.

перро́н platform.

перс Persian. **перси́дский** Persian.

пе́рсик peach.

персия́нка Persian woman.

персо́на person; со́бственной персо́ной in person. **персона́ж** character; personage. **персона́л** personnel, staff. **персона́льный** personal.

перспекти́ва perspective; vista; prospect. **перспекти́вный** prospective; long-term; promising.

пе́рстень (-тня) *m* ring.

перфока́рта punched card.

пе́рхоть dandruff.

перча́тка glove.

пе́рчить (-чу) *impf* (*pf* по~) pepper.

пёс (пса) dog.

пе́сенник song-book; (choral) singer; song-writer. **пе́сенный** song; of songs.

песе́ц (-сца́) (polar) fox.

песнь (*gen pl* -ей) song; canto. **пе́сня** (*gen pl* -сен) song.

песо́к (-ска́) sand. **песо́чный** sand; sandy.

пессими́зм pessimism. **пессими́ст** pessimist. **пессимисти́ческий** pessimistic.

пестрота́ diversity of colours; diversity. **пёстрый** variegated; diverse; colourful.

песча́ник sandstone. **песча́ный** sandy. **песчи́нка** grain of sand.

петербу́ргский (of) St Petersburg.

пети́ция petition.

петли́ца buttonhole; tab. **пе́тля** (*gen pl* -тель) loop; noose; but-

tonhole; stitch; hinge.

петру́шка[1] parsley.

петру́шка[2] *m* Punch; *f* Punch-and-Judy show.

пету́х (-á) cock. **петушо́к** (-шка́) cockerel.

петь (пою́, поёшь) *impf* (*pf* про~, с~) sing.

пехо́та infantry, foot. **пехоти́нец** (-нца) infantryman. **пехо́тный** infantry.

печа́лить *impf* (*pf* о~) sadden; ~ся grieve, be sad. **печа́ль** sorrow. **печа́льный** sad.

печа́тать *impf* (*pf* на~, от~) print; ~ся write, be published; be at the printer's. **печа́тный** printing; printer's; printed; ~ые бу́квы block capitals; ~ый стано́к printing-press. **печа́ть** seal, stamp; print; printing; press.

пече́ние baking.

печёнка liver.

печёный baked.

пе́чень liver.

пече́нье pastry; biscuit. **пе́чка** stove. **печно́й** stove; oven; kiln. **печь** (*loc* -и́; *gen pl* -е́й) stove; oven; kiln. **печь** (пеку́, -чёшь; пёк, -ла́) *impf* (*pf* ис~) bake; ~ся bake.

пешехо́д pedestrian. **пешехо́дный** *neut indecl* pedestrian; foot-. **пе́шка** pawn. **пешко́м** *adv* on foot.

пеще́ра cave. **пеще́рный** cave; ~ челове́к cave-dweller.

пиани́но *neut indecl* (upright) piano. **пиани́ст**, ~ка pianist.

пивна́я *sb* pub. **пивно́й** beer. **пи́во** beer. **пивова́р** brewer.

пигме́й pygmy.

пиджа́к (-á) jacket.

пижа́ма pyjamas.

пижо́н dandy.

пик peak; часы́ пик rush-hour.

пи́ка lance.

пика́нтный piquant; spicy.

пика́п pick-up (van).

пике́ *neut indecl* dive.

пике́т picket. **пике́тчик** picket.

пи́ки (пик) *pl* (*cards*) spades.

пики́ровать *impf & pf* (*pf also* с~) dive.

пикиро́вщик, пики́рующий бомбардиро́вщик dive-bomber.

пикни́к (-á) picnic.

пи́кнуть (-ну) *pf* squeak; make a sound.

пи́ковый of spades.

пила́ (*pl* -ы) saw; nagger. **пи́леный** sawed, sawn. **пили́ть** (-лю́, -лишь) *impf* saw; nag (at). **пи́лка** sawing; fret-saw; nail-file.

пило́т pilot.

пило́тка forage-cap.

пилоти́ровать *impf* pilot.

пилю́ля pill.

пина́ть *impf* (*pf* пнуть) kick. **пино́к** (-нка́) kick.

пингви́н penguin.

пинце́т tweezers.

пио́н peony.

пионе́р pioneer. **пионе́рский** pioneer.

пипе́тка pipette.

пир (*loc* -у́; *pl* -ы́) feast, banquet. **пирова́ть** *impf* feast.

пирами́да pyramid.

пира́т pirate.

пиро́г (-á) pie. **пиро́жное** *sb* cake, pastry. **пирожо́к** (-жка́) pasty.

пирс pier.

пируэ́т pirouette.

пи́ршество feast; celebration.

пи́саный handwritten. **писа́рь** (*pl* -я́) *m* clerk. **писа́тель** *m*, пи-

са́тельница writer, author. **писа́ть** (пишу́, пи́шешь) *impf* (*pf* на~) write; paint; ~ **ма́слом** paint in oils; ~**ся** be spelt.

писк squeak, chirp. **пи́скнуть** (-ну) *pf of* **пища́ть**

пистоле́т pistol; gun; ~**пулемёт** sub-machine gun.

писто́н (percussion-)cap; piston.

писчебума́жный stationery. **пи́счая бума́га** writing paper. **пи́сьменно** *adv* in writing. **пи́сьменность** literature. **пи́сьменный** writing, written. **письмо́** (*pl* -а, -сем) letter.

пита́ние nourishment; feeding. **пита́тельный** nutritious; alimentary; feed. **пита́ть** (*pf* ~**ся**) feed; nourish; supply; ~**ся** feed; eat; live; +*instr* feed on.

пито́мец (-мца) charge; pupil; alumnus. **пито́мник** nursery.

пить (пью, пьёшь; пил, -а́, -о) *impf* (*pf* вы́~) drink. **питьево́й** drinkable; drinking.

пиха́ть *impf*, **пихну́ть** (-ну́, -нёшь) *pf* push, shove.

пи́хта (silver) fir.

пи́чкать *impf* (*pf* на~) stuff.

пи́шущий writing; ~**ая маши́нка** typewriter.

пи́ща food.

пища́ть (-щу́) *impf* (*pf* пи́скнуть) squeak; cheep.

пищеваре́ние digestion. **пищево́д** oesophagus, gullet. **пищево́й** food.

пия́вка leech.

ПК *abbr* (*of* персона́льный компью́тер) PC (*personal computer*).

пла́вание swimming; sailing; voyage. **пла́вательный** swimming; ~ **бассе́йн** swimming-

---

pool. **пла́вать** *impf* swim; float; sail. **плавба́за** depot ship, factory ship.

плави́льный melting, smelting. **плави́льня** foundry. **пла́вить** (-влю) *impf* (*pf* рас~) melt, smelt; ~**ся** melt. **пла́вка** fusing; melting.

пла́вки (-вок) *pl* bathing trunks.

пла́вкий fusible; fuse. **плавле́ние** melting.

плавни́к (-а́) fin; flipper. **пла́вный** smooth, flowing; liquid. **плаву́чий** floating.

плагиа́т plagiarism. **плагиа́тор** plagiarist.

пла́зма plasma.

плака́т poster; placard.

пла́кать (-а́чу) *impf* cry, weep; ~**ся** complain, lament; +**на**+*acc* complain of; bemoan.

пла́кса cry-baby. **плакси́вый** whining. **плаку́чий** weeping.

пла́менный flaming; ardent. **пла́мя** (-мени) *neut* flame; blaze.

план plan

планёр glider. **планери́зм** gliding. **планери́ст** glider-pilot.

плане́та planet. **плане́тный** planetary.

плани́рование¹ planning.

плани́рование² gliding; glide.

плани́ровать¹ *impf* (*pf* за~) plan.

плани́ровать² *impf* (*pf* с~) glide (down).

пла́нка lath, slat.

пла́новый planned, systematic; planning. **планоме́рный** systematic, planned.

планта́ция plantation.

пласт (-á) layer; stratum. **пласти́на** plate. **пласти́нка** plate; (*gramophone*) record.

пласти́ческий, пласти́чный plastic. **пластма́сса** plastic. **пластма́ссовый** plastic.

пла́стырь *m* plaster.

пла́та pay; charge; fee. **платёж** (-á) payment. **платёжеспосо́бный** solvent. **платёжный** pay.

пла́тина platinum.

плати́ть (-ачу́, -а́тишь) *impf* (*pf* за~, у~) pay; ~ся (*pf* по~) за+*acc* pay for. **пла́тный** paid; requiring payment.

плато́к (-тка́) shawl; head-scarf; handkerchief.

платони́ческий platonic.

платфо́рма platform; truck.

пла́тье (*gen pl* -ьев) clothes, clothing; dress; gown. **платяно́й** clothes.

плафо́н ceiling; lamp shade.

плацда́рм bridgehead; beach-head; base; springboard.

плацка́рта reserved-seat ticket.

плач weeping. **плаче́вный** lamentable. **пла́чу** *etc.: see* **пла́кать**

плачу́ *etc.: see* **плати́ть**

плашмя́ *adv* flat, prone.

плащ (-á) cloak; raincoat.

плебе́й plebeian.

плева́тельница spittoon. **плева́ть** (плюю́, плюёшь) *impf* (*pf* на~, плю́нуть) spit; *inf+dat*: мне ~ I don't give a damn (на+*acc* about); ~ся spit. **плево́к** (-вка́) spit, spittle.

плеври́т pleurisy.

плед rug; plaid.

плёл *etc.: see* **плести́**

племенно́й tribal; pedigree. **пле́мя** (-мени; *pl* -мена́, -мён) *neut* tribe. **племя́нник** nephew. **племя́нница** niece.

плен (*loc* -ý) captivity.

плена́рный plenary.

плени́тельный captivating.

плени́ть *pf* (*impf* пленя́ть) captivate; ~ся be captivated.

плёнка film; tape; pellicle.

пле́нник prisoner. **пле́нный** captive.

пле́нум plenary session.

пленя́ть(ся *impf of* плени́ть(ся

пле́сень mould.

плеск splash, lapping. **плеска́ть** (-ещу́, -е́щешь) *impf* (*pf* плесну́ть) splash; lap; ~ся splash; lap.

плесневе́ть (-еет) *impf* (*pf* за~) go mouldy, grow musty.

плесну́ть (-ну́, -нёшь) *pf of* плеска́ть

плести́ (-ету́, -етёшь; плёл, -á) *impf* (*pf* с~) plait; weave; ~сь trudge along. **плете́ние** plaiting; wickerwork. **плетёный** wattled; wicker. **плете́нь** (-тня́) *m* wattle fencing. **плётка, плеть** (*gen pl* -éй) lash.

пле́чико (*pl* -и, -ов) shoulder-strap; *pl* coat-hanger. **плечи́стый** broad-shouldered. **плечо́** (*pl* -и, -а́м) shoulder.

плеши́вый bald. **плеши́на, плешь** bald patch.

плещу́ *etc.: see* плеска́ть

плинтус plinth; skirting-board.

плис velveteen.

плиссирова́ть *impf* pleat.

плита́ (*pl* -ы) slab; flag-(stone); stove, cooker; моги́льная ~ gravestone. **пли́тка** tile; (thin) slab; stove, cooker; ~ шокола́да bar of chocolate. **пли́точный** tiled.

плове́ц (-вца́) **пловчи́ха** swimmer. **плову́чий** floating; buoyant.

плод (-á) fruit. **плоди́ть** (-ожу́) *impf* (*pf* рас~) produce, procreate; ~ся propagate.

плодо- *in comb* fruit-. **плодо-**

ви́тый fruitful, prolific; fertile. **~во́дство** fruit-growing. **~но́сный** fruit-bearing, fruitful. **~овощно́й** fruit and vegetable. **~ро́дный** fertile. **~тво́рный** fruitful.

пло́мба seal; filling. **пломбирова́ть** *impf* (*pf* **за~, о~**) fill; seal.

пло́ский (-сок, -ска́, -о) flat; trivial.

плоско- *in comb* flat. **плоского́рье** plateau. **~гу́бцы** (-ев) *pl* pliers. **~до́нный** flat-bottomed.

пло́скость (*gen pl* -е́й) flatness; plane; platitude.

плот (-а́) raft.

плоти́на dam; weir; dyke.

пло́тник carpenter.

пло́тность solidity; density. **пло́тный** (-тен, -тна́, -о) thick; compact; dense; solid, strong; hearty.

плотоя́дный carnivorous. **плоть** flesh.

плохо́й bad; poor.

площа́дка area, (sports) ground, court, playground; site; landing; platform. **пло́щадь** (*gen pl* -е́й) area; space; square.

плуг (*pl* -и́) plough.

плут (-а́) cheat, swindler; rogue. **плутова́тый** cunning. **плутовско́й** roguish; picaresque.

плуто́ний plutonium.

плыть (-ыву́, -ывёшь; плыл, -а́, -о) *impf* swim; float; sail.

плю́нуть (-ну) *pf of* **плева́ть**

плюс plus; advantage.

плюш (-а́) plush.

плющ (-а́) ivy.

плюю́ *etc.*: *see* **плева́ть**

пляж beach.

пляса́ть (-яшу́, -я́шешь) *impf* (*pf*

с~) dance. **пля́ска** dance; dancing.

пневмати́ческий pneumatic.

пневмони́я pneumonia.

пнуть (пну, пнёшь) *pf of* **пина́ть**

пня *etc.*: *see* **пень**

по *prep* I. +*dat* on; along; round, about; by; over; according to; in accordance with; for; in; at; by (reason of); on account of; from; **по понеде́льникам** on Mondays; **по профе́ссии** by profession; **по ра́дио** over the radio. II. +*dat or acc of cardinal number, forms distributive number:* **по́ два, по́ двое** in twos, two by two; **по пять рубле́й шту́ка** at five roubles each. III. +*acc* to, up to; for, to get; **идти́ по во́ду** go to get water; **по пе́рвое сентября́** up to (and including) 1st September. IV. +*prep* on, (immediately) after; **по прибы́тии** on arrival.

по- *pref* I. *in comb* +*dat of adjs, or with advs in* -и, *indicates manner, use of a named language, or accordance with the opinion or wish of:* **говори́ть по-ру́сски** speak Russian; **жить по-ста́рому** live in the old style; **по-мо́ему** in my opinion. II. *in comb with adjs and nn, indicates situation along or near a thing:* **помо́рье** seaboard, coastal region. III. *in comb with comp of adjs indicates a smaller degree of comparison:* **поме́ньше** a little less.

побаива́ться *impf* be rather afraid.

побе́г[1] flight; escape.

побе́г[2] shoot; sucker.

побегу́шки: быть на побегу́шках run errands.

побе́да victory. **победи́тель** *m* victor; winner. **победи́ть** *pf*

(*impf* **побежда́ть**) conquer; win. **побе́дный, победоно́сный** victorious, triumphant.

по|бежа́ть *pf*.

побежда́ть *impf of* **победи́ть**

побеле́ть (-е́ю) *pf.* **по|бели́ть** *pf.* **побе́лка** whitewashing.

побере́жье coastal. **побере́жье** (sea-)coast.

по|беспоко́ить(ся *pf.*

побира́ться *impf* beg; live by begging.

по|би́ть(ся (-бью́(сь, -бьёшь(ся) *pf.* **по|благодари́ть(ся** *pf.*

побла́жка indulgence.

по|бледне́ть (-е́ю) *pf.*

поблёскивать *impf* gleam.

побли́зости *adv* nearby.

побо́и (-ев) *pl* beating. **побо́ище** slaughter; bloody battle.

побо́рник champion, advocate. **поборо́ть** (-рю́, -решь) *pf* overcome.

побо́чный secondary; done on the side; ~ **проду́кт** by-product.

по|брани́ться *pf*. **побрати́м** twin town.

по|брата́ться *pf*. **побрати́м** twin town.

по|бре́згать *pf*. **по|бри́ть(ся** (-бре́ю(сь) *pf*.

побуди́тельный stimulating. **побуди́ть** (-ужу́) *pf*, **побужда́ть** *impf* induce, prompt. **побужде́ние** motive; inducement.

побыва́ть *pf* have been, have visited; look in, visit. **побы́вка** leave. **побы́ть** (-бу́ду, -дешь; по́был, -á, -о) *pf* stay (for a short time).

побью́(сь *etc.*: *see* **поби́ть(ся**

пова́диться (-а́жусь) get into the habit (of). **пова́дка** habit.

по|вали́ть(ся (-лю́(сь, -лишь(ся) *pf*.

пова́льно *adv* without exception. **пова́льный** general; mass.

по́вар (*pl* -á) cook, chef. **поваре́нный** culinary; cookery; cooking.

по-ва́шему *adv* in your opinion.

пове́дать *pf* disclose; relate.

поведе́ние behaviour.

поведу́ *etc.*: *see* **повести́**. **по|везти́** (-зу́, -зёшь; -вёз, -ла́) *pf.* **повёл** *etc.*: *see* **повести́**

повелева́ть *impf* +*instr* rule (over); +*dat* command. **повеле́ние** command. **повели́тельный** imperious; imperative.

по|венча́ть(ся *pf*.

поверга́ть *impf*, **пове́ргнуть** (-ну, -вéрг) *pf* throw down; plunge.

пове́ренная *sb* confidante. **пове́ренный** *sb* attorney; confidant; ~ **в дела́х** chargé d'affaires. **пове́рить¹** *pf see* **ве́рить**. **пове́рить²** *pf* (*impf* **поверя́ть**) check; confide. **пове́рка** check; roll-call.

поверну́ть (-ну́, -нёшь) *pf*, **повёртывать** *impf* (*impf also* **повора́чивать**) turn; ~**ся** turn.

пове́рх *prep*+*gen* over. **пове́рхностный** surface, superficial. **пове́рхность** surface.

пове́рье (*gen pl* -ий) popular belief, superstition. **поверя́ть** *impf of* **пове́рить²**

пове́са playboy.

по|весели́ть (-е́ю) *pf*.

повесели́ть *pf* cheer (up), amuse; ~**ся** have fun.

пове́сить(ся (-е́шу(сь) *pf of* **ве́шать(ся**

повествова́ние narrative, narration. **повествова́тельный** narrative. **повествова́ть** *impf*

+о+*prep* narrate, relate.

по|вести (-еду́, -едёшь, -вёл, -á) *pf* (*impf* **поводи́ть**) +*instr* move.

пове́стка notice; summons; ~ (дня) agenda.

по́весть (*gen pl* -е́й) story, tale.

пове́тpие epidemic; craze.

пове́шу *etc.*: *see* **пове́сить**.

по|вздо́рить *pf*.

повзросле́ть (-е́ю) *pf* grow up.

по|вида́ть(ся *pf*.

по-ви́димому apparently.

повидло jam.

по|вини́ться *pf*.

пови́нность duty, obligation; во́инская ~ conscription. **пови́нный** guilty.

повинова́ться *impf & pf* obey. **повинове́ние** obedience.

повиса́ть *impf*, **по|ви́снуть** (-ну; -ви́с) *pf* hang (on); hang down, droop.

повле́чь (-еку́, -ечёшь, -ёк, -ла́) *pf* (**за собо́й**) entail, bring in its train.

по|влия́ть *pf*.

по́вод[1] occasion, cause; по ~у+*gen* as regards, concerning.

по́вод[2] (*loc* -ý; *pl* -о́дья, -ьев) rein; быть на ~ý y+*gen* be under the thumb of. **поводи́ть** (-ожу́, -о́дишь) *impf of* **повести́**. **пово́док** (-дка́) leash. **поводы́рь** (-я́) *m* guide.

пово́зка cart; vehicle.

повора́чивать(ся *impf of* **повернуть(ся, повороти́ть(ся; повора́чивайся, -айтесь!** get a move on!

поворо́т turn, turning; bend; turning-point. **повороти́ть(ся** (-рочу́(сь, -ро́тишь(ся) *pf* (*impf* **повора́чивать(ся**) turn. **поворо́тливый** agile, nimble; man-

oeuvrable. **поворо́тный** turning; rotary; revolving.

по|вреди́ть (-ежу́) *pf*, **повре-жда́ть** *impf* damage; injure; ~ся be damaged; be injured. **поврежде́ние** damage, injury.

повремени́ть (-ню́) *pf* wait a little; +*c*+*instr* delay over.

повседне́вный daily; everyday.

повсеме́стно *adv* everywhere. **повсеме́стный** universal, general.

повста́нец (-нца) rebel, insurgent. **повста́нческий** rebel; insurgent.

повсю́ду *adv* everywhere.

повторе́ние repetition. **повтори́ть** *pf*, **повторя́ть** *impf* repeat; ~ся repeat o.s.; be repeated; recur. **повто́рный** repeated.

повы́сить (-ы́шу) *pf*, **повы-ша́ть** *impf* raise, heighten; ~ся rise. **повыше́ние** rise; promotion. **повы́шенный** heightened, high.

повяза́ть (-яжу́, -я́жешь) *pf*, **по-вя́зывать** *impf* tie. **повя́зка** band; bandage.

по|гада́ть *pf*.

пога́нка toadstool. **пога́ный** foul; unclean.

погаси́ть *impf*, **по|га́снуть** (-ну) *pf* go out, be extinguished. **по|гаси́ть** (-ашу́, -а́сишь) *pf*. **погаша́ть** *impf* liquidate, cancel. **пога́шенный** used, cancelled; cashed.

погиба́ть *impf*, **по|ги́бнуть** (-ну; -ги́б) *pf* perish; be lost. **поги́бель** ruin. **поги́бший** lost; ruined; killed.

по|гла́дить (-а́жу) *pf*.

поглоти́ть (-ощу́, -о́тишь) *pf*, **по-глоща́ть** *impf* swallow up; ab-

sorb. **поглоще́ние** absorption.
по|**глупе́ть** (-е́ю) *pf.*
по|**гляде́ть** (-яжу́) *pf.* **погля́ды-вать** *impf* glance (from time to time); ~**за**+*instr* keep an eye on.
погна́ть (-гоню́, -го́нишь; -гна́л, -а́, -о) *pf* drive; ~**ся за**+*instr* run after; start in pursuit of.
по|**гну́ть**(**ся**) (-ну́(сь, -нёшь(ся)) *pf.* **по**|**гнуша́ться** *pf.*
поговори́ть *pf* have a talk.
погово́рка saying, proverb.
пого́да weather.
погоди́ть (-ожу́) *pf* wait a little; **немно́го погодя́** a little later.
поголо́вно *adv* one and all. **по-голо́вный** general; capitation. **поголо́вье** number.
пого́н (*gen pl* -о́н) shoulder-strap.
пого́нщик driver. **погоню́** *etc.*: *see* **погна́ть. пого́ня** pursuit, chase. **погоня́ть** *impf* urge on, drive.
погорячи́ться (-чу́сь) *pf* get worked up.
пого́ст graveyard.
погра́ничник frontier guard. **погра́ничный** frontier.
по́греб (*pl* -а́) cellar. **погреба́льный** funeral. **погреба́ть** *impf of* **погрести́. погребе́ние** burial.
погрему́шка rattle.
погрести́¹ (-ебу́, -ебёшь; -рёб, -ла́) *pf* (*impf* **погреба́ть**) bury.
погрести́² (-ебу́, -ебёшь; -рёб, -ла́) *pf* row for a while.
погре́ть (-е́ю) *pf* warm; ~**ся** warm o.s.
по|**греши́ть** (-шу́) *pf* sin; err. **по-гре́шность** error, mistake.
по|**грози́ться** (-ожу́сь) *pf.* **по**|**грубе́ть** (-е́ю) *pf.*

погружа́ть *impf*, **по**|**грузи́ть** (-ужу́, -у́зи́шь) *pf* load; ship; dip, plunge, immerse; ~**ся** sink, plunge; dive; be plunged, absorbed. **погруже́ние** submergence; immersion; dive. **погру́зка** loading; shipment.
погряза́ть *impf*, **по**|**гря́знуть** (-ну; -яз) *pf* be bogged down; wallow.
по|**губи́ть** (-блю́, -бишь) *pf.* **по**|**гуля́ть** *pf.*
под, подо *prep* I. +*acc or instr* under; near, close to; **взять под ру́ку**+*acc* take the arm of; ~ **ви́дом**+*gen* under the guise of; **под го́ру** downhill; ~ **Москво́й** in the environs of Moscow. II. +*instr* occupied by, used as; (meant, implied) by; in, with; **говя́дина** ~ **хре́ном** beef with horseradish. III. +*acc* towards; to (the accompaniment of); in imitation of; for, to serve as; **ему́** ~ **пятьдеся́т (лет)** he is getting on for fifty.
подава́ть(**ся** (-даю́(сь, -даёшь(ся)) *impf of* **пода́ть**(**ся**
подави́ть (-влю́, -вишь) *pf*, **подавля́ть** *impf* suppress; depress; overwhelm. **по**|**дави́ться** (-влю́сь, -вишься) *pf.* **подавле́ние** suppression; repression. **пода́вленность** depression. **пода́вленный** suppressed; depressed. **подавля́ющий** overwhelming.
пода́вно *adv* all the more.
пода́гра gout.
пода́льше *adv* a little further.
по|**дари́ть** (-рю́, -ришь) *pf.* **пода́рок** (-рка) present.
пода́тливый pliant, pliable.
пода́ть (*gen pl* -е́й) tax. **пода́ть** (-а́м, -а́шь, -а́ст, -ади́м; по́дал, -а́, -о) *pf* (*impf* **подава́ть**) serve;

give; put, move, turn; put forward, present, hand in; **~ся** move; give way; yield; **+на**+*acc* set out for. **пода́ча** giving, presenting; serve; feed, supply. **да́чка** handout, crumb. **подаю́** *etc.: see* **подава́ть. подая́ние** alms.

подбега́ть *impf*, **подбежа́ть** (**-егу́**) *pf* come running (up).

подбива́ть *impf of* **подби́ть**

подберу́ *etc.: see* **подобра́ть. подбива́ть(ся** *impf of* **подобра́ть(ся**

подби́ть (**-добью́, -добьёшь**) *pf* (*impf* **подбива́ть**) line; re-sole; bruise; put out of action; incite.

подбодри́ть *pf*, **подбодря́ть** *impf* cheer up, encourage; **~ся** cheer up, take heart.

подбо́р selection, assortment.

подборо́док (**-дка**) chin.

подбоче́нившись *adv* with hands on hips.

подбра́сывать *impf*, **подбро́сить** (**-ро́шу**) *pf* throw up.

подва́л cellar; basement. **подва́льный** basement, cellar.

подведу́ *etc.: see* **подвести́**

подвезти́ (**-зу́, -зёшь, -вёз, -ла́**) *pf* (*impf* **подвози́ть**) bring, take; give a lift.

подвене́чный wedding.

подверга́ть *impf*, **подве́ргнуть** (**-ну; -вёрг**) *pf* subject; expose; **~ся** +*dat* undergo. **подве́рженный** subject, liable.

подверну́ть (**-ну́, -нёшь**) *pf*, **подвёртывать** *impf* turn up; tuck under; sprain; tighten; **~ся** be sprained; be turned up; be tucked under.

подве́сить (**-е́шу**) *pf* (*impf* **подве́шивать**) hang up, suspend.

подвесно́й hanging, suspended.

подвести́ (**-еду́, -едёшь; -вёл, -а́**) *pf* (*impf* **подводи́ть**) lead up, bring up; place (under); bring under, subsume; let down; **~ ито́ги** reckon up; sum up.

подве́шивать *impf of* **подве́сить**

по́двиг exploit, feat.

подвига́ть(ся *pf of* **подви́нуть(ся**

подви́жник religious ascetic; champion.

подвижно́й mobile; **~ соста́в** rolling-stock. **подви́жность** mobility. **подви́жный** mobile; lively; agile.

подвиза́ться *impf* (**в** *or* **на** +*prep*) work (in).

подви́нуть (**-ну**) *pf* (*impf* **подвига́ть**) move; push; advance; **~ся** move; advance.

подвла́стный +*dat* subject to; under the control of.

подво́да cart. **подводи́ть** (**-ожу́, -о́дишь**) *impf of* **подвести́**

подво́дный submarine; underwater; **~ая скала́** reef.

подво́з transport; supply. **подвози́ть** (**-ожу́, -о́зишь**) *impf of* **подвезти́**

подворо́тня (*gen pl* **-тен**) gateway.

подво́х trick.

подвы́пивший tipsy.

подвяза́ть (**-яжу́, -я́жешь**) *pf*, **подвя́зывать** *impf* tie up. **подвя́зка** garter; suspender.

подгиба́ть *impf of* **подогну́ть**

подгляде́ть (**-яжу́**) *pf*, **подгля́дывать** *impf* peep; spy.

подгова́ривать *impf*, **подговори́ть** *pf* incite.

подгоню́ *etc.: see* **подогна́ть.**

подгоня́ть *impf of* **подогна́ть**

подгора́ть *impf,* **подгоре́ть** (-ри́т) *pf* get a bit burnt. **подгоре́лый** slightly burnt.

подготови́тельный preparatory. **подгото́вить** (-влю) *pf,* **подгота́вливать** *impf* prepare; **~ся** prepare, get ready. **подгото́вка** preparation, training.

поддава́ться (-даю́сь, -даёшься) *impf of* **подда́ться**

подда́кивать *impf* agree, assent.

по́дданный *sb* subject; citizen. **по́дданство** citizenship. **подда́ться** (-а́мся, -а́шься, -а́стся, -ади́мся; -а́лся, -ла́сь) *pf (impf* **поддава́ться)** yield, give way.

подде́лать, подде́лывать *impf* counterfeit; forge. **подде́лка** falsification; forgery; imitation. **подде́льный** false, counterfeit.

поддержа́ть (-жу́, -жишь) *pf,* **подде́рживать** *impf* support; maintain. **подде́ржка** support.

поде́йствовать *pf.*

поде́лать *pf* do; **ничего́ не поде́лаешь** it can't be helped.

по|дели́ть(ся (-лю́(сь, -лишь(ся) *pf.*

поде́лка *pl* small (hand-made) articles.

поде́лом *adv:* **~ ему́** (*etc.*) it serves him (*etc.*) right.

подённый by the day. **подённик, -ица** day-labourer.

подёргивать *impf* twitch.

поде́ржанный second-hand.

подёрнуть (-нет) *pf* cover. **поде́шеве́ть** (-ёет) *pf.*

поджа́ривать(ся *impf,* **поджа́рить(ся** *pf* fry, roast, grill; toast. **поджа́ристый** brown(ed).

поджа́рый lean, wiry.

поджа́ть (-дожму́, -дожмёшь) *pf (impf* **поджима́ть)** draw in, draw under; **~ гу́бы** purse one's lips.

подже́чь (-дожгу́, -ожжёшь; -жёг, -дожгла́) *pf,* **поджига́ть** *impf* set fire to; burn. **поджига́тель** *m* arsonist; instigator.

поджида́ть *impf* (+*gen*) wait (for).

поджима́ть *impf of* **поджа́ть**

поджо́г arson.

подзаголо́вок (-вка) subtitle, sub-heading.

подзащи́тный *sb* client.

подземе́лье (*gen pl* -лий) cave; dungeon. **подзе́мный** underground.

подзову́ *etc.: see* **подозва́ть**

подзо́рная труба́ telescope.

подзыва́ть *impf of* **подозва́ть**

поди́виться (-влю́сь) *pf.*

подка́пывать(ся *impf of* **подкопа́ть(ся**

подкара́уливать *impf,* **подкарау́лить** *pf* be on the watch (for).

подкати́ть (-ачу́, -а́тишь) *pf,* **подка́тывать** *impf* roll up, drive up; roll.

подка́шивать(ся *impf of* **подкоси́ть(ся**

подки́дывать *impf,* **подки́нуть** (-ну) *pf* throw up. **подки́дыш** foundling.

подкла́дка lining. **подкла́дывать** *impf of* **подложи́ть**

подкле́ивать *impf,* **подкле́ить** *pf* glue (up); mend.

подко́ва (horse-)shoe. **подко́ва́ть** (-кую́, -ёшь) *pf,* **подко́вывать** *impf* shoe.

подко́жный hypodermic.

подкоми́ссия, подкомите́т sub-committee.

подко́п undermining; underground passage. **подкопа́ть** pf (impf **подка́пывать**) undermine; **~ся под**+acc undermine; burrow under.

подкоси́ть (-ошу́, -о́сишь) pf (impf **подка́шивать**) cut down; **~ся** give way.

подкра́дываться impf of **подкра́сться**

подкра́сить (-а́шу) pf (impf **подкра́шивать**) touch up; **~ся** make up lightly.

подкра́сться (-аду́сь, -адёшься) pf (impf **подкра́дываться**) sneak up.

подкра́шивать(ся **подкра́шу** etc.: see **подкра́сить**

подкрепи́ть (-плю́) pf, **подкрепля́ть** impf reinforce; support; corroborate; fortify; **~ся** fortify o.s. **подкрепле́ние** confirmation; sustenance; reinforcement.

подкрути́ть (-учу́, -у́тишь) pf (impf **подкру́чивать**) tighten up.

по́дкуп bribery. **подкупа́ть** impf, **подкупи́ть** (-плю́, -пишь) pf bribe; win over.

подлади́ться (-а́жусь) pf, **подла́живаться** impf +к+dat adapt o.s. to; make up to.

подла́мываться impf of **подломи́ться**

по́дле prep+gen by the side of, beside.

подлежа́ть (-жу́) impf +dat be subject to; **не подлежи́т сомне́нию** it is beyond doubt. **подлежа́щее** sb subject. **подлежа́щий**+dat subject to.

подле́зть impf, **подле́зть** (-зу, -ез) pf crawl (under).

подле́сок (-ска) undergrowth.

подле́ц (-а́) scoundrel.

подлива́ть impf of **подли́ть**. **подли́вка** sauce, dressing, gravy.

подли́за m & f toady. **подлиза́ться** (-ижу́сь, -и́жешься) pf, **подли́зываться** impf +к+dat suck up to.

по́длинник original. **по́длинно** adv really. **по́длинный** genuine; authentic; original; real.

подли́ть (-долью́, -дольёшь; по́длил, -а́, -о) pf (impf **подлива́ть**) pour; add.

подло́г forgery.

подло́дка submarine.

подложи́ть (-жу́, -о́жишь) pf (impf **подкла́дывать**) add; **под**+acc lay under; line.

подло́жный false, spurious; counterfeit, forged.

подлоко́тник arm (of chair).

подломи́ться (-о́мится) pf (impf **подла́мываться**) break; give way.

по́длость meanness, baseness; mean trick. **по́длый** (подл, -а́, -о) mean, base.

подма́зать (-а́жу) pf, **подма́зывать** impf grease; bribe.

подмасте́рье (gen pl -ьев) m apprentice.

подме́н, **подме́на** replacement. **подме́нивать** impf, **подмени́ть** (-ню́, -нишь) pf, **подменя́ть** impf replace.

подмести́ (-ету́, -етёшь; -мёл, -а́) pf, **подмета́ть**[1] impf sweep.

подмета́ть[2] pf (impf **подмётывать**) tack.

подме́тить (-е́чу) pf (impf **подмеча́ть**) notice.

подмётка sole.

подмётывать impf of **подме-**

та́ть². подмеча́ть *impf of* под-
ме́тить

подмеша́ть *pf*, подме́шивать
impf mix in, stir in.

подми́гивать *impf*, подмиг-
ну́ть (-ну́, -нёшь) *pf* +*dat*
wink at.

подмо́га help.

подмока́ть *impf*, подмо́кнуть
(-нет; -мо́к) *pf* get damp, get
wet.

подмора́живать *impf*, подморо́-
зить *impf* freeze.

подмоско́вный (situated) near
Moscow.

подмо́стки (-ов) *pl* scaffolding;
stage.

подмо́ченный damp; tar-
nished.

подмыва́ть *impf*, подмы́ть
(-о́ю) *pf* wash; wash away; его́
так и подмыва́ет he feels an
urge (to).

подмы́шка armpit.

поднево́льный dependent;
forced.

поднести́ (-су́, -сёшь; -ёс, -ла́) *pf*
(*impf* подноси́ть) present; take,
bring.

поднима́ть(ся *impf of* под-
ня́ть(ся

поднови́ть (-влю́) *pf*, подно-
вля́ть *impf* renew, renovate.

подного́тная *sb* ins and outs.

подно́жие foot; pedestal. под-
но́жка running-board. подно́ж-
ный корм pasture.

подно́с tray. подноси́ть (-ошу́,
-о́сишь) *impf of* поднести́. под-
ноше́ние giving; present.

подня́тие raising. подня́ть
(-ниму́, -ни́мешь; по́дня́л, -а́, -о)
pf (*impf* поднима́ть, подыма́ть)
raise; lift (up); rouse; ~ся rise,
go up.

подо́ *see* под

подоба́ть *impf* befit, become.
подоба́ющий proper.

подо́бие likeness; similarity.
подо́бный like, similar; и тому́
~ое and so on, and such like;
ничего́ ~ого! nothing of the
sort!

подобостра́стие servility.
подобостра́стный servile.

подобра́ть (-дберу́, -дберёшь;
-бра́л, -а́, -о) *pf* (*impf* подбира́ть)
pick up; tuck up, put up; pick;
~ся steal up.

подобью́ *etc.: see* подби́ть

подогна́ть (-дгоню́, -дго́нишь;
-а́л, -а́, -о) *pf* (*impf* подгоня́ть)
drive; urge on; adjust.

подогну́ть (-ну́, -нёшь) *pf* (*impf*
подгиба́ть) tuck in; bend
under.

подогрева́ть *impf*, подогре́ть
(-е́ю) *pf* warm up.

пододвига́ть *impf*, пододви́-
нуть (-ну) *pf* move up.

пододея́льник blanket cover;
top sheet.

подожгу́ *etc.: see* подже́чь

подожда́ть (-ду́, -дёшь; -а́л, -а́,
-о) *pf* wait (+*gen or acc* for).

подожму́ *etc.: see* поджа́ть

подозва́ть (-дзову́, -дзовёшь;
-а́л, -а́, -о) *pf* (*impf* подзыва́ть)
call to; beckon.

подозрева́емый suspected;
suspect. подозрева́ть *impf* suspect. подозре́ние suspicion.
подозри́тельный suspicious.

пои́до́йть (-ою́, -о́ишь) *pf*

подойти́ (-йду́, -йдёшь; -ошёл,
-шла́) *pf* (*impf* подходи́ть) approach; come up; +*dat* suit, fit.

подоко́нник window-sill.

подо́л hem and ends.

подо́лгу *adv* for ages; for hours
(*etc.*) on end.

подолью́ *etc.*: see **подли́ть**

подо́нки (-ов) *pl* dregs; scum.

подопле́ка underlying cause.

подопру́ *etc.*: see **подпере́ть**

подо́пытный experimental.

подорва́ть (-ву́, -вёшь; -а́л, -а́, -о) *pf* (*impf* **подрыва́ть**) undermine; blow up.

подоро́жать *pf*.

подоро́жник plantain. **подоро́жный** roadside.

подосла́ть (-ошлю́, -ошлёшь) *pf* (*impf* **подсыла́ть**) send (secretly).

подоспева́ть *impf*, **подоспе́ть** (-е́ю) *pf* arrive, appear (in time).

подостла́ть (-дстелю́, -дсте́лешь) *pf* (*impf* **подстила́ть**) lay under.

подотде́л section, subdivision.

подотру́ *etc.*: see **подтере́ть**

подотчётный accountable.

подо́хнуть (-ну) *pf* (*impf* also **подыха́ть**).

подохо́дный нало́г income-tax.

подо́шва sole; foot.

подошёл *etc.*: see **подойти́**. **подошлю́** *etc.*: see **подосла́ть** **подошью́** *etc.*: see **подши́ть**.

подпада́ть *impf*, **подпа́сть** (-аду́, -адёшь; -а́л) *pf* **под**+*acc* fall under.

подпева́ть *impf* (+*dat*) sing along (with).

подпере́ть (-допру́; -пёр) *pf* (*impf* **подпира́ть**) prop up.

подпи́ливать *impf*, **подпили́ть** (-лю́, -пи́лишь) *pf* saw; saw a little off.

подпира́ть *impf of* **подпере́ть**

подписа́ние signing. **подписа́ть** (-ишу́, -и́шешь) *pf*, **подпи́сывать** *impf* sign; ~**ся** sign; subscribe. **подпи́ска** subscrip-

tion. **подписно́й** subscription. **подпи́счик** subscriber. **по́дпись** signature.

подплыва́ть *impf*, **подплы́ть** (-ыву́, -ывёшь; -ы́л, -а́, -о) *pf* **к**+*dat* swim *or* sail up to.

подполза́ть *impf*, **подползти́** (-зу́, -зёшь; -по́лз, -ла́) *pf* creep up (**к**+*dat* to); +**под**+*acc* crawl under.

подполко́вник lieutenant-colonel.

подпо́лье cellar; underground. **подпо́льный** underfloor; underground.

подпо́ра, подпо́рка prop, support.

подпо́чва subsoil.

подпра́вить (-влю) *pf*, **подправля́ть** *impf* touch up, adjust.

подпры́гивать *impf*, **подпры́гнуть** (-ну) *pf* jump up (and down).

подпуска́ть *impf*, **подпусти́ть** (-ущу́, -у́стишь) *pf* allow to approach.

подраба́тывать *impf*, **подрабо́тать** *pf* earn on the side; work up.

подра́внивать *impf of* **подровня́ть**

подража́ние imitation. **подража́ть** *impf* imitate.

подразделе́ние subdivision. **подраздели́ть** *pf*, **подразделя́ть** *impf* subdivide.

подразумева́ть *impf* imply, mean; ~**ся** be meant, be understood.

подраста́ть *impf*, **подрасти́** (-ту́, -тёшь; -ро́с, -ла́) *pf* grow.

подра́ть(ся (-деру́(сь, -дерёшь(ся, -а́л(ся, -ла́(сь, -ó(сь *or* -о́(сь) *pf*.

подре́зать (-е́жу) *pf*, **подреза́ть** *impf* cut; clip, trim.

подро́бно *adv* in detail. подро́бность detail. подро́бный detailed.

подровня́ть *pf* (*impf* подра́внивать) level, even; trim.

подро́с *etc.: see* подрасти́. подро́сток (-тка) adolescent; youth.

подро́ю *etc.: see* подры́ть

подруба́ть¹ *impf*, подруби́ть (-блю́, -бишь) *pf* chop down; cut short(er).

подруба́ть² *impf*, подруби́ть (-блю́, -бишь) *pf* hem.

подру́га friend; girlfriend. по-дру́жески *adv* in a friendly way. подружи́ться (-жу́сь) *pf* make friends.

по-друго́му *adv* differently.

подру́чный at hand; improvised; *sb* assistant.

подры́в undermining; injury.

подрыва́ть¹ *impf of* подорва́ть

подрыва́ть² *impf*, подры́ть (-ро́ю) *pf* undermine, sap. подрывно́й blasting, demolition; subversive.

подря́д¹ *adv* in succession.

подря́д² contract. подря́дчик contractor.

подса́живаться *impf of* подсе́сть

подса́ливать *impf of* подсоли́ть

подсве́чник candlestick.

подсе́сть (-ся́ду; -се́л) *pf* (*impf* подса́живаться) sit down (к+*dat* near).

подсказа́ть (-ажу́, -а́жешь) *pf*, подска́зывать *impf* prompt; suggest. подска́зка prompting.

подска́кивать *impf*, подскочи́ть (-чу́, -чишь) *pf* jump (up); soar; come running.

подсласти́ть (-ащу́) *pf*, подсла́щивать *impf* sweeten.

подсле́дственный under investigation.

подслу́шать *pf*, подслу́шивать *impf* overhear; eavesdrop, listen.

подсма́тривать *impf*, подсмотре́ть (-рю́, -ришь) *pf* spy (on).

подсне́жник snowdrop.

подсо́бный subsidiary; auxiliary.

подсо́вывать *impf of* подсу́нуть

подсозна́ние subconscious (mind). подсозна́тельный subconscious.

подсоли́ть (-со́лишь) *pf* (*impf* подса́ливать) add salt to.

подсо́лнечник sunflower. подсо́лнечный sunflower.

подсо́хнуть (-ну) *pf* (*impf* подсыха́ть) dry out a little.

подспо́рье help.

подста́вить (-влю) *pf*, подставля́ть *impf* put (under); bring up; expose; ∼ но́жку +*dat* trip up. подста́вка stand; support. подставно́й false.

подстака́нник glass-holder.

подстелю́ *etc.: see* подостла́ть

подстерега́ть *impf*, подстере́чь (-егу́, -ежёшь; -рёг, -ла́) *pf* lie in wait for.

подстила́ть *impf of* подостла́ть. подсти́лка litter.

подстра́ивать *impf of* подстро́ить

подстрека́тель *m* instigator. подстрека́тельство instigation. подстрека́ть *impf*, подстрекну́ть (-ну́, -нёшь) *pf* instigate, incite.

подстре́ливать *impf*, под-

стрели́ть (-лю́, -лишь) *pf* wound.

подстригáть *impf*, **подстри́чь** (-игу́, -ижёшь; -и́г) *pf* cut; clip, trim; ~**ся** have a hair-cut.

подстро́ить *pf* (*impf* **подстрáивать**) build on; cook up.

подстро́чный *literal*; ~**ое примечáние** footnote.

пóдступ approach. **подступáть** *impf*, **подступи́ть** (-плю́, -пишь) *pf* approach; ~**ся к**+*dat* approach.

подсуди́мый *sb* defendant; the accused. **подсýдный**+*dat* under the jurisdiction of.

подсýнуть (-ну) *pf* (*impf* **подсóвывать**) put, shove; palm off.

подсчёт calculation; count. **подсчитáть** *pf*, **подсчи́тывать** *impf* count (up); calculate.

подсылáть *impf* of **подослáть**. **подсыхáть** *impf* of **подсóхнуть**. **подся́ду** *etc.*: *see* **подсéсть**. **подтáлкивать** *impf* of **подтолкну́ть**

подтáскивать *impf* of **подтащи́ть**

подтасовáть *pf*, **подтасóвывать** *impf* shuffle unfairly; juggle with.

подтáчивать *impf* of **подточи́ть**

подтащи́ть (-щу́, -щишь) *pf* (*impf* **подтáскивать**) drag up.

подтверди́ть (-ржу́) *pf*, **подтверждáть** *impf* confirm; corroborate. **подтвержде́ние** confirmation, corroboration.

подтёк bruise. **подтекáть** *impf* of **подте́чь**; leak.

подтере́ть (-дотру́, -дотрёшь; подтёр) *pf* (*impf* **подтирáть**) wipe (up).

подте́чь (-ечёт; -тёк, -лá) *pf*

(*impf* **подтекáть**) **под**+*acc* flow under.

подтирáть *impf* of **подтере́ть**

подтолкну́ть (-ну́, -нёшь) *pf* (*impf* **подтáлкивать**) push; urge on.

подточи́ть (-чу́, -чишь) *pf* (*impf* **подтáчивать**) sharpen; eat away; undermine.

подтру́нивать *impf*, **подтруни́ть** *pf* **над**+*instr* tease.

подтя́гивать *impf*, **подтяну́ть** (-ну́, -нешь) *pf* tighten; pull up; move up; ~**ся** tighten one's belt *etc.*; move up; pull o.s. together.

подтя́жки (-жек) *pl* braces, suspenders. **подтя́нутый** smart.

поду́мать *pf* think (for a while). **поду́мывать** *impf*+*inf* or **о**+*prep* think about.

поду́ть (-у́ю) *pf*.

поду́шка pillow; cushion.

подхали́м *m* toady. **подхали́мство** grovelling.

подхвати́ть (-ачу́, -áтишь) *pf*, **подхвáтывать** *impf* catch (up), pick up, take up.

подхлестну́ть (-ну́, -нёшь) *pf*, **подхлёстывать** *impf* whip up.

подхóд approach. **подходи́ть** (-ожу́, -óдишь) *impf* of **подойти́**. **подходя́щий** suitable.

подцепи́ть (-плю́, -пишь) *pf*, **подцепля́ть** *impf* hook on; pick up.

подчáс *adv* sometimes.

подчёркивать *impf*, **подчеркну́ть** (-ну́, -нёшь) *pf* underline; emphasize.

подчине́ние subordination; submission. **подчинённый** subordinate. **подчини́ть** *pf*, **подчиня́ть** *impf* subordinate, subject; ~**ся**+*dat* submit to.

подшивáть *impf* of **подши́ть**.

подши́вка hemming; lining; soling.

подши́пник bearing.

подши́ть (-дошью́, -дошьёшь) pf (impf подшива́ть) hem, line; sole.

подшути́ть (-учу́, -у́тишь) pf, подшу́чивать impf над+instr mock; play a trick on.

подъе́ду etc.: see подъе́хать

подъе́зд entrance, doorway; approach. подъезжа́ть impf of подъе́хать

подъём lifting; raising; ascent; climb; enthusiasm; instep; reveille. подъёмник lift, elevator, hoist. подъёмный lifting; ~ кран crane; ~ мост drawbridge.

подъе́хать (-е́ду) pf (impf подъезжа́ть) drive up.

подыма́ть(ся) impf of подня́ть(ся)

подыска́ть (-ыщу́, -ы́щешь) pf, поды́скивать impf seek (out).

подыто́живать impf, подыто́жить (-жу) sum up.

подыха́ть impf of подо́хнуть

подыша́ть (-шу́, -шишь) pf breathe.

поеда́ть impf of пое́сть

поеди́нок (-нка) duel.

по́езд (pl -а́) train. пое́здка trip.

пое́сть (-е́м, -е́шь, -е́ст, -еди́м; -е́л) pf (impf поеда́ть) eat, eat up; have a bite to eat.

пое́хать (-е́ду) pf go; set off.

пожале́ть (-е́ю) pf.

пожа́ловать(ся pf. пожа́луй adv perhaps. пожа́луйста partl please; you're welcome.

пожа́р fire. пожа́рище scene of a fire. пожа́рник, пожа́рный sb fireman. пожа́рный fire; ~ая кома́нда fire-brigade; ~ая лест-

ница fire-escape; ~ая маши́на fire-engine.

пожа́тие handshake. пожа́ть[1] (-жму́, -жмёшь) pf (impf пожима́ть) press; ~ ру́ку+dat shake hands with; ~ плеча́ми shrug one's shoulders.

пожа́ть[2] (-жну́, -жнёшь) pf (impf пожина́ть) reap.

пожела́ние wish, desire. пожела́ть pf.

пожелте́ть (-е́ю) pf.

пожени́ть (-ню́, -нишь) pf. пожени́ться (-же́нимся) pf get married.

поже́ртвование donation. поже́ртвовать pf.

пожива́ть impf live; как (вы) пожива́ете? how are you (getting on)? пожи́зненный life(long). пожило́й elderly.

пожима́ть impf of пожа́ть[1]. пожина́ть impf of пожа́ть[2]. пожира́ть impf of пожра́ть

пожи́тки (-ов) pl belongings.

пожи́ть (-иву́, -ивёшь; по́жил, -а́, -о) pf. live for a while; stay.

пожму́ etc.: see пожа́ть[1]. пожну́ etc.: see пожа́ть[2]

пожра́ть (-ру́, -рёшь; -а́л, -а́, -о) pf (impf пожира́ть) devour.

по́за pose.

позабо́титься (-о́чусь) pf.

позабыва́ть impf, позабы́ть (-у́ду) pf forget all about.

позави́довать pf. поза́втракать pf.

позавчера́ adv the day before yesterday.

позади́ adv & prep+gen behind.

поза́имствовать pf.

позапро́шлый before last.

позва́ть (-зову́, -зовёшь; -а́л, -а́, -о) pf.

позволе́ние permission. поз-

воли́тельный permissible.
позво́лить pf, **позволя́ть** impf +dat allow, permit; **позво́ль(те)** allow me; excuse me.
по|**звони́ть** pf.
позвоно́к (-нка́) vertebra. **позвоно́чник** spine. **позвоно́чный** spinal; vertebrate; **~ые** sb pl vertebrates.
поздне́е adv later. **по́здний** late; **по́здно** it is late.
по|**здоро́ваться** pf. **поздра́вить** (-влю) pf, **поздравля́ть** impf c+instr congratulate on. **поздравле́ние** congratulation.
по|**зелене́ть** (-е́ет) pf.
по́зже adv later (on).
пози́ровать impf pose.
позити́в positive. **позити́вный** positive.
пози́ция position.
познава́тельный cognitive. **познава́ть** (-наю́, -наёшь) impf of **позна́ть**
по|**знако́мить(ся** (-млю(сь) pf.
позна́ние cognition. **позна́ть** pf (impf **познава́ть**) get to know.
позоло́та gilding. **по**|**золоти́ть** (-лочу́) pf.
позо́р shame, disgrace. **позо́рить** impf (pf o~) disgrace; **~ся** disgrace o.s. **позо́рный** shameful.
поигра́ть pf play for a while).
поимённо adv by name.
по́имка capture.
поинтересова́ться pf be curious.
поиска́ть (-ищу́, -и́щешь) pf look for. **по́иски** (-ов) pl search.
пои́стине adv indeed.
пои́ть (пою́, по́ишь) impf (pf на~) give something to drink; water.

пойду́ etc.: see **пойти́**
по́йло swill.
пойма́ть pf of **лови́ть**. **пойму́** etc.: see **поня́ть**
пойти́ (-йду́, -йдёшь, пошёл, -шла́) pf of **идти́**, **ходи́ть**; go, walk; begin to walk; +inf begin; **пошёл!** off you go! I'm off; **пошёл вон!** be off!
пока́ adv for the present; cheerio; **~ что** in the meanwhile. **пока́** conj while; **~ не** until.
пока́з showing, demonstration. **показа́ние** testimony, evidence; reading. **показа́тель** m index. **показа́тельный** significant; model; demonstration. **показа́ть** (-ажу́, -а́жешь) pf, **пока́зывать** impf show. **показа́ться** (-ажу́сь, -а́жешься) pf, **пока́зываться** impf show o.s.; appear. **показно́й** for show; ostentatious. **показу́ха** show.
по|**кале́чить(ся** (-чу(сь) pf.
пока́мест adv & conj for the present; while; meanwhile.
по|**кара́ть** pf.
по|**ката́ться** pf.
покати́ть (-чу́, -тишь) pf start (rolling); **~ся** start rolling.
пока́тый sloping; slanting.
покача́ть pf rock, swing; **~ голово́й** shake one's head. **пока́чивать** rock slightly; **~ся** rock; stagger. **покачну́ть** (-ну́, -нёшь) pf shake; rock; **~ся** sway, totter, lurch.
пока́шливать impf have a slight cough.
покая́ние confession; repentance. **по**|**ка́яться** pf.
поквита́ться pf be quits; get even.
покида́ть impf, **поки́нуть** (-ну

pf leave; abandon. **поки́нутый** deserted.

поклада́я: не ~ рук untiringly.

покла́дистый complaisant, obliging.

покло́н bow; greeting; regards. **поклоне́ние** worship. **поклони́ться** (-ню́сь, -ни́шься) *pf of* **кла́няться. покло́нник** admirer; worshipper. **поклоня́ться** *impf* +*dat* worship.

по|кля́сться (-яну́сь, -нёшься; -я́лся, -ла́сь) *pf*.

поко́иться *impf* rest, repose. **поко́й** rest, peace; room. **поко́йник, -ица** the deceased. **поко́йный** calm, quiet; deceased.

по|колеба́ть(ся (-е́блю(сь), -о́тишь(ся) *pf*.

поколе́ние generation.

по|колоти́ть(ся (-очу́(сь), -о́тишь(ся) *pf*.

поко́нчить (-чу) *pf* с+*instr* finish; put an end to; **~ с собо́й** commit suicide.

покоре́ние conquest. **покори́ть** *pf* (*impf* **покоря́ть**) subdue; conquer; **~ся** submit.

по|корми́ть(ся (-млю́(сь), -мишь(ся) *pf*.

поко́рный humble; submissive, obedient.

по|коро́бить(ся (-блю(сь) *pf*.

покоря́ть(ся *impf of* **покори́ть(ся**

поко́с mowing; meadow(-land). **покоси́вшийся** rickety, ramshackle. **по|коси́ть(ся** (-ошу́(сь) *pf*.

по|кра́сить (-а́шу) *pf*. **покра́ска** painting, colouring. **по|красне́ть** (-е́ю) *pf*. **по|криви́ть(ся** (-влю́(сь) *pf*.

покро́в cover. **покрови́тель** *m*, **покрови́тельница** patron; sponsor. **покрови́тельственный** protective; patronizing.

покрови́тельство protection, patronage. **покрови́тельствовать** *impf* +*dat* protect, patronize.

покро́й cut.

покроши́ть (-шу́, -шишь) *pf* crumble; chop.

по|крути́ть (-учу́, -у́тишь) *pf* twist.

покрыва́ло cover; bedspread; veil. **по|кры́ть** (-ро́ю) *pf* cover; **~ся** cover o.s.; get covered. **покры́тие** covering; surfacing; payment. **покры́шка** cover; tyre.

покупа́тель *m* buyer; customer. **покупа́ть** *impf of* **купи́ть. поку́пка** purchase. **покупно́й** bought, purchased; purchase.

по|кури́ть (-рю́, -ришь) *pf* have a smoke.

по|ку́шать *pf*.

покуше́ние +**на**+*acc* attempted assassination of.

пол[1] (*loc* -ý; *pl* -ы́) floor.

пол[2] sex.

пол- *in comb with n in gen, in oblique cases usu* **полу-**, half.

пола́ (*pl* -ы) flap; **из-под полы́** on the sly.

полага́ть *impf* suppose, think. **полага́ться** *impf of* **положи́ться; полага́ется** *impers* one is supposed to; +*dat* it is due to.

по|лако́мить(ся (-млю(сь) *pf*.

полго́да (полуго́да) *m* half a year.

по́лдень (-дня *or* -лу́дня) *m* noon. **полдне́вный** *adj*.

по́ле (*pl* -я́, -е́й) field; ground; margin; brim. **полево́й** field; **~ые цветы́** wild flowers.

полежа́ть (-жу́) *pf* lie down for a while.

поле́зн|ый useful; helpful; good, wholesome; **~ая нагру́зка** payload.

по|ле́зть (-зу; -ле́з) *pf.*

полемизи́ровать *impf* debate, engage in controversy. **поле́мика** controversy; polemics. **полеми́ческий** polemical.

по|лени́ться (-ню́сь, -нишься) *pf.*

поле́но (*pl* -е́нья, -ьев) log.

полёт flight. **по|лете́ть** (-лечу́) *pf.*

по́лзать *indet impf*, **ползти́** (-зу́, -зёшь; полз, -ла́) *det impf* crawl, creep; ooze; fray. **ползу́чий** creeping.

поли- *in comb* poly-.

полива́ть(ся *impf of* **поли́ть(ся, поли́вка** watering.

полига́мия polygamy.

полигло́т polyglot.

полиграфи́ческий printing. **полигра́фия** printing.

полиго́н range.

поликли́ника polyclinic.

полиме́р polymer.

поли́ня|лый faded. **по|линя́ть** *pf.*

полиомиели́т poliomyelitis

полирова́ть *impf* (*pf* **от~**) polish. **полиро́вка** polishing; polish.

полит- *abbr in comb* (*of* **полити́ческий**) political. **политзаключённый** *sb* political prisoner.

политехни́ческий polytechnic.

поли́тик politician. **поли́тика** policy; politics. **полити́ческий** political; **полити́чески корре́ктный** politically correct.

поли́ть (-лью́, -льёшь; по́ли́л, -а́, -о) *pf* (*impf* **полива́ть**) pour

over; water; **~ся** +*instr* pour over o.s.

полице́йский police; *sb* policeman. **поли́ция** police.

поли́чн|ое *sb*: **с ~ым** red-handed.

полк (-а́, *loc* -ý) regiment.

по́лка berth; berth.

полко́вник colonel. **полково́дец** (-дца) commander; general. **полково́й** regimental.

пол-ли́тра half a litre.

полне́ть (-е́ю) *impf* (*pf* **по~**) put on weight.

по́лно *adv* that's enough! stop it!

полно- *in comb* full; completely. **полнолу́ние** full moon. **~метра́жный** full-length. **~пра́вный** enjoying full rights; competent. **~це́нный** of full value.

полномо́чи|е (*usu pl*) authority, power. **полномо́чный** plenipotentiary.

по́лностью *adv* in full; completely. **полнота́** completeness; corpulence.

по́лночь (-л(ý)ночи) midnight.

по́лн|ый (-лон, -лна́, по́лно́) full; complete; plump.

полови́к (-а́) mat, matting.

полови́на half; **два с полови́ной** two and a half; **~ шесто́го** half-past five. **полови́нка** half.

полови́ца floor-board.

полово́дье high water.

полово́й[1] floor.

полово́й[2] sexual.

поло́гий gently sloping.

положе́ние position; situation; status; regulations; thesis; provisions. **поло́женный** agreed; determined. **поло́жим** let us assume; suppose. **положи́тельный** positive. **положи́ть** (-жу́,

-жишь) *pf* (*impf* **класть**) put; lay (down); **~ся** (*impf* **полага́ться**) rely.

по́лоз (*pl* -о́зья, -ьев) runner.

полома́ть(ся *pf.* **поло́мка** breakage.

полоса́ (*acc* по́лосу; *pl* по́лосы, -ло́с, -а́м) stripe; strip; band; region; belt; period. **полоса́тый** striped.

полоска́ть (-ощу́, -о́щешь) *impf* (*pf* вы́~, от~, про~) rinse; **~ го́рло** gargle; **~ся** paddle; flap.

по́лость[1] (*gen pl* -е́й) cavity.

по́лость[2] (*gen pl* -е́й) travelling rug.

полоте́нце (*gen pl* -нец) towel.

полотёр floor-polisher.

поло́тнище width; panel. **поло́тно** (*pl* -а, -тен) linen; canvas. **полотня́ный** linen.

поло́ть (-лю́, -лешь) *impf* (*pf* вы́~) weed.

полощу́ *etc.: see* **полоска́ть**

полти́нник fifty copecks.

полтора́ (-ра́ра) *m & neut*, **полторы́** (-ра́ра) *f* one and a half. **полтора́ста** (полут-) a hundred and fifty.

полу-[1] *see* **пол**

полу-[2] *in comb* half-, semi-, demi-. **полуботи́нок** (-нка; *gen pl* -нок) shoe. **~го́дие** half a year. **~годи́чный** six months', lasting six months. **~годова́лый** six-month-old. **~годово́й** half-yearly, six-monthly. **~гра́мотный** semi-literate. **~защи́тник** half-back. **~круг** semi-circle. **~кру́глый** semicircular. **~ме́сяц** crescent (moon). **~мра́к** semi-darkness. **~но́чный** midnight. **~о́стров** peninsula. **~откры́тый** ajar. **~прово́дник** (-а́) semi-conductor, transistor. **~ста́нок** (-нка) halt.

~тьма́ semi-darkness. **~фабрика́т** semi-finished product, convenience food. **~фина́л** semi-final. **~часово́й** half-hourly. **~шу́бок** (-бка) sheepskin coat.

получа́тель *m* recipient. **получа́ть** *impf*, **получи́ть** (-чу́, -чишь) *pf* get, receive, obtain; **~ся** come, turn up; turn out; **из э́того ничего́ не получи́лось** nothing came of it. **получе́ние** receipt. **полу́чка** receipt; pay(-packet).

полу́чше *adv* a little better.

полчаса́ (получа́са) *m* half an hour.

по́лчище horde.

по́лый hollow; flood.

по|лысе́ть (-е́ю) *pf*.

по́льза benefit, profit; **в по́льзу**+*gen* in favour of, on behalf of. **по́льзование** use. **по́льзоваться** *impf* (*pf* вос~) +*instr* make use of, utilize; profit by; enjoy.

по́лька Pole; polka. **по́льский** Polish; *sb* polonaise.

по|льсти́ть(ся (-льщу́(сь)

польщу́ *etc. see* **польти́ть**

По́льша Poland.

полюби́ть (-блю́, -бишь) *pf* come to like; fall in love with.

по|любова́ться (-бу́юсь) *pf.*

полюбо́вный amicable.

по|любопы́тствовать *pf.*

по́люс pole.

поля́к Pole.

поля́на glade, clearing.

поляриза́ция polarization. **поля́рник** polar explorer. **поля́рный** polar; **~ая звезда́** pole-star.

пом- *abbr in comb* (*of* помощ-

ник) assistant. **∼на́ч** assistant chief, assistant head.

пома́да pomade; lipstick.

помаза́ние anointment. **по|ма́зать(ся** (-а́жу(сь)) *pf.* **помазо́к** (-зка́) small brush.

помале́ньку *adv* gradually; gently; modestly; so-so.

пома́лкивать *impf* hold one's tongue.

по|мани́ть (-ню́, -нишь) *pf.*

пома́рка blot; pencil mark; correction.

по|ма́слить *pf.*

помаха́ть (-машу́, -ма́шешь) *pf*, **пома́хивать** *impf +instr* wave; wag.

помедли́ть *pf +с+instr* delay.

поме́ньше a little smaller; a little less.

по|меня́ть(ся *pf.*

помере́ть (-мру́, -мрёшь; -мер, -ла́, -ло) *pf* (*impf* **помира́ть**) die.

по|мере́щиться (-щусь) *pf.* **по|ме́рить** *pf.*

помертве́лый deathly pale. **по|мертве́ть** (-е́ю) *pf.*

помести́ть (-ещу́) *pf* (*impf* **помеща́ть**) accommodate; place, locate; invest; **∼ся** lodge; find room. **поме́стье** (*gen pl* -тий, -тьям) estate.

по́месь cross(-breed), hybrid.

помёт dung; droppings; litter, brood.

поме́та, поме́тка mark, note. **по|ме́тить** (-е́чу) *pf* (*impf also* **помеча́ть**) mark; date; **∼ га́лочкой** tick.

поме́ха hindrance; obstacle; *pl* interference.

помеча́ть *impf of* **поме́тить**

поме́шанный mad; *sb* lunatic. **помеша́тельство** madness; craze. **по|меша́ть** *pf.* **поме-**

ша́ться *pf* go mad.

помеща́ть *impf of* **помести́ть**. **помеща́ться** *impf of* **помести́ться**; be (situated); be accommodated, find room. **помеще́ние** premises; apartment, room, lodging; location; investment. **поме́щик** landowner.

помидо́р tomato.

помилова́ние forgiveness. **по|ми́ловать** *pf* forgive.

поми́мо *prep+gen* apart from; besides; without the knowledge of.

помина́ть *impf of* **помяну́ть**; **не ∼ ли́хом** remember kindly. **поми́нки** (-нок) *pl* funeral repast.

помира́ть *impf of* **помере́ть**. **по|мири́ть(ся** *pf.*

по́мнить *impf* remember.

помога́ть *impf of* **помо́чь**.

по-мо́ему *adv* in my opinion.

помо́и (-ев) *pl* slops. **помо́йка** (*gen pl* -о́ек) rubbish dump. **помо́йный** slop.

помо́л grinding.

помо́лвка betrothal.

по|моли́ться (-лю́сь, -лишься) *pf.* **по|молоде́ть** (-е́ю) *pf.*

помолча́ть (-чу́) *pf* be silent for a time.

помо́рье: *see* **по-** II.

по|мо́рщиться (-щусь) *pf.*

помо́ст dais; rostrum.

по|мочи́ться (-чу́сь, -чишься) *pf.*

помо́чь (-огу́, -о́жешь; -о́г, -ла́) *pf* (*impf* **помога́ть**) (+*dat*) help. **помо́щник, помо́щница** assistant. **по́мощь** help; **на ∼!** help!

помо́ю *etc.: see* **помы́ть**

по́мпа pump.

помутне́ние dimness, clouding.

помча́ться (-чу́сь) *pf* rush; dart off.

помыка́ть *impf* +*instr* order about.

по́мысел (-сла) intention; thought.

по|мы́ть(ся (-мо́ю(сь)) *pf.*

помяну́ть (-ну́, -нешь) *pf* (*impf* помина́ть) mention; pray for.

помя́тый crumpled. **по|мя́ться** (-мнётся) *pf.*

по|наде́яться (-е́юсь) *pf* count, rely.

пона́добиться (-блюсь) *pf* be or become necessary; **е́сли пона́добится** if necessary.

понапра́сну *adv* in vain.

понаслы́шке *adv* by hearsay.

по-настоя́щему *adv* properly, truly.

понача́лу *adv* at first.

понево́ле *adv* willynilly; against one's will.

понеде́льник Monday.

понемно́гу, понемно́жку *adv* little by little.

по|нести́(сь (-су́(сь, -сёшь(ся; -нёс(ся, -ла́(сь) *pf.*

понижа́ть *impf*, **пони́зить** (-ни́жу) *pf* lower; reduce; **~ся** fall, drop, go down. **пониже́ние** fall; lowering; reduction.

поника́ть *impf*, **пони́кнуть** (-ну; -ник) *pf* droop, wilt.

понима́ние understanding. **понима́ть** *impf* of поня́ть

по-но́вому *adv* in a new fashion.

поно́с diarrhoea.

поноси́ть¹ (-ошу́, -о́сишь) *pf* carry; wear.

поноси́ть² (-ошу́, -о́сишь) *impf* abuse (*verbally*).

поно́шенный worn; threadbare.

по|нра́виться (-влюсь) *pf.*

понто́н pontoon.

пону́дить (-у́жу) *pf*, **понужда́ть** *impf* compel.

понука́ть *impf* urge on.

пону́рить *pf*: **~ го́лову** hang one's head. **пону́рый** downcast.

по|ню́хать *pf*. **поню́шка**: **~ табаку́** pinch of snuff.

поня́тие concept; notion, idea. **поня́тливый** bright, quick. **поня́тный** understandable, comprehensible; clear; **~о** naturally; **~о?** (do you) see? **поня́ть** (пойму́, -мёшь; по́нял, -а́, -о) *pf* (*impf* понима́ть) understand; realize.

по|обе́дать *pf*. **по|обеща́ть** *pf.*

поо́даль *adv* at some distance.

поодино́чке *adv* one by one.

поочерёдно *adv* in turn.

поощре́ние encouragement. **поощри́ть** *pf*, **поощря́ть** *impf* encourage.

поп (-á) priest.

попада́ние hit. **попада́ть(ся** *impf* of попа́сть(ся

попадья́ priest's wife.

попа́ло: see попа́сть. **по|па́риться** *pf.*

попа́рно *adv* in pairs, two by two.

попа́сть (-аду́, -адёшь; -а́л) *pf* (*impf* попада́ть) +в+*acc* hit; get (in)to, find o.s. in; +на+*acc* hit upon, come on; **не туда́ ~** get the wrong number; **~ся** be caught; find o.s.; turn up; **что попадётся** anything. **попа́ло** with *prons* & *advs*: **где ~** anywhere; **как ~** anyhow; **что ~** the first thing to hand.

поперёк *adv* & *prep*+*gen* across.

попереме́нно *adv* in turns.

попере́чник diameter. **попере́чный** transverse, diamet-

rical, cross; **∼ый разре́з, ∼ое сече́ние** cross-section.

поперхну́ться (-ну́сь, -нёшься) *pf* choke.

по|пе́рчить (-чу) *pf*.

попече́ние care; charge; **на попече́нии**+*gen* in the care of. **попечи́тель** *m* guardian, trustee.

попира́ть *impf* (*pf* **попра́ть**) trample on; flout.

попи́ть (-пью́, -пьёшь; по́пи́л, -ла́, по́пи́ло) *pf* have a drink.

поплаво́к (-вка́) float.

попла́кать (-а́чу) *pf* cry a little.

по|плати́ться (-чу́сь, -тишься) *pf*.

попльíть (-ывý, -ывёшь; -ы́л, -ыла́, -о) *pf* start swimming.

попо́йка drinking-bout.

попола́м *adv* in two, in half; half-and-half.

поползнове́ние half a mind; pretension(s).

пополне́ние replenishment; reinforcement. **попо́лнить** (-ню) *pf*. **пополня́ть** *impf* replenish; re-stock; reinforce.

пополу́дни *adv* in the afternoon; p.m.

попо́на horse-cloth.

по|по́тчевать (-чую) *pf*.

поправи́мый rectifiable. **попра́вить** (-влю) *pf*, **поправля́ть** *impf* repair; correct; put right; set straight; **∼ся** correct o.s.; get better, recover; improve. **попра́вка** correction; repair; adjustment; recovery.

попра́ть *pf* of **попира́ть**

по-пре́жнему *adv* as before.

попрёк reproach. **попрека́ть** *impf*, **попрекну́ть** (-нý, -нёшь) *pf* reproach.

по́прище field; walk of life.

по|про́бовать *pf*. **по|проси́ть(ся** (-ошý(сь, -о́сишь(ся) *pf*.

по́просту *adv* simply; without ceremony.

попроша́йка *m* & *f* cadger. **попроша́йничать** *impf* cadge.

попроща́ться *pf* (+с+*instr*) say goodbye (to).

попры́гать *pf* jump, hop.

попуга́й parrot.

популя́рность popularity. **популя́рный** popular.

попусти́тельство connivance.

по-пусто́му, по́пусту *adv* in vain.

попу́тно *adv* at the same time; in passing. **попу́тный** passing. **попу́тчик** fellow-traveller.

по|пыта́ться *pf*. **попы́тка** attempt.

по|пя́титься (-я́чусь) *pf*. **попя́тный** backward; **идти́ на ∼** go back on one's word.

по́ра¹ pore.

пора́² (*acc* -у; *pl* -ы, пор, -а́м) time; it is time; **до каки́х пор?** till when?; **до сих пор** till now; **с каки́х пор?** since when?

порабо́тать *pf* do some work.

порабо́тить (-ощý) *pf*, **порабоща́ть** *impf* enslave. **порабоще́ние** enslavement.

поравня́ться *pf* come alongside.

по|ра́доваться(ся *pf*.

поража́ть *impf*, **по|рази́ть** (-ажý) *pf* hit; strike; defeat; affect; astonish; **∼ся** be astounded. **пораже́ние** defeat. **порази́тельный** striking; astonishing.

по-ра́зному *adv* differently.

пора́нить *pf* wound; injure.

порва́ть (-вý, -вёшь; -ва́л, -á, -о) *pf* (*impf* **порыва́ть**) tear (up)

поредеть break, break off; ~ся tear; break (off).

по|редеть (-еет) *pf.*

порез cut. **порезать** (-ежу) *pf* cut; ~ся cut o.s.

порей leek.

по|рекомендовать *pf.*

по|ржаветь (-еет) *pf.*

пористый porous.

порицание reprimand. **порицать** *impf* reprimand.

порка flogging.

поровну *adv* equally.

порог threshold; rapids.

порода breed, race, species; (*also* горная порода) rock. **породистый** thoroughbred. **породить** (-ожу) *pf* (*impf* порождать) give birth to; give rise to.

по|роднить(ся *pf.* **породный** pedigree.

порождать *impf of* породить.

порознь *adv* separately, apart.

порой, порою *adv* at times.

порок vice; defect.

поросёнок (-нка; *pl* -сята, -сят) piglet.

поросль shoots; young wood.

пороть[1] (-рю, -решь) *impf* (*pf* вы~) thrash; whip.

пороть[2] (-рю, -решь) *impf* (*pf* рас~) undo, unpick; ~ся come unstitched.

порох (*pl* -á) gunpowder, powder. **пороховой** powder.

порочить (-чу) *impf* (*pf* о~) discredit; smear. **порочный** vicious, depraved; faulty.

порошить (-шит) *impf* snow slightly.

порошок (-шка) powder.

порт (*loc* -ý; *pl* -ы, -óв) port.

портативный portable; ~ компьютер laptop; ~ телефон mobile phone.

портвейн port (wine...

портить (-чу) *impf* (... spoil; corrupt; ~ся deter... go bad.

портниха dressmaker. **портновский** tailor's. **портной** *sb* tailor.

портовый port.

портрет portrait.

портсигар cigarette-case.

португалец (-льца), -лка Portuguese. **Португалия** Portugal. **португальский** Portuguese.

портфель *m* brief-case; portfolio.

портьера curtain(s), portière.

портянка foot-binding; puttee

поругание desecration. **поруганный** desecrated; outraged. **поругать** *pf* scold, swear at; ~ся swear; fall out.

порука bail; guarantee; surety; на поруки on bail.

по-русски *adv* (in) Russian.

поручать *impf of* поручить. **поручение** assignment; errand; message.

поручень (-чня) *m* handrail.

поручительство guarantee; bail.

поручить (-чу, -чишь) *pf* (*impf* поручать) entrust; instruct. **поручиться** (-чусь, -чишься) *pf of* ручаться

порхать *impf*, **порхнуть** (-нý, -нёшь) *pf* flutter, flit.

порция portion; helping.

порча spoiling; damage; curse.

поршень *m* piston.

порыв[1] gust; rush; fit

порыв[2] breaking. **порывать(ся**[1] *impf of* порвать(ся

порываться[2] *impf* make jerky movements; endeavour. **порывистый** gusty; jerky; impetuous; fitful.

ы|ва́ть

l. поря́док
e; manner,
t; ~ дня
the day. поря́-
honest; re-
considerable.

...ку) -ады́шь) *pf of*
сади́ть, сажа́ть. поса́дка planting; embarkation; boarding;
landing. поса́дочный planting;
landing.

посажу́ *etc.: see* посади́ть.
по|сва́тать(ся *pf.* по|свеже́ть
(-е́ет) *pf.* по|свети́ть (-ечу́,
-е́тишь) *pf.* по|светле́ть (-е́ет)
pf.

посви́стывать *impf* whistle.

по-сво́ему *adv* (in) one's own
way.

посвяти́ть (-ящу́) *pf,* посвя-
ща́ть *impf* devote; dedicate; let
in; ordain. посвяще́ние dedication; initiation; ordination.

посе́в sowing; crops. посевно́й
sowing; ~áя пло́щадь area
under crops.

по|седе́ть (-е́ю) *pf.*

поселе́нец (-нца) settler; exile.
поселе́ние settlement; exile.
по|сели́ть (ся) *pf,* поселя́ть *impf*
settle; lodge; arouse; ~ся settle,
take up residence. посёлок
(-лка) settlement; housing
estate.

посеребрённый (-рён, -á)
silver-plated. по|серебри́ть *pf.*

посереди́не *adv & prep+gen* in
the middle (of).

посети́тель *m* visitor. посе-
ти́ть (-ещу́) *pf* (*impf* посеща́ть)
visit; attend.

по|се́товать *pf.*

посеща́емость attendance.
посеща́ть *impf of* посети́ть.
посеще́ние visit.

по|се́ять (-е́ю) *pf.*

посиде́ть (-ижу́) *pf* sit (for a
while).

поси́льный within one's powers; feasible.

посине́лый gone blue. по|си-
не́ть (-е́ю) *pf.*

по|скака́ть (-ачу́, -а́чешь) *pf.*

поскользну́ться (-ну́сь,
-нёшься) *pf* slip.

поско́льку *conj* as far as, (in) so
far as.

по|скро́мничать *pf.* по|ску-
пи́ться (-плю́сь) *pf.*

посла́нец (-нца) messenger;
envoy. посла́ние message; epistle. посла́нник envoy, minister.
посла́ть (-шлю́, -шлёшь) *pf*
(*impf* посыла́ть) send.

по́сле *adv & prep+gen* after;
afterwards.

после- *in comb* post-; after-. по-
слевое́нный post-war. ~за́в-
тра *adv* the day after tomorrow.
~родово́й post-natal. ~сло́-
вие epilogue; concluding remarks.

после́дний last; recent; latest;
latter. после́дователь *m* follower. после́довательность
sequence; consistency. после́-
довательный consecutive;
consistent. по|сле́довать *pf.* по-
сле́дствие consequence. по-
сле́дующий subsequent; consequent.

посло́вица proverb, saying.
по|служи́ть (-жу́, -жишь) *pf.* по-
служно́й service.

послуша́ние obedience.
по|слу́шать(ся *pf.* послу́шный
obedient.

по|слы́шаться (-шится) *pf.*

посма́тривать *impf* look from
time to time.

посме́иваться *impf* chuckle.
посме́ртный posthumous.

по|сме́ть (-е́ю) *pf.*

посмея́ние ridicule. по|смея́ться (-ею́сь, -еёшься *pf* laugh; +над+*instr* laugh at.

по|смотре́ть(ся (-рю́(сь, -ришь)ся *pf.*

посо́бие (-я) aid; allowance, benefit; textbook. посо́бник accomplice.

по|сове́товать(ся *pf.* по|содействовать *pf.*

посо́л (-сла́) ambassador.

по|соли́ть (-олю́, -о́лишь) *pf.*

посо́льство embassy.

поспа́ть (-сплю́; -а́л, -а́, -о) *pf* sleep; have a nap.

поспева́ть[1] *impf,* по|спе́ть[1] (-е́ет) *pf* ripen.

поспева́ть[2] *impf,* поспе́ть[2] (-е́ю) *pf* have time; be in time (к+*dat,* на+*acc* for); +за+*instr* keep up with.

по|спеши́ть (-шу́) *pf.* поспе́шный hasty, hurried.

по|спо́рить *pf.* по|спосо́бствовать *pf.*

посрами́ть (-млю́) *pf,* посрамля́ть *impf* disgrace.

посреди́, посреди́не *adv &* *prep*+*gen* in the middle (of). посре́дник mediator. посре́дничество mediation. посре́дственный mediocre. посре́дством *prep*+*gen* by means of.

по|ссо́рить(ся *pf.*

пост[1] (-а́, *loc* -у́) post.

пост[2] (-а́, *loc* -у́) fast(ing).

по|ста́вить[1] (-влю) *pf.*

поста́вить[2] (-влю) *pf,* поставля́ть *impf* supply. поста́вка delivery. поставщи́к (-а́) supplier.

постаме́нт pedestal.

постанови́ть (-влю́, -вишь) *pf* (*impf* постановля́ть) decree; decide.

постано́вка production; arrangement; putting, placing.

постановле́ние decree; decision. постановля́ть *impf of* постанови́ть

постано́вщик producer; (film) director.

по|стара́ться *pf.*

по|старе́ть (-е́ю) *pf.* по-ста́рому *adv* as before.

посте́ль bed. посте́лю *etc.: see* постла́ть

постепе́нный gradual.

по|стесня́ться *pf.*

постига́ть *impf of* пости́чь. постига́ть *see* пости́чь. постиже́ние comprehension, grasp. постижи́мый comprehensible.

постила́ть *impf of* постла́ть

постира́ть *pf* do some washing.

пости́ться (-щу́сь) *impf* fast.

пости́чь, постигну́ть (-и́гну, -и́г(нул) *pf* (*impf* постига́ть) comprehend, grasp; befall.

по|стла́ть (-стелю́, -сте́лешь) *pf* (*impf also* постила́ть) spread; make (*bed*).

по́стный lenten; lean; glum; ~ое ма́сло vegetable oil.

постово́й on point duty.

посто́й billeting.

посто́льку: ~, поско́льку *conj* to that extent, insofar as.

по|сторони́ться (-ню́сь, -ни́шься) *pf.* посторо́нний strange; foreign; extraneous; outside; *sb* stranger, outsider.

постоя́нный permanent; constant; continual; ~ый ток direct current. постоя́нство constancy.

по|стоя́ть (-ою́) *pf* stand (for a while); +за+*acc* stand up for.

пострада́вший *sb* victim.

постригаться *impf*, **постр*и*чься** (-игусь, -ижёшься; - игся) *pf* get monastic vows; get one's hair cut.

постро*е*ние construction; building; formation. **по|стр*о*ить(ся** (-*о*ю(сь) *pf*. **постр*о*йка** building.

постскр*и*птум postscript.

постул*и*ровать *impf & pf* postulate.

поступ*а*тельный forward. **поступ*а*ть** *impf*, **поступ*и*ть** (-плю, -пишь) *pf* act; do; be received; **+в** or **на**+*acc* enter, join; **+с**+*instr* treat; **~ся** +*instr* waive, forgo. **поступл*е*ние** entering, joining; receipt. **пост*у*пок** (-пка) act, deed. **п*о*ступь** gait; step.

по|стуч*а*ть(ся (-чу(сь) *pf*.

по|стыд*и*ться (-ыжусь) *pf*. **пост*ы*дный** shameful.

пос*у*да crockery; dishes. **пос*у*дный** china; dish.

по|сул*и*ть *pf*.

посчастл*и*виться *pf impers* (+*dat*) be lucky; **ей посчастл*и*вилось** +*inf* she had the luck to.

посчит*а*ть *pf* count (up). **по|счит*а*ться** *pf*.

посыл*а*ть *impf* of **посл*а*ть**. **пос*ы*лка** sending; parcel; errand; premise. **пос*ы*льный** *sb* messenger.

пос*ы*пать (-плю, -плешь) *pf*, **посып*а*ть** *impf* strew. **посып*а*ться** (-плется) *pf* begin to fall; rain down.

посяг*а*тельство encroachment; infringement. **посяг*а*ть** *impf*, **посягн*у*ть** (-ну, -нёшь) *pf* encroach, infringe.

пот (*loc* -*у*; *pl* -ы́) sweat.

пот*а*йной secret.

потак*а*ть *impf* +*dat* indulge.

потас*о*вка brawl.

пот*а*ш (-а́) potash.

по-тв*о*ему *adv* in your opinion.

потв*о*рствовать *impf* (+*dat*) be indulgent (towards), pander (to).

пот*ё*к damp patch.

потёмки (-мок) *pl* darkness. **по|темн*е*ть** (-*е*ет) *pf*.

потенци*а*л potential. **потенци*а*льный** potential.

по|тепл*е*ть (-*е*ет) *pf*.

потерп*е*вший *sb* victim. **по|терп*е*ть** (-плю, -пишь) *pf*.

пот*е*ря loss; waste; *pl* casualties. **по|тер*я*ть(ся** *pf*.

потесн*и*ть *pf*. **потесн*и*ться** *pf* sit closer, squeeze up.

пот*е*ть (-*е*ю) *impf* (*pf* вс~, за~) sweat; mist over.

пот*е*ха fun. **по|т*е*шить(ся** (-шу(сь) *pf*. **пот*е*шный** amusing.

пот*е*чь (-чёт, -тёк, -ла́) *pf* begin to flow.

потир*а*ть *impf* rub.

потих*о*ньку *adv* softly; secretly; slowly.

п*о*тный (-тен, -тна́, -тно) sweaty.

пот*о*к stream; torrent; flood.

потол*о*к (-лка́) ceiling.

по|толст*е*ть (-*е*ю) *pf*.

пот*о*м *adv* later (on); then. **пот*о*мок** (-мка) descendant. **пот*о*мство** posterity.

потом*у́ *adv* that is why; **~ что** *conj* because.

по|тон*у*ть (-ну, -нешь) *pf*. **пот*о*п** flood, deluge. **по|топ*и*ть** (-плю, -пишь) *pf*, **потопл*я*ть** *impf* sink.

по|топт*а*ть (-пчу, -пчешь) *pf*. **по|тороп*и*ть(ся** (-плю(сь, -пишь(ся) *pf*.

пото́чный continuous; production-line.

по|тра́тить (-а́чу) *pf.*

потреби́тель *m* consumer, user. **потреби́тельский** consumer; consumers'. **потреби́ть** (-блю́) *pf*, **потребля́ть** *impf* consume. **потребле́ние** consumption. **потре́бность** need, requirement. **по|тре́бовать(ся)** *pf.*

по|трево́жить(ся) (-жу(сь)) *pf.*

потрёпанный shabby; tattered. **по|трепа́ть(ся)** (-плю́(сь), -плешь(ся)) *pf.*

по|тре́скаться *pf.* **потре́скивать** *impf* crackle.

потро́гать *pf* touch, feel, finger.

потроха́ (-о́в) *pl* giblets. **потроши́ть** (-шу́) *impf* (*pf* вы́~) disembowel, clean.

потруди́ться (-ужу́сь, -у́дишься) *pf* do some work; take the trouble.

потряса́ть *impf*, **потрясти́** (-су́, -сёшь; -я́с, -ла́) *pf* shake; stagger; +*acc or instr* brandish, shake. **потряса́ющий** staggering, tremendous. **потрясе́ние** shock.

поту́ги *f pl* vain attempts; родо́вые ~ labour.

поту́пить (-плю) *pf*, **потупля́ть** *impf* lower; ~ся look down.

по|тускне́ть (-е́ет) *pf.*

потусторо́ний мир the next world.

потуха́ть *impf*, **по|ту́хнуть** (-нет, -ух) *pf* go out; die out. **поту́хший** extinct; lifeless.

по|тче́вать (-чую) *impf* (*pf* по~) +*instr* treat to.

потя́гиваться *impf*, **потяну́ться** (-ну́сь, -нешься) *pf* stretch o.s. **по|тяну́ть** (-ну́, -нешь) *pf.*

по|у́жинать *pf.* **по|умне́ть** (-е́ю) *pf.*

поуча́ть *impf* preach at. **поучи́тельный** instructive.

поха́бный obscene.

похвала́ praise. **по|хвали́ть(ся)** (-лю́(сь, -лишь(ся)) *pf.* **похва́льный** laudable; laudatory.

по|хва́стать(ся) *pf.*

похити́тель *m* kidnapper; abductor; thief. **похи́тить** (-и́щу) *pf*, **похища́ть** *impf* kidnap; abduct; steal. **похище́ние** theft; kidnapping; abduction.

похлёбка broth, soup.

похло́пать *pf* slap; clap.

по|хлопота́ть (-очу́, -о́чешь) *pf.*

похме́лье hangover.

похо́д campaign; march; hike; excursion.

по|хода́тайствовать *pf.*

походи́ть (-ожу́, -о́дишь) *impf* на+*acc* resemble.

похо́дка gait, walk. **похо́дный** mobile, field; marching. **похожде́ние** adventure.

похо́жий alike; ~ на like.

похолода́ние drop in temperature.

по|хорони́ть (-ню́, -нишь) *pf.* **похоро́нный** funeral. **по́хороны** (-ро́н, -рона́м) *pl* funeral.

по|хороше́ть (-е́ю) *pf.*

по́хоть lust.

по|худе́ть (-е́ю) *pf.*

по|целова́ть(ся *pf.* **поцелу́й** kiss.

поча́ток (-тка) ear; (corn) cob.

по́чва soil; ground; basis. **по́чвенный** soil; ~ покро́в topsoil.

почём *adv* how much; how; ~ знать? who can tell? ~ я зна́ю?

how should I know?

почему́ *adv* why. **почему́-либо, -нибудь** *advs* for some reason or other. **почему́-то** *adv* for some reason.

по́черк hand(writing).

почерне́лый blackened, darkened. **по|черне́ть** (-е́ю) *pf*.

почерпну́ть (-ну́, -нёшь) *pf* draw, scoop up; glean.

по|черстве́ть (-е́ю) *pf*. **по|чеса́ть(ся** (-ешу́(сь, -е́шешь(ся) *pf*.

по́честь honour. **почёт** honour; respect. **почётный** of honour; honourable; honorary.

по́чечный renal; kidney.

почива́ть *impf of* почи́ть

почи́н initiative.

по|чини́ть (-ню́, -нишь) *pf*, **чини́ть** *impf* repair, mend. **по-чи́нка** repair.

по|чи́стить(ся (-и́щу(сь) *pf*.

почита́ть[1] honour; revere.

почита́ть[2] *pf* read for a while.

почи́ть (-и́ю, -и́ешь) *pf* (*impf* почива́ть) rest; pass away; ~ на ла́врах rest on one's laurels.

по́чка[1] bud.

по́чка[2] kidney.

по́чта post, mail; post-office. **почтальо́н** postman. **почта́мт** (*main*) post-office.

почте́ние respect. **почте́нный** venerable; considerable.

почти́ *adv* almost.

почти́тельный respectful. **по|чти́ть** (-чту́) *pf* honour.

почто́вый postal; ~ая ка́рточка postcard; ~ый перево́д postal order; ~ый я́щик letter-box.

по|чу́вствовать *pf*. **по|чу́диться** (-ишься) *pf*.

пошатну́ть (-ну́, -нёшь) *pf* shake; ~ся shake; stagger.

по|шевели́ть(ся (-елю́(сь, -е́ли́шь(ся) *pf*. **пошёл** *etc.*: *see* пойти́

поши́вочный sewing.

по́шлина duty.

по́шлость vulgarity; banality. **по́шлый** vulgar; banal.

поштучный by the piece.

по|шути́ть (-учу́, -у́тишь) *pf*.

поща́да mercy. **по|щади́ть** (-ажу́) *pf*.

по|щекота́ть (-очу́, -о́чешь) *pf*.

пощёчина slap in the face.

по|щу́пать *pf*.

поэ́зия poetry. **поэ́ма** poem. **поэ́т** poet. **поэти́ческий** poetic.

поэ́тому *adv* therefore.

пою́ *etc.*: *see* петь, пои́ть

появи́ться (-влю́сь, -вишься) *pf*, **появля́ться** *impf* appear. **по-явле́ние** appearance.

по́яс (*pl* -а́) belt; girdle; waist-band; waist; zone.

поясне́ние explanation. **поясни́тельный** explanatory. **поясни́ть** (*impf* поясня́ть) explain, elucidate.

поясни́ца small of the back. **поясно́й** waist; to the waist; zonal.

поясня́ть *impf of* поясни́ть

пра- *pref* first; great-. **пра́ба́бушка** great-grandmother.

пра́вда (the) truth. **правди́вый** true; truthful. **правдоподо́бный** likely; plausible. **пра́ведный** righteous; just.

пра́вило rule; principle.

пра́вильный right, correct; regular; ~о! that's right!

прави́тель *m* ruler. **прави́тельственный** government(al). **прави́тельство** government. **пра́вить**[1] (-влю) +*instr*

rule, govern; drive.

пра́вить² (-влю) *impf* correct. **пра́вка** correcting.

правле́ние board; administration; government.

пра́внук, ~**вну́чка** great-grandson, -granddaughter.

пра́во¹ (*pl* -á) law; right. (води́тельские) права́ driving licence; **на права́х**+*gen* in the capacity of, as.

пра́во² *adv* really.

пра́во-¹ *in comb* law; right. **правове́рный** orthodox. ~**ме́рный** lawful, rightful. ~**мо́чный** competent. ~**наруше́ние** infringement of the law, offence. ~**наруши́тель** *m* offender, delinquent. ~**писа́ние** spelling, orthography. ~**сла́вный** orthodox; *sb* member of the Orthodox Church. ~**су́дие** justice.

пра́во-² *in comb* right, right-hand. **правосторо́нний** right; right-hand.

правово́й legal.

правота́ rightness; innocence.

пра́вый¹ right; right-hand; right-wing.

пра́вый² (прав, -á, -о) right, correct; just.

пра́вящий ruling.

пра́дед great-grandfather; *pl* ancestors. **прадеду́шка** *m* great-grandfather.

пра́здник (public) holiday. **пра́здничный** festive. **пра́зднование** celebration. **пра́здновать** *impf* (*pf* **от**~) celebrate. **пра́здность** idleness. **пра́здный** idle; useless.

пра́ктика practice; practical work. **практикова́ть** *impf* practise; ~**ся** (*pf* **на**~ся) be practised; +**в**+*prep* practise. **практи́ческий**, **практи́чный** practical.

пра́отец (-тца) forefather.

пра́порщик ensign.

прапра́дед great-great-grandfather. **прароди́тель** *m* forefather.

прах dust; remains.

пра́чечная *sb* laundry. **пра́чка** laundress.

пребыва́ние stay. **пребыва́ть** *impf* be; reside.

превзойти́ (-йду́, -йдёшь; -ошёл, -шла́) *pf* (*impf* **превосходи́ть**) surpass; excel.

превозмога́ть *impf*, **превозмо́чь** (-огу́, -о́жешь; -о́г, -ла́) *pf* overcome.

превознести́ (-су́, -сёшь; -ёс, -ла́) *pf*, **превозноси́ть** (-ошу́, -о́сишь) *impf* extol, praise.

превосходи́тельство Excellency. **превосходи́ть** (-ожу́, -о́дишь) *impf of* **превзойти́**. **превосхо́дный** superlative; superb, excellent. **превосхо́дство** superiority. **превосходя́щий** superior.

преврати́ть (-ащу́) *pf*, **превраща́ть** *impf* convert, turn, reduce; ~**ся** turn, change. **превра́тный** wrong; changeful. **превраще́ние** transformation.

превы́сить (-ы́шу) *pf*, **превыша́ть** *impf* exceed. **превыше́ние** exceeding, excess.

прегра́да obstacle; barrier. **прегради́ть** (-ажу́) *pf*, **прегражда́ть** *impf* bar, block.

пред *prep*+*instr: see* **пе́ред**

предава́ть(ся (-даю́(сь, -даёшь(ся) *impf of* **преда́ть(ся**

преда́ние legend; tradition; handing over, committal. **пре́данность** devotion. **пре́данный** devoted. **преда́тель** *m*, ~**ница** betrayer, traitor. **преда́тельский** treacherous. **пре-**

да́тельство treachery. **преда́ть** (-а́м, -а́шь, -а́ст, -ади́м; пре́дал, -а́, -о) pf (impf **преда-ва́ть**) hand over, commit; betray; **~ся** abandon o.s.; give way, indulge.

предаю́ etc.: see **предава́ть**

предвари́тельный preliminary; prior. **предвари́ть** pf, **предваря́ть** impf forestall, anticipate.

предве́стник forerunner; harbinger. **предвеща́ть** impf portend; augur.

предвзя́тый preconceived; biased.

предви́деть (-и́жу) impf foresee.

предвкуси́ть (-ушу́, -у́сишь) pf, **предвкуша́ть** impf look forward to.

предводи́тель m leader. **предводи́тельствовать** impf +instr lead.

предвое́нный pre-war.

предвосхи́тить (-и́щу) pf, **предвосхища́ть** impf anticipate.

предвы́борный (pre-)election.

предго́рье foothills.

преддве́рие threshold.

преде́л limit; bound. **преде́льный** boundary; maximum; utmost.

предзнаменова́ние omen, augury.

предисло́вие preface.

предлага́ть impf of **предложи́ть. предло́г[1]** pretext.

предло́г[2] preposition.

предложе́ние[1] sentence; clause.

предложе́ние[2] offer; proposition; proposal; motion; suggestion; supply. **предложи́ть** (-жу́,

-жишь) pf (impf **предлага́ть**) offer; propose; suggest; order.

предло́жный prepositional.

предме́стье suburb.

предме́т object; subject.

предназнача́ть impf, **предназна́чить** (-чу) pf destine, intend; earmark.

преднаме́ренный premeditated.

пре́до: see **пе́ред**

пре́док (-дка) ancestor.

предопределе́ние predetermination. **предопредели́ть** pf, **предопределя́ть** impf predetermine, predestine.

предоста́вить (-влю) pf, **предоставля́ть** impf grant; leave; give.

предостерега́ть impf, **предостере́чь** (-егу́, -ежёшь; -ёг, -ла́) pf warn. **предостереже́ние** warning. **предосторо́жность** precaution.

предосуди́тельный reprehensible.

предотврати́ть (-ащу́) pf, **предотвраща́ть** impf avert, prevent.

предохране́ние protection; preservation. **предохрани́тель** m guard; safety device, safety-catch; fuse. **предохрани́тельный** preservative; preventive; safety. **предохрани́ть** pf, **предохраня́ть** impf preserve, protect.

предписа́ние order; pl directions, instructions. **предписа́ть** (-ишу́, -и́шешь) pf, **предпи́сывать** impf order, direct; prescribe.

предпле́чье forearm.

предполага́емый supposed. **предполага́ется** impers it is proposed. **предполага́ть** impf, **предположи́ть** (-жу́, -о́жишь) pf

suppose, assume. **предположе́ние** supposition, assumption. **предположи́тельный** conjectural; hypothetical.

предпосле́дний penultimate, last-but-one.

предпосы́лка precondition; premise.

предпоче́сть (-чту́, -чтёшь; -чёл, -чла́) *pf*, **предпочита́ть** *impf* prefer. **предпочте́ние** preference. **предпочти́тельный** preferable.

предприи́мчивый enterprising.

предпринима́тель *m* owner; entrepreneur; employer. **предпринима́тельство**: свобо́дное ~ free enterprise. **предпринима́ть** *impf*, **предприня́ть** (-иму́, -и́мешь; -и́нял, -а́, -о) *pf* undertake. **предприя́тие** undertaking, enterprise.

предрасположе́ние predisposition.

предрассу́док (-дка) prejudice.

предрека́ть *impf*, **предре́чь** (-еку́, -ечёшь; -рёк, -ла́) *pf* foretell.

предреша́ть *impf*, **предреши́ть** (-шу́) *pf* decide beforehand; predetermine.

председа́тель *m* chairman.

предсказа́ние prediction. **предсказа́ть** (-ажу́, -а́жешь) *pf*, **предска́зывать** *impf* predict; prophesy.

предсме́ртный dying.

представле́ние representative. **представи́тельный** representative; imposing. **представи́тельство** representation; representatives.

предста́вить (-влю) *pf*, **предста-**

ставля́ть *impf* present; submit; introduce; represent; ~ себе́ imagine; **представля́ть собо́й** represent, be; ~ся present itself; occur; seem; introduce o.s.; +*instr* pretend to be. **представле́ние** presentation; performance; idea, notion.

предста́ть (-а́ну) *pf* (*impf* **представа́ть**) appear.

предстоя́ть (-ои́т) *impf* be in prospect, lie ahead. **предстоя́щий** forthcoming; imminent.

предте́ча *m & f* forerunner, precursor.

предубежде́ние prejudice.

предугада́ть *pf*, **предуга́дывать** *impf* guess; foresee.

предупреди́тельный preventive; warning; courteous, obliging. **предупреди́ть** (-ежу́) *pf*, **предупрежда́ть** *impf* warn; give notice; prevent; anticipate. **предупрежде́ние** notice; warning; prevention.

предусма́тривать *impf*, **предусмотре́ть** (-рю́, -ришь) *pf* envisage, foresee; provide for. **предусмотри́тельный** prudent; far-sighted.

предчу́вствие presentiment; foreboding. **предчу́вствовать** *impf* have a presentiment (about).

предше́ственник predecessor. **предше́ствовать** *impf* +*dat* precede.

предъяви́тель *m* bearer. **предъяви́ть** (-влю́, -вишь) *pf*, **предъявля́ть** *impf* show, produce; bring (*lawsuit*); ~ пра́во на+*acc* lay claim to.

предыду́щий previous.

прее́мник successor. **прее́мственность** succession; continuity.

пре́жде *adv* first; formerly; *prep+gen* before; ~ всего́ first of all; first and foremost; ~ чем *conj* before. **преждевре́менный** premature. **пре́жний** previous, former.

презервати́в condom.

президе́нт president. **президе́нтский** presidential. **прези́диум** presidium.

презира́ть *impf* despise. **презре́ние** contempt. **презре́нный** contemptible. **презри́тельный** scornful.

преиму́щественно *adv* mainly, chiefly, principally. **преиму́щественный** main, primary; preferential. **преиму́щество** advantage; preference; по преиму́ществу for the most part.

преиспо́дняя *sb* the underworld.

прейскура́нт price list, catalogue.

преклоне́ние admiration. **преклони́ть** (-ню́), **преклоня́ть** *impf* bow, bend; ~ся bow down; +*dat or* пе́ред+*instr* admire, worship. **прекло́нный**: ~ во́зраст old age.

прекра́сный beautiful; fine; excellent.

прекрати́ть (-ащу́) *pf*, **прекраща́ть** *impf* stop, discontinue; ~ся cease, end. **прекраще́ние** halt; cessation.

преле́стный delightful. **пре́лесть** charm, delight.

преломи́ть (-млю́, -мишь) *pf*, **преломля́ть** *impf* refract. **преломле́ние** refraction.

прельсти́ть (-льщу́) *pf*, **прельща́ть** *impf* attract; entice; ~ся be attracted; fall (+*instr* for).

прелюбодея́ние adultery.

прелю́дия prelude.

прему́нуть (-ну) *pf with neg* not fail.

премирова́ть *impf & pf* award a prize to; give a bonus. **пре́мия** prize; bonus; premium.

премье́р prime minister; lead(ing actor). **премье́ра** première. **премье́р-мини́стр** prime minister. **премье́рша** leading lady.

пренебрега́ть *impf*, **пренебре́чь** (-егу́, -ежёшь; -ёг, -ла́) *pf* +*instr* scorn; neglect. **пренебреже́ние** scorn; neglect. **пренебрежи́тельный** scornful.

пре́ния (-ий) *pl* debate.

преоблада́ние predominance. **преоблада́ть** *impf* predominate; prevail.

преобража́ть *impf*, **преобрази́ть** (-ажу́) *pf* transform. **преображе́ние** transformation; Transfiguration. **преобразова́ние** transformation; reform. **преобразова́ть** *pf*, **преобразо́вывать** *impf* transform; reform, reorganize.

преодолева́ть *impf*, **преодоле́ть** (-е́ю) *pf* overcome.

препара́т preparation.

препина́ние: зна́ки препина́ния punctuation marks.

препира́тельство altercation, wrangling.

преподава́ние teaching. **преподава́тель** *m*, **~ница** teacher. **преподава́тельский** teaching. **преподава́ть** (-даю́, -даёшь) *impf* teach.

преподнести́ (-су́, -сёшь; -ёс, -ла́) *pf*, **преподноси́ть** (-ошу́, -о́сишь) present with, give.

препроводи́ть (-вожу́, -во́дишь) *pf*, **препровожда́ть** *impf* send, forward.

препя́тствие obstacle; hurdle. препя́тствовать *impf* (*pf* вос~) +*dat* hinder.

прерва́ть (-ву́, -вёшь; -а́л, -а́, -о) *pf* (*impf* прерыва́ть) interrupt; break off; ~ся be interrupted; break.

пререка́ние argument. пререка́ться *impf* argue.

прерыва́ть(ся *impf of* прерва́ть(ся

пресека́ть *impf*, пресе́чь (-еку́, -ечёшь; -е́к, -екла́) *pf* stop; put an end to; ~ся stop; break.

пресле́дование pursuit; persecution; prosecution. пресле́довать *impf* pursue; haunt; persecute; prosecute.

пресло́вутый notorious.

пресмыка́ться *impf* grovel. пресмыка́ющееся *sb* reptile.

пресново́дный freshwater. пре́сный fresh; unleavened; insipid; bland.

пресс press. пре́сса the press. пресс-конфере́нция press-conference.

престаре́лый aged.

прести́ж prestige.

престо́л throne.

преступле́ние crime. престу́пник criminal. престу́пность criminality; crime, delinquency. престу́пный criminal.

пресы́титься (-ы́щусь) *pf*, пресыща́ться *impf* be satiated. пресыще́ние surfeit, satiety.

претвори́ть *pf*, претворя́ть *impf* (в+*acc*) turn, change, convert; ~ в жизнь realize, carry out.

претенде́нт claimant; candidate; pretender. претендова́ть *impf* на+*acc* lay claim to; have pretensions to. прете́нзия claim; pretension; быть в пре-

те́нзии на+*acc* have a grudge, a grievance, against.

претерпева́ть *impf*, претерпе́ть (-плю́, -пишь) *pf* undergo; suffer.

преть (пре́ет) *impf* (*pf* со~) rot.

преувеличе́ние exaggeration. преувели́чивать *impf*, преувели́чить (-чу) *pf* exaggerate.

преуменьша́ть *impf*, преуме́ньшить (-еньшу) *pf* underestimate; understate.

преуспева́ть *impf*, преуспе́ть (-е́ю) *pf* be successful; thrive.

преходя́щий transient.

прецеде́нт precedent.

при *prep* +*prep* by, at; in the presence of; attached to, affiliated to; with; about; on; in the time of; under; during; when, in case of; ~ всём том for all that.

приба́вить (-влю) *pf*, прибавля́ть add; increase; ~ся increase; rise; wax; день прибыл the days are getting longer. приба́вка addition; increase. прибавле́ние addition; supplement; appendix. приба́вочный additional; surplus.

Приба́лтика the Baltic States.

прибау́тка humorous saying.

прибега́ть[1] *impf of* прибежа́ть

прибега́ть[2] *impf*, прибе́гнуть (-ну; -бе́г) *pf* +к+*dat* resort to.

прибежа́ть (-егу́) *pf* (*impf* прибега́ть) come running.

прибе́жище refuge.

прибере́гать *impf*, прибере́чь (-егу́, -ежёшь; -ёг, -ла́) *pf* save (up), reserve.

прибе́ру *etc.*: *see* приба́ть. прибива́ть *impf of* приби́ть. прибира́ть *impf of* прибра́ть. приби́ть (-бью́, -бьёшь) *pf* (*impf* прибива́ть) nail; flatten; drive

приближа́ть *impf*, **прибли́-зить** (-и́жу) *pf* bring *or* move nearer. ~ся approach; draw nearer. **приближе́ние** approach. **приблизи́тельный** approximate.

прибо́й surf, breakers.

прибо́р instrument, device, apparatus; set. **прибо́рная доска́** instrument panel; dashboard.

прибра́ть (-беру́, -берёшь; -а́л, -а́, -о) *pf* (*impf* **прибира́ть**) tidy (up); put away.

прибре́жный coastal; offshore.

прибыва́ть *impf*, **прибы́ть** (-бу́ду; при́был, -а́, -о) *pf* arrive; increase, grow; rise; wax. **при́быль** profit, gain; increase, rise. **при́быльный** profitable. **прибы́тие** arrival.

прибью́ *etc.*: *see* **прибы́ть**

прива́л halt.

прива́ривать *impf*, **привари́ть** (-рю́, -ришь) *pf* weld on.

приватиза́ция privatization. **приватизи́ровать** *impf & pf* privatize.

приведу́ *etc.*: *see* **привести́**

привезти́ (-зу́, -зёшь; -ёз, -ла́) (*impf* **привози́ть**) bring.

привере́дливый pernickety.

приве́рженец (-нца) adherent. **приве́рженный** devoted.

приве́сить (-е́шу) *pf* (*impf* **приве́шивать**) hang up, suspend.

привести́ (-еду́, -едёшь; -ёл, -а́) *pf* (*impf* **приводи́ть**) bring; lead; take; reduce; cite; put in(to); set.

приве́т greeting(s); regards; hi! **приве́тливый** friendly; affable. **приве́тствие** greeting; speech of welcome. **приве́тствовать** *impf & pf* greet, salute; welcome.

приве́шивать *impf of* **приве́сить**

привива́ть (ся *impf of* **приви́ть** (ся. **приви́вка** inoculation.

привиде́ние ghost; apparition. **при|ви́деться** (-дится) *pf*.

привилегиро́ванный privileged. **привиле́гия** privilege.

привинти́ть (-нчу́) *pf*, **приви́нчивать** *impf* screw on.

приви́ть (-вью́, -вьёшь; -и́л, -а́, -о) *pf* (*impf* **привива́ть**) inoculate; graft; inculcate; foster; ~ся take; become established.

при́вкус after-taste; smack.

привлека́тельный attractive. **привлека́ть** *impf*, **привле́чь** (-еку́, -ечёшь; -ёк, -ла́) *pf* attract; draw; draw in, win over; (*law*) have up; ~ к суду́ sue. **привлече́ние** attraction.

приво́д drive, gear. **приводи́ть** (-ожу́, -о́дишь) *impf of* **привести́**. **приводно́й** driving.

привожу́ *etc.*: *see* **приводи́ть**, **привози́ть**

приво́з bringing; importation; load. **привози́ть** (-ожу́, -о́зишь) *impf of* **привезти́**. **привозно́й**, **приво́зный** imported.

приво́льный free.

привстава́ть (-таю́, -таёшь) *impf*, **привста́ть** (-а́ну) *pf* half-rise; rise.

привыка́ть *impf*, **привы́кнуть** (-ну; -ык) *pf* get accustomed. **привы́чка** habit. **привы́чный** habitual, usual.

привью́ *etc.*: *see* **приви́ть**

привя́занность attachment; affection. **привяза́ть** (-яжу́, -я́жешь) *pf*, **привя́зывать** *impf* attach; tie; bind; ~ся become attached; attach o.s.; +к+*dat* pester. **привя́зчивый** annoying; affectionate. **при́вязь** tie;

lead, leash; tether.

пригиба́ть *impf of* **пригну́ть**

пригласи́ть (-ашу́) *pf,* **пригла-ша́ть** *impf* invite. **приглаше́ние** invitation.

пригляде́ться (-яжу́сь) *pf,* **при-гля́дываться** *impf* look closely; +к+*dat* scrutinize; get used to.

пригна́ть (-гоню́, -го́нишь; -а́л, -а́, -о) *pf (impf* **пригоня́ть)** bring in; fit, adjust.

пригну́ть (-ну́, -нёшь) *pf (impf* **пригиба́ть)** bend down.

пригова́ривать[1] *impf* keep saying.

приговоа́ривать[2] *impf,* **пригово-ри́ть** *pf* sentence, condemn. **пригово́р** verdict, sentence.

пригоди́ться (-ожу́сь) *pf* prove useful. **приго́дный** fit, suitable.

пригоня́ть *impf of* **пригна́ть**

пригора́ть *impf,* **пригоре́ть** (-ри́т) *pf* be burnt.

при́город suburb. **при́город-ный** suburban.

приго́рок (-рка) hillock.

при́горшня (*gen pl* -ей) handful.

приготови́тельный prepara-tory. **пригото́вить** (-влю) *pf,* **приготовля́ть** *impf* prepare; **∼ся** prepare. **приготовле́ние** preparation.

пригрева́ть *impf,* **пригре́ть** (-е́ю) *pf* warm; cherish.

пригрози́ть (-ожу́) *pf*

прида́ное *sb* dowry. **прида́ток** (-тка) appendage.

придвига́ть *impf,* **придви́нуть** (-ну) *pf* move up, draw up; **∼ся** move up, draw near.

придво́рный court.

приде́лать *pf,* **приде́лывать** *impf* attach.

приде́рживаться *impf* hold on, hold; +*gen* keep to.

придира́ться *etc.: see* **при-дра́ться. придира́ться** *impf of* **придра́ться. приди́рка** quibble; fault-finding. **приди́рчивый** fault-finding.

придоро́жный roadside.

придра́ться (-деру́сь, -дерёшься; -а́лся, -ась, -а́ло́сь) *pf (impf* **придира́ться)** find fault.

приду́ *etc.: see* **прийти́**

приду́мать *pf,* **приду́мывать** *impf* think up, invent.

прие́ду *etc.: see* **прие́хать. прие́зд** arrival. **приезжа́ть** *impf of* **прие́хать. прие́зжий** newly ar-rived; *sb* newcomer.

прие́м receiving; reception; sur-gery; welcome; admittance; dose; go; movement; method, way; trick. **приёмлемый** ac-ceptable. **приёмная** *sb* waiting-room; reception room. **приёмник** (radio) receiver. **приёмный** receiving; reception; entrance; foster, adopted.

прие́хать (-е́ду) *pf (impf* **приезжа́ть)** arrive, come.

прижа́ть (-жму́, -жмёшь) *pf (impf* **прижима́ть)** press; clasp; **∼ся** nestle up.

приже́чь (-жгу́, -жжёшь; -жёг, -жгла́) *pf (impf* **прижига́ть)** caut-erize.

прижива́ться *impf of* **при-жи́ться**

прижига́ние cauterization.

прижига́ть *impf of* **прижéчь**

прижима́ть(ся *impf of* **при-жа́ть(ся**

прижи́ться (-иву́сь, -ивёшься; -жи́лся, -а́сь, -о́сь) *pf* (*impf* **прижива́ться**) become acclimatized.

прижму́ *etc.: see* **прижа́ть**

приз (*pl* -ы́) prize.

призва́ние vocation. **призва́ть** (-зову́, -зовёшь; -а́л, -а́, -о) *pf* (*impf* **призыва́ть**) call; call upon; call up.

призе́мистый stocky, squat.

приземлéние landing. **приземли́ться** *pf*, **приземля́ться** *impf* land.

призёр prizewinner.

при́зма prism.

признава́ть (-наю́, -наёшь) *impf*, **призна́ть** *pf* recognize; admit; **~ся** confess. **при́знак** sign, symptom; indication. **призна́ние** confession, declaration; acknowledgement; recognition. **при́знанный** acknowledged, recognized. **призна́тельный** grateful.

призову́ *etc.: see* **призва́ть**

при́зрак spectre, ghost. **при́зрачный** ghostly; illusory; imagined.

призы́в call, appeal; slogan; call-up. **призыва́ть** *impf of* **призва́ть**. **призывно́й** conscription.

при́иск mine.

прийти́ (приду́, -дёшь; пришёл, -шла́) *pf* (*impf* **приходи́ть**) come; arrive; **~** в себя́ regain consciousness; **~сь** +*no*+*dat* fit; suit; +*на*+*acc* fall on; *impers*+*dat* have to; happen (to), fall to the lot (of).

прика́з order, command. **прика́зание** order, command. **прика-за́ть** (-ажу́, -а́жешь) *pf*, **прика-**

зывать *impf* order, command.

прика́лывать *impf of* **приколо́ть. прикаса́ться** *impf of* **прикосну́ться**

прика́нчивать *impf of* **прикончить**

прикати́ть (-ачу́, -а́тишь) *pf*, **прика́тывать** *impf* roll up.

прики́дывать *impf*, **прики́нуть** *pf* throw in, add; weigh; estimate; **~ся** +*instr* pretend (to be).

прикла́д[1] butt.

прикла́д[2] trimmings. **прикладно́й** applied. **прикла́дывать(ся** *impf of* **приложи́ть(ся**

прикле́ивать *impf*, **прикле́ить** *pf* stick; glue.

приключа́ться *impf*, **приключи́ться** *pf* happen, occur. **приключе́ние** adventure. **приключе́нческий** adventure.

прикова́ть (-кую́, -куёшь) *pf*, **прико́вывать** *impf* chain; rivet.

прикола́чивать *impf*, **приколоти́ть** (-очу́, -о́тишь) *pf* nail.

приколо́ть (-лю́, -лешь) *pf* (*impf* **прика́лывать**) pin; stab.

прикомандирова́ть *pf*, **прикомандиро́вывать** *impf* attach.

прико́нчить (-чу) *pf* (*impf* **прика́нчивать**) use up; finish off.

прикоснове́ние touch; concern. **прикосну́ться** (-ну́сь, -нёшься) *pf* (*impf* **прикаса́ться**) к+*dat* touch.

прикрепи́ть (-плю́) *pf*, **прикрепля́ть** *impf* fasten, attach. **прикрепле́ние** fastening; registration.

прикрыва́ть *impf*, **прикры́ть** (-ро́ю) *pf* cover; screen; shelter. **прикры́тие** cover; escort.

прику́ривать *impf*, **прикури́ть**

(-рю́, -ришь) *pf* get a light.
прикуси́ть (-ушу́, -у́сишь) *pf*, **прику́сывать** *impf* bite.
прила́вок (-вка) counter.
прилага́тельное *sb* adjective. **прилага́ть** *impf of* приложи́ть
прила́дить (-а́жу) *pf*, **прила́живать** *impf* fit, adjust.
приласка́ть *pf* caress, pet; ~**ся** snuggle up.
прилега́ть *impf* (*pf* приле́чь) к+*dat* fit; adjoin. **прилега́ющий** close-fitting; adjoining, adjacent.
приле́жный diligent.
прилепи́ть(ся) (-плю́(сь), -пишь(ся)) *pf*, **прилепля́ть(ся)** *impf* stick.
приле́т arrival. **прилета́ть** *impf*, **прилете́ть** (-ечу́) *pf* arrive, fly in; come flying.
приле́чь (-ля́гу, -ля́жешь; -ёг, -гла́) *pf* **прилега́ть** lie down.
прили́в flow, flood; rising tide; surge. **прилива́ть** *impf of* прили́ть. **прили́вный** tidal.
прилипа́ть *impf*, **прили́пнуть** (-нет; -ли́п) *pf* stick.
прили́ть (-лье́т; -и́л, -á, -o) *pf* (*impf* **прилива́ть**) flow; rush.
прили́чие decency. **прили́чный** decent.
приложе́ние application; enclosure; supplement; appendix. **приложи́ть** (-жу́, -жишь) *pf* (*impf* **прикла́дывать**, **прилага́ть**) put; apply; affix; add; enclose; ~**ся** take aim; +*instr* apply; +к+*dat* kiss.
прилье́т *etc.: see* прили́ть.
прилью́(ть) (-ну́, -нёшь) *pf.* **приля́гу** *etc.: see* приле́чь
прима́нивать *impf*, **прима́ни́ть** (-ню́, -нишь) *pf* lure; entice.
прима́нка bait, lure.

примене́ние application; use. **примени́ть** (-ню́, -нишь) *pf*, **применя́ть** *impf* apply; use; ~**ся** adapt o.s., conform.
приме́р example.
при|ме́рить *pf* (*impf also* **примеря́ть**) try on. **приме́рка** fitting.
приме́рно *adv* approximately. **приме́рный** exemplary; approximate.
примеря́ть *impf of* приме́рить
при́месь admixture.
приме́та sign, token. **приме́тный** perceptible; conspicuous.
примеча́ние note, footnote; *pl* comments. **примеча́тельный** notable.
примеша́ть *pf*, **приме́шивать** *impf* add, mix in.
примина́ть *impf of* примя́ть
примире́ние reconciliation. **примири́тельный** conciliatory. **при|мири́ть** *pf*, **примиря́ть** *impf* reconcile; conciliate; ~**ся** be reconciled.
примити́вный primitive.
примкну́ть (-ну́, -нёшь) *pf* (*impf* **примыка́ть**) join; fix, attach.
приму́ *etc.: see* приня́ть
примо́рский seaside; maritime. **примо́рье** seaside.
примо́чка wash, lotion.
приму́ *etc.: see* приня́ть
примча́ться (-чу́сь) *pf* come tearing along.
примыка́ть *impf of* примкну́ть; +к+*dat* adjoin. **примыка́ющий** affiliated.
примя́ть (-мну́, -мнёшь) *pf* (*impf* **примина́ть**) crush; trample down.
принадлежа́ть (-жу́) *impf* belong. **принадле́жность** belonging; membership; *pl* acces-

sories; equipment.

принести́ (-су́, -сёшь; -нёс, -ла́) *pf* (*impf* приноси́ть) bring; fetch.

принижа́ть *impf*, **прини́зить** (-и́жу) *pf* humiliate; belittle.

принима́ть(ся *impf of* **приня́ть(ся**

приноси́ть (-ошу́, -о́сишь) *impf of* принести́. **приноше́ние** gift, offering.

при́нтер (*comput*) printer.

принуди́тельный compulsory. **прину́дить** (-у́жу) *pf*, **принужда́ть** *impf* compel. **принужде́ние** compulsion, coercion. **принуждённый** constrained, forced.

принц prince. **принце́сса** princess.

при́нцип principle. **принципиа́льно** *adv* on principle; in principle. **принципиа́льный** of principle; general.

приня́тие taking; acceptance; admission. **при́нято** it is accepted, it is usual; **не ~** it is not done. **приня́ть** (-иму́, -и́мешь; при́нял, -а́, -о) *pf* (*impf* принима́ть) take; accept; take over; receive; **+за**+*acc* take for; **~ уча́стие** take part; **~ на себя́** take; **~ за рабо́ту** set to work.

приободри́ть *pf*, **приободря́ть** *impf* cheer up; **~ся** cheer up.

приобрести́ (-ету́, -етёшь; -рёл, -а́) *pf*, **приобрета́ть** *impf* acquire. **приобрете́ние** acquisition.

приобща́ть *impf*, **приобщи́ть** (-щу́) *pf* join, attach, unite; **~ся к**+*dat* join in.

приорите́т priority.

приостана́вливать *impf*, **приостанови́ть** (-влю́, -вишь) *pf* stop, suspend; **~ся** stop. **приостано́вка** halt, suspension.

приоткрыва́ть *impf*, **приоткры́ть** (-ро́ю) *pf* open slightly.

припа́док (-дка) fit; attack.

припа́сы (-ов) *pl* supplies.

припе́в refrain.

приписа́ть (-ишу́, -и́шешь) *pf*, **припи́сывать** *impf* add; attribute. **припи́ска** postscript; codicil.

припло́д offspring; increase.

приплыва́ть *impf*, **приплы́ть** (-ыву́, -ывёшь; -ы́л, -а, -о) *pf* swim up; sail up.

приплю́снуть (-ну) *pf*, **приплю́щивать** *impf* flatten.

приподнима́ть *impf*, **приподня́ть** (-ниму́, -ни́мешь; -о́дня́л, -а́, -о) *pf* raise (a little); **~ся** raise o.s. (a little).

припо́й solder.

приполза́ть *impf*, **приползти́** (-зу́, -зёшь; -по́лз, -ла́) *pf* creep up, crawl up.

припомина́ть *impf*, **припо́мнить** *pf* recollect.

припра́ва seasoning, flavouring. **приправля́ть** (-влю) *pf*, **приправля́ть** *impf* season, flavour.

припря́тать (-я́чу) *pf*, **припря́тывать** *impf* secrete, put by.

припу́гивать *impf*, **припугну́ть** (-ну́, -нёшь) *pf* scare.

прираба́тывать *impf*, **прирабо́тать** *pf* earn ... extra. **прирабо́ток** (-тка) additional earnings.

прира́внивать *impf*, **приравня́ть** *pf* equate (with **к**+*dat*).

прираста́ть *impf*, **прирасти́** (-тёт; -ро́с, -ла́) *pf* adhere; take; increase; accrue.

приро́да nature. **приро́дный**

natural; by birth; innate. **при-рождённый** innate; born.

приро́с *etc*.: *see* прирасти́. **при-ро́ст** increase.

прируча́ть *impf*, **приручи́ть** (-чу́) *pf* tame; domesticate.

приса́живаться *impf of* при-се́сть

присва́ивать *impf*, **присво́ить** *pf* appropriate; award.

приседа́ть *impf*, **присе́сть** (-ся́ду) *pf* (*impf also* приса́живаться) sit down, take a seat.

прискака́ть (-ачу́, -а́чешь) *pf* come galloping.

прискорбный sorrowful.

присла́ть (-ишлю́, -ишлёшь) *pf* (*impf* присыла́ть) send.

прислони́ть(ся (-оню́(сь, -о́ни́шь(ся) *pf*, **прислоня́ть(ся** *impf* lean, rest.

прислу́га servant; crew. **при-слу́живать** *impf* (+*dat*) wait (on), attend.

прислу́шаться *pf*, **прислу́шиваться** *impf* listen; +к+*dat* listen to; heed.

присма́тривать *impf*, **при-смотре́ть** (-рю́, -ришь) *pf* +за +*instr* look after, keep an eye on; ∼ся (к+*dat*) look closely (at). **присмо́тр** supervision.

при|**сни́ться** *pf*.

присоедине́ние joining; addition; annexation. **присоедини́ть** *pf*, **присоединя́ть** *impf* join; add; annex; ∼ся +к+*dat* join; subscribe to (*an opinion*).

приспосо́бить (-блю) *pf*, **приспоса́бливать** *impf* fit, adjust, adapt; ∼ся adapt o.s. **приспособле́ние** adaptation; device; appliance. **приспособля́емость** adaptability.

приставать (-таю́, -таёшь) *impf of* приста́ть

приста́вить (-влю) *pf* (*impf* приставля́ть) к+*dat* place, set, *or* lean against; add; appoint to look after.

приста́вка prefix.

приставля́ть *impf of* приста́вить

при́стальный intent.

приста́нище refuge, shelter.

при́стань (*gen pl* -е́й) landing-stage; pier; wharf.

приста́ть (-а́ну) *pf* (*impf* приставать) к+*dat* stick, adhere (к+*dat* to); pester.

пристёгивать *impf*, **пристег-ну́ть** (-ну́, -нёшь) *pf* fasten.

присто́йный decent, proper.

пристра́ивать(ся *impf of* при-стро́ить(ся

пристра́стие predilection, passion; bias. **пристра́стный** biased.

пристре́ливать *impf*, **при-стрели́ть** *pf* shoot (down).

пристро́ить (-о́ю) *pf* (*impf* пристра́ивать) add, build on; fix up; ∼ся be fixed up, get a place. **пристро́йка** annexe, extension.

при́ступ assault, fit, attack. **приступа́ть** *impf*, **приступи́ть** (-плю́, -пишь) *pf* к+*dat* set about, start.

при|**стыди́ть** (-ыжу́) *pf*.

при|**стыкова́ться** *pf*.

присуди́ть (-ужу́, -у́дишь) *pf*, **присужда́ть** *impf* sentence, condemn; award; confer. **при-сужде́ние** awarding; conferment.

прису́тствие presence. **при-су́тствовать** *impf* be present, attend. **прису́тствующие** *sb pl* those present.

прису́щий inherent; characteristic.

присыла́ть *impf of* присла́ть

прися́га oath. **присяга́ть** *impf*, **присягну́ть** (-ну́, -нёшь) *pf* swear.

прися́ду *etc.*: *see* **присе́сть**

прися́жный *sb* juror.

притаи́ть *pf* hide.

прита́птывать *impf of* **притопта́ть**

прита́скивать *impf*, **притащи́ть** (-ащу́, -а́щишь) *pf* bring, drag, haul; **~ся** drag o.s.

притвори́ться *pf*, **притворя́ться** *impf* +*instr* pretend to be. **притво́рный** pretended, feigned. **притво́рство** pretence, sham. **притво́рщик** sham; hypocrite.

притека́ть *impf of* **прите́чь**

притесне́ние oppression. **притесни́ть** *pf*, **притесня́ть** *impf* oppress.

прите́чь (-ечёт, -еку́т; -ёк, -ла́) *pf* (*impf* **притека́ть**) pour in.

притиха́ть *impf*, **прити́хнуть** (-ну; -и́х) *pf* quiet down.

прито́к tributary; influx.

при́толока lintel.

прито́м *conj* (and) besides.

прито́н den, haunt.

притопта́ть (-пчу́, -пчешь) *pf* (*impf* **прита́птывать**) trample down.

при́торный sickly-sweet, luscious, cloying.

притра́гиваться *impf*, **притро́нуться** (-нусь) *pf* touch.

притупи́ть (-плю́, -пишь) *pf*, **притупля́ть** *impf* blunt, dull; deaden; **~ся** become blunt or dull.

при́тча parable.

притяга́тельный attractive, magnetic. **притя́гивать** *impf of* **притяну́ть**

притяжа́тельный possessive.

притяже́ние attraction.

притяза́ние claim, pretension. **притяза́тельный** demanding.

притя́нутый far-fetched. **притяну́ть** (-ну́, -нешь) *pf* (*impf* **притя́гивать**) attract; drag (up).

приуро́чивать *impf*, **приуро́чить** (-чу) *pf* к+*dat* time for.

приуса́дебный: ~ уча́сток individual plot (in *kolkhoz*).

приуча́ть *impf*, **приучи́ть** (-чу́, -чишь) *pf* train, school.

прихлеба́тель *m* sponger.

прихо́д coming, arrival; receipts; parish. **приходи́ть(ся** (-ожу́(сь, -о́дишь(ся) *impf of* **прийти́(сь. прихо́дный** receipt. **приходя́щий** non-resident; ~ больно́й outpatient. **прихожа́нин** (*pl* -а́не, -а́н) **-а́нка** parishioner.

прихо́жая *sb* hall, lobby.

прихотли́вый capricious; fanciful, intricate. **при́хоть** whim, caprice.

прихра́мывать limp (slightly).

прице́л sight; aiming. **прице́ливаться** *impf*, **прице́литься** *pf* take aim.

прице́ниваться *impf*, **прицени́ться** (-ню́сь, -нишься) *pf* (к+*dat*) ask the price (of).

прице́п trailer. **прицепи́ть** (-плю́, -пишь) *pf*, **прицепля́ть** *impf* hitch, hook on; **~ся** stick to, cling to. **прице́пка** hitching, hooking on; quibble. **прицепно́й**: ~ ваго́н trailer.

прича́л mooring; mooring line. **прича́ливать** *impf*, **прича́лить** *pf* moor.

прича́стие¹ participle. **прича́стие²** communion. **причасти́ть** (-ащу́) *pf* (*impf* **причаща́ть**) give communion to; **~ся** receive communion.

причáстный¹ participial. причáстный² concerned; privy.

причащáть impf of причасти́ть

причём conj moreover, and.

причеса́ть (-ешу́, -е́шешь) pf, причёсывать impf comb; do the hair (of); ~ся do one's hair, have one's hair done. причёска hair-do; haircut.

причи́на cause; reason. причини́ть pf, причиня́ть impf cause.

причи́|слить pf, причисля́ть impf number, rank (к+dat among); add on.

причита́ние lamentation. причита́ть impf lament.

причита́ться impf be due.

причмо́кивать impf, причмо́кнуть (-ну) pf smack one's lips.

причу́да caprice, whim.

при|чу́диться pf.

причу́дливый odd; fantastic; whimsical.

пришвартова́ть pf. пришёл etc.: see прийти́

пришле́ц (-еца́) newcomer.

прише́ствие coming; advent.

пришива́ть impf, приши́ть (-шью́, -шьёшь) pf sew on.

пришлю́ etc.: see присла́ть

пришпи́ливать impf, пришпи́лить pf pin on.

пришпо́ривать impf, пришпо́рить pf spur (on).

прищеми́ть (-млю́) pf, прищемля́ть impf pinch.

прищу́риваться impf, прищу́риться pf screw up one's eyes.

прию́т shelter, refuge. приюти́ть (-ючу́) pf shelter; ~ся take shelter.

прия́тель m, прия́тельница friend. прия́тельский friendly.

прия́тный nice, pleasant.

про prep+acc about; for; ~ себя́ to o.s.

проанализи́ровать pf.

про́ба test; hallmark; sample.

пробе́г run; race. пробега́ть impf, пробежа́ть (-егу́) pf run; cover; learn. run past. пробе́жка run.

пробе́л blank, gap; flaw.

проберу́ etc.: see пробра́ть. пробива́ть(ся impf of проби́ть(ся. пробира́ть(ся impf of пробра́ть(ся

проби́рка test-tube. проби́ровать impf test, assay.

про|би́ть (-бью́, -бьёшь) pf (impf also пробива́ть) make a hole in; pierce; punch; ~ся force, make, one's way.

про́бка cork; stopper; fuse; (traffic) jam, congestion. про́бковый cork.

пробле́ма problem.

про́блеск flash; gleam, ray.

про́бный trial, test; ~ ка́мень touchstone. про́бовать impf (pf ис~, по~) try; attempt.

пробо́ина hole.

пробо́р parting.

про|бормота́ть (-очу́, -о́чешь) pf.

пробра́ть (-беру́, -берёшь; -а́л, -а́, -о) pf (impf пробира́ть) penetrate; scold; ~ся make or force one's way.

пробу́ду etc.: see пробы́ть

про|буди́ть (-ужу́, -у́дишь) pf, пробужда́ть impf wake (up); arouse; ~ся wake up. пробужде́ние awakening.

про|бура́вить (-влю) pf, пробура́вливать impf bore (through), drill.

про|бури́ть pf.

пробы́ть (-бу́ду; про́бы́л, -а́, -о) pf stay; be.

пробью́ *etc.*: *see* **проби́ть**

прова́л failure; downfall; gap. **прова́ливать** (-лю, -лишь) *pf* bring down; ruin; reject; fail; ~ся collapse; fall in; fail; disappear.

прове́дать *pf*, **прове́дывать** *impf* call on; learn.

проведе́ние conducting; construction; installation.

провезти́ (-зу́, -зёшь; -ёз, -ла́) *pf* (*impf* **провози́ть**) convey, transport.

прове́рить *pf*, **проверя́ть** *impf* check; test. **прове́рка** checking, check; testing.

прове|сти́ (-еду́, -едёшь; -ёл, -а́) *pf* (*impf also* **проводи́ть**) lead, take; build; install; carry out; conduct; pass; draw; spend; +*instr* pass over.

прове́тривать *impf*, **прове́трить** *pf* air.

прове́ять (-е́ю) *pf*.

провиде́ние Providence.

прови́зия provisions.

провини́ться *pf* be guilty; do wrong.

провинциа́льный provincial. **прови́нция** province; the provinces.

про́вод (*pl* -á) wire, lead, line. **проводи́мость** conductivity. **проводи́ть**[1] (-ожу́, -о́дишь) *impf of* **провести́**; conduct. **проводи́ть**[2] (-ожу́, -о́дишь) *impf* (*impf* **провожа́ть**) accompany; see off.

прово́дка leading; taking; building; installation; wiring, wires.

проводни́к[1] (-а́) guide; conductor.

проводни́к[2] (-а́) conductor; bearer; transmitter. **про́воды** (-ов) *pl* send-off. **про-**

вожа́тый *sb* guide, escort. **провожа́ть** *impf of* **проводи́ть**

провоз conveyance, transport.

провозгласи́ть (-ашу́) *pf*, **провозглаша́ть** *impf* proclaim; propose. **провозглаше́ние** proclamation.

провози́ть (-ожу́, -о́зишь) *impf of* **провезти́**

провока́тор agent provocateur. **провока́ция** provocation.

про́волока wire. **про́волочный** wire.

прово́рный quick; agile. **прово́рство** quickness; agility.

провоци́ровать *impf & pf* (*pf* **с~**) provoke.

прогада́ть *pf*, **прога́дывать** *impf* miscalculate.

прога́лина glade; space.

прогиба́ть(ся *impf of* **прогну́ть(ся**

прогла́тывать *impf*, **проглоти́ть** (-очу́, -о́тишь) *pf* swallow.

прогляде́ть (-яжу́) *pf*, **прогля́дывать**[1] *impf* overlook; look through. **прогляну́ть** (-я́нет) *pf*, **прогля́дывать**[2] *impf* show, peep through; appear.

прогна́ть (-гоню́, -го́нишь; -а́л, -а́, -о) *pf* (*impf* **прогоня́ть**) drive away; banish; drive; sack.

прогнива́ть *impf*, **прогни́ть** (-иёт; -и́л, -а́, -о) *pf* rot through.

прогно́з prognosis; (weather) forecast.

прогну́ть (-ну́, -нёшь) *pf* (*impf* **прогиба́ть**) cause to sag; ~ся sag, bend.

progова́ривать *impf*, **проговори́ть** *pf* say, utter; talk; ~ся let the cat out of the bag.

проголода́ться *pf* get hungry.

проголосова́ть *pf*.

прого́н purlin; girder; stairwell.

прогоня́ть *impf of* **прогна́ть**

прогора́ть *impf*, **прогоре́ть** (-рю́) *pf* burn (through); burn out; go bankrupt.

прого́рклый rancid, rank.

програ́мма programme; syllabus. **программи́ровать** *impf* (*pf* **за**~) programme. **программи́ст** (computer) programmer.

прогрева́ть *impf*, **прогре́ть** (-е́ю) *pf* heat; warm up; ~**ся** warm up.

про|греме́ть (-млю́) *pf*. **про|грохота́ть** (-очу́, -о́чешь) *pf*.

прогре́сс progress. **прогресси́вный** progressive. **прогресси́ровать** *impf* progress.

прогрыза́ть *impf*, **прогры́зть** (-зу́, -зёшь; -ы́з) *pf* gnaw through.

про|гуде́ть (-гужу́) *pf*.

прогу́л truancy; absenteeism. **прогу́ливать** *impf*, **прогуля́ть** *pf* play truant, be absent, (from); miss; take a walk. ~**ся** take a walk. **прогу́лка** walk, stroll; outing. **прогу́льщик** absentee, truant.

продава́ть (-даю́, -даёшь) *impf*, **прода́ть** (-а́м, -а́шь, -а́ст, -ади́м; про́дал, -а́, -о) *pf* sell. **продава́ться** (-даётся) *impf* be for sale; sell. **продаве́ц** (-вца́) seller, vendor; salesman. **продавщи́ца** seller, vendor; saleswoman. **прода́жа** sale. **прода́жный** for sale; corrupt.

продвига́ть *impf*, **продви́нуть** (-ну) *pf* move on, push forward; advance; ~**ся** advance; move forward; push on. **продвиже́ние** advancement.

продева́ть *impf of* **проде́ть**

про|деклами́ровать *pf*.

проде́лать *pf*, **проде́лывать** *impf* do, perform, make. **про-** **де́лка** trick; prank.

продемонстри́ровать *pf* demonstrate, show.

продёргивать *impf of* **продёрнуть**

продержа́ть (-жу́, -жишь) *pf* hold; keep; ~**ся** hold out.

продёрнуть (-ну, -нешь) *pf* (*impf* **продёргивать**) pass, run; criticize severely.

проде́ть (-е́ну) *pf* (*impf* **продева́ть**) pass; ~ **ни́тку в иго́лку** thread a needle.

продешеви́ть (-влю́) *pf* sell too cheap.

про|диктова́ть *pf*.

продлева́ть *impf*, **продли́ть** *pf* prolong. **продле́ние** extension. **про|дли́ться** *pf*.

продма́г grocery. **продово́льственный** food. **продово́льствие** food; provisions.

продолгова́тый oblong.

продолжа́тель *m* continuer. **продолжа́ть** *impf*, **продо́лжить** (-жу) *pf* continue; prolong; ~**ся** continue, last, go on. **продолже́ние** continuation; sequel; **в** ~+*gen* in the course of. **продолжи́тельность** duration. **продолжи́тельный** long; prolonged.

продо́льный longitudinal.

продро́гнуть (-ну; -ог) *pf* be chilled to the bone.

продтова́ры (-ов) *pl* food products.

продува́ть *impf* **проду́ть**

проду́кт product; *pl* food-stuffs. **продукти́вность** productivity. **продукти́вный** productive. **проду́ктовый** food. **проду́кция** production.

проду́манный well thought-out. **проду́мать** *pf*, **проду́мы-**

вать *impf* think over; think out.

проду́ть (-ýю, -ýешь) *pf* (*impf* **продува́ть**) blow through.

продыря́вить (-влю) *pf* make a hole in.

проеда́ть *impf of* **прое́сть. прое́ду** *etc.: see* **прое́хать**

прое́зд passage, thoroughfare; trip. **прое́здить** (-зжу) *pf* (*impf* **проезжа́ть**) spend travelling. **проездно́й** travelling; ~о́й биле́т ticket; ~а́я пла́та fare; ~ы́е *sb pl* travelling expenses. **проезжа́ть** *impf of* **прое́здить, прое́хать. прое́зжий** passing (by); *sb* passer-by.

прое́кт project, plan, design; draft. **проекти́ровать** *impf* (*pf* **с~**) project; plan. **прое́ктный** planning; planned. **прое́ктор** projector.

проекцио́нный фона́рь projector. **прое́кция** projection.

прое́сть (-е́м, -е́шь, -е́ст, -еди́м; -е́н) *pf* (*impf* **проеда́ть**) eat through, corrode; spend on food.

прое́хать (-е́ду) *pf* (*impf* **проезжа́ть**) pass, ride, drive (by, through); cover.

прожа́ренный (*cul*) well-done.

прожева́ть (-жую́, -жуёшь) *pf*, **прожёвывать** *impf* chew well.

прожёктор (*pl* -ы *or* -á) searchlight.

проже́чь (-жгý, -жжёшь; -жёг, -жгла́) *pf* (*impf* **прожига́ть**) burn (through).

прожива́ть *impf of* **прожи́ть. прожига́ть** *impf of* **проже́чь**

прожи́точный ми́нимум living wage. **прожи́ть** (-ивý, -ивёшь; про́жил, -á, -о) *pf* (*impf* **прожива́ть**) live; spend.

прожо́рливый gluttonous.

про́за prose. **проза́ический** prose; prosaic.

прозва́ние, про́звище nickname. **прозва́ть** (-зову́, -зовёшь; -áл, -á, -о) *pf* (*impf* **прозыва́ть**) nickname, name.

прозвуча́ть *pf*.

прозева́ть *pf*. **про**|**зимова́ть** *pf*. **прозову́** *etc.: see* **прозва́ть**

прозорли́вый perspicacious.

прозра́чный transparent.

прозре́ть *impf*, **прозре́ть** *pf* regain one's sight; see clearly. **прозре́ние** recovery of sight; insight.

прозыва́ть *impf of* **прозва́ть**

прозя́бнуть vegetation. **прозя́-ба́ть** *impf* vegetate.

проигра́ть *pf*, **прои́грывать** *impf* lose; play; **~ся** gamble away all one's money. **прои́гры-ватель** *m* record-player. **про́-игрыш** loss.

произведе́ние work; production; product. **произвести́** (-едý, -едёшь; -ёл, -á) *pf*, **произ-води́ть** (-ожу́, -о́дишь) *impf* make; carry out; produce; +**в**+*acc/nom pl* promote to the rank of. **производи́тель** *m* producer. **производи́тель-ность** productivity. **произво-ди́тельный** productive. **произ-во́дный** derivative. **произво́дственный** industrial; production. **произво́дство** production.

произво́л arbitrariness; arbitrary rule. **произво́льный** arbitrary.

произнести́ (-сý, -сёшь; -ёс, -лá) *pf*, **произноси́ть** (-ошу́, -о́сишь) *impf* pronounce; utter. **произ-ноше́ние** pronunciation.

произойти́ (-ойдёт; -оше́л, -шлá) *pf* (*impf* **происходи́ть**) happen,

occur; result; be descended.
произраста́ть *impf*, **произрасти́** (-ту́; -тёшь; -ро́с, -ла́) *pf* sprout; grow.
про́иски (-ов) *pl* intrigues.
проистека́ть *impf*, **происте́чь** (-ечёт; -ёк, -ла́) *pf* spring, result.
происходи́ть (-ожу́, -о́дишь) *impf of* **произойти́**. **происхожде́ние** origin; birth.
происше́ствие event, incident.
пройдо́ха *m & f* sly person.
пройти́ (-йду́, -йдёшь; -ошёл, -шла́) *pf* (*impf* **проходи́ть**) pass; go; go past; cover; study; get through; ~сь (*impf* **проха́живаться**) take a stroll.
прок use, benefit.
прокажённый *sb* leper. **прока́за¹** leprosy.
прока́за² mischief, prank. **прока́зничать** *impf* (*pf* на~) be up to mischief. **прока́зник** prankster.
прока́лывать *impf of* **проколо́ть**
прока́пывать *impf of* **прокопа́ть**
прока́т hire.
прокати́ться (-ачу́сь, -а́тишься) *pf* roll; go for a drive.
прока́тный rolling; rolled.
прокипяти́ть (-ячу́) *pf* boil (thoroughly).
прокиса́ть *impf*, **про|ки́снуть** (-нет) *pf* turn (sour).
прокла́дка laying; construction; washer; packing. **прокла́дывать** *impf of* **проложи́ть**
проклама́ция leaflet.
проклина́ть *impf*, **прокля́сть** (-яну́, -яня́шь; -о́клял, -а́, -о) *pf* curse, damn. **прокля́тие** curse; damnation. **про́клятый** (-ят, -а́, -о) damned.

проко́л puncture.
проколо́ть (-лю́, -лешь) *pf* (*impf* **прока́лывать**) prick, pierce.
прокомменти́ровать *pf* comment (upon).
про|компости́ровать *pf*.
про|конспекти́ровать *pf*.
про|консульти́ровать(ся *pf*.
про|контроли́ровать *pf*.
прокопа́ть *pf* (*impf* **прока́пывать**) dig, dig through.
проко́рм nourishment, sustenance. **про|корми́ть(ся** (-млю́(сь, -мишь(ся) *pf*.
про|корректи́ровать *pf*.
прокра́дываться *impf*, **прокра́сться** (-аду́сь, -адёшься) *pf* steal in.
прокурату́ра office of public prosecutor. **прокуро́р** public prosecutor.
прокуси́ть (-ушу́, -у́сишь) *pf*, **проку́сывать** *impf* bite through.
прокути́ть (-учу́, -у́тишь) *pf*, **проку́чивать** *impf* squander; go on a binge.
пролага́ть *impf of* **проложи́ть**
прола́мывать *impf of* **пролома́ть**
пролега́ть *impf* lie, run.
пролеза́ть *impf*, **проле́зть** (-зу; -лез) *pf* get through, climb through.
про|лепета́ть (-ечу́, -е́чешь) *pf*.
пролёт span; stairwell; bay.
пролетариа́т proletariat. **пролета́рий** proletarian. **пролета́рский** proletarian.
пролета́ть *impf*, **пролете́ть** (-ечу́) *pf* fly; cover; fly by, past, through.
проли́в strait. **пролива́ть** *impf*, **проли́ть** (-лью́, -льёшь; -о́ли́л, -а́, -о) *pf* spill, shed; ~ся be spilt.

проло́г prologue.

проложи́ть (-жу́, -жишь) pf (impf **прокла́дывать, пролага́ть**) lay; build; interlay.

проло́м breach, break. **прола́мть, проломи́ть** (-млю́, -мишь) pf (impf **прола́мывать**) break (through).

пролью́ etc.: see **проли́ть**

про|ма́зать (-а́жу) pf. **прома́тывать(ся** impf of **промота́ть(ся**

про́мах miss; slip, blunder. **прома́хиваться** impf, **промахну́ться** (-ну́сь, -нёшься) pf miss; make a blunder.

прома́чивать impf of **промочи́ть**

промедле́ние delay. **проме́длить** pf delay; procrastinate.

промежу́ток (-тка) interval; space. **промежу́точный** intermediate

промелькну́ть (-ну́, -нёшь) pf flash (past, by).

проме́нивать impf, **проме́нять** pf exchange.

промерза́ть impf, **промёрзнуть** (-ну; -ёрз) pf freeze through. **промёрзлый** frozen.

промока́ть impf, **промо́кнуть** (-ну; -мо́к) pf get soaked; let water in.

промо́лвить (-влю) pf say, utter.

промолча́ть (-чу́) pf keep silent.

про|мота́ть pf (impf also **прома́тывать**) squander.

промочи́ть (-чу́, -чишь) pf (impf **прома́чивать**) soak, drench.

промою́ etc.: see **промы́ть**

промтова́ры (-ов) pl manufactured goods.

промча́ться (-чу́сь) pf rush by.

промыва́ть impf of **промы́ть**

про́мысел (-сла) trade, business; pl works. **промысло́вый** producers'; business; game.

промы́ть (-мо́ю) pf (impf **промыва́ть**) wash (thoroughly); bathe; ~ **мозги́**+dat brainwash.

про|мыча́ть (-чу́) pf.

промы́шленник industrialist. **промы́шленность** industry. **промы́шленный** industrial.

пронести́ (-су́, -сёшь; -ёс, -ла́) pf (impf **проноси́ть**) carry (past, through); pass (over); ~**сь** rush past, through; scud (past); fly; spread.

пронза́ть impf, **пронзи́ть** (-нжу́) pf pierce, transfix. **пронзи́тельный** piercing.

прониза́ть (-ижу́, -и́жешь) pf, **прони́зывать** impf pierce; permeate.

проника́ть impf, **прони́кнуть** (-ну; -и́к) pf penetrate; percolate; ~**ся** be imbued. **проникнове́ние** penetration; feeling. **проникнове́нный** heartfelt.

проница́емый permeable. **проница́тельный** perspicacious.

проноси́ть(ся (-ошу́(сь, -о́сишь(ся) impf of **пронести́(сь. про|нумерова́ть** pf.

проню́хать pf, **проню́хивать** impf smell out, get wind of.

прообраз prototype.

пропага́нда propaganda. **пропаганди́ст** propagandist.

пропада́ть impf of **пропа́сть. пропа́жа** loss.

пропа́лывать impf of **пропо́лоть**

про́пасть precipice; abyss; lots of.

пропа́сть (-аду́, -адёшь) pf (impf

пропада́ть) be missing; be lost; disappear; be done for, die; be wasted. пропа́щий lost; hopeless.

пропека́ть(ся *impf* of пропе́чь(ся. про|пе́ть (-пою́, -поёшь) *pf*.

пропе́чь (-еку́, -ечёшь; -ёк, -ла́) *pf* (*impf* пропека́ть) bake thoroughly; ~ся get baked through.

пропива́ть *impf* of пропи́ть

прописа́ть (-ишу́, -и́шешь) *pf*, пропи́сывать *impf* prescribe; register; ~ся register. пропи́ска registration; residence permit. пропи́сно́й: ~а́я бу́ква capital letter; ~а́я и́стина truism. про́писью *adv* in words.

пропита́ние subsistence; sustenance. пропита́ть *pf*, пропи́тывать *impf* impregnate, saturate.

пропи́ть (-пью, -пьёшь; -о́пи́л, -а́, -о) *pf* (*impf* пропива́ть) spend on drink.

проплыва́ть *impf*, проплы́ть (-ыву́, -ывёшь; -ы́л, -а́, -о) *pf* swim, sail, *or* float past *or* through.

пропове́дник preacher; advocate. пропове́довать *impf* preach; advocate. про́поведь sermon; advocacy.

прополза́ть *impf*, проползти́ (-зу́, -зёшь; -по́лз, -ла́) *pf* crawl, creep.

пропо́лка weeding. прополо́ть (-лю́, -лешь) *pf* (*impf* пропа́лывать) weed.

про|полоска́ть (-ощу́, -о́щешь) *pf*.

пропорциона́льный proportional, proportionate. пропо́рция proportion.

про́пуск (*pl* -а́ *or* -и, -о́в *or* -ов)

pass, permit; password; admission; omission; non-attendance; blank, gap. пропуска́ть *impf*, пропусти́ть (-ущу́, -у́стишь) *pf* let pass; let in; pass; leave out; miss. пропускно́й admission.

про|пылесо́сить *pf*.

пропью́ *etc*.: *see* пропи́ть

прора́б works superintendent.

пораба́тывать *impf*, прораба́ботать *pf* work (through, at); study; pick holes in.

прораста́ние germination; sprouting. прораста́ть *impf*, прорасти́ (-тёт; -ро́с, -ла́) *pf* germinate, sprout.

прорва́ть (-ву́, -вёшь; -а́л, -а́, -о) *pf* (*impf* прорыва́ть) break through; ~ся burst open; break through.

про|реаги́ровать *pf*.

проре́дить (-ежу́) *pf*, проре́живать *impf* thin out.

проре́з cut; slit; notch. проре́зать (-е́жу) *pf*, прореза́ть *impf* (*impf also* прорезы́вать) cut through; ~ся be cut, come through.

прорезы́вать(ся *impf* of проре́зать(ся. про|репети́ровать *pf*.

проре́ха tear, slit; flies; deficiency.

про|рецензи́ровать *pf*.

проро́к prophet.

пророни́ть *pf* utter.

проро́с *etc*.: *see* прорасти́

проро́ческий prophetic. проро́чество prophecy.

проро́ю *etc*.: *see* проры́ть

прору́бать *impf*, проруби́ть (-блю́, -бишь) *pf* cut *or* hack through. прору́бь ice-hole.

проры́в break; break-through; hitch. прорыва́ть[1](ся *impf* of прорва́ть(ся

прорыва́ть² *impf*, проры́ть (-ро́ю) *pf* dig through; ~ся dig one's way through.

проса́чиваться *impf of* просочи́ться

просве́рливать *impf*, просверли́ть *pf* drill, bore; perforate.

просве́т (clear) space; shaft of light; ray of hope; opening. просвети́тельный educational. просвети́ть¹ (-ещу́) *pf* (*impf* просвеща́ть) enlighten.

просвети́ть² (-ечу́, -е́тишь) *pf* (*impf* просве́чивать) X-ray.

просветле́ние brightening (up); lucidity. про|светле́ть (-е́ет)

просве́чивание radioscopy. просве́чивать *impf of* просвети́ть; be translucent; be visible.

просвеща́ть *impf of* просвети́ть. просвеще́ние enlightenment.

просви́ра communion bread.

про́седь streak(s) of grey.

просе́ивать *impf of* просе́ять

просёлок (-лка) country road.

просе́ять (-е́ю) *pf* (*impf* просе́ивать) sift.

про|сигнализи́ровать *pf*.

просиде́ть (-ижу́) *pf*, проси́живать *impf* sit.

проси́тельный pleading. проси́ть (-ошу́, -о́сишь) *impf* (*pf* по~) ask; beg; invite; ~ся ask; apply.

проска́кивать *impf of* проскочи́ть

проска́льзывать *impf*, проскользну́ть (-ну́, -нёшь) *pf* slip, creep.

проскочи́ть (-чу́, -чишь) *pf* (*impf* проска́кивать) rush by;

slip through; creep in.

просла́вить (-влю) *pf*, прославля́ть *impf* glorify; make famous; ~ся become famous. просла́вленный renowned.

проследи́ть (-ежу́) *pf*, просле́живать *impf* track (down); trace.

прослези́ться (-ежу́сь) *pf* shed a few tears.

просло́йка layer, stratum.

прослужи́ть (-жу́, -жишь) *pf* serve (for a certain time).

прослу́шать *pf*, прослу́шивать *impf* hear; listen to; miss, not catch.

про|слы́ть (-ыву́, -ывёшь; -ы́л, -а́, -о) *pf*.

просма́тривать *impf*, просмотре́ть (-рю́, -ришь) *pf* look over; overlook. просмо́тр survey; view, viewing; examination.

просну́ться (-ну́сь, -нёшься) *pf* (*impf* просыпа́ться) wake up.

про́со millet.

просо́вывать(ся *impf of* просу́нуть(ся

про|со́хнуть (-ну; -о́х) *pf* (*impf also* просыха́ть) dry out.

просочи́ться (-и́тся) *pf* (*impf* проса́чиваться) percolate; seep (out); leak (out).

проспа́ть (-плю́; -а́л, -а́, -о) *pf* (*impf* просыпа́ть) sleep (through); oversleep.

проспе́кт avenue.

про|спряга́ть *pf*.

просро́ченный overdue; expired. просро́чить (-чу) *pf* allow to run out; be behind with; overstay. просро́чка delay; expiry of time limit.

проста́ивать *impf of* простоя́ть

проста́к (-а́) simpleton.

простёнок (-нка) pier (*between windows*).

простере́ться (-трётся; -тёрся) *pf*, **простира́ться** *impf* extend.

прости́тельный pardonable, excusable. **прости́ть** (-ощу́) *pf* (*impf* **проща́ть**) forgive; excuse; ~ся (c+*instr*) say goodbye (to).

проститу́тка prostitute. **проститу́ция** prostitution.

про́сто *adv* simply.

простоволо́сый bare-headed. **простоду́шный** simple-hearted; ingenuous.

просто́й[1] downtime.

просто́й[2] simple; plain; mere; ~ым гла́зом with the naked eye; ~о́е число́ prime number.

простоква́ша thick sour milk.

про́сто-на́просто *adv* simply.

простонаро́дный of the common people.

просто́р spaciousness; space. **просто́рный** spacious.

просторе́чие popular speech. **простосерде́чный** simple-hearted.

простота́ simplicity.

простоя́ть (-ою́) *pf* (*impf* **проста́ивать**) stand (idle).

простра́нный extensive, vast. **простра́нственный** spatial. **простра́нство** space.

простре́л lumbago. **простре́ливать** *impf*, **прострели́ть** (-лю́, -лишь) *pf* shoot through.

про|стро́чить (-очу́, -о́чишь) *pf*.

просту́да cold. **простуди́ться** (-ужу́сь, -у́дишься) *pf*, **простужа́ться** *impf* catch (a) cold.

проступа́ть *impf*, **проступи́ть** (-ит) *pf* appear.

просту́пок (-пка) misdemeanour.

простыня́ (*pl* про́стыни, -ы́нь, -ня́м) sheet.

прости́ть (-ы́ну) *pf* get cold.

просу́нуть (-ну) *pf* (*impf* **просо́вывать**) push, thrust.

просу́шивать *impf*, **просуши́ть** (-шу́, -шишь) *pf* dry out; ~ся (get) dry.

просуществова́ть *pf* exist; endure.

просчёт error. **просчита́ться** *pf*, **просчи́тываться** *impf* miscalculate.

просыпа́ть (-плю) *pf*, **просыпа́ть**[1] *impf* spill; ~ся get spilt.

просыпа́ть[2] *impf* of **проспа́ть**. **просыпа́ться** *impf* of **просну́ться**. **просыха́ть** *impf* of **просо́хнуть**

про́сьба request.

прота́лкивать(ся *impf* of **протолкну́ть(ся**. **прота́пливать** *impf* of **протопи́ть**

прота́птывать *impf* of **протопта́ть**

прота́скивать *impf*, **протащи́ть** (-щу́, -щишь) *pf* drag, push (through).

проте́з artificial limb, prosthesis; зубно́й ~ denture.

протеи́н protein.

протека́ть *impf* of **проте́чь**.

проте́кция patronage.

протере́ть (-тру́, -трёшь; -тёр) *pf* (*impf* **протира́ть**) wipe (over); wear (through).

проте́ст protest. **протеста́нт**, ~ка Protestant. **протестова́ть** *impf* protest.

проте́чь (-ечёт; -тёк, -ла́) *pf* (*impf* **протека́ть**) flow; leak; seep; pass; take its course.

про́тив *prep*+*gen* against; opposite; contrary to, as against.

проти́вень (-вня) *m* baking-tray; meat-pan.

проти́виться (-влюсь) *impf* (*pf* **вос~**) +*dat* oppose; resist. **про-**

ти́вник opponent; the enemy. **проти́вный**[1] opposite; contrary. **проти́вный**[2] nasty, disgusting.

противо- in comb anti-, contra-, counter-. **противове́с** counterbalance. **~возду́шный** anti-aircraft. **~га́з** gas-mask. **~де́йствие** opposition. **~де́йствовать** impf +dat oppose, counteract. **~есте́ственный** unnatural. **~зако́нный** illegal. **~зача́точный** contraceptive. **~поло́жность** opposite; opposition, contrast. **~поло́жный** opposite; contrary. **~поста́вить** pf, **~поставля́ть** impf oppose; contrast. **~речи́вый** contradictory; conflicting. **~ре́чие** contradiction. **~ре́чить** (-чу) impf +dat contradict. **~стоя́ть** (-ою́) impf +dat resist, withstand. **~та́нковый** anti-tank. **~я́дие** antidote.

протира́ть impf of протере́ть
проти́скивать impf, **проти́скнуть** (-ну) pf force, squeeze (through, into).

проткну́ть (-ну́, -нёшь) pf (impf **протыка́ть**) pierce.

протоко́л minutes; report; protocol.

протолкну́ть (-ну́, -нёшь) pf (impf **прота́лкивать**) push through; **~ся** push one's way through.

прото́н proton.

протопи́ть (-плю́, -пишь) pf (impf **прота́пливать**) heat (thoroughly).

протопта́ть (-пчу́, -пчешь) pf (impf **прота́птывать**) tread; wear out.

проторённый beaten, well-trodden.

прототи́п prototype.

прото́чный flowing, running.

протра́ pf. **протру́** etc.: see протере́ть. **протруби́ть** (-блю́) pf

протрезви́ть (-влю́сь) pf, **протрезвля́ться** impf sober up.

протуха́ть impf, **проту́хнуть** (-нет, -ух) pf become rotten; go bad.

протыка́ть impf of проткну́ть
протя́гивать impf, **протяну́ть** (-ну́, -нешь) pf stretch; extend; hold out; **~ся** stretch out; extend; last. **протяже́ние** extent, stretch; period. **протя́жный** long-drawn-out; drawling.

проу́чивать impf, **проучи́ть** (-чу́, -чишь) pf study; teach a lesson.

профа́н ignoramus.

профана́ция profanation.

профессиона́л professional. **профессиона́льный** professional; occupational. **профе́ссия** profession. **профе́ссор** (pl -á) professor.

профила́ктика prophylaxis; preventive measures.

про́филь m profile; type.

профильтрова́ть pf.

профсою́з trade-union.

проха́живаться impf of пройти́сь

прохво́ст scoundrel.

прохла́да coolness. **прохлади́тельный** refreshing, cooling. **прохла́дный** cool, chilly.

прохо́д passage; gangway, aisle; duct. **проходи́мец** (-мца) rogue. **проходи́мый** passable. **проходи́ть** (-ожу́, -о́дишь) impf of пройти́. **проходно́й** entrance; communicating. **проходя́щий** passing. **прохо́жий**

passing, in transit; *sb* passer-by.

процвета́ние prosperity. **процвета́ть** *impf* prosper, flourish.

процеди́ть (-ежу́, -е́дишь) *pf* (*impf* **проце́живать**) filter, strain.

процеду́ра procedure; (*usu in pl*) treatment.

проце́живать *pf of* **процеди́ть**

проце́нт percentage; per cent; interest.

проце́сс process; trial; legal proceedings. **проце́ссия** procession.

процити́ровать *pf*.

прочёска screening; combing.

проче́сть (-чту́, -чтёшь; -чёл, -чла́) *pf of* **чита́ть**

про́чий other.

прочи́стить (-и́щу) *pf* (*impf* **прочища́ть**) clean; clear.

прочита́ть *pf*, **прочи́тывать** *impf* read (through).

прочища́ть *impf of* **прочи́стить**

про́чность firmness, stability, durability. **про́чный** (-чен, -чна́, -о) firm, sound, solid; durable.

прочте́ние reading. **прочту́** *etc.: see* **проче́сть**

прочу́вствовать *pf* feel deeply; experience, go through.

прочь *adv* away, off; averse to.

проше́дший past; last. **прошёл** *etc.: see* **пройти́**

проше́ние application, petition.

прошепта́ть (-пчу́, -пчешь) *pf* whisper.

проше́ствие: по проше́ствии +*gen* after.

прошива́ть *impf*, **проши́ть** (-шью́, -шьёшь) *pf* sew, stitch.

прошлого́дний last year's. **про́шлый** past; last; **~ое** *sb* the past.

прошнурова́ть *pf*. **прошту|ди́ровать** *pf*. **прошью́** *etc.: see* **проши́ть**

проща́й(те) goodbye. **проща́льный** parting; farewell. **проща́ние** farewell; parting. **проща́ть(ся** *impf of* **прости́ть(ся**

про́ще simpler, plainer.

проще́ние forgiveness, pardon.

прощу́пать *pf*, **прощу́пывать** *impf* feel.

проэкзаменова́ть *pf*.

прояви́тель *m* developer. **прояви́ть** (-влю́, -вишь) *pf*, **проявля́ть** *impf* show, display; develop; **~ся** reveal itself. **проявле́ние** display; manifestation; developing.

проясни́ться, **проясня́ться** *impf* clear, clear up.

пруд (-а́, *loc* -у́) pond. **пруди́ть** (-ужу́, -у́ди́шь) *impf* (*pf* **за~**) dam.

пружи́на spring. **пружи́нистый** springy. **пружи́нный** spring.

пру́сский Prussian.

прут (-а *or* -а́; *pl* -тья) twig.

пры́гать *impf*, **пры́гнуть** (-ну) *pf* jump, leap; bounce; ~ с шесто́м pole-vault. **прыгу́н** (-а́), **прыгу́нья** (*gen pl* -ний) jumper. **прыжо́к** (-жка́) jump; leap; **прыжки́** jumping; **прыжки́ в во́ду** diving; ~ **в высоту́** high jump; ~ **в длину́** long jump.

пры́скать *impf*, **пры́снуть** (-ну) *pf* spurt; sprinkle; burst out laughing.

прыть speed; energy.

прыщ (-а́), **пры́щик** pimple.

пряди́льный spinning. **пряди́льня** (*gen pl* -лен) (spinning-)mill. **пряди́льщик** spinner. **пряду́** *etc.: see* **прясть**

прядь lock; strand. **пря́жа** yarn, thread.

пря́жка buckle, clasp.

пря́лка distaff; spinning-wheel.

пряма́я *sb* straight line. **прямо** *adv* straight; straight on; frankly; really.

прямоду́шие directness, straightforwardness. **∼ду́шный** direct, straightforward.

прямо́й (-ям, -á, -о) straight; upright, erect; through; direct; straightforward; real.

прямолине́йный rectilinear; straightforward. **прямоуго́льник** rectangle. **прямоуго́льный** rectangular.

пря́ник spice cake. **пря́ность** spice. **пря́ный** spicy; heady.

прясть (-яду́, -ядёшь; -ял, -яла́, -о) *impf* (*pf* с∼) spin.

пря́тать (-ячу) *impf* (*pf* с∼) hide; **∼ся** hide. **пря́тки** (-ток) *pf* hide-and-seek.

пса *etc.*: *see* **пёс**

псало́м (-лма́) psalm. **псалты́рь** Psalter.

псевдони́м pseudonym.

псих madman, lunatic. **психиатри́я** psychiatry. **психика** psyche; psychology. **психи́ческий** mental, psychical.

психоана́лиз psychoanalysis. **психо́з** psychosis. **психо́лог** psychologist. **психологи́ческий** psychological. **психоло́гия** psychology. **психопа́т** psychopath. **психопати́ческий** psychopathic. **психосомати́ческий** psychosomatic. **психотерапе́вт** psychotherapist. **психотерапи́я** psychotherapy. **психоти́ческий** psychotic.

птене́ц (-нца́) nestling; fledgeling. **пти́ца** bird. **птицефе́рма** poultry-farm. **пти́чий** bird,

bird's, poultry. **пти́чка** bird; tick.

пу́блика public; audience. **публика́ция** publication; notice, advertisement. **публикова́ть** *impf* (*pf* о∼) publish. **публици́стика** writing on current affairs. **публи́чность** publicity. **публи́чный** public; **∼ дом** brothel.

пуга́ло scarecrow. **пуга́ть** *impf* (*pf* ис∼, на∼) frighten, scare; **∼ся** (+*gen*) be frightened (of). **пуга́ч** (-á) toy pistol. **пугли́вый** fearful.

пуд (*pl* -ы́) pood (= *16.38 kg*). **пудово́й, пудо́вый** one pood in weight.

пу́дель *m* poodle.

пу́динг blancmange.

пу́дра powder. **пу́дреница** powder compact. **пу́дреный** powdered. **пу́дриться** *impf* (*pf* на∼) powder one's face.

пуза́тый pot-bellied.

пузырёк (-рька́) vial; bubble. **пузы́рь** (-я́) *m* bubble; blister; bladder.

пук (*pl* -и́) bunch, bundle; tuft.

пу́кать *impf*, **пу́кнуть** *pf* fart.

пулемёт machine-gun. **пулемётчик** machine-gunner. **пуленепробива́емый** bullet-proof.

пульвериза́тор atomizer; spray.

пульс pulse. **пульса́р** pulsar. **пульси́ровать** *impf* pulsate.

пульт desk, stand; control panel.

пу́ля bullet.

пункт point; spot; post; item. **пункти́р** dotted line. **пункти́рный** dotted, broken.

пунктуа́льный punctual.

пунктуа́ция punctuation.

пунцо́вый crimson.

пуп (-а́) navel. **пупови́на** umbilical cord. **пупо́к** (-пка́) navel; gizzard.

пурга́ blizzard.

пурита́нин (pl -та́не, -та́н), **-а́нка** Puritan.

пу́рпур purple, crimson. **пурпу́рный, ~овый** purple.

пуск starting (up). **пуска́й** see **пусть. пуска́ть(ся** impf of **пусти́ть(ся. пусково́й** starting.

пусте́ть (-е́ет) impf (pf о~) empty; become empty.

пусти́ть (пущу́, пу́стишь) pf (impf **пуска́ть)** let go; let in; let; start; send; set in motion; throw; put forth; **~ся** set out; start.

пустова́ть impf be or stand empty. **пусто́й** (-ст, -а́, -о) empty; uninhabited; idle; shallow. **пустота́** (pl -ы) emptiness; void; vacuum; futility. **пустоте́лый** hollow.

пусты́нный uninhabited; deserted; desert. **пусты́ня** desert. **пусты́рь** (-я́) m waste land; vacant plot.

пусты́шка blank; hollow object; dummy.

пусть, пуска́й partl let; all right; though, even if.

пустя́к (-а́) trifle. **пустяко́вый** trivial.

пу́таница muddle, confusion. **пу́таный** muddled, confused. **пу́тать** impf (pf за~, пере~, с~) tangle; confuse; mix up; **~ся** get confused or mixed up.

путёвка pass; place on a group tour. **путеводи́тель** m guide, guide-book. **путево́й** travelling; road. **путём** prep+gen by means of. **путеше́ственник** traveller. **путеше́ствие** journey; voyage.

путеше́ствовать impf travel; voyage.

пу́ты (пут) pl shackles.

путь (-и́, instr -ём, prep -и́) way; track; path; course; journey; voyage; means; **в пути́** en route, on one's way.

пух (loc -у́) down; fluff.

пу́хлый (-хл, -а́, -о) plump. **пу́хнуть** (-ну; пух) impf (pf вс~, о~) swell.

пухови́к (-а́) feather-bed. **пухо́вка** powder-puff. **пухо́вый** downy.

пучи́на abyss; the deep.

пучо́к (-чка́) bunch, bundle.

пу́шечный gun, cannon.

пуши́нка bit of fluff. **пуши́стый** fluffy.

пу́шка gun, cannon.

пушни́на furs, pelts. **пушно́й** fur; fur-bearing.

пу́ще adv more; **~ всего́** most of all.

пущу́ etc.: see **пусти́ть**

пчела́ (pl -ёлы) bee. **пчели́ный** bee, bees'. **пчелово́д** bee-keeper. **пче́льник** apiary.

пшени́ца wheat. **пшени́чный** wheat(en).

пшённый millet. **пшено́** millet.

пыл (loc -у́) heat, ardour. **пыла́ть** impf blaze; burn.

пылесо́с vacuum cleaner. **пылесо́сить** impf (pf про~) vacuum(-clean). **пыли́нка** speck of dust. **пыли́ть** impf (pf за~, на~) raise a dust; cover with dust; **~ся** get dusty.

пы́лкий ardent; fervent.

пыль (loc -и́) dust. **пы́льный** (-лен, -льна́, -о) dusty. **пыльца́** pollen.

пыре́й couch grass.

пырну́ть (-ну́, -нёшь) pf jab.

пыта́ть *impf* torture. **пыта́ться** *impf* (*pf* по~) try. **пы́тка** torture, torment. **пытли́вый** inquisitive.

пыхте́ть (-хчу́) *impf* puff, pant.

пы́шка bun.

пы́шность splendour. **пы́шный** (-шен, -шна́, -шно) splendid; lush.

пьедеста́л pedestal.

пье́са play; piece.

пью *etc.*: see пить

пьяне́ть (-е́ю) *impf* (*pf* о~) get drunk. **пьяни́ть** *impf* (*pf* о~) intoxicate, make drunk. **пья́ница** *m* & *f* drunkard. **пья́нство** drunkenness. **пья́нствовать** *impf* drink heavily. **пья́ный** drunk.

пюпи́тр lectern; stand.

пюре́ *neut indecl* purée.

пядь (*gen pl* -е́й) span; ни пя́ди not an inch.

па́льцы (-лец) *pl* embroidery frame.

пята́ (*pl* -ы, -а́м) heel.

пята́к (-а́), **пятачо́к** (-чка́) five-copeck piece. **пятёрка** five; figure 5; No. 5; fiver (5-*rouble note*).

пяти- *in comb* five; penta-. **пятибо́рье** pentathlon. ~**десятиле́тие** fifty years; fiftieth anniversary, birthday. П~**деся́тница** Pentecost. ~**деся́тый** fiftieth. ~**деся́тые го́ды** the fifties. ~**коне́чный** five-pointed. ~**ле́тие** five years; fifth anniversary. ~**ле́тка** five-year plan. ~**со́тый** five-hundredth. ~**уго́льник** pentagon. ~**уго́льный** pentagonal.

пя́титься (-ячусь) *impf* (*pf* по~) move backwards; back.

пя́тка heel.

пятна́дцатый fifteenth. **пятна́дцать** fifteen.

пятна́ть *impf* (*pf* за~) spot, stain. **пятна́шки** (-шек) *pl* tag. **пятни́стый** spotted.

пя́тница Friday.

пятно́ (*pl* -а, -тен) stain; spot; blot; **роди́мое ~** birth-mark.

пя́тый fifth. **пять** (-й, *instr* -ью́) five. **пятьдеся́т** (-и́десяти, *instr* -ьюдесятью́) fifty. **пятьсо́т** (-тисо́т, -тиста́м) five hundred. **пя́тью** *adv* five times.

Р

раб (-а́), **раба́** slave. **рабовладе́лец** (-льца) slave-owner. **раболе́пие** servility. **раболе́пный** servile. **раболе́пствовать** cringe, fawn.

рабо́та work; job; functioning. **рабо́тать** *impf* work; function; be open; ~ **над**+*instr* work on. **рабо́тник**, -ица worker. **работоспосо́бность** capacity for work, efficiency. **работоспосо́бный** able-bodied, hard-working. **рабо́тящий** hard-working. **рабо́чий** *sb* worker. **рабо́чий** worker's; working; ~**ая си́ла** manpower.

ра́бский slave; servile. **ра́бство** slavery. **рабы́ня** female slave.

равви́н rabbi.

ра́венство equality. **равне́ние** alignment. **равни́на** plain.

равно́ *adv* alike; equally; ~ **как** as well as. **равно́** *predic*: see **ра́вный**

равно- *in comb* equi-, iso-. **равнобе́дренный** isosceles. ~**ве́сие** equilibrium; balance. ~**де́нствие** equinox. ~**ду́шие**

indifference. ~ду́шный indifferent. ~ме́рный even; uniform. ~пра́вие equality of rights. ~пра́вный having equal rights. ~си́льный of equal strength; equal, equivalent, tantamount. ~сторо́нний equilateral. ~це́нный of equal value; equivalent.

ра́вный (-вен, -вна́) equal. равно́ *predic* make(s), equals; всё ~о́ (it is) all the same. равня́ть *impf* (*pf* с~) make even; treat equally; +c+*instr* compare with, treat as equal to; ~ся compete, compare; be equal; be tantamount.

рад (-а, -о) *predic* glad.

рада́р radar.

ра́ди *prep*+*gen* for the sake of.

радиа́тор radiator. радиа́ция radiation.

ра́дий radium.

радика́льный radical.

ра́дио *neut indecl* radio.

ра́дио- *in comb* radio-; radioactive. радиоакти́вный radioactive. ~веща́ние broadcasting. ~волна́ radio-wave. ~гра́мма radio-telegram. ~дио́лог radiologist. ~ло́гия radiology. ~люби́тель *m* radio amateur, ham. ~мая́к (-а́) radio beacon. ~переда́тчик transmitter. ~переда́ча broadcast. ~приёмник radio (set). ~связь radio communication. ~слу́шатель *m* listener. ~ста́нция radio station. ~электро́ника radioelectronics.

радио́ла radiogram.

ради́ровать *impf* & *pf* radio. ради́ст radio operator.

ра́диус radius.

ра́довать *impf* (*pf* об~, по~) gladden, make happy; ~ся be glad, rejoice. ра́достный joyful. ра́дость gladness, joy.

ра́дуга rainbow. ра́дужный iridescent; cheerful; ~ая оболо́чка iris.

раду́шие cordiality. раду́шный cordial.

ражу́ *etc.*: *see* рази́ть

раз (*pl* -ы́, раз) time, occasion; one; ещё ~ (once) again; как ~ just, exactly; не ~ more than once; ни ~у not once. раз *adv* once, one day. раз *conj* if; since.

разба́вить (-влю) *pf*, разбавля́ть *impf* dilute.

разбаза́ривать *impf*, разбаза́рить *pf* squander.

разба́лтывать(ся *impf* *see* разболта́ть(ся

разбе́г running start. разбега́ться *impf*, разбежа́ться (-егу́сь) *pf* take a run, run up; scatter.

разберу́ *etc.*: *see* разобра́ть

разбива́ть(ся *impf* *see* разби́ть(ся. разби́вка laying out; spacing (out).

разбинтова́ть *pf*, разбинто́вывать *impf* unbandage.

разбира́тельство investigation. разбира́ть *impf* of разобра́ть; ~ся *impf* of разобра́ться

разби́ть (-зобью́, -зобьёшь) *pf* (*impf* разбива́ть) break; smash; divide (up); damage; defeat; mark out; space (out); ~ся break, get broken; hurt o.s. разби́тый broken; jaded.

разбогате́ть (-е́ю) *pf*.

разбо́й robbery. разбо́йник robber. разбо́йничий robber.

разболе́ться[1] (-лю́сь) *pf* begin to ache badly.

разболе́ться² (-е́юсь) *pf* become ill.

разболта́ть¹ *pf* (*impf* **разба́лтывать**) divulge, give away.

разболта́ть² *pf* (*impf* **разба́лтывать**) shake up; loosen; **~ся** work loose; get out of hand.

разбомби́ть (-блю́) *pf* bomb, destroy by bombing.

разбо́р analysis; critique; discrimination; investigation. **разбо́рка** sorting out; dismantling. **разбо́рный** collapsible. **разбо́рчивый** legible; discriminating.

разбра́сывать *impf of* **разбросать**

разбреда́ться *impf*, **разбрести́сь** (-едётся, -ёлся, -ла́сь) *pf* disperse; straggle. **разбро́д** disorder.

разбро́санный scattered; disconnected, incoherent. **разброса́ть** *pf* (*impf* **разбра́сывать**) throw about; scatter.

разбуди́ть (-ужу́, -у́дишь) *pf*.

разбуха́ть *impf*, **разбу́хнуть** (-нет, -бу́х) *pf* swell.

разбушева́ться (-шу́юсь) *pf* fly into a rage; blow up; rage.

разва́л breakdown, collapse. **разва́ливать** *impf*, **развали́ть** (-лю́, -лишь) *pf* pull down; mess up; **~ся** collapse; go to pieces; tumble down; sprawl. **разва́лина** ruin; wreck.

ра́зве *partl* really?; **~ (то́лько)**, **~ (что)** except that, only.

развева́ться *impf* fly, flutter.

разве́дать *pf* (*impf* **разве́дывать**) find out; reconnoitre.

разведе́ние breeding; cultivation.

разведённый divorced; **~ый**, **~ая** *sb* divorcee.

разве́дка intelligence (service); reconnaissance; prospecting. **разве́дочный** prospecting, exploratory.

разведу́ *etc.: see* **развести́**

разве́дчик intelligence officer; scout; prospector. **разве́дывать** *impf of* **разве́дать**

развезти́ (-зу́, -зёшь; -ёз, -ла́) *pf* (*impf* **развози́ть**) convey, transport; deliver.

разве́ивать(ся *impf of* **разве́ять(ся. разве́ял** *etc.: see* **развести́**

развенча́ть *pf*, **разве́нчивать** *impf* dethrone; debunk.

развёрнутый extensive, all-out; detailed. **разверну́ть** (-ну́, -нёшь) *pf* (*impf* **развёртывать**, **развора́чивать**) unfold, unwrap; unroll; unfurl; deploy; expand; turn; scan; display; **~ся** unfold, unroll, come unwrapped; deploy; develop; spread; turn.

развёрстка allotment, apportionment.

развёртывать(ся *impf of* **развернуть(ся**

раз|весели́ть *pf* cheer up, amuse; **~ся** cheer up.

разве́сить¹ (-е́шу) *pf* (*impf* **разве́шивать**) spread; hang (out).

разве́сить² (-е́шу) *pf* (*impf* **разве́шивать**) weigh out. **разве́ска** weighing. **развесно́й** sold by weight.

развести́ (-еду́, -едёшь; -ёл, -а́) *pf* (*impf* **разводи́ть**) take; separate; divorce; dilute; dissolve; start; breed; cultivate; **~сь** get divorced; breed, multiply.

разветви́ться (-ви́тся) *pf*, **разветвля́ться** *impf* branch; fork. **разветвле́ние** branching, forking; branch; fork.

разве́шать *pf*, **разве́шивать** *impf* hang.

разве́шивать *impf of* **разве́сить, разве́шать. разве́шу** *etc.*: *see* **разве́сить**

разве́ять (-е́ю) *pf* (*impf* **разве́ивать**) scatter, disperse; dispel; ~ся disperse; be dispelled.

развива́ть(ся *impf of* **разви́ть(ся**

разви́лка fork.

развинти́ть (-нчу́) *pf*, **разви́нчивать** *impf* unscrew.

разви́тие development. **разви́той** (ра́звит, -а́, -о) developed; mature. **разви́ть** (-зовью́; -зовье́шь; -л, -а́, -о) *pf* (*impf* **развива́ть**) develop; unwind; ~ся develop.

развлека́ть *impf*, **развле́чь** (-еку́, -ече́шь; -ёк, -ла́) *pf* entertain, amuse; ~ся have a good time; amuse o.s. **развлече́ние** entertainment, amusement.

разво́д divorce. **разводи́ть(ся** (-ожу́(сь, -о́дишь(ся) *impf of* **развести́(сь. разво́дка** separation. **разводно́й**: ~ ключ adjustable spanner; ~ мост drawbridge.

развози́ть (-ожу́, -о́зишь) *impf of* **развезти́**

разволнова́ть(ся *pf* get excited; be agitated.

развора́чивать(ся *impf of* **разверну́ть(ся**

разворова́ть *pf*, **разворо́вывать** *impf* loot; steal.

разворо́т U-turn; turn; development.

развра́т depravity, corruption. **разврати́ть** (-ащу́) *pf*. **развраща́ть** *impf* corrupt; deprave. **развра́тничать** *impf* lead a depraved life. **развра́тный** (-тен, -тна́) corrupt. **развращённый** (-ён, -а́) corrupt.

развяза́ть (-яжу́, -я́жешь) *pf*, **развя́зывать** *impf* untie; unleash; ~ся come untied; ~ся с+*instr* rid o.s. of. **развя́зка** dénouement; outcome. **развя́зный** overfamiliar.

разгада́ть *pf*, **разга́дывать** *impf* solve, guess, interpret. **разга́дка** solution.

разга́р height, climax.

разгиба́ть(ся *impf of* **разогну́ть(ся**

разглаго́льствовать *impf* hold forth.

разгла́дить (-а́жу) *pf*, **разгла́живать** *impf* smooth out; iron (out).

разгласи́ть (-ашу́) *pf*, **разглаша́ть** *impf* divulge; +о+*prep* trumpet. **разглаше́ние** disclosure.

разгляде́ть (-яжу́) *pf*, **разгля́дывать** *impf* make out, discern.

разгне́вать *pf* anger. **раз|гне́ваться** *pf*.

разгова́ривать *impf* talk, converse. **разгово́р** conversation. **разгово́рник** phrase-book. **разгово́рный** colloquial. **разгово́рчивый** talkative.

разго́н dispersal; running start; distance. **разгоня́ть(ся** *impf of* **разогна́ть(ся**

разгоня́жи́вать *impf of* **разгороди́ть**

разгора́ться *impf*, **разгоре́ться** (-рю́сь) *pf* flare up.

разгороди́ть (-ожу́, -о́дишь) *pf* (*impf* **разгора́живать**) partition off.

раз|горячи́ть(ся (-чу́(сь) *pf*.

разгра́бить (-блю) *pf* plunder, loot. **разграбле́ние** plunder, looting.

разграниче́ние demarcation;

differentiation. **разграни́чивать** *impf*, **разграни́чить** (-чу) *pf* delimit; differentiate.

разгреба́ть *impf*, **разгрести́** (-ебу́, -ебёшь; -ёб, -ла́) *pf* rake *or* shovel (away).

разгро́м crushing defeat; devastation; havoc. **разгроми́ть** (-млю́) *pf* rout, defeat.

разгружа́ть *impf*, **разгрузи́ть** (-ужу́, -у́зи́шь) *pf* unload; relieve; ∼ся unload; be relieved. **разгру́зка** unloading; relief.

разгрыза́ть *impf*, **разгры́зть** (-зу́, -зёшь; -ы́з) *pf* crack.

разгу́л revelry; outburst. **разгу́ливать** *impf* stroll about. **разгу́ливаться** *impf*, **разгуля́ться** *pf* spread o.s.; become wide awake; clear up. **разгу́льный** wild, rakish.

раздава́ть(ся (-даю́(сь, -даёшь(ся) *impf of* **разда́ть(ся**

разда́вить (-влю́, -вишь) *pf*. **разда́вливать** *impf* crush; run over.

разда́ть (-а́м, -а́шь, -а́ст, -ади́м; ро́з- *or* разда́л, -а́, -о) *pf* (*impf* **раздава́ть**) distribute, give out; ∼ся be heard; resound; ring out; make way; expand; put on weight. **разда́ча** distribution.

раздаю́ *etc.*: *see* **раздава́ть**

раздва́ивать(ся *impf of* **раздво́ить(ся**

раздвига́ть *impf*, **раздви́нуть** (-ну) *pf* move apart; ∼ся move apart. **раздвижно́й** expanding; sliding.

раздвое́ние division; split; ∼ ли́чности split personality. **раздво́енный** forked; cloven; split. **раздво́ить** *pf* (*impf* **раздва́ивать**) divide into two; bisect; ∼ся fork; split.

раздева́лка cloakroom. **раз**

дева́ть(ся *impf of* **разде́ть(ся**

разде́л division; section.

разде́латься *pf* +c+*instr* finish with; settle accounts with.

разделе́ние division. **раздели́мый** divisible. **раздели́ть** (-лю́, -лишь) *pf*, **разделя́ть** *impf* divide; separate; share; ∼ся be divided; be divisible; separate. **разде́льный** separate.

разде́ну *etc.*: *see* **разде́ть. раздеру́** *etc.*: *see* **раздира́ть**

разде́ть (-де́ну) *pf* (*impf* **раздева́ть**) undress; ∼ся undress; take off one's coat.

раздира́ть *impf of* **разодра́ть**

раздобыва́ть *impf*, **раздобы́ть** (-бу́ду) *pf* get, get hold of.

раздо́лье expanse; liberty. **раздо́льный** free.

раздо́р discord. **раздоса́довать** *pf* vex.

раздража́ть *impf*, **раздражи́ть** (-жу́) *pf* irritate; annoy; ∼ся get annoyed. **раздраже́ние** irritation. **раздражи́тельный** irritable.

раздроби́ть (-блю́) *pf*, **раздробля́ть** *impf* break; smash to pieces.

раздува́ть(ся *impf of* **разду́ть(ся**

разду́мать *pf*, **разду́мывать** *impf* change one's mind; ponder. **разду́мье** meditation; thought.

разду́ть (-у́ю) *pf* (*impf* **раздува́ть**) blow; fan; exaggerate; whip up; swell; ∼ся swell.

развева́ть *impf of* **разви́нуть**

разжа́лобить (-блю) *pf* move (to pity).

разжа́ловать *pf* demote.

разжа́ть (-зожму́, -мёшь) *pf* (*impf* **разжима́ть**) unclasp; open; release.

разжева́ть (-жую́, -жуёшь) pf, **разжёвывать** impf chew.

разже́чь (-зожгу́, -зожжёшь; -жёг, -зожгла́) pf, **разжига́ть** impf kindle; rouse.

разжима́ть impf of **разжа́ть**. **раз|жире́ть** (-е́ю) pf.

рази́нуть (-ну) pf (impf **разева́ть**) open; ~ рот gape. **рази́ня** m & f scatter-brain.

рази́тельный striking. **рази́ть** (ражу́) impf (pf по~) strike.

разлага́ть(ся impf of **разложи́ть(ся**

разла́д discord; disorder.

разла́мывать(ся impf of **разломи́ть(ся**, **разломи́ть(ся**. **разлёгся** etc.: see **разле́чься**

разлеза́ться impf, **разле́зться** (-зется; -ле́зся) pf come to pieces; fall apart.

разлета́ться impf, **разлете́ться** (-лечу́сь) pf fly away; scatter; shatter; rush.

разле́чься (-ля́гусь; -лёгся, -гла́сь) pf stretch out.

разли́в bottling; flood; overflow. **разлива́ть** impf, **разли́ть** (-золью́, -зольёшь; -и́л, -а́, -о) pf pour out; spill; flood (with); ~ся spill; overflow; spread. **разливно́й** draught.

различа́ть impf, **различи́ть** (-чу́) pf distinguish; discern; ~ся differ. **разли́чие** distinction; difference. **различи́тельный** distinctive, distinguishing. **разли́чный** different.

разложе́ние decomposition; decay; disintegration. **разложи́ть** (-жу́, -жишь) pf (impf **разлага́ть**, **раскла́дывать**) put away; spread (out); distribute; break down; decompose; resolve; corrupt; ~ся decompose; become demoralized; be cor-

rupted; disintegrate, go to pieces.

разло́м breaking; break. **разлома́ть**, **разломи́ть** (-млю́, -мишь) pf (impf **разла́мывать**) break to pieces; pull down; ~ся break to pieces.

разлу́ка separation. **разлуча́ть** impf, **разлучи́ть** (-чу́) pf separate, part; ~ся separate, part.

разлюби́ть (-блю́, -бишь) pf stop loving or liking.

разля́гусь etc.: see **разле́чься**

размажу etc.: see **разма́зать**

разма́зать (-а́жу) pf, **разма́зывать** impf spread, smear.

разма́лывать impf of **размоло́ть**

разма́тывать impf of **размота́ть**

разма́х sweep; swing; span; scope. **разма́хивать** impf +instr swing; brandish. **разма́хиваться** impf, **размахну́ться** (-ну́сь, -нёшься) pf swing one's arm. **разма́шистый** sweeping.

размежева́ние demarcation, delimitation. **размежева́ть** (-жу́ю) pf, **размежёвывать** impf delimit.

размёл etc.: see **размести́**

размельча́ть impf, **размельчи́ть** (-чу́) pf crush, pulverize.

размелю́ etc.: see **размоло́ть**

разме́н exchange. **разме́нивать** impf, **разменя́ть** pf change; ~ся +instr exchange; dissipate. **разме́нная моне́та** (small) change.

разме́р size; measurement; amount; scale, extent; pl proportions. **разме́ренный** measured. **разме́рить** pf, **размеря́ть** impf measure.

размести́ (-ету́, -етёшь; -мёл, -а́) pf (impf **размета́ть**) sweep clear; sweep away.

размести́ть (-ещу́) *pf* (*impf* размеща́ть) place, accommodate; distribute; ∼ся take one's seat.

размета́ть *impf of* размести́

размеча́ть (-е́чу) *pf*, размеча́ть *impf* mark.

размеша́ть *pf*, разме́шивать *impf* stir (in).

размеща́ть(ся *impf of* размести́ть(ся. размеще́ние placing; accommodation; distribution.

размещу́ *etc.*: *see* размести́ть

размина́ть(ся *impf of* размя́ть(ся

разми́нка limbering up.

размину́ться (-ну́сь, -нёшься) *pf*; +c+*instr* pass; miss.

размножа́ть *impf*, размно́жить (-жу) *pf* multiply, duplicate; breed; ∼ся multiply; breed.

размозжи́ть (-жу́) *pf* smash.

размо́лвка tiff.

размоло́ть (-мелю́, -ме́лешь) *pf* (*impf* разма́лывать) grind.

размора́живать *impf*, разморо́зить (-о́жу) *pf* unfreeze, defrost; ∼ся unfreeze; defrost.

размота́ть *pf* (*impf* разма́тывать) unwind.

размыва́ть *impf*, размы́ть (-о́ет) *pf* wash away; erode.

размыка́ть *impf of* размкну́ть

размышле́ние reflection; meditation. размышля́ть *impf* reflect, ponder.

размягча́ть *impf*, размягчи́ть (-чу́) *pf* soften; ∼ся soften.

размя́кать *impf*, размя́кнуть (-ну; -мя́к) *pf* soften.

раз|**мя́ть** (-зомну́, -зомнёшь) *pf* (*impf also* размина́ть) knead; mash; ∼ся stretch one's legs; limber up.

разна́шивать *impf of* разноси́ть

разнести́ (-су́, -сёшь; -ёс, -ла́) *pf* (*impf* разноси́ть) carry; deliver; spread; note down; smash; scold; scatter; *impers* make puffy, swell.

разнима́ть *impf of* разня́ть

ра́зниться *impf* differ. ра́зница difference.

разно- *in comb* different, vari-, hetero-. разнобо́й lack of co-ordination; difference. ∼ви́дность variety. ∼гла́сие disagreement; discrepancy. ∼обра́зие variety, diversity. ∼обра́зный various, diverse. ∼речи́вый contradictory. ∼ро́дный heterogeneous. ∼сторо́нний many-sided; versatile. ∼цве́тный variegated. ∼шёрстный of different colours; ill-assorted.

разноси́ть¹ (-ошу́, -о́сишь) *pf* (*impf* разна́шивать) wear in.

разноси́ть² (-ошу́, -о́сишь) *impf of* разнести́. разно́ска delivery.

ра́зность difference.

разно́счик pedlar.

разношу́ *etc.*: *see* разноси́ть

разнузда́нный unbridled.

ра́зн|**ый** different; various; ∼ое *sb* various things.

разню́хать *pf*, разню́хивать *impf* smell out.

разня́ть (-ниму́, -ни́мешь; ро́знял, -а́, -о) *pf* (*impf* разнима́ть) take to pieces; separate.

разоблача́ть *impf*, разоблачи́ть (-чу́) *pf* expose. разоблаче́ние exposure.

разобра́ть (-зберу́, -рёшь; -а́л, -а́, -о) *pf* (*impf* разбира́ть) take to pieces; buy up; sort out; investigate; analyse; understand; ∼ся sort things out; +в+*prep* investigate, look into; understand.

разобща́ть *impf*, разобщи́ть

(-щу́) *pf* separate; estrange, alienate.

разобью́ *etc.*: *see* **разби́ть**.
разовью́ *etc.*: *see* **разви́ть**.
ра́зовый single.

разогна́ть (-згоню́, -о́нишь; -гна́л, -а́, -о) *pf* (*impf* **разгоня́ть**) scatter; disperse; dispel; drive fast; ∼ся gather speed.

разогну́ть (-ну́, -нёшь) *pf* (*impf* **разгиба́ть**) unbend, straighten; ∼ся straighten up.

разогрева́ть *impf*, **разогре́ть** (-е́ю) *pf* warm up.

разоде́ть(ся (-е́ну(сь) *pf* dress up.

разодра́ть (-здеру́, -рёшь; -ал, -а́, -о) *pf* (*impf* **раздира́ть**) tear (up); lacerate.

разожгу́ *etc.*: *see* **разже́чь**.
разожму́ *etc.*: *see* **разжа́ть**.
разозли́ть *pf*.

разойти́сь (-йду́сь, -йдёшься; -ошёлся, -ошла́сь) *pf* (*impf* **расходи́ться**) disperse; diverge; radiate; differ; conflict; part; be spent; be sold out.

разолью́ *etc.*: *see* **разли́ть**.
ра́зом *adv* at once, at one go.

разомкну́ть (-ну́, -нёшь) *pf* (*impf* **размыка́ть**) open; break.
разомну́ *etc.*: *see* **размя́ть**.

разорва́ть (-ву́, -вёшь; -а́л, -а́, -о) *pf* (*impf* **разрыва́ть**) tear (off); blow up; ∼ся tear; break; explode.

разоре́ние ruin; destruction. **разори́тельный** ruinous; wasteful. **разори́ть** *pf* (*impf* **разоря́ть**) ruin; destroy; ∼ся ruin o.s.

разоружа́ть *impf*, **разоружи́ть** (-жу́) *pf* disarm; ∼ся disarm. **разоруже́ние** disarmament.
разоря́ть(ся *impf of* **разори́ть(ся**

разосла́ть (-ошлю́, -ошлёшь) *pf* (*impf* **рассыла́ть**) distribute, circulate.

разостла́ть, **расстели́ть** (-стелю́, -те́лешь) *pf* (*impf* **расстила́ть**) spread (out); lay; ∼ся spread.

разотру́ *etc.*: *see* **растере́ть**.

разочарова́ние disappointment.

разочарова́ть *pf*, **разочаро́вывать** *impf* disappoint; ∼ся be disappointed.

разочту́ *etc.*: *see* **расче́сть**.
разошёлся *etc.*: *see* **разойти́сь**.
разошлю́ *etc.*: *see* **разосла́ть**.
разошью́ *etc.*: *see* **расши́ть**.

разраба́тывать *impf*, **разрабо́тать** *pf* cultivate; work, exploit; work out; develop. **разрабо́тка** cultivation; exploitation; working out; mining; quarry.

разража́ться *impf*, **разрази́ться** (-ажу́сь) *pf* break out; burst out.

разраста́ться *impf*, **разрасти́сь** (-тётся; -ро́сся, -ла́сь) *pf* grow; spread.

разреже́нный (-ён, -а́) rarefied.

разре́з cut; section; point of view. **разре́зать** (-е́жу) *pf*, **разреза́ть** *impf* cut; slit.

разреша́ть *impf*, **разреши́ть** (-шу́) *pf* (+dat) allow; solve; settle; ∼ся be allowed; be solved; be settled. **разреше́ние** permission; permit; solution; settlement. **разреши́мый** solvable.

разро́зненный uncoordinated; odd; incomplete.

разрослось *etc.*: *see* **разрасти́сь**.
разро́ю *etc.*: *see* **разры́ть**.

разруба́ть *impf*, **разруби́ть** (-блю́, -бишь) *pf* cut; chop up.

разру́ха ruin, collapse. **разруша́ть** *impf*, **разру́шить** (-шу) *pf*

destroy; demolish; ruin; ~ся go to ruin, collapse. **разрушéние** destruction. **разруши́тельный** destructive.

разры́в break; gap; rupture; burst. **разрыва́ть**[1]**(ся** impf of **разорва́ть(ся**

разрыва́ть[2] impf of **разры́ть**
разрывнóй explosive.
разрыда́ться pf burst into tears.
разры́ть (-рóю) pf (impf **разрыва́ть**) dig (up).
раз|рыхли́ть pf, **разрыхля́ть** impf loosen; hoe.
разря́д[1] category; class.
разря́д[2] discharge. **разряди́ть** (-яжý, -я́дишь) pf (impf **разряжа́ть**) unload; discharge; space out; ~ся run down; clear, ease. **разря́дка** spacing (out); discharging; unloading; relieving. **разряжа́ть(ся** impf of **разряди́ть(ся**
разубеди́ть (-ежý) pf, **разубежда́ть** impf dissuade; ~ся change one's mind.
разува́ться impf of **разу́ться**
разуве́рить pf, **разуверя́ть** impf dissuade, undeceive; ~ся (в+prep) lose faith (in).
разузнава́ть (-наю́, -наёшь) impf, **разузна́ть** pf (try to) find out.
разукра́сить (-áшу) pf, **разукра́шивать** impf adorn, embellish.
рáзум reason; intellect. **разумé́ться** (-éется) impf be understood, be meant; (самó собóй) **разумéется** of course; it goes without saying. **разу́мный** rational, intelligent; sensible; reasonable; wise.
разу́ться (-у́юсь) pf (impf **разува́ться**) take off one's shoes.

разу́чивать impf, **разучи́ть** (-чý, -чишь) pf learn (up). **разу́чиваться** impf, **разучи́ться** (-чýсь, -чишься) pf forget (how to)
разъеда́ть impf of **разъéсть**
разъедини́ть pf, **разъединя́ть** impf separate; disconnect.
разъéдусь etc.: see **разъéхаться**
разъéзд departure; siding (track); mounted patrol; pl travel; journeys. **разъездной** travelling. **разъезжа́ть** impf drive or ride about; travel; ~ся impf of **разъéхаться**
разъéсть (-éст, -едя́т; -éл) pf (impf **разъеда́ть**) eat away; corrode.
разъéхаться (-éдусь) pf (impf **разъезжа́ться**) depart; separate; pass (one another); miss one another.
разъярённый (-ён, -á) furious. **разъяри́ть** pf, **разъяря́ть** impf infuriate; ~ся get furious.
разъяснéние explanation; interpretation. **разъясни́тельный** explanatory.
разъясни́ть pf, **разъясня́ть** impf explain; interpret; ~ся become clear, be cleared up.
разыгра́ть pf, **разы́грывать** impf perform; draw; raffle; play a trick on; ~ся get up; run high.
разыска́ть (-ыщý, -ы́щешь) pf find. **разы́скивать** impf search for.
рай (loc -ю́) paradise; garden of Eden.
райкóм district committee.
райóн region. **райóнный** district.
рáйский heavenly.
рак crayfish; cancer; Cancer.

раке́та[1], **раке́тка** racket.

раке́та[2] rocket; missile; flare.

ра́ковина shell; sink.

ра́ковый cancer; cancerous.

раку́шка cockle-shell, mussel.

ра́ма frame. **ра́мка** frame; pl framework.

ра́мпа footlights.

ра́на wound. **ране́ние** wounding; wound. **ра́неный** wounded; injured.

ранг rank.

ра́нец (-нца) knapsack; satchel.

ра́нить impf & pf wound; injure.

ра́нний early. **ра́но** adv early. **ра́ньше** adv earlier; before; formerly.

рапи́ра foil.

ра́порт report. **рапортова́ть** impf & pf report.

ра́са race. **раси́зм**, racism. **раси́стский** racist.

раска́иваться impf of **раска́яться**

раскалённый (-ён, -а́) scorching; incandescent. **раскали́ть** pf (impf **раска́ливать**) make red-hot; **~ся** become red-hot. **раска́лывать(ся** impf of **расколо́ть(ся. раскаля́ть(ся** impf of **раскали́ть(ся. раска́пывать** impf of **раскопа́ть**

раска́т roll, peal. **раската́ть** pf, **раска́тывать** impf roll (out), smooth out; level; drive or roll (about). **раска́тистый** rolling, booming. **раскати́ться** (-ачу́сь, -а́тишься) pf, **раска́тываться** impf gather speed; roll away; peal, boom.

раскача́ть pf, **раска́чивать** impf swing; rock; **~ся** swing, rock.

раска́яние repentance. **раска́-**

-яться pf (impf also **раска́-иваться**) repent.

расквита́ться pf settle accounts.

раски́дывать impf, **раски́нуть** (-ну) pf stretch (out); spread; pitch; **~ся** spread out; sprawl.

раскладно́й folding. **раскладу́шка** camp-bed. **раскла́дывать** impf of **разложи́ть**

раскла́няться pf bow; take leave.

раскле́ивать impf, **раскле́ить** pf unstick; stick (up); **~ся** come unstuck.

раско́л split; schism. **расколо́ть** (-лю́, -лешь) pf (impf also **раска́лывать**) split; break; disrupt; **~ся** split. **раско́льник** dissenter.

раскопа́ть pf (impf **раска́пывать**) dig up, unearth, excavate. **раско́пки** (-пок) pf excavations.

раско́сый slanting.

раскра́ивать impf of **раскрои́ть**

раскра́сить (-а́шу) pf, impf **раскра́шивать** paint, colour. **раскрепости́ть** (-ощу́) pf, impf **раскрепоща́ть** liberate. **раскрепоще́ние** emancipation.

раскритикова́ть pf criticize harshly.

раскрои́ть pf (impf **раскра́ивать**) cut out.

раскро́ю etc.: see **раскры́ть**

раскрути́ть (-учу́, -у́тишь) pf, **раскру́чивать** impf untwist; **~ся** come untwisted.

раскрыва́ть impf, **раскры́ть** (-о́ю) pf open; expose; reveal; discover; **~ся** open; uncover o.s.; come to light.

раскупа́ть impf, **раскупи́ть** (-упит) pf buy up.

раску́поривать impf, **раску́-**

поро́рить pf uncork, open.
раскуси́ть (-ушу́, -у́сишь) pf, **раску́сывать** impf bite through; see through.
ра́совый racial.
распа́д disintegration; collapse.
распада́ться impf of **распа́сться**
распакова́ть pf, **распако́вывать** impf unpack.
распа́рывать(ся impf of **распоро́ть(ся**
распа́сться (-адётся) pf (impf **распада́ться**) disintegrate, fall to pieces.
распаха́ть (-ашу́, -а́шешь) pf, **распа́хивать**[1] impf plough up.
распа́хивать[2] impf, **распахну́ть** (-ну́, -нёшь) pf throw open; ~ся fly open, swing open.
распашо́нка baby's vest.
распева́ть impf sing.
распеча́тать pf, **распеча́тывать** impf open; unseal.
распи́ливать impf, **распили́ть** (-лю́, -лишь) pf saw up.
распина́ть impf of **распя́ть**
расписа́ние time-table. **расписа́ть** (-ишу́, -и́шешь) pf, **распи́сывать** impf enter; assign; paint; ~ся sign; register one's marriage; +в+prep sign for; acknowledge. **распи́ска** receipt. **расписно́й** painted, decorated. **распи́хать** pf, **распи́хивать** impf push, shove, stuff.
распла́вить (-влю) pf, **расплавля́ть** impf melt, fuse. **распла́вленный** molten.
распла́каться (-а́чусь) pf burst into tears.
распласта́ть pf, **распла́стывать** impf spread; flatten; split; ~ся sprawl.
расплати́ть (-ачу́сь,

-а́тишься) pf, **распла́чиваться** impf (+с+instr) pay off; get even; +за+acc pay for.
расплеска́ть(ся (-ещу́(сь, -е́щешь(ся) pf, **расплёскивать(ся** impf spill.
расплести́ (-ету́, -етёшь; -ёл, -а́) pf, **расплета́ть** impf unplait; untwist.
распло́дить(ся (-ожу́(сь) pf.
расплыва́ться impf, **расплы́ться** (-ывётся; -ы́лся, -а́сь) pf run. **расплы́вчатый** indistinct; vague.
расплю́щивать impf, **расплю́щить** (-щу) pf flatten out, hammer out.
распну́ etc.: see **распя́ть**
распознава́ть (-наю́, -наёшь) impf, **распозна́ть** pf recognize, identify; diagnose.
располага́ть impf +instr have at one's disposal. **располага́ться** impf of **расположи́ться**
располза́ться impf, **расползти́сь** (-зётся; -о́лзся, -зла́сь) pf crawl (away); give at the seams.
расположе́ние disposition; arrangement; situation; tendency; liking; mood. **расположе́нный** disposed, inclined. **расположи́ть** (-жу́, -жишь) pf (impf **располага́ть**) dispose; set out; win over; ~ся settle down.
распо́рка cross-bar, strut.
распоро́ть (-рю́, -решь) pf (impf also **распа́рывать**) unpick; rip; ~ся rip, come undone.
распоряди́тель m manager. **распоряди́тельный** capable; efficient. **распоряди́ться** (-яжу́сь) pf, **распоряжа́ться** impf order, give orders; see; +instr manage, deal with. **распоря́док** (-дка) order; routine. **распоряже́ние** order; instruc-

tion; disposal, command.

распра́ва violence; reprisal.

распра́вить (-влю) *pf*, **расправля́ть** *impf* straighten; smooth out; spread.

распра́виться (влюсь) *pf*, **расправля́ться** *impf* c+*instr* deal with severely; make short work of.

распределе́ние distribution; allocation. **распредели́тель** *m* distributor. **распредели́тельный** distributive, distributing; ∼ щит switchboard. **распредели́ть** *pf*, **распределя́ть** *impf* distribute; allocate.

распродава́ть (-даю́, -даёшь) *impf*, **распрода́ть** (-а́м, -а́шь, -а́ст, -ади́м; -о́дал, -а́, -о) *pf* sell off; sell out of. **распрода́жа** (clearance) sale.

распростёртый outstretched; prostrate.

распростране́ние spreading; dissemination. **распространённый** (-ён, -а́) widespread, prevalent. **распространи́ть** *pf*, **распространя́ть** *impf* spread; ∼ся spread.

ра́спря (*gen pl* -ей) quarrel.

распряга́ть *impf*, **распря́чь** (-яту́, -яжёшь; -я́г, -ла́) *pf* unharness.

распрями́ться *pf*, **распрямля́ться** *impf* straighten up.

распуска́ть *impf*, **распусти́ть** (-ущу́, -у́стишь) *pf* dismiss; dissolve; let out; relax; let get out of hand; melt; spread; ∼ся open; come loose; dissolve; melt; get out of hand; let o.s. go.

распу́тать *pf* (*impf* **распу́тывать**) untangle; unravel.

распу́тица season of bad roads.

распу́тный dissolute. **распу́тство** debauchery.

распу́тывать *impf of* **распу́тать**

распу́тье crossroads.

распуха́ть *impf*, **распу́хнуть** (-ну; -у́х) *pf* swell (up).

распу́щенный undisciplined; spoilt; dissolute.

распыли́тель *m* spray, atomizer. **распыли́ть** *pf*, **распыля́ть** *impf* spray; pulverize; disperse.

распя́тие crucifixion; crucifix. **распя́ть** (-пну́, -пнёшь) *pf* (*impf* **распина́ть**) crucify.

расса́да seedlings. **рассади́ть** (-ажу́, -а́дишь) *pf*, **расса́живать** *impf* plant out; seat; separate, seat separately.

расса́живаться *impf of* рас**се́сться**. **рассаса́сываться** *impf of* **рассоса́ться**

рассвести́ (-етёт; -ело́) *pf*, **рассвета́ть** *impf* dawn. **рассве́т** dawn.

рас|свирепе́ть (-е́ю) *pf*.

расседла́ть *pf* unsaddle.

рассе́ивание dispersal, scattering. **рассе́ивать(ся** *impf of* **рассе́ять(ся**

рассека́ть *impf of* **рассе́чь**

расселе́ние settling, resettlement; separation.

рассе́лина cleft, fissure.

рассели́ть *pf*, **расселя́ть** *impf* settle, resettle; separate.

рас|серди́ть(ся   (-жу́сь, -рди́шь(ся) *pf*.

рассе́сться (-ся́дусь) *pf* (*impf* **расса́живаться**) take seats.

рассе́чь (-еку́, -ечёшь; -ёк, -ла́) *pf* (*impf* **рассека́ть**) cut (through); cleave.

рассе́янность   absent-

mindedness; dispersion. рассе́янный absent-minded; diffused; scattered. рассе́ять (-е́ю)
pf (*impf* рассе́ивать) disperse,
scatter; dispel; ∼ся disperse,
scatter; clear; divert o.s.

расска́з story; account. рассказа́ть
(-ажу́, -а́жешь) *pf*, расска́
зывать *impf* tell, recount. расска́зчик story-teller, narrator.

рассла́бить (-блю) *pf*, расслабля́ть (-я́ю) *impf* weaken; ∼ся relax.

рассла́ивать(ся *impf of* расслои́ть(ся

рассле́дование investigation,
examination; inquiry; произвести́ ∼+gen hold an inquiry into.
рассле́довать *impf & pf* investigate, look into, hold an inquiry into.

расслои́ть *pf* (*impf* рассла́ивать) divide into layers; ∼ся become stratified; flake off.

рассльпша́ть (-шу) *pf* catch.

рассма́тривать *impf of* рассмотре́ть; examine; consider.

рас|смеши́ть (-шу́) *pf*

рассмея́ться (-ею́сь, -её́шься)
pf burst out laughing.

рассмотре́ние examination;
consideration. рассмотре́ть
(-рю́, -ришь) *pf* (*impf* рассма́тривать) examine, consider; discern, make out.

рассова́ть (-сую́, -суёшь) *pf*,
рассо́вывать *impf* по+*dat*
shove into.

рассо́л brine; pickle.

рассо́риться *pf* c+*instr* fall out
with.

рас|сортирова́ть *pf*, рассортиро́вывать *impf* sort out.

рассоса́ться (-сётся) *pf* (*impf*
расса́сываться) resolve.

рассо́хнуться (-нется, -о́хся) *pf*
(*impf* рассыха́ться) crack.

расспра́шивать *impf*, расспроси́ть (-ошу́, -о́сишь) *pf*
question; make inquiries of.

рассро́чить (-чу) *pf* spread
(over a period). рассро́чка instalment.

расстава́ние parting. расстава́ться (-таю́сь, -таёшься) *impf*
of расста́ться

расста́вить (-влю) *pf*, расставля́ть *impf* place, arrange;
move apart. расстано́вка arrangement; pause.

расста́ться (-а́нусь) *pf* (*impf*
расстава́ться) part, separate.

расстёгивать *impf*, расстегну́ть (-ну́, -нёшь) *pf* undo, unfasten; ∼ся come undone; undo
one's coat.

расстели́ть(ся, *etc.*: *see* разостла́ть(ся. расстила́ть(ся,
-а́ю(сь *impf of* разостла́ть(ся

расстоя́ние distance.

расстра́ивать(ся *impf of* расстро́ить(ся

расстре́л execution by firing
squad. расстре́ливать *impf*,
расстреля́ть *pf* shoot.

расстро́енный disordered;
upset; out of tune. расстро́ить
pf (*impf* расстра́ивать) upset;
thwart; disturb; throw into confusion; put out of tune; ∼ся be
upset; get out of tune; fall into
confusion; fall through. расстро́йство upset; disarray;
confusion; frustration.

расступа́ться *impf*, расступи́ться (-у́пится) *pf* part, make
way.

рассуди́тельный reasonable;
sensible. рассуди́ть (-ужу́,
-у́дишь) *pf* judge; think; decide.
рассу́док (-дка) reason; intellect. рассужда́ть *impf* reason;
+о+*prep* discuss. рассужде́ние

reasoning; discussion; argument.

рассую́ *etc.: see* **рассова́ть**

рассчи́танный deliberate; intended. **рассчита́ть** *pf*, **рассчи́тывать** *impf*, **расче́сть** (разочту́, -тёшь; расчёл, разочла́) *pf* calculate; count; depend; ∼ся settle accounts.

рассыла́ть *impf of* **разосла́ть**. **рассы́лка** distribution. **рассы́льный** *sb* delivery man.

рассы́пать (-плю) *pf*, **рассыпа́ть** *impf* spill; scatter; ∼ся spill, scatter; spread out; crumble. **рассы́пчатый** friable, crumbly.

рассыха́ться *impf of* **рассо́хнуться**. **рассяду́сь** *etc.: see* **рассе́сться**. **раста́лкивать** *impf of* **растолка́ть**. **раста́пливать(ся** *impf of* **растопи́ть(ся**

растаска́ть *pf*, **раста́скивать** *impf*, **растащи́ть** (-щу́, -щишь) *pf* pilfer, filch.

растащи́ть *see* **растаска́ть**. **раста́ять** (-а́ю) *pf*.

раство́р² opening, span. **раство́р¹** solution; mortar. **раствори́мый** soluble. **раствори́тель** *m* solvent. **раствори́ть¹** *pf* (*impf* **растворя́ть**) dissolve; ∼ся dissolve.

раствори́ть² (-рю́, -ришь) *pf* (*impf* **растворя́ть**) open; ∼ся open.

растворя́ть(ся *impf of* **раствори́ть(ся**. **растека́ться** *impf of* **расте́чься**

расте́ние plant.

растере́ть (разотру́, -трёшь; растёр) *pf* (*impf* **растира́ть**) grind; spread; rub; massage.

растерза́ть *pf*, **расте́рзывать** *impf* tear to pieces.

расте́рянность confusion, dis-

may. **расте́рянный** confused, dismayed. **растеря́ть** *pf* lose; ∼ся get lost; lose one's head.

расте́чься (-ечётся, -еку́тся; -тёкся, -ла́сь) *pf* (*impf* **растека́ться**) run; spread.

расти́ (-ту́, -тёшь; рос, -ла́) *impf* grow; grow up.

растира́ние grinding; rubbing, massage. **растира́ть(ся** *impf of* **растере́ть(ся**

расти́тельность vegetation; hair. **расти́тельный** vegetable. **расти́ть** (ращу́) *impf* bring up; train; grow.

растлева́ть *impf*, **растли́ть** *pf* seduce; corrupt.

растолка́ть *pf* (*impf* **раста́лкивать**) push apart; shake.

растолкова́ть *pf*, **растолко́вывать** *impf* explain.

расто́лочь (-лку́, -лчёшь; -ло́к, -лкла́) *pf*.

растолсте́ть (-е́ю) *pf* put on weight.

растопи́ть¹ (-плю́, -пишь) *pf* (*impf* **раста́пливать**) melt; thaw; ∼ся melt.

растопи́ть² (-плю́, -пишь) *pf* (*impf* **раста́пливать**) light, kindle; ∼ся begin to burn.

растопта́ть (-пчу́, -пчешь) *pf* trample, stamp on.

расторга́ть *impf*, **расто́ргнуть** (-ну; -о́рг) *pf* annul, dissolve. **расторже́ние** annulment, dissolution.

растаро́пный quick; efficient.

расточа́ть *impf*, **расточи́ть** (-чу́) *pf* squander, dissipate. **расточи́тельный** extravagant, wasteful.

растрави́ть (-влю́, -вишь) *pf*, **растравля́ть** *impf* irritate.

растра́та spending; waste; embezzlement. **растра́тить** (-а́чу)

pf, **растра́чивать** *impf* spend; waste; embezzle.

растрёпанный dishevelled; tattered. **растрепа́ть** (-плю́, -плешь) *pf* disarrange; tatter.

растре́скаться, **растре́скиваться** *impf* crack, chap.

растро́гать *pf* move, touch; ~ся be moved.

расту́щий growing.

растя́гивать *impf*, **растяну́ть** (-ну́, -нешь) *pf* stretch (out); strain, sprain; drag out; ~ся stretch; drag on; sprawl. **растяже́ние** tension; strain, sprain. **растяжи́мый** tensile; stretchable. **растя́нутый** stretched; long-winded.

расфасова́ть *pf*.

расформирова́ть *pf*, **расформиро́вывать** *impf* break up; disband.

расха́живать *impf* walk about; pace up and down.

расхва́ливать *impf*, **расхвали́ть** (-лю́, -лишь) *pf* lavish praises on.

расхвата́ть *pf*, **расхва́тывать** *impf* seize on, buy up.

расхити́тель *m* embezzler. **расхити́ть** (-ищу́) *pf*, **расхища́ть** *impf* steal, misappropriate. **расхище́ние** misappropriation.

расхля́банный loose; lax.

расхо́д expenditure; consumption; *pl* expenses, outlay. **расходи́ться** (-ожу́сь, -о́дишься) *impf of* разойти́сь. **расхо́дование** expense, expenditure. **расхо́довать** *impf* (*pf* из~) spend; consume. **расхожде́ние** divergence.

расхола́живать *impf*, **расхолоди́ть** (-ожу́) *pf* damp the ardour of.

расхоте́ть (-очу́, -о́чешь, -оти́м) *pf* no longer want.

расхохота́ться (-очу́сь, -о́чешься) *pf* burst out laughing.

расцара́пать *pf* scratch (all over).

расцвести́ (-ету́, -етёшь; -ёл, -а́) *pf*, **расцвета́ть** *impf* blossom; flourish. **расцве́т** blossoming (out); flowering, heyday.

расцве́тка colours; colouring.

расце́нивать *impf*, **расцени́ть** (-ню́, -нишь) *pf* estimate, value; consider. **расце́нка** valuation; price; (wage-)rate.

расцепи́ть (-плю́, -пишь) *pf*, **расцепля́ть** *impf* uncouple, unhook.

расчеса́ть (-ешу́, -е́шешь) *pf* (*impf* **расчёсывать**) comb; scratch. **расчёска** comb.

расчёсть *etc.: see* рассчита́ть. **расчёсывать** *impf of* расчеса́ть

расчёт[1] calculation; estimate; gain; settlement. **расчётливый** thrifty; careful. **расчётный** calculated; pay; accounts; calculated.

расчи́стить (-и́щу) *pf*, **расчища́ть** *impf* clear; ~ся clear. **расчи́стка** clearing.

расчлени́ть *pf*, **расчленя́ть** *impf* dismember; divide.

расшата́ть *pf*, **расша́тывать** *impf* shake loose, make rickety; impair.

расшевели́ть (-лю́, -ели́шь) *pf* stir; rouse.

расшиба́ть *impf*, **расшиби́ть** (-бу́, -бёшь; -и́б) *pf* smash to pieces; hurt; stub; ~ся hurt o.s.

расшива́ть *impf of* расши́ть

расшире́ние widening; expansion; dilation, dilatation. **рас-**

ши́рить *pf*, **расширя́ть** *impf* widen; enlarge; expand; **~ся** broaden, widen; expand, dilate.

расши́ть (разошью́, -шьёшь) *pf* (*impf* **расшива́ть**) embroider; unpick.

расшифрова́ть *pf*, **расшифро́вывать** *impf* decipher.

расшнурова́ть *pf*, **расшнуро́вывать** *impf* unlace.

расще́лина crevice.

расщепи́ть (-плю́) *pf*, **расщепля́ть** *impf* split; **~ся** split. **расщепле́ние** splitting; fission.

ратифици́ровать *impf* & *pf* ratify.

рать army, battle.

ра́унд round.

рафини́рованный refined.

рацио́н ration.

рационализа́ция rationalization. **рационализи́ровать** *impf* & *pf* rationalize. **рациона́льный** rational; efficient.

ра́ция walkie-talkie.

рвану́ться (-ну́сь, -нёшься) *pf* dart, dash.

рва́ный torn; lacerated. **рвать**[1] (рву, рвёшь; рвал, -а, -о) *impf* tear (out); pull out; pick; blow up; break off; **~ся** break; tear; burst, explode; be bursting.

рвать[2] (рвёт; рва́ло) *impf* (*pf* **вы́~**) *impers+acc* vomit.

рвач (-а́) self-seeker.

рве́ние zeal.

рво́та vomiting.

реабилита́ция rehabilitation. **реабилити́ровать** *impf* & *pf* rehabilitate.

реаги́ровать *impf* (*pf* **от~**, **про~**) react.

реакти́в reagent. **реакти́вный** reactive; jet-propelled. **реа́ктор** reactor.

реакционе́р reactionary. **реакцио́нный** reactionary. **реа́кция** reaction.

реализа́ция realization. **реали́зм** realism. **реализова́ть** *impf* & *pf* realize. **реали́ст** realist. **реалисти́ческий** realistic.

реа́льность reality; practicability. **реа́льный** real; practicable.

ребёнок (-нка; *pl* ребя́та, -я́т *and* де́ти, -е́й) child; infant.

ребро́ (*pl* рёбра, -бер) rib; edge.

ребя́та (-я́т) *pl* children; guys; lads. **ребя́ческий** child's; childish. **ребя́чество** childishness. **ребя́читься** (-чусь) *impf* be childish.

рёв roar; howl.

рева́нш revenge; return match.

ревера́нс curtsey.

реве́ть (-ву́, -вёшь) *impf* roar; bellow; howl.

ревизио́нный inspection; auditing. **реви́зия** inspection; audit; revision. **ревизо́р** inspector.

ревмати́зм rheumatism.

ревни́вый jealous. **ревнова́ть** *impf* (*pf* **при~**) be jealous. **ре́вностный** zealous. **ре́вность** jealousy.

револьве́р revolver.

революционе́р revolutionary. **революцио́нный** revolutionary. **револю́ция** revolution.

рега́та regatta.

ре́гби *neut indecl* rugby.

ре́гент regent.

регио́н region. **региона́льный** regional.

регистра́тор registrar. **регистрату́ра** registry. **регистра́ция** registration. **регистри́ровать** *impf* & *pf* (*pf also* **за~**)

register, record; **~ся** register; register one's marriage.

регла́мент standing orders; time-limit. **регламента́ция** regulation. **регламенти́ровать** *impf & pf* regulate.

регресси́ровать *impf* regress.

регули́ровать *impf* (*pf* от~, у~) regulate; adjust. **регули́ровщик** traffic controller. **регуля́рный** regular. **регуля́тор** regulator.

редакти́ровать *impf* (*pf* от~) edit. **реда́ктор** editor. **реда́кторский** editorial. **редакцио́нный** editorial, editing. **реда́кция** editorial staff; editorial office; editing.

реде́ть (-е́ет) *impf* (*pf* по~) thin (out).

реди́с radishes. **реди́ска** radish.

ре́дкий (-док, -дка́, -о) thin; sparse; rare. **ре́дко** *adv* sparsely, rarely, seldom. **ре́дкость** rarity.

редколле́гия editorial board.

рее́стр register.

режи́м régime; routine; procedure; regimen; conditions.

режиссёр-(постано́вщик) producer; director.

ре́жущий cutting, sharp. **ре́зать** (ре́жу) *impf* (*pf* за~, про~, с~) cut; engrave; kill, slaughter.

резви́ться (-влю́сь) *impf* gambol, play. **ре́звый** frisky, playful.

резе́рв reserve. **резе́рвный** reserve; back-up.

резервуа́р reservoir.

резе́ц (-зца́) cutter; chisel; incisor.

резиде́нция residence.

рези́на rubber. **рези́нка** rubber; elastic band. **рези́новый** rubber.

ре́зкий sharp; harsh; abrupt; shrill. **резно́й** carved. **резня́** carnage.

резолю́ция resolution.

резона́нс resonance; response.

результа́т result.

резьба́ carving, fretwork.

резюме́ *neut indecl* résumé.

рейд[1] roads, roadstead.

рейд[2] raid.

ре́йка lath, rod.

рейс trip; voyage; flight.

рейту́зы (-уз) *pl* leggings; riding breeches.

река́ (*acc* ре́ку; *pl* -и, ре́кам) river.

ре́квием requiem.

реквизи́т props.

рекла́ма advertising, advertisement. **реклами́ровать** *impf & pf* advertise. **рекла́мный** publicity.

рекоменда́тельный of recommendation. **рекоменда́ция** recommendation; reference. **рекомендова́ть** *impf & pf* (*pf also* от~, по~) recommend; **~ся** introduce o.s.; be advisable.

реконструи́ровать *impf & pf* reconstruct. **реконстру́кция** reconstruction.

реко́рд record. **реко́рдный** record, record-breaking. **рекордсме́н, -е́нка** record-holder.

ре́ктор principal (*of university*).

реле́ (*electr*) *neut indecl* relay.

религио́зный religious. **рели́гия** religion.

рели́квия relic.

релье́ф relief. **релье́фный** relief; raised, bold.

рельс rail.

ремáрка stage direction.

ремéнь (-мня́) *m* strap; belt.

ремéсленник artisan, crafts-man. **ремéсленный** handi-craft; mechanical. **ремесло́** (*pl* -ёсла, -ёсел) craft; trade.

ремóнт repair(s); maintenance. **ремонти́ровать** *impf & pf* (*pf also* от~) repair; recondition. **ремóнтный** repair.

рéнта rent; income. **рентáбель-ный** paying, profitable.

рентгéн X-rays. **рентгéнов-ский** X-ray. **рентгенóлог** radi-ologist. **рентгенолóгия** radi-ology.

реорганизáция reorganiza-tion. **реорганизовáть** *impf & pf* reorganize.

рéпа turnip.

репатрии́ровать *impf & pf* re-patriate.

репертуáр repertoire.

репети́ровать (*pf* от~, про~, с~) rehearse; coach. **ре-пети́тор** coach. **репети́ция** re-hearsal.

рéплика retort; cue.

репортáж report; reporting. **ре-портёр** reporter.

репрéссия repression.

репродýктор loud-speaker. **ре-продýкция** reproduction.

репутáция reputation.

ресни́ца eyelash.

респýблика republic. **респу-бликáнский** republican.

рессóра spring.

реставрáция restoration. **рес-таври́ровать** *impf & pf* (*pf also* от~) restore.

ресторáн restaurant.

ресýрс resort; *pl* resources.

ретранслятор (radio-)relay.

реферáт synopsis, abstract; paper, essay.

референдум referendum.

рефлéкс reflex. **рефлéктор** re-flector.

рефóрма reform. **реформи́ро-вать** *impf & pf* reform.

рефрижерáтор refrigerator.

рецензи́ровать *impf* (*pf* про~) review. **рецéнзия** re-view.

рецéпт prescription; recipe.

рециди́в relapse. **рецидиви́ст** recidivist.

речевóй speech; vocal.

рéчка river. **речнóй** river.

речь (*gen pl* -éй) speech.

решáть(ся *impf of* **реши́ть(ся. решáющий** decisive, deciding. **решéние** decision; solution.

решётка grating; grille, railing; lattice, trellis; fender, (fire-)guard; (fire-)grate; tail. **реше-тó** (*pl* -ёта) sieve. **решётчатый** lattice, latticed.

реши́мость resoluteness; re-solve. **реши́тельно** *adv* reso-lutely; definitely; absolutely. **реши́тельность** determin-ation. **реши́тельный** definite; decisive. **реши́ть** (-шý) *pf* (*impf* **решáть**) decide; solve; ~ся make up one's mind.

ржавéть (-éет) *impf* (*pf* за~, по~) rust. **ржáвчина** rust. **ржá-вый** rusty.

ржанóй rye.

ржать (ржу, ржёшь) *impf* neigh.

ри́млянин (*pl* -яне, -ян), **ри́м-лянка** Roman. **ри́мский** Roman.

ринг boxing ring.

ри́нуться (-нусь) *pf* rush, dart.

рис rice.

риск risk. **рискóванный** risky;

risqué. **рискова́ть** *impf*, **рискну́ть** *pf* run risks; +*instr or inf* risk.

рисова́ние drawing. **рисова́ть** *impf* (*pf* на∼) draw; paint, depict; ∼**ся** be silhouetted; appear; pose.

ри́совый rice.

рису́нок (-нка) drawing; figure; pattern, design.

ритм rhythm. **ритми́ческий**, **ритми́чный** rhythmic.

ритуа́л ritual.

риф reef.

ри́фма rhyme. **рифмова́ть** *impf* rhyme; ∼**ся** rhyme.

робе́ть (-е́ю) *impf* (*pf* о∼) be timid. **ро́бкий** (-бок, -бка́, -о) timid, shy. **ро́бость** shyness.

ро́бот robot.

ров (рва, *loc* -у́) ditch.

рове́сник coeval. **ро́вно** *adv* evenly; exactly; absolutely. **ро́вный** flat; even; level; equable; exact; equal. **ровня́ть** *impf* (*pf* с∼) even, level.

рог (*pl* -а́, -о́в) horn; antler. **рога́тка** catapult. **рога́тый** horned. **рогови́ца** cornea. **рогово́й** horn; horny; horn-rimmed.

род (*loc* -у́; *pl* -ы́) family, kin, clan; birth, origin, stock; generation; genus; sort, kind. **роди́льный** maternity. **ро́дина** native land; homeland. **роди́нка** birth-mark. **роди́тели** (-ей) *pl* parents. **роди́тельный** genitive. **роди́тельский** parental. **роди́ть** (рожу́, -и́л, -и́ла́, -о) *impf & pf* (*impf also* **рожа́ть**, **рожда́ть**) give birth to; ∼**ся** be born.

родни́к (-а́) spring.

родни́ть *impf* (*pf* по∼) make related, link; ∼**ся** become re-lated. **родн|о́й** own; native; home; ∼о́й брат brother; ∼ы́е *sb pl* relatives. **родня́** relative(s); kinsfolk. **родово́й** tribal; ancestral; generic; gender. **родонача́льник** ancestor; father. **родосло́вн|ый** genealogical; ∼ая *sb* genealogy, pedigree. **ро́дственник** relative. **ро́дственный** related. **родство́** relationship, kinship. **ро́ды** (-ов) *pl* childbirth; labour.

ро́жа (ugly) mug.

рожа́ть, **рожда́ть(ся** *impf of* **роди́ть(ся**. **рожда́емость** birth-rate. **рожде́ние** birth. **рожде́ственский** Christmas. **Рождество́** Christmas.

рожь (ржи) rye.

ро́за rose.

ро́зга (*gen pl* -зог) birch.

ро́здал *etc.*: *see* **разда́ть**

розе́тка electric socket, power point; rosette.

ро́зница retail; в ∼у retail. **ро́зничный** retail. **рознь** difference; dissension.

ро́знил *etc.*: *see* **разни́ть**

ро́зовый pink.

ро́зыгрыш draw; drawn game.

ро́зыск search; inquiry.

ро́иться swarm. **рой** (*loc* -ю́; *pl* -и́, -ёв) swarm.

рок fate.

рокиро́вка castling.

рок-му́зыка rock music.

роково́й fateful; fatal.

ро́кот roar, rumble. **рокота́ть** (-о́чет) *impf* roar, rumble.

ро́лик roller; castor; *pl* roller skates.

роль (*gen pl* -е́й) role.

ром rum.

рома́н novel; romance. **рома-ни́ст** novelist.

рома́нс (*mus*) romance.

рома́нтик romantic. **рома́нтика** romance. **романти́ческий, романти́чный** romantic.

рома́шка camomile.

ромб rhombus.

роня́ть *impf* (*pf* **урони́ть**) drop.

ро́пот murmur, grumble. **ропта́ть** (-пщу́, -пщешь) *impf* murmur, grumble.

рос *etc.*: *see* **расти́**

роса́ (*pl* -ы) dew. **роси́стый** dewy.

роско́шный luxurious; luxuriant. **ро́скошь** luxury; luxuriance.

ро́слый strapping.

ро́спись painting(s), mural(s).

ро́спуск dismissal; disbandment.

росси́йский Russian. **Росси́я** Russia.

ро́ссыпи *f pl* deposit.

рост growth; increase; height, stature.

ро́стбиф roast beef.

ростовщи́к (-а́) usurer, money-lender.

росто́к (-тка́) sprout, shoot.

ро́счерк flourish.

рот (рта, *loc* рту) mouth.

ро́та company.

рота́тор duplicator.

ро́тный company; *sb* company commander.

ротозе́й, -зе́йка gaper, rubberneck; scatter-brain.

ро́ща grove.

ро́ю *etc.*: *see* **рыть**

роя́ль *m* (grand) piano.

ртуть *f* mercury.

руба́нок (-нка) plane.

руба́ха, руба́шка shirt.

рубе́ж (-а́) boundary, border(line); line; **за ~о́м** abroad.

рубе́ц (-бца́) scar; weal; hem; tripe.

руби́н ruby. **руби́новый** ruby; ruby-coloured.

руби́ть (-блю́, -бишь) *impf* (*pf* **с~**) fell; hew, chop; mince; build (of logs).

ру́бище rags.

ру́бка[1] felling; chopping; mincing.

ру́бка[2] deck house; **боева́я ~** conning-tower; **рулева́я ~** wheelhouse.

рублёвка one-rouble note.

рублёвый (one-)rouble.

ру́бленый minced, chopped; of logs.

рубль (-я́) *m* rouble.

ру́брика rubric, heading.

ру́бчатый ribbed. **ру́бчик** scar; rib.

ру́гань abuse, swearing. **руга́тельный** abusive. **руга́тельство** oath, swear-word. **руга́ть** *impf* (*pf* **вы́~, об~, от~**) curse, swear at; abuse; **~ся** curse, swear; swear at one another.

руда́ (*pl* -ы) ore. **рудни́к** (-а́) mine, pit. **рудни́чный** mine, pit; **~ газ** fire-damp. **рудоко́п** miner.

руже́йный rifle, gun. **ружьё** (*pl* -ья, -жей, -ьям) gun, rifle.

руи́на *usu pl* ruin.

рука́ (*acc* -у; *pl* ру́ки, рук, -а́м) hand; arm; **идти́ по́д руку** с+*instr* walk arm in arm with; **под руко́й** at hand; **руко́й пода́ть** a stone's throw away; **это мне на́ руку** that suits me.

рука́в (-а́; *pl* -а́, -о́в) sleeve. **рукави́ца** mitten; gauntlet.

руководи́тель *m* leader; manager; instructor; guide. **руководи́ть** (-ожу́) *impf* +*instr* lead; guide; manage.

во́дство leadership; guidance; direction; guide; handbook, manual; leaders. **руково́дствоваться**+*instr* follow; be guided by. **руководя́щий** leading; guiding.

рукоде́лие needlework.

рукомо́йник washstand.

рукопа́шный hand-to-hand.

рукопи́сный manuscript. **ру́копись** manuscript.

рукоплеска́ние applause. **рукоплеска́ть** (-ещу́, -е́щешь) *impf* +*dat* applaud.

рукопожа́тие handshake.

рукоя́тка handle.

рулево́й steering; *sb* helmsman.

руле́тка tape-measure; roulette.

рули́ть *impf* (*pf* вы́~) taxi.

руль (-я́) *m* rudder; helm; (steering-)wheel; handlebar.

румы́н (*gen pl* -ы́н), ~ка Romanian. **Румы́ния** Romania. **румы́нский** Romanian.

румя́на (-я́н) *pl* rouge. **румя́нец** (-нца) (high) colour; flush; blush. **румя́ный** rosy, ruddy.

ру́пор megaphone; mouthpiece.

руса́к (-á) hare.

руса́лка mermaid.

ру́сло river-bed; course.

ру́сский Russian; *sb* Russian.

ру́сый light brown.

Русь (*hist*) Russia.

рути́на routine.

ру́хлядь junk.

ру́хнуть (-ну) *pf* crash down.

руча́тельство guarantee. **руча́ться** *impf* (*pf* поручи́ться) +*за*+*acc* vouch for, guarantee.

руче́й (-чья́) brook.

ру́чка handle; (door-)knob; (chair-)arm; pen; **ручн**|**о́й** hand; arm; manual; tame; ~**ы́е часы́** wrist-watch.

ру́шить (-у) *impf* (*pf* об~) pull down; ~**ся** collapse.

РФ *abbr* (*of* Росси́йская Федера́ция) Russian Federation.

ры́ба fish. **рыба́к** (-á) fisherman. **рыба́лка** fishing. **рыба́цкий, рыба́чий** fishing. **ры́бий** fish; fishy; ~ **жир** cod-liver oil. **ры́бный** fish. **рыболо́в** fisherman. **рыболо́вный** fishing.

рыво́к (-вка́) jerk.

рыда́ние sobbing. **рыда́ть** *impf* sob.

ры́жий (рыж, -á, -е) red, red-haired; chestnut.

ры́ло snout; mug.

ры́нок (-нка) market; marketplace. **ры́ночный** market.

рыса́к (-á) trotter.

рысь[1] (*loc* -и́) trot; ~ю, на рыся́х at a trot.

рысь[2] lynx.

ры́твина rut, groove. **ры́ть**(**ся** (ро́ю(сь) *impf* (*pf* вы́~, от~) dig; rummage.

рыхли́ть *impf* (*pf* вз~, раз~) loosen. **ры́хлый** (-л, -á, -о) friable; loose.

ры́царский chivalrous. **ры́царь** *m* knight.

рыча́г (-á) lever.

рыча́ть (-чу́) *impf* growl, snarl.

рья́ный zealous.

рюкза́к (*gen* -á) rucksack.

рю́мка wineglass.

ряби́на[1] rowan, mountain ash. **ряби́на**[2] pit, pock. **ряби́ть** (-и́т) *impf* ripple; *impers*: **у меня́ ряби́т в глаза́х** I am dazzled. **рябо́й** pock-marked. **ра́бчик** hazel hen, hazel grouse. **рябь** ripples; dazzle.

ря́вкать *impf*, **ря́вкнуть** (-ну) *pf* bellow, roar.

ряд (*loc* -у́; *pl* -ы́) row; line; file,

rank; series; number. **рядово́й** ordinary; common; ~ **соста́в** rank and file; *sb* private. **ря́дом** *adv* alongside; close by; +c+*instr* next to.

ря́са cassock.

С

с, со *prep* **I.** +*gen* from; since; off; for; with; on; by; **с ра́дости** for joy; **с утра́** since morning. **II.** +*acc* about; the size of; **с неде́лю** for about a week. **III.** +*instr* with; and; **мы с ва́ми** you and I; **что с ва́ми?** what is the matter?

са́бля (*gen pl* -бель) sabre.

сабота́ж sabotage. **саботи́ровать** *impf* & *pf* sabotage.

са́ван shroud; blanket.

с|агити́ровать *pf.*

сад (*loc* -у́; *pl* -ы́) garden. **сади́ть** (сажу́, са́дишь) *impf* (*pf* по~) plant. **сади́ться** (сажу́сь) *impf of* сесть. **садово́д, -ница** gardener. **садово́дство** gardening; horticulture. **садо́вый** garden; cultivated.

сади́зм sadism. **сади́ст** sadist. **сади́стский** sadistic.

са́жа soot.

сажа́ть *impf* (*pf* посади́ть) plant; seat; set, put. **са́женец** (-нца) seedling; sapling.

са́жень (*pl* -и, -жен *or* -жёней) sazhen (2.13 metres).

сажу́ *etc.: see* сади́ть

са́йка roll.

сайт (*comput*) (web)site.

саксофо́н saxophone.

сала́зки (-зок) *pl* toboggan.

сала́т lettuce; salad.

са́ло fat, lard; suet; tallow.

сало́н salon; saloon.

салфе́тка napkin.

са́льный greasy; tallow; obscene.

салю́т salute. **салютова́ть** *impf* & *pf* (*pf* also от~) +*dat* salute.

сам (-ого́) *m*, **сама́** (-о́й, *acc* -оё) *f*, **само́** (-ого́) *neut*, **са́ми** (-и́х) *pl*, *pron* -self, -selves; myself, *etc.*, ourselves, *etc.*; ~ **по себе́** in itself; by o.s.; ~ **собо́й** of itself, of its own accord; ~**о́ собо́й (разуме́ется)** of course; it goes without saying.

са́мбо *neut indecl abbr* (*of* самозащи́та без ору́жия) unarmed combat.

саме́ц (-мца́) male. **са́мка** female.

само- *in comb* self-, auto-. **самобы́тный** original, distinctive. **~возгора́ние** spontaneous combustion. **~во́льный** wilful; unauthorized. **~де́льный** home-made. **~держа́вие** autocracy. **~держа́вный** autocratic. **~де́ятельность** amateur work, amateur performance; initiative. **~дово́льный** self-satisfied. **~ду́р** petty tyrant. **~ду́рство** highhandedness. **~забве́ние** selflessness. **~забве́нный** selfless. **~защи́та** self-defence. **~зва́нец** (-нца) impostor, pretender. **~ка́т** scooter. **~кри́тика** selfcriticism. **~люби́вый** proud; touchy. **~любие** pride, selfesteem. **~мне́ние** conceit, self-importance. **~наде́янный** presumptuous. **~облада́ние** self-control. **~обма́н** selfdeception. **~оборо́на** selfdefence. **~образова́ние** selfeducation. **~обслу́живание** self-service. **~определе́ние** self-determination. **~отве́р-**

же́нность selflessness. **∼отве́р-**
женный selfless. **∼поже́рт-**
вование self-sacrifice.
∼ро́док (-дка) nugget; person
with natural talent. **∼сва́л**
tip-up lorry. **∼созна́ние**
(self-)consciousness. **∼сохра-**
не́ние self-preservation.
∼стоя́тельность independence. **∼стоя́тельный** independent. **∼су́д** lynch law, mob
law. **∼тёк** drift. **∼тёком** adv by
gravity; of its own accord.
∼уби́йственный suicidal.
∼уби́йство suicide. **∼уби́йца**
m & f suicide. **∼уваже́ние** self-
respect. **∼уве́ренность** self-
confidence. **∼уве́ренный** self-
confident. **∼униже́ние** self-
abasement. **∼управле́ние**
self-government. **∼управля́ю-**
щийся self-governing. **∼упра́в-**
ный arbitrary. **∼учи́тель** m
self-instructor, manual. **∼у́чка**
m & f self-taught person. **∼хо́д-**
ный self-propelled. **∼чу́вствие**
general state; **как ва́ше ∼чу́в-**
ствие? how do you feel?

самова́р samovar.

самого́н home-made vodka.

самолёт aeroplane.

самоцве́т semi-precious stone.

са́мый pron (the) very, (the)
right; (the) same; (the) most.

сан dignity, office.

санато́рий sanatorium.

санда́лия sandal.

са́ни (-е́й) pl sledge, sleigh.

санита́р medical orderly;
stretcher-bearer. **санита́рка** nurse.
санита́рн|ый medical; health;
sanitary; **∼ая маши́на** ambulance; **∼ый у́зел = сану́зел.**

са́нки (-нок) pl sledge; toboggan.

санкциони́ровать impf & pf
sanction. **са́нкция** sanction.

сано́вник dignitary.

санпу́нкт medical centre.

санскри́т Sanskrit.

санте́хник plumber.

сантиме́тр centimetre; tape-
measure.

сану́зел (-зла́) sanitary arrange-
ments; WC.

санча́сть (gen pl -е́й) medical
unit.

сапёр sapper.

сапо́г (-а́; gen pl -о́г) boot. **са-**
по́жник shoemaker; cobbler.
сапо́жный shoe.

сапфи́р sapphire.

сара́й shed; barn.

саранча́ locust(s).

сарафа́н sarafan; pinafore
dress.

сарде́лька small fat sausage.

сарди́на sardine.

сарка́зм sarcasm. **саркасти́че-**
ский sarcastic.

сатана́ m Satan. **сатани́нский**
satanic.

сателли́т satellite.

сати́н sateen.

сати́ра satire. **сати́рик** satirist.
сатири́ческий satirical.

Сау́довская Ара́вия Saudi
Arabia.

сафья́н morocco. **сафья́но-**
вый morocco.

са́хар sugar. **сахари́н** sacchar-
ine. **са́харистый** sugary. **са́-**
харница sugar-basin. **са́хар-**
н|ый sugar; sugary; **∼ый заво́д**
sugar-refinery; **∼ый песо́к**
granulated sugar; **∼ая пу́дра**
castor sugar; **∼ая свёкла** sugar-
beet.

сачо́к (-чка́) net.

сба́вить (-влю) pf, **сбавля́ть**

impf take off; reduce.

с|баланси́ровать *pf.*

сбега́ть[1] *pf* run; +за+*instr* run for. сбега́ть[2] *impf*, сбежа́ть (-егу́) *pf* run down (from); run away; disappear; ∼ся come running.

сберега́тельная ка́сса savings bank. сберега́ть *impf*, сбере́чь (-егу́, -ежёшь; -ёг, -ла́) *pf* save; save up; preserve. сбере-же́ние economy; saving; savings. сберка́сса savings bank.

сбива́ть *impf*, сбить (собью, -бьёшь) *pf* bring down, knock down; knock off; distract; wear down; knock together; churn; whip, whisk; ∼ся be dislodged; slip; go wrong; be confused; ∼ся с пути́ lose one's way; ∼ся с ног be run off one's feet. сби́вчивый confused; inconsistent.

сближа́ть *impf*, сбли́зить (-и́жу) *pf* bring (closer) together, draw together; ∼ся draw together; become good friends. сближе́ние rapprochement; closing in.

сбо́ку *adv* from one side; on one side.

сбор collection; duty; fee, toll; takings; gathering. сбо́рище crowd, mob. сбо́рка assembling, assembly; gather. сбо́рник collection. сбо́рный assembly; mixed, combined; prefabricated; detachable. сбо́рочный assembly. сбо́рщик collector; assembler.

сбра́сывать(ся *impf of* сбро́сить(ся

сбрива́ть *impf*, сбрить (сбре́ю) *pf* shave off.

сброд riff-raff.

сброс fault, break. сбро́сить (-о́шу) *pf* (*impf* сбра́сывать)

throw down, drop; throw off; shed; discard.

сбру́я (collect) (riding) tack.

сбыва́ть *impf*, сбыть (сбу́ду; сбыл, -á, -o) *pf* sell, market; get rid of; ∼ся come true, be realized. сбыт (*no pl*) sale; market.

св. *abbr* (*of* свято́й) Saint.

сва́дебный wedding. сва́дьба (*gen pl* -деб) wedding.

сва́ливать *impf*, с|вали́ть (-лю́, -лишь) *pf* throw down; overthrow; pile up; ∼ся fall (down), collapse. сва́лка dump; scuffle.

с|валя́ть *pf.*

сва́ривать *impf*, с|вари́ть (-рю́, -ришь) *pf* boil; cook; weld. сва́рка welding.

сварли́вый cantankerous.

сварно́й welded. сва́рочный welding. сва́рщик welder.

сва́стика swastika.

сва́тать *impf* (*pf* по∼, со∼) propose as a husband or wife; propose to; ∼ся к+*dat or* за+*acc* propose to.

свая pile.

све́дение piece of information; knowledge; *pl* information, intelligence; knowledge. све́дущий knowledgeable; versed.

сведу́ *etc.: see* свести́

свежезаморо́женный freshfrozen; chilled. све́жесть freshness. свеже́ть (-е́ет) *impf* (*pf* по∼) become cooler; freshen. све́жий (-еж, -á, -ó, -и) fresh; new.

свезти́ (-зу́, -зёшь; свёз, -лá) *pf* (*impf* свози́ть) take; bring *or* take down *or* away.

свёкла beet, beetroot.

свёкор (-кра) father-in-law. све-кро́вь mother-in-law.

свёл *etc.: see* свести́

сверга́ть *impf*, све́ргнуть (-ну;

сверг) *pf* throw down, overthrow. **сверже́ние** overthrow.

све́рить *pf* (*impf* **сверя́ть**) collate.

сверка́ть *impf* sparkle, twinkle; glitter; gleam. **сверкну́ть** (-ну́, -нёшь) *pf* flash.

сверли́льный drill, drilling; boring. **сверли́ть** *impf* (*pf* про~) drill; bore (through); nag. **сверло́** drill. **сверля́щий** gnawing, piercing.

сверну́ть (-ну́, -нёшь) *pf* (*impf* **свёртывать, свора́чивать**) roll (up); turn; curtail, cut down; ~ ше́ю+*dat* wring the neck of; ~ся roll up, curl up; curdle, coagulate; contract.

све́рстник contemporary.

свёрток (-тка) package, bundle. **свёртывание** rolling (up); curdling; coagulation; curtailment, cuts. **свёртывать(ся** *impf of* **сверну́ть(ся**

сверх *prep*+*gen* over, above, on top of; beyond; in addition to; ~ того́ moreover.

сверх- *in comb* super-, over-, hyper-. **сверхзвуково́й** supersonic. ~**пла́новый** over and above the plan. ~**при́быль** excess profit. ~**проводни́к** (-а́) superconductor. ~**секре́тный** top secret. ~**уро́чный** overtime. ~**уро́чные** *sb pl* overtime. ~**челове́к** superman. ~**челове́ческий** superhuman. ~**есте́ственный** supernatural.

све́рху *adv* from above; ~ до́низу from top to bottom.

сверчо́к (-чка́) cricket.

сверше́ние achievement.

сверя́ть *impf of* **све́рить**

све́сить (-е́шу) *pf* (*impf* **све́шивать**) let down, lower; ~ся hang over, lean over.

свести́ (-еду́, -еде́шь; -ёл, -а́) *pf* (*impf* **своди́ть**) take; take down; take away; remove; bring together; reduce, bring; cramp.

свет[1] light; daybreak.

свет[2] world; society.

света́ть *impf impers* dawn. **свети́ло** luminary. **свети́ть** (-ечу́, -е́тишь) *impf* (*pf* по~) shine; +*dat* light; light the way for; ~ся shine, gleam. **светле́ть** (-е́ет) *impf* (*pf* по~, про~) brighten (up); grow lighter. **све́тлость** brightness; Grace. **све́тлый** light; bright; joyous. **светлячо́к** (-чка́) glow-worm.

свето- *in comb* light, photo-. **светонепроница́емый** light-proof. ~**фи́льтр** light filter. ~**фо́р** traffic light(s).

светово́й light; luminous; ~ день daylight hours.

светопреставле́ние end of the world.

све́тский fashionable; refined; secular.

светя́щийся luminous, fluorescent. **свеча́** (*pl* -и, -е́й) candle; (spark-)plug. **свече́ние** luminescence, fluorescence. **све́чка** candle. **свечу́** *etc.*: *see* **свети́ть**

с|ве́шать *pf*. **све́шивать(ся** *impf of* **све́сить(ся. свива́ть** *impf of* **свить**

свида́ние meeting; appointment; до свида́ния! goodbye!

свиде́тель *m*, **-ница** witness. **свиде́тельство** evidence; testimony; certificate. **свиде́тельствовать** *impf* (*pf* за~), give evidence, testify; be evidence (of); witness.

свина́рник pigsty.

свине́ц (-нца́) lead.

свини́на pork. **сви́нка** mumps. **свино́й** pig; pork. **сви́нство**

despicable act; outrage; squalor.

свинцо́вый lead; leaden.

свинья́ (pl -ньи, -не́й, -ньям) pig, swine.

свире́ль (reed-)pipe.

свирепе́ть (-е́ю) impf (pf рас∼) grow savage; become violent. **свире́пствовать** impf rage; be rife. **свире́пый** fierce, ferocious.

свиса́ть impf, **сви́снуть** (-ну; -ис) pf hang down, dangle; trail.

свист whistle; whistling. **свиста́ть** (-ищу́, -и́щешь) impf whistle. **свисте́ть** (-ищу́) impf, **сви́стнуть** (-ну) pf whistle; hiss. **свисто́к** (-тка́) whistle.

сви́та suite; retinue.

сви́тер sweater.

сви́ток (-тка) roll, scroll. **с|вить** (совью́, совьёшь; -ил, -а́, -о) pf (impf also **свива́ть**) twist, wind; ∼ся roll up.

свихну́ться (-ну́сь, -нёшься) impf go mad; go astray.

свищ (-а́) flaw; (knot-)hole; fistula.

свищу́ etc.: see **свиста́ть**, **свисте́ть**

свобо́да freedom. **свобо́дно** adv freely; easily; fluently; loose(ly). **свобо́дный** free; easy; vacant; spare; loose; flowing. **свободолюби́вый** freedom-loving. **свободомы́слие** free-thinking.

свод code; collection; arch, vault.

своди́ть (-ожу́, -о́дишь) impf of **свести́**

сво́дка summary; report. **сво́дный** composite; step-.

сво́дчатый arched, vaulted.

своево́лие self-will, wilfulness.

своево́льный wilful.

своевре́менно adv in good time; opportunely. **своевре́менный** timely, opportune.

своенра́вие capriciousness. **своенра́вный** wilful, capricious.

своеобра́зие originality; peculiarity. **своеобра́зный** original; peculiar.

свожу́ etc.: see **своди́ть**, **свози́ть**. **свози́ть** (-ожу́, -о́зишь) impf of **свезти́**

свой (своего́) m, **своя́** (свое́й) f, **своё** (своего́) neut, **свои́** (свои́х) pl, pron one's (own); my, his, her, its; our, your, their. **сво́йственный** peculiar, characteristic. **сво́йство** property, attribute, characteristic.

сво́лочь swine; riff-raff.

сво́ра leash; pack.

свора́чивать impf of **сверну́ть**, **свороти́ть**. **с|ворова́ть** pf.

свороти́ть (-очу́, -о́тишь) pf (impf **свора́чивать**) dislodge; shift; turn; twist.

своя́к brother-in-law (husband of wife's sister). **своя́ченица** sister-in-law (wife's sister).

свыка́ться impf, **свы́кнуться** (-нусь, -ыкся) pf get used.

свысока́ adv haughtily. **свы́ше** adv from above. **свы́ше** prep+gen over; beyond.

свя́занный constrained; combined; bound; coupled. **с|вя-за́ть** (-яжу́, -я́жешь) pf, **свя́зывать** impf tie, bind; connect; ∼ся get in touch; get involved. **связи́ст**, **-и́стка** signaller; worker in communication services. **свя́зка** sheaf, bundle; ligament. **свя́зный** connected, coherent. **связь** (loc -и́) connection; link, bond; liaison;

communication(s).

святи́лище sanctuary. **свя́тки** (-ток) *pl* Christmas-tide. **свя́то** *adv* piously; religiously. **свят|о́й** (-я́т, -á, -о) holy; ~**о́й**, ~**áя** *sb* saint. **святы́ня** sacred object *or* place. **свяще́нник** priest. **свяще́нный** sacred.

сгиб bend. **сгиба́ть** *impf of* **согну́ть**

сгла́дить (-áжу) *pf*, **сгла́живать** *impf* smooth out; smooth over, soften.

сгла́зить (-áжу) *pf* put the evil eye on.

сгнива́ть *impf*, **с|гнить** (-ию́, -иёшь; -ил, -á, -о) *pf* rot.

с|гнои́ться *pf*.

сгова́риваться *impf*, **сгово-ри́ться** *pf* come to an arrange-ment; arrange. **сго́вор** agree-ment. **сгово́рчивый** com-pliant.

сгоня́ть *impf of* **согна́ть**

сгора́ние combustion; **дви́га-тель вну́треннего сгора́ния** internal-combustion engine. **сгора́ть** *impf of* **сгоре́ть**

с|горбить(ся (-блю(сь) *pf*.

с|горе́ть (-рю́) *pf* (*impf also* **сгора́ть**) burn down; be burnt down; be used up; burn; burn o.s. out. **сгоряча́** *adv* in the heat of the moment.

с|гото́вить(ся (-влю(сь) *pf*.

сгреба́ть *impf*, **с|грести́** (-ебу́, -ебёшь; -ёб, -лá) *pf* rake up, rake together.

сгружа́ть *impf*, **сгрузи́ть** (-ужу́, -у́зишь) *pf* unload.

с|группирова́ть(ся *pf*.

сгусти́ть (-ущу́) *pf*, **сгуща́ть** *impf* thicken; condense; ~**ся** thicken; condense; clot. **сгу́сток** (-тка) clot. **сгуще́ние** thicken-ing, condensation; clotting.

сдава́ть (сдаю́, сдаёшь) *impf of* **сдать**; ~ **экза́мен** take an exam-ination; ~**ся** *impf of* **сда́ться**

сдави́ть (-влю́, -вишь) *pf*, **сда́-вливать** *impf* squeeze.

сдать (-ам, -ашь, -аст, -ади́м; -ал, -á, -о) *pf* (*impf* **сдава́ть**) hand in, hand over; pass; let, hire out; surrender, give up; deal; ~**ся** surrender, yield. **сда́ча** handing over; hiring out; surrender; change; deal.

сдвиг displacement; fault; change, improvement. **сдви-га́ть** *impf*, **сдви́нуть** (-ну) *pf* shift, move; move together; ~**ся** move, budge; come together.

с|де́лать(ся *pf*. **сде́лка** trans-action; deal, bargain. **сде́ль-ный** piece-work; ~**ая рабо́та** piece-work. **сде́льщина** piece-work.

сдёргивать *impf of* **сдёрнуть**

сде́ржанный restrained, re-served. **сдержа́ть** (-жу́, -жишь) *pf*, **сде́рживать** *impf* hold back; restrain; keep.

сдёрнуть (-ну) *pf* (*impf* **сдёрги-вать**) pull off.

сдеру́ *etc.: see* **содра́ть**. **сди-ра́ть** *impf of* **содра́ть**

сдо́ба shortening; fancy bread, bun(s). **сдо́бный** (-бен, -бнá, -о) rich, short.

с|до́хнуть (-нет; сдох) *pf* die; kick the bucket.

сдружи́ться (-жу́сь) *pf* become friends.

сдува́ть *impf*, **сду́нуть** (-ну) *pf*, **сдуть** (-у́ю) *pf* blow away *or* off.

сеа́нс performance; showing; sitting.

себесто́имость prime cost; cost (price).

себя́ (*dat & prep* себе́, *instr*

собой or **собою** *refl pron* oneself; myself, yourself, himself, *etc.*; **ничего себе** not bad; **собой** -looking, in appearance.

себялюбие selfishness.

сев sowing.

север north. **северный** north, northerly. **северо-восток** north-east **северо-восточный** north-east(ern). **северо-запад** north-west. **северо-западный** north-west(ern). **северянин** (*pl* -яне, -ян) northerner.

севооборот crop rotation.

сего *see* **сей. сегодня** *adv* today. **сегодняшний** of today, to-day's.

седеть (-ею) *impf* (*pf* по~) turn grey. **седина** (*pl* -ы) grey hair(s).

седлать *impf* (*pf* о~) saddle. **седло** (*pl* сёдла, -дел) saddle.

седобородый grey-bearded. **седоволосый** grey-haired. **седой** (сед, -а, -о) grey(-haired).

седок (-а) passenger; rider.

седьмой seventh.

сезон season. **сезонный** seasonal.

сей (сего) *m*, **сия** (сей) *f*, **сие** (сего) *neut*, **сий** (сих) *pl*, this; these; **сию минуту** at once, instantly.

сейсмический seismic.

сейф safe.

сейчас *adv* (just) now; soon; immediately.

сёк *etc.*: *see* **сечь**

секрет secret.

секретариат secretariat.

секретарский secretarial. **секретарша**, **секретарь** (-я) *m* secretary.

секретный secret.

секс sex. **сексуальный** sexual; sexy.

секстет sextet.

секта sect. **сектант** sectarian.

сектор sector.

секу *etc.*: *see* **сечь**

секуляризация secularization.

секунда second. **секундант** second. **секундный** second. **секундомер** stop-watch.

секционный sectional. **секция** section.

селёдка herring.

селезёнка spleen.

селезень (-зня) *m* drake.

селекция breeding.

селение settlement, village.

селитра saltpetre, nitre.

селить(ся *impf* (*pf* по~) settle. **село** (*pl* сёла) village.

сельдерей celery.

сельдь (*pl* -и, -ей) herring.

сельский rural; village; ~ое хозяйство agriculture. **сельскохозяйственный** agricultural.

сельсовет village soviet.

семантика semantics. **семантический** semantic.

семафор semaphore; signal.

сёмга (smoked) salmon.

семейный family; domestic. **семейство** family.

семени *etc.*: *see* **семя**

семенить *impf* mince.

семениться *impf* seed. **семенник** (-а) testicle; seed-vessel. **семенной** seed; seminal.

семёрка seven; figure 7; No. 7. **семеро** (-ых) seven.

семестр term, semester.

семечко (*pl* -и) seed; *pl* sun-flower seeds.

семидесятилетие seventy

years; seventieth anniversary, birthday. **семидеся́тый** seventieth; **~ые го́ды** the seventies.

семиле́тка seven-year school. **семиле́тний** seven-year; seven-year-old.

семина́р seminar. **семина́рия** seminary.

семисо́тый seven-hundredth. **семна́дцатый** seventeenth. **семна́дцать** seventeen. **семь** (-ми́, -мью) seven. **се́мьдесят** (-ми́десяти, -мью́десятью) seventy. **семьсо́т** (-мисо́т, instr -мьюста́ми) seven hundred. **се́мью** adv seven times.

семья́ (pl -мьи, -ме́й, -мьям) family. **семьяни́н** family man.

се́мя (-мени; pl -мена́, -мя́н, -мена́м) seed; semen, sperm.

сена́т senate. **сена́тор** senator.

се́ни (-е́й) pl (entrance-)hall.

се́но hay. **сенова́л** hayloft. **сеноко́с** haymaking; hayfield.

сенсацио́нный sensational. **сенса́ция** sensation.

сенте́нция maxim.

сентимента́льный sentimental.

сентя́брь (-я́) m September. **сентя́брьский** September.

се́псис sepsis.

се́ра sulphur; ear-wax.

серб, ~ка Serb. **Се́рбия** Serbia. **се́рбский** Serb(ian). **се́рбско-хорва́тский** Serbo-Croat(ian).

серва́нт sideboard.

се́рвер (comput) server.

серви́з service, set. **сервирова́ть** impf & pf serve; lay (a table). **сервиро́вка** laying; table lay-out.

серде́чник core. **серде́чность** cordiality; warmth. **серде́чный** heart; cardiac; cordial; warm-hearted). **серди́тый** angry. **сер-**

ди́ть (-ржу́, -рдишь) impf (pf рас~) anger; **~ся** be angry. **сердобо́льный** tender-hearted. **се́рдце** (pl -á, -де́ц) heart; **в се́рдцах** in anger; **от всего́ се́рдца** from the bottom of one's heart. **сердцебие́ние** palpitation. **сердцеви́дный** heart-shaped. **сердцеви́на** core, pith, heart.

серебрёный silver-plated. **серебри́стый** silvery. **серебри́ть** impf (pf по~) silver, silver-plate; **~ся** become silvery. **серебро́** silver. **сере́бряный** silver.

середи́на middle.

Серёжка earring; catkin.

серена́да serenade.

сере́нький grey; dull.

сержа́нт sergeant.

сери́йный serial; mass. **се́рия** series; part.

се́рный sulphur; sulphuric.

серогла́зый grey-eyed.

се́рость uncouthness; ignorance.

серп (-á) sickle; **~ луны́** crescent moon.

серпанти́н streamer.

сертифика́т certificate.

се́рый (сер, -á, -о) grey; dull; un-educated.

серьга́ (pl -и, -рёг) earring.

серьёзность seriousness. **серьёзный** serious.

се́ссия session.

сестра́ (pl сёстры, сестёр, сёстрам) sister.

сесть (ся́ду) pf (impf сади́ться) sit down; land; set; shrink; **+на+acc** board, get on.

се́тка net, netting; (luggage-) rack; string bag; grid.

се́товать impf (pf по~) complain.

сетча́тка retina. **сеть** (loc -и́; pl -и, -е́й) net; network.

сече́ние section. **сечь** (секу́, сечёшь; сёк) impf (pf вы́∼) cut to pieces; flog, ∼ся cut oneself.

се́ялка seed drill. **се́ять** (се́ю) impf (pf по∼) sow.

сжа́литься pf take pity (над +instr) on.

сжа́тие pressure; grasp, grip; compression. **сжа́тый** compressed; compact; concise.

сжа́ть[1] (сожну́, -нёшь) pf.

сжа́ть[2] (сожму́, -мёшь) pf (impf сжима́ть) squeeze; compress; grip; clench; ∼ся tighten, clench; shrink, contract.

сжечь (сожгу́, сожжёшь; сжёг, сожгла́) pf (impf сжига́ть) burn (down); cremate.

сжива́ться impf of сжи́ться

сжига́ть impf of сжечь

сжима́ть(ся impf of сжа́ть[2]

сжи́ться (-иву́сь, -ивёшься; -и́лся, -а́сь) pf (impf сжива́ться) с+instr get used to.

сжу́льничать pf.

сза́ди adv from behind; behind. **сза́ди** prep+gen behind.

сзыва́ть impf of созва́ть

сиби́рский Siberian. **Сиби́рь** Siberia. **сибиря́к** (-а́), **сибиря́чка** Siberian.

сига́ра cigar. **сигаре́та** cigarette.

сигна́л signal. **сигнализа́ция** signalling. **сигнализи́ровать** impf & pf (pf also про∼) signal. **сигна́льный** signal. **сигна́льщик** signal-man.

сиде́лка sick-nurse. **сиде́ние** sitting. **сиде́нье** seat. **сиде́ть** (-ижу́) impf sit; be; fit. **сидя́чий** sitting; sedentary.

сие́ etc.: see сей

си́зый (сиз, -а́, -о) (blue-)grey.

сий see сей

си́ла strength; force; power; в си́лу +gen on the strength of, because of; не по ∼ам beyond one's powers; си́лой by force. **сила́ч** (-а́) strong man. **си́литься** impf try, make efforts. **силово́й** power; of force.

сило́к (-лка́) noose, snare.

си́лос silo; silage.

силуэ́т silhouette.

си́льно adv strongly, violently; very much, greatly. **си́льный** (-лен or -лён, -льна́, -о) strong; powerful; intense, hard.

симбио́з symbiosis.

си́мвол symbol. **символизи́ровать** impf symbolize. **символи́зм** symbolism. **символи́ческий** symbolic.

сим-ка́рта SIM (card).

симме́три́я symmetry.

симпатизи́ровать impf +dat like, sympathize with. **симпати́чный** likeable, nice. **симпа́тия** liking; sympathy.

симпо́зиум symposium.

симпто́м symptom.

симули́ровать impf & pf simulate, feign. **симуля́нт** malingerer, sham. **симуля́ция** simulation, pretence.

симфо́ния symphony.

синаго́га synagogue.

синева́ blue. **синева́тый** bluish. **синегла́зый** blue-eyed. **сине́ть** (-е́ю) impf (pf по∼) turn blue; show blue. **си́ний** (синь, -ня, -не) (dark) blue.

сини́ца titmouse.

сино́д synod. **сино́ним** synonym. **си́нтаксис** syntax.

си́нтез synthesis. **синтези́ровать** impf & pf synthesize. **син-**

тети́ческий synthetic.

си́нус sine; sinus.

синхронизи́ровать *impf & pf* synchronize.

синь[1] blue. **синь**[2] *see* **си́ний**. **си́нька** blueing; blue-print. **синя́к** (-á) bruise.

сиони́зм Zionism.

си́плый hoarse, husky. **си́пнуть** (-ну; сип) *impf* (*pf* о~) become hoarse, husky.

сире́на siren; hooter.

сире́невый lilac(-coloured). **сире́нь** lilac.

Си́рия Syria.

сиро́п syrup.

сирота́ (*pl* -ы) *m & f* orphan. **сироти́вый** lonely.

систе́ма system. **систематизи́ровать** *impf & pf* systematize. **системати́ческий**, **системати́чный** systematic.

си́тец (-тца) (printed) cotton; chintz.

си́то sieve.

ситуа́ция situation.

си́тцевый print, chintz.

сифили́с syphilis.

сифо́н siphon.

сия́ *see* **сей**

сия́ние radiance. **сия́ть** *impf* shine, beam.

сказ tale. **сказа́ние** story, legend. **сказа́ть** (-ажу́, -а́жешь) *pf* (*impf* **говори́ть**) say; speak; tell. **сказа́ться** (-ажу́сь, -а́жешься) *pf*, **ска́зываться** *impf* tell (on); declare o.s. **скази́тель** *m* storyteller. **ска́зка** (fairy-)tale; fib. **ска́зочный** fairy-tale; fantastic. **сказу́емое** *sb* predicate.

скака́лка skipping-rope. **ска́кать** (-ачу́, -а́чешь) *impf* (*pf* по~) skip; jump; gallop. **скаково́й** race, racing.

скала́ (*pl* -ы) rock; cliff. **скали́стый** rocky.

скали́ть *impf* (*pf* о~); ~ зу́бы bare one's teeth; grin; ~ся bare one's teeth.

ска́лка rolling-pin.

скалола́з rock-climber.

ска́лывать *impf of* **сколо́ть**

скальп scalp.

ска́льпель *m* scalpel.

скаме́ечка footstool; small bench. **скаме́йка** bench. **скамья́** (*pl* скамьи́, -е́й) bench; ~ подсуди́мых dock.

сканда́л scandal; brawl; rowdy scene. **скандали́ст** trouble-maker. **скандали́ться** *impf* (*pf* о~) disgrace o.s. **сканда́льный** scandalous.

скандина́вский Scandinavian.

сканди́ровать *impf & pf* declaim.

ска́нер (*comput, med*) scanner.

ска́пливать(ся *impf of* **скопи́ть(ся**

скарб goods and chattels.

ска́редный stingy.

скарлати́на scarlet fever.

скат slope; pitch.

ската́ть *pf* (*impf* **ска́тывать**) roll (up).

ска́терть (*pl* -и, -е́й) table-cloth.

скати́ть (-ачу́, -а́тишь) *pf*, **ска́тывать**[1] *impf* roll down; ~ся roll down; rush, slide, slither. **ска́тывать**[2] *impf of* **ската́ть**

скафа́ндр diving-suit; space-suit.

скачка́ gallop, galloping. **ска́чки** (-чек) *pl* horse-race; races. **скачо́к** (-чка́) jump, leap.

ска́шивать *impf of* **скоси́ть**

сква́жина slit, chink; well.

сквер public garden.

скве́рно badly; bad. **скверно-сло́вить** (-влю) *impf* use foul language. **скве́рный** foul; bad.

сквози́ть *impf* be transparent; show through; **сквози́т** *impers* there is a draught. **сквозно́й** through; transparent. **сквозня́к** (-á) draught. **сквозь** *prep*+acc through.

скворе́ц (-рца́) starling.

скеле́т skeleton.

ске́птик sceptic. **скептици́зм** scepticism. **скепти́ческий** sceptical.

скетч sketch.

ски́дка reduction. **ски́дывать** *impf*, **ски́нуть** (-ну) *pf* throw off or down; knock off.

ски́петр sceptre.

скипида́р turpentine.

скирд (-á; *pl* -ы́), **скирда́** (*pl* -ы, -áм) stack, rick.

скиса́ть *impf*, **ски́снуть** (-ну; скис) *pf* go sour.

скита́лец (-льца) wanderer. **скита́ться** *impf* wander.

скиф Scythian.

склад[1] depot; store.

склад[2] mould; turn; logical connection; ~ ума́ mentality.

скла́дка fold; pleat; crease; wrinkle.

скла́дно *adv* smoothly.

складно́й folding, collapsible.

скла́дный (-ден, -дна́, -о) well-knit, well-built; smooth, coherent.

скла́дчина: в скла́дчину by clubbing together. **скла́дывать(ся** *impf of* сложи́ть(ся

скле́ивать *impf*, **скле́ить** *pf* stick together; ~ся stick together.

склеп (burial) vault, crypt.

склепа́ть *pf*, **склёпывать** *impf*

rivet. **склёпка** riveting.

склеро́з sclerosis.

скло́ка squabble.

склон slope; на ~е лет in one's declining years. **склоне́ние** inclination; declension. **склони́ть** (-ню, -нишь) *pf*, **склоня́ть** *impf* incline; bow; win over; decline; ~ся bend, bow; yield; be declined. **скло́нность** inclination; tendency. **скло́нный** (-нен, -нна́, -нно) inclined, disposed. **склоня́емый** declinable.

скля́нка phial; bottle; (*naut*) bell.

скоба́ (*pl* -ы, -áм) cramp, clamp, staple.

ско́бка *dim of* скоба́; bracket; *pl* parenthesis, parentheses.

скобли́ть (-облю́, -о́бли́шь) *impf* scrape, plane.

ско́ванность constraint. **ско́ванный** constrained; bound. **скова́ть** (скую́, скуёшь) *pf* (*impf* **ско́вывать**) forge; chain; fetter; pin down, hold, contain.

сковорода́ (*pl* ско́вороды, -ро́д, -áм), **сковоро́дка** frying-pan.

ско́вывать *impf of* скова́ть

скола́чивать *impf*, **сколоти́ть** (-очу́, -о́тишь) *pf* knock together.

сколо́ть (-лю́, -лешь) *pf* (*impf* **ска́лывать**) chop off; pin together.

скольже́ние sliding, slipping; glide. **скользи́ть** (-льжу́) *impf*, **скользну́ть** (-ну́, -нёшь) *pf* slide; slip; glide. **ско́льзкий** (-зок, -зка́, -о) slippery. **скользя́щий** sliding.

ско́лько *adv* how much; how many; as far as.

с|кома́ндовать *pf*. **с|комбини́ровать** *pf*. **с|ко́мкать** *pf*. **с|ком-**

плектова́ть pf. с|компромети́ровать pf. с|конструи́ровать pf.

сконфу́женный embarrassed, confused, disconcerted. с|конфу́зить(ся -у́жу(сь) pf.

с|концентри́ровать pf.

сконча́ться pf pass away, die.

с|копи́ровать pf.

скопи́ть (-плю́, -пишь) pf (impf ска́пливать) save (up); amass; ~ся accumulate. скопле́ние accumulation; crowd.

ско́пом adv in a crowd, en masse.

скорбе́ть (-блю́) impf grieve. ско́рбный sorrowful. скорбь (pl -и, -е́й) sorrow.

скоре́е, скоре́й comp of ско́ро, ско́рый; adv rather, sooner; как мо́жно ~ as soon as possible; ~ всего́ most likely.

скорлупа́ (pl -ы) shell.

скорня́к (-а́) furrier.

ско́ро adv quickly; soon.

ско́ро- in comb quick-, fast-. скорова́рка pressure-cooker. ~гово́рка patter; tongue-twister. ско́ропись cursive; shorthand. ~по́ртящийся perishable. ~пости́жный sudden. ~спе́лый early; fast-ripening; premature; hasty. ~сшива́тель m binder, file. ~те́чный transient, short-lived.

скоростно́й high-speed. ско́рость (gen pl -е́й) speed; gear.

скорпио́н scorpion; Scorpio.

с|корректи́ровать pf. с|корти́ть(ся -чу(сь) pf.

ско́рый (скор, -а́, -о) quick, fast; near; forthcoming; ~ая по́мощь first-aid; ambulance.

с|коси́ть¹ (-ошу́, -о́сишь) pf (impf also ска́шивать) mow.

с|коси́ть² (-ошу́) pf (impf also ска́шивать) squint; cut on the cross.

скот (-а́), скоти́на cattle; livestock; beast. ско́тный cattle.

ското- in comb cattle. ското-бо́йня (gen pl -о́ен) slaughter-house. ~во́д cattle-breeder. ~во́дство cattle-raising.

ско́тский cattle; brutish. ско́тство brutish condition; brutality.

с|краси́ть (-а́шу) pf, скра́шивать impf smooth over; relieve.

скребо́к (-бка́) scraper. скребу́ etc.: see скрести́

скре́жет grating; gnashing. скрежета́ть (-ещу́, -е́щешь) impf grate; +instr gnash.

скре́па clamp, brace; counter-signature.

скрепи́ть (-плю́) pf, скрепля́ть impf fasten (together); make fast; clamp; countersign, ratify; скрепя́ се́рдце reluctantly. скре́пка paper-clip. скрепле́ние fastening; clamping; tie, clamp.

скрести́ (-ебу́, -ебёшь; -ёб, -ла́) impf scrape; scratch; ~сь scratch.

скрести́ть (-ещу́) pf, скре́щивать impf cross; interbreed. скреще́ние crossing. скре́щивание crossing; interbreeding.

с|криви́ть(ся -влю(сь) pf.

скрип squeak, creak. скрипа́ч (-а́) violinist. скрипе́ть (-плю́) impf, скри́пнуть (-ну) pf squeak, creak; scratch. скри́пичный violin; ~ ключ treble clef. скри́пка violin. скрипу́чий squeaky, creaking.

скро́ить pf.

скро́мничать impf (pf по-) be (too) modest. скро́мность

modesty. **скро́мный** (-мен, -мна́, -о) modest.

скро́ю *etc.: see* **скрыть. скрою́** *etc.: see* **скрои́ть**

скрупулёзный scrupulous.

скрути́ть (-учу́, -у́тишь) *pf*, **скру́чивать** *impf* twist; roll; tie up.

скрыва́ть *impf*, **скрыть** (-о́ю) *pf* hide, conceal; **~ся** hide, go into hiding, be hidden; steal away; disappear. **скры́тничать** *impf* be secretive. **скры́тный** secretive. **скры́тый** secret, hidden; latent.

скря́га *m & f* miser.

ску́дный (-ден, -дна́, -о) scanty; meagre. **ску́дость** scarcity, paucity.

ску́ка boredom.

скула́ (*pl* -ы) cheek-bone. **скула́стый** with high cheek-bones. **скули́ть** *impf* whine, whimper.

ску́льптор sculptor. **скульпту́ра** sculpture.

ску́мбрия mackerel.

скунс skunk.

скупа́ть *impf of* **скупи́ть**

скупе́ц (-пца́) miser.

скупи́ть (-плю́, -пишь) *pf* (*impf* **скупа́ть**) buy (up).

скупи́ться (-плю́сь) *impf* (*pf* **по~**) be stingy; skimp; be sparing (of +**на**+*acc*).

ску́пка buying (up).

ску́по *adv* sparingly. **скупо́й** (-п, -а́, -о) stingy, meagre. **ску́пость** stinginess.

ску́пщик buyer(-up).

ску́тер (*pl* -а́) outboard speedboat.

скуча́ть *impf* be bored; **+по** +*dat* miss, yearn for.

ску́ченность density, overcrowding. **ску́ченный** dense,

overcrowded. **ску́чить** (-чу) *pf* crowd (together); **~ся** cluster, crowd together.

ску́чный (-чен, -чна́, -о) boring; **мне ску́чно** I'm bored.

с|ку́шать *pf.* **скую́** *etc.: see* **скова́ть**

слабе́ть (-е́ю) *impf* (*pf* **о~**) weaken, grow weak. **слаби́тельный** laxative; **~ое** *sb* laxative. **сла́бить** *impf impers:* **его́ сла́бит** he has diarrhoea.

слабо- *in comb* weak, feeble, slight. **слабово́лие** weakness of will. **~во́льный** weak-willed. **~не́рвный** nervy, nervous. **~разви́тый** underdeveloped. **~у́мие** feeble-mindedness. **~у́мный** feeble-minded.

сла́бость weakness. **сла́бый** (-б, -а́, -о) weak.

сла́ва glory; fame; **на сла́ву** wonderfully well. **сла́вить** (-влю) *impf* celebrate, sing the praises of; **~ся** (+*instr*) be famous (for). **сла́вный** glorious, renowned; nice.

славяни́н (*pl* -я́не, -я́н), **славя́нка** Slav. **славянофи́л** Slavophil(e). **славя́нский** Slav, Slavonic.

слага́емое *sb* component, term, member. **слага́ть** *impf of* **сложи́ть**

сла́дить (-а́жу) *pf* +*instr* cope with, handle; arrange.

сла́дкий (-док, -дка́, -о) sweet; **~ое** *sb* sweet course. **сладостра́стник** voluptuary. **сладостра́стный** voluptuous. **сла́дость** joy; sweetness; *pl* sweets.

сла́женность harmony. **сла́женный** co-ordinated, harmonious.

сла́мывать *impf of* **сломи́ть**

сла́нец (-нца) shale, slate.

сластёна m & f person with a sweet tooth (pl -ы, -ей) delight; pl sweets, sweet things.

слать (шлю, шлёшь) impf send.

слаща́вый sugary, sickly-sweet. **сла́ще** comp of **сла́дкий**

сле́ва adv to or on the left; ~ на-пра́во from left to right.

слёг etc.: see **слечь**

слегка́ adv slightly; lightly.

след (следа́, dat -у, loc -ý; pl -ы́) track; footprint; trace. **следи́ть**[1] (-ежу́) impf +за+instr watch; follow; keep up with; look after; keep an eye on. **следи́ть**[2] (-ежу́) impf (pf на~) leave footprints. **сле́дование** movement. **сле́дователь** m investigator. **сле́довательно** adv consequently. **сле́довать** impf (pf по~) I. +dat or за+instr follow; go, be bound; II. impers (+dat) ought; be owing, be owed; **вам сле́дует** +inf you ought to; **как сле́дует** properly; as it should be; **ско́лько с меня́ сле́дует?** how much do I owe (you)? **сле́дом** adv (за+instr) immediately after, close behind. **сле́дственный** investigation, inquiry. **сле́дствие**[1] consequence. **сле́дствие**[2] investigation. **сле́дующий** following; next. **слёжка** shadowing.

слеза́ (pl -ёзы, -а́м) tear.

слеза́ть impf of **слезть**

слези́ться (-и́тся) impf water. **слези́вый** tearful. **слёзный** tear; tearful. **слезоточи́вый** watering; ~ **газ** tear-gas.

слезть (-зу; слез) pf (impf **слеза́ть**) climb or get down; dismount; get off; come off.

слепе́нь (-пня́) m horse-fly.

слепе́ц (-пца́) blind man. **сле-**

пи́ть[1] impf blind; dazzle.

слепи́ть[2] (-плю́, -пишь) pf stick together.

сле́пнуть (-ну; слеп) impf (pf о~) go blind. **сле́по** adv blindly. **слепо́й** (-п, -а́, -о) blind; ~ые sb pl the blind.

слепо́к (-пка) cast.

слепота́ blindness.

сле́сарь (pl -я́ or -и) m metal-worker; locksmith.

слёт gathering; rally. **слета́ть** impf, **слете́ть** (-ечу́) pf fly down or away; fall down or off; ~ся fly together; congregate.

слечь (сля́гу, -я́жешь; слёг, -ла́) pf take to one's bed.

сли́ва plum; plum-tree.

слива́ть(ся impf of **сли́ть(ся.** **сли́вки** (-вок) pl cream. **сли́вочный** cream; creamy; ~ое ма́сло butter; ~ое моро́женое dairy ice-cream.

сли́зистый slimy. **слизня́к** (-á) slug. **слизь** mucus; slime.

с|линя́ть pf.

слипа́ться impf, **сли́пнуться** (-нется; -и́пся) pf stick together.

сли́тно adv together, as one word. **сли́ток** (-тка) ingot, bar. **слить** (солью́, -ьёшь; -ил, -á, -о) pf (impf also **слива́ть**) pour, pour out or off; fuse, amalgamate; ~ся flow together; blend; merge.

слича́ть impf, **сличи́ть** (-чу́) pf collate; check. **сличе́ние** collation, checking.

сли́шком adv too; too much.

слия́ние confluence; merging; merger.

слова́к, -а́чка Slovak. **слова́цкий** Slovak.

слова́рный lexical; dictionary. **слова́рь** (-я́) m dictionary; vocabulary. **слове́сность** litera-

ture; philology. **слове́сный** verbal, oral. **сло́вно** *conj* as if; like, as. **сло́во** (*pl* -á) word; **одни́м** ~**м** in a word. **сло́вом** *adv* in a word. **словообразова́ние** word-formation. **словоохо́тливый** talkative. **словосочета́ние** word combination, phrase. **словоупотребле́ние** usage.

слог¹ style.

слог² (*pl* -и́, -óв) syllable.

слоёный flaky.

сложе́ние composition; addition; build, constitution. **сложи́ть** (-жу́, -жишь) *pf* (*impf* **класть**, **скла́дывать**, **слага́ть**) put or lay (together); pile, stack; add, add up; fold (up); compose; take off, put down; lay down; ~**ся** turn out; take shape; arise; club together. **сло́жность** complication; complexity. **сло́жный** (-жен, -жна́, -о) complicated; complex; compound.

слои́стый stratified; flaky. **слой** (*pl* -и́, -ёв) layer; stratum.

слом demolition, pulling down. **с|лома́ть(ся** *pf*. **сломи́ть** (-млю́, -мишь) *pf* (*impf* **сла́мывать**) break (off); overcome; **сломя́ го́лову** at breakneck speed; ~**ся** break.

слон (-á) elephant; bishop. **слони́ха** she-elephant. **слоно́вый** elephant; ~**ая кость** ivory.

слоня́ться *impf* loiter, mooch (about).

слуга́ (*pl* -и) *m* (man) servant. **служа́нка** servant, maid. **слу́жащий** *sb* employee. **слу́жба** service; work. **служе́бный** official; auxiliary; secondary. **служе́ние** service, serving. **служи́ть** (-жу́, -жишь) *impf* (*pf*

по~) serve; work.

с|лука́вить (-влю) *pf*.

слух hearing; ear; rumour; по ~у by ear. **слухово́й** acoustic, auditory, aural; ~**о́й аппара́т** hearing aid; ~**о́е окно́** dormer (window).

слу́чай incident, event; case; opportunity; chance; **ни в ко́ем слу́чае** in no circumstances. **случа́йно** *adv* by chance, accidentally; by any chance. **случа́йность** chance. **случа́йный** accidental; chance; incidental. **случа́ться** *impf*, **случи́ться** *pf* happen.

слу́шание listening; hearing. **слу́шатель** *m* listener; student; *pl* audience. **слу́шать** *impf* (*pf* по~, про~) listen (to); hear; attend lectures on; (я) **слу́шаю!** hello!; very well; ~**ся** +*acc* obey, +*gen* heed.

слыть (-ыву́, -ывёшь; -ыл, -á, -о) *impf* (*pf* про~) have the reputation (+*instr* or за+*acc* for).

слыха́ть *impf*, **слы́шать** (-шу) *impf* (*pf* y~) hear; sense. **слы́шаться** (-шится) *impf* (*pf* по~) be heard. **слы́шимость** audibility. **слы́шимый** audible. **слы́шный** (-шен, -шна́, -шно) audible.

слюда́ mica.

слюна́ (*pl* -и, -éй) saliva; spit; *pl* spittle. **слюня́вый** dribbling.

слягу *etc.*: *see* **слечь**

сля́коть slush.

см. *abbr* (*of* смотри́) see, vide.

сма́зать (-áжу) *pf*, **сма́зывать** *impf* lubricate; grease; slur over. **сма́зка** lubrication; greasing; grease. **сма́зочный** lubricating.

смак relish. **смакова́ть** *impf* relish; savour.

с|маневри́ровать *pf*.

сма́нивать *impf*, **смани́ть** (-ню́, -нишь) *pf* entice.

с|мастери́ть *pf*. **сма́тывать** *impf of* смота́ть

сма́хивать *impf*, **смахну́ть** (-ну́, -нёшь) *pf* brush away or off.

сма́чивать *impf of* смочи́ть

смежный adjacent.

смека́лка native wit.

смёл *etc.: see* смести́

смеле́ть (-е́ю) *impf* (*pf* о∼) grow bolder. **сме́лость** boldness, courage. **сме́лый** (-л, -ла́, -ло) bold, courageous. **смельча́к** (-а́) daredevil.

смелю́ *etc.: see* смоло́ть

сме́на changing; change; replacement(s); relief; shift. **смени́ть** (-ню́, -нишь) *pf*, **сменя́ть**[1] *impf* change; replace; relieve; ∼ся hand over; be relieved; take turns; *+instr* give place to. **сме́нный** shift; changeable. **сме́нщик** relief; *pl* new shift. **сменя́ть**[2] *pf* exchange.

с|ме́рить *pf*.

смерка́ться *impf*, **смеркнуться** (-нется) *pf* get dark.

смерте́льный mortal, fatal; death; extreme. **сме́ртность** mortality. **сме́ртный** mortal; death; deadly, extreme. **смерть** (*gen pl* -е́й) death.

смерч whirlwind; waterspout.

смеси́тельный mixing. **смеси́ть** (-ешу́, -е́сишь) *pf*.

смести́ (-ету́, -етёшь; -ёл, -а́) *pf* (*impf* смета́ть) sweep off, away.

смести́ть (-ещу́) *pf* (*impf* смеща́ть) displace; remove.

смесь mixture; medley.

сме́та estimate.

смета́на sour cream.

с|мета́ть[1] *pf* (*impf also* смёты-

вать) tack (together).

смета́ть[2] *impf of* смести́

смётливый quick, sharp.

смету́ *etc.: see* смести́. **смёты-вать** *impf of* смета́ть

сметь (-е́ю) *impf* (*pf* по∼) dare.

смех laughter; laugh. **смехотво́рный** laughable.

сме́шанный mixed; combined.

с|меша́ть *pf*, **сме́шивать** *impf* mix, blend; confuse; ∼ся mix, (inter)blend; get mixed up. **сме́шение** mixture; mixing up.

смеши́ть (-шу́) *impf* (*pf* на∼, рас∼) make laugh. **смешли́вый** given to laughing. **смешно́й** (-шо́н, -шна́) funny; ridiculous.

смешу́ *etc.: see* смеси́ть, сме-ши́ть

смеща́ть(ся *impf of* смести́ть(ся. **смеще́ние** displacement, removal. **смещу́** *etc.: see* смести́ть

смея́ться (-ею́сь, -еёшься) *impf* laugh (at *+над+instr*).

смире́ние humility, meekness. **смире́нный** humble, meek. **смири́тельный**: ∼ая руба́шка straitjacket. **смири́ть** *pf*, **смиря́ть** *impf* restrain, subdue; ∼ся submit; resign o.s. **сми́рно** *adv* quietly; ∼! attention! **сми́рный** quiet; submissive.

смогу́ *etc.: see* смочь

смола́ (*pl* -ы) resin; pitch, tar; rosin. **смоли́стый** resinous.

смолка́ть *impf*, **смо́лкнуть** (-ну; -олк) *pf* fall silent.

смо́лоду *adv* from one's youth.

с|молоти́ть (-очу́, -о́тишь) *pf*. **с|моло́ть** (смелю́, сме́лешь) *pf*.

смоляно́й resin, pitch, tar.

с|монти́ровать *pf*.

сморка́ть *impf* (*pf* вы́∼) blow;

~ся blow one's nose.

сморо́дина (no pl; usu collect) currant; currants; currant-bush

смо́рщенный wrinkled. **смо́рщить(ся** (-щу(сь) pf.

смота́ть pf (impf **сма́тывать**) wind, reel.

смотр (loc -ý; pl -о́тры) review, inspection. **смотре́ть** (-рю́, -ришь) impf (pf по~) look (at на+acc); see; watch; look through; examine; ~за+instr look after; +в+acc, на+acc look on to; +instr look (like); смотри́(те)! take care!; смотря́ it depends; смотря́ how depending on; ~ся look at o.s. **смотрово́й** observation, inspection.

смочи́ть (-чý, -чишь) pf (impf **сма́чивать**) moisten.

смочь (-огý, -о́жешь; смог, -ла́) pf.

с|моше́нничать pf. смо́ю etc.: see **смыть**

смрад stench. **смра́дный** stinking.

СМС-сообще́ние text message.

сму́глый (-гл, -а́, -о) dark-complexioned, swarthy.

смути́ть (-ущý) pf, **смуща́ть** impf embarrass, confuse; ~ся be embarrassed, be confused. **сму́тный** vague; dim; troubled. **смуще́ние** embarrassment, confusion. **смущённый** (-ён, -á) embarrassed, confused.

смыва́ть impf of **смыть**

смыка́ть(ся impf of **сомкну́ть(ся**

смысл sense; meaning. **смы́слить** impf understand. **смыслово́й** semantic.

смыть (смо́ю) pf (impf **смыва́ть**) wash off, away.

смычо́к (-чка́) bow.

смышлёный clever.

смягчи́ть impf, **смягчи́ть** (-чý) pf soften; alleviate; ~ся soften; relent; grow mild.

смяте́ние confusion; commotion. **с|мя́ть(ся** (сомнý(сь, -нёшь(ся) pf.

снабди́ть (-бжý) pf, **снабжа́ть** impf +instr supply with. **снабже́ние** supply, supplying.

сна́йпер sniper.

снару́жи adv on or from the outside.

снаря́д projectile, missile; shell; contrivance; tackle, gear. **снаряди́ть** (-яжý) pf, **снаряжа́ть** impf equip, fit out. **снаряже́ние** equipment, outfit.

снасть (gen pl -е́й) tackle; pl rigging.

снача́ла adv at first; all over again.

сна́шивать impf of **сноси́ть**

СНГ abbr (of Содру́жества незави́симых госуда́рств) CIS.

снег (loc -ý; pl -á) snow.

снеги́рь (-я́) bullfinch.

снегово́й snow. **снегопа́д** snowfall. **Снегу́рочка** Snow Maiden. **снежи́нка** snow-flake. **сне́жный** snow(y); ~ая ба́ба snowman. **снежо́к** (-жка́) light snow; snowball.

снести́[1] (-сý, -сёшь; -ёс, -ла́) pf (impf **сноси́ть**) take; bring together; bring or fetch down; carry away; blow off; demolish; endure; ~сь communicate (с+instr with).

с|нести́[2](сь (-сý(сь, -сёшь(ся; снёс(ся, -сла́(сь) pf.

снижа́ть impf, **сни́зить** (-и́жу) pf lower; bring down; reduce; ~ся come down; fall. **сниже́ние** lowering; loss of height.

снизойти́ (-йду́, -йдёшь; -ошёл, -шла́) *pf* (*impf* **снисходи́ть**) condescend.

сни́зу *adv* from below.

снима́ть(ся *impf of* **сня́ть(ся. сни́мок** (-мка) photograph. **сниму́** *etc.: see* **снять**

снискать (-ищу́, -и́щешь) *pf*, **сни́скивать** *impf* gain, win.

снисходи́тельность condescension; leniency. **снисходи́тельный** condescending; lenient. **снисходи́ть** (-ожу́, -о́дишь) *impf of* **снизойти́. снисхожде́ние** indulgence, leniency.

сни́ться *impf* (*pf* **при~**) *impers+dat* dream.

сноби́зм snobbery.

сно́ва *adv* again, anew.

снова́ть (сную́, снуёшь) *impf* rush about.

сновиде́ние dream.

сноп (-а́) sheaf.

сноро́вка knack, skill.

снос demolition; drift; wear. **сноси́ть**[1] (-ошу́, -о́сишь) *pf* (*impf* **сна́шивать**) wear out. **сноси́ть**[2] **(ся** (-ошу́(сь, -о́сишь(ся) *impf of* **снести́(сь. сно́ска** footnote. **сно́сно** *adv* tolerably, so-so. **сно́сный** tolerable; fair.

снотво́рный soporific.

сноха́ (*pl* -и) daughter-in-law.

сноше́ние intercourse; relations, dealings.

сношу́ *etc.: see* **сноси́ть**

сня́тие taking down; removal; making. **снять** (сниму́, -и́мешь; -ял, -а́, -о) *pf* (*impf* **снима́ть**) take off; take down; gather in; remove; rent; take; make; photograph; **~ся** come off; move off; be photographed.

со *see* **с** *prep*.

со- *pref* со-, joint. **соа́втор** co-author.

соба́ка dog. **соба́чий** dog's; canine. **соба́чка** little dog; trigger.

соберу́ *etc.: see* **собра́ть**

собе́с *abbr* (*of* социа́льное обеспе́чение) social security (department).

собесе́дник interlocutor, companion. **собесе́дование** conversation.

собира́тель *m* collector. **собира́ть(ся** *impf of* **собра́ть(ся**

соблазни́тель *m*, **~ница** tempter; seducer. **соблазни́тельный** tempting; seductive. **соблазни́ть** *pf*, **соблазня́ть** *impf* tempt; seduce.

соблюда́ть *impf*, **со|блюсти́** (-юду́, -юдёшь; -юл, -а́) *pf* observe; keep (to). **соблюде́ние** observance; maintenance.

собо́й, собо́ю *see* **себя́**

соболе́знование sympathy, condolence(s). **соболе́зновать** *impf +dat* sympathize or commiserate with.

со́боль (*pl* -и *or* -я́) *m* sable.

собо́р cathedral; council, synod. **собо́рный** cathedral.

собра́ние meeting; assembly; collection. **со́бранный** collected; concentrated.

собра́т (*pl* -ья, -ьев) colleague.

собра́ть (-беру́, -берёшь; -ал, -а́, -о) *pf* (*impf* **собира́ть**) gather; collect; **~ся** gather; prepare; intend, be going; **+c+**instr collect.

со́бственник owner, proprietor. **со́бственнический** proprietary; proprietorial. **со́бственно** *adv*: **~** (говоря́) strictly speaking, as a matter of fact. **собственнору́чно** *adv* personally, with one's own hand. **со́б-**

ственность property; ownership. **со́бственный** (one's) own; proper; true; **и́мя ~ое** proper name; **~ои персо́ной** in person.

собы́тие event.

собью́ *etc.*: *see* сбить

сова́ (*pl* -ы) owl.

сова́ть (сую́, -ёшь) *impf* (*pf* су́нуть) thrust, shove; **~ся** push, push in; butt in.

соверша́ть *impf*, **соверши́ть** (-шу́) *pf* accomplish; carry out; commit; complete; **~ся** happen; be accomplished. **соверше́ние** accomplishment; perpetration. **соверше́нно** *adv* perfectly; absolutely, completely. **совершенноле́тие** majority. **совершенноле́тний** of age. **соверше́нный**[1] perfect; absolute, complete. **соверше́нный**[2] perfective. **соверше́нство** perfection. **соверше́нствование** perfecting; improvement. **соверше́нствовать** *impf* (*pf* у~) perfect; improve; **~ся** в+*instr* perfect o.s. in; improve.

со́вестливый conscientious. **со́вестно** *impers+dat* be ashamed. **со́весть** conscience.

сове́т advice, counsel; opinion; council; soviet, Soviet. **сове́тник** adviser. **сове́товать** *impf* (*pf* по~) advise; **~ся** с+*instr* consult, ask advice of. **сове́толог** Kremlinologist. **сове́тский** Soviet; **~ая** власть the Soviet regime; **~ий** Сою́з the Soviet Union. **сове́тчик** adviser.

совеща́ние conference. **совеща́тельный** consultative, deliberative. **совеща́ться** *impf* deliberate; consult.

совлада́ть *pf* с+*instr* control, cope with.

совмести́мый compatible. **совмести́тель** *m* person holding more than one office. **совмести́ть** (-ещу́) *pf*, **совмеща́ть** *impf* combine; **~ся** coincide; be combined, combine. **совме́стно** jointly. **совме́стный** joint, combined.

сово́к (-вка́) shovel; scoop; dustpan.

совокупи́ться (-плю́сь) *pf*, **совокупля́ться** *impf* copulate. **совокупле́ние** copulation. **совоку́пно** *adv* jointly. **совоку́пность** aggregate, sum total.

совпада́ть *impf*, **совпа́сть** (-адёт) *pf* coincide; agree, tally. **совпаде́ние** coincidence.

соврати́ть (-ащу́) *pf* (*impf* совраща́ть) pervert, seduce.

совра́ть (-ру́, -рёшь; -а́л, -а́, -о) *pf*

совраща́ть(ся *impf of* соврати́ть(ся. **совраще́ние** perverting, seduction.

совреме́нник contemporary. **совреме́нность** the present (time); contemporaneity. **совреме́нный** contemporary; modern.

совру́ *etc.*: *see* совра́ть

совсе́м *adv* quite; entirely.

совхо́з State farm.

совью́ *etc.*: *see* свить

согла́сие consent; assent; agreement; harmony. **согласи́ться** (-ашу́сь) *pf* (*impf* согла-ша́ться) consent; agree. **согла́сно** *adv* in accord, in harmony; *prep+dat* in accordance with. **согла́сный**[1] agreeable (to); in agreement; harmonious. **согла́сный**[2] consonant(al); *sb* consonant.

согласова́ние co-ordination; agreement. **согласо́ванность** co-ordination. **согласова́ть** *pf*, **согласо́вывать** *impf* co-ordinate; make agree; **~ся** conform; agree.

соглаша́ться *impf of* **согласи́ться**. **соглаше́ние** agreement. **соглашу́** *etc.*: *see* **согласи́ть**

согна́ть (сгоню́, сго́нишь; -а́л, -а́, -о) *pf* (*impf* **сгоня́ть**) drive away; drive together.

со|гну́ть (-ну́, -нёшь) *pf* (*impf also* **сгиба́ть**) bend, curve; **~ся** bend (down).

согрева́ть *impf*, **согре́ть** (-е́ю) *pf* warm, heat; **~ся** get warm; warm o.s.

со|греши́ть (-шу́) *pf*.

со́да soda.

соде́йствие assistance. **соде́йствовать** *impf & pf* (*pf also* **по~**) +*dat* assist; promote; contribute to.

содержа́ние maintenance, upkeep; content(s); pay. **содержа́тельный** rich in content; pithy. **содержа́ть** (-жу́, -жишь) *impf* keep; maintain; contain; **~ся** be kept; be maintained; be; be contained. **содержи́мое** *sb* contents.

со|дра́ть (сдеру́, -рёшь; -а́л, -а́, -о) *pf* (*impf also* **сдира́ть**) tear off, strip off; fleece.

содрога́ние shudder. **содрога́ться** *impf*, **содрогну́ться** (-ну́сь, -нёшься) *pf* shudder.

содру́жество concord; commonwealth.

соедине́ние joining, combination; joint; compound; formation. **Соединённое Короле́вство** United Kingdom. **Соединённые Шта́ты (Аме́рики)**

m pl United States (of America). **соединённый** (-ён, -а́) united, joint. **соедини́тельный** connective, connecting. **соедини́ть** *pf*, **соединя́ть** *impf* join, unite; connect; combine; **~ся** join, unite; combine.

сожале́ние regret; pity; **к сожале́нию** unfortunately. **сожале́ть** (-е́ю) *impf* regret, deplore.

сожгу́ *etc.*: *see* **сжечь**. **сожже́ние** burning; cremation.

сожи́тель *m*, **~ница** roommate, flat-mate; lover. **сожи́тельство** co-habitation.

сожму́ *etc.*: *see* **сжать²**. **сожну́** *etc.*: *see* **сжать¹**. **созва́ниваться** *impf of* **созвони́ться**

со|зва́ть (-зову́, -зовёшь; -а́л, -а́, -о) *pf* (*impf* **сзыва́ть**, **созыва́ть**) call together; call; invite.

созве́здие constellation.

созвони́ться *pf* (*impf* **созва́ниваться**) ring up; speak on the telephone.

созву́чие accord; assonance. **созву́чный** harmonious; +*dat* in keeping with.

создава́ть (-даю́, -даёшь) *impf*, **созда́ть** (-а́м, -а́шь, -а́ст, -ади́м; со́здал, -а́, -о) *pf* create; establish; **~ся** be created; arise, spring up. **созда́ние** creation; work; creature. **созда́тель** *m* creator; originator.

созерца́ние contemplation. **созерца́тельный** contemplative. **созерца́ть** *impf* contemplate.

созида́ние creation. **созида́тельный** creative.

сознава́ть (-наю́, -наёшь) *impf*, **созна́ть** *pf* be conscious of, realize; acknowledge; **~ся** confess. **созна́ние** consciousness; acknowledgement; confession.

созна́тельность awareness, consciousness. **созна́тельный** conscious; deliberate.

созову́ etc.: see **созва́ть**

созрева́ть impf, **со|зре́ть** (-е́ю) pf ripen, mature.

созы́в summoning, calling. **созыва́ть** impf of **созва́ть**

соизмери́мый commensurable.

соиска́ние competition. **соиска́тель** m, **~ница** competitor, candidate.

сойти́ (-йду́, -йдёшь; сошёл, -шла́) pf (impf **сходи́ть**) go or come down; get off; leave; come off; pass, go off; ~ **с ума́** go mad, go out of one's mind; **~сь** meet; gather; become friends; become intimate; agree.

сок (loc -ý) juice.

со́кол falcon.

сократи́ть (-ащу́) pf, **сокра|ща́ть** impf shorten; abbreviate; reduce; **~ся** grow shorter; decrease; contract. **сокраще́ние** shortening; abridgement; abbreviation; reduction.

сокрове́нный secret; innermost. **сокро́вище** treasure. **сокро́вищница** treasure-house.

сокруша́ть impf, **сокруши́ть** (-шу́) pf shatter; smash; distress; **~ся** grieve, be distressed. **сокруше́ние** smashing; grief. **сокрушённый** (-ён, -а́) griefstricken. **сокруши́тельный** shattering.

сокры́тие concealment.

со|лга́ть (-лгу́, -лжёшь; -а́л, -а́, -о) pf.

солда́т (gen pl -а́т) soldier. **солда́тский** soldier's.

соле́ние salting; pickling. **солёный** (со́лон, -а́, -о) salt(y);

salted; pickled. **соле́нье** salted food(s); pickles.

солида́рность solidarity. **соли́дный** solid; strong; reliable; respectable; sizeable.

соли́ст, соли́стка soloist.

соли́ть (-лю́, со́лишь) impf (pf по~) salt; pickle.

со́лнечный sun; solar; sunny; ~ **свет** sunlight; sunshine; ~ **уда́р** sunstroke. **со́лнце** sun. **солнцепёк: на ~е** in the sun. **солнцестоя́ние** solstice.

со́ло neut indecl solo; adv solo.

солове́й (-вья́) nightingale.

со́лод malt.

соло́дковый liquorice.

соло́ма straw; thatch. **соло́менный** straw; thatch. **соло́минка** straw.

со́лон etc.: see **солёный**. **солони́на** corned beef. **соло́нка** salt-cellar. **солонча́к** (-а́) saline soil; pl salt marshes. **соль** (pl -и, -е́й) salt.

со́льный solo.

солью́ etc.: see **слить**

соля́ной, соляно́й salt, saline; **соляна́я кислота́** hydrochloric acid.

со́мкнутый close. **сомкну́ть** (-ну́, -нёшь) pf (impf **смыка́ть**) close; **~ся** close.

сомнева́ться impf doubt, have doubts. **сомне́ние** doubt. **сомни́тельный** doubtful.

сомну́ etc.: see **смять**

сон (сна) sleep; dream. **сонли́вость** sleepiness; somnolence. **сонли́вый** sleepy. **со́нный** sleepy; sleeping.

сона́та sonata.

соне́т sonnet.

соображáть impf, **сообрази́ть** (-ажу́) pf consider, think out;

weigh; understand. **соображе́ние** consideration; understanding; notion. **сообрази́тельный** quick-witted.

сообра́зный adv c+instr conforming to, in keeping with.

сообща́ adv together. **сообща́ть** impf, **сообщи́ть** (-щу́) pf communicate, report, announce; impart; pf inform. **сообще́ние** communication, report; announcement. **сообще́ство** association. **сообщни́к** accomplice.

сооруди́ть (-ужу́) pf, **сооружа́ть** impf build, erect. **сооруже́ние** building; structure.

соотве́тственно adv accordingly, correspondingly; prep +dat according to, in accordance with. **соотве́тственный** corresponding. **соотве́тствие** accordance, correspondence. **соотве́тствовать** impf correspond, conform. **соотве́тствующий** corresponding; suitable.

соотéчественник fellow-countryman.

соотноше́ние correlation.

сопе́рник rival. **сопе́рничать** impf compete, vie. **сопе́рничество** rivalry.

сопе́ть (-плю́) impf wheeze; snuffle.

со́пка hill, mound.

сопли́вый snotty.

сопоста́вить (-влю) pf, **сопоставля́ть** impf compare. **сопоставле́ние** comparison.

сопреде́льный contiguous.

со|пре́ть pf.

соприкаса́ться impf, **соприкосну́ться** (-ну́сь, -нёшься) pf adjoin; come into contact. **соприкоснове́ние** contact.

сопроводи́тельный accompanying. **сопроводи́ть** (-ожу́) pf, **сопровожда́ть** impf accompany; escort. **сопровожде́ние** accompaniment; escort.

сопротивле́ние resistance. **сопротивля́ться** impf +dat resist, oppose.

сопу́тствовать impf +dat accompany.

сопью́сь etc.: see **спи́ться**

сор litter, rubbish.

соразме́рить pf, **соразмеря́ть** impf balance, match. **соразме́рный** proportionate, commensurate.

сора́тник comrade-in-arms.

сорва́ть (-ву́, -вёшь; -а́л, -а́, -о) pf (impf **срыва́ть**) tear off, away, down; break off; pick; get; break; ruin, spoil; vent; ~ся break away, break loose; fall, come down; fall through.

с|организова́ть pf.

соревнова́ние competition; contest. **соревнова́ться** impf compete.

сори́ть impf (pf **на**~) +acc or instr litter; throw about. **со́рный** rubbish, refuse; ~ая трава́ weed(s). **сорня́к** (-а́) weed.

со́рок (-а́) forty.

соро́ка magpie.

сорокова́|ой fortieth; ~ые го́ды the forties.

соро́чка shirt; blouse; shift.

сорт (pl -а́) grade, quality; sort. **сортирова́ть** impf (pf рас~) sort, grade. **сортиро́вка** sorting. **сортиро́вочный** sorting; ~ая sb marshalling-yard. **сортиро́вщик** sorter. **со́ртный** high quality.

соса́ть (-су́, -сёшь) impf suck.

со|сва́тать pf.

сосе́д (*pl* -и, -е́й, -я́м), **сосе́дка** neighbour. **сосе́дний** neighbouring; adjacent, next. **сосе́дский** neighbours'. **сосе́дство** neighbourhood. **соси́ска** frankfurter, sausage.

со́ска (*baby's*) dummy.

соска́кивать *impf of* **соскочи́ть**

соска́льзывать *impf*, **соскользну́ть** (-ну́, -нёшь) *pf* slide down, slide off.

соскочи́ть (-чу́, -чишь) *pf* (*impf* **соска́кивать**) jump off *or* down; come off.

соску́читься (-чусь) *pf* get bored; **~по**+*dat* miss.

сослага́тельный subjunctive.

сосла́ть (сошлю́, -лёшь) *pf* (*impf* **ссыла́ть**) exile, deport; **~ся на**+*acc* refer to; cite; plead, allege.

сосло́вие estate; class.

сослужи́вец (-вца) colleague.

сосна́ (*pl* -ы, -сен) pine(-tree). **сосно́вый** pine; deal.

сосо́к (-ска́) nipple, teat.

сосредото́ченный concentrated. **сосредото́чивать** *impf*, **сосредото́чить** (-чу) *pf* concentrate; focus; **~ся** concentrate.

соста́в composition; structure; compound; staff; strength; train; в **~е** +*gen* consisting of. **составитель** *m* compiler. **соста́вить** (-влю) *pf*, **составля́ть** *impf* put together; make (up); draw up; compile; be, constitute; total; **~ся** form, be formed. **составно́й** compound; component, constituent.

со|ста́рить(ся *pf*.

состоя́ние state, condition; fortune. **состоя́тельный** well-to-do; well-grounded. **со-**

стоя́ть (-ою́) *impf* be; +*из*+*gen* consist of; +*в*+*prep* consist in, be. **состоя́ться** (-о́йтся) *pf* take place.

сострада́ние compassion. **сострада́тельный** compassionate.

с|остри́ть *pf*. **со|стря́пать** *pf*.

со|стыкова́ться *pf*, **состыко́вываться** *impf* dock.

состяза́ние competition, contest. **состяза́ться** *impf* compete.

сосу́д vessel.

сосу́лька icicle.

сосуществова́ние co-existence.

со|счита́ть *pf*. **сот** *see* **сто**.

сотворе́ние creation. **со|твори́ть** *pf*.

сотка́ть (-ку́, -кёшь; -а́л, -ала́, -о) *pf*.

со́тня (*gen pl* -тен) a hundred.

со́товый cellular; **~ телефо́н** mobile phone, cell phone.

сотру́ *etc.*: *see* **стере́ть**

сотру́дник collaborator; colleague; employee. **сотру́дничать** *impf* collaborate; +*в*+*prep* contribute to. **сотру́дничество** collaboration.

сотряса́ть *impf*, **сотрясти́** (-су́, -сёшь; -я́с, -ла́) *pf* shake; **~ся** tremble. **сотрясе́ние** shaking; concussion.

со́ты (-ов) *pl* honeycomb.

со́тый hundredth.

со́ус sauce; gravy; dressing.

соуча́стие participation; complicity. **соуча́стник** participant; accomplice.

софа́ (*pl* -ы) sofa.

соха́ (*pl* -и) (*wooden*) plough.

со́хнуть (-ну; сох) *impf* (*pf* **вы́-**, **за-**, **про-**) (get) dry; wither.

сохране́ние preservation; con-

servation; (safe)keeping; retention. **сохрани́ть** pf, **сохраня́ть** impf preserve, keep; ~ся remain (intact); last out; be well preserved. **сохра́нный** safe.

социа́л-демокра́т Social Democrat. **социа́л-демократи́ческий** Social Democratic. **социали́зм** socialism. **социали́ст** socialist. **социалисти́ческий** socialist. **социа́льный** social; ~ое обеспе́чение social security. **социо́лог** sociologist. **социоло́гия** sociology.

соцреали́зм socialist realism.

сочета́ние combination. **сочета́ть** impf & pf combine; ~ся combine; harmonize; match.

сочине́ние composition; work. **сочини́ть** pf, **сочиня́ть** impf compose; write; make up.

сочи́ться (-и́тся) impf ooze (out), trickle; ~ кро́вью bleed.

со́чный (-чен, -чна́, -о) juicy; rich.

сочту́ etc.: see **счесть**

сочу́вствие sympathy. **сочу́вствовать** impf +dat sympathize with.

сошёл etc.: see **сойти́**. **сошлю́** etc.: see **сосла́ть**. **сошью́** etc.: see **сшить**

сощу́ривать impf, **сощу́рить** pf screw up, narrow; ~ся screw up one's eyes; narrow.

сою́з[1] union; alliance; league. **сою́з**[2] conjunction. **сою́зник** ally. **сою́зный** allied; Union.

спад recession; abatement. **спада́ть** impf of **спасть**

спазм spasm.

спа́ивать impf of **спая́ть**, **спои́ть**

спа́йка soldered joint; solidarity, unity.

спали́ть pf.

спа́льный sleeping; ~ый ваго́н sleeping car; ~ое ме́сто berth. **спа́льня** (gen pl -лен) bedroom.

спа́ржа asparagus.

спартакиа́да sports meeting.

спаса́тельный rescue; ~ жиле́т life jacket; ~ круг lifebuoy; ~ по́яс lifebelt. **спаса́ть(ся** impf of **спасти́(сь**. **спасе́ние** rescue, escape; salvation.

спаси́бо thank you. **спаси́тель** m rescuer; saviour. **спаси́тельный** saving; salutary.

спасти́ (-су́, -сёшь; спас, -ла́) pf (impf **спаса́ть**) save; rescue; ~сь be saved.

спасть (-адёт) pf (impf **спада́ть**) fall (down); abate.

спать (сплю; -ал, -а́, -о) impf sleep; лечь ~ go to bed.

спа́янность cohesion, unity. **спа́янный** united. **спая́ть** pf (impf **спа́ивать**) solder, weld; unite.

спекта́кль m performance; show.

спектр spectrum.

спекули́ровать impf speculate. **спекуля́нт** speculator, profiteer. **спекуля́ция** speculation; profiteering.

спе́лый ripe.

сперва́ adv at first; first.

спе́реди adv in front, from the front; prep+gen (from) in front of.

спёртый close, stuffy.

спеси́вый arrogant, haughty. **спесь** arrogance, haughtiness.

спеть[1] (-е́ет) impf (pf по~) ripen.

спеть[2] (спою́, споёшь) pf.

спец- abbr in comb (of спе-

циа́льный) special. **спецко́р** special correspondent. ∼**оде́жда** protective clothing; overalls.

специализа́ция specialization. **специализи́роваться** *impf & pf* specialize. **специали́ст, -ка** specialist, expert. **специа́льность** speciality; profession. **специа́льный** special; specialist.

специфика specific character. **специфи́ческий** specific.

спе́ция spice.

спецо́вка protective clothing; overall(s).

спеши́ть (-шу́) *impf* (*pf* по∼) hurry, be in a hurry; be fast. **спе́шка** hurry, haste. **спе́шный** urgent.

спива́ться *impf of* спи́ться

СПИД *abbr* (*of* синдром приобре́тенного имму́нного дефици́та) Aids.

спики́ровать *pf.*

спи́ливать *impf*, **спили́ть** (-лю́, -лишь) *pf* saw down, off.

спина́ (*acc* -у; *pl* -ы) back. **спи́нка** back. **спинно́й** spinal; ∼ **мозг** spinal cord.

спира́ль spiral.

спирт alcohol, spirit(s). **спиртно́й** alcoholic; ∼**о́е** *sb* alcohol. **спиртовка** spirit-stove. **спиртово́й** spirit, alcoholic.

списа́ть (-ишу́, -и́шешь) *pf*, **спи́сывать** *impf* copy; ∼**ся** exchange letters. **спи́сок** (-ска) list; record.

спи́ться (сопью́сь, -ьёшься; -и́лся, -а́сь) *pf* (*impf* спива́ться) take to drink.

спи́хивать *impf*, **спихну́ть** (-ну́, -нёшь) *pf* push aside, down. **спи́ца** knitting-needle; spoke.

спи́чечн|ый match; ∼**ая ко-**

ро́бка match-box. **спи́чка** match.

спишу́ *etc.: see* списа́ть

сплав[1] floating. **сплав**[2] alloy. **спла́вить**[1] (-влю) *pf*, **спла-вля́ть**[1] *impf* float; raft; get rid of. **спла́вить**[2] (-влю) *pf*, **спла-вля́ть**[2] *impf* alloy; ∼**ся** fuse.

с|плани́ровать *pf*. **спла́чи-вать(ся** *impf of* сплоти́ть(ся.

сплеву́ть *impf of* сплю́нуть

с|плести́ (-ету́, -етёшь; -ёл, -á) *pf*, **сплета́ть** *impf* weave; plait; interlace. **сплете́ние** interlacing; plexus.

спле́тник, -ница gossip, scandalmonger. **спле́тничать** *impf* (*pf* на∼) gossip. **спле́тня** (*gen pl* -тен) gossip, scandal.

сплоти́ть (-очу́) *pf* (*impf* спла́-чивать) join; unite, rally; ∼**ся** unite, rally; close ranks. **спло-че́ние** uniting. **сплочённость** cohesion, unity. **сплочённый** (-ён, -á) united; firm; unbroken.

сплошно́й solid; complete; continuous; utter. **сплошь** *adv* all over; completely; ∼ **да ря́дом** pretty often.

сплю *see* спать

сплю́нуть (-ну) *pf* (*impf* сплёвывать) spit; spit out.

сплю́щивать(ся *impf*, **сплю́щить** (-щу) *pf* flatten; ∼**ся** become flat.

с|пляса́ть (-яшу́, -я́шешь) *pf*.

сподви́жник comrade-in-arms.

спо́ить (-ою́, -о́ишь) *pf* (*impf* спа́ивать) make a drunkard of.

споко́йн|ый quiet; calm; ∼**ой но́чи** good night! **споко́йствие** quiet; calm, serenity.

спола́скивать *impf of* сполосну́ть

сполза́ть *impf*, **сползти́** (-зу́,

-зёшь; -олз, -ла́) pf climb down; slip (down); fall away.

сполна́ adv in full.

сполосну́ть (-ну́, -нёшь) pf (impf спола́скивать) rinse.

спо́нсор sponsor, backer.

спор argument; controversy; dispute. **спо́рить** (pf по~) argue; dispute; debate. **спо́рный** debatable, questionable; disputed; moot.

спо́ра spore.

спорт sport. **спорти́вный** sports; ~ **зал** gymnasium. **спортсме́н**, **~ка** athlete, player.

спо́соб way, method; таки́м ~ом in this way. **спосо́бность** ability, aptitude; capacity. **спосо́бный** able; clever; capable. **спосо́бствовать** impf (pf по~) +dat assist; further.

споткну́ться (-ну́сь, -нёшься) pf, **спотыка́ться** impf stumble.

спохвати́ться (-ачу́сь, -а́тишься) pf, **спохва́тываться** impf remember suddenly.

спою́ etc.: see **спеть, спои́ть**

спра́ва adv to or on the right.

справедли́вость justice; fairness; truth. **справедли́вый** just; fair; justified.

спра́вить (-влю) pf, **справля́ть** impf celebrate. **спра́виться** (-влюсь) pf, **справля́ться** impf с+instr cope with, manage. **спра́виться²** (-влюсь) pf, **справля́ться** impf inquire; +в+prep consult. **спра́вка** information; reference; certificate; наводи́ть **спра́вку** make inquiries. **спра́вочник** reference-book, directory. **спра́вочный** inquiry, reference.

спра́шивать(ся impf of **спроси́ть(ся**

спринт sprint. **спри́нтер** sprinter.

с|провоци́ровать pf. с|проекти́ровать pf.

спрос demand; asking; без ~у without permission. **спроси́ть** (-ошу́, -о́сишь) pf (impf спра́шивать) ask (for); inquire; ~ся ask permission.

спрут octopus.

спры́гивать impf, **спры́гнуть** (-ну) pf jump off, jump down.

спры́скивать impf, **спры́снуть** (-ну) pf sprinkle.

спряга́ть (pf про~) conjugate. **спряже́ние** conjugation.

с|прясть (-яду́, -ядёшь; -ял, -а́ла, -о) pf. с|пря́таться(ся (-я́чу(сь) pf.

спу́гивать impf, **спугну́ть** (-ну́, -нёшь) pf frighten off.

спуск lowering; descent; slope. **спуска́ть** impf, **спусти́ть** (-ущу́, -у́стишь) pf let down, lower; release; let out; send out; go down; forgive; squander; ~ кора́бль launch a ship; ~ куро́к pull the trigger; ~ пе́тлю drop a stitch; ~ся go down, descend. **спускно́й** drain. **спусково́й** trigger. **спустя́** prep+acc after; adv later.

с|пу́тать(ся pf.

спу́тник satellite, sputnik; (travelling) companion.

спущу́ etc.: see **спусти́ть**

спя́чка hibernation; sleepiness.

ср. abbr (of **сравни́**) cf.

сраба́тывать impf, **срабо́тать** pf make; work, operate.

сравне́ние comparison; simile. **сра́внивать** impf of **сравни́ть, сравня́ть**. **сравни́мый** comparable. **сравни́тельно** adv comparatively. **сравни́тельный** comparative. **сравни́ть** pf (impf **сра́внивать**) compare; ~ся

с+*instr* compare with. с|рав-
ня́ть *pf* (*impf also* сра́внивать)
make even, equal; level.

сража́ть *impf*, срази́ть (-ажу́) *pf*
strike down; overwhelm, crush;
~ся fight. сраже́ние battle.

сра́зу *adv* at once.

срам shame. срами́ть (-млю)
impf (*pf* o~) shame; ~ся cover
o.s. with shame. срамота́
shame.

сраста́ние growing together.
сраста́ться *impf*, срасти́сь
(-тётся; сро́сся, -ла́сь) *pf* grow
together; knit.

среда́¹ (*pl* -ы) environment, surroundings; medium. среда́²
(*acc* -у; *pl* -ы, -ам *or* -ам) Wednesday. среди́ *prep*+*gen* among; in
the middle of; ~ бе́ла дня in
broad daylight. средиземно-
мо́рский Mediterranean.
сре́дне *adv* so-so. средневеко́-
вый *medieval*. средневеко́вье
the Middle Ages. сре́дний middle;
medium; mean; average;
middling; secondary; neuter;
~ее *sb* mean, average. средо-
то́чие focus. сре́дство means;
remedy.

срез cut; section; slice. с|ре́зать
(-е́жу) *pf*, среза́ть *impf* cut off;
slice; fail; ~ся fail.

с|репети́ровать *pf*.

срисова́ть *pf*, сри́совывать
impf copy.

с|ровня́ть *pf*.

сро́дно etc.: *see* срасти́сь

сро́чно *adv* urgently. сро́ч-
ность urgency. сро́чный urgent; for a fixed period.

сро́ю etc.: *see* срыть

сруб felling; framework. сру-

ба́ть *impf*, с|руби́ть (-блю́,
-бишь) *pf* cut down; build (*of*
logs).

срыв disruption; breakdown;
ruining. срыва́ть¹(ся *impf of*
сорва́ть(ся

срыва́ть² *impf*, срыть (сро́ю)
pf raze to the ground.

сря́ду *adv* running.

сса́дина scratch. ссади́ть
(-ажу́, -а́дишь) *pf*, сса́живать
impf set down; help down; turn
off.

ссо́ра quarrel. ссо́рить *impf*
(*pf* по~) cause to quarrel; ~ся
quarrel.

СССР *abbr* (*of* Сою́з Сове́тских
Социалисти́ческих Респу́блик)
USSR.

ссу́да loan. ссуди́ть (-ужу́,
-у́дишь) *pf*, ссужа́ть *impf* lend,
loan.

ссыла́ть(ся *impf of* сосла́ть(ся.
ссы́лка¹ exile. ссы́лка² reference. ссы́льный, ссы́льная *sb*
exile.

ссыпа́ть (-плю) *pf*, ссыпа́ть
impf pour.

стабилиза́тор stabilizer; tail-
plane. стабилизи́ровать(ся
impf & pf stabilize. стаби́ль-
ность stability. стаби́льный
stable, firm.

ста́вень (-вня; *gen pl* -вней) *m*,
ста́вня (*gen pl* -вен) shutter.

ста́вить (-влю) *impf* (*pf* по~)
put, place, set; stand; station;
erect; install; apply; present,
stage. ста́вка¹ rate; stake.
ста́вка² headquarters.

ста́вня *see* ста́вень

стадио́н stadium.

ста́дия stage.

ста́дность herd instinct. ста́д-
ный gregarious. ста́до (*pl* -а́)
herd, flock.

стаж length of service; probation. **стажёр** probationer; student on a special non-degree course. **стажиро́вка** period of training.

стака́н glass.

сталелите́йный steel-founding; ~ заво́д steel foundry. **сталепла́вильный** steelmaking; ~ заво́д steel works. **сталепрока́тный** (steel-)rolling; ~ стан rolling-mill.

ста́лкивать(ся impf of **столкну́ть(ся**

ста́ло быть conj consequently.

сталь steel. **стально́й** steel.

стаме́ска chisel.

стан¹ figure, torso.

стан² camp.

стан³ mill.

станда́рт standard. **станда́ртный** standard.

стани́ца Cossack village.

станкостроє́ние machine-tool engineering.

станови́ться (-влю́сь, -вишься) impf of **стать¹**

стано́к (-нка́) machine tool, machine.

ста́ну etc.: see **стать²**

станцио́нный station. **ста́нция** station.

ста́пель (pl -я́) m stocks.

ста́птывать(ся impf of **стопта́ть(ся**

стара́ние effort. **стара́тельность** diligence. **стара́тельный** diligent. **стара́ться** impf (pf по~) try.

старе́ть impf (pf по~, у~) grow old. **ста́рец** (-рца) elder, (venerable) old man. **старик** (-а́) old man. **старина́** antiquity, olden times; antique(s); old fellow.

стари́нный ancient; old; antique. **ста́рить** impf (pf co~) age, make old; ~ся age, grow old.

старо- in comb old. **старове́р** Old Believer. ~жи́л old resident. ~мо́дный old-fashioned. ~славя́нский Old Slavonic. ~ста́рть starting.

ста́роста head; monitor; churchwarden. **ста́рость** old age.

старт start; на ~! on your marks! **старте́р** starter. **стартова́ть** impf & pf start. **ста́ртовый** starting.

стару́ха, стару́шка old woman. **ста́рческий** old man's; senile. **ста́рше** comp of **ста́рый**. **ста́рший** oldest; elder, elder; senior; head; ~ие sb pl (one's) elders; ~ий sb chief; man in charge. **старшина́** m sergeant-major; petty officer; leader. **ста́рый** (-ар, -á, -o) old. **старьё** old things, junk.

ста́скивать impf of **стащи́ть**

с|тасова́ть pf.

стати́ст extra.

стати́стика statistics. **стати́стический** statistical.

ста́тный stately.

ста́тский civil, civilian.

ста́тус status. **ста́тус-кво** neut indecl status quo.

статуэ́тка statuette.

ста́туя statue.

стать¹ (-а́ну) pf (impf станови́ться) stand; take up position; stop; cost; begin; +instr become; +c+instr become of; не ~ impers+gen cease to be; disappear; его́ не ста́ло he is no more; ~ на коле́ни kneel.

стать² physique, build.

ста́ться (-а́нется) pf happen.

статья́ (gen pl -е́й) article;

clause; item; matter.

стациона́р permanent establishment; hospital. **стациона́рный** stationary; permanent; ∼ **больно́й** in-patient.

ста́чечник striker. **ста́чка** strike.

стащи́ть (-щу́, -щишь) *pf* (*impf also* **ста́скивать**) drag off, pull off.

ста́я flock; school, shoal; pack.

ствол (-á) trunk; barrel.

ство́рка leaf, fold.

сте́бель (-бля; *gen pl* -бле́й) *m* stem, stalk.

стёган|ый quilted; ∼**ое одея́ло** quilt, duvet. **стега́ть¹** *impf* (*pf* **вы́∼**) quilt.

стега́ть² *impf*, **стегну́ть** (-ну́) *pf* (*pf also* **от∼**) whip, lash.

стежо́к (-жка́) stitch.

стезя́ path, way.

стёк *etc.: see* **стечь**. **стека́ть(ся** *impf of* **стечь(ся**

стекло́ (*pl* -ёкла, -кол) glass; lens; (window-)pane.

стекло- *in comb* glass. **стекло-воло́кно** glass fibre. ∼**очисти́тель** *m* windscreen-wiper. ∼**ре́з** glass-cutter. ∼**ткань** fibreglass.

стекля́нный glassy, glassy. **стеко́льщик** glazier.

стели́ть *see* **стлать**

стелла́ж (-á) shelves, shelving.

сте́лька insole.

стелю́ *etc.: see* **стлать**

стемне́ть (-е́ет) *pf*

стена́ (*acc* -у; *pl* -ы, -áм) wall.

стенгазе́та wall newspaper.

стенд stand.

сте́нка wall; side. **стенно́й** wall.

стеногра́мма shorthand record. **стено́граф**, **стеногра́фист**, ∼**ка** stenographer. **сте-**

нографи́ровать *impf* & *pf* take down in shorthand. **стеногра-фи́ческий** shorthand. **стено-гра́фия** shorthand.

стенокарди́я angina.

степе́нный staid; middle-aged.

сте́пень (*gen pl* -éй) degree; extent; power.

степно́й steppe. **степь** (*loc* -и́; *gen pl* -éй) steppe.

стервя́тник vulture.

стерегу́ *etc.: see* **стере́чь**

сте́рео *indecl adj* stereo. **сте́рео-** *in comb* stereo. **стерео-ти́п** stereotype. **стереоти́пный** stereotype(d). **стереофони́ческий** stereo(phonic). ∼**фо́ния** stereo(phony).

стере́ть (сотру́, сотрёшь; стёр) *pf* (*impf* **стира́ть¹**) wipe off, rub out, rub sore; ∼**ся** rub off; wear down; be effaced.

стере́чь (-регу́, -режёшь; -ёг, -ла́) *impf* guard; watch for.

сте́ржень (-жня) *m* pivot; rod; core.

стерилизова́ть *impf* & *pf* sterilize. **стери́льный** sterile.

стерлинг sterling.

стерля́дь (*gen pl* -éй) sterlet.

стерпе́ть (-плю́, -пишь) *pf* bear, endure.

стёртый worn, effaced.

стесне́ние constraint. **стесни́тельный** shy; inconvenient. **стесни́ть** *pf*, **стесня́ть** *impf* constrain; hamper; inhibit. **стесни́ться** *pf*, **стесня́ться** *impf* (*pf also* **по∼**) +*inf* feel too shy (to), be ashamed to.

стече́ние confluence; gathering; combination. **стечь** (-чёт, -ёк, -ла́) *pf* (*impf* **стека́ть**) flow down; ∼**ся** flow together; gather.

стилисти́ческий stylistic.

стиль *m* style. сти́льный stylish; period.

сти́мул stimulus, incentive. стимули́ровать *impf & pf* stimulate.

стипе́ндия grant.

стира́льный washing.

стира́ть¹(ся *impf of* стере́ть(ся

стира́ть² *impf* (*pf* вы́~) wash, launder; ~ся wash. сти́рка washing, wash, laundering.

сти́скивать *impf*, сти́снуть (-ну) *pf* squeeze; clench; hug.

стих (-á) verse; line; *pl* poetry.

стиха́ть *impf of* сти́хнуть

стихи́йный elemental; spontaneous. стихи́я element.

сти́хнуть (-ну; стих) *pf* (*impf* стиха́ть) subside; calm down.

стихотворе́ние poem. стихотво́рный in verse form.

стлать, стели́ть (стелю́, сте́лешь) *impf* (*pf* по~) spread; ~ постель make a bed; ~ся spread; creep.

сто (ста; *gen pl* сот) a hundred.

стог (*loc* -е & -ý; *pl* -á) stack, rick.

сто́имость cost; value. сто́ить *impf* cost; be worth(while); deserve.

стой *see* стоя́ть

сто́йка counter, bar; prop; upright; strut. сто́йкий firm; stable; steadfast. сто́йкость firmness, stability; steadfastness. сто́йло stall. стоймя́ *adv* upright.

сток flow; drainage; drain, gutter; sewer.

стол (-á) table; desk; cuisine.

столб (-á) post, pole, pillar, column. столбене́ть (-е́ю) *impf* (*pf* о~) be rooted to the ground. столбня́к (-á) stupor; tetanus.

столе́тие century; centenary. столе́тний hundred-year-old; of a hundred years.

столи́ца capital; metropolis. столи́чный (of the) capital.

столкнове́ние collision; clash. столкну́ть (-ну́, -нёшь) *pf* (*impf* ста́лкивать) push off, away; cause to collide; bring together; ~ся collide, clash; +с+*instr* run into.

столо́вая *sb* dining-room; canteen. столо́вый table.

столп (-á) pillar.

столпи́ться *pf* crowd.

столь *adv* so. сто́лько *adv* so much, so many.

столя́р (-á) joiner, carpenter. столя́рный joiner's.

стомато́лог dentist.

стометро́вка (the) hundred metres.

стон groan. стона́ть (-ну́, -нешь) *impf* groan.

стоп! *int* stop!

стопа́¹ foot.

стопа́² (*pl* -ы) ream; pile.

сто́пка¹ pile.

сто́пка² small glass.

сто́пор stop, catch. сто́пориться *impf* (*pf* за~) come to a stop.

стопроце́нтный hundred-percent.

стоп-сигна́л brake-light.

стопта́ть (-пчу́, -пчешь) *pf* (*impf* ста́птывать) wear down; ~ся wear down.

с|торгова́ть(ся *pf*.

сто́рож (*pl* -á) watchman, guard. сторожево́й watch; patrol-. сторожи́ть (-жу́) *impf* guard, watch (over).

сторона́ (*acc* сто́рону; *pl* сто́роны, -ро́н, -áм) side; direction; hand; feature; part; land; в сто́-

рону aside; **с мое́й стороны́** for my part; **с одно́й стороны́** on the one hand. **сторони́ться** (-ню́сь, -ни́шься) *impf* (*pf* по~) stand aside; +*gen* avoid. **сто́ронник** supporter, advocate.

сто́чный sewage, drainage.

стоя́нка stop; parking; stopping place, parking space; stand; rank. **стоя́ть** (-ою́) *impf* stand; be; stay; stop; have stopped; +*за*+*acc* stand up for; ~ **на коле́нях** kneel. **стоя́чий** standing; upright; stagnant.

стоя́щий deserving; worthwhile.

стр. *abbr* (*of* страни́ца) page.

страда́ (*pl* -ды) (hard work at harvest time).

страда́лец (-льца) sufferer. **страда́ние** suffering. **страда́тельный** passive. **страда́ть** (-а́ю *or* -ра́жду) *impf* (*pf* по~) suffer; ~ **за** +*gen* feel for.

стра́жа guard, watch; **под стра́жей** under arrest, in custody; **стоя́ть на стра́же** +*gen* guard.

страна́ (*pl* -ы) country; land; ~ **све́та** cardinal point.

страни́ца page.

стра́нник, **стра́нница** wanderer.

стра́нно *adv* strangely. **стра́нность** strangeness; eccentricity. **стра́нн ый** (-а́нен, -анна́, -о) strange.

стра́нствие wandering. **стра́нствовать** *impf* wander.

Страстн о́й of Holy Week; ~ **а́я пя́тница** Good Friday.

стра́стный (-тен, -тна́, -о) passionate. **страсть**[1] (*pl* -и) passion. **страсть**[2] *adv* awfully, frightfully.

стратеги́ческий strategic(al). **страте́гия** strategy.

стратосфе́ра stratosphere.

стра́ус ostrich.

страх fear.

страхова́ние insurance; ~ **жи́зни** life insurance. **страхова́ть** *impf* (*pf* за~) insure (**от**+*gen* against); ~**ся** insure o.s. **страхо́вка** insurance.

страши́ться (-шу́сь) *impf* +*gen* be afraid of. **стра́шно** *adv* awfully. **стра́шн ый** (-шен, -шна́, -о) terrible, awful.

стрекоза́ (*pl* -ы) dragonfly.

стрекота́ть (-очу́, -о́чешь) *impf* chirr.

стрела́ (*pl* -ы) arrow; boom. **стреле́ц** (-льца́) Sagittarius. **стре́лка** pointer; hand; needle; arrow; spit; hand. **стрелко́вый** rifle; shooting; infantry. **стрело́к** (-лка́) shot; rifleman, gunner. **стре́лочник** pointsman. **стрельба́** (*pl* -ы) shooting, firing. **стре́льчатый** lancet; arched. **стреля́ть** *impf* shoot; fire; ~**ся** shoot o.s.; fight a duel.

стремгла́в *adv* headlong.

стреми́тельный swift; impetuous. **стреми́ться** (-млю́сь) *impf* strive. **стремле́ние** striving, aspiration. **стремни́на** rapid(s).

стре́мя (-мени; *pl* -мена́, -мя́н, -а́м) *neut* stirrup. **стремя́нка** step-ladder.

стресс stress. **стре́ссовый** stressful, stressed.

стри́женый short; short-haired; cropped; shorn. **стри́жка** hair-cut; shearing. **стричь** (-игу́, -иже́шь; -иг) *impf* (*pf* о~) cut, clip the hair of; shear; ~**ся** have one's hair cut.

строга́ть *impf* (*pf* вы́~) plane, shave.

стро́гий strict; severe. **стро́-**

гость strictness.

строево́й combatant; line; drill.

строе́ние building; structure; composition.

строжа́йший, стро́же superl & comp of **стро́гий**

строи́тель m builder. **строи́тельный** building, construction. **строи́тельство** building, construction; building site. **стро́ить** impf (pf **по~**) build; construct; make; base; draw up; **~ся** be built, be under construction; draw up; **стро́йся!** fall in! **строй** (loc -ю́; pl -и or -й, -ев or -ёв) system; régime; structure; pitch; formation. **стро́йка** building; building-site. **стро́йность** proportion; harmony; balance, order. **стро́йный** (-о́ен, -о́йна́, -о) harmonious, orderly, well-proportioned, shapely.

строка́ (acc -о́ку́; pl -и, -а́м) line; **кра́сная ~** new paragraph.

строп, стро́па sling; shroud line.

стропи́ло rafter, beam.

стропти́вый refractory.

строфа́ (pl -ы, -) stanza.

строчи́ть (-чу́, -о́чи́шь) impf (pf **на~, про~**) stitch; scribble, dash off. **стро́чка** stitch; line.

стро́ю etc.: see **стро́ить**

струга́ть impf (pf **вы~**) plane. **стру́жка** shaving.

струи́ться impf stream.

структу́ра structure.

струна́ (pl -ы) string. **стру́нный** stringed.

струп (pl -пья, -пьев) scab.

с|тру́сить (-у́шу) pf.

стручо́к (-чка́) pod.

струя́ (pl -и, -уй) jet, spurt, stream.

стря́пать impf (pf **со~**) cook; concoct. **стря́пня** cooking.

стря́хивать impf, **стряхну́ть** (-ну́, -нёшь) pf shake off.

студени́стый jelly-like.

студе́нт, студе́нтка student. **студе́нческий** student.

студе́нь (-дня) m jelly; aspic.

студи́ть (-ужу́, -у́дишь) impf (pf **о~**) cool.

сту́дия studio.

стужа severe cold, hard frost.

стук knock, clatter. **сту́кать** impf, **сту́кнуть** (-ну) pf knock; bang; strike; **~ся** knock (o.s.), bang. **стука́ч** (-а́) informer.

стул (pl -лья, -льев) chair. **стульча́к** (-а́) (lavatory) seat. **сту́льчик** stool.

сту́па mortar.

ступа́ть impf, **ступи́ть** (-плю́, -пишь) pf step; tread. **ступе́нчатый** stepped, graded. **ступе́нь** (gen pl -е́ней) step, rung; stage, grade. **ступе́нька** step. **ступня́** foot; sole.

стуча́ть (-чу́) impf (pf **по~**) knock; chatter; pound; **~ся** knock; **~ся в+acc** knock at.

стушева́ться (-шу́юсь) pf, **стушёвываться** impf efface o.s.

стыд (-а́) shame. **стыди́ть** (-ыжу́) impf (pf **при~**) put to shame; **~ся** (pf **по~ся**) be ashamed. **стыдли́вый** bashful. **сты́дный** shameful; **~о!** shame! **~о** impers ему́ **~о** he is ashamed; **как тебе́ не ~о!** you ought to be ashamed of yourself!

стык joint; junction. **стыкова́ть** impf (pf **со~**) join end to end; **~ся** (pf **при~ся**) dock. **стыко́вка** docking.

сты́нуть, стыть (-ы́ну) impf cool; get cold.

сты́чка skirmish; squabble.

стюарде́сса stewardess.

стя́гивать *impf*, **стяну́ть** (-ну́, -нешь) *pf* tighten; pull together; assemble; pull off; steal; **~ся** tighten; assemble.

стяжа́тель (-я) *m* money-grubber. **стяжа́ть** *impf & pf* gain, win.

суббо́та Saturday.

субсиди́ровать *impf & pf* subsidize. **субси́дия** subsidy.

субъе́кт subject; ego; person; character, type. **субъекти́вный** subjective.

сувени́р souvenir.

суверените́т sovereignty. **суверенный** sovereign.

сугли́нок (-нка) loam.

сугро́б snowdrift.

сугу́бо *adv* especially.

суд (-á) court; trial; verdict.

суда́ *etc.*: *see* **суд, су́дно¹**

суда́к (-á) pike-perch.

суде́бный judicial; legal; forensic. **суде́йский** judge's; referee's, umpire's. **суди́мость** previous convictions. **суди́ть** (сужу́, су́дишь) *impf* judge; try; referee, umpire; try; judge; **~ся** go to law.

су́дно¹ (*pl* -да́, -о́в) vessel, craft. **су́дно²** (*gen pl* -ден) bed-pan.

судово́й ship's; marine.

судомо́йка kitchen-maid; scullery.

судопроизво́дство legal proceedings.

су́дорога cramp, convulsion. **су́дорожный** convulsive.

судострое́ние shipbuilding. **судострои́тельный** shipbuilding. **судохо́дный** navigable; shipping.

судьба́ (*pl* -ы, -деб) fate, destiny.

судья́ (*pl* -дьи, -де́й, -дьям) *m* judge; referee; umpire.

суеве́рие superstition. **суеве́рный** superstitious.

суета́ bustle, fuss. **суети́ться** (-ечу́сь) *impf* bustle, fuss. **суетли́вый** fussy, bustling.

сужде́ние opinion; judgement.

суже́ние narrowing; constriction. **сужа́ть** *impf*, **су́зить** (-у́жу) *pf* narrow, contract; **~ся** narrow; taper.

сук (-á, *loc* -ý; *pl* сучья, -ьев *or* -и́, -о́в) bough.

су́ка bitch. **су́кин** *adj*: **~ сын** son of a bitch.

сукно́ (*pl* -а, -кон) cloth; **положи́ть под ~** shelve. **суко́нный** cloth; clumsy, crude.

сули́ть *impf* (*pf* **по~**) promise.

султа́н plume.

сумасбро́д, **сумасбро́дка** nutcase. **сумасбро́дный** wild, mad. **сумасбро́дство** wild behaviour. **сумасше́дший** mad; **~ий** *sb*, **~ая** *sb* lunatic. **сумасше́ствие** madness.

сумато́ха turmoil; bustle.

сумбу́р confusion. **сумбу́рный** confused.

су́меречный twilight. **су́мерки** (-рек) *pl* twilight, dusk.

суме́ть (-е́ю) *pf* + *inf* be able to, manage to.

су́мка bag.

су́мма sum. **сумма́рный** summary; total. **сумми́ровать** *impf & pf* add up; summarize.

су́мрак twilight; murk. **су́мрачный** gloomy.

су́мчатый marsupial.

сунду́к (-á) trunk, chest.

су́нуть(ся (-ну(сь) *pf* of **со́вать(ся**

суп (*pl* -ы́) soup.

суперма́ркет supermarket.
суперобло́жка dust-jacket.
супру́г husband, spouse; *pl* husband and wife, (*married*) couple. **супру́га** wife, spouse. **супру́жеский** conjugal. **супру́жество** matrimony.
сургу́ч (-á) sealing-wax.
сурди́нка mute; **под сурди́нку** on the sly.
суро́вость severity, sternness. **суро́вый** severe, stern; bleak; unbleached.
суро́к (-рка́) marmot.
суррога́т substitute.
су́слик ground-squirrel.
суста́в joint, articulation.
су́тки (-ток) *pl* twenty-four hours; a day.
су́толока commotion.
су́точн|ый daily; round-the-clock; ~**ые** *sb pl* per diem allowance.
суту́литься *impf* stoop. **суту́лый** round-shouldered.
суть essence, main point.
суфлёр prompter. **суфли́ровать** *impf +dat* prompt.
су́ффикс suffix.
суха́рь (-я́) *m* rusk; *pl* bread-crumbs. **су́хо** *adv* drily; coldly.
сухожи́лие tendon.
сухо́й (сух, -á, -о) dry; cold. **сухопу́тный** land. **су́хость** dryness; coldness. **сухоща́вый** lean, skinny.
сучкова́тый knotty; gnarled. **сучо́к** (-чка́) twig; knot.
су́ша (dry) land. **су́ше** *comp of* **сухо́й**. **сушёный** dried. **су́шилка** dryer; drying-room. **суши́ть** (-шу́, -шишь) *impf* (*pf* вы́~) dry, dry out, up; ~**ся** (get) dry.
суще́ственный essential, vital.
существи́тельное *sb* noun.

существо́ being, creature; essence. **существова́ние** existence. **существова́ть** *impf* exist.
су́щий absolute, downright.
сую́ etc.: *see* **сова́ть**. **с|фабрикова́ть** *pf.* **с|фальши́вить** (-влю) *pf.*
с|фантази́ровать *pf.*
сфе́ра sphere. **сфери́ческий** spherical.
сфинкс sphinx.
с|формирова́ть(ся *pf.* **с|формова́ть** *pf.* **с|формули́ровать** *pf.* **с|фотографи́ровать(ся** *pf.*
схвати́ть (-ачу́, -а́тишь) *pf,* **схва́тывать** *impf* (*impf also* **хвата́ть**) seize; catch; grasp; ~**ся** snatch, catch; grapple. **схва́тка** skirmish; *pl* contractions.
схе́ма diagram; outline, plan; circuit. **схемати́ческий** schematic; sketchy. **схемати́чный** sketchy.
с|хитри́ть *pf.*
схлы́нуть (-нет) *pf* (break and) flow back; subside.
сход coming off; descent; gathering. **сходи́ть**[1](**ся** (-ожу́сь, -о́дишься(ся) *impf of* **сойти́(сь. сходи́ть**[2] (-ожу́, -о́дишь) *pf go;* +**за**+*instr* to fetch. **схо́дный** gathering, meeting. **схо́дный** (-ден, -дна́, -о) similar; reasonable. **сходня** (*gen pl* -ей) (*usu pl*) gang-plank. **схо́дство** similarity.
с|хорони́ть(ся (-ню́(сь, -нишь-ся) *pf.*
сцеди́ть (-ежу́, -е́дишь) *pf,* **сце́живать** *impf* strain off, decant.
сце́на stage; scene. **сцена́рий** scenario; script. **сценари́ст** script-writer. **сцени́ческий** stage.

сцепи́ть (-плю́, -пишь) *pf*, **сцепля́ть** *impf* couple; ~**ся** be coupled; grapple. **сце́пка** coupling. **сцепле́ние** coupling; clutch.

счастли́вец (-вца), **счастли́вчик** lucky man. **счастли́вица** lucky woman. **счастли́вый** (счастли́в) happy; lucky; ~о! all the best!; ~ого пути́ bon voyage. **сча́стье** happiness; good fortune.

счесть(ся (сочту́(сь, -тёшь(ся; счёл(ся, сочла́(сь) *pf of* счита́ть(ся. **счёт** (*loc* -у́; *pl* -а́) bill; account; counting, calculation; score; expense. **счётный** calculating; accounts. **счетово́д** book-keeper, accountant. **счётчик** counter; meter. **счёты** (-ов) *pl* abacus.

счи́стить (-и́щу) *pf* (*impf* **счища́ть**) clean off; clear away.

счита́ть *impf* (*pf* **со**~, **счесть**) count; reckon; consider; ~**ся** (*pf also* **по**~**ся**) settle accounts; be considered; +с+*instr* take into consideration; reckon with.

счища́ть *impf of* счи́стить

США *pl indecl abbr* (*of* Соединённые Шта́ты Аме́рики) USA.

сшиба́ть *impf*, **сшиби́ть** (-бу́, -бёшь; сшиб) *pf* strike, hit, knock (off); ~ **с ног** knock down; ~**ся** collide; come to blows.

сшива́ть *impf*, **сшить** (сошью́, -ьёшь) *pf* sew (together).

съеда́ть *impf of* съесть. **съедо́бный** edible; nice.

съе́ду *etc.: see* съе́хать

съёживаться *impf*, **съёжиться** (-жусь) *pf* shrivel, shrink.

съезд congress; conference; arrival. **съе́здить** (-зжу) *pf* go, drive, travel.

съезжа́ть(ся *impf of* съе́хать(ся. съел *etc.: see* съесть

съёмка removal; surveying; shooting. **съёмный** detachable, removable. **съёмщик**, **съёмщица** tenant; surveyor.

съестно́й food; ~**о́е** *sb* food (supplies). **съесть** (-ем, -ешь, -ест, -еди́м; съел) *pf* (*impf also* **съеда́ть**)

съе́хать (-е́ду) *pf* (*impf* **съезжа́ть**) go down; come down; move; ~**ся** meet; assemble.

съязви́ть (-влю) *pf*.

сы́воротка whey; serum.

сыгра́ть *pf of* игра́ть; ~**ся** play (well) together.

сын (*pl* сыновья́, -ве́й, -вьям *or* -ы́, -ов) son. **сыно́вний** filial. **сыно́к** (-нка́) little son; sonny.

сы́пать (-плю) *impf* pour; pour forth; ~**ся** fall; pour out; rain down; fray. **сыпно́й тиф** typhus. **сы́пучий** friable; free-flowing; shifting. **сыпь** rash, eruption.

сыр (*loc* -у́; *pl* -ы́) cheese.

сыре́ть (-е́ю) *impf* (*pf* **от**~) become damp.

сыре́ц (-рца́) raw product.

сыро́й (сыр, -а́, -о) damp; raw; uncooked; unboiled; unfinished; unripe. **сы́рость** dampness. **сырьё** raw material(s).

сыска́ть (сыщу́, сы́щешь) *pf* find.

сы́тный (-тен, -тна́, -о) filling. **сы́тость** satiety. **сы́тый** (сыт, -а́, -о) full.

сыч (-а́) little owl.

сы́щик detective.

сэконо́мить (-млю) *pf*.

сэр sir.

сюда adv here, hither.

сюжет subject; plot; topic. **сюжетный** subject; having a theme.

сюита suite.

сюрприз surprise.

сюрреализм surrealism. **сюрреалистический** surrealist.

сюртук (-а) frock-coat.

сяк adv: see **так**. **сям** adv: see **там**

Т

та see **тот**

табак (-а) tobacco. **табакерка** snuff-box. **табачный** tobacco.

табель (-я; pl -и, -ей or -я, -ей) m table, list. **табельный** table; time.

таблетка tablet.

таблица table; ~ умножения multiplication table.

табор (gipsy) camp.

табун (-а) herd.

табурет, табуретка stool.

тавро (pl -а, -ам) brand.

тавтология tautology.

таджик, -ичка Tadzhik.

Таджикистан Tadzhikistan.

таёжный taiga.

таз (loc -ý; pl -ы) basin; pelvis. **тазобедренный** hip. **тазовый** pelvic.

таинственный mysterious; secret. **таить** impf hide, harbour; ~ся hide; lurk.

Тайвань m Taiwan.

тайга taiga.

тайком adv secretly, surreptitiously; ~ от+gen behind the back of.

тайм half; period of play.

тайна secret; mystery. **тайник** (-á) hiding-place; pl recesses. **тайный** secret; privy.

тайфун typhoon.

так adv so; like this; as it should be; just like that; и ~ even so; as it is; и ~ далее and so on; ~ и сяк this way and that; не ~ wrong; ~ же in the same way; же... как as ... as; ~ и есть I thought so!; ~ ему и надо serves him right; ~ или иначе one way or another; ~ себе so-so. **так** conj then; so; ~ как as, since; ~ что so.

такелаж rigging.

также adv also, too, as well.

таков m (-á f, -ó neut, -ы́ pl) pron such.

такой pron such (a); в том случае in that case; кто он ~ой? who is he?; ~ой же the same; ~им образом in this way; что это ~ое? what is this? **такой-то** pron so-and-so; such-and-such.

такса fixed rate; tariff.

таксёр taxi-driver. **такси** neut indecl taxi. **таксист** taxi-driver. **таксопарк** taxi depot.

такт time; bar; beat; tact. **так-таки** after all, really.

тактика tactics. **тактический** tactical.

тактичность tact. **тактичный** tactful.

тактовый time, timing; ~ая черта bar-line. **талант** talent. **талантливый** talented.

талисман talisman.

талия waist.

талон, талончик coupon.

талый thawed, melted.

тальк talc; talcum powder.

там adv there; ~ и сям here and

there; ∼ же in the same place; ibid.

тамада́ *m* toast-master.

та́мбур¹ tambour; lobby; platform. **та́мбур²** chain-stitch.

тамо́женник customs official. **тамо́женный** customs. **тамо́жня** custom-house.

та́мошний of that place, local.

тампо́н tampon.

та́нгенс tangent.

та́нго *neut indecl* tango.

та́нец (-нца) dance; dancing.

тани́н tannin.

танк tank. **та́нкер** tanker. **танки́ст** member of a tank crew. **та́нковый** tank, armoured.

танцева́льный dancing; ∼ ве́чер dance. **танцева́ть** (-цу́ю) *impf* dance. **танцо́вщик, танцо́вщица** (ballet) dancer. **танцо́р, танцо́рка** dancer.

та́пка, та́почка slipper.

та́ра packing; tare.

тарака́н cockroach.

тара́н battering-ram.

тара́нтул tarantula.

таре́лка plate; cymbal; satellite dish.

тари́ф tariff.

таска́ть *impf* drag, lug; carry; pull; take; pull out; swipe; wear; ∼ся drag; hang about.

тасова́ть *impf* (*pf* с∼) shuffle.

ТАСС *abbr* (*of* Телегра́фное аге́нтство Сове́тского Сою́за) Tass (Telegraph Agency of the Soviet Union).

тата́рин, тата́рка Tatar.

татуиро́вка tattooing, tattoo.

тафта́ taffeta.

тахта́ ottoman.

та́чка wheelbarrow.

тащи́ть (-щу́, -щишь) *impf* (*pf* вы́∼, с∼) pull; drag; lug; carry;

take; pull out; swipe; ∼ся drag o.s. along; drag.

та́ять (та́ю) *impf* (*pf* рас∼) melt; thaw; dwindle.

ТВ *abbr* (*of* телеви́дение) TV, television.

тварь creature(s); wretch.

тверде́ть (-е́ет) *impf* (*pf* за∼) harden, become hard. **тверди́ть** (-ржу́) *impf* (*pf* вы́∼) repeat, say again and again; memorize. **твёрдо** *adv* hard; firmly, firm. **твердоло́бый** thick-skulled; diehard. **твёрдый** hard; firm; solid; steadfast; ∼ знак hard sign, ъ; ∼ое те́ло solid. **тверды́ня** stronghold.

твой (-его́) *m*, **твоя́** (-е́й) *f*, **твоё** (-его́) *neut*, **твой** (-и́х) *pl* your, yours.

творе́ние creation, work; creature. **творе́ц** (-рца́) creator. **твори́тельный** instrumental. **твори́ть** *impf* (*pf* со∼) create; do; make; ∼ся happen.

творо́г (-а́) curds; cottage cheese.

тво́рческий creative. **тво́рчество** creation; creative work; work.

те *see* тот

т.е. *abbr* (*of* то есть) that is, i.e.

теа́тр theatre. **театра́льный** theatre; theatrical.

тебя́ *etc.*: *see* ты

те́зис thesis.

тёзка *m* & *f* namesake.

тёк *see* течь

текст text; libretto, lyrics.

тексти́ль *m* textiles. **тексти́льный** textile.

тексту́ра texture.

теку́чий fluid; unstable. **теку́щий** current; routine.

теле- in *comb* tele-; television.

телеви́дение television. **~визио́нный** television. **~ви́зор** television (set). **~гра́мма** telegram. **~гра́ф** telegraph (office). **~графи́ровать** *impf* & *pf* telegraph. **~гра́фный** telegraph(ic). **~зри́тель** *m* (television) viewer. **~объекти́в** telephoto lens. **~пати́ческий** telepathic. **~па́тия** telepathy. **~ско́п** telescope. **~ста́нция** television station. **~сту́дия** television studio. **~фо́н** telephone; (telephone) number; (по)звони́ть по **~фо́ну** +*dat* ring up. **~фон-автома́т** public telephone, call-box. **~фони́ст, -и́стка** (telephone) operator. **~фо́нный** telephone; **~фо́нная кни́га** telephone directory; **~фо́нная ста́нция** telephone exchange; **~фо́нная тру́бка** receiver. **~фон-отве́тчик** answering machine. **~центр** television centre.

теле́га cart, wagon. **теле́жка** small cart; trolley.

те́лекс telex.

телёнок (-нка; *pl* -я́та, -я́т) calf.

теле́сный bodily; corporal; **~ого цве́та** flesh-coloured.

Теле́ц (-льца́) Taurus.

тели́ться *impf* (*pf* о**~**) calve. **тёлка** heifer.

те́ло (*pl* -а́) body. **телогре́йка** padded jacket. **телосложе́ние** build. **телохрани́тель** *m* bodyguard.

теля́та etc.: see **телёнок**. **теля́тина** veal. **теля́чий** calf; veal.

тем *conj* (so much) the; **~ лу́чше** so much the better; **~ не ме́нее** nevertheless.

тем see **тот, тьма**.

те́ма subject; theme. **тема́тика** subject-matter; themes. **тема́ти-**ческий subject; thematic.

тембр timbre.

темне́ть (-е́ет) *impf* (*pf* по**~**, с**~**) become dark. **темни́ца** dungeon. **темно́** *predic* it is dark. **темноко́жий** dark-skinned, swarthy. **тёмно-си́ний** dark blue. **темнота́** darkness. **тёмный** dark.

темп tempo; rate.

темпера́мент temperament. **темпера́ментный** temperamental.

температу́ра temperature.

те́мя (-мени) *neut* crown, top of the head.

тенде́нция tendency; bias.

теневой, тени́стый shady.

те́ннис tennis. **тенниси́ст, -и́стка** tennis-player. **те́ннисный** tennis; **~ая площа́дка** tennis-court.

те́нор (*pl* -а́) tenor.

тент awning.

тень (*loc* -и́; *pl* -и, -е́й) shade; shadow; phantom; ghost; particle, vestige, atom; suspicion; **те́ни для век** *pl* eyeshadow.

тео́лог theologian. **теологи́ческий** theological. **теоло́гия** theology.

теоре́ма theorem. **теоре́тик** theoretician. **теорети́ческий** theoretical. **тео́рия** theory.

тепе́решний *adj* present. **тепе́рь** *adv* now; today.

тепли́ться (-е́ет) *impf* (*pf* по**~**) be warm. **тепли́ться** (-ится) *impf* flicker; glimmer. **тепли́ца** greenhouse, conservatory. **тепли́чный** hothouse. **тепло́** heat; warmth. **тепло́** *adv* warmly; *predic* it is warm.

тепло- in comb heat; thermal; thermo-. **теплово́з** diesel locomotive. **~кро́вный** warm-

blooded. ∼обмéн heat exchange. ∼провóдный heat-conducting. ∼стóйкий heat-resistant. ∼хóд motor ship. ∼центрáль heat and power station.

теплово́й heat; thermal. **теплота́** heat; warmth. **тёплый** (-пел, -пла́, тёпло) warm.

теракт terrorist act.

терапéвт therapeutist. **терапи́я** therapy.

тереби́ть (-блю) *impf* pull (at); pester.

тере́ть (тру, трёшь; тёр) *impf* rub; grate; ∼ся rub o.s.; ∼ся óколо+*gen* hang about, hang around; ∼ся среди́ +*gen* mix with.

терза́ть *impf* tear to pieces; torment; ∼ся +*instr* suffer; be a prey to.

тёрка grater.

тéрмин term. **терминоло́гия** terminology.

терми́ческий thermic, thermal. **термóметр** thermometer. **тéрмос** thermos (flask). **термостáт** thermostat. **термоя́дерный** thermonuclear.

терно́вник sloe, blackthorn. **терни́стый** thorny.

терпели́вый patient. **терпéние** patience. **терпéть** (-плю́, -пишь) *impf* (*pf* по∼) bear, endure. **терпéться** (-пится) *impf impers+dat:* ему́ не тéрпится +*inf* he is impatient to. **терпи́мость** tolerance. **терпи́мый** tolerant; tolerable.

тéрпкий (-пок, -пка́, -о) astringent; tart.

терра́са terrace.

территориáльный territorial. **террито́рия** territory.

терро́р terror. **терроризи́ро-** вать *impf & pf* terrorize. **террори́ст** terrorist.

тёртый grated; experienced.

терьéр terrier.

теря́ть *impf* (*pf* по∼, у∼) lose; shed; ∼ся get lost; disappear; fail, decline; become flustered.

тёс boards, planks. **теса́ть** (тешу́, тéшешь) *impf* cut, hew.

тесёмка ribbon, braid.

тесни́ть *impf* (*pf* по∼, с∼) crowd; squeeze, constrict; be too tight; ∼ся press through; move up; crowd, jostle. **теснота́** crowded state; crush. **тéсный** crowded; (too) tight; close; compact; ∼о it is crowded.

тесо́вый board, plank.

тест test.

тéсто dough; pastry.

тесть *m* father-in-law.

тесьма́ ribbon, braid.

тéтерев (*pl* -а́) black grouse. **тетёрка** grey hen.

тётка aunt.

тетра́дка, тетра́дь exercise book.

тётя (*gen pl* -ей) aunt.

тех- *abbr in comb of* техни́ческий) technical.

тéхник technician. **тéхника** technical equipment; technology; technique. **тéхникум** technical college. **техни́ческий** technical; ∼ие услóвия specifications. **техно́лог** technologist. **технологи́ческий** technological. **техноло́гия** technology. **техперсонáл** technical personnel.

течéние flow; course; current, stream; trend.

течь[1] (-чёт, тёк, -ла́) *impf* flow; stream; leak. **течь**[2] leak.

тéшить (-шу) *impf* (*pf* по∼)

amuse; gratify; ~**ся** (+*instr*) amuse o.s. (with).

тешу́ *etc.: see* теса́ть

тёща mother-in-law.

тигр tiger. **тигри́ца** tigress.

тик¹ tic.

тик² teak.

ти́на slime, mud.

тип type. **типи́чный** typical. **типово́й** standard; model. **типогра́фия** printing-house, press. **типогра́фский** typographical.

тир shooting-range, -gallery. **тира́ж** (-а́) draw; circulation; edition.

тира́н tyrant. **тира́нить** *impf* tyrannize. **тирани́ческий** tyrannical. **тира́ния** tyranny.

тире́ *neut indecl* dash.

ти́скать, **ти́снуть** (-ну) *impf* press, squeeze. **тиски́** (-о́в) *pl* vice; **в тиска́х** +*gen* in the grip of. **тисне́ние** stamping; imprint; design. **тиснёный** stamped.

тита́н¹ titanian.

тита́н² boiler.

тита́н³ titan.

титр title, sub-title.

ти́тул title; title-page. **ти́тульный** title.

тиф (*loc* -у́) typhus.

ти́хий (тих, -а́, -о) quiet; silent; calm; slow. **тихоокеа́нский** Pacific. **ти́ше** *comp of* ти́хий, ти́хо; ти́ше! quiet! **тишина́** quiet, silence.

т. к. *abbr* (*of* так как) as, since.

тка́ный woven. **ткань** fabric; cloth; tissue. **ткать** (тку, ткёшь; -ал, -ала́, -о) *impf* (*pf* со~) weave. **тка́цкий** weaving; ~ **стано́к** loom. **ткач**, **ткачи́ха** weaver.

ткну́ть(**ся** (-у(сь, -ёшь(ся) *pf of* **ты́кать**(**ся**

тле́ние decay; smouldering. **тлеть** (-е́ет) *impf* rot, decay; smoulder. ~**ся** smoulder.

тля aphis.

тмин caraway(-seeds).

то *pron* that; **а не то́** or else, otherwise; (**да**) **и то́** and even then, and that; **то́ есть** that is (to say); **то и де́ло** every now and then. **то** *conj* then; **не то..., не то** either ... or; half ... half; **то..., то** now ..., now; **то ли..., то ли** whether ... or.

-то *partl* just, exactly; **в то́м-то и де́ло** that's just it.

тобо́й *see* **ты**

това́р goods; commodity.

това́рищ comrade; friend; colleague. **това́рищеский** comradely; friendly.

това́рищество comradeship; company; association.

това́рный goods; commodity.

товаро́- *in comb* commodity; goods. **товарообме́н** barter. ~**оборо́т** (sales) turnover. ~**отправи́тель** *m* consignor. ~**получа́тель** *m* consignee.

тогда́ *adv* then; ~ **как** whereas. **тогда́шний** of that time.

того́ *see* **тот**

тожде́ственный identical. **тожде́ство** identity.

то́же *adv* also, too.

ток (*pl* -и) current.

тока́рный turning; ~ **стано́к** lathe. **то́карь** (*pl* -я́, -е́й *or* -и, -ей) *m* turner, lathe operator.

токси́ческий toxic.

толк sense; use; **без** ~**у** senselessly; **знать** ~ **в**+*prep* know well; **сбить с** ~**у** confuse; **с** ~**ом** intelligently.

толка́ть *impf* (*pf* **толкну́ть**) push, shove; jog; ~**ся** jostle.

то́лки (-ов) *pl* rumours, gossip.

толкну́ть(ся (-ну́(сь, -нёшь(ся) *pf of* **толка́ть(ся**

толкова́ние interpretation; *pl* commentary. **толкова́ть** *impf* interpret; explain; talk. **толко́вый** intelligent; clear; ~ **слова́рь** defining dictionary. **то́лком** *adv* plainly; seriously.

толкотня́ crush, squash.

толку́ *etc.: see* **толо́чь**

толку́чка crush, squash; second-hand market.

толокно́ oatmeal.

толо́чь (-лку́, -лчёшь; -ло́к, -лкла́) *impf* (*pf* ис~, рас~) pound, crush.

толпа́ (*pl* -ы) crowd. **толпи́ться** *impf* crowd; throng.

толсте́ть (-е́ю) *impf* (*pf* по~) grow fat; put on weight. **толстоко́жий** thick-skinned; pachydermatous. **то́лстый** (-á, -о) fat; thick. **толстя́к** (-á) fat man *or* boy.

толчёный crushed; ground. **толчёт** *etc.: see* **толо́чь**

толчея́ crush, squash.

толчо́к (-чка́) push, shove; (*sport*) put; jolt; shock, tremor.

то́лща thickness; thick. **то́лще** *comp of* **то́лстый**. **толщина́** thickness; fatness.

толь *m* roofing felt.

то́лько *adv* only, merely; ~ **что** (only) just; *conj* only but; (как) ~, (пишь) as soon as; ~ бы if only.

том (*pl* -á) volume. **то́мик** small volume.

тома́т tomato. **тома́тный** tomato.

томи́тельный tedious, wearing; agonizing. **томи́ть** (-млю́) *impf* (*pf* ис~) tire; torment; ~ся languish; be tormented.

томле́ние languor. **то́мный** (-мен, -мна́, -о) languid, languorous.

тон (*pl* -á *or* -ы, -óв) tone; note; shade; form. **тона́льность** key.

то́ненький thin; slim. **то́нкий** (-нок, -нка́, -о) thin; slim; fine; refined; subtle; keen. **то́нкость** thinness; slimness; fineness; subtlety.

то́нна ton.

тонне́ль *see* **тунне́ль**

то́нус tone.

тону́ть (-ну́, -нешь) *impf* (*pf* по~, у~) sink; drown.

то́ньше *comp of* **то́нкий**

то́пать *impf* (*pf* то́пнуть) stamp.

топи́ть¹ (-плю́, -пишь) *impf* (*pf* по~, у~) sink; drown; ruin; ~ся drown o.s.

топи́ть² (-плю́, -пишь) *impf* stoke; heat; melt (down); ~ся burn; melt. **то́пка** stoking; heating; melting (down); furnace.

то́пкий boggy, marshy.

то́пливный fuel. **то́пливо** fuel.

то́пнуть (-ну) *pf of* **то́пать**

топографи́ческий topographical. **топогра́фия** topography.

то́поль (*pl* -я́ *or* -и) *m* poplar.

топо́р (-á) axe. **топо́рик** hatchet. **топо́рище** axe-handle. **топо́рный** axe; clumsy, crude.

то́пот tramp; clatter. **топта́ть** (-пчу́, -пчешь) *impf* (*pf* по~) trample (down); ~ся stamp; ~ся на ме́сте mark time.

топча́н (-á) trestle-bed.

топь bog, marsh.

торг (*loc* -ý; *pl* -и́) trading; bargaining; *pl* auction. **торгова́ть** *impf* (*pf* с~) trade; ~ся bargain, haggle. **торго́вец** (-вца)

merchant; tradesman. **торго́вка** market-woman; stall-holder. **торго́вля** trade. **торго́вый** trade, commercial; merchant. **торгпре́д** *abbr* trade representative.

торе́ц (-рца́) butt-end; wooden paving-block.

торже́ственный solemn; ceremonial. **торжество́** celebration; triumph. **торжествова́ть** *impf* celebrate; triumph.

торможе́ние braking. **то́рмоз** (*pl* -а́ *or* -ы) brake. **тормози́ть** (-ожу́) *impf* (*pf* за~) brake; hamper.

тормоши́ть (-шу́) *impf* pester; bother.

торопи́ть (-плю́, -пишь) *impf* (*pf* по~) hurry; hasten; ~**ся** hurry. **торопли́вый** hasty.

торпе́да torpedo.

торс torso.

торт cake.

торф peat. **торфяно́й** peat.

торча́ть (-чу́) *impf* stick out; protrude; hang about.

торше́р standard lamp.

тоска́ melancholy; boredom; nostalgia; ~ **по**+*dat* longing for. **тоскли́вый** melancholy; depressed; dreary. **тоскова́ть** *impf* be melancholy, depressed; long; ~ **по**+*dat* miss.

тост toast.

тот *m* (та *f*, то *neut*, те *pl*) *pron* that; the former; the other; the one; the same; the right; и ~ и друго́й both; к тому́ же moreover; не ~ the wrong; ни ~ ни друго́й neither; тот, кто the one who, the person who. **то́тчас** *adv* immediately.

тоталитари́зм totalitarianism. **тоталита́рный** totalitarian. **тота́льный** total.

точи́лка sharpener; pencil-sharpener. **точи́ло** whetstone, grindstone. **точи́льный** grinding, sharpening; ~ **ка́мень** whetstone, grindstone. **точи́льщик** (knife-)grinder. **точи́ть** (-чу́, -чишь) *impf* (*pf* вы~, на~) sharpen; hone; turn; eat away; gnaw at.

то́чка spot; dot; full stop; point; ~ **зре́ния** point of view; ~ **с запято́й** semicolon. **то́чно**[1] *adv* exactly, precisely; punctually. **то́чно**[2] *conj* as though, as if. **то́чность** punctuality; precision; accuracy; **в то́чности** exactly, precisely. **то́чный** (-чен, -чна́, -о) exact, precise; accurate; punctual. **точь-в-то́чь** *adv* exactly; word for word.

тошни́ть *impf impers*: меня́ **тошни́т** I feel sick. **тошнота́** nausea. **тошнотво́рный** sickening, nauseating.

то́щий (тощ, -а́, -е) gaunt, emaciated; skinny; empty; poor.

трава́ (*pl* -ы) grass; herb. **трави́нка** blade of grass.

трави́ть (-влю́, -вишь) *impf* (*pf* вы~, за~) exterminate, destroy; etch; hunt; torment; badger. **травле́ние** extermination; etching. **тра́вля** hunting; persecution; badgering.

тра́вма trauma, injury.

травоя́дный herbivorous. **травяни́стый**, **травяно́й** grass; herbaceous; grassy.

траге́дия tragedy. **тра́гик** tragedian. **траги́ческий**, **траги́чный** tragic.

традицио́нный traditional. **тради́ция** tradition.

траекто́рия trajectory.

тракта́т treatise; treaty.

тракти́р inn, tavern.

трактова́ть *impf* interpret; treat, discuss. **трактовка** treatment; interpretation.

тра́ктор tractor. **тракторист** tractor driver.

трал trawl. **тра́лить** *impf* (*pf* про~) trawl; sweep. **тра́льщик** trawler; mine-sweeper.

трамбова́ть *impf* (*pf* у~) ram, tamp.

трамва́й tram. **трамва́йный** tram.

трампли́н spring-board; ski-jump.

транзи́стор transistor; transistor radio.

транзи́тный transit.

транс trance.

трансатланти́ческий transatlantic.

трансли́ровать *impf* & *pf* broadcast, transmit. **трансляцио́нный** transmission; broadcasting. **трансля́ция** broadcast, transmission.

тра́нспорт transport; consignment. **транспортёр** conveyor. **транспорти́р** protractor. **транспорти́ровать** *impf* & *pf* transport. **тра́нспортный** transport.

трансформа́тор transformer.

транше́я trench.

трап ladder.

тра́пеза meal.

трапе́ция trapezium; trapeze.

тра́сса line, course, direction; route, road.

тра́та expenditure; waste. **тра́тить** (-а́чу) *impf* (*pf* ис~, по~) spend, expend; waste.

тра́улер trawler.

тра́ур mourning. **тра́урный** mourning; funeral; mournful.

трафаре́т stencil; stereotype;

cliché. **трафаре́тный** stencilled; conventional, stereotyped.

тра́чу *etc.*: *see* **тра́тить**

тре́бование demand; request; requirement; requisition, order; *pl* needs. **тре́бовательный** demanding. **тре́бовать** *impf* (*pf* по~) summon; +*gen* demand, require; need; ~ся be needed, be required.

трево́га alarm; anxiety. **трево́жить** (-жу) *impf* (*pf* вс~, по~) alarm; disturb; worry; ~ся worry, be anxious; trouble o.s. **трево́жный** worried, anxious; alarming; alarm.

тре́звенник teetotaller. **трезве́ть** (-е́ю) *impf* (*pf* о~) sober up.

трезво́н peal (*of bells*); rumours; row.

тре́звость sobriety. **тре́звый** (-зв, -á, -о) sober; teetotal.

тре́йлер trailer.

трель trill; warble.

тре́нер trainer, coach.

тре́ние friction.

трениро́вать *impf* (*pf* на~) train, coach; ~ся be in training. **трениро́вка** training, coaching. **трениро́вочный** training.

трепа́ть (-плю́, -плешь) *impf* (*pf* ис~, по~, рас~) blow about; dishevel; wear out; pat; ~ся fray; wear out; flutter. **тре́пет** trembling; trepidation. **трепета́ть** (-ещу́, -ещешь) *impf* tremble; flicker; palpitate. **тре́петный** trembling; flickering; palpitating; timid.

треск crack; crackle; fuss.

треска́ cod.

тре́скаться[1] *impf* (*pf* по~) crack; chap.

тре́скаться² *impf of* **тре́снуться**

тре́снуть (-нет) *pf* snap, crackle; crack; chap; bang; **~ся** (*impf* **тре́скаться**) +*instr* bang.

трест trust.

тре́тий (-ья, -ье) third; **~ье** *sb* sweet (course).

третьи́ровать *impf* slight.

треть (*gen pl* -е́й) third. **тре́тье** *etc.*: *see* **тре́тий**. **треуго́льник** triangle. **треуго́льный** triangular.

тре́фы (треф) *pl* clubs.

трёх- *in comb* three-, tri-. **трёхгоди́чный** three-year. **~голо́сный** three-part. **~гра́нный** three-edged; trihedral. **~колёсный** three-wheeled. **~ле́тний** three-year; three-year old. **~ме́рный** three-dimensional. **~ме́сячный** three-month; quarterly; three-month-old. **~по́лье** three-field system. **~со́тый** three-hundredth. **~сторо́нний** three-sided; trilateral; tripartite. **~эта́жный** three-storeyed.

треща́ть (-щу́) *impf* crack; crackle; creak; chirr; crack up; chatter. **тре́щина** crack, split; fissure; chap.

три (трёх, -ём, -емя́, -ёх) three.

трибу́на platform, rostrum; stand. **трибуна́л** tribunal.

тригономе́трия trigonometry.

тридцатиле́тний thirty-year; thirty-year old. **тридца́тый** thirtieth. **три́дцать** (-й, *instr* -ью) thirty. **три́жды** *adv* three times; thrice.

трико́ *neut indecl* tricot; tights; knickers. **трикота́ж** knitted fabric; knitwear. **трикота́жный** jersey, tricot; knitted.

трина́дцатый thirteenth. **три-**

на́дцать thirteen. **трио́ль** triplet.

три́ппер gonorrhoea.

три́ста (трёхсо́т, -ёмста́м, -емяста́ми, -ёхста́х) three hundred.

трито́н *zool* triton.

триу́мф triumph.

тро́гательный touching, moving. **тро́гать(ся** *impf of* **тро́нуть(ся**

тро́е (-и́х) *pl* three. **троебо́рье** triathlon. **троекра́тный** thrice-repeated. **Тро́ица** Trinity; **тро́ица** trio. **Тро́ицын день** Whit Sunday. **тро́йка** three; figure 3; troika; No. 3; three-piece suit. **тройно́й** triple, treble; three-ply. **тро́йственный** triple; tripartite.

тролле́йбус trolley-bus.

тромб blood clot.

тромбо́н trombone.

трон throne.

тро́нуть (-ну) *pf* (*impf* **тро́гать**) touch; disturb; affect; **~ся** start, set out; be touched; be affected.

тропа́ path.

тро́пик tropic.

тропи́нка path.

тропи́ческий tropical.

трос rope, cable.

тростни́к (-а́) reed, rush. **тро́сточка, трость** (*gen pl* ~е́й) cane, walking-stick.

тротуа́р pavement.

трофе́й trophy; *pl* spoils (*of war*), booty.

трою́родн|ый: ~ый брат, ~ая сестра́ second cousin.

тру *etc.*: *see* **тере́ть**

труба́ (*pl* -ы) pipe; chimney; funnel; tube. **труба́ч** (-а́) trumpeter; trumpet-player.

труби́ть (-блю́) *impf* (*pf* про-) blow, sound; blare. **тру́бка** tube; pipe; (*telephone*) receiver. **трубопрово́д** pipe-line; piping; manifold. **трубочи́ст** chimney-sweep. **тру́бочный** pipe. **тру́бчатый** tubular.

труд (-á) labour; work; effort; с ~о́м with difficulty. **труди́ться** (-ужу́сь, -у́дишься) *impf* toil, labour, work; trouble. **тру́дно** *predic* it is difficult. **тру́дность** difficulty. **тру́дный** (-ден, -дна́, -о) difficult; hard.

трудо- *in comb* labour, work. **трудоде́нь** (-дня́) *m* work-day (*unit*). **~ёмкий** labour-intensive. **~люби́вый** industrious. **~лю́бие** industry. **~спосо́бность** ability to work. **~спосо́бный** able-bodied; capable of working.

трудово́й work; working; earned; hard-earned. **трудя́щийся** working; ~иеся *sb pl* the workers. **тру́женик, тру́женица** toiler.

труп corpse; carcass.

тру́ппа troupe, company.

трус coward.

тру́сики (-ов) *pl* shorts; trunks; pants.

труси́ть¹ (-ушу́) *impf* trot, jog along.

труси́ть² (-ушу́) *impf* (*pf* с~) be a coward; lose one's nerve; be afraid. **труси́ха** coward. **трусли́вый** cowardly. **тру́сость** cowardice.

трусы́ (-о́в) *pl* shorts; trunks; pants.

труха́ dust; trash.

тру́щу *etc.: see* труси́ть¹, тру́сить²

трущо́ба slum; godforsaken hole.

трюк stunt; trick.

трюм hold.

трюмо́ *neut indecl* pier-glass.

трю́фель (*gen pl* -ле́й) *m* truffle.

тря́пка rag; spineless creature; *pl* clothes. **тряпьё** rags; clothes.

тряси́на quagmire. **тря́ска** shaking, jolting. **трясти́** (-су́, -сёшь; -яс, -ла) *impf*, **тряхну́ть** (-ну́, -нёшь) (*pf also* вы~) shake; shake out; jolt; ~сь shake; tremble, shiver; jolt.

тсс *int* sh! hush!

туале́т dress; toilet. **туале́тный** toilet.

туберкулёз tuberculosis.

ту́го *adv* tight(ly), taut; with difficulty. **туго́й** (туг, -á, -о) tight; taut; tightly filled; difficult.

туда́ *adv* there, thither; that way; to the right place; ни ~ ни сюда́ neither one way nor the other; ~ и обра́тно there and back.

ту́же *comp of* ту́го, туго́й

тужу́рка (double-breasted) jacket.

туз (-á, *acc* -á) ace; bigwig.

тузе́мец (-мца) **-мка** native.

ту́ловище trunk; torso.

тулу́п sheepskin coat.

тума́н fog; mist; haze. **тума́нить** *impf* (*pf* за~) dim, cloud, obscure; ~ся grow misty; be befogged. **тума́нность** fog, mist; nebula; obscurity. **тума́нный** foggy; misty; hazy; obscure, vague.

ту́мба post; bollard; pedestal. **ту́мбочка** bedside table.

ту́ндра tundra.

туне́ядец (-дца) sponger.

туни́ка tunic.

тунне́ль *m*, **тонне́ль** *m* tunnel.

тупе́ть (-е́ю) *impf* (*pf* о~) be-

come blunt; grow dull. **тупи́к** (-á) cul-de-sac, dead end; impasse; **поста́вить** в ∼ stump, nonplus. **тупи́ться** (-ится) *impf* (*pf* за∼, ис∼) become blunt. **тупи́ца** *m* & *f* blockhead, dimwit. **тупо́й** (туп, -á, -о) blunt; obtuse; dull; vacant, stupid. **ту́пость** bluntness; vacancy; dullness, slowness.

тур turn; round.

тура́ rook, castle.

турба́за holiday village, campsite.

турби́на turbine.

туре́цкий Turkish; ∼ бараба́н bass drum.

тури́зм tourism. **тури́ст, -и́стка** tourist. **тури́ст(и́че)ский** tourist.

туркме́н (*gen pl* -ме́н), ∼ка Turkmen. **Туркмениста́н** Turkmenistan.

турне́ *neut indecl* tour.

турне́пс swede.

турни́р tournament.

турóк (-рка) Turk. **турча́нка** Turkish woman. **Тýрция** Turkey.

тýсклый dim, dull; lacklustre. **тускне́ть** (-е́ет) *impf* (*pf* по∼) grow dim.

тут *adv* here; now; ∼ же here and then.

тýфля shoe.

тýхлый (-хл, -á, -о) rotten, bad. **тýхнуть**[1] (-нет; тух) go bad.

тýхнуть[2] (-нет; тух) *impf* (*pf* по∼) go out.

тýча cloud; storm-cloud.

тýчный (-чен, -чнá, -чно) fat; rich, fertile.

туш flourish.

тýша carcass.

тушева́ть (-шýю) *impf* (*pf* за∼) shade.

тушёный stewed. **туши́ть**[1] (-шý, -шишь) *impf* (*pf* с∼) stew.

туши́ть[2] (-шý, -шишь) *impf* (*pf* за∼, по∼) extinguish.

тушýю *etc.*: *see* **тушева́ть**. **тушь** Indian ink; ∼ (для ресни́ц) mascara.

тща́тельность care. **тща́тельный** careful; painstaking.

тщеду́шный feeble, frail.

тщесла́вие vanity, vainglory. **тщесла́вный** vain. **тщета́** vanity. **тще́тный** vain, futile.

ты (тебя́, тебе́, тобо́й, тебе́) you; thou; **быть на ты** с+*instr* be on intimate terms with.

ты́кать (ты́чу) *impf* (*pf* ткнуть) poke; prod; stick.

ты́ква pumpkin; gourd.

тыл (*loc* -ý; *pl* -ы́) back; rear. **ты́льный** back; rear.

тын paling; palisade.

ты́сяча (*instr* -ей *or* -ью) thousand. **тысячеле́тие** millennium; thousandth anniversary. **ты́сячный** thousandth; of (many) thousands.

тычи́нка stamen.

тьма[1] dark, darkness.

тьма[2] host, multitude.

тюбете́йка skull-cap.

тю́бик tube.

тюк (-á) bale, package.

тюле́нь *m* seal.

тюльпа́н tulip.

тюре́мный prison. **тюре́мщик** gaoler. **тюрьма́** (*pl* -ы, -рем) prison, gaol.

тюфя́к (-á) mattress.

тя́га traction; thrust; draught; attraction; craving. **тяга́ться** *impf* vie, contend. **тяга́ч** (-á) tractor.

тя́гостный burdensome; painful. **тя́гость** burden. **тяготе́ние**

gravity, gravitation; bent, inclination. **тяготе́ть** (-е́ю) *impf* gravitate; be attracted; ~ **над** hang over. **тяготи́ть** (-ощу́) *impf* be a burden on; oppress.

тягу́чий malleable, ductile; viscous; slow.

тя́жба lawsuit; competition.

тяжело́ *adv* heavily; seriously. **тяжело́** *predic* it is hard; it is painful. **тяжелоатле́т** weightlifter. **тяжелове́с** heavyweight. **тяжелове́сный** heavy; ponderous. **тяжёлый** (-ёл, -а́) heavy; hard; serious; painful. **тя́жесть** gravity; weight; heaviness; severity. **тя́жкий** heavy; severe; grave.

тяну́ть (-ну́, -нешь) *impf* (*pf* по~) pull; draw; drag; drag out; weigh; *impers* attract; be tight; ~**ся** stretch; extend; stretch out; stretch o.s.; drag on; crawl; drift; move along one after another; last out; reach.

тяну́чка toffee.

У

у *prep+gen* by; at; with; from, of; belonging to; **у меня́ (есть)** I have; **у нас** at our place; in our country.

уба́вить (-влю) *pf*, **убавля́ть** *impf* reduce, diminish.

у/баю́кать *pf*, **убаю́кивать** *impf* lull (to sleep).

убега́ть *impf of* **убежа́ть**

убеди́тельный convincing; earnest. **убеди́ть** (-и́шь) (*pf of* **убежда́ть**) convince; persuade; ~**ся** be convinced; make certain.

убежа́ть (-егу́) *pf* (*impf* **убега́ть**)

run away; escape; boil over.

убежда́ть(ся *impf of* **убеди́ть(ся.** **убежде́ние** persuasion; conviction; belief. **убеждённость** conviction. **убеждённый** (-ён, -á) convinced; staunch.

убе́жище refuge, asylum; shelter.

уберега́ть *impf*, **убере́чь** (-регу́, -режёшь; -рёг, -гла́) *pf* protect, preserve; ~**ся от**+*gen* protect o.s. against.

уберу́ *etc.*: *see* **убра́ть**

убива́ть *impf of* **уби́ть.** **уби́йственный** deadly; murderous; killing. **уби́йство** murder. **уби́йца** *m & f* murderer.

убира́ть(ся *impf of* **убра́ть(ся;** **убира́йся!** clear off!

уби́тый killed; crushed; *sb* dead man. **уби́ть** (убью́, -ьёшь) *pf* (*impf* **убива́ть**) kill; murder; ~**ся** hurt o.s.

убо́гий wretched. **убо́жество** poverty; squalor.

убо́й slaughter.

убо́р dress, attire.

убо́рка harvesting; clearing up. **убо́рная** *sb* lavatory; dressing-room. **убо́рочный** harvesting; ~**ая маши́на** harvester. **убо́рщик, убо́рщица** cleaner.

убра́нство furniture. **убра́ть** (уберу́, -рёшь; -а́л, -á, -о) *pf* (*impf* **убира́ть**) take away; put away; harvest; clear up; decorate; ~ **посте́ль** make a bed; ~ **со стола́** clear the table; ~**ся** tidy up, clean up; clear off.

убыва́ть *impf*, **убы́ть** (убу́ду; у́был, -а́, -о) *pf* diminish; subside; wane; leave. **убыль** diminution; casualties. **убы́ток** (-тка) loss; *pl* damages. **убы́точный** unprofitable.

убью́ *etc.*: *see* уби́ть

уважа́емый respected; dear. **уважа́ть** *impf* respect. **уваже́ние** respect; с ~м yours sincerely. **уважи́тельный** valid; respectful.

уве́домить (-млю) *pf*, **уведомля́ть** *impf* inform. **уведомле́ние** notification.

уведу́ *etc.*: *see* увести́

увезти́ (-зу́, -зёшь; увёз, -ла́) *pf* (*impf* **увози́ть**) take (away); steal; abduct.

увекове́чивать *impf*, **увекове́чить** (-чу) *pf* immortalize; perpetuate.

увёл *etc.*: *see* увести́

увеличе́ние increase; magnification; enlargement. **увели́чивать** *impf*, **увели́чить** (-чу) *pf* increase; magnify; enlarge; ~ся increase, grow. **увеличи́тель** *m* enlarger. **увеличи́тельный** magnifying; enlarging; ~ое стекло́ magnifying glass.

у|венча́ть *pf*, **увенчивать** *impf* crown; ~ся be crowned.

увере́нность confidence; certainty. **уве́ренный** confident; sure; certain. **уве́рить** *pf* (*impf* **уверя́ть**) assure; convince; ~ся satisfy o.s.; be convinced.

уверну́ться (-нусь, -нёшься) *pf*, **увёртываться** *impf* от+*gen* evade. **увёртка** dodge, evasion; subterfuge; *pl* wiles. **увёртливый** evasive, shifty.

увертю́ра overture.

уверя́ть(ся *impf of* уве́рить(ся

увеселе́ние amusement, entertainment. **увесели́тельный** entertainment; pleasure. **увеселя́ть** *impf* amuse, entertain.

уве́систый weighty.

увести́ (-еду́, -едёшь; -ёл, -а́) *pf*

(*impf* **уводи́ть**) take (away); walk off with.

уве́чить (-чу) *impf* maim, cripple. **уве́чный** maimed, crippled; *sb* cripple. **уве́чье** maiming; injury.

уве́шать *pf*, **уве́шивать** *impf* hang (+*instr* with).

увеща́ть *impf*, **увещева́ть** *impf* exhort, admonish.

у|ви́деть *pf* *see*. **у|ви́деть(ся** (-и́жу(сь) *pf*.

увили́вать *impf*, **увильну́ть** (-ну́, -нёшь) *pf* от+*gen* dodge; evade.

увлажни́ть *pf*, **увлажня́ть** *impf* moisten.

увлека́тельный fascinating. **увлека́ть** *impf*, **увле́чь** (-еку́, -ечёшь; -ёк, -ла́) *pf* carry away; fascinate; ~ся be carried away; become mad (+*instr* about). **увлече́ние** animation; passion; crush.

уво́д withdrawal; stealing. **уводи́ть** (-ожу́, -о́дишь) *impf of* увести́

увози́ть (-ожу́, -о́зишь) *impf of* увезти́

уво́лить *pf*, **увольня́ть** *impf* discharge, dismiss; retire; ~ся be discharged, retire. **увольне́ние** discharge, dismissal.

увы́ *int* alas!

увяда́ть *impf of* увя́нуть. **увя́дший** withered.

увяза́ть¹ *impf of* увя́знуть

увяза́ть² (-яжу́, -я́жешь) *pf* (*impf* **увя́зывать**) tie up; pack up; co-ordinate; ~ся pack; tag along. **увя́зка** tying up; co-ordination.

у|вя́знуть (-ну; -я́з) *pf* (*impf also* **увяза́ть**¹) get bogged down.

увя́зывать(ся *impf of* увяза́ть(ся

у|вя́нуть (-ну) *pf* (*impf also* **увя-да́ть**) fade, wither.

угада́ть *pf*, **уга́дывать** *impf* guess.

уга́р carbon monoxide (poisoning); ecstasy. **уга́рный газ** carbon monoxide.

угаса́ть *impf*, **уга́снуть** (-нет, -ас) *pf* go out; die down.

угле- *in comb* coal; charcoal; carbon. **углево́д** carbohydrate. **~водоро́д** hydrocarbon. **~добы́ча** coal extraction. **~кислота́** carbonic acid; carbon dioxide. **~ки́слый** carbonate (of). **~ро́д** carbon.

углово́й corner; angular.

углуби́ть (-блю́) *pf*, **углубля́ть** *impf* deepen; **~ся** deepen; delve deeply; become absorbed. **углубле́ние** depression, dip; deepening. **углублённый** deepened; profound; absorbed.

угна́ть (угоню́, -о́нишь; -а́л, -а́, -о) *pf* (*impf* **угоня́ть**) drive away; despatch; steal; **~ся за**+*instr* keep pace with.

угнета́тель *m* oppressor. **угнета́ть** *impf* oppress; depress. **угнете́ние** oppression; depression. **угнетённый** oppressed; depressed.

угова́ривать *impf*, **уговори́ть** *pf* persuade; **~ся** arrange, agree. **угово́р** persuasion; agreement.

уго́да: в уго́ду +*dat* to please. **угоди́ть** (-ожу́) *pf*, **угожда́ть** *impf* fall; bang; (+*dat*) hit; +*dat or* на+*acc* please. **угодли́вый** obsequious. **уго́дно** *predic*+*dat*: как вам ~ as you wish; что вам ~? what would you like?; *partl* кто ~ anyone (you like); что ~ anything (you like).

уго́дье (*gen pl* -ий) land.

у́гол (угла́, *loc* -у́) corner; angle.

уголо́вник criminal. **уголо́вный** criminal.

уголо́к (-лка́, *loc* -у́) corner.

у́голь (у́гля́; *pl* у́гли, -ей *or* -е́й) *m* coal; charcoal.

у́гольник set square.

у́гольный coal; carbonic.

угомони́ть *pf* calm down; **~ся** calm down.

уго́н driving away; stealing. **уго́нять** *impf of* **угна́ть**

угора́ть *impf*, **угоре́ть** (-рю́) *pf* get carbon monoxide poisoning; be mad. **угоре́лый** mad; possessed.

у́горь[1] (угря́) *m* eel.

у́горь[2] (угря́) *m* blackhead.

угости́ть (-ощу́) *pf*, **угоща́ть** *impf* entertain; treat. **угоще́ние** entertaining; treating; refreshments.

угрожа́ть *impf* threaten. **угро́за** threat, menace.

угро́зыск *abbr* criminal investigation department.

угрызе́ние pangs.

угрю́мый sullen, morose.

удава́ться (удаётся) *impf of* **уда́ться**

у|дави́ть(ся) (-влю́(сь), -вишь(ся) *pf*. **уда́вка** running-knot, half hitch.

удале́ние removal; sending away; moving off. **удали́ть** *pf* (*impf* **удаля́ть**) remove; send away; move away; **~ся** move off, away; retire.

удало́й, уда́лый (-а́л, -а́, -о) daring, bold. **у́даль, уда́льство** daring, boldness.

удаля́ть(ся) *impf of* **удали́ть(ся)**

уда́р blow; stroke; attack; kick; thrust; seizure; bolt. **ударе́ние**

accent; stress; emphasis. **уда́рить** pf, **ударя́ть** impf (impf also **бить**) strike; hit; beat; ~ **в** +acc strike, hit; ~**в** +acc break into; burst into them. **уда́рник, -ница** shock-worker. **уда́рный** percussion; shock; stressed; urgent.

уда́ться (-а́стся, -аду́тся; -а́лся, -ла́сь) pf (impf **удава́ться**) succeed, be a success; impers +dat +inf succeed, manage; **мне удало́сь найти́ рабо́ту** I managed to find a job. **уда́ча** good luck; success. **уда́чный** successful; felicitous.

удава́ть impf, **удво́ить** (-о́ю) pf double, redouble. **удвое́ние** (re)doubling.

уде́л lot, destiny.

удели́ть pf (impf **уделя́ть**) spare, give.

уделя́ть impf of **удели́ть**

удержа́ние deduction; retention, keeping. **удержа́ть** (-жу́, -жишь) pf, **уде́рживать** impf hold (on to); retain; restrain; suppress; deduct; ~**ся** hold out; stand firm; refrain (from).

удеру́ etc.: see **удра́ть**

удешеви́ть (-влю́) pf, **удешевля́ть** impf reduce the price of.

удиви́тельный surprising, amazing; wonderful. **удиви́ть** (-влю́) pf, **удивля́ть** impf surprise, amaze; ~**ся** be surprised, be amazed. **удивле́ние** surprise, amazement.

удила́ (-и́л) pl bit.

уди́лище fishing-rod.

удира́ть impf of **удра́ть**

уди́ть (ужу́, у́дишь) impf fish for; ~ **ры́бу** fish; ~**ся** bite.

удлине́ние lengthening; extension. **удлини́ть** pf, **удлиня́ть** impf lengthen; extend; ~**ся** be-

come longer; be extended.

удо́бно adv comfortably; conveniently. **удо́бный** comfortable; convenient.

удобовари́мый digestible.

удобре́ние fertilization; fertilizer. **удо́брить** pf, **удобря́ть** impf fertilize. **удо́бство** comfort; convenience.

удовлетворе́ние satisfaction; gratification. **удовлетво́рённый** (-рён, -а́) satisfied. **удовлетвори́тельный** satisfactory. **удовлетворя́ть** pf, **удовлетворя́ть** impf satisfy; +dat meet; +instr supply with; ~**ся** be satisfied.

удово́льствие pleasure. **удово́льствоваться** pf.

удо́й milk-yield; milking.

удоста́ивать(ся impf of **удосто́ить(ся**

удостовере́ние certification; certificate; ~ **ли́чности** identity card. **удостове́рить** pf, **удостоверя́ть** impf certify, witness; ~**ся** make sure (**в** +prep of), assure o.s.

удосто́ить pf (impf **удоста́ивать**) make an award to; +gen award; +instr favour with; ~**ся** +gen be awarded; be favoured with.

у́дочка (fishing-)rod.

удра́ть (удеру́, -ёшь; удра́л, -а́, -о) pf (impf **удира́ть**) make off.

удруча́ть impf, **удручи́ть** (-чу́) pf depress. **удручённый** (-чён, -а́) depressed.

удуша́ть impf, **удуши́ть** (-шу́, -шишь) pf stifle, suffocate. **удуше́ние** suffocation. **уду́шливый** stifling. **уду́шье** asthma; asphyxia.

уедине́ние solitude; seclusion.

уединённый secluded; lonely. **уедини́ться** *pf*, **уединя́ться** *impf* seclude o.s.

уе́зд uyezd, District.

уезжа́ть *impf*, **уе́хать** (уе́ду) *pf* go away, depart.

уж¹ (-á) grass-snake.

уж²: *see* **уже́²**, **уж³**, **уже́³** *partl* indeed; really.

ужа́лить *pf*.

у́жас horror, terror; *predic* it is awful. **ужаса́ть** *impf*, **ужасну́ть** (-ну́, -нёшь) *pf* horrify; **~ся** be horrified; be terrified. **ужа́сно** *adv* terribly; awfully. **ужа́сный** awful, terrible.

уже́¹ *comp of* **у́зкий**

уже́², **уж²** *adv* already; **~** не no longer. **уже́³**: *see* **уж³**

уже́ние fishing.

ужива́ться *impf of* **ужи́ться**. **ужи́вчивый** easy to get on with.

ужи́мка grimace.

у́жин supper. **у́жинать** *impf* (*pf* по**~**) have supper.

ужи́ться (-иву́сь, -ивёшься; -и́лся, -ла́сь) *pf* (*impf* **ужива́ться**) get on.

ужу́ *see* **уди́ть**

узако́нивать *impf*, **узако́нить** *pf* legalize.

узбе́к, -е́чка Uzbek. **Узбеки́ста́н** Uzbekistan.

узда́ (*pl* -ы) bridle.

у́зел (узла́) knot; junction; centre; node; bundle.

у́зкий (у́зок, узка́, -о) narrow; tight; narrow-minded. **узкоколе́йка** narrow-gauge railway.

узлова́тый knotty. **узлов|о́й** junction; main, key; **~а́я ста́нция** junction.

узнава́ть (-наю́, -наёшь) *impf*, **узна́ть** *pf* recognize; get to know; find out.

у́зник, у́зница prisoner.

узо́р pattern, design. **узо́рчатый** patterned.

у́зость narrowness; tightness.

узурпа́тор usurper. **узурпи́ровать** *impf* & *pf* usurp.

у́зы (уз) *pl* bonds, ties.

уйду́ *etc.*: *see* **уйти́**

уйма́ lots (of).

уйму́ *etc.*: *see* **уня́ть**

уйти́ (уйду́, -дёшь; ушёл, ушла́) *pf* (*impf* **уходи́ть**) go away, leave, depart; escape; retire; bury o.s.; be used up; pass away.

ука́з decree; edict. **указа́ние** indication; instruction. **ука́занный** appointed, stated. **указа́тель** *m* indicator; gauge; index; directory. **указа́тельный** indicating; demonstrative; **~ па́лец** index finger. **указа́ть** (-ажу́, -а́жешь) *pf*, **ука́зывать** *impf* show; indicate; point; point out. **ука́зка** pointer; orders.

ука́лывать *impf of* **уколо́ть**

уката́ть *pf*, **ука́тывать¹** *impf* roll; flatten; wear out. **укати́ть** (-ачу́, -а́тишь) *pf*, **ука́тывать²** *impf* roll away; drive off; **~ся** roll away.

укача́ть *pf*, **ука́чивать** *impf* rock to sleep; make sick.

укла́д structure; style; organization. **укла́дка** packing; stacking; laying; setting. **укла́дчик** packer; layer. **укла́дывать(ся)** *impf of* **уложи́ть(ся)**

укла́дываться² *impf of* **уле́чься**

укло́н slope; incline; gradient; bias; deviation. **уклоне́ние** deviation; digression. **уклони́ться** (-ню́сь, -ни́шься) *pf*, **уклоня́ться** *impf* deviate; +*от*+*gen* turn (off, aside); avoid; evade. **укло́нчивый** evasive.

уклю́чина rowlock.

уко́л prick; injection; thrust.

уколо́ть (-лю́, -лешь) pf (impf **ука́лывать**) prick; wound.

у|комплектова́ть pf, **у|комплекто́вывать** impf complete; bring up to (full) strength; man; +instr equip with.

уко́р reproach.

укора́чивать impf of **укороти́ть**

укорени́ть pf, **укореня́ть** impf implant, inculcate; ~ся take root.

укори́зна reproach. **укори́зненный** reproachful. **укори́ть** pf (impf **укоря́ть**) reproach (в+prep in).

укороти́ть (-очу́) pf (impf **укора́чивать**) shorten.

укоря́ть impf of **укори́ть**

уко́с (hay-)crop.

укра́дкой adv stealthily. **украду́** etc.: see **укра́сть**

Украи́на Ukraine. **украи́нец** (-нца), **украи́нка** Ukrainian. **украи́нский** Ukrainian.

укра́сить (-а́шу) pf (impf **украша́ть**) adorn, decorate; ~ся be decorated; adorn o.s.

у|кра́сть (-аду́, -дёшь) pf.

украша́ть(ся impf of **укра́сить(ся**. **украше́ние** decoration; adornment.

укрепи́ть (-плю́) pf, **укрепля́ть** impf strengthen; fix; fortify; ~ся become stronger; fortify one's position. **укрепле́ние** strengthening; reinforcement; fortification.

укро́мный secluded, cosy.

укро́п dill.

укроти́тель m (animal-)tamer. **укроти́ть** (-ощу́) pf, **укроща́ть** impf tame; curb; ~ся become

tame; calm down. **укроще́ние** taming.

укро́ю etc.: see **укры́ть**

укрупне́ние enlargement; amalgamation. **укрупни́ть** pf, **укрупня́ть** impf enlarge; amalgamate.

укрыва́тель m harbourer. **укрыва́тельство** harbouring; receiving. **укрыва́ть** impf, **укры́ть** (-ро́ю) pf cover; conceal; harbour; shelter; receive; ~ся cover o.s.; take cover. **укры́тие** cover; shelter.

у́ксус vinegar.

уку́с bite; sting. **укуси́ть** (-ушу́, -у́сишь) pf bite; sting.

уку́тать pf, **уку́тывать** impf wrap up; ~ся wrap o.s. up.

укушу́ etc.: see **укуси́ть**

ул. abbr (of **у́лица**) street, road.

ула́вливать impf of **улови́ть**

ула́дить (-а́жу) pf, **ула́живать** impf settle, arrange.

у́лей (у́лья) m (bee)hive.

улета́ть impf, **улете́ть** (улечу́) pf fly (away). **улету́чиваться**, impf, **улету́читься** (-чусь) pf evaporate; vanish.

уле́чься (уля́гусь, -я́жешься; улёгся, -гла́сь) pf (impf **укла́дываться**) lie down; settle; subside.

ули́ка clue; evidence.

ули́тка snail.

у́лица street; **на у́лице** in the street; outside.

улича́ть impf, **уличи́ть** (-чу́) pf establish the guilt of.

у́личный street.

уло́в catch. **улови́мый** perceptible; audible. **улови́ть** (-влю́, -вишь) pf (impf **ула́вливать**) catch; seize. **уло́вка** trick, ruse.

уложе́ние code. **уложи́ть** (-жу́,

-жишь) pf (impf укла́дывать) lay; pack; pile; ~ спать put to bed; ~ся pack (up); fit in.

улуча́ть impf, **улучи́ть** (-чу́) pf find, seize.

улучша́ть impf, **улу́чшить** (-шу) pf improve; better; ~ся improve; get better. **улучше́ние** improvement.

улыба́ться impf, **улыбну́ться** (-ну́сь, -нёшься) pf smile. **улы́бка** smile.

ультима́тум ultimatum.

ультра- in comb ultra-. **ультразвуково́й** supersonic. ~**фиоле́товый** ultra-violet.

уля́гусь etc.: see **уле́чься**

ум (-а́) mind, intellect; head; **сойти́ с ~а́** go mad.

умали́ть pf (impf умаля́ть) belittle.

умалишённый mad; sb lunatic.

ума́лчивать impf of умолча́ть

умаля́ть impf of умали́ть

уме́лец (-льца) skilled craftsman. **уме́лый** able, skilful. **уме́ние** ability, skill.

уменьша́ть impf, **уме́ньшить** (-шу) pf reduce, diminish, decrease; ~ся diminish, decrease; abate. **уменьше́ние** decrease, reduction; abatement. **уменьши́тельный** diminutive.

уме́ренность moderation. **уме́ренный** moderate; temperate.

умере́ть (умру́, -рёшь; у́мер, -ла́, -о) pf (impf умира́ть) die.

уме́рить pf (impf умеря́ть) moderate; restrain.

умертви́ть (-рщвлю́, -ртви́шь) pf, **умерщвля́ть** impf kill, destroy; mortify. **у́мерший** dead; sb the deceased. **умерщвле́ние**

killing, destruction; mortification.

умеря́ть impf of уме́рить

умести́ть (-ещу́) pf (impf умеща́ть) fit in, find room for; ~ся fit in. **уме́стный** appropriate; pertinent; timely.

уме́ть (-е́ю) impf be able, know how.

умеща́ть(ся impf of умести́ть(ся

умиле́ние tenderness; emotion. **умили́ть** pf, **умиля́ть** impf move, touch; ~ся be moved.

умира́ние dying. **умира́ть** impf of умере́ть. **умира́ющий** dying; sb dying person.

умиротворе́ние pacification; appeasement. **умиротвори́ть** pf, **умиротворя́ть** impf pacify; appease.

умне́ть (-е́ю) impf (pf по~) grow wiser. **у́мница** good girl; m & f clever person.

умножа́ть impf, **у́мно́жить** (-жу) pf multiply; increase; ~ся increase, multiply. **умноже́ние** multiplication; increase. **умножи́тель** m multiplier.

у́мный (умён, умна́, у́мно́) clever, wise, intelligent. **умозаключе́ние** deduction; conclusion.

умоли́ть pf (impf умоля́ть) move by entreaties.

умолка́ть impf, **умо́лкнуть** (-ну; -о́лк) pf fall silent; stop.

умолча́ть (-чу́) pf (impf ума́лчивать) fail to mention; hush up.

умоля́ть impf of умоли́ть; beg, entreat.

умопомеша́тельство derangement.

умори́тельный incredibly funny, killing. **у|мори́ть** pf kill; exhaust.

умо́ю *etc.*: *see* **умы́ть. умру́** *etc.*: *see* **умере́ть**.

у́мственный mental, intellectual.

умудри́ть *pf*, **умудря́ть** *impf* make wiser; **~ся** contrive.

умыва́льная *sb* wash-room. **умыва́льник** wash-stand, wash-basin. **умыва́ть(ся** *impf of* **умы́ть(ся**

у́мысел (-сла) design, intention.

умы́ть (умо́ю) *pf* (*impf* **умыва́ть**) wash; **~ся** wash (o.s.).

умышленный intentional.

у|насле́довать *pf*.

унести́ (-су́, -сёшь; -ёс, -ла́) *pf* (*impf* **уноси́ть**) take away; carry off, make off with; **~сь** speed away; fly by; be carried (away).

универма́г *abbr* department store. **универса́льный** universal; all-round; versatile; all-purpose; **~ магази́н** department store; **~ое сре́дство** panacea. **универса́м** *abbr* supermarket.

университе́т university. **университе́тский** university.

унижа́ть *impf*, **уни́зить** (-и́жу) *pf* humiliate; **~ся** humble o.s.; stoop. **униже́ние** humiliation. **уни́женный** humble. **унизи́тельный** humiliating. **уника́льный** unique.

унима́ть(ся *impf of* **уня́ть(ся**

унисо́н unison.

унита́з lavatory pan.

унифици́ровать *impf & pf* standardize.

уничижи́тельный pejorative.

уничтожа́ть *impf*, **уничто́жить** (-жу) *pf* destroy, annihilate; abolish; do away with. **уничтоже́ние** destruction, annihilation; abolition.

уноси́ть(ся *impf of* **унести́(сь**

у́нция ounce.

уныва́ть *impf* be dejected. **уны́лый** dejected; doleful, cheerless. **уны́ние** dejection, despondency.

уня́ть (уйму́, -мёшь; -я́л, -а́, -о) *pf* (*impf* **унима́ть**) calm, soothe; **~ся** calm down.

упа́док (-дка) decline; decay; **~ ду́ха** depression. **упа́дочнический** decadent. **упа́дочный** depressive; decadent. **упаду́** *etc.*: *see* **упа́сть**.

у|пако́вывать *impf* pack (up). **упако́вка** packing; wrapping. **упако́вщик** packer.

упа́сть (-аду́, -адёшь) *pf of* **па́дать**

упере́ть (упру́, -рёшь; -ёр) *pf*, **упира́ть** *impf* rest, lean; **~ на+**acc stress; **~ся** rest, lean; resist; **+в+**acc come up against.

упи́танный well-fed; fattened.

упла́та payment. **уплати́ть** (-ачу́, -а́тишь) *pf*, **упла́чивать** *impf* pay.

уплотне́ние compression; condensation; consolidation; sealing. **уплотни́ть** *pf*, **уплотня́ть** *impf* condense; compress; pack more into.

уплыва́ть *impf*, **уплы́ть** (-ыву́ -ывёшь; -ы́л, -а́, -о) *pf* swim or sail away; pass.

упова́ть *impf* +на+acc put one's trust in.

уподо́биться (-блюсь) *pf*, **уподобля́ться** *impf* +dat become like.

упое́ние ecstasy, rapture. **упои́тельный** intoxicating, ravishing.

уполза́ть *impf*, **уползти́** (-зу́,

-зёшь; -о́лз, -зла́) *pf* creep away, crawl away.

уполномо́ченный *sb* (authorized) agent, representative, proxy. **уполномо́чивать, уполномо́чить** (-чу) *pf* authorize, empower.

упомина́ние mention. **упомина́ть** *impf*, **упомяну́ть** (-ну́, -нешь) *pf* mention, refer to.

упо́р prop, support; в ~ point-blank; сде́лать ~ на+*acc* or *prep* lay stress on. **упо́рный** stubborn; persistent. **упо́рство** stubbornness; persistence. **упо́рствовать** *impf* be stubborn; persist (в+*prep* in).

упоря́дочивать *impf*, **упоря́дочить** (-чу) *pf* regulate, put in order.

употреби́тельный (widely-)used; common. **употреби́ть** (-блю́) *pf*, **употребля́ть** *impf* use. **употребле́ние** use; usage.

упра́ва justice.

управдо́м *abbr* manager (*of block of flats*). **упра́виться** (-влюсь) *pf*, **управля́ться** *impf* cope, manage; +*c*+*instr* deal with. **управле́ние** management; administration; direction; control; driving, steering; government. **управля́емый снаря́д** guided missile. **управля́ть** *impf* +*instr* manage, direct, run; govern; be in control of; operate; drive. **управля́ющий** *sb* manager.

упражне́ние exercise. **упражня́ть** *impf* exercise, train; ~ся practise, train.

упраздни́ть *pf*, **упраздня́ть** *impf* abolish.

упра́шивать *impf of* упроси́ть

упрёк reproach. **упрека́ть** *impf*,

упрекну́ть (-ну́, -нёшь) *pf* reproach.

упроси́ть (-ошу́, -о́сишь) *pf* (*impf* упра́шивать) entreat; prevail upon.

упрости́ть (-ощу́) *pf* (*impf* упроща́ть) (over-)simplify.

упро́чить *impf*, **упро́чить** (-чу) *pf* strengthen, consolidate; ~ся be firmly established.

упрошу́ *etc.: see* упроси́ть

упроща́ть *impf of* упрости́ть. **упрощённый** (-щён, -а́) (over-)simplified.

упру́ *etc.: see* упере́ть

упру́гий elastic; springy. **упру́гость** elasticity; spring. **упру́же** *comp of* упру́гий

упря́жка harness; team. **упряжно́й** draught. **упря́жь** harness.

упря́миться (-млюсь) *impf* be obstinate; persist. **упря́мство** obstinacy. **упря́мый** obstinate; persistent.

упуска́ть *impf*, **упусти́ть** (-ущу́, -у́стишь) *pf* let go, let slip; miss. **упуще́ние** omission; slip; negligence.

ура́ *int* hurrah!

уравне́ние equalization; equation. **ура́внивать** *impf*, **уравня́ть** *pf* equalize. **уравни́тельный** equalizing, levelling. **уравнове́сить** (-е́шу) *pf*, **уравнове́шивать** *impf* balance; counterbalance. **уравнове́шенность** composure. **уравнове́шенный** balanced, composed.

урага́н hurricane; storm.

ура́льский Ural.

ура́н uranium; Uranus. **ура́новый** uranium.

урва́ть (-ву́, -вёшь; -а́л, -а́, -о) *pf* (*impf* урыва́ть) snatch.

урегули́рование regulation;

settlement. у**регули́ровать** pf.

у**ре́зать** (-е́жу) pf, уреза́ть, уре́зывать impf cut off; shorten; reduce.

у́рка m & f (sl) lag, convict.

у́рна urn; litter-bin.

у́ровень (-вня) m level; standard.

уро́д freak, monster.

уроди́ться (-ожу́сь) pf ripen; grow.

уро́дливость deformity; ugliness. **уро́дливый** deformed; ugly; bad. **уро́довать** impf (pf из~) disfigure; distort. **уро́дство** disfigurement; ugliness.

урожа́й harvest; crop; abundance. **урожа́йность** yield; productivity. **урожа́йный** productive, high-yield.

урождённый née. **уроже́нец** (-нца), **уроже́нка** native. **урожу́сь** see **уроди́ться**

уро́к lesson.

уро́н losses; damage. **урони́ть** (-ню́, -нишь) pf of **роня́ть**

урча́ть (-чу́) impf rumble.

урыва́ть impf of **урва́ть**. **уры́вками** adv in snatches, by fits and starts.

ус (pl -ы́) whisker; tendril; pl moustache.

усади́ть (-ажу́, -а́дишь) pf, **уса́живать** impf seat, offer a seat; plant. **уса́дьба** (gen pl -деб or -дьб) country estate; farmstead. **уса́живаться** impf of **усе́сться**

усы́тый moustached; whiskered.

усва́ивать impf, **усво́ить** pf master; assimilate; adopt. **усвое́ние** mastering; assimilation; adoption.

усе́рдие zeal; diligence. **усе́рдный** zealous; diligent.

усе́сться (уся́дусь, -е́лся) pf

(impf уса́живаться) take a seat; settle down (to).

усиде́ть (-ижу́) pf remain seated; hold down a job. **уси́дчивый** assiduous.

у́сик tendril; runner; antenna; pl small moustache.

усиле́ние strengthening; reinforcement; intensification; amplification. **уси́ленный** intensified, increased; earnest. **уси́ливать** impf, **уси́лить** pf intensify, increase; amplify; strengthen, reinforce; ~ся increase, intensify; become stronger. **уси́лие** effort. **уси́литель** m amplifier; booster.

ускака́ть (-ачу́, -а́чешь) pf skip off; gallop off.

ускольза́ть impf, **ускользну́ть** (-ну́, -нёшь) pf slip off; steal away; escape.

ускоре́ние acceleration. **ускоренный** accelerated; rapid; crash. **ускори́тель** m accelerator.

уско́рить pf, **ускоря́ть** impf quicken; accelerate; hasten; ~ся accelerate, be accelerated; quicken.

усло́вие condition. **усло́виться** (-влюсь) pf, **усло́вливаться**, **усла́вливаться** impf agree; arrange. **усло́вленный** agreed, fixed. **усло́вность** convention. **усло́вный** conditional; conditioned; conventional; agreed; relative.

усложне́ние complication. **усложни́ть** pf, **усложня́ть** impf complicate; ~ся become complicated.

услу́га service; good turn. **услу́жливый** obliging.

услыха́ть (-ы́шу) pf, у**слы́шать** (-ы́шу) pf hear; sense; scent.

усматривать *impf of* усмотреть

усмехаться *impf*, **усмехнуться** (-нусь, -нёшься) *pf* smile; grin; smirk. **усмешка** smile; grin; sneer.

усмирение pacification; suppression. **усмирить** *pf*, **усмирять** *impf* pacify; calm; suppress.

усмотрение discretion, judgement. **усмотреть** (-рю, -ришь) *pf* (*impf* усматривать) perceive; see; regard; +за+*instr* keep an eye on.

уснуть (-ну, -нёшь) *pf* go to sleep.

усовершенствование advanced studies; improvement, refinement. **у|совершенствовать(ся** *impf*.

усомниться *pf* doubt.

успеваемость progress. **успевать** *impf*, **успеть** (-ею) *pf* have time; manage; succeed. **успех** success; progress. **успешный** successful.

успокаивать *impf*, **успокоить** *pf* calm, quiet, soothe; ~**ся** calm down; abate. **успокаивающий** calming, sedative. **успокоение** calming, soothing; calm; peace. **успокоительный** calming; reassuring; ~**ое** *sb* sedative, tranquillizer.

уста (-т, -там) *pl* mouth.

устав regulations, statutes; charter.

уставать (-таю, -ёшь) *impf of* устать; не уставая incessantly.

уставить (-влю) *impf* set, arrange; cover, fill; direct; ~**ся** find room, go in; stare.

усталость tiredness. **усталый** tired.

устанавливать *impf*, **установить** (-влю, -вишь) *pf* put, set up; install; set; establish; fix; ~**ся** dispose o.s.; be established; set in. **установка** putting, setting up; installation; setting; plant, unit; directions. **установление** establishment. **установленный** established, prescribed.

устану *etc.*: *see* устать

устаревать *impf*, **у|старе́ть** (-ею) *pf* become obsolete; become antiquated. **устаре́лый** obsolete; antiquated, out-of-date.

устать (-ану) *pf* (*impf* уставать) get tired.

устилать *impf*, **устлать** (-телю, -телешь) *pf* cover; pave.

устный oral, verbal.

устой abutment; foundation; support. **устойчивость** stability, steadiness. **устойчивый** stable, steady. **устоять** (-ою) *pf* keep one's balance; stand firm; ~**ся** settle; become fixed.

устраивать(ся *impf of* устроить(ся

устранение removal, elimination. **устранить** *pf*, **устранять** *impf* remove; eliminate; ~**ся** resign, retire.

устрашать *impf*, **устрашить** (-шу) *pf* frighten; ~**ся** be frightened.

устремить (-млю) *pf*, **устремлять** *impf* direct, fix; ~**ся** rush; be directed; concentrate. **устремление** rush; aspiration.

устрица oyster.

устроитель *m*, ~**ница** organizer. **устроить** *pf* (*impf* устраивать) arrange, organize; make; cause; settle, put in order; place; fix up; get; suit; ~**ся** work out; manage; settle down; be found,

get fixed up. **устро́йство** arrangement; construction; mechanism, device; system.

усту́п shelf, ledge. **уступа́ть** *impf*, **уступи́ть** (-плю́, -пишь) *pf* yield; give up; ~ **доро́гу** make way. **усту́пка** concession. **усту́пчивый** pliable; compliant.

устыди́ть(ся) (-ыжу́сь) *pf* (+*gen*) be ashamed (of).

у́стье (*gen pl* -ьев) mouth; estuary.

усугуби́ть (-у́блю) *pf*, **усугубля́ть** *impf* increase; aggravate.

усы́ *see* ус

усынови́ть (-влю́) *pf*, **усыновля́ть** *impf* adopt. **усыновле́ние** adoption.

усы́пать (-плю) *pf*, **усыпа́ть** *impf* strew, scatter.

усыпи́тельный soporific. **усыпи́ть** (-плю́) *pf*, **усыпля́ть** *impf* put to sleep; lull; weaken.

уся́дусь *etc.*: *see* усе́сться

ута́ивать *impf*, **утаи́ть** *pf* conceal; keep secret.

ута́птывать *impf of* утопта́ть

ута́скивать *impf*, **утащи́ть** (-щу́, -щишь) *pf* drag off.

у́тварь utensils.

утверди́тельный affirmative. **утверди́ть** (-ржу́) *pf*, **утвержда́ть** *impf* confirm; approve; ratify; establish; assert; ~**ся** gain a foothold; become established; be confirmed. **утвержде́ние** approval; confirmation; ratification; assertion; establishment.

утека́ть *impf of* уте́чь

утёнок (-нка; *pl* утя́та, -я́т) duckling.

утепли́ть *pf*, **утепля́ть** *impf* warm.

утере́ть (утру́, -рёшь; утёр) *pf* (*impf* утира́ть) wipe (off, dry).

утерпе́ть (-плю́, -пишь) *pf* restrain o.s.

утёс cliff, crag.

уте́чка leak, leakage; escape; loss. **уте́чь** (-еку́, -ечёшь; утёк, -ла́) *pf* (*impf* утека́ть) leak, escape; pass.

утеша́ть *impf*, **уте́шить** (-шу) *pf* console; ~**ся** console o.s. **утеше́ние** consolation. **утеши́тельный** comforting.

утилизи́ровать *impf & pf* utilize.

ути́ль *m*, утильсырьё scrap.

ути́ный duck, duck's.

утира́ть(ся) *impf of* утере́ть(ся)

утиха́ть *impf*, **ути́хнуть** (-ну; -и́х) *pf* abate, subside; calm down.

у́тка duck; canard.

уткну́ть (-ну́, -нёшь) *pf* bury; fix; ~**ся** bury o.s.

утоли́ть *pf* (*impf* утоля́ть) quench; satisfy; relieve.

утолще́ние thickening; bulge.

утоля́ть *impf of* утоли́ть

утоми́тельный tedious; tiring. **утоми́ть** (-млю́) *pf*, **утомля́ть** *impf* tire, fatigue; ~**ся** get tired. **утомле́ние** weariness. **утомлённый** weary.

утону́ть (-ну́, -нешь) *pf* drown, be drowned; sink.

утончённый refined.

утопи́ть(ся) (-плю́(сь), -пишь(ся)) *pf*. **утопле́нник** drowned man.

утопи́ческий utopian. **уто́пия** Utopia.

утопта́ть (-пчу́, -пчешь) *pf* (*impf* ута́птывать) trample down.

уточне́ние more precise definition; amplification. **уточни́ть** *pf*, **уточня́ть** *impf* define more precisely; amplify.

утра́ивать *impf of* утро́ить

у|трамбова́ть pf, утрамбо́вы-вать impf ram, tamp; ~ся be-come flat.

утра́та loss. утра́тить (-а́чу) pf, утра́чивать impf lose.

у́тренний morning. у́тренник morning performance; early-morning frost.

утри́ровать impf & pf exag-gerate.

у́тро (-а or -а́, -у or -у́; pl -а, -ам or -а́м) morning.

утро́ба womb; belly.

утро́ить pf (impf утра́ивать) triple, treble.

утру́ etc.: see утере́ть, у́тро

утружда́ть impf trouble, tire.

утю́г (-а́) iron. утю́жить (-жу) impf (pf вы́~, от~) iron.

ух int oh, ooh, ah.

уха́ fish soup.

уха́б pot-hole. уха́бистый bumpy.

уха́живать impf за+instr tend; look after; court.

ухвати́ть (-ачу́, -а́тишь) pf, хвата́ть impf seize; grasp; ~ся за+acc grasp, lay hold of; set to; seize; jump at. ухва́тка grip; skill; trick; manner.

ухитри́ться pf, ухитря́ться impf manage, contrive. ухищре́-ние device, trick.

ухмы́лка smirk. ухмыль-ну́ться (-ну́сь, -нёшься) pf, ух-мыля́ться impf smirk.

у́хо (pl у́ши, уше́й) ear; ear-flap.

ухо́д[1] за+instr care of; tend-ing, looking after.

ухо́д[2] leaving, departure. ухо-ди́ть (-ожу́, -о́дишь) impf of уйти́

ухудша́ть impf, уху́дшить (-шу) pf make worse; ~ся get worse. ухудше́ние deterior-ation.

уцеле́ть (-е́ю) pf remain intact; survive.

уце́нивать impf, уцени́ть (-ню́, -нишь) pf reduce the price of.

уцепи́ть (-плю́, -пишь) pf catch hold of, seize; ~ся за+acc catch hold of, seize; jump at.

уча́ствовать impf take part; hold shares. уча́ствующий sb participant. уча́стие participa-tion; share; sympathy.

участи́ть (-ащу́) pf (impf уча-ща́ть) make more frequent; ~ся become more frequent, quicken.

уча́стливый sympathetic. уча́стник participant. уча́сток (-тка) plot; part; section; sector; district; field, sphere. у́часть lot, fate.

учаща́ть(ся impf of уча-сти́ть(ся

уча́щийся sb student; pupil. уче́ба studies; course; training. уче́бник text-book. уче́бный educational; school; training. уче́ние learning; studies; ap-prenticeship; teaching; doc-trine; exercise.

учени́к (-а́), учени́ца pupil; ap-prentice; disciple. учени́ческий pupil('s); apprentice('s); un-skilled; crude. учёность learn-ing, erudition. учёный learned; scholarly; academic; scientific; ~ая сте́пень (university) degree; ~ый sb scholar; scientist.

уче́сть (учту́, -тёшь; учёл, учла́) pf (impf учи́тывать) take stock of; take into account; discount. учёт stock-taking; calculation; taking into account; discount; без ~а +gen dis-regarding; взять на ~ register. учётный registration; dis-count.

учи́лище (specialist) school.

учини́ть pf, **учиня́ть** impf make; carry out; commit.

учи́тель (pl -я́) m, **учи́тельница** teacher. **учи́тельск|ий** teacher's; teachers'; **~ая** sb staff-room.

учи́тывать impf of **уче́сть**

учи́ть (учу́, у́чишь) impf (pf **вы́~**, **на~**, **об~**) teach; be a teacher; learn; **~ся** be a student; +dat or inf learn, study.

учреди́тельный constituent. **учреди́ть** (-ежу́) pf, **учрежда́ть** impf found, establish. **учрежде́ние** founding; establishment; institution.

учти́вый civil, courteous.

учту́ etc.: see **уче́сть**

уша́нка hat with ear-flaps.

ушёл etc.: see **уйти́**. **у́ши** etc.: see **у́хо**

уши́б injury; bruise. **ушиба́ть** impf, **ушиби́ть** (-бу́, -бёшь; уши́б) pf injure; bruise; hurt; **~ся** hurt o.s.

ушко́ (pl -и́, -о́в) eye; tab.

ушно́й ear, aural.

уще́лье ravine, gorge, canyon.

ущеми́ть (-млю́) pf, **ущемля́ть** impf pinch, jam; limit; encroach on; hurt. **ущемле́ние** pinching, jamming; limitation; hurting.

уще́рб detriment; loss; damage; prejudice. **уще́рбный** waning.

ущипну́ть (-ну́, -нёшь) pf of **щипа́ть**

Уэ́льс Wales. **уэ́льский** Welsh.

ую́т cosiness, comfort. **ую́тный** cosy, comfortable.

уязви́мый vulnerable. **уязви́ть** (-влю́) pf, **уязвля́ть** impf wound, hurt.

уясни́ть (-ню́) pf, **уясня́ть** impf understand, make out.

Ф

фа́брика factory. **фабрика́нт** manufacturer. **фабрика́т** finished product, manufactured product. **фабрикова́ть** impf (pf **с~**) fabricate, forge. **фабри́чн|ый** factory; manufacturing; factory-made; **~ая ма́рка**, **~ое клеймо́** trade-mark.

фа́була plot, story.

фаго́т bassoon.

фа́за phase; stage.

фаза́н pheasant.

фа́зис phase.

файл (comput) file.

фа́кел torch, flare.

факс fax.

факси́миле neut indecl facsimile.

факт fact; **соверши́вшийся ~** fait accompli. **факти́чески** adv in fact; virtually. **факти́ческий** actual; real; virtual.

факту́ра texture; style, execution.

фа́ктор factor.

факультати́вный optional. **факульте́т** faculty, department.

фа́лда tail (of coat).

фальсифика́тор falsifier, forger. **фальсифика́ция** falsification; adulteration; forgery. **фальсифици́ровать** impf & pf falsify; forge; adulterate. **фальши́вить** (-влю) impf (pf **с~**) be a hypocrite; sing or play out of tune. **фальши́вка** forged document. **фальши́вый** false; spurious; forged; artificial; out of tune. **фальшь** deception; falseness.

фами́лия surname. **фами́льярничать** be over-familiar.

фамилья́рность (over-)familiarity. **фамилья́рный** (over-)familiar; unceremonious.

фанати́зм fanaticism. **фана́тик** fanatic.

фане́ра veneer; plywood.

фантазёр dreamer, visionary. **фантази́ровать** impf (pf c~) dream; make up, dream up; improvise. **фанта́зия** fantasy; fancy; imagination; whim. **фанта́стика** fiction, fantasy. **фантасти́ческий**, **фантасти́чный** fantastic.

фа́ра headlight.

фарао́н pharaoh; faro.

фарва́тер fairway, channel.

фармазо́н freemason.

фармаце́вт pharmacist.

фарс farce.

фа́ртук apron.

фарфо́р china; porcelain. **фарфо́ровый** china.

фарцо́вщик currency speculator.

фарш stuffing; minced meat. **фарширова́ть** impf (pf за~) stuff.

фаса́д façade.

фасова́ть impf (pf рас~) package.

фасо́ль kidney bean(s), French bean(s); haricot beans.

фасо́н cut; fashion; style; manner. **фасо́нный** shaped.

фата́ veil.

фатали́зм fatalism. **фата́льный** fatal.

фаши́зм Fascism. **фаши́ст** Fascist. **фаши́стский** Fascist.

фая́нс faience, pottery.

февра́ль (-я́) m February. **февра́льский** February.

федера́льный federal. **федера́ция** federation.

феери́ческий fairy-tale. **фейерве́рк** firework(s).

фе́льдшер (pl -а́), **-ери́ца** (partly-qualified) medical assistant.

фельето́н feuilleton, feature.

feminíзм feminism. **feminíстический**, **feminíстский** feminist.

фен (hair-)dryer.

феноме́н phenomenon. **феномена́льный** phenomenal.

феода́л feudal lord. **феодали́зм** feudalism. **феода́льный** feudal.

ферзь (-я́) m queen.

фе́рма¹ farm.

фе́рма² girder, truss.

ферма́та (mus) pause.

ферме́нт ferment.

фе́рмер farmer.

фестива́ль m festival.

фетр felt. **фе́тровый** felt.

фехтова́льщик, **-щица** fencer. **фехтова́ние** fencing. **фехтова́ть** impf fence.

фе́я fairy.

фиа́ско neut indecl fiasco.

фи́бра fibre.

фигля́р buffoon.

фигу́ра figure; court-card; (chess-)piece. **фигура́льный** figurative, metaphorical. **фигури́ровать** impf figure, appear. **фигури́ст**, **-и́стка** figure-skater. **фигу́рка** figurine, statuette; figure. **фигу́рный** figured; ~ое ката́ние figure-skating.

фи́зик physicist. **фи́зика** physics. **физио́лог** physiologist. **физиологи́ческий** physiological. **физиоло́гия** physiology. **физионо́мия** physiognomy; face,

expression. **физиотерапе́вт** physiotherapist. **физи́ческий** physical; physics. **физкульту́ра** *abbr* P.E.; gymnastics. **физкульту́рный** *abbr* gymnastic; athletic; ~ зал gymnasium.

фикса́ж fixer. **фикса́ция** fixing. **фикси́ровать** *impf & pf* (*pf also* за~) fix; record.

фикти́вный fictitious. ~ брак marriage of convenience. **фи́кция** fiction.

филантро́п philanthropist. **филантро́пия** philanthropy.

филармо́ния philharmonic society; concert hall.

филатели́ст philatelist.

филе́ *neut indecl* sirloin; fillet.

филиа́л branch.

фили́стер philistine.

фило́лог philologist. **филологи́ческий** philological. **филоло́гия** philology.

фило́соф philosopher. **филосо́фия** philosophy. **филосо́фский** philosophical.

фильм film. **фильмоско́п** projector.

фильтр filter. **фильтрова́ть** *impf* (*pf* про~) filter.

фина́л finale; final. **фина́льный** final.

финанси́ровать *impf & pf* finance. **фина́нсовый** financial. **фина́нсы** (-ов) *pl* finance, finances.

фи́ник date.

фи́ниш finish; finishing post.

фи́нка Finn. **Финля́ндия** Finland. **финля́ндский** Finnish. **финн** Finn. **фи́нский** Finnish.

фиоле́товый violet.

фи́рма firm; company. **фи́рменное блю́до** speciality of the house.

фисгармо́ния harmonium.

фити́ль (-я́) *m* wick; fuse.

флаг flag. **фла́гман** flagship.

флако́н bottle, flask.

фланг flank; wing.

флане́ль flannel.

флегмати́чный phlegmatic.

фле́йта flute.

фле́ксия inflexion. **флекти́вный** inflected.

фли́гель (*pl* -я́) *m* wing; annexe.

флирт flirtation. **флиртова́ть** *impf* flirt.

фломастер felt-tip pen.

фло́ра flora.

флот fleet. **фло́тский** naval.

флю́гер (*pl* -а́) weather-vane.

флюоресце́нтный fluorescent.

флюс[1] gumboil, abscess.

флюс[2] (*pl* -ы́) flux.

фля́га flask; churn. **фля́жка** flask.

фойе́ *neut indecl* foyer.

фо́кус[1] trick.

фо́кус[2] focus. **фокуси́ровать** *impf* focus.

фо́кусник conjurer, juggler.

фолиа́нт folio.

фольга́ foil.

фолькло́р folklore.

фон background.

фона́рик small lamp; torch. **фона́рный** lamp; ~ столб lamp-post. **фона́рь** (-я́) *m* lantern; lamp; light.

фонд fund; stock; reserves.

фоне́тика phonetics. **фонети́ческий** phonetic.

фонта́н fountain.

форе́ль trout.

фо́рма form; shape; mould; cast; uniform. **форма́льность** formality. **форма́льный** for-

mal. **форма́т** format. **форма́ция** structure; stage; formation; mentality. **фо́рменный** uniform; proper, regular. **формирова́ние** forming; unit, formation. **формирова́ть** impf (pf c~) form; organize; ~ся form, develop. **формова́ть** impf (pf c~) form, shape; mould, cast.

фо́рмула formula. **формули́ровать** impf & pf (pf also c~) formulate. **формулиро́вка** formulation; wording; formula. **формуля́р** log-book; library card.

форси́ровать impf & pf force; speed up.

форсу́нка sprayer; injector.

фортепья́но neut indecl piano.

фо́рточка small hinged (window-)pane.

форту́на fortune.

фо́рум forum.

фо́сфор phosphorus.

фо́то neut indecl photo(graph).

фото- in comb photo-, photoelectric. **фотоаппара́т** camera. **~бума́га** photographic paper. **~гени́чный** photogenic. **фото́граф** photographer. **~графи́ровать** impf (pf c~) photograph. **~графи́роваться** have one's photograph taken. **~графи́ческий** photographic. **~гра́фия** photography; photograph; photographer's studio. **~ко́пия** photocopy. **~люби́тель** m amateur photographer. **~объекти́в** (camera) lens. **~репортёр** press photographer. **~хро́ника** news in pictures. **~элеме́нт** photoelectric cell.

фрагме́нт fragment.

фра́за sentence; phrase. **фразеоло́гия** phraseology.

фрак tail-coat, tails.

фракцио́нный fractional; factional. **фра́кция** fraction; faction.

франк franc.

франкмасо́н Freemason.

франт dandy.

Фра́нция France. **францу́женка** Frenchwoman. **францу́з** Frenchman. **францу́зский** French.

фрахт freight. **фрахтова́ть** impf (pf за~) charter.

фрега́т frigate.

фре́ска fresco.

фронт (pl -ы, -о́в) front. **фронтови́к** (-á) front-line soldier. **фронтово́й** front(-line).

фронто́н pediment.

фрукт fruit. **фру́ктовый** fruit; ~ сад orchard.

ФСБ abbr (of Федера́льная слу́жба безопа́сности) Federal Security Service.

фтор fluorine. **фто́ристый** fluorine; fluoride. ~ ка́льций calcium fluoride.

фу int ugh! oh!

фуга́нок (-нка) smoothing-plane.

фуга́с landmine. **фуга́сный** high-explosive.

фунда́мент foundation. **фундамента́льный** solid, sound; main; basic.

функциона́льный functional. **функциони́ровать** impf function. **фу́нкция** function.

фунт pound.

фура́ж (-á) forage, fodder. **фура́жка** peaked cap, forage-cap.

фурго́н van; caravan.

фут foot; foot-rule. **футбо́л** football. **футболи́ст** footballer. **футбо́лка** T-shirt, sports shirt.

футбо́льный football; ~ мяч football.

футля́р case, container.

футури́зм futurism.

фуфа́йка jersey; sweater.

фы́ркать *impf*, **фы́ркнуть** (-ну) *pf* snort.

фюзеля́ж fuselage.

X

хала́т dressing-gown. **хала́тный** careless, negligent.

халту́ра pot-boiler; hackwork; money made on the side. **халту́рщик** hack.

хам boor, lout. **ха́мский** boorish, loutish. **ха́мство** boorishness, loutishness.

хамелео́н chameleon.

хан khan.

хандра́ depression. **хандри́ть** *impf* be depressed.

ханжа́ hypocrite. **ха́нжеский** sanctimonious, hypocritical.

хао́с chaos. **хаоти́ческий** chaotic.

хара́ктер character. **характеризова́ть** *impf* & *pf* (*pf also* o~) describe; characterize; ~ся be characterized. **характери́стика** reference; description. **характе́рный** characteristic; distinctive; character.

ха́ркать *impf*, **ха́ркнуть** (-ну) *pf* spit.

ха́ртия charter.

ха́та peasant hut.

хвала́ praise. **хвале́бный** laudatory. **хвалёный** highly-praised. **хвали́ть** (-лю́, -лишь) *impf* (*pf* по~) praise; ~ся boast.

хва́стать(ся *impf* (*pf* по~)

boast. **хвастли́вый** boastful. **хвастовство́** boasting. **хвасту́н** (-á) boaster.

хвата́ть[1] *impf*, **хвати́ть** (-ачу́, -а́тишь) *pf* (*pf also* **схвати́ть**) snatch, seize; grab; ~ся remember; +*gen* realize the absence of; +за+*acc* snatch at, clutch at; take up.

хвата́ть[2] *impf*, **хвати́ть** (-а́тит) *pf*, *impers* (+*gen*) suffice, be enough; last out; **вре́мени не хвата́ло** there was not enough time; **у нас не хвата́ет де́нег** we haven't enough money; **хва́тит!** that will do!; **э́того ещё не хвата́ло!** that's all we needed! **хва́тка** grasp, grip; method; skill.

хво́йн|**ый** coniferous; ~ые *sb pl* conifers.

хвора́ть *impf* be ill.

хво́рост brushwood; (*pastry*) straws. **хворости́на** stick, switch.

хвост (-á) tail; tail-end. **хво́стик** tail. **хвоя́** needle(s); (*coniferous*) branch(es).

херуви́м cherub.

хиба́р(к)а shack, hovel.

хи́жина shack, hut.

хи́лый (-л, -á, -о) sickly.

химе́ра chimera.

хи́мик chemist. **химика́т** chemical. **хими́ческий** chemical. **хи́мия** chemistry.

химчи́стка dry-cleaning; dry-cleaner's.

хи́на, хини́н quinine.

хиру́рг surgeon. **хирурги́ческий** surgical. **хирурги́я** surgery.

хитре́ц (-á) cunning person. **хитри́ть** *impf* (*pf* с~) use cunning, be crafty. **хи́трость** cun-

ning; ruse; skill; intricacy. **хи́т-рый** cunning; skilful; intricate.

хихи́кать *impf*, **хихи́кнуть** (-ну) *pf* giggle, snigger.

хище́ние theft; embezzlement. **хи́щник** predator, bird *or* beast of prey. **хи́щнический** predatory. **хи́щный** predatory; rapacious; **~ые пти́цы** birds of prey.

хладнокро́вие coolness, composure. **хладнокро́вный** cool, composed.

хлам rubbish.

хлеб (*pl* -ы, -ов *or* -á, -óв) bread; loaf; grain. **хлеба́ть** *impf*, **хлебну́ть** (-ну́, -нёшь) *pf* gulp down. **хле́бный** bread; baker's; grain. **хлебозаво́д** bakery. **хлебопека́рня** (*gen pl* -рен) bakery.

хлев (*loc* -ý; *pl* -á) cow-shed.

хлеста́ть (-ещу́, -е́щешь) *impf*, **хлестну́ть** (-ну́, -нёшь) *pf* lash; whip.

хлоп *int* bang! **хло́пать** *impf* (*pf* **хло́пнуть**) bang; slap; **~ (в ладо́ши)** clap.

хлопково́дство cotton-growing. **хло́пковый** cotton.

хло́пнуть (-ну) *pf of* **хло́пать**

хлопо́к[1] (-пка́) clap.

хло́пок[2] (-пка) cotton.

хлопота́ть (-очу́, -о́чешь) *impf* (*pf* **по~**) busy o.s.; bustle about; take trouble; **+о**+*prep or* **за**+*acc* petition for. **хлопотли́вый** troublesome; exacting; busy, bustling. **хло́поты** (-о́т) *pl* trouble; efforts.

хлопчатобума́жный cotton. **хло́пья** (-ьев) *pl* flakes.

хлор chlorine. **хло́ристый**, **хло́рный** chlorine; chloride. **хло́рка** bleach. **хлорофи́лл**

chlorophyll. **хлорофо́рм** chloroform.

хлы́нуть (-нет) *pf* gush, pour.

хлыст (-á) whip, switch.

хмеле́ть (-е́ю) *impf* (*pf* **за~, о~**) get tipsy. **хмель** (*loc* -ю́) *m* hop, hops; drunkenness; **во хмелю́** tipsy. **хмельно́й** (-ён, -льна́) drunk; intoxicating.

хму́рить *impf* (*pf* **на~**): **~ бро́ви** knit one's brows; **~ся** frown; become gloomy; be overcast. **хму́рый** gloomy; overcast.

хны́кать (-ы́чу *or* -аю) *impf* whimper, snivel.

хо́бби *neut indecl* hobby.

хо́бот trunk. **хобото́к** (-тка́) proboscis.

ход (*loc* -ý; *pl* -ы, -ов *or* -ы́ *or* -á, -óв) motion; going; speed; course; operation; stroke; move; manoeuvre; entrance; passage; **в ~ý** in demand; **дать за́дний ~** reverse; **дать ~** set in motion; **на ~ý** in transit, on the move; in motion; in operation; **по́лным ~ом** at full speed; **пусти́ть в ~** start, set in motion; **три часа́ ~у** three hours' journey.

хода́тайство petitioning; application. **хода́тайствовать** *impf* (*pf* **по~**) petition, apply.

ходи́ть (хожу́, хо́дишь) *impf* walk; go; run; pass, go round; lead; play; move; **+в**+*prep* wear; **+за**+*instr* look after. **хо́дкий** (-док, -дка́, -о) fast; marketable; popular. **ходьба́** walking; walk. **ходя́чий** walking; able to walk; popular; current.

хозрасчёт *abbr* (*of* **хозя́йственный расчёт**) self-financing system.

хозя́ин (*pl* -я́ева, -я́ев) owner, proprietor; master; boss; land-

lord; host; **хозя́ева по́ля** home team. **хозя́йка** owner; mistress; hostess; landlady. **хозя́йничать** *impf* keep house; be in charge; lord it. **хозя́йственный** financial manager. **хозя́йственный** economic; household; economical. **хозя́йство** economy; housekeeping; equipment; farm; **дома́шнее ~** housekeeping; **се́льское ~** agriculture.

хоккеи́ст (ice-)hockey-player. **хокке́й** hockey, ice-hockey.

холе́ра cholera.

холестери́н cholesterol.

холл hall, vestibule.

холм (-á) hill. **холми́стый** hilly.

хо́лод (-á, -о́в) cold; coldness; cold weather. **холоди́льник** refrigerator. **хо́лодно** *adv* coldly. **холо́дн|ый** (хо́лоден, -дна́, -о) cold; inadequate, thin; **~ое ору́жие** cold steel.

холо́п serf.

холосто́й (хо́лост, -á) unmarried, single; bachelor; idle; blank. **холостя́к** (-á) bachelor.

холст (-á) canvas; linen.

холу́й (-нуя́) *m* lackey.

хому́т (-á) (horse-)collar; burden.

хомя́к (-á) hamster.

хор (*pl* -ы́(-а́)) choir; chorus.

хорва́т, **~ка** Croat. **Хорва́тия** Croatia. **хорва́тский** Croatian.

хорёк (-рька́) polecat.

хореографи́ческий choreographic. **хореогра́фия** choreography.

хори́ст member of a choir or chorus.

хорони́ть (-ню́, -нишь) *impf* (*pf* за-, по-, с~) bury.

хоро́шенький pretty; nice. **хоро́шенько** *adv* properly, thoroughly. **хороше́ть** (-е́ю) *impf* (*pf* по~) grow prettier. **хоро́ший** (-о́ш, -а́, -о́) good; nice; pretty, nice-looking; **хорошо́** *predic* it is good; it is nice. **хорошо́** *adv* well; nicely; all right! good.

хо́ры (хор *or* -о́в) *pl* gallery.

хоте́ть (хочу́, хо́чешь, хоти́м) *impf* (*pf* за~) wish; +*gen*, *acc* want; **~ пить** be thirsty; **~ сказа́ть** mean; *impers* +*dat* want; **мне хоте́лось бы** I should like; **мне хо́чется** I want.

хоть *conj* although; even if; *partl* at least, if only; for example; **~ бы** if only. **хотя́** *conj* although; **~ бы** even if; if only.

хо́хот loud laugh(ter). **хохота́ть** (-очу́, -о́чешь) *impf* laugh loudly.

хочу́ *etc.*: *see* **хоте́ть**

храбре́ц (-á) brave man. **хра́бриться** make a show of bravery; pluck up courage. **хра́брость** bravery. **хра́брый** brave.

храм temple, church.

хране́ние keeping; storage; **ка́мера хране́ния** cloakroom, left-luggage office. **храни́лище** storehouse, depository. **храни́тель** *m* keeper, custodian; curator. **храни́ть** *impf* keep; preserve; **~ся** be, be kept.

храпе́ть (-плю́) *impf* snore; snort.

хребе́т (-бта́) spine; (mountain) range; ridge.

хрен horseradish.

хрестома́тия reader.

хрип wheeze. **хрипе́ть** (-плю́) *impf* wheeze. **хри́плый** (-пл, -á, -о) hoarse. **хри́пнуть** (-ну; *impf* (*pf* о~) become hoarse. **хрипота́** hoarseness.

христиани́н (*pl* -а́не, -а́н), **христиа́нка** Christian. **христиа́нский** Christian. **христиа́нство** Christianity. **Христо́с** (-иста́) Christ.

хром chromium; chrome.

хромати́ческий chromatic.

хрома́ть *impf* limp; be poor. **хромо́й** (хром, -а́, -о) lame; *sb* lame person.

хромосо́ма chromosome.

хромота́ lameness.

хро́ник chronic invalid. **хро́ника** chronicle; news items; newsreel. **хрони́ческий** chronic.

хронологи́ческий chronological. **хроноло́гия** chronology.

хру́пкий (-пок, -пка́, -о) fragile; frail. **хру́пкость** fragility; frailness.

хруст crunch; crackle.

хруста́ль (-я́) *m* cut glass; crystal. **хруста́льный** cut-glass; crystal; crystal-clear.

хрусте́ть (-ущу́) *impf*, **хру́стнуть** (-ну) *pf* crunch; crackle.

хрю́кать *impf*, **хрю́кнуть** (-ну) *pf* grunt.

хрящ (-а́) cartilage, gristle. **хрящево́й** cartilaginous, gristly.

худе́ть (-е́ю) *impf* (*pf* по~) grow thin.

ху́до harm; evil. **ху́до** *adv* ill, badly.

худоба́ thinness.

худо́жественный art, arts; artistic; ~ **фильм** feature film. **худо́жник** artist.

худо́й[1] (худ, -а́, -о) thin, lean.

худо́й[2] (худ, -а́, -о) full of holes; worn; **ему́ ху́до** he feels bad.

худоща́вый thin, lean.

ху́дший *superl of* худо́й, плохо́й

(the) worst. **ху́же** *comp of* худо́й, ху́до, плохо́й, пло́хо worse.

хула́ abuse, criticism.

хулига́н hooligan. **хулига́нить** *impf* behave like a hooligan. **хулига́нство** hooliganism.

ху́нта junta.

ху́тор (*pl* -а́) farm; small village.

Ц

ца́пля (*gen pl* -пель) heron.

цара́пать *impf*, **цара́пнуть** (-ну) *pf* (*pf also* на~, о~) scratch; scribble; ~**ся** scratch; scratch one another. **цара́пина** scratch.

цари́зм tsarism. **цари́ть** *impf* reign, prevail. **цари́ца** tsarina; queen. **ца́рский** tsar's; royal; tsarist; regal. **ца́рство** kingdom, realm; reign. **ца́рствование** reign. **ца́рствовать** *impf* reign. **царь** (-я́) *m* tsar; king.

цвести́ (-ету́, -ете́шь; -ёл, -а́) *impf* flower, blossom; flourish.

цвет[1] (*pl* -а́) colour; ~ лица́ complexion.

цвет[2] (*loc* -у́; *pl* -ы́) flower; prime; **в цвету́** in blossom. **цветни́к** (-а́) flower-bed, flower-garden.

цветн|о́й coloured; colour; non-ferrous; ~**а́я капу́ста** cauliflower; ~**о́е стекло́** stained glass.

цветов|о́й colour; ~**а́я слепота́** colour-blindness.

цвето́к (-тка́; *pl* цветы́ *or* цветки́, -о́в) flower. **цвето́чный** flower. **цвету́щий** flowering, prosperous.

цеди́ть (цежу́, це́дишь) *impf* strain, filter.

целе́бный curative, healing.

целево́й earmarked for a specific purpose. **целенапра́вленный** purposeful. **целесообра́зный** expedient. **целеустремлённый** (-ён, -ённа *or* -ена́) purposeful.

целико́м *adv* entirely.

целина́ virgin lands, virgin soil. **цели́нный** virgin; ~ые зе́мли virgin lands.

цели́тельный healing, medicinal.

це́лить(ся *impf* (*pf* на~) aim, take aim.

целлофа́н cellophane.

целова́ть *impf* (*pf* по~) kiss; ~ся kiss.

це́лое *sb* whole; integer. **цело́мудренный** chaste. **цело́мудрие** chastity. **це́лостность** integrity, **це́лый** (цел, -á, -о) whole; safe, intact.

цель target; aim, object, goal.

це́льный (-лен, -льна́, -о) *of one* piece, solid; whole; integral; single. **це́льность** wholeness.

цеме́нт cement. **цементи́ровать** *impf & pf* cement. **цеме́нтный** cement.

цена́ (*acc* -у; *pl* -ы) price, cost; worth.

ценз qualification. **це́нзор** censor. **цензу́ра** censorship.

цени́тель *m* judge, connoisseur. **цени́ть** (-ню́, -нишь) *impf* value; appreciate. **це́нность** value; price; *pl* valuables; values. **це́нный** valuable.

цент cent. **це́нтнер** centner (*100kg*).

центр centre. **централиза́ция** centralization. **централизова́ть** *impf & pf* centralize. **цен-**

тра́льный central. **центробе́жный** centrifugal.

цепене́ть (-е́ю) *impf* (*pf* о~) freeze; become rigid. **це́пкий** tenacious; prehensile; sticky; obstinate. **це́пкость** tenacity. **цепля́ться** *impf* за+*acc* clutch at; cling to.

цепно́й chain. **цепо́чка** chain; file. **цепь** (*loc* -и́; *gen pl* -е́й) chain; series; circuit.

церемо́ниться *impf* (*pf* по~) stand on ceremony. **церемо́ния** ceremony.

церковнославя́нский Church Slavonic. **церко́вный** church; ecclesiastical. **це́рковь** (-кви; *pl* -и, -е́й, -а́м) church.

цех (*loc* -у; *pl* -и *or* -а́) shop; section; guild.

цивилиза́ция civilization. **цивилизо́ванный** civilized. **цивилизова́ть** *impf & pf* civilize.

циге́йка beaver lamb.

цикл cycle.

цико́рий chicory.

цили́ндр *m* cylinder; top hat. **цилиндри́ческий** cylindrical.

цимба́лы (-а́л) *pl* cymbals.

цини́зм cynicism. **ци́ник** cynic. **цини́чный** cynical.

цинк zinc. **ци́нковый** zinc.

цино́вка mat.

цирк circus.

циркули́ровать *impf* circulate. **ци́ркуль** *m* (pair of) compasses; dividers. **циркуля́р** circular. **циркуля́ция** circulation.

цисте́рна cistern, tank.

цитаде́ль citadel.

цита́та quotation. **цити́ровать** *impf* (*pf* про~) quote.

ци́трус citrus. **ци́трусовый** citrous; ~ые *sb pl* citrus plants.

цифербла́т dial, face.
ци́фра figure; number, numeral. **цифрово́й** numerical, digital.
цо́коль *m* socle, plinth.
цыга́н (*pl* -е, -а́н *or* -ы, -ов), **цыга́нка** gipsy. **цыга́нский** gipsy.
цыплёнок (-нка *pl* -ля́та, -ля́т) chicken; chick.
цы́почки: на ~, на цы́почках on tip-toe.

Ч

чаба́н (-а́) shepherd.
чад (*loc* -у́) fumes, smoke.
чадра́ yashmak.
чай (*pl* -и́, -ёв) tea. **чаевы́е** (-ы́х) *sb pl* tip.
ча́йка (*gen pl* ча́ек) (sea-)gull.
ча́йная *sb* tea-shop. **ча́йник** tea-pot; kettle. **ча́йный** tea. **чай-хана́** tea-house.
чалма́ turban.
чан (*loc* -у́; *pl* -ы́) vat, tub.
чарова́ть *impf* bewitch; charm.
час (*with numerals* -а́, *loc* -у́; *pl* -ы́) hour; *pl* guard-duty; кото́рый час? what's the time? ~ one o'clock; в два ~а́ at two o'clock; стоя́ть на ~а́х stand guard; ~ы́ пик rush-hour. ча-со́вня (*gen pl* -вен) chapel. часово́й *sb* sentry. часово́й clock, watch; of one hour, hour-long. часовщи́к (-а́) watch-maker.
части́ца small part; particle. **части́чно** *adv* partly, partially. **части́чный** partial.
ча́стник private trader.
ча́стность detail; в ча́стности in particular. **ча́стный** private; personal; particular, individual.
ча́сто *adv* often; close, thickly.

частоко́л paling, palisade. **ча-стота́** (*pl* -ы) frequency. **ча-сто́тный** frequency. **часту́шка** ditty. **ча́стый** (част, -а́, -о) frequent; close (together); dense; close-woven; rapid.
часть (*gen pl* -е́й) part; department; field; unit.
часы́ (-о́в) *pl* clock, watch.
чат (*comput*) IRC (Internet Relay Chat).
ча́хлый stunted; sickly, puny. **чахо́тка** consumption.
ча́ша bowl; chalice; ~ весо́в scale, pan. **ча́шка** cup; scale, pan.
ча́ща thicket.
ча́ще *comp of* ча́сто, ча́стый; ~ всего́ most often, mostly.
ча́яние expectation; hope. **ча́ять** (ча́ю) hope, expect.
чва́нство conceit, arrogance.
чего́ *see* что
чей *m*, **чья** *f*, **чьё** *neut*, **чьи** *pl pron* whose. **чей-либо**, **чей-нибудь** anyone's. **чей-то** someone's.
чек (-а́) cheque; receipt.
чека́нить *impf* (*pf* вы́~, от~) mint, coin; stamp. **чека́нка** coinage, minting. **чека́нный** stamped, engraved.
чёлка fringe; forelock.
чёлн (-а́; *pl* чёлны) dug-out (canoe); boat. **челно́к** (-а́) dug-out (canoe); shuttle.
челове́к (*pl* лю́ди; *with numerals*, *gen* -ве́к, -ам) man, person.
челове́ко- *in comb* man-, anthropo-. **человеколюби́вый** philanthropic. ~**лю́бие** philanthropy. ~**ненави́стнический** misanthropic. **челове́ко-ча́с** (*pl* -ы́) man-hour.
челове́чек (-чка) little man. **че-**

ловеческий human; humane. **человечество** mankind. **человечность** humaneness. **человечный** humane.

челюсть jaw(-bone); dentures, false teeth.

чем, чём *see* что. **чем** *conj* than; ~..., **тем**...+*comp* the more ..., the more.

чемодан suitcase.

чемпион, ~ка champion, title-holder. **чемпионат** championship.

чему *see* что

чепуха nonsense; trifle.

чепчик cap; bonnet.

черви (-ей), **червы** (черв) *pl* hearts. **червонный** of hearts; ~ое золото pure gold.

червь (-я́; *pl* -и, -ей) *m* worm; bug. **червяк** (-á) worm.

чердак (-á) attic, loft.

черёд (-á, *loc* -у́) turn; идти́ свои́м ~о́м take its course. **чередование** alternation. **чередовать** *impf* alternate; ~ся alternate, take turns.

через, чрез *prep+acc* across; over; through; via; in; after; every other.

черёмуха bird cherry.

черенок (-нка́) handle; graft, cutting.

череп (*pl* -á) skull.

черепаха tortoise; turtle; tortoiseshell. **черепаховый** tortoise; tortoiseshell. **черепаший** tortoise; turtle; very slow.

черепица tile. **черепичный** tile; tiled.

черепок (-пка́) potsherd, fragment of pottery.

чересчур *adv* too; too much.

черешневый cherry. **черешня** (*gen pl* -шен) cherry(-tree).

черкес, черкешенка Circassian.

черкнуть (-ну́, -нёшь) *pf* scrape; leave a mark on; scribble.

чернеть (-е́ю) *impf* (*pf* по~) turn black; show black. **черника** (*no pl; usu collect*) bilberry; bilberries. **чернила** (-и́л) *pl* ink. **чернильный** ink. **чернить** *impf* (*pf* о~) blacken; slander.

черно- *in comb* black; unskilled; rough. **~-белый** black-and-white. **~-бурый** dark-brown; **~бурая лиса́** silver fox. **~волосый** black-haired. **~глазый** black-eyed. **~зём** chernozem, black earth. **~кожий** black; *sb* black. **~морский** Black-Sea. **~рабочий** unskilled worker, labourer. **~сли́в** prunes. **~смородинный** blackcurrant.

черновик (-á) rough copy, draft. **черновой** rough; draft.

чернота blackness; darkness. **чёрный** (-рен, -рна́) black; back; unskilled; ferrous; gloomy; *sb* (*derog*) black person; **~ая сморо́дина** (*no pl; usu collect*) blackcurrant.

черпак (-á) scoop. **черпать** *impf*, **черпнуть** (-ну́, -нёшь) *pf* draw; scoop; extract.

черстветь (-е́ю) *impf* (*pf* за~, о~, по~) get stale; become hardened. **чёрствый** (чёрств, -á, -о) stale; hard.

чёрт (*pl* черти, -ей) devil.

черта line; boundary; trait, characteristic. **чертёж** (-á) drawing; blueprint, plan. **чертёжник** draughtsman. **чертёжный** drawing. **чертить** (-рчу́, -ртишь) *impf* (*pf* на~) draw.

чёртов adj devil's; devilish. **чертóвский** devilish.

чертополóх thistle.

чёрточка line; hyphen. **черчéние** drawing. **черчý** etc.: see **черти́ть**

чесáть (чешý, -шешь) impf (pf по~) scratch; comb; card; ~ся scratch o.s.; itch; comb one's hair.

чеснóк (-á) garlic.

чéствование celebration. **чéствовать** impf celebrate; honour. **чéстность** honesty. **чéстный** (-тен, -тнá, -о) honest. **честолюби́вый** ambitious. **честолю́бие** ambition. **честь** (loc -и) honour; **отдáть** ~ +dat salute.

четá pair, couple.

четвéрг (-á) Thursday. **четверéньки: на** ~, **на четверéньках** on hands and knees. **четвёрка** four; figure 4; No. 4. **чéтверо** (-ы́х) four. **четвероно́гий** four-legged; ~**ое** sb quadruped. **четверости́шие** quatrain. **четвёртый** fourth. **чéтверть** (gen pl -éй) quarter; quarter of an hour; **без четверти час а** quarter to one. **четвертьфинáл** quarter-final.

чёткий (-ток, -ткá, -о) precise; clear-cut; clear; distinct. **чёткость** precision; clarity.

чётный even.

четы́ре (-рёх, -рьмя́, -рёх) four. **четы́реста** (-рёхсо́т, -мьстáми, -ёхстáх) four hundred.

четырёх- in comb four-, tetra-. **~мéстный** four-seater. **~со́тый** four-hundredth. **~уго́льник** quadrangle. **~уго́льный** quadrangular. **четы́рнадцатый** fourteenth.

четы́рнадцать fourteen.

чех Czech.

чехóл (-хлá) cover, case.

чечеви́ца lentil; lens.

чéшка Czech. **чéшский** Czech.

чешý etc.: see **чесáть**

чешýйка scale. **чешуя́** scales.

чи́бис lapwing.

чиж (-á) siskin.

чин (pl -ы́) rank.

чини́ть¹ (-ню́, -нишь) impf (pf по~) repair, mend.

чини́ть² impf (pf у~) carry out; cause; ~ **препя́тствия** +dat put obstacles in the way of.

чино́вник civil servant; official.

чип (micro)chip.

чи́псы (-ов) pl (potato) crisps.

чири́кать impf, **чири́кнуть** (-ну) pf chirp.

чи́ркать impf, **чи́ркнуть** (-ну) pf +instr strike.

чи́сленность numbers; strength. **чи́сленный** numerical. **числи́тель** m numerator. **числи́тельное** sb numeral. **чи́слить** impf count, reckon; ~**ся** be; +instr be reckoned. **число́** (pl -a, -сел) number; date, day; **в числé** +gen among; **в том числé** including; **еди́нственное** ~ singular; **мно́жественное** ~ plural. **числово́й** numerical.

чи́стилище purgatory.

чи́стильщик cleaner. **чи́стить** (чи́щу) impf (pf вы́~, о~, по~) clean; peel; clear. **чи́стка** cleaning; purge. **чи́сто** adv cleanly, clean; purely; completely. **чистови́й** fair, clean. **чисто-кро́вный** thoroughbred. **чисто-писа́ние** calligraphy. **чисто-пло́тный** neat; decent. **чистосердéчный** frank, sincere. **чистотá** cleanness; neat-

ness; purity. **чи́стый** clean; neat; pure; complete.

чита́емый widely-read, popular. **чита́льный** reading. **чита́тель** *m* reader. **чита́ть** *impf* (*pf* про~, прочесть) read; recite; ~ ле́кции lecture; ~ся be legible; be discernible. **чи́тка** reading.

чиха́ть *impf*, **чихну́ть** (-ну́, -нёшь) *pf* sneeze.

чи́ще *comp of* чи́сто, чи́стый

чи́щу *etc.*: *see* чи́стить

член member; limb; term; part; article. **члени́ть** *impf* (*pf* рас~) divide; articulate. **член-корреспонде́нт** corresponding member, associate. **членоразде́льный** articulate. **чле́нский** membership. **чле́нство** membership.

чмо́кать *impf*, **чмо́кнуть** (-ну) *pf* smack; squelch; kiss noisily; ~ губа́ми smack one's lips.

чо́каться *impf*, **чо́кнуться** (-нусь) *pf* clink glasses.

чо́порный prim; stand-offish.

чрева́тый +*instr* fraught with. **чре́во** belly, womb. **чревовеща́тель** *m* ventriloquist.

чрез *see* че́рез. **чрезвыча́йный** extraordinary; extreme; ~ое положе́ние state of emergency. **чрезме́рный** excessive.

чте́ние reading. **чтец** (-а́) reader; reciter.

чтить (чту) *impf* honour.

что, чего́, чему́, чем, о чём *pron* what?; how?; why?; how much?; which, what, who; anything; в чём де́ло? what is the matter? для чего́? what … for? why?; ~ ему́ до э́того? what does it matter to him?; ~ с тобо́й? what's the matter (with you)?; ~ за so what? what sort of?; what (a) …!; **что** *conj* that. **что (бы) ни**

pron whatever, no matter what.

чтоб, **что́бы** *conj* in order (to); so as; that; to. **что-ли́бо**, **что-нибудь** *prons* anything. **что-то¹** *pron* something. **что-то²** *adv* somewhat, slightly; somehow; for some reason.

чу́вственность sensuality. **чу́вствительность** sensitivity; perceptibility; sentimentality. **чу́вствительный** sensitive; perceptible; sentimental. **чу́вство** feeling; sense; senses; прийти́ в ~ come round. **чу́вствовать** *impf* (*pf* по~) feel; realize; appreciate; ~ себя́ +*adv or instr* feel a certain way; ~ся be perceptible; make itself felt.

чугу́н (-а́) cast iron. **чугу́нный** cast-iron.

чуда́к (-а́), **чуда́чка** eccentric, crank. **чуда́чество** eccentricity.

чудеса́ *etc.*: *see* чу́до. **чуде́сный** miraculous; wonderful.

чу́диться (-ишься) *impf* (*pf* по~, при~) seem.

чу́дно *adv* wonderfully; wonderful! **чудно́й** (-дён, -дна́) odd, strange. **чу́дный** wonderful; magical. **чу́до** (*pl* -деса́) miracle; wonder. **чудо́вище** monster. **чудо́вищный** monstrous. **чудоде́йственный** miracleworking; miraculous. **чу́дом** *adv* miraculously. **чудотво́рный** miraculous, miracleworking.

чужби́на foreign land. **чужда́ться** *impf* +*gen* avoid; stand aloof from. **чу́ждый** (-жд, -а́, -о) alien (to); +*gen* free from, devoid of. **чужезе́мец** (-мца), **-зе́мка** foreigner. **чужезе́мный** foreign. **чужо́й** someone else's, others'; strange, alien; foreign.

чула́н store-room; larder.

чуло́к (-лка́; *gen pl* -ло́к) stocking.

чума́ plague.

чума́зый dirty.

чурба́н block. **чу́рка** block, lump.

чу́ткий (-ток, -тка́, -о) keen; sensitive; sympathetic; delicate. **чу́ткость** keenness; delicacy.

чу́точка: **ни чу́точки** not in the least; **чу́точку** a little (bit).

чу́тче *comp of* **чу́ткий**

чуть *adv* hardly; just; very slightly; **~ не** almost; **~чуть** a tiny bit.

чутьё scent; flair.

чу́чело stuffed animal, stuffed bird; scarecrow.

чушь nonsense.

чу́ять (чу́ю) *impf* scent; sense.

чьё *etc.*: *see* **чей**

Ш

ша́баш sabbath.

шабло́н template; mould; stencil; cliché. **шабло́нный** stencil; trite; stereotyped.

шаг (with numerals -á, *loc* -ý; *pl* -и́) step; footstep; pace. **шага́ть** *impf*, **шагну́ть** (-ну́, -нёшь) *pf* step; stride; pace; make progress. **ша́гом** *adv* at walking pace.

ша́йба washer; puck.

ша́йка[1] tub.

ша́йка[2] gang, band.

шака́л jackal.

шала́ш (-á) cabin, hut.

шали́ть *impf* be naughty; play up. **шаловли́вый** mischievous, playful. **ша́лость** prank; *pl* mischief. **шалу́н** (-á), **шалу́нья**

(*gen pl* -ний) naughty child.

шаль shawl.

шально́й mad, crazy.

ша́мкать *impf* mumble.

шампа́нское *sb* champagne.

шампиньо́н field mushroom.

шампу́нь *m* shampoo.

шанс chance.

шанта́ж (-á) blackmail. **шантажи́ровать** *impf* blackmail.

ша́пка hat; banner headline. **ша́почка** hat.

шар (with numerals -á; *pl* -ы́) sphere; ball; balloon.

шара́хать *impf*, **шара́хнуть** (-ну) hit; **~ся** dash; shy.

шарж caricature.

ша́рик ball; corpuscle. **ша́риковый**: **~ая (а́вто)ру́чка** ball-point pen; **~ый подши́пник** ball-bearing. **шарикоподши́пник** ball-bearing.

ша́рить *impf* grope; sweep.

ша́ркать *impf*, **ша́ркнуть** (-ну) *pf* shuffle; scrape.

шарлата́н charlatan.

шарма́нка barrel-organ. **шарма́нщик** organ-grinder.

шарни́р hinge, joint.

шарова́ры (-áр) *pl* (wide) trousers.

шарови́дный spherical. **шарово́й** ball; globular. **шарообра́зный** spherical.

шарф scarf.

шасси́ *neut indecl* chassis.

шата́ть *impf* rock, shake; *impers* +*acc* **его́ шата́ет** he is reeling; **~ся** sway; reel, stagger; come loose, be loose; be unsteady; loaf about.

шатёр (-тра́) tent; marquee.

ша́ткий unsteady; shaky.

шату́н (-á) connecting-rod.

ша́фер (*pl* -á) best man.

шах check; ~ и мат checkmate. **шахмати́ст** chess-player. **ша́хматы** (-ат) *pl* chess; chessmen.

ша́хта mine, pit; shaft. **шахтёр** miner. **шахтёрский** miner's; mining.

ша́шка¹ draught; *pl* draughts.

ша́шка² sabre.

шашлы́к (-á) kebab; barbecue.

шва *etc.*: *see* шов

шва́бра mop.

шваль rubbish; riff-raff.

шварто́в mooring-line; *pl* moorings. **швартова́ть** *impf* (*pf* при~) moor; ~ся moor.

швед, ~ка Swede. **шве́дский** Swedish.

шве́йный sewing; ~ая маши́на sewing-machine.

швейца́р porter, doorman.

швейца́рец (-рца), -ца́рка Swiss. **Швейца́рия** Switzerland. **швейца́рский** Swiss.

Шве́ция Sweden.

швея́ seamstress.

швырну́ть (-ну́, -нёшь) *pf*, **швыря́ть** *impf* throw, fling; ~ся +*instr* throw (about); treat carelessly.

шевели́ть (-елю́, -éли́шь) *impf*, **шевельну́ть** (-ну́, -нёшь) *pf* (*pf also* по~) (+*instr*) move, stir; ~ся move, stir.

шеде́вр masterpiece.

ше́йка (*gen pl* ше́ек) neck.

шёл *see* идти́

ше́лест rustle. **шелесте́ть** (-сти́шь) *impf* rustle.

шёлк (*loc* -у́; *pl* -á) silk. **шелкови́стый** silky. **шелкови́ца** mulberry(-tree). **шелкови́чный** mulberry; ~ червь silkworm. **шёлковый** silk.

шелохну́ть (-ну́, -нёшь) *pf* stir, agitate; ~ся stir, move.

шелуха́ skin; peelings; pod. **шелуши́ть** (-шу́) peel; shell; ~ся peel (off), flake off.

шепеля́вить (-влю) *impf* lisp. **шепеля́вый** lisping.

шепну́ть (-ну́, -нёшь) *pf*, **шепта́ть** (-пчу́, -пчешь) *impf* whisper; ~ся whisper (together). **шёпотом** *adv* in a whisper.

шере́нга rank; file.

шерохова́тый rough; uneven.

шерсть wool; hair, coat. **шерстяно́й** wool(len).

верша́вый rough.

шест (-á) pole; staff.

ше́ствие procession. **ше́ствовать** *impf* process; march.

шестёрка six; figure 6; No. 6.

шестерня́ (*gen pl* -рён) gear-wheel, cogwheel.

ше́стеро (-ы́х) six.

шести- *in comb* six-, hexa-, sex(i)-. **шестигра́нник** hexahedron. **~дне́вка** six-day (*working*) week. **~деся́тый** sixtieth; six-month-old. **~со́тый** six-hundredth. **~уго́льник** hexagon.

шестнадцатиле́тний sixteen-year; sixteen-year-old. **шестна́дцатый** sixteenth. **шестна́дцать** sixteen. **шесто́й** sixth.

шесть (-и́, *instr* -ью) six. **шестьдеся́т** (-и́десяти, *instr* -ью́десятью) sixty. **шестьсо́т** (-исо́т, -иста́м, -ьюста́ми, -иста́х) six hundred. **шестью** *adv* six times.

шеф boss, chief; patron, sponsor. **шеф-по́вар** chef. **ше́фство** patronage, adoption. **ше́фствовать** *impf* +над+*instr* adopt; sponsor.

ше́я neck.

ши́ворот collar.

шика́рный chic, smart; splendid.

ши́ло (*pl* -ья, -ьев) awl.

шимпанзе́ *m indecl* chimpanzee.

ши́на tyre; splint.

шине́ль overcoat.

шинкова́ть *impf* shred, chop.

ши́нный tyre.

шип (-á) thorn, spike, crampon; pin; tenon.

шипе́ние hissing; sizzling. **шипе́ть** (-плю́) *impf* hiss; sizzle; fizz.

шипо́вник dog-rose.

шипу́чий sparkling; fizzy. **шипу́чка** fizzy drink. **шипя́щий** sibilant.

ши́ре *comp of* **широ́кий**, **широко́**. **ширина́** width; gauge. **ши́рить** *impf* extend; expand; **~ся** spread, expand.

ши́рма screen.

широ́кий (-о́к, -á, -о́ко́) wide; broad; **това́ры ~ого потребле́ния** consumer goods. **широко́** *adv* wide, widely, broadly. **широко-** *in comb* wide-, broad-. **широкове́щание** broadcasting. **~веща́тельный** broadcasting. **~экра́нный** wide-screen.

широта́ (*pl* -ы) width, breadth; latitude. **широ́тный** of latitude; latitudinal. **широча́йший** *superl of* **широ́кий**. **ширпотре́б** *abbr* consumption; consumer goods. **ширь** (wide) expanse.

шить (шью, шьёшь) *impf* (*pf* с~) sew; make; embroider. **шитьё** sewing; embroidery.

ши́фер slate.

шифр cipher, code; shelf mark. **шифро́ванный** coded. **шифрова́ть** *impf* (*pf* за~) encipher.

шифро́вка enciphering; coded communication.

ши́шка cone; bump; lump; (*sl*) big shot.

шкала́ (*pl* -ы) scale; dial.

шкату́лка box, casket, case.

шкаф (*loc* -у́; *pl* -ы́) cupboard; wardrobe. **шка́фчик** cupboard, locker.

шквал squall.

шкив (*pl* -ы́) pulley.

шко́ла school. **шко́льник** schoolboy. **шко́льница** schoolgirl. **шко́льный** school.

шку́ра skin, hide, pelt. **шку́рка** skin; rind; sandpaper.

шла *see* **идти́**

шлагба́ум barrier.

шлак slag; dross; clinker. **шлакобло́к** breeze-block.

шланг hose.

шлейф train.

шлем helmet.

шлёпать *impf*, **шлёпнуть** (-ну) *pf* smack, spank; shuffle; tramp; **~ся** fall flat, plop down.

шли *see* **идти́**

шлифова́льный polishing; grinding. **шлифова́ть** *impf* (*pf* от~) polish; grind. **шлифо́вка** polishing.

шло *see* **идти́**. **шлю** *etc.*: *see* **слать**

шлюз lock, sluice.

шлю́пка boat.

шля́па hat. **шля́пка** hat; head.

шмель (-я́) *m* bumble-bee.

шмон *sl* search, frisking.

шмы́гать *impf*, **шмыгну́ть** (-ыгну́, -ыгнёшь) *pf* dart, rush; +*instr* rub, brush; **~ но́сом** sniff.

шни́цель *m* schnitzel.

шнур (-á) cord; lace; flex, cable. **шнурова́ть** *impf* (*pf* за~,

про~) lace up; tie. шнуро́к
(-рка́) lace.

шов (шва) seam; stitch; joint.

шовини́зм chauvinism. шови-
ни́ст chauvinist. шовинисти́-
ческий chauvinistic.

шок shock. шоки́ровать *impf*
shock.

шокола́д chocolate. шоко-
ла́дка chocolate, bar of chocolate. шокола́дный chocolate.

шо́рох rustle.

шо́рты (шорт) *pl* shorts.

шо́ры (шор) *pl* blinkers.

шоссе́ *neut indecl* highway.

шотла́ндец (-дца) Scotsman,
Scot. Шотла́ндия Scotland.
шотла́ндка¹ Scotswoman. шот-
ла́ндка² tartan. шотла́ндский
Scottish, Scots.

шо́у *neut indecl* show; ~ -би́знес
show business.

шофёр driver; chauffeur.
шофёрский driver's; driving.

шпа́га sword.

шпага́т cord; twine; string;
splits.

шпаклева́ть (-лю́ю) *impf* (*pf*
за~) caulk; fill, putty.
шпаклёвка filling, puttying;
putty.

шпа́ла sleeper.

шпана́ (*sl*) hooligan(s); riff-raff.

шпарга́лка crib.

шпа́рить *impf* (*pf* о~) scald.

шпат spar.

шпиль *m* spire; capstan.
шпи́лька hairpin; hat-pin; tack;
stiletto heel.

шпина́т spinach.

шпинга́ле́т (vertical) bolt;
catch, latch.

шпио́н spy. шпиона́ж espionage. шпио́нить *impf* spy (за
+*instr* on). шпио́нский spy's;
espionage.

шпо́ра spur.

шприц syringe.

шпрота sprat.

шпу́лька spool, bobbin.

шрам scar.

шрапне́ль shrapnel.

шрифт (*pl* -ы́) type, print.

шт. *abbr* (*of* шту́ка) item, piece.

штаб (*pl* -ы́) staff; headquarters.

шта́бель (*pl* -я́) *m* stack.

штабно́й staff; headquarters.

штамп die, punch; stamp; cliché.
штампо́ванный punched,
stamped, pressed; stock.

шта́нга bar, rod, beam; weight.
штанги́ст weight-lifter.

штани́шки (-шек) *pl* (*child's*)
shorts. штаны́ (-о́в) trousers.

штат¹ State.

штат², шта́ты (-ов) *pl* staff, establishment.

штати́в tripod, base, stand.

шта́тный staff; established.

шта́тск|ий civilian; ~ое
(пла́тье) civilian clothes; ~ий *sb*
civilian.

ште́мпель (*pl* -я́) *m* stamp; по-
что́вый ~ postmark.

ште́псель (*pl* -я́) *m* plug,
socket.

штиль *m* calm.

штифт (-а́) pin, dowel.

што́льня (*gen pl* -лен) gallery.

што́пать *impf* (*pf* за~) darn.
што́пка darning; darning wool.

што́пор corkscrew; spin.

што́ра blind.

шторм gale.

штраф fine. штрафно́й penal;
penalty. штрафова́ть *impf* (*pf*
о~) fine.

штрих (-а́) stroke; feature.
штрихова́ть *impf* (*pf* за~)
shade, hatch.

штуди́ровать *impf* (*pf* **про~**) study.

шту́ка item, one; piece; trick.

штукату́р plasterer. **штукату́рить** *impf* (*pf* **от~, о~**) plaster. **штукату́рка** plastering; plaster.

штурва́л (steering-)wheel, helm.

штурм storm, assault.

шту́рман (*pl* **-ы** *or* **-а́**) navigator.

штурмова́ть *impf* storm, assault. **штурмово́й** assault; storming; **~а́я авиа́ция** ground-attack aircraft. **штурмовщи́на** rushed work.

шту́чный piece, by the piece.

штык (**-а́**) bayonet.

штырь (**-я́**) *m* pintle, pin.

шу́ба fur coat.

шу́лер (*pl* **-а́**) card-sharper.

шум noise; uproar; racket; stir. **шуме́ть** (**-млю́**) *impf* make a noise; row; make a fuss. **шу́мный** (**-мен, -мна́, -о**) noisy; loud; sensational.

шумово́й sound; **~ы́е эффе́кты** sound effects. **шумо́к** (**-мка́**) noise; **под ~** on the quiet.

шу́рин brother-in-law (*wife's brother*).

шурф prospecting shaft.

шурша́ть (**-шу́**) *impf* rustle.

шу́стрый (**-тёр, -тра́, -о**) smart, bright, sharp.

шут (**-а́**) fool; jester. **шути́ть** (**-чу́, -тишь**) *impf* (*pf* **по~**) joke; play, trifle; **+над**+*instr* make fun of. **шу́тка** joke, jest. **шутли́вый** humorous; joking, light-hearted. **шу́точный** comic; joking. **шутя́** *adv* for fun, in jest; easily.

шушу́каться *impf* whisper together.

шху́на schooner.

шью *etc.: see* **шить**

Щ

щаве́ль (**-я́**) *m* sorrel.

щади́ть (**щажу́**) *impf* (*pf* **по~**) spare.

щебёнка, ще́бень (**-бня**) *m* crushed stone, ballast; road-metal.

щебе́т twitter, chirp. **щебета́ть** (**-ечу́, -е́чешь**) *impf* twitter, chirp.

щего́л (**-гла́**) goldfinch.

щёголь *m* dandy, fop. **щегольну́ть** (**-ну́, -нёшь**), **щеголя́ть** *impf* dress fashionably; strut about; **+**instr show off, flaunt. **щегольско́й** foppish.

ще́дрость generosity. **ще́дрый** (**-др, -а́, -о**) generous; liberal.

щека́ (*acc* **щёку**; *pl* **щёки, -а́м**) cheek.

щеко́лда latch, catch.

щекота́ть (**-очу́, -о́чешь**) *impf* (*pf* **по~**) tickle. **щеко́тка** tickling; tickle. **щекотли́вый** ticklish, delicate.

щёлкать *impf*, **щёлкнуть** (**-ну**) *pf* crack; flick; trill; **+**instr click, snap, pop.

щёлок bleach. **щелочно́й** alkaline. **щёлочь** (*gen pl* **-е́й**) alkali.

щелчо́к (**-чка́**) flick; slight; blow.

щель (*gen pl* **-е́й**) crack; chink; slit; crevice; slit trench.

щеми́ть (**-млю́**) *impf* constrict; ache; oppress.

щено́к (**-нка́**; *pl* **-нки́, -о́в** *or* **-ня́та, -я́т**) pup; cub.

щепа́ (*pl* **-ы, -а́м**), **ще́пка** splinter, chip; kindling.

щепети́льный punctilious.

щепка *see* щепа́

щепо́тка, **щепо́ть** pinch.

щети́на bristle; stubble. **щети́нистый** bristly. **щети́ниться** *impf* (*pf* o∼) bristle. **щётка** brush; fetlock.

щи (щей *or* щец, щам, ща́ми) *pl* shchi, cabbage soup.

щи́колотка ankle.

щипа́ть (-плю́, -плешь) *impf*, **щипну́ть** (-ну́, -нёшь) *pf* (*pf also* об∼, o∼, ущипну́ть) pinch, nip; sting, bite; burn; pluck; nibble; ∼ся pinch. **щипко́м** *adv* pizzicato. **щипо́к** (-пка́) pinch, nip. **щипцы́** (-о́в) *pl* tongs, pincers, pliers; forceps.

щит (-а́) shield; screen; sluice-gate; (tortoise-)shell; board; panel. **щитови́дный** thyroid. **щито́к** (-тка́) dashboard.

щу́ка pike.

щуп probe. **щу́пальце** (*gen pl* -лец) tentacle; antenna. **щу́пать** *impf* (*pf* по∼) feel, touch.

щу́плый (-пл, -á, -o) weak, puny.

щу́рить *impf* (*pf* co∼) screw up, narrow; ∼ся screw up one's eyes; narrow.

Э

эбе́новый ebony.

эвакуа́ция evacuation. **эвакуи́рованный** *sb* evacuee. **эвакуи́ровать** *impf & pf* evacuate.

эвкали́пт eucalyptus.

эволюциони́ровать *impf & pf* evolve. **эволюцио́нный** evolutionary. **эволю́ция** evolution.

эги́да aegis.

эгои́зм egoism, selfishness. **эгои́ст**, **∼ка** egoist. **эгоисти́че-**ский, **эгоисти́чный** egoistic, selfish.

эй *int* hi! hey!

эйфори́я euphoria.

эква́тор equator.

эквивале́нт equivalent.

экзальта́ция exaltation.

экза́мен examination. **∼ держа́ть, сдать ∼** pass an examination. **экзамена́тор** examiner. **экзаменова́ть** *impf* (*pf* про∼) examine; ∼ся take an examination.

экзеку́ция (corporal) punishment.

экзе́ма eczema.

экземпля́р specimen; copy.

экзистенциали́зм existentialism.

экзоти́ческий exotic.

э́кий *which* what.

экипа́ж[1] carriage.

экипа́ж[2] crew. **экипирова́ть** *impf & pf* equip. **экипиро́вка** equipping; equipment.

эклекти́зм eclecticism.

эклер éclair.

экологи́ческий ecological. **эколо́гия** ecology.

эконо́мика economics; economy. **эконо́мист** economist. **эконо́мить** (-млю) *impf* (*pf* c∼) use sparingly; save; economize. **экономи́ческий** economic; economical. **экономи́чный** economical; saving. **эконо́мия** economy; saving. **эконо́мка** housekeeper. **эконо́мный** economical; thrifty.

экра́н screen. **экраниза́ция** filming; film version.

экскава́тор excavator.

эксклюзи́вный exclusive.

экскурса́нт tourist. **экскурсио́нный** excursion. **экску́рсия**

(conducted) tour; excursion. **экскурсово́д** guide.

экспанси́вный effusive.

экспатриа́нт expatriate.

экспеди́тор shipping agent. **экспеди́ция** expedition; dispatch; forwarding office.

экспериме́нт experiment. **экспериме́нта́льный** experimental. **эксперименти́ровать** *impf* experiment.

экспе́рт expert. **эксперти́за** (expert) examination; commission of experts.

эксплуата́тор exploiter. **эксплуатацио́нный** operating. **эксплуата́ция** exploitation; operation. **эксплуати́ровать** *impf* exploit; operate, run.

экспози́ция lay-out; exposition; exposure. **экспона́т** exhibit. **экспоно́метр** exposure meter.

э́кспорт export. **экспорти́ровать** *impf & pf* export. **э́кспортный** export.

экспре́сс express (*train etc.*).

экспро́мт impromptu. **экспро́мтом** *adv* impromptu.

экспроприа́ция expropriation. **экспроприи́ровать** *impf & pf* expropriate.

экста́з ecstasy.

экстравага́нтный eccentric, bizarre.

экстра́кт extract.

экстреми́ст extremist. **экстреми́стский** extremist.

э́кстренный urgent; emergency; special.

эксцентри́чный eccentric.

эксце́сс excess.

эласти́чный elastic; supple. **элева́тор** grain elevator; hoist. **элега́нтный** elegant, smart.

эле́гия elegy.

электризова́ть *impf* (*pf* на∼) electrify. **эле́ктрик** electrician. **электрифика́ция** electrification. **электрифици́ровать** *impf & pf* electrify. **электри́ческий** electric(al). **электри́чество** electricity. **электри́чка** electric train.

электро́- *in comb* electro-, electric, electrical. **электробыто́вой** electrical. **∼во́з** electric locomotive. **электро́лиз** electrolysis. **∼магни́тный** electromagnetic. **∼монтёр** electrician. **∼оде́ло** electric blanket. **∼по́езд** electric train. **∼прибо́р** electrical appliance. **∼про́вод** (*pl* -á) electric cable. **∼прово́дка** electric wiring. **∼ста́нция** power-station. **∼те́хник** electrical engineer. **∼те́хника** electrical engineering. **∼шо́к** electric shock, electric-shock treatment. **∼эне́ргия** electrical energy.

электро́д electrode.

электро́н electron. **электро́ника** electronics.

электро́нный electron; electronic; **∼ая по́чта** email; **∼ое письмо́** email (letter); **∼ый а́дрес** email address.

элеме́нт element; cell; character. **элемента́рный** elementary.

эли́та élite.

э́ллипс elipse.

эма́левый enamel. **эмали́рова́ть** *impf* enamel. **эма́ль** enamel.

эмансипа́ция emancipation.

эмба́рго *neut indecl* embargo.

эмбле́ма emblem.

эмбрио́н embryo.

эмигра́нт emigrant, émigré.

эмигра́ция emigration. **эмигри́ровать** *impf & pf* emigrate.

эмоциона́льный emotional. **эмо́ция** emotion.

эмпири́ческий empirical.

эму́льсия emulsion.

э́ндшпиль *m* end-game.

энерге́тика power engineering. **энергети́ческий** energy. **энерги́чный** energetic. **эне́ргия** energy.

энтомоло́гия entomology.

энтузиа́зм enthusiasm. **энтузиа́ст** enthusiast.

энциклопеди́ческий encyclopaedic. **энциклопе́дия** encyclopaedia.

эпигра́мма epigram. **эпи́граф** epigraph.

эпиде́мия epidemic.

эпизо́д episode. **эпизоди́ческий** episodic; sporadic.

эпиле́псия epilepsy. **эпиле́птик** epileptic.

эпило́г epilogue. **эпита́фия** epitaph. **эпи́тет** epithet. **эпице́нтр** epicentre.

эпопе́я epic.

эпо́ха epoch, era.

э́ра era; до на́шей э́ры ВС; на́шей э́ры AD.

эре́кция erection.

эро́зия erosion.

эроти́зм eroticism. **эро́тика** sensuality. **эроти́ческий, эроти́чный** erotic, sensual.

эруди́ция erudition.

эска́дра (*naut*) squadron. **эскадри́лья** (*gen pl* -лий) (*aeron*) squadron. **эскадро́н** (*mil*) squadron.

эскала́тор escalator. **эскала́ция** escalation.

эски́з sketch; draft. **эски́зный** sketch; draft.

эскимо́с, эскимо́ска Eskimo.

эско́рт escort.

эсми́нец (-нца) *abbr* (*of* эска́дренный миноно́сец) destroyer.

эссе́нция essence.

эстака́да trestle bridge; overpass; pier, boom.

эста́мп print, engraving, plate.

эстафе́та relay race; baton.

эсте́тика aesthetics. **эстети́ческий** aesthetic.

эсто́нец (-нца), **эсто́нка** Estonian. **Эсто́ния** Estonia. **эсто́нский** Estonian.

эстра́да stage, platform; variety. **эстра́дный** stage; variety; ~ конце́рт variety show.

эта́ж (-а́) storey, floor. **этаже́рка** shelves.

э́так *adv* so, thus; about. **э́такий** such (a), what (a).

этало́н standard.

эта́п stage; halting-place.

э́тика ethics.

этике́т etiquette.

этике́тка label.

эти́л ethyl.

этимоло́гия etymology.

эти́ческий, эти́чный ethical.

этни́ческий ethnic. **этногра́фия** ethnography.

э́то *partl* this (is), that (is), it (is). **э́тот** *m*, **э́та** *f*, **э́то** *neut*, **э́ти** *pl* *pron* this, these.

этю́д study, sketch; étude.

эфеме́рный ephemeral.

эфио́п, ~ка Ethiopian. **эфио́пский** Ethiopian.

эфи́р ether; air. **эфи́рный** ethereal; ether, ester.

эффе́кт effect. **эффекти́вность** effectiveness. **эффекти́вный** effective. **эффе́ктный** effective; striking.

эх *int* eh! oh!

э́хо echo.

эшафо́т scaffold.

эшело́н echelon; special train.

Ю

юбиле́й anniversary; jubilee. **юбиле́йный** jubilee.

ю́бка skirt. **ю́бочка** short skirt.

ювели́р jeweller. **ювели́рный** jeweller's, jewellery; fine, intricate.

юг south; **на ~е** in the south. **ю́го-восто́к** south-east. **ю́го-за́пад** south-west. **югосла́в, ~ка** Yugoslav. **Югосла́вия** Yugoslavia. **югосла́вский** Yugoslav.

юдофо́б anti-Semite. **юдофо́бство** anti-Semitism.

южа́нин (pl -а́не, -а́н), **южа́нка** southerner. **ю́жный** south, southern; southerly.

юла́ top; fidget. **юли́ть** impf fidget.

ю́мор humour. **юмори́ст** humourist. **юмористи́ческий** humorous.

ю́ность youth. **ю́ноша** (gen pl -шей) m youth. **ю́ношеский** youthful. **ю́ношество** youth; young people. **ю́ный** (юн, -а́, о) young; youthful.

юпи́тер floodlight.

юриди́ческий legal, juridical. **юриско́нсульт** legal adviser. **юри́ст** lawyer.

ю́ркий (-рок, -рка́, -рко) quick-moving, brisk; smart.

юро́дивый crazy.

ю́рта yurt, nomad's tent.

юсти́ция justice.

юти́ться (ючу́сь) impf huddle (together).

Я

я (меня́, мне, мной (-о́ю), (обо) мне) pron I.

я́беда m & f, tell-tale; informer.

я́блоко (pl -и, -ок) apple; **глазно́е ~** eyeball. **я́блоневый**, **я́блочный** apple. **я́блоня** apple-tree.

яви́ться (явлю́сь, я́вишься) pf, **явля́ться** impf appear; arise; +instr be, serve as. **я́вка** appearance, attendance; secret rendezvous. **явле́ние** phenomenon; appearance; occurrence; scene. **я́вный** obvious; overt. **я́вственный** clear. **я́вствовать** be clear, be obvious.

ягнёнок (-нка; pl -ня́та, -я́т) lamb.

я́года berry; berries. **я́годица** buttock(s).

ягуа́р jaguar.

яд poison; venom.

я́дерный nuclear.

ядови́тый poisonous; venomous.

ядрёный healthy; bracing; juicy. **ядро́** (pl -а, я́дер) kernel, core; nucleus; (cannon-) ball; shot.

я́зва ulcer, sore. **я́звенный** ulcerous; **~ая боле́знь** ulcers. **язви́тельный** caustic, sarcastic. **язви́ть** (-влю́) impf (pf съ~) be sarcastic.

язы́к (-а́) tongue; clapper; language. **языкове́д** linguist. **языкове́дение, языкозна́ние** linguistics. **языково́й** linguistic. **языко́вый** tongue; lingual. **язы́ческий** heathen, pagan. **язычо́к** (-чка́) tongue; reed; catch.

я́йчко (pl -и, -чек) egg; testicle.

яи́чник ovary. **яи́чница** fried eggs. **яйцо́** (*pl* я́йца, яи́ц) egg; ovum.

я́кобы *conj* as if; *partl* supposedly.

я́корн|**ый** anchor; **~ая стоя́нка** anchorage. **я́корь** (*pl* -я́) *m* anchor.

я́лик skiff.

я́ма pit, hole.

ямщи́к (-а́) coachman.

янва́рский January. **янва́рь** (-я́) *m* January.

янта́рный amber. **янта́рь** (-я́) *m* amber.

япо́нец (-нца), **япо́нка** Japanese. **Япо́ния** Japan. **япо́нский** Japanese.

ярд yard.

я́ркий (я́рок, ярка́, -o) bright; colourful, striking.

ярлы́к (-а́) label; tag.

я́рмарка fair.

ярмо́ (*pl* -a) yoke.

яровой spring.

я́ростный furious, fierce. **я́рость** fury.

я́рус circle; tier; layer.

я́рче *comp of* я́ркий

я́рый fervent; furious; violent.

я́сли (-ей) *pl* manger; crèche, day nursery.

яснеть (-е́ет) *impf* become clear, clear. **я́сно** *adv* clearly. **ясно-ви́дение** clairvoyance. **ясно-ви́дец** (-дца), **ясновидица** clairvoyant. **я́сность** clarity; clearness. **я́сный** (я́сен, ясна́, -o) clear; bright; fine.

я́ства (яств) *pl* victuals.

я́сень *m* ash(-tree).

я́стреб (*pl* -á) hawk.

я́хта yacht.

яче́йка cell.

ячме́нь[1] (-я́) *m* barley.

ячме́нь[2] (-я́) *m* stye.

я́щерица lizard.

я́щик box; drawer.

ящу́р foot-and-mouth (disease).

Phrasefinder/
Разгово́рник

Useful phrases

Поле́зные фра́зы

yes, please	да, пожа́луйста
no, thank you	нет, спаси́бо
sorry	прости́те
excuse me	извини́те (меня́)
I'm sorry, I don't understand	прости́те, я не понима́ю

Meeting people

Встре́ча

hello/goodbye	здра́вствуйте/до свида́ния
how are you?	как пожива́ете?
nice to meet you	рад/ра́да с ва́ми познако́миться

Asking questions

Вопро́сы

do you speak English/Russian?	вы говори́те по-англи́йски/по-ру́сски?
what's your name?	как вас зову́т?/как ва́ше и́мя?
where are you from?	отку́да вы?
how much is it?	ско́лько э́то сто́ит?
where is…?	где…?
can I have…?	мо́жно мне…?
would you like…?	не хоти́те ли…?

Statements about yourself

Немно́го о себе́

my name is…	меня́ зову́т…, моё и́мя…
I'm American/Russian	я америка́нец/америка́нка/ру́сский/ру́сская
I don't speak Russian/English	я не говорю́ по-ру́сски/по-англи́йски
I live near Chester/Moscow	я живу́ недалеко́ от Че́стера/Москвы́
I'm a student	я студе́нт/студе́нтка
I work in an office	я рабо́таю на фи́рме

Emergencies

Экстренные слу́чаи

can you help me, please?	не могли́ бы вы мне помо́чь?
I'm lost	я заблуди́лся/заблуди́лась
I'm ill	я бо́лен/больна́
call an ambulance	вы́зовите ско́рую по́мощь

Reading signs

Чита́ем на́дписи

no entry	нет вхо́да
no smoking	не кури́те
fire exit	запа́сный вы́ход
for sale	продаётся

❶ Going Places

On the road

Where's the nearest service station?

what's the best way to get there?

I've got a puncture

I'd like to hire a bike/car

there's been an accident

my car's broken down

the car won't start

На шоссе

где ближа́йшая бензозапра́вочная ста́нция?/где ближа́йший автосе́рвис?

как быстре́е туда́ добра́ться?

у меня́ проко́л ши́ны

я хоте́л/хоте́ла бы взять напрока́т велосипе́д/автомоби́ль

произошла́ ава́рия/произошло́ ДТП

у меня́ слома́лась маши́на

мото́р не заво́дится

By rail

where can I buy a ticket?

what time is the next train to Orel/Oxford?

do I have to change?

can I take my bike on the train?

which platform for the train to Kiev/London?

there's a train to London at 10 o'clock

a single/return to Leeds/Zvenigorod, please

I'd like an all-day ticket

I'd like to reserve a seat

По́езд

где я могу́ купи́ть биле́т?

когда́ сле́дующий по́езд на Орёл/О́ксфорд?

ну́жно ли мне де́лать переса́дку?

меня́ пу́стят в ваго́н с велосипе́дом?

с како́й платфо́рмы идёт по́езд на Ки́ев/Ло́ндон?

по́езд на Ло́ндон отправля́ется в 10 часо́в

биле́т в оди́н коне́ц/биле́т туда́ и обра́тно до Ли́дса/Звени́города, пожа́луйста

мне ну́жен биле́т на су́тки

я хоте́л/хоте́ла бы зарезерви́ровать ме́сто

At the airport

when's the next flight to Vladivostok/
Manchester?

where do I check in?

I'd like to confirm my flight

I'd like a window seat/an aisle seat

I want to change/cancel my reservation

В аэропорту́

когда́ сле́дующий рейс во
Владивосто́к/в Ма́нчестер?

где регистра́ция пассажи́ров?

я хоте́л/хоте́ла бы подтверди́ть
свой рейс

мне хоте́лось бы взять ме́сто у
окна́/у прохо́да

я хочу́ измени́ть/отмени́ть зака́з
биле́та

Getting there

could you tell me the way to the castle
(*on foot/by transport*)?

how long will it take to get there?

how far is it from here?

which bus do I take for the cathedral?

can you tell me where to get off?

what time is the last bus?

how do I get to the airport?

where's the nearest underground
station, (*Amer.*) subway station?

I'll take a taxi

can you call me a taxi?

take the first turning on the right

turn left at the traffic lights/just past the
church

Как прое́хать?

не подска́жете мне, как пройти́/
прое́хать к за́мку?

до́лго ли туда́ добира́ться?

как далеко́ э́то отсю́да?

како́й авто́бус идёт до собо́ра?

вы ска́жете мне, где вы́йти?

до како́го ча́са хо́дит авто́бус?

как мне прое́хать до аэропо́рта?

где ближа́йшая ста́нция метро́?

я возьму́ такси́

мо́жете мне вы́звать такси́?

поверни́те на пе́рвом поворо́те
напра́во

поверни́те нале́во у светофо́ра/
сра́зу за це́рковью

❷ Keeping in touch

On the phone

may I use your phone?	мо́жно позвони́ть по ва́шему телефо́ну?
do you have a mobile, (*Amer.*) cell phone?	у вас есть моби́льный телефо́н?
what is the code for St Petersburg/Edinburgh?	како́й код (телефо́на) в Санкт-Петербу́рг/Эдинбу́рг?
I want to make a phone call	мне ну́жно сде́лать звоно́к
I'd like to reverse the charges, (*Amer.*) call collect	мне ну́жно, что́бы звоно́к оплати́ла вызыва́емая сторона́
I need to top up my mobile, (*Amer.*) cell phone	мне ну́жно доплати́ть за моби́льный телефо́н
the line's engaged, (*Amer.*) busy	ли́ния занята́
there's no answer	отве́та нет
hello, this is John/Igor	алло́, э́то Джон/И́горь
is Oleg/Richard there, please?	пожа́луйста, позови́те Оле́га/Ри́чарда
who's calling?	кто говори́т?
sorry, wrong number	извини́те, не туда́ попа́ли
just a moment, please	одну́ мину́тку, пожа́луйста
please hold the line	не ве́шайте тру́бку, пожа́луйста
please tell him/her I called	пожа́луйста, переда́йте ему́/ей, что я звони́л/звони́ла
I'd like to leave a message for him/her	я хоте́л/хоте́ла бы оста́вить сообще́ние для него́/неё
...I'll try again later	...я ещё поздне́е позвоню́
please tell him/her that Elena called	пожа́луйста, переда́йте ему́/ей, что звони́ла Еле́на
can he/she ring me back?	мо́жет он/она́ мне перезвони́ть?
my home number is...	мой дома́шний телефо́н...
my business number is...	мой рабо́чий телефо́н...
my mobile, (*Amer.*) cell phone number is...	но́мер моего́ моби́льного...
we were cut off	нас прерва́ли

Говори́м по телефо́ну

Средства связи. Отношения ❷

Writing

Пишем письмо

what's your address?

ваш áдрес?

where is the nearest post office?

где ближáйшая пóчта?

could I have a stamp for Russia, please?

пожáлуйста, дáйте мне мáрку для письмá в Россию

I'd like to send a parcel/a fax

я хотéл/хотéла бы послáть посылку/факс

On line

Он-лáйн

are you on the Internet?

вы подключены́ к Интернéту?

what's your email address?

какóй ваш электрóнный áдрес?

we could send it by email

мы моглú бы послáть э́то по электрóнной пóчте

I'll email it to you on Tuesday

я пошлю́ э́то вам по электрóнной пóчте во втóрник

I looked it up on the Internet

я посмотрéл/посмотрéла э́то по Интернéту

the information is on their website

информáция есть на их веб-сáйте

Meeting up

Встрéчи

what shall we do this evening?

что мы бýдем дéлать сегóдня вéчером?

where shall we meet?

где мы встрéтимся?

I'll see you outside the cafe at 6 o'clock

я вас встрéчу у кафé в 6 часóв

see you later

до встрéчи

I can't today, I'm busy

сегóдня не могý, я зáнят/занятá

❸ Food and Drink

Reservations

can you recommend a good restaurant?

I'd like to reserve a table for four

a reservation for tomorrow evening at eight o'clock

Ordering

could we see the menu/wine list, please?

do you have a vegetarian/children's menu?

as a starter… and to follow…

could we have some more bread/rice?

what would you recommend?

I'd like a
…white coffee, (*Amer.*) coffee with cream
…black coffee
…a decaffeinated coffee
…a liqueur

could I have the bill, (*Amer.*) check

You will hear

вы гото́вы зака́зывать?

хоти́те заказа́ть аперити́в?

бу́дете зака́зывать заку́ску?

како́е блю́до бу́дете зака́зывать?

зака́зываете десе́рт?

ко́фе?/ликёр?

что ещё зака́жете?

прия́тного аппети́та!

обслу́живание (не) включено́

Зака́з в рестора́не

мо́жете ли порекомендова́ть хоро́ший рестора́н?

я хоте́л/хоте́ла бы заказа́ть сто́лик на четверы́х

зака́з на за́втра на во́семь часо́в ве́чера

Зака́з блюд

мо́жно нам меню́/ка́рту вин?

у вас есть вегетариа́нское/де́тское меню́?

на заку́ску… и зате́м…

мо́жно ещё хле́ба/ри́са?

что вы порекоменду́ете?

я хоте́л/хоте́ла бы заказа́ть
…ко́фе с молоко́м
…чёрный ко́фе
…ко́фе без кофеи́на
…ликёр

счёт, пожа́луйста

Что вы слы́шите

are you ready to order?

would you like an aperitif?

would you like a starter?

what will you have for the main course?

would you like a dessert?

would you like coffee/liqueurs?

anything else?

enjoy your meal!

service is (not) included

The menu	Меню́	Меню́	The menu
starters	**заку́ски**	**заку́ски**	**starters**
hors d'oeuvres	заку́ски	заку́ски	hors d'oeuvres
omelette	омле́т	омле́т	omelette
soup	суп	суп	soup
fish	**ры́ба**	**ры́ба**	**fish**
bass	морско́й о́кунь	кальма́р	squid
cod	треска́	карп	carp
eel	у́горь	кефа́ль	mullet
hake	хек	креве́тки	prawns, shrimps
herring	сельдь	лосо́сь	salmon
monkfish	морско́й чёрт	ми́дии	mussels
mullet	кефа́ль	морско́й о́кунь	bass
mussels	ми́дии	морско́й язы́к	sole
oyster	у́стрица	осетри́на	sturgeon
prawns	короле́вские	па́лтус	turbot
	креве́тки	сарди́ны	sardines
salmon	лосо́сь, сёмга	сельдь	herring
sardines	сарди́ны	сёмга	salmon
shrimps	креве́тки	треска́	cod
sole	морско́й язы́к	туне́ц	tuna
squid	кальма́р	хек	hake
trout	форе́ль	у́горь	eel
tuna	туне́ц	у́стрица	oyster
turbot	па́лтус	форе́ль	trout
meat	**мя́со**	**мя́со**	**meat**
beef	говя́дина	(молода́я)	lamb
chicken	цыплёнок	бара́нина	
chop	отбивна́я	бифште́кс	steak
duck	у́тка	ветчина́	ham
goose	гусь	вы́резка	steak
hare	за́яц	говя́дина	beef
ham	ветчина́	гусь	goose
kidneys	по́чки	колба́ски	sausages
lamb	(молода́я) бара́нина	оле́нина	venison
liver	печёнка	отбивна́я	chop
pork	свини́на	печёнка	liver
rabbit	кролья́тина	по́чки	kidneys
sirloin	филе́	свини́на	pork
steak	бифште́кс, вы́резка	теля́тина	veal
turkey	инде́йка	у́тка	duck
veal	теля́тина	филе́	sirloin steak
venison	оле́нина	цыплёнок	chicken

❸ Food and Drink

vegetables	о́вощи	о́вощи	vegetables
asparagus	спа́ржа	баклажа́н	aubergine
aubergine	баклажа́н	бобы́	beans
beans	бобы́; фасо́ль	горо́шек	peas
beetroot	свёкла	грибы́	mushrooms
broccoli	бро́кколи	зелёный лук	spring onions
carrots	морко́вь	капу́ста	cabbage
cabbage	капу́ста	карто́фель	potatoes
celery	сельдере́й	лук	onions
courgettes (Br.)	цуки́ни	морко́вь	carrots
French beans (Br.)	стручко́вая фасо́ль	огуре́ц	cucumber
lettuce	сала́т-лату́к	(сла́дкий) пе́рец	(sweet) pepper
mushrooms	грибы́	помидо́р	tomato
peas	горо́шек	реди́с	radish
(sweet) pepper	сла́дкий пе́рец	свёкла	beetroot
potatoes	карто́фель	сельдере́й	celery
runner beans	вью́щаяся фасо́ль	спа́ржа	asparagus
		фасо́ль	beans
tomato	помидо́р	цветна́я капу́ста	cauliflower
sweet potato	сла́дкий карто́фель, бата́т		
zucchini (Amer.)	цуки́ни		

the way it's cooked	как э́то пригото́влено	как э́то пригото́влено	the way it's cooked
baked	запечённый	варёный	boiled
boiled	отварно́й, варёный	в горшо́чке	casseroled
		жа́реный	(в духо́вке)
fried	жа́реный		roast;
griddled	пригото́вленный на пло́ской сковороде́		(на сковороде́) fried
		жа́реный на гри́ле	grilled
grilled	(жа́реный) на гри́ле		
		запечённый	baked
poached	припу́щенный	отварно́й	boiled
pureed	пюре́, пюри́рованный	пригото́вленный на пло́ской сковороде́	griddled
rare	с кро́вью (о мя́се)		
roast	жа́реный	припу́щенный	poached
stewed	тушёный	с кро́вью (о мя́се)	rare
well done	хорошо́ прожа́ренный	тушёный	stewed
		хорошо́ прожа́ренный	well done

desserts	десе́рты	десе́рты	desserts
ice cream	моро́женое	моро́женое	ice cream
fruit	фру́кты	пиро́г	pie
gateau	торт	торт	gateau
pie	пиро́г	фру́кты	fruit

other	друго́е	друго́е	other
bread	хлеб	горчи́ца	mustard
butter	сли́вочное ма́сло	майоне́з	mayonnaise
cheese	сыр	оли́вковое ма́сло	olive oil
cheeseboard	доска́/блю́до с	пе́рец	pepper
	сы́ром	припра́ва	seasoning
garlic	чесно́к	сли́вочное ма́сло	butter
mayonnaise	майоне́з	соль	salt
mustard	горчи́ца	со́ус	sauce
olive oil	оли́вковое ма́сло	сыр	cheese
pepper	пе́рец	у́ксус	vinegar
rice	рис	хлеб	bread
salt	соль	хрен	horseradish
sauce	со́ус	чесно́к	garlic
seasoning	припра́ва		
vinegar	у́ксус		

drinks	напи́тки	напи́тки	drinks
beer	пи́во	безалкого́льный	soft drink
bottle	буты́лка	напи́ток	
carbonated	газиро́ванный	бе́лое вино́	white wine
fizzy	шипу́чий	буты́лка	bottle
half-bottle	полбуты́лки	вино́	wine
liqueur	likёр	водопрово́дная	tap water
mineral water	минера́льная вода́	вода́	
red wine	кра́сное вино́	газиро́ванный	carbonated
rosé	ро́зовое вино́	дома́шнее вино́	house wine
soft drink	безалкого́льный	кра́сное вино́	red wine
	напи́ток	likёр	liqueur
still	негазиро́ванный	минера́льная вода́	mineral water
house wine	дома́шнее вино́	негазиро́ванный	still
table wine	столо́вое вино́	пи́во	beer
tap water	водопрово́дная вода́	полбуты́лки	half-bottle
white wine	бе́лое вино́	ро́зовое вино́	rosé
wine	вино́	столо́вое вино́	table wine
		шипу́чий	fizzy

❹ Places to stay

Camping

can we pitch our tent here?	мы мо́жем здесь разби́ть пала́тку?
can we park our caravan here?	мо́жем здесь припаркова́ть наш карава́н?
what are the facilities like?	каки́е здесь усло́вия?
how much is it per night?	ско́лько здесь беру́т за су́тки?
where do we park the car?	где мо́жно припаркова́ть маши́ну?
we're looking for a campsite	мы и́щем ке́мпинг
this is a list of local campsites	вот спи́сок ме́стных ке́мпингов
we go on a camping holiday every year	мы ка́ждый год отдыха́ем в ке́мпинге

Ке́мпинг

At the hotel

I'd like a double/single room with bath	мне ну́жен двухме́стный/одноме́стный но́мер с ва́нной
we have a reservation in the name of Morris	мы зарезерви́ровали но́мер на фами́лию Мо́ррис
we'll be staying three nights, from Friday to Sunday	мы бу́дем здесь тро́е су́ток, с пя́тницы по воскресе́нье
how much does the room cost?	ско́лько сто́ит но́мер?
I'd like to see the room	я хоте́л/хоте́ла бы посмотре́ть но́мер
what time is breakfast?	когда́ здесь за́втрак?
can I leave this in your safe?	могу́ я э́то оста́вить в ва́шем се́йфе?
bed and breakfast	ночле́г и за́втрак
we'd like to stay another night	мы хоте́ли бы оста́ться ещё на су́тки
please call me at 7.30	пожа́луйста, позвони́те мне в 7.30
are there any messages for me?	есть ли мне сообще́ние?

В гости́нице

Hostels	**Молодёжные гости́ницы**
could you tell me where the youth hostel is?	скажи́те мне, пожа́луйста, где молодёжная гости́ница?
what time does the hostel close?	когда́ молодёжную гости́ницу закрыва́ют?
I'll be staying in a hostel	я останови́лось в молодёжной гости́нице
the hostel we're staying in is great value	молодёжная гости́ница, где мы останови́лись, недорога́я и о́чень удо́бная
I know a really good hostel in Dublin	я зна́ю в Ду́блине весьма́ прили́чную молодёжную гости́ницу
I'd like to go backpacking in Australia	я хоте́л/хоте́ла бы попутеше́ствовать с рюкзако́м по Австра́лии

Rooms to rent	**Жильё внаём**
I'm looking for a room with a reasonable rent	я ищу́ ко́мнату за уме́ренную це́ну
I'd like to rent an apartment for a few weeks	я хоте́л/хоте́ла бы снять кварти́ру на не́сколько неде́ль
where do I find out about rooms to rent?	где мне узна́ть о ко́мнатах, кото́рые сдаю́тся?
what's the weekly rent?	ско́лько плати́ть за жильё в неде́лю?
I'm staying with friends at the moment	я сейча́с живу́ у друзе́й
I rent an apartment on the outskirts of town	я снима́ю кварти́ру на окра́ине го́рода
the room's fine—I'll take it	ко́мната мне подхо́дит—я сниму́ её
the deposit is one month's rent in advance	зада́ток вперёд в су́мме ме́сячной опла́ты

❺ Shopping and money

Banking

I'd like to change some money	я хоте́л/хоте́ла бы поменя́ть де́ньги
I want to change some dollars into euros	я хочу́ поменя́ть до́ллары на е́вро
do you need identification?	вам ну́жно удостовере́ние ли́чности?
what's the exchange rate today?	како́й курс обме́на на сего́дня?
Do you accept traveller's cheques, (Amer.) traveler's checks	вы принима́ете доро́жные че́ки?
I'd like to transfer some money from my account	я хоте́л/хоте́ла бы перевести́ не́которую су́мму с моего́ счёта
Where is there an ATM/a cash machine?	где здесь банкома́т?
I'd like high denomination notes, (Amer.) bills	мне нужны́ кру́пные купю́ры
I'm with another bank	у меня́ счёт в друго́м ба́нке

В ба́нке

Finding the right shop

where's the main shopping district?	где здесь торго́вый центр?
where can I buy batteries/postcards?	где я могу́ купи́ть батаре́йки/ откры́тки?
where's the nearest pharmacy/ bookshop?	где ближа́йшая апте́ка/ ближа́йший кни́жный магази́н?
is there a good food shop around here?	есть здесь побли́зости хоро́ший продово́льственный магази́н?
what time do the shops open/close?	когда́ магази́ны открыва́ются/ закрыва́ются?
where did you get those?	где вы э́то купи́ли?
I'm looking for presents for my family	я ищу́ пода́рки для мои́х родны́х
we'll do our shopping on Saturday	мы пойдём по магази́нам в суббо́ту
I love shopping	я люблю́ ходи́ть по магази́нам

Ну́жный магази́н

Покупки и де́ньги ❺

Are you being served?

how much does that cost?	ско́лько э́то сто́ит?
can I try it on?	могу́ я э́то приме́рить?
could you wrap it for me, please?	заверни́те, пожа́луйста
can I pay by credit card?	я могу́ плати́ть креди́тной ка́ртой?
do you have this in another colour, (Amer.) color?	есть у вас э́то друго́й расцве́тки?
could I have a bag, please?	бу́дьте добры́, да́йте мне паке́т
I'm just looking	я про́сто смотрю́
I'll think about it	я до́лжен/должна́ поду́мать
I'd like a receipt, please	мне нужна́ квита́нция/мне ну́жен чек
I need a bigger/smaller size	мне ну́жен бо́льший/ме́ньший разме́р
I take a size 10/a medium	ношу́ разме́р 10/сре́дний разме́р
it doesn't suit me	мне э́то не подхо́дит
I'm sorry, I don't have any change/anything smaller	прости́те, у меня́ нет ме́лочи/ме́лких де́нег
that's all, thank you	э́то всё, спаси́бо

Вас обслу́живают?

Changing things

I'd like to change it, please	я хоте́л/хоте́ла бы э́то поменя́ть
I bought this here yesterday	я купи́л/купи́ла э́то здесь вчера́
can I have a refund?	могу́ я рассчи́тывать на возмеще́ние?/мне верну́т де́ньги?
can you mend it for me?	мо́жете э́то испра́вить/почини́ть?
it doesn't work	э́то не рабо́тает
can I speak to the manager?	могу́ я поговори́ть с ме́неджером?

Заме́на това́ра

❻ Sport and leisure

Keeping fit

Занятия спортом

where can we play football/squash? — где мы можем поиграть в футбол/сквош?

where is the local sports centre, (*Amer.*) center? — где здесь местный спортивный центр?

what's the charge per day? — сколько стоит день занятий?

is there a reduction for children/ a student discount? — есть ли скидка для детей/ студентов?

I'm looking for a swimming pool/ tennis court — я ищу бассейн/теннисный корт

you have to be a member — вы должны быть членом (клуба)

I play tennis on Mondays — я играю в теннис по понедельникам

I would like to go fishing/riding — я хотел/хотела бы заняться рыбной ловлей/верховой ездой

I want to do aerobics — я хочу заняться аэробикой

I love swimming/rollerskating — я люблю плавание/катание на роликовых коньках

we want to hire skis/snowboards — мы хотели бы взять напрокат лыжи/сноуборды

Watching sport

Спортивные зрелища

is there a football match on Saturday? — есть футбольный матч в воскресенье?

which teams are playing? — какие команды играют?

where can I get tickets? — где я могу купить билеты?

I'd like to see a rugby/football match — я хотел/хотела бы попасть на регби/футбол

my favourite, (*Amer.*) favorite team is... — моя любимая команда...

let's watch the game on TV — давайте посмотрим игру по телевизору

Going out in the evening	В теа́тре, на конце́рте
what's on?	что идёт?
when does the box office open/close?	когда́ открыва́ется/закрыва́ется биле́тная ка́сса?
what time does the concert/performance start?	когда́ нача́ло конце́рта/спекта́кля?
when does it finish?	когда́ конча́ется (спекта́кль)?
are there any seats left for tonight?	есть ли свобо́дные места́ на сего́дня?
how much are the tickets?	ско́лько сто́ят биле́ты?
where can I get a programme, (*Amer.*) program?	где я могу́ купи́ть програ́мму?
I want to book tickets for tonight's performance	я хочу́ заказа́ть биле́ты на сего́дняшний конце́рт/спекта́кль
I'll book seats in the circle	я закажу́ биле́ты на балко́н
I'd rather have seats in the stalls	я бы хоте́л/хоте́ла купи́ть биле́ты на места́ в парте́ре
somewhere in the middle, but not too far back	где-нибудь в середи́не, но не о́чень далеко́
four, please	четы́ре биле́та, пожа́луйста
for Saturday	на суббо́ту
we'd like to go to a club	мы бы хоте́ли сходи́ть в ночно́й клуб
I go clubbing every weekend	я хожу́ в ночно́й клуб ка́ждый уи́к-э́нд

Hobbies	Хо́бби
what do you do at the weekend?	что вы де́лаете по суббо́там и воскресе́ньям?
I like yoga/listening to music	мне нра́вится занима́ться йо́гой/слу́шать му́зыку
I spend a lot of time surfing the Net	я мно́го вре́мени провожу́ в Интерне́те/я мно́го брожу́ по Интерне́ту
I read a lot	я мно́го чита́ю
I collect old coins	я собира́ю стари́нные моне́ты

❼ Time

Telling the time

what time is it?	ско́лько вре́мени?
it's 2 o'clock	два часа́
at about 8 o'clock	о́коло 8 (восьми́) часо́в
from 10 o'clock onwards	по́сле 10 (десяти́) часо́в
at 5 o'clock in the morning/afternoon	в 5 (пять) (часо́в) утра́/ве́чера
it's five past/quarter past/half past one	пять мину́т/че́тверть/полови́на второ́го
it's twenty-five to/quarter to one	без двадцати́ пяти́/че́тверти час
a quarter/three quarters of an hour	че́тверть часа́/со́рок пять мину́т

Ско́лько вре́мени?

Days and dates

Sunday, Monday, Tuesday, Wednesday, Thursday, Friday, Saturday	воскресе́нье, понеде́льник, вто́рник, среда́, четве́рг, пя́тница, суббо́та
January, February, March, April, May, June, July, August, September, October, November, December	янва́рь, февра́ль, март, апре́ль, май, ию́нь, ию́ль, а́вгуст, сентя́брь, октя́брь, ноя́брь, дека́брь
what's the date?	како́е сего́дня число́?
it's the second of June	сего́дня второ́е ию́ня
we meet up every Monday	мы ви́димся ка́ждый понеде́льник
we're going away in August	мы уезжа́ем в а́вгусте
on November 8th	восьмо́го ноября́

Дни и чи́сла

Public holidays and special days

bank holiday	нерабо́чий день
bank holiday Monday	нерабо́чий понеде́льник
New Year's Day (1 Jan.)	Но́вый год (1-е января́)
Epiphany (6 Jan.)	Креще́ние Госпо́дне, Богоявле́ние (19-е января́)
St Valentine's Day (14 Feb.)	День свято́го Валенти́на (14-е февраля́)

Пра́здники, нерабо́чие дни

Day of the Defender of the Fatherland	День защи́тника Оте́чества (*23-е февраля́*)
Shrove Tuesday/Pancake Day	вто́рник на ма́сленой неде́ле
Ash Wednesday	пе́рвый день Вели́кого поста́
International Woman's Day (*8 March*)	Восьмо́е ма́рта, Междунаро́дный же́нский день (*8-е ма́рта*)
Maundy Thursday	Вели́кий четве́рг (на Страстно́й неде́ле)
Good Friday	Страстна́я пя́тница
Easter	Па́сха
May Day (*1 May*)	Пе́рвое ма́я (*1-е ма́я*)
VE Day (*8 May*)	День Побе́ды (*9-е ма́я*)
Whit Sunday, Pentecost (*7th Sunday after Easter*)	Тро́ица, Тро́ицын день
Russian Defenders' Memorial Day (*marking the beginning of the Great Patriotic War (1941–45)*)	День па́мяти защи́тников Оте́чества (22-е ию́ня)
Fourth of July/Independence Day (US)	День незави́симости
Assumption/Dormition of the Virgin Mary (*15 August*)	Успе́ние Пресвято́й Богоро́дицы (*28-е а́вгуста*)
Protecting Veil/Intercession of the Virgin Mary (*people pray for protection from evil and hardships and help in view of the long winter ahead*)	Покро́в Пресвято́й Богоро́дицы (*14-е октября́*)
Halloween (*31 Oct.*)	Кану́н Дня Всех Святы́х
All Saints' Day (*1 Nov.*)	День Всех Святы́х
Guy Fawkes Day/Bonfire Night (*5 Nov., UK*)	день Га́я Фо́кса, день годовщи́ны раскры́тия "порохово́го за́говора"
National Unity Day	День наро́дного еди́нства (*4-е ноября́*)
Remembrance Sunday (*anniversary of the armistice of 11 November 1918*)	Помина́льное воскресе́нье
Thanksgiving (*4th Thursday in November, US*)	День благодаре́ния
Christmas Eve (*24 Dec.*)	Рожде́ственский соче́льник (*6-е января́*)
Christmas Day (*25 Dec.*)	Рождество́ Христо́во (*7-е января́*)
New Year's Eve (*31 Dec.*)	Нового́дняя ночь (*31-е декабря́*)

❽ Weights and measures/ Ме́ры длины́, ве́са, объёма

Length/Длина́

inches/дю́ймы	0.39	3.9	7.8	11.7	15.6	19.5	39
centimetres/сантиме́тры	1	10	20	30	40	50	100

Distance/Расстоя́ние

miles/ми́ли	0.62	6.2	12.4	18.6	24.8	31	62
kilometres/киломе́тры	1	10	20	30	40	50	100

Weight/Вес

pounds/фу́нты	2.2	22	44	66	88	110	220
kilos/килогра́ммы	1	10	20	30	40	50	100

Capacity/Объём

(Br.) gallons/галло́ны	0.22	2.2	4.4	6.6	8.8	11	22
(US) gallons/галло́ны	0.26	2.64	5.28	7.92	10.56	13.2	26.4
litres/ли́тры	1	10	20	30	40	50	100

Temperature/Температу́ра

°C (Celsius)/ °C (по Це́льсию)	0	5	10	15	20	25	30	37	38	40
°F (Fahrenheit)/ °F (по Фаренге́йту)	32	41	50	59	68	77	86	98.4	100	104

Clothing and shoe sizes/Разме́ры оде́жды и о́буви

Women's clothing sizes/Же́нская оде́жда

UK	8	10	12	14	16	18
US	6	8	10	12	14	16
Russia	40	42	44	46	48	50

Men's clothing sizes (chest sizes)/Мужска́я оде́жда (костю́мы, пиджаки́)

UK/US	36	38	40	42	44	46
Russia	46	48	50	52	54	56

Women's shoes/Же́нская о́бувь

UK	2.5	3	3.5	4	4.5	5	5.5	6	6.5	7	7.5	8
US	5	5.5	6	6.5	7	7.5	8	8.5	9	9.5	10	10.5
Russia	35	35.5	36	37	37.5	38	39	39.5	40	40.5	41	42

Men's shoes/Мужска́я о́бувь

UK	6	6.5	7	7.5	8	8.5	9	9.5	10	10.5	11	11.5	12
US	6.5	7	7.5	8	8.5	9	9.5	10	10.5	11	11.5	12	12.5
Russia	39.5	40	40.5	41	42	42.5	43	44	44.5	45	46	46.5	47

A

a /ə, eɪ/, **an** /æn, ən/ indef article, not usu translated; **twice a week** два раза в неделю.

aback /ə'bæk/ adv: **take ~** озадачивать impf, озадачить pf.

abacus /'æbəkəs/ n счёты pl.

abandon /ə'bænd(ə)n/ vt покидать impf, покинуть pf; (give up) отказываться impf, отказаться pf от+gen; **~ o.s. to** предаваться impf, предаться pf +dat. **abandoned** /ə'bænd(ə)nd/ adj покинутый; (profligate) распутный.

abase /ə'beɪs/ vt унижать impf, унизить pf. **abasement** /-mənt/ n унижение.

abate /ə'beɪt/ vi затихать impf, затихнуть pf.

abattoir /'æbə,twɑ:(r)/ n скотобойня.

abbey /'æbɪ/ n аббатство.

abbreviate /ə'bri:vɪ,eɪt/ vt сокращать impf, сократить pf. **abbreviation** /-'eɪʃ(ə)n/ n сокращение.

abdicate /'æbdɪ,keɪt/ vi отрекаться impf, отречься pf от престола. **abdication** /-'keɪʃ(ə)n/ n отречение (от престола).

abdomen /'æbdəmən/ n брюшная полость. **abdominal** /-'dɒmɪn(ə)l/ adj брюшной.

abduct /əb'dʌkt/ vt похищать impf, похитить pf. **abduction** /-'dʌkʃ(ə)n/ n похищение.

aberration /,æbə'reɪʃ(ə)n/ n (mental) помутнение рассудка.

abet /ə'bet/ vt подстрекать impf, подстрекнуть pf (к совершению преступления etc.)

abhor /əb'hɔ:(r)/ vt ненавидеть impf. **abhorrence** /-'hɒrəns/ n отвращение. **abhorrent** /-'hɒrənt/ adj отвратительный.

abide /ə'baɪd/ vt (tolerate) выносить impf, вынести pf; **~ by** (rules etc.) следовать impf, по~ pf.

ability /ə'bɪlɪtɪ/ n способность.

abject /'æbdʒekt/ adj (wretched) жалкий; (humble) униженный; **~ poverty** крайняя нищета.

ablaze /ə'bleɪz/ predic охваченный огнём.

able /'eɪb(ə)l/ adj способный, умелый; **be ~ to** мочь impf, с~ pf; (know how to) уметь impf, с~ pf.

abnormal /æb'nɔ:m(ə)l/ adj ненормальный. **abnormality** /-'mælɪtɪ/ n ненормальность.

aboard /ə'bɔ:d/ adv на борт(ý); (train) в поезд(е).

abode /ə'bəʊd/ n жилище; **of no fixed ~** без постоянного местожительства.

abolish /ə'bɒlɪʃ/ vt отменять impf, отменить pf. **abolition** /,æbə'lɪʃ(ə)n/ n отмена.

abominable /ə'bɒmɪnəb(ə)l/ adj отвратительный. **abomination** /-'neɪʃ(ə)n/ n мерзость.

aboriginal /,æbə'rɪdʒɪn(ə)l/ adj коренной; n абориген, коренной житель m. **aborigine** /-nɪ/ n

абориге́н, коренно́й жи́тель *m*.

abort /ə'bɔːt/ *vi* (*med*) выки́дывать *impf*, вы́кинуть *pf*; *vt* (*terminate*) прекраща́ть *impf*, прекрати́ть *pf*. **abortion** /ə'bɔː-ʃ(ə)n/ *n* або́рт; **have an** ~ де́лать *impf*, с~ *pf* або́рт. **abortive** /-tɪv/ *adj* безуспе́шный.

abound /ə'baʊnd/ *vi* быть в изоби́лии; ~ **in** изоби́ловать *impf* +*instr*.

about /ə'baʊt/ *adv & prep* (*approximately*) о́коло+*gen*; (*concerning*) о+*prep*, насчёт+*gen*; (*up and down*) по+*dat*; (*in the vicinity*) круго́м; **be** ~ to собира́ться *impf*, собра́ться *pf* +*inf*.

above /ə'bʌv/ *adv* наверху́; (*higher up*) вы́ше; **from** ~ све́рху; *prep* над+*instr*; (*more than*) свы́ше+*gen*. **above-board** *adj* че́стный. **above-mentioned** *adj* вы́шеупомя́нутый.

abrasion /ə'breɪʒ(ə)n/ *n* истира́ние; (*wound*) сса́дина. **abrasive** /-sɪv/ *adj* абрази́вный; (*manner*) колю́чий; *n* абрази́вный материа́л.

abreast /ə'brest/ *adv* в ряд; **keep** ~ **of** идти́ в но́гу с+*instr*.

abridge /ə'brɪdʒ/ *vt* сокраща́ть *impf*, сократи́ть *pf*. **abridgement** /-mənt/ *n* сокраще́ние.

abroad /ə'brɔːd/ *adv* за грани́цей, за грани́цу; **from** ~ из-за грани́цы.

abrupt /ə'brʌpt/ *adj* (*steep*) круто́й; (*sudden*) внеза́пный; (*curt*) ре́зкий.

abscess /'æbsɪs/ *n* абсце́сс.

abscond /əb'skɒnd/ *vi* скрыва́ться *impf*, скры́ться *pf*.

absence /'æbs(ə)ns/ *n* отсу́тствие. **absent** /-s(ə)nt/ *adj*

отсу́тствующий; **be** ~ отсу́тствовать *impf*; *vt*: ~ **o.s.** отлуча́ться *impf*, отлучи́ться *pf*. **absentee** /ˌæbsən'tiː/ *n* отсу́тствующий *sb*. **absenteeism** *n* /-'tiːɪz(ə)m/ прогу́л. **absent-minded** *adj* рассе́янный.

absolute /'æbsəˌluːt/ *adj* абсолю́тный; (*complete*) по́лный, соверше́нный. **absolution** /ˌæbsə'luːʃ(ə)n/ *n* отпуще́ние грехо́в. **absolve** /əb'zɒlv/ *vt* проща́ть *impf*, прости́ть *pf*.

absorb /əb'zɔːb/ *vt* впи́тывать *impf*, впита́ть *pf*. **absorbed** /əb'zɔːbd/ *adj* поглощённый. **absorbent** /əb'zɔːbənt/ *adj* вса́сывающий. **absorption** /əb'zɔːpʃ(ə)n/ *n* впи́тывание; (*mental*) погружённость.

abstain /əb'steɪn/ *vi* возде́рживаться *impf*, воздержа́ться *pf* (**from** от+*gen*). **abstemious** /əb'stiːmɪəs/ *adj* возде́ржанный. **abstention** /əb'stenʃ(ə)n/ *n* воздержа́ние; (*person*) воздержа́вшийся *sb*. **abstinence** /'æbstɪnəns/ *n* воздержа́ние.

abstract /'æbstrækt/ *adj* абстра́ктный, отвлечённый; *n* рефера́т.

absurd /əb'sɜːd/ *adj* абсу́рдный. **absurdity** /-dɪtɪ/ *n* абсу́рд.

abundance /ə'bʌnd(ə)ns/ *n* оби́лие. **abundant** /-(ə)nt/ *adj* оби́льный.

abuse *vt* /ə'bjuːz/(*insult*) руга́ть *impf*, вы́~, об~, от~ *pf*; (*misuse*) злоупотребля́ть *impf*, злоупотреби́ть *pf*; *n* /ə'bjuːs/ (*curses*) руга́нь, руга́тельства *neut pl*; (*misuse*) злоупотребле́ние. **abusive** /-sɪv/ *adj* оскорби́тельный, руга́тельный.

abut /ə'bʌt/ *vi* примыка́ть *impf* (**on** к+*dat*).

abysmal /ə'bɪzm(ə)l/ adj (extreme) безграни́чный; (bad) ужа́сный. **abyss** /ə'bɪs/ n бе́здна.

academic /ækə'demɪk/ adj академи́ческий. **academician** /ə,kædə'mɪʃ(ə)n/ n акаде́мик. **academy** /ə'kædəmɪ/ n акаде́мия.

accede /ək'si:d/ vi вступа́ть impf, вступи́ть pf (to в, на+acc); (assent) соглаша́ться impf, согласи́ться pf.

accelerate /ək'seləreɪt/ vt & i ускоря́ть(ся) impf, ускори́ть(ся) pf; (motoring) дава́ть impf, дать pf газ. **acceleration** /-'reɪʃ(ə)n/ n ускоре́ние. **accelerator** /-,reɪtə(r)/ n ускори́тель m; (pedal) акселера́тор.

accent n /'æksent/ акце́нт; (stress) ударе́ние; vt /æk'sent/ де́лать impf, c~ pf ударе́ние на+acc. **accentuate** /æk'sentjueɪt/ vt акценти́ровать impf & pf.

accept /ək'sept/ vt принима́ть impf, приня́ть pf. **acceptable** /-təb(ə)l/ adj прие́млемый. **acceptance** /-t(ə)ns/ n приня́тие.

access /'ækses/ n до́ступ. **accessible** /ək'sesɪb(ə)l/ adj досту́пный. **accession** /ək'seʃ(ə)n/ n вступле́ние (на престо́л). **accessories** /ək'sesərɪz/ n pl принадле́жности f pl. **accessory** /ək'sesərɪ/ n (accomplice) соуча́стник, -ица.

accident /'æksɪd(ə)nt/ n (chance) случа́йность; (mishap) несча́стный слу́чай; (crash) ава́рия; by ~ случа́йно. **accidental** /-'dent(ə)l/ adj случа́йный.

acclaim /ə'kleɪm/ vt (praise) восхваля́ть impf, восхвали́ть pf; n восхвале́ние.

acclimatization /ə,klaɪmətaɪ'zeɪʃ(ə)n/ n акклиматиза́ция. **acclimatize** /ə'klaɪmə,taɪz/ vt акклиматизи́ровать impf & pf.

accommodate /ə'kɒmə,deɪt/ vt помеща́ть impf, помести́ть pf; (hold) вмеща́ть impf, вмести́ть pf. **accommodating** /-,deɪtɪŋ/ adj услу́жливый. **accommodation** /-'deɪʃ(ə)n/ n (hotel) но́мер; (home) жильё.

accompaniment /ə'kʌmpənɪmənt/ n сопровожде́ние; (mus) аккомпанеме́нт. **accompanist** /-nɪst/ n аккомпаниа́тор. **accompany** /-nɪ/ vt сопровожда́ть impf, сопроводи́ть pf; (escort) провожа́ть impf, проводи́ть pf; (mus) аккомпани́ровать impf +dat.

accomplice /ə'kʌmplɪs/ n соуча́стник, -ица.

accomplish /ə'kʌmplɪʃ/ vt соверша́ть impf, соверши́ть pf. **accomplished** /-plɪʃt/ adj зако́нченный. **accomplishment** /-plɪʃmənt/ n выполне́ние; (skill) соверше́нство.

accord /ə'kɔ:d/ n согла́сие; of one's own ~ доброво́льно; of its own ~ сам собо́й, сам по себе́. **accordance** /-dəns/ n: in ~ with в соотве́тствии c+instr, согла́сно+dat. **according** /-dɪŋ/ adv: ~ to по+dat, ~ to him по его́ слова́м. **accordingly** /-dɪŋlɪ/ adv соотве́тственно. **accordion** /ə'kɔ:dɪən/ n аккордео́н.

accost /ə'kɒst/ vt пристава́ть impf, приста́ть pf к+dat.

account /ə'kaʊnt/ n (comm) счёт; (report) отчёт; (description) описа́ние; on no ~ ни в ко́ем слу́чае; on ~ of из-за+gen, по причи́не+gen; take into ~ принима́ть impf,

приня́ть *pf* в расчёт; *vi*: ~ for объясня́ть *impf*, объясни́ть *pf*.

accountable /ə'təb(ə)l/ *adj* отве́тственный.

accountancy /ə'kaʊntənsɪ/ *n* бухгалте́рия. **accountant** /-tənt/ *n* бухга́лтер.

accrue /ə'kru:/ *vi* нараста́ть *impf*, нарасти́ *pf*.

accumulate /ə'kju:mjʊ,leɪt/ *vt & i* нака́пливать(ся) *impf*, копи́ть(ся) *impf*, на~ *pf*. **accumulation** /-'leɪʃ(ə)n/ *n* накопле́ние. **accumulator** /-,leɪtə(r)/ *n* аккумуля́тор.

accuracy /'ækjʊrəsɪ/ *n* то́чность. **accurate** /-rət/ *adj* то́чный.

accusation /,ækju:'zeɪʃ(ə)n/ *n* обвине́ние. **accusative** /ə'kju:zətɪv/ *adj* (*n*) вини́тельный (паде́ж). **accuse** /ə'kju:z/ *vt* обвиня́ть *impf*, обвини́ть *pf* (of в+*prep*); **the ~d** обвиня́емый *sb*.

accustom /ə'kʌstəm/ *vt* приуча́ть *impf*, приучи́ть *pf* (to к+*dat*). **accustomed** /-təmd/ *adj* привы́чный; **be, get ~** привыка́ть *impf*, привы́кнуть *pf* (to к+*dat*).

ace /eɪs/ *n* туз; (*pilot*) ас.

ache /eɪk/ *n* боль; *vi* боле́ть *impf*.

achieve /ə'tʃi:v/ *vt* достига́ть *impf*, дости́чь & дости́гнуть *pf* +*gen*. **achievement** /-mənt/ *n* достиже́ние.

acid /'æsɪd/ *n* кислота́; *adj* ки́слый; **~ rain** кисло́тный дождь. **acidity** /ə'sɪdɪtɪ/ *n* кислота́.

acknowledge /ək'nɒlɪdʒ/ *vt* признава́ть *impf*, призна́ть *pf*; (*receipt of*) подтвержда́ть *impf*, подтверди́ть *pf* получе́ние +*gen*. **acknowledgement** /-mənt/ *n* призна́ние; подтвер-

жде́ние.

acne /'æknɪ/ *n* прыщи́ *m pl*.

acorn /'eɪkɔ:n/ *n* жёлудь *m*.

acoustic /ə'ku:stɪk/ *adj* акусти́ческий. **acoustics** /-stɪks/ *n pl* аку́стика.

acquaint /ə'kweɪnt/ *vt* знако́мить *impf*, по~ *pf*. **acquaintance** /-t(ə)ns/ *n* знако́мство; (*person*) знако́мый *sb*. **acquainted** /-tɪd/ *adj* знако́мый.

acquiesce /,ækwɪ'es/ *vi* соглаша́ться *impf*, согласи́ться *pf*. **acquiescence** /-s(ə)ns/ *n* согла́сие.

acquire /ə'kwaɪə(r)/ *vt* приобрета́ть *impf*, приобрести́ *pf*. **acquisition** /,ækwɪ'zɪʃ(ə)n/ *n* приобрете́ние. **acquisitive** /ə'kwɪzɪtɪv/ *adj* стяжа́тельский.

acquit /ə'kwɪt/ *vt* опра́вдывать *impf*, оправда́ть *pf*; ~ **o.s.** вести́ *impf* себя́. **acquittal** /-t(ə)l/ *n* оправда́ние.

acre /'eɪkə(r)/ *n* акр.

acrid /'ækrɪd/ *adj* е́дкий.

acrimonious /,ækrɪ'məʊnɪəs/ *adj* язви́тельный.

acrobat /'ækrə,bæt/ *n* акроба́т. **acrobatic** /-'bætɪk/ *adj* акробати́ческий.

across /ə'krɒs/ *adv & prep* че́рез+*acc*; (*athwart*) поперёк (+*gen*); (*to, on, other side*) на ту сто́рону (+*gen*), на той стороне́ (+*gen*); (*crosswise*) кресткре́ст.

acrylic /ə'krɪlɪk/ *n* акри́л; *adj* акри́ловый.

act /ækt/ *n* (*deed*) акт, посту́пок; (*law*) акт, зако́н; (*of play*) де́йствие; (*item*) но́мер; *vi* посту́пать *impf*, поступи́ть *pf*; де́йствовать *impf*, по~ *pf*; *vi* игра́ть *impf*, сыгра́ть *pf*. **acting** /'æktɪŋ/ *n* игра́; (*profession*) актёрство; *adj* исполня́ющий

обя́занности+*gen.* **action** /'ækʃ(ə)n/ *n* де́йствие, посту́пок; (*law*) иск, проце́сс; (*battle*) бой; ~ **replay** повто́р; **be out of** ~ не рабо́тать *impf.* **activate** /'æktɪ,veɪt/ *vt* приводи́ть *impf*, привести́ *pf* в де́йствие. **active** /'æktɪv/ *adj* акти́вный; ~ **service** действи́тельная слу́жба; ~ **voice** действи́тельный зало́г. **activity** /æk'tɪvɪtɪ/ *n* де́ятельность. **actor** /'æktə(r)/ *n* актёр. **actress** /'æktrɪs/ *n* актри́са.

actual /'æktʃʊəl/ *adj* действи́тельный. **actuality** /-'ælɪtɪ/ *n* действи́тельность. **actually** /'æktʃʊəlɪ/ *adv* на са́мом де́ле, факти́чески.

acumen /'ækjʊmən/ *n* проница́тельность.

acupuncture /'ækju:,pʌŋktʃə(r)/ *n* иглоука́лывание.

acute /ə'kju:t/ *adj* о́стрый.

AD *abbr* н.э. (на́шей э́ры).

adamant /'ædəmənt/ *adj* непреклонный.

adapt /ə'dæpt/ *vt* приспособля́ть *impf*, приспосо́бить *pf*; (*theat*) инсцени́ровать *impf* & *pf*; ~ **o.s.** приспособля́ться *impf*, приспосо́биться *pf*. **adaptable** /-təb(ə)l/ *adj* приспособля́ющийся. **adaptation** /,ædæp'teɪʃ(ə)n/ *n* приспособле́ние; (*theat*) инсцениро́вка. **adapter** /-tə(r)/ *n* ада́птер.

add /æd/ *vt* прибавля́ть *impf*, приба́вить *pf*; (*say*) добавля́ть *impf*, доба́вить *pf*; ~ **together** скла́дывать *impf*, сложи́ть *pf*; ~ **up** сумми́ровать *impf* & *pf*; ~ **up to** составля́ть *impf*, соста́вить *pf*; (*fig*) своди́ться *impf*, свести́сь *pf* к+*dat.* **addenda** /ə'dendə/ *n* в приложе́ния *pl.*

adder /'ædə(r)/ *n* гадю́ка.

addict /'ædɪkt/ *n* наркома́н, ~ка. **addicted** /ə'dɪktɪd/ *adj*: **be** ~ **to** быть рабо́м+*gen*; **become** ~ **to** пристрасти́ться *pf* к+*dat.* **addiction** /ə'dɪkʃ(ə)n/ *n* (*passion*) пристра́стие; (*to drugs*) наркома́ния.

addition /ə'dɪʃ(ə)n/ *n* прибавле́ние; дополне́ние; (*math*) сложе́ние; **in** ~ вдоба́вок, кро́ме того́. **additional** /-n(ə)l/ *adj* доба́вочный. **additive** /'ædɪtɪv/ *n* доба́вка.

address /ə'dres/ *n* а́дрес; (*speech*) речь; ~ **book** записна́я кни́жка; *vt* адресова́ть *impf* & *pf*; (*speak to*) обраща́ться *impf*, обрати́ться *pf* к+*dat*; ~ **a meeting** выступа́ть *impf*, вы́ступить *pf* на собра́нии. **addressee** /,ædre'si:/ *n* адреса́т.

adept /'ædept/ *adj* све́дущий; *n* ма́стер.

adequate /'ædɪkwət/ *adj* доста́точный.

adhere /əd'hɪə(r)/ *vi* прилипа́ть *impf*, прили́пнуть *pf* (**to** к+*dat*); (*fig*) приде́рживаться *impf* +*gen.* **adherence** /-rəns/ *n* приве́рженность. **adherent** /-rənt/ *n* приве́рженец. **adhesive** /əd'hi:sɪv/ *adj* ли́пкий; *n* кле́йкое вещество́.

ad hoc /æd 'hɒk/ *adj* специа́льный.

ad infinitum /æd ,ɪnfɪ'naɪtəm/ *adv* до бесконе́чности.

adjacent /ə'dʒeɪs(ə)nt/ *adj* сме́жный.

adjective /'ædʒɪktɪv/ *n* (и́мя) прилага́тельное.

adjoin /ə'dʒɔɪn/ *vt* прилега́ть *impf* к+*dat.*

adjourn /ə'dʒɜːn/ *vt* откла́дывать *impf*, отложи́ть *pf*; *vi* объявля́ть *impf*, объяви́ть *pf*

перерыв; (*move*) переходить *impf*, перейти *pf*.

adjudicate /ə'dʒuːdɪˌkeɪt/ *vi* выносить *impf*, вынести *pf* решение (in по+*dat*); судить *impf*.

adjust /ə'dʒʌst/ *vt* & *i* приспособлять(ся) *impf*, приспособить(ся) *pf*; (*regulate*) регулировать *impf*, от~ *pf*. **adjustable** /-təb(ə)l/ *adj* регулируемый. **adjustment** /-mənt/ *n* регулирование, подгонка.

ad lib /æd 'lɪb/ *vt* & *i* импровизировать *impf*, сымпровизировать *pf*.

administer /əd'mɪnɪstə(r)/ *vt* (*manage*) управлять *impf* +*instr*; (*give*) давать *impf*, дать *pf*. **administration** /-'streɪʃ(ə)n/ *n* управление; (*government*) правительство. **administrative** /-strətɪv/ *adj* административный. **administrator** /-ˌstreɪtə(r)/ *n* администратор.

admirable /'ædmərəb(ə)l/ *adj* похвальный.

admiral /'ædmər(ə)l/ *n* адмирал.

admiration /ˌædmɪ'reɪʃ(ə)n/ *n* восхищение. **admire** /əd'maɪə(r)/ *vt* (*look at*) любоваться *impf* +*instr*, на+*acc*; (*respect*) восхищаться *impf*, восхититься *pf* +*instr*. **admirer** /əd'maɪərə(r)/ *n* поклонник.

admissible /əd'mɪsɪb(ə)l/ *adj* допустимый. **admission** /əd'mɪʃ(ə)n/ *n* (*access*) доступ; (*entry*) вход; (*confession*) признание. **admit** /əd'mɪt/ *vt* (*allow in*) впускать *impf*, впустить *pf*; (*confess*) признавать *impf*, признать *pf*. **admittance** /əd'mɪt(ə)ns/ *n* доступ. **admittedly** /əd'mɪtɪdli/ *adv* признаться.

admixture /æd'mɪkstʃə(r)/ *n* примесь.

adolescence /ˌædə'les(ə)ns/ *n* отрочество. **adolescent** /-s(ə)nt/ *adj* подростковый *n* подросток.

adopt /ə'dɒpt/ *vt* (*child*) усыновлять *impf*, усыновить *pf*; (*thing*) усваивать *impf*, усвоить *pf*; (*accept*) принимать *impf*, принять *pf*. **adoptive** /-tɪv/ *adj* приёмный. **adoption** /ə'dɒpʃ(ə)n/ *n* усыновление; принятие.

adorable /ə'dɔːrəb(ə)l/ *adj* прелестный. **adoration** /ˌædə'reɪʃ(ə)n/ *n* обожание. **adore** /ə'dɔː(r)/ *vt* обожать *impf*.

adorn /ə'dɔːn/ *vt* украшать *impf*, украсить *pf*. **adornment** /-mənt/ *n* украшение.

adrenalin /ə'drenəlɪn/ *n* адреналин.

adroit /ə'drɔɪt/ *adj* ловкий.

adulation /ˌædjʊ'leɪʃ(ə)n/ *n* преклонение.

adult /'ædʌlt/ *adj* & *n* взрослый (*sb*).

adulterate /ə'dʌltəˌreɪt/ *vt* фальсифицировать *impf* & *pf*.

adultery /ə'dʌltəri/ *n* супружеская измена.

advance /əd'vɑːns/ *n* (*going forward*) продвижение (вперёд); (*progress*) прогресс; (*mil*) наступление; (*of pay etc.*) аванс; **in ~** заранее; *pl* (*overtures*) авансы *m pl*; *vi* (*go forward*) продвигаться *impf*, продвинуться *pf* вперёд; идти *impf* вперёд; (*mil*) наступать *impf*; *vt* продвигать *impf*, продвинуть *pf*; (*put forward*) выдвигать *impf*, выдвинуть *pf*. **advanced** /əd'vɑːnst/ *adj* (*modern*) передовой. **advancement** /-mənt/ *n* продвижение.

advantage /əd'vɑ:ntɪdʒ/ n преимущество; (*profit*) выгода, польза; **take** ~ of пользоваться *impf*, вос~ *pf* +*instr*. **advantageous** /ˌædvən'teɪdʒəs/ adj выгодный.

adventure /əd'ventʃə(r)/ n приключение. **adventurer** /-rə(r)/ n искатель m приключений. **adventurous** /-rəs/ adj предприимчивый.

adverb /'ædvɜːb/ n наречие.

adversary /'ædvəsərɪ/ n противник. **adverse** /'ædvɜːs/ adj неблагоприятный. **adversity** /əd'vɜːsɪtɪ/ n несчастье.

advertise /'ædvətaɪz/ vt (*publicize*) рекламировать *impf* & *pf*; vt & i (~ for) дать *impf*, дать *pf* объявление о+*prep*. **advertisement** /əd'vɜːtɪsmənt/ n объявление, реклама.

advice /əd'vaɪs/ n совет. **advisable** /əd'vaɪzəb(ə)l/ adj желательный. **advise** /əd'vaɪz/ vt советовать *impf*, по~ *pf* +*dat* & *inf*; (*notify*) уведомлять *impf*, уведомить *pf*. **advisedly** /əd'vaɪzɪdlɪ/ adv намеренно. **adviser** /əd'vaɪzə(r)/ n советник. **advisory** /əd'vaɪzərɪ/ adj совещательный.

advocate n (*supporter*) сторонник; vt /'ædvəkeɪt/ выступать *impf* за+*acc*; (*advise*) советовать *impf*, по~ *pf*.

aegis /'iːdʒɪs/ n эгида.

aerial /'eərɪəl/ n антенна; adj воздушный.

aerobics /eə'rəʊbɪks/ n аэробика.

aerodrome /'eərədrəʊm/ n аэродром. **aerodynamics** /-daɪ'næmɪks/ n аэродинамика. **aeroplane** /-ˌpleɪn/ n самолёт. **aerosol** /-ˌsɒl/ n аэрозоль m.

aesthetic /iːs'θetɪk/ adj эстетический. **aesthetics** /-tɪks/ n эстетика.

afar /ə'fɑː(r)/ adv: from ~ издалека.

affable /'æfəb(ə)l/ adj приветливый.

affair /ə'feə(r)/ n (*business*) дело; (*love*) роман.

affect /ə'fekt/ vt влиять *impf*, по~ *pf* на+*acc*; (*touch*) трогать *impf*, тронуть *pf*; (*concern*) затрагивать *impf*, затронуть *pf*. **affectation** /ˌæfek'teɪʃ(ə)n/ n жеманство. **affected** /-tɪd/ adj жеманный. **affection** /ə'fekʃ(ə)n/ n привязанность. **affectionate** /ə'fekʃənət/ adj нежный.

affiliated /ə'fɪlɪˌeɪtɪd/ adj связанный (**to** c+*instr*).

affinity /ə'fɪnɪtɪ/ n (*relationship*) родство; (*resemblance*) сходство; (*attraction*) влечение.

affirm /ə'fɜːm/ vt утверждать *impf*. **affirmation** /ˌæfə'meɪʃ(ə)n/ n утверждение. **affirmative** /ə'fɜːmətɪv/ adj утвердительный.

affix /ə'fɪks/ vt прикреплять *impf*, прикрепить *pf*.

afflict /ə'flɪkt/ vt постигать *impf*, постичь *pf*; **be afflicted with** страдать *impf* +*instr*. **affliction** /ə'flɪkʃ(ə)n/ n бедствие.

affluence /'æfluəns/ n богатство. **affluent** /-ənt/ adj богатый.

afford /ə'fɔːd/ vt позволять *impf*, позволить *pf* себе; (*supply*) предоставлять *impf*, предоставить *pf*.

affront /ə'frʌnt/ n оскорбление; vt оскорблять *impf*, оскорбить *pf*.

afield /ə'fiːld/ adv: far ~ далеко; farther ~ дальше.

afloat /ə'fləʊt/ adv & predic на воде.

afoot /ə'fʊt/ predic: be ~ гото́-
виться impf.

aforesaid /ə'fɔːsed/ adj вы́ше-
упомя́нутый.

afraid /ə'freid/ predic: be ~
боя́ться impf.

afresh /ə'freʃ/ adv сно́ва.

Africa /'æfrikə/ n А́фрика. **African** /-kən/ n африка́нец,
-ка́нка; adj африка́нский.

after /'ɑːftə(r)/ adv пото́м; prep
по́сле +gen; (time) че́рез+acc;
(behind) за+acc, instr; ~ all в
конце́ концо́в; conj по́сле того́,
как.

aftermath /'ɑːftəmæθ/ n после́д-
ствия neut pl. **afternoon** /-'nuːn/
n втора́я полови́на дня; **in the
~** днём. **aftershave** /-ʃeiv/ n
лосьо́н по́сле бритья́. **after-
thought** /-θɔːt/ n запозда́лая
мысль.

afterwards /'ɑːftəwədz/ adv
пото́м.

again /ə'gen/ adv опя́ть; (once
more) ещё раз; (anew) сно́ва.

against /ə'genst/ prep (opposing)
про́тив+gen; (touching) к+dat;
(hitting) о+acc.

age /eidʒ/ n во́зраст; (era) век,
эпо́ха; vt ста́рить impf, co~ pf;
vi старе́ть impf, no~ pf. **aged**
/'eidʒid/ adj престаре́лый.

agency /'eidʒənsi/ n аге́нтство.
agenda /ə'dʒendə/ n пове́стка
дня. **agent** /'eidʒ(ə)nt/ n аге́нт.

aggravate /'ægrəveit/ vt ухудш-
а́ть impf, уху́дшить pf;
(annoy) раздража́ть impf, раз-
дражи́ть pf.

aggregate /'ægrigət/ adj сово-
ку́пный; n совоку́пность.

aggression /ə'greʃ(ə)n/ n агре́с-
сия. **aggressive** /-siv/ adj агр-
есси́вный. **aggressor** /-sə(r)/ n
агре́ссор.

aggrieved /ə'griːvd/ adj оби́-

же́нный.

aghast /ə'gɑːst/ predic в у́жасе
(at от +gen).

agile /'ædʒail/ adj прово́рный.
agility /-'dʒiliti/ n прово́рство.

agitate /'ædʒiteit/ vt волнова́ть
impf, вз~ pf; vi агити́ровать
impf. **agitation** /-'teiʃ(ə)n/ n вол-
не́ние; агита́ция.

agnostic /æg'nɒstik/ n агно́-
стик. **agnosticism** /-ti,siz(ə)m/ n
агностици́зм.

ago /ə'gəʊ/ adv (тому́) наза́д;
long ~ давно́.

agonize /'ægə,naiz/ vi му́читься
impf. **agonizing** /-ziŋ/ adj му́чи-
тельный. **agony** /'ægəni/ n
аго́ния.

agrarian /ə'greəriən/ adj аг-
ра́рный.

agree /ə'griː/ vi соглаша́ться
impf, согласи́ться pf; (arrange)
догова́риваться impf, догово-
ри́ться pf. **agreeable** /-əb(ə)l/
adj (pleasant) прия́тный.
agreement /-mənt/ n согла́сие;
(treaty) соглаше́ние; **in ~** со-
гла́сен (-сна).

agricultural /ægri'kʌltʃər(ə)l/ adj
сельскохозя́йственный. **agriculture** /'ægri,kʌltʃə(r)/ n се́ль-
ское хозя́йство.

aground /ə'graʊnd/ predic на
мели́; adv: **run ~** сади́ться
impf, сесть pf на мель.

ahead /ə'hed/ adv (forward)
вперёд; (in front) впереди́; **~ of
time** досро́чно.

aid /eid/ vt помога́ть impf, по-
мо́чь pf +dat; n по́мощь;
(teaching) посо́бие; **in ~ of** в
по́льзу +gen.

Aids /eidz/ n СПИД.

ailing /'eiliŋ/ adj (ill) больно́й.
ailment /'eilmənt/ n неду́г.

aim /eim/ n цель, наме́рение;
take ~ прице́ливаться impf,

прицелиться *pf* (at в+*acc*); *vi* целиться *impf*, на~ *pf* (at в+*acc*); (*also fig*) метить *impf*, на~ *pf* (at в+*acc*); *vt* нацеливать *impf*, нацелить *pf*; (*also fig*) наводить *impf*, навести *pf.* **aimless** /'eɪmlɪs/ *adj* бесцельный.

air /eə(r)/ *n* воздух; (*look*) вид; by ~ самолётом; on the ~ в эфире; *attrib* воздушный; *vt* (*ventilate*) проветривать *impf*, проветрить *pf*; (*make known*) выставлять *impf*, выставить *pf* напоказ. **air-conditioning** *n* кондиционирование воздуха. **aircraft** *n* самолёт. **aircraft-carrier** *n* авианосец **airfield** *n* аэродром. **air force** *n* ВВС военно-воздушные силы *pl*. **air hostess** *n* стюардесса. **airless** /-l(ə)s/ *adj* душный. **airlift** *n* воздушные перевозки *pl*; *vt* перевозить *impf*, перевезти *pf* по воздуху. **airline** *n* авиакомпания. **airlock** *n* воздушная пробка. **airmail** *n* авиа(почта). **airman** *n* лётчик. **airport** *n* аэропорт. **air raid** *n* воздушный налёт. **airship** *n* дирижабль *m.* **airstrip** *n* взлётно-посадочная полоса. **airtight** *adj* герметичный. **air traffic controller** *n* диспетчер. **airwaves** *n pl* радиоволны *f pl.* **aisle** /aɪl/ *n* боковой неф; (*passage*) проход.

ajar /ə'dʒɑː(r)/ *predic* приоткрытый.

akin /ə'kɪn/ *predic* (*similar*) похожий; **be ~ to** быть сродни к+*dat.*

alabaster /'æləˌbæstə(r)/ *n* алебастр.

alacrity /ə'lækrɪtɪ/ *n* быстрота.

alarm /ə'lɑːm/ *n* тревога; *vt* тревожить *impf*, вс~ *pf*; ~ **clock**

будильник. **alarming** /-mɪŋ/ *adj* тревожный. **alarmist** /-mɪst/ *n* паникёр; *adj* паникёрский.

alas /ə'læs/ *int* увы!

album /'ælbəm/ *n* альбом.

alcohol /'ælkəˌhɒl/ *n* алкоголь *m*, спирт; спиртные напитки *m pl.* **alcoholic** /ˌælkə'hɒlɪk/ *adj* алкогольный; *n* алкоголик, -ичка.

alcove /'ælkəʊv/ *n* альков.

alert /ə'lɜːt/ *adj* бдительный; *n* тревога; *vt* предупреждать *impf*, предупредить *pf.*

algebra /'ældʒɪbrə/ *n* алгебра.

alias /'eɪlɪəs/ *adv* иначе (называемый); *n* кличка, вымышленное имя *neut.*

alibi /'ælɪˌbaɪ/ *n* алиби *neut indecl.*

alien /'eɪlɪən/ *n* иностранец, -нка; *adj* иностранный; ~ **to** чуждый +*dat.* **alienate** /-ˌneɪt/ *vt* отчуждать *impf*, отчудить *pf.* **alienation** /-'neɪʃ(ə)n/ *n* отчуждение.

alight[1] /ə'laɪt/ *vi* сходить *impf*, сойти *pf*; (*bird*) садиться *impf*, сесть *pf.*

alight[2] /ə'laɪt/ *predic*: **be ~** гореть *impf*; (*shine*) сиять *impf.*

align /ə'laɪn/ *vt* выравнивать *impf*, выровнять *pf.* **alignment** /-mənt/ *n* выравнивание.

alike /ə'laɪk/ *predic* похож; *adv* одинаково.

alimentary /ˌælɪ'mentərɪ/ *adj*: ~ **canal** пищеварительный канал.

alimony /'ælɪmənɪ/ *n* алименты *m pl.*

alive /ə'laɪv/ *predic* жив, в живых.

alkali /'ælkəˌlaɪ/ *n* щёлочь. **alkaline** /-ˌlaɪn/ *adj* щелочной.

all /ɔːl/ *adj* весь; *n* всё, *pl* все; совсем, совершенно; ~ **along** всё время; ~ **right** хорошо;

ла́дно; (*not bad*) та́к себе; непло́хо; ~ **the same** всё равно́; **in** ~ всего́; **two** ~ по́ два; **not at** ~ ниско́лько.

allay /əˈleɪ/ *vt* успока́ивать *impf*, успоко́ить *pf*.

allegation /ˌælɪˈɡeɪʃ(ə)n/ *n* утвержде́ние. **allege** /əˈledʒ/ *vt* утвержда́ть *impf*. **allegedly** /əˈledʒɪdlɪ/ *adv* я́кобы.

allegiance /əˈliːdʒ(ə)ns/ *adv* ве́рность.

allegorical /ˌælɪˈɡɒrɪk(ə)l/ *adj* аллегори́ческий. **allegory** /ˈælɪɡərɪ/ *n* аллего́рия.

allergic /əˈlɜːdʒɪk/ *adj* аллерги́ческий; **be** ~ **to** име́ть аллерги́ю к+*dat*. **allergy** /ˈælədʒɪ/ *n* аллерги́я.

alleviate /əˈliːvɪˌeɪt/ *vt* облегча́ть *impf*, облегчи́ть *pf*. **alleviation** /-ˈeɪʃ(ə)n/ *n* облегче́ние.

alley /ˈælɪ/ *n* переу́лок.

alliance /əˈlaɪəns/ *n* сою́з. **allied** /ˈælaɪd/ *adj* сою́зный.

alligator /ˈælɪˌɡeɪtə(r)/ *n* аллига́тор.

allocate /ˈæləˌkeɪt/ *vt* (*distribute*) распределя́ть *impf*, распредели́ть *pf*; (*allot*) выделя́ть *impf*, вы́делить *pf*. **allocation** /-ˈkeɪʃ(ə)n/ *n* распределе́ние; выделе́ние.

allot /əˈlɒt/ *vt* выделя́ть *impf*, вы́делить *pf*; (*distribute*) распределя́ть *impf*, распредели́ть *pf*. **allotment** /-mənt/ *n* выделе́ние; (*land*) уча́сток.

allow /əˈlaʊ/ *vt* разреша́ть *impf*, разреши́ть *pf*; (*let happen*; *concede*) допуска́ть *impf*, допусти́ть *pf*; ~ **for** учи́тывать *impf*, уче́сть *pf*. **allowance** /-əns/ *n* (*financial*) посо́бие; (*deduction, also fig*) ски́дка; **make** ~**(s) for** учи́тывать *impf*, уче́сть *pf*.

alloy /ˈælɔɪ/ *n* сплав.

all-round /ˈɔːlraʊnd/ *adj* разносторо́нний.

allude /əˈluːd/ *vi* ссыла́ться *impf*, сосла́ться *pf* (**to** на+*acc*).

allure /əˈljʊə(r)/ *vt* замани́вать *impf*, замани́ть *pf*. **allure(ment)** /-mənt/ *n* прима́нка. **alluring** /-rɪŋ/ *adj* зама́нчивый.

allusion /əˈluːʒ(ə)n/ *n* ссы́лка.

ally *n* /ˈælaɪ/ сою́зник; *vt* /əˈlaɪ/ соединя́ть *impf*, соедини́ть *pf*; ~ **oneself with** вступа́ть *impf*, вступи́ть *pf* в сою́з с+*instr*.

almighty /ɔːlˈmaɪtɪ/ *adj* всемогу́щий.

almond /ˈɑːmənd/ *n* (*tree*; *pl collect*) минда́ль *m*; (*nut*) минда́льный оре́х.

almost /ˈɔːlməʊst/ *adv* почти́, едва́ не.

alms /ɑːmz/ *n pl* ми́лостыня.

aloft /əˈlɒft/ *adv* наве́рх(-у́).

alone /əˈləʊn/ *predic* оди́н; (*lonely*) одино́к; *adv* то́лько; **leave** ~ оставля́ть *impf*, оста́вить *pf* в поко́е; **let** ~ не говоря́ уже́ о+*prep*.

along /əˈlɒŋ/ *prep* по+*dat*, (*position*) вдоль+*gen*; *adv* (*onward*) да́льше; **all** ~ всё вре́мя; ~ **with** вме́сте с+*instr*. **alongside** /əˌlɒŋˈsaɪd/ *adv & prep* ря́дом (с +*instr*).

aloof /əˈluːf/ *predic & adv* (*distant*) сде́ржанный; (*apart*) в стороне́.

aloud /əˈlaʊd/ *adv* вслух.

alphabet /ˈælfəˌbet/ *n* алфави́т. **alphabetical** /ˌælfəˈbetɪk(ə)l/ *adj* алфави́тный.

alpine /ˈælpaɪn/ *adj* альпи́йский.

already /ɔːlˈredɪ/ *adv* уже́.

also /ˈɔːlsəʊ/ *adv* та́кже, то́же.

altar /ˈɔːltə(r)/ *n* алта́рь *m*.

alter /ˈɔːltə(r)/ *vt* (*modify*) переде́лывать *impf*, переде́лать *pf*.

vt & i (*change*) изменя́ть(ся) *impf*, измени́ть(ся) *pf*. **alteration** /ˌɔːltəˈreɪʃ(ə)n/ *n* переде́лка; измене́ние.

alternate *adj* /ɔːlˈtɜːnət/ череду́ющийся; *vt & i* /ˈɔːltəˌneɪt/ чередова́ть(ся) *impf*; **alternating current** переме́нный ток; **on ~ days** че́рез день. **alternation** /ˌɔːltəˈneɪʃ(ə)n/ *n* чередова́ние. **alternative** /ɔːlˈtɜːnətɪv/ *n* альтернати́ва; *adj* альтернати́вный.

although /ɔːlˈðəʊ/ *conj* хотя́.

altitude /ˈæltɪˌtjuːd/ *n* высота́.

alto /ˈæltəʊ/ *n* альт.

altogether /ˌɔːltəˈɡeðə(r)/ *adv* (*fully*) совсе́м; (*in total*) всего́.

altruistic /ˌæltruˈɪstɪk/ *adj* альтруисти́ческий.

aluminium /ˌæljʊˈmɪniəm/ *n* алюми́ний.

always /ˈɔːlweɪz/ *adv* всегда́; (*constantly*) постоя́нно.

Alzheimer's disease /ˈæltsˌhaɪməz/ *n* боле́знь Альцге́ймера.

a.m. *abbr* (*morning*) утра́; (*night*) но́чи.

amalgamate /əˈmælɡəˌmeɪt/ *vt & i* слива́ть(ся) *impf*, сли́ть(ся) *pf*; (*chem*) амальгами́ровать(ся) *impf & pf*. **amalgamation** /-ˈmeɪʃ(ə)n/ *n* слия́ние; (*chem*) амальгами́рование.

amass /əˈmæs/ *vt* копи́ть *impf*, на~ *pf*.

amateur /ˈæmətə(r)/ *n* люби́тель *m*, ~ница; *adj* люби́тельский. **amateurish** /-rɪʃ/ *adj* дилета́нтский.

amaze /əˈmeɪz/ *vt* изумля́ть *impf*, изуми́ть *pf*. **amazement** /-mənt/ *n* изумле́ние. **amazing** /-zɪŋ/ *adj* изуми́тельный.

ambassador /æmˈbæsədə(r)/ *n* посо́л.

amber /ˈæmbə(r)/ *n* янта́рь *m*.

ambience /ˈæmbɪəns/ *n* среда́; атмосфе́ра.

ambiguity /ˌæmbɪˈɡjuːɪtɪ/ *n* двусмы́сленность. **ambiguous** /æmˈbɪɡjuəs/ *adj* двусмы́сленный.

ambition /æmˈbɪʃ(ə)n/ *n* (*quality*) честолю́бие; (*aim*) мечта́. **ambitious** /-ˈbɪʃəs/ *adj* честолюби́вый.

amble /ˈæmb(ə)l/ *vi* ходи́ть *indet*, идти́ *det* неторопли́вым ша́гом.

ambulance /ˈæmbjʊləns/ *n* маши́на ско́рой по́мощи.

ambush /ˈæmbʊʃ/ *n* заса́да; *vt* напада́ть *impf*, напа́сть *pf* из заса́ды на+*acc*.

ameliorate /əˈmiːlɪəˌreɪt/ *vt & i* улучша́ть(ся) *impf*, улу́чшить(ся) *pf*. **amelioration** /-ˈreɪʃ(ə)n/ *n* улучше́ние.

amen /eɪˈmen/ *int* ами́нь!

amenable /əˈmiːnəb(ə)l/ *adj* сгово́рчивый (**to** +*dat*)

amend /əˈmend/ *vt* (*correct*) исправля́ть *impf*, испра́вить *pf*; (*change*) вноси́ть *impf*, внести́ *pf* попра́вки в+*acc*. **amendment** /-mənt/ *n* попра́вка, исправле́ние. **amends** /əˈmendz/ *n pl*: **make ~ for** загла́живать *impf*, загла́дить *pf*.

amenities /əˈmiːnɪtɪz/ *n pl* удо́бства *neut pl*.

America /əˈmerɪkə/ *n* Аме́рика. **American** /-kən/ *adj* америка́нский; *n* америка́нец, -нка. **Americanism** /-kəˌnɪz(ə)m/ *n* американи́зм.

amiable /ˈeɪmɪəb(ə)l/ *adj* любе́зный. **amicable** /ˈæmɪkəb(ə)l/ *adj* дружелю́бный.

amid(st) /əˈmɪdst/ *prep* среди́+*gen*.

amino acid /əˌmiːnəʊ ˈæsɪd/ *n* аминокислота́.

amiss /ə'mɪs/ adv неладный; **take ~** обижаться impf, обидеться pf на+acc.

ammonia /ə'məʊnɪə/ n аммиак; (liquid ~) нашатырный спирт.

ammunition /ˌæmjʊ'nɪʃ(ə)n/ n боеприпасы m pl.

amnesia /æm'niːzɪə/ n амнезия.

amnesty /'æmnɪstɪ/ n амнистия.

among(st) /ə'mʌŋ(st)/ prep (amidst) среди+gen, (between) между+instr.

amoral /eɪ'mɒr(ə)l/ adj аморальный.

amorous /'æmərəs/ adj влюбчивый.

amorphous /ə'mɔːfəs/ adj бесформенный.

amortization /əˌmɔːtaɪ'zeɪʃ(ə)n/ n амортизация.

amount /ə'maʊnt/ n количество; vi: **~ to** составлять impf, составить pf; (be equivalent to) быть равносильным+dat.

ampere /'æmpeə(r)/ n ампер.

amphetamine /æm'fetəmiːn/ n амфетамин.

amphibian /æm'fɪbɪən/ n амфибия. **amphibious** /-'fɪbɪəs/ adj земноводный; (mil) плавающий.

amphitheatre /'æmfɪˌθɪətə(r)/ n амфитеатр.

ample /'æmp(ə)l/ adj достаточный. **amplification** /ˌæmplɪfɪ'keɪʃ(ə)n/ n усиление. **amplifier** /'æmplɪˌfaɪə(r)/ n усилитель m. **amplify** /'æmplɪˌfaɪ/ vt усиливать impf, усилить pf. **amply** /'æmplɪ/ adv достаточно.

amputate /'æmpjʊˌteɪt/ vt ампутировать impf & pf. **amputation** /-'teɪʃ(ə)n/ n ампутация.

amuse /ə'mjuːz/ vt забавлять impf; развлекать impf, развлечь pf. **amusement** /-mənt/ n забава, развлечение; pl ат-

тракционы m pl. **amusing** /-zɪŋ/ adj забавный; (funny) смешной.

anachronism /ə'nækrəˌnɪz(ə)m/ n анахронизм. **anachronistic** /-'nɪstɪk/ adj анахронический.

anaemia /ə'niːmɪə/ n анемия. **anaemic** /-mɪk/ adj анемичный.

anaesthesia /ˌænɪs'θiːzɪə/ n анестезия. **anaesthetic** /-'θetɪk/ n обезболивающее средство. **anaesthetist** /ə'niːsθətɪst/ n анестезиолог. **anaesthetize** /ə'niːsθəˌtaɪz/ vt анестезировать impf & pf.

anagram /'ænəˌɡræm/ n анаграмма.

analogous /ə'næləɡəs/ adj аналогичный. **analogue** /'ænəˌlɒɡ/ n аналог. **analogy** /ə'næləʤɪ/ n аналогия.

analyse /'ænəˌlaɪz/ vt анализировать impf & pf. **analysis** /ə'nælɪsɪs/ n анализ. **analyst** /'ænəlɪst/ n аналитик; психоаналитик. **analytical** /ˌænə'lɪtɪk(ə)l/ adj аналитический.

anarchic /ə'nɑːkɪk/ adj анархический. **anarchist** /'ænəkɪst/ n анархист, ~ка; adj анархистский; **anarchy** /'ænəkɪ/ n анархия.

anathema /ə'næθəmə/ n анафема.

anatomical /ˌænə'tɒmɪk(ə)l/ adj анатомический. **anatomy** /ə'nætəmɪ/ n анатомия.

ancestor /'ænsestə(r)/ n предок. **ancestry** /-strɪ/ n происхождение.

anchor /'æŋkə(r)/ n якорь m; vt ставить impf, по~ pf на якорь; vi становиться impf, стать pf на якорь. **anchorage** /'æŋkərɪʤ/ n якорная стоянка.

anchovy /'æntʃəvɪ/ n анчоус.

ancient /'eɪnʃ(ə)nt/ *adj* дре́вний, стари́нный.

and /ænd, ənd/ *conj* и, (*but*) а; c+*instr*; you ~ I мы с ва́ми; my wife ~ I мы с жено́й.

anecdote /'ænɪkˌdəʊt/ *n* анекдо́т.

anew /ə'njuː/ *adv* сно́ва.

angel /'eɪndʒ(ə)l/ *n* а́нгел. **angelic** /æn'dʒelɪk/ *adj* а́нгельский.

anger /'æŋgə(r)/ *n* гнев; *vt* серди́ть *impf*, рас~ *pf*.

angina /æn'dʒaɪnə/ *n* стенокарди́я.

angle[1] /'æŋg(ə)l/ *n* у́гол; (*fig*) то́чка зре́ния.

angle[2] /'æŋg(ə)l/ *vi* уди́ть *impf* ры́бу. **angler** /-glə(r)/ *n* рыболо́в.

angry /'æŋgrɪ/ *adj* серди́тый.

anguish /'æŋgwɪʃ/ *n* страда́ние, му́ка. **anguished** /-gwɪʃt/ *adj* отча́янный.

angular /'æŋgjʊlə(r)/ *adj* углово́й; (*sharp*) углова́тый.

animal /'ænɪm(ə)l/ *n* живо́тное *sb*; *adj* живо́тный. **animate** /-mət/ *adj* живо́й. **animated** /-meɪtɪd/ *adj* оживлённый; ~ cartoon мультфи́льм. **animation** /-'meɪʃ(ə)n/ *n* оживле́ние.

animosity /ˌænɪ'mɒsɪtɪ/ *n* враждебность.

ankle /'æŋk(ə)l/ *n* лоды́жка.

annals /'æn(ə)lz/ *n pl* ле́топись.

annex /ə'neks/ *vt* аннекси́ровать *impf* & *pf*. **annexation** /-'seɪʃ(ə)n/ *n* анне́ксия. **annexe** /'æneks/ *n* пристро́йка.

annihilate /ə'naɪəˌleɪt/ *vt* уничтожа́ть *impf*, уничто́жить *pf*. **annihilation** /-'leɪʃ(ə)n/ *n* уничтоже́ние.

anniversary /ˌænɪ'vɜːsərɪ/ *n* годовщи́на.

annotate /'ænəˌteɪt/ *vt* коммен-

ти́ровать *impf* & *pf*. **annotated** /-tɪd/ *adj* снабжённый коммента́риями. **annotation** /ˌænə'teɪʃ(ə)n/ *n* анно-та́ция.

announce /ə'naʊns/ *vt* объявля́ть *impf*, объяви́ть *pf*; заявля́ть *impf*, заяви́ть *pf*; (*radio*) сообща́ть *impf*, сообщи́ть *pf*. **announcement** /-mənt/ *n* объявле́ние; сообще́ние. **announcer** /-sə(r)/ *n* ди́ктор.

annoy /ə'nɔɪ/ *vt* досажда́ть *impf*, досади́ть *pf*; раздража́ть *impf*, раздражи́ть *pf*. **annoyance** /-əns/ *n* доса́да. **annoying** /-ɪŋ/ *adj* доса́дный.

annual /'ænjʊəl/ *adj* ежего́дный, (*of a given year*) годово́й; (*book*) ежего́дник; (*bot*) одноле́тник. **annually** /-lɪ/ *adv* еже-го́дно. **annuity** /ə'njuːɪtɪ/ *n* (ежего́дная) ре́нта.

annul /ə'nʌl/ *vt* аннули́ровать *impf* & *pf*. **annulment** /-mənt/ *n* аннули́рование.

anoint /ə'nɔɪnt/ *vt* пома́зывать *impf*, пома́зать *pf*.

anomalous /ə'nɒmələs/ *adj* анома́льный. **anomaly** /-lɪ/ *n* анома́лия.

anonymous /ə'nɒnɪməs/ *adj* анони́мный. **anonymity** /ˌænə'nɪmɪtɪ/ *n* анони́мность.

anorak /'ænəˌræk/ *n* ку́ртка.

anorexia /ˌænə'reksɪə/ *n* анорекси́я.

another /ə'nʌðə(r)/ *adj, pron* друго́й; ~ one ещё (оди́н); in ~ ten years ещё че́рез де́сять лет.

answer /'ɑːnsə(r)/ *n* отве́т; *vt* от-веча́ть *impf*, отве́тить *pf* (*person*) +*dat*, (*question*) на+*acc*; ~ the door отворя́ть *impf*, отвори́ть *pf* дверь; ~ the phone подходи́ть *impf*, подойти́ *pf* к

телефо́ну. **answerable** /-rəb(ə)l/ *adj* отве́тственный. **answering machine** *n* телефо́н-отве́тчик.

ant /ænt/ *n* мураве́й.

antagonism /ænˈtægə,nɪz(ə)m/ *n* антагони́зм. **antagonistic** /æn‚tægəˈnɪstɪk/ *adj* антагонисти́ческий. **antagonize** /ænˈtægə,naɪz/ *vt* настра́ивать *impf*, настро́ить *pf* про́тив *+gen*.

Antarctic /ænˈtɑːktɪk/ *n* Анта́рктика.

antelope /ˈæntɪ,ləʊp/ *n* антило́па.

antenna /ænˈtenə/ *n* у́сик; (*also radio*) анте́нна.

anthem /ˈænθəm/ *n* гимн.

anthology /ænˈθɒlədʒɪ/ *n* антоло́гия.

anthracite /ˈænθrə,saɪt/ *n* антраци́т.

anthropological /‚ænθrəpəˈlɒdʒɪk(ə)l/ *adj* антропологи́ческий. **anthropologist** /‚ænθrəˈpɒlədʒɪst/ *n* антрополо́г. **anthropology** /‚ænθrəˈpɒlədʒɪ/ *n* антрополо́гия.

anti-aircraft /‚æntɪˈeəkrɑːft/ *adj* зени́тный. **antibiotic** /‚æntɪbaɪˈɒtɪk/ *n* антибио́тик. **antibody** /ˈæntɪ,bɒdɪ/ *n* антите́ло. **anticlimax** /-ˈklaɪmæks/ *n* разочарова́ние. **anticlockwise** /-ˈklɒkwaɪz/ *adj & adv* про́тив часово́й стре́лки. **antidepressant** /-dɪˈpres(ə)nt/ *n* антидепресса́нт. **antidote** /ˈæntɪ,dəʊt/ *n* противоя́дие. **antifreeze** /ˈæntɪ,friːz/ *n* антифри́з.

antipathy /ænˈtɪpəθɪ/ *n* антипа́тия. **anti-Semitic** /‚æntɪsɪˈmɪtɪk/ *adj* антисеми́тский. **anti-Semitism** /‚æntɪˈsemɪ,tɪz(ə)m/ *n* антисемити́зм. **antiseptic** /‚æntɪˈseptɪk/ *adj* антисепти́ческий; *n* антисе́птик. **antisocial** /‚æntɪˈsəʊʃ(ə)l/ *adj* асоциа́льный. **anti-**

tank /‚æntɪˈtæŋk/ *adj* противота́нковый. **antithesis** /ænˈtɪθɪsɪs/ *n* противополо́жность; (*philos*) антите́зис.

anticipate /ænˈtɪsɪ,peɪt/ *vt* ожида́ть *impf* +*gen*; (*with pleasure*) предвкуша́ть *impf*, предвкуси́ть *pf*; (*forestall*) предупрежда́ть *impf*, предупреди́ть *pf*. **anticipation** /-ˈpeɪʃ(ə)n/ *n* ожида́ние; предвкуше́ние; предупрежде́ние.

antics /ˈæntɪks/ *n* вы́ходки *f pl*.

antiquarian /‚æntɪˈkweərɪən/ *adj* антиква́рный. **antiquated** /ˈæntɪ,kweɪtɪd/ *adj* устаре́лый. **antique** /ænˈtiːk/ *adj* стари́нный; *n* антиква́рная вещь; ~ **shop** антиква́рный магази́н. **antiquity** /ænˈtɪkwɪtɪ/ *n* дре́вность.

antler /ˈæntlə(r)/ *n* оле́ний рог.

anus /ˈeɪnəs/ *n* за́дний прохо́д.

anvil /ˈænvɪl/ *n* накова́льня.

anxiety /æŋˈzaɪətɪ/ *n* беспоко́йство. **anxious** /ˈæŋkʃ(ə)s/ *adj* беспоко́йный; **be** ~ беспоко́иться *impf*; трево́житься *impf*.

any /ˈenɪ/ *adj, pron* (*some*) како́й-нибудь; ско́лько-нибудь; (*every*) вся́кий, любо́й; (*anybody*) кто́-нибудь, (*anything*) что́-нибудь; (*with neg*) никако́й, ни оди́н; ниско́лько; никто́, ничто́; *adv* ско́лько-нибудь; (*with neg*) ниско́лько, ничу́ть. **anybody, anyone** *pron* кто́-нибудь; (*everybody*) вся́кий, любо́й; (*with neg*) никто́. **anyhow** *adv* ка́к-нибудь; ко́е-ка́к; (*with neg*) ника́к; *conj* во вся́ком слу́чае; всё равно́. **anyone** *see* **anybody**. **anything** *pron* что́-нибудь; всё (что уго́дно); (*with neg*) ничего́. **anyway** *adv* во вся́ком слу́чае; как бы то

ни́ было. **anywhere** *adv* где́/ куда́ уго́дно; (*with neg, interrog*) где́-нибудь, куда́-нибудь.

apart /ə'pɑːt/ *adv* (*aside*) в стороне́, в сто́рону; (*separately*) врозь; (*distant*) друг от дру́га; (*into pieces*) на ча́сти; ~ **from** кро́ме+*gen*.

apartheid /ə'pɑːteɪt/ *n* апарте́йд.

apartment /ə'pɑːtmənt/ *n* (*flat*) кварти́ра.

apathetic /ˌæpə'θetɪk/ *adj* апати́чный. **apathy** /'æpəθɪ/ *n* апа́тия.

ape /eɪp/ *n* обезья́на; *vt* обезья́нничать *impf*, с~ *pf* c+*gen*.

aperture /'æpə'tjʊə(r)/ *n* отве́рстие.

apex /'eɪpeks/ *n* верши́на.

aphorism /'æfə'rɪz(ə)m/ *n* афори́зм.

apiece /ə'piːs/ *adv* (*per person*) на ка́ждого; (*per thing*) за шту́ку; (*amount*) по+*dat or acc with numbers*.

aplomb /ə'plɒm/ *n* апло́мб.

Apocalypse /ə'pɒkəlɪps/ *n* Апока́липсис. **apocalyptic** /-'lɪptɪk/ *adj* апокалипти́ческий.

apologetic /ˌə'pɒlə'dʒetɪk/ *adj* извиня́ющийся; **be** ~ извиня́ться *impf*. **apologize** /ə'pɒlə'dʒaɪz/ *vi* извиня́ться *impf*, извини́ться *pf* (**to** пе́ред +*instr*; **for** за+*acc*). **apology** /ə'pɒlədʒɪ/ *n* извине́ние.

apostle /ə'pɒs(ə)l/ *n* апо́стол.

apostrophe /ə'pɒstrəfɪ/ *n* апостро́ф.

appal /ə'pɔːl/ *vi* ужаса́ть *impf*, ужасну́ть *pf*. **appalling** /-lɪŋ/ *adj* ужа́сный.

apparatus /ˌæpə'reɪtəs/ *n* аппара́т; прибо́р; (*gymnastic*) гимнасти́ческие снаря́ды *pl*.

apparel /ə'pær(ə)l/ *n* оде́яние.

apparent /ə'pærənt/ *adj* (*seeming*) ви́димый; (*manifest*) очеви́дный. **apparently** /-lɪ/ *adv* ка́жется, по-ви́димому.

apparition /ˌæpə'rɪʃ(ə)n/ *n* виде́ние.

appeal /ə'piːl/ *n* (*request*) призы́в, обраще́ние; (*law*) апелля́ция, обжа́лование; (*attraction*) привлека́тельность; ~ **court** апелляцио́нный суд; *vi* (*request*) взыва́ть *impf*, воззва́ть *pf* (**to** к+*dat*; **for** о+*prep*); обраща́ться *impf*, обрати́ться *pf* (с призы́вом); апелли́ровать *impf* & *pf*; ~ **to** (*attract*) привлека́ть *impf*, привле́чь *pf*.

appear /ə'pɪə(r)/ *vi* появля́ться *impf*, появи́ться *pf*; (*in public*) выступа́ть *impf*, вы́ступить *pf*; (*seem*) каза́ться *impf*, по~ *pf*. **appearance** /-rəns/ *n* появле́ние; выступле́ние; (*aspect*) вид.

appease /ə'piːz/ *vt* умиротворя́ть *impf*, умиротвори́ть *pf*.

append /ə'pend/ *vt* прилага́ть *impf*, приложи́ть *pf*. **appendicitis** /ˌə'pendɪ'saɪtɪs/ *n* аппендици́т. **appendix** /ə'pendɪks/ *n* приложе́ние; (*anat*) аппе́ндикс.

appertain /ˌæpə'teɪn/ *vi*: ~ **to** относи́ться *impf* +*dat*.

appetite /'æpɪˌtaɪt/ *n* аппети́т. **appetizing** /-ˌtaɪzɪŋ/ *adj* аппети́тный.

applaud /ə'plɔːd/ *vt* аплоди́ровать *impf* +*dat*. **applause** /-'plɔːz/ *n* аплодисме́нты *m pl*.

apple /'æp(ə)l/ *n* я́блоко; *adj* я́блочный; ~ **tree** я́блоня.

appliance /ə'plaɪəns/ *n* прибо́р. **applicable** /ə'plɪkəb(ə)l/ *adj* примени́мый. **applicant** /'æplɪkənt/ *n* кандида́т. **application** /ˌæplɪ'keɪʃ(ə)n/ *n* (*use*) примене́ние;

(*putting on*) наложе́ние; (*request*) заявле́ние. **applied** /ə'plaɪd/ *adj* прикладно́й. **apply** /ə'plaɪ/ *vt* (*use*) применя́ть *impf*, примени́ть *pf*; (*put on*) накла́дывать *impf*, наложи́ть *pf*; *vi* (*request*) обраща́ться *impf*, обрати́ться *pf* to к+*dat*; **for as** to +*acc*; ~ **for** (*job*) подава́ть *impf*, пода́ть *pf* заявле́ние на+*acc*; ~ **to** относи́ться *impf* к+*dat*.

appoint /ə'pɔɪnt/ *vt* назнача́ть *impf*, назна́чить *pf*. **appointment** /-mənt/ *n* назначе́ние; (*job*) до́лжность; (*meeting*) свида́ние.

apposite /'æpəzɪt/ *adj* уме́стный.

appraise /ə'preɪz/ *vt* оце́нивать *impf*, оцени́ть *pf*.

appreciable /ə'priːʃəb(ə)l/ *adj* заме́тный; (*considerable*) значи́тельный. **appreciate** /ə'priːʃɪˌeɪt/ *vt* цени́ть *impf*; (*understand*) понима́ть *impf*, поня́ть *pf*; *vi* повыша́ться *impf*, повы́ситься *pf* в цене́. **appreciation** /əˌpriːʃɪ'eɪʃ(ə)n/ *n* (*estimation*) оце́нка; (*gratitude*) призна́тельность; (*rise in value*) повыше́ние цены́. **appreciative** /ə'priːʃətɪv/ *adj* призна́тельный (*of* за+*acc*).

apprehension /ˌæprɪ'henʃ(ə)n/ *n* (*fear*) опасе́ние. **apprehensive** /-'hensɪv/ *adj* опаса́ющийся.

apprentice /ə'prentɪs/ *n* учени́к; *vt* отдава́ть *impf*, отда́ть *pf* в уче́ние. **apprenticeship** /-ʃɪp/ *n* учени́чество.

approach /ə'prəʊtʃ/ *vt & i* подходи́ть *impf*, подойти́ *pf* (к+*dat*); приближа́ться *impf*, прибли́зиться *pf* (к+*dat*); (*apply to*) обраща́ться *impf*, обрати́ться *pf* к+*dat*; *n* при-

ближе́ние; подхо́д; подъе́зд; (*access*) до́ступ.

approbation /ˌæprə'beɪʃ(ə)n/ *n* одобре́ние.

appropriate *adj* /ə'prəʊprɪət/ подходя́щий; *vt* /ə'prəʊprɪˌeɪt/ присва́ивать *impf*, присво́ить *pf*. **appropriation** /-'eɪʃ(ə)n/ *n* присвое́ние.

approval /ə'pruːv(ə)l/ *n* одобре́ние; **on** ~ на про́бу. **approve** /ə'pruːv/ *vt* утвержда́ть *impf*, утверди́ть *pf*; *vt & i* (~ **of**) одобря́ть *impf*, одо́брить *pf*.

approximate *adj* /ə'prɒksɪmət/ приблизи́тельный; *vi* /ə'prɒksɪmeɪt/ приближа́ться *impf* (**to** к+*dat*). **approximation** /əˌprɒksɪ'meɪʃ(ə)n/ *n* приближе́ние.

apricot /'eɪprɪˌkɒt/ *n* абрико́с.

April /'eɪprɪl/ *n* апре́ль *m*; *adj* апре́льский.

apron /'eɪprən/ *n* пере́дник.

apropos /ˌæprə'pəʊ/ *adv:* ~ **of** по по́воду+*gen*.

apt /æpt/ *adj* (*suitable*) уда́чный; (*inclined*) скло́нный. **aptitude** /'æptɪˌtjuːd/ *n* спосо́бность.

aqualung /'ækwəˌlʌŋ/ *n* аквала́нг. **aquarium** /ə'kweərɪəm/ *n* аква́риум. **Aquarius** /ə'kweərɪəs/ *n* Водоле́й. **aquatic** /ə'kwætɪk/ *adj* водяно́й; (*of sport*) во́дный. **aqueduct** /'ækwɪˌdʌkt/ *n* акведу́к.

aquiline /'ækwɪˌlaɪn/ *adj* орли́ный.

Arab /'ærəb/ *n* ара́б, ~ка; *adj* ара́бский. **Arabian** /ə'reɪbɪən/ *adj* арави́йский. **Arabic** /'ærəbɪk/ *adj* ара́бский.

arable /'ærəb(ə)l/ *adj* па́хотный.

arbitrary /'ɑːbɪtrərɪ/ *adj* произво́льный. **arbitrate** /-ˌtreɪt/ *vi* де́йствовать *impf* в ка́честве трете́йского судьи́. **arbitration**

arc /-'treɪʃ(ə)n/ *n* арбитра́ж, трете́йское реше́ние. **arbitrator** /-,treɪtə(r)/ *n* арби́тр, тре́тейский судья́ *m*.

arc /ɑːk/ *n* дуга́. **arcade** /ɑː'keɪd/ *n* арка́да, (*shops*) пасса́ж.

arch¹ /ɑːtʃ/ *n* а́рка, свод; (*of foot*) свод стопы́; *vt & i* выгиба́ть(ся) *impf*, вы́гнуть(ся) *pf*.

arch² /ɑːtʃ/ *adj* игри́вый.

archaeological /,ɑːkɪə'lɒdʒɪk(ə)l/ *adj* археологи́ческий. **archaeologist** /,ɑːkɪ'ɒlədʒɪst/ *n* архео́лог. **archaeology** /,ɑːkɪ'ɒlədʒɪ/ *n* археоло́гия.

archaic /ɑː'keɪɪk/ *adj* архаи́ческий.

archangel /'ɑːk,eɪndʒ(ə)l/ *n* арха́нгел.

archbishop /ɑːtʃ'bɪʃəp/ *n* архиепи́скоп.

arched /ɑːtʃt/ *adj* сво́дчатый.

arch-enemy /ɑːtʃ'enəmɪ/ *n* закля́тый враг.

archer /'ɑːtʃə(r)/ *n* стрело́к из лу́ка. **archery** /-rɪ/ *n* стрельба́ из лу́ка.

archipelago /ɑːkɪ'peləˌgəʊ/ *n* архипела́г.

architect /'ɑːkɪˌtekt/ *n* архите́ктор. **architectural** /-'tektʃər(ə)l/ *adj* архитекту́рный. **architecture** /'ɑːkɪˌtektʃə(r)/ *n* архитекту́ра.

archive(s) /'ɑːkaɪv(z)/ *n* архи́в.

archway /'ɑːtʃweɪ/ *n* сво́дчатый прохо́д.

Arctic /'ɑːktɪk/ *adj* аркти́ческий; *n* А́рктика.

ardent /'ɑːd(ə)nt/ *adj* горя́чий. **ardour** /'ɑːdə(r)/ *n* пыл.

arduous /'ɑːdjʊəs/ *adj* тру́дный.

area /'eərɪə/ *n* (*extent*) пло́щадь; (*region*) райо́н; (*sphere*) о́бласть.

arena /ə'riːnə/ *n* аре́на.

argue /'ɑːgjuː/ *vt* (*maintain*) утвержда́ть *impf*; дока́зывать *impf*; *vi* спо́рить *impf*, по~ *pf*. **argument** /-mənt/ *n* (*dispute*) спор; (*reason*) до́вод. **argumentative** /ɑːgjuː'mentətɪv/ *adj* любя́щий спо́рить.

aria /'ɑːrɪə/ *n* а́рия.

arid /'ærɪd/ *adj* сухо́й.

Aries /'eəriːz/ *n* Ове́н.

arise /ə'raɪz/ *vi* возника́ть *impf*, возни́кнуть *pf*.

aristocracy /ˌærɪ'stɒkrəsɪ/ *n* аристокра́тия. **aristocrat** /'ærɪstəˌkræt/ *n* аристокра́т, ~ка. **aristocratic** /ˌærɪstə'krætɪk/ *adj* аристократи́ческий.

arithmetic /ə'rɪθmətɪk/ *n* арифме́тика. **arithmetical** /ærɪθ'metɪk(ə)l/ *adj* арифмети́ческий.

ark /ɑːk/ *n* (Но́ев) ковче́г.

arm¹ /ɑːm/ *n* (*of body*) рука́; (*of chair*) ру́чка; ~ **in** ~ по́д руку; **at** ~**s length** (*fig*) на почти́тельном расстоя́нии; **with open** ~**s** с распростёртыми объя́тиями.

arm² /ɑːm/ *n pl* (*weapons*) ору́жие; *vt* вооружа́ть *impf*, вооружи́ть *pf*. **armaments** /'ɑːməmənts/ *n pl* вооруже́ние.

armchair /'ɑːmtʃeə(r)/ *n* кре́сло.

Armenia /ɑː'miːnɪə/ *n* Арме́ния. **Armenian** /-ən/ *n* армяни́н, армя́нка; *adj* армя́нский.

armistice /'ɑːmɪstɪs/ *n* переми́рие.

armour /'ɑːmə(r)/ *n* (*for body*) доспе́хи *m pl*; (*for vehicles; fig*) броня́. **armoured** /'ɑːməd/ *adj* брониро́ванный; (*vehicles etc.*) бронета́нковый, броне-; ~ **car** броневи́к. **armoury** /'ɑːmərɪ/ *n* арсена́л.

armpit /'ɑːmpɪt/ *n* подмы́шка.

army /'ɑːmɪ/ *n* а́рмия; *adj* ар-

мейский.

aroma /ə'rəʊmə/ n аромат.

aromatherapy /ər,əʊmə'θerəpı/ n ароматерапия. **aromatic** /,ærə'mætık/ adj ароматичный.

around /ə'raʊnd/ adv кругом; prep вокруг+gen; all ~ повсюду.

arouse /ə'raʊz/ vt (wake up) будить impf, раз~ pf; (stimulate) возбуждать impf, возбудить pf.

arrange /ə'reındʒ/ vt расставлять impf, расставить pf; (plan) устраивать impf, устроить pf; (mus) аранжировать impf & pf; vi: ~ to договариваться impf, договориться pf +inf. **arrangement** /-mənt/ n расположение; устройство; (agreement) соглашение; (mus) аранжировка; pl приготовления neut pl.

array /ə'reı/ vt выставлять impf, выставить pf; n (dress) наряд; (display) коллекция.

arrears /ə'rıəz/ n pl задолженность.

arrest /ə'rest/ vt арестовывать impf, арестовать pf; n арест.

arrival /ə'raıv(ə)l/ n прибытие, приезд; (new ~) вновь прибывший sb. **arrive** /ə'raıv/ vi прибывать impf, прибыть pf; приезжать impf, приехать pf.

arrogance /'ærəgəns/ n высокомерие. **arrogant** /-gənt/ adj высокомерный.

arrow /'ærəʊ/ n стрела; (pointer) стрелка.

arsenal /'ɑːsən(ə)l/ n арсенал. **arsenic** /'ɑːsənık/ n мышьяк. **arson** /'ɑːs(ə)n/ n поджог.

art /ɑːt/ n искусство; pl гуманитарные науки f pl; adj художественный. **arterial** /ɑː'tıərıəl/ adj: ~ road

магистраль. **artery** /'ɑːtərı/ n артерия.

artful /'ɑːtfʊl/ adj хитрый. **arthritis** /ɑː'θraıtıs/ n артрит. **article** /'ɑːtık(ə)l/ n (literary) статья; (clause) пункт; (thing) предмет; (gram) артикль m.

articulate vt /ɑː'tıkjʊ,leıt/ произносить impf, произнести pf; (express) выражать impf, выразить pf; adj /ɑː'tıkjʊlət/ (of speech) членораздельный; be ~ чётко выражать impf свои мысли. **articulated lorry** /ɑː'tıkjʊ,leıtıd 'lɒrı/ n грузовой автомобиль с прицепом.

artifice /'ɑːtıfıs/ n хитрость. **artificial** /,ɑːtı'fıʃ(ə)l/ adj искусственный.

artillery /ɑː'tılərı/ n артиллерия.

artisan /,ɑːtı'zæn/ n ремесленник.

artist /'ɑːtıst/ n художник. **artiste** /ɑː'tiːst/ n артист, ~ка. **artistic** /ɑː'tıstık/ adj художественный.

artless /'ɑːtlıs/ adj простодушный.

as /æz, əz/ adv как; conj (when) когда; в то время как; (because) так как; (manner) как; (though, however) как ни; rel pron какой; который; что; as ... as так (же)... как; **as for, to** относительно+gen; что касается +gen; **as if** как будто; **as it were** как бы; так сказать; **as soon as** как только; **as well** также; тоже.

asbestos /æs'bestɒs/ n асбест. **ascend** /ə'send/ vt (go up) подниматься impf, подняться pf по+dat; (throne) всходить impf, взойти pf на+acc; vi восходить impf, взойти pf. **ascendancy** /ə'send(ə)nsı/ n

власть. **Ascension** /ə'senʃ(ə)n/ n (eccl) Вознесе́ние. **ascent** /ə'sent/ n восхожде́ние (**of** на+acc).

ascertain /ˌæsə'tein/ vt устана́вливать impf, установи́ть pf.

ascetic /ə'setik/ adj аскети́ческий; n аске́т. **asceticism** /ə'setiˌsiz(ə)m/ n аскети́зм.

ascribe /ə'skraib/ vt припи́сывать impf, приписа́ть pf (**to** +dat).

ash[1] /æʃ/ n (tree) я́сень m.

ash[2] /æʃ/, **ashes** /'æʃiz/ n зола́, пе́пел; (human remains) прах. **ashtray** n пе́пельница.

ashamed /ə'ʃeimd/ predic: he is ~ ему́ сты́дно; **be, feel,** ~ of стыди́ться impf, по~ pf +gen.

ashen /'æʃ(ə)n/ adj (pale) ме́ртвенно-бле́дный.

ashore /ə'ʃɔː(r)/ adv на бе́рег(у́).

Asia /'eiʃə/ n А́зия. **Asian, Asiatic** /'eiʃ(ə)n, ˌeiʃi'ætik/ adj азиа́тский; n азиа́т, ~ка.

aside /ə'said/ adv в сто́рону.

ask /ɑːsk/ vt & i (enquire of) спра́шивать impf, спроси́ть pf; (request) проси́ть impf, по~ pf (**for** acc, gen, o+prep); (invite) приглаша́ть impf, пригласи́ть pf; (demand) тре́бовать impf +gen (**of** от+gen); ~ **after** осведомля́ться impf, осве́домиться pf o+prep; ~ **a question** задава́ть impf, зада́ть pf вопро́с.

askance /ə'skɑːns/ adv ко́со.

askew /ə'skjuː/ adv кри́во.

asleep /ə'sliːp/ predic & adv: **be** ~ спать impf; **fall** ~ засыпа́ть impf, засну́ть pf.

asparagus /ə'spærəgəs/ n спа́ржа.

aspect /'æspekt/ n вид; (side) сторона́.

aspersion /ə'spɜːʃ(ə)n/ n клевета́.

asphalt /'æsfælt/ n асфа́льт.

asphyxiate /æs'fiksi,eit/ vt удуша́ть impf, удуши́ть.

aspiration /ˌæspi'reiʃ(ə)n/ n стремле́ние. **aspire** /ə'spaiə(r)/ vi стреми́ться impf (**to** к+dat).

aspirin /'æsprin/ n аспири́н; (tablet) табле́тка аспири́на.

ass /æs/ n осёл.

assail /ə'seil/ vt напада́ть impf, напа́сть pf на+acc; (with questions) забра́сывать impf, бро́сить pf вопро́сами. **assailant** /-lənt/ n напада́ющий sb.

assassin /ə'sæsin/ n уби́йца m & f. **assassinate** /-ˌneit/ vt убива́ть impf, уби́ть pf. **assassination** /-'neiʃ(ə)n/ n уби́йство.

assault /ə'sɔːlt/ n нападе́ние; (mil) штурм; ~ **and battery** оскорбле́ние де́йствием; vt напада́ть impf, напа́сть pf на+acc.

assemblage /ə'semblidʒ/ n сбо́рка. **assemble** /ə'semb(ə)l/ vt & i собира́ть(ся) impf, собра́ть(ся) pf. **assembly** /ə'sembli/ n собра́ние; (of machine) сбо́рка.

assent /ə'sent/ vi соглаша́ться impf, согласи́ться pf (**to** на+acc); n согла́сие.

assert /ə'sɜːt/ vt утвержда́ть impf, ~ **o.s.** отста́ивать impf, отстоя́ть pf свои́ права́. **assertion** /ə'sɜːʃ(ə)n/ n утвержде́ние. **assertive** /ə'sɜːtiv/ adj насто́йчивый.

assess /ə'ses/ vt (amount) определя́ть impf, определи́ть pf; (value) оце́нивать impf, оцени́ть pf. **assessment** /-mənt/ n определе́ние; оце́нка.

asset /'æset/ n це́нное ка́чество; (comm; also pl) акти́в.

assiduous /ə'sɪdjʊəs/ adj прилéжный.

assign /ə'saɪn/ vt (appoint) назначáть impf, назнáчить pf; (allot) отводить impf, отвести pf. **assignation** /ˌæsɪg'neɪʃ(ə)n/ n свидáние. **assignment** /ə'saɪnmənt/ n (task) задáние; (mission) командирóвка.

assimilate /ə'sɪmɪ,leɪt/ vt усвáивать impf, усвóить pf. **assimilation** /-'leɪʃ(ə)n/ n усвоéние.

assist /ə'sɪst/ vt помогáть impf, помóчь pf +dat. **assistance** /-təns/ n пóмощь. **assistant** /-tənt/ n помóщник, ассистéнт.

associate vt /ə'səʊsɪ,eɪt/ ассоции́ровать impf & pf; vi общáться impf (with c+instr); n /ə'səʊʃɪət/ коллéга m & f. **association** /əˌsəʊsɪ'eɪʃ(ə)n/ n óбщество, ассоциáция.

assorted /ə'sɔːtɪd/ adj рáзный. **assortment** /ə'sɔːtmənt/ n ассортимéнт.

assuage /ə'sweɪdʒ/ vt (calm) успокáивать impf, успокóить pf; (alleviate) смягчáть impf, смягчить pf.

assume /ə'sjuːm/ vt (take on) принимáть impf, принять pf; (suppose) предполагáть impf, предположить pf; **~d name** вымышленное имя neut; **let us ~** допустим. **assumption** /ə'sʌmpʃ(ə)n/ n (taking on) принятие на себя; (supposition) предположéние.

assurance /ə'ʃʊərəns/ n заверéние; (self-~) самоувéренность. **assure** /ə'ʃʊə(r)/ vt уверять impf, увéрить pf.

asterisk /'æstərɪsk/ n звёздочка.

asthma /'æsmə/ n áстма. **asthmatic** /æs'mætɪk/ adj астматический.

astonish /ə'stɒnɪʃ/ vt удивлять impf, удивить pf. **astonishing** /-ʃɪŋ/ adj удивительный. **astonishment** /-mənt/ n удивлéние.

astound /ə'staʊnd/ vt изумлять impf, изумить pf. **astounding** /-dɪŋ/ adj изумительный.

astray /ə'streɪ/ adv: **go ~** сбивáться impf, сбиться pf с пути; **lead ~** сбивáть impf, сбить pf с пути.

astride /ə'straɪd/ prep верхóм на+prep.

astringent /ə'strɪndʒ(ə)nt/ adj вяжущий; тéрпкий.

astrologer /ə'strɒlədʒə(r)/ n астрóлог. **astrology** /-dʒɪ/ n астролóгия. **astronaut** /'æstrə,nɔːt/ n астронáвт. **astronomer** /ə'strɒnəmə(r)/ n астронóм. **astronomical** /ˌæstrə'nɒmɪk(ə)l/ adj астрономический. **astronomy** /ə'strɒnəmɪ/ n астронóмия.

astute /ə'stjuːt/ adj проницáтельный.

asunder /ə'sʌndə(r)/ adv (apart) врозь; (in pieces) на чáсти.

asylum /ə'saɪləm/ n сумасшéдший дом; (refuge) убéжище; **~ seeker** претендéнт, ~ка на получéние (политического) убéжища.

asymmetrical /ˌeɪsɪ'metrɪk(ə)l/ adj асимметричный.

at /æt, unstressed ət/ prep (position) на+prep, в+prep, у+gen: **at a concert** на концéрте; **at the cinema** в кинó; **at the window** у окнá; (time) в+acc: **at two o'clock** в два часá; **at+acc**: at Easter на Пáсху; (price) по+dat: **at 5p a pound** по пяти пéнсов за фунт; (speed): **at 60 mph** со скóростью шестьдесят миль в час; **~ first** сна-

ча́ла, сперва́; ~ home до́ма; ~ last наконе́ц; ~ least по кра́йней ме́ре; ~ that на том; (moreover) к тому́ же.

atheism /'eɪθɪ,ɪz(ə)m/ n атеи́зм. **atheist** /-ɪst/ n атеи́ст, ~ка.

athlete /'æθliːt/ n спортсме́н, ~ка. **athletic** /æθ'letɪk/ adj атлети́ческий. **athletics** /æθ'letɪks/ n (лёгкая) атле́тика.

atlas /'ætləs/ n а́тлас.

atmosphere /'ætməs,fɪə(r)/ n атмосфе́ра. **atmospheric** /,ætməs'ferɪk/ adj атмосфе́рный.

atom /'ætəm/ n а́том; ~ bomb а́томная бо́мба. **atomic** /ə'tɒmɪk/ adj а́томный.

atone /ə'təʊn/ vi искупа́ть impf, искупи́ть pf (for +acc). **atonement** /-mənt/ n искупле́ние.

atrocious /ə'trəʊʃəs/ adj ужа́сный. **atrocity** /ə'trɒsɪtɪ/ n зве́рство.

attach /ə'tætʃ/ vt (fasten) прикрепля́ть impf, прикрепи́ть pf; (append) прилага́ть impf, приложи́ть pf; (attribute) придава́ть impf, прида́ть pf; **attached to** (devoted) привя́занный к+dat. **attaché** /ə'tæʃeɪ/ n атташе́ m indecl. **attachment** /ə'tætʃmənt/ n прикрепле́ние; привя́занность; (tech) принадле́жность.

attack /ə'tæk/ vt напада́ть impf, напа́сть pf на+acc; n нападе́ние; (of illness) припа́док.

attain /ə'teɪn/ vt достига́ть impf, дости́чь & дости́гнуть pf +gen. **attainment** /-mənt/ n достиже́ние.

attempt /ə'tempt/ vt пыта́ться impf, по~ pf +inf; n попы́тка.

attend /ə'tend/ vt & i (be present at) прису́тствовать impf (at +prep); vt (accompany) сопровожда́ть impf, сопроводи́ть pf;

(go to regularly) посеща́ть impf, посети́ть pf; ~ to занима́ться impf, заня́ться pf. **attendance** /-dəns/ n (presence) прису́тствие; (number) посеща́емость. **attendant** /-dənt/ adj сопровожда́ющий; sb (escort) провожа́тый sb.

attention /ə'tenʃ(ə)n/ n внима́ние; pay ~ обраща́ть impf, обрати́ть pf внима́ние (to на+acc); int (mil) сми́рно! **attentive** /ə'tentɪv/ adj внима́тельный; (solicitous) забо́тливый.

attest /ə'test/ vt & i (also ~ to) заверя́ть impf, заве́рить pf; свиде́тельствовать impf, за~ pf (to +prep).

attic /'ætɪk/ n черда́к.

attire /ə'taɪə(r)/ vt наряжа́ть impf, наряди́ть pf; n наря́д.

attitude /'ætɪ,tjuːd/ n (posture) по́за; (opinion) отноше́ние (towards к+dat).

attorney /ə'tɜːnɪ/ n пове́ренный sb; power of ~ дове́ренность.

attract /ə'trækt/ vt привлека́ть impf, привле́чь pf. **attraction** /ə'trækʃ(ə)n/ n привлека́тельность; (entertainment) аттракцио́н. **attractive** /-ɪv/ adj привлека́тельный.

attribute /ə'trɪbjuːt/ vt припи́сывать impf, приписа́ть pf; /'ætrɪ,bjuːt/ (quality) сво́йство. **attribution** /,ætrɪ'bjuːʃ(ə)n/ n /,ætrɪ,bjuːt/ припи́сывание. **attributive** /ə'trɪbjuːtɪv/ adj атрибути́вный.

attrition /ə'trɪʃ(ə)n/ n: war of ~ война́ на истоще́ние.

aubergine /'əʊbə,ʒiːn/ n бакла́жан.

auburn /'ɔːbən/ adj тёмно-ры́жий.

auction /'ɔːkʃ(ə)n/ n аукцио́н; vt продава́ть impf, прода́ть pf с аукцио́на. **auctioneer** /ˌɔːkʃə'nɪə(r)/ n аукциони́ст.

audacious /ɔː'deɪʃəs/ adj (bold) сме́лый; (impudent) де́рзкий. **audacity** /ɔː'dæsɪtɪ/ n сме́лость; де́рзость.

audible /'ɔːdɪb(ə)l/ adj слы́шный. **audience** /'ɔːdɪəns/ n пу́блика, аудито́рия; (listeners) слу́шатели m pl, (viewers, spectators) зри́тели m pl; (interview) аудие́нция. **audit** /'ɔːdɪt/ n прове́рка счето́в, реви́зия; vt проверя́ть impf, прове́рить pf (счета́+gen). **audition** /ɔː'dɪʃ(ə)n/ n про́ба; vt устра́ивать impf, устро́ить pf про́бу +gen. **auditor** /'ɔːdɪtə(r)/ n реви́зор. **auditorium** /ˌɔːdɪ'tɔːrɪəm/ n зри́тельный зал.

augment /ɔːg'ment/ n увели́чивать impf, увели́чить pf.

augur /'ɔːgə(r)/ vt & i предвеща́ть impf.

August /'ɔːgəst/ n а́вгуст; adj а́вгустовский. **august** /ɔː'gʌst/ adj вели́чественный.

aunt /ɑːnt/ n тётя, тётка.

au pair /əʊ 'peə(r)/ n домрабо́тница иностра́нного происхожде́ния.

aura /'ɔːrə/ n орео́л.

auspices /'ɔːspɪsɪz/ n pl покрови́тельство. **auspicious** /ɔː'spɪʃ(ə)s/ adj благоприя́тный.

austere /ɒ'stɪə(r)/ adj стро́гий. **austerity** /ɒ'sterɪtɪ/ n стро́гость.

Australia /ɒ'streɪlɪə/ n Австра́лия. **Australian** /-ən/ n австрали́ец, -и́йка; adj австрали́йский.

Austria /'ɒstrɪə/ n А́встрия. **Austrian** /-ən/ n австри́ец, -и́йка; adj австри́йский.

authentic /ɔː'θentɪk/ adj по́длинный. **authenticate** /-ˌkent/ vt устана́вливать impf, установи́ть pf по́длинность+gen. **authenticity** /-'tɪsɪtɪ/ n по́длинность.

author /'ɔːθə(r)/ n а́втор.

authoritarian /ɔːˌθɒrɪ'teərɪən/ adj авторита́рный. **authoritative** /ɔː'θɒrɪtətɪv/ adj авторите́тный. **authority** /ɔː'θɒrɪtɪ/ n (power) власть, полномо́чие; (weight; expert) авторите́т; (source) авторите́тный исто́чник. **authorization** /ˌɔːθəraɪ'zeɪʃ(ə)n/ n уполномо́чивание; (permission) разреше́ние. **authorize** /'ɔːθəˌraɪz/ vt (action) разреша́ть impf, разреши́ть pf; (person) уполномо́чивать impf, уполномо́чить pf. **authorship** /'ɔːθəʃɪp/ n а́вторство.

autobiographical /ˌɔːtəˌbaɪə'græfɪk(ə)l/ adj автобиографи́ческий. **autobiography** /ˌɔːtəbaɪ'ɒgrəfɪ/ n автобиогра́фия. **autocracy** /ɔː'tɒkrəsɪ/ n автокра́тия. **autocrat** /'ɔːtəˌkræt/ n автокра́т. **autocratic** /ˌɔːtə'krætɪk/ adj автократи́ческий. **autograph** /'ɔːtəˌgrɑːf/ n авто́граф. **automatic** /ˌɔːtə'mætɪk/ adj автомати́ческий. **automation** /ˌɔːtə'meɪʃ(ə)n/ n автоматиза́ция. **automaton** /ɔː'tɒmət(ə)n/ n автома́т. **automobile** /'ɔːtəməˌbiːl/ n автомоби́ль m. **autonomous** /ɔː'tɒnəməs/ adj автоно́мный. **autonomy** /ɔː'tɒnəmɪ/ n автоно́мия. **autopilot** /'ɔːtəʊˌpaɪlət/ n автопило́т. **autopsy** /'ɔːtɒpsɪ/ n вскры́тие; а́утопсия.

autumn /'ɔːtəm/ n о́сень. **autumn(al)** /ɔː'tʌmn(ə)l/ adj осе́нний.

auxiliary /ɔːg'zɪljərɪ/ adj вспомога́тельный; n помо́щник,

-ица.

avail /ə'veɪl/ n: to no ~ напра́сно; vt: ~ o.s. of по́льзоваться impf, вос~ pf +instr. **available** /-ləb(ə)l/ adj досту́пный, нали́чный.

avalanche /'ævəlɑ:ntʃ/ n лави́на.

avant-garde /,ævɑ̃'gɑ:d/ n аванга́рд; adj авангáрдный.

avarice /'ævərɪs/ n жа́дность. **avaricious** /-'rɪʃ(ə)s/ adj жа́дный.

avenge /ə'vendʒ/ vt мстить impf, ото~ pf за+acc. **avenger** /-dʒə(r)/ n мсти́тель m.

avenue /'ævə,nju:/ n (of trees) алле́я; (wide street) проспе́кт; (means) путь m.

average /'ævərɪdʒ/ n сре́днее число́, сре́днее sb; on ~ в сре́днем; adj сре́дний; vt де́лать impf в сре́днем & vi: ~ (out at) составля́ть impf, соста́вить pf в сре́днем.

averse /ə'vɜ:s/ adj: not ~ to не прочь +inf, не про́тив+gen. **aversion** /ə'vɜ:ʃ(ə)n/ n отвраще́ние. **avert** /ə'vɜ:t/ vt (ward off) предотвраща́ть impf, предотврати́ть pf; (turn away) отводи́ть impf, отвести́ pf.

aviary /'eɪvɪərɪ/ n пти́чник.

aviation /,eɪvɪ'eɪʃ(ə)n/ n авиа́ция.

avid /'ævɪd/ adj жа́дный; (keen) стра́стный.

avocado /,ævə'kɑ:dəʊ/ n авока́до neut indecl.

avoid /ə'vɔɪd/ vt избега́ть impf, избежа́ть pf +gen; (evade) уклоня́ться impf, уклони́ться pf от+gen. **avoidance** /-dəns/ n избежа́ние, уклоне́ние.

avowal /ə'vaʊ(ə)l/ n призна́ние. **avowed** /ə'vaʊd/ adj при́знанный.

await /ə'weɪt/ vt ждать impf +gen.

awake /ə'weɪk/ predic: be ~ не спать impf. **awake(n)** /-kən/ vt пробужда́ть impf, пробуди́ть pf; vi просыпа́ться impf, просну́ться pf.

award /ə'wɔːd/ vt присужда́ть impf, присуди́ть pf (person dat, thing acc); награжда́ть impf, награди́ть pf (person acc, thing instr); n награ́да.

aware /ə'weə(r)/ predic: be ~ сознава́ть impf; знать impf. **awareness** /-n(ə)s/ n созна́ние.

away /ə'weɪ/ adv прочь; be ~ отсу́тствовать impf; far ~ (from) далеко́ (от+gen); 5 miles ~ в пяти́ ми́лях отсю́да; ~ game игра́ на чужо́м по́ле.

awe /ɔː/ n благогове́йный страх. **awful** /'ɔːfʊl/ adj ужа́сный. **awfully** /'ɔːfʊlɪ/ adv ужа́сно.

awhile /ə'waɪl/ adv не́которое вре́мя.

awkward /'ɔːkwəd/ adj нело́вкий. **awkwardness** /-nɪs/ n нело́вкость.

awning /'ɔːnɪŋ/ n наве́с, тент.

awry /ə'raɪ/ adv ко́со.

axe /æks/ n топо́р; vt урезы́вать, уреза́ть impf, уре́зать pf от+gen.

axiom /'æksɪəm/ n аксио́ма. **axiomatic** /-'mætɪk/ adj аксиомати́ческий.

axis /'æksɪs/ n ось.

axle /'æks(ə)l/ n ось.

ay /aɪ/ int да!; n (in vote) го́лос «за».

Azerbaijan /,æzəbaɪ'dʒɑːn/ n Азербайджа́н. **Azerbaijani** /-nɪ/ n азербайджа́нец (-нца, -ница), -а́нка) pl азербайджа́нский.

azure /'æʒə(r)/ n лазу́рь; adj лазу́рный.

B

BA *abbr* (*univ*) бакалáвр.

babble /'bæb(ə)l/ *n* (*voices*) болтовня; (*water*) журчáние; *vi* болтáть *impf*; (*water*) журчáть *impf*.

baboon /bə'buːn/ *n* павиáн.

baby /'beɪbɪ/ *n* ребёнок; ~-**sit** присмáтривать за детьми́ в отсу́тствие роди́телей; ~-**sitter** приходя́щая ня́ня. **babyish** /'beɪbɪʃ/ *adj* ребя́ческий.

bachelor /'bætʃələ(r)/ *n* холостя́к; (*univ*) бакалáвр.

bacillus /bə'sɪləs/ *n* баци́лла.

back /bæk/ *n* (*of body*) спинá; (*rear*) зáдняя часть; (*reverse*) оборóт; (*of seat*) спи́нка; (*sport*) защи́тник; *adj* зáдний; *vt* (*support*) поддéрживать *impf*, поддержáть *pf*; (*car*) отодвигáть *impf*, отодви́нуть *pf*; (*horse*) стáвить *impf*, по~ *pf* на+*acc*; (*finance*) финанси́ровать *impf* & *pf*; *vi* отодви́гаться *impf*, отодви́нуться *pf* назáд; **backed out of the garage** вы́ехал зáдом из гарáжа; ~ **down** уступáть *impf*, уступи́ть *pf*; ~ **out** уклоня́ться *impf*, уклони́ться *pf* (of от+*gen*); ~ **up** (*support*) поддéрживать *impf*, поддержáть *pf*; (*confirm*) подкрепля́ть *impf*, подкрепи́ть *pf*. **backbiting** *n* сплéтня. **backbone** *n* позвонóчник; (*support*) глáвная опóра; (*firmness*) твёрдость харáктера. **backcloth**, **backdrop** *n* зáдник; (*fig*) фон. **backer** /'bækə(r)/ *n* (*sponsor*) спóнсор; (*supporter*) сторóнник. **backfire** *vi* давáть *impf*, дать *pf* отсéчку. **background** *n* фон, зáдний план; (*person's*) происхождéние. **backhand(er)** *n* удáр

слéва. **backhanded** *adj* (*fig*) сомни́тельный. **backhander** *n* (*bribe*) взя́тка. **backing** /'bækɪŋ/ *n* поддéржка. **backlash** *n* реáкция. **backlog** *n* задóлженность. **backside** *n* зад. **backstage** *adv* за кули́сами; *adj* закули́сный. **backstroke** *n* плáвание на спинé. **backup** *n* поддéржка; (*copy*) резéрвная кóпия; *adj* вспомогáтельный. **backward** /'bækwəd/ *adj* отстáлый. **backward(s)** /'bækwəd(z)/ *adv* назáд. **backwater** *n* заво́дь. **back yard** *n* зáдний двор.

bacon /'beɪkən/ *n* бекóн.

bacterium /bæk'tɪərɪəm/ *n* бактéрия.

bad /bæd/ *adj* плохóй; (*food etc.*) испóрченный; (*language*) гру́бый; ~-**mannered** невоспи́танный; ~ **taste** безвку́сица; ~-**tempered** раздражи́тельный.

badge /bædʒ/ *n* значóк.

badger /'bædʒə(r)/ *n* барсу́к; *vt* трави́ть *impf*, за~ *pf*.

badly /'bædlɪ/ *adv* плóхо; (*very much*) óчень.

badminton /'bædmɪnt(ə)n/ *n* бадминтóн.

baffle /'bæf(ə)l/ *vt* озадáчивать *impf*, озадáчить *pf*.

bag /bæg/ *n* (*handbag*) су́мка; (*plastic* ~, *sack*, *under eyes*) мешóк; (*paper* ~) бумáжный пакéт; *pl* (*luggage*) багáж.

baggage /'bægɪdʒ/ *n* багáж.

baggy /'bægɪ/ *adj* мешковáтый.

bagpipe /'bægpaɪp/ *n* волы́нка.

bail[1] /beɪl/ *n* (*security*) поручи́тельство; **release on** ~ отпускáть *impf*, отпусти́ть *pf* на пору́ки; *vt* (*out*) брать *impf*, взять *pf* на пору́ки; (*help*) выруча́ть *impf*, вы́ручить *pf*.

bail[2] /beɪl/, **bale**[2] /beɪl/ *vt* вычéр-

пывать *impf*, вы́черпнуть *pf* (во́ду из+*gen*); ~ **out** *vi* выбра́сываться *impf*, вы́броситься *pf* с парашю́том.

bailiff /'beɪlɪf/ *n* суде́бный исполни́тель.

bait /beɪt/ *n* нажи́вка; прима́нка (*also fig*); *vt* (*torment*) трави́ть *impf*, за~ *pf*.

bake /beɪk/ *vt & i* пе́чь(ся) *impf*, ис~ *pf*. **baker** /'beɪkə(r)/ *n* пе́карь *m*, бу́лочник *m*. **bakery** /'beɪkərɪ/ *n* пека́рня; (*shop*) бу́лочная *sb*.

balalaika /ˌbælə'laɪkə/ *n* балала́йка.

balance /'bæləns/ *n* (*scales*) весы́ *m pl*; (*equilibrium*) равнове́сие; (*econ*) бала́нс; (*remainder*) оста́ток; ~ **sheet** бала́нс; *vt* (*make equal*) уравнове́шивать *impf*, уравнове́сить *pf*; *& i* (*econ*; *hold steady*) баланси́ровать *impf*, с~ *pf*.

balcony /'bælkənɪ/ *n* балко́н.

bald /bɔːld/ *adj* лы́сый; ~ **patch** лы́сина. **balding** /'bɔːldɪŋ/ *adj* лысе́ющий. **baldness** /'bɔːldnɪs/ *n* плеши́вость.

bale[1] /beɪl/ *n* (*bundle*) ки́па.

bale[2] *see* **bail**[2]

balk /bɔːlk/ *vi* арта́читься *impf*, за~ *pf*; **she balked at the price** цена́ её испуга́ла.

ball[1] /bɔːl/ *n* (*in games*) мяч; (*sphere*; *billiards*) шар; (*wool*) клубо́к; ~**-bearing** шарикоподши́пник; ~**-point** (*pen*) ша́риковая ру́чка.

ball[2] /bɔːl/ *n* (*dance*) бал.

ballad /'bæləd/ *n* балла́да.

ballast /'bæləst/ *n* балла́ст.

ballerina /ˌbælə'riːnə/ *n* балери́на.

ballet /'bæleɪ/ *n* бале́т. **balletdancer** *n* арти́ст, ~ка, бале́та.

balloon /bə'luːn/ *n* возду́шный шар.

ballot /'bælət/ *n* голосова́ние. **ballot-paper** *n* избира́тельный бюллете́нь *m*; *vt* держа́ть *impf* голосова́ние ме́жду+*instr*.

balm /bɑːm/ *n* бальза́м. **balmy** /'bɑːmɪ/ *adj* (*soft*) мя́гкий.

Baltic /'bɔːltɪk/ *n* Балти́йское мо́ре; ~ **States** прибалти́йские госуда́рства, Приба́лтика.

balustrade /ˌbælə'streɪd/ *n* балюстра́да.

bamboo /bæm'buː/ *n* бамбу́к.

bamboozle /bæm'buːz(ə)l/ *vt* наду́вать *impf*, наду́ть *pf*.

ban /bæn/ *n* запре́т; *vt* запреща́ть *impf*, запрети́ть *pf*.

banal /bə'nɑːl/ *adj* бана́льный. **banality** /bə'nælɪtɪ/ *n* бана́льность.

banana /bə'nɑːnə/ *n* бана́н.

band /bænd/ *n* (*stripe*, *strip*) полоса́; (*braid*, *tape*) тесьма́; (*category*) катего́рия; (*of people*) гру́ппа; (*gang*) ба́нда; (*mus*) орке́стр; (*radio*) диапазо́н; *vi*: ~ **together** объединя́ться *impf*, объедини́ться *pf*.

bandage /'bændɪdʒ/ *n* бинт; *vt* бинтова́ть *impf*, за~ *pf*.

bandit /'bændɪt/ *n* банди́т.

bandstand /'bændstænd/ *n* эстра́да для орке́стра.

bandwagon /'bændwægən/ *n*: **jump on the** ~ по́льзоваться *impf*, вос~ *pf* благоприя́тными обстоя́тельствами.

bandy-legged /'bændɪˌlegd/ *adj* кривоно́гий.

bane /beɪn/ *n* отра́ва.

bang /bæŋ/ *n* (*blow*) уда́р; (*noise*) стук; (*of gun*) вы́стрел; *vt* (*strike*) ударя́ть *impf*, уда́рить *pf*; *vi* хло́пать *impf*, хло́пнуть *pf*; (*slam shut*) захло́пываться *impf*, захло́пнуться *pf*; ~ **one's head** ударя́ться *impf*, уда́-

риться *pf* голово́й; ~ **the door** хло́пать *impf*, хло́пнуть *pf* две́рью.

bangle /'bæŋg(ə)l/ *n* брасле́т.

banish /'bænɪʃ/ *vt* изгоня́ть *impf*, изгна́ть *pf*.

banister /'bænɪstə(r)/ *n* пери́ла *neut pl*.

banjo /'bændʒəʊ/ *n* ба́нджо *neut indecl*.

bank¹ /bæŋk/ *n* (*of river*) бе́рег; (*of earth*) вал; *vt* сгреба́ть *impf*, сгрести́ *pf* в ку́чу; *vi* (*aeron*) накреня́ться *impf*, накрени́ться *pf*.

bank² /bæŋk/ *n* (*econ*) банк; ~ **account** счёт в ба́нке; ~ **holiday** устано́вленный пра́здник; *vt* (*keep money*) держа́ть *impf* де́ньги (в ба́нке); *vt* (*put in* ~) класть *impf*, положи́ть *pf* в банк; ~ **on** полага́ться *impf*, положи́ться *pf* на+*acc*. **banker** /'bæŋkə(r)/ *n* банки́р. **banknote** *n* банкно́та.

bankrupt /'bæŋkrʌpt/ *n* банкро́т; *adj* обанкро́тившийся; *vt* доводи́ть *impf*, довести́ *pf* до банкро́тства. **bankruptcy** /-sɪ/ *n* банкро́тство.

banner /'bænə(r)/ *n* зна́мя *neut*.

banquet /'bæŋkwɪt/ *n* банке́т, пир.

banter /'bæntə(r)/ *n* подшу́чивание.

baptism /'bæptɪz(ə)m/ *n* креще́ние. **baptize** /bæp'taɪz/ *vt* крести́ть *impf*, о~ *pf*.

bar /bɑː(r)/ *n* (*beam*) брус; (*of cage*) решётка; (*of chocolate*) пли́тка; (*of soap*) кусо́к; (*barrier*) прегра́да; (*law*) адвокату́ра; (*counter*) сто́йка; (*room*) бар; (*mus*) такт; *vt* (*obstruct*) прегражда́ть *impf*, прегради́ть *pf*; (*prohibit*) запреща́ть *impf*, запрети́ть *pf*.

barbarian /bɑː'beərɪən/ *n* ва́рвар. **barbaric** /bɑː'bærɪk/, **barbarous** /'bɑːbərəs/ *adj* ва́рварский.

barbecue /'bɑːbɪˌkjuː/ *n* (*party*) шашлы́к; *vt* жа́рить *impf*, за~ *pf* на ве́ртеле.

barbed wire /ˌbɑːbd 'waɪə(r)/ *n* колю́чая про́волока.

barber /'bɑːbə(r)/ *n* парикма́хер; ~'s **shop** парикма́херская *sb*.

bar code /bɑː kəʊd/ *n* марки́ро́вка.

bard /bɑːd/ *n* бард.

bare /beə(r)/ *adj* (*naked*) го́лый; (*empty*) пусто́й; (*small*) минима́льный; *vt* обнажа́ть *impf*, обнажи́ть *pf*; ~ **one's teeth** оска́лить *impf*, о~ *pf* зу́бы. **barefaced** *adj* на́глый. **barefoot** *adv* босо́й. **barely** /'beəlɪ/ *adv* едва́.

bargain /'bɑːgɪn/ *n* (*deal*) сде́лка; (*good buy*) вы́годная сде́лка; *vi* торгова́ться *impf*, с~ *pf*; ~ **for, on** (*expect*) ожида́ть *impf*+*gen*.

barge /bɑːdʒ/ *n* ба́ржа; *vi*: ~ **into** (*room etc.*) вырыва́ться *impf*, ворва́ться *pf* в+*acc*.

baritone /'bærɪˌtəʊn/ *n* барито́н.

bark¹ /bɑːk/ *n* (*of dog*) лай; *vi* ла́ять *impf*.

bark² /bɑːk/ *n* (*of tree*) кора́.

barley /'bɑːlɪ/ *n* ячме́нь *m*.

barmaid /'bɑːmeɪd/ *n* буфе́тчица. **barman** /'bɑːmən/ *n* буфе́тчик.

barmy /'bɑːmɪ/ *adj* тро́нутый.

barn /bɑːn/ *n* амба́р.

barometer /bə'rɒmɪtə(r)/ *n* баро́метр.

baron /'bærən/ *n* баро́н. **baroness** /-nɪs/ *n* бароне́сса.

baroque /bə'rɒk/ *n* баро́кко *neut indecl*; *adj* баро́чный.

barrack¹ /'bærək/ *n* каза́рма.

barrack² /'bærək/ *vt* осв#ст-

вать *impf*, освиста́ть *pf*.

barrage /'bærɑːʒ/ *n* (*in river*) запру́да; (*gunfire*) огнево́й вал; (*fig*) град.

barrel /'bær(ə)l/ *n* бо́чка; (*of gun*) дуло́.

barren /'bærən/ *adj* бесплóдный.

barricade *n* /ˌbærɪˌkeɪd/ баррикáда; *vt* /ˌbærɪˈkeɪd/ баррикади́ровать *impf*, за~ *pf*.

barrier /'bærɪə(r)/ *n* барье́р.

barring /'bɑːrɪŋ/ *prep* исключа́я.

barrister /'bærɪstə(r)/ *n* адвока́т.

barrow /'bærəʊ/ *n* теле́жка.

barter /'bɑːtə(r)/ *n* ба́ртер, товарообме́н; *vi* обме́ниваться *impf*, обменя́ться *pf* това́рами.

base[1] /beɪs/ *adj* ни́зкий; (*metal*) неблагоро́дный.

base[2] /beɪs/ *n* осно́ва; (*also mil*) ба́за; *vt* осно́вывать *impf*, основа́ть *pf*. **baseball** *n* бейсбо́л. **baseless** /'beɪslɪs/ *adj* необосно́ванный. **basement** /'beɪsmənt/ *n* подва́л.

bash /bæʃ/ *vt* тре́снуть *pf*; *n*: **have a ~!** попро́бу(йте)!

bashful /'bæʃfʊl/ *adj* засте́нчивый.

basic /'beɪsɪk/ *adj* основно́й. **basically** /-kəlɪ/ *adv* в основно́м.

basin /'beɪs(ə)n/ *n* таз; (*geog*) бассе́йн.

basis /'beɪsɪs/ *n* осно́ва, ба́зис.

bask /bɑːsk/ *vi* гре́ться *impf*; (*fig*) наслажда́ться *impf*, насла́ди́ться *pf* (**in** +*instr*).

basket /'bɑːskɪt/ *n* корзи́на. **basketball** *n* баскетбо́л.

bass /beɪs/ *n* бас; *adj* басо́вый.

bassoon /bə'suːn/ *n* фаго́т.

bastard /'bɑːstəd/ *n* (*sl*) него́дяй.

baste /beɪst/ *vt* (*cul*) полива́ть

impf, поли́ть *pf* жи́ром.

bastion /'bæstɪən/ *n* бастио́н.

bat[1] /bæt/ *n* (*zool*) летучая мышь.

bat[2] /bæt/ *n* (*sport*) бита́; *vi* бить *impf*, по~ *pf* по мячу́.

bat[3] /bæt/ *vt*: **he didn't ~ an eyelid** он и гла́зом не моргну́л.

batch /bætʃ/ *n* па́чка; (*of loaves*) вы́печка.

bated /'beɪtɪd/ *adj*: **with ~ breath** затаи́в дыха́ние.

bath /bɑːθ/ *n* (*vessel*) ва́нна; *pl* пла́вательный бассе́йн; **have a bath** принима́ть *impf*, приня́ть *pf* ва́нну; *vt* купа́ть *impf*, вы́-, ис~ *pf*. **bathe** /beɪð/ *vi* купа́ться *impf*, вы́-, ис~ *pf*; *vt* омыва́ть *impf*, омы́ть *pf*. **bather** /'beɪðə(r)/ *n* купа́льщик, -ица. **bath-house** *n* ба́ня. **bathing** /'beɪðɪŋ/ *n*: **~ cap** купа́льная ша́почка; **~ costume** купа́льный костю́м. **bathroom** *n* ва́нная *sb*.

baton /'bæt(ə)n/ *n* (*staff of office*) жезл; (*sport*) эстафе́та; (*mus*) (дирижёрская) па́лочка.

battalion /bə'tælɪən/ *n* батальо́н.

batten /'bæt(ə)n/ *n* ре́йка.

batter /'bætə(r)/ *n* взби́тое те́сто; *vt* колоти́ть *impf*, по~ *pf*. **battery** /'bætərɪ/ *n* батаре́я.

battle /'bæt(ə)l/ *n* би́тва; (*fig*) борьба́; *vi* боро́ться *impf*. **battlefield** *n* по́ле бо́я. **battlement** /-mənt/ *n* зубча́тая стена́. **battleship** *n* лине́йный кора́бль *m*.

bawdy /'bɔːdɪ/ *adj* непристо́йный.

bawl /bɔːl/ *vi* ора́ть *impf*.

bay[1] /beɪ/ *n* (*bot*) лавр; *adj* ла́вровый.

bay[2] /beɪ/ *n* (*geog*) зали́в.

bay[3] /beɪ/ *n* (*recess*) пролёт; **~**

window фона́рь *m*.

bay⁴ /beɪ/ *v* 1 (bark) ла́ять *impf*; (howl) выть *impf*.

bay⁵ /beɪ/ *adj* (colour) гнедо́й.

bayonet /ˈbeɪənet/ *n* штык.

bazaar /bəˈzɑː(r)/ *n* база́р.

BC *abbr* до н.э. (до на́шей э́ры).

be¹ /biː/ *v* 1. быть: *usually omitted in pres*: **he is a teacher** он учи́тель. 2. (*exist*) существова́ть *impf*. 3. (*frequentative*) быва́ть *impf*. 4. (~ *situated*) находи́ться *impf*; (*stand*) стоя́ть *impf*; (*lie*) лежа́ть *impf*. 5. (*in general definitions*) явля́ться *impf +instr*: **Moscow is the capital of Russia** столи́цей Росси́и явля́ется го́род Москва́. 6.: **there is, are** име́ется, име́ются (*impf*) есть.

be² /biː/ *v aux* 1. be+inf, *expressing duty, plan*: до́лжен+inf. 2. be+past participle passive, *expressing passive*: быть+past participle passive *in short form*: **it was done** бы́ло сде́лано; *impers construction of 3 pl+acc*: **I was beaten** меня́ би́ли; *reflexive construction*: **music was heard** слы́шалась му́зыка. 3. be+present participle active, *expressing continuous tenses: imperfective aspect*: **I am reading** я чита́ю.

beach /biːtʃ/ *n* пляж.

beacon /ˈbiːkən/ *n* мая́к, сигна́льный ого́нь *m*.

bead /biːd/ *n* бу́сина; (*drop*) ка́пля; *pl* бу́сы *f pl*.

beak /biːk/ *n* клюв.

beaker /ˈbiːkə(r)/ *n* (*child's*) ча́шка с но́сиком; (*chem*) мензу́рка.

beam /biːm/ *n* ба́лка; (*ray*) луч; *vi* (*shine*) сия́ть *impf*.

bean /biːn/ *n* фасо́ль, боб.

bear² /beə(r)/ *n* медве́дь *m*.

bear² /beə(r)/ *vt* (*carry*) носи́ть *indet*, нести́ *det*, по~ *pf*; (*endure*) терпе́ть *impf*; (*child*) роди́ть *impf & pf*; ~ **out** подтвержда́ть *impf*, подтверди́ть *pf*; ~ **up** держа́ться *impf*.

bearable /ˈbeərəb(ə)l/ *adj* терпи́мый.

beard /bɪəd/ *n* борода́. **bearded** /-dɪd/ *adj* борода́тый.

bearer /ˈbeərə(r)/ *n* носи́тель *m*; (*of cheque*) предъяви́тель *m*; (*of letter*) пода́тель *m*.

bearing /ˈbeərɪŋ/ *n* (*deportment*) оса́нка; (*relation*) отноше́ние; (*position*) пеленг; (*tech*) подши́пник; **get one's ~s** ориенти́роваться *impf & pf*; **lose one's ~s** потеря́ть *pf* ориентиро́вку.

beast /biːst/ *n* живо́тное *sb*; (*fig*) скоти́на *m & f*. **beastly** /ˈbiːstlɪ/ *adj* (*coll*) проти́вный.

beat /biːt/ *n* бой; (*round*) обхо́д; (*mus*) такт; *vt* бить *impf*, по~ *pf*; (*sport*) выи́грывать *impf*, вы́играть *pf y+gen*; взбива́ть *impf*, взбить *pf*; *vi* би́ться *impf*, ~ **off** отбива́ть *impf*, отби́ть *pf*; ~ **up** избива́ть *impf*, изби́ть *pf*. **beating** /ˈbiːtɪŋ/ *n* битьё; (*defeat*) пораже́ние; (*of heart*) бие́ние.

beautiful /ˈbjuːtɪfʊl/ *adj* краси́вый. **beautify** /-ˌfaɪ/ *vt* украша́ть *impf* укра́сить *pf*. **beauty** /ˈbjuːtɪ/ *n* красота́; (*person*) краса́вица.

beaver /ˈbiːvə(r)/ *n* бобр.

because /bɪˈkɒz/ *conj* потому́, что; так как; *adv*: ~ **of** из-за+*gen*.

beckon /ˈbekən/ *vt* мани́ть *impf*, по~ *pf* к себе́.

become /bɪˈkʌm/ *vi* станови́ться *impf*, стать *pf +instr*; ~ **of** ста́ться *pf* c+*instr*. **becom-**

ing /-mɪŋ/ *adj* (*dress*) идущий к лицу+*dat*.

bed /bed/ *n* кровать, постель; (*garden*) грядка; (*sea*) дно; (*river*) русло; (*geol*) пласт; **go to** ~ ложиться *impf*, лечь *pf* спать; **make the** ~ стелить *impf*, по~ *pf* постель. **bed and breakfast** *n* (*hotel*) маленькая гостиница. **bedclothes** *n pl*, **bedding** /'bedɪŋ/ *n* постельное бельё. **bedridden** /'bedrɪd(ə)n/ *adj* прикованный к постели. **bedroom** *n* спальня. **bedside table** *n* тумбочка. **bedsitter** /'bedsɪtə(r)/ *n* однокомнатная квартира. **bedspread** *n* покрывало. **bedtime** *n* время *neut* ложиться спать.

bedlam /'bedləm/ *n* бедлам. **bedraggled** /bɪ'dræg(ə)ld/ *adj* растрёпанный.

bee /biː/ *n* пчела. **beehive** *n* улей.

beech /biːtʃ/ *n* бук.

beef /biːf/ *n* говядина. **beefburger** *n* котлета.

beer /bɪə(r)/ *n* пиво.

beetle /'biːt(ə)l/ *n* жук.

beetroot /'biːtruːt/ *n* свёкла.

befall /bɪ'fɔːl/ *vt & i* случаться *impf*, случиться *pf* (+*dat*).

befit /bɪ'fɪt/ *vt* подходить *impf*, подойти *pf* +*dat*.

before /bɪ'fɔː(r)/ *adv* раньше; *prep* перед+*instr*, до+*gen*; *conj* до того как; прежде чем; (*rather than*) скорее чем; **the day ~ yesterday** позавчера. **beforehand** *adv* заранее.

befriend /bɪ'frend/ *vt* дружить *impf*, по~ *pf* c+*instr*.

beg /beg/ *vt* (*ask*) очень просить *impf*, по~ *pf* (*person*+*acc*; *thing*+*acc or gen*); *vi* нищенствовать *impf*; (*of dog*) служить *impf*; ~ **for** просить *impf*,

по~ *pf* +*acc or gen*; ~ **pardon** просить *impf* прощение.

beggar /'begə(r)/ *n* нищий *sb*.

begin /bɪ'gɪn/ *vt* (& *i*) начинать(ся) *impf*, начать(ся) *pf*. **beginner** /-'gɪnə(r)/ *n* начинающий *sb*. **beginning** /-'gɪnɪŋ/ *n* начало.

begrudge /bɪ'grʌdʒ/ *vt* (*give reluctantly*) жалеть *impf*, со~ *pf* o+*prep*.

beguile /bɪ'gaɪl/ *vt* (*charm*) очаровывать *impf*, очаровать *pf*; (*seduce, delude*) обольщать *impf*, обольстить *pf*.

behalf /bɪ'hɑːf/ *n*: **on ~ of** от имени +*gen*; (*in interest of*) в пользу +*gen*.

behave /bɪ'heɪv/ *vi* вести *impf* себя. **behaviour** /-'heɪvjə(r)/ *n* поведение.

behest /bɪ'hest/ *n* завет.

behind /bɪ'haɪnd/ *adv* сзади (+*gen*), позади (+*gen*), за (+*acc, instr*); *n* зад; **be, fall, ~** отставать *impf*, отстать *pf*.

behold /bɪ'həʊld/ *vt* смотреть *impf*, по~ *pf*. **beholden** /-d(ə)n/ *predic*: ~ **to** обязан+*dat*.

beige /beɪʒ/ *adj* бежевый.

being /'biːɪŋ/ *n* (*existence*) бытие; (*creature*) существо.

Belarus /,belə'ruːs/ *n* Беларусь.

belated /bɪ'leɪtɪd/ *adj* запоздалый.

belch /beltʃ/ *vi* рыгать *impf*, рыгнуть *pf*; *vt* извергать *impf*, извергнуть *pf*.

beleaguer /bɪ'liːgə(r)/ *vt* осаждать *impf*, осадить *pf*.

belfry /'belfrɪ/ *n* колокольня.

Belgian /'beldʒ(ə)n/ *n* бельгиец, -гийка; *adj* бельгийский. **Belgium** /-dʒəm/ *n* Бельгия.

belie /bɪ'laɪ/ *vt* противоречить *impf* +*dat*.

belief /bɪ'liːf/ *n* (*faith*) вера;

(*confidence*) убеждение. **believable** /-'li:vəb(ə)l/ *adj* вероятный, правдоподобный. **believe** /-'li:v/ *vt* верить *impf*, по~ *pf* +*dat*; ~ **in** верить *impf* в+*acc*. **believer** /-'li:və(r)/ *n* верующий *sb*.

belittle /bɪ'lɪt(ə)l/ *vt* умалять *impf*, умалить *pf*.

bell /bel/ *n* колокол; (*doorbell*) звонок; ~ **tower** колокольня.

bellicose /'belɪ,kəʊz/ *adj* воинственный. **belligerence** /bɪ'lɪdʒər(ə)ns/ *n* воинственность. **belligerent** /bɪ'lɪdʒərənt/ *adj* воюющий; (*aggressive*) воинственный.

bellow /'beləʊ/ *vt & i* реветь *impf*.

bellows /'beləʊz/ *n pl* мехи *m pl*.

belly /'belɪ/ *n* живот.

belong /bɪ'lɒŋ/ *vi* принадлежать *impf* (**to** к+*dat*). **belongings** /-ɪŋz/ *n pl* пожитки (-ков) *pl*.

Belorussian /,beləʊ'rʌʃ(ə)n/ *n* белорус, ~ка; *adj* белорусский.

beloved /bɪ'lʌvɪd/ *adj & sb* возлюбленный.

below /bɪ'ləʊ/ *adv* (*position*) внизу; *prep* (*position*) под+*instr*; (*less than*) ниже+*gen*.

belt /belt/ *n* (*strap*) пояс, (*also tech*) ремень; (*zone*) зона, полоса.

bench /bentʃ/ *n* скамейка; (*for work*) станок.

bend /bend/ *n* изгиб; *vt* (*& i*, ~ **down**) сгибать(ся) *impf*, согнуть(ся) *pf*; ~ **over** склоняться *impf*, склониться *pf* над+*instr*.

beneath /bɪ'ni:θ/ *prep* под+*instr*.

benediction /,benɪ'dɪkʃ(ə)n/ *n* благословение.

benefactor /'benɪ,fæktə(r)/ *n*

благодетель *m*. **benefactress** /-,fæktrɪs/ *n* благодетельница

beneficial /,benɪ'fɪʃ(ə)l/ *adj* полезный. **beneficiary** /-'fɪʃərɪ/ *n* получатель *m*; (*law*) наследник. **benefit** /'benɪfɪt/ *n* польза; (*allowance*) пособие; (*theat*) бенефис; *vt* приносить *impf*, принести *pf* пользу +*dat*; *vi* извлекать *impf*, извлечь *pf* выгоду.

benevolence /bɪ'nevəl(ə)ns/ *n* благожелательность. **benevolent** /-l(ə)nt/ *adj* благожелательный.

benign /bɪ'naɪn/ *adj* добрый, мягкий; (*tumour*) доброкачественный.

bent /bent/ *n* склонность.

bequeath /bɪ'kwi:ð/ *vt* завещать *impf & pf* +*dat*. **bequest** /bɪ'kwest/ *n* посмертный дар.

berate /bɪ'reɪt/ *vt* ругать *impf*, вы~ *pf*.

bereave /bɪ'ri:v/ *vt* лишать *impf*, лишить *pf* (**of** +*gen*). **bereavement** /-mənt/ *n* тяжёлая утрата.

berry /'berɪ/ *n* ягода.

berserk /bə'sɜ:k/ *adj*: **go** ~ взбеситься *pf*.

berth /bɜ:θ/ *n* (*bunk*) койка; (*naut*) стоянка; *vi* причаливать *impf*, причалить *pf*.

beseech /bɪ'si:tʃ/ *vt* умолять *impf*, умолить *pf*.

beset /bɪ'set/ *vt* осаждать *impf*, осадить *pf*.

beside /bɪ'saɪd/ *prep* около+*gen*, рядом с+*instr*; ~ **the point** некстати; ~ **o.s.** вне себя. **besides** /bɪ'saɪdz/ *adv* кроме того; *prep* кроме+*gen*.

besiege /bɪ'si:dʒ/ *vt* осаждать *impf*, осадить *pf*.

besotted /bɪ'sɒtɪd/ *adj* одурманенный.

bespoke /bɪ'spəʊk/ adj сдéланный на закáз.

best /best/ adj лýчший, сáмый лýчший; adv лýчше всегó, бóльше всегó; all the ~l всегó наилýчшего; at ~ в лýчшем слýчае; do one's ~ дéлать impf, с~ pf всё возмóжное; ~ man шáфер.

bestial /'bestɪəl/ adj звéрский. **bestiality** /,bestɪ'ælɪtɪ/ n звéрство.

bestow /bɪ'stəʊ/ vt даровáть impf & pf.

bestseller /,best'selə(r)/ n бестсéллер.

bet /bet/ n парú neut indecl; (stake) стáвка; vi держáть impf парú (on на+acc); vt (stake) стáвить impf, по~ pf; he bet me £5 он поспóрил со мной на 5 фýнтов.

betray /bɪ'treɪ/ vt изменя́ть impf, изменúть pf+dat. **betrayal** /-'treɪəl/ n измéна.

better /'betə(r)/ adj лýчший; adv лýчше; (more) бóльше; vt улучшáть impf, улýчшить pf; the ~ тем лýчше; ~ off бóлее состоя́тельный; ~ o.s. выдвигáться impf, вы́двинуться pf; get ~ (health) поправля́ться impf, попрáвиться pf; get the ~ of брать impf, взять pf верх над+instr; had you ~ go you had ~ go вам (dat) лýчше бы пойтú; think ~ of передýмывать impf, передýмать pf. **betterment** /-mənt/ n улучшéние.

between /bɪ'twi:n/ prep мéжду +instr.

bevel /'bev(ə)l/ vt скáшивать impf, скосúть pf.

beverage /'bevərɪdʒ/ n напúток.

bevy /'bevɪ/ n стáйка.

beware /bɪ'weə(r)/ vi остерегáться impf, остерéчься pf (of

+gen).

bewilder /bɪ'wɪldə(r)/ vt сбивáть impf, сбить pf с тóлку. **bewildered** /-dəd/ adj озадáченный. **bewilderment** /-mənt/ n замешáтельство.

bewitch /bɪ'wɪtʃ/ vt заколдóвывать impf, заколдовáть pf; (fig) очарóвывать impf, очаровáть pf. **bewitching** /-tʃɪŋ/ adj очаровáтельный.

beyond /bɪ'jɒnd/ prep за+acc & instr; по ту стóрону+gen; (above) сверх+gen; (outside) вне+gen; the back of ~ край свéта.

bias /'baɪəs/ n (inclination) уклóн; (prejudice) предупреждéние. **biased** /'baɪəst/ adj предупреждённый.

bib /bɪb/ n нагрýдник.

Bible /'baɪb(ə)l/ n Бúблия. **biblical** /'bɪblɪk(ə)l/ adj библéйский.

bibliographical /,bɪblɪə'græfɪk(ə)l/ adj библиографúческий. **bibliography** /,bɪblɪ'ɒɡrəfɪ/ n библиогрáфия.

bicarbonate (of soda) /baɪ'kɑ:bənɪt/ n питьевáя сóда.

biceps /'baɪseps/ n бúцепс.

bicker /'bɪkə(r)/ vi пререкáться impf.

bicycle /'baɪsɪk(ə)l/ n велосипéд.

bid /bɪd/ n предложéние цены́; (attempt) попы́тка; vt & i предлагáть impf, предложúть pf (цéну) (for за+acc); vt (command) прикáзывать impf, приказáть pf +dat. **bidding** /'bɪdɪŋ/ n предложéние цены́; (command) приказáние.

bide /baɪd/ vt: ~ one's time ожидáть impf благоприя́тного слýчая.

biennial /baɪ'enɪəl/ adj двухлéт-

ний; n двухлётник.

bier /bɪə(r)/ n катафáлк.

bifocals /baɪˈfəʊk(ə)lz/ n pl бифокáльные очки́ pl.

big /bɪg/ adj большóй; (also important) кру́пный.

bigamist /ˈbɪgəmɪst/ n (man) двоежéнец; (woman) двуму́жница. **bigamy** /-mɪ/ n двубрáчие.

bigwig /ˈbɪgwɪg/ n ши́шка.

bike /baɪk/ n велосипéд. **biker** /ˈbaɪkə(r)/ n мотоцикли́ст.

bikini /bɪˈkiːnɪ/ n бики́ни neut indecl.

bilateral /baɪˈlætər(ə)l/ adj двусторóнний.

bilberry /ˈbɪlbərɪ/ n черни́ка (no pl; usu collect).

bile /baɪl/ n жёлчь. **bilious** /ˈbɪljəs/ adj жёлчный.

bilingual /baɪˈlɪŋgw(ə)l/ adj двуязы́чный.

bill¹ /bɪl/ n счёт; (parl) законопрóект; (~ of exchange) вéксель; (poster) афи́ша; vt (announce) объявля́ть impf, объяви́ть pf в афи́шах; (charge) присылáть impf, присла́ть pf счёт+dat.

bill² /bɪl/ n (beak) клюв.

billet /ˈbɪlɪt/ n раскварти́ровывать impf, раскварти́ровáть pf.

billiards /ˈbɪljədz/ n билья́рд.

billion /ˈbɪljən/ n биллиóн.

billow /ˈbɪləʊ/ n вал; vi вздыма́ться impf.

bin /bɪn/ n му́сорное ведрó.

bind /baɪnd/ vt (tie) свя́зывать impf, связáть pf; (oblige) обя́зывать impf, обязáть pf; (book) переплетáть impf, переплести́ pf. **binder** /ˈbaɪndə(r)/ n (person) переплётчик; (for papers) пáпка. **binding** /ˈbaɪndɪŋ/ n переплёт.

binge /bɪndʒ/ n кутёж; ~ drinking попóйка.

binoculars /bɪˈnɒkjʊləz/ n pl бинóкль n.

biochemistry /ˌbaɪəʊˈkemɪstrɪ/ n биохи́мия. **biographer** /baɪˈɒgrəfə(r)/ n биóграф. **biographical** /ˌbaɪəˈgræfɪk(ə)l/ adj биографи́ческий. **biography** /baɪˈɒgrəfɪ/ n биогрáфия. **biological** /ˌbaɪəˈlɒdʒɪk(ə)l/ adj биологи́ческий. **biologist** /baɪˈɒlədʒɪst/ n биóлог. **biology** /baɪˈɒlədʒɪ/ n биолóгия.

bipartisan /ˌbaɪpɑːtɪˈzæn/ adj двухпарти́йный.

birch /bɜːtʃ/ n берёза; (rod) рóзга.

bird /bɜːd/ n пти́ца; ~ flu пти́чий грипп; ~ of prey хи́щная пти́ца.

birth /bɜːθ/ n рождéние; (descent) происхождéние; ~ certificate метри́ка; ~ control противозачáточные мéры f pl. **birthday** n день m рождéния; **fourth** ~ четырёхлéтие. **birthplace** n мéсто рождéния. **birthright** n прáво по рождéнию.

biscuit /ˈbɪskɪt/ n печéнье.

bisect /baɪˈsekt/ vt разрезáть impf, разрéзать pf пополáм.

bisexual /baɪˈseksjʊəl/ adj бисексуáльный.

bishop /ˈbɪʃəp/ n епи́скоп; (chess) слон.

bit¹ /bɪt/ n (piece) кусóчек; **a** ~ немнóго; **not a** ~ ничу́ть.

bit² /bɪt/ n (tech) сверлó; (bridle) удилá (-л) pl.

bitch /bɪtʃ/ n (coll) стéрва. **bitchy** /ˈbɪtʃɪ/ adj стервóзный.

bite /baɪt/ n уку́с; (snack) заку́ска; (fishing) клёв; vt кусáть impf, укуси́ть pf; vi (fish) клевáть impf, клю́нуть pf. **biting** /ˈbaɪtɪŋ/ adj éдкий.

bitter /ˈbɪtə(r)/ adj гóрький. **bit-**

terness /-nɪs/ n го́речь.

bitumen /'bɪtjʊmɪn/ n биту́м.

bivouac /'bɪvʊˌæk/ n бива́к.

bizarre /bɪ'zɑ:(r)/ adj стра́нный.

black /blæk/ adj чёрный; ~ **eye** подби́тый глаз; ~ **market** чёрный ры́нок; v: ~ **out** затемня́ть impf, затемни́ть pf; (vi) теря́ть impf, по~ pf созна́ние; n (colour) чёрный цвет; (person) негр; ~интя́жка; (mourning) тра́ур. **blackberry** n ежеви́ка (no pl; usu collect). **blackbird** n чёрный дрозд. **blackboard** n доска́. **blackcurrant** n чёрная сморо́дина (no pl; usu collect). **blacken** /'blækən/ vt (fig) черни́ть impf, о~ pf. **blackleg** n штрейкбре́хер. **blacklist** n вноси́ть impf, внести́ p в чёрный спи́сок. **blackmail** n шанта́ж; vt шантажи́ровать impf. **blackout** n затемне́ние; (faint) поте́ря созна́ния. **blacksmith** n кузне́ц.

bladder /'blædə(r)/ n пузы́рь m.

blade /bleɪd/ n (knife) ле́звие; (oar) ло́пасть; (grass) были́нка.

blame /bleɪm/ n вина́, порица́ние; vt вини́ть impf, (for в+prep); **to be ~** быть винова́тым. **blameless** /'bleɪmlɪs/ adj безупре́чный.

blanch /blɑ:ntʃ/ vt (vegetables) ошпа́ривать impf, ошпа́рить pf; vi бледне́ть impf, по~ pf.

bland /blænd/ adj мя́гкий; (dull) пре́сный.

blandishments /'blændɪʃmənts/ n pl лесть.

blank /blæŋk/ adj (look) отсу́тствующий; (paper) чи́стый; n (space) про́пуск; (form) бланк; (cartridge) холосто́й патро́н; ~ **cheque** n незапо́лненный чек.

blanket /'blæŋkɪt/ n одея́ло.

blare /bleə(r)/ vi труби́ть impf, про~ pf.

blasé /'blɑ:zeɪ/ adj пресы́щенный.

blasphemous /'blæsfəməs/ adj богоху́льный. **blasphemy** /-fəmɪ/ n богоху́льство.

blast /blɑ:st/ n (wind) поры́в ве́тра; (explosion) взрыв; vt взрыва́ть impf, взорва́ть pf; ~**off** стартова́ть impf & pf. **blastfurnace** n до́менная печь.

blatant /'bleɪt(ə)nt/ adj я́вный.

blaze /bleɪz/ n (flame) пла́мя neut; (fire) пожа́р; vi пыла́ть impf.

blazer /'bleɪzə(r)/ n лёгкий пиджа́к.

bleach /bli:tʃ/ n хло́рка, отбе́ливатель m; vt отбе́ливать impf, отбели́ть pf.

bleak /bli:k/ adj пусты́нный; (dreary) уны́лый.

bleary-eyed /'blɪərɪˌaɪd/ adj с затума́ненными глаза́ми.

bleat /bli:t/ vi бле́ять impf.

bleed /bli:d/ vi кровоточи́ть impf.

bleeper /'bli:pə(r)/ n персона́льный сигнализа́тор.

blemish /'blemɪʃ/ n пятно́.

blend /blend/ n смесь; vt сме́шивать impf, смеша́ть pf; vi гармони́ровать impf. **blender** /'blendə(r)/ n ми́ксер.

bless /bles/ vt благословля́ть impf, благослови́ть pf. **blessed** /'blesɪd, bles/ adj благослове́нный. **blessing** /'blesɪŋ/ n (action) благослове́ние; (object) бла́го.

blight /blaɪt/ vt губи́ть impf, по~ pf.

blind /blaɪnd/ adj слепо́й; ~ **alley** тупи́к; n што́ра; vt ослепля́ть impf, ослепи́ть pf. **blindfold**

завя́зывать *impf*, завяза́ть *pf* глаза́+*dat*. **blindness** /'blaɪndnɪs/ *n* слепота́.

blink /blɪŋk/ *vi* мига́ть *impf*, мигну́ть *pf*. **blinkers** /'blɪŋkəz/ *n pl* шо́ры (-p) *pl*.

bliss /blɪs/ *n* блаже́нство. **blissful** /'blɪsful/ *adj* блаже́нный.

blister /'blɪstə(r)/ *n* пузы́рь *m*, волды́рь *m*.

blithe /blaɪð/ *adj* весёлый; (*carefree*) беспе́чный.

blitz /blɪts/ *n* бомбёжка.

blizzard /'blɪzəd/ *n* мете́ль.

bloated /'bləʊtɪd/ *adj* взду́тый.

blob /blɒb/ *n* (*liquid*) ка́пля; (*colour*) кля́кса.

bloc /blɒk/ *n* блок.

block /blɒk/ *n* (*wood*) чурба́н; (*stone*) глы́ба; (*flats*) жило́й дом; *vt* прегражда́ть *impf*, прегради́ть *pf*; ~ **up** забива́ть *impf*, заби́ть *pf*.

blockade /blɒ'keɪd/ *n* блока́да; *vt* блоки́ровать *impf* & *pf*.

blockage /'blɒkɪdʒ/ *n* зато́р.

bloke /bləʊk/ *n* па́рень *m*.

blond /blɒnd/ *n* блонди́н, ~ка; *adj* белоку́рый.

blood /blʌd/ *n* кровь; ~ **donor** до́нор; ~**poisoning** *n* зараже́ние кро́ви; ~ **pressure** кровяно́е давле́ние; ~ **relation** бли́зкий ро́дственник, -ая ро́дственница; ~ **transfusion** перелива́ние кро́ви. **bloodhound** *n* ище́йка. **bloodshed** *n* кровопроли́тие. **bloodshot** *adj* нали́тый кро́вью. **bloodthirsty** *adj* кровожа́дный. **bloody** /'blʌdɪ/ *adj* крова́вый.

bloom /blu:m/ *n* расцве́т; *vi* цвести́ *pf*.

blossom /'blɒsəm/ *n* цвет; **in** ~ в цвету́.

blot /blɒt/ *n* кля́кса; пятно́; *vt* (*dry*) промока́ть *impf*, промок-

кну́ть *pf*; (*smudge*) па́чкать *impf*, за~ *pf*.

blotch /blɒtʃ/ *n* пятно́.

blotting-paper /'blɒtɪŋˌpeɪpə(r)/ *n* промока́тельная бума́га.

blouse /blaʊz/ *n* ко́фточка, блу́зка.

blow[1] /bləʊ/ *n* уда́р.

blow[2] /bləʊ/ *vt* & *i* дуть *impf*, по~ *pf*; ~ **away** сноси́ть *impf*, снести́ *pf*; ~ **down** вали́ть *impf*, по~ *pf*; ~ **one's nose** сморка́ться *impf*, сморкну́ться *pf*; ~ **out** задува́ть *impf*, заду́ть *pf*; ~ **over** (*fig*) проходи́ть *impf*, пройти́ *pf*; ~ **up** взрыва́ть *impf*, взорва́ть *pf*; (*inflate*) надува́ть *impf*, наду́ть *pf*. **blowlamp** *n* пая́льная ла́мпа.

blubber[1] /'blʌbə(r)/ *n* во́рвань.

blubber[2] /'blʌbə(r)/ *vi* реве́ть *impf*.

bludgeon /'blʌdʒ(ə)n/ *vt* (*compel*) вынужда́ть *impf*, вы́нудить *pf*.

blue /blu:/ *adj* (*dark*) си́ний; (*light*) голубо́й; *n* си́ний, голубо́й, цвет. **bluebell** *n* колоко́льчик. **bluebottle** *n* си́няя му́ха. **blueprint** *n* си́нька, светоко́пия; (*fig*) прое́кт.

bluff /blʌf/ *n* блеф; *vi* блефова́ть *impf*.

blunder /'blʌndə(r)/ *n* опло́шность; *vi* оплоша́ть *pf*.

blunt /blʌnt/ *adj* тупо́й; (*person*) прямо́й; *vt* тупи́ть *impf*, за~, ис~ *pf*.

blur /blɜː(r)/ *vt* затума́нивать *impf*, затума́нить *pf*. **blurred** /blɜːd/ *adj* распльíвчатый.

blurt /blɜːt/ *vt* ~ **out** выба́лтывать *impf*, вы́болтать *pf*.

blush /blʌʃ/ *vi* красне́ть *impf*, по~ *pf*.

bluster /'blʌstə(r)/ *vi* бушева́ть *impf*; *n* пусты́е слова́ *neut pl*.

boar /bɔː(r)/ n бо́ров; (wild) каба́н.

board /bɔːd/ n доска́; (committee) правле́ние, сове́т; on ~ на борт(у́); vt сади́ться impf, сесть pf (на кора́бль, в по́езд и т.д.); ~ up забива́ть impf, заби́ть pf impf. **boarder** n /ˈbɔːdə(r)/ n пансионе́р. **boarding-house** /ˈbɔːdɪŋˌhaʊs/ n пансио́н. **boarding-school** n интерна́т.

boast /bəʊst/ vi хва́статься impf, по~pf; vt горди́ться impf +instr. **boaster** /ˈbəʊstə(r)/ n хвасту́н. **boastful** /ˈbəʊstfʊl/ adj хвастли́вый.

boat /bəʊt/ n (small) ло́дка; (large) кора́бль m.

bob /bɒb/ vi подпры́гивать impf, подпры́гнуть pf.

bobbin /ˈbɒbɪn/ n кату́шка.

bobsleigh /ˈbɒbsleɪ/ n бо́бслей.

bode /bəʊd/ vt: ~well/ill предвеща́ть impf хоро́шее/недо́брое.

bodice /ˈbɒdɪs/ n лиф, корса́ж.

bodily /ˈbɒdɪlɪ/ adv целико́м; adj теле́сный.

body /ˈbɒdɪ/ n те́ло, ту́ловище; (corpse) труп; (group) о́рган; (main part) основна́я часть. **bodyguard** n телохрани́тель m. **bodywork** n ку́зов.

bog /bɒg/ n боло́та; get ~ged down увяза́ть impf, увя́знуть pf. **boggy** /ˈbɒgɪ/ adj боло́тистый.

bogus /ˈbəʊgəs/ adj подде́льный.

boil¹ /bɔɪl/ n (med) фуру́нкул.

boil² /bɔɪl/ vi кипе́ть impf, вс~ pf; vt кипяти́ть impf, вс~ pf; (cook) вари́ть impf, с~ pf; ~ down to сходи́ться impf, сойти́сь pf к тому́, что; ~ over выкипа́ть impf, вы́кипеть pf; n кипе́ние; bring to the ~ дово-

ди́ть impf, довести́ pf до кипе́ния. **boiled** /bɔɪld/ adj варёный.

boiler /ˈbɔɪlə(r)/ n котёл; ~ suit комбинезо́н. **boiling** /ˈbɔɪlɪŋ/ adj кипя́щий; ~ point то́чка кипе́ния; ~ water кипято́к.

boisterous /ˈbɔɪstərəs/ adj шумли́вый.

bold /bəʊld/ adj сме́лый; (type) жи́рный.

bollard /ˈbɒləd/ n (in road) столб; (on quay) пал.

bolster /ˈbəʊlstə(r)/ n ва́лик; vt: ~ up подпира́ть impf, подпере́ть pf.

bolt /bəʊlt/ n засо́в, (tech) болт; vt запира́ть impf, запере́ть pf на засо́в; скрепля́ть impf, скрепи́ть pf болта́ми; vi (flee) удира́ть impf, удра́ть pf; (horse) понести́ pf.

bomb /bɒm/ n бо́мба; vt бомби́ть impf, bombard. **bombard** /bɒmˈbɑːd/ vt бомбарди́ровать impf. **bombardment** n /bɒmˈbɑːdmənt/ n бомбардиро́вка. **bomber** /ˈbɒmə(r)/ n бомбарди́ровщик.

bombastic /bɒmˈbæstɪk/ adj напы́щенный.

bond /bɒnd/ n (econ) облига́ция; (link) связь; pl око́вы (-в) pl, (fig) у́зы (уз) pl.

bone /bəʊn/ n кость.

bonfire /ˈbɒnˌfaɪə(r)/ n костёр.

bonnet /ˈbɒnɪt/ n ка́пор; (car) капо́т.

bonus /ˈbəʊnəs/ n пре́мия.

bony /ˈbəʊnɪ/ adj кости́стый.

boo /buː/ vt осви́стывать impf, освиста́ть pf; vi улюлю́кать impf.

booby trap /ˈbuːbɪ ˌtræp/ n лову́шка.

book /bʊk/ n кни́га; vt (order) зака́зывать impf, заказа́ть pf; (reserve) брони́ровать impf, за~ pf. **bookbinder** n пере-

плётчик. **bookcase** *n* книжный шкаф. **booking** /ˈbʊkɪŋ/ *n* заказ; ~ **office** касса. **bookkeeper** /ˈbʊk,kiːpə(r)/ *n* бухгалтер. **bookmaker** /ˈbʊk,meɪkə(r)/ *n* букмекер. **bookshop** *n* книжный магазин.

boom¹ /buːm/ *n* (*barrier*) бон.
boom² /buːm/ *n* (*sound*) гул; (*econ*) бум; *vi* гудеть *impf*; (*fig*) процветать *impf*.
boorish /ˈbʊərɪʃ/ *adj* хамский.
boost /buːst/ *n* содействие; *vt* увеличивать *impf*, увеличить *pf*.
boot /buːt/ *n* ботинок; (*high*) сапог; (*football*) бутса; (*car*) багажник.
booth /buːð/ *n* киоск, будка; (*polling*) кабина.
booty /ˈbuːti/ *n* добыча.
booze /buːz/ *n* выпивка; *vi* выпивать *impf*.
border /ˈbɔːdə(r)/ *n* (*frontier*) граница; (*trim*) кайма; (*gardening*) бордюр; *vi* граничить *impf* (on с +*instr*). **borderline** *n* граница.
bore¹ /bɔː(r)/ *n* (*calibre*) канал (ствола); *vt* сверлить *impf*, про~ *pf*.
bore² /bɔː(r)/ *n* (*thing*) скука; (*person*) скучный человек; *vt* надоедать *impf*, надоесть *pf* +*dat*. **bored** /bɔːd/ *impers*: **I'm** ~ мне скучно; **we were** ~ нам было скучно. **boredom** /ˈbɔːdəm/ *n* скука.
boring /ˈbɔːrɪŋ/ *adj* скучный.
born /bɔːn/ *adj* прирождённый; **be** ~ родиться *impf* & *pf*.
borough /ˈbʌrə/ *n* район.
borrow /ˈbɒrəʊ/ *vt* одолжать *impf*, одолжить *pf* (**from** у +*gen*).
Bosnia /ˈbɒznɪə/ *n* Босния. **Bosnian** /-ən/ *n* босниец, -ийка; *adj*

боснийский.
bosom /ˈbʊz(ə)m/ *n* грудь.
boss /bɒs/ *n* начальник; *vt* командовать *impf*, с~ *pf* +*instr*. **bossy** /ˈbɒsi/ *adj* командирский.
botanical /bəˈtænɪk(ə)l/ *adj* ботанический. **botanist** /ˈbɒtənɪst/ *n* ботаник. **botany** /ˈbɒtəni/ *n* ботаника.
botch /bɒtʃ/ *vt* залатывать *impf*, залатать *pf*.
both /bəʊθ/ *adj* & *pron* оба *m* & *neut*, обе *f*; ~ **... and ...** и ... и.
bother /ˈbɒðə(r)/ *n* досада; *vt* беспокоить *impf*.
bottle /ˈbɒt(ə)l/ *n* бутылка; *vt* разливать *impf*, разлить *pf* по бутылкам; ~ **up** сдерживать *impf*, сдержать *pf*.
bottom /ˈbɒtəm/ *n* (*of river, container, etc.*) дно; (*of mountain*) подножие; (*buttocks*) зад; **at the** ~ **of** (*stairs, page*) внизу +*gen*; **get to the** ~ **of** добираться *impf*, добраться *pf* до сути +*gen*; *adj* нижний. **bottomless** /-lɪs/ *adj* бездонный.
bough /baʊ/ *n* сук.
boulder /ˈbəʊldə(r)/ *n* валун.
bounce /baʊns/ *vi* подпрыгивать *impf*, подпрыгнуть *pf*; (*cheque*) вернуться *pf*.
bound¹ /baʊnd/ *n* (*limit*) предел; *vt* ограничивать *impf*, ограничить *pf*.
bound² /baʊnd/ *n* (*spring*) прыжок; *vi* прыгать *impf*, прыгнуть *pf*.
bound³ /baʊnd/ *adj*: **he is** ~ **to be there** он обязательно там будет.
bound⁴ /baʊnd/ *adj*: **to be** ~ **for** направляться *impf* в+*acc*.
boundary /ˈbaʊndəri/ *n* граница.

boundless /'baʊndlɪs/ *adj* безграни́чный.

bountiful /'baʊntɪfʊl/ *adj* (*generous*) ще́дрый; (*ample*) оби́льный. **bounty** /'baʊntɪ/ *n* ще́дрость; (*reward*) пре́мия.

bouquet /buːˈkeɪ/ *n* буке́т.

bourgeois /'bʊəʒwɑː/ *adj* буржуа́зный. **bourgeoisie** /ˌbʊəʒwɑːˈziː/ *n* буржуази́я.

bout /baʊt/ *n* (*med*) при́ступ; (*sport*) схва́тка.

bow[1] /baʊ/ *n* (*weapon*) лук; (*knot*) бант; (*mus*) смычо́к.

bow[2] /baʊ/ *n* (*obeisance*) покло́н; *vi* кла́няться *impf*, поклони́ться *pf*; *vt* склоня́ть *impf*, склони́ть *pf*.

bow[3] /baʊ/ *n* (*naut*) нос.

bowel /'baʊəl/ *n* кишка́; (*depths*) не́дра (-р) *pl*.

bowl[1] /baʊl/ *n* ми́ска.

bowl[2] /baʊl/ *n* (*ball*) шар; *vi* подава́ть *impf*, пода́ть *pf* мяч. **bowler** /'baʊlə(r)/ *n* подаю́щий *sb* мяч; (*hat*) котело́к. **bowling-alley** /'baʊlɪŋ 'ælɪ/ *n* кегельба́н. **bowls** /baʊlz/ *n* игра́ в ша́ры.

box[1] /bɒks/ *n* коро́бка, я́щик; (*theat*) ло́жа; ~ **office** ка́сса.

box[2] /bɒks/ *vi* бокси́ровать *impf*. **boxer** /'bɒksə(r)/ *n* боксёр.

boxing /'bɒksɪŋ/ *n* бокс. **Boxing Day** *n* второ́й день Рождества́.

boy /bɔɪ/ *n* ма́льчик. **boyfriend** *n* друг, молодо́й челове́к. **boyhood** /'bɔɪhʊd/ *n* о́трочество. **boyish** /'bɔɪʃ/ *adj* мальчи́шеский.

boycott /'bɔɪkɒt/ *n* бойко́т; *vt* бойкоти́ровать *impf & pf*.

bra /brɑː/ *n* ли́фчик.

brace /breɪs/ *n* (*clamp*) скре́па; *pl* подтя́жки *f pl*; (*dental*) ши́на; *vt* скрепля́ть *impf*, скрепи́ть *pf*; ~ **o.s.** собира́ться *impf*, со-

бра́ться *pf* с си́лами.

bracelet /'breɪslɪt/ *n* брасле́т.

bracing /'breɪsɪŋ/ *adj* бодря́щий.

bracket /'brækɪt/ *n* (*support*) кронште́йн; *pl* ско́бки *f pl*; (*category*) катего́рия.

brag /bræg/ *vi* хва́статься *impf*, по~ *pf*.

braid /breɪd/ *n* тесьма́.

braille /breɪl/ *n* шрифт Бра́йля.

brain /breɪn/ *n* мозг. **brainstorm** *n* припа́док безу́мия. **brainwash** *vt* промыва́ть *impf*, промы́ть *pf* мозги́+*dat*. **brainwave** *n* блестя́щая иде́я.

braise /breɪz/ *vt* туши́ть *impf*, с~ *pf*.

brake /breɪk/ *n* то́рмоз; *vt* тормози́ть *impf*, за~ *pf*.

bramble /'bræmb(ə)l/ *n* ежеви́ка.

bran /bræn/ *n* о́труби (-бе́й) *pl*.

branch /brɑːntʃ/ *n* ве́тка; (*fig*) о́трасль; (*comm*) филиа́л; *vi* разветвля́ться *impf*, разветви́ться *pf* ~ **out** (*fig*) расширя́ть *impf*, расши́рить *pf* де́ятельность.

brand /brænd/ *n* (*mark*) клеймо́; (*make*) ма́рка; (*sort*) сорт; *vt* клейми́ть *impf*, за~ *pf*.

brandish /'brændɪʃ/ *vt* разма́хивать *impf+instr*.

brandy /'brændɪ/ *n* конья́к.

brash /bræʃ/ *adj* наха́льный.

brass /brɑːs/ *n* лату́нь, жёлтая медь; (*mus*) ме́дные инструме́нты *m pl*; *adj* лату́нный, ме́дный; ~ **band** ме́дный духово́й орке́стр; **top** ~ вы́сшее нача́льство.

brassière /'bræzɪə(r)/ *n* бюстга́льтер.

brat /bræt/ *n* чертёнок.

bravado /brəˈvɑːdəʊ/ *n* брава́да.

brave /breɪv/ adj хра́брый; vt покоря́ть impf, покори́ть pf.
bravery /'breɪvərɪ/ n хра́брость.

bravo /brɑː'vəʊ/ int бра́во.

brawl /brɔːl/ n сканда́л; vi дра́ться impf, по~ pf.

brawny /'brɔːnɪ/ adj му́скулистый.

bray /breɪ/ n крик осла́; vi крича́ть impf.

brazen /'breɪz(ə)n/ adj бессты́дный.

brazier /'breɪzɪə(r)/ n жаро́вня.

breach /briːtʃ/ n наруше́ние; (break) проло́м; (mil) брешь; vt прорыва́ть impf, прорва́ть pf; (rule) наруша́ть impf, нару́шить pf.

bread /bred/ n хлеб; (white) бу́лка. **breadcrumb** n кро́шка. **breadwinner** n корми́лец.

breadth /bredθ/ n ширина́; (fig) широта́.

break /breɪk/ n проло́м, разры́в; (pause) переры́в, па́уза; vt (& i) лома́ть(ся) impf, с~ pf; разбива́ть(ся) impf, разби́ть(ся) pf; vt (violate) наруша́ть impf, нару́шить pf; ~ **away** вырыва́ться impf, вы́рваться pf; ~ **down** (vi) (tech) лома́ться impf, с~ pf; (talks) срыва́ться impf, сорва́ться pf; (vt) (door) выла́мывать impf, вы́ломать pf; ~ **in(to)** вла́мываться impf, вломи́ться pf в+acc; ~ **off** (vt & i) отла́мывать(ся) impf, отломи́ть(ся) pf; (vi) (speaking) замолча́ть pf; (vt) (relations) порыва́ть impf, порва́ть pf; ~ **out** вырыва́ться impf, вы́рваться pf; (fire, war) вспы́хнуть pf; ~ **through** пробива́ть impf, проби́ть pf; ~ **up** (vi) (marriage) распада́ться impf, распа́сться pf;

(meeting) прерыва́ться impf, прерва́ться pf; (vt) (disperse) разгоня́ть impf, разогна́ть pf; (vt & i) разбива́ть(ся) impf, разби́ть(ся) pf; ~ **with** порыва́ть impf, порва́ть pf с+instr. **breakage** /'breɪkɪdʒ/ n поло́мка. **breakdown** n поло́мка; (med) не́рвный срыв. **breakfast** /'brekfəst/ n за́втрак; vi за́втракать impf, по~ pf. **breakneck** adj: **at** ~ **speed** сломя́ го́лову. **breakthrough** n проры́в. **breakwater** n волноре́з.

breast /brest/ n грудь; ~**-feeding** n кормле́ние гру́дью; ~ **stroke** n брасс.

breath /breθ/ n дыха́ние; **be out of** ~ запыха́ться impf & pf. **breathe** /briːð/ vi & vt дыша́ть impf; ~ **in** вдыха́ть impf, вдохну́ть pf; ~ **out** выдыха́ть impf, вы́дохнуть pf. **breather** /'briːðə(r)/ n переды́шка. **breathless** /'breθlɪs/ adj запыха́вшийся.

breeches /'brɪtʃɪz/ n pl бри́джи (-жей) pl.

breed /briːd/ n поро́да; vi размножа́ться impf, размножи́ться pf; vt разводи́ть impf, развести́ pf. **breeder** /'briːdə(r)/ n -во́д: **cattle** ~ скотово́д. **breeding** /'briːdɪŋ/ n разведе́ние, -во́дство; (upbringing) воспи́танность.

breeze /briːz/ n ве́тер(ок); (naut) бриз. **breezy** /'briːzɪ/ adj све́жий.

brevity /'brevɪtɪ/ n кра́ткость.

brew /bruː/ n (beer) вари́ть impf, с~ pf; (tea) зава́ривать impf, завари́ть pf; (beer) ва́рка; (tea) зава́рка. **brewer** /'bruːə(r)/ n пивова́р. **brewery** /'bruːərɪ/ n пивова́ренный заво́д.

bribe /braɪb/ n взя́тка; vt подку-

пать *impf*, подкупи́ть *pf*. **bribery** /'braɪbərɪ/ *n* по́дкуп.

brick /brɪk/ *n* кирпи́ч; *adj* кирпи́чный. **bricklayer** *n* ка́менщик.

bridal /'braɪd(ə)l/ *adj* сва́дебный. **bride** /braɪd/ *n* неве́ста. **bridegroom** /'braɪdgru:m/ *n* жени́х. **bridesmaid** /'braɪdzmeɪd/ *n* подру́жка неве́сты.

bridge[1] /brɪdʒ/ *n* мост; (*of nose*) перено́сица; *vt* (*gap*) заполня́ть *impf*, заполни́ть *pf*; (*overcome*) преодолева́ть *impf*, преодоле́ть *pf*.

bridge[2] /brɪdʒ/ *n* (*game*) бридж.

bridle /'braɪd(ə)l/ *n* узда́; *vi* возмуща́ться *impf*, возмути́ться *pf*.

brief /bri:f/ *adj* недо́лгий; (*concise*) кра́ткий; *n* инстру́кция; *vt* инструкти́ровать *impf* & *pf*. **briefcase** *n* портфе́ль *m*. **briefing** /'bri:fɪŋ/ *n* инструкта́ж. **briefly** /'bri:flɪ/ *adv* кра́тко. **briefs** /bri:fs/ *n pl* трусы́ (-со́в) *pl*.

brigade /brɪ'geɪd/ *n* брига́да. **brigadier** /brɪgə'dɪə(r)/ *n* генера́л-майо́р.

bright /braɪt/ *adj* я́ркий. **brighten** /'braɪt(ə)n/ (*also* ~ **up**) *vi* проясня́ться *impf*, проясни́ться *pf*; *vt* оживля́ть *impf*, оживи́ть *pf*. **brightness** /'braɪtnɪs/ *n* я́ркость.

brilliant /'brɪljənt/ *adj* блестя́щий.

brim /brɪm/ *n* край; (*hat*) поля́ (-ле́й) *pl*.

brine /braɪn/ *n* рассо́л.

bring /brɪŋ/ *vt* (*carry*) приноси́ть *impf*, принести́ *pf*; (*lead*) приводи́ть *impf*, привести́ *pf*; (*transport*) привози́ть *impf*, привезти́ *pf*; ~ **about** приноси́ть *impf*, принести́ *pf*; ~ **back** возвраща́ть *impf*, возврати́ть *pf*; ~ **down** сва́ливать *impf*, свали́ть *pf*; ~ **round** (*unconscious person*) приводи́ть *impf*, привести́ *pf* в себя́; (*deliver*) привози́ть *impf*, привезти́ *pf*; ~ **up** (*educate*) воспи́тывать *impf*, воспита́ть *pf*; (*question*) поднима́ть *impf*, подня́ть *pf*.

brink /brɪŋk/ *n* край.

brisk /brɪsk/ *adj* (*air etc.*) све́жий; (*quick*) бы́стрый.

bristle /'brɪs(ə)l/ *n* щети́на; *vi* щети́ниться *impf*, o~ *pf*.

Britain /'brɪt(ə)n/ *n* Великобрита́ния, А́нглия. **British** /'brɪtɪʃ/ *adj* брита́нский, англи́йский; ~ **Isles** Брита́нские острова́ *m pl*. **Briton** /'brɪt(ə)n/ *n* брита́нец, -нка; англича́нин, -а́нка.

brittle /'brɪt(ə)l/ *adj* хру́пкий.

broach /brəʊtʃ/ *vt* затра́гивать *impf*, затро́нуть *pf*.

broad /brɔːd/ *adj* широ́кий; in ~ **daylight** средь бе́ла дня; in ~ **outline** в о́бщих черта́х. **broadband** (*comput*) широкополо́сная переда́ча да́нных. **broad-minded** /ˌbrɔːd'maɪndɪd/ *adj* с широ́кими взгля́дами. **broadly** /'brɔːdlɪ/ *adv*: ~ **speaking** вообще́ говоря́.

broadcast /'brɔːdkɑːst/ *n* переда́ча; *vt* передава́ть *impf*, переда́ть *pf* по ра́дио, по телеви́дению; (*seed*) се́ять *impf*, по~ *pf* вразбро́с. **broadcaster** /-stə(r)/ *n* ди́ктор. **broadcasting** /-stɪŋ/ *n* ра́дио-, телевеща́ние.

brocade /brə'keɪd/ *n* парча́.

broccoli /'brɒkəlɪ/ *n* бро́кколи *neut indecl*.

brochure /'brəʊʃə(r)/ *n* брошю́ра.

broke /brəʊk/ *predic* без гроша́.

broken /'brəʊk(ə)n/ *adj* сло́ман-

ный; ~-**hearted** с разби́тым се́рдцем.

broker /'brəʊkə(r)/ n бро́кер, ма́клер.

bronchitis /brɒŋ'kaɪtɪs/ n бронхи́т.

bronze /brɒnz/ n бро́нза; adj бро́нзовый.

brooch /brəʊtʃ/ n брошь, бро́шка.

brood /bru:d/ n вы́водок; vi мра́чно размышля́ть impf.

brook¹ /brʊk/ n ручей.

brook² /brʊk/ vt терпе́ть impf.

broom /bru:m/ n метла́. **broom-stick** n (witches) помело́.

broth /brɒθ/ n бульо́н.

brothel /'brɒθ(ə)l/ n публи́чный дом.

brother /'brʌðə(r)/ n брат; ~-**in-law** n (sister's husband) зять; (husband's brother) де́верь; (wife's brother) шу́рин; (wife's sister's husband) своя́к. **brotherhood** /'brʌðəhʊd/ n бра́тство. **brotherly** /'brʌðəlɪ/ adj бра́тский.

brow /braʊ/ n (eyebrow) бровь; (forehead) лоб; (of hill) гре́бень m. **browbeaten** /'braʊbi:t(ə)n/ adj запу́ганный.

brown /braʊn/ adj кори́чневый; (eyes) ка́рий; n кори́чневый цвет; vt (cul) подрумя́нивать impf, подрумя́нить pf.

browse /braʊz/ vi (look around) осма́триваться impf, осмотре́ться pf; (in book) просма́тривать impf просмотре́ть pf кни́гу.

bruise /bru:z/ n синя́к; vt уши́бать impf, ушиби́ть pf.

brunette /bru:'net/ n брюне́тка.

brunt /brʌnt/ n основна́я тя́жесть.

brush /brʌʃ/ n щётка; (paint) кисть; vt (clean) чи́стить impf,

вы~, по~ pf (щёткой); (touch) легко́ каса́ться impf, косну́ться pf +gen; (hair) расчёсывать impf, расчеса́ть pf щёткой; ~ **aside, off** отма́хиваться impf, отмахну́ться pf от+gen; ~ **up** смета́ть impf, смести́ pf; (renew) подчища́ть impf, подчи́стить pf.

brushwood /'brʌʃwʊd/ n хво́рост.

Brussels sprouts /ˌbrʌs(ə)lz 'spraʊts/ n pl брюссе́льская капу́ста.

brutal /'bru:t(ə)l/ adj жесто́кий. **brutality** /bru:'tælɪtɪ/ n жесто́кость. **brutalize** /'bru:tə,laɪz/ vt ожесточа́ть impf, ожесточи́ть pf. **brute** /bru:t/ n живо́тное sb; (person) скоти́на. **brutish** /'bru:tɪʃ/ adj ха́мский.

B.Sc. abbr бакала́вр нау́к.

bubble /'bʌb(ə)l/ n пузы́рь m; vi пузы́риться impf; кипе́ть impf, вс~ pf.

buck /bʌk/ n саме́ц оле́ня, кро́лика etc.; vi брыка́ться impf.

bucket /'bʌkɪt/ n ведро́.

buckle /'bʌk(ə)l/ n пря́жка; vt застёгивать impf, застегну́ть pf (пря́жкой); vi (warp) коро́биться impf, по~, с~ pf.

bud /bʌd/ n по́чка.

Buddhism /'bʊdɪz(ə)m/ n будди́зм. **Buddhist** /'bʊdɪst/ n будди́ст; adj будди́йский.

budge /bʌdʒ/ vt & i шеве-ли́ть(ся) impf, по~ pf.

budget /'bʌdʒɪt/ n бюдже́т; vi: ~ **for** предусма́тривать impf, предусмотре́ть pf в бюдже́те.

buff /bʌf/ adj све́тло-кори́чневый.

buffalo /'bʌfə,ləʊ/ n бу́йвол.

buffet¹ /'bʊfeɪ/ n буфе́т.

buffet² /'bʌfɪt/ vt броса́ть impf (impers).

buffoon /bə'fu:n/ *n* шут.

bug /bʌg/ *n* (*insect*) бука́шка; (*germ*) инфе́кция; (*comput*) оши́бка в програ́мме; (*microphone*) потайно́й микрофо́н; *vt* (*install ~*) устана́вливать *impf*, установи́ть *pf* аппарату́ру для подслу́шивания в+*prep*; (*listen*) подслу́шивать *impf*.

bugle /'bju:g(ə)l/ *n* горн.

build /bɪld/ *n* (*of person*) телосложе́ние; *vt* стро́ить *impf*, по~ *pf*; ~ on пристра́ивать *impf*, пристро́ить *pf* (*to к*+*dat*); ~ up (*vt*) создава́ть *impf*, созда́ть *pf*; (*vi*) накопля́ться *impf*, накопи́ться *pf*. builder /'bɪldə(r)/ *n* строи́тель *m*. building /'bɪldɪŋ/ *n* (*edifice*) зда́ние; (*action*) строи́тельство; ~ site стро́йка; ~ society жили́щно-строи́тельный кооперати́в.

built-up area *n* застро́енный райо́н.

bulb /bʌlb/ *n* (*electric*) лампо́чка. bulbous /'bʌlbəs/ *adj* лу́ковичный.

Bulgaria /bʌl'geərɪə/ *n* Болга́рия. Bulgarian /-ən/ *n* болга́рин, -га́рка; *adj* болга́рский.

bulge /bʌldʒ/ *n* вы́пуклость; *vi* выпя́чиваться *impf*, вы́пятиться *impf*. bulging /'bʌldʒɪŋ/ *adj* разбу́хший, оттопы́ривающийся.

bulk /bʌlk/ *n* (*size*) объём; (*greater part*) бо́льшая часть; in ~ гурто́м. bulky /'bʌlkɪ/ *adj* громо́здкий.

bull /bʊl/ *n* бык; (*male*) саме́ц. bulldog *n* бульдо́г. bulldozer /-dəuz/ *vt* расчища́ть *impf*, расчи́стить *pf* бульдо́зером. bulldozer /-dəuzə(r)/ *n* бульдо́зер. bullfinch *n* снеги́рь *m*. bullock /'bʊlək/ *n* вол. bull's-eye *n* я́блоко.

bullet /'bʊlɪt/ *n* пу́ля. bullet-

proof *adj* пулесто́йкий.

bulletin /'bʊlɪtɪn/ *n* бюллете́нь *m*.

bullion /'bʊlɪən/ *n*: gold ~ зо́лото в сли́тках.

bully /'bʊlɪ/ *n* зади́ра *m* & *f*; *vt* запу́гивать *impf*, запуга́ть *pf*.

bum /bʌm/ *n* зад.

bumble-bee /'bʌmb(ə)l,bi:/ *n* шмель *m*.

bump /bʌmp/ *n* (*blow*) уда́р, толчо́к; (*swelling*) ши́шка; (*in road*) уха́б; *vi* ударя́ться *impf*, уда́риться *pf*; ~ into ната́лкиваться *impf*, натолкну́ться *pf* на+*acc*. bumper /'bʌmpə(r)/ *n* ба́мпер.

bumpkin /'bʌmpkɪn/ *n* дереве́нщина *m* & *f*.

bumptious /'bʌmpʃəs/ *adj* самоуве́ренный.

bumpy /'bʌmpɪ/ *adj* уха́бистый.

bun /bʌn/ *n* сдо́бная бу́лка; (*hair*) пучо́к.

bunch /bʌntʃ/ *n* (*of flowers*) буке́т; (*grapes*) гроздь; (*keys*) свя́зка.

bundle /'bʌnd(ə)l/ *n* у́зел; *vt* свя́зывать *impf*, связа́ть *pf* в у́зел; ~ off спрова́живать *impf*, спрова́дить *pf*.

bungalow /'bʌŋgə,ləʊ/ *n* бу́нгало *neut indecl*.

bungle /'bʌŋg(ə)l/ *vt* по́ртить *impf*, ис~ *pf*.

bunk /bʌŋk/ *n* ко́йка.

bunker /'bʌŋkə(r)/ *n* бу́нкер.

buoy /bɔɪ/ *n* буй. buoyancy /'bɔɪənsɪ/ *n* плаву́честь; (*fig*) бо́дрость. buoyant /'bɔɪənt/ *adj* плаву́чий; (*fig*) бо́дрый.

burden /'bɜːd(ə)n/ *n* бре́мя *neut*; *vt* обременя́ть *impf*, обремени́ть *pf*.

bureau /'bjʊərəʊ/ *n* бюро́ *neut indecl*. bureaucracy /,bjʊə'rɒkrəsɪ/ *n* бюрокра́тия. bur-

eaucrat /'bjːʊərəˌkræt/ *n* бюрократ. **bureaucratic** /ˌbjʊərə'krætɪk/ *adj* бюрократический.

burger /'bɜːgə(r)/ *n* котлета.

burglar /'bɜːglə(r)/ *n* взломщик. **burglary** /-rɪ/ *n* кража со взломом. **burgle** /'bɜːg(ə)l/ *vt* грабить *impf*, o~ *pf*.

burial /'berɪəl/ *n* погребение.

burly /'bɜːlɪ/ *adj* здоровенный.

burn /bɜːn/ *n* ожёг; *vt* & *i* (*injure*) обжигать(ся) *impf*, обжечь(ся) *pf*; *vi* гореть *impf*, c~ *pf*; (*by sun*) загорать *impf*, загореть *pf*; o~ ожёг. **burner** /'bɜːnə(r)/ *n* горелка.

burnish /'bɜːnɪʃ/ *vt* полировать *impf*, oт~ *pf*.

burp /bɜːp/ *vi* рыгать *impf*, рыгнуть *pf*.

burrow /'bʌrəʊ/ *n* нора; *vi* рыть *impf*, вы~ *pf* нору; (*fig*) рыться *impf*.

bursar /'bɜːsə/ *n* казначей. **bursary** /-rɪ/ *n* стипендия.

burst /bɜːst/ *n* разрыв, вспышка; *vi* разрываться *impf*, разорваться *pf*; (*bubble*) лопаться *impf*, лопнуть *pf*; *vt* разрывать *impf*, разорвать *pf*; ~ **into tears** расплакаться *pf*.

bury /'berɪ/ *vt* (*dead*) хоронить *impf*, по~ *pf*; (*hide*) зарывать *impf*, зарыть *pf*.

bus /bʌs/ *n* автобус; ~ **stop** автобусная остановка.

bush /bʊʃ/ *n* куст. **bushy** /'bʊʃɪ/ *adj* густой.

busily /'bɪzɪlɪ/ *adv* энергично.

business /'bɪznɪs/ *n* (*affair*, *dealings*) дело; (*firm*) предприятие; **mind your own** ~ не ваше дело; **on** ~ по делу. **businesslike** *adj* деловой. **businessman** *n* бизнесмен.

busker /'bʌskə(r)/ *n* уличный музыкант.

bust /bʌst/ *n* бюст; (*bosom*) грудь.

bustle /'bʌs(ə)l/ *n* суета; *vi* суетиться *impf*.

busy /'bɪzɪ/ *adj* занятой; *vt*: ~ **o.s.** заниматься *impf*, заняться *pf* (**with** +*instr*). **busybody** *n* назойливый человек.

but /bʌt/ *conj* но, а; **then** зато; *prep* кроме+*gen*.

butcher /'bʊtʃə(r)/ *n* мясник; *vt* резать *impf*, за~ *pf*; ~'s **shop** мясная *sb*.

butler /'bʌtlə(r)/ *n* дворецкий *sb*.

butt[1] /bʌt/ *n* (*cask*) бочка.

butt[2] /bʌt/ *n* (*of gun*) приклад; (*cigarette*) окурок.

butt[3] /bʌt/ *n* (*target*) мишень.

butt[4] /bʌt/ *vt* бодать *impf*, за~ *pf*; ~ **in** вмешиваться *impf*, вмешаться *pf*.

butter /'bʌtə(r)/ *n* (*slivochnoe*) масло; *vt* намазывать *impf*, намазать *pf* маслом; ~ **up** льстить *impf*, по~ *pf*. **buttercup** *n* лютик. **butterfly** *n* бабочка.

buttock /'bʌtək/ *n* ягодица.

button /'bʌt(ə)n/ *n* пуговица; (*knob*) кнопка; *vt* застёгивать *impf*, застегнуть *pf*. **buttonhole** *n* петля.

buttress /'bʌtrɪs/ *n* контрфорс; *vt* подпирать *impf*, подпереть *pf*.

buxom /'bʌksəm/ *adj* полногрудая.

buy /baɪ/ *n* покупка; *vt* покупать *impf*, купить *pf*. **buyer** /'baɪə(r)/ *n* покупатель *m*.

buzz /bʌz/ *n* жужжание; *vi* жужжать *impf*.

buzzard /'bʌzəd/ *n* канюк.

buzzer /'bʌzə(r)/ *n* зуммер.

by /baɪ/ *adv* мимо; *prep* (*near*) около+*gen*, у+*gen*; (*beside*)

ря́дом c+*instr*; (*past*) ми́мо +*gen*; (*time*) к+*dat*; (*means*) *instr without prep*; **~ and large** в це́лом.

bye /baɪ/ *int* пока́!

by-election /'baɪɪ,lekʃ(ə)n/ *n* дополни́тельные вы́боры *pl*.

Byelorussian /,bjelɔʊ'rʌʃ(ə)n/ *see* Belorussian

bygone /'baɪɡɒn/ *adj* мину́вший; **let ~s be ~s** что прошло́, то прошло́. **by-law** *n* постановле́ние. **bypass** *n* обхо́д; *vt* обходи́ть *impf*, обойти́ *pf*. **by-product** *n* побо́чный проду́кт. **byroad** *n* небольша́я доро́га. **bystander** /'baɪ,stændə(r)/ *n* свиде́тель *m*. **byway** *n* просёлочная доро́га. **byword** *n* олицетворе́ние (**for** +*gen*).

Byzantine /bɪ'zæntaɪn/ *adj* византи́йский.

C

cab /kæb/ *n* (*taxi*) такси́ *neut indecl*; (*of lorry*) каби́на.

cabaret /'kæbə,reɪ/ *n* кабаре́ *neut indecl*.

cabbage /'kæbɪdʒ/ *n* капу́ста.

cabin /'kæbɪn/ *n* (*hut*) хи́жина; (*aeron*) каби́на; (*naut*) каю́та.

cabinet /'kæbɪnɪt/ *n* шкаф; (*Cabinet*) кабине́т; **~-maker** краснодере́вец; **~-minister** мини́стр-член кабине́та.

cable /'keɪb(ə)l/ *n* (*rope*) кана́т; (*electric*) ка́бель *m*; (*cablegram*) телегра́мма; *vt & i* телеграфи́ровать *impf & pf*.

cache /kæʃ/ *n* пота́йной склад.

cackle /'kæk(ə)l/ *vi* гогота́ть *impf*.

cactus /'kæktəs/ *n* ка́ктус.

caddy /'kædɪ/ *n* (*box*) ча́йница.

cadet /kə'det/ *n* новобра́нец.

cadge /kædʒ/ *vt* стреля́ть *impf*, стрельну́ть *pf*.

cadres /'kɑːdəz/ *n pl* ка́дры *m pl*.

Caesarean (section) /sɪ'zeərɪən 'sekʃ(ə)n)/ *n* ке́сарево сече́ние.

cafe /'kæfeɪ/ *n* кафе́ *neut indecl*.

cafeteria /,kæfɪ'tɪərɪə/ *n* кафете́рий.

caffeine /'kæfiːn/ *n* кофеи́н.

cage /keɪdʒ/ *n* кле́тка.

cajole /kə'dʒəʊl/ *vt* заба́лтывать *impf*, задо́брить *pf*.

cake /keɪk/ *n* (*large*) торт, (*small*) пиро́жное *sb*; (*fruit-~*) кекс; *vt*: **~d** обле́пленный (**in** +*instr*).

calamitous /kə'læmɪtəs/ *adj* бе́дственный. **calamity** /-'læmɪtɪ/ *n* бе́дствие.

calcium /'kælsɪəm/ *n* ка́льций.

calculate /'kælkjʊ,leɪt/ *vt* вычисля́ть *impf*, вы́числить *pf*; *vi* рассчи́тывать *impf*, рассчита́ть *pf* (**on** на+*acc*). **calculation** /,kælkjʊ'leɪʃ(ə)n/ *n* вычисле́ние, расчёт. **calculator** /'kælkjʊ,leɪtə(r)/ *n* калькуля́тор.

calendar /'kælɪndə(r)/ *n* календа́рь *m*.

calf¹ /kɑːf/ *n* (*cow*) телёнок.

calf² /kɑːf/ *n* (*leg*) икра́.

calibrate /'kælɪ,breɪt/ *vt* калиброва́ть *impf*. **calibre** /-bə(r)/ *n* кали́бр.

call /kɔːl/ *v* звать *impf*, по~ *pf*; (*name*) называ́ть *impf*, назва́ть *pf*; (*cry*) крича́ть *impf*, кри́кнуть *pf*; (*wake*) буди́ть *impf*, раз~ *pf*; (*visit*) заходи́ть *impf*, зайти́ *pf* (**on** к+*dat*; **at** в+*acc*); (*stop at*) остана́вливаться *impf*, останови́ться *pf* (**at** в, на, +*prep*); (*summon*) вызыва́ть *impf*, вы́звать *pf*; (*ring up*) зво-

ни́ть *impf*, по~ *pf* +*dat*; ~ **for** (*require*) тре́бовать *impf*, по~ *pf* +*gen*; (*fetch*) заходи́ть *impf*, зайти́ *pf* за+*instr*; ~ **off** отменя́ть *impf*, отмени́ть *pf*; ~ **out** вскри́кивать *impf*, вскри́кнуть *pf*; ~ **up** призыва́ть *impf*, призва́ть *pf*; *n* (*cry*) крик; (*summons*) зов, при́зыв; (*telephone*) (телефо́нный) вы́зов, разгово́р; (*visit*) визи́т; (*signal*) сигна́л; ~**-box** телефо́н-автома́т; ~ **centre** колл-це́нтр, информацио́нно-спра́вочная слу́жба; ~**up** при́зыв. **caller** /'kɔːlə(r)/ *n* посети́тель *m*, ~ница; (*tel*) позвони́вший *sb*. **calling** /'kɔːlɪŋ/ *n* (*vocation*) призва́ние.

callous /'kæləs/ *adj* (*person*) чёрствый.

callus /'kæləs/ *n* мозо́ль.

calm /kɑːm/ *adj* споко́йный; *n* споко́йствие; *vt & i* (~ **down**) успока́ивать(ся) *impf*, успоко́ить(ся) *pf*.

calorie /'kælərɪ/ *n* кало́рия.

camber /'kæmbə(r)/ *n* скат.

camcorder /'kæm,kɔːdə(r)/ *n* камко́рдер.

camel /'kæm(ə)l/ *n* верблю́д.

camera /'kæmrə/ *n* фотоаппара́т. **cameraman** *n* кинооперра́тор.

camouflage /'kæməˌflɑːʒ/ *n* камуфля́ж; *vt* маскирова́ть *impf*, за~ *pf*.

camp /kæmp/ *n* ла́герь *m*; *vi* (*set up* ~) располага́ться *impf*, расположи́ться *pf* ла́герем; (*go camping*) жить *impf* в пала́тках; ~**bed** раскладу́шка; ~**fire** костёр.

campaign /kæm'peɪn/ *n* кампа́ния; *vi* проводи́ть *impf*, провести́ *pf* кампа́нию.

campsite /'kæmpsaɪt/ *n* ла́герь

m, ке́мпинг.

campus /'kæmpəs/ *n* университе́тский городо́к.

can¹ /kæn/ *n* ба́нка; *vt* консерви́ровать *impf*, за~ *pf*.

can² /kæn/ *v aux* (*be able*) мочь *impf*, c~ *pf* +*inf*; (*know how*) уме́ть *impf*, c~ *pf* +*inf*.

Canada /'kænədə/ *n* Кана́да. **Canadian** /kə'neɪdɪən/ *n* кана́дец, -дка; *adj* кана́дский.

canal /kə'næl/ *n* кана́л.

canary /kə'neərɪ/ *n* канаре́йка.

cancel /'kæns(ə)l/ *vt* (*make void*) аннули́ровать *impf & pf*; (*call off*) отменя́ть *impf*, отмени́ть *pf*; (*stamp*) гаси́ть *impf*, по~ *pf*. **cancellation** /ˌkænsə'leɪʃ(ə)n/ *n* аннули́рование; отме́на.

cancer /'kænsə(r)/ *n* рак; (**C**~) Рак. **cancerous** /'kænsərəs/ *adj* ра́ковый.

candelabrum /ˌkændɪ'lɑːbrəm/ *n* канделя́бр.

candid /'kændɪd/ *adj* открове́нный.

candidate /'kændɪdət/ *n* кандида́т.

candied /'kændɪd/ *adj* заса́харенный.

candle /'kænd(ə)l/ *n* свеча́. **candlestick** /*n* подсве́чник.

candour /'kændə(r)/ *n* открове́нность.

candy /'kændɪ/ *n* сла́дости *pl fpl*.

cane /keɪn/ *n* (*plant*) тростни́к; (*stick*) трость, па́лка; *vt* бить *impf*, по~ *pf* па́лкой.

canine /'keɪnaɪn/ *adj* соба́чий; *n* (*tooth*) клык.

canister /'kænɪstə(r)/ *n* ба́нка.

cannabis /'kænəbɪs/ *n* гаши́ш.

cannibal /'kænɪb(ə)l/ *n* людое́д. **cannibalism** /-ˌlɪz(ə)m/ *n* людое́дство.

cannon /'kænən/ *n* пу́шка. ~**ball** пу́шечное ядро́.

canoe /kə'nuː/ *n* кано́э *neut in-*

decl; *vi* пла́вать *indet*, плыть *det* на кано́э.

canon /'kænən/ *n* кано́н; (*person*) кано́ник. **canonize** /-,naɪz/ *vt* канонизова́ть *impf & pf*.

canopy /'kænəpɪ/ *n* балдахи́н.

cant /kænt/ *n* (*hypocrisy*) ха́нжество; (*jargon*) жарго́н.

cantankerous /kæn'tæŋkərəs/ *adj* сварли́вый.

cantata /kæn'tɑːtə/ *n* канта́та.

canteen /kæn'tiːn/ *n* столо́вая *sb*.

canter /'kæntə(r)/ *n* лёгкий гало́п; *vi* (*rider*) е́здить *indet*, е́хать *det* лёгким гало́пом; (*horse*) ходи́ть *indet*, идти́ *det* лёгким гало́пом.

canvas /'kænvəs/ *n* (*art*) холст; (*naut*) паруси́на; (*tent material*) брезе́нт.

canvass /'kænvəs/ *vi* агити́ровать *impf*, *c∼ pf* (*for* за+*acc*); *n* собира́ние голосо́в; агита́ция. **canvasser** /'kænvəsə(r)/ *n* собира́тель *m* голосо́в.

canyon /'kænjən/ *n* каньо́н.

cap /kæp/ *n* (*of uniform*) фура́жка; (*cloth*) ке́пка; (*woman's*) чепе́ц; (*lid*) кры́шка; *vt* превосходи́ть *impf*, превзойти́ *pf*.

capability /,keɪpə'bɪlɪtɪ/ *n* спосо́бность. **capable** /'keɪpəb(ə)l/ *adj* спосо́бный (*of* на+*acc*).

capacious /kə'peɪʃəs/ *adj* вмести́тельный. **capacity** /kə'pæsɪtɪ/ *n* ёмкость; (*ability*) спосо́бность; **in the ∼ of** в ка́честве +*gen*.

cape[1] /keɪp/ *n* (*geog*) мыс.

cape[2] /keɪp/ *n* (*cloak*) наки́дка.

caper /'keɪpə(r)/ *vi* скака́ть *impf*.

capers /'keɪpəz/ *n pl* (*cul*) ка́персы *m pl*.

capillary /kə'pɪlərɪ/ *adj* капилля́рный.

capital /'kæpɪt(ə)l/ *adj* (*letter*) прописно́й; ∼ **punishment** сме́ртная казнь; *n* (*town*) столи́ца; (*letter*) прописна́я бу́ква; (*econ*) капита́л. **capitalism** /-,lɪz(ə)m/ *n* капитали́зм. **capitalist** /-lɪst/ *n* капитали́ст; *adj* капиталисти́ческий. **capitalize** /-,laɪz/ *vt* извлека́ть *impf*, извле́чь *pf* вы́году (*on* из+*gen*).

capitulate /kə'pɪtjʊ,leɪt/ *vi* капитули́ровать *impf & pf*. **capitulation** /-'leɪʃ(ə)n/ *n* капитуля́ция.

caprice /kə'priːs/ *n* капри́з. **capricious** /-'prɪʃəs/ *adj* капри́зный.

Capricorn /'kæprɪ,kɔːn/ *n* Козеро́г.

capsize /kæp'saɪz/ *vt & i* опроки́дывать(ся) *impf*, опроки́нуть(ся) *pf*.

capsule /'kæpsjuːl/ *n* ка́псула.

captain /'kæptɪn/ *n* капита́н; *vt* быть капита́ном +*gen*.

caption /'kæpʃ(ə)n/ *n* по́дпись; (*cin*) титр.

captious /'kæpʃəs/ *adj* придирчи́вый.

captivate /'kæptɪ,veɪt/ *vt* пленя́ть *impf*, плени́ть *pf*. **captivating** /'kæptɪ,veɪtɪŋ/ *adj* плени́тельный. **captive** /'kæptɪv/ *adj & n* пле́нный. **captivity** /kæp'tɪvɪtɪ/ *n* нево́ля; (*esp mil*) плен. **capture** /'kæptʃə(r)/ *n* взя́тие, захва́т, пои́мка; *vt* (*person*) брать *impf*, взять *pf* в плен; (*seize*) захва́тывать *impf*, захвати́ть *pf*.

car /kɑː(r)/ *n* маши́на; автомоби́ль *m*; ∼ **park** стоя́нка.

carafe /kə'ræf/ *n* графи́н.

caramel(s) /'kærə,mel(z)/ *n* караме́ль.

carat /'kærət/ *n* кара́т.

caravan /'kærə,væn/ *n* фурго́н;

(convoy) карава́н.

caraway (seeds) /'kærəˌweɪ (siːdz)/ n тмин.

carbohydrate /ˌkɑːbə'haɪdreɪt/ n углево́д. **carbon** /'kɑːb(ə)n/ n углеро́д; ~ **copy** ко́пия; ~ **dioxide** углекислота́; ~ **monoxide** о́кись углеро́да; ~ **paper** копирова́льная бума́га.

carburettor /ˌkɑːbjʊ'retə(r)/ n карбюра́тор.

carcass /'kɑːkəs/ n ту́ша.

card /kɑːd/ n (stiff paper) карто́н; (visiting ~) ка́рточка; (playing ~) ка́рта; (greetings ~) откры́тка; (ticket) биле́т. **cardboard** n карто́н; attrib карто́нный.

cardiac /'kɑːdɪæk/ adj серде́чный.

cardigan /'kɑːdɪɡən/ n кардига́н.

cardinal /'kɑːdɪn(ə)l/ adj кардина́льный; ~ **number** коли́чественное числи́тельное sb; n кардина́л.

care /keə(r)/ n (trouble) забо́та; (caution) осторо́жность; (tending) ухо́д; **in the** ~ **of** на попече́нии +gen; **take** ~ осторо́жно!; смотри́(те)!; **take** ~ **of** забо́титься impf, по~ pf o+prep; vi: **I don't** ~ мне всё равно́; ~ **for** (look after) уха́живать impf за +instr; (like) нра́виться impf, по~ pf impers +dat.

career /kə'rɪə(r)/ n карье́ра.

carefree /'keəfriː/ adj беззабо́тный. **careful** /-fʊl/ adj (cautious) осторо́жный; (thorough) тща́тельный. **careless** /-lɪs/ adj (negligent) небре́жный; (incautious) неосторо́жный.

caress /kə'res/ n ла́ска; vt ласка́ть impf.

caretaker /'keəteɪkə(r)/ n смотри́тель m, ~ница; attrib вре-

менный.

cargo /'kɑːɡəʊ/ n груз.

caricature /'kærɪkətjʊə(r)/ n карикату́ра; vt изобража́ть impf, изобрази́ть pf в карикату́рном ви́де.

carnage /'kɑːnɪdʒ/ n резня́.

carnal /'kɑːn(ə)l/ adj пло́тский.

carnation /kɑː'neɪʃ(ə)n/ n гвозди́ка.

carnival /'kɑːnɪv(ə)l/ n карнава́л.

carnivorous /kɑː'nɪvərəs/ adj плотоя́дный.

carol /'kær(ə)l/ n (рожде́ственский) гимн.

carouse /kə'raʊz/ vi кути́ть impf, кутну́ть pf.

carp¹ /kɑːp/ n карп.

carp² /kɑːp/ vi придира́ться impf, придра́ться pf (at к+dat).

carpenter /'kɑːpɪntə(r)/ n пло́тник. **carpentry** /-trɪ/ n пло́тничество.

carpet /'kɑːpɪt/ n ковёр; vt покрыва́ть impf, покры́ть pf ковро́м.

carping /'kɑːpɪŋ/ adj придирчивый.

carriage /'kærɪdʒ/ n (vehicle) каре́та; (rly) ваго́н; (conveyance) перево́зка; (bearing) оса́нка. **carriageway** n прое́зжая часть доро́ги. **carrier** /'kærɪə(r)/ n (on bike) бага́жник; (firm) тра́нспортная кампа́ния; (med) бацилоноси́тель m.

carrot /'kærət/ n морко́вка; pl морко́вь (collect).

carry /'kærɪ/ vt (by hand) носи́ть indet, нести́ det; перено́сить impf, перенести́ pf; (in vehicle) вози́ть indet, везти́ det; (sound) передава́ть impf, переда́ть pf; vi (sound) быть слы́шен; **be carried away** увлека́ться impf,

увлечься *pf*; ~ **on** (*continue*)
продолжа́ть *impf*; ~ **out** вы-
полня́ть *impf*, вы́полнить *pf*; ~
over переноси́ть *impf*, перене-
сти́ *pf*.

cart /kɑːt/ *n* теле́га; *vt* (*lug*) та-
щи́ть *impf*.

cartilage /'kɑːtɪlɪdʒ/ *n* хрящ.

carton /'kɑːt(ə)n/ *n* карто́нка.

cartoon /kɑː'tuːn/ *n* карикату́ра;
(*cin*) мультфи́льм. **cartoonist**
/-nɪst/ *n* карикатури́ст, ~ка.

cartridge /'kɑːtrɪdʒ/ *n* патро́н;
(*for printer*) ка́ртридж.

carve /kɑːv/ *vt* ре́зать *impf*
по+*dat*; (*in wood*) выреза́ть
impf, вы́резать *pf*; (*in stone*)
высека́ть *impf*, вы́сечь *pf*; (*slice*)
нареза́ть *impf*, наре́зать *pf*.
carving /'kɑːvɪŋ/ *n* резьба́; ~
knife нож для наре́зания
мя́са.

cascade /kæs'keɪd/ *n* каска́д; *vi*
па́дать *impf*.

case[1] /keɪs/ *n* (*instance*) слу́чай;
(*law*) де́ло; (*med*) больно́й *sb*;
(*gram*) паде́ж; **in ~** (в слу́чае)
е́сли; **in any ~** во вся́ком слу́-
чае; **in no ~** ни в ко́ем слу́чае;
just in ~ на вся́кий слу́чай.

case[2] /keɪs/ *n* (*box*) я́щик; (*suitcase*) чемода́н; (*small box*) футля́р;
(*cover*) на́лепень; (*display* ~)
витри́на.

cash /kæʃ/ *n* нали́чные *sb*;
(*money*) де́ньги *pl*; ~ **on delivery**
нало́женным платежо́м; ~
desk, register ка́сса; ~ **machine**
банкома́т; *vt*: ~ **a cheque** полу-
ча́ть *impf*, получи́ть *pf* де́ньги
по че́ку. **cashier** /kæ'ʃɪə(r)/ *n*
касси́р.

casing /'keɪsɪŋ/ *n* (*tech*) кожу́х.

casino /kə'siːnəʊ/ *n* казино́ *neut
indecl*.

cask /kɑːsk/ *n* бо́чка.

casket /'kɑːskɪt/ *n* шкату́лка.

casserole /'kæsərəʊl/ *n* (*pot*)
ла́тка; (*stew*) рагу́ *neut indecl*.

cassette /kə'set/ *n* кассе́та; ~ **recorder** кассе́тный магни-
тофо́н.

cassock /'kæsək/ *n* ря́са.

cast /kɑːst/ *vt* (*throw*) броса́ть
impf, бро́сить *pf*; (*shed*) сбра́-
сывать *impf*, сбро́сить *pf*;
(*theat*) распределя́ть *impf*, рас-
предели́ть *pf* ро́ли *+dat*;
(*found*) лить *impf*, с~ *pf*; ~ **off**
(*knitting*) спуска́ть *impf*, спу-
сти́ть *pf* пе́тли; (*naut*) отплы-
ва́ть *impf*, отплы́ть *pf*; ~ **on**
(*knitting*) набира́ть *impf*, на-
бра́ть *pf* пе́тли; *n* (*of mind etc.*)
склад; (*mould*) фо́рма;
(*moulded object*) слепо́к; (*med*)
ги́псовая повя́зка; (*theat*) дей-
ствующие ли́ца -(ц) *pl*.
castaway /'kɑːstəweɪ/ *n*
потерпе́вший *sb* кораблекру-
ше́ние. **cast iron** *n* чугу́н. **cast-
iron** *adj* чугу́нный. **cast-offs** *n
pl* ноше́ное пла́тье.

castanet /ˌkæstə'net/ *n* каста-
нье́та.

caste /kɑːst/ *n* ка́ста.

castigate /'kæstɪˌɡeɪt/ *vt* бичева́ть *impf*.

castle /'kɑːs(ə)l/ *n* за́мок; (*chess*)
ладья́.

castor /'kɑːstə(r)/ *n* (*wheel*)
ро́лик; ~ **sugar** са́харная
пу́дра.

castrate /kæ'streɪt/ *vt* кастри́ро-
вать *impf* & *pf*. **castration**
/-'streɪʃ(ə)n/ *n* кастра́ция.

casual /'kæʒʊəl/ *adj* (*chance*)
случа́йный; (*offhand*) небре́ж-
ный; (*clothes*) обыде́нный; (*unofficial*) неофициа́льный; (*informal*) лёгкий; (*labour*)
подённый; ~ **labourer**
подёнщик, -ица. **casualty**
/'kæʒʊəltɪ/ *n* (*wounded*) ра́не-

ный sb; (killed) убитый sb; pl потери (-рь) pl; ~ ward палата скорой помощи.

cat /kæt/ n кошка; (tom) кот; ~'s-eye (on road) (дорожный) рефлектор.

catalogue /'kætəˌlɒg/ n каталог; (price list) прейскурант; vt каталогизировать impf & pf.

catalyst /'kætəlıst/ n катализатор. catalytic /ˌkætə'lıtık/ adj каталитический.

catapult /'kætəˌpʌlt/ n (toy) рогатка; (hist, aeron) катапульта; vt & i катапультировать(ся) impf & pf.

cataract /'kætəˌrækt/ n (med) катаракта.

catarrh /kə'tɑ:(r)/ n катар.

catastrophe /kə'tæstrəfɪ/ n катастрофа. catastrophic /ˌkætə'strɒfɪk/ adj катастрофический.

catch /kætʃ/ vt (ball, fish, thief) ловить impf, поймать pf; (surprise) заставать impf, застать pf; (disease) заражаться impf, заразиться pf +instr; (be in time for) успевать impf, успеть pf на+acc; vt & i (snag) зацепляться(ся) impf, зацепиться pf (on за+acc); ~ on (become popular) прививаться impf, привиться pf; ~ up with догонять impf, догнать pf n (of fish) улов; (trick) уловка; (on door etc.) защёлка. catching /'kætʃɪŋ/ adj заразный. catchword n модное словечко. catchy /'kætʃɪ/ adj прилипчивый.

categorical /ˌkætɪ'gɒrɪk(ə)l/ adj категорический. category /'kætɪgərɪ/ n категория.

cater /'keɪtə(r)/ vi: ~ for поставлять impf, поставить pf провизию для+gen; (satisfy) удовлетворять impf, удовлетворить pf. caterer /'keɪtərə(r)/ n поставщик (провизии).

caterpillar /'kætəˌpɪlə(r)/ n гусеница.

cathedral /kə'θiːdr(ə)l/ n собор.

catheter /'kæθɪtə(r)/ n катетер.

Catholic /'kæθəlɪk/ adj католический; n католик, -ичка. Catholicism /kə'θɒlɪˌsɪz(ə)m/ n католичество.

cattle /'kæt(ə)l/ n скот.

Caucasus /'kɔːkəsəs/ n Кавказ.

cauldron /'kɔːldrən/ n котёл.

cauliflower /'kɒlɪˌflaʊə(r)/ n цветная капуста.

cause /kɔːz/ n причина, повод; (law etc.) дело; vt причинять impf, причинить pf; вызывать impf, вызвать pf; (induce) заставлять impf, заставить pf.

caustic /'kɔːstɪk/ adj едкий.

cauterize /'kɔːtəˌraɪz/ vt прижигать impf, прижечь pf.

caution /'kɔːʃ(ə)n/ n осторожность; (warning) предостережение; vt предостерегать impf, предостеречь pf. cautious /'kɔːʃəs/ adj осторожный. cautionary /'kɔːʃənərɪ/ adj предостерегающий.

cavalcade /ˌkævəl'keɪd/ n кавалькада. cavalier /ˌkævə'lɪə(r)/ adj бесцеремонный. cavalry /'kævəlrɪ/ n кавалерия.

cave /keɪv/ n пещера; vi: ~ in обваливаться impf, обвалиться pf; (yield) сдаваться impf, сдаться pf. caveman n пещерный человек. cavern /'kæv(ə)n/ n пещера. cavernous /'kævə(ə)nəs/ adj пещеристый.

caviare /'kævɪˌɑː(r)/ n икра.

cavity /'kævɪtɪ/ n впадина, полость; (in tooth) дупло.

cavort /kə'vɔːt/ vi скакать impf.

caw /kɔː/ vi каркать impf, кар-

кнуть *pf.*

CD *abbr (of compact disc)* компа́кт-ди́ск; ~ **player** проигрыватель *m* компа́кт-ди́сков.

cease /siːs/ *vt & i* прекраща́ть(ся) *impf*, прекрати́ть(ся) *pf*; *vt* переставать *impf*, переста́ть *pf* (+*inf*); ~**fire** прекраще́ние огня́. **ceaseless** /'siːslɪs/ *adj* непреста́нный.

cedar /'siːdə(r)/ *n* кедр.

cede /siːd/ *vt* уступа́ть *impf*, уступи́ть *pf.*

ceiling /'siːlɪŋ/ *n* потоло́к; (*fig*) максима́льный у́ровень *m*.

celebrate /'selɪˌbreɪt/ *vt & i* пра́здновать *impf*, от~ *pf*; (*extol*) прославля́ть *impf*, просла́вить *pf*. **celebrated** /-tɪd/ *adj* знамени́тый. **celebration** /-'breɪʃ(ə)n/ *n* пра́зднование. **celebrity** /sɪ'lebrɪtɪ/ *n* знамени́тость.

celery /'selərɪ/ *n* сельдере́й.

celestial /sɪ'lestɪəl/ *adj* небе́сный.

celibacy /'selɪbəsɪ/ *n* безбра́чие. **celibate** /'selɪbət/ *adj* холосто́й; *n* холостя́к.

cell /sel/ *n* (*prison*) ка́мера; (*biol*) кле́тка; ~ **phone** со́товый телефо́н.

cellar /'selə(r)/ *n* подва́л.

cello /'tʃeləʊ/ *n* виолонче́ль.

cellophane /'seləˌfeɪn/ *n* целлофа́н. **cellular** /'seljʊlə(r)/ *adj* кле́точный.

Celt /kelt/ *n* кельт. **Celtic** /'keltɪk/ *adj* ке́льтский.

cement /sɪ'ment/ *n* цеме́нт; *vt* цементи́ровать *impf*, за~ *pf.*

cemetery /'semɪtərɪ/ *n* кла́дбище.

censor /'sensə(r)/ *n* це́нзор; *vt* подверга́ть *impf*, подве́ргнуть *pf* цензу́ре. **censorious** /sen'sɔːrɪəs/ *adj* сверхкрити́ческий.

censorship /'sensəʃɪp/ *n* цензу́ра. **censure** /'senʃə(r)/ *n* порица́ние; *vt* порица́ть *impf.*

census /'sensəs/ *n* пе́репись.

cent /sent/ *n* цент; **per** ~ проце́нт.

centenary /sen'tiːnərɪ/ *n* столе́тие. **centennial** /-'tenɪəl/ *adj* столе́тний. **centigrade** /'sentɪˌɡreɪd/ *adj*: **10°** = 10° по Це́льсию. **centimetre** /'sentɪˌmiːtə(r)/ *n* сантиме́тр. **centipede** /'sentɪˌpiːd/ *n* сороконо́жка.

central /'sentr(ə)l/ *adj* центра́льный; ~ **heating** центра́льное отопле́ние. **centralization** /ˌsentrəlaɪ'zeɪʃ(ə)n/ *n* централиза́ция. **centralize** /'sentrəˌlaɪz/ *vt* централизова́ть *impf & pf.* **centre** /'sentə(r)/ *n* центр; середи́на; ~ **forward** центр нападе́ния; *vi & i*: ~ **on** сосредото́чивать(ся) *impf*, сосредото́чить(ся) *pf* на+*prep*. **centrifugal** /ˌsentrɪ'fjuːɡ(ə)l/ *adj* центробе́жный.

century /'sentʃərɪ/ *n* столе́тие, век.

ceramic /sɪ'ræmɪk/ *adj* керами́ческий. **ceramics** /-mɪks/ *n pl* кера́мика.

cereals /'stərɪəlz/ *n pl* хле́бные зла́ки *m pl*; **breakfast** ~ зерновые хло́пья (-ев) *pl.*

cerebral /'serɪbr(ə)l/ *adj* мозгово́й.

ceremonial /ˌserɪ'məʊnɪəl/ *adj* церемониа́льный; *n* церемониа́л. **ceremonious** /-nɪəs/ *adj* церемо́нный. **ceremony** /'serɪmənɪ/ *n* церемо́ния.

certain /'sɜːt(ə)n/ *adj* (*confident*) уве́рен (-нна); (*undoubted*) несомне́нный; (*unspecified*) изве́стный; (*inevitable*) ве́рный; **for** ~ наверняка́. **certainly** /-lɪ/ *adv* (*of course*) коне́чно, безус-

ло́вно; (*without doubt*) несомне́нно; ~ not! ни в ко́ем слу́чае. **certainty** /-tɪ/ *n* (*conviction*) уве́ренность; (*fact*) несомне́нный факт.

certificate /sə'tɪfɪkət/ *n* свиде́тельство; сертифика́т. **certify** /'sɜːtɪfaɪ/ *vt* удостоверя́ть *impf*, удостове́рить *pf*.

cervical /sɜː'vaɪk(ə)l/ *n* ше́йный. **cervix** /'sɜːvɪks/ *n* ше́йка ма́тки.

cessation /se'seɪʃ(ə)n/ *n* прекраще́ние.

cf. *abbr* ср., сравни́.

CFCs *abbr* (*of* **chlorofluorocarbons**) хлори́рованные фторуглеро́ды *m pl*.

chafe /tʃeɪf/ *vt* (*rub*) тере́ть *impf*; (*rub sore*) натира́ть *impf*, натере́ть *pf*.

chaff /tʃɑːf/ *n* (*husks*) мяки́на; (*straw*) се́чка.

chaffinch /'tʃæfɪntʃ/ *n* зя́блик.

chagrin /'ʃæɡrɪn/ *n* огорче́ние.

chain /tʃeɪn/ *n* цепь; ~ **reaction** цепна́я реа́кция; ~ **smoker** зая́длый кури́льщик.

chair /tʃeə(r)/ *n* стул, (*armchair*) кре́сло; (*univ*) ка́федра; *vt* (*preside*) председа́тельствовать *impf* на+*prep*. **chairman, -woman** *n* председа́тель *m*, -ница.

chalice /'tʃælɪs/ *n* ча́ша.

chalk /tʃɔːk/ *n* мел. **chalky** /'tʃɔːkɪ/ *adj* мелово́й.

challenge /'tʃælɪndʒ/ *n* (*summons*, *fig*) вы́зов; (*sentry's*) о́клик; (*law*) отво́д; *vt* вызыва́ть *impf*, вы́звать *pf*; (*sentry*) оклика́ть *impf*, окли́кнуть *pf*; (*law*) отводи́ть *impf*, отвести́ *pf*. **challenger** /-dʒə(r)/ *n* претенде́нт. **challenging** /-dʒɪŋ/ *adj* интригу́ющий.

chamber /'tʃeɪmbə(r)/ *n* (*cavity*)

ка́мера; (*hall*) зал; (*parl*) пала́та; *pl* (*law*) адвока́тская конто́ра, (*judge's*) кабине́т (судьи́); ~ **music** ка́мерная му́зыка; ~ **pot** ночно́й горшо́к. **chambermaid** *n* го́рничная *sb*.

chameleon /kə'miːliən/ *n* хамелео́н.

chamois /'ʃæmwɑː/ *n* (*animal*) се́рна; (~-*leather*) за́мша.

champagne /ʃæm'peɪn/ *n* шампа́нское *sb*.

champion /'tʃæmpiən/ *n* чемпио́н, ~ка; (*upholder*) побо́рник, -ица; *vt* боро́ться *impf* за +*acc*. **championship** *n* пе́рвенство, чемпиона́т.

chance /tʃɑːns/ *n* случа́йность; (*opportunity*) возмо́жность; (*favourable*) слу́чай; (*likelihood*) ша́нс (*usu pl*); **by** ~ случа́йно; *adj* случа́йный; *vi*: ~ **it** рискну́ть *pf*.

chancellery /'tʃɑːnsələri/ *n* канцеля́рия. **chancellor** /'tʃɑːnsələ(r)/ *n* ка́нцлер; (*univ*) ре́ктор; **C~ of the Exchequer** ка́нцлер казначе́йства.

chancy /'tʃɑːnsɪ/ *adj* риско́ванный.

chandelier /ʃændɪ'lɪə(r)/ *n* лю́стра.

change /tʃeɪndʒ/ *n* переме́на; измене́ние; (*of clothes etc.*) сме́на; (*money*) сда́ча; (*trains etc.*) переса́дка; **for a** ~ для разнообра́зия; *vt* и *i* меня́ть(ся) *impf*, изменя́ть(ся) *impf*, измени́ть(ся) *pf*; *vi* (*one's clothes*) переодева́ться *impf*, переоде́ться *pf*; (*trains etc.*) переса́живаться *impf*, пересе́сть *pf*; *vt* (*a baby*) перепелёнывать *impf*, перепелена́ть *pf*; (*money*) обме́нивать *impf*, обменя́ть *pf*; (*give ~ for*) разме́нивать *impf*, разменя́ть *pf*; ~ **into** превраща́ться *impf*,

превратиться *pf* в+*acc*; ~ over to переходить *impf*, перейти *pf* на+*acc*. **changeable** /'tʃeɪndʒəb(ə)l/ *adj* изменчивый.

channel /'tʃæn(ə)l/ *n* (water) пролив; (also TV) канал; *m* путь *m*; the (English) C~ Ла-Манш; *vt* (fig) направлять *impf*.

chant /tʃɑːnt/ *n* (eccl) песнопение; *vt* & *i* петь *impf*; (slogans) скандировать *impf* & *pf*.

chaos /'keɪɒs/ *n* хаос. **chaotic** /-'ɒtɪk/ *adj* хаотичный.

chap /tʃæp/ *n* (person) парень *m*.

chapel /'tʃæp(ə)l/ *n* часовня; (Catholic) капелла.

chaperone /'ʃæpərəʊn/ *n* компаньонка.

chaplain /'tʃæplɪn/ *n* капеллан.

chapped /tʃæpt/ *adj* потрескавшийся.

chapter /'tʃæptə(r)/ *n* глава.

char /tʃɑː(r)/ *vt* & *i* обугливать(ся) *impf*, обуглить(ся) *pf*.

character /'kærɪktə(r)/ *n* характер; (theat) действующее лицо; (letter) буква; (Chinese etc.) иероглиф. **characteristic** /ˌkærɪktə'rɪstɪk/ *adj* характерный; *n* свойство; (of person) черта характера. **characterize** /'kærɪktəraɪz/ *vt* характеризовать *impf* & *pf*.

charade /ʃə'rɑːd/ *n* шарада.

charcoal /'tʃɑːkəʊl/ *n* древесный уголь *m*.

charge /tʃɑːdʒ/ *n* (for gun; electr) заряд; (fee) плата; (person) питомец, -мица; (accusation) обвинение; (mil) атака; be in ~ of заведовать *impf* +*instr*; in the ~ of на попечении +*gen*; *vt* (gun; electr) заряжать *impf*, зарядить *pf*; (accuse) об-

винять *impf*, обвинить *pf* (with в+*prep*); (mil) атаковать *impf* & *pf*; *vi* бросаться *impf*, броситься *pf* в атаку; (for) брать *impf*, взять *pf* (за+*acc*); ~ to (the account of) записывать *impf*, записать *pf* на счёт+*gen*.

chariot /'tʃærɪət/ *n* колесница.

charisma /kə'rɪzmə/ *n* обаяние. **charismatic** /ˌkærɪz'mætɪk/ *adj* обаятельный.

charitable /'tʃærɪtəb(ə)l/ *adj* благотворительный; (kind, merciful) милосердный. **charity** /'tʃærɪtɪ/ *n* (kindness) милосердие; (organization) благотворительная организация.

charlatan /'ʃɑːlət(ə)n/ *n* шарлатан.

charm /tʃɑːm/ *n* очарование. прелесть; (spell) заговор; *pl* чары (чар) *pl*; (amulet) талисман; (trinket) брелок; *vt* очаровывать *impf*, очаровать *pf*. **charming** /-mɪŋ/ *adj* очаровательный, прелестный.

chart /tʃɑːt/ *n* (naut) морская карта; (table) график; *vt* наносить *impf*, нанести *pf* на график. **charter** /-tə(r)/ *n* (document) хартия; (statutes) устав; *vt* нанимать *impf*, нанять *pf*.

charwoman /'tʃɑːwʊmən/ *n* приходящая уборщица.

chase /tʃeɪs/ *vt* гоняться *indet*, гнаться *det* за+*instr*; *n* погоня; (hunting) охота.

chasm /'kæz(ə)m/ *n* (abyss) бездна.

chassis /'ʃæsɪ/ *n* шасси *neut indecl*.

chaste /tʃeɪst/ *adj* целомудренный.

chastise /tʃæs'taɪz/ *vt* карать *impf*, по~ *pf*.

chastity /'tʃæstɪtɪ/ *n* целому-

дрие.

chat /tʃæt/ *n* бесе́да; *vi* бесе́довать *impf*; **~ room** (*comput*) разде́л ча́та; **~ show** телевизио́нная бесе́да-интервью́ f.

chatter /'tʃætə(r)/ *n* болтовня́; *vi* болта́ть *impf*; (*teeth*) стуча́ть *impf*. **chatterbox** *n* болту́н. **chatty** /'tʃætɪ/ *adj* разгово́рчивый.

chauffeur /'ʃəʊfə(r)/ *n* шофёр.

chauvinism /'ʃəʊvɪ,nɪz(ə)m/ *n* шовини́зм. **chauvinist** /-nɪst/ *n* шовини́ст; *adj* шовинисти́ческий.

cheap /tʃi:p/ *adj* дешёвый. **cheapen** /'tʃi:pən/ *vt* (*fig*) опошля́ть *impf*, опо́шлить *pf*. **cheaply** /'tʃi:plɪ/ *adv* дёшево.

cheat /tʃi:t/ *vt* обма́нывать *impf*, обману́ть *pf*; *vi* плутова́ть *impf*, на~, с~ *pf*; *n* обма́нщик, -ица; плут.

check[1] /tʃek/ *n* контро́ль *m*, прове́рка; (*chess*) шах, **~mate** шах и мат; *vt* (*examine*) проверя́ть *impf*, прове́рить *pf*; контроли́ровать *impf*, про~ *pf*; (*restrain*) сде́рживать *impf*, сдержа́ть *pf*; **~ in** регистри́роваться *impf*, за~ *pf*; **~ out** выпи́сываться *impf*, вы́писаться *pf*; **~-out** ка́сса; **~up** осмо́тр.

check[2] /tʃek/ *n* (*pattern*) кле́тка. **check(ed)** /tʃekt/ *adj* кле́тчатый.

cheek /tʃi:k/ *n* щека́; (*impertinence*) на́глость. **cheeky** /'tʃi:kɪ/ *adj* на́глый.

cheep /tʃi:p/ *vi* пища́ть *impf*, пи́скнуть *pf*.

cheer /tʃɪə(r)/ *n* ободря́ющий во́зглас; **~s!** за (ва́ше) здоро́вье!; *vt* (*applaud*) приве́тствовать *impf* & *pf*; **~ up** ободря́ть(ся) *impf*, ободри́ть(ся) *pf*. **cheerful** /'tʃɪəfʊl/

adj весёлый. **cheerio** /,tʃɪərɪ'əʊ/ *int* пока́. **cheerless** /'tʃɪəlɪs/ *adj* уны́лый.

cheese /tʃi:z/ *n* сыр; **~-cake** ватру́шка.

cheetah /'tʃi:tə/ *n* гепа́рд.

chef /ʃef/ *n* (шеф-)по́вар.

chemical /'kemɪk(ə)l/ *adj* хими́ческий; *n* химика́т. **chemist** /'kemɪst/ *n* хи́мик; (*druggist*) апте́карь *m*; **~'s (shop)** апте́ка. **chemistry** /'kemɪstrɪ/ *n* хи́мия.

cheque /tʃek/ *n* чек; **~-book** че́ковая кни́жка.

cherish /'tʃerɪʃ/ *vt* (*foster*) леле́ять *impf*; (*hold dear*) дорожи́ть *impf* +*instr*; (*love*) не́жно люби́ть *impf*.

cherry /'tʃerɪ/ *n* ви́шня; *adj* вишнёвый.

cherub /'tʃerəb/ *n* херуви́м.

chess /tʃes/ *n* ша́хматы (-т) *pl*; **~-board** ша́хматная доска́; **~-men** ша́хматы (-т) *pl*.

chest /tʃest/ *n* сунду́к; (*anat*) грудь; **~ of drawers** комо́д.

chestnut /'tʃesnʌt/ *n* кашта́н; (*horse*) гнеда́я sb.

chew /tʃu:/ *vt* жева́ть *impf*. **chewing-gum** /'tʃu:ɪŋ gʌm/ *n* жева́тельная рези́нка.

chic /ʃi:k/ *adj* элега́нтный.

chick /tʃɪk/ *n* цыплёнок. **chicken** /'tʃɪkɪn/ *n* ку́рица; цыплёнок; *adj* трусли́вый; **~ out** тру́сить *impf*, с~ *pf*. **chicken-pox** /'tʃɪkɪn pɒks/ *n* ветря́нка.

chicory /'tʃɪkərɪ/ *n* цико́рий.

chief /tʃi:f/ *n* глава́ *m* & *f*; (*boss*) нача́льник; (*of tribe*) вождь *m*; *adj* гла́вный. **chiefly** /'tʃi:flɪ/ *adv* гла́вным о́бразом. **chieftain** /'tʃi:ft(ə)n/ *n* вождь *m*.

chiffon /'ʃɪfɒn/ *n* шифо́н.

child /tʃaɪld/ *n* ребёнок; **~-birth** ро́ды (-дов) *pl*. **childhood**

/ˈtʃaɪldhʊd/ n де́тство. **childish**
/ˈtʃaɪldɪʃ/ adj де́тский. **childless**
/ˈtʃaɪldlɪs/ adj безде́тный. **child-like** /ˈtʃaɪldlaɪk/ adj де́тский.
childrens' /ˈtʃaɪldr(ə)nz/ adj де́тский.

chili /ˈtʃɪlɪ/ n стручко́вый
пе́рец.

chill /tʃɪl/ n хо́лод; (ailment)
просту́да; vt охлажда́ть impf,
охлади́ть pf. **chilly** /ˈtʃɪlɪ/ adj
прохла́дный.

chime /tʃaɪm/ n (set of bells)
набо́р колоко́лов; pl (sound)
перезво́н; (of clock) бой; vt & i
(clock) бить impf, про~ pf; vi
(bell) звони́ть impf, по~ pf.

chimney /ˈtʃɪmnɪ/ n труба́;
~**sweep** трубочи́ст.

chimpanzee /ˌtʃɪmpænˈziː/ n
шимпанзе́ n indecl.

chin /tʃɪn/ n подборо́док.

china /ˈtʃaɪnə/ n фарфо́р.

China /ˈtʃaɪnə/ n Кита́й. **Chinese** /tʃaɪˈniːz/ n кита́ец,
-ая́нка; adj кита́йский.

chink¹ /tʃɪŋk/ n (sound) звон; vi
звене́ть impf, про~ pf.

chink² /tʃɪŋk/ n (crack) щель.

chintz /tʃɪnts/ n си́тец.

chip /tʃɪp/ vt & i отка́лывать(ся)
impf, отколо́ть(ся) pf; n (of
wood) ще́пка; (in games) фи́шка;
(in cul.) карто́фель-соло́мка
(collect); (electron) чип, микросхе́ма.

chiropodist /kɪˈrɒpədɪst/ n челове́к, занима́ющийся педикю́ром. **chiropody** /-ˈrɒpədɪ/ n
педикю́р.

chirp /tʃɜːp/ vi чири́кать impf.

chisel /ˈtʃɪz(ə)l/ n (wood) стаме́ска; (masonry) зуби́ло; vt
высека́ть impf, вы́сечь pf.

chit /tʃɪt/ n (note) запи́ска.

chivalrous /ˈʃɪvəlrəs/ adj ры́царский. **chivalry** /-rɪ/ n ры́цар-

ство.

chlorine /ˈklɔːriːn/ n хлор.
chlorophyll /ˈklɒrəfɪl/ n хлорофи́лл.

chock-full /ˈtʃɒkfʊl/ adj битко́м
наби́тый.

chocolate /ˈtʃɒkələt/ n шокола́д; (sweet) шокола́дная конфе́та; ~ **bar** шокола́дка.

choice /tʃɔɪs/ n вы́бор; adj отбо́рный.

choir /ˈkwaɪə(r)/ n хор m; ~**boy**
пе́вчий sb.

choke /tʃəʊk/ n (valve) дро́ссель
m; vi дави́ться impf, по~ pf;
(with anger etc.) задыха́ться
impf, задохну́ться pf (with
от+gen); vt (suffocate) души́ть
impf, за~ pf; (of plants) заглуша́ть, глуши́ть impf, заглуши́ть pf.

cholera /ˈkɒlərə/ n холе́ра.

cholesterol /kəˈlestərɒl/ n холестери́н.

choose /tʃuːz/ vt (select) выбира́ть impf, вы́брать pf; (decide)
реша́ть impf, реши́ть pf.
choosy /ˈtʃuːzɪ/ adj разбо́рчивый.

chop /tʃɒp/ vt (also ~ down) рубить impf, рубну́ть
pf; ~ **off** отруба́ть impf, отруби́ть pf; n (cul) отбивна́я котле́та.

chopper /ˈtʃɒpə(r)/ n топо́р.
choppy /ˈtʃɒpɪ/ adj бурли́вый.

chop-sticks /ˈtʃɒpstɪks/ n па́лочки f pl для еды.

choral /ˈkɔːr(ə)l/ adj хорово́й.
chorale /kɒˈrɑːl/ n хора́л.

chord /kɔːd/ n (mus) акко́рд.

chore /tʃɔː(r)/ n обя́занность.

choreographer /ˌkɒrɪˈɒɡrəfə(r)/
n хорео́граф. **choreography**
/-ɡrəfɪ/ n хореогра́фия.

chorister /ˈkɒrɪstə(r)/ n пе́вчий sb.

chortle /'tʃɔːt(ə)l/ *vi* фы́ркать *impf*, фы́ркнуть *pf*.

chorus /'kɔːrəs/ *n* хор; (*refrain*) припе́в.

christen /'krɪs(ə)n/ *vt* крести́ть *impf* & *pf*. **Christian** /'krɪstɪən/ *n* христиани́н, -а́нка; *adj* христиа́нский; ~ **name** и́мя *neut*. **Christianity** /ˌkrɪstɪ'ænɪtɪ/ *n* христиа́нство. **Christmas** /'krɪsməs/ *n* Рождество́; ~ **Day** пе́рвый день Рождества́; ~ **Eve** соче́льник; ~ **tree** ёлка.

chromatic /krə'mætɪk/ *adj* хромати́ческий. **chrome** /krəʊm/ *n* хром. **chromium** /'krəʊmɪəm/ *n* хром. **chromosome** /'krəʊməˌsəʊm/ *n* хромосо́ма.

chronic /'krɒnɪk/ *adj* хрони́ческий.

chronicle /'krɒnɪk(ə)l/ *n* хро́ника, ле́топись.

chronological /ˌkrɒnə'lɒdʒɪk(ə)l/ *adj* хронологи́ческий.

chrysalis /'krɪsəlɪs/ *n* ку́колка.

chrysanthemum /krɪ'sænθəməm/ *n* хризанте́ма.

chubby /'tʃʌbɪ/ *adj* пу́хлый.

chuck /tʃʌk/ *vt* броса́ть *impf*, бро́сить *pf*; ~ **out** вышиба́ть *impf*, вы́шибить *pf*.

chuckle /'tʃʌk(ə)l/ *vi* посме́иваться *impf*.

chum /tʃʌm/ *n* това́рищ.

chunk /tʃʌŋk/ *n* ломо́ть *m*.

church /tʃɜːtʃ/ *n* це́рковь. **churchyard** *n* кла́дбище.

churlish /'tʃɜːlɪʃ/ *adj* грубы́й.

churn /tʃɜːn/ *n* масло́бойка; *vt* сбива́ть *impf*, сбить *pf*; *vi* (*foam*) пе́ниться *impf*; ~ **out** выпека́ть *impf*, вы́печь *pf*; ~ **up** взбить *pf*.

chute /ʃuːt/ *n* жёлоб.

cider /'saɪdə(r)/ *n* сидр.

cigar /sɪ'gɑː(r)/ *n* сига́ра. **cigar-ette** /ˌsɪgə'ret/ *n* сигаре́та; папиро́са; ~ **lighter** зажига́лка.

cinder /'sɪndə(r)/ *n* шлак; *pl* зола́.

cine-camera /'sɪnɪˌkæmrə/ *n* киноаппара́т. **cinema** /'sɪnɪˌmɑː/ *n* кино́ *neut indecl*.

cinnamon /'sɪnəmən/ *n* кори́ца.

cipher /'saɪfə(r)/ *n* нуль *m*; (*code*) шифр.

circle /'sɜːk(ə)l/ *n* круг; (*theatre*) я́рус; *vi* кружи́ться *impf*; *vt* (*walking*) обходи́ть *impf*, обойти́ *pf*; (*flying*) облета́ть *impf*, облете́ть *pf*. **circuit** /'sɜːkɪt/ *n* кругооборо́т; объе́зд, обхо́д; (*electron*) схе́ма; (*electr*) цепь. **circuitous** /sɜː'kjuːɪtəs/ *adj* окру́жный. **circular** /'sɜːkjʊlə(r)/ *adj* кру́глый; (*moving in a circle*) круговой; *n* циркуля́р. **circulate** /'sɜːkjʊˌleɪt/ *vi* циркули́ровать *impf*; *vt* распространя́ть *impf*, распространи́ть *pf*. **circulation** /ˌsɜːkjʊ'leɪʃ(ə)n/ *n* (*air*) циркуля́ция; (*distribution*) распростране́ние; (*of newspaper*) тира́ж; (*med*) кровообраще́ние.

circumcise /'sɜːkəmˌsaɪz/ *vt* обреза́ть *impf*, обре́зать *pf*. **circumcision** /-'sɪʒ(ə)n/ *n* обреза́ние.

circumference /sɜː'kʌmfərəns/ *n* окру́жность.

circumspect /'sɜːkəmˌspekt/ *adj* осмотри́тельный.

circumstance /'sɜːkəmstəns/ *n* обстоя́тельство; **under the ~s** при да́нных обстоя́тельствах, в тако́м слу́чае; **under no ~** ни при каки́х обстоя́тельствах, ни в ко́ем слу́чае.

circumvent /ˌsɜːkəm'vent/ *vt* обходи́ть *impf*, обойти́ *pf*.

circus /'sɜːkəs/ *n* цирк.

cirrhosis /sɪ'rəʊsɪs/ *n* цирро́з.

CIS abbr (of **Commonwealth of Independent States**) СНГ.

cistern /'sɪst(ə)n/ n бачо́к.

citadel /'sɪtəd(ə)l/ n цитаде́ль.

cito /saɪt/ vt ссыла́ться impf, со-сла́ться pf на+acc.

citizen /'sɪtɪz(ə)n/ n граждани́н, -а́нка. **citizenship** /'sɪtɪz(ə)nʃɪp/ n гражда́нство.

citrus /'sɪtrəs/ n ци́трус; adj ци́трусовый.

city /'sɪtɪ/ n го́род.

civic /'sɪvɪk/ adj гражда́нский. **civil** /-v(ə)l/ adj гражда́нский; (polite) ве́жливый; ~ **engineer** гражда́нский инжене́р; ~-**engineering** гражда́нское строи́тельство; C~ **Servant** госуда́рственный служащий sb; чино́вник; C~ **Service** госуда́рственная слу́жба. **civilian** /sɪ'vɪlɪən/ n шта́тский sb; adj шта́тский. **civility** /sɪ'vɪlɪtɪ/ n ве́жливость. **civilization** /ˌsɪvɪlaɪ'zeɪʃ(ə)n/ n цивилиза́ция. **civilize** /'sɪvɪlaɪz/ vt цивилизова́ть impf & pf. **civilized** /'sɪvɪlaɪzd/ adj цивилизо́ванный.

clad /klæd/ adj оде́тый.

claim /kleɪm/ n (demand) тре́бование, притяза́ние; (assertion) утвержде́ние; vt (demand) тре́бовать impf +gen; (assert) утвержда́ть impf, утверди́ть pf. **claimant** /'kleɪmənt/ n прете́ндент.

clairvoyant /kleə'vɔɪənt/ n ясно-ви́дец, -дица; adj яснови́дящий.

clam /klæm/ n моллю́ск; vi: ~ **up** отка́зываться impf, отка-за́ться pf разгова́ривать.

clamber /'klæmbə(r)/ vi кара́б-каться impf, вс-~ pf.

clammy /'klæmɪ/ adj вла́жный.

clamour /'klæmə(r)/ n шум; vi: ~

for шу́мно тре́бовать impf, по-~ pf +gen.

clamp /klæmp/ n зажи́м; vt скрепля́ть impf, скрепи́ть pf; ~ **down on** прижа́ть pf.

clan /klæn/ n клан.

clandestine /klæn'destɪn/ adj та́йный.

clang, clank /klæŋ, klæŋk/ n лязг; vt & i ля́згать impf, ля́зг-нуть pf (+instr).

clap /klæp/ vt & i хло́пать impf, хло́пнуть pf +dat; n хлопо́к; (thunder) уда́р.

claret /'klærət/ n бордо́ neut indecl.

clarification /ˌklærɪfɪ'keɪʃ(ə)n/ n (explanation) разъясне́ние. **clarify** /'klærɪfaɪ/ vt разъясня́ть impf, разъясни́ть pf.

clarinet /klærɪ'net/ n кларне́т.

clarity /'klærɪtɪ/ n я́сность.

clash /klæʃ/ n (conflict) столкно-ве́ние; (disharmony) дисгармо́-ния; vi ста́лкиваться impf, столкну́ться pf; (coincide) совпада́ть impf, совпа́сть pf; не гармони́ровать impf.

clasp /klɑːsp/ n застёжка; (embrace) объя́тие; vt обхва́ты-вать impf, обхвати́ть pf; ~ **one's hands** сплести́ pf па́льцы рук.

class /klɑːs/ n класс; ~-**room** класс; vt классифици́ровать impf & pf.

classic /'klæsɪk/ adj класси́че-ский; n кла́ссик; pl (literature) кла́ссика. (Latin and Greek) класси́ческие языки́ m pl. **classical** /-k(ə)l/ adj класси́ческий.

classification /ˌklæsɪfɪ'keɪʃ(ə)n/ n классифика́ция. **classified** /'klæsɪfaɪd/ adj засекре́ченный. **classify** /'klæsɪfaɪ/ vt классифи-ци́ровать impf & pf.

classy /'klɑːsɪ/ adj кла́ссный.

clatter /'klætə(r)/ n стук; vi стуча́ть impf, по~ pf.

clause /klɔːz/ n статья́; (gram) предложе́ние.

claustrophobia /ˌklɔːstrə'fəʊbɪə/ n клаустрофо́бия.

claw /klɔː/ n ко́готь; vt цара́пать impf когтя́ми.

clay /kleɪ/ n гли́на; adj гли́няный.

clean /kliːn/ adj чи́стый; adv (fully) соверше́нно; ~-**shaven** гла́дко вы́бритый; vt чи́стить impf, вы~, по~ pf. **cleaner** /'kliːnə(r)/ n убо́рщик, -ица. **cleaner's** /'kliːnəz/ n хими́чистка. **clean(li)ness** /'klenlɪnɪs/ n чистота́. **cleanse** /klenz/ vt очища́ть impf, очи́стить pf.

clear /klɪə(r)/ adj я́сный; (transparent) прозра́чный; (distinct) отчётливый; (free) свобо́дный (**of** от+gen); (pure) чи́стый; vt & i очища́ть(ся) impf, очи́стить(ся) pf; vt (jump over) перепры́гивать impf, перепры́гнуть pf; (acquit) опра́вдывать impf, оправда́ть pf; ~ **away** убира́ть impf, убра́ть pf со стола́; ~ **off** (go away) убира́ться impf, убра́ться pf; ~ **out** (vt) вычища́ть impf, вы́чистить pf; (vi) (make off) убира́ться impf, убра́ться pf; ~ **up** (tidy away) убира́ть impf, убра́ть pf; (weather) проясня́ться impf, проясни́ться pf; (explain) выясня́ть impf, вы́яснить pf. **clearance** /'klɪərəns/ n расчи́стка; (permission) разреше́ние. **clearing** /'klɪərɪŋ/ n (glade) поля́на. **clearly** /'klɪəlɪ/ adv я́сно.

cleavage /'kliːvɪdʒ/ n разре́з груди́.

clef /klef/ n (mus) ключ.

cleft /kleft/ n тре́щина.

clemency /'klemənsɪ/ n милосе́рдие.

clench /klentʃ/ vt (fist) сжима́ть impf, сжать pf; (teeth) сти́скивать impf, сти́снуть pf.

clergy /'klɜːdʒɪ/ n духове́нство. **clergyman** n свяще́нник. **clerical** /'klerɪk(ə)l/ adj (eccl) духо́вный; (of clerk) канцеля́рский.

clerk /klɑːk/ n конто́рский слу́жащий sb.

clever /'klevə(r)/ adj у́мный. **cleverness** /-nɪs/ n уме́ние.

cliche /'kliːʃeɪ/ n кли́ше neut indecl.

click /klɪk/ vt щёлкать impf, щёлкнуть pf +instr.

client /'klaɪənt/ n клие́нт. **clientele** /ˌkliːɒn'tel/ n клиенту́ра.

cliff /klɪf/ n утёс.

climate /'klaɪmɪt/ n кли́мат. **climatic** /'mætɪk/ adj климати́ческий.

climax /'klaɪmæks/ n кульмина́ция.

climb /klaɪm/ vt & i ла́зить indet, лезть det на+acc; влеза́ть impf, влезть pf на+acc; поднима́ться impf, подня́ться pf на+acc; ~ **down** (tree) слезть pf (c+gen); (mountain) спуска́ться impf, спусти́ться pf (c+gen); (give in) отступа́ть impf, отступи́ть pf; n подъём. **climber** /-m(ə)(r)/ n альпини́ст, ~ка; (plant) вью́щееся расте́ние. **climbing** /-mɪŋ/ n альпини́зм.

clinch /klɪntʃ/ vt: ~ **a deal** закрепи́ть pf сде́лку.

cling /klɪŋ/ vi (stick) прилипа́ть impf, прили́пнуть pf (**to** к+dat); (grasp) цепля́ться impf, (**to** за+acc).

clinic /'klɪnɪk/ n кли́ника. **clinical** /-k(ə)l/ adj клини́ческий.

clink /klɪŋk/ vt & i звене́ть impf,

про~ *pf* (+*instr*); ~ **glasses** чо́каться *impf*, чо́кнуться *pf*; *n* звон.

clip[1] /klɪp/ *n* скре́пка; зажи́м; *vt* скрепля́ть *impf*, скрепи́ть *pf*.

clip[2] /klɪp/ *vt* (*cut*) подстрига́ть *impf*, подстри́чь *pf*. **clippers** /-pəz/ *n pl* но́жницы *f pl*. **clipping** /-pɪŋ/ *n* (*extract*) вы́резка.

clique /kliːk/ *n* кли́ка.

cloak /kləʊk/ *n* плащ. **cloakroom** *n* гардеро́б; (*lavatory*) убо́рная *sb*.

clock /klɒk/ *n* часы́ *m pl*; ~**wise** /-waɪz/ по часово́й стре́лке; ~**work** часово́й механи́зм; *vt*: ~ **in, out** отмеча́ться *impf*, отме́титься *pf* приходя́ на рабо́ту/уходя́ с рабо́ты.

clod /klɒd/ *n* ком.

clog /klɒg/ *vt*: ~ **up** засоря́ть *impf*, засори́ть *pf*.

cloister /ˈklɔɪstə(r)/ *n* арка́да.

clone /kləʊn/ *n* клон.

close *adj* /kləʊs/ (*near*) бли́зкий; (*stuffy*) ду́шный; *vt & i* /kləʊz/ (*also* ~ **down**) закрыва́ть(ся) *impf*, закры́ть(ся) *pf*; (*conclude*) зака́нчивать *impf*, зако́нчить *pf*; *adv* бли́зко (*to* от+*gen*). **closed** /kləʊzd/ *adj* закры́тый. **closet** /ˈklɒzɪt/ *n* (*stennoi*) шкаф. **close-up** *n* фотогра́фия сня́тая кру́пным пла́ном. **closing** /ˈkləʊzɪŋ/ *n* закры́тие; *adj* заключи́тельный. **closure** /ˈkləʊʒə(r)/ *n* закры́тие.

clot /klɒt/ *n* сгу́сток; *vi* сгуща́ться *impf*, сгусти́ться *pf*.

cloth /klɒθ/ *n* ткань; (*duster*) тря́пка; (*table-*~) ска́терть.

clothe /kləʊð/ *vt* одева́ть *impf*, оде́ть (*in* +*instr*, в+*acc*) *pf*. **clothes** /kləʊðz/ *n pl* оде́жда, пла́тье.

cloud /klaʊd/ *n* о́блако; (*rain* ~) ту́ча; *vt* затемня́ть *impf*, за-

темни́ть *pf*; омрача́ть *impf*, омрачи́ть *pf*; ~ **over** покрыва́ться *impf*, покры́ться *pf* облака́ми, ту́чами. **cloudy** /-dɪ/ *adj* о́блачный; (*liquid*) му́тный.

clout /klaʊt/ *vt* ударя́ть *impf*, уда́рить *pf*; *n* затре́щина; (*fig*) влия́ние.

clove /kləʊv/ *n* гвозди́ка; (*of garlic*) зубо́к.

cloven /ˈkləʊv(ə)n/ *adj* раздвоённый.

clover /ˈkləʊvə(r)/ *n* кле́вер.

clown /klaʊn/ *n* кло́ун.

club /klʌb/ *n* (*stick*) дуби́нка; *pl* (*cards*) тре́фы (треф) *pl*; (*association*) клуб; *vt* колоти́ть *impf*, по~ *pf* дуби́нкой; *vi*: ~ **together** скла́дываться *impf*, сложи́ться *pf*.

cluck /klʌk/ *vi* куда́хтать *impf*.

clue /kluː/ *n* (*evidence*) ули́ка; (*to puzzle*) ключ; (*hint*) намёк.

clump /klʌmp/ *n* гру́ппа.

clumsiness /ˈklʌmzɪnɪs/ *n* неуклю́жесть. **clumsy** /ˈklʌmzɪ/ *adj* неуклю́жий.

cluster /ˈklʌstə(r)/ *n* гру́ппа; *vi* собира́ться *impf*, собра́ться *pf* гру́ппами.

clutch /klʌtʃ/ *n* (*grasp*) хва́тка; ко́гти *m pl*; (*tech*) сцепле́ние; *vt* зажима́ть *impf*, зажа́ть *pf*; *vi*: ~ **at** хвата́ться *impf*, хвати́ться *pf* за+*acc*.

clutter /ˈklʌtə(r)/ *n* беспоря́док; *vt* загроможда́ть *impf*, загромозди́ть *pf*.

c/o *abbr* (*of care of*) по а́дресу +*gen*; че́рез+*acc*.

coach /kəʊtʃ/ *n* (*horse-drawn*) каре́та; (*rly*) ваго́н; (*bus*) авто́бус; (*tutor*) репети́тор; (*sport*) тре́нер; *vt* репети́ровать *impf*, тренирова́ть *impf*, на~ *pf*.

coagulate /kəʊˈægjʊˌleɪt/ *vi* сгу-

щаться *impf*, сгуститься *pf*.

coal /kəʊl/ *n* у́голь *m*; **~mine** у́гольная ша́хта.

coalition /ˌkəʊəˈlɪʃ(ə)n/ *n* коали́ция.

coarse /kɔːs/ *adj* грубы́й.

coast /kəʊst/ *n* побере́жье, бе́рег; **~ guard** берегова́я охра́на; *vi* (*move without power*) дви́гаться *impf*, дви́нуться *pf* по ине́рции. **coastal** /-t(ə)l/ *adj* берегово́й, прибре́жный.

coat /kəʊt/ *n* пальто́ *neut indecl*; (*layer*) слой; (*animal*) шерсть, мех; **~ of arms** герб; *vt* покрыва́ть *impf*, покры́ть *pf*.

coax /kəʊks/ *vt* угова́ривать *impf*, уговори́ть *pf*.

cob /kɒb/ *n* (*corn-*~) поча́ток кукуру́зы.

cobble /ˈkɒb(ə)l/ *n* булы́жник (*also collect*). **cobbled** /-b(ə)ld/ *adj* булы́жный.

cobbler /ˈkɒblə(r)/ *n* сапо́жник.

cobweb /ˈkɒbweb/ *n* паути́на.

Coca-Cola /ˌkəʊkəˈkəʊlə/ *n* (*propr*) ко́ка-ко́ла.

cocaine /kəˈkeɪn/ *n* кокаи́н.

cock /kɒk/ *n* (*bird*) пету́х; (*tap*) кран; (*of gun*) куро́к; *vt* (*gun*) взводи́ть *impf*, взвести́ *pf* куро́к+*gen*.

cockerel /ˈkɒkər(ə)l/ *n* петушо́к.

cockle /ˈkɒk(ə)l/ *n* серде́цеви́дка.

cockpit /ˈkɒkpɪt/ *n* (*aeron*) каби́на.

cockroach /ˈkɒkrəʊtʃ/ *n* тарака́н.

cocktail /ˈkɒkteɪl/ *n* кокте́йль *m*.

cocky /ˈkɒki/ *adj* чва́нный.

cocoa /ˈkəʊkəʊ/ *n* кака́о *neut indecl*.

coco(a)nut /ˈkəʊkənʌt/ *n* коко́с.

cocoon /kəˈkuːn/ *n* ко́кон.

cod /kɒd/ *n* треска́.

code /kəʊd/ *n* (*of laws*) ко́декс; (*cipher*) код; *vt* шифрова́ть *impf*, за~ *pf*. **codify** /ˈkəʊdɪfaɪ/ *vt* кодифици́ровать *impf & pf*.

co-education /ˌkəʊedjuˈkeɪʃ(ə)n/ *n* совме́стное обуче́ние.

coefficient /ˌkəʊɪˈfɪʃ(ə)nt/ *n* коэффицие́нт.

coerce /kəʊˈɜːs/ *vt* принужда́ть *impf*, прину́дить *pf*. **coercion** /kəʊˈɜːʃ(ə)n/ *n* принужде́ние.

coexist /ˌkəʊɪɡˈzɪst/ *vi* сосуществова́ть *impf*. **coexistence** /-ˈzɪstəns/ *n* сосуществова́ние.

coffee /ˈkɒfi/ *n* ко́фе *m indecl*; **~mill** *n* кофе́йница; **~pot** *n* кофе́йник.

coffer /ˈkɒfə(r)/ *n pl* казна́.

coffin /ˈkɒfɪn/ *n* гроб.

cog /kɒɡ/ *n* зубе́ц. **cogwheel** *n* зубча́тое колесо́.

cogent /ˈkəʊdʒ(ə)nt/ *adj* убеди́тельный.

cohabit /kəʊˈhæbɪt/ *vi* сожи́тельствовать *impf*.

coherent /kəʊˈhɪərənt/ *adj* свя́зный. **cohesion** /kəʊˈhiːʒ(ə)n/ *n* сплочённость. **cohesive** /kəʊˈhiːsɪv/ *adj* сплочённый.

coil /kɔɪl/ *vt & i* свёртывать(ся) *impf*, сверну́ть(ся) *pf* кольцо́м; *n* кольцо́; (*electr*) кату́шка.

coin /kɔɪn/ *n* моне́та; *vt* чека́нить *impf*, от~ *pf*.

coincide /ˌkəʊɪnˈsaɪd/ *vi* совпада́ть *impf*, совпа́сть *pf*. **coincidence** /kəʊˈɪnsɪdəns/ *n* совпаде́ние. **coincidental** /kəʊˌɪnsɪˈdent(ə)l/ *adj* случа́йный.

coke /kəʊk/ *n* кокс.

colander /ˈkʌləndə(r)/ *n* дуршла́г.

cold /kəʊld/ *n* хо́лод; (*med*) просту́да, на́сморк; *adj* холо́дный; **~-blooded** *adj* жесто́кий; (*zool*)

холоднокро́вный.

colic /'kɒlık/ n ко́лики f pl.

collaborate /kə'læbə,reɪt/ vi сотру́дничать pf. **collaboration** /kə,læbə'reɪʃ(ə)n/ n сотру́дничество. **collaborator** /kə'læbə ,reɪtə(r)/ n сотру́дник, -ица; (traitor) коллаборациони́ст, -и́стка.

collapse /kə'læps/ vi ру́хнуть pf; n паде́ние; круше́ние.

collar /'kɒlə(r)/ n воротни́к; (dog's) оше́йник; ~**bone** ключи́ца.

colleague /'kɒli:g/ n колле́га m & f.

collect /kə'lekt/ vt собира́ть impf, собра́ть pf; (as hobby) коллекциони́ровать impf; (fetch) забира́ть impf, забра́ть pf. **collected** /-'lektıd/ adj (calm) со́бранный; ~ **works** собра́ние сочине́ний. **collection** /-'lekʃ(ə)n/ n (stamps etc.) колле́кция; (church etc.) сбор; (post) вы́емка. **collective** /-'lektıv/ n коллекти́в; adj коллекти́вный; ~ **farm** колхо́з; ~ **noun** собира́тельное существи́тельное sb. **collectivization** /kə,lektıvaɪ'zeɪʃ(ə)n/ n коллективиза́ция. **collector** /-'lektə(r)/ n сбо́рщик; коллекционе́р.

college /'kɒlıdʒ/ n колле́дж, учи́лище.

collide /kə'laɪd/ vi ста́лкиваться impf, столкну́ться pf. **collision** /-'lıʒ(ə)n/ n столкнове́ние.

colliery /'kɒlıərı/ n каменноуго́льная ша́хта.

colloquial /kə'ləʊkwıəl/ adj разгово́рный. **colloquialism** /-,lız(ə)m/ n разгово́рное выраже́ние.

collusion /kə'lu:ʒ(ə)n/ n та́йный сго́вор.

colon[1] /'kəʊlən/ n (anat) то́лстая кишка́.

colon[2] /'kəʊlən/ n (gram) двоето́чие.

colonel /'kɜ:n(ə)l/ n полко́вник.

colonial /kə'ləʊnıəl/ adj колониа́льный. **colonialism** /-,lız(ə)m/ n колониали́зм. **colonize** /'kɒlə,naɪz/ vt колонизова́ть impf & pf. **colony** /'kɒlənı/ n коло́ния.

colossal /kə'lɒs(ə)l/ adj колосса́льный.

colour /'kʌlə(r)/ n цвет, кра́ска; (pl) (flag) зна́мя neut; ~**blind** страда́ющий дальтони́змом; ~ **film** цветна́я плёнка; vt раскра́шивать impf, раскра́сить pf; vi красне́ть impf, по~ pf. **coloured** /-ləd/ adj цветно́й. **colourful** /-fʊl/ adj я́ркий. **colourless** /-lıs/ adj бесцве́тный.

colt /kəʊlt/ n жеребёнок.

column /'kɒləm/ n (archit, mil) коло́нна; (of smoke etc.) столб; (of print) столбе́ц. **columnist** /'kɒləmnıst/ n журнали́ст.

coma /'kəʊmə/ n ко́ма.

comb /kəʊm/ n гребёнка; vt причёсывать impf, причеса́ть pf.

combat /'kɒmbæt/ n бой; vt боро́ться impf c+instr, про́тив+gen.

combination /,kɒmbı'neɪʃ(ə)n/ n сочета́ние; комбина́ция. **combine** /'kɒmbaın/ n комбина́т; (~-harvester) комба́йн; vt & i /kəm'baın/ совмеща́ть(ся) impf, совмести́ть(ся) pf. **combined** /kəm'baınd/ adj совме́стный.

combustion /kəm'bʌstʃ(ə)n/ n горе́ние.

come /kʌm/ vi (on foot) приходи́ть impf, прийти́ pf; (by transport) приезжа́ть impf, прие́хать pf; ~ **about** случа́ться

impf, случи́ться *pf*; ~ **across** случа́йно наталкиваться *impf*, натолкну́ться *pf* на+*acc*; ~ **back** возвраща́ться *impf*, возврати́ться *pf*; ~ **in** входи́ть *impf*, войти́ *pf*; ~ **out** выходи́ть *impf*, вы́йти *pf*; ~ **round** (*revive*) приходи́ть *impf*, прийти́ *pf* в себя́; (*visit*) заходи́ть *impf*, зайти́ *pf*; (*agree*) соглаша́ться *impf*, согласи́ться *pf*; ~ **up to** (*approach*) подходи́ть *impf*, подойти́ *pf* к+*dat*; (*reach*) доходи́ть *impf*, дойти́ *pf* до+*gen*. **come-back** *n* возвраще́ние. **come-down** *n* униже́ние.

comedian /kə'mi:diən/ *n* коме-диа́нт. **comedy** /'kɒmidi/ *n* коме́дия.

comet /'kɒmit/ *n* коме́та.

comfort /'kʌmfət/ *n* комфо́рт; (*convenience*) удо́бство; (*consolation*) утеше́ние; *vt* утеша́ть *impf*, уте́шить *pf*. **comfortable** /'kʌmftəb(ə)l/ *adj* удо́бный.

comic /'kɒmik/ *adj* коми́ческий; *n* ко́мик; (*magazine*) ко́микс. **comical** /-k(ə)l/ *adj* смешно́й.

coming /'kʌmiŋ/ *adj* сле́дующий.

comma /'kɒmə/ *n* запята́я *sb*.

command /kə'mɑːnd/ *n* (*order*) прика́з; (*order, authority*) кома́нда; **have** ~ **of** (*master*) владе́ть *impf* +*instr*; *vt* прика́зывать *impf*, приказа́ть *pf* +*dat*; ~ *pf* +*instr*. **commandant** /ˌkɒmən'dænt/ *n* комен-да́нт. **commandeer** /ˌkɒmən'dɪə(r)/ *vt* реквизи́ровать *impf* & *pf*. **commander** /kə'mɑːndə(r)/ *n* команди́р; ~**in-chief** главнокома́ндующий *sb*. **commandment** /kə'mɑːndmənt/ *n* за́поведь. **commando** /kə'mɑːndəʊ/ *n* деса́нтник.

commemorate /kə'meməˌreɪt/ *vt* ознамено́вывать *impf*, ознамено́вать *pf*. **commemoration** /kəˌmemə'reɪʃ(ə)n/ *n* ознаменова́ние. **commemorative** /kə'memərətɪv/ *adj* па́мятный.

commence /kə'mens/ *vt* & *i* начина́ть(ся) *impf*, нача́ть(ся) *pf*. **commencement** /-mənt/ *n* нача́ло.

commend /kə'mend/ *vt* хвали́ть *impf*, по~ *pf*; (*recommend*) рекомендова́ть *impf* & *pf*. **commendable** /-dəb)l/ *adj* похва́льный. **commendation** /ˌkɒmen'deɪʃ(ə)n/ *n* похвала́.

commensurate /kə'menʃərət/ *adj* соразме́рный.

comment /'kɒment/ *n* заме́чание; *vi* де́лать *impf*, с~ *pf* замеча́ния; ~ **on** комменти́ровать *impf* & *pf*, про~ *pf*. **commentary** /-məntəri/ *n* коммента́рий. **commentator** /-ˌteɪtə(r)/ *n* комментатор.

commerce /'kɒmɜːs/ *n* комме́рция. **commercial** /kə'mɜːʃ(ə)l/ *adj* торго́вый; *n* рекла́ма.

commiserate /kə'mɪzəreɪt/ *vi*: ~ **with** соболе́зновать *impf* +*dat*. **commiseration** /-'reɪʃ(ə)n/ *n* соболе́знование.

commission /kə'mɪʃ(ə)n/ *n* (*order for work*) зака́з; (*agent's fee*) комиссио́нные *sb*; (*of inquiry etc.*) коми́ссия; (*mil*) офице́рское зва́ние; *vt* зака́зывать *impf*, заказа́ть *pf*. **commissionaire** /kəˌmɪʃ(ə)'neə(r)/ *n* швейца́р. **commissioner** /kə'mɪʃənə(r)/ *n* комисса́р.

commit /kə'mɪt/ *vt* соверша́ть *impf*, соверши́ть *pf*; ~ **o.s.** обя́зываться *impf*, обяза́ться *pf*. **commitment** /-mənt/ *n* обяза́тельство.

committee /kə'mɪtɪ/ *n* комитéт.

commodity /kə'mɒdɪtɪ/ *n* товáр.

commodore /'kɒmədɔː(r)/ *n* (*officer*) коммодóр.

common /'kɒmən/ *adj* óбщий; (*ordinary*) простóй; *n* общинная земля; ~ **sense** здрáвый смысл. **commonly** /-lɪ/ *adv* обычно. **commonplace** *adj* банáльный. **commonwealth** *n* содрýжество.

commotion /kə'məʊʃ(ə)n/ *n* сумáтоха.

communal /'kɒmjʊn(ə)l/ *adj* общинный, коммунáльный. **commune** *n* /'kɒmjuːn/ коммýна; *vi* /kə'mjuːn/ общáться *impf*.

communicate /kə'mjuːnɪˌkeɪt/ *vt* передавáть *impf*, передáть *pf*; сообщáть *impf*, сообщить *pf*. **communication** /-'keɪʃ(ə)n/ *n* сообщéние; связь. **communicative** /kə'mjuːnɪkətɪv/ *adj* разговóрчивый.

communion /kə'mjuːnɪən/ *n* (*eccl*) причáстие.

communiqué /kə'mjuːnɪkeɪ/ *n* коммюникé *neut indecl*.

Communism /'kɒmjʊˌnɪz(ə)m/ *n* коммунизм. **Communist** /'kɒmjʊnɪst/ *n* коммунист, ~ка; *adj* коммунистический.

community /kə'mjuːnɪtɪ/ *n* общинá.

commute /kə'mjuːt/ *vt* заменять *impf*, заменить *pf*; (*travel*) добирáться *impf*, добрáться *pf* трáнспортом. **commuter** /-tə(r)/ *n* регулярный пассажир.

compact¹ /'kɒmpækt/ *n* (*agreement*) соглашéние.

compact² /kəm'pækt/ *adj* компáктный; ~ **disc** /'kɒmpækt/ *n* компáкт-диск. **compact** /'kɒmpækt/ *n* пýдреница.

companion /kəm'pænjən/ *n* товáрищ; (*handbook*) спрáвочник. **companionable** /-nəb(ə)l/ *adj* общительный. **companionship** /-ʃɪp/ *n* дрýжеское общéние. **company** /'kʌmpənɪ/ *n* óбщество, (*also firm*) компáния; (*theat*) трýппа; (*mil*) рóта.

comparable /'kɒmpərəb(ə)l/ *adj* сравнимый. **comparative** /kəm'pærətɪv/ *adj* сравнительный; *n* сравнительная стéпень. **compare** /kəm'peə(r)/ *vt & i* сравнивать(ся) *impf*, сравнить(ся) *pf* (**to, with** *c+instr*). **comparison** /kəm'pærɪs(ə)n/ *n* сравнéние.

compartment /kəm'pɑːtmənt/ *n* отделéние; (*rly*) купé *neut indecl*.

compass /'kʌmpəs/ *n* кóмпас; *pl* циркуль *m*.

compassion /kəm'pæʃ(ə)n/ *n* сострадáние. **compassionate** /-nət/ *adj* сострадáтельный.

compatibility /kəm,pætə'bɪlɪtɪ/ *n* совместимость. **compatible** /kəm'pætəb(ə)l/ *adj* совместимый.

compatriot /kəm'pætrɪət/ *n* соотéчественник, -ница.

compel /kəm'pel/ *vt* заставлять *impf*, застáвить *pf*.

compensate /'kɒmpenˌseɪt/ *vt* компенсировать *impf & pf* (**for** за+*acc*). **compensation** /-'seɪʃ(ə)n/ *n* компенсáция.

compete /kəm'piːt/ *vi* конкурировать *impf*, соревновáться *impf*.

competence /'kɒmpɪtəns/ *n* компетéнтность. **competent** /-tənt/ *adj* компетéнтный.

competition /ˌkɒmpə'tɪʃ(ə)n/ *n* (*contest*) соревновáние, состязáние; (*rivalry*) конкурéнция. **competitive** /kəm'petɪtɪv/ *adj*

(*comm*) конкурентоспосо́бный. **competitor** /kəm'petɪtə(r)/ *n* конкуре́нт, ~ка.

compilation /ˌkɒmpɪ'leɪʃ(ə)n/ *n* (*result*) компиля́ция; (*act*) составле́ние. **compile** /kəm'paɪl/ *vt* составля́ть *impf*, соста́вить *pf*. **compiler** /kəm'paɪlə(r)/ *n* состави́тель *m*, ~ница.

complacency /kəm'pleɪsənsɪ/ *n* самодово́льство. **complacent** /kəm'pleɪs(ə)nt/ *adj* самодово́льный.

complain /kəm'pleɪn/ *vi* жа́ловаться *impf*, по~ *pf*. **complaint** /-'pleɪnt/ *n* жа́лоба.

complement /'kɒmplɪmənt/ *n* дополне́ние; (*full number*) (ли́чный) соста́в; *vt* дополня́ть *impf*, допо́лнить *pf*. **complementary** /ˌkɒmplɪ'mentərɪ/ *adj* дополни́тельный.

complete /kəm'pliːt/ *vt* заверша́ть *impf*, заверши́ть *pf*; *adj* (*entire, thorough*) по́лный; (*finished*) зако́нченный. **completion** /-'pliːʃ(ə)n/ *n* заверше́ние.

complex /'kɒmpleks/ *adj* сло́жный; *n* ко́мплекс. **complexity** /kəm'pleksɪtɪ/ *n* сло́жность.

complexion /kəm'plekʃ(ə)n/ *n* цвет лица́.

compliance /kəm'plaɪəns/ *n* усту́пчивость. **compliant** /-'plaɪənt/ *adj* усту́пчивый.

complicate /'kɒmplɪˌkeɪt/ *vt* осложня́ть *impf*, осложни́ть *pf*. **complicated** /-tɪd/ *adj* сло́жный. **complication** /ˌkɒmplɪ'keɪʃ(ə)n/ *n* осложне́ние.

complicity /kəm'plɪsɪtɪ/ *n* соуча́стие.

compliment /'kɒmplɪmənt/ *n* комплиме́нт; *pl* приве́т; говори́ть *impf* комплиме́нт(ы) +*dat*; хвали́ть *impf*, по~ *pf*. **complimentary** /ˌkɒmplɪ-

'mentərɪ/ *adj* ле́стный; (*free*) беспла́тный.

comply /kəm'plaɪ/ *vi*: ~ with (*fulfil*) исполня́ть *impf*, испо́лнить *pf*; (*submit to*) подчиня́ться *impf*, подчини́ться *pf* +*dat*.

component /kəm'pəʊnənt/ *n* дета́ль; *adj* составно́й.

compose /kəm'pəʊz/ *vt* (*music etc.*) сочиня́ть *impf*, сочини́ть *pf*; (*constitute*) составля́ть *impf*, соста́вить *pf*. **composed** /-'pəʊzd/ *adj* споко́йный; be ~ of состоя́ть *impf* из+*gen*. **composer** /-'pəʊzə(r)/ *n* компози́тор. **composition** /ˌkɒmpə'zɪʃ(ə)n/ *n* сочине́ние; (*make-up*) соста́в.

compost /'kɒmpɒst/ *n* компо́ст. **composure** /kəm'pəʊʒə(r)/ *n* самооблада́ние.

compound[1] /'kɒmpaʊnd/ *n* (*chem*) соедине́ние; *adj* сло́жный.

compound[2] /'kɒmpaʊnd/ *n* (*enclosure*) огоро́женное ме́сто.

comprehend /ˌkɒmprɪ'hend/ *vt* понима́ть *impf*, поня́ть *pf*. **comprehensible** /-'hensɪb(ə)l/ *adj* поня́тный. **comprehension** /-'henʃ(ə)n/ *n* понима́ние. **comprehensive** /-'hensɪv/ *adj* все-объе́млющий; ~ school общеобразова́тельная шко́ла.

compress /kəm'pres/ *vt* сжима́ть *impf*, сжать *pf*. **compressed** /-'prest/ *adj* сжа́тый.

comprise /kəm'praɪz/ *vt* состоя́ть *impf* из+*gen*.

compromise /'kɒmprəˌmaɪz/ *n* компроми́сс; *vt* компромети́ровать *impf*, с~ *pf*; *vi* идти́ *impf*, пойти́ *pf* на компроми́сс.

compulsion /kəm'pʌlʃ(ə)n/ *n* принужде́ние. **compulsory**

/-'pʌlsəri/ adj обязательный.
озабоченный; as far as I'm ~
что касается меня. concerning
/-'sɜːnɪŋ/ prep относительно+gen.

compunction /kəm'pʌŋkʃ(ə)n/ n
угрызение совести.

computer /kəm'pjuːtə(r)/ n
компьютер. ~ game компьютерная игра; ~ science электронно-вычислительная наука.

comrade /'kɒmreɪd/ n товарищ.
comradeship n товарищество.

con¹ /kɒn/ see pro¹

con² /kɒn/ vt надувать impf, надуть pf.

concave /'kɒnkeɪv/ adj вогнутый.

conceal /kən'siːl/ vt скрывать impf, скрыть pf.

concede /kən'siːd/ vt уступать impf, уступить pf; (admit) признавать impf, признать pf; (goal) пропускать impf, пропустить pf.

conceit /kən'siːt/ n самомнение.
conceited /kən'siːtɪd/ adj самовлюблённый.

conceivable /kən'siːvəb(ə)l/ adj
мыслимый. **conceive** /kən'siːv/
vt (plan, imagine) задумывать
impf, задумать pf; (biol) зачинать impf зачать pf; vi забеременеть pf.

concentrate /'kɒnsən,treɪt/ vt & i
сосредоточивать(ся) impf, сосредоточить(ся) pf (on на
+prep); vt (also chem) концентрировать impf, с~ pf. **concentration** /,kɒnsən'treɪʃ(ə)n/ n
сосредоточенность, концентрация.

concept /'kɒnsept/ n понятие.
conception /kən'sepʃ(ə)n/ n понятие; (biol) зачатие.

concern /kən'sɜːn/ n (worry) забота; (comm) предприятие; vt
касаться impf +gen; ~ o.s. with
заниматься impf, заняться pf
+instr. **concerned** /-'sɜːnd/ adj

concert /'kɒnsət/ n концерт.
concerted /kən'sɜːtɪd/ adj согласованный.

concertina /,kɒnsə'tiːnə/ n гармоника.

concession /kən'seʃ(ə)n/ n уступка; (econ) концессия. **concessionary** /-nəri/ adj
концессионный.

conciliation /kən,sɪlɪ'eɪʃ(ə)n/ n
примирение. **conciliatory** /kən'sɪliətəri/ adj примирительный.

concise /kən'saɪs/ adj краткий.
conciseness /-nɪs/ n краткость.

conclude /kən'kluːd/ vt заключать impf, заключить pf.
concluding /-dɪŋ/ adj
заключительный. **conclusion**
/-'kluːʒ(ə)n/ n заключение; (deduction) вывод. **conclusive**
/-'kluːsɪv/ adj решающий.

concoct /kən'kɒkt/ vt стряпать
impf, с~ pf. **concoction**
/-'kɒkʃ(ə)n/ n стряпня.

concourse /'kɒŋkɔːs/ n зал.

concrete /'kɒŋkriːt/ n бетон; adj
бетонный; (fig) конкретный.

concur /kən'kɜː(r)/ vi соглашаться impf, согласиться pf.
concurrent /-'kʌrənt/ adj одновременный.

concussion /kən'kʌʃ(ə)n/ n сотрясение.

condemn /kən'dem/ vt осуждать impf, осудить pf; (as
unfit for use) браковать impf,
за~ pf. **condemnation**
/,kɒndem'neɪʃ(ə)n/ n осуждение.

condensation /,kɒnden'seɪʃ(ə)n/
n конденсация. **condense** /kən'dens/ vt (liquid etc.) конденсировать impf & pf; (text etc.) со-

краща́ть *impf*, сократи́ть *pf*.
condensed /kən'denst/ *adj* сжа́тый; (*milk*) сгущённый. **condenser** /kən'densə(r)/ *n* конденса́тор.

condescend /ˌkɒndɪ'send/ *vi* снисходи́ть *impf*, снизойти́ *pf*. **condescending** /-'sendɪŋ/ *adj* снисходи́тельный. **condescension** /-'senʃ(ə)n/ *n* снисхожде́ние.

condiment /'kɒndɪmənt/ *n* припра́ва.

condition /kən'dɪʃ(ə)n/ *n* усло́вие; (*state*) состоя́ние; *vt* (*determine*) обусло́вливать *impf*, обусло́вить *pf*; (*psych*) приуча́ть *impf*, приучи́ть *pf*. **conditional** /-'dɪʃən(ə)l/ *adj* усло́вный.

condolence /kən'dəʊləns/ *n*: pl соболе́знование.

condom /'kɒndɒm/ *n* презервати́в.

condone /kən'dəʊn/ *vt* закрыва́ть *impf*, закры́ть *pf* глаза́ на+*acc*.

conducive /kən'dju:sɪv/ *adj* спосо́бствующий (**to** +*dat*).

conduct /'kɒndʌkt/ *n* (*behaviour*) поведе́ние; *vt* /kən'dʌkt/ вести́ *impf*, по~, про~ *pf*; (*mus*) дирижи́ровать *impf* +*instr*; (*phys*) проводи́ть *impf*. **conduction** /kən'dʌkʃ(ə)n/ *n* проводи́мость. **conductor** /kən'dʌktə(r)/ *n* (*bus*) конду́ктор; (*phys*) проводни́к; (*mus*) дирижёр.

conduit /'kɒndɪt/ *n* трубопрово́д.

cone /kəʊn/ *n* ко́нус; (*bot*) ши́шка.

confectioner /kən'fekʃənə(r)/ *n* конди́тер; ~**'s** (*shop*) конди́терская *sb*. **confectionery** /-nərɪ/ *n* конди́терские изде́лия

neut pl.

confederation /kənˌfedə'reɪʃ(ə)n/ *n* конфедера́ция.

confer /kən'fɜ:(r)/ *vt* присужда́ть *impf*, присуди́ть (**on** +*dat*) *pf*; *vi* совеща́ться *impf*. **conference** /'kɒnfərəns/ *n* совеща́ние; конфере́нция.

confess /kən'fes/ *vt* & *i* (*acknowledge*) признава́ть(ся) *impf*, призна́ть(ся) *pf* (**to** в+*prep*); (*eccl*) испове́доваться(ся) *impf* & *pf*. **confession** /-'feʃ(ə)n/ *n* призна́ние; и́споведь. **confessor** /-'fesə(r)/ *n* духовни́к.

confidant(e) /ˌkɒnfɪ'dænt/ *n* бли́зкий собесе́дник. **confide** /kən'faɪd/ *vt* доверя́ть *impf*, дове́рить *pf*; ~ **in** дели́ться *impf*, по~ *pf* c+*instr*. **confidence** /'kɒnfɪd(ə)ns/ *n* (*trust*) дове́рие; (*certainty*) уве́ренность; (*self*-~) самоуве́ренность. **confident** /'kɒnfɪd(ə)nt/ *adj* уве́ренный. **confidential** /ˌkɒnfɪ'denʃ(ə)l/ *adj* секре́тный.

confine /kən'faɪn/ *vt* ограни́чивать *impf*, ограни́чить *pf*; (*shut in*) заключа́ть *impf*, заключи́ть *pf*. **confinement** /-mənt/ *n* заключе́ние. **confines** /'kɒnfaɪnz/ *n pl* преде́лы *m pl*.

confirm /kən'fɜ:m/ *vt* подтвержда́ть *impf*, подтверди́ть *pf*. **confirmation** /ˌkɒnfə'meɪʃ(ə)n/ *n* подтвержде́ние; (*eccl*) конфирма́ция. **confirmed** /-'fɜ:md/ *adj* закорене́лый.

confiscate /'kɒnfɪˌskeɪt/ *vt* конфискова́ть *impf* & *pf*. **confiscation** /ˌkɒnfɪ'skeɪʃ(ə)n/ *n* конфиска́ция.

conflict *n* /'kɒnflɪkt/ конфли́кт; противоре́чие; *vi*: /kən'flɪkt/ ~ **with** противоре́чить *impf* +*dat*. **conflicting** /kən'flɪktɪŋ/ *adj* противоречи́вый.

conform /kən'fɔːm/ *vi*: ~ **to** подчиня́ться *impf*, подчини́ться *pf* +dat. **conformity** /-'fɔːmɪtɪ/ *n* соотве́тствие; (*compliance*) подчине́ние.

confound /kən'faʊnd/ *vt* сбива́ть *impf*, сбить *pf* с то́лку. **confounded** /-dɪd/ *adj* прокля́тый.

confront /kən'frʌnt/ *vt* стоя́ть *impf* лицо́м к лицу́ с+*instr*; ~ (*person*) **with** ста́вить *impf*, по~ *pf* лицо́м к лицу́ с+*instr*. **confrontation** /ˌkɒnfrʌn'teɪʃ(ə)n/ *n* конфронта́ция.

confuse /kən'fjuːz/ *vt* смуща́ть *impf*, смути́ть *pf*; (*also mix up*) пу́тать *impf*, за~, с~ *pf*. **confusion** /-'fjuːʒ(ə)n/ *n* смуще́ние; пу́таница.

congeal /kən'dʒiːl/ *vi* густе́ть *impf*, за~ *pf*; (*blood*) свёртываться *impf*, сверну́ться *pf*.

congenial /kən'dʒiːnɪəl/ *adj* прия́тный.

congenital /kən'dʒenɪt(ə)l/ *adj* врождённый.

congested /kən'dʒestɪd/ *adj* переполненный. **congestion** /-'dʒestʃ(ə)n/ *n* (*traffic*) зато́р.

congratulate /kən'grætjʊˌleɪt/ *vt* поздравля́ть *impf*, поздра́вить *pf* (**on** с+*instr*). **congratulation** /-'leɪʃ(ə)n/ *n* поздравле́ние; ~**s!** поздравля́ю!

congregate /'kɒŋgrɪˌgeɪt/ *vi* собира́ться *impf*, собра́ться *pf*. **congregation** /-'geɪʃ(ə)n/ *n* (*eccl*) прихожа́не (-н) *pl*.

congress /'kɒŋgres/ *n* съезд. **Congressman** *n* конгрессме́н.

conic(al) /'kɒnɪk(ə)l/ *adj* кони́ческий.

conifer /'kɒnɪfə(r)/ *n* хво́йное де́рево. **coniferous** /kə'nɪfərəs/ *adj* хво́йный.

conjecture /kən'dʒektʃə(r)/ *n* до-га́дка; *vt* гада́ть *impf*.

conjugal /'kɒndʒʊg(ə)l/ *adj* супру́жеский.

conjugate /'kɒndʒʊˌgeɪt/ *vt* спряга́ть *impf*, про~ *pf*. **conjugation** /-'geɪʃ(ə)n/ *n* спряже́ние.

conjunction /kən'dʒʌŋkʃ(ə)n/ *n* (*gram*) сою́з; **in** ~ **with** совме́стно с+*instr*.

conjure /'kʌndʒə(r)/ *vi*: ~ **up** (*in mind*) вызыва́ть *impf*, вы́звать *pf* в воображе́нии. **conjurer** /-rə(r)/ *n* фо́кусник. **conjuring trick** /-rɪŋ/ *n* фо́кус.

connect /kə'nekt/ *vt & i* свя́зывать(ся) *impf*, связа́ть(ся) *pf*; соединя́ть(ся) *impf*, соедини́ть(ся) *pf*. **connected** /-'nektɪd/ *adj* свя́занный. **connection, -exion** /-'nekʃ(ə)n/ *n* связь; (*rly etc.*) переса́дка.

connivance /kə'naɪv(ə)ns/ *n* попусти́тельство. **connive** /kə'naɪv/ *vi*: ~ **at** попусти́тельствовать *impf* +dat.

connoisseur /ˌkɒnə'sɜː(r)/ *n* знато́к.

conquer /'kɒŋkə(r)/ *vt* (*country*) завоёвывать *impf*, завоева́ть *pf*; (*enemy*) побежда́ть *impf*, победи́ть *pf*; (*habit*) преодолева́ть *impf*, преодоле́ть *pf*. **conqueror** /'kɒŋkərə(r)/ *n* завоева́тель *m*. **conquest** /'kɒŋkwest/ *n* завоева́ние.

conscience /'kɒnʃ(ə)ns/ *n* со́весть. **conscientious** /ˌkɒnʃɪ'enʃ(ə)s/ *adj* добросо́вестный. **conscious** /'kɒnʃəs/ *adj* созна́тельный; *predic* в созна́нии; **be** ~ **of** сознава́ть *impf* +acc. **consciousness** /'kɒnʃəsnɪs/ *n* созна́ние.

conscript *vt* /kən'skrɪpt/ призыва́ть *impf*, призва́ть *pf* на вое́нную слу́жбу; *n* /'kɒnskrɪpt/ призывни́к. **conscription** /kən

'skrɪpʃ(ə)n/ n воинская повинность.

consecrate /'kɒnsɪˌkreɪt/ vt освящать impf, освятить pf. **consecration** /-'kreɪʃ(ə)n/ n освящение.

consecutive /kən'sekjʊtɪv/ adj последовательный.

consensus /kən'sensəs/ n согласие.

consent /kən'sent/ vi соглашаться impf, согласиться pf (to +inf, на+acc); n согласие.

consequence /'kɒnsɪkwəns/ n последствие; of great ~ большого значения; of some ~ довольно важный. **consequent** /-kwənt/ adj вытекающий. **consequential** /ˌkɒnsɪ'kwenʃ(ə)l/ adj важный. **consequently** /'kɒnsɪˌkwəntlɪ/ adv следовательно.

conservation /ˌkɒnsə'veɪʃ(ə)n/ n сохранение; (of nature) охрана природы. **conservative** /kən'sɜːvətɪv/ adj консервативный; n консерватор. **conservatory** /kən'sɜːvətərɪ/ n оранжерея. **conserve** /kən'sɜːv/ vt сохранять impf, сохранить pf.

consider /kən'sɪdə(r)/ vt (think over) обдумывать impf, обдумать pf; (examine) рассматривать impf, рассмотреть pf; (regard as, be of opinion that) считать impf, счесть pf +instr, за+acc, что; (take into account) считаться impf c+instr. **considerable** /-'sɪdərəb(ə)l/ adj значительный. **considerate** /-'sɪdərət/ adj внимательный. **consideration** /kənˌsɪdə'reɪʃ(ə)n/ n рассмотрение; внимание; (factor) фактор; take into ~ принимать impf, принять pf во внимание. **considering** /-'sɪdərɪŋ/ prep принимая +acc во внимание.

consign /kən'saɪn/ vt передавать impf, передать pf. **consignment** /-'saɪnmənt/ n (goods) партия; (consigning) отправка товаров.

consist /kən'sɪst/ vi: ~ of состоять impf из+gen. **consistency** /-'sɪstənsɪ/ n последовательность; (density) консистенция. **consistent** /-'sɪstənt/ adj последовательный; ~ with совместимый c+instr.

consolation /ˌkɒnsə'leɪʃ(ə)n/ n утешение. **console¹** /kən'səʊl/ vt утешать impf, утешить pf. **console²** /'kɒnsəʊl/ n (control panel) пульт управления.

consolidate /kən'sɒlɪˌdeɪt/ vt укреплять impf, укрепить pf. **consolidation** /-'deɪʃ(ə)n/ n укрепление.

consonant /'kɒnsənənt/ n согласный sb.

consort /'kɒnsɔːt/ n супруг, ~a.

conspicuous /kən'spɪkjʊəs/ adj заметный.

conspiracy /kən'spɪrəsɪ/ n заговор. **conspirator** /-'spɪrətə(r)/ n заговорщик, -ица. **conspiratorial** /-ˌspɪrə'tɔːrɪəl/ adj заговорщицкий. **conspire** /-'spraɪə(r)/ vi устраивать impf, устроить pf заговор.

constable /'kʌnstəb(ə)l/ n полицейский sb.

constancy /'kɒnstənsɪ/ n постоянство. **constant** /-st(ə)nt/ adj постоянный. **constantly** /-st(ə)ntlɪ/ adv постоянно.

constellation /ˌkɒnstə'leɪʃ(ə)n/ n созвездие.

consternation /ˌkɒnstə'neɪʃ(ə)n/ n тревога.

constipation /ˌkɒnstɪ'peɪʃ(ə)n/ n запор.

constituency /kən'stɪtjʊənsɪ/

избира́тельный о́круг. con-
stituent /-'stɪtjʊənt/ n (component) составна́я часть; (voter)
избира́тель m; adj составно́й.
constitute /'kɒnstɪtjuːt/ vt со-
ставля́ть impf, соста́вить pf.
constitution /ˌkɒnstɪ'tjuːʃ(ə)n/ n
(polit, med) конститу́ция;
(composition) составле́ние.
constitutional /ˌkɒnstɪ
'tjuːʃən(ə)l/ adj (polit) консти-
туцио́нный.
constrain /kən'streɪn/ vt прину-
жда́ть impf, прину́дить pf. con-
strained /-'streɪnd/ adj
(inhibited) стеснённый. con-
straint /-'streɪnt/ n принужде́-
ние; (inhibition) стесне́ние.
constrict /kən'strɪkt/ vt (compress) сжима́ть impf, сжать pf;
(narrow) сужа́ть impf, су́зить
pf. **constriction** /-'strɪkʃ(ə)n/ n
сжа́тие; суже́ние.
construct /kən'strʌkt/ vt
стро́ить impf, по~ pf. con-
struction /-'strʌkʃ(ə)n/ n стро́и-
тельство; (also gram)
констру́кция; (interpretation)
истолкова́ние; ~ site стро́йка.
constructive /-'strʌktɪv/ adj
конструкти́вный.
construe /kən'struː/ vt истолко́-
вывать impf, истолкова́ть pf.
consul /'kɒns(ə)l/ n ко́нсул. con-
sulate /'kɒnsjʊlət/ n ко́нсуль-
ство.
consult /kən'sʌlt/ vt сове́то-
ваться impf, по~ pf c+instr.
consultant /-'sʌlt(ə)nt/ n кон-
сульта́нт. **consultation** /ˌkɒnsəl
'teɪʃ(ə)n/ n консульта́ция.
consume /kən'sjuːm/ vt потреб-
ля́ть impf, потреби́ть pf; (eat
or drink) съеда́ть impf, съесть
pf. **consumer** /-'sjuːmə(r)/ n по-
треби́тель m; ~ **goods** това́ры
m pl широ́кого потребле́ния.

consummate /'kɒnsjʊˌmeɪt/ vt
заверша́ть impf, заверши́ть pf;
~ **a marriage** осуществля́ть
impf, осуществи́ть pf бра́чные
отноше́ния. **consummation**
/-'meɪʃ(ə)n/ n заверше́ние; (of
marriage) осуществле́ние.
consumption /kən'sʌmpʃ(ə)n/ n
потребле́ние.
contact /'kɒntækt/ n конта́кт;
(person) связь; ~ **lens** конта́кт-
ная ли́нза; vt свя́зываться
impf, связа́ться pf c+instr.
contagious /kən'teɪdʒəs/ adj за-
ра́зный.
contain /kən'teɪn/ vt содержа́ть
impf; (restrain) сде́рживать
impf, сдержа́ть pf. **container**
/-nə(r)/ n (vessel) сосу́д; (transport) контéйнер.
contaminate /kən'tæmɪˌneɪt/ vt
загрязня́ть impf, загрязни́ть
pf. **contamination** /-'neɪʃ(ə)n/ n
загрязне́ние.
contemplate /'kɒntəmˌpleɪt/ vt
(gaze) созерца́ть impf; размы-
шля́ть impf; (consider) предпо-
лага́ть impf, предположи́ть pf.
contemplation /-'pleɪʃ(ə)n/ n co-
зерца́ние; размышле́ние. con-
templative /kən'templətɪv/ adj
созерца́тельный.
contemporary /kən'tempərərɪ/ n
совреме́нник; adj совреме́н-
ный.
contempt /kən'tempt/ n презре́-
ние; ~ **of court** неуваже́ние к
суду́; **hold in** ~ презира́ть impf.
contemptible /-'temptɪb(ə)l/ adj
презре́нный. **contemptuous**
/-'temptjʊəs/ adj презри́-
тельный.
contend /kən'tend/ vi (compete)
состяза́ться impf; ~ **for** оспа́-
ривать impf; ~ **with** справ-
ля́ться impf, спра́виться pf
c+instr; vt утвержда́ть impf.

contender /-də(r)/ *n* претенде́нт.

content¹ /'kɒntent/ *n* содержа́ние; *pl* содержи́мое *sb*; (**table of**) ~s содержа́ние.

content² /kən'tent/ *predic adj* дово́лен (-льна); *vt*: ~ **o.s. with** довольствоваться *impf*, у~ *pf* +*instr*. **contented** /-'tentid/ *adj* дово́льный.

contention /kən'tenʃ(ə)n/ *n* (*claim*) утвержде́ние. **contentious** /-'tenʃəs/ *adj* спо́рный.

contest *n* /'kɒntest/ состяза́ние; *vt* /kən'test/ (*dispute*) оспа́ривать *impf*, оспо́рить *pf*. **contestant** /kən'test(ə)nt/ *n* уча́стник, -ица, состяза́ния.

context /'kɒntekst/ *n* конте́кст.

continent /'kɒntinənt/ *n* матери́к. **continental** /ˌkɒnti'nent(ə)l/ *adj* материко́вый.

contingency /kən'tindʒənsi/ *n* возмо́жный слу́чай; ~ **plan** вариа́нт пла́на. **contingent** /-'tindʒənt/ *adj* случа́йный; *n* континге́нт.

continual /kən'tinjʊəl/ *adj* непреста́нный. **continuation** /-ˌtinjʊ'eiʃ(ə)n/ *n* продолже́ние. **continue** /-'tinjuː/ *vt* & *i* продолжа́ть(ся) *impf*, продо́лжить(ся) *pf*. **continuous** /-'tinjʊəs/ *adj* непреры́вный.

contort /kən'tɔːt/ *vt* искажа́ть *impf*, искази́ть *pf*. **contortion** /-'tɔːʃ(ə)n/ *n* искаже́ние.

contour /'kɒntʊə(r)/ *n* ко́нтур; ~ **line** горизонта́ль.

contraband /'kɒntrəˌbænd/ *n* контраба́нда.

contraception /ˌkɒntrə'sepʃ(ə)n/ *n* предупрежде́ние зача́тия. **contraceptive** /-'septiv/ *n* противозача́точное сре́дство; *adj* противозача́точный.

contract *n* /'kɒntrækt/ контра́кт,

догово́р; *vi* /kən'trækt/ (*make a* ~) заключа́ть *impf*, заключи́ть *pf* контра́кт; *vt* & *i* /kən'trækt/ (*shorten, reduce*) сокраща́ть(ся) *impf*, сократи́ть(ся) *pf*; *vt* (*illness*) заболева́ть *impf*, заболе́ть *pf* +*instr*. **contraction** /kən'trækʃ(ə)n/ *n* сокраще́ние; *pl* (*med*) схва́тки *f pl*. **contractor** /kən'træktə(r)/ *n* подря́дчик.

contradict /ˌkɒntrə'dikt/ *vt* противоре́чить *impf* +*dat*. **contradiction** /-'dikʃ(ə)n/ *n* противоре́чие. **contradictory** /-'diktəri/ *adj* противоречи́вый.

contraflow /'kɒntrəfləʊ/ *n* встре́чный пото́к.

contralto /kən'træltəʊ/ *n* контра́льто (*voice*) *neut* & (*person*) *f indecl*.

contraption /kən'træpʃ(ə)n/ *n* приспособле́ние.

contrary *adj* (*opposite*) противополо́жный; ~ **to** вопреки́ +*dat*; (*perverse*) /kən'treəri/ капри́зный; *n* /'kɒntrəri/: **on the** ~ наоборо́т.

contrast *n* /'kɒntrɑːst/ *n* контра́ст, противополо́жность; *vt* противопоставля́ть *impf*, противопоста́вить *pf* (**with** +*dat*); *vi* контрасти́ровать (*impf*).

contravene /ˌkɒntrə'viːn/ *vt* наруша́ть *impf*, нару́шить *pf*. **contravention** /-'venʃ(ə)n/ *n* нарушение.

contribute /kən'tribjuːt/ *vt* (*to fund etc.*) же́ртвовать *impf*, по~ *pf* (**to** в+*acc*); ~ **to** (*further*) соде́йствовать *impf* & *pf* +*dat*; (*write for*) сотру́дничать *impf* в+*prep*. **contribution** /ˌkɒntri'bjuːʃ(ə)n/ *n* (*money*) поже́ртвование; (*fig*) вклад. **contributor** /kən'tribjʊtə(r)/ *n* (*donor*) же́ртвователь —

(*writer*) сотру́дник.

contrite /'kɒntraɪt/ *adj* ка́ющийся.

contrivance /kən'traɪv(ə)ns/ n приспособле́ние. **contrive** /kən'traɪv/ *vt* ухитря́ться *impf*, ухитри́ться *pf* +*inf*.

control /kən'trəʊl/ n (*mastery*) контро́ль m; (*operation*) управле́ние; pl управле́ния pl; *vt* (*dominate, verify*) контроли́ровать *impf*, про~ *pf*; (*regulate*) управля́ть *impf* +*instr*; ~ o.s. сде́рживаться *impf*, сдержа́ться *pf*.

controversial /ˌkɒntrə'vɜ:ʃ(ə)l/ *adj* спо́рный. **controversy** /'kɒntrə,vɜ:sɪ/ n спор.

convalesce /ˌkɒnvə'les/ *vi* выздора́вливать *impf*. **convalescence** /-'les(ə)ns/ n выздоровле́ние.

convection /kən'vekʃ(ə)n/ n конве́кция. **convector** /-'vektə(r)/ n конве́ктор.

convene /kən'vi:n/ *vt* созыва́ть *impf*, созва́ть *pf*.

convenience /kən'vi:nɪəns/ n удо́бство; (*public* ~) убо́рная sb. **convenient** /-'vi:nɪənt/ *adj* удо́бный.

convent /'kɒnv(ə)nt/ n же́нский монасты́рь m.

convention /kən'venʃ(ə)n/ n (*assembly*) съезд; (*agreement*) конве́нция; (*custom*) обы́чай; (*conventionality*) усло́вность. **conventional** /-ʃən(ə)l/ *adj* общепри́нятый; (*also mil*) обы́чный.

converge /kən'vɜ:dʒ/ *vi* сходи́ться *impf*, сойти́сь *pf*. **convergence** /-dʒəns/ n схо́димость.

conversant /kən'vɜ:s(ə)nt/ *predic*: ~ with знако́м c+*instr*.

conversation /ˌkɒnvə'seɪʃ(ə)n/ n разгово́р. **conversational** /-'seɪʃən(ə)l/ *adj* разгово́рный.

converse[1] /kən'vɜ:s/ *vi* разгова́ривать *impf*.

converse[2] /'kɒnvɜ:s/ n обра́тное sb. **conversely** /'kɒnvɜ:slɪ/ *adv* наоборо́т. **conversion** /kən'vɜ:ʃ(ə)n/ n (*change*) превраще́ние; (*of faith*) обраще́ние; (*of building*) перестро́йка. **convert** /kən'vɜ:t/ *vt* (*change*) превраща́ть *impf*, преврати́ть *pf* (*into* в+*acc*); (*to faith*) обраща́ть *impf*, обрати́ть *pf* (*to* в+*acc*); (*a building*) перестра́ивать *impf*, перестро́ить *pf*. **convertible** /kən'vɜ:tɪb(ə)l/ *adj* обрати́мый; n автомоби́ль m со снима́ющейся кры́шей.

convex /'kɒnveks/ *adj* вы́пуклый.

convey /kən'veɪ/ *vt* (*transport*) перевози́ть *impf*, перевезти́ *pf*; (*communicate*) передава́ть *impf*, переда́ть *pf*. **conveyance** /-'veɪəns/ n перево́зка; переда́ча. **conveyancing** /-'veɪənsɪŋ/ n нотариа́льная переда́ча. **conveyor belt** /-'veɪə(r)/ n транспортёрная ле́нта.

convict /kən'vɪkt/ n осуждённый sb; *vt* признава́ть *impf*, осуди́ть *pf*. **conviction** /kən'vɪkʃ(ə)n/ n (*law*) осужде́ние; (*belief*) убежде́ние. **convince** /kən'vɪns/ *vt* убежда́ть *impf*, убеди́ть *pf*. **convincing** /kən'vɪnsɪŋ/ *adj* убеди́тельный.

convivial /kən'vɪvɪəl/ *adj* весёлый.

convoluted /'kɒnvə,lu:tɪd/ *adj* изви́листый; (*fig*) запу́танный.

convoy /'kɒnvɔɪ/ n конво́й.

convulse /kən'vʌls/ *vt*: be ~d with содрога́ться *impf*, содрог-

нуться *pf* от+*gen.* **convulsion** /-ˈvʌlʃ(ə)n/ *n* (*med*) конвульсия.

cook /kʊk/ *n* кухарка, повар; *vt* готовить *impf*; c~ *pf.* **cooker** /ˈkʊkə(r)/ *n* плита, печь. **cookery** /ˈkʊkərɪ/ *n* кулинария.

cool /kuːl/ *adj* прохладный; (*calm*) хладнокровный; (*unfriendly*) холодный; *vt* охлаждать *impf*, охладить *pf*; ~ **down, off** остывать *impf*, остыть (-ну)ть *pf.* **coolness** /ˈkuːlnɪs/ *n* прохлада; (*calm*) хладнокровие; (*manner*) холодок.

coop /kuːp/ *n* курятник; *vt*: ~ **up** держать *impf* взаперти.

cooperate /kəʊˈɒpə̩reɪt/ *vi* сотрудничать *impf*. **cooperation** /kəʊˌɒpə̩ˈreɪʃ(ə)n/ *n* сотрудничество. **cooperative** /kəʊˈɒpə̩rətɪv/ *n* кооператив; *adj* кооперативный; (*helpful*) услужливый.

co-opt /kəʊˈɒpt/ *vt* кооптировать *impf* & *pf.*

coordinate *vt* /kəʊˈɔːdɪˌneɪt/ координировать *impf* & *pf*; *n* /kəʊˈɔːdɪnət/ координата. **coordination** /kəʊˌɔːdɪˈneɪʃ(ə)n/ *n* координация.

cope /kəʊp/ *vi*: ~ **with** справляться *impf*, справиться *pf* c+*instr.*

copious /ˈkəʊpɪəs/ *adj* обильный.

copper /ˈkɒpə(r)/ *n* (*metal*) медь; *adj* медный.

coppice, copse /ˈkɒpɪs, kɒps/ *n* рощица.

copulate /ˈkɒpjʊˌleɪt/ *vi* совокупляться *impf*, совокупиться *pf.*

copy /ˈkɒpɪ/ *n* копия; (*book*) экземпляр; *vt* (*reproduce*) копировать *impf*, c~ *pf*; (*transcribe*) переписывать *impf*, переписать *pf*; (*imitate*) подражать

impf +*dat.* **copyright** *n* авторское право.

coral /ˈkɒr(ə)l/ *n* коралл.

cord /kɔːd/ *n* (*string*) верёвка; (*electr*) шнур.

cordial /ˈkɔːdɪəl/ *adj* сердечный.

corduroy /ˈkɔːdə̩rɔɪ/ *n* рубчатый вельвет.

core /kɔː(r)/ *n* сердцевина; (*fig*) суть.

cork /kɔːk/ *n* (*material*; *stopper*) пробка; (*float*) поплавок. **corkscrew** *n* штопор.

corn[1] /kɔːn/ *n* зерно; (*wheat*) пшеница; (*maize*) кукуруза. **cornflakes** *pl* *n* кукурузные хлопья (-ьев) *pl.* **cornflour** *n* кукурузная мука. **corny** /ˈkɔːnɪ/ *adj* (*coll*) банальный.

corn[2] /kɔːn/ *n* (*med*) мозоль.

cornea /ˈkɔːnɪə/ *n* роговая оболочка.

corner /ˈkɔːnə(r)/ *n* угол; ~**stone** *n* краеугольный камень *m*; *vt* загонять *impf*, загнать *pf* в угол.

cornet /ˈkɔːnɪt/ *n* (*mus*) корнет; (*ice-cream*) рожок.

cornice /ˈkɔːnɪs/ *n* карниз.

coronary (*thrombosis*) /ˈkɒrənərɪ (θrɒmˈbəʊsɪs)/ *n* коронаротромбоз. **coronation** /ˌkɒrəˈneɪʃ(ə)n/ *n* коронация. **coroner** /ˈkɒrənə(r)/ *n* медик судебной экспертизы.

corporal[1] /ˈkɔːp(ə)r(ə)l/ *n* капрал. **corporal**[2] /ˈkɔːp(ə)r(ə)l/ *adj* телесный; ~ **punishment** телесное наказание.

corporate /ˈkɔːpərət/ *adj* корпоративный. **corporation** /ˌkɔːpəˈreɪʃ(ə)n/ *n* корпорация.

corps /kɔː(r)/ *n* корпус.

corpse /kɔːps/ *n* труп.

corpulent /ˈkɔːpjʊlənt/ *adj* тучный.

corpuscle /ˈkɔːpʌs(ə)l/ *n* кровя-

ной шáрик.

correct /kə'rekt/ adj прáвильный; (*conduct*) коррéктный; vt исправля́ть *impf*, испрáвить *pf* **correction** /-'rekʃ(ə)n/ n исправлéние.

correlation /ˌkɒrɪ'leɪʃ(ə)n/ n соотношéние.

correspond /ˌkɒrɪ'spɒnd/ vi соотвéтствовать *impf* (**to, with** +*dat*); (*by letter*) переписываться *impf* **correspondence** /-dəns/ n соотвéтствие; (*letters*) корреспондéнция. **correspondent** /-dənt/ n корреспондéнт. **corresponding** /-dɪŋ/ adj соотвéтствующий (**to** +*dat*).

corridor /ˌkɒrɪˌdɔː(r)/ n коридóр.

corroborate /kə'rɒbəˌreɪt/ vt подтверждáть *impf*, подтвердить *pf*.

corrode /kə'rəʊd/ vt разъедáть *impf*, разъéсть *pf* **corrosion** /-'rəʊʒ(ə)n/ n коррóзия. **corrosive** /-'rəʊsɪv/ adj éдкий.

corrugated iron /ˈkɒrʊˌɡeɪtɪd 'aɪən/ n рифлёное желéзо.

corrupt /kə'rʌpt/ adj (*person*) развращённый; (*government*) продáжный; vt развращáть *impf*, развратить *pf* **corruption** /-'rʌpʃ(ə)n/ n развращéние; коррýпция.

corset /'kɔːsɪt/ n корсéт.

cortège /kɔː'teɪʒ/ n кортéж.

cortex /'kɔːteks/ n корá.

corundum /kə'rʌndəm/ n корýнд.

cosmetic /kɒz'metɪk/ adj космети́ческий. **cosmetics** /-tɪks/ n pl космéтика.

cosmic /'kɒzmɪk/ adj коcми́ческий. **cosmonaut** /'kɒzməˌnɔːt/ n космонáвт.

cosmopolitan /ˌkɒzmə'pɒlɪt(ə)n/ adj космополити́ческий.

cosmos /'kɒzmɒs/ n кóсмос.

Cossack /'kɒsæk/ n казáк, -áчка.

cosset /'kɒsɪt/ vt нéжить *impf*.

cost /kɒst/ n стóимость, ценá; vt стóить *impf*.

costly /'kɒstlɪ/ adj дорогóй.

costume /'kɒstjuːm/ n костю́м.

cosy /'kəʊzɪ/ adj ую́тный.

cot /kɒt/ n дéтская кровáтка.

cottage /'kɒtɪdʒ/ n коттéдж; ~ **cheese** творóг.

cotton /'kɒt(ə)n/ n хлóпок; (*cloth*) хлопчатобумáжная ткань; (*thread*) ни́тка; ~ **wool** вáта; adj хлóпковый; хлопчатобумáжный.

couch /kaʊtʃ/ n дивáн.

couchette /kuː'ʃet/ n спáльное мéсто.

cough /kɒf/ n кáшель m; vi кáшлять *impf*.

council /'kaʊns(ə)l/ n совéт; ~ **tax** мéстный налóг; ~ **house** жильё из обще́ственного фóнда. **councillor** /'kaʊnsələ(r)/ n член совéта.

counsel /'kaʊns(ə)l/ n (*advice*) совéт; (*lawyer*) адвокáт; vt совéтовать *impf*, по~ *pf* +*dat*.

count[1] /kaʊnt/ vt считáть *impf*, со~, счесть *pf*; ~ **on** рассчи́тывать *impf* на+*acc*; n счёт. **countdown** n отсчёт врéмени.

count[2] /kaʊnt/ n (*title*) граф.

countenance /'kaʊntənəns/ n лицó; vt одобря́ть *impf*, одóбрить *pf*.

counter[1] /'kaʊntə(r)/ n прилáвок; (*token*) фи́шка; adv: **run ~ to** идти́ *impf* вразрéз с+*instr*; vt пари́ровать *impf*, от~ *pf*.

counteract vt противодéйствовать *impf* +*dat*. **counterbalance** n противовéс; vt уравновéшивать *impf*, уравновéсить *pf*. **counterfeit** /-fɪt/ adj

подде́льный. **counterpart** *n* соотве́тственная часть. **counterpoint** *n* контрапу́нкт. **counter-revolutionary** *n* контрреволюционе́р; *adj* контрреволюцио́нный. **countersign** *vt* поста́вить *impf*, по~ *pf* втору́ю по́дпись на+*prep*.

countess /ˈkaʊntɪs/ *n* графи́ня.

countless /ˈkaʊntlɪs/ *adj* бесчи́сленный.

country /ˈkʌntrɪ/ *n* (*nation*) страна́; (*native land*) ро́дина; (*rural areas*) дере́вня; *adj* дереве́нский, се́льский. **countryman** *n* (*compatriot*) соотéчественник; сéльский жи́тель *m*. **countryside** *n* приро́дный ландша́фт.

county /ˈkaʊntɪ/ *n* гра́фство.

coup /kuː/ *n* (*polit*) переворо́т.

couple /ˈkʌp(ə)l/ *n* па́ра; (*a few*) не́сколько +*gen*; *vt* сцепля́ть *impf*, сцепи́ть *pf*.

coupon /ˈkuːpɒn/ *n* купо́н; тало́н; ва́учер.

courage /ˈkʌrɪdʒ/ *n* хра́брость. **courageous** /kəˈreɪdʒəs/ *adj* хра́брый.

courier /ˈkʊrɪə(r)/ *n* (*messenger*) курье́р; (*guide*) гид.

course /kɔːs/ *n* курс; (*process*) ход, тече́ние; (*of meal*) блю́до; **of ~** коне́чно.

court /kɔːt/ *n* двор; (*sport*) корт, площа́дка; (*law*) суд; ~ **martial** вое́нный суд; *vt* уха́живать *impf* за+*instr*. **courteous** /ˈkɜːtɪəs/ *adj* ве́жливый. **courtesy** /ˈkɜːtɪsɪ/ *n* ве́жливость. **courtier** /ˈkɔːtɪə(r)/ *n* придво́рный *sb*. **courtyard** *n* двор.

cousin /ˈkʌz(ə)n/ *n* двою́родный брат, -ная сестра́.

cove /kəʊv/ *n* бу́хточка.

covenant /ˈkʌvənənt/ *n* догово́р.

cover /ˈkʌvə(r)/ *n* (*covering*; *lid*) покры́шка; (*shelter*) укры́тие; (*chair ~*; *soft case*) чехо́л; (*bed*) покрыва́ло; (*book*) переплёт, обло́жка; **under separate ~** в отде́льном конве́рте; *vt* покрыва́ть *impf*, покры́ть *pf*; (*hide*, *protect*) закрыва́ть *impf*, закры́ть *pf*. **coverage** /-rɪdʒ/ *n* освеще́ние. **covert** /ˈkʌvɜːt/ *adj* скры́тый.

covet /ˈkʌvɪt/ *vt* пожела́ть *pf* +*gen*.

cow[1] /kaʊ/ *n* коро́ва. **cowboy** *n* ковбо́й. **cowshed** *n* хлев.

cow[2] /kaʊ/ *vt* запу́гивать *impf*, запуга́ть *pf*.

coward /ˈkaʊəd/ *n* трус. **cowardice** /-dɪs/ *n* тру́сость. **cowardly** /-lɪ/ *adj* трусли́вый.

cower /ˈkaʊə(r)/ *vi* съёживаться *impf*, съёжиться *pf*.

cox(swain) /ˈkɒks(weɪn)/ *n* рулево́й *m*.

coy /kɔɪ/ *adj* жема́нно стыдли́вый.

crab /kræb/ *n* краб.

crack /kræk/ *n* (*in cup*, *ice*) тре́щина; (*in wall*) щель; (*noise*) треск; *adj* первокла́ссный; *vt* (*break*) коло́ть *impf*, рас~ *pf*; (*china*) де́лать *impf*, с~ *pf* тре́щину +*acc*; *vi* тре́снуть *pf*. **crackle** /ˈkræk(ə)l/ *vi* потре́скивать *impf*.

cradle /ˈkreɪd(ə)l/ *n* колыбе́ль.

craft /krɑːft/ *n* (*trade*) ремесло́; (*boat*) су́дно. **craftiness** /ˈkrɑːftɪnɪs/ *n* хи́трость. **craftsman** *n* реме́сленник. **crafty** /ˈkrɑːftɪ/ *adj* хи́трый.

crag /kræg/ *n* утёс. **craggy** /ˈkrægɪ/ *adj* скали́стый.

cram /kræm/ *vt* (*fill*) набива́ть *impf*, наби́ть *pf*; (*stuff in*) впи́хивать *impf*, впихну́ть *pf*; *vi* (*study*) зубри́ть *impf*.

cramp[1] /kræmp/ n (med) су́дорога.

cramp[2] /kræmp/ vt стесня́ть impf, стесни́ть pf. **cramped** /kræmpt/ adj те́сный.

cranberry /'krænbərı/ n клю́ква.

crane /kreın/ n (bird) жура́вль m; (machine) кран; vt (one's neck) вытя́гивать impf, вы́тянуть pf (ше́ю).

crank[1] /kræŋk/ n заводна́я ру́чка; ~-shaft коле́нчатый вал; vt заводи́ть impf, завести́ pf.

crank[2] /kræŋk/ n (eccentric) чуда́к.

cranny /'krænı/ n щель.

crash /kræʃ/ n (noise) гро́хот, треск; (accident) ава́рия; (financial) крах; ~ course ускоренный курс; ~ helmet защи́тный шлем; ~ landing авари́йная поса́дка; vi (~ into) вреза́ться impf, вре́заться pf в+acc; (aeron) разбива́ться impf, разби́ться pf; (fall with ~) гро́хнуться pf; (comput) зависа́ть impf, зави́снуть pf; (bang down) гро́хнуть pf.

crass /kræs/ adj гру́бый.

crate /kreıt/ n я́щик.

crater /'kreıtə(r)/ n кра́тер.

crave /kreıv/ vi: ~ for жа́ждать impf +gen. **craving** /'kreıvıŋ/ n стра́стное жела́ние.

crawl /krɔːl/ vi по́лзать indet, ползти́ det; ~ with кише́ть +instr; n (sport) кроль m.

crayon /'kreıən/ n цветно́й каранда́ш.

craze /kreız/ n ма́ния. **crazy** /'kreızı/ adj поме́шанный (about на+prep).

creak /kriːk/ n скрип; vi скрипе́ть impf.

cream /kriːm/ n сли́вки (-вок)

pl; (cosmetic; cul) крем; ~ cheese сли́вочный сыр; **soured** ~ смета́на; vt сбива́ть impf, сбить pf; adj (of cream) сли́вочный; (colour) кре́мовый. **creamy** /'kriːmı/ adj сли́вочный, кре́мовый.

crease /kriːs/ n скла́дка; vt мять impf, из-, с~ pf. **creased** /kriːst/ adj мя́тый.

create /krıː'eıt/ vt создава́ть impf, созда́ть pf. **creation** /-'eıʃ(ə)n/ n созда́ние. **creative** /-'eıtıv/ adj тво́рческий. **creator** /-'eıtə(r)/ n созда́тель m. **creature** /'kriːtʃə(r)/ n созда́ние.

crèche /kreʃ/ n (де́тские) я́сли (-лей) pl.

credence /'kriːd(ə)ns/ n ве́ра; **give** ~ ве́рить impf (to +dat).

credentials /krı'denʃ(ə)lz/ n pl удостовере́ние; (diplomacy) вери́тельные гра́моты f pl.

credibility /,kredı'bılıtı/ n правдоподо́бие; (of person) спосо́бность вызыва́ть дове́рие. **credible** /'kredıb(ə)l/ adj (of thing) правдоподо́бный; (of person) заслу́живающий дове́рия.

credit /'kredıt/ n дове́рие; (comm) креди́т; (honour) честь; **give** ~ кредитова́ть impf & pf +acc; отдава́ть impf, отда́ть pf до́лжное+dat; ~ card креди́тная ка́рточка; vt: ~ with припи́сывать impf, приписа́ть pf +dat. **creditable** /-təb(ə)l/ adj похва́льный. **creditor** /-tə(r)/ n кредито́р.

credulity /krı'djuːlıtı/ n легкове́рие. **credulous** /'kredjʊləs/ adj легкове́рный.

creed /kriːd/ n убежде́ния neut pl; (eccl) вероиспове́дание.

creep /kriːp/ vi по́лзать indet, ползти́ det. **creeper** /'kriːpə(r)/ n

(*plant*) ползу́чее расте́ние.

cremate /krɪ'meɪt/ *vt* кремйрова́ть *impf & pf.* **cremation** /-'meɪʃ(ə)n/ *n* крема́ция. **crematorium** /ˌkremə'tɔːrɪəm/ *n* кремато́рий.

crêpe /kreɪp/ *n* креп.

crescendo /krɪ'ʃendəʊ/ *adv, adj, & n* креще́ндо *indecl.*

crescent /'krez(ə)nt/ *n* полуме́сяц.

crest /krest/ *n* гре́бень *m*; (*heraldry*) герб.

crevasse, crevice /krə'væs, 'krevɪs/ *n* расще́лина, рассе́лина.

crew /kruː/ *n* брига́да; (*of ship, plane*) экипа́ж.

crib /krɪb/ *n* (*bed*) де́тская крова́тка; *vi* спи́сывать *impf*, списа́ть *pf.*

crick /krɪk/ *n* растяже́ние мышц.

cricket[1] /'krɪkɪt/ *n* (*insect*) сверчо́к.

cricket[2] /'krɪkɪt/ *n* (*sport*) кри́кет; ~ **bat** бита́.

crime /kraɪm/ *n* преступле́ние.

Crimea /kraɪ'mɪə/ *n* Крым. **Crimean** /-ən/ *adj* крымский.

criminal /'krɪmɪn(ə)l/ *n* престу́пник; *adj* престу́пный; (*of crime*) уголо́вный.

crimson /'krɪmz(ə)n/ *adj* мали́новый.

cringe /krɪndʒ/ *vi* (*cower*) съёживаться *impf*, съёжиться *pf.*

crinkle /'krɪŋk(ə)l/ *n* морщи́на; *vt & i* мо́рщить(ся) *impf*, на~, с~ *pf.*

cripple /'krɪp(ə)l/ *n* кале́ка *m & f*; *vt* кале́чить *impf*, ис~ *pf*; (*fig*) расша́тывать *impf*, расшата́ть *pf.*

crisis /'kraɪsɪs/ *n* кри́зис.

crisp /krɪsp/ *adj* (*brittle*) хрустя́щий; (*fresh*) све́жий. **crisps**

/krɪsps/ *n pl* хрустя́щий карто́фель *m.*

criss-cross /'krɪskrɒs/ *adv* крест-на́крест.

criterion /kraɪ'tɪərɪən/ *n* крите́рий.

critic /'krɪtɪk/ *n* кри́тик. **critical** /-k(ə)l/ *adj* крити́ческий. **critically** /-kəlɪ/ *adv* (*ill*) тяжело́. **criticism** /-ˌtɪsɪz(ə)m/ *n* кри́тика. **criticize** /-ˌtɪsaɪz/ *vt* критикова́ть *impf.* **critique** /krɪ'tiːk/ *n* кри́тика.

croak /krəʊk/ *vi* ква́кать *impf*, ква́кнуть *pf*; хрипе́ть *impf.*

Croat /'krəʊæt/ *n* хорва́т, ~ка. **Croatia** /krəʊ'eɪʃə/ *n* Хорва́тия. **Croatian** /krəʊ'eɪʃ(ə)n/ *adj* хорва́тский.

crochet /'krəʊʃeɪ/ *n* вяза́ние крючко́м; *vt* вяза́ть *impf*, с~ *pf* (крючко́м).

crockery /'krɒkərɪ/ *n* посу́да.

crocodile /'krɒkədaɪl/ *n* кро코ди́л.

crocus /'krəʊkəs/ *n* кро́кус.

crony /'krəʊnɪ/ *n* закады́чный друг.

crook /krʊk/ *n* (*staff*) по́сох; (*swindler*) моше́нник. **crooked** /'krʊkɪd/ *adj* криво́й; (*dishonest*) нече́стный.

crop /krɒp/ *n* (*yield*) урожа́й; (*bird's*) зоб; *vt* (*cut*) подстрига́ть *impf*, подстри́чь *pf*; ~ **up** возника́ть *impf*, возни́кнуть *pf.*

croquet /'krəʊkeɪ/ *n* кроке́т.

cross /krɒs/ *n* крест; (*biol*) по́месь; *adj* (*angry*) злой; *vt* (*on foot*) переходи́ть *impf*, перейти́ *pf* (че́рез *+acc*; (*by transport*) переезжа́ть *impf*, перее́хать *pf* (че́рез) *+acc*; (*biol*) скре́щивать *impf*, скрести́ть *pf*; ~ **off, out** вычёркивать *impf*, вы́черкнуть *pf*; ~ **o.s.** крести́ться

impf, пере~ *pf;* ~ **over** переходи́ть *impf,* перейти́ *pf* (че́рез) +*acc.* ~**bar** попере́чина. ~**breed** по́месь. ~**country race** кросс; ~**examination** перекрёстный допро́с; ~**examine,** ~**question** подверга́ть *impf,* подве́ргнуть *pf* перекрёстному допро́су; ~**eyed** косогла́зый; ~**legged: sit** ~ сиде́ть *impf* по-туре́цки; ~**reference** перекрёстная ссы́лка; ~**road(s)** перекрёсток; ~**section** перекрёстное сече́ние; ~**word (puzzle)** кроссво́рд.

crossing /'krɒsɪŋ/ *n* (*intersection*) перекрёсток; (*foot*) перехо́д; (*transport; rly*) перее́зд.

crotch /krɒtʃ/ *n* (*anat*) промежность.

crotchet /'krɒtʃɪt/ *n* (*mus*) четвертна́я но́та.

crotchety /'krɒtʃɪtɪ/ *adj* раздражи́тельный.

crouch /krautʃ/ *vi* приседа́ть *impf,* присе́сть *pf.*

crow /krəʊ/ *n* воро́на; **as the** ~ **flies** по прямо́й ли́нии; *vi* кука́рекать *impf.* **crowbar** *n* лом.

crowd /kraʊd/ *n* толпа́; *vi* тесни́ться *impf,* с~ *pf;* ~ **into** вти́скиваться *impf,* вти́снуться *pf.* **crowded** /'kraʊdɪd/ *adj* перепо́лненный.

crown /kraʊn/ *n* коро́на; (*tooth*) коро́нка; (*head*) те́мя *n;* (*hat*) ту́лья; *vt* коронова́ть *impf* & *pf.*

crucial /'kru:ʃ(ə)l/ *adj* (*important*) о́чень ва́жный; (*decisive*) реша́ющий; (*critical*) крити́ческий.

crucifix /'kru:sɪˌfɪks/ *n* распя́тие. **crucifixion** /-'fɪkʃ(ə)n/ *n* распя́тие. **crucify** /'kru:sɪˌfaɪ/ *vt* распина́ть *impf,* распя́ть *pf.*

crude /kru:d/ *adj* (*rude*) гру́бый;

(*raw*) сыро́й. **crudity** /'kru:dɪtɪ/ *n* гру́бость.

cruel /'kru:əl/ *adj* жесто́кий. **cruelty** /-tɪ/ *n* жесто́кость.

cruise /kru:z/ *n* круи́з; *vi* крейси́ровать *impf.* **cruiser** /'kru:zə(r)/ *n* кре́йсер.

crumb /krʌm/ *n* кро́шка.

crumble /'krʌmb(ə)l/ *vt* кроши́ть *impf,* рас~ *pf;* *vi* обва́ливаться *impf,* обвали́ться *pf.* **crumbly** /'krʌmblɪ/ *adj* рассы́пчатый.

crumple /'krʌmp(ə)l/ *vt* мять *impf,* с~ *pf;* (*intentionally*) ко́мкать *impf,* с~ *pf.*

crunch /krʌntʃ/ *n* (*fig*) реша́ющий моме́нт; *vt* грызть *impf,* раз~ *pf;* *vi* хрусте́ть *impf,* хру́стнуть *pf.*

crusade /kru:'seɪd/ *n* кресто́вый похо́д; (*fig*) кампа́ния. **crusader** /-'seɪdə(r)/ *n* кресто-но́сец; (*fig*) боре́ц (**for** за+*acc*).

crush /krʌʃ/ *n* да́вка; (*infatuation*) си́льное увлече́ние; *vt* дави́ть *impf,* за~, раз~ *pf;* (*crease*) мять *impf,* с~ *pf;* (*fig*) подавля́ть *impf,* подави́ть *pf.*

crust /krʌst/ *n* (*of earth*) кора́; (*bread etc.*) ко́рка.

crutch /krʌtʃ/ *n* косты́ль *m.*

crux /krʌks/ *n:* ~ **of the matter** суть де́ла.

cry /kraɪ/ *n* крик; **a far** ~ **from** далеко́ от+*gen;* *vi* (*weep*) пла́кать *impf;* (*shout*) крича́ть *impf,* кри́кнуть *pf.*

crypt /krɪpt/ *n* склеп. **cryptic** /'krɪptɪk/ *adj* зага́дочный.

crystal /'krɪst(ə)l/ *n* криста́лл; (*glass*) хруста́ль *m.* **crystallize** /-laɪz/ *vt* & *i* кристаллизова́ть(ся) *impf* & *pf.*

cub /kʌb/ *n* детёныш; **bear** ~ медвежо́нок; **fox** ~ лисёнок; **lion** ~ львёнок; **wolf** ~

волчо́нок

cube /kjuːb/ n куб. **cubic** /'kjuːbɪk/ adj куби́ческий.

cubicle /'kjuːbɪk(ə)l/ n каби́на.

cuckoo /'kʊkuː/ n куку́шка.

cucumber /'kjuːkʌmbə(r)/ n огуре́ц.

cuddle /'kʌd(ə)l/ vt обнима́ть impf, обня́ть pf; vi обнима́ться impf, обня́ться pf; ~ **up** прижима́ться impf, прижа́ться pf (**to** к+ dat).

cudgel /'kʌdʒ(ə)l/ n дуби́нка.

cue[1] /kjuː/ n (theat) ре́плика.

cue[2] /kjuː/ n (billiards) кий.

cuff[1] /kʌf/ n манже́та; **off the ~** экспро́мтом; **~link** за́понка.

cuff[2] /kʌf/ vt (hit) шлёпать impf, шлёпнуть pf.

cul-de-sac /'kʌldəˌsæk/ n тупи́к.

culinary /'kʌlɪnərɪ/ adj кулина́рный.

cull /kʌl/ vt (select) отбира́ть impf, отобра́ть pf; (slaughter) бить impf.

culminate /'kʌlmɪˌneɪt/ vi конча́ться impf, ко́нчиться pf (**in** +instr). **culmination** /-'neɪʃ(ə)n/ n кульминацио́нный пункт.

culpability /ˌkʌlpə'bɪlɪtɪ/ n вино́вность. **culpable** /'kʌlpəb(ə)l/ adj вино́вный. **culprit** /'kʌlprɪt/ n вино́вный.

cult /kʌlt/ n культ.

cultivate /'kʌltɪˌveɪt/ vt (land) обраба́тывать impf, обрабо́тать pf; (crops) выра́щивать impf, вы́растить pf; (develop) развива́ть impf, разви́ть pf.

cultural /'kʌltʃər(ə)l/ adj культу́рный. **culture** /'kʌltʃə(r)/ n культу́ра. **cultured** /'kʌltʃəd/ adj культу́рный.

cumbersome /'kʌmbəsəm/ adj громо́здкий.

cumulative /'kjuːmjʊlətɪv/ adj кумуляти́вный.

cunning /'kʌnɪŋ/ n хи́трость; adj хи́трый.

cup /kʌp/ n ча́шка; (prize) ку́бок.

cupboard /'kʌbəd/ n шкаф.

cupola /'kjuːpələ/ n ку́пол.

curable /'kjʊərəb(ə)l/ adj излечи́мый.

curative /'kjʊərətɪv/ adj целе́бный.

curator /kjʊə'reɪtə(r)/ n храни́тель m.

curb /kɜːb/ vt обу́здывать impf, обузда́ть pf.

curd /kɜːd/ n (cheese) творо́г. **curdle** /'kɜːd(ə)l/ vt & i свёртывать(ся) impf, сверну́ть(ся) pf.

cure /kjʊə(r)/ n сре́дство pf про́тив+gen; vt вылечивать impf, вы́лечить pf; (smoke) копти́ть impf, за~ pf; (salt) соли́ть impf, по~ pf.

curfew /'kɜːfjuː/ n комендантский час.

curiosity /ˌkjʊərɪ'ɒsɪtɪ/ n любопы́тство. **curious** /'kjʊərɪəs/ adj любопы́тный.

curl /kɜːl/ n ло́кон; vt завива́ть impf, зави́ть pf; ~ **up** свёртываться impf, сверну́ться pf. **curly** /'kɜːlɪ/ adj кудря́вый.

currants /'kʌrənts/ n pl (dried) изю́м (collect).

currency /'kʌrənsɪ/ n валю́та; (prevalence) хожде́ние. **current** /'kʌrənt/ adj теку́щий; n тече́ние; (air) струя́; (water, electr) ток.

curriculum /kə'rɪkjələm/ n курс обуче́ния; ~ **vitae** /'viːtaɪ/ автобиогра́фия.

curry[1] /'kʌrɪ/ n ке́рри neut indecl.

curry[2] /'kʌrɪ/ vt: ~ **favour with** зайскивать impf пе́ред+instr.

curse /kɜːs/ n прокля́тие; (oath) руга́тельство; vt проклина́ть

impf, прокля́сть *pf*; *vi* руга́ться *impf*, по~ *pf*.

cursor /'kɜːsə(r)/ *n* (*comput*) курсо́р.

cursory /'kɜːsərɪ/ *adj* бе́глый.

curt /kɜːt/ *adj* ре́зкий.

curtail /kɜː'teɪl/ *vt* сокраща́ть *impf*, сократи́ть *pf*.

curtain /'kɜːt(ə)n/ *n* занаве́ска.

curts(e)y /'kɜːtsɪ/ *n* реве́ранс; *vi* де́лать *impf*, с~ *pf* реве́ранс.

curve /kɜːv/ *n* изги́б; (*line*) крива́я *sb*; *vi* изгиба́ться *impf*, изогну́ться *pf*.

cushion /'kʊʃ(ə)n/ *n* поду́шка; *vt* смягча́ть *impf*, смягчи́ть *pf*.

custard /'kʌstəd/ *n* сла́дкий зава́рно́й крем.

custodian /kʌ'stəʊdɪən/ *n* храни́тель *m*. **custody** /'kʌstədɪ/ *n* опе́ка; (*of police*) аре́ст; **to take into** ~ арестова́ть *pf*.

custom /'kʌstəm/ *n* обы́чай; (*comm*) клиенту́ра; *pl* (*duty*) тамо́женные по́шлины *f pl*; **go through** ~**s** проходи́ть *impf*, пройти́ *pf* тамо́женный осмо́тр; ~**-house** тамо́жня; ~**officer** тамо́женник. **customary** /'kʌstəmərɪ/ *adj* обы́чный. **customer** /'kʌstəmə(r)/ *n* клие́нт; покупа́тель *m*.

cut /kʌt/ *vt* ре́зать *impf*, по~ *pf*; (*hair*) стричь *impf*, о~ *pf*; (*mow*) коси́ть *impf*, с~ *pf*; (*price*) снижа́ть *impf*, сни́зить *pf*; (*cards*) снима́ть *impf*, снять *pf* коло́ду; ~ **back** (*prune*) подреза́ть *impf*, подре́зать *pf*; (*reduce*) сокраща́ть *impf*, сократи́ть *pf*; ~ **down** сруби́ть *pf*; ~ **off** отреза́ть *impf*, отре́зать *pf*; (*interrupt*) прерыва́ть *impf*, прерва́ть *pf*; (*disconnect*) отключа́ть *impf*, отключи́ть *pf*; ~ **out** выреза́ть *impf*, вы́резать *pf*; ~ **out for** со́зданный

для+*gen*; ~ **up** разреза́ть *impf*, разре́зать *pf* в (*gash*) поре́з; (*clothes*) покро́й; (*reduction*) сниже́ние; ~ **glass** хруста́ль *m*.

cute /kjuːt/ *adj* симпати́чный.

cutlery /'kʌtlərɪ/ *n* ножи́, ви́лки и ло́жки *pl*.

cutlet /'kʌtlɪt/ *n* отбивна́я котле́та.

cutting /'kʌtɪŋ/ *n* (*press*) вы́резка; (*plant*) черено́к; *adj* ре́зкий.

CV *abbr* (*of* **curriculum vitae**) автобиогра́фия.

cycle /'saɪk(ə)l/ *n* цикл; (*bicycle*) велосипе́д; *vi* е́здить *impf* на велосипе́де. **cyclic(al)** /'sɪklɪk((ə)l)/ *adj* цикли́ческий. **cyclist** /'saɪklɪst/ *n* велосипеди́ст.

cylinder /'sɪlɪndə(r)/ *n* цили́ндр. **cylindrical** /sɪ'lɪndrɪk(ə)l/ *adj* цилиндри́ческий.

cymbals /'sɪmb(ə)lz/ *n pl* таре́лки *f pl*.

cynic /'sɪnɪk/ *n* ци́ник. **cynical** /-k(ə)l/ *adj* цини́чный. **cynicism** /'sɪnɪsɪz(ə)m/ *n* цини́зм.

cypress /'saɪprəs/ *n* кипари́с.

Cyrillic /sɪ'rɪlɪk/ *n* кири́ллица.

cyst /sɪst/ *n* киста́.

Czech /tʃek/ *n* чех, че́шка; *adj* че́шский; ~ **Republic** Че́шская Респу́блика.

D

dab /dæb/ *n* мазо́к; *vt* (*eyes etc.*) прикла́дывать *impf* плато́к к+*dat*; ~ **on** накла́дывать *impf*, наложи́ть *pf* ма́зками.

dabble /'dæb(ə)l/ *vi*: ~ **in** пове́рхностно занима́ться *impf*, заня́ться *pf* +*instr*.

dachshund /'dækʃʊnd/ *n* тákca.

dad, daddy /dæd, 'dædɪ/ *n* пáпа; ~long-legs *n* долгонóжка.

daffodil /'dæfədɪl/ *n* жёлтый нарцисс.

daft /dɑ:ft/ *adj* глýпый.

dagger /'dægə(r)/ *n* кинжáл.

dahlia /'deɪlɪə/ *n* геóргин.

daily /'deɪlɪ/ *adv* ежеднéвно; *adj* ежеднéвный; *n* (*charwoman*) приходящая убóрщица; (*newspaper*) ежеднéвная газéта.

dainty /'deɪntɪ/ *adj* изящный.

dairy /'deərɪ/ *n* маслобóйня; (*shop*) молóчная *sb*; *adj* молóчный.

dais /'deɪs/ *n* помóст.

daisy /'deɪzɪ/ *n* маргарúтка.

dale /deɪl/ *n* долúна.

dally /'dælɪ/ *vi* (*dawdle*) мéшкать *impf*; (*toy*) игрáть *impf* +*instr*; (*flirt*) флиртовáть *impf*.

dam /dæm/ *n* (*barrier*) плотúна; *vt* запрýживать *impf*, запрудúть *pf*.

damage /'dæmɪdʒ/ *n* поврежлéние; *pl* убытки *m pl*; *vt* поврежлáть *impf*, повредúть *pf*.

damn /dæm/ *vt* (*curse*) проклинáть *impf*, проклясть *pf*; (*censure*) осуждáть *impf*, осудúть *pf*; *int* чёрт возьмú!; **I don't give a ~** мне наплевáть. **damnation** /-'neɪʃ(ə)n/ *n* проклятие. **damned** /dæmd/ *adj* проклятый.

damp /dæmp/ *n* сырость; *adj* сырóй; *vt* (*also* **dampen**) смáчивать *impf*, смочúть *pf*; (*fig*) охлаждáть *impf*, охладúть *pf*.

dance /dɑ:ns/ *vi* & *t* танцевáть *impf*; *n* тáнец; (*party*) танцевáльный вéчер. **dancer** /-sə(r)/ *n* танцóр, ~ка; (*ballet*) танцóвщик, -ица; балерúна.

dandelion /'dændɪˌlaɪən/ *n* одувáнчик.

dandruff /'dændrʌf/ *n* пéрхоть.

Dane /deɪn/ *n* датчáнин, -áнка; **Great ~** дог. **Danish** /'deɪnɪʃ/ *adj* дáтский.

danger /'deɪndʒə(r)/ *n* опáсность. **dangerous** /-rəs/ *adj* опáсный.

dangle /'dæŋɡ(ə)l/ *vt* & *i* покáчивать(ся) *impf*.

dank /dæŋk/ *adj* промóзглый.

dapper /'dæpə(r)/ *adj* выхоленный.

dare /deə(r)/ *vi* (*have courage*) мéливаться *impf*, осмéлиться *pf*; (*have impudence*) сметь *impf*, по~ *pf*; *vt* вызывáть *impf*, вызвать *pf*; *n* вызов. **daredevil** *n* лихáч; *adj* отчáянный. **daring** /'deərɪŋ/ *n* отвáга; *adj* отчáянный.

dark /dɑ:k/ *adj* тёмный; ~ **blue** тёмно-сúний; *n* темнотá. **darken** /-kən/ *vt* затемнять *impf*, затемнúть *pf*; *vi* темнéть *impf*, по~ *pf*; **darkly** /-lɪ/ *adv* мрáчно. **darkness** /-nɪs/ *n* темнотá.

darling /'dɑ:lɪŋ/ *n* дорогóй *sb*, мúлый *sb*; *adj* дорогóй.

darn /dɑ:n/ *vt* штóпать *impf*, за~ *pf*.

dart /dɑ:t/ *n* стрелá; (*for game*) метáтельная стрелá; (*tuck*) вытáчка; *vi* бросáться *pf*.

dash /dæʃ/ *n* (*hyphen*) тире *neut indecl*; (*admixture*) прúмесь; *vt* швырять *impf*, швырнýть *pf*; *vi* бросáться *impf*, брóситься *pf*. **dashboard** *n* прибóрная доскá. **dashing** /'dæʃɪŋ/ *adj* лихóй.

data /'deɪtə/ *n pl* дáнные *sb pl*. **database** *n* бáза дáнных.

date¹ /deɪt/ *n* (*fruit*) фúник.

date² /deɪt/ *n* числó, дáта; (*engagement*) свидáние; **out of ~**

устаре́лый; **up to ~** совреме́нный; **в ку́рсе де́ла**; ~ да́тировать *impf* & *pf*; **(go out with)** встреча́ться *impf* с+*instr*; **vi (originate)** относи́ться *impf* **(from** к+*instr*)

dative /'deɪtɪv/ *adj* (*n*) да́тельный (паде́ж).

daub /dɔ:b/ *vt* ма́зать *impf*, на~ *pf* **(with** +*instr*).

daughter /'dɔ:tə(r)/ *n* дочь; **~-in-law** неве́стка **(in relation to mother)**, сноха́ **(in relation to father)**.

daunting /'dɔ:ntɪŋ/ *adj* угрожа́ющий.

dawdle /'dɔ:d(ə)l/ *vi* ме́шкать *impf*.

dawn /dɔ:n/ *n* рассве́т; **(also fig)** заря́; *vi* **(day)** рассвета́ть *impf*, рассвести́ *pf impers*; **(up)on** осеня́ть *impf*, осени́ть *pf*; **it ~ed on me** меня́ осени́ло.

day /deɪ/ *n* день *m*; **(24 hours)** су́тки *pl*; *pl* **(period)** пери́од, вре́мя *neut*; **~ after** изо дня́ в день; **the ~ after tomorrow** послеза́втра; **the ~ before** накану́не; **the ~ before yesterday** позавчера́; **the other ~** на днях; **by ~** днём; **every other ~** че́рез день; **~ off** выходно́й день *m*; **one ~** одна́жды; **these ~s** в на́ши дни. **daybreak** *n* рассве́т. **day-dreams** *n* пусты́е мечты́ *f pl*. **daylight** *n* дневно́й свет; **in broad ~** средь бе́ла дня́. **daytime** *n*: **in the ~** днём.

daze /deɪz/ *n*: **in a ~, dazed** /deɪzd/ *adj* оглушён (-ена́).

dazzle /'dæz(ə)l/ *vt* ослепля́ть *impf*, ослепи́ть *pf*.

deacon /'di:kən/ *n* дья́кон.

dead /ded/ *adj* мёртвый; **(animals)** до́хлый; **(plants)** увя́дший; **(numb)** онеме́вший; *n*: **the ~** мёртвые *sb pl*; **at ~ of night**

глубо́кой но́чью; *adv* соверше́нно; **~ end** тупи́к; **~ heat** одновреме́нный фи́ниш; **~line** преде́льный срок; **~lock** тупи́к.

deaden /'ded(ə)n/ *vt* заглуша́ть *impf*, заглуши́ть *pf*.

deadly /'dedlɪ/ *adj* сме́ртельный.

deaf /def/ *adj* глухо́й; **~ and dumb** глухонемо́й. **deafen** /-f(ə)n/ *vt* оглуша́ть *impf*, оглуши́ть *pf*. **deafness** /-nɪs/ *n* глухота́.

deal[1] /di:l/ *n*: **a great, good, ~** мно́го (+*gen*); **(with comp)** гора́здо.

deal[2] /di:l/ *n* **(bargain)** сде́лка; **(cards)** сда́ча; *vt* **(cards)** сдава́ть *impf*, сдать *pf*; **(blow)** наноси́ть *impf*, нанести́ *pf*; **~ in** торгова́ть *impf* +*instr*; **~ out** распределя́ть *impf*, распредели́ть *pf*; **~ with (take care of)** занима́ться *impf*, заня́ться *pf* +*instr*; **(handle a person)** поступа́ть *impf*, поступи́ть *pf* с+*instr*; **(treat a subject)** рассма́тривать *impf*, рассмотре́ть *pf*; **(cope)** справля́ться *impf*, спра́виться *pf* с+*instr*. **dealer** /'di:lə(r)/ *n* торго́вец (**in** +*instr*).

dean /di:n/ *n* дека́н.

dear /dɪə(r)/ *adj* дорого́й; **(also n)** ми́лый **(sb)**.

dearth /dɜ:θ/ *n* недоста́ток.

death /deθ/ *n* смерть; **put to ~** казни́ть *impf* & *pf*; **~bed** *n* сме́ртное ло́же; **~ certificate** свиде́тельство о сме́рти; **~ penalty** сме́ртная казнь. **deathly** /'deθlɪ/ *adj* сме́ртельный.

debar /dɪ'bɑ:(r)/ *vt*: **~ from** допуска́ть *impf* до+*gen*.

debase /dɪ'beɪs/ *vt* унижа́ть

impf, уни́зить *pf*; (*coinage*) понижа́ть *impf*, пони́зить *pf* ка́чество +*gen*.

debatable /dɪˈbeɪtəb(ə)l/ *adj* спо́рный. **debate** /dɪˈbeɪt/ *n* пре́ния (-ий) *pl*; *vt* обсужда́ть *impf*, обсуди́ть *pf*.

debauched /dɪˈbɔːtʃt/ *adj* развра́щенный. **debauchery** /-ˈbɔːtʃərɪ/ *n* разврат.

debilitate /dɪˈbɪlɪˌteɪt/ *vt* ослабля́ть; *impf*, осла́бить *pf*. **debility** /-ˈbɪlɪtɪ/ *n* сла́бость.

debit /ˈdebɪt/ *n* де́бет; *vt* дебетова́ть *impf* & *pf*.

debris /ˈdebriː/ *n* обло́мки *m pl*.

debt /det/ *n* долг. **debtor** /ˈdetə(r)/ *n* должни́к.

début /ˈdeɪbjuː/ *n* дебю́т; **make one's ~** дебюти́ровать *impf* & *pf*.

decade /ˈdekeɪd/ *n* десятиле́тие.

decadence /ˈdekəd(ə)ns/ *n* декаде́нтство. **decadent** /-d(ə)nt/ *adj* декаде́нтский.

decaffeinated /diːˈkæfɪˌneɪtɪd/ *adj* без кофеи́на.

decant /dɪˈkænt/ *vt* перелива́ть *impf*, перели́ть *pf*. **decanter** /-ˈkæntə(r)/ *n* графи́н.

decapitate /dɪˈkæpɪˌteɪt/ *vt* обезгла́вливать *impf*, обезгла́вить *pf*.

decay /dɪˈkeɪ/ *vi* гнить *impf*, с~ *pf*; (*tooth*) разруша́ться *impf*, разру́шиться *pf*; *n* гние́ние; (*tooth*) разруше́ние.

decease /dɪˈsiːs/ *n* кончи́на. **deceased** /-ˈsiːst/ *adj* поко́йный; *n* поко́йник, -ица.

deceit /dɪˈsiːt/ *n* обма́н. **deceitful** /-ˈsiːtfʊl/ *adj* лжи́вый. **deceive** /-ˈsiːv/ *vt* обма́нывать *impf*, обману́ть *pf*.

deceleration /diːˌseləˈreɪʃ(ə)n/ *n* замедле́ние.

December /dɪˈsembə(r)/ *n* дека́брь *m*; *adj* дека́брьский.

decency /ˈdiːsənsɪ/ *n* прили́чие. **decent** /-s(ə)nt/ *adj* прили́чный.

decentralization /diːˌsentrəlaɪˈzeɪʃ(ə)n/ *n* децентрализа́ция. **decentralize** /diːˈsentrəˌlaɪz/ *vt* децентрализова́ть *impf* & *pf*.

deception /dɪˈsepʃ(ə)n/ *n* обма́н. **deceptive** /-ˈseptɪv/ *adj* обма́нчивый.

decibel /ˈdesɪˌbel/ *n* дециба́л.

decide /dɪˈsaɪd/ *vt* реша́ть *impf*, реши́ть *pf*. **decided** /-ˈsaɪdɪd/ *adj* реши́тельный.

deciduous /dɪˈsɪdjʊəs/ *adj* листопа́дный.

decimal /ˈdesɪm(ə)l/ *n* десяти́чная дробь; *adj* десяти́чный; **~ point** запята́я *sb*.

decimate /ˈdesɪˌmeɪt/ *vt* (*fig*) коси́ть *impf*, с~ *pf*.

decipher /dɪˈsaɪfə(r)/ *vt* расшифро́вывать *impf*, расшифрова́ть *pf*.

decision /dɪˈsɪʒ(ə)n/ *n* реше́ние. **decisive** /dɪˈsaɪsɪv/ *adj* (*firm*) реши́тельный, (*deciding*) реша́ющий.

deck /dek/ *n* па́луба; (*bus etc.*) эта́ж; **~-chair** *n* шезло́нг; *vt*: **~ out** украша́ть *impf*, укра́сить *pf*.

declaim /dɪˈkleɪm/ *vt* деклами́ровать *impf*, про~ *pf*.

declaration /ˌdekləˈreɪʃ(ə)n/ *n* объявле́ние; (*document*) деклара́ция. **declare** /dɪˈkleə(r)/ *vt* объявля́ть *impf*, объяви́ть *pf*; (*assert*) заявля́ть *impf*, заяви́ть *pf*.

declension /dɪˈklenʃ(ə)n/ *n* склоне́ние. **decline** /dɪˈklaɪn/ *n* упа́док; *vi* приходи́ть *impf*, прийти́ *pf* в упа́док; *vt* отклоня́ть *impf*, отклони́ть *pf*;

(*gram*) склоня́ть *impf*, про~ *pf*.

decode /diːˈkəʊd/ *vt* расшифро́вывать *impf*, расшифрова́ть *pf*.

decompose /ˌdiːkəmˈpəʊz/ *vi* разлага́ться *impf*, разложи́ться *pf*.

décor /ˈdeɪkɔː(r)/ *n* эстети́ческое оформле́ние. **decorate** /ˈdekəˌreɪt/ *vt* украша́ть *impf*, укра́сить *pf* (*room*) ремонти́ровать *impf*, от~ *pf*; (*with medal etc.*) награжда́ть *impf*, награди́ть *pf*. **decoration** /ˌdekəˈreɪʃ(ə)n/ *n* украше́ние; (*medal*) о́рден. **decorative** /ˈdekərətɪv/ *adj* декорати́вный. **decorator** /ˈdekəˌreɪtə(r)/ *n* маля́р.

decorous /ˈdekərəs/ *adj* прили́чный. **decorum** /dɪˈkɔːrəm/ *n* прили́чие.

decoy /ˈdiːkɔɪ/ *n* (*bait*) прима́нка; *vt* зама́нивать *impf*, замани́ть *pf*.

decrease *vt & i* /dɪˈkriːs/ уменьша́ть(ся) *impf*, уме́ньшить(ся) *pf*; *n* /ˈdiːkriːs/ уменьше́ние.

decree /dɪˈkriː/ *n* ука́з; *vt* постановля́ть *impf*, постанови́ть *pf*.

decrepit /dɪˈkrepɪt/ *adj* дря́хлый.

dedicate /ˈdediˌkeɪt/ *vt* посвяща́ть *impf*, посвяти́ть *pf*. **dedication** /ˌdediˈkeɪʃ(ə)n/ *n* посвяще́ние.

deduce /dɪˈdjuːs/ *vt* заключа́ть *impf*, заключи́ть *pf*.

deduct /dɪˈdʌkt/ *vt* вычита́ть *impf*, вы́честь *pf*. **deduction** /-ˈdʌkʃ(ə)n/ *n* (*subtraction*) вы́чет; (*inference*) вы́вод.

deed /diːd/ *n* посту́пок; (*heroic*) по́двиг; (*law*) акт.

deem /diːm/ *vt* счита́ть *impf*, счесть *pf* +*acc & instr*.

deep /diːp/ *adj* глубо́кий;

(*colour*) тёмный; (*sound*) ни́зкий; ~ **freeze** морози́льник.

deepen /-pən/ *vt & i* углубля́ть(ся) *impf*, углуби́ть(ся) *pf*.

deer /dɪə(r)/ *n* оле́нь *m*.

deface /dɪˈfeɪs/ *vt* обезобра́живать *impf*, обезобра́зить *pf*.

defamation /ˌdefəˈmeɪʃ(ə)n/ *n* диффама́ция. **defamatory** /dɪˈfæmətərɪ/ *adj* клеветни́ческий.

default /dɪˈfɔːlt/ *n* (*failure to pay*) неупла́та; (*failure to appear*) нея́вка; (*comput*) автомати́ческий вы́бор; *vi* не выполня́ть *impf* обяза́тельств.

defeat /dɪˈfiːt/ *n* пораже́ние; *vt* побежда́ть *impf*, победи́ть *pf*. **defeatism** /-tɪz(ə)m/ *n* пораже́нчество. **defeatist** /-tɪst/ *n* пораже́нец; *adj* пораже́нческий.

defecate /ˈdefiˌkeɪt/ *vi* испражня́ться *impf*, испражни́ться *pf*.

defect *n* /ˈdiːfekt/ дефе́кт; *vi* /dɪˈfekt/ перебега́ть *impf*, перебежа́ть *pf*. **defective** /dɪˈfektɪv/ *adj* неиспра́вный. **defector** /dɪˈfektə(r)/ *n* перебе́жчик.

defence /dɪˈfens/ *n* защи́та. **defenceless** /-ˈfensləs/ *adj* беззащи́тный. **defend** /-ˈfend/ *vt* защища́ть *impf*, защити́ть *pf*. **defendant** /-ˈfend(ə)nt/ *n* подсуди́мый *sb*. **defender** /-ˈfendə(r)/ *n* защи́тник. **defensive** /-ˈfensɪv/ *adj* оборони́тельный.

defer¹ /dɪˈfɜː(r)/ *vt* (*postpone*) отсро́чить *pf*.

defer² /dɪˈfɜː(r)/ *vi*: ~ **to** подчиня́ться *impf* +*dat*. **deference** /ˈdefərəns/ *n* уваже́ние. **deferential** /ˌdefəˈrenʃ(ə)l/ *adj* почти́тельный.

defiance /dɪˈfaɪəns/ *n* неповинове́ние; **in** ~ **of** вопреки́ +*dat*. **defiant** /-ˈfaɪənt/ *adj* вызыва́ющий.

deficiency /dɪˈfɪʃənsɪ/ n недостаток. **deficient** /-ˈfɪʃ(ə)nt/ adj недостаточный. **deficit** /ˈdefɪsɪt/ n дефицит.

defile /dɪˈfaɪl/ vt осквернять impf, осквернить pf.

define /dɪˈfaɪn/ vt определять impf, определить pf. **definite** /ˈdefɪnɪt/ adj определённый. **definitely** /ˈdefɪnɪtlɪ/ adv несомненно. **definition** /defɪˈnɪʃ(ə)n/ n определение. **definitive** /dɪˈfɪnɪtɪv/ adj окончательный.

deflate /dɪˈfleɪt/ vt & i спускать impf, спустить pf; vt (person) сбивать спесь c+gen. **deflation** /-ˈfleɪʃ(ə)n/ n дефляция.

deflect /dɪˈflekt/ vt отклонять impf, отклонить pf.

deforestation /diːˌfɒrɪˈsteɪʃ(ə)n/ n обезлесение.

deformed /dɪˈfɔːmd/ adj уродливый. **deformity** /-ˈfɔːmɪtɪ/ n уродство.

defraud /dɪˈfrɔːd/ vt обманывать impf, обмануть pf; ~ of выманивать impf, выманить pf +acc & y+gen of person).

defray /dɪˈfreɪ/ vt оплачивать impf, оплатить pf.

defrost /diːˈfrɒst/ vt размораживать impf, разморозить pf.

deft /deft/ adj ловкий.

defunct /dɪˈfʌŋkt/ adj больше не существующий.

defy /dɪˈfaɪ/ vt (challenge) вызывать impf, вызвать pf; (disobey) идти impf, по~ pf против+acc; (fig) не поддаваться impf +dat.

degenerate vi /dɪˈdʒenəˌreɪt/ вырождаться impf, выродиться pf; adj /dɪˈdʒenərət/ выродившийся.

degradation /ˌdegrəˈdeɪʃ(ə)n/ n унижение. **degrade** /dɪˈgreɪd/

унижать impf, унизить pf. **degrading** /dɪˈgreɪdɪŋ/ adj унизительный.

degree /dɪˈgriː/ n степень; (math etc.) градус; (univ) учёная степень.

dehydrate /diːˈhaɪdreɪt/ vt обезвоживать impf, обезводить pf. **dehydration** /-ˈdreɪʃ(ə)n/ n обезвоживание.

deign /deɪn/ vi снисходить impf, снизойти pf.

deity /ˈdiːɪtɪ/ n божество.

dejected /dɪˈdʒektɪd/ adj удручённый.

delay /dɪˈleɪ/ n задержка; without ~ немедленно; vt задерживать impf, задержать pf.

delegate n /ˈdelɪgət/ делегат; vt /ˈdelɪˌgeɪt/ делегировать impf & pf. **delegation** /-ˈgeɪʃ(ə)n/ n делегация.

delete /dɪˈliːt/ vt вычёркивать impf, вычеркнуть pf.

deliberate adj /dɪˈlɪbərət/ (intentional) преднамеренный; (careful) осторожный; vt & i /dɪˈlɪbəˌreɪt/ размышлять impf, размыслить pf (o+prep); (discuss) совещаться impf (o+prep). **deliberation** /dɪˌlɪbəˈreɪʃ(ə)n/ n размышление; (discussion) совещание.

delicacy /ˈdelɪkəsɪ/ n (tact) деликатность; (dainty) лакомство. **delicate** /-kət/ adj тонкий; (tactful, needing tact) деликатный; (health) болезненный. **delicatessen** /ˌdelɪkəˈtes(ə)n/ n гастроном.

delicious /dɪˈlɪʃəs/ adj очень вкусный.

delight /dɪˈlaɪt/ n наслаждение; (delightful thing) прелесть. **delightful** /-fʊl/ adj прелестный.

delinquency /dɪˈlɪŋkwənsɪ/ n преступность. **delinquent**

/-wənt/ *n* правонаруши́тель *m*, ~ница; *adj* вино́вный.

delirious /dɪ'lɪrɪəs/ *adj*: be ~ бре́дить *impf*. **delirium** /-rɪəm/ *n* бред.

deliver /dɪ'lɪvə(r)/ *vt* (*goods*) доставля́ть *impf*, доста́вить *pf*; (*save*) избавля́ть *impf*, изба́вить *pf* (*from* +*gen*); (*lecture*) прочита́ть *impf*, прочесть *pf*; (*letters*) разноси́ть *impf*, разнести́ *pf*; (*speech*) произноси́ть *impf*, произнести́ *pf*; (*blow*) наноси́ть *impf*, нанести́ *pf*. **deliverance** /-'lɪvərəns/ *n* избавле́ние. **delivery** /-'lɪvərɪ/ *n* доста́вка.

delta /'deltə/ *n* де́льта.

delude /dɪ'luːd/ *vt* вводи́ть *impf*, ввести́ *pf* в заблужде́ние.

deluge /'deljuːdʒ/ *n* (*flood*) пото́п; (*rain*) ли́вень *m*; (*fig*) пото́к.

delusion /dɪ'luːʒ(ə)n/ *n* заблужде́ние; ~s of grandeur ма́ния вели́чия.

de luxe /də 'lʌks/ *adj* -люкс (*added to noun*).

delve /delv/ *vi* углубля́ться *impf*, углуби́ться *pf* (*into* в+*acc*).

demand /dɪ'mɑːnd/ *n* тре́бование; (*econ*) спрос (*for* на+*acc*); *vt* тре́бовать *impf*, по— *pf* +*gen*. **demanding** /-dɪŋ/ *adj* тре́бовательный.

demarcation /ˌdiːmɑː'keɪʃ(ə)n/ *n* демарка́ция.

demean /dɪ'miːn/ *vt*: ~ o.s. унижа́ться *impf*, уни́зиться *pf*.

demeanour /dɪ'miːnə(r)/ *n* мане́ра вести́ себя́.

demented /dɪ'mentɪd/ *adj* сумасше́дший. **dementia** /-'menʃə/ *n* слабоу́мие.

demise /dɪ'maɪz/ *n* кончи́на.

demobilize /ˌdiː'məʊbɪˌlaɪz/ *vt* демобилизова́ть *impf & pf*.

democracy /dɪ'mɒkrəsɪ/ *n* демокра́тия. **democrat** /'deməˌkræt/ *n* демокра́т. **democratic** /ˌdeməˈkrætɪk/ *adj* демократи́ческий. **democratization** /dɪˌmɒkrətaɪ'zeɪʃ(ə)n/ *n* демократиза́ция.

demolish /dɪ'mɒlɪʃ/ *vt* (*destroy*) разруша́ть *impf*, разру́шить *pf*; (*building*) сноси́ть *impf*, снести́ *pf*; (*refute*) опроверга́ть *impf*, опрове́ргнуть *pf*. **demolition** /ˌdeməˈlɪʃ(ə)n/ *n* разруше́ние; снос.

demon /'diːmən/ *n* де́мон.

demonstrable /'demənstrəb(ə)l/ *adj* доказу́емый. **demonstrably** /dɪ'mɒnstrəblɪ/ *adv* нагля́дно. **demonstrate** /'demənˌstreɪt/ *vt impf & pf*; *vi* уча́ствовать *impf* в демонстра́ции. **demonstration** /ˌdemənˈstreɪʃ(ə)n/ *n* демонстра́ция. **demonstrative** /dɪ'mɒnstrətɪv/ *adj* экспанси́вный; (*gram*) указа́тельный. **demonstrator** /'demənˌstreɪtə(r)/ *n* демонстра́тор; (*polit*) демонстра́нт.

demoralize /dɪ'mɒrəˌlaɪz/ *vt* деморализова́ть *impf & pf*.

demote /dɪ'məʊt/ *vt* понижа́ть *impf*, пони́зить *pf* в до́лжности.

demure /dɪ'mjʊə(r)/ *adj* скро́мный.

den /den/ *n* берло́га.

denial /dɪ'naɪəl/ *n* отрица́ние; (*refusal*) отка́з.

denigrate /'denɪˌɡreɪt/ *vt* черни́ть *impf*, о— *pf*.

denim /'denɪm/ *adj* джинсо́вый; *n* джинсо́вая ткань.

Denmark /'denmɑːk/ *n* Да́ния.

denomination /dɪˌnɒmɪ'neɪʃ(ə)n/ *n* (*money*) досто́инство; (*relig*) вероиспове́дание. **denominator** /dɪ'nɒmɪˌneɪtə(r)/ *n* знаме-

нátель *m.*

denote /dɪ'nəʊt/ *vt* означáть *impf,* означить *pf.*

denounce /dɪ'naʊns/ *vt* (*condemn*) осуждáть *impf,* осудить *pf*; (*inform on*) доносить *impf,* донести *pf* на+*acc.*

dense /dens/ *adj* густóй; (*stupid*) тупóй. **density** /'densɪtɪ/ *n* плóтность.

dent /dent/ *n* вмятина; *vt* дéлать *impf,* с~ *pf* вмятину в+*prep.*

dental /'dent(ə)l/ *adj* зубнóй. **dentist** /'dentɪst/ *n* зубнóй врач. **dentures** /'dentʃəz/ *n pl* зубнóй протéз.

denunciation /dɪˌnʌnsɪ'eɪʃ(ə)n/ *n* (*condemnation*) осуждéние; (*informing*) донóс.

deny /dɪ'naɪ/ *vt* отрицáть *impf*; (*refuse*) откáзывать *impf,* отказáть *pf* +*dat* (*person*) в+*prep.*

deodorant /dɪ'əʊdərənt/ *n* дезодорáнт.

depart /dɪ'pɑːt/ *vi* отбывáть *impf,* отбыть *pf*; (*deviate*) отклоняться *impf,* отклониться *pf* (*from* от+*gen*).

department /dɪ'pɑːtmənt/ *n* отдéл; (*univ*) кáфедра; ~ **store** универмáг.

departure /dɪ'pɑːtʃə(r)/ *n* отбытие; (*deviation*) отклонéние.

depend /dɪ'pend/ *vi* зависеть *impf* (*on* от+*gen*); (*rely*) полагáться *impf,* положиться *pf* (*on* на+*acc*). **dependable** /-'pendəb(ə)l/ *adj* надёжный. **dependant** /-'pend(ə)nt/ *n* иждивéнец **dependence** /-'pend(ə)ns/ *n* зависимость. **dependent** /-'pend(ə)nt/ *adj* зависимый.

depict /dɪ'pɪkt/ *vt* изображáть *impf,* изобразить *pf.*

deplete /dɪ'pliːt/ *vt* истощáть

impf, истощить *pf.* **depleted** /-'pliːtɪd/ *adj* истощённый. **depletion** /-'pliːʃ(ə)n/ *n* истощéние.

deplorable /dɪ'plɔːrəb(ə)l/ *adj* плачéвный. **deplore** /dɪ'plɔː(r)/ *vt* сожалéть *impf* о+*prep.*

deploy /dɪ'plɔɪ/ *vt* развёртывать *impf,* развернуть *pf.* **deployment** /-mənt/ *n* развёртывание.

deport /dɪ'pɔːt/ *vt* депортировать *impf & pf*; высылáть *impf,* выслать *pf.* **deportation** /diːpɔː'teɪʃ(ə)n/ *n* депортáция; высылка.

deportment /dɪ'pɔːtmənt/ *n* осáнка.

depose /dɪ'pəʊz/ *vt* свергáть *impf,* свергнуть *pf.* **deposit** /-'pɒzɪt/ *n* (*econ*) вклад; (*advance*) задáток; (*sediment*) осáдок; (*coal etc.*) месторождéние; *vt* (*econ*) вносить *impf,* внести *pf.*

depot /'depəʊ/ *n* (*transport*) депó *neut indecl*; (*store*) склад.

deprave /dɪ'preɪv/ *vt* развращáть *impf,* развратить *pf.* **depraved** /-'preɪvd/ *adj* развращённый. **depravity** /-'prævɪtɪ/ *n* разврáт.

deprecate /'deprɪˌkeɪt/ *vt* осуждáть *impf,* осудить *pf.*

depreciate /dɪ'priːʃɪeɪt/ *vt & i* (*econ*) обесцéнивать *impf,* обесцéнить(ся) *pf.* **depreciation** /-'eɪʃ(ə)n/ *n* обесцéнение.

depress /dɪ'pres/ *vt* (*dispirit*) удручáть *impf,* удручить *pf.* **depressed** /-'prest/ *adj* удручённый. **depressing** /-'presɪŋ/ *adj* угнетáющий. **depression** /-'preʃ(ə)n/ *n* (*hollow*) впáдина; (*econ, med, meteorol, etc.*) депрéссия.

deprivation /ˌdeprɪ'veɪʃ(ə)n/ *n*

лише́ние. **deprive** /dɪˈpraɪv/ vt лиша́ть impf, лиши́ть pf (of +gen).

depth /depθ/ n глубина́; **in the ~ of winter** в разга́ре зимы́.

deputation /ˌdepjʊˈteɪʃ(ə)n/ n депута́ция. **deputize** /ˈdepjʊˌtaɪz/ vi замеща́ть impf, замести́ть pf (**for** +acc). **deputy** /ˈdepjʊtɪ/ n замести́тель m; (parl) депута́т.

derail /dɪˈreɪl/ vt: **be derailed** сходи́ть impf, сойти́ pf с ре́льсов. **derailment** /-mənt/ n сход с ре́льсов.

deranged /dɪˈreɪndʒd/ adj сумасше́дший.

derelict /ˈderəlɪkt/ adj забро́шенный.

deride /dɪˈraɪd/ vt высме́ивать impf, вы́смеять pf. **derision** /-ˈrɪʒ(ə)n/ n высме́ивание. **derisive** /-ˈraɪsɪv/ adj (mocking) насме́шливый. **derisory** /-ˈraɪsərɪ/ adj (ridiculous) смехотво́рный.

derivation /ˌderɪˈveɪʃ(ə)n/ n происхожде́ние. **derivative** /dəˈrɪvətɪv/ n произво́дное sb; adj произво́дный. **derive** /dɪˈraɪv/ vt извлека́ть impf, извле́чь pf; vi: **~ from** происходи́ть impf, произойти́ pf от+gen.

derogatory /dɪˈrɒɡətərɪ/ adj рица́тельный.

descend /dɪˈsend/ vi (& t) (go down) спуска́ться impf, спусти́ться pf (c+gen); **be descended from** происходи́ть impf, произойти́ pf из, от, +gen. **descendant** /-ˈsend(ə)nt/ n пото́мок. **descent** /-ˈsent/ n спуск; (lineage) происхожде́ние.

describe /dɪˈskraɪb/ vt опи́сывать impf, описа́ть pf. **description** /-ˈskrɪpʃ(ə)n/ n описа́ние. **descriptive** /-ˈskrɪptɪv/ adj описа́тельный.

desecrate /ˈdesɪˌkreɪt/ vt оскверня́ть impf, оскверни́ть pf. **desecration** /ˌdesɪˈkreɪʃ(ə)n/ n оскверне́ние.

desert[1] /ˈdezət/ n (waste) пусты́ня.

desert[2] /dɪˈzɜːt/ vt покида́ть impf, поки́нуть pf; (mil) дезерти́ровать impf & pf. **deserter** /-ˈzɜːtə(r)/ n дезерти́р. **desertion** /-ˈzɜːʃ(ə)n/ n дезерти́рство.

deserts /dɪˈzɜːts/ n pl заслу́ги f pl. **deserve** /-ˈzɜːv/ vt заслу́живать impf, заслужи́ть pf. **deserving** /-ˈzɜːvɪŋ/ adj досто́йный (of +gen).

design /dɪˈzaɪn/ n (pattern) узо́р; (of car etc.) констру́кция, прое́кт; (industrial) диза́йн; (aim) у́мысел; vt проекти́ровать impf, c~ pf; (intend) предназнача́ть impf, предназна́чить pf.

designate /ˈdezɪɡˌneɪt/ vt (indicate) обознача́ть impf, обозна́чить pf; (appoint) назнача́ть impf, назна́чить pf.

designer /dɪˈzaɪnə(r)/ n (tech) констру́ктор; (industrial) диза́йнер; (of clothes) моделье́р.

desirable /dɪˈzaɪərəb(ə)l/ adj жела́тельный. **desire** /-ˈzaɪə(r)/ n жела́ние; vt жела́ть impf, по~ pf +gen.

desist /dɪˈzɪst/ vi (refrain) возде́рживаться impf, воздержа́ться pf (**from** от+gen).

desk /desk/ n пи́сьменный стол; (school) па́рта.

desolate /ˈdesələt/ adj забро́шенный. **desolation** /ˌdesəˈleɪʃ(ə)n/ n забро́шенность.

despair /dɪˈspeə(r)/ n отча́яние; vi отча́иваться impf, отча́яться pf. **desperate** /ˈdespərət/ adj отча́янный. **desperation**

/ˌdespəˈreɪʃ(ə)n/ n отчáяние.

despicable /dɪˈspɪkəb(ə)l/ adj
презрéнный. **despise** /dɪˈspaɪz/
vt презирáть impf, пре-
зрéть pf.

despite /dɪˈspaɪt/ prep несмотря
на+acc.

despondency /dɪˈspɒndənsɪ/ n
уныние. **despondent** /-d(ə)nt/
adj унылый.

despot /ˈdespɒt/ n дéспот.

dessert /dɪˈzɜːt/ n десéрт.

destination /ˌdestɪˈneɪʃ(ə)n/ n (of
goods) мéсто назначéния; (of
journey) цель f. **destiny** /ˈdestɪnɪ/
n судьбá.

destitute /ˈdestɪtjuːt/ adj без
всяких средств.

destroy /dɪˈstrɔɪ/ vt разрушáть
impf, разрýшить pf. **destroyer**
/-ˈstrɔɪə(r)/ n (naut) эсминец.
destruction /-ˈstrʌkʃ(ə)n/ n
разрушéние. **destructive**
/-ˈstrʌktɪv/ adj разруши-
тельный.

detach /dɪˈtætʃ/ vt отделять
impf, отделить pf. **detached**
/-ˈtætʃt/ adj отдельный; (objective) беспристрáстный; ~
house особняк. **detachment**
/-ˈtætʃmənt/ n (objectivity) бес-
пристрáстие; (mil) отряд.

detail /ˈdiːteɪl/ n детáль, под-
рóбность; in detail подрóбно;
vt подрóбно рассказывать
impf, рассказáть pf. **detailed**
/-teɪld/ adj подрóбный.

detain /dɪˈteɪn/ vt задéрживать
impf, задержáть pf. **detainee**
/ˌdiːteɪˈniː/ n задéржанный sb.

detect /dɪˈtekt/ vt обнарýживать impf, обнарýжить pf.
detection /-ˈtekʃ(ə)n/ n
обнаружéние; (crime) расслé-
дование. **detective** /-tɪv/ n
детектив; ~ film, story, etc. детектив. **detector** /-ˈtektə(r)/ n

детéктор.

detention /dɪˈtenʃ(ə)n/ n задер-
жáние; (school) задéржка в
наказáние.

deter /dɪˈtɜː(r)/ vt удéрживать
impf, удержáть pf (from
от+gen).

detergent /dɪˈtɜːdʒ(ə)nt/ n мóю-
щее срéдство.

deteriorate /dɪˈtɪərɪəˌreɪt/ vi
ухудшáться impf, ухýдшиться
pf. **deterioration** /-ˈreɪʃ(ə)n/ n
ухудшéние.

determination /dɪˌtɜːmɪˈneɪʃ(ə)n/
n решимость. **determine** /dɪ-
ˈtɜːmɪn/ vt (ascertain) устанá-
вливать impf, установить pf;
(be decisive factor) определять
impf, определить pf; (decide)
решáть impf, решить pf. **determined** /dɪˈtɜːmɪnd/ adj решительный.

deterrent /dɪˈterənt/ n срéдство
устрашéния.

detest /dɪˈtest/ vt ненавидеть
impf. **detestable** /-ˈtestəb(ə)l/ adj
отвратительный.

detonate /ˈdetəˌneɪt/ vt & i взры-
вáть(ся) impf, взорвáть(ся) pf.
detonator /-ˈtet(r)/ n детонáтор.

detour /ˈdiːtʊə(r)/ n объéзд.

detract /dɪˈtrækt/ vi: ~ from умa-
лять impf, умалить pf+acc.

detriment /ˈdetrɪmənt/ n ущéрб.
detrimental /-ˈment(ə)l/ adj
врéдный.

deuce /djuːs/ n (tennis) рáвный
счёт.

devaluation /diːˌvæljuːˈeɪʃ(ə)n/ n
девальвáция. **devalue** /diː-
ˈvæljuː/ vt девальвировать impf
& pf.

devastate /ˈdevəˌsteɪt/ vt опустошáть impf, опустошить pf.
devastated /-ˌsteɪtɪd/ adj
потрясённый. **devastating**
/-ˌsteɪtɪŋ/ adj уничтожáющий.

devastation /ˌdevəˈsteɪʃ(ə)n/ n опустошéние.

develop /dɪˈveləp/ vt & i развивáть(ся) impf, развить(ся) pf; vt (phot) проявлять impf, проявить pf. **developer** /-pə(r)/ n (of land etc.) застрóйщик. **development** /-mənt/ n развитие.

deviant /ˈdiːvɪənt/ adj ненормáльный. **deviate** /-vɪeɪt/ vi отклоняться impf, отклониться pf (from от+gen). **deviation** /ˌdiːvɪˈeɪʃ(ə)n/ n отклонéние.

device /dɪˈvaɪs/ n прибóр.

devil /ˈdev(ə)l/ n чёрт. **devilish** /ˈdevəlɪʃ/ adj чертóвский.

devious /ˈdiːvɪəs/ adj (circuitous) окружнóй; (person) непорядочный.

devise /dɪˈvaɪz/ vt придумывать impf, придумать pf.

devoid /dɪˈvɔɪd/ adj лишённый (of +gen).

devolution /ˌdiːvəˈluːʃ(ə)n/ n передáча (власти).

devote /dɪˈvəʊt/ vt посвящáть impf, посвятить pf. **devoted** /-ˈvəʊtɪd/ adj прéданный. **devotee** /ˌdevəˈtiː/ n поклóнник. **devotion** /dɪˈvəʊʃ(ə)n/ n прéданность.

devour /dɪˈvaʊə(r)/ vt пожирáть impf, пожрáть pf.

devout /dɪˈvaʊt/ adj нáбожный.

dew /djuː/ n росá.

dexterity /dekˈsterɪtɪ/ n лóвкость. **dext(e)rous** /ˈdekstrəs/ adj лóвкий.

diabetes /ˌdaɪəˈbiːtiːz/ n диабéт. **diabetic** /ˌdaɪəˈbetɪk/ n диабéтик; adj диабетический.

diabolic(al) /ˌdaɪəˈbɒlɪk((ə)l)/ adj дьявольский.

diagnose /ˈdaɪəɡnəʊz/ vt диагностировать impf & pf. **diagnosis** /ˌdaɪəɡˈnəʊsɪs/ n диагнóз.

diagonal /daɪˈæɡən(ə)l/ n диагонáль; adj диагонáльный. **diagonally** /-ˈæɡənəlɪ/ adv по диагонáли.

diagram /ˈdaɪəɡræm/ n диаграмма.

dial /ˈdaɪ(ə)l/ n (clock) циферблáт; (tech) шкалá; vt набирáть impf, набрáть pf.

dialect /ˈdaɪəlekt/ n диалéкт.

dialogue /ˈdaɪəlɒɡ/ n диалóг.

diameter /daɪˈæmɪtə(r)/ n диáметр. **diametric(al)** /ˌdaɪə-ˈmetrɪk((ə)l)/ adj диаметрáльный; ~ly opposed диаметрáльно противополóжный.

diamond /ˈdaɪəmənd/ n алмáз; (shape) ромб; pl (cards) бубны (-бён, -бнáм) pl.

diaper /ˈdaɪəpə(r)/ n пелёнка.

diaphragm /ˈdaɪəfræm/ n диафрáгма.

diarrhoea /ˌdaɪəˈrɪə/ n понóс.

diary /ˈdaɪərɪ/ n дневник.

dice /daɪs/ see die¹

dicey /ˈdaɪsɪ/ adj рискóванный.

dictate /dɪkˈteɪt/ vt диктовáть impf, про~ pf. **dictation** /-ˈteɪʃ(ə)n/ n диктóвка. **dictator** /-ˈteɪtə(r)/ n диктáтор. **dictatorial** /ˌdɪktəˈtɔːrɪəl/ adj диктáторский. **dictatorship** /dɪkˈteɪtəʃɪp/ n диктатýра.

diction /ˈdɪkʃ(ə)n/ n дикция.

dictionary /ˈdɪkʃənrɪ/ n словáрь m.

didactic /dɪˈdæktɪk/ adj дидактический.

die¹ /daɪ/ n (pl dice /daɪs/) игрáльная кость; (pl dies /daɪz/) (stamp) штамп.

die² /daɪ/ vi (person) умирáть impf, умерéть pf; (animal) дóхнуть impf, из~, по~ pf; (plant) вянуть impf, за~ pf; be dying to óчень хотéть impf; ~ down (fire, sound) угасáть impf,

угаснуть *pf*; ~ out вымирать *impf*, вымереть *pf*.

diesel /'diːz(ə)l/ *n* (*engine*) дизель *m*; *attrib* дизельный.

diet /'daɪət/ *n*; (*habitual food*) пища; *vi* быть на диете. **dietary** /'daɪətrɪ/ *adj* диетический.

differ /'dɪfə(r)/ *vi* отличаться *impf*; различаться *impf*; (*disagree*) расходиться *impf*, разойтись *pf*. **difference** /'dɪfrəns/ *n* разница; (*disagreement*) разногласие. **different** /'dɪfrənt/ *adj* различный, разный. **differential** /dɪfə'renʃ(ə)l/ *n* (*in difference*) разница. **differentiate** /dɪfə'renʃɪeɪt/ *vt* различать *impf*, различить *pf*.

difficult /'dɪfɪkəlt/ *adj* трудный. **difficulty** /-kəltɪ/ *n* трудность; (*difficult situation*) затруднение; without ~ без труда.

diffidence /'dɪfɪdəns/ *n* неуверенность в себе; **diffident** /-d(ə)nt/ *adj* неуверенный в себе.

diffused /dɪ'fjuːzd/ *adj* рассеянный.

dig /dɪg/ *n* (*archael*) раскопки *f pl*; (*poke*) тычок; (*gibe*) шпилька; *pl* (*lodgings*) квартира; give a ~ in the ribs ткнуть *pf* локтем под ребро; *vt* копать *impf*, вы~ *pf*; рыть *impf*, вы~ *pf*; ~ up (*bone*) выкапывать *impf*, выкопать *pf*; (*land*) вскапывать *impf*, вскопать *pf*.

digest /daɪ'dʒest/ *vt* переваривать *impf*, переварить *pf*. **digestible** /-'dʒestɪb(ə)l/ *adj* удобоваримый. **digestion** /-'dʒestʃ(ə)n/ *n* пищеварение.

digger /'dɪgə(r)/ *n* (*tech*) экскаватор.

digit /'dɪdʒɪt/ *n* (*math*) знак. **digital** /'dɪdʒɪt(ə)l/ *adj* циф-

фровой.

dignified /'dɪgnɪfaɪd/ *adj* величавый. **dignitary** /-nɪtərɪ/ *n* сановник. **dignity** /-nɪtɪ/ *n* достоинство.

digress /daɪ'gres/ *vi* отклоняться *impf*, отклониться *pf*. **digression** /-'greʃ(ə)n/ *n* отклонение.

dike /daɪk/ *n* дамба; (*ditch*) ров.

dilapidated /dɪ'læpɪˌdeɪtɪd/ *adj* ветхий.

dilate /daɪ'leɪt/ *vt & i* расширять(ся) *impf*, расширить(ся) *pf*.

dilemma /daɪ'lemə/ *n* дилемма.

dilettante /ˌdɪlɪ'tæntɪ/ *n* дилетант.

diligence /'dɪlɪdʒəns/ *n* прилежание; **diligent** /-lɪdʒ(ə)nt/ *adj* прилежный.

dilute /daɪ'ljuːt/ *vt* разбавлять *impf*, разбавить *pf*.

dim /dɪm/ *adj* (*not bright*) тусклый; (*vague*) смутный; (*stupid*) тупой.

dimension /daɪ'menʃ(ə)n/ *n* (*pl*) размеры *m pl*; (*math*) измерение. **-dimensional** /-'menʃən(ə)l/ *in comb* -мерный; **three-**~ трёхмерный.

diminish /dɪ'mɪnɪʃ/ *vt & i* уменьшать(ся) *impf*, уменьшить(ся) *pf*. **diminutive** /-'mɪnjʊtɪv/ *adj* маленький *n* уменьшительное *sb*.

dimness /'dɪmnɪs/ *n* тусклость.

dimple /'dɪmp(ə)l/ *n* ямочка.

din /dɪn/ *n* грохот; (*voices*) гам.

dine /daɪn/ *vi* обедать *impf*, по~ *pf*. **diner** /'daɪnə(r)/ *n* обедающий *sb*.

dinghy /'dɪŋɪ/ *n* шлюпка; (*rubber* ~) надувная лодка.

dingy /'dɪndʒɪ/ *adj* (*drab*) тусклый; (*dirty*) грязный.

dining-car /'daɪnɪŋ kɑː/ *n* вагон-ресторан. **dining-room** /-to-

ло́вая *sb.* dinner /'dɪnə(r)/ *n* обе́д; ~-jacket смо́кинг.

dinosaur /'daɪnəsɔː(r)/ *n* диноза́вр.

diocese /'daɪəsɪs/ *n* епа́рхия.

dip /dɪp/ *vt* (*immerse*) окуна́ть *impf*, окуну́ть *pf*; (*partially*) обма́кивать *impf*, обмакну́ть *pf*; *vi* (*slope*) понижа́ться *impf*, пони́зиться *pf*; *n* (*depression*) впа́дина; (*slope*) укло́н; have a ~ (*bathe*) купа́ться *impf*, вы́~ *pf*.

diphtheria /dɪf'θɪərɪə/ *n* дифтери́я.

diphthong /'dɪfθɒŋ/ *n* дифто́нг.

diploma /dɪ'pləʊmə/ *n* дипло́м. diplomacy /dɪ'pləʊməsɪ/ *n* дипломати́я. diplomat /'dɪpləmæt/ *n* диплома́т. diplomatic /ˌdɪplə'mætɪk/ *adj* дипломати́ческий.

dire /'daɪə(r)/ *adj* стра́шный; (*ominous*) злове́щий.

direct /daɪ'rekt/ *adj* прямо́й; ~ current постоя́нный ток; *vt* направля́ть *impf*, напра́вить *pf*; (*guide*, *manage*) руководи́ть *impf* +*instr*; (*film*) режиссёровать *impf*. direction /dɪ'rek(ʃ)n/ *n* направле́ние; (*guidance*) руково́дство; (*instruction*) указа́ние; (*film*) режиссу́ра; stage ~ рема́рка. directive /dɪ'rektɪv/ *n* директи́ва. directly /dɪ'rektlɪ/ *adv* прямо́; (*at once*) сра́зу. director /dɪ'rektə(r)/ *n* дире́ктор; (*film etc.*) режиссёр(-постано́вщик). directory /dɪ'rektərɪ/ *n* спра́вочник, указа́тель *m*; (*tel*) телефо́нная кни́га.

dirt /dɜːt/ *n* грязь. dirty /'dɜːtɪ/ *adj* гря́зный; *vt* па́чкать *impf*, за~ *pf*.

disability /ˌdɪsə'bɪlɪtɪ/ *n* физи́ческий/психи́ческий недоста́ток; (*disablement*) инвали́дность. disabled /dɪs'eɪb(ə)ld/

adj: he is ~ он инвали́д.

disadvantage /ˌdɪsəd'vɑːntɪdʒ/ *n* невы́годное положе́ние; (*defect*) недоста́ток. disadvantageous /ˌdɪsˌædvən'teɪdʒəs/ *adj* невы́годный.

disaffected /ˌdɪsə'fektɪd/ *adj* недово́льный.

disagree /ˌdɪsə'griː/ *vi* не соглаша́ться *impf*, согласи́ться *pf*; (*not correspond*) не соотве́тствовать *impf* +*dat*. disagreeable /-'grɪəb(ə)l/ *adj* неприя́тный. disagreement /-'griːmənt/ *n* разногла́сие; (*quarrel*) ссо́ра.

disappear /ˌdɪsə'pɪə(r)/ *vi* исчеза́ть *impf*, исче́знуть *pf*. disappearance /-'pɪərəns/ *n* исчезнове́ние.

disappoint /ˌdɪsə'pɔɪnt/ *vt* разоча́ровывать *impf*, разочарова́ть *pf*. disappointed /-'pɔɪntɪd/ *adj* разоча́рованный. disappointing /-'pɔɪntɪŋ/ *adj* разочаро́вывающий. disappointment /-'pɔɪntmənt/ *n* разочарова́ние.

disapproval /ˌdɪsə'pruːv(ə)l/ *n* неодобре́ние. disapprove /ˌdɪsə'pruːv/ *vt & i* не одобря́ть *impf*.

disarm /dɪs'ɑːm/ *vt* (*mil*) разоружа́ть *impf*, разоружи́ть *pf*; (*criminal*; *also fig*) обезору́живать *impf*, обезору́жить *pf*. disarmament /-'ɑːməmənt/ *n* разоруже́ние.

disarray /ˌdɪsə'reɪ/ *n* беспоря́док.

disaster /dɪ'zɑːstə(r)/ *n* бе́дствие. disastrous /-'zɑːstrəs/ *adj* катастрофи́ческий.

disband /dɪs'bænd/ *vt* распуска́ть *impf*, распусти́ть *pf*; *vi* расходи́ться *impf*, разойти́сь *pf*.

disbelief /ˌdɪsbɪ'liːf/ *n* неве́рие.

disc, disk /dɪsk/ *n* диск; ~ **drive** (*comput*) дисково́д; ~ **jockey** диск-жоке́й, диджже́й.

discard /dɪ'skɑːd/ *vt* отбра́сывать *impf*, отбро́сить *pf*.

discern /dɪ'sɜːn/ *vt* различа́ть *impf*, различи́ть *pf*. **discernible** /-'sɜːnɪb(ə)l/ *adj* различи́мый. **discerning** /-'sɜːnɪŋ/ *adj* проница́тельный.

discharge *vt* /dɪs'tʃɑːdʒ/ (*gun*; *electr*) разряжа́ть *impf*, разряди́ть *pf*; (*dismiss*) увольня́ть *impf*, уво́лить *pf*; (*prisoner*) освобожда́ть *impf*, освободи́ть *pf*; (*debt*; *duty*) выполня́ть *impf*, вы́полнить *pf*; (*from hospital*) выпи́сывать *impf*, вы́писать *pf*; *n* /'dɪstʃɑːdʒ/ разгру́зка; (*electr*) разря́д; увольне́ние; освобожде́ние; выполне́ние; (*med*) выделе́ния *neut pl*.

disciple /dɪ'saɪp(ə)l/ *n* учени́к.

disciplinarian /ˌdɪsɪplɪ'neərɪən/ *n* сторо́нник дисципли́ны. **disciplinary** /ˌdɪsɪ'plɪnərɪ/ *adj* дисциплина́рный. **discipline** /'dɪsɪplɪn/ *n* дисципли́на; *vt* дисциплини́ровать *impf* & *pf*.

disclaim /dɪs'kleɪm/ *vt* (*deny*) отрица́ть *impf*; ~ **responsibility** слага́ть *impf*, сложи́ть *pf* с себя́ отве́тственность.

disclose /dɪs'kləʊz/ *vt* обнару́живать *impf*, обнару́жить *pf*. **disclosure** /-'kləʊʒə(r)/ *n* обнаруже́ние.

discoloured /dɪs'kʌləd/ *adj* обесцве́ченный.

discomfit /dɪs'kʌmfɪt/ *vt* смуща́ть *impf*, смути́ть *pf*. **discomfiture** /-'kʌmfɪtʃə(r)/ *n* смуще́ние.

discomfort /dɪs'kʌmfət/ *n* неудо́бство.

disconcert /ˌdɪskən'sɜːt/ *vt* смуща́ть *impf*, смути́ть *pf*.

disconnect /ˌdɪskə'nekt/ *vt* разъединя́ть *impf*, разъедини́ть *pf*; (*switch off*) выключа́ть *impf*, вы́ключить *pf*. **disconnected** /-tɪd/ *adj* (*incoherent*) бессвя́зный.

disconsolate /dɪs'kɒnsələt/ *adj* неуте́шный.

discontent /ˌdɪskən'tent/ *n* недово́льство. **discontented** /-'tentɪd/ *adj* недово́льный.

discontinue /ˌdɪskən'tɪnjuː/ *vt* прекраща́ть *impf*, прекрати́ть *pf*.

discord /'dɪskɔːd/ *n* разногла́сие; (*mus*) диссона́нс. **discordant** /-'skɔːd(ə)nt/ *adj* несогласу́ющийся; диссони́рующий.

discotheque /'dɪskəˌtek/ *n* дискоте́ка.

discount *n* /'dɪskaʊnt/ ски́дка; *vt* /dɪs'kaʊnt/ (*disregard*) не принима́ть *impf*, приня́ть *pf* в расчёт.

discourage /dɪs'kʌrɪdʒ/ *vt* обескура́живать *impf*, обескура́жить *pf*; (*dissuade*) отгова́ривать *impf*, отговори́ть *pf*.

discourse /'dɪskɔːs/ *n* речь.

discourteous /dɪs'kɜːtɪəs/ *adj* неве́жливый.

discover /dɪ'skʌvə(r)/ *vt* открыва́ть *impf*, откры́ть *pf*; (*find out*) обнару́живать *impf*, обнару́жить *pf*. **discovery** /-'skʌvərɪ/ *n* откры́тие.

discredit /dɪs'kredɪt/ *n* позо́р; *vt* дискредити́ровать *impf* & *pf*.

discreet /dɪs'kriːt/ *adj* такти́чный. **discretion** /-'skreʃ(ə)n/ *n* (*judgement*) благоразу́мие; (*prudence*) благоразу́мие; **at one's** ~ по своему́ усмотре́нию.

discrepancy /dɪs'krepənsɪ/ *n* не-

соответствие.

discriminate /dɪˈskrɪmɪˌneɪt/ vt различа́ть impf, различи́ть pf; ~ **against** дискримини́ровать impf & pf. **discrimination** /-ˈneɪʃ(ə)n/ n (taste) разбо́рчивость; (bias) дискримина́ция.

discus /ˈdɪskəs/ n диск.

discuss /dɪˈskʌs/ vt обсужда́ть impf, обсуди́ть pf. **discussion** /-ˈkʌʃ(ə)n/ n обсужде́ние.

disdain /dɪsˈdeɪn/ n презре́ние. **disdainful** /-fʊl/ adj презри́тельный.

disease /dɪˈziːz/ n боле́знь. **diseased** /-ziːzd/ adj больно́й.

disembark /ˌdɪsɪmˈbɑːk/ vi выса́живаться impf, вы́садиться pf.

disenchantment /ˌdɪsɪnˈtʃɑːntmənt/ n разочарова́ние.

disengage /ˌdɪsɪnˈgeɪdʒ/ vt освобожда́ть impf, освободи́ть pf; (clutch) отпуска́ть impf, отпусти́ть pf.

disentangle /ˌdɪsɪnˈtæŋg(ə)l/ vt распу́тывать impf, распу́тать pf.

disfavour /dɪsˈfeɪvə(r)/ n неми́лость.

disfigure /dɪsˈfɪgə(r)/ vt уро́довать impf, из~ pf.

disgrace /dɪsˈgreɪs/ n позо́р; (disfavour) неми́лость; vt позо́рить impf, о~ pf. **disgraceful** /-ˈgreɪsfʊl/ adj позо́рный.

disgruntled /dɪsˈɡrʌnt(ə)ld/ adj недово́льный.

disguise /dɪsˈgaɪz/ n маскиро́вка; vt маскирова́ть impf, за~ pf; (conceal) скрыва́ть impf, скрыть pf. **disguised** /-ˈgaɪzd/ adj замаскиро́ванный.

disgust /dɪsˈgʌst/ n отвраще́ние; vt внуша́ть impf, внуши́ть pf. отвраще́ние +dat. **disgusting** /-ˈgʌstɪŋ/ adj отврати-

тельный.

dish /dɪʃ/ n блю́до; pl посу́да collect; ~**washer** посудомо́ечная маши́на; vt: ~ **up** подава́ть impf, пода́ть pf.

dishearten /dɪsˈhɑːt(ə)n/ vt обескура́живать impf, обескура́жить pf.

dishevelled /dɪˈʃev(ə)ld/ adj растрёпанный.

dishonest /dɪsˈɒnɪst/ adj нече́стный. **dishonesty** /-ˈɒnɪsti/ n нече́стность. **dishonour** /-ˈɒnə(r)/ n бесче́стие; vt бесче́стить impf, о~ pf. **dishonourable** /-ˈɒnərəb(ə)l/ adj бесче́стный.

disillusion /ˌdɪsɪˈluːʒ(ə)n/ vt разочаро́вывать impf, разочарова́ть pf. **disillusionment** /-mənt/ n разочаро́ванность.

disinclination /ˌdɪsɪnklɪˈneɪʃ(ə)n/ n нескло́нность, неохо́та. **disinclined** /-ˈklaɪnd/ adj **be** ~ не хоте́ться impers +dat.

disinfect /ˌdɪsɪnˈfekt/ vt дезинфици́ровать impf & pf. **disinfectant** /-t(ə)nt/ n дезинфици́рующее сре́дство.

disingenuous /ˌdɪsɪnˈdʒenjʊəs/ adj нейскренний.

disinherit /ˌdɪsɪnˈherɪt/ vt лиша́ть impf, лиши́ть pf насле́дства.

disintegrate /dɪsˈɪntɪˌgreɪt/ vi распада́ться impf, распа́сться pf. **disintegration** /-ˈgreɪʃ(ə)n/ n распа́д.

disinterested /dɪsˈɪntrɪstɪd/ adj беско́рыстный.

disjointed /dɪsˈdʒɔɪntɪd/ adj бессвя́зный.

disk /dɪsk/ see disc

dislike /dɪsˈlaɪk/ n нелюбо́вь (**for** к+dat); vt не люби́ть impf.

dislocate /ˈdɪsləˌkeɪt/ vt (med) вы́вихнуть pf.

dislodge /dɪsˈlɒdʒ/ vt смеща́ть

impf, смести́ть *pf.*

disloyal /dɪs'lɔɪəl/ *adj* нелоя́льный. **disloyalty** /-tɪ/ *n* нелоя́льность.

dismal /'dɪzm(ə)l/ *adj* мра́чный.

dismantle /dɪs'mænt(ə)l/ *vt* разбира́ть *impf,* разобра́ть *pf.*

dismay /dɪs'meɪ/ *vt* смуща́ть *impf,* смути́ть *pf; n* смуще́ние.

dismiss /dɪs'mɪs/ *vt* (*sack*) увольня́ть *impf,* уво́лить *pf;* (*disband*) распуска́ть *impf,* распусти́ть *pf.* **dismissal** /-səl/ *n* увольне́ние; ро́спуск.

dismount /dɪs'maʊnt/ *vi* спе́шиваться *impf,* спе́шиться *pf.*

disobedience /ˌdɪsə'biːdɪəns/ *n* непослуша́ние. **disobedient** /-ənt/ *adj* непослу́шный. **disobey** /ˌdɪsə'beɪ/ *vt* не слу́шаться *impf* +*gen.*

disorder /dɪs'ɔːdə(r)/ *n* беспоря́док. **disorderly** /-lɪ/ *adj* (*untidy*) беспоря́дочный; (*unruly*) бу́йный.

disorganized /dɪs'ɔːgənaɪzd/ *adj* неорганизо́ванный.

disorientation /dɪsˌɔːrɪən'teɪʃ(ə)n/ *n* дезориента́ция. **disoriented** /dɪs'ɔːrɪəntɪd/ *adj:* I am /was ~ я потеря́л(а) направле́ние.

disown /dɪs'əʊn/ *vt* отка́зываться *impf,* отказа́ться *pf* от+*gen.*

disparaging /dɪ'spærɪdʒɪŋ/ *adj* оскорби́тельный.

disparity /dɪ'spærɪtɪ/ *n* нера́венство.

dispassionate /dɪ'spæʃənət/ *adj* беспристра́стный.

dispatch /dɪ'spætʃ/ *vt* (*send*) отправля́ть *impf,* отпра́вить *pf;* (*deal with*) распра́виться *impf* с c+*instr;* *n* отпра́вка; (*message*) донесе́ние; (*rapidity*) быстрота́; **~-rider**

мотоцикли́ст свя́зи.

dispel /dɪ'spel/ *vt* рассе́ивать *impf,* рассе́ять *pf.*

dispensable /dɪ'spensəb(ə)l/ *adj* необяза́тельный.

dispensary /dɪ'spensərɪ/ *n* апте́ка.

dispensation /ˌdɪspen'seɪʃ(ə)n/ *n* (*exemption*) освобожде́ние (от обяза́тельства). **dispense** /dɪ'spens/ *vt* (*distribute*) раздава́ть *impf,* разда́ть *pf;* ~ **with** обходи́ться *impf,* обойти́сь *pf* без+*gen.*

dispersal /dɪ'spɜːsəl/ *n* распростране́ние. **disperse** /-'spɜːs/ *vt* (*drive away*) разгоня́ть *impf,* разогна́ть *pf;* (*scatter*) рассе́ивать *impf,* рассе́ять *pf; vi* расходи́ться *impf,* разойти́сь *pf.*

dispirited /dɪ'spɪrɪtɪd/ *adj* удручённый.

displaced /dɪs'pleɪst/ *adj:* ~ **persons** перемещённые ли́ца *neut pl.*

display /dɪs'pleɪ/ *n* пока́з; *vt* пока́зывать *impf,* показа́ть *pf.*

displeased /dɪs'pliːzd/ *predic* недово́лен (-льна). **displeasure** /-'pleʒə(r)/ *n* недово́льство.

disposable /dɪs'pəʊzəb(ə)l/ *adj* одноразо́вый. **disposal** /-'spəʊz(ə)l/ *n* удале́ние; **at your** ~ в ва́шем распоряже́нии. **dispose** /-'spəʊz/ *vi:* ~ **of** избавля́ться *impf,* изба́виться *pf* от+*gen.* **disposed** /-'spəʊzd/ *predic:* ~ **to** располо́жен (-ена) к+*dat* or +*inf.* **disposition** /ˌdɪspə'zɪʃ(ə)n/ *n* расположе́ние; (*temperament*) нрав.

disproportionate /ˌdɪsprə'pɔːʃənət/ *adj* непропорциона́льный.

disprove /dɪs'pruːv/ *vt* опроверга́ть *impf,* опрове́ргнуть *pf.*

dispute /dɪ'spjuːt/ *n* (*debate*)

спор; (*quarrel*) ссо́ра; *vt* оспа́ривать *impf*, оспо́рить *pf*.

disqualification /dɪs,kwɒlɪfɪ'keɪʃ(ə)n/ *n* дисквалифика́ция.

disqualify /dɪs'kwɒlɪ,faɪ/ *vt* дисквалифици́ровать *impf* & *pf*.

disquieting /dɪs'kwaɪətɪŋ/ *adj* трево́жный.

disregard /,dɪsrɪ'gɑːd/ *n* пренебреже́ние +*instr*; *vt* игнори́ровать *impf* & *pf*; пренебрега́ть *impf*, пренебре́чь *pf* +*instr*.

disrepair /,dɪsrɪ'peə(r)/ *n* неиспра́вность.

disreputable /dɪs'repjʊtəb(ə)l/ *adj* по́льзующийся дурно́й сла́вой. **disrepute** /,dɪsrɪ'pjuːt/ *n* дурна́я сла́ва.

disrespect /,dɪsrɪ'spekt/ *n* неуваже́ние. **disrespectful** /-fʊl/ *adj* непочти́тельный.

disrupt /dɪs'rʌpt/ *vt* срыва́ть *impf*, сорва́ть *pf*. **disruptive** /tɪv/ *adj* подрывно́й.

dissatisfaction /,dɪsætɪs'fækʃ(ə)n/ *n* недово́льство. **dissatisfied** /dɪ'sætɪsfaɪd/ *adj* недово́льный.

dissect /dɪ'sekt/ *vt* разреза́ть *impf*, разре́зать *pf*; (*med*) вскрыва́ть *impf*, вскрыть *pf*.

disseminate /dɪ'semɪ,neɪt/ *vt* распространя́ть *impf*, распространи́ть *pf*; **dissemination** /-'neɪʃ(ə)n/ *n* распростране́ние.

dissension /dɪ'senʃ(ə)n/ *n* раздо́р. **dissent** /-'sent/ *n* расхожде́ние; (*eccl*) раско́л.

dissertation /,dɪsə'teɪʃ(ə)n/ *n* диссерта́ция.

disservice /dɪs'sɜːvɪs/ *n* плоха́я услу́га.

dissident /'dɪsɪd(ə)nt/ *n* дисси-де́нт.

dissimilar /dɪ'sɪmɪlə(r)/ *adj* несхо́дный.

dissipate /'dɪsɪ,peɪt/ *vt* (*dispel*)

рассе́ивать *impf*, рассе́ять *pf*; (*squander*) прома́тывать *impf*, промота́ть *pf*. **dissipated** /-tɪd/ *adj* распу́тный.

dissociate /dɪ'səʊʃɪ,eɪt/ *vt*: ~ o.s. отмежёвываться *impf*, отмежева́ться *pf* (*from* +*gen*).

dissolute /'dɪsə,luːt/ *adj* распу́тный. **dissolution** /-'luːʃ(ə)n/ *n* (*parl*) ро́спуск. **dissolve** /dɪ'zɒlv/ *vt* & *i* (*in liquid*) растворя́ть(ся) *impf*, раствори́ть(ся) *pf*; *vt* (*annul*) расторга́ть *impf*, расто́ргнуть *pf*; (*parl*) распуска́ть *impf*, распусти́ть *pf*.

dissonance /'dɪsənəns/ *n* диссона́нс. **dissonant** /-nənt/ *adj* диссони́рующий.

dissuade /dɪ'sweɪd/ *vt* отгова́ривать *impf*, отговори́ть *pf*.

distance /'dɪst(ə)ns/ *n* расстоя́ние; *from a* ~ и́здали; *in the* ~ вдалеке́. **distant** /-'t(ə)nt/ *adj* далёкий, (*also of relative*) да́льний; (*reserved*) сде́ржанный.

distaste /dɪs'teɪst/ *n* отвраще́ние. **distasteful** /-fʊl/ *adj* проти́вный.

distended /dɪ'stendɪd/ *adj* наду́тый.

distil /dɪ'stɪl/ *vt* (*whisky*) перегоня́ть *impf*, перегна́ть *pf*; (*water*) дистилли́ровать *impf* & *pf*. **distillation** /-'leɪʃ(ə)n/ *n* перего́нка; дистилля́ция. **distillery** /dɪ'stɪlərɪ/ *n* перего́нный заво́д.

distinct /dɪ'stɪŋkt/ *adj* (*different*) отли́чный; (*clear*) отчётливый; (*evident*) заме́тный. **distinction** /-'stɪŋkʃ(ə)n/ *n* (*difference*) ра́зница; (*excellence*) отли́чие; (*discrimination*) разли́чие. **distinctive** /-'stɪŋktɪv/ *adj* отличи́тельный. **distinctly** /-'stɪŋktlɪ/ *adv* я́сно.

distinguish /dɪ'stɪŋgwɪʃ/ *vt* раз-

личáть *impf*, различи́ть *pf*; ~ **o.s.** отличáться *impf*, отличи́ться *pf*. **distinguished** /-'stɪŋwɪʃt/ *adj* выдаю́щийся.

distort /dɪ'stɔːt/ *vt* искажáть *impf*, искази́ть *pf*; (*misrepresent*) извращáть *impf*, извратáть *pf*. **distortion** /-'stɔːʃ(ə)n/ *n* искажéние; извращéние.

distract /dɪ'strækt/ *vt* отвлекáть *impf*, отвлéчь *pf*. **distraction** /-'stræk∫(ə)n/ *n* (*amusement*) развлечéние; (*madness*) безýмие.

distraught /dɪ'strɔːt/ *adj* обезýмевший.

distress /dɪ'stres/ *n* (*suffering*) огорчéние; (*danger*) бéдствие; *vt* огорчáть *impf*, огорчи́ть *pf*.

distribute /dɪ'strɪbjuːt/ *vt* (*hand out*) раздавáть *impf*, раздáть *pf*; (*allocate*) распределя́ть *impf*, распредели́ть *pf*. **distribution** /ˌdɪstrɪ'bjuːʃ(ə)n/ *n* распределéние. **distributor** /dɪ'strɪbjʊtə(r)/ *n* распределитель *m*.

district /'dɪstrɪkt/ *n* райóн.

distrust /dɪs'trʌst/ *n* недовéрие; *vt* не довéря́ть *impf*. **distrustful** /-fʊl/ *adj* недовéрчивый.

disturb /dɪ'stɜːb/ *vt* беспокóить *impf*, о~ *pf*. **disturbance** /-bəns/ *n* нарушéние покóя; *pl* (*polit etc*.) беспорядки *m pl*.

disuse /dɪs'juːs/ *n* неупотреблéние; **fall into** ~ выйти́ *pf* из употреблéния. **disused** /-'juːzd/ *adj* заброшенный.

ditch /dɪtʃ/ *n* канáва, ров.

dither /'dɪðə(r)/ *vi* колебáться *impf*.

ditto /'dɪtəʊ/ *n* то же сáмое; *adv* так же.

divan /dɪ'væn/ *n* дивáн.

dive /daɪv/ *vi* ныря́ть *impf*, нырнýть *pf*; (*aeron*) пики́ровать *impf* & *pf*; *n* нырóк, прыжóк в вóду. **diver** /-və(r)/ *n* водолáз.

diverge /daɪ'vɜːdʒ/ *vi* расходи́ться *impf*, разойти́сь *pf*. **divergent** /-dʒ(ə)nt/ *adj* расходя́щийся.

diverse /daɪ'vɜːs/ *adj* разнообрáзный. **diversification** /-vɜːsɪfɪ'keɪʃ(ə)n/ *n* расширéние ассортимéнта. **diversify** /-'vɜːsɪˌfaɪ/ *vt* разнообрáзить *impf*. **diversion** /-'vɜːʃ(ə)n/ *n* (*detour*) объéзд; (*amusement*) развлечéние. **diversity** /-'vɜːsɪtɪ/ *n* разнообрáзие. **divert** /-'vɜːt/ *vt* отклоня́ть *impf*, отклони́ть *pf*; (*amuse*) развлекáть *impf*, развлéчь *pf*. **diverting** /-'vɜːtɪŋ/ *adj* забáвный.

divest /daɪ'vest/ *vt* (*deprive*) лишáть *impf*, лиши́ть *pf* (of +*gen*); ~ **o.s.** отказываться *impf*, отказáться *pf* (of от+*gen*).

divide /dɪ'vaɪd/ *vt* (*share*; *math*) дели́ть *impf*, по~ *pf*; (*separate*) разделя́ть *impf*, раздели́ть *pf*.

dividend /'dɪvɪˌdend/ *n* дивидéнд.

divine /dɪ'vaɪn/ *adj* божéственный.

diving /'daɪvɪŋ/ *n* ныря́ние; ~**board** трамплин.

divinity /dɪ'vɪnɪtɪ/ *n* (*quality*) божéственность; (*deity*) божествó; (*theology*) богослóвие.

divisible /dɪ'vɪzɪb(ə)l/ *adj* дели́мый. **division** /-'vɪʒ(ə)n/ *n* (*dividing*) делéние, разделéние; (*section*) отдéл; (*mil*) дивизия.

divorce /dɪ'vɔːs/ *n* развóд; *vt* разводи́ться *impf*, развести́сь *pf*. **divorced** /-'vɔːst/ *adj* разведённый.

divulge /daɪ'vʌldʒ/ *vt* разглашáть *impf*, разгласи́ть *pf*.

DIY abbr (of do-it-yourself): he is good at ~ у него золотые руки; ~ shop магазин «сделай сам».

dizziness /'dɪzɪnɪs/ n головокружение. **dizzy** /'dɪzɪ/ adj (causing dizziness) головокружительный; I am ~ у меня кружится голова.

DNA abbr (of deoxyribonucleic acid) ДНК.

do /duː/ vt делать impf, c~ pf; vi (be suitable) годиться impf; (suffice) быть достаточным; ~-it-yourself see DIY; that will ~! хватит!; how ~ you ~? здравствуйте!; как вы поживаете?; ~ away with (abolish) уничтожать impf, уничтожить pf; ~ in (kill) убивать impf, убить pf; ~ up (restore) ремонтировать impf, от~ pf; (wrap up) завёртывать impf, завернуть pf; (fasten) застёгивать impf, застегнуть pf; ~ without обходиться impf, обойтись pf без+gen.

docile /'dəʊsaɪl/ adj покорный. **docility** /'sɪlɪtɪ/ n покорность.

dock¹ /dɒk/ n (naut) док; vt ставить impf, по~ pf в док; vi входить impf, войти pf в док; vi (spacecraft) стыковаться impf, co~ pf. **docker** /-kə(r)/ n докер. **dockyard** n верфь.

dock² /dɒk/ n (law) скамья подсудимых.

docket /'dɒkɪt/ n квитанция; (label) ярлык.

doctor /'dɒktə(r)/ n врач; (also univ) доктор; vt (castrate) кастрировать impf & pf; (spay) удалять impf, удалить pf яичники y+gen; (falsify) фальсифицировать impf & pf. **doctorate** /-rət/ n степень доктора.

doctrine /'dɒktrɪn/ n доктрина.

document /'dɒkjʊmənt/ n документ; vt документировать impf & pf. **documentary** /,dɒkjʊ'mentərɪ/ n документальный фильм. **documentation** /,dɒkjʊmen'teɪʃ(ə)n/ n документация.

doddery /'dɒdərɪ/ adj дряхлый.

dodge /dɒdʒ/ n увертка; vt уклоняться impf, уклониться pf от+gen; (jump to avoid) отскакивать impf, отскочить pf (от+gen). **dodgy** /'dɒdʒɪ/ adj каверзный.

doe /dəʊ/ n самка.

dog /dɒg/ n собака, пёс; (fig) преследовать impf. **dog-eared** /'dɒgɪəd/ adj захватанный.

dogged /'dɒgɪd/ adj упорный.

dogma /'dɒgmə/ n догма. **dogmatic** /-'mætɪk/ adj догматический.

doings /'duːɪŋz/ n pl дела neut pl.

doldrums /'dɒldrəmz/ n: be in the ~ хандрить impf.

dole /dəʊl/ n пособие по безработице; vt (~ out) выдавать impf, выдать pf.

doleful /'dəʊlfʊl/ adj скорбный.

doll /dɒl/ n кукла.

dollar /'dɒlə(r)/ n доллар.

dollop /'dɒləp/ n солидная порция.

dolphin /'dɒlfɪn/ n дельфин.

domain /də'meɪn/ n (estate) владение; (field) область.

dome /dəʊm/ n купол.

domestic /də'mestɪk/ adj (of household; animals) домашний; (of family) семейный; (polit) внутренний; n прислуга. **domesticate** /-'mestɪ,keɪt/ vt приручать impf, приручить pf. **domesticity** /,dəmə'stɪsɪtɪ/ n домашняя, семейная, жизнь.

domicile /'dɒmɪ,saɪl/ n место-

жи́тельство.

dominance /'dɒmɪnəns/ n госпо́дство. **dominant** /-mɪnənt/ adj преоблада́ющий; госпо́дствующий. **dominate** /-mɪˌneɪt/ vt госпо́дствовать impf над +instr. **domineering** /-mɪ'nɪərɪŋ/ adj вла́стный.

dominion /də'mɪnɪən/ n влады́чество; (realm) владе́ние.

domino /'dɒmɪˌnəʊ/ n кость доми́но; pl (game) доми́но neut indecl.

don /dɒn/ vt надева́ть impf, наде́ть pf.

donate /dəʊ'neɪt/ vt же́ртвовать impf, по~ pf. **donation** /-'neɪʃ(ə)n/ n поже́ртвование.

donkey /'dɒŋkɪ/ n осёл.

donor /'dəʊnə(r)/ n же́ртвователь m; (med) до́нор.

doom /duːm/ n (ruin) ги́бель; vt обрека́ть impf, обре́чь pf.

door /dɔː(r)/ n дверь. **doorbell** n (дверно́й) звоно́к. **doorman** n швейца́р. **doormat** n полови́к. **doorstep** n поро́г. **doorway** n дверно́й проём.

dope /dəʊp/ n (drug) нарко́тик; vt дурма́нить impf, о~ pf.

dormant /'dɔːmənt/ adj (sleeping) спя́щий; (inactive) безде́йствующий.

dormer window /'dɔːmə 'wɪndəʊ/ n слухово́е окно́.

dormitory /'dɔːmɪtərɪ/ n о́бщая спа́льня.

dormouse /'dɔːmaʊs/ n со́ня.

dorsal /'dɔːs(ə)l/ adj спинно́й.

dosage /'dəʊsɪdʒ/ n дозиро́вка. **dose** /dəʊs/ n до́за.

dossier /'dɒsɪə(r)/ n досье́ neut indecl.

dot /dɒt/ n то́чка; vt ста́вить impf, по~ pf то́чки на+асс; (scatter) усе́ивать impf, усе́ять pf (with +instr). **~ted line**

пункти́р.

dote /dəʊt/ vi: ~ on обожа́ть impf.

double /'dʌb(ə)l/ adj двойно́й; (doubled) удвоенный; **~bass** контраба́с; **~ bed** двуспа́льная крова́ть; **~breasted** двубо́ртный; **~cross** обма́нывать impf, обману́ть pf; **~dealing** двуру́шничество; **~decker** двухэта́жный авто́бус; **~edged** обоюдоо́стрый; **~ glazing** двойны́е ра́мы f pl; **~room** ко́мната на двои́х; adv вдво́е; (two together) вдвоём; (person's) двойно́е коли́чество; **~** двойни́к; pl (sport) па́рная игра́; vt & i удва́ивать(ся) impf, удво́ить(ся) pf; **~ back** возвраща́ться impf, верну́ться pf наза́д; **~ up** (in pain) скрю́чиваться impf, скрю́читься pf; (share a room) помеща́ться impf, помести́ться pf вдвоём в одно́й ко́мнате; (~ up as) рабо́тать impf + instr по совмести́тельству.

doubt /daʊt/ n сомне́ние; vt сомнева́ться impf в+prep. **doubtful** /-fʊl/ adj сомни́тельный; (~ up as). **doubtless** /-lɪs/ adv несомне́нно.

dough /dəʊ/ n те́сто. **doughnut** n по́нчик.

douse /daʊs/ vt (drench) залива́ть impf, зали́ть pf.

dove /dʌv/ n го́лубь m. **dovetail** n ла́сточкин хвост.

dowdy /'daʊdɪ/ adj неэлега́нтный.

down¹ /daʊn/ n (fluff) пух.

down² /daʊn/ adv (motion) вниз; (position) внизу́; be ~ with (ill) impf + instr; prep вниз с+gen, по+dat; (along) (вдоль по+dat; vt: (gulp) опроки́дывать impf, опроки́нуть pf.

~-and-out бродя́га *m*; ~cast, ~-hearted уны́лый. **downfall** *n* ги́бель. **downhill** *adv* под го́ру. **download** *vt* (*comput*) загружа́ть *impf*, загрузи́ть *pf*. **downpour** *n* ли́вень *m*. **downright** *adj* я́вный; *adv* соверше́нно. **downstairs** *adv* (*motion*) вниз; (*position*) внизу́. **downstream** *adv* вниз по тече́нию. **down-to-earth** *adj* реали́стичный. **downtrodden** /'daʊn,trɒd(ə)n/ *adj* угнетённый.

dowry /'daʊərɪ/ *n* прида́ное *sb*. **doze** /dəʊz/ *vi* дрема́ть *impf*. **dozen** /'dʌz(ə)n/ *n* дю́жина. **drab** /dræb/ *adj* бесцве́тный. **draft** /drɑːft/ *n* (*outline, rough copy*) набро́сок; (*document*) прое́кт; (*econ*) тра́тта; *see also* **draught**; *vt* составля́ть *impf*, соста́вить *pf* план, прое́кт +*gen*.

drag /dræg/ *vt* тащи́ть *impf*; (*river etc.*) драги́ровать *impf* & *pf*; ~ **on** (*vi*) затя́гиваться *impf*, затяну́ться *pf*; *n* (*burden*) обу́за; (*on cigarette*) затя́жка; **in** ~ в же́нской оде́жде.

dragon /'dræg(ə)n/ *n* драко́н. **dragonfly** *n* стрекоза́. **drain** /dreɪn/ *n* водосто́к; (*leakage; fig*) уте́чка; *vt* осуша́ть *impf*, осуши́ть *pf*; *vi* спуска́ться *impf*, спусти́ться *pf*. **drainage** /'dreɪnɪdʒ/ *n* дрена́ж; (*system*) канализа́ция.

drake /dreɪk/ *n* се́лезень *m*. **drama** /'drɑːmə/ *n* дра́ма; (*quality*) драмати́зм. **dramatic** /drə-'mætɪk/ *adj* драмати́ческий. **dramatist** /'dræmətɪst/ *n* драмату́рг. **dramatize** /'dræmə,taɪz/ *vt* драматизи́ровать *impf* & *pf*. **drape** /dreɪp/ *vt* драпирова́ть *impf*, за~ *pf*; *n* драпиро́вка.

drastic /'dræstɪk/ *adj* ради́кальный.

draught /drɑːft/ *n* (*air*) сквозня́к; (*traction*) тя́га; *pl* (*game*) ша́шки *f pl*; *see also* **draft**; **there is a** ~ сквози́т; ~ **beer** пи́во из бо́чки. **draughtsman** /'drɑːftsmən/ *n* чертёжник. **draughty** /'drɑːftɪ/ *adj*: **it is** ~ **here** здесь ду́ет.

draw /drɔː/ *n* (*in lottery*) ро́зыгрыш; (*attraction*) прима́нка; (*drawn game*) ничья́; *vt* (*pull*) тяну́ть *impf*, по~ *pf*; таска́ть *indet*, тащи́ть *det*; (*curtains*) задёргивать *impf*, задёрнуть *pf* (занаве́ски); (*attract*) привлека́ть *impf*, привле́чь *pf*; (*pull out*) выта́скивать *impf*, вы́тащить *pf*; (*sword*) обнажа́ть *impf*, обнажи́ть *pf*; (*lots*) броса́ть *impf*, бро́сить *pf* (жре́бий); (*water; inspiration*) че́рпать *impf*, черпну́ть *pf*; (*evoke*) вызыва́ть *impf*, вы́звать *pf*; (*conclusion*) выводи́ть *impf*, вы́вести *pf* (заключе́ние); (*diagram*) черти́ть *impf*, на~ *pf*; (*picture*) рисова́ть *impf*, на~ *pf*; *vi* (*sport*) сыгра́ть *impf* вничью́, отвести́ *pf* в сто́рону; ~ **aside** отводи́ть *impf*, отвести́ *pf* в сто́рону; ~ **back** (*withdraw*) отступа́ть *impf*, отступи́ть *pf*; ~ **in** втя́гивать *impf*, втяну́ть *pf*; (*train*) входи́ть *impf*, войти́ в ста́нцию; (*car*) подходи́ть *impf*, подойти́ *pf* (**to** к + *dat*); (*days*) станови́ться *impf* коро́че; ~ **out** выта́гивать *impf*, вы́тянуть *pf*; (*money*) выпи́сывать *impf*, вы́писать *pf* (*train/car*) выходи́ть *impf*, вы́йти *pf* (со ста́нции/на доро́гу); ~ **up** (*car*) подходи́ть *impf*, подойти́ *pf* (**to** к + *dat*); (*document*) составля́ть *impf*, соста́вить *pf*;

drawback n недоста́ток. **draw-bridge** n подъёмный мост. **drawer** /drɔː(r)/ n я́щик. **drawing** /ˈdrɔːɪŋ/ n (action) рисова́ние, черче́ние; (object) рису́нок, чертёж; ~**-board** чертёжная доска́; ~**-pin** кно́пка; ~**-room** гости́ная sb.

drawl /drɔːl/ n протя́жное произноше́ние.

dread /dred/ n страх; vt боя́ться impf +gen. **dreadful** /ˈdredfʊl/ adj ужа́сный.

dream /driːm/ n сон; (fantasy) мечта́; vi ви́деть impf, у~ pf сон; ~ **of** ви́деть impf, у~ pf во сне́; (fig) мечта́ть impf о+prep.

dreary /ˈdrɪərɪ/ adj (weather) па́смурный; (boring) ску́чный.

dredge /dredʒ/ vt (river etc.) драги́ровать impf & pf. **dredger** /-dʒə(r)/ n дра́га.

dregs /dregz/ n pl оса́дки (-ков) pl.

drench /drentʃ/ vt прома́чивать impf, промочи́ть pf; **get ~ed** промока́ть impf, промо́кнуть pf.

dress /dres/ n пла́тье; (apparel) оде́жда; ~ **circle** бельэта́ж; ~**-maker** портни́ха; ~ **rehearsal** генера́льная репети́ция; vt & i одева́ть(ся) impf, оде́ть(ся) pf; vt (cul) приправля́ть impf, припра́вить pf; (med) перевя́зывать impf, перевяза́ть pf; ~ **up** наряжа́ться impf, наряди́ться pf (as + instr).

dresser /ˈdresə(r)/ n ку́хонный шкаф.

dressing /ˈdresɪŋ/ n (cul) припра́ва; (med) перевя́зка; ~**-gown** хала́т; ~**-room** убо́рная sb; ~**-table** туале́тный сто́лик.

dribble /ˈdrɪb(ə)l/ vi (person) пу-

ска́ть impf, пусти́ть pf слю́ни; (sport) вести́ impf мяч.

dried /draɪd/ adj сушёный. **drier** /ˈdraɪə(r)/ n суши́лка.

drift /drɪft/ n (meaning) смысл; (snow) сугро́б; vi плыть impf по тече́нию; (naut) дрейфова́ть impf; (snow etc.) скопля́ться impf, скопи́ться pf; ~ **apart** расходи́ться impf, разойти́сь pf.

drill¹ /drɪl/ n сверло́; (dentist's) бур; vt сверли́ть impf, про~ pf.

drill² /drɪl/ n (mil) обуча́ть impf, обучи́ть pf стро́ю; vi проходи́ть impf, пройти́ pf строеву́ю подгото́вку; n строева́я подгото́вка.

drink /drɪŋk/ n напи́ток; vt пить impf, вы́~ pf; ~**-driving** вожде́ние в нетре́звом состоя́нии. **drinking-water** /ˈdrɪŋkɪŋ ˈwɔːtə(r)/ n питьева́я вода́.

drip /drɪp/ n (action) ка́панье; (drop) ка́пля; vi ка́пать impf, ка́пнуть pf.

drive /draɪv/ n (journey) езда́; (excursion) прогу́лка; (campaign) похо́д, кампа́ния; (energy) эне́ргия; (tech) при́вод; (driveway) подъездна́я доро́га; vt (urge; chase) гоня́ть indet, гнать det; (vehicle) води́ть indet, вести́ det; управля́ть impf +instr, (convey) вози́ть indet, везти́ det, по~ pf; (travel) е́здить indet, е́хать det, по~ pf pf управля́ть impf, довести́ pf (**to** до+gen); (nail etc.) вбива́ть impf, вбить pf (**into** в+acc); ~ **away** vt прогоня́ть impf, прогна́ть pf; vi уезжа́ть impf, уе́хать pf; ~ **up** подъезжа́ть impf, подъе́хать pf (**to** к+dat).

driver /ˈdraɪvə(r)/ n (of vehicle)

водитель *m*, шофёр. **driving**
/'draɪvɪŋ/ *adj* (*force*) движу́-
щий; (*rain*) проливно́й; **~li-
cence** экза́мен на получе-
ние води́тельских прав; **~test** экза́мен на получе́-
ние води́тельских прав; **~wheel** веду́щее колесо́.

drizzle /'drɪz(ə)l/ *n* ме́лкий
дождь *m*; *vi* мороси́ть *impf.*

drone /drəʊn/ *n* (*bee; idler*) тру́-
тень *m*; (*of voice*) жужжа́ние;
(*of engine*) гул; *vi* (*buzz*) жуж-
жа́ть *impf.* (~ *on*) буби́ть
impf.

drool /druːl/ *vi* пуска́ть *impf*, пу-
сти́ть *pf* слю́ни.

droop /druːp/ *vi* поника́ть *impf*,
пони́кнуть *pf.*

drop /drɒp/ *n* (*of liquid*) ка́пля;
(*fall*) паде́ние, пониже́ние; *vt*
& *i* (*price*) снижа́ть(ся) *impf*,
сни́зить(ся) *pf*; *vi* (*fall*) па́дать
impf, упа́сть *pf*; *vt* (*let fall*) ро-
ня́ть *impf*, урони́ть *pf*; (*abandon*) броса́ть *impf*, бро́сить *pf*;
~ **behind** отстава́ть *impf*, от-
ста́ть *pf*; ~ **in** заходи́ть *impf*,
зайти́ *pf* (**on** к+*dat*); ~ **off** (*fall
asleep*) засыпа́ть *impf*, засну́ть
pf; (*from car*) выса́живать
impf, вы́садить *pf*; ~ **out** выбы-
ва́ть *impf*, вы́быть *pf* (**of** из
+*gen*). **droppings** /'drɒpɪŋz/ *n pl*
помёт.

drought /draʊt/ *n* за́суха.

droves /drəʊvz/ *n pl*: **in** ~ то́л-
пами.

drown /draʊn/ *vt* топи́ть *impf*,
у~ *pf*; (*sound*) заглуша́ть
impf, заглуши́ть *pf*; *vi* тону́ть
impf, у~ *pf.*

drowsy /'draʊzɪ/ *adj* со́нливый.

drudgery /'drʌdʒərɪ/ *n* ну́дная
рабо́та.

drug /drʌɡ/ *n* медикаме́нт; (*narcotic*) нарко́тик; ~ **addict**
наркома́н, ~ка; *vt* дава́ть

impf, дать *pf* нарко́тик+*dat.*

drum /drʌm/ *n* бараба́н; *vi* бить
impf в бараба́н; бараба́нить
impf; ~ **sth into s.o.** вда́лбли-
вать *impf*, вдолби́ть *pf* + *dat of
person* в го́лову. **drummer**
/'drʌmə(r)/ *n* бараба́нщик.

drunk /drʌŋk/ *adj* пья́ный.
drunkard /'drʌŋkəd/ *n* пья́ница
m & f. **drunken** /'drʌŋkən/ *adj*
пья́ный; ~ **driving** вожде́ние в
нетре́звом состоя́нии. **drunkenness** /'drʌŋkənnɪs/ *n* пья́н-
ство.

dry /draɪ/ *adj* сухо́й; ~ **land**
су́ша; *vt* суши́ть *impf*, вы́~ *pf*;
(*wipe dry*) вытира́ть *impf*, вы́-
тереть *pf*; *vi* со́хнуть *impf*,
вы́~, про~ *pf*. **dry-cleaning**
/draɪ'kliːnɪŋ/ *n* химчи́стка. **dryness** /'draɪnɪs/ *n* сухость.

dual /'djuːəl/ *adj* двойно́й;
(*joint*) совме́стный; **~purpose**
двойно́го назначе́ния.

dub¹ /dʌb/ *vt* (*nickname*) прозы-
ва́ть *impf*, прозва́ть *pf.*

dub² /dʌb/ *vt* (*cin*) дубли́ровать
impf & pf.

dubious /'djuːbɪəs/ *adj* сомни́-
тельный.

duchess /'dʌtʃɪs/ *n* герцоги́ня.

duchy /'dʌtʃɪ/ *n* ге́рцогство.

duck¹ /dʌk/ *n* (*bird*) у́тка.

duck² /dʌk/ *vt* (*immerse*) оку-
на́ть *impf*, окуну́ть *pf*; (*one's
head*) нагну́ть *pf*; (*evade*)
увёртываться *impf*, увер-
ну́ться *pf* от+*gen*; (~ **down**)
наклоня́ться *impf*, накло-
ни́ться *pf.*

duckling /'dʌklɪŋ/ *n* утёнок

duct /dʌkt/ *n* прохо́д; (*anat*)
прото́к.

dud /dʌd/ *n* (*forgery*) подде́лка;
(*shell*) неразорва́вшийся сна-
ря́д; *adj* подде́льный; (*worthless*) него́дный.

due /dju:/ n (credit) до́лжное sb; pl взно́сы m pl; adj (proper) до́лжный, надлежа́щий; predic (expected) до́лжен (-жна́); in ~ course со вре́менем; ~ south пря́мо на юг; ~ to благодаря́+dat.

duel /dju:əl/ n дуэ́ль.

duet /dju:'et/ n дуэ́т.

duke /dju:k/ n ге́рцог.

dull /dʌl/ adj (tedious) ску́чный; (colour) ту́склый, (weather) па́смурный; (not sharp; stupid) тупо́й; vt притупля́ть impf, притупи́ть pf.

duly /dju:lɪ/ adv надлежа́щим о́бразом; (punctually) своевре́менно.

dumb /dʌm/ adj немо́й. **dumbfounded** /'dʌmfaʊndɪd/ adj ошара́шенный.

dummy /'dʌmɪ/ n (tailor's) манеке́н; (baby's) со́ска; ~ **run** испыта́тельный рейс.

dump /dʌmp/ n сва́лка; vt сва́ливать impf, свали́ть pf.

dumpling /'dʌmplɪŋ/ n клёцка.

dumpy /'dʌmpɪ/ adj призе́мистый.

dune /dju:n/ n дю́на.

dung /dʌŋ/ n наво́з.

dungarees /ˌdʌŋgə'ri:z/ n pl комбинезо́н.

dungeon /'dʌndʒ(ə)n/ n темни́ца.

duo /'dju:əʊ/ n па́ра; (mus) дуэ́т.

dupe /dju:p/ vt надува́ть impf, наду́ть pf; n простофи́ля m & f.

duplicate n /'dju:plɪkət/ n ко́пия; **in** ~ в двух экземпля́рах; adj запасно́й; vt /'dju:plɪkeɪt/ размножа́ть impf, размно́жить pf.

duplicity /dju:'plɪsɪtɪ/ n двули́чность.

durability /ˌdjʊərə'bɪlɪtɪ/ n про́ч-

ность. **durable** /'djʊərəb(ə)l/ adj про́чный. **duration** /djʊə'reɪʃ(ə)n/ n продолжи́тельность.

duress /djʊə'res/ n принужде́ние; **under** ~ под давле́нием.

during /'djʊərɪŋ/ prep во вре́мя +gen; (throughout) в тече́ние +gen.

dusk /dʌsk/ n су́мерки (-рек) pl.

dust /dʌst/ n пыль; ~**bin** му́сорный я́щик; ~**jacket** суперобло́жка; ~**man** му́сорщик; ~**pan** сово́к; vt & i (clean) стира́ть impf, стере́ть pf пыль (с+gen); (sprinkle) посыпа́ть impf, посы́пать pf sth +acc, with +instr. **duster** /'dʌstə(r)/ n пы́льная тря́пка. **dusty** /'dʌstɪ/ adj пы́льный.

Dutch /dʌtʃ/ adj голла́ндский; n: **the** ~ голла́ндцы m pl. **Dutchman** n голла́ндец. **Dutchwoman** n голла́ндка.

dutiful /'dju:tɪfʊl/ adj послу́шный. **duty** /dju:tɪ/ n (obligation) долг; обя́занность; (office) дежу́рство; (tax) по́шлина; **be on** ~ дежу́рить impf; ~-**free** беспо́шлинный.

duvet /'du:veɪ/ n стёганое одея́ло.

DVD abbr (of digital versatile disk) DVD; ~ **player** DVD-пле́ер.

dwarf /dwɔ:f/ n ка́рлик; vt (tower above) возвыша́ться impf, возвы́ситься pf над+instr.

dwell /dwel/ vi обита́ть impf; ~ **upon** остана́вливаться impf на+prep. **dweller** /'dwelə(r)/ n жи́тель. **dwelling** /'dwelɪŋ/ n жили́ще.

dwindle /'dwɪnd(ə)l/ vi убыва́ть impf, убы́ть pf.

dye /daɪ/ n краси́тель m; vt ок-

ра́шивать *impf*, окра́сить *pf*.

dynamic /daɪˈnæmɪk/ *adj* динами́ческий. **dynamics** /-mɪks/ *n pl* дина́мика.

dynamite /ˈdaɪnəmaɪt/ *n* динами́т.

dynamo /ˈdaɪnəˌməʊ/ *n* дина́мо *neut indecl*.

dynasty /ˈdɪnəsti/ *n* дина́стия.

dysentery /ˈdɪsəntəri/ *n* дизентери́я.

dyslexia /dɪsˈleksɪə/ *n* дисле́ксия. **dyslexic** /-ˈleksɪk/ *adj*: **he is ~** он дисле́ктик.

E

each /iːtʃ/ *adj & pron* ка́ждый; **~ other** друг дру́га (*dat* - гу, *etc.*).

eager /ˈiːɡə(r)/ *adj* (*pupil*) усе́рдный; **I am ~ to** мне не те́рпится +*inf*: о́чень жела́ю +*inf*. **eagerly** /-lɪ/ *adv* с нетерпе́нием; жа́дно. **eagerness** /-nɪs/ *n* си́льное жела́ние.

eagle /ˈiːɡ(ə)l/ *n* орёл.

ear¹ /ɪə(r)/ *n* (*corn*) ко́лос.

ear² /ɪə(r)/ *n* (*anat*) у́хо; (*sense*) слух; **~-ache** боль в у́хе; **~drum** бараба́нная перепо́нка; **~mark** (*assign*) предназна́чить *pf*; **~phone** нау́шник; **~ring** серьга́; (*clip-on*) кли́пс; **~shot: within/out of ~** в преде́лах/вне преде́лов слы́шимости.

earl /ɜːl/ *n* граф.

early /ˈɜːlɪ/ *adj* ра́нний; *adv* ра́но.

earn /ɜːn/ *vt* зараба́тывать *impf*, зарабо́тать *pf*; (*deserve*) заслу́живать *impf*, заслужи́ть *pf*. **earnings** /ˈɜːnɪŋz/ *n pl* за́работок.

earnest /ˈɜːnɪst/ *adj* серьёзный;

n: **in ~** всерьёз.

earth /ɜːθ/ *n* земля́; (*soil*) по́чва; *vt* заземля́ть *impf*, заземли́ть *pf*. **earthenware** /ˈɜːθ(ə)nˌweə(r)/ *adj* гли́няный. **earthly** /ˈɜːθlɪ/ *adj* земно́й. **earthquake** /ˈɜːθkweɪk/ *n* землетрясе́ние. **earthy** /ˈɜːθɪ/ *adj* земли́стый; (*coarse*) гру́бый.

earwig /ˈɪəwɪg/ *n* уховёртка.

ease /iːz/ *n* (*facility*) лёгкость; (*unconstraint*) непринуждённость; **with ~** непринуждённо; *vt* облегча́ть *impf*, облегчи́ть *pf*; *vi* успока́иваться *impf*, успоко́иться *pf*.

easel /ˈiːz(ə)l/ *n* мольбе́рт.

east /iːst/ *n* восто́к; (*naut*) ост; *adj* восто́чный. **easterly** /ˈiːstəlɪ/ *adj* восто́чный. **eastern** /ˈiːst(ə)n/ *adj* восто́чный. **eastward(s)** /ˈiːstwəd(z)/ *adv* на восто́к, к восто́ку.

Easter /ˈiːstə(r)/ *n* Па́сха.

easy /ˈiːzɪ/ *adj* лёгкий; (*unconstrained*) непринуждённый; **~-going** уживчивый.

eat /iːt/ *vt* есть *impf*, с~ *pf*; ку́шать *impf*, по~, с~ *pf*; **~ away** разъеда́ть *impf*, разъе́сть *pf*; **~ into** въеда́ться *impf*, въе́сться *pf* в +*acc*; **~ up** доеда́ть *impf*, дое́сть *pf*. **eatable** /ˈiːtəb(ə)l/ *adj* съедо́бный.

eaves /iːvz/ *n pl* стреха́. **eavesdrop** /ˈiːvzdrɒp/ *vi* подслу́шивать *impf*.

ebb /eb/ *n* (*tide*) отли́в; (*fig*) упа́док.

ebony /ˈebənɪ/ *n* чёрное де́рево.

ebullient /ɪˈbʌlɪənt/ *adj* кипу́чий.

EC *abbr* (*European Community*) Европе́йское соо́бщество.

eccentric /ɪkˈsentrɪk/ *n* чуда́к; *adj* эксцентри́чный.

ecclesiastical /ɪˌkliːzɪˈæstɪk(ə)l/ *adj* церко́вный.

echo /'ekəʊ/ *n* эхо; *vi* (*resound*) отража́ться *impf*, отрази́ться *pf*; *vt* (*repeat*) повторя́ть *impf*, повтори́ть *pf*.

eclipse /ɪ'klɪps/ *n* затме́ние; *vt* затмева́ть *impf*, затми́ть *pf*.

ecological /ˌiːkə'lɒdʒɪk(ə)l/ *adj* экологи́ческий. **ecology** /ɪ'kɒlədʒɪ/ *n* эколо́гия.

economic /ˌiːkə'nɒmɪk/ *adj* экономи́ческий. **economical** /ˌiːkə'nɒmɪk(ə)l/ *adj* эконо́мный. **economist** /ɪ'kɒnəmɪst/ *n* экономи́ст. **economize** /ɪ'kɒnəˌmaɪz/ *vt & i* эконо́мить *impf*, с∼ *pf*. **economy** /ɪ'kɒnəmɪ/ *n* эконо́мика; (*saving*) эконо́мия.

ecstasy /'ekstəsɪ/ *n* экста́з. **ecstatic** /ek'stætɪk/ *adj* экстати́ческий.

eddy /'edɪ/ *n* водоворо́т.

edge /edʒ/ *n* край; (*blade*) ле́звие; **on ∼** в не́рвном состоя́нии; **have the ∼ on** име́ть *impf* преиму́щество над+*instr*; *vt* (*border*) окаймля́ть *impf*, окайми́ть *pf*; *vi* пробира́ться *impf*, пробра́ться *pf*. **edging** /'edʒɪŋ/ *n* кайма́. **edgy** /'edʒɪ/ *adj* раздражи́тельный.

edible /'edɪb(ə)l/ *adj* съедо́бный.

edict /'iːdɪkt/ *n* ука́з.

edifice /'edɪfɪs/ *n* зда́ние. **edifying** /'edɪfaɪɪŋ/ *adj* назида́тельный.

edit /'edɪt/ *vt* редакти́ровать *impf*, от∼ *pf*; (*cin*) монти́ровать *impf*, с∼ *pf*. **edition** /ɪ'dɪʃ(ə)n/ *n* изда́ние; (*number of copies*) тира́ж. **editor** /'edɪtə(r)/ *n* реда́ктор. **editorial** /ˌedɪ'tɔːrɪəl/ *n* передова́я статья́; *adj* реда́кторский, редакцио́нный.

educate /'edjʊˌkeɪt/ *vt* дава́ть *impf*, дать *pf* образова́ние

+*dat*; **where was he educated?** где он получи́л образова́ние? **educated** /-ˌkeɪtɪd/ *adj* образо́ванный. **education** /-'keɪʃ(ə)n/ *n* образова́ние. **educational** /-'keɪʃən(ə)l/ *adj* образова́тельный; (*instructive*) уче́бный.

eel /iːl/ *n* у́горь *m*.

eerie /'ɪərɪ/ *adj* жу́ткий.

effect /ɪ'fekt/ *n* (*result*) сле́дствие; (*validity; influence*) де́йствие; (*impression; theat*) эффе́кт; **in ∼** факти́чески; **take ∼** вступа́ть *impf*, вступи́ть *pf* в си́лу; (*medicine*) начина́ть *impf*, нача́ть *pf* де́йствовать; *vt* производи́ть *impf*, произвести́ *pf* про. **effective** /-'fektɪv/ *adj* эффекти́вный; (*striking*) эффе́ктный; (*actual*) факти́ческий. **effectiveness** /-'fektɪvnɪs/ *n* эффекти́вность.

effeminate /ɪ'femɪnət/ *adj* женоподо́бный.

effervesce /ˌefə'ves/ *vi* пузы́риться *impf*. **effervescent** /-'ves(ə)nt/ *adj* (*fig*) искря́щийся.

efficiency /ɪ'fɪʃ(ə)nsɪ/ *n* эффекти́вность. **efficient** /-'fɪʃ(ə)nt/ *adj* эффекти́вный; (*person*) организо́ванный.

effigy /'efɪdʒɪ/ *n* изображе́ние.

effort /'efət/ *n* уси́лие.

effrontery /ɪ'frʌntərɪ/ *n* на́глость.

effusive /ɪ'fjuːsɪv/ *adj* экспанси́вный.

e.g. *abbr* напр.

egalitarian /ɪˌɡælɪ'teərɪən/ *adj* эгалита́рный.

egg[1] /eɡ/ *n* яйцо́; **∼cup** рю́мка для яйца́; **∼shell** яи́чная скорлупа́.

egg[2] /eɡ/ *vt*: **∼ on** подстрека́ть *impf*, подстрекну́ть *pf*.

ego /'iːɡəʊ/ *n* «Я». **egocentric** /ˌiːɡəʊ'sentrɪk/ *adj* эгоцентри-

ский. **egoism** /'iːɡəʊ,ɪz(ə)m/ *n* эгои́зм. **ego(t)ist** /'iːɡəʊ,tɪst/ *n* эгои́ст, ~ка. **ego(t)istical** /,iːɡəʊ 't(ɪ)stɪk(ə)l/ *adj* эгоцентри́ческий. **egotism** /'iːɡəʊ,tɪz(ə)m/ *n* эготи́зм.

Egypt /'iːdʒɪpt/ *n* Еги́пет. **Egyptian** /ɪ'dʒɪpʃ(ə)n/ *n* египтя́нин, -я́нка; *adj* еги́петский.

eiderdown /'aɪdə,daʊn/ *n* пухо́вое одея́ло.

eight /eɪt/ *adj & n* во́семь; (*number* 8) восьмёрка. **eighteen** /eɪ 'tiːn/ *adj & n* восемна́дцать. **eighteenth** /eɪ'tiːnθ/ *adj & n* восемна́дцатый. **eighth** /eɪtθ/ *adj & n* восьмо́й; (*fraction*) восьма́я *sb.* **eightieth** /'eɪtɪθ/ *adj & n* восьмидеся́тый. **eighty** /'eɪtɪ/ *adj & n* во́семьдесят; *pl* (*decade*) восьмидеся́тые го́ды (-до́в) *m pl.*

either /'aɪðə(r)/ *adj & pron* (*one of two*) оди́н из двух, тот и́ли друго́й; (*both*) и тот, и друго́й; оба; (*one or other*) любо́й; *adv & conj:* ~ ... **or** и́ли... и́ли, ли́бо... ли́бо.

eject /ɪ'dʒekt/ *vt* выбра́сывать *impf*, вы́бросить *pf; vi* (*pilot*) катапульти́роваться *impf & pf.*

eke /iːk/ *vt:* ~ **out a living** переби́ваться *impf*, переби́ться *pf* ко́е-как.

elaborate *adj* /ɪ'læbərət/ (*ornate*) витиева́тый; (*detailed*) подро́бный; *vt* /ɪ'læbə,reɪt/ разраба́тывать *impf*, разрабо́тать *pf;* (*detail*) уточня́ть *impf*, уточни́ть *pf.*

elapse /ɪ'læps/ *vi* проходи́ть *impf*, пройти́ *pf;* (*expire*) исте́ка́ть *impf*, исте́чь *pf.*

elastic /ɪ'læstɪk/ *n* рези́нка; *adj* эласти́чный; ~ **band** рези́нка. **elasticity** /-'stɪsɪtɪ/ *n* эласти́ч-

ность.

elated /ɪ'leɪtɪd/ *adj* в восто́рге. **elation** /ɪ'leɪʃ(ə)n/ *n* восто́рг.

elbow /'elbəʊ/ *n* ло́коть *m; vt:* ~ (**one's way**) **through** прота́лкиваться *impf*, протолкну́ться *pf* че́рез+*acc.*

elder[1] /'eldə(r)/ *n* (*tree*) бузина́. **elder**[2] /'eldə(r)/ *n* (*person*) ста́рец; *pl* ста́ршие *sb; adj* ста́рший. **elderly** /'eldəlɪ/ *adj* пожило́й. **eldest** /'eldɪst/ *adj* ста́рший.

elect /ɪ'lekt/ *adj* и́збранный; *vt* избира́ть *impf*, избра́ть *pf.* **election** /ɪ'lekʃ(ə)n/ *n* вы́боры *m pl.* **elector** /ɪ'lektə(r)/ *n* избира́тель *m.* **electoral** /ɪ'lektər(ə)l/ *adj* избира́тельный. **electorate** /ɪ'lektərət/ *n* избира́тели *m pl.*

electric(al) /ɪ'lektrɪk(ə)l/ *adj* электри́ческий; ~ **shock** уда́р электри́ческим то́ком. **electrician** /ˌɪlek'trɪʃ(ə)n/ *n* эле́ктрик. **electricity** /ˌɪlek'trɪsɪtɪ/ *n* электри́чество. **electrify** /ɪ'lektrɪ,faɪ/ *vt* (*convert to electricity*) электрифици́ровать *impf & pf;* (*charge with electricity; fig*) электризова́ть *impf*, на~ *pf.* **electrode** /ɪ'lektrəʊd/ *n* электро́д. **electron** /ɪ'lektrɒn/ *n* электро́н. **electronic** /ˌɪlek 'trɒnɪk/ *adj* электро́нный. **electronics** /ˌɪlek'trɒnɪks/ *n* электро́ника.

electrocute /ɪ'lektrə,kjuːt/ *vt* убива́ть *impf*, уби́ть *pf* электри́ческим то́ком; (*execute*) казни́ть *impf & pf* на электри́ческом сту́ле. **electrolysis** /ˌɪlek 'trɒlɪsɪs/ *n* электро́лиз.

elegance /'elɪɡəns/ *n* элега́нтность. **elegant** /-ɡənt/ *adj* элега́нтный.

elegy /'elɪdʒɪ/ *n* эле́гия.

element /'elɪmənt/ *n* элеме́нт;

(*earth, wind, etc.*) стихи́я; **be in one's ~** быть в свое́й стихи́и.
elemental /ˌelɪˈment(ə)l/ *adj* стихи́йный. **elementary** /-ˈmentərɪ/ *adj* элемента́рный; (*school etc.*) нача́льный.

elephant /ˈelɪfənt/ *n* слон.
elevate /ˈelɪˌveɪt/ *vt* поднима́ть *impf*, подня́ть *pf*. **elevated** /-ˌveɪtɪd/ *adj* возвы́шенный. **elevation** /-ˈveɪʃ(ə)n/ *n* (*height*) высота́. **elevator** /-ˌveɪtə(r)/ *n* (*lift*) лифт.
eleven /ɪˈlev(ə)n/ *adj & n* оди́ннадцать. **eleventh** /-ˈlevənθ/ *adj & n* оди́ннадцатый; **at the ~ hour** в после́днюю мину́ту.
elf /elf/ *n* эльф.
elicit /ɪˈlɪsɪt/ *vt* (*obtain*) выявля́ть *impf*, вы́явить *pf*; (*evoke*) вызыва́ть *impf*, вы́звать *pf*.
eligible /ˈelɪdʒɪb(ə)l/ *adj* име́ющий пра́во (**for** на+*acc*); (*bachelor*) подходя́щий.
eliminate /ɪˈlɪmɪˌneɪt/ *vt* устраня́ть *impf*, устрани́ть *pf*; (*rule out*) исключа́ть *impf*, исключи́ть *pf*.
élite /eɪˈliːt/ *n* эли́та.
ellipse /ɪˈlɪps/ *n* э́ллипс. **elliptic(al)** /ɪˈlɪptɪk(ə)l)/ *adj* эллипти́ческий.
elm /elm/ *n* вяз.
elongate /ˈiːlɒŋˌɡeɪt/ *vt* удлиня́ть *impf*, удлини́ть *pf*.
elope /ɪˈləʊp/ *vi* бежа́ть *det* (с возлю́бленным).
eloquence /ˈeləkwəns/ *n* красноре́чие. **eloquent** /-kwənt/ *adj* красноречи́вый.
else /els/ *adv* (*besides*) ещё; (*instead*) друго́й; (*with neg*) бо́льше; **nobody ~** никто́ бо́льше; **or ~** ина́че; а (не) то; и́ли же; **s.o. ~** кто-нибудь другой; **something ~?** ещё что́-ни-

будь? **elsewhere** *adv* (*place*) в друго́м ме́сте; (*direction*) в друго́е ме́сто.
elucidate /ɪˈluːsɪˌdeɪt/ *vt* разъясня́ть *impf*, разъясни́ть *pf*.
elude /ɪˈluːd/ *vt* избега́ть *impf* +*gen*. **elusive** /-ˈluːsɪv/ *adj* неулови́мый.
emaciated /ɪˈmeɪsɪˌeɪtɪd/ *adj* исто́щённый.
email /ˈiːmeɪl/ *n* (*system, letters*) электро́нная по́чта; (*letter*) электро́нное письмо́; **~ address** электро́нный а́дрес
emanate /ˈeməˌneɪt/ *vi* исходи́ть *impf* (**from** из, от, +*gen*).
emancipate /ɪˈmænsɪˌpeɪt/ *vt* эмансипи́ровать *impf & pf*. **emancipation** /-ˈpeɪʃ(ə)n/ *n* эмансипа́ция.
embankment /ɪmˈbæŋkmənt/ *n* (*river*) на́бережная *sb*; (*rly*) на́сыпь.
embargo /emˈbɑːɡəʊ/ *n* эмба́рго *neut indecl*.
embark /ɪmˈbɑːk/ *vi* сади́ться *impf*, сесть *pf* на кора́бль; **~ upon** предпринима́ть *impf*, предприня́ть *pf*. **embarkation** /ˌembɑːˈkeɪʃ(ə)n/ *n* поса́дка (на кора́бль).
embarrass /ɪmˈbærəs/ *vt* смуща́ть *impf*, смути́ть *pf*; **be ~ed** чу́вствовать *impf* себя́ неудо́бно. **embarrassing** /-sɪŋ/ *adj* неудо́бный. **embarrassment** /-mənt/ *n* смуще́ние.
embassy /ˈembəsɪ/ *n* посо́льство.
embedded /ɪmˈbedɪd/ *adj* вре́занный.
embellish /ɪmˈbelɪʃ/ *vt* (*adorn*) украша́ть *impf*, укра́сить *pf*; (*story*) прикра́шивать *impf*, прикра́сить *pf*. **embellishment** /-mənt/ *n* украше́ние.
embers /ˈembəz/ *n pl* тле́ющие

угольки́ *m pl.*

embezzle /ɪmˈbez(ə)l/ *vt* растра́-
чивать *impf*, растра́тить *pf*.
embezzlement /-mənt/ *n* рас-
тра́та.

embittered /ɪmˈbɪtəd/ *adj* озло́-
бленный.

emblem /ˈembləm/ *n* эмбле́ма.

embodiment /ɪmˈbɒdɪmənt/ *n*
воплоще́ние. **embody** /ɪmˈbɒdɪ/
vt воплоща́ть *impf*, вопло-
ти́ть *pf*.

emboss /ɪmˈbɒs/ *vt* чека́нить
impf, вы́~, от~ *pf*.

embrace /ɪmˈbreɪs/ *n* объя́тие; *vi*
обнима́ться *impf*, обня́ться *pf*;
vt обнима́ть *impf*, обня́ть *pf*;
(*accept*) принима́ть *impf*, при-
ня́ть *pf*; (*include*) охва́тывать
impf, охвати́ть *pf*.

embroider /ɪmˈbrɔɪdə(r)/ *vt* вы-
шива́ть *impf*, вы́шить *pf*;
(*story*) прикра́шивать *impf*,
прикра́сить *pf*. **embroidery**
/-dərɪ/ *n* вы́шивка.

embroil /ɪmˈbrɔɪl/ *vt* впу́тывать
impf, впу́тать *pf*.

embryo /ˈembrɪəʊ/ *n* эмбрио́н.

emerald /ˈemər(ə)ld/ *n* изумру́д.

emerge /ɪˈmɜːdʒ/ *vi* появля́ться
impf, появи́ться *pf*. **emergence**
/-dʒəns/ *n* появле́ние. **emergency** /-dʒənsɪ/ *n* кра́йняя не-
обходи́мость; **state of ~**
чрезвыча́йное положе́ние; **~
exit** запасно́й вы́ход.

emery paper /ˈeməri ˈpeɪpə(r)/ *n*
нажда́чная бума́га.

emigrant /ˈemɪɡrənt/ *n* эми-
гра́нт, **~ка**. **emigrate**
/ˈemɪɡreɪt/ *vi* эмигри́ровать
impf & *pf*. **emigration** /ˌemɪ
ˈɡreɪʃ(ə)n/ *n* эмигра́ция.

eminence /ˈemɪnəns/ *n* (*fame*)
знамени́тость. **eminent** /-nənt/
adj выдаю́щийся. **eminently**
/-nəntlɪ/ *adv* чрезвыча́йно.

emission /ɪˈmɪʃ(ə)n/ *n* испуска́-
ние. **emit** /ɪˈmɪt/ *vt* испуска́ть
impf, испусти́ть *pf*; (*light*) излу-
ча́ть *impf*, излучи́ть *pf*; (*sound*)
издава́ть *impf*, изда́ть *pf*.

emotion /ɪˈməʊʃ(ə)n/ *n* эмо́ция,
чу́вство. **emotional** /-n(ə)l/ *adj*
эмоциона́льный.

empathize /ˈempəˌθaɪz/ *vt* сопе-
режива́ть *impf*, сопережи́ть *pf*.
empathy /-pəθɪ/ *n* эмпа́тия.

emperor /ˈempərə(r)/ *n* импе-
ра́тор.

emphasis /ˈemfəsɪs/ *n* ударе́ние.
emphasize /ˈemfəsaɪz/ *vt*
подчёркивать *impf*, подчерк-
ну́ть *pf*. **emphatic** /ɪmˈfætɪk/
adj вырази́тельный; категори́-
ческий.

empire /ˈempaɪə(r)/ *n* импе́рия.

empirical /ɪmˈpɪrɪk(ə)l/ *adj* эм-
пири́ческий.

employ /ɪmˈplɔɪ/ *vt* (*use*) по́льзо-
ваться *impf* +*instr*; (*person*) на-
нима́ть *impf*, наня́ть *pf*.
employee /ˌemplɔɪˈiː/ *n* сотру́д-
ник, рабо́чий *sb*. **employer** /ɪm
ˈplɔɪə(r)/ *n* работода́тель *m*.
employment /ɪmˈplɔɪmənt/ *n*
рабо́та, слу́жба; (*use*)
испо́льзование.

empower /ɪmˈpaʊə(r)/ *vt* упол-
номо́чивать *impf*, уполномо́-
чить *pf* (**to** на+*acc*).

empress /ˈemprɪs/ *n* императ-
ри́ца.

emptiness /ˈemptɪnɪs/ *n* пу-
стота́. **empty** /ˈemptɪ/ *adj* пу-
сто́й; **~-headed** пустоголо́вый;
vt (*container*) опорожня́ть
impf, опорожни́ть *pf*; (*solid*)
высыпа́ть *impf*, вы́сыпать *pf*;
(*liquid*) вылива́ть *impf*, вы́лить
pf; *vi* пусте́ть *impf*, о~ *pf*.

emulate /ˈemjʊˌleɪt/ *vt* достига́ть
impf, дости́гнуть, до-
сти́чь *pf* +*gen*; (*copy*)

подража́ть *impf* +*dat.*

emulsion /ɪˈmʌlʃ(ə)n/ *n* эму́льсия.

enable /ɪˈneɪb(ə)l/ *vt* дава́ть *impf*, дать *pf* возмо́жность +*dat* & *inf.*

enact /ɪˈnækt/ *vt* (*law*) принима́ть *impf*, приня́ть *pf*; (*theat*) разы́грывать *impf*, разыгра́ть *pf.* **enactment** /-ˈnæktmənt/ *n* (*law*) постановле́ние; (*theat*) игра́.

enamel /ɪˈnæm(ə)l/ *n* эма́ль; *adj* эма́левый; *vt* эмалирова́ть *impf* & *pf.*

encampment /ɪnˈkæmpmənt/ *n* ла́герь *m.*

enchant /ɪnˈtʃɑːnt/ *vt* очаро́вывать *impf*, очарова́ть *pf.* **enchanting** /-tɪŋ/ *adj* очарова́тельный. **enchantment** /-mənt/ *n* очарова́ние.

encircle /ɪnˈsɜːk(ə)l/ *vt* окружа́ть *impf*, окружи́ть *pf.*

enclave /ˈenkleɪv/ *n* анкла́в.

enclose /ɪnˈkləʊz/ *vt* огора́живать *impf*, огороди́ть *pf*; (*in letter*) прикла́дывать *impf*, приложи́ть *pf*; **please find ~d** прилага́ется (-а́ются) +*nom.* **enclosure** /ɪnˈkləʊʒə(r)/ *n* огоро́женное ме́сто; (*in letter*) приложе́ние.

encode /ɪnˈkəʊd/ *vt* шифрова́ть *impf*, за- *pf.*

encompass /ɪnˈkʌmpəs/ *vt* (*encircle*) окружа́ть *impf*, окружи́ть *pf*; (*contain*) заключа́ть *impf*, заключи́ть *pf.*

encore /ˈɒŋkɔː(r)/ *int* бис!; *n* вы́зов на бис.

encounter /ɪnˈkaʊntə(r)/ *n* встре́ча; (*in combat*) столкнове́ние; *vt* встреча́ть *impf*, встре́тить *pf*; (*fig*) ста́лкиваться *impf*, столкну́ться *pf* с+*instr.*

encourage /ɪnˈkʌrɪdʒ/ *vt* ободря́ть *impf*, ободри́ть *pf.* **encouragement** /-mənt/ *n* ободре́ние. **encouraging** /-dʒɪŋ/ *adj* ободри́тельный.

encroach /ɪnˈkrəʊtʃ/ *vi* втога́ться *impf*, вто́гнуться *pf* (**on** в+*acc*). **encroachment** /-mənt/ *n* вторже́ние.

encumber /ɪnˈkʌmbə(r)/ *vt* обременя́ть *impf*, обремени́ть *pf.* **encumbrance** /-brəns/ *n* обу́за.

encyclopaedia /en,saɪkləˈpiːdɪə/ *n* энциклопе́дия. **encyclopaedic** /-ˈpiːdɪk/ *adj* энциклопеди́ческий.

end /end/ *n* коне́ц; (*death*) смерть; (*purpose*) цель; **an ~ in itself** самоце́ль; **in the ~** в конце́ концо́в; **make ~s meet** своди́ть *impf*, свести́ *pf* концы́ с конца́ми; **no ~ of** ма́сса+*gen*; **on ~** (*upright*) стоймя́, дыбо́м; (*continuously*) подря́д; **put an ~to** класть *impf*, положи́ть *pf* коне́ц +*dat*; *vi* конча́ть *impf*, ко́нчить *pf*; (*halt*) прекраща́ть *impf*, прекрати́ть *pf*; *vi* конча́ться *impf*, ко́нчиться *pf.*

endanger /ɪnˈdeɪndʒə(r)/ *vt* подверга́ть *impf*, подве́ргнуть *pf* опа́сности.

endearing /ɪnˈdɪərɪŋ/ *adj* привлека́тельный. **endearment** /-ˈdɪəmənt/ *n* ла́ска.

endeavour /ɪnˈdevə(r)/ *n* попы́тка; (*exertion*) уси́лие; (*undertaking*) де́ло; *vi* стара́ться *impf*, по-~ *pf.*

endemic /enˈdemɪk/ *adj* энде-ми́ческий.

ending /ˈendɪŋ/ *n* оконча́ние. **endless** /ˈendlɪs/ *adj* бесконе́чный.

endorse /ɪnˈdɔːs/ *vt* (*document*) подпи́сывать *impf*, подписа́ть *pf*; (*support*) подде́рживать

impf, поддержа́ть *pf*. **endorsement** /-mənt/ *n* по́дпись; подде́ржка; (*on driving licence*) проко́л.

endow /ɪnˈdaʊ/ *vt* обеспе́чивать *impf*, обеспе́чить *pf* постоя́нным дохо́дом, (*fig*) одаря́ть *impf*, одари́ть *pf*. **endowment** /-mənt/ *n* поже́ртвование; (*talent*) дарова́ние.

endurance /ɪnˈdjʊərəns/ *n* (*of person*) выно́сливость; (*of object*) про́чность. **endure** /ɪˈdjʊə(r)/ *vt* выноси́ть *impf*, вы́нести *pf*; терпе́ть *impf*, по~ *pf*; *vi* продолжа́ться *impf*, продо́лжиться *pf*.

enemy /ˈenəmɪ/ *n* враг; *adj* вра́жеский.

energetic /ˌenəˈdʒetɪk/ *adj* энерги́чный. **energy** /ˈenədʒɪ/ *n* эне́ргия; *pl* си́лы *f pl*.

enforce /ɪnˈfɔːs/ *vt* (*law etc.*) следи́ть *impf* за выполне́нием +*gen*. **enforcement** /-mənt/ *n* наблюде́ние за выполне́нием +*gen*.

engage /ɪnˈgeɪdʒ/ *vt* (*hire*) нанима́ть *impf*, наня́ть *pf*; (*tech*) сцепля́ть *impf*, зацепи́ть *pf*. **engaged** /-ˈgeɪdʒd/ *adj* (*occupied*) за́нятый; **be ~ in** занима́ться *impf*, заня́ться *pf* +*instr*; **become ~** обруча́ться *impf*, обручи́ться *pf* (*to* c+*instr*). **engagement** /-ˈgeɪdʒmənt/ *n* (*appointment*) свида́ние; (*betrothal*) обруче́ние; (*battle*) бой; **~ ring** обруча́льное кольцо́. **engaging** /-ˈgeɪdʒɪŋ/ *adj* привлека́тельный.

engender /ɪnˈdʒendə(r)/ *vt* порожда́ть *impf*, породи́ть *pf*.

engine /ˈendʒɪn/ *n* дви́гатель *m*; (*rly*) локомоти́в, **~-driver** (*rly*) маши́нист. **engineer** /ˌendʒɪ-

'nɪə(r)/ *n* инжене́р; *vt* (*fig*) организова́ть *impf* & *pf*. **engineering** /ˌendʒɪˈnɪərɪŋ/ *n* инжене́рное де́ло, те́хника.

England /ˈɪŋglənd/ *n* А́нглия. **English** /ˈɪŋglɪʃ/ *adj* англи́йский; *n*: **the ~** *pl* англича́не (-н) *pl*. **Englishman, -woman** *n* англича́нин, -а́нка.

engrave /ɪnˈgreɪv/ *vt* гравирова́ть *impf*, вы́~ *pf*; (*fig*) вреза́ть *impf*, вре́зать *pf*. **engraver** /-ˈgreɪvə(r)/ *n* гравёр. **engraving** /-ˈgreɪvɪŋ/ *n* гравю́ра.

engross /ɪnˈgrəʊs/ *vt* поглоща́ть *impf*, поглоти́ть *pf*; **be ~ed in** быть поглощённым +*instr*.

engulf /ɪnˈgʌlf/ *vt* поглоща́ть *impf*, поглоти́ть *pf*.

enhance /ɪnˈhɑːns/ *vt* увели́чивать *impf*, увели́чить *pf*.

enigma /ɪˈnɪgmə/ *n* зага́дка. **enigmatic** /ˌenɪgˈmætɪk/ *adj* зага́дочный.

enjoy /ɪnˈdʒɔɪ/ *vt* получа́ть *impf*, получи́ть *pf* удово́льствие от+*gen*; наслажда́ться *impf*, наслади́ться *pf* +*instr*; (*health etc.*) облада́ть *impf* +*instr*; **~ o.s.** хорошо́ проводи́ть *impf*, провести́ *pf* вре́мя. **enjoyable** /-əb(ə)l/ *adj* прия́тный. **enjoyment** /-mənt/ *n* удово́льствие.

enlarge /ɪnˈlɑːdʒ/ *vt* увели́чивать *impf*, увели́чить *pf*; **~ upon** распространя́ться *impf*, распространи́ться *pf* o+*prep*. **enlargement** /-mənt/ *n* увеличе́ние.

enlighten /ɪnˈlaɪt(ə)n/ *vt* просвеща́ть *impf*, просвети́ть *pf*. **enlightenment** /-mənt/ *n* просвеще́ние.

enlist /ɪnˈlɪst/ *vi* поступа́ть *impf*, поступи́ть *pf* на вое́нную слу́жбу; *vt* (*mil*) вербова́ть

impf, за~ *pf*; (*support etc.*) заручáться *impf*, заручи́ться *pf* +*instr*.

enliven /ɪn'laɪv(ə)n/ *vt* оживля́ть *impf*, оживи́ть *pf*.

enmity /'enmɪtɪ/ *n* вражда́.

ennoble /ɪ'nəʊb(ə)l/ *vt* облагорáживать *impf*, облагоро́дить *pf*.

ennui /ɒn'wiː/ *n* тоскá.

enormity /ɪ'nɔːmɪtɪ/ *n* чудо́вищность. **enormous** /-'nɔːməs/ *adj* огро́мный. **enormously** /-'nɔːməslɪ/ *adv* чрезвычáйно.

enough /ɪ'nʌf/ *adj* достáточно +*gen*; *adv* достáточно, дово́льно; **be** ~ хватáть *impf*, хвати́ть *pf impers*+*gen*.

enquire, **enquiry** /ɪn'kwaɪə(r), m 'kwaɪərɪ/ *see* **inquire**, **inquiry**

enrage /ɪn'reɪdʒ/ *vt* беси́ть *impf*, вз~ *pf*.

enrapture /ɪn'ræptʃə(r)/ *vt* восхищáть *impf*, восхити́ть *pf*.

enrich /ɪn'rɪtʃ/ *vt* обогащáть *impf*, обогати́ть *pf*.

enrol /ɪn'rəʊl/ *vt* & *i* запи́сывать(ся) *impf*, записáть(ся) *pf*. **enrolment** /-mənt/ *n* за́пись.

en route /ɑ̃ 'ruːt/ *adv* по пути́ (**to**, **for** в+*acc*).

ensconce /ɪn'skɒns/ *vt*: ~ o.s. засáживаться *impf*, засéсть *pf* (**with** за+*acc*).

ensemble /ɒn'sɒmb(ə)l/ *n* (*mus*) ансáмбль *m*.

enshrine /ɪn'ʃraɪn/ *vt* (*fig*) охранять *impf*, охрани́ть *pf*.

ensign /'ensaɪn/ *n* (*flag*) флаг.

enslave /ɪn'sleɪv/ *vt* порабощáть *impf*, поработи́ть *pf*.

ensue /ɪn'sjuː/ *vi* слéдовать *impf*. **ensuing** /-'sjuːɪŋ/ *adj* послéдующий.

ensure /ɪn'ʃʊə(r)/ *vt* обеспéчивать *impf*, обеспéчить *pf*.

entail /ɪn'teɪl/ *vt* (*necessitate*)

влечь *impf* за собо́й.

entangle /ɪn'tæŋɡ(ə)l/ *vt* запу́тывать *impf*, запутáть *pf*.

enter /'entə(r)/ *vt* & *i* входи́ть *impf*, войти́ *pf* в+*acc*; (*by transport*) въезжáть *impf*, въéхать *pf* в+*acc*; *vt* (*join*) поступáть *impf*, поступи́ть *pf* в, на, +*acc*; (*competition*) вступáть *impf*, вступи́ть *pf* в+*acc*; (*in list*) вноси́ть *impf*, внести́ *pf* в+*acc*.

enterprise /'entəpraɪz/ *n* (*undertaking*) предприя́тие; (*initiative*) предприи́мчивость. **enterprising** /-zɪŋ/ *adj* предприи́мчивый.

entertain /ˌentə'teɪn/ *vt* (*amuse*) развлекáть *impf*, развлéчь *pf*; (*guests*) принимáть *impf*, приня́ть *pf*; угощáть *impf*, угости́ть *pf* (**to** +*instr*); (*hopes*) питáть *impf*. **entertaining** /-ɪŋ/ *adj* занимáтельный. **entertainment** /-mənt/ *n* развлечéние; (*show*) представлéние.

enthral /ɪn'θrɔːl/ *vt* порабощáть *impf*, поработи́ть *pf*.

enthusiasm /ɪn'θjuːzɪˌæz(ə)m/ *n* энтузиáзм. **enthusiast** /-ˌæst/ *n* энтузиáст, ~ка. **enthusiastic** /-'æstɪk/ *adj* восто́рженный, по́лный энтузиáзма.

entice /ɪn'taɪs/ *vt* замáнивать *impf*, замани́ть *pf*. **enticement** /-mənt/ *n* примáнка. **enticing** /-sɪŋ/ *adj* замáнчивый.

entire /ɪn'taɪə(r)/ *adj* по́лный, цéлый, весь. **entirely** /-'taɪəlɪ/ *adv* вполнé, совершéнно; (*solely*) исключи́тельно. **entirety** /-'taɪərətɪ/ *n*: **in its** ~ по́лностью.

entitle /ɪn'taɪt(ə)l/ *vt* (*authorize*) давáть *impf*, дать *pf* прáво+*dat* (**to** на+*acc*); **be** ~d (*book*) называ́ться *impf*; **be** ~d **to** имéть *impf* прáво на+*acc*.

entity /'entɪtɪ/ n объе́кт; фено́мен.

entomology /ˌentə'mɒlədʒɪ/ n энтомоло́гия.

entourage /ˌɒntʊ'rɑːʒ/ n сви́та.

entrails /'entreɪlz/ n pl вну́тренности (-тей) pl.

entrance[1] /'entrəns/ n вход, въезд; (theat) вы́ход; ~ **exam** вступи́тельный экза́мен; ~ **hall** вестибю́ль m.

entrance[2] /ɪn'trɑːns/ vt (charm) очаро́вывать impf, очарова́ть pf. **entrancing** /-'trɑːnsɪŋ/ adj очарова́тельный.

entrant /'entrənt/ n уча́стник (for +gen).

entreat /ɪn'triːt/ vt умоля́ть impf, умоли́ть pf. **entreaty** /-'triːtɪ/ n мольба́.

entrench /ɪn'trentʃ/ vt be, become ~ed (fig) укореня́ться impf, укрени́ться pf.

entrepreneur /ˌɒntrəprə'nɜː(r)/ n предпринима́тель m.

entrust /ɪn'trʌst/ vt (secret) вверя́ть impf, вве́рить pf (to +dat); (object; person) поруча́ть impf, поручи́ть pf (to +dat).

entry /'entrɪ/ n вход, въезд; вступле́ние; (theat) вы́ход; (note) за́пись; (in reference book) статья́.

entwine /ɪn'twaɪn/ vt (interweave) сплета́ть impf, сплести́ pf; (wreathe) обвива́ть impf, обви́ть pf.

enumerate /ɪ'njuːmə,reɪt/ vt перечисля́ть impf, перечи́слить pf.

enunciate /ɪ'nʌnsɪ,eɪt/ vt (express) излага́ть impf, изложи́ть pf; (pronounce) произноси́ть impf, произнести́ pf. **enunciation** /-'eɪʃ(ə)n/ n изложе́ние; произноше́ние.

envelop /ɪn'veləp/ vt оку́тывать

impf, оку́тать pf. **envelope** /'envə,ləʊp/ n конве́рт.

enviable /'envɪəb(ə)l/ adj зави́дный. **envious** /'envɪəs/ adj зави́стливый.

environment /ɪn'vaɪərənmənt/ n среда́; (the ~) окружа́ющая среда́. **environs** /ɪn'vaɪərənz/ n pl окре́стности f pl.

envisage /ɪn'vɪzɪdʒ/ vt предусма́тривать impf, предусмотре́ть pf.

envoy /'envɔɪ/ n посла́нник, аге́нт.

envy /'envɪ/ n за́висть; vt зави́довать impf, по~ pf +dat.

enzyme /'enzaɪm/ n энзи́м.

ephemeral /ɪ'femər(ə)l/ adj эфеме́рный.

epic /'epɪk/ n эпопе́я; adj эпи́ческий.

epidemic /ˌepɪ'demɪk/ n эпиде́мия.

epilepsy /'epɪ,lepsɪ/ n эпиле́псия. **epileptic** /-'leptɪk/ n эпиле́птик; adj эпилепти́ческий.

epilogue /'epɪ,lɒg/ n эпило́г.

episode /'epɪ,səʊd/ n эпизо́д. **episodic** /-'sɒdɪk/ adj эпизоди́ческий.

epistle /ɪ'pɪs(ə)l/ n посла́ние.

epitaph /'epɪ,tɑːf/ n эпита́фия.

epithet /'epɪ,θet/ n эпи́тет.

epitome /ɪ'pɪtəmɪ/ n воплоще́ние. **epitomize** /-,maɪz/ vt воплоща́ть impf, воплоти́ть pf.

epoch /'iːpɒk/ n эпо́ха.

equal /'iːkw(ə)l/ adj ра́вный, одина́ковый; (capable of) спосо́бный (to на+acc, +inf); n ра́вный sb; vt равня́ться impf +dat. **equality** /ɪ'kwɒlɪ/ n ра́венство. **equalize** /'iːkwə,laɪz/ vt ура́внивать impf, уравня́ть pf; vi (sport) равня́ть impf, с~ pf счёт. **equally** /'iːkwəlɪ/ adv равно́, ра́вным о́бразом.

equanimity /ˌekwəˈnɪmɪtɪ/ *n* хладнокро́вие.

equate /ɪˈkweɪt/ *vt* прира́внивать *impf*, приравня́ть *pf* (with k+*dat*).

equation /ɪˈkweɪʒ(ə)n/ *n* (*math*) уравне́ние.

equator /ɪˈkweɪtə(r)/ *n* эква́тор.

equatorial /ˌekwəˈtɔːrɪəl/ *adj* экваториа́льный.

equestrian /ɪˈkwestrɪən/ *adj* ко́нный.

equidistant /ˌiːkwɪˈdɪst(ə)nt/ *adj* равноотстоя́щий. **equilibrium** /ˌiːkwɪˈlɪbrɪəm/ *n* равнове́сие.

equip /ɪˈkwɪp/ *vt* обору́довать *impf* & *pf*; (*person*) снаряжа́ть *impf*, снаряди́ть *pf*; (*fig*) вооружа́ть *impf*, вооружи́ть *pf*. **equipment** /-mənt/ *n* обору́дование, снаряже́ние.

equitable /ˈekwɪtəb(ə)l/ *adj* справедли́вый. **equity** /ˈekwɪtɪ/ *n* справедли́вость; *pl* (*econ*) обыкнове́нные а́кции *f pl*.

equivalent /ɪˈkwɪvələnt/ *adj* эквивале́нтный; *n* эквивале́нт.

equivocal /ɪˈkwɪvək(ə)l/ *adj* двусмы́сленный.

era /ˈɪərə/ *n* э́ра.

eradicate /ɪˈrædɪˌkeɪt/ *vt* искореня́ть *impf*, искорени́ть *pf*.

erase /ɪˈreɪz/ *vt* стира́ть *impf*, стере́ть *pf*; (*from memory*) вычёркивать *impf*, вы́черкнуть *pf* (из па́мяти). **eraser** /-zə(r)/ *n* ла́стик.

erect /ɪˈrekt/ *adj* прямо́й; *vt* сооружа́ть *impf*, сооруди́ть *pf*. **erection** /ɪˈrekʃ(ə)n/ *n* сооруже́ние; (*biol*) эре́кция.

erode /ɪˈrəʊd/ *vt* разруша́ть *impf*, разру́шить *pf*. **erosion** /ɪˈrəʊʒ(ə)n/ *n* эро́зия; (*fig*) разруше́ние.

erotic /ɪˈrɒtɪk/ *adj* эроти́ческий.

err /ɜː/ *vi* ошиба́ться *impf*,

ошиба́ться *pf*; (*sin*) греши́ть *impf*, co—*pf*.

errand /ˈerənd/ *n* поруче́ние; **run —s** быть на посы́лках (for y+*gen*).

erratic /ɪˈrætɪk/ *adj* неро́вный.

erroneous /ɪˈrəʊnɪəs/ *adj* оши́бочный. **error** /ˈerə(r)/ *n* оши́бка.

erudite /ˈeruːˌdaɪt/ *adj* учёный. **erudition** /ˌeruːˈdɪʃ(ə)n/ *n* эруди́ция.

erupt /ɪˈrʌpt/ *vi* взрыва́ться *impf*, взорва́ться *pf*; (*volcano*) изверга́ться *impf*, изве́ргнуться *pf* (of). **eruption** /ɪˈrʌpʃ(ə)n/ *n* изверже́ние.

escalate /ˈeskəˌleɪt/ *vi* возраста́ть *impf*, возрасти́ *pf*; *vt* интенсифици́ровать *impf* & *pf*.

escalator /ˈeskəˌleɪtə(r)/ *n* эскала́тор.

escapade /ˈeskəˌpeɪd/ *n* вы́ходка. **escape** /ɪˈskeɪp/ *n* (*from prison*) побе́г; (*from danger*) спасе́ние; (*leak*) уте́чка; **have a narrow —** едва́ спасти́сь; *vi* (*flee*) бежа́ть *impf* & *pf*; (*save o.s.*) спаса́ться *impf*, спасти́сь *pf*; (*leak*) утека́ть *impf*, уте́чь *pf*; *vt* избега́ть *impf*, избежа́ть *pf* +*gen*; (*groan*) вырыва́ться *impf*, вы́рваться *pf* из, y, +*gen*.

escort /n ˈeskɔːt/ (*mil*) эско́рт; (*of lady*) кавале́р; /ɪˈskɔːt/ *vt* сопровожда́ть *impf*, сопроводи́ть *pf*; (*mil*) эскорти́ровать *impf* & *pf*.

Eskimo /ˈeskɪˌməʊ/ *n* эскимо́с, —ка.

esoteric /ˌiːsəʊˈterɪk/ *adj* эзотери́ческий.

especially /ɪˈspeʃəlɪ/ *adv* осо́бенно.

espionage /ˈespɪəˌnɑːʒ/ *n* шпиона́ж.

espousal /ɪˈspaʊz(ə)l/ *n* поддержка. **espouse** /ɪˈspaʊz/ *vt* (*fig*) поддерживать *impf*, поддержать *pf*.

essay /ˈeseɪ/ *n* очерк; (*in school*) сочинение.

essence /ˈes(ə)ns/ *n* (*philos*) сущность; (*gist*) суть; (*extract*) эссенция. **essential** /ɪˈsenʃ(ə)l/ *adj* (*fundamental*) существенный; (*necessary*) необходимый; *n pl* (*necessities*) необходимое *sb*; (*crux*) суть; (*fundamentals*) основы *f pl*. **essentially** /ɪˈsenʃəlɪ/ *adv* по существу.

establish /ɪˈstæblɪʃ/ *vt* (*set up*) учреждать *impf*, учредить *pf*; (*fact etc.*) устанавливать *impf*, установить *pf*. **establishment** /-mənt/ *n* (*action*) учреждение, установление; (*institution*) учреждение.

estate /ɪˈsteɪt/ *n* (*property*) имение; (*after death*) наследство; (*housing ~*) жилой массив; **~ agent** агент по продаже недвижимости; **~ car** автомобиль *m* с кузовом «универсал».

esteem /ɪˈstiːm/ *n* уважение; *vt* уважать *impf*. **estimate** *n* /ˈestɪmət/ (*of quality*) оценка; (*of cost*) смета; *vt* /ˈestɪˌmeɪt/ оценивать *impf*, оценить *pf*. **estimation** /ˌestɪˈmeɪʃ(ə)n/ *n* оценка, мнение.

Estonia /ɪˈstəʊnɪə/ *n* Эстония. **Estonian** /-nɪən/ *n* эстонец, -нка; *adj* эстонский.

estranged /ɪˈstreɪndʒd/ *adj* отчуждённый.

estuary /ˈestjʊərɪ/ *n* устье.

etc. *abbr* и т.д. **etcetera** /it ˈsetərə/ и так далее.

etch /etʃ/ *vt* травить *impf*, выˉ *pf*. **etching** /ˈetʃɪŋ/ *n* (*action*) травление; (*object*) офорт.

eternal /ɪˈtɜːn(ə)l/ *adj* вечный. **eternity** /-nɪtɪ/ *n* вечность.

ether /ˈiːθə(r)/ *n* эфир. **ethereal** /ɪˈθɪərɪəl/ *adj* эфирный.

ethical /ˈeθɪk(ə)l/ *adj* этический, этичный. **ethics** /ˈeθɪks/ *n* этика.

ethnic /ˈeθnɪk/ *adj* этнический.

etiquette /ˈetɪˌket/ *n* этикет.

etymology /ˌetɪˈmɒlədʒɪ/ *n* этимология.

EU *abbr* (*of* European Union) ЕС.

eucalyptus /ˌjuːkəˈlɪptəs/ *n* эвкалипт.

Eucharist /ˈjuːkərɪst/ *n* причастие.

eulogy /ˈjuːlədʒɪ/ *n* похвала.

euphemism /ˈjuːfɪˌmɪz(ə)m/ *n* эвфемизм. **euphemistic** /-ˈmɪstɪk/ *adj* эвфемистический.

euro /ˈjʊərəʊ/ *n* евро *neut indecl*.

Europe /ˈjʊərəp/ *n* Европа. **European** /-ˈpɪən/ *n* европеец; *adj* европейский; **~ Community** Европейское сообщество; **~ Union** Европейский союз.

evacuate /ɪˈvækjʊˌeɪt/ *vt* (*person, place*) эвакуировать *impf & pf*. **evacuation** /-ˈeɪʃ(ə)n/ *n* эвакуация.

evade /ɪˈveɪd/ *vt* уклоняться *impf*, уклониться *pf* от+*gen*.

evaluate /ɪˈvæljʊˌeɪt/ *vt* оценивать *impf*, оценить *pf*. **evaluation** /-ˈeɪʃ(ə)n/ *n* оценка.

evangelical /ˌiːvænˈdʒelɪk(ə)l/ *adj* евангельский. **evangelist** /ɪˈvændʒəlɪst/ *n* евангелист.

evaporate /ɪˈvæpəˌreɪt/ *vt & i* испарять(ся) *impf*, испарить(ся) *pf*. **evaporation** /-ˈreɪʃ(ə)n/ *n* испарение.

evasion /ɪˈveɪʒ(ə)n/ *n* уклонение (**of** от+*gen*). **evasive** /ɪˈveɪsɪv/ *adj* уклончивый.

eve /iːv/ *n* кану́н; on the ∼ накану́не.

even /ˈiːv(ə)n/ *adj* ро́вный; (*number*) чётный; get ∼ расквита́ться *pf* (with с+*instr*); *adv* да́же; (*just*) как раз; (with *comp*) ещё; ∼ if да́же е́сли; ∼ though хотя́; ∼ so всё-таки; not ∼ да́же не; *vt* выра́внивать *impf*, вы́ровнять *pf*.

evening /ˈiːvnɪŋ/ *n* ве́чер; *adj* вече́рний; ∼ class вече́рние ку́рсы *m pl*.

evenly /ˈiːvənlɪ/ *adv* по́ровну, ро́вно. **evenness** /ˈiːvənnɪs/ *n* ро́вность.

event /ɪˈvent/ *n* собы́тие, происше́ствие; in the ∼ of в слу́чае +*gen*; in any ∼ во вся́ком слу́чае; in the ∼ в коне́чном счёте. **eventful** /ɪˈventfʊl/ *adj* по́лный собы́тий. **eventual** /ɪˈventjʊəl/ *adj* коне́чный. **eventuality** /ɪˌventjʊˈælɪtɪ/ *n* возмо́жность. **eventually** /ɪˈventjʊəlɪ/ *adv* в конце́ концо́в.

ever /ˈevə(r)/ *adv* (*at any time*) когда́-либо, когда́-нибудь; (*always*) всегда́; (*emph*) же; ∼ since с тех пор (как); ∼ so о́чень; for ∼ навсегда́; hardly ∼ почти́ никогда́. **evergreen** *adj* вечнозелёный; *n* вечнозелёное расте́ние. **everlasting** /ˌevəˈlɑːstɪŋ/ *adj* ве́чный. **evermore** *adv*: for ∼ навсегда́.

every /ˈevrɪ/ *adj* ка́ждый, вся́кий, все (*pl*); ∼ now and then вре́мя от вре́мени; ∼ other ка́ждый второ́й; ∼ other day че́рез день. **everybody**, **everyone** *pron* ка́ждый, все (*pl*). **everyday** *adj* (*daily*) ежедне́вный; (*commonplace*) повседне́вный. **everything** *pron* всё. **everywhere** *adv* всю́ду, везде́.

evict /ɪˈvɪkt/ *vt* выселя́ть *impf*, вы́селить *pf*. **eviction** /ɪˈvɪkʃ(ə)n/ *n* выселе́ние.

evidence /ˈevɪdəns/ *n* свиде́тельство, доказа́тельство; give ∼ свиде́тельствовать *impf* (о+*prep*; +*acc*; +что). **evident** /-d(ə)nt/ *adj* очеви́дный.

evil /ˈiːv(ə)l/ *n* зло; *adj* злой.

evoke /ɪˈvəʊk/ *vt* вызыва́ть *impf*, вы́звать *pf*.

evolution /ˌiːvəˈluːʃ(ə)n/ *n* эволю́ция. **evolutionary** /-nərɪ/ *adj* эволюцио́нный. **evolve** /ɪˈvɒlv/ *vt & i* развива́ть(ся) *impf*, разви́ть(ся) *pf*.

ewe /juː/ *n* овца́.

ex- /eks/ *in comb* бы́вший.

exacerbate /ekˈsæsəˌbeɪt/ *vt* обостря́ть *impf*, обостри́ть *pf*.

exact /ɪgˈzækt/ *adj* то́чный; *vt* взы́скивать *impf*, взыска́ть *pf* (from, с+*gen*). **exacting** /-ˈzæktɪŋ/ *adj* тре́бовательный. **exactitude, exactness** /ɪgˈzæktɪˌtjuːd, -ˈzæktnɪs/ *n* то́чность. **exactly** /-ˈzæktlɪ/ *adv* то́чно; (*just*) как раз; (*precisely*) и́менно.

exaggerate /ɪgˈzædʒəˌreɪt/ *vt* преувели́чивать *impf*, преувели́чить *pf*. **exaggeration** /-ˈreɪʃ(ə)n/ *n* преувеличе́ние.

exalt /ɪgˈzɔːlt/ *vt* возвыша́ть *impf*, возвы́сить *pf*; (*extol*) превозноси́ть *impf*, превознести́ *pf*.

examination /ɪgˌzæmɪˈneɪʃ(ə)n/ *n* (*inspection*) осмо́тр; (*exam*) экза́мен; (*law*) допро́с. **examine** /ɪgˈzæmɪn/ *vt* (*inspect*) осма́тривать *impf*, осмотре́ть *pf*; (*test*) экзаменова́ть *impf*, про-∼ *pf*; (*law*) допра́шивать *impf*, допроси́ть *pf*. **examiner** /ɪgˈzæmɪnə/ *n* экзамена́тор.

example /ɪgˈzɑːmp(ə)l/ *n* приме́р; for ∼ наприме́р.

exasperate /ɪgˈzɑːspəˌreɪt/ *vt* раздражáть *impf*, раздражи́ть *pf*. **exasperation** /-ˈreɪʃ(ə)n/ *n* раздражéние.

excavate /ˈekskəˌveɪt/ *vt* раскáпывать *impf*, раскопáть *pf*. **excavations** /-ˈveɪʃ(ə)nz/ *n pl* раскóпки *f pl*. **excavator** /ˈekskəˌveɪtə(r)/ *n* экскавáтор.

exceed /ɪkˈsiːd/ *vt* превышáть *impf*, превы́сить *pf*. **exceedingly** /-dɪŋlɪ/ *adv* чрезвычáйно.

excel /ɪkˈsel/ *vt* превосходи́ть *impf*, превзойти́ *pf*; *vi* отличáться *impf*, отличи́ться *pf* (**at**, **in** в+*prep*). **excellence** /ˈeksələns/ *n* превосхóдство. **excellency** /ˈeksələnsɪ/ *n* превосходи́тельство. **excellent** /ˈeksələnt/ *adj* отли́чный.

except /ɪkˈsept/ *vt* исключáть *impf*, исключи́ть *pf*; *prep* крóме+*gen*. **exception** /-ˈsepʃ(ə)n/ *n* исключéние; **take** ~ **to** возражáть *impf*, возрази́ть *pf* прóтив+*gen*. **exceptional** /-ˈsepʃən(ə)l/ *adj* исключи́тельный.

excerpt /ˈeksɜːpt/ *n* отры́вок.

excess /ɪkˈses/ *n* избы́ток. **excessive** /-sɪv/ *adj* чрезмéрный.

exchange /ɪksˈtʃeɪndʒ/ *vt n* обмéн (**of** +*instr*); (*of currency*) размéн; (*building*) би́ржа; (*telephone*) центрáльная телефóнная стáнция; ~ **rate** курс; *vt* обмéнивать *impf*, обменя́ть *pf* (**for** на+*acc*); обмéниваться *impf*, обменя́ться *pf* +*instr*.

excise[1] /ˈeksaɪz/ *n* (*duty*) акци́з(ный).

excise[2] /ekˈsaɪz/ *vt* (*cut out*) выре́зать *impf*, вы́резать *pf*.

excitable /ɪkˈsaɪtəb(ə)l/ *adj* возбуди́мый. **excite** /-ˈsaɪt/ *vt* (*cause*, *arouse*) возбуждáть *impf*, возбуди́ть *pf*; (*thrill*, *agitate*) волновáть *impf*, вз~ *pf*. **excitement** /-ˈsaɪtmənt/ *n* возбуждéние; волнéние.

exclaim /ɪkˈskleɪm/ *vi* восклицáть *impf*, воскли́кнуть *pf*. **exclamation** /ˌekskləˈmeɪʃ(ə)n/ *n* восклицáние; ~ **mark** восклицáтельный знак.

exclude /ɪkˈskluːd/ *vt* исключáть *impf*, исключи́ть *pf*. **exclusion** /-ˈskluːʒ(ə)n/ *n* исключéние. **exclusive** /-ˈskluːsɪv/ *adj* исключи́тельный; (*high-class*) эксклюзи́вный.

excommunicate /ˌekskəˈmjuːnɪˌkeɪt/ *vt* отлучáть *impf*, отлучи́ть *pf* (**от** цéркви).

excrement /ˈekskrɪmənt/ *n* экскремéнты (-тов).

excrete /ɪkˈskriːt/ *vt* выделя́ть *impf*, вы́делить *pf*. **excretion** /-ˈskriːʃ(ə)n/ *n* выделéние.

excruciating /ɪkˈskruːʃɪˌeɪtɪŋ/ *adj* мучи́тельный.

excursion /ɪkˈskɜːʃ(ə)n/ *n* экскýрсия.

excusable /ɪkˈskjuːzəb(ə)l/ *adj* прости́тельный. **excuse** /-ˈskjuːs/ *n* оправдáние; (*pretext*) отговóрка; /-ˈskjuːz/ *vt* (*forgive*) извиня́ть *impf*, извини́ть *pf*; (*justify*) опрáвдывать *impf*, оправдáть *pf*; (*release*) освобождáть *impf*, освободи́ть *pf* (**from** от+*gen*); ~ **me!** извини́те!; прости́те!

execute /ˈeksɪˌkjuːt/ *vt* исполня́ть *impf*, испóлнить *pf*; (*criminal*) казни́ть *impf* & *pf*. **execution** /-ˈkjuːʃ(ə)n/ *n* исполнéние; казнь. **executioner** /-ˈkjuːʃ(ə)nə(r)/ *n* палáч. **executive** /ɪgˈzekjʊtɪv/ *n* исполни́тельный óрган; (*person*) руководи́тель *m*; *adj* исполни́тельный.

exemplary /ɪɡ'zemplərɪ/ *adj* примéрный. **exemplify** /-'zemplɪˌfaɪ/ *vt* (*illustrate by example*) приводи́ть *impf*, привести́ *pf* пример +*gen*; (*serve as example*) служи́ть *impf*, по~ *pf* примéром +*gen*.

exempt /ɪɡ'zempt/ *adj* освобождённый; *vt* освобожда́ть *impf*, освободи́ть *pf* (**from** от+*gen*). **exemption** /-'zempʃ(ə)n/ *n* освобождéние.

exercise /'eksəˌsaɪz/ *n* (*use*) примене́ние; (*physical* ~; *task*) упражне́ние; **take** ~ упражня́ться *impf*; ~ **book** тетра́дь; *vt* (*use*) применя́ть *impf*, примени́ть *pf*; (*dog*) прогу́ливать *impf*; (*train*) упражня́ть *impf*.

exert /ɪɡ'zɜːt/ *vt* ока́зывать *impf*, оказа́ть *pf*; ~ **o.s.** стара́ться *impf*, по~ *pf*. **exertion** /-'zɜːʃ(ə)n/ *n* напряже́ние.

exhale /eks'heɪl/ *vt* выдыха́ть *impf*, вы́дохнуть *pf*.

exhaust /ɪɡ'zɔːst/ *n* вы́хлоп; ~ **fumes** выхлопны́е га́зы *m pl*; ~ **pipe** выхлопна́я труба́; *vt* (*use up*) истоща́ть *impf*, истощи́ть *pf*; (*person*) изнуря́ть *impf*, изнури́ть *pf*; (*subject*) исчéрпывать *impf*, исчéрпать *pf*. **exhausted** /-stɪd/ *adj*: **be** ~ (*person*) быть изможде́нным. **exhausting** /-stɪŋ/ *adj* изнури́тельный. **exhaustion** /-stʃ(ə)n/ *n* изнуре́ние; (*depletion*) истоще́ние. **exhaustive** /-stɪv/ *adj* исчéрпывающий.

exhibit /ɪɡ'zɪbɪt/ *n* экспона́т; (*law*) веще́ственное доказа́тельство; *vt* (*manifest*) проявля́ть *impf*, прояви́ть *pf*; (*publicly*) выставля́ть *impf*, вы́ставить *pf*. **exhibition** /ˌeksɪ'bɪʃ(ə)n/ *n* вы́ставка. **exhibitor** /ɪɡ'zɪbɪtə(r)/ *n* экспоне́нт.

exhilarated /ɪɡ'zɪləˌreɪtɪd/ *adj* в припо́днятом настрое́нии. **exhilarating** /-ˌreɪtɪŋ/ *adj* возбужда́ющий. **exhilaration** /-'reɪʃ(ə)n/ *n* возбужде́ние.

exhort /ɪɡ'zɔːt/ *vt* увещева́ть *impf*. **exhortation** /ˌeɡzɔː'teɪʃ(ə)n/ *n* увещева́ние.

exhume /eks'hjuːm/ *vt* выка́пывать *impf*, вы́копать *pf*.

exile /'eksaɪl/ *n* изгна́ние; (*person*) изгна́нник; *vt* изгоня́ть *impf*, изгна́ть *pf*.

exist /ɪɡ'zɪst/ *vi* существова́ть *impf*. **existence** /-st(ə)ns/ *n* существова́ние. **existing** /-stɪŋ/ *adj* существу́ющий.

exit /'eksɪt/ *n* вы́ход; (*for vehicles*) вы́езд; (*theat*) ухо́д (со сце́ны); ~ **visa** выездна́я ви́за; *vi* уходи́ть *impf*, уйти́ *pf*.

exonerate /ɪɡ'zɒnəˌreɪt/ *vt* опра́вдывать *impf*, опра́вдать *pf*.

exorbitant /ɪɡ'zɔːbɪt(ə)nt/ *adj* непоме́рный.

exorcize /'eksɔːˌsaɪz/ *vt* (*spirits*) изгоня́ть *impf*, изгна́ть *pf*.

exotic /ɪɡ'zɒtɪk/ *adj* экзоти́ческий.

expand /ɪk'spænd/ *vt & i* расширя́ть(ся) *impf*, расши́рить(ся) *pf*; ~ **on** распространя́ться *impf*, распространи́ться *pf* o+*prep*. **expanse** /-'spæns/ *n* простра́нство. **expansion** /-'spænʃ(ə)n/ *n* расшире́ние. **expansive** /-'spænsɪv/ *adj* экспанси́вный.

expatriate /eks'pætrɪət/ *n* экспатриа́нт, ~ка.

expect /ɪk'spekt/ *vt* (*await*) ожида́ть *impf* +*gen*; ждать *impf* +*gen*, что; (*suppose*) полага́ть *impf*; (*require*) тре́бовать *impf* +*gen*, что́бы. **expectant** /-t(ə)nt/ *adj* выжида́тельный;

mother бере́менная же́нщина.

expectation /ˌekspekˈteɪʃ(ə)n/ n ожида́ние.

expediency /ɪkˈspiːdɪənsɪ/ n целесообра́зность. **expedient** /-ənt/ n приём; adj целесообра́зный. **expedite** /ˈekspɪˌdaɪt/ vt ускоря́ть impf, уско́рить pf. **expedition** /ˌekspɪˈdɪʃ(ə)n/ n экспеди́ция. **expeditionary** /ˌekspɪˈdɪʃənərɪ/ adj экспедицио́нный.

expel /ɪkˈspel/ vt (drive out) выгоня́ть impf, вы́гнать pf; (from school etc.) исключа́ть impf, исключи́ть pf; (from country etc.) изгоня́ть impf, изгна́ть pf.

expend /ɪkˈspend/ vt тра́тить impf, из~, по~ pf. **expendable** /-ˈspendəb(ə)l/ adj необяза́тельный. **expenditure** /-ˈspendɪtʃə(r)/ n расхо́д. **expense** /-ˈspens/ n расхо́д; pl расхо́ды m pl, at the ~ of за счёт+gen; (fig) цено́ю+gen. **expensive** /-ˈspensɪv/ adj дорого́й.

experience /ɪkˈspɪərɪəns/ n о́пыт; (incident) пережива́ние; vt испы́тывать impf, испыта́ть pf; (undergo) пережива́ть impf, пережи́ть pf. **experienced** /-ənst/ adj о́пытный.

experiment /ɪkˈsperɪmənt/ n экспериме́нт; vi эксперименти́ровать impf (on, with над, c+instr). **experimental** /-ˈment(ə)l/ adj эксперимента́льный.

expert /ˈekspɜːt/ n экспе́рт; adj о́пытный. **expertise** /-ˈtiːz/ n специа́льные зна́ния neut pl.

expire /ɪkˈspaɪə(r)/ vi (period) истека́ть impf, исте́чь pf. **expiry** /-rɪ/ n истече́ние.

explain /ɪkˈspleɪn/ vt объясня́ть impf, объясни́ть pf. **explanation** /ˌekspləˈneɪʃ(ə)n/ n объяс-

не́ние. **explanatory** /ɪkˈsplænətərɪ/ adj объясни́тельный.

expletive /ɪkˈspliːtɪv/ n (oath) бра́нное сло́во.

explicit /ɪkˈsplɪsɪt/ adj я́вный; (of person) прямо́й.

explode /ɪkˈspləʊd/ vt & i взрыва́ть(ся) impf, взорва́ть(ся) pf; vt (discredit) опроверга́ть impf, опрове́ргнуть pf; vi (with anger etc.) разража́ться impf, разрази́ться pf.

exploit /ˈeksplɔɪt/ n по́двиг; vt /ɪkˈsplɔɪt/ эксплуати́ровать impf; (use to advantage) испо́льзовать impf & pf. **exploitation** /ˌeksplɔɪˈteɪʃ(ə)n/ n эксплуата́ция. **exploiter** /ɪkˈsplɔɪtə(r)/ n эксплуата́тор.

exploration /ˌeksplɔˈreɪʃ(ə)n/ n иссле́дование. **exploratory** /ɪkˈsplɔrətərɪ/ adj иссле́довательский. **explore** /ɪkˈsplɔː(r)/ vt иссле́довать impf & pf. **explorer** /ɪkˈsplɔːrə(r)/ n иссле́дователь m.

explosion /ɪkˈspləʊʒ(ə)n/ n взрыв. **explosive** /-ˈspləʊsɪv/ n взры́вчатое вещество́; adj взры́вчатый; (fig) взрывно́й.

exponent /ɪkˈspəʊnənt/ n (interpreter) истолкова́тель m; (advocate) сторо́нник.

export /ˈekspɔːt/ n вы́воз, э́кспорт; vt /ekˈspɔːt/ вывози́ть impf, вы́вести pf; экспорти́ровать impf & pf. **exporter** /ekˈspɔːtə(r)/ n экспортёр.

expose /ɪkˈspəʊz/ vt (bare) раскрыва́ть impf, раскры́ть pf; (subject) подверга́ть impf, подве́ргнуть pf (to +dat); (discredit) разоблача́ть impf, разоблачи́ть pf; (phot) экспони́ровать impf & pf. **exposition** /ˌekspəˈzɪʃ(ə)n/ n из-

ложéние.

exposure /ɪkˈspəʊʒə(r)/ n подвергáние (**to** +dat); (phot) выдержка; (unmasking) разоблачéние; (med) хóлод.

expound /ɪkˈspaʊnd/ vt излагáть impf, изложи́ть pf.

express /ɪkˈspres/ n (train) экспрéсс; adj (clear) тóчный; (purpose) специáльный; (urgent) срóчный; vt выразить impf, вырaзить pf. **expression** /-ˈspreʃ(ə)n/ n выражéние; (expressiveness) выразительность. **expressive** /-ˈspresɪv/ adj выразительный. **expressly** adv (clearly) я́сно; (specifically) специáльно.

expropriate /eksˈprəʊprɪeɪt/ vt экспроприи́ровать impf & pf. **expropriation** /-ˈeɪʃ(ə)n/ n экспроприáция.

expulsion /ɪkˈspʌlʃ(ə)n/ n (from school etc.) исключéние; (from country etc.) изгнáние.

exquisite /ˈekskwɪzɪt/ adj утончённый.

extant /ekˈstænt/ adj сохрани́вшийся.

extempore /ɪkˈstempərɪ/ adj экспрóмптом. **extemporize** /-ˈstempəˌraɪz/ vt & i импровизи́ровать impf, сымпровизи́ровать pf.

extend /ɪkˈstend/ vt (stretch out) протя́гивать impf, протяну́ть pf; (enlarge) расширя́ть impf, расши́рить pf; (prolong) продлевáть impf, продли́ть pf; vi простирáться impf, простерéться pf. **extension** /-ˈstenʃ(ə)n/ n (enlarging) расшире́ние; (time) продлéние; (to house) пристрóйка; (tel) добáвочный. **extensive** /-ˈstensɪv/ adj обши́рный. **extent** /-ˈstent/ n (degree) стéпень.

extenuating /ɪkˈstenjʊˌeɪtɪŋ/ adj ~ **circumstances** смягчáющие вину́ обстоя́тельства neut pl.

exterior /ɪkˈstɪərɪə(r)/ n внéшность; adj внéшний.

exterminate /ɪkˈstɜːmɪˌneɪt/ vt истребля́ть impf, истреби́ть pf. **extermination** /-ˈneɪʃ(ə)n/ n истреблéние.

external /ɪkˈstɜːn(ə)l/ adj внéшний.

extinct /ɪkˈstɪŋkt/ adj (volcano) потухший; (species) вымерший; **become** ~ вымирáть impf, вымереть pf. **extinction** /-ˈstɪŋkʃ(ə)n/ n вымирáние.

extinguish /ɪkˈstɪŋgwɪʃ/ vt гаси́ть impf, по~ pf. **extinguisher** /-ˈstɪŋgwɪʃə(r)/ n огнетуши́тель m.

extol /ɪkˈstəʊl/ vt превозноси́ть impf, превознести́ pf.

extort /ɪkˈstɔːt/ vt вымогáть impf (**from** y+gen). **extortion** /-ˈstɔːʃ(ə)n/ n вымогáтельство. **extortionate** /-ˈstɔːʃənət/ adj вымогáтельский.

extra /ˈekstrə/ n (theat) стати́ст, ~ка; (payment) приплáта; adj дополни́тельный; (special) осóбый; adv осóбенно.

extract n /ˈekstrækt/ экстрáкт; (from book etc.) вы́держка /ɪkˈstrækt/ извлекáть impf, извлéчь pf. **extraction** /-ˈstrækʃ(ə)n/ n извлечéние; (origin) происхождéние. **extradite** /ˈekstrəˌdaɪt/ vt выдавáть impf, вы́дать pf. **extradition** /-ˈdɪʃ(ə)n/ n вы́дача.

extramarital /ˌekstrəˈmærɪt(ə)l/ adj внебрáчный.

extraneous /ɪkˈstreɪnɪəs/ adj постóронний.

extraordinary /ɪkˈstrɔːdɪnərɪ/ adj чрезвычáйный.

extrapolate /ɪkˈstræpəˌleɪt/ vt & i

экстраполи́ровать *impf & pf.*

extravagant /ik'strævəgəns/ *n* расточи́тельность. **extravagant** /-gənt/ *adj* расточи́тельный; *(fantastic)* сумасбро́дный.

extreme /ik'stri:m/ *n* кра́йность; *adj* кра́йний. **extremity** /-'stremiti/ *n (end)* край; *(adversity)* кра́йность; *pl (hands & feet)* коне́чности *f pl.*

extricate /'ekstri,keit/ *vt* вы́пу́тывать *impf*, вы́путать *pf.*

exuberance /ig'zju:bərəns/ *n* жизнера́достность. **exuberant** /-rənt/ *adj* жизнера́достный.

exude /ig'zju:d/ *vt & i* выделя́ть(ся) *impf*, вы́делить(ся) *pf*; *(fig)* излуча́ть(ся) *impf*, излучи́ть(ся) *pf.*

exult /ig'zʌlt/ *vi* ликова́ть *impf.* **exultant** /-tənt/ *adj* лику́ющий. **exultation** /ig,zʌl'teiʃ(ə)n/ *n* ликова́ние.

eye /ai/ *n* глаз; *(needle etc.)* ушко́; *vt* разгля́дывать *impf*, разгляде́ть *pf.* **eyeball** *n* глазно́е я́блоко. **eyebrow** *n* бровь. **eyelash** *n* ресни́ца. **eyelid** *n* ве́ко. **eyeshadow** *n* те́ни *f pl* для век. **eyesight** *n* зре́ние. **eyewitness** *n* очеви́дец.

F

fable /'feib(ə)l/ *n* ба́сня.

fabric /'fæbrik/ *n (structure)* структу́ра; *(cloth)* ткань. **fabricate** /-,keit/ *vt (invent)* выду́мывать *impf*, вы́думать *pf.* **fabrication** /-'keiʃ(ə)n/ *n* вы́думка.

fabulous /'fæbjuləs/ *adj* ска́зочный.

façade /fə'sɑ:d/ *n* фаса́д.

face /feis/ *n* лицо́; *(expression)* выраже́ние; *(grimace)* грима́са; *(side)* сторона́; *(surface)* пове́рхность; *(clock etc.)* цифербла́т; **make ~s** ко́рчить *impf* ро́жи; **~ down** лицо́м вниз; **~ to ~** лицо́м к лицу́; **the ~ of** пе́ред лицо́м+*gen*, вопреки́+*dat*; **on the ~ of it** на пе́рвый взгляд; *vt (be turned towards)* быть обращённым к+*dat*; *(of person)* стоя́ть *impf* лицо́м к+*dat*; *(meet firmly)* смотре́ть *impf* в лицо́+*dat*; *(cover)* облицо́вывать *impf*, облицева́ть *pf*; **I can't ~ it** я не в состоя́нии об э́том ду́мать. **faceless** /'feislis/ *adj* безли́чный.

facet /'fæsit/ *n* грань; *(fig)* аспе́кт.

facetious /fə'si:ʃəs/ *adj* шутли́вый.

facial /'feiʃ(ə)l/ *adj* лицево́й.

facile /'fæsail/ *adj* пове́рхностный. **facilitate** /fə'sili,teit/ *vt* облегча́ть *impf*, облегчи́ть *pf.* **facility** /fə'siliti/ *n (ease)* лёгкость; *(ability)* спосо́бность; *pl (conveniences)* удо́бства *neut pl*, *(opportunities)* возмо́жности *f pl.*

facing /'feisiŋ/ *n* облицо́вка; *(of garment)* отде́лка.

facsimile /fæk'simili/ *n* факси́миле *neut indecl.*

fact /fækt/ *n* факт; **the ~ is that** … де́ло в том, что…; **as a matter of ~** со́бственно говоря́; **in ~** на са́мом де́ле.

faction /'fækʃ(ə)n/ *n* фра́кция.

factor /'fæktə(r)/ *n* фа́ктор.

factory /'fæktəri/ *n* фа́брика, заво́д.

factual /'fæktjuəl/ *adj* факти́ческий.

faculty /'fækəlti/ *n* спосо́бность; *(univ)* факульте́т.

fade /feɪd/ vi (wither) вянуть impf, за~ pf; (colour) выцветать impf, выцвести pf; (sound) замирать impf, замереть pf.

faeces /ˈfiːsiːz/ n pl кал.

fag /fæg/ n (cigarette) сигаретка.

fail /feɪl/ n: without ~ обязательно; vi (weaken) слабеть impf; (break down) отказывать impf, отказать pf; (not succeed) терпеть impf, по~ pf неудачу; не удаваться impf, удаться pf impers+dat; vt & i (exam) проваливать(ся) impf, провалить(ся) pf; vt (disappoint) подводить impf, подвести pf.

failing /ˈfeɪlɪŋ/ n недостаток; prep за неимением +gen. **failure** /ˈfeɪljə(r)/ n неудача; (person) неудачник, -ица.

faint /feɪnt/ n обморок; adj (weak) слабый; (pale) бледный; **I feel ~** мне дурно; **~-hearted** малодушный; vi падать impf, упасть pf в обморок.

fair¹ /feə(r)/ n ярмарка.

fair² /feə(r)/ adj (hair, skin) светлый; (weather) ясный; (just) справедливый; (average) сносный; **a ~ amount** довольно много +gen. **fairly** /ˈfeəlɪ/ adv довольно.

fairy /ˈfeərɪ/ n фея; **~-tale** сказка.

faith /feɪθ/ n вера; (trust) доверие. **faithful** /ˈfeɪθfʊl/ adj верный; **yours ~ly** с уважением.

fake /feɪk/ n подделка; vt подделывать impf, подделать pf.

falcon /ˈfɔːlkən/ n сокол.

fall /fɔːl/ n падение; vi падать impf, упасть pf, распадаться pf; **~ apart** распадаться pf; **~ asleep** засыпать impf, заснуть pf; **~ back on** прибегать impf,

прибегнуть pf к+dat; **~ down** падать impf, упасть pf; в руху́лся pf; **~ in love with** влюбляться impf, влюбиться pf в+acc; **~ off** отпадать impf, отпасть pf; **~ out** выпадать impf, выпасть pf; (quarrel) поссориться pf; **~ over** опрокидываться impf, опрокинуться pf; **~ through** проваливаться impf, провалиться pf; **~-out** радиоактивные осадки (-ков) pl.

fallacy /ˈfæləsɪ/ n ошибка.

fallible /ˈfælɪb(ə)l/ adj подверженный ошибкам.

fallow /ˈfæləʊ/ n: **lie ~** лежать impf под паром.

false /fɔːls/ adj ложный; (teeth) искусственный; **~ start** неверный старт. **falsehood** /ˈfɔːlshʊd/ n ложь. **falsification** /ˌfɔːlsɪfɪˈkeɪʃ(ə)n/ n фальсификация. **falsify** /ˈfɔːls̩faɪ/ vt фальсифицировать impf & pf. **falsity** /ˈfɔːlsɪtɪ/ n ложность.

falter /ˈfɔːltə(r)/ vi спотыкаться impf, споткнуться pf; (stammer) запинаться impf, запнуться pf.

fame /feɪm/ n слава.

familiar /fəˈmɪlɪə(r)/ adj (well known) знакомый; (usual) обычный; (informal) фамильярный. **familiarity** /fəˌmɪlɪˈærɪtɪ/ n знакомство; фамильярность. **familiarize** /fəˈmɪlɪəˌraɪz/ vt ознакомлять impf, ознакомить pf (with c+instr).

family /ˈfæmɪlɪ/ n семья; attrib семейный; **~ tree** родословная sb.

famine /ˈfæmɪn/ n голод. **famished** /ˈfæmɪʃd/ adj: **be ~** голодать impf.

famous /ˈfeɪməs/ adj знаменитый.

fan¹ /fæn/ n веер; (ventilator)

вентиля́тор; ~-belt реме́нь *m* вентиля́тора; *vt* обма́хивать *impf*, обмахну́ть *pf*; (*flame*) раздува́ть *impf*, разду́ть *pf*.

fan² /fæn/ *n* покло́нник, -ица; (*sport*) боле́льщик. **fanatic** /fə'nætɪk/ *n* фана́тик. **fanatical** /fə'nætɪkəl/ *adj* фанати́ческий.

fanciful /'fænsɪfʊl/ *adj* причу́дливый. **fancy** /'fænsɪ/ *n* фанта́зия; (*whim*) причу́да; take a ~ to увлека́ться *impf*, увле́чься *pf* +*instr*; *adj* витиева́тый; *vt* (*imagine*) представля́ть *impf*, предста́вить *pf* себе́; (*suppose*) полага́ть *impf*; (*like*) нра́виться *impf*, по~ *pf impers* +*dat*; ~ dress маскара́дный костю́м; ~-dress костюми́рованный.

fanfare /'fænfeə(r)/ *n* фанфа́ра.

fang /fæŋ/ *n* клык; (*serpent's*) ядови́тый зуб.

fantasize /'fæntəsaɪz/ *vi* фантази́ровать *impf*. **fantastic** /fæn'tæstɪk/ *adj* фантасти́ческий. **fantasy** /'fæntəsɪ/ *n* фанта́зия.

far /fɑ:(r)/ *adj* да́льний; Russia is ~ away Росси́я о́чень далеко́; *adv* далеко́; (*fig*) намно́го; as ~ as (*prep*) до+*gen*; (*conj*) поско́льку; by ~ намно́го; (in) so ~ as поско́льку; so ~ до сих пор; ~-fetched притя́нутый за́ волосы; ~-reaching далеко́ иду́щий; ~-sighted дальнови́дный.

farce /fɑ:s/ *n* фарс. **farcical** /'fɑ:sɪk(ə)l/ *adj* смехотво́рный.

fare /feə(r)/ *n* (*price*) проездна́я пла́та; (*food*) пи́ща; *vi* пожива́ть *impf*. **farewell** /feə'wel/ *int* проща́й(те)!; *n* проща́ние; *attrib* проща́льный; bid ~ проща́ться *impf*, прости́ться *pf* (to с+*instr*).

farm /fɑ:m/ *n* фе́рма. **farmer** /'fɑ:mə(r)/ *n* фе́рмер; ~s' market; ры́нок сельскохозя́йственной проду́кции. **farming** /'fɑ:mɪŋ/ *n* се́льское хозя́йство.

fart /fɑ:t/ *n* (*vulg*) пука́ние; *vi* пу́кать *impf*, пу́кнуть *pf*.

farther /'fɑ:ðə(r)/ *see* further. **farthest** /'fɑ:ðɪst/ *see* furthest.

fascinate /'fæsɪneɪt/ *vt* очаро́вывать *impf*, очарова́ть *pf*. **fascinating** /-,neɪtɪŋ/ *adj* очарова́тельный. **fascination** /-'neɪʃ(ə)n/ *n* очарова́ние.

Fascism /'fæʃɪz(ə)m/ *n* фаши́зм. **Fascist** /-ʃɪst/ *n* фаши́ст, ~ка; *adj* фаши́стский.

fashion /'fæʃ(ə)n/ *n* мо́да; (*manner*) мане́ра; after a ~ не́которым о́бразом; *vt* придава́ть *impf*, прида́ть *pf* фо́рму +*dat*. **fashionable** /'fæʃnəb(ə)l/ *adj* мо́дный.

fast¹ /fɑ:st/ *n* пост; *vi* пости́ться *impf*.

fast² /fɑ:st/ *adj* (*rapid*) ско́рый, бы́стрый; (*colour*) сто́йкий; (*shut*) пло́тно закры́тый; be ~ (*timepiece*) спеши́ть *impf*.

fasten /'fɑ:s(ə)n/ *vt* (*attach*) прикрепля́ть *impf*, прикрепи́ть *pf* (to к+*dat*); (*tie*) привя́зывать *impf*, привяза́ть *pf* (to к+*dat*); (*garment*) застёгивать *impf*, застегну́ть *pf*. **fastener, fastening** /'fɑ:s(ə)nə(r), 'fɑ:snɪŋ/ *n* запо́р, задви́жка; (*on garment*) застёжка.

fastidious /fæ'stɪdɪəs/ *adj* брезгли́вый.

fat /fæt/ *n* жир; *adj* (*greasy*) жи́рный; (*plump*) то́лстый; get ~ толсте́ть *impf*, по~ *pf*.

fatal /'feɪt(ə)l/ *adj* роково́й; (*deadly*) смерте́льный. **fatalism** /'feɪtə,lɪz(ə)m/ *n* фатали́зм. **fatality** /fə'tælɪtɪ/ *n* (*death*)

смерте́льный слу́чай. **fate**
/feɪt/ n судьба́. **fateful** /'feɪtfʊl/
adj роково́й.

father /'fɑːðə(r)/ n оте́ц; **~-in-law**
(husband's ~) свёкор; (wife's ~)
тесть m. **fatherhood** n отцо́в-
ство. **fatherland** n оте́чество.
fatherly /'fɑːðəlɪ/ adj отече́-
ский.

fathom /'fæð(ə)m/ n морска́я са́-
жень; vt (fig) понима́ть impf,
поня́ть pf.

fatigue /fə'tiːɡ/ n утомле́ние; vt
утомля́ть impf, утоми́ть pf.

fatten /'fæt(ə)n/ vt отка́рмли-
вать impf, откорми́ть pf; vi
толсте́ть impf, по~ pf. **fatty**
/'fætɪ/ adj жи́рный.

fatuous /'fætjʊəs/ adj глу́пый.

fault /fɔːlt/ n недоста́ток; (blame)
вина́; (geol) сброс. **faultless**
/-lɪs/ adj безупре́чный. **faulty**
/-tɪ/ adj дефе́ктный.

fauna /'fɔːnə/ n фа́уна.

favour /'feɪvə(r)/ n любе́з-
ность; (goodwill) благо-
скло́нность; in (s.o.'s) ~ в
по́льзу +gen; be in ~ of быть
за+acc; (support) благоприя́т-
ствовать impf +dat; (treat
with partiality) ока́зывать impf,
оказа́ть pf предпочте́ние +dat.
favourable /-rəb(ə)l/ adj (propitious) благоприя́тный; (approving) благоскло́нный. **favourite**
/-rɪt/ n люби́мец, -мица; (also
sport) фавори́т, ~ка; adj люби́-
мый.

fawn¹ /fɔːn/ n оленёнок; adj
желтова́то-кори́чневый.

fawn² /fɔːn/ vi подли́зываться
impf, подлиза́ться pf (on
к+dat).

fax /fæks/ n факс; vt посыла́ть
impf, посла́ть pf по фа́ксу.

fear /fɪə(r)/ n страх, боя́знь,
опасе́ние; vt & i боя́ться impf

+gen; опаса́ться impf +gen.
fearful /-fʊl/ adj (terrible)
стра́шный; (timid) пугли́вый.
fearless /-lɪs/ adj бесстра́шный.
fearsome /-səm/ adj гро́зный.

feasibility /ˌfiːzɪ'bɪlɪtɪ/ n осуще-
сти́мость. **feasible** /'fiːzɪb(ə)l/
adj осуществи́мый.

feast /fiːst/ n (meal) пир; (festival) пра́здник; vi пирова́ть
impf.

feat /fiːt/ n по́двиг.

feather /'feðə(r)/ n перо́.

feature /'fiːtʃə(r)/ n черта́; (newspaper) (темати́ческая) статья́;
~ film худо́жественный
фильм; vt помеща́ть impf, по-
мести́ть pf на ви́дном ме́сте;
(in film) пока́зывать impf, по-
каза́ть pf; vi игра́ть impf сы-
гра́ть pf роль.

February /'febrʊərɪ/ n февра́ль
m; adj февра́льский.

feckless /'feklɪs/ adj безала́-
берный.

federal /'fedər(ə)l/ adj федера́ль-
ный. **federation** /-'reɪʃ(ə)n/ n
федера́ция.

fee /fiː/ n гонора́р; (entrance ~
etc.) взнос; pl (regular payment,
school, etc.) пла́та.

feeble /'fiːb(ə)l/ adj сла́бый.

feed /fiːd/ n корм; vt корми́ть
impf, на~, по~ pf; vi кор-
ми́ться impf, по~ pf; ~ up от-
ка́рмливать impf, откорми́ть
pf; **I am fed up with** мне надое́л
(-а, -о; -и) +nom. **feedback** n
обра́тная связь.

feel /fiːl/ vt чу́вствовать impf,
по~ pf; (think) счита́ть impf,
счесть pf; vi (~ bad etc.) чу́в-
ствовать impf, по~ pf себя́
+adv, +instr; ~ like хоте́ться
impf impers+dat. **feeling** /-lɪŋ/ n
(sense) ощуще́ние; (emotion)
чу́вство; (impression) впечатлі-

ние; (*mood*) настрое́ние.

feign /feɪn/ *vt* притворя́ться *impf*, притвори́ться *pf* +*instr*.

feigned /feɪnd/ *adj* притво́рный.

feline /ˈfiːlaɪn/ *adj* коша́чий.

fell /fel/ *vt* (*tree*) сруба́ть *impf*, сруби́ть *pf*; (*person*) сбива́ть *impf*, сбить *pf* с ног.

fellow /ˈfeləʊ/ *n* па́рень *m*; (*of society etc.*) член; ~ **countryman** соотече́ственник. **fellowship** /-ʃɪp/ *n* това́рищество.

felt /felt/ *n* фетр; *adj* фе́тровый; ~**tip pen** флома́стер.

female /ˈfiːmeɪl/ *n* (*animal*) са́мка; (*person*) же́нщина; *adj* же́нский. **feminine** /ˈfemɪnɪn/ *adj* же́нский, же́нственный; (*gram*) же́нского ро́да. **femininity** /-ˈnɪnɪtɪ/ *n* же́нственность. **feminism** /ˈfemɪnɪz(ə)m/ *n* фемини́зм. **feminist** /-nɪst/ *n* фемини́ст, ~ка; *adj* фемини́стский.

fence /fens/ *n* забо́р; *vt*: ~ **in** огора́живать *impf*, огороди́ть *pf*; ~ **off** отгора́живать *impf*, отгороди́ть *pf*; *vi* (*sport*) фехтова́ть *impf*. **fencer** /-sə(r)/ *n* фехтова́льщик, -и́ца. **fencing** /-sɪŋ/ *n* (*enclosure*) забо́р; (*sport*) фехтова́ние.

fend /fend/ *vt*: ~ **off** отража́ть *impf*, отрази́ть *pf*; *vi*: ~ **for o.s.** забо́титься *impf*, по~ *pf* о себе́. **fender** /-də(r)/ *n* реше́тка.

fennel /ˈfen(ə)l/ *n* фе́нхель *m*.

ferment *n* /ˈfɜːment/ броже́ние; *vi* /fəˈment/ броди́ть *impf*; *vt* ква́сить *impf*, за~ *pf*; (*excite*) возбужда́ть *impf*, возбуди́ть *pf*. **fermentation** /ˌfɜːmen-ˈteɪʃ(ə)n/ *n* броже́ние; (*excitement*) возбужде́ние.

fern /fɜːn/ *n* па́поротник.

ferocious /fəˈrəʊʃəs/ *adj* свире́-

пый. **ferocity** /-ˈrɒsɪtɪ/ *n* свире́пость.

ferret /ˈferɪt/ *n* хорёк; *vt*: ~ **out** (*search out*) разню́хивать *impf*, разню́хать *pf*; *vi*: ~ **about** (*rummage*) ры́ться *impf*.

ferry /ˈferɪ/ *n* паро́м; *vt* перево-зи́ть *impf*, перевезти́ *pf*.

fertile /ˈfɜːtaɪl/ *adj* плодоро́д-ный. **fertility** /fəˈtɪlɪtɪ/ *n* плодоро́дие. **fertilize** /ˈfɜːtɪˌlaɪz/ *vt* (*soil*) удобря́ть *impf*, удобри́ть *pf*; (*egg*) оплодотворя́ть *impf*, оплодотвори́ть *pf*. **fertilizer** /ˈfɜːtɪˌlaɪzə(r)/ *n* удобре́ние.

fervent /ˈfɜːv(ə)nt/ *adj* горя́чий. **fervour** /-və(r)/ *n* жар.

fester /ˈfestə(r)/ *vi* гнои́ться *impf*.

festival /ˈfestɪv(ə)l/ *n* пра́здник, (*music etc.*) фестива́ль *m*. **festive** /ˈfestɪv/ *adj* пра́здничный. **festivities** /feˈstɪvɪtɪz/ *n pl* торже-ства́ *neut pl*.

festoon /feˈstuːn/ *vt* украша́ть *impf*, укра́сить *pf*.

fetch /fetʃ/ *vt* (*carrying*) приноси́ть *impf*, принести́ *pf*; (*leading*) приводи́ть *impf*, привести́ *pf*; (*go and come back with*) (*on foot*) идти́ *impf*, по~ *pf* за +*instr*; (*by vehicle*) заезжа́ть *impf*, зае́хать *pf* за+*instr*; (*price*) выруча́ть *impf*, вы́ручить *pf*. **fetching** /ˈfetʃɪŋ/ *adj* привлека́тельный.

fetid /ˈfetɪd/ *adj* злово́нный.

fetish /ˈfetɪʃ/ *n* фети́ш.

fetter /ˈfetə(r)/ *vt* ско́вывать *impf*, скова́ть *pf*; *n*: *pl* кандалы́ (-ло́в) *pl*; (*fig*) око́вы (-в) *pl*.

fettle /ˈfet(ə)l/ *n* состоя́ние.

feud /fjuːd/ *n* кро́вная месть.

feudal /ˈfjuːd(ə)l/ *adj* феода́льный. **feudalism** /-dəˌlɪz(ə)m/ *n* феодали́зм.

fever /ˈfiːvə(r)/ *n* лихора́дка. **fe-**

verish /-rɪʃ/ *adj* лихора́дочный.

few /fjuː/ *adj & pron* немно́гие *pl*; ма́ло+*gen*; **a ~** не́сколько +*gen*; **quite a ~** нема́ло +*gen*.

fiancé /fɪˈɒnseɪ/ *n* жени́х. **fiancée** /fɪˈɒnseɪ/ *n* неве́ста.

fiasco /fɪˈæskəʊ/ *n* прова́л.

fib /fɪb/ *n* привра́ть *impf*, привра́ть *pf*.

fibre /ˈfaɪbə(r)/ *n* волокно́. **fibreglass** *n* стекловолокно́. **fibrous** /-brəs/ *adj* волокни́стый.

fickle /ˈfɪk(ə)l/ *adj* непостоя́нный.

fiction /ˈfɪk(ə)n/ *n* худо́жественная литерату́ра; (*invention*) вы́думка. **fictional** /ˈfɪkʃən(ə)l/ *adj* беллетристи́ческий. **fictitious** /fɪkˈtɪʃəs/ *adj* вы́мышленный.

fiddle /ˈfɪd(ə)l/ *n* (*violin*) скри́пка; (*swindle*) обма́н; *vi*: **~ about** безде́льничать *impf*; **~ with** верте́ть *impf*; *vt* (*falsify*) подде́лывать *impf*, подде́лать *pf*; (*cheat*) жи́лить *impf*, **y~** *pf*.

fidelity /fɪˈdelɪtɪ/ *n* ве́рность.

fidget /ˈfɪdʒɪt/ *n* непосе́да *m & f*; *vi* ёрзать *impf*; не́рвничать *impf*. **fidgety** /-tɪ/ *adj* непосе́дливый.

field /fiːld/ *n* по́ле; (*sport*) площа́дка; (*sphere*) о́бласть (*f*). **~-glasses** полево́й бино́кль *m*. **~work** полевы́е рабо́ты *f pl*.

fiend /fiːnd/ *n* дья́вол. **fiendish** /ˈfiːndɪʃ/ *adj* дья́вольский.

fierce /fɪəs/ *adj* свире́пый; (*strong*) си́льный.

fiery /ˈfaɪərɪ/ *adj* о́гненный.

fifteen /fɪfˈtiːn/ *adj & n* пятна́дцать. **fifteenth** /fɪfˈtiːnθ/ *adj & n* пятна́дцатый. **fifth** /fɪfθ/ *adj & n* пя́тый; (*fraction*) пя́тая *sb*. **fiftieth** /ˈfɪftɪɪθ/ *adj & n* пятиде-

ся́тый. **fifty** /ˈfɪftɪ/ *adj & n* пятьдеся́т; *pl* (*decade*) пятидеся́тые го́ды (-до́в) *m pl*.

fig /fɪg/ *n* инжи́р.

fight /faɪt/ *n* дра́ка; (*battle*) бой; (*fig*) борьба́; *vt* боро́ться *impf* с+*instr*; *vi* дра́ться *impf*; *vt & i* (*wage war*) воева́ть *impf* с+*instr*. **fighter** /-tə(r)/ *n* (*aeron*) истреби́тель *m*. **fighting** /-tɪŋ/ *n* бой *m*, дра́ка.

figment /ˈfɪgmənt/ *n* плод воображе́ния.

figurative /ˈfɪgjʊrətɪv/ *adj* перено́сный. **figure** /ˈfɪgə(r)/ *n* (*form, body, person*) фигу́ра; (*number*) ци́фра; (*diagram*) рису́нок; (*image*) изображе́ние; (*of speech*) оборо́т ре́чи; **~head** (*naut*) носово́е украше́ние; (*person*) номина́льная глава́; *vt* (*think*) полага́ть *impf*; *vi* фигури́ровать *impf*; **~ out** вычисля́ть *impf*, вы́числить *pf*.

filament /ˈfɪləmənt/ *n* волокно́; (*electr*) нить.

file¹ /faɪl/ *n* (*tool*) напи́льник; *vt* подпи́ливать *impf*, подпили́ть *pf*.

file² /faɪl/ *n* (*folder*) па́пка; (*comput*) файл; *vt* подшива́ть *impf*, подши́ть *pf*; (*complaint*) подава́ть *impf*, пода́ть *pf*.

file³ /faɪl/ *n* (*row*) ряд; *n*: **in** (*single*) **~** гусько́м.

filigree /ˈfɪlɪgriː/ *adj* филигра́нный.

fill /fɪl/ *vt & i* (*also* **~ up**) наполня́ть(ся) *impf*, напо́лнить(ся) *pf*; *vt* заполня́ть *impf*, запо́лнить *pf*; (*tooth*) пломбирова́ть *impf*, за~ *pf*; (*occupy*) занима́ть *impf*, заня́ть *pf*; (*satiate*) насыща́ть *impf*, насы́тить *pf*; **~ in** (*vt*) заполня́ть *impf*, запо́лнить *pf*; (*vi*) замеща́ть *impf*,

замести́ть *pf.*

fillet /'fɪlɪt/ *n* (*cul*) филе́ *neut indecl.*

filling /'fɪlɪŋ/ *n* (*tooth*) пло́мба; (*cul*) начи́нка.

filly /'fɪlɪ/ *n* кобы́лка.

film /fɪlm/ *n* (*layer; phot*) плёнка; (*cin*) фильм; ~ **star** ки+ звезда́; *vt* снима́ть *impf*, снять *pf.*

filter /'fɪltə(r)/ *n* фильтр; *vt* фильтрова́ть *impf*, про~ *pf*; ~ **through, out** проса́чиваться *impf*, просочи́ться *pf.*

filth /fɪlθ/ *n* грязь. **filthy** /-θɪ/ *adj* гря́зный.

fin /fɪn/ *n* плавни́к.

final /'faɪn(ə)l/ *n* фина́л; *pl* выпускны́е экза́мены *m pl*; *adj* после́дний; (*decisive*) оконча́тельный. **finale** /fɪ'nɑːlɪ/ *n* фина́л. **finalist** /'faɪnəlɪst/ *n* финали́ст. **finality** /faɪ'nælɪtɪ/ *n* зако́нченность. **finalize** /'faɪnəlaɪz/ *vt* (*complete*) заверша́ть *impf*, заверши́ть *pf*; (*settle*) ула́живать *impf*, ула́дить *pf*. **finally** /'faɪnəlɪ/ *adv* (*at last*) наконе́ц; (*in the end*) в конце́ концо́в.

finance /'faɪnæns/ *n* фина́нсы (-сов) *pl*; *vt* финанси́ровать *impf* & *pf*. **financial** /-'nænʃ(ə)l/ *adj* фина́нсовый. **financier** /-'nænsɪə(r)/ *n* финанси́ст.

finch /fɪntʃ/ *n see comb*, e.g. **bullfinch**

find /faɪnd/ *n* нахо́дка; *vt* находи́ть *impf*, найти́ *pf*; (*person*) застава́ть *impf*, заста́ть *pf*; ~ **out** узнава́ть *impf*, узна́ть *pf*; ~ **fault with** придира́ться *impf*, придра́ться *pf* к+*dat.* **finding** /-dɪŋ/ *n pl* (*of inquiry*) вы́воды *m pl.*

fine[1] /faɪn/ *n* (*penalty*) штраф; *vt* штрафова́ть *impf*, о~ *pf.*

fine[2] /faɪn/ *adj* (*weather*) я́сный; (*excellent*) прекра́сный; (*delicate*) то́нкий; (*of sand etc.*) ме́лкий; ~ **arts** изобрази́тельные иску́сства *neut pl*; *adv* хорошо́.

finery /-nərɪ/ *n* наря́д. **finesse** /fɪ'nes/ *n* то́нкость.

finger /'fɪŋgə(r)/ *n* па́лец; ~**nail** но́готь; ~**print** отпеча́ток па́льца; ~**tip** ко́нчик па́льца; **have at (one's)** ~**tips** знать как свои́ пять па́льцев; *vt* щу́пать *impf*, по~ *pf.*

finish /'fɪnɪʃ/ *n* коне́ц; (*polish*) отде́лка; (*sport*) фи́ниш; *vt* & *i* конча́ть(ся) *impf*, ко́нчить(ся) *pf*; *vt* ока́нчивать *impf*, око́нчить *pf.*

finite /'faɪnaɪt/ *adj* коне́чный.

Finland /'fɪnlənd/ *n* Финля́ндия. **Finn** /fɪn/ *n* финн, фи́нка. **Finnish** /'fɪnɪʃ/ *adj* фи́нский.

fir /fɜː(r)/ *n* ель, пи́хта.

fire /'faɪə(r)/ *n* (*bake*) обжига́ть *impf*, обже́чь *pf*; (*excite*) воспламеня́ть *impf*, воспламени́ть *pf*; (*gun*) стреля́ть *impf* из+*gen* (*at* в+*acc*, по+*dat*); (*dismiss*) увольня́ть *impf*, уво́лить *pf*; *on*+*gen* *m*; (*grate*) ками́н; (*conflagration*) пожа́р; (*bonfire*) костёр; (*fervour*) пыл; **be on** ~ горе́ть *impf*; **catch** ~ загора́ться *impf*, загоре́ться *pf*; **set** ~ **to, set on** ~ поджига́ть *impf*, подже́чь *pf*; ~**alarm** пожа́рная трево́га; ~**arm(s)** огнестре́льное ору́жие; ~ **brigade** пожа́рная кома́нда; ~**engine** пожа́рная маши́на; ~**escape** пожа́рная ле́стница; ~ **extinguisher** огнетуши́тель *m*; ~**guard** ками́нная решётка; ~**man** пожа́рный *sb*; ~**place** ками́н; ~**side** ме́сто у ками́на; ~ **station** пожа́рное депо́ *neut indecl*; ~**wood** дрова́ (-в) *pl*;

~**work** фейерве́рк. **firing**
/'faɪərɪŋ/ n (shooting) стрельба́.

firm[1] /fɜːm/ n (business) фи́рма.
firm[2] /fɜːm/ adj твёрдый. **firmness** /-nɪs/ n твёрдость.

first /fɜːst/ adj пе́рвый; n пе́рвый
sb; adv спе́рва, снача́ла; (for
the ~ time) впервы́е; **in the ~
place** во-пе́рвых; at ~ all пре́ж-
де всего́; at ~ sight на пе́р-
вый взгляд; ~ **aid** пе́рвая
по́мощь; ~**class** первокла́сс-
ный; ~ **hand** из пе́рвых рук;
~**rate** первокла́ссный. **first-
ly** /-lɪ/ adv во-пе́рвых.

fiscal /'fɪsk(ə)l/ adj фина́н-
совый.

fish /fɪʃ/ n ры́ба; adj ры́бный; vi
лови́ть impf ры́бу; ~ **out** выта́-
скивать impf, вы́таскать pf.
fisherman /'fɪʃəmən/ n рыба́к.
fishery /'fɪʃərɪ/ n рыбный про́-
мысел. **fishing** /'fɪʃɪŋ/ n рыбная
ло́вля; ~ **boat** рыболо́вное
су́дно; ~ **line** леса́; ~ **rod**
у́дочка. **fishmonger** /'fɪʃ-
mʌŋgə(r)/ n торго́вец ры́бой.
fishmonger's /'fɪʃmʌŋgəz/ n
ры́бный магази́н. **fishy** /'fɪʃɪ/
adj ры́бный; (dubious) подо-
зри́тельный.

fissure /'fɪʃə(r)/ n тре́щина.

fist /fɪst/ n кула́к.

fit[1] /fɪt/ n: **be a good** ~ хорошо́
сиде́ть impf; adj (suitable) под-
ходя́щий, го́дный; (healthy)
здоро́вый; vt (be suitable) го-
ди́ться impf +dat, на+acc, на
+gen; vt & i (be the right size
(for)) подходи́ть impf, подой-
ти́ pf (+dat); (adjust) прила́-
живать impf, прила́дить pf (to
к+dat); (be small enough for)
входи́ть impf, войти́ pf в+acc;
~ **out** снабжа́ть impf, снаб-
ди́ть pf.

fit[2] /fɪt/ n (attack) припа́док.

(fig) поры́в. **fitful** /-fʊl/ adj по-
ры́вистый.

fitter /'fɪtə(r)/ n монтёр. **fitting**
/'fɪtɪŋ/ n (of clothes) приме́рка; n
армату́ра; adj подходя́щий.

five /faɪv/ adj & n пять; (number
5) пятёрка; ~**year plan** пяти-
ле́тка.

fix /fɪks/ n (dilemma) переде́лка;
(drugs) уко́л; vt (repair) чини́ть
impf, по~ pf; (settle) назнача́ть
impf, назна́чить pf; (fasten)
укрепля́ть impf, укрепи́ть pf;
~ **up** (organize) организо́вы-
вать impf & pf; (install) устана́вли-
вать impf, установи́ть pf. **fix-
ation** /-'seɪʃ(ə)n/ n фикса́ция.
fixed /fɪkst/ adj устано́влен-
ный. **fixture** /'fɪkstʃə(r)/ n (sport)
предстоя́щее спорти́вное ме-
роприя́тие; (fitting) приспособ-
ле́ние.

fizz, fizzle /fɪz, fɪz(ə)l/ vi шипе́ть
impf; **fizzle out** выды́хаться
impf, вы́дохнуться pf. **fizzy**
/'fɪzɪ/ adj шипу́чий.

flabbergasted /'flæbəgɑːstɪd/
adj ошеломлённый.

flabby /'flæbɪ/ adj дря́блый.

flag[1] /flæg/ n флаг, зна́мя neut;
vt: ~ **down** остана́вливать
impf, останови́ть pf.

flag[2] /flæg/ vi (weaken) ослабе-
ва́ть impf, ослабе́ть pf.

flagon /'flægən/ n кувши́н.

flagrant /'fleɪgrənt/ adj во-
пию́щий.

flagship /'flægʃɪp/ n фла́гман.

flagstone /'flægstəʊn/ n плита́.

flair /fleə(r)/ n чутьё.

flake /fleɪk/ n слой; pl хло́пья
(-ьев) pl; vi шелуши́ться impf.
flaky /'fleɪkɪ/ adj слои́стый.

flamboyant /flæm'bɔɪənt/ adj
цвети́стый.

flame /fleɪm/ n пла́мя neut,
ого́нь m; vi пыла́ть impf.

flange /flændʒ/ n фла́нец.

flank /flæŋk/ n (of body) бок; (mil) фланг; vt быть сбо́ку +gen.

flannel /ˈflæn(ə)l/ n фланс́ль; (for face) мочалка для лица́.

flap /flæp/ n (board) откидна́я доска́; (pocket, tent ~) кла́пан; (panic) па́ника; vt взма́хивать impf, взмахну́ть pf +instr; vi развева́ться impf.

flare /fleə(r)/ n вспы́шка; (signal) сигна́льная раке́та; vi вспы́хивать impf, вспы́хнуть pf; ~ up (fire) возгора́ться impf, возгоре́ться pf; (fig) вспы́хнуть pf.

flash /flæʃ/ n вспы́шка; in a ~ ми́гом; vi сверка́ть impf, сверкну́ть pf. **flashback** n ретроспе́кция. **flashy** /ˈflæʃɪ/ adj показно́й.

flask /flɑːsk/ n фля́жка.

flat¹ /flæt/ n (dwelling) кварти́ра.

flat² /flæt/ n (mus) бемо́ль m; (tyre) спу́щенная ши́на; on the ~ на пло́скости; adj пло́ский; ~-**fish** ка́мбала. **flatly** /-lɪ/ adv наотре́з. **flatten** /-t(ə)n/ vt & vi выра́внивать impf, вы́ровнять(ся) impf, вы́ровнять(ся) pf. **flatmate** /ˈflætmeɪt/ n сосе́д, ~ка по кварти́ре. **flatter** /ˈflætə(r)/ vt льстить impf, по~ +dat. **flattering** /-rɪŋ/ adj льсти́вый. **flattery** /-rɪ/ n лесть.

flaunt /flɔːnt/ vt щеголя́ть, щегольну́ть pf +instr.

flautist /ˈflɔːtɪst/ n флейти́ст.

flavour /ˈfleɪvə(r)/ n вкус; (fig) при́вкус; vt припра́вить, припра́вить pf.

flaw /flɔː/ n изъя́н.

flax /flæks/ n лён. **flaxen** /ˈflæks(ə)n/ adj (colour) соло́менный.

flea /fliː/ n блоха́; ~ market барахо́лка.

fleck /flek/ n кра́пинка.

flee /fliː/ vi бежа́ть impf & impf (from от+gen); vt бежа́ть impf из+gen.

fleece /fliːs/ n руно́; vt (fig) обдира́ть impf, ободра́ть pf. **fleecy** /-sɪ/ adj шерсти́стый.

fleet /fliːt/ n флот; (vehicles) парк.

fleeting /ˈfliːtɪŋ/ adj мимолётный.

flesh /fleʃ/ n (as opposed to mind) плоть; (meat) мя́со; in the ~ во плоти́. **fleshy** /-ʃɪ/ adj мяси́стый.

flex /fleks/ n шнур; vt сгиба́ть impf, согну́ть pf. **flexibility** /ˌfleksɪˈbɪlɪtɪ/ n ги́бкость. **flexible** /ˈfleksɪb(ə)l/ adj ги́бкий.

flick /flɪk/ n & vt щёлкать impf, щёлкнуть pf (+instr); ~ **through** пролиста́ть pf.

flicker /ˈflɪkə(r)/ n мерца́ние; vi мерца́ть impf.

flier /ˈflaɪə(r)/ see flyer

flight¹ /flaɪt/ n (fleeing) бе́гство; **put (take) to** ~ обраща́ть(ся) impf, обрати́ть(ся) pf в бе́гство.

flight² /flaɪt/ n (flying) полёт; (trip) рейс; ~ **of stairs** ле́стничный марш. **flighty** /-tɪ/ adj ве́треный.

flimsy /ˈflɪmzɪ/ adj (fragile) непро́чный; (dress) лёгкий; (excuse) сла́бый.

flinch /flɪntʃ/ vi (recoil) отпря́дывать impf, отпря́нуть pf; (fig) уклоня́ться impf, уклони́ться pf (from от+gen).

fling /flɪŋ/ n vt швыря́ть impf, швырну́ть pf; vi (also ~ o.s.) броса́ться impf, бро́ситься pf.

flint /flɪnt/ n креме́нь m.

flip /flɪp/ vt щёлкать impf,

щёлкнуть pf +instr.

flippant /'flɪpənt/ adj легкомы́сленный.

flipper /'flɪpə(r)/ n ласт.

flirt /flɜːt/ n коке́тка; vi флиртова́ть impf (**with** +instr). **flirtation** /-'teɪʃ(ə)n/ n флирт.

flit /flɪt/ vi порха́ть impf, порхну́ть pf.

float /fləʊt/ n поплаво́к; vi пла́вать indet, плыть det; vt (company) пуска́ть impf, пусти́ть pf в ход.

flock /flɒk/ n (animals) ста́до; (birds) ста́я; vi стека́ться impf, сте́чься pf.

flog /flɒɡ/ vt сечь impf, вы́~ pf.

flood /flʌd/ n наводне́ние; (bibl) пото́п; (fig) пото́к; vi (river etc.) выступа́ть impf, вы́ступить pf из берего́в; vt затопля́ть impf, затопи́ть pf. **floodgate** n шлюз. **floodlight** n прожектор.

floor /flɔː(r)/ n пол; (storey) эта́ж; ~**board** полови́ца; vt (confound) ста́вить impf, по~ pf в тупи́к.

flop /flɒp/ vi (fall) плю́хаться impf, плю́хнуться pf; (fail) прова́ливаться impf, провали́ться pf.

flora /'flɔːrə/ n фло́ра. **floral** /-r(ə)l/ adj цвето́чный.

florid /'flɒrɪd/ adj цвети́стый; (ruddy) румя́ный. **florist** /'flɒrɪst/ n торго́вец цвета́ми.

flounce¹ /flaʊns/ vi броса́ться impf, бро́ситься pf.

flounce² /flaʊns/ n (of skirt) обо́рка.

flounder¹ /'flaʊndə(r)/ n (fish) ка́мбала.

flounder² /'flaʊndə(r)/ vi бара́хтаться impf.

flour /'flaʊə(r)/ n мука́.

flourish /'flʌrɪʃ/ n (movement)

разма́хивание (+instr); (of pen) ро́счерк; vi (thrive) процвета́ть impf; vt (wave) разма́хивать impf, размахну́ть pf +instr.

flout /flaʊt/ vt попира́ть impf, попра́ть pf.

flow /fləʊ/ n течь impf; ли́ться impf; n тече́ние.

flower /'flaʊə(r)/ n цвето́к; ~**bed** клу́мба; ~**pot** цвето́чный горшо́к; vi цвести́ impf. **flowery** /-rɪ/ adj цвети́стый.

flu /fluː/ n грипп.

fluctuate /'flʌktjʊeɪt/ vi колеба́ться impf, по~ pf. **fluctuation** /-'eɪʃ(ə)n/ n колеба́ние.

flue /fluː/ n дымохо́д.

fluent /'fluːənt/ adj бе́глый. **fluently** /-lɪ/ adv свобо́дно.

fluff /flʌf/ n пух. **fluffy** /-fɪ/ adj пуши́стый.

fluid /'fluːɪd/ n жи́дкость; adj жи́дкий.

fluke /fluːk/ n случа́йная уда́ча.

fluorescent /flʊə'res(ə)nt/ adj флюоресце́нтный.

fluoride /'flʊəraɪd/ n фтори́д.

flurry /'flʌrɪ/ n (squall) шквал; (fig) волна́.

flush /flʌʃ/ n (redness) румя́нец; vi (redden) красне́ть impf, по~ pf; vt спуска́ть impf, спусти́ть pf во́ду в+acc.

flustered /'flʌstəd/ adj сконфу́женный.

flute /fluːt/ n фле́йта.

flutter /'flʌtə(r)/ vi (flit) порха́ть impf, порхну́ть pf; (wave) разве́ваться impf.

flux /flʌks/ n: **in a state of ~** в состоя́нии измене́ния.

fly¹ /flaɪ/ n (insect) му́ха.

fly² /flaɪ/ vi лета́ть indet, лете́ть det, по~ pf; (flag) развева́ться impf; (hasten) нести́сь impf, по~ pf; vt (aircraft) управля́ть impf +instr; (transport) перево-

зи́ть *impf*, перевезти́ *pf* (самолётом); *(flag)* поднима́ть *impf*, подня́ть *pf*. **flyer, flier** /'flaɪə(r)/ *n* лётчик. **flying** /'flaɪɪŋ/ *n* полёт.

foal /fəʊl/ *n (horse)* жеребёнок.

foam /fəʊm/ *n* пе́на; ~ **plastic** пенопла́ст; ~ **rubber** пенорезина; *vi* пе́ниться *impf*, вс~ *pf*. **foamy** /-mɪ/ *adj* пе́нистый.

focal /'fəʊk(ə)l/ *adj* фо́кусный.

focus /'fəʊkəs/ *n* фо́кус; *(fig)* центр; *vt* фокуси́ровать *impf*, с~ *pf*. (*concentrate*) сосредото́чивать *impf*, сосредото́чить *pf*.

fodder /'fɒdə(r)/ *n* корм.

foe /fəʊ/ *n* враг.

foetus /'fiːtəs/ *n* заро́дыш.

fog /fɒg/ *n* тума́н. **foggy** /-gɪ/ *adj* тума́нный.

foible /'fɔɪb(ə)l/ *n* сла́бость.

foil[1] /fɔɪl/ *n (metal)* фольга́; *(contrast)* контра́ст.

foil[2] /fɔɪl/ *vt (thwart)* расстра́ивать *impf*, расстро́ить *pf*.

foil[3] /fɔɪl/ *n (sword)* рапи́ра.

foist /fɔɪst/ *vt* нава́зывать *impf*, навяза́ть *pf* (**on** +*dat*).

fold[1] /fəʊld/ *n (sheep-~)* овча́рня.

fold[2] /fəʊld/ *n* скла́дка, сгиб; *vt* скла́дывать *impf*, сложи́ть *pf*. **folder** /-də(r)/ *n* па́пка. **folding** /-dɪŋ/ *adj* складно́й.

foliage /'fəʊlɪɪdʒ/ *n* листва́.

folk /fəʊk/ *n* наро́д, лю́ди *pl*; *(relatives)* родня́ *collect*; *attrib* наро́дный. **folklore** /'fəʊklɔː(r)/ *n* фолькло́р.

follow /'fɒləʊ/ *vt* сле́довать *impf*, по~ *pf* +*dat*, за+*instr*; *(walk behind)* идти́ *det* за+*instr*; *(fig)* следи́ть *impf* за+*instr*. **follower** /'fɒləʊə(r)/ *n* после́дователь *m*. **following** /'fɒləʊɪŋ/ *adj* сле́дующий.

folly /'fɒlɪ/ *n* глу́пость.

fond /fɒnd/ *adj* не́жный; **be ~ of** люби́ть *impf* +*acc*.

fondle /'fɒnd(ə)l/ *vt* ласка́ть *impf*.

fondness /'fɒndnɪs/ *n* любо́вь.

font /fɒnt/ *n (eccl)* купе́ль.

food /fuːd/ *n* пи́ща, еда́. **foodstuff** *n* пищево́й проду́кт.

fool /fuːl/ *n* дура́к, ду́ра; *vt* дура́чить *impf*, о~ *pf*; *vi:* ~ **about** дура́читься *impf*. **foolhardy** /'fuːlhɑːdɪ/ *adj* безрассу́дно хра́брый. **foolish** /'fuːlɪʃ/ *adj* глу́пый. **foolishness** /'fuːlɪʃnɪs/ *n* глу́пость. **foolproof** /'fuːlpruːf/ *adj* абсолю́тно надёжный.

foot /fʊt/ *n* нога́; *(measure)* фут; *(of hill etc.)* подно́жие; **on ~** пешко́м; **put one's ~ in it** сесть *pf* в лу́жу. **foot-and-mouth (disease)** *n* я́щур. **football** *n* футбо́л; *attrib* футбо́льный. **footballer** /'fʊtbɔːlə(r)/ *n* футболи́ст. **foothills** *n pl* предго́рье. **footing** /'fʊtɪŋ/ *n (fig)* ба́зис; **lose one's ~** оступи́ться *pf*; **on an equal ~** на ра́вной ноге́. **footlights** *n pl* ра́мпа. **footman** *n* лаке́й. **footnote** *n* сно́ска. **footpath** *n* тропи́нка; *(pavement)* тротуа́р. **footprint** *n* след. **footstep** *n (sound)* шаг; *(footprint)* след. **footwear** *n* обувь.

for /fɔː(r)/ *prep (of time)* в тече́ние +*gen*, на+*acc*; *(of purpose)* для+*gen*, за+*acc* +*instr*; *(price)* за+*acc*; *(on account of)* из-за +*gen*; *(in place of)* вме́сто+*gen*; ~ **the sake of** ра́ди +*gen*; **as** ~ что каса́ется+*gen*; *conj* так как.

forage /'fɒrɪdʒ/ *n* фура́ж; *vi:* ~ **for** разы́скивать *impf*.

foray /'fɒreɪ/ *n* набе́г.

forbearance /fɔː'beərəns/ n воздержанность.

forbid /fə'bɪd/ vt запрещать impf, запретить pf (+dat (person) & acc (thing)). **forbidding** /-dɪŋ/ adj грозный.

force /fɔːs/ n сила; pl (armed ~) вооружённые силы f pl; by ~ силой; vt (compel) заставлять impf, заставить pf; (lock etc.) взламывать impf, взломать pf. **forceful** /-fʊl/ adj сильный; (speech) убедительный. **forcible** /'fɔːsɪb(ə)l/ adj насильственный.

forceps /'fɔːseps/ n щипцы (-цо́в) pl.

ford /fɔːd/ n брод; vt переходить impf, перейти pf вброд+acc.

fore /fɔː(r)/ n: come to the ~ выдвигаться impf, выдвинуться pf на передний план.

forearm /n 'fɔːrɑːm/ предплечье.

foreboding /fɔː'bəʊdɪŋ/ n предчувствие. **forecast** /'fɔːkɑːst/ n предсказание; (of weather) прогноз; vt /fɔː'rɑːm/ предсказывать impf, предсказать pf. **forecourt** n передний двор. **forefather** n предок. **forefinger** n указательный палец. **forefront** n (foreground) передний план; (leading position) авангард. **foregone** /'fɔːgɒn/ adj: ~ conclusion предрешённый исход. **foreground** n передний план. **forehead** /'fɒrɪd/ n лоб.

foreign /'fɒrɪn/ adj (from abroad) иностранный; (alien) чуждый; (external) внешний; ~ body инородное тело; ~ currency валюта. **foreigner** /'fɒrɪnə(r)/ n иностранец, -нка.

foreman /'fɔːmən/ n мастер.

foremost /'fɔːməʊst/ adj выдающийся; **first and** ~ прежде всего.

forename /'fɔːneɪm/ n имя.

forensic /fə'rensɪk/ adj судебный.

forerunner /'fɔːrʌnə(r)/ n предвестник. **foresee** /fɔː'siː/ vt предвидеть impf. **foreshadow** /fɔː'ʃædəʊ/ vt предвещать impf. **foresight** /'fɔːsaɪt/ n предвидение; (caution) предусмотрительность.

forest /'fɒrɪst/ n лес.

forestall /fɔː'stɔːl/ vt предупреждать impf, предупредить pf.

forester /'fɒrɪstə(r)/ n лесничий sb. **forestry** /'fɒrɪstrɪ/ n лесоводство.

foretaste /'fɔːteɪst/ n предвкушение; vt предвкушать impf, предвкусить pf. **foretell** /fɔː'tel/ vt предсказывать impf, предсказать pf. **forethought** /'fɔːθɔːt/ n предусмотрительность.

forewarn /fɔː'wɔːn/ vt предостерегать impf, предостеречь pf. **foreword** /'fɔːwɜːd/ n предисловие.

forfeit /'fɔːfɪt/ n (in game) фант; vt лишаться impf, лишиться pf +gen.

forge¹ /fɔːdʒ/ n (smithy) кузница; (furnace) горн; vt ковать impf, вы~ pf; (fabricate) подделывать impf, подделать pf.

forge² /fɔːdʒ/ vi: ~ ahead продвигаться impf, продвинуться pf вперёд.

forger /'fɔːdʒə(r)/ n фальшивомонетчик. **forgery** /-rɪ/ n подделка.

forget /fə'get/ vt забывать impf, забыть pf. **forgetful** /-fʊl/ adj забывчивый.

forgive /fə'gɪv/ vt прощать impf, простить pf. **forgiveness** /-nɪs/ n прощение.

forgo /fɔː'gəʊ/ vt воздерживаться impf, воздержаться pf от+gen.

fork /fɔːk/ n (*eating*) вилка; (*digging*) вилы (-л) pl; (*in road*) разветвление; vi (*road*) разветвляться *impf*, разветвиться *pf*.

forlorn /fə'lɔːn/ adj жалкий.

form /fɔːm/ n (*shape*; *kind*) форма; (*class*) класс; (*document*) анкета; vt (*make, create*) образовывать *impf*, образовать *pf*; (*develop*; *make up*) составлять *impf*, составить *pf*; vi образовываться *impf*, образоваться *pf*. **formal** /'fɔːm(ə)l/ adj формальный; (*official*) официальный. **formality** /fɔː'mælɪtɪ/ n формальность. **format** /'fɔːmæt/ n формат. **formation** /fɔː'meɪʃ(ə)n/ n образование. **formative** /'fɔːmətɪv/ adj: ~ **years** молодые годы (-дов) m pl.

former /'fɔːmə(r)/ adj (*earlier*) прежний; (*ex*) бывший; the ~ (*of two*) первый. **formerly** /'fɔːməlɪ/ adv прежде.

formidable /'fɔːmɪdəb(ə)l/ adj (*dread*) грозный; (*arduous*) трудный.

formless /'fɔːmlɪs/ adj бесформенный.

formula /'fɔːmjʊlə/ n формула. **formulate** /-leɪt/ vt формулировать *impf*, с~ *pf*. **formulation** /-'leɪʃ(ə)n/ n формулировка.

forsake /fə'seɪk/ vt (*desert*) покидать *impf*, покинуть *pf*; (*renounce*) отказываться *impf*, отказаться *pf* от+gen.

fort /fɔːt/ n форт.

forth /fɔːθ/ adv вперёд, дальше; **back and** ~ взад и вперёд; **and so** ~ и так далее. **forthcoming** /fɔːθ'kʌmɪŋ/ adj предстоящий; **be** ~ (*available*) поступать *impf*, поступить *pf*. **forthwith** /fɔːθ'wɪθ/ adv немедленно.

fortieth /'fɔːtɪɪθ/ adj & n сороковой.

fortification /ˌfɔːtɪfɪ'keɪʃ(ə)n/ n укрепление. **fortify** /'fɔːtɪfaɪ/ vt укреплять *impf*, укрепить *pf*; (*fig*) подкреплять *impf*, подкрепить *pf*. **fortitude** /'fɔːtɪˌtjuːd/ n стойкость.

fortnight /'fɔːtnaɪt/ n две недели f pl. **fortnightly** /-lɪ/ adj двухнедельный; adv раз в две недели.

fortress /'fɔːtrɪs/ n крепость.

fortuitous /fɔː'tjuːɪtəs/ adj случайный.

fortunate /'fɔːtʃənət/ adj счастливый. **fortunately** /-lɪ/ adv к счастью. **fortune** /'fɔːtjuːn/ n (*destiny*) судьба; (*good* ~) счастье; (*wealth*) состояние.

forty /'fɔːtɪ/ adj & n сорок; (*decade*) сороковые годы (-дов) m pl.

forward /'fɔːwəd/ adj передний; (*presumptuous*) развязный; n (*sport*) нападающий sb; adv вперёд; vt (*letter*) пересылать *impf*, переслать *pf*.

fossil /'fɒs(ə)l/ n ископаемое sb; adj ископаемый. **fossilized** /'fɒsɪˌlaɪzd/ adj ископаемый.

foster /'fɒstə(r)/ vt (*child*) приютить *pf*; (*idea*) вынашивать *impf*, выносить *pf*; (*create*) создавать *impf*, создать *pf*; (*cherish*) лелеять *impf*; ~**child** приёмыш.

foul /faʊl/ adj (*dirty*) грязный; (*repulsive*) отвратительный; (*obscene*) непристойный; n (*sport*) нарушение правил; vt (*dirty*) пачкать *impf*, за~, из~ *pf*; (*entangle*) запутывать *impf*, запутать *pf*.

found /faʊnd/ vt основывать *impf*, основать *pf*.

foundation /faʊn'deɪʃ(ə)n/ n (*of*

building) фунда́мент; (*basis*) осно́ва; (*institution*) учрежде́ние; (*fund*) фонд. **founder¹** /'faʊndə(r)/ n основа́тель *m*.

founder² /'faʊndə(r)/ vi (*naut, fig*) тону́ть *impf*, по~ *pf*.

foundry /'faʊndrɪ/ n лите́йная sb.

fountain /'faʊntɪn/ n фонта́н. ~pen авторучка.

four /fɔː(r)/ adj & n четы́ре; (*number 4*) четвёрка; **on all** ~s на четвере́ньках. **fourteen** /fɔː-'tiːn/ adj & n четы́рнадцать. **fourteenth** /fɔː'tiːnθ/ adj & n четы́рнадцатый. **fourth** /fɔːθ/ adj & n четвёртый; (*quarter*) че́тверть.

fowl /faʊl/ n (*domestic*) дома́шняя пти́ца; (*wild*) дичь collect.

fox /fɒks/ n лиса́, лиси́ца; vt озада́чивать *impf*, озада́чить *pf*.

foyer /'fɔɪeɪ/ n фойе́ neut indecl.

fraction /'frækʃ(ə)n/ n (*math*) дробь; (*portion*) ча́стица.

fractious /'frækʃəs/ adj раздражи́тельный.

fracture /'fræktʃə(r)/ n перело́м; vt & i лома́ть(ся) *impf*, с~ *pf*.

fragile /'frædʒaɪl/ adj ло́мкий.

fragment /'frægmənt/ n обло́мок; (*of conversation*) отры́вок; (*of writing*) фрагме́нт. **fragmentary** /-tərɪ/ adj отры́вочный.

fragrance /'freɪɡrəns/ n арома́т. **fragrant** /-ɡrənt/ adj арома́тный, души́стый.

frail /freɪl/ adj хру́пкий.

frame /freɪm/ n о́стов; (*build*) телосложе́ние; (*picture*) ра́ма; (*cin*) кадр; ~ **of mind** настрое́ние; vt (*devise*) создава́ть *impf*, созда́ть *pf*; (*formulate*) формули́ровать *impf*, с~ *pf*; (*picture*) вставля́ть *impf*, вста́вить *pf* в ра́му; (*incriminate*) фабрико-

ва́ть *impf*, с~ *pf* обвине́ние про́тив+*gen*. **framework** n о́стов; (*fig*) ра́мки *f pl*.

franc /fræŋk/ n франк.

France /frɑːns/ n Фра́нция.

franchise /'fræntʃaɪz/ n (*comm*) привиле́гия; (*polit*) пра́во го́лоса.

frank¹ /fræŋk/ adj открове́нный.

frank² /fræŋk/ vt (*letter*) франки́ровать *impf* & *pf*.

frantic /'fræntɪk/ adj неи́стовый.

fraternal /frə'tɜːn(ə)l/ adj бра́тский. **fraternity** /-'tɜːnɪtɪ/ n бра́тство.

fraud /frɔːd/ n обма́н; (*person*) обма́нщик. **fraudulent** /'frɔːdjʊlənt/ adj обма́нный.

fraught /frɔːt/ adj: ~ **with** чрева́тый +*instr*.

fray¹ /freɪ/ vt & i обтрёпывать(ся) *impf*, обтрепа́ть(ся) *pf*.

fray² /freɪ/ n бой.

freak /friːk/ n уро́д; *attrib* необы́чный.

freckle /'frek(ə)l/ n весну́шка. **freckled** /'frekəld/ adj весну́шчатый.

free /friː/ adj свобо́дный; (*gratis*) беспла́тный; ~ **kick** штрафно́й уда́р; ~ **speech** свобо́да сло́ва; vt освобожда́ть *impf*, освободи́ть *pf*. **freedom** /'friːdəm/ n свобо́да. **freehold** n неограни́ченное пра́во со́бственности на недви́жимость. **freelance** /'friːlɑːns/ adj внешта́тный. **Freemason** n франкмасо́н.

freeze /friːz/ vi замерза́ть *impf*, мёрзнуть *impf*, замёрзнуть *pf*; vt замора́живать *impf*, заморо́зить *pf*. **freezer** /-zə(r)/ n моро́зильник; (*compartment*)

морозилка. **freezing** /-zɪŋ/ adj морозный; **below** ~ ниже нуля.

freight /freɪt/ n фрахт. **freighter** /-tə(r)/ n (ship) грузовое судно.

French /frentʃ/ adj французский; ~ **bean** фасоль; ~ **horn** валторна; ~ **windows** двустворчатое окно в пол. **Frenchman** n француз. **Frenchwoman** n француженка.

frenetic /frə'netɪk/ adj нейстовый.

frenzied /'frenzɪd/ adj нейстовый. **frenzy** /-zɪ/ n нейстовство.

frequency /'fri:kwənsɪ/ n частота. **frequent** adj /'fri:kwənt/ частый; vt /frɪ'kwent/ часто посещать impf.

fresco /'freskəʊ/ n фреска.

fresh /freʃ/ adj свежий; (new) новый; ~ **water** пресная вода. **freshen** /-ʃ(ə)n/ vt освежать impf, освежить pf; vi свежеть impf, по~ pf. **freshly** /-lɪ/ adv свежо; (recently) недавно. **freshness** /-nɪs/ n свежесть. **freshwater** adj пресноводный.

fret[1] /fret/ vi мучиться impf. **fretful** /-fʊl/ adj раздражительный.

fret[2] /fret/ n (mus) лад.

fretsaw /'fretsɔ:/ n лобзик.

friar /fraɪə(r)/ n монах.

friction /'frɪkʃ(ə)n/ n трение; (fig) трения neut pl.

Friday /'fraɪdeɪ/ n пятница.

fridge /frɪdʒ/ n холодильник.

fried /fraɪd/ adj: ~ **egg** яичница.

friend /frend/ n друг, подруга; приятель m, ~ница. **friendly** /-lɪ/ adj дружеский. **friendship** n дружба.

frieze /fri:z/ n фриз.

frigate /'frɪgɪt/ n фрегат.

fright /fraɪt/ n испуг. **frighten** /-t(ə)n/ vt пугать impf, ис~, на~ pf. **frightful** /-fʊl/ adj страшный.

frigid /'frɪdʒɪd/ adj холодный.

frill /frɪl/ n оборка.

fringe /frɪndʒ/ n бахрома; (of hair) чёлка; (edge) край.

frisk /frɪsk/ vi (frolic) резвиться impf; vt (search) шмонать impf. **frisky** /-kɪ/ adj резвый.

fritter /'frɪtə(r)/ vt: ~ **away** растрачивать impf, растратить pf.

frivolity /frɪ'vɒlɪtɪ/ n легкомысленность. **frivolous** /'frɪvələs/ adj легкомысленный.

fro /frəʊ/ adv: **to and** ~ взад и вперёд.

frock /frɒk/ n платье.

frog /frɒg/ n лягушка.

frolic /'frɒlɪk/ vi резвиться impf.

from /frɒm/ prep от+gen; (~ off, down ~; in time) с+gen; (out of) из+gen; (according to) по+dat; (because of) из-за+gen; ~ **above** сверху; ~ **abroad** из-за границы; ~ **afar** издали; ~ **among** из числа+gen; ~ **behind** из-за+gen; ~ **day to day** изо дня в день; ~ **everywhere** отовсюду; ~ **here** отсюда; ~ **memory** по памяти; ~ **now on** отныне; ~ **there** оттуда; ~ **time to time** время от времени; ~ **under** из-под+gen.

front /frʌnt/ n фасад, передняя сторона; (mil) фронт; **in** ~ впереди+gen, впереди+instr; adj передний; (first) первый.

frontier /'frʌntɪə(r)/ n граница.

frost /frɒst/ n мороз; ~**bite** отморожение; ~**bitten** отмороженный. **frosted** /-tɪd/ adj: ~ **glass** матовое стекло. **frosty** /-tɪ/ adj морозный; (fig) ледяной.

froth /frɒθ/ n пе́на; vi пе́ниться impf, вс~ pf. **frothy** /-θɪ/ adj пе́нистый.

frown /fraʊn/ n хму́рый взгляд; vi хму́риться impf, на~ pf.

frugal /ˈfruːg(ə)l/ adj (careful) бережли́вый; (scanty) ску́дный.

fruit /fruːt/ n плод; collect фру́кты m pl; adj фрукто́вый. **fruitful** /-fʊl/ adj плодотво́рный. **fruition** /fruːˈɪʃ(ə)n/ n: come to ~ осуществля́ться impf. **fruitless** /ˈfruːtlɪs/ adj беспло́дный.

frustrate /frʌˈstreɪt/ vt фрустри́ровать impf & pf. **frustrating** /-ˈstreɪtɪŋ/ adj фрустри́рующий. **frustration** /-ˈstreɪʃ(ə)n/ n фрустра́ция.

fry[1] /fraɪ/ n: small ~ мелюзга́.

fry[2] /fraɪ/ vt & i жа́рить(ся) impf, за~, из~ pf. **frying-pan** /ˈfraɪɪŋ pæn/ n сковорода́.

fuel /ˈfjuːəl/ n то́пливо.

fugitive /ˈfjuːdʒɪtɪv/ n бегле́ц.

fulcrum /ˈfʊlkrəm/ n то́чка опо́ры.

fulfil /fʊlˈfɪl/ vt (perform) выполня́ть impf, вы́полнить pf; (dreams) осуществля́ть impf, осуществи́ть pf. **fulfilling** /-lɪŋ/ adj удовлетворя́ющий. **fulfilment** /-mənt/ n выполне́ние; осуществле́ние; удовлетворе́ние.

full /fʊl/ adj по́лный (of +gen, instr); (replete) сы́тый; ~ stop то́чка; ~ time: I work ~ time я рабо́таю на по́лную ста́вку; in ~ по́лностью; to the ~ в по́лной ме́ре. **fullness** /ˈfʊlnɪs/ n полнота́. **fully** /ˈfʊlɪ/ adv вполне́.

fulsome /ˈfʊlsəm/ adj чрезме́рный.

fumble /ˈfʌmb(ə)l/ vi: ~ for нащу́пывать impf +acc; ~ with

вози́ться impf c+instr.

fume /fjuːm/ vi (with anger) кипе́ть impf, вс~ pf гне́вом. **fumes** /fjuːmz/ n pl испаре́ния neut pl. **fumigate** /ˈfjuːmɪɡeɪt/ vt окури́вать impf, окури́ть pf.

fun /fʌn/ n заба́ва; it was ~ бы́ло заба́вно; have ~ забавля́ться impf; make ~ of смея́ться impf, по~ pf над +instr.

function /ˈfʌŋkʃ(ə)n/ n фу́нкция; (event) ве́чер; vi функциони́ровать impf; де́йствовать impf. **functional** /-n(ə)l/ adj функциона́льный. **functionary** /-nərɪ/ n чино́вник.

fund /fʌnd/ n фонд; (store) запа́с.

fundamental /ˌfʌndəˈment(ə)l/ adj основно́й; n: pl осно́вы f pl.

funeral /ˈfjuːnər(ə)l/ n по́хороны (-о́н, -она́м) pl.

fungus /ˈfʌŋɡəs/ n гриб.

funnel /ˈfʌn(ə)l/ n воро́нка; (chimney) дымова́я труба́.

funny /ˈfʌnɪ/ adj смешно́й; (odd) стра́нный.

fur /fɜː(r)/ n мех; ~ coat шу́ба. **furious** /ˈfjʊərɪəs/ adj бе́шеный.

furnace /ˈfɜːnɪs/ n горн, печь.

furnish /ˈfɜːnɪʃ/ vt (provide) снабжа́ть impf, снабди́ть pf (with +instr); (house) обставля́ть impf, обста́вить pf. **furniture** /ˈfɜːnɪtʃə(r)/ n ме́бель.

furrow /ˈfʌrəʊ/ n борозда́.

furry /ˈfɜːrɪ/ adj пуши́стый.

further /ˈfɜːðə(r)/, **farther** /ˈfɑːðə(r)/ comp adj да́льнейший; adv да́льше; vt продвига́ть impf, продви́нуть pf. **furthermore** adv к тому́ же. **furthest**, **farthest** /ˈfɜːðɪst, ˈfɑːðɪst/ superl adj са́мый да́льний.

furtive /ˈfɜːtɪv/ adj скры́тый,

тайный.

fury /'fjʊərɪ/ n я́рость.

fuse¹ /fjuːz/ vt & i (of metal) сплавля́ть(ся) impf, спла́вить(ся) pf.

fuse² /fjuːz/ n (in bomb) запа́л; (detonating device) взрыва́тель m.

fuse³ /fjuːz/ n (electr) про́бка; vi перегора́ть impf, перегоре́ть pf.

fuselage /'fjuːzəlɑːʒ/ n фюзеля́ж.

fusion /'fjuːʒ(ə)n/ n пла́вка, слия́ние.

fuss /fʌs/ n суета́; vi суети́ться impf. **fussy** /-sɪ/ adj суетли́вый; (fastidious) разбо́рчивый.

futile /'fjuːtaɪl/ adj тще́тный. **futility** /-'tɪlɪtɪ/ n тще́тность.

future /'fjuːtʃə(r)/ n бу́дущее sb; (gram) бу́дущее вре́мя neut; adj бу́дущий. **futuristic** /ˌfjuːtʃə'rɪstɪk/ adj футуристи́ческий.

fuzzy /'fʌzɪ/ adj (hair) пуши́стый; (blurred) расплы́вчатый.

G

gabble /'gæb(ə)l/ vi тарато́рить impf.

gable /'geɪb(ə)l/ n щипе́ц.

gad /gæd/ vi: ~ about шата́ться impf.

gadget /'gædʒɪt/ n приспособле́ние.

gaffe /gæf/ n опло́шность.

gag /gæg/ n кляп; vt засо́вывать impf, засу́нуть pf кляп в рот+dat.

gaiety /'geɪətɪ/ n весёлость. **gaily** /'geɪlɪ/ adv ве́село.

gain /geɪn/ n при́быль; pl дохо́ды m pl; (increase) приро́ст;

vt (acquire) получа́ть impf, получи́ть pf; ~ on нагоня́ть impf, нагна́ть pf.

gait /geɪt/ n похо́дка.

gala /'gɑːlə/ n пра́зднество; adj пра́здничный.

galaxy /'gæləksɪ/ n гала́ктика; (fig) плея́да.

gale /geɪl/ n бу́ря, шторм.

gall¹ /gɔːl/ n (bile) жёлчь; (cheek) на́глость; ~-bladder жёлчный пузы́рь m.

gall² /gɔːl/ vt (vex) раздража́ть impf, раздражи́ть pf.

gallant /'gælənt/ adj (brave) хра́брый; (courtly) гала́нтный. **gallantry** /-trɪ/ n хра́брость; гала́нтность.

gallery /'gælərɪ/ n галере́я.

galley /'gælɪ/ n (ship) гале́ра; (kitchen) ка́мбуз.

gallon /'gælən/ n галло́н.

gallop /'gæləp/ n гало́п; vi галопи́ровать impf.

gallows /'gæləʊz/ n pl ви́селица.

gallstone /'gɔːlstəʊn/ n жёлчный ка́мень m.

galore /gə'lɔː(r)/ adv в изоби́лии.

galvanize /'gælvənaɪz/ vt гальванизи́ровать impf & pf.

gambit /'gæmbɪt/ n гамби́т.

gamble /'gæmb(ə)l/ n (undertaking) риско́ванное предприя́тие; vi игра́ть impf в аза́ртные и́гры; (fig) рискова́ть impf (with +instr); ~ away проѝгрывать impf, проигра́ть pf. **gambler** /-blə(r)/ n игро́к. **gambling** /-blɪŋ/ n аза́ртные и́гры f pl.

game /geɪm/ n игра́; (single ~) па́ртия; (collect, animals) дичь; adj (ready) гото́вый. **gamekeeper** /-ˌkiːpə(r)/ n лесни́к.

gammon /'gæmən/ n о́корок.

gamut /'gæmət/ n га́мма.

gang /gæŋ/ n бáнда; (*workmen*) бригáда.

gangrene /'gæŋgriːn/ n гангрéна.

gangster /'gæŋstə(r)/ n гáнгстер.

gangway /'gæŋweɪ/ n (*passage*) прохóд; (*naut*) схóдни (-ней) pl.

gaol /dʒeɪl/ n тюрьмá; vt заключáть impf, заключить pf в тюрьмý. **gaoler** /-lə(r)/ n тюрéмщик.

gap /gæp/ n (*empty space; deficiency*) пробéл; (*in wall etc.*) брешь; (*fig*) разрыв.

gape /geɪp/ vi (*person*) зевáть impf (*at* на+acc); (*chasm*) зиять impf.

garage /'gærɑːʒ/ n гарáж.

garb /gɑːb/ n одеяние.

garbage /'gɑːbɪdʒ/ n мýсор.

garbled /'gɑːbl̩d/ adj искажённый.

garden /'gɑːd(ə)n/ n сад; attrib садóвый. **gardener** /'gɑːdnə(r)/ n садóвник. **gardening** /'gɑːdnɪŋ/ n садовóдство.

gargle /'gɑːg(ə)l/ vi полоскáть impf, про~ pf гóрло.

gargoyle /'gɑːgɔɪl/ n горгýлья.

garish /'geərɪʃ/ adj кричáщий.

garland /'gɑːlənd/ n гирлянда.

garlic /'gɑːlɪk/ n чеснóк.

garment /'gɑːmənt/ n предмéт одéжды.

garnish /'gɑːnɪʃ/ n гарнир; vt гарнировáть impf & pf.

garret /'gærɪt/ n мансáрда.

garrison /'gærɪs(ə)n/ n гарнизóн.

garrulous /'gærʊləs/ adj болтливый.

gas /gæs/ n газ; attrib гáзовый; vt отравлять impf, отравить pf гáзом. **gaseous** /'gæsɪəs/ adj газообрáзный.

gash /gæʃ/ n порéз; vt порéзать pf.

gasket /'gæskɪt/ n проклáдка.

gasp /gɑːsp/ vi задыхáться impf, задохнýться pf.

gastric /'gæstrɪk/ adj желýдочный.

gate /geɪt/ n (*large*) ворóта (-т) pl; (*small*) калитка. **gateway** n (*gate*) ворóта (-т) pl; (*entrance*) вход.

gather /'gæðə(r)/ vt & i собирáть(ся) impf, собрáть(ся) pf; vt заключáть impf, заключить pf. **gathering** /-rɪŋ/ n (*assembly*) собрáние.

gaudy /'gɔːdɪ/ adj кричáщий.

gauge /geɪdʒ/ n (*measure*) мéра; (*instrument*) калибр, измерительный прибóр; (*rly*) колея; (*criterion*) критéрий; vt измерять impf, измéрить pf; (*estimate*) оцéнивать impf, оценить pf.

gaunt /gɔːnt/ adj тóщий.

gauntlet /'gɔːntlɪt/ n рукавица.

gauze /gɔːz/ n мáрля.

gay /geɪ/ adj весёлый; (*bright*) пёстрый; (*homosexual*) гомосексуáльный.

gaze /geɪz/ n пристáльный взгляд; vi пристáльно глядéть impf (*at* на+acc).

gazelle /gə'zel/ n газéль.

GCSE abbr (of General Certificate of Secondary Education) аттестáт о срéднем образовáнии.

gear /gɪə(r)/ n (*equipment*) принадлéжности f pl; (*in car*) скóрость; ~ **lever** рычáг; vt приспосáбливать impf, приспосóбить pf (*to* к+dat). **gearbox** n корóбка передáч.

gel /dʒel/ n косметическое желé neut indecl. **gelatine** /'dʒelə,tiːn/ n желатин.

gelding /'geldɪŋ/ n мéрин.

gelignite /'dʒelɪgˌnaɪt/ n гелигнит.

gem /dʒem/ n драгоцéнный кáмень m.

Gemini /'dʒemɪˌnaɪ/ n Близнецы́ m pl.

gender /'dʒendə(r)/ n род.

gene /dʒiːn/ n ген.

genealogy /ˌdʒiːnɪˈælədʒɪ/ n генеалóгия.

general /'dʒenər(ə)l/ n генерáл; adj óбщий; (nationwide) всеóбщий; in ~ в óбщем. **generalization** /ˌdʒenərəˌlaɪˈzeɪʃ(ə)n/ n обобщéние. **generalize** /'dʒenərəˌlaɪz/ vi обобщáть impf, обобщи́ть pf. **generally** /'dʒenərəlɪ/ adv (usually) обы́чно; (in general) вообщé.

generate /'dʒenəˌreɪt/ vt порождáть impf, породи́ть pf. **generation** /-'reɪʃ(ə)n/ n (in descent) поколéние. **generator** /'dʒenəˌreɪtə(r)/ n генерáтор.

generic /dʒɪˈnerɪk/ adj родовóй; (general) óбщий.

generosity /ˌdʒenəˈrɒsɪtɪ/ n (magnanimity) великодýшие; (munificence) щéдрость. **generous** /'dʒenərəs/ adj великодýшный; щéдрый.

genesis /'dʒenɪsɪs/ n происхождéние; (G~) Кни́га Бытия́.

genetic /dʒɪˈnetɪk/ adj генети́ческий. **genetics** /-tɪks/ n генéтика.

genial /'dʒiːnɪəl/ adj (of person) добродýшный.

genital /'dʒenɪt(ə)l/ adj половóй. **genitals** /-t(ə)lz/ n pl половы́е óрганы m pl.

genitive /'dʒenɪtɪv/ adj (n) роди́тельный (падéж).

genius /'dʒiːnɪəs/ n (person) гéний; (ability) гениáльность.

genocide /'dʒenəˌsaɪd/ n геноци́д.

genome /'dʒiːnəʊm/ n генóм.

genre /'ʒɑːrə/ n жанр.

genteel /dʒenˈtiːl/ adj благовоспи́танный.

gentile /'dʒentaɪl/ n нееврéй, ~ка.

gentility /dʒenˈtɪlɪtɪ/ n благовоспи́танность.

gentle /'dʒent(ə)l/ adj (mild) мя́гкий; (quiet) ти́хий; (light) лёгкий. **gentleman** n джентльмéн. **gentleness** /-nɪs/ n мя́гкость. **gents** /dʒents/ n pl мужскáя убóрная sb.

genuine /'dʒenjʊɪn/ adj (authentic) пóдлинный; (sincere) и́скренний.

genus /'dʒiːnəs/ n род.

geographical /ˌdʒiːəˈɡræfɪk(ə)l/ adj географи́ческий. **geography** /dʒɪˈɒɡrəfɪ/ n геогрáфия.

geological /ˌdʒiːəˈlɒdʒɪk(ə)l/ adj геологи́ческий. **geologist** /dʒɪˈɒlədʒɪst/ n геóлог. **geology** /dʒɪˈɒlədʒɪ/ n геолóгия. **geometric(al)** /ˌdʒiːəˈmetrɪk((ə)l)/ adj геометри́ческий. **geometry** /dʒɪˈɒmɪtrɪ/ n геомéтрия.

Georgia /'dʒɔːdʒə/ n Грýзия. **Georgian** /'dʒɔːdʒən/ n грузи́н, ~ка; adj грузи́нский.

geranium /dʒəˈreɪnɪəm/ n герáнь.

geriatric /ˌdʒerɪˈætrɪk/ adj гериатри́ческий.

germ /dʒɜːm/ n микрóб.

German /'dʒɜːmən/ n нéмец, нéмка; adj немéцкий; ~ **measles** краснýха.

germane /dʒɜːˈmeɪn/ adj умéстный.

Germanic /dʒɜːˈmænɪk/ adj гермáнский.

Germany /'dʒɜːmənɪ/ n Гермáния.

germinate /'dʒɜːmɪˌneɪt/ vi прорастáть impf, прорасти́ pf.

gesticulate /dʒeˈstɪkjʊˌleɪt/ *vi* жестикулировать *impf.* **gesture** /ˈdʒestʃə(r)/ *n* жест.

get /get/ *vt* (*obtain*) доставать *impf*, достать *pf*; (*receive*) получать *impf*, получить *pf*; (*understand*) понимать *impf*, понять *pf*; (*disease*) заражаться *impf*, заразиться *pf* +*instr*; (*induce*) уговаривать *impf*, уговорить *pf* (*to do* +*inf*); (*fetch*) приносить *impf*, принести *pf*; *vi* (*become*) становиться *impf*, стать *pf* +*instr*; **have got** (*have*) иметь *impf*; **have got to** быть должен (-жна) +*inf*; ~ **about** (*spread*) распространяться *impf*, распространиться *pf*; (*move around*) передвигаться *impf*; (*travel*) разъезжать *impf*; ~ **at** (*mean*) хотеть *impf* сказать; ~ **away** (*slip off*) ускользать *impf*, ускользнуть *pf*; (*escape*) убегать *impf*, убежать *pf*; (*leave*) уезжать *impf*, уехать *pf*; ~ **away with** избегать *impf*, избежать *pf* ответственности за+*acc*; ~ **back** (*recover*) получать *impf*, получить *pf* обратно; (*return*) возвращаться *impf*, вернуться *pf*; ~ **by** (*manage*) справляться *impf*, справиться *pf*; ~ **down** сходить *impf*, сойти *pf*; ~ **down to** приниматься *impf*, приняться *pf* за+*acc*; ~ **off** слезать *impf*, слезть *pf* c+*gen*; (*alight*) выходить *impf*, выйти *pf* из+*gen*; ~ **on** (*prosper*) преуспевать *impf*, преуспеть *pf*; ~ **on with** (*person*) уживаться *impf*, ужиться *pf* +*instr*; ~ **out of** (*avoid*) избавляться *impf*, избавиться *pf* от+*gen*; (*car*) выходить *impf*, выйти *pf* из+*gen*; ~ **round to** успевать *impf*, успеть *pf*; ~ **to** (*reach*) достигать *impf*, до-

стигнуть & достичь *pf* +*gen*; ~ **up** (*from bed*) вставать *impf*, встать *pf*.

geyser /ˈgiːzə(r)/ *n* (*spring*) гейзер; (*water-heater*) колонка.

ghastly /ˈgɑːstlɪ/ *adj* ужасный.

gherkin /ˈgɜːkɪn/ *n* огурец.

ghetto /ˈgetəʊ/ *n* гетто *neut indecl.*

ghost /gəʊst/ *n* привидение. **ghostly** /-lɪ/ *adj* призрачный.

giant /ˈdʒaɪənt/ *n* гигант; *adj* гигантский.

gibberish /ˈdʒɪbərɪʃ/ *n* тарабарщина.

gibbet /ˈdʒɪbɪt/ *n* виселица.

gibe /dʒaɪb/ *n* насмешка; *vi* насмехаться *impf* (*at* над+*instr*).

giblets /ˈdʒɪblɪts/ *n pl* потроха (-хов) *pl.*

giddiness /ˈgɪdɪnɪs/ *n* головокружение. **giddy** /ˈgɪdɪ/ *predic:* I feel ~ у меня кружится голова.

gift /gɪft/ *n* (*present*) подарок; (*donation; ability*) дар. **gifted** /-tɪd/ *adj* одарённый.

gig /gɪg/ *n* (*theat*) выступление.

gigantic /dʒaɪˈgæntɪk/ *adj* гигантский.

giggle /ˈgɪg(ə)l/ *n* хихиканье; *vi* хихикать *impf*, хихикнуть *pf.*

gild /gɪld/ *vt* золотить *impf*, вы~, по~ *pf.*

gill /gɪl/ *n* (*of fish*) жабра.

gilt /gɪlt/ *n* позолота; *adj* золочёный.

gimmick /ˈgɪmɪk/ *n* трюк.

gin /dʒɪn/ *n* (*spirit*) джин.

ginger /ˈdʒɪndʒə(r)/ *n* имбирь *m*; *adj* (*colour*) рыжий.

gingerly /ˈdʒɪndʒəlɪ/ *adv* осторожно.

gipsy /ˈdʒɪpsɪ/ *n* цыган, ~ка.

giraffe /dʒɪˈrɑːf/ *n* жираф.

girder /ˈgɜːdə(r)/ *n* балка. **girdle** /ˈgɜːd(ə)l/ *n* пояс.

girl 477 glorify

girl /gɜːl/ n (child) де́вочка; (young woman) де́вушка. **girlfriend** n подру́га. **girlish** /-lɪʃ/ adj де́вичий.

girth /gɜːθ/ n обхва́т; (on saddle) подпру́га.

gist /dʒɪst/ n суть.

give /gɪv/ vt дава́ть impf, дать pf; ~ **away** выдава́ть impf, вы́дать pf; ~ **back** возвраща́ть impf, возврати́ть pf; (yield, vi) уступа́ть impf, уступи́ть pf (to +dat); (hand in, vt) вруча́ть impf, вручи́ть pf; ~ **out** (emit) издава́ть impf, изда́ть pf; (distribute) раздава́ть impf, разда́ть pf; ~ **up** отка́зываться impf, отказа́ться pf от+gen; (habit etc.) броса́ть impf, бро́сить pf; ~ **o.s. up** сдава́ться impf, сда́ться pf. **given** /'gɪv(ə)n/ predic (inclined) скло́нен (-онна́, -о́нно) (to k+dat).

glacier /'glæsɪə(r)/ n ледни́к.

glad /glæd/ adj ра́достный; predic рад. **gladden** /-d(ə)n/ vt ра́довать impf, об~ pf.

glade /gleɪd/ n поля́на.

gladly /'glædlɪ/ adv охо́тно.

glamorous /'glæmərəs/ adj я́ркий; (attractive) привлека́тельный.

glamour /'glæmə(r)/ n я́ркость; привлека́тельность.

glance /glɑːns/ n (look) бе́глый взгляд; vi: ~ **at** взгля́дывать impf, взгляну́ть pf на+acc.

gland /glænd/ n железа́. **glandular** /-djʊlə(r)/ adj желе́зистый.

glare /gleə(r)/ n (light) ослепи́тельный блеск; (look) свире́пый взгляд; vi свире́по смотре́ть impf (at на+acc). **glaring** /-rɪŋ/ adj (dazzling) ослепи́тельный; (mistake) гру́бый.

glasnost /'glæznɒst/ n гла́сность.

glass /glɑːs/ n (substance) стекло́; (drinking vessel) стака́н; (wine ~) рю́мка, (mirror) зе́ркало; pl (spectacles) очки́ (-ко́в) pl; attrib стекля́нный. **glassy** /-sɪ/ adj (look) ту́склый.

glaze /gleɪz/ n глазу́рь; vt (with glass) застекля́ть impf, застекли́ть pf; (pottery) глазурова́ть impf & pf; (cul) глази́ровать impf & pf. **glazier** /-zjə(r)/ n стекольщик.

gleam /gliːm/ n про́блеск; vi свети́ться impf.

glean /gliːn/ vt собира́ть impf, собра́ть pf по крупи́цам.

glee /gliː/ n весе́лье. **gleeful** /-fʊl/ adj лику́ющий.

glib /glɪb/ adj бо́йкий.

glide /glaɪd/ vi скользи́ть impf; (aeron) плани́ровать impf, с~ pf. **glider** /-də(r)/ n планёр.

glimmer /'glɪmə(r)/ n мерца́ние; vi мерца́ть impf.

glimpse /glɪmps/ vt мелько́м ви́деть impf, у~ pf.

glint /glɪnt/ n блеск; vi блесте́ть impf.

glisten, glitter /'glɪs(ə)n, 'glɪtə(r)/ vi блесте́ть impf.

gloat /gləʊt/ vi злора́дствовать impf.

global /'gləʊb(ə)l/ adj (worldwide) глоба́льный; (total) всео́бщий. **globe** /gləʊb/ n (sphere) шар; (the earth) земно́й шар; (chart) гло́бус. **globule** /'glɒbjuːl/ n ша́рик.

gloom /gluːm/ n мрак. **gloomy** /-mɪ/ adj мра́чный.

glorify /'glɔːrɪfaɪ/ vt прославля́ть impf, просла́вить pf. **glorious** /'glɔːrɪəs/ adj сла́вный; (splendid) великоле́пный. **glory** /'glɔːrɪ/ n сла́ва; vi торжествова́ть impf.

gloss /glɒs/ n лоск; vi: ~ **over** замазывать impf, замазать pf.

glossary /'glɒsərɪ/ n глоссарий.

glove /glʌv/ n перчатка.

glow /gləʊ/ n зарево; (of cheeks) румянец; vi (incandesce) накаляться impf, накалиться pf; (shine) сиять impf.

glucose /'gluːkəʊs/ n глюкоза.

glue /gluː/ n клей; vt приклеивать impf, приклеить pf (**to** k+dat).

glum /glʌm/ adj угрюмый.

glut /glʌt/ n избыток.

glutton /'glʌt(ə)n/ n обжора m & f. **gluttonous** /-nəs/ adj обжорливый. **gluttony** /-nɪ/ n обжорство.

GM abbr (of **genetically modified**) генетически модифицированный.

gnarled /nɑːld/ adj (hands) шишковатый; (tree) сучковатый.

gnash /næʃ/ vt скрежетать impf +instr.

gnat /næt/ n комар.

gnaw /nɔː/ vt грызть impf.

gnome /nəʊm/ n гном.

go /gəʊ/ n (try) попытка; **be on the** ~ быть в движении; **have a** ~ пытаться impf, по~ pf; vi (on foot) ходить indet, идти det, пойти pf; (by transport) ездить indet, ехать det, по~ pf; (work) работать impf; (become) становиться impf, стать pf +instr; (belong) идти impf; **be** ~**ing** (to do) собираться impf (+inf); ~ **about** (set to work at) браться impf, взяться pf за+acc; (wander) бродить indet; ~ **away** (on foot) уходить impf, уйти pf; (by transport) уезжать impf, уехать pf; ~ **down** спускаться impf, спуститься pf (c+gen); ~ **in(to)** (enter) входить impf, войти pf

(в+acc); (investigate) расследовать impf & pf; ~ **off** (go away) уходить impf, уйти pf; (deteriorate) портиться impf, ис~ pf; ~ **on** (continue) продолжать(ся) impf, продолжить(ся) pf; ~ **out** выходить impf, выйти pf; (flame etc.) гаснуть impf, по~ pf; ~ **over** (inspect) пересматривать impf, пересмотреть pf; (rehearse) повторять impf, повторить pf; (change allegiance etc.) переходить impf, перейти pf (**to** в, на, +acc, k+dat); ~ **through** (scrutinize) разбирать impf, разобрать pf; ~ **through with** доводить impf, довести pf до конца; ~ **without** обходиться impf, обойтись pf без+gen; ~-**ahead** предприимчивый; ~-**between** посредник.

goad /gəʊd/ vt (provoke) подстрекать impf, подстрекнуть pf (**into** k+dat).

goal /gəʊl/ n (aim) цель; (sport) ворота (-т) pl; (point won) гол. **goalkeeper** n вратарь m.

goat /gəʊt/ n коза; (male) козёл.

gobble /'gɒb(ə)l/ vt (eat) жрать impf; ~ **up** пожирать impf, пожрать pf.

goblet /'gɒblɪt/ n бокал, кубок.

god /gɒd/ n бог; (**G**~) Бог. **godchild** n крёстник, -ица. **goddaughter** n крёстница. **goddess** /'gɒdɪs/ n богиня. **godfather** n крёстный sb. **godfearing** /'gɒdfɪərɪŋ/ adj богобоязненный. **godless** /'gɒdlɪs/ adj безбожный. **godly** /'gɒdlɪ/ adj набожный. **godmother** n крёстная sb. **godparent** n крёстный sb. **godsend** n божий дар. **godson** n крёстник.

goggle /'gɒg(ə)l/ vi таращить impf глаза (**at** на+acc); n: pl за-

щи́тные очки́ (-ко́в) pl.

going /'ɡəʊɪŋ/ adj действу́ющий. **goings-on** /ˌɡəʊɪŋ'zɒn/ n pl дела́ neut pl.

gold /ɡəʊld/ n зо́лото; adj золото́й; **~-plated** накладно́го зо́лота; **~-smith** золоты́х дел ма́стер. **golden** /-d(ə)n/ adj золото́й; **~ eagle** берку́т. **goldfish** n золота́я ры́бка.

golf /ɡɒlf/ n гольф; **~ club** (implement) клю́шка; **~ course** площа́дка для го́льфа. **golfer** /'ɡɒlfə(r)/ n игро́к в гольф.

gondola /'ɡɒndələ/ n гондо́ла.

gong /ɡɒŋ/ n гонг.

gonorrhoea /ˌɡɒnə'rɪə/ n три́ппер.

good /ɡʊd/ n добро́; pl (wares) това́р(ы); do **~** (benefit) идти́ impf, пойти́ pf на по́льзу +dat; adj хоро́ший, до́брый; **~-humoured** добро́душный; **~-looking** краси́вый; **~ morning** до́брое у́тро!; **~ night** споко́йной но́чи! **goodbye** /ɡʊd'baɪ/ int проща́й(те); до свида́ния! **goodness** /'ɡʊdnɪs/ n добро́та. **goose** /ɡuːs/ n гусь m; **~-flesh** гуси́ная ко́жа.

gooseberry /'ɡʊzbərɪ/ n крыжо́вник.

gore¹ /ɡɔː(r)/ n (blood) запёкшаяся кровь.

gore² /ɡɔː(r)/ vt (pierce) бода́ть impf, за~ pf.

gorge /ɡɔːdʒ/ n (geog) уще́лье; vi & t объеда́ться impf, объе́сться pf (on +instr).

gorgeous /'ɡɔːdʒəs/ adj великоле́пный.

gorilla /ɡə'rɪlə/ n гори́лла.

gorse /ɡɔːs/ n утёсник.

gory /'ɡɔːrɪ/ adj крова́вый.

gosh /ɡɒʃ/ int бо́же мой!

Gospel /'ɡɒspəl/ n Ева́нгелие.

gossip /'ɡɒsɪp/ n спле́тня; (per-

son) спле́тник, -ица; vi спле́тничать impf, на~ pf.

Gothic /'ɡɒθɪk/ adj готи́ческий.

gouge /ɡaʊdʒ/ vt: **~ out** выда́лбливать impf, вы́долбить pf; (eyes) выка́лывать impf, вы́колоть pf.

goulash /'ɡuːlæʃ/ n гуля́ш.

gourmet /'ɡʊəmeɪ/ n гурма́н.

gout /ɡaʊt/ n пода́гра.

govern /'ɡʌv(ə)n/ vt пра́вить impf +instr; (determine) определя́ть impf, определи́ть pf. **governess** /'ɡʌvənɪs/ n гуверна́нтка. **government** /'ɡʌvənmənt/ n прави́тельство. **governmental** /ˌɡʌvən'ment(ə)l/ adj прави́тельственный. **governor** /'ɡʌvənə(r)/ n губерна́тор; (of school etc.) член правле́ния.

gown /ɡaʊn/ n пла́тье; (official's) ма́нтия.

grab /ɡræb/ vt хвата́ть impf, схвати́ть pf.

grace /ɡreɪs/ n (gracefulness) гра́ция; (refinement) изя́щество; (favour) ми́лость; (at meal) моли́тва; **have the ~** to быть насто́лько такти́чным, что; **with bad ~** нелюбе́зно; **with good ~** с досто́инством; (adorn) украша́ть impf, укра́сить pf; (favour) удоста́ивать impf, удосто́ить pf (**with** +gen). **graceful** /-fʊl/ adj грацио́зный.

gracious /'ɡreɪʃəs/ adj ми́лостивый.

gradation /ɡrə'deɪʃ(ə)n/ n града́ция.

grade /ɡreɪd/ n (level) сте́пень; (quality) сорт; vt сортирова́ть impf, рас~ pf.

gradient /'ɡreɪdɪənt/ n укло́н.

gradual /'ɡrædjʊəl/ adj постепе́нный.

graduate n /ˈgrædjuət/ окончивший sb университет, вуз; vi /ˈgrædjuˌeɪt/ кончать impf, окончить pf (университет, вуз); vt градуи́ровать impf & pf.

graffiti /grəˈfiːtiː/ n на́дписи f pl.

graft /grɑːft/ n (bot) черено́к; (med) переса́дка (живо́й тка́ни); vt (bot) прививать impf, приви́ть pf (to +dat); (med) переса́живать impf, пересади́ть pf.

grain /greɪn/ n (seed; collect) зерно́; (particle) крупи́нка; (of sand) песчи́нка; (of wood) (древе́сное) волокно́; against the ~ не по нутру́.

gram(me) /græm/ n грамм.

grammar /ˈgræmə(r)/ n грамма́тика; ~ school шко́ла. **grammatical** /grəˈmætɪk(ə)l/ adj граммати́ческий.

gramophone /ˈgræməˌfəʊn/ n прои́грыватель m; ~ record грампласти́нка.

granary /ˈgrænərɪ/ n амба́р.

grand /grænd/ adj великоле́пный; ~ piano роя́ль m. **grandchild** n внук, вну́чка. **granddaughter** n вну́чка. **grandfather** n де́душка m. **grandmother** n ба́бушка. **grandparents** n ба́бушка и де́душка. **grandson** n внук. **grandstand** n трибу́на.

grandeur /ˈgrændjə(r)/ n вели́чие.

grandiose /ˈgrændɪˌəʊs/ adj грандио́зный.

granite /ˈgrænɪt/ n грани́т.

granny /ˈgrænɪ/ n ба́бушка.

grant /grɑːnt/ n (financial) грант, ассигнова́ние; (univ) стипе́ндия; vt дарова́ть impf & pf; (concede) допуска́ть impf, допусти́ть pf; take for ~ed (assume) счита́ть impf, счесть pf само́ собо́й разуме́ющимся; (not appreciate) принима́ть impf как до́лжное.

granular /ˈgrænjʊlə(r)/ adj зерни́стый.

granulated /ˈgrænəˌleɪtɪd/ adj: ~ sugar са́харный песо́к.

granule /ˈgrænjuːl/ n зёрнышко.

grape /greɪp/ n (single grape) виногра́дина; (collect виногра́д. **grapefruit** n гре́йпфрут.

graph /grɑːf/ n гра́фик. **graphic** /ˈgræfɪk/ adj графи́ческий; (vivid) я́ркий. **graphite** /ˈgræfaɪt/ n графи́т.

grapple /ˈgræp(ə)l/ vi (struggle) боро́ться impf (with c+instr).

grasp /grɑːsp/ n (grip) хва́тка; (comprehension) понима́ние; vt (clutch) хвата́ть impf, схвати́ть pf; (comprehend) понима́ть impf, поня́ть pf. **grasping** /-spɪŋ/ adj жа́дный.

grass /grɑːs/ n трава́. **grasshopper** /ˈgrɑːsˌhɒpə(r)/ n кузне́чик. **grassy** /ˈgrɑːsɪ/ adj травяни́стый.

grate[1] /greɪt/ n (fireplace) решётка.

grate[2] /greɪt/ vt (rub) тере́ть impf, на~ pf; vi (sound) скрипе́ть impf; ~ (up)on (irritate) раздража́ть impf, раздражи́ть pf.

grateful /ˈgreɪtfʊl/ n благода́рный.

grater /ˈgreɪtə(r)/ n тёрка.

gratify /ˈgrætɪˌfaɪ/ vt удовлетворя́ть impf, удовлетвори́ть pf.

grating /ˈgreɪtɪŋ/ n решётка.

gratis /ˈgrɑːtɪs/ adv беспла́тно.

gratitude /ˈgrætɪˌtjuːd/ n благода́рность.

gratuitous /grəˈtjuːɪtəs/ adj (free) даровой; (motiveless) беспричи́нный.

gratuity /grə'tju:ɪtɪ/ n (tip) чаевые sb pl.

grave¹ /greɪv/ n моги́ла. **gravedigger** /'greɪvdɪgə(r)/ n моги́льщик. **gravestone** n надгро́бный ка́мень m. **graveyard** n кла́дбище.

grave² /greɪv/ adj серьёзный.

gravel /'grævl/ n гра́вий.

gravitate /'grævɪteɪt/ vi тяготе́ть impf (towards к+dat). **gravitational** /-'teɪʃənl/ adj гравитацио́нный. **gravity** /'grævɪtɪ/ n (seriousness) серьёзность; (force) тя́жесть.

gravy /'greɪvɪ/ n (мясна́я) подли́вка.

graze¹ /greɪz/ vi (feed) пасти́сь impf.

graze² /greɪz/ n (abrasion) цара́пина; vt (touch) заде́ть impf, заде́ть impf; (abrade) цара́пать impf, o~ pf.

grease /gri:s/ n жир; (lubricant) сма́зка; ~-paint грим; vt сма́зывать impf, сма́зать pf. **greasy** /-sɪ/ adj жи́рный.

great /greɪt/ adj (large) большо́й; (eminent) вели́кий; (splendid) замеча́тельный; to a ~ extent в большо́й сте́пени; a ~ deal мно́го (+gen); a ~ many мно́гие; ~-aunt двою́родная ба́бушка; ~-granddaughter пра́внучка; ~-grandfather пра́дед; ~-grandmother праба́бка; ~-grandson пра́внук; ~-uncle двою́родный де́душка m. **greatly** /-lɪ/ adv о́чень.

Great Britain /greɪt 'brɪt(ə)n/ n Великобрита́ния.

Greece /gri:s/ n Гре́ция.

greed /gri:d/ n жа́дность (for к+dat). **greedy** /-dɪ/ adj жа́дный (for к+dat).

Greek /gri:k/ n грек, греча́нка; adj гре́ческий.

green /gri:n/ n (colour) зелёный цвет; (grassy area) лужа́йка; n зе́лень collect; adj зелёный. **greenery** /-nərɪ/ n зе́лень. **greenfly** n тля. **greengrocer** n зеленщи́к. **greengrocer's** n овощно́й магази́н. **greenhouse** n тепли́ца; ~ effect парнико́вый эффе́кт.

greet /gri:t/ vt здоро́ваться impf, по~ pf с+instr; (meet) встреча́ть impf, встре́тить pf. **greeting** n (-tɪŋ) n приве́т(ствие).

gregarious /grɪ'geərɪəs/ adj общи́тельный.

grenade /grɪ'neɪd/ n грана́та.

grey /greɪ/ adj се́рый; (hair) седо́й. **greyhound** /'greɪhaʊnd/ n борза́я sb.

grid /grɪd/ n (grating) решётка; (electr) сеть; (map) координа́тная се́тка.

grief /gri:f/ n го́ре; come to ~ терпе́ть impf, по~ pf неуда́чу. **grievance** /'gri:v(ə)ns/ n жа́лоба, оби́да. **grieve** /gri:v/ vt огорча́ть impf, огорчи́ть pf; vi горева́ть impf (for o+prep). **grievous** /'gri:vəs/ adj тя́жкий.

grill /grɪl/ n ра́шпер; vt жа́рить impf, за~, из~ pf (на ра́шпере); (question) допра́шивать impf, допроси́ть pf.

grille /grɪl/ n (grating) решётка.

grim /grɪm/ adj (stern) суро́вый; (unpleasant) неприя́тный.

grimace /grɪ'meɪs/ n грима́са; vi грима́сничать impf.

grime /graɪm/ n грязь. **grimy** /-mɪ/ adj гря́зный.

grin /grɪn/ n усме́шка; vi усмеха́ться impf, усмехну́ться pf.

grind /graɪnd/ vt (flour etc.) моло́ть impf, с~ pf; (axe) точи́ть

impf, на~ *pf*; ~ one's teeth скрежета́ть *impf* зуба́ми.

grip /grɪp/ *n* хва́тка; *vt* схва́тывать *impf*, схвати́ть *pf*.

gripe /graɪp/ *vi* ворча́ть *impf*.

gripping /ˈɡrɪpɪŋ/ *adj* захва́тывающий.

grisly /ˈɡrɪzlɪ/ *adj* жу́ткий.

gristle /ˈɡrɪs(ə)l/ *n* хрящ.

grit /grɪt/ *n* песо́к; (*for building*) гра́вий; (*firmness*) вы́держка.

grizzle /ˈɡrɪz(ə)l/ *vi* хны́кать *impf*.

groan /ɡrəʊn/ *n* стон; *vi* стона́ть *impf*.

grocer /ˈɡrəʊsə(r)/ *n* бакале́йщик; ~'s (**shop**) бакале́йная ла́вка, гастроно́м. **groceries** /-sərɪz/ *n pl* бакале́я collect.

groggy /ˈɡrɒɡɪ/ *adj* разби́тый.

groin /ɡrɔɪn/ *n* (*anat*) пах.

groom /ɡruːm/ *n* ко́нюх; (*bridegroom*) жени́х; *vt* (*horse*) чи́стить *impf*, по~ *pf*; (*prepare*) гото́вить *impf*, под~ *pf* (**for** к+*dat*); **well-groomed** хорошо́ вы́глядящий.

groove /ɡruːv/ *n* желобо́к.

grope /ɡrəʊp/ *vi* нащу́пывать *impf* (**for**, **after** +*acc*).

gross¹ /ɡrəʊs/ *n* (12 dozen) гросс.

gross² /ɡrəʊs/ *adj* (*fat*) ту́чный; (*coarse*) гру́бый; (*total*) валово́й; ~ **weight** вес бру́тто.

grotesque /ɡrəʊˈtesk/ *adj* гроте́скный.

grotto /ˈɡrɒtəʊ/ *n* грот.

ground /ɡraʊnd/ *n* земля́; (*earth*) по́чва; *pl* (*dregs*) гу́ща; (*sport*) площа́дка; *pl* (*of house*) парк; (*reason*) основа́ние; ~ **floor** пе́рвый эта́ж; *vt* (*instruct*) обуча́ть *impf*, обучи́ть *pf* осно́вам (**in** +*gen*); (*aeron*) запреща́ть *impf*, запрети́ть *pf* полёты +*gen*; *vi* (*naut*) са-

ди́ться *impf*, сесть *pf* на мель.

groundless /-lɪs/ *adj* необосно́ванный. **groundwork** *n* фунда́мент.

group /ɡruːp/ *n* гру́ппа; *vt & i* группирова́ть(ся) *impf*, с~ *pf*.

grouse¹ /ɡraʊs/ *n* шотла́ндская куропа́тка.

grouse² /ɡraʊs/ *vi* (*grumble*) ворча́ть *impf*.

grove /ɡrəʊv/ *n* ро́ща.

grovel /ˈɡrɒv(ə)l/ *vi* пресмыка́ться *impf* (**before** пе́ред +*instr*).

grow /ɡrəʊ/ *vi* расти́ *impf*; (*become*) станови́ться *impf*, стать *pf* +*instr*; *vt* (*cultivate*) выра́щивать *impf*, вы́растить *pf*; (*hair*) отра́щивать *impf*, отрасти́ть *pf*; ~ **up** (*person*) выраста́ть *impf*, вы́расти *pf*; (*custom*) возника́ть *impf*, возни́кнуть *pf*.

growl /ɡraʊl/ *n* ворча́ние; *vi* ворча́ть *impf* (**at** на+*acc*).

grown-up /ˈɡrəʊnʌp/ *adj* взро́слый *sb*.

growth /ɡrəʊθ/ *n* рост; (*med*) о́пухоль.

grub /ɡrʌb/ *n* (*larva*) личи́нка; (*food*) жратва́; *vi*: ~ **about** ры́ться *impf*. **grubby** /ˈɡrʌbɪ/ *adj* запа́чканный.

grudge /ɡrʌdʒ/ *n* зло́ба; **have a** ~ **against** име́ть *impf* зуб про́тив+*gen*; *vt* жале́ть *impf*, по~ *pf* +*acc*, +*gen*. **grudgingly** /-dʒɪŋlɪ/ *adv* неохо́тно.

gruelling /ˈɡruːəlɪŋ/ *adj* изнури́тельный.

gruesome /ˈɡruːsəm/ *adj* жу́ткий.

gruff /ɡrʌf/ *adj* (*surly*) грубова́тый; (*voice*) хри́плый.

grumble /ˈɡrʌmb(ə)l/ *vi* ворча́ть *impf* (**at** на+*acc*).

grumpy /ˈɡrʌmpɪ/ *adj* брюзгли́вый.

grunt /grʌnt/ n хрю́канье; vi хрю́кать impf, хрю́кнуть pf.

guarantee /ˌɡærənˈtiː/ n гара́нтия; vt гаранти́ровать impf & pf (**against** от+gen). **guarantor** /-'tɔː(r)/ n поручи́тель m.

guard /ɡɑːd/ n (device) предохрани́тель; (watch; soldiers) карау́л; (sentry) часово́й sb; (watchman) сто́рож; (rly) конду́ктор; pl (prison) надзира́тель m; vt охраня́ть impf, охрани́ть pf; vi: ~ **against** остерега́ться impf, остере́чься pf +gen, inf.

guardian /ˈɡɑːdɪən/ n храни́тель m; (law) опеку́н.

guer(r)illa /ɡəˈrɪlə/ n партиза́н; ~ **warfare** партиза́нская война́.

guess /ɡes/ n дога́дка; vt & i дога́дываться impf, догада́ться pf (о+prep); vt (~ correctly) уга́дывать impf, угада́ть pf. **guesswork** n дога́дки f pl.

guest /ɡest/ n гость m; ~ **house** ма́ленькая гости́ница.

guffaw /ɡʌˈfɔː/ n хо́хот; vi хохота́ть impf.

guidance /ˈɡaɪd(ə)ns/ n руково́дство. **guide** /ɡaɪd/ n проводни́к, гид; (guidebook) путеводи́тель m; vt води́ть indet, вести́ det; (direct) руководи́ть impf +instr. ~**ed missile** управля́емая раке́та. **guidelines** n pl инстру́кции f pl; (advice) сове́т.

guild /ɡɪld/ n ги́льдия, цех.

guile /ɡaɪl/ n кова́рство. **guileless** /-lɪs/ adj простоду́шный.

guillotine /ˈɡɪləˌtiːn/ n гильоти́на.

guilt /ɡɪlt/ n вина́; (guiltiness) вино́вность. **guilty** /-tɪ/ adj (of crime) вино́вный (**of** в+prep); (of wrong) винова́тый.

guinea-pig /ˈɡɪnɪpɪɡ/ n морска́я сви́нка; (fig) подо́пытный кро́лик.

guise /ɡaɪz/ n: **under the ~ of** под ви́дом+gen.

guitar /ɡɪˈtɑː(r)/ n гита́ра. **guitarist** /-rɪst/ n гитари́ст.

gulf /ɡʌlf/ n (geog) зали́в; (chasm) про́пасть.

gull /ɡʌl/ n ча́йка.

gullet /ˈɡʌlɪt/ n (oesophagus) пищево́д; (throat) го́рло.

gullible /ˈɡʌlɪb(ə)l/ adj легкове́рный.

gully /ˈɡʌlɪ/ n (ravine) овра́г.

gulp /ɡʌlp/ n глото́к; vt жа́дно глота́ть impf.

gum[1] /ɡʌm/ n (anat) десна́.

gum[2] /ɡʌm/ n каме́дь; (glue) клей; vt скле́ивать impf, скле́ить pf.

gumption /ˈɡʌmpʃ(ə)n/ n инициати́ва.

gun /ɡʌn/ n (piece of ordnance) ору́дие, пу́шка; (rifle etc.) ружьё; (pistol) пистоле́т; vt: ~ **down** расстре́ливать impf, расстреля́ть pf. **gunner** /-nə(r)/ n артиллери́ст. **gunpowder** n по́рох.

gurgle /ˈɡɜːɡ(ə)l/ vi булька́ть impf.

gush /ɡʌʃ/ vi хлы́нуть pf.

gusset /ˈɡʌsɪt/ n клин.

gust /ɡʌst/ n поры́в. **gusty** /-stɪ/ adj поры́вистый.

gusto /ˈɡʌstəʊ/ n смак.

gut /ɡʌt/ n кишка́; pl (entrails) кишки́ f pl; pl (bravery) му́жество; vt потроши́ть impf, вы́~ pf; (devastate) опустоша́ть impf, опустоши́ть pf.

gutter /ˈɡʌtə(r)/ n (of roof) (водосто́чный) жёлоб; (of road) сто́чная кана́ва.

guttural /ˈɡʌtərəl/ adj горта́нный.

guy¹ /gaɪ/ n (rope) оття́жка.

guy² /gaɪ/ n (fellow) па́рень m.

guzzle /ˈgʌz(ə)l/ vt (food) пожира́ть impf, пожра́ть pf; (liquid) хлеба́ть impf, хлебну́ть pf.

gym /dʒɪm/ n (gymnasium) тим-насти́ческий зал; (gymnastics) гимна́стика. **gymnasium** /dʒɪmˈneɪzɪəm/ n гимнасти́ческий зал. **gymnast** /ˈdʒɪmnæst/ n гимна́ст. **gymnastic** /dʒɪmˈnæstɪk/ adj гимнасти́ческий. **gymnastics** /dʒɪmˈnæstɪks/ n гимна́стика.

gynaecologist /ˌgaɪnɪˈkɒlədʒɪst/ n гинеко́лог. **gynaecology** /-dʒɪ/ n гинеколо́гия.

gyrate /ˌdʒaɪˈreɪt/ vi враща́ться impf.

H

haberdashery /ˈhæbədæʃərɪ/ n галантере́я; (shop) галанте-ре́йный магази́н.

habit /ˈhæbɪt/ n привы́чка; (monk's) ря́са.

habitable /ˈhæbɪtəb(ə)l/ adj приго́дный для жилья́. **habitat** /-tæt/ n есте́ственная среда́. **habitation** /-ˈteɪʃ(ə)n/ n: unfit for ~ неприго́дный для жилья́.

habitual /həˈbɪtjʊəl/ adj привы́чный.

hack¹ /hæk/ vt руби́ть impf; ~saw ножо́вка.

hack² /hæk/ n (hired horse) наёмная ло́шадь; (writer) халту́рщик **hackneyed** /ˈhæknɪd/ adj.

haddock /ˈhædək/ n пи́кша.

haemophilia /ˌhiːməˈfɪlɪə/ n гемофили́я. **haemorrhage** /ˈhemərɪdʒ/ n кровотече́ние. **haemorrhoids** /ˈheməˌrɔɪdz/ n pl геморро́й collect.

hag /hæg/ n карга́.

haggard /ˈhægəd/ adj из-можде́нный.

haggle /ˈhæg(ə)l/ vi торгова́ться impf, c~ pf.

hail¹ /heɪl/ n град; vi it is ~ing идёт град. **hailstone** n гра́дина.

hail² /heɪl/ vt (greet) приве́т-ствовать impf (& pf in past); (taxi) подзыва́ть impf, подо-зва́ть pf.

hair /heə(r)/ n (single ~) во́лос; collect (human) во́лосы (-о́с, -оса́м) pl; (animal) шерсть. **hairbrush** n щётка для воло́с. **haircut** n стри́жка; have a ~ по-стри́чься pf. **hair-do** /ˈheəduː/ n причёска. **hairdresser** /ˈheədresə(r)/ n парикма́хер. **hair-dresser's** /ˈheədresəz/ n парикма́херская sb. **hair-dryer** /ˈheəˌdraɪə(r)/ n фен. **hairstyle** n причёска. **hairy** /ˈheərɪ/ adj волоса́тый.

hale /heɪl/ adj: ~ and hearty здоро́вый и бо́дрый.

half /hɑːf/ n полови́на; (sport) тайм; adj полови́нный; in ~ попола́м; one and a ~ полтора́; ~ past (one etc.) полови́на (вто-ро́го и т.д.); ~-hearted равно-ду́шный; ~ an hour полчаса́; ~-time переры́в ме́жду тай-мами; ~way на полпути́; ~-witted слабоу́мный.

hall /hɔːl/ n (large room) зал; (en-trance ~) холл, вестибю́ль m; (~ of residence) общежи́тие.

hallmark n про́бирное клеймо́; (fig) при́знак.

hallo /həˈləʊ/ int здра́вствуй(те), приве́т; (on telephone) алло́.

hallucination /həˌluːsɪˈneɪʃ(ə)n/ n галлюцина́ция.

halo /ˈheɪləʊ/ n (around Saint)

нимб.

halt /hɒlt/ n остано́вка; vt & i остана́вливать(ся) impf, останови́ть(ся) pf; int (mil) стой(те)! **halting** /-tɪŋ/ adj запина́ющий.

halve /hɑːv/ vt дели́ть impf, раз~ pf попола́м.

ham /hæm/ n (cul) ветчина́.

hamburger /'hæm,bɜːɡə(r)/ n котле́та.

hamlet /'hæmlɪt/ n дереву́шка.

hammer /'hæmə(r)/ n молото́к; vt бить impf молотко́м.

hammock /'hæmək/ n гама́к.

hamper[1] /'hæmpə(r)/ n (basket) корзи́на с кры́шкой.

hamper[2] /'hæmpə(r)/ vt (hinder) меша́ть impf, по~ pf +dat.

hamster /'hæmstə(r)/ n хомя́к.

hand /hænd/ n рука́; (worker) рабо́чий sb; (writing) по́черк; (clock ~) стре́лка; **at** ~ под руко́й; **on ~s and knees** на четвере́ньках; vt передава́ть impf, переда́ть pf; ~ **in** подава́ть impf, пода́ть pf; ~ **out** раздава́ть impf, разда́ть pf. **handbag** n су́мка. **handbook** n руково́дство. **handcuffs** /-kʌfs/ n pl нару́чники pl. **handful** /-fʊl/ n горсть.

handicap /'hændɪ,kæp/ n (sport) гандика́п; (hindrance) поме́ха. **handicapped** /-,kæpt/ adj: ~ **person** инвали́д.

handicraft /'hændɪ,krɑːft/ n ремесло́.

handiwork /'hændɪ,wɜːk/ n ручна́я рабо́та.

handkerchief /'hæŋkə,tʃiːf/ n носово́й плато́к.

handle /'hænd(ə)l/ n ру́чка, рукоя́тка; vt (people) обраща́ться impf c+instr; (situations) справля́ться impf, спра́виться pf c+instr; (touch)

тро́гать impf, тро́нуть pf руко́й, рука́ми. **handlebar(s)** /'hændl,bɑːz/ n руль m.

handmade /'hændmeɪd/ adj ручно́й рабо́ты.

handout /'hændaʊt/ n пода́чка; (document) лифлёт.

handrail /'hændreɪl/ n пери́ла (-л) pl.

handshake /'hændʃeɪk/ n рукопожа́тие.

handsome /'hænsəm/ adj краси́вый; (generous) ще́дрый.

handwriting /'hænd,raɪtɪŋ/ n по́черк.

handy /'hændɪ/ adj (convenient) удо́бный; (skilful) ло́вкий; **come in** ~ пригоди́ться pf.

hang /hæŋ/ vt ве́шать impf, пове́сить pf; vi висе́ть impf; ~ **about** слоня́ться impf; ~ **on** (cling) держа́ться impf; (tel) не ве́шать impf тру́бку; (persist) упо́рствовать impf; ~ **out** выве́шивать impf, вы́весить pf; (spend time) болта́ться impf; ~ **up** ве́шать impf, пове́сить pf; (tel) ве́шать impf, пове́сить pf тру́бку. **hanger** /'hæŋə(r)/ n ве́шалка. **hanger-on** /,hæŋə'rɒn/ n прилипа́ла m & f. **hangman** n пала́ч.

hangar /'hæŋə(r)/ n анга́р.

hangover /'hæŋəʊvə(r)/ n похме́лье.

hang-up /'hæŋʌp/ n ко́мплекс.

hanker /'hæŋkə(r)/ vi: ~ **after** мечта́ть impf o+prep.

haphazard /hæp'hæzəd/ adj случа́йный.

happen /'hæpən/ vi (occur) случа́ться impf, случи́ться pf; (transpire) происходи́ть impf, произойти́ pf; ~ **upon** ната́лкиваться impf, натолкну́ться pf на+acc.

happiness /'hæpɪnɪs/ n сча́стье.

happy /'hæpɪ/ adj счастли́вый;

~-**go-lucky** беззаботный.

harass /'hærəs/ vt (pester) дёргать impf; (persecute) преследовать impf. **harassment** /-mənt/ n травля; преследование.

harbinger /'ha:bɪndʒə(r)/ n предвестник.

harbour /'ha:bə(r)/ n гавань, порт; vt (person) укрывать impf, укрыть pf; (thoughts) затаивать impf, затаить pf.

hard /ha:d/ adj твёрдый; (difficult) трудный; (difficult to bear) тяжёлый; (severe) суровый; adv (work) много; (hit) сильно; (try) очень; ~-**boiled egg** яйцо вкрутую; ~ **disk** (comput) жёсткий диск; ~-**headed** практичный; ~-**hearted** жестокосердный; ~-**up** стеснённый в средствах; ~-**working** трудолюбивый. **hardboard** n строительный картон.

harden /'ha:d(ə)n/ vi затвердевать impf, затвердеть pf; (fig) ожесточаться impf, ожесточиться pf.

hardly /'ha:dlɪ/ adv едва (ли).

hardship /'ha:dʃɪp/ n (privation) нужда.

hardware /'ha:dweə(r)/ n скобяные изделия neut pl; (comput) аппаратура.

hardy /'ha:dɪ/ adj (robust) выносливый; (plant) морозостойкий.

hare /heə(r)/ n заяц.

hark /ha:k/ vi: ~ **back to** возвращаться impf, вернуться pf к+dat; ~ ты слушай(те)!

harm /ha:m/ n вред; vt вредить impf, по~ pf +dat. **harmful** /-fʊl/ adj вредный. **harmless** /-lɪs/ adj безвредный.

harmonic /ha:'mɒnɪk/ adj гармонический. **harmonica**

/-'mɒnɪkə/ n губная гармоника.

harmonious /-'məʊnɪəs/ adj гармоничный. **harmonize** /'ha:mənaɪz/ vi гармонировать impf (with c+instr). **harmony** /'ha:mənɪ/ n гармония.

harness /'ha:nɪs/ n упряжь; vt запрягать impf, запрячь pf; (fig) использовать impf & pf.

harp /ha:p/ n арфа; vi: ~ **on** твердить impf o+prep.

harpoon /ha:'pu:n/ n гарпун.

harpsichord /'ha:psɪ,kɔ:d/ n клавесин.

harrowing /'hærəʊɪŋ/ adj душераздирающий.

harsh /ha:ʃ/ adj (sound, colour) резкий; (cruel) суровый.

harvest /'ha:vɪst/ n жатва, сбор (плодов); (yield) урожай; (fig) плоды m pl; vt & abs собирать impf, собрать pf (урожай).

hash /hæʃ/ n: **make a ~ of** напутать pf +acc, в+prep.

hashish /'hæʃi:ʃ/ n гашиш.

hassle /'hæs(ə)l/ n беспокойство.

hassock /'hæsək/ n подушечка.

haste /heɪst/ n спешка. **hasten** /'heɪs(ə)n/ vi спешить impf, по~ pf; vt & i торопить(ся) impf, по~ pf; vt ускорять impf, ускорить pf. **hasty** /'heɪstɪ/ adj (hurried) поспешный; (quick-tempered) вспыльчивый.

hat /hæt/ n шапка; (stylish) шляпа.

hatch¹ /hætʃ/ n люк; ~-**back** машина-пикап.

hatch² /hætʃ/ vi вылупливаться, вылупляться impf, вылупиться pf.

hatchet /'hætʃɪt/ n топорик.

hate /heɪt/ n ненависть; vt ненавидеть impf. **hateful** /-fʊl/ adj ненавистный. **hatred** /-trɪd/ n

не́нависть.

haughty /'hɔːtɪ/ *adj* надме́нный.

haul /hɔːl/ *n* (*fish*) уло́в; (*loot*) добы́ча; (*distance*) езда́; *vt* (*drag*) тяну́ть *impf*; таска́ть *indet*, тащи́ть *det*. **haulage** /-lɪdʒ/ *n* перево́зка.

haunt /hɔːnt/ *n* люби́мое ме́сто; *vt* (*ghost*) обита́ть *impf*; (*memory*) пресле́довать *impf*. **haunted** /-tɪd/ *adj*: ~ **house** дом с привиде́ниями. **haunting** /-tɪŋ/ *adj* навя́зчивый.

have /hæv/ *vt* име́ть *impf*; I ~ (*possess*) у меня́ (есть; был, -а́, -о) +*nom*; I ~ **not** у меня́ не (*past* не́ было) +*gen*; I ~ (**got) to** я до́лжен +*inf*; **you had better** вам лу́чше бы +*inf*; ~ **on** (*wear*) быть оде́тым в +*prep*; (*be engaged in*) быть за́нятым +*instr*.

haven /'heɪv(ə)n/ *n* (*refuge*) убе́жище.

haversack /'hævəˌsæk/ *n* рюкза́к.

havoc /'hævək/ *n* (*devastation*) опустоше́ние; (*disorder*) беспоря́док.

hawk[1] /hɔːk/ *n* (*bird*) я́стреб.

hawk[2] /hɔːk/ *vt* (*trade*) торгова́ть *impf* вразно́с+*instr*. **hawker** /-kə(r)/ *n* разно́счик.

hawser /'hɔːzə(r)/ *n* трос.

hawthorn /'hɔːθɔːn/ *n* боя́рышник.

hay /heɪ/ *n* се́но; **make** ~ коси́ть *impf*; с~ се́но; ~ **fever** се́нная лихора́дка. **haystack** *n* стог.

hazard /'hæzəd/ *n* риск; *vt* рискова́ть *impf* +*instr*. **hazardous** /-dəs/ *adj* риско́ванный.

haze /heɪz/ *n* ды́мка.

hazel /'heɪz(ə)l/ *n* лещи́на. **hazelnut** *n* лесно́й оре́х.

hazy /'heɪzɪ/ *adj* тума́нный; (*vague*) сму́тный.

he /hiː/ *pron* он.

head /hed/ *n* голова́; (*mind*) ум; (~ *of coin*) лицева́я сторона́ моне́ты; ~**s or tails?** орёл и́ли ре́шка?; (*chief*) глава́ *m*, нача́льник; *attrib* гла́вный; *vt* (*lead*) возглавля́ть *impf*, возгла́вить *pf*; (*ball*) забива́ть *impf*, заби́ть *pf* голово́й; *vi*: ~ **for** направля́ться *impf*, напра́виться *pf* в, на, +*acc*, к+*dat*. **headache** *n* головна́я боль. **head-dress** *n* головно́й убо́р. **header** /-də(r)/ *n* уда́р голово́й. **heading** /-dɪŋ/ *n* (*title*) заголо́вок. **headland** *n* мыс. **headlight** *n* фа́ра. **headline** *n* заголо́вок. **headlong** *adv* стремгла́в. **headmaster, -mistress** *n* дире́ктор шко́лы, -тор дире́кторша. **head-on** *adj* столкове́ние; *adv* в лоб. **headphone** *n* нау́шник. **headquarters** *n* штаб-кварти́ра. **headscarf** *n* косы́нка. **headstone** *n* надгро́бный ка́мень *m*. **headstrong** *adj* своево́льный. **headway** *n* движе́ние вперёд. **heady** /-dɪ/ *adj* опьяня́ющий.

heal /hiːl/ *vt* изле́чивать *impf*, излечи́ть *pf*; *vi* зажива́ть *impf*, зажи́ть *pf*. **healing** /-lɪŋ/ *adj* целе́бный.

health /helθ/ *n* здоро́вье; ~ **care** здравоохране́ние. **healthy** /-θɪ/ *adj* здоро́вый; (*beneficial*) поле́зный.

heap /hiːp/ *n* ку́ча; *vt* нагромождать *impf*, нагромозди́ть *pf*.

hear /hɪə(r)/ *vt* слы́шать *impf*, у~ *pf*; (*listen to*) слу́шать *impf*, по~ *pf*; ~ **out** выслу́шивать *impf*, вы́слушать *pf*. **hearing** /-rɪŋ/ *n* слух; (*law*) слу́шание. **hearsay** *n* слух.

hearse /hɜːs/ *n* катафа́лк.

heart /hɑːt/ n се́рдце; (*essence*) суть; pl (*cards*) че́рви (-ве́й) pl; by ~ наизу́сть; ~ **attack** серде́чный при́ступ. **heartburn** n изжо́га. **hearten** /-t(ə)n/ vt ободря́ть impf, ободри́ть pf. **heartfelt** adj серде́чный. **heartless** /-lɪs/ adj бессерде́чный. **heart-rending** /-ˌrendɪŋ/ adj душераздира́ющий. **hearty** /-tɪ/ adj (*cordial*) серде́чный; (*vigorous*) здоро́вый.

hearth /hɑːθ/ n оча́г.

heat /hiːt/ n жара́; (*phys*) теплота́; (*of feeling*) пыл; (*sport*) забе́г, заёзд; vt & i (*heat up*) нагрева́ть(ся) impf, нагре́ть(ся) pf; vt (*house*) топи́ть impf. **heater** /-tə(r)/ n нагрева́тель m. **heating** /-tɪŋ/ n отопле́ние.

heath /hiːθ/ n пу́стошь.

heathen /ˈhiːð(ə)n/ n язы́чник; adj язы́ческий.

heather /ˈheðə(r)/ n ве́реск.

heave /hiːv/ vt (*lift*) поднима́ть impf, подня́ть pf; (*pull*) тяну́ть impf, по~ pf.

heaven /ˈhev(ə)n/ n (*sky*) не́бо; (*paradise*) рай; pl небеса́ neut pl. **heavenly** /-lɪ/ adj небе́сный; (*divine*) боже́ственный.

heavy /ˈhevɪ/ adj тяжёлый; (*strong, intense*) си́льный. **heavyweight** n тяжелове́с.

Hebrew /ˈhiːbruː/ adj (дре́вне)евре́йский.

heckle /ˈhek(ə)l/ vt пререка́ться impf c+instr.

hectic /ˈhektɪk/ adj лихора́дочный.

hedge /hedʒ/ n жива́я и́згородь. **hedgerow** n шпале́ра.

hedgehog /ˈhedʒhɒg/ n ёж.

heed /hiːd/ vt обраща́ть impf, обрати́ть pf внима́ние на+acc. **heedless** /-lɪs/ adj небре́жный.

heel¹ /hiːl/ n (*of foot*) пята́; (*of foot, sock*) пя́тка; (*of shoe*) каблу́к.

heel² /hiːl/ vi крени́ться impf, на~ pf.

hefty /ˈheftɪ/ adj дю́жий.

heifer /ˈhefə(r)/ n тёлка.

height /haɪt/ n высота́; (*of person*) рост. **heighten** /-t(ə)n/ vt (*strengthen*) усили́вать impf, уси́лить pf.

heinous /ˈheɪnəs/ adj гну́сный.

heir /eə(r)/ n насле́дник. **heiress** /ˈeərɪs/ n насле́дница. **heirloom** /ˈeəluːm/ n фами́льная вещь.

helicopter /ˈhelɪˌkɒptə(r)/ n вертолёт.

helium /ˈhiːlɪəm/ n ге́лий.

hell /hel/ n ад. **hellish** /-lɪʃ/ adj а́дский.

hello /həˈləʊ/ see **hallo**

helm /helm/ n руль.

helmet /ˈhelmɪt/ n шлем.

help /help/ n по́мощь; vt помога́ть impf, помо́чь pf +dat; (*can't ~*) не мочь impf не +inf; ~ **o.s.** брать impf, взять pf себе́; ~ **yourself** бери́те! **helpful** /-fʊl/ adj поле́зный; (*obliging*) услу́жливый. **helping** /-pɪŋ/ n (*of food*) по́рция. **helpless** /-lɪs/ adj беспомо́щный.

helter-skelter /ˌheltəˈskeltə(r)/ adv как попа́ло.

hem /hem/ n рубе́ц; vt подруба́ть impf, подруби́ть pf; ~ **in** окружа́ть impf, окружи́ть pf.

hemisphere /ˈhemɪˌsfɪə(r)/ n полуша́рие.

hemp /hemp/ n (*plant*) конопля́; (*fibre*) пенька́.

hen /hen/ n (*female bird*) са́мка; (*domestic fowl*) ку́рица.

hence /hens/ adv (*from here*) отсю́да; (*as a result*) сле́довательно; **3 years** ~ че́рез три го́да. **henceforth** /-ˈfɔːθ/ adv отны́не.

henchman /'hentʃmən/ n приспе́шник.

henna /'henə/ n хна.

hepatitis /ˌhepə'taɪtɪs/ n гепати́т.

her /hɜː(r)/ poss pron её; свой.

herald /'herəld/ n ве́стник; vt возвеща́ть impf, возвести́ть pf.

herb /hɜːb/ n трава́. **herbaceous** /hɜː'beɪʃəs/ adj травяно́й; ~ **border** цвето́чный бордю́р. **herbal** /'hɜːb(ə)l/ adj травяно́й.

herd /hɜːd/ n ста́до; (people) толпи́ться impf, c~ pf; (tend) пасти́ impf; (drive) загоня́ть impf, загна́ть pf в ста́до.

here /hɪə(r)/ adv (position) здесь, тут; (direction) сюда́; ~ **is** ~ вот (+nom); ~ **and there** там и сям; ~ **you are!** пожа́луйста. **hereabout(s)** /ˌhɪərə'baʊts/ adv поблизости. **hereafter** /ˌhɪər'ɑːftə(r)/ adv в бу́дущем. **hereby** /ˌhɪə'baɪ/ adv э́тим. **hereupon** /ˌhɪərə'pɒn/ adv (in consequence) всле́дствие э́того; (after) по́сле э́того. **herewith** /ˌhɪə'wɪð/ adv при сём.

hereditary /hɪ'redɪtərɪ/ adj насле́дственный. **heredity** /hɪ'redɪtɪ/ n насле́дственность.

heresy /'herəsɪ/ n е́ресь. **heretic** /'herətɪk/ n ерети́к. **heretical** /hɪ'retɪk(ə)l/ adj ерети́ческий.

heritage /'herɪtɪdʒ/ n насле́дие.

hermetic /hɜː'metɪk/ adj гермети́ческий.

hermit /'hɜːmɪt/ n отше́льник.

hernia /'hɜːnɪə/ n гры́жа.

hero /'hɪərəʊ/ n геро́й. **heroic** /hɪ'rəʊɪk/ adj герои́ческий. **heroin** /'herəʊɪn/ n герои́н. **heroine** /'herəʊɪn/ n геро́йня. **heroism** /'herəʊɪz(ə)m/ n герои́зм.

heron /'herən/ n ца́пля.

herpes /'hɜːpiːz/ n лиша́й.

herring /'herɪŋ/ n сельдь; (food) селёдка.

hers /hɜːz/ poss pron её; свой. **herself** /hɜː'self/ pron (emph) (она́) сама́; (refl) себя́.

hertz /hɜːts/ n герц.

hesitant /'hezɪt(ə)nt/ adj нереши́тельный. **hesitate** /-ˌteɪt/ vi колеба́ться impf, по~ pf; (in speech) запина́ться impf, запну́ться pf. **hesitation** /-'teɪʃ(ə)n/ n колеба́ние.

hessian /'hesɪən/ n мешкови́на.

heterogeneous /ˌhetərə'dʒiːnɪəs/ adj разноро́дный.

heterosexual /ˌhetərəʊ'seksjʊəl/ adj гетеросексуа́льный.

hew /hjuː/ vt руби́ть impf.

hexagon /'heksəgən/ n шестиуго́льник.

hey /heɪ/ int эй!

heyday /'heɪdeɪ/ n расцве́т.

hi /haɪ/ int приве́т!

hiatus /haɪ'eɪtəs/ n пробе́л.

hibernate /'haɪbəˌneɪt/ vi быть impf в спя́чке; впада́ть impf, впасть pf в спя́чку. **hibernation** /-'neɪʃ(ə)n/ n спя́чка.

hiccup /'hɪkʌp/ vi ика́ть impf, и́кнуть pf; n: pl ико́та.

hide[1] /haɪd/ n (skin) шку́ра.

hide[2] /haɪd/ vt & i (conceal) пря́тать(ся) impf, c~ pf; скрыва́ть(ся) impf, скрыть(ся) pf.

hideous /'hɪdɪəs/ adj отврати́тельный.

hideout /'haɪdaʊt/ n укры́тие.

hiding /'haɪdɪŋ/ n (flogging) по́рка.

hierarchy /'haɪəˌrɑːkɪ/ n иера́рхия.

hieroglyphics /ˌhaɪərə'glɪfɪks/ n pl иеро́глифы m pl.

hi-fi /'haɪfaɪ/ n с высокока́чественным воспроизведе́нием зву́ка за́писи.

higgledy-piggledy /ˌhɪgəldɪ ˈpɪgəldɪ/ adv как придётся.

high /haɪ/ adj высо́кий; (wind) си́льный; (on drugs) в наркоти́ческом дурма́не; ~er education вы́сшее образова́ние; ~-handed своево́льный; ~-heeled на высо́ких каблука́х; ~ jump прыжо́к в высоту́; ~-minded благоро́дный, иде́йный; ~-pitched высо́кий; ~-rise высо́тный. highbrow adj интеллектуа́льный. highland(s) n го́рная страна́. highlight n (fig) вы́сшая то́чка; n vt обраща́ть impf, обрати́ть pf внима́ние на+acc. highly /-lɪ/ adv весьма́; ~-strung легко́ возбужда́емый. highness n (title) высо́чество. highstreet n гла́вная у́лица. highway n маги́страль.

hijack /ˈhaɪdʒæk/ vt похища́ть impf, похи́тить pf. hijacker /-kə(r)/ n похити́тель m.

hike /haɪk/ n похо́д.

hilarious /hɪˈleərɪəs/ adj умори́тельный. hilarity /-ˈlærɪtɪ/ n весе́лье.

hill /hɪl/ n холм. hillock /ˈhɪlək/ n хо́лмик. hillside n склон холма́. hilly /ˈhɪlɪ/ adj холми́стый.

hilt /hɪlt/ n рукоя́тка.

himself /hɪmˈself/ pron (emph) (он) сам; (refl) себя́.

hind /haɪnd/ adj (rear) за́дний.

hinder /ˈhɪndə(r)/ vt меша́ть impf, по~ pf +dat. hindrance /-drəns/ n поме́ха.

Hindu /ˈhɪnduː/ n инду́с; adj инду́сский.

hinge /hɪndʒ/ n шарни́р; vi (fig) зави́сеть impf от+gen.

hint /hɪnt/ n намёк; vi намека́ть impf, намекну́ть pf (at на+acc)

hip /hɪp/ n (anat) бедро́.

hippie /ˈhɪpɪ/ n хи́ппи neut indecl.

hippopotamus /ˌhɪpəˈpɒtəməs/ n гиппопота́м.

hire /ˈhaɪə(r)/ n наём, прока́т; ~-purchase поку́пка в рассро́чку; vt нанима́ть impf, наня́ть pf; ~ out сдава́ть impf, сдать pf напрока́т.

his /hɪz/ poss pron его́; свой.

hiss /hɪs/ n шипе́ние; vi шипе́ть impf; vt (performer) освисты́вать impf, освиста́ть pf.

historian /hɪˈstɔːrɪən/ n исто́рик. historic(al) /hɪˈstɒrɪk(ə)l/ adj истори́ческий. history /ˈhɪstərɪ/ n исто́рия.

histrionic /ˌhɪstrɪˈɒnɪk/ adj театра́льный.

hit /hɪt/ n (blow) уда́р; (on target) попада́ние (в цель); (success) успе́х; vt (strike) ударя́ть impf, уда́рить pf; (target) попада́ть impf, попа́сть pf (в цель); ~ (up)on находи́ть impf, найти́ pf.

hitch /hɪtʃ/ n (stoppage) заде́ржка; vt (fasten) привя́зывать impf, привяза́ть pf; ~ up подтя́гивать impf, подтяну́ть pf; ~-hike е́здить impf, е́хать det, автосто́пом.

hither /ˈhɪðə(r)/ adv сюда́. hitherto /ˈhɪðətuː/ adv до сих пор.

HIV abbr (of human immunodeficiency virus) ВИЧ.

hive /haɪv/ n у́лей.

hoard /hɔːd/ n запа́с; vt ска́пливать impf, скопи́ть pf.

hoarding /ˈhɔːdɪŋ/ n рекла́мный щит.

hoarse /hɔːs/ adj хри́плый.

hoax /həʊks/ n надува́тельство.

hobble /ˈhɒb(ə)l/ vi ковыля́ть impf.

hobby /ˈhɒbɪ/ n хо́бби neut indecl.

decl.

hock /hɒk/ *n* (*wine*) рейнвейн.

hockey /'hɒkɪ/ *n* хоккей.

hoe /həʊ/ *n* мотыга; *vt* мотыжить *impf.*

hog /hɒg/ *n* боров.

hoist /hɔɪst/ *n* подъёмник; *vt* поднимать *impf*, поднять *pf*.

hold[1] /həʊld/ *n* (*naut*) трюм.

hold[2] /həʊld/ *n* (*grasp*) захват; (*influence*) влияние (on на+*acc*); **catch** *or* **get** ~ **of** ухватиться *pf* за+*acc*; *vt* (*grasp*) держать *impf*, (*contain*) вмещать *impf*, вместить *pf*; (*possess*) владеть *impf* +*instr*; (*conduct*) проводить *impf*, провести *pf*; (*consider*) считать *impf*, счесть *pf* (+*acc* & *instr*, за+*acc*); *vi* держаться *impf*; (*weather*) продерживаться *impf*, продержаться *pf*; ~ **back** сдерживать(ся) *impf*, сдержать(ся) *pf*; ~ **forth** разглагольствовать *impf*; ~ **on** (*wait*) подождать *pf*; (*tel*) не вешать *impf* трубку; (*grip*) держаться *impf* (**to** за+*acc*); ~ **out** (*stretch out*) протягивать *impf*, протянуть *pf*; (*resist*) не сдаваться *impf*; ~ **up** (*support*) поддерживать *impf*, поддержать *pf*; (*impede*) задерживать *impf*, задержать *pf*. **holdall** *n* сумка. **hold-up** *n* (*robbery*) налёт; (*delay*) задержка.

hole /həʊl/ *n* дыра; (*animal's*) нора; (*golf*) лунка.

holiday /'hɒlɪdeɪ/ *n* (*day off*) выходной день; (*festival*) праздник; (*annual leave*) отпуск; *pl* (*school*) каникулы (-л) *pl*; ~**maker** турист; **on** ~ в отпуске.

holiness /'həʊlɪnɪs/ *n* святость.

Holland /'hɒlənd/ *n* Голландия.

hollow /'hɒləʊ/ *n* впадина; (*valley*) лощина; *adj* пустой;

(*sunken*) впалый; (*sound*) глухой; *vt* (~ **out**) выдалбливать *impf*, выдолбить *pf*.

holly /'hɒlɪ/ *n* остролист.

holocaust /'hɒləkɔːst/ *n* массовое уничтожение.

holster /'həʊlstə(r)/ *n* кобура.

holy /'həʊlɪ/ *adj* святой, священный.

homage /'hɒmɪdʒ/ *n* почтение; **pay** ~ **to** преклоняться *impf*, преклониться *pf* перед+*instr*.

home /həʊm/ *n* дом; (*also* **homeland**) родина; **at** ~ дома; **feel at** ~ чувствовать *impf* себя как дома; *adj* домашний; (*native*) родной; **H**~ **Affairs** внутренние дела *neut pl*; *adv* (*direction*) домой; (*position*) дома. **homeless** /-lɪs/ *adj* бездомный. **home-made** *adj* (*food*) домашний; (*object*) самодельный. **homesick** *adj*: **be** ~ скучать *impf* по дому. **homewards** /-wədz/ *adv* домой. **homework** *n* домашние задания *neut pl.*

homely /'həʊmlɪ/ *adj* простой.

homicide /'hɒmɪˌsaɪd/ *n* (*action*) убийство.

homogeneous /ˌhɒməʊˈdʒiːnɪəs/ *adj* однородный.

homosexual /ˌhɒməʊˈseksjʊəl/ *n* гомосексуалист; *adj* гомосексуальный.

honest /'ɒnɪst/ *n* честный. **honesty** /-tɪ/ *n* честность.

honey /'hʌnɪ/ *n* мёд. **honeymoon** *n* медовый месяц. **honeysuckle** *n* жимолость.

honk /hɒŋk/ *vi* гудеть *impf.*

honorary /'ɒnərərɪ/ *adj* почётный.

honour /'ɒnə(r)/ *n* честь; *vt* (*respect*) почитать *impf*; (*confer*) удостаивать *impf*, удостоить *pf* (**with** +*gen*); (*fulfil*) выпол-

нять *impf*, вы́полнить *pf*. **honourable** /-rəb(ə)l/ *adj* че́стный.

hood /hʊd/ *n* капюшо́н; (*tech*) капо́т.

hoodwink /ˈhʊdwɪŋk/ *vt* обма́нывать *impf*, обману́ть *pf*.

hoof /huːf/ *n* копы́то.

hook /hʊk/ *n* крючо́к; *vt* (*hitch*) зацепля́ть *impf*, зацепи́ть *pf*; (*fasten*) застёгивать *impf*, застегну́ть *pf*.

hooligan /ˈhuːlɪɡən/ *n* хулига́н.

hoop /huːp/ *n* о́бруч.

hoot /huːt/ *vi* (*owl*) у́хать *impf*, у́хнуть *pf*; (*horn*) гуде́ть *impf*. **hooter** /ˈhuːtə(r)/ *n* гудо́к.

hop[1] /hɒp/ *n* (*plant*; *collect*) хмель *m*.

hop[2] /hɒp/ *n* (*jump*) прыжо́к; *vi* пры́гать *impf*, пры́гнуть *pf* (на одно́й ноге́).

hope /həʊp/ *n* наде́жда; *vi* наде́яться *impf*, по~ *pf* (**for** на+*acc*). **hopeful** /-fʊl/ *adj* (*promising*) обнадёживающий; **I am** ~ я наде́юсь. **hopefully** /-fʊlɪ/ *adv* с наде́ждой; (*it is hoped*) на́до наде́яться. **hopeless** /-lɪs/ *adj* безнадёжный.

horde /hɔːd/ *n* (*hist*; *fig*) орда́.

horizon /həˈraɪz(ə)n/ *n* горизо́нт.

horizontal /ˌhɒrɪˈzɒnt(ə)l/ *adj* горизонта́льный.

hormone /ˈhɔːməʊn/ *n* гормо́н.

horn /hɔːn/ *n* рог; (*French horn*) валто́рна; (*car*) гудо́к.

hornet /ˈhɔːnɪt/ *n* ше́ршень *m*.

horny /ˈhɔːnɪ/ *adj* (*calloused*) мозо́листый.

horoscope /ˈhɒrəˌskəʊp/ *n* гороско́п.

horrible, **horrid** /ˈhɒrɪb(ə)l/, /ˈhɒrɪd/ *adj* ужа́сный. **horrify** /ˈhɒrɪfaɪ/ *vt* ужаса́ть *impf*, ужасну́ть *pf*. **horror** /ˈhɒrə(r)/ *n* у́жас.

hors-d'oeuvre /ɔːˈdɜːv/ *n* заку́ска.

horse /hɔːs/ *n* ло́шадь. **horse-chestnut** *n* ко́нский кашта́н. **horseman**, **-woman** *n* вса́дник, -ица. **horseplay** *n* возня́. **horsepower** *n* лошади́ная си́ла. **horse-racing** /ˈhɔːsˌreɪsɪŋ/ *n* ска́чки (-чек) *pl*. **horse-radish** *n* хрен. **horseshoe** *n* подко́ва.

horticulture /ˈhɔːtɪˌkʌltʃə(r)/ *n* садово́дство.

hose /həʊz/ *n* (~**pipe**) шланг.

hosiery /ˈhəʊzɪərɪ/ *n* чуло́чные изде́лия *neut pl*.

hospitable /ˈhɒspɪtəb(ə)l/ *adj* гостеприи́мный.

hospital /ˈhɒspɪt(ə)l/ *n* больни́ца.

hospitality /ˌhɒspɪˈtælɪtɪ/ *n* гостеприи́мство.

host[1] /həʊst/ *n* (*multitude*) мно́жество.

host[2] /həʊst/ *n* (*entertaining*) хозя́ин.

hostage /ˈhɒstɪdʒ/ *n* зало́жник.

hostel /ˈhɒst(ə)l/ *n* общежи́тие.

hostess /ˈhəʊstɪs/ *n* хозя́йка; (*air* ~) стюарде́сса.

hostile /ˈhɒstaɪl/ *adj* вражде́бный. **hostility** /hɒˈstɪlɪtɪ/ *n* вражде́бность; *pl* вое́нные де́йствия *neut pl*.

hot /hɒt/ *adj* горя́чий, жа́ркий; (*pungent*) о́стрый; ~**headed** вспы́льчивый; ~**-water bottle** гре́лка. **hotbed** *n* (*fig*) оча́г. **hothouse** *n* тепли́ца. **hotplate** *n* пли́тка.

hotel /həʊˈtel/ *n* гости́ница.

hound /haʊnd/ *n* охо́тничья соба́ка; *vt* трави́ть *impf*, за~ *pf*.

hour /aʊə(r)/ *n* час. **hourly** /ˈaʊəlɪ/ *adj* ежеча́сный.

house /haʊs/ *n* дом; (*parl*) пала́та; *attrib* дома́шний; *vt* /haʊz/ помеща́ть *impf*, поме-

стить *pf.* household *n* семья́; *adj* хозя́йственный; дома́шний. **house-keeper** /ˈhaʊsˌkiːpə(r)/ *n* эконо́мка. **house-warming** /ˈhaʊsˌwɔːmɪŋ/ *n* новосе́лье. **housewife** *n* хозя́йка. **housework** *n* дома́шняя рабо́та. **housing** /ˈhaʊzɪŋ/ *n* (*accommodation*) жильё; (*casing*) кожу́х; ~ **estate** жило́й масси́в.

hovel /ˈhɒv(ə)l/ *n* лачу́га. **hover** /ˈhɒvə(r)/ *vi* (*bird*) пари́ть *impf*; (*helicopter*) висе́ть *impf*; (*person*) мая́чить *impf*. **hovercraft** *n* су́дно на возду́шной поду́шке, СВП.

how /haʊ/ *adv* как, каки́м о́бразом; ~ **do you do?** здра́вствуйте!; ~ **many,** ~ **much** ско́лько (+*gen*). **however** /haʊˈevə(r)/ *adv* как бы ни (+*past*); *conj* одна́ко, тем не ме́нее; ~ **much** ско́лько бы ни (+*gen & past*).

howl /haʊl/ *n* вой; *vi* выть *impf*. **howler** /ˈhaʊlə(r)/ *n* грубе́йшая оши́бка.

hub /hʌb/ *n* (*of wheel*) ступи́ца; (*fig*) центр, средото́чие.

hubbub /ˈhʌbʌb/ *n* шум, гам.

huddle /ˈhʌd(ə)l/ *vi*: ~ **together** прижима́ться *impf*, прижа́ться *pf* друг к дру́гу.

hue /hjuː/ *n* (*tint*) отте́нок.

huff /hʌf/ *n*: **in a** ~ оскорблённый.

hug /hʌɡ/ *n* объя́тие; *vt* (*embrace*) обнима́ть *impf*, обня́ть *pf*.

huge /hjuːdʒ/ *adj* огро́мный.

hulk /hʌlk/ *n* ко́рпус (корабля́). **hulking** /-kɪŋ/ *adj* (*bulky*) грома́дный; (*clumsy*) неуклю́жий.

hull /hʌl/ *n* (*of ship*) ко́рпус.

hum /hʌm/ *n* жужжа́ние; *vi* (*buzz*) жужжа́ть *impf*; *vt & i*

(*person*) напева́ть *impf*.

human /ˈhjuːmən/ *adj* челове́ческий, людско́й; *n* челове́к. **humane, humanitarian** /hjuːˈmeɪn, hjuːˌmænɪˈteəriən/ *adj* гума́нный. **humanity** /hjuːˈmænɪtɪ/ *n* (*human race*) челове́чество; (*humaneness*) гума́нность; **the Humanities** гуманита́рные нау́ки *f pl*.

humble /ˈhʌmb(ə)l/ *adj* (*person*) смире́нный; (*abode*) скро́мный; *vt* унижа́ть *impf*, уни́зить *pf*.

humdrum /ˈhʌmdrʌm/ *adj* однообра́зный.

humid /ˈhjuːmɪd/ *adj* вла́жный. **humidity** /hjuːˈmɪdɪtɪ/ *n* вла́жность.

humiliate /hjuːˈmɪlɪˌeɪt/ *vt* унижа́ть *impf*, уни́зить *pf*. **humiliation** /-ˈeɪʃ(ə)n/ *n* униже́ние.

humility /hjuːˈmɪlɪtɪ/ *n* смире́ние.

humorous /ˈhjuːmərəs/ *adj* юмористи́ческий. **humour** /ˈhjuːmə(r)/ *n* юмор; (*mood*) настрое́ние; *vt* потака́ть *impf* +*dat*.

hump /hʌmp/ *n* горб; (*of earth*) буго́р.

humus /ˈhjuːməs/ *n* перегно́й.

hunch /hʌntʃ/ *n* (*idea*) предчу́вствие; *vt* го́рбить *impf*, с~ *pf*. **hunchback** *n* (*person*) горбу́н, ~ья. **hunchbacked** /ˈhʌntʃbækt/ *adj* горба́тый.

hundred /ˈhʌndrəd/ *adj & n* сто; ~**s of** со́тни *f pl* +*gen*; **two** ~ две́сти; **three** ~ три́ста; **four** ~ четы́реста; **five** ~ пятьсо́т. **hundredth** /ˈhʌndrədθ/ *adj & n* со́тый.

Hungarian /hʌŋˈɡeəriən/ *n* венгр, венге́рка; *adj* венге́рский. **Hungary** /ˈhʌŋɡəri/ *n* Ве́нгрия.

hunger /'hʌŋgə(r)/ *n* го́лод; *(fig)* жа́жда (for +*gen*); ~ **strike** голодо́вка; *vi* голода́ть *impf*; ~ **for** жа́ждать *impf* +*gen*. **hungry** /'hʌŋgrɪ/ *adj* голо́дный.

hunk /hʌŋk/ *n* ломо́ть *m*.

hunt /hʌnt/ *n* охо́та; *(fig)* по́иски *m pl* (for +*gen*); *vt* охо́титься *impf* на+*acc*, за+*instr*; *(persecute)* трави́ть *impf*, за~ *pf*; ~ **down** вы́следить *pf*; ~ **for** иска́ть *impf* +*acc or gen*; ~ **out** отыска́ть *pf*. **hunter** /-tə(r)/ *n* охо́тник. **hunting** /-tɪŋ/ *n* охо́та.

hurdle /'hɜːd(ə)l/ *n* (sport; fig) барье́р. **hurdler** /'hɜːdlə(r)/ *n* барьери́ст. **hurdles** /'hɜːd(ə)lz/ *n pl* (sport) барье́рный бег.

hurl /hɜːl/ *vt* ~ швыря́ть *impf*, швырну́ть *pf*.

hurly-burly /'hɜːlɪˌbɜːlɪ/ *n* сумато́ха.

hurrah, hurray /hʊˈrɑː, hʊˈreɪ/ *int* ура́!

hurricane /'hʌrɪkən/ *n* урага́н.

hurried /'hʌrɪd/ *adj* торопли́вый. **hurry** /'hʌrɪ/ *n* спе́шка; **be in a** ~ спеши́ть *impf*; *vt & i* торопи́ть(ся) *impf*, по~ *pf*; *vi* спеши́ть *impf*, по~ *pf*.

hurt /hɜːt/ *n* уще́рб; *vi* боле́ть *impf*; *vt* повреди́ть *impf*, повреди́ть *pf*; *(offend)* обижа́ть *impf*, оби́деть *pf*.

hurtle /'hɜːt(ə)l/ *vi* нести́сь *impf*, по~ *pf*.

husband /'hʌzbənd/ *n* муж.

hush /hʌʃ/ *n* тишина́; *vt*: ~ **up** замина́ть *impf*, замя́ть *pf*; *int* ти́ше!

husk /hʌsk/ *n* шелуха́.

husky /'hʌskɪ/ *adj* (voice) хри́плый.

hustle /'hʌs(ə)l/ *n* толкотня́; *vt* (push) затолка́ть *impf*, затолкну́ть *pf*; (herd people) заго-

ня́ть *impf*, загна́ть *pf*; *vt & i* (hurry) торопи́ть(ся) *impf*, по~ *pf*.

hut /hʌt/ *n* хи́жина.

hutch /hʌtʃ/ *n* кле́тка.

hyacinth /'haɪəsɪnθ/ *n* гиаци́нт.

hybrid /'haɪbrɪd/ *n* гибри́д; *adj* гибри́дный.

hydrangea /haɪˈdreɪndʒə/ *n* горте́нзия.

hydrant /'haɪdrənt/ *n* гидра́нт.

hydraulic /haɪˈdrɒlɪk/ *adj* гидравли́ческий.

hydrochloric acid /ˌhaɪdrə'klɔːrɪk 'æsɪd/ *n* соляна́я кислота́. **hydroelectric** /ˌhaɪdrəʊɪ'lektrɪk/ *adj* гидроэлектри́ческий; ~ **power station** гидроэлектроста́нция, ГЭС *f indecl*. **hydrofoil** /'haɪdrə‚fɔɪl/ *n* су́дно на подво́дных кры́льях, СПК. **hydrogen** /'haɪdrədʒ(ə)n/ *n* водоро́д.

hyena /haɪˈiːnə/ *n* гие́на.

hygiene /'haɪdʒiːn/ *n* гигие́на. **hygienic** /-'dʒiːnɪk/ *adj* гигиени́ческий.

hymn /hɪm/ *n* гимн.

hyperbole /haɪˈpɜːbəlɪ/ *n* гипе́рбола.

hyphen /'haɪf(ə)n/ *n* дефи́с. **hyphen(ate)** /'haɪfəˌneɪt/ *vt* писа́ть *impf*, на~ *pf* че́рез дефи́с.

hypnosis /hɪp'nəʊsɪs/ *n* гипно́з. **hypnotic** /hɪp'nɒtɪk/ *adj* гипноти́ческий. **hypnotism** /'hɪpnəˌtɪz(ə)m/ *n* гипноти́зм. **hypnotist** /'hɪpnətɪst/ *n* гипнотизёр. **hypnotize** /'hɪpnəˌtaɪz/ *vt* гипнотизи́ровать *impf*, за~ *pf*.

hypochondria /ˌhaɪpə'kɒndrɪə/ *n* ипохо́ндрия. **hypochondriac** /-rɪˌæk/ *n* ипохо́ндрик.

hypocrisy /hɪ'pɒkrɪsɪ/ *n* лицеме́рие. **hypocrite** /'hɪpəkrɪt/ *n* лицеме́р. **hypocritical** /ˌhɪpə'krɪtɪk(ə)l/ *adj* лицеме́рный.

hypodermic /ˌhaɪpəˈdɜːmɪk/ adj подкожный.

hypothesis /haɪˈpɒθɪsɪs/ n гипотеза. **hypothesize** /-ˈpɒθɪˌsaɪz/ vi строить impf, по~ pf гипотезу. **hypothetical** /ˌhaɪpəˈθetɪk(ə)l/ adj гипотетический.

hysterectomy /ˌhɪstəˈrektəmɪ/ n гистерэктомия, удаление матки.

hysteria /hɪˈstɪərɪə/ n истерия. **hysterical** /-ˈsterɪk(ə)l/ adj истерический. **hysterics** /-ˈsterɪks/ n pl истерика.

I

I /aɪ/ pron я.

ibid(em) /ˈɪbɪˌd(em)/ adv там же.

ice /aɪs/ n лёд; ~age ледниковый период; ~axe ледоруб; ~cream мороженое sb; ~hockey хоккей (с шайбой); ~rink каток; ~ skate конёк; vi кататься impf на коньках; pf (chill) замораживать impf, заморозить pf; (cul) глазировать impf & pf; vi: ~ over, up обледеневать impf, обледенеть pf. **iceberg** /ˈaɪsbɜːg/ n айсберг. **icicle** /ˈaɪsɪk(ə)l/ n сосулька. **icing** /ˈaɪsɪŋ/ n (cul) глазурь. **icy** /ˈaɪsɪ/ adj ледяной.

icon /ˈaɪkɒn/ n икона.

ID abbr (of identification) удостоверение личности.

idea /aɪˈdɪə/ n идея, мысль; (conception) понятие.

ideal /aɪˈdɪːəl/ n идеал; adj идеальный. **idealism** /-ˈdɪːəˌlɪz(ə)m/ n идеализм. **idealist** /-ˈdɪːəlɪst/ n идеалист. **idealize** /-ˈdɪːəˌlaɪz/ vt идеализировать

impf & pf.

identical /aɪˈdentɪk(ə)l/ adj тождественный, одинаковый. **identification** /aɪˌdentɪfɪˈkeɪʃ(ə)n/ n (recognition) опознание; (of person) установление личности. **identify** /aɪˈdentɪˌfaɪ/ vt опознавать impf, опознать pf. **identity** /aɪˈdentɪtɪ/ n (of person) личность; ~ card удостоверение личности.

ideological /ˌaɪdɪəˈlɒdʒɪk(ə)l/ adj идеологический. **ideology** /ˌaɪdɪˈɒlədʒɪ/ n идеология.

idiom /ˈɪdɪəm/ n идиома. **idiomatic** /-ˈmætɪk/ adj идиоматический.

idiosyncrasy /ˌɪdɪəˈsɪŋkrəsɪ/ n идиосинкразия.

idiot /ˈɪdɪət/ n идиот. **idiotic** /-ˈɒtɪk/ adj идиотский.

idle /ˈaɪd(ə)l/ adj (unoccupied; lazy; purposeless) праздный; (vain) тщетный; (empty) пустой; (machine) недействующий; vi бездельничать impf; (engine) работать impf вхолостую; vt: ~ away праздно проводить impf, провести pf. **idleness** /-nɪs/ n праздность.

idol /ˈaɪd(ə)l/ n идол. **idolatry** /aɪˈdɒlətrɪ/ n идолопоклонство; (fig) обожание. **idolize** /ˈaɪdəˌlaɪz/ vt боготворить impf.

idyll /ˈɪdɪl/ n идиллия. **idyllic** /ɪˈdɪlɪk/ adj идиллический.

i.e. abbr т.е., то есть.

if /ɪf/ conj если, если бы; (whether) ли; as ~ как будто; even ~ даже если; ~ only если бы только.

ignite /ɪgˈnaɪt/ vt зажигать impf, зажечь pf; vi загораться impf, загореться pf. **ignition** /-ˈnɪʃ(ə)n/ n зажигание.

ignoble /ɪgˈnəʊb(ə)l/ adj низкий.

ignominious /ˌɪgnəˈmɪnɪəs/ adj позо́рный.

ignoramus /ˌɪgnəˈreɪməs/ n невѣжда m. **ignorance** /ˈɪgnərəns/ n невѣжество, (of certain facts) невѣдение. **ignorant** /ˈɪgnərənt/ adj невѣжественный, (uninformed) несвѣдущий (of в+prep).

ignore /ɪgˈnɔː(r)/ vt не обраща́ть impf внима́ния на+acc; игнори́ровать impf & pf.

ilk /ɪlk/ n: of that ~ тако́го ро́да.

ill /ɪl/ n (evil) зло; (harm) вред; pl (misfortunes) несча́стья (-тий) pl; (sick) больно́й; (bad) дурно́й; adv пло́хо, ду́рно; fall ~ заболѣва́ть impf, заболѣ́ть pf; **~-advised** неблагоразу́мный; **~-mannered** невѣ́жливый; **~-treat** vt пло́хо обраща́ться impf c+instr.

illegal /ɪˈliːg(ə)l/ adj нелега́льный. **illegality** /ˌɪliːˈgælɪtɪ/ n незако́нность, нелега́льность.

illegible /ɪˈledʒɪb(ə)l/ adj неразбо́рчивый.

illegitimacy /ˌɪlɪˈdʒɪtɪməsɪ/ n незако́нность, (of child) незаконноро́жденность. **illegitimate** /-mət/ adj незако́нный, незаконноро́жденный.

illicit /ɪˈlɪsɪt/ adj незако́нный, недозво́ленный.

illiteracy /ɪˈlɪtərəsɪ/ n негра́мотность. **illiterate** /-rət/ adj негра́мотный.

illness /ˈɪlnɪs/ n болѣ́знь.

illogical /ɪˈlɒdʒɪk(ə)l/ adj нелоги́чный.

illuminate /ɪˈluːmɪneɪt/ vt освѣща́ть impf, освѣти́ть pf. **illumination** /-ˈneɪʃ(ə)n/ n освѣще́ние.

illusion /ɪˈluːʒ(ə)n/ n иллю́зия. **illusory** /ɪˈluːsərɪ/ adj иллю́зорный.

illustrate /ˈɪləˌstreɪt/ vt иллюстри́ровать impf & pf, про-~ pf. **illustration** /-ˈstreɪʃ(ə)n/ n иллюстра́ция. **illustrative** /ˈɪləstrətɪv/ adj иллюстрати́вный.

illustrious /ɪˈlʌstrɪəs/ adj знамени́тый.

image /ˈɪmɪdʒ/ n (phys; statue etc.) изображе́ние; (optical ~) отраже́ние; (likeness) ко́пия; (metaphor, conception) о́браз; (reputation) репута́ция. **imagery** /-dʒərɪ/ n о́бразность.

imaginable /ɪˈmædʒɪnəb(ə)l/ adj вообрази́мый. **imaginary** /-ˈmædʒɪnərɪ/ adj вообража́емый. **imagination** /-ˈneɪʃ(ə)n/ n воображе́ние. **imagine** /ɪˈmædʒɪn/ vt вообража́ть impf, вообрази́ть pf; (conceive) представля́ть impf, предста́вить pf себе́.

imbecile /ˈɪmbɪˌsiːl/ n слабоу́мный sb; (fool) глупе́ц.

imbibe /ɪmˈbaɪb/ vt (absorb) впи́тывать impf, впита́ть pf.

imbue /ɪmˈbjuː/ vt внуша́ть impf, внуши́ть pf +dat (with +acc).

imitate /ˈɪmɪˌteɪt/ vt подража́ть impf +dat. **imitation** /-ˈteɪʃ(ə)n/ n подража́ние (of +dat); attrib иску́сственный. **imitative** /ˈɪmɪtətɪv/ adj подража́тельный.

immaculate /ɪˈmækjʊlət/ adj безупре́чный.

immaterial /ˌɪməˈtɪərɪəl/ adj (unimportant) несуще́ственный.

immature /ˌɪməˈtjʊə(r)/ adj незрѣ́лый.

immeasurable /ɪˈmeʒərəb(ə)l/ adj неизмери́мый.

immediate /ɪˈmiːdɪət/ adj (direct) непосре́дственный; (swift) немѣ́дленный. **immediately** /-lɪ/

adv тотчас, сразу.

immemorial /ˌɪmɪ'mɔːrɪəl/ *adj*: from time ~ с незапамятных времён.

immense /ɪ'mens/ *adj* огромный.

immerse /ɪ'mɜːs/ *vt* погружать *impf*, погрузить *pf*. **immersion** /ɪ'mɜːʃ(ə)n/ *n* погружение.

immigrant /'ɪmɪɡrənt/ *n* иммигрант, ~ка. **immigration** /-'ɡreɪʃ(ə)n/ *n* иммиграция.

imminent /'ɪmɪnənt/ *adj* надвигающийся; (*danger*) грозящий.

immobile /ɪ'məʊbaɪl/ *adj* неподвижный. **immobilize** /-bɪˌlaɪz/ *vt* парализовать *impf & pf*.

immoderate /ɪ'mɒdərət/ *adj* неумеренный.

immodest /ɪ'mɒdɪst/ *adj* нескромный.

immoral /ɪ'mɒr(ə)l/ *adj* безнравственный. **immorality** /ˌɪmə' rælɪtɪ/ *n* безнравственность.

immortal /ɪ'mɔːt(ə)l/ *adj* бессмертный. **immortality** /ˌɪmɔː'tælɪtɪ/ *n* бессмертие. **immortalize** /ɪ'mɔːtəˌlaɪz/ *vt* обессмертить *pf*.

immovable /ɪ'muːvəb(ə)l/ *adj* неподвижный; (*fig*) непоколебимый.

immune /ɪ'mjuːn/ *adj* (*to illness*) невосприимчивый (**to** к+*dat*); (*free from*) свободный (**from** от+*gen*). **immunity** /ɪ'mjuːnɪtɪ/ *n* иммунитет (**from** к+*dat*); освобождение (**from** от+*gen*). **immunize** /'ɪmjuːˌnaɪz/ *vt* иммунизировать *impf & pf*.

immutable /ɪ'mjuːtəb(ə)l/ *adj* неизменный.

imp /ɪmp/ *n* бесёнок.

impact /'ɪmpækt/ *n* удар; (*fig*) влияние.

impair /ɪm'peə(r)/ *vt* вредить *impf*, по~ *pf*.

impale /ɪm'peɪl/ *vt* протыкать *impf*, проткнуть *pf*.

impart /ɪm'pɑːt/ *vt* делиться *impf*, по~ *pf* +*instr* (**to** с+*instr*).

impartial /ɪm'pɑːʃ(ə)l/ *adj* беспристрастный.

impassable /ɪm'pɑːsəb(ə)l/ *adj* непроходимый; (*for vehicles*) непроезжий.

impasse /'æmpæs/ *n* тупик.

impassioned /ɪm'pæʃ(ə)nd/ *adj* страстный.

impassive /ɪm'pæsɪv/ *adj* бесстрастный.

impatience /ɪm'peɪʃəns/ *n* нетерпение. **impatient** /-ʃənt/ *adj* нетерпеливый.

impeach /ɪm'piːtʃ/ *vt* обвинять *impf*, обвинить *pf* (**for** в+*prep*).

impeccable /ɪm'pekəb(ə)l/ *adj* безупречный.

impecunious /ˌɪmpɪ'kjuːnɪəs/ *adj* безденежный.

impedance /ɪm'piːd(ə)ns/ *n* полное сопротивление. **impede** /-'piːd/ *vt* препятствовать *impf*, вос~ *pf* +*dat*. **impediment** /-'pedɪmənt/ *n* препятствие; (*in speech*) заикание.

impel /ɪm'pel/ *vt* побуждать *impf*, побудить *pf* (**to** +*inf*, к+*dat*).

impending /ɪm'pendɪŋ/ *adj* предстоящий.

impenetrable /ɪm'penɪtrəb(ə)l/ *adj* непроницаемый.

imperative /ɪm'perətɪv/ *adj* необходимый; *n* (*gram*) повелительное наклонение.

imperceptible /ˌɪmpə'septɪb(ə)l/ *adj* незаметный.

imperfect /ɪm'pɜːfɪkt/ *n* имперфект; *adj* несовершенный. **imperfection** /ˌɪmpə'fekʃ(ə)n/ *n* несовершенство; (*fault*) недостаток. **imperfective** /ˌɪmpə

'fektɪv/ *adj* (*n*) несовершённый (вид).

imperial /ɪm'pɪərɪəl/ *adj* импéрский. **imperialism** /-'pɪərɪə,lɪz(ə)n/ *n* империали́зм. **imperialist** /-'pɪərɪəlɪst/ *n* империали́ст; *attrib* империалисти́ческий.

imperil /ɪm'perɪl/ *vt* подверга́ть *impf*, подве́ргнуть *pf* опа́сности.

imperious /ɪm'pɪərɪəs/ *adj* вла́стный.

impersonal /ɪm'pɜːsən(ə)l/ *adj* безли́чный.

impersonate /ɪm'pɜːsə,neɪt/ *vt* (*imitate*) подража́ть *impf*; (*pretend to be*) выдава́ть *impf*, вы́дать *pf* себя́ за+*acc*. **impersonation** /-'neɪʃ(ə)n/ *n* подража́ние.

impertinence /ɪm'pɜːtɪnəns/ *n* де́рзость. **impertinent** /-nənt/ *adj* де́рзкий.

imperturbable /,ɪmpə'tɜːbəb(ə)l/ *adj* невозмути́мый.

impervious /ɪm'pɜːvɪəs/ *adj* (*fig*) глухо́й (**to** к+*dat*).

impetuous /ɪm'petjʊəs/ *adj* стреми́тельный.

impetus /'ɪmpɪtəs/ *n* дви́жущая си́ла.

impinge /ɪm'pɪndʒ/ *vi*: ~ (**up)on** ока́зывать *impf*, оказа́ть *pf* (отрица́тельный) эффéкт на+*acc*.

implacable /ɪm'plækəb(ə)l/ *adj* неумоли́мый.

implant /ɪm'plɑːnt/ *vt* вводи́ть *impf*, ввести́ *pf*; (*fig*) се́ять *impf*, по~ *pf*.

implement¹ /'ɪmplɪmənt/ *n* ору́дие, инструме́нт.

implement² /'ɪmplɪ,ment/ *vt* (*fulfil*) выполня́ть *impf*, вы́полнить *pf*.

implicate /'ɪmplɪ,keɪt/ *vt* впу́ты-

вать *impf*, впу́тать *pf*. **implication** /-'keɪʃ(ə)n/ *n* (*inference*) намёк; *pl* значе́ние.

implicit /ɪm'plɪsɪt/ *adj* подразумева́емый; (*absolute*) безоговóрочный.

implore /ɪm'plɔː(r)/ *vt* умоля́ть *impf*.

imply /ɪm'plaɪ/ *vt* подразумева́ть *impf*.

impolite /,ɪmpə'laɪt/ *adj* невéжливый.

imponderable /ɪm'pɒndərəb(ə)l/ *adj* неопределённый.

import *n* /'ɪmpɔːt/ (*meaning*) значе́ние; (*of goods*) и́мпорт; *vt* /ɪm'pɔːt/ импорти́ровать *impf* & *pf*. **importer** /ɪm'pɔːtə(r)/ *n* импортёр.

importance /ɪm'pɔːt(ə)ns/ *n* ва́жность. **important** /-t(ə)nt/ *adj* ва́жный.

impose /ɪm'pəʊz/ *vt* (*tax*) облага́ть *impf*, обложи́ть *pf* +*instr* (**on** +*acc*); (*obligation*) налага́ть *impf*, наложи́ть *pf* (**on** на+*acc*); ~ (**o.s.**) **on** налега́ть *impf* на+*acc*. **imposing** /-'pəʊzɪŋ/ *adj* внуши́тельный. **imposition** /,ɪmpə'zɪʃ(ə)n/ *n* обложе́ние, наложе́ние.

impossibility /ɪm,pɒsɪ'bɪlɪtɪ/ *n* невозмо́жность. **impossible** /ɪm'pɒsɪb(ə)l/ *adj* невозмо́жный.

impostor /ɪm'pɒstə(r)/ *n* самозва́нец.

impotence /'ɪmpət(ə)ns/ *n* бесси́лие; (*med*) импотéнция. **impotent** /-t(ə)nt/ *adj* бесси́льный; (*med*) импотéнтный.

impound /ɪm'paʊnd/ *vt* (*confiscate*) конфискова́ть *impf* & *pf*.

impoverished /ɪm'pɒvərɪʃt/ *adj* обедне́вший.

impracticable /ɪm'præktɪkəb(ə)l/

adj невыполни́мый.

imprecise /ˌɪmprɪˈsaɪs/ *n* неточный.

impregnable /ɪmˈpregnəb(ə)l/ *adj* непристу́пный.

impregnate /ˈɪmpregˌneɪt/ *vt* (*fertilize*) оплодотвори́ть *impf*, оплодотвори́ть *pf*; (*saturate*) пропи́тывать *impf*, пропита́ть *pf*.

impresario /ˌɪmprɪˈsɑːrɪəʊ/ *n* аге́нт.

impress *vt* /ɪmˈpres/ производи́ть *impf*, произвести́ *pf* (како́е-либо) впечатле́ние на+*acc*; ~ **upon** (s.o.) внуша́ть *impf*, внуши́ть *pf* (+*dat*). **impression** /-ˈpreʃ(ə)n/ *n* впечатле́ние; (*imprint*) отпеча́ток; (*reprint*) (стереоти́пное) изда́ние.

impressionism /ɪmˈpreʃənɪz(ə)m/ *n* импрессиони́зм. **impressionist** /-nɪst/ *n* импрессиони́ст.

impressive /ɪmˈpresɪv/ *adj* впечатля́ющий.

imprint *n* /ˈɪmprɪnt/ отпеча́ток; *vt* /ɪmˈprɪnt/ отпеча́тывать *impf*, отпеча́тать *pf*; (*on memory*) запечатлева́ть *impf*, запечатле́ть *pf*.

imprison /ɪmˈprɪz(ə)n/ *vt* заключа́ть *impf*, заключи́ть *pf* (в тюрьму́). **imprisonment** /-mənt/ *n* тюре́мное заключе́ние.

improbable /ɪmˈprɒbəb(ə)l/ *adj* невероя́тный.

impromptu /ɪmˈprɒmptjuː/ *adj* импровизи́рованный; *adv* без подгото́вки, экспро́мтом.

improper /ɪmˈprɒpə(r)/ *adj* (*incorrect*) непра́вильный; (*indecent*) неприли́чный. **impropriety** /ˌɪmprəˈpraɪətɪ/ *n* неуме́стность.

improve /ɪmˈpruːv/ *vt* & *i* улучша́ть(ся) *impf*, улу́чшить(ся) *pf*. **improvement** /-mənt/ *n* улучше́ние.

improvisation /ˌɪmprəvaɪˈzeɪʃ(ə)n/ *n* импровиза́ция. **improvise** /ˈɪmprəˌvaɪz/ *vt* импровизи́ровать *impf*, сымпровизи́ровать *pf*.

imprudent /ɪmˈpruːd(ə)nt/ *adj* неосторо́жный.

impudence /ˈɪmpjʊd(ə)ns/ *n* на́глость. **impudent** /-d(ə)nt/ *adj* на́глый.

impulse /ˈɪmpʌls/ *n* толчо́к, и́мпульс; (*sudden tendency*) поры́в. **impulsive** /ɪmˈpʌlsɪv/ *adj* импульси́вный.

impunity /ɪmˈpjuːnɪtɪ/ *n*: **with** ~ безнака́занно.

impure /ɪmˈpjʊə(r)/ *adj* нечи́стый.

impute /ɪmˈpjuːt/ *vt* припи́сывать *impf*, приписа́ть *pf* (**to** +*dat*).

in /ɪn/ *prep* (*place*) в+*prep*, на +*prep*; (*into*) в+*acc*, на+*acc*; (*point in time*) в+*prep*, на+*prep*; **in the morning** (*etc.*) у́тром (*instr*); **in spring** (*etc.*) весно́й (*instr*); (*at some stage in*: *throughout*) во вре́мя +*gen*; (*duration*) за+*acc*; (*after interval of*) че́рез+*acc*; (*during course of*) в тече́ние+*gen*; (*circumstance*) в+*prep*, при+*prep*; *adv* (*place*) внутри́; (*motion*) внутрь; (*at home*) до́ма; (*in fashion*) в мо́де; **in here, there** (*place*) здесь, там; (*motion*) сюда́, туда́; *adj* вну́тренний; (*fashionable*) мо́дный; *n*: **the ins and outs** все ходы́ и вы́ходы.

inability /ˌɪnəˈbɪlɪtɪ/ *n* неспосо́бность.

inaccessible /ˌɪnækˈsesɪb(ə)l/ *adj* недосту́пный.

inaccurate /ɪn'ækjʊrət/ adj неточный.

inaction /ɪn'ækʃ(ə)n/ n бездействие. **inactive** /-'æktɪv/ adj бездействующий. **inactivity** /ˌɪnæk'tɪvɪtɪ/ n бездействие.

inadequate /ɪn'ædɪkwət/ adj недостаточный.

inadmissible /ˌɪnəd'mɪsɪb(ə)l/ adj недопустимый.

inadvertent /ˌɪnəd'vɜːt(ə)nt/ adj нечаянный.

inalienable /ɪn'eɪlɪənəb(ə)l/ adj неотъемлемый.

inane /ɪ'neɪn/ adj глупый.

inanimate /ɪn'ænɪmət/ adj неодушевлённый.

inappropriate /ˌɪnə'prəʊprɪət/ adj неуместный.

inarticulate /ˌɪnɑː'tɪkjʊlət/ adj (person) косноязычный; (indistinct) невнятный.

inasmuch /ˌɪnəz'mʌtʃ/ adv: ~ **as** так как; ввиду того, что.

inattentive /ˌɪnə'tentɪv/ adj невнимательный.

inaudible /ɪn'ɔːdɪb(ə)l/ adj неслышный.

inaugural /ɪ'nɔːɡjʊr(ə)l/ adj вступительный. **inaugurate** /-reɪt/ vt (admit to office) торжественно вводить impf, ввести pf в должность; (open) открывать impf, открыть pf; (introduce) вводить impf, ввести pf. **inauguration** /-'reɪʃ(ə)n/ n введение в должность; открытие; начало.

inauspicious /ˌɪnɔː'spɪʃəs/ adj неблагоприятный.

inborn, inbred /'ɪnbɔːn, 'ɪnbred/ adj врождённый.

incalculable /ɪn'kælkjʊləb(ə)l/ adj неисчислимый.

incandescent /ˌɪnkæn'des(ə)nt/ adj накалённый.

incantation /ˌɪnkæn'teɪʃ(ə)n/ n заклинание.

incapability /ˌɪnˌkeɪpə'bɪlɪtɪ/ n неспособность. **incapable** /ɪn'keɪpəb(ə)l/ adj неспособный (of к+dat, на+acc).

incapacitate /ˌɪnkə'pæsɪˌteɪt/ vt делать impf, с~ pf неспособным. **incapacity** /-'pæsɪtɪ/ n неспособность.

incarcerate /ɪn'kɑːsəˌreɪt/ vt заключать impf, заключить pf в тюрьму. **incarceration** /-'reɪʃ(ə)n/ n заключение (в тюрьму).

incarnate /ɪn'kɑːnət/ adj воплощённый. **incarnation** /-'neɪʃ(ə)n/ n воплощение.

incendiary /ɪn'sendɪərɪ/ adj зажигательный.

incense[1] /'ɪnsens/ n фимиам, ладан.

incense[2] /ɪn'sens/ vt разгневать pf.

incentive /ɪn'sentɪv/ n побуждение.

inception /ɪn'sepʃ(ə)n/ n начало.

incessant /ɪn'ses(ə)nt/ adj непрестанный.

incest /'ɪnsest/ n кровосмешение.

inch /ɪntʃ/ n дюйм; ~ **by** ~ мало-помалу; vi ползти impf.

incidence /'ɪnsɪd(ə)ns/ n (phys) падение; (prevalence) распространение. **incident** /-d(ə)nt/ n случай, инцидент. **incidental** /ˌɪnsɪ'dent(ə)l/ adj (casual) случайный; (inessential) несущественный. **incidentally** /-lɪ/ adv между прочим.

incinerate /ɪn'sɪnəˌreɪt/ vt испепелять impf, испепелить pf. **incinerator** /-tə(r)/ n мусоросжигательная печь.

incipient /ɪn'sɪpɪənt/ adj начинающийся.

incision /ɪn'sɪʒ(ə)n/ *n* надре́з (**in** на+*acc*). **incisive** /ɪn'saɪsɪv/ *adj* (*fig*) о́стрый. **incisor** /ɪn'saɪzə(r)/ *n* резе́ц.

incite /ɪn'saɪt/ *vt* подстрека́ть *impf*, подстрекну́ть *pf* (**to** к+*dat*). **incitement** /-mənt/ *n* подстрека́тельство.

inclement /ɪn'klemənt/ *adj* суро́вый.

inclination /ˌɪnklɪ'neɪʃ(ə)n/ *n* (*slope*) накло́н; (*propensity*) скло́нность (**for, to** к+*dat*). **incline** *n* /'ɪnklaɪn/ накло́н; *vt & i* /ɪn'klaɪn/ склоня́ть(ся) *impf*, склони́ть(ся) *pf*. **inclined** /ɪn'klaɪnd/ *predic* (*disposed*) скло́нен (-онна́, -о́нно) (**to** к+*dat*).

include /ɪn'kluːd/ *vt* включа́ть *impf*, включи́ть *pf* (**in** в+*acc*); (*contain*) заключа́ть *impf*, заключи́ть *pf* в себе́. **including** /-'kluːdɪŋ/ *prep* включа́я+*acc*. **inclusion** /-'kluːʒ(ə)n/ *n* включе́ние. **inclusive** /-'kluːsɪv/ *adj* включа́ющий (в себе́); *adv* включи́тельно.

incognito /ˌɪnkɒg'niːtəʊ/ *adv* инко́гнито.

incoherent /ˌɪnkəʊ'hɪərənt/ *adj* бессвя́зный.

income /'ɪnkʌm/ *n* дохо́д; ~ **tax** подохо́дный нало́г.

incommensurate /ˌɪnkə'menʃərət/ *adj* несоразме́рный.

incomparable /ɪn'kɒmpərəb(ə)l/ *adj* несравни́мый (**to, with** с+*instr*); (*matchless*) несравне́нный.

incompatible /ˌɪnkəm'pætɪb(ə)l/ *adj* несовмести́мый.

incompetence /ɪn'kɒmpɪt(ə)ns/ *n* некомпете́нтность. **incompetent** /-t(ə)nt/ *adj* некомпете́нтный.

incomplete /ˌɪnkəm'pliːt/ *adj* непо́лный, незако́нченный.

incomprehensible /ˌɪnkɒmprɪ'hensɪb(ə)l/ *adj* непоня́тный.

inconceivable /ˌɪnkən'siːvəb(ə)l/ *adj* невообрази́мый.

inconclusive /ˌɪnkən'kluːsɪv/ *adj* (*evidence*) недоста́точный; (*results*) неопределённый.

incongruity /ˌɪnkɒn'gruːɪtɪ/ *n* несоотве́тствие. **incongruous** /ɪn'kɒŋgrʊəs/ *adj* несоотве́тствующий.

inconsequential /ˌɪnkɒnsɪ'kwenʃ(ə)l/ *adj* незначи́тельный.

inconsiderable /ˌɪnkən'sɪdərəb(ə)l/ *adj* незначи́тельный.

inconsiderate /ˌɪnkən'sɪdərət/ *adj* невнима́тельный.

inconsistency /ˌɪnkən'sɪst(ə)nsɪ/ *n* непосле́довательность. **inconsistent** /-t(ə)nt/ *adj* непосле́довательный.

inconsolable /ˌɪnkən'səʊləb(ə)l/ *adj* безуте́шный.

inconspicuous /ˌɪnkən'spɪkjʊəs/ *adj* незаме́тный.

incontinence /ɪn'kɒntɪnəns/ *n* (*med*) недержа́ние. **incontinent** /-nənt/ *adj*: **be** ~ страда́ть *impf* недержа́нием.

incontrovertible /ˌɪnkɒntrə'vɜːtɪb(ə)l/ *adj* неопроверж́имый.

inconvenience /ˌɪnkən'viːnɪəns/ *n* неудо́бство; *vt* затрудня́ть *impf*, затрудни́ть *pf*. **inconvenient** /-ənt/ *adj* неудо́бный.

incorporate /ɪn'kɔːpəˌreɪt/ *vt* (*include*) включа́ть *impf*, включи́ть *pf*; (*unite*) объединя́ть *impf*, объедини́ть *pf*.

incorrect /ˌɪnkə'rekt/ *adj* непра́вильный.

incorrigible /ɪn'kɒrɪdʒɪb(ə)l/ *adj* неисправи́мый.

incorruptible /ˌɪnkə'rʌptɪb(ə)l/

adj неподку́пный.

increase *n* /'ɪnkriːs/ рост, увеличе́ние; (*in pay etc.*) приба́вка; *vt* & *i* /ɪn'kriːs/ увели́чивать(ся) *impf*, увели́чить(ся) *pf*.

incredible /ɪn'kredɪb(ə)l/ *adj* невероя́тный.

incredulous /ɪn'kredjʊləs/ *adj* недове́рчивый.

increment /'ɪnkrɪmənt/ *n* приба́вка.

incriminate /ɪn'krɪmɪˌneɪt/ *vt* изоблича́ть *impf*, изоблачи́ть *pf*.

incubate /'ɪŋkjʊbeɪt/ *vt* (*eggs*) выводи́ть *impf*, вы́вести *pf* (в инкуба́тор). **incubator** /-tə(r)/ *n* инкуба́тор.

inculcate /'ɪnkʌlˌkeɪt/ *vt* внедря́ть *impf*, внедри́ть *pf*.

incumbent /ɪn'kʌmbənt/ *adj* (*in office*) стоя́щий у вла́сти; **it is ~ (up)on you** вы обя́заны.

incur /ɪn'kɜː(r)/ *vt* навлека́ть *impf*, навле́чь *pf* на себя́.

incurable /ɪn'kjʊərəb(ə)l/ *adj* неизлечи́мый.

incursion /ɪn'kɜːʃ(ə)n/ *n* (*invasion*) вторже́ние; (*attack*) набе́г.

indebted /ɪn'detɪd/ *predic* в долгу́ (**to** *to*+*gen*).

indecency /ɪn'diːs(ə)nsɪ/ *n* неприли́чие. **indecent** /-'diːs(ə)nt/ *adj* неприли́чный.

indecision /ˌɪndɪ'sɪʒ(ə)n/ *n* нереши́тельность. **indecisive** /-'saɪsɪv/ *adj* нереши́тельный.

indeclinable /ˌɪndɪ'klaɪnəb(ə)l/ *adj* несклоня́емый.

indeed /ɪn'diːd/ *adv* в са́мом де́ле, действи́тельно; (*interrog*) неужели?

indefatigable /ˌɪndɪ'fætɪɡəb(ə)l/ *adj* неутоми́мый.

indefensible /ˌɪndɪ'fensɪb(ə)l/ *adj* не име́ющий оправда́ния.

indefinable /ˌɪndɪ'faɪnəb(ə)l/ *adj* неопредели́мый. **indefinite** /ɪn'defɪnɪt/ *adj* неопределённый.

indelible /ɪn'delɪb(ə)l/ *adj* несмыва́емый.

indemnify /ɪn'demnɪˌfaɪ/ *vt*: **~ against** страхова́ть *impf*, за~ от+*gen*; **~ for** (*compensate*) компенси́ровать *impf* & *pf*. **indemnity** /-'demnɪtɪ/ *n* (*against loss*) гара́нтия от убы́тков; (*compensation*) компенса́ция.

indent /ɪn'dent/ *vt* (*printing*) писа́ть *impf*, c~ *pf* с отсту́пом. **indentation** /-'teɪʃ(ə)n/ *n* (*notch*) зубе́ц; (*printing*) отсту́п.

independence /ˌɪndɪ'pend(ə)ns/ *n* незави́симость, самостоя́тельность. **independent** /-d(ə)nt/ *adj* незави́симый, самостоя́тельный.

indescribable /ˌɪndɪ'skraɪbə b(ə)l/ *adj* неопису́емый.

indestructible /ˌɪndɪ'strʌktɪb(ə)l/ *adj* неразруши́мый.

indeterminate /ˌɪndɪ'tɜːmɪnət/ *adj* неопределённый.

index /'ɪndeks/ *n* (*alphabetical*) указа́тель *m*; (*econ*) и́ндекс; (*pointer*) стре́лка; **~ finger** указа́тельный па́лец.

India /'ɪndɪə/ *n* Индия. **Indian** /-ən/ *n* инди́ец, индиа́нка; (*American*) инде́ец, индиа́нка; *adj* инди́йский; (*American*) инде́йский; **~ summer** ба́бье ле́то.

indicate /'ɪndɪˌkeɪt/ *vt* ука́зывать *impf*, указа́ть *pf*; (*be a sign of*) свиде́тельствовать *impf* о+*prep*. **indication** /-'keɪʃ(ə)n/ *n* указа́ние; (*sign*) при́знак. **indicative** /ɪn'dɪkətɪv/ *adj* изъяви́тельный; *n* изъяви́тельное наклоне́ние /'ɪndɪ ˌkeɪtə(r)/ *n* указа́тель *m*.

indict /ɪn'daɪt/ *vt* обвиня́ть

обвини́ть pf (for в+prep).
indifference /ɪnˈdɪfrəns/ n равноду́шие. **indifferent** /-frənt/ adj равноду́шный; (mediocre) посре́дственный.

indigenous /ɪnˈdɪdʒɪnəs/ adj тузе́мный.

indigestible /ˌɪndɪˈdʒestɪb(ə)l/ adj неудобовари́мый. **indigestion** /-ˈdʒestʃ(ə)n/ n несваре́ние желу́дка.

indignant /ɪnˈdɪgnənt/ adj негоду́ющий; be ~ негодова́ть impf (with на+acc). **indignation** /-ˈneɪʃ(ə)n/ n негодова́ние.

indignity /ɪnˈdɪgnɪtɪ/ n оскорбле́ние.

indirect /ˌɪndɪˈrekt/ adj непрямо́й; (econ; gram) ко́свенный.

indiscreet /ˌɪndɪˈskriːt/ adj нескро́мный. **indiscretion** /-ˈskreʃ(ə)n/ n нескро́мность.

indiscriminate /ˌɪndɪˈskrɪmɪnət/ adj неразбо́рчивый. **indiscriminately** /-lɪ/ adv без разбо́ра.

indispensable /ˌɪndɪˈspensəb(ə)l/ adj необходи́мый.

indisposed /ˌɪndɪˈspəʊzd/ predic (unwell) нездоро́в.

indisputable /ˌɪndɪˈspjuːtəb(ə)l/ adj бесспо́рный.

indistinct /ˌɪndɪˈstɪŋkt/ adj нея́сный.

indistinguishable /ˌɪndɪˈstɪŋgwɪʃəb(ə)l/ adj неразличи́мый.

individual /ˌɪndɪˈvɪdjʊəl/ n ли́чность; adj индивидуа́льный. **individualism** /-ˈvɪdjʊəˌlɪz(ə)m/ n индивидуали́зм. **individualist** /-ˈvɪdjʊəlɪst/ n индивидуали́ст. **individualistic** /ˌɪndɪˌvɪdjʊəˈlɪstɪk/ adj индивидуалисти́ческий. **individuality** /ˌɪndɪˌvɪdjʊˈælɪtɪ/ n индивидуа́льность.

indivisible /ˌɪndɪˈvɪzɪb(ə)l/ adj недели́мый.

indoctrinate /ɪnˈdɒktrɪˌneɪt/ vt внуша́ть impf, внуши́ть pf +dat (with +acc).

indolence /ˈɪndələns/ n ле́ность. **indolent** /-lənt/ adj лени́вый.

indomitable /ɪnˈdɒmɪtəb(ə)l/ adj неукроти́мый.

Indonesia /ˌɪndəʊˈniːzɪə/ n Индоне́зия.

indoor /ˈɪndɔː(r)/ adj ко́мнатный. **indoors** /ɪnˈdɔːz/ adv (position) в до́ме; (motion) в дом.

induce /ɪnˈdjuːs/ vt (prevail on) убежда́ть impf, убеди́ть pf; (bring about) вызыва́ть impf, вы́звать pf. **inducement** /-mənt/ n побужде́ние.

induction /ɪnˈdʌkʃ(ə)n/ n (logic, electr) инду́кция; (in post) введе́ние в до́лжность.

indulge /ɪnˈdʌldʒ/ vt потво́рствовать impf +dat; vi предава́ться impf, преда́ться pf (in +dat). **indulgence** /-dʒ(ə)ns/ n потво́рство; (tolerance) снисходи́тельность. **indulgent** /-dʒ(ə)nt/ adj снисходи́тельный.

industrial /ɪnˈdʌstrɪəl/ adj промы́шленный. **industrialist** /-ˈdʌstrɪəlɪst/ n промы́шленник. **industrious** /ɪnˈdʌstrɪəs/ adj трудолюби́вый. **industry** /ˈɪndəstrɪ/ n промы́шленность; (zeal) трудолю́бие.

inebriated /ɪˈniːbrɪˌeɪtɪd/ adj пья́ный.

inedible /ɪnˈedɪb(ə)l/ adj несъедо́бный.

ineffective, ineffectual /ˌɪnɪˈfektɪv, ˌɪnɪˈfektjʊəl/ adj безрезульта́тный; (person) неспосо́бный.

inefficiency /ˌɪnɪˈfɪʃ(ə)nsɪ/ n неэффекти́вность. **inefficient** /-ˈfɪʃ(ə)nt/ adj неэффекти́вный.

ineligible /ɪnˈelɪdʒɪb(ə)l/ adj не

имеющий пра́во (**на**+*acc*).
inept /ɪ'nept/ *adj* неуме́лый.
inequality /,ɪnɪ'kwɒlɪtɪ/ *n* нера́-
венство.
inert /ɪ'nɜːt/ *adj* ине́ртный. **inertia** /ɪ'nɜːʃə/ *n* (*phys*) ине́рция;
(*sluggishness*) ине́ртность.
inescapable /,ɪnɪ'skeɪpəb(ə)l/ *adj*
неизбе́жный.
inevitability /ɪn,evɪtə'bɪlɪtɪ/ *n* не-
избе́жность. **inevitable** /ɪn-
'evɪtəb(ə)l/ *adj* неизбе́жный.
inexact /,ɪnɪg'zækt/ *adj* не-
то́чный.
inexcusable /,ɪnɪk'skjuːzəb(ə)l/
adj непрости́тельный.
inexhaustible /,ɪnɪg'zɔːstɪb(ə)l/
adj неистощи́мый.
inexorable /ɪn'eksərəb(ə)l/ *adj*
неумоли́мый.
inexpensive /,ɪnɪk'spensɪv/ *adj*
недорого́й.
inexperience /,ɪnɪk'spɪərɪəns/ *n*
нео́пытность. **inexperienced**
/-ənst/ *adj* нео́пытный.
inexplicable /,ɪnɪk'splɪkəb(ə)l/
adj необъясни́мый.
infallible /ɪn'fælɪb(ə)l/ *adj* непо-
греши́мый.
infamous /'ɪnfəməs/ *adj* позо́р-
ный. **infamy** /-mɪ/ *n* позо́р.
infancy /'ɪnfənsɪ/ *n* младе́нче-
ство. **infant** /'ɪnfənt/ *n* младе́-
нец. **infantile** /'ɪnfən,taɪl/ *adj*
де́тский.
infantry /'ɪnfəntrɪ/ *n* пехо́та.
infatuate /ɪn'fætjʊ,eɪt/ *vt* вскру-
жи́ть *pf* го́лову +*dat*. **infatuation** /-'eɪʃ(ə)n/ *n* увлече́ние.
infect /ɪn'fekt/ *vt* заража́ть *impf*,
зарази́ть *pf* (**with** +*instr*). **infection** /-'fekʃ(ə)n/ *n* зара́за, ин-
фе́кция. **infectious** /-'fekʃəs/ *adj*
зара́зный; (*fig*) зарази́-
тельный.
infer /ɪn'fɜː(r)/ *vt* заключа́ть
impf, заключи́ть *pf*. **inference**

/'ɪnfərəns/ *n* заключе́ние.

inferior /ɪn'fɪərɪə(r)/ *adj* (*in rank*)
ни́зший; (*in quality*) ху́дший,
плохо́й; *n* подчинённый sb. **inferiority** /ɪn,fɪərɪ'ɒrɪtɪ/ *n* бо́лее
ни́зкое ка́чество; ~ **complex**
ко́мплекс неполноце́нности.
infernal /ɪn'fɜːn(ə)l/ *adj* а́дский.
inferno /-nəʊ/ *n* ад.
infertile /ɪn'fɜːtaɪl/ *adj* непло́до-
ро́дный.
infested /ɪn'festɪd/ *adj*: **be ~ with**
кише́ть *impf* +*instr*.
infidelity /,ɪnfɪ'delɪtɪ/ *n* неве́р-
ность.
infiltrate /'ɪnfɪl,treɪt/ *vt* посте-
пе́нно проника́ть *impf*, прони́к-
нуть *pf* в+*acc*.
infinite /'ɪnfɪnɪt/ *adj* бесконе́ч-
ный. **infinitesimal** /,ɪnfɪnɪ-
'tesɪməl/ *adj* бесконе́чно
ма́лый. **infinitive** /ɪn'fɪnɪtɪv/ *n*
инфинити́в. **infinity** /ɪn'fɪnɪtɪ/ *n*
бесконе́чность.
infirm /ɪn'fɜːm/ *adj* не́мощный.
infirmary /-mərɪ/ *n* больни́ца.
infirmity /-mɪtɪ/ *n* не́мощь.
inflame /ɪn'fleɪm/ *vt & i* (*excite*)
возбужда́ть(ся) *impf*, возбу-
ди́ть(ся) *pf*; (*med*) воспа-
ля́ть(ся) *impf*, воспали́ть(ся)
pf. **inflammable** /-'flæməb(ə)l/
adj огнеопа́сный. **inflammation** /,ɪnflə'meɪʃ(ə)n/ *n* воспале́-
ние. **inflammatory** /ɪn'flæmətərɪ/
adj подстрека́тельский.
inflate /ɪn'fleɪt/ *vt* надува́ть
impf, наду́ть *pf*. **inflation** /-
'fleɪʃ(ə)n/ *n* (*econ*) инфля́ция.
inflection /ɪn'flekʃ(ə)n/ *n* (*gram*)
фле́ксия.
inflexible /ɪn'fleksɪb(ə)l/ *adj* не-
ги́бкий; (*fig*) непрекло́нный.
inflict /ɪn'flɪkt/ *vt* (*blow*) нано-
си́ть *impf*, нанести́ *pf* ((up)on
+*dat*); (*suffering*) причиня́ть
impf, причини́ть *pf* ((up)on

+dat); (penalty) налага́ть impf, наложи́ть pf ((up)on на+acc); ~ o.s. (up)on навя́зываться impf, навяза́ться pf +dat.

inflow /ˈɪnfləʊ/ n втека́ние, прито́к.

influence /ˈɪnfluəns/ n влия́ние; vt влия́ть impf, по~ pf на+acc.
influential /ˌɪnfluˈenʃ(ə)l/ adj влия́тельный.

influenza /ˌɪnfluˈenzə/ n грипп.

influx /ˈɪnflʌks/ n (fig) наплы́в.

inform /ɪnˈfɔːm/ vt сообща́ть impf, сообщи́ть pf +dat (of, about на+acc, o+prep); vi доноси́ть impf, донести́ pf (against на+acc).

informal /ɪnˈfɔːm(ə)l/ adj (unofficial) неофициа́льный; (casual) обыде́нный.

informant /ɪnˈfɔːmənt/ n осведоми́тель m. **information** /ˌɪnfəˈmeɪʃ(ə)n/ n информа́ция. **informative** /ɪnˈfɔːmətɪv/ adj поучи́тельный. **informer** /ɪnˈfɔːmə(r)/ n доно́счик.

infra-red /ˌɪnfrəˈred/ adj инфракра́сный.

infrequent /ɪnˈfriːkwənt/ adj ре́дкий.

infringe /ɪnˈfrɪndʒ/ vt (violate) наруша́ть impf, нару́шить pf; vi: ~ (up)on посяга́ть impf, посягну́ть pf на+acc. **infringement** /-mənt/ n наруше́ние; посяга́тельство.

infuriate /ɪnˈfjʊərɪˌeɪt/ vt разъяря́ть impf, разъяри́ть pf.

infuse /ɪnˈfjuːz/ vt (fig) внуша́ть impf, внуши́ть pf (into +dat). **infusion** /-ˈfjuːʒ(ə)n/ n (fig) внуше́ние; (herbs etc) насто́й.

ingenious /ɪnˈdʒiːnɪəs/ adj изобрета́тельный. **ingenuity** /ˌɪndʒɪˈnjuːɪtɪ/ n изобрета́тельность.

ingenuous /ɪnˈdʒenjʊəs/ adj бесхи́тростный.

ingot /ˈɪŋɡɒt/ n сли́ток.

ingrained /ɪnˈɡreɪnd/ adj закоренёлый.

ingratiate /ɪnˈɡreɪʃɪˌeɪt/ vt ~ o.s. вкра́дываться impf, вкра́сться pf в ми́лость (with +dat).

ingratitude /ɪnˈɡrætɪˌtjuːd/ n неблагода́рность.

ingredient /ɪnˈɡriːdɪənt/ n ингредие́нт, составля́ющее sb.

inhabit /ɪnˈhæbɪt/ vt жить impf в, на, +prep; обита́ть impf в, на, +prep. **inhabitant** /-t(ə)nt/ n жи́тель m, ~ница.

inhalation /ˌɪnhəˈleɪʃ(ə)n/ n вдыха́ние. **inhale** /ɪnˈheɪl/ vt вдыха́ть impf, вдохну́ть pf.

inherent /ɪnˈhɪərənt/ adj прису́щий (in +dat).

inherit /ɪnˈherɪt/ vt насле́довать impf & pf, y~ pf. **inheritance** /-təns/ n насле́дство.

inhibit /ɪnˈhɪbɪt/ vt стесня́ть impf, стесни́ть pf. **inhibited** /-tɪd/ adj стесни́тельный. **inhibition** /ˌɪnhɪˈbɪʃ(ə)n/ n стесне́ние.

inhospitable /ˌɪnhɒˈspɪtəb(ə)l/ adj негостеприи́мный; (fig) недружелю́бный.

inhuman(e) /ɪnˈhjuːmən, ˌɪnhjuːˈmeɪn/ adj бесчелове́чный.

inimical /ɪˈnɪmɪk(ə)l/ adj вражде́бный; (harmful) вре́дный.

inimitable /ɪˈnɪmɪtəb(ə)l/ adj неподража́емый.

iniquity /ɪˈnɪkwɪtɪ/ n несправедли́вость.

initial /ɪˈnɪʃ(ə)l/ adj (перво)нача́льный; n нача́льная бу́ква; pl инициа́лы m pl; vt ста́вить impf, по~ pf инициа́лы на+acc. **initially** /-ʃəlɪ/ adv в нача́ле.

initiate /ɪˈnɪʃɪˌeɪt/ vt вводи́ть impf, ввести́ pf (into в+acc). **initiation** /-ˈeɪʃ(ə)n/ n введе́ние.

initiative /ɪ'nɪʃətɪv/ n инициати́ва.

inject /ɪn'dʒekt/ vt вводи́ть impf, ввести́ pf (person +dat, substance +acc). **injection** /-'dʒekʃ(ə)n/ n уко́л; (fig) инъе́кция.

injunction /ɪn'dʒʌŋkʃ(ə)n/ n (law) суде́бный запре́т.

injure /'ɪndʒə(r)/ vt поврежда́ть impf, повреди́ть pf. **injury** /'ɪndʒərɪ/ n ра́на.

injustice /ɪn'dʒʌstɪs/ n несправедли́вость.

ink /ɪŋk/ n черни́ла (-л).

inkling /'ɪŋklɪŋ/ n представле́ние.

inland /'ɪnlənd/ adj вну́тренний; adv (motion) внутрь страны́; (place) внутри́ страны́; I~ **Revenue** управле́ние нало́говых сбо́ров.

in-laws /'ɪnlɔːz/ n pl ро́дственники m pl супру́га, -ги.

inlay /'ɪnleɪ/ n инкруста́ция; /-'leɪ/ vt инкрусти́ровать impf & pf.

inlet /'ɪnlet/ n (of sea) у́зкий зали́в.

inmate /'ɪnmeɪt/ n (prison) заключённый sb; (hospital) больно́й sb.

inn /ɪn/ n гости́ница.

innate /ɪ'neɪt/ adj врождённый.

inner /'ɪnə(r)/ adj вну́тренний. **innermost** adj глубоча́йший; (fig) сокрове́ннейший.

innocence /'ɪnəs(ə)ns/ n неви́нность; (guiltlessness) невино́вность. **innocent** /-s(ə)nt/ adj неви́нный; (not guilty) невино́вный (of в+prep).

innocuous /ɪ'nɒkjʊəs/ adj безвре́дный.

innovate /'ɪnəveɪt/ vi вводи́ть impf, ввести́ pf но́вшества. **innovation** /-'veɪʃ(ə)n/ n нововведе́ние. **innovative** /'ɪnəvətɪv/ adj

нова́торский. **innovator** /'ɪnə,veɪtə(r)/ n нова́тор.

innuendo /,ɪnjʊ'endəʊ/ n намёк, инсинуа́ция.

innumerable /ɪ'njuːmərəb(ə)l/ adj бесчи́сленный.

inoculate /ɪ'nɒkjʊ,leɪt/ vt привива́ть impf, приви́ть pf +dat (against +acc). **inoculation** /-'leɪʃ(ə)n/ n приви́вка.

inoffensive /,ɪnə'fensɪv/ adj безоби́дный.

inopportune /ɪn'ɒpə,tjuːn/ adj несвоевре́менный.

inordinate /ɪn'ɔːdɪnət/ adj чрезме́рный.

inorganic /,ɪnɔː'gænɪk/ adj неоргани́ческий.

in-patient /'ɪn,peɪʃ(ə)nt/ n стациона́рный больно́й sb.

input /'ɪnpʊt/ n ввод.

inquest /'ɪnkwest/ n суде́бное сле́дствие, дозна́ние.

inquire /ɪn'kwaɪə(r)/ vt спра́шивать impf, спроси́ть pf; vi справля́ться impf, спра́виться pf (about о+prep); рассле́довать impf & pf (into +acc). **inquiry** /-'kwaɪərɪ/ n вопро́с, спра́вка; (investigation) рассле́дование.

inquisition /,ɪnkwɪ'zɪʃ(ə)n/ n инквизи́ция. **inquisitive** /ɪn'kwɪzɪtɪv/ adj пытли́вый, любозна́тельный.

inroad /'ɪnrəʊd/ n (attack) набе́г; (fig) посяга́тельство (on, into на+acc).

insane /ɪn'seɪn/ adj безу́мный. **insanity** /ɪn'sænɪtɪ/ n безу́мие.

insatiable /ɪn'seɪʃəb(ə)l/ adj ненасы́тный.

inscribe /ɪn'skraɪb/ vt надпи́сывать impf, надписа́ть pf; (engrave) выреза́ть impf, вы́резать pf. **inscription** /-'skrɪpʃ(ə)n/ n на́дпись.

inscrutable /ɪn'skruːtəb(ə)l/ adj

непостижи́мый, непроница́емый.

insect /'ɪnsekt/ *n* насеко́мое *sb*.

insecticide /ɪn'sektɪsaɪd/ *n* инсектици́д.

insecure /ˌɪnsɪ'kjʊə(r)/ *adj* (*unsafe*) небезопа́сный; (*not confident*) неуве́ренный (в себе́).

insemination /ɪnˌsemɪ'neɪʃ(ə)n/ *n* оплодотворе́ние.

insensible /ɪn'sensɪb(ə)l/ *adj* (*unconscious*) потеря́вший созна́ние.

insensitive /ɪn'sensɪtɪv/ *adj* нечувстви́тельный.

inseparable /ɪn'sepərəb(ə)l/ *adj* неотдели́мый; (*people*) неразлучи́й.

insert /ɪn'sɜːt/ *vt* вставля́ть *impf*, вста́вить *pf*; вкла́дывать *impf*, вложи́ть *pf*; (*coin*) опуска́ть *impf*, опусти́ть *pf*. **insertion** /-'sɜːʃ(ə)n/ *n* (*inserting*) вставле́ние, вкла́дывание; (*thing inserted*) вста́вка.

inshore /ɪn'ʃɔː(r)/ *adj* прибре́жный; *adv* бли́зко к бе́регу.

inside /ɪn'saɪd/ *n* вну́тренняя часть; *pl* (*anat*) вну́тренности *f pl*; turn ~ out выве́ртывать *impf*, вы́вернуть *pf* наизна́нку; *adj* вну́тренний; *adv* (*place*) внутри́; (*motion*) внутрь; (*place*) внутри́+*gen*, в+*prep*; (*motion*) внутрь+*gen*, в+*acc*.

insidious /ɪn'sɪdɪəs/ *adj* кова́рный.

insight /'ɪnsaɪt/ *n* проница́тельность.

insignia /ɪn'sɪɡnɪə/ *n* зна́ки *m pl* разли́чия.

insignificant /ˌɪnsɪɡ'nɪfɪkənt/ *adj* незначи́тельный.

insincere /ˌɪnsɪn'sɪə(r)/ *adj* неи́скренний.

insinuate /ɪn'sɪnjʊˌeɪt/ *vt* (*hint*) намека́ть *impf*, намекну́ть *pf*

на+*acc*. **insinuation** /-'eɪʃ(ə)n/ *n* инсинуа́ция.

insipid /ɪn'sɪpɪd/ *adj* пре́сный.

insist /ɪn'sɪst/ *vt* & *i* наста́ивать *impf*, настоя́ть *pf* (on **+**prep). **insistence** /-t(ə)ns/ *n* настойчивость. **insistent** /-t(ə)nt/ *adj* насто́йчивый.

insolence /'ɪnsələns/ *n* на́глость. **insolent** /-lənt/ *adj* на́глый.

insoluble /ɪn'sɒljʊb(ə)l/ *adj* (*problem*) неразреши́мый; (*in liquid*) нераствори́мый.

insolvent /ɪn'sɒlv(ə)nt/ *adj* несостоя́тельный.

insomnia /ɪn'sɒmnɪə/ *n* бессо́нница.

inspect /ɪn'spekt/ *vt* инспекти́ровать *impf*, про~ *pf*. **inspection** /-'spekʃ(ə)n/ *n* инспе́кция. **inspector** /-'spektə(r)/ *n* инспе́ктор; (*ticket* ~) контролёр.

inspiration /ˌɪnspɪ'reɪʃ(ə)n/ *n* вдохнове́ние. **inspire** /ɪn'spaɪə(r)/ *vt* вдохновля́ть *impf*, вдохнови́ть *pf*; внуша́ть *impf*, внуши́ть *pf* **+**dat (with **+**acc).

instability /ˌɪnstə'bɪlɪtɪ/ *n* неусто́йчивость; (*of character*) неуравнове́шенность.

install /ɪn'stɔːl/ *vt* (*person in office*) вводи́ть *impf*, ввести́ *pf* в до́лжность; (*apparatus*) устана́вливать *impf*, установи́ть *pf*. **installation** /ˌɪnstə'leɪʃ(ə)n/ *n* введе́ние в до́лжность; устано́вка; *pl* сооруже́ния *neut pl*.

instalment /ɪn'stɔːlmənt/ *n* (*comm*) взнос; (*publication*) вы́пуск; часть; by ~s в рассро́чку.

instance /'ɪnst(ə)ns/ *n* (*example*) приме́р; (*case*) слу́чай; for ~ наприме́р.

instant /'ɪnst(ə)nt/ *n* мгнове́ние, моме́нт; *adj* неме́дленный;

(*coffee etc.*) раствори́мый. **instantaneous** /ˌɪnstən'teɪnɪəs/ *adj* мгнове́нный. **instantly** /'ɪnstəntlɪ/ *adv* неме́дленно, то́тчас.

instead /ɪn'sted/ *adv* вме́сто (*of* +*gen*); ~ **of going** вме́сто того́, что́бы пойти́.

instep /'ɪnstep/ *n* подъём.

instigate /'ɪnstɪˌgeɪt/ *vt* подстрека́ть *impf*, подстрекну́ть *pf* (**to** к+*dat*). **instigation** /-'geɪʃ(ə)n/ *n* подстрека́тельство. **instigator** /'ɪnstɪˌgeɪtə(r)/ *n* подстрека́тель *m*, ~ница.

instil /ɪn'stɪl/ *vt* (*ideas etc.*) внуша́ть *impf*, внуши́ть *pf* (**into** +*dat*).

instinct /'ɪnstɪŋkt/ *n* инсти́нкт. **instinctive** /ɪn'stɪŋktɪv/ *adj* инстинкти́вный.

institute /'ɪnstɪˌtjuːt/ *n* институ́т; *vt* (*establish*) устана́вливать *impf*, установи́ть *pf*; (*introduce*) вводи́ть *impf*, ввести́ *pf*; (*reforms*) проводи́ть *impf*, провести́ *pf*. **institution** /-'tjuːʃ(ə)n/ *n* учрежде́ние.

instruct /ɪn'strʌkt/ *vt* (*teach*) обуча́ть *impf*, обучи́ть *pf* (**in** +*dat*); (*inform*) сообща́ть *impf*, сообщи́ть *pf* +*dat*; (*command*) прика́зывать *impf*, приказа́ть *pf* +*dat*. **instruction** /-'strʌkʃ(ə)n/ *n* (*in pl*) инстру́кция; (*teaching*) обуче́ние. **instructive** /-'strʌktɪv/ *adj* поучи́тельный. **instructor** /-'strʌktə(r)/ *n* инстру́ктор.

instrument /'ɪnstrəmənt/ *n* ору́дие, инструме́нт. **instrumental** /-'ment(ə)l/ *adj* (*mus*) инструмента́льный; (*gram*) твори́тельный; **be** ~ **in** спосо́бствовать *impf*, по~ *pf* +*dat*; *n* (*gram*) твори́тельный паде́ж. **instrumentation**

/ˌɪnstrəmen'teɪʃ(ə)n/ *n* (*mus*) инструменто́вка.

insubordinate /ˌɪnsə'bɔːdɪnət/ *adj* неподчиня́ющийся.

insufferable /ɪn'sʌfərəb(ə)l/ *adj* невыноси́мый.

insular /'ɪnsjʊlə(r)/ *adj* (*fig*) ограни́ченный.

insulate /'ɪnsjʊˌleɪt/ *vt* изоли́ровать *impf & pf*. **insulation** /-'leɪʃ(ə)n/ *n* изоля́ция. **insulator** /'ɪnsjʊˌleɪtə(r)/ *n* изоля́тор.

insulin /'ɪnsjʊlɪn/ *n* инсули́н.

insult /ɪn'sʌlt/ *n* оскорбле́ние; /ɪn'sʌlt/ *vt* оскорбля́ть *impf*, оскорби́ть *pf*. **insulting** /ɪn'sʌltɪŋ/ *adj* оскорби́тельный.

insuperable /ɪn'suːpərəb(ə)l/ *adj* непреодоли́мый.

insurance /ɪn'ʃʊərəns/ *n* страхова́ние; *attrib* страхово́й. **insure** /-'ʃʊə(r)/ *vt* страхова́ть *impf*, за~ *pf* (*against* от+*gen*).

insurgent /ɪn'sɜːdʒ(ə)nt/ *n* повста́нец.

insurmountable /ˌɪnsə'maʊntəb(ə)l/ *adj* непреодоли́мый.

insurrection /ˌɪnsə'rekʃ(ə)n/ *n* восста́ние.

intact /ɪn'tækt/ *adj* це́лый.

intake /'ɪnteɪk/ *n* (*of persons*) набо́р; (*consumption*) потребле́ние.

intangible /ɪn'tændʒɪb(ə)l/ *adj* неосяза́емый.

integral /'ɪntɪgr(ə)l/ *adj* неотъе́млемый. **integrate** /-ˌgreɪt/ *vt & i* интегри́роваться *impf & pf*. **integration** /-'greɪʃ(ə)n/ *n* интегра́ция.

integrity /ɪn'tegrɪtɪ/ *n* (*honesty*) че́стность.

intellect /'ɪntɪˌlekt/ *n* интелле́кт. **intellectual** /-'lektjʊəl/ *n* интеллиге́нт; *adj* интеллектуа́льный.

intelligence /ɪnˈtelɪdʒ(ə)ns/ n (*intellect*) ум; (*information*) сведения neut pl; (~ *service*) разведка. **intelligent** /-dʒ(ə)nt/ adj умный.

intelligentsia /ɪnˌtelɪˈdʒentsɪə/ n интеллигенция.

intelligible /ɪnˈtelɪdʒɪb(ə)l/ adj понятный.

intemperate /ɪnˈtempərət/ adj невоздержанный.

intend /ɪnˈtend/ vt собираться impf, собраться pf; (*design*) предназначать impf, предназначить pf (for для+gen, на+acc).

intense /ɪnˈtens/ adj сильный. **intensify** /-ˈtensɪˌfaɪ/ vt & i усиливать(ся) impf, усилить(ся) pf. **intensity** /-ˈtensɪtɪ/ n интенсивность, сила. **intensive** /-ˈtensɪv/ adj интенсивный.

intent /ɪnˈtent/ n намерение; adj (*resolved*) стремящийся (on к+dat); (*occupied*) погружённый (on в+acc); (*earnest*) внимательный. **intention** /-ˈtenʃ(ə)n/ n намерение. **intentional** /-ˈtenʃən(ə)l/ adj намеренный.

inter /ɪnˈtɜː(r)/ vt хоронить impf, по~ pf.

interact /ˌɪntərˈækt/ vi взаимодействовать impf. **interaction** /-ˈæk(ʃ)ən/ n взаимодействие. **interactive** /-tɪv/ adj (*comput*) интерактивный.

intercede /ˌɪntəˈsiːd/ vi ходатайствовать impf, по~ pf (for за+acc; with перед+instr).

intercept /ˌɪntəˈsept/ vt перехватывать impf, перехватить pf. **interception** /-ˈsep(ʃ)ən/ n перехват.

interchange /ˈɪntəˌtʃeɪndʒ/ n обмен (of +instr); (*junction*) транспортная развязка; vt об-

мениваться impf, обменяться pf +instr. **interchangeable** /ˌtʃeɪndʒəb(ə)l/ adj взаимозаменяемый.

inter-city /ˌɪntəˈsɪtɪ/ adj междугородный.

intercom /ˈɪntəˌkɒm/ n селектор; (*to get into house*) домофон.

interconnected /ˌɪntəkəˈnektɪd/ adj взаимосвязанный.

intercourse /ˈɪntəˌkɔːs/ n (*social*) общение; (*trade*; *sexual*) сношения neut pl.

interdisciplinary /ˌɪntədɪsɪˈplɪnərɪ/ adj межотраслевой.

interest /ˈɪntrəst/ n интерес (in к+dat); (*econ*) проценты m pl. vt интересовать impf; (~ *person in*) заинтересовывать impf, заинтересовать pf (in +instr); be ~ed in интересоваться impf +instr. **interesting** /-stɪŋ/ adj интересный.

interfere /ˌɪntəˈfɪə(r)/ vi вмешиваться impf, вмешаться pf (in в+acc). **interference** /-ˈfɪərəns/ n вмешательство; (*radio*) помехи f pl.

interim /ˈɪntərɪm/ n: in the ~ тем временем; adj промежуточный; (*temporary*) временный.

interior /ɪnˈtɪərɪə(r)/ n (of building) интерьер; (of object) внутренность; adj внутренний.

interjection /ˌɪntəˈdʒekʃ(ə)n/ n восклицание; (*gram*) междометие.

interlock /ˌɪntəˈlɒk/ vt & i сцепляться impf, сцепиться pf.

interloper /ˈɪntəˌləʊpə(r)/ n незваный гость m.

interlude /ˈɪntəˌluːd/ n (*theat*) антракт; (*mus*, fig) интерлюдия.

intermediary /ˌɪntəˈmiːdɪərɪ/ n посредник.

intermediate /ˌɪntəˈmiːdɪət/ adj промежуточный.

interminable /ɪn'tɜːmɪnəb(ə)l/ *adj* бесконе́чный.

intermission /ˌɪntə'mɪʃ(ə)n/ *n* (*theat*) антра́кт.

intermittent /ˌɪntə'mɪt(ə)nt/ *adj* & pf. прерыви́стый.

intern /ɪn'tɜːn/ *vt* интерни́ровать *impf* & pf.

internal /ɪn'tɜːn(ə)l/ *adj* вну́тренний; ~ combustion engine дви́гатель *m* вну́треннего сгора́ния.

international /ˌɪntə'næʃən(ə)l/ *adj* междунаро́дный; *n* (*contest*) междунаро́дные состяза́ния *neut pl*.

Internet /ɪntə.net/ *n* Интерне́т; on the ~ в Интерне́те.

internment /ɪn'tɜːnmənt/ *n* интерни́рование.

interplay /'ɪntə.pleɪ/ *n* взаимоде́йствие.

interpret /ɪn'tɜːprɪt/ *vt* (*explain*) толкова́ть *impf*; (*understand*) истолко́вывать *impf*, истолкова́ть pf; *vi* переводи́ть *impf*, перевести́ pf. **interpretation** /-'teɪʃ(ə)n/ *n* толкова́ние. **interpreter** /ɪn'tɜːprɪtə(r)/ *n* перево́дчик, -ица.

interrelated /ˌɪntərɪ'leɪtɪd/ *adj* взаимосвя́занный.

interrogate /ɪn'terə.geɪt/ *vt* допра́шивать *impf*, допроси́ть pf. **interrogation** /-'geɪʃ(ə)n/ *n* допро́с. **interrogative** /ˌɪntə'rɒɡətɪv/ *adj* вопроси́тельный.

interrupt /ˌɪntə'rʌpt/ *vt* прерыва́ть *impf*, прерва́ть pf. **interruption** /-'rʌpʃ(ə)n/ *n* переры́в.

intersect /ˌɪntə'sekt/ *vt* & *i* пересека́ть(ся) *impf*, пересе́чь(ся) pf. **intersection** /-'sekʃ(ə)n/ *n* пересече́ние.

intersperse /ˌɪntə'spɜːs/ *vt* (*scatter*) рассыпа́ть *impf*, рассы́пать pf (**between, among**

ме́жду+*instr*, среди́+*gen*).

intertwine /ˌɪntə'twaɪn/ *vt* & *i* переплета́ть(ся) *impf*, переплести́(сь) pf.

interval /'ɪntəv(ə)l/ *n* интерва́л; (*theat*) антра́кт.

intervene /ˌɪntə'viːn/ *vi* (*occur*) происходи́ть *impf*, произойти́ pf; ~ in вме́шиваться *impf*, вмеша́ться pf в+*acc*. **intervention** /-'venʃ(ə)n/ *n* вмеша́тельство; (*polit*) интерве́нция.

interview /'ɪntə.vjuː/ *n* интервью́ *neut indecl*; *vt* интервьюи́ровать *impf* & pf, про~ pf. **interviewer** /-.vjuːə(r)/ *n* интервью́ер.

interweave /ˌɪntə'wiːv/ *vt* вотка́ть pf.

intestate /ɪn'testeɪt/ *adj* без завеща́ния.

intestine /ɪn'testɪn/ *n* кишка́; *pl* кише́чник.

intimacy /'ɪntɪməsɪ/ *n* инти́мность. **intimate**[1] /'ɪntɪmət/ *adj* инти́мный.

intimate[2] /'ɪntɪ.meɪt/ *vt* (*hint*) намека́ть *impf*, намекну́ть pf на+*acc*. **intimation** /-'meɪʃ(ə)n/ *n* намёк.

intimidate /ɪn'tɪmɪ.deɪt/ *vt* запу́гивать *impf*, запуга́ть pf.

into /'ɪntu/ *prep* в, во+*acc*.

intolerable /ɪn'tɒlərəb(ə)l/ *adj* невыноси́мый. **intolerance** /-rəns/ *n* нетерпи́мость. **intolerant** /-rənt/ *adj* нетерпи́мый.

intonation /ˌɪntə'neɪʃ(ə)n/ *n* интона́ция.

intoxicated /ɪn'tɒksɪ.keɪtɪd/ *adj* пья́ный. **intoxication** /-'keɪʃ(ə)n/ *n* опьяне́ние.

intractable /ɪn'træktəb(ə)l/ *adj* неподатливый.

intransigent /ɪn'trænsɪdʒ(ə)nt/

adj непримири́мый.

intransitive /ɪnˈtrænsɪtɪv/ *adj* непереходный.

intrepid /ɪnˈtrepɪd/ *adj* неустрашимый.

intricacy /ˈɪntrɪkəsɪ/ *n* запу́танность. **intricate** /ˈɪntrɪkət/ *adj* запу́танный.

intrigue /ˈɪntriːg/ *n* интри́га; *vi* интригова́ть *impf*; *vt* интригова́ть *impf*, за~ *pf*.

intrinsic /ɪnˈtrɪnzɪk/ *adj* прису́щий; (*value*) вну́тренний.

introduce /ˌɪntrəˈdjuːs/ *vt* вводи́ть *impf*, ввести́ *pf*; (*person*) представля́ть *impf*, предста́вить *pf*. **introduction** /-ˈdʌkʃ(ə)n/ *n* введе́ние; представле́ние; (*to book*) предисло́вие. **introductory** /-ˈdʌktərɪ/ *adj* вступи́тельный.

introspection /ˌɪntrəˈspekʃ(ə)n/ *n* интроспе́кция.

intrude /ɪnˈtruːd/ *vi* вторга́ться *impf*, вто́ргнуться *pf* (**into** в+*acc*); (*disturb*) меша́ть *impf*, по~ *pf*. **intruder** /ɪnˈtruːdə(r)/ *n* (*burglar*) граби́тель *m*. **intrusion** /ɪnˈtruːʒ(ə)n/ *n* вторже́ние.

intuition /ˌɪntjuːˈɪʃ(ə)n/ *n* интуи́ция. **intuitive** /ɪnˈtjuːɪtɪv/ *adj* интуити́вный.

inundate /ˈɪnʌndeɪt/ *vt* наводня́ть *impf*, наводни́ть *pf*. **inundation** /-ˈdeɪʃ(ə)n/ *n* наводне́ние.

invade /ɪnˈveɪd/ *vt* вторга́ться *impf*, вто́ргнуться *pf* в+*acc*. **invader** /-də(r)/ *n* захва́тчик.

invalid[1] /ˈɪnvəlɪd/ *n* (*person*) инвали́д.

invalid[2] /ɪnˈvælɪd/ *adj* недействи́тельный. **invalidate** /-ˈvælɪdeɪt/ *vt* де́лать *impf*, с~ *pf* недействи́тельным.

invaluable /ɪnˈvæljʊəb(ə)l/ *adj* неоцени́мый.

invariable /ɪnˈveərɪəb(ə)l/ *adj* неизме́нный.

invasion /ɪnˈveɪʒ(ə)n/ *n* вторже́ние.

invective /ɪnˈvektɪv/ *n* брань.

invent /ɪnˈvent/ *vt* изобрета́ть *impf*, изобрести́ *pf*; (*think up*) выду́мывать *impf*, вы́думать *pf*. **invention** /-ˈvenʃ(ə)n/ *n* изобрете́ние; вы́думка. **inventive** /-ˈventɪv/ *adj* изобрета́тельный. **inventor** /-ˈventə(r)/ *n* изобрета́тель *m*.

inventory /ˈɪnvəntərɪ/ *n* инвента́рь *m*.

inverse /ˈɪnvɜːs/ *adj* обра́тный; *n* противополо́жность. **invert** /ɪnˈvɜːt/ *vt* перевора́чивать *impf*, переверну́ть *pf*. **inverted commas** *n pl* кавы́чки *f pl*.

invest /ɪnˈvest/ *vt* & *i* (*econ*) вкла́дывать *impf*, вложи́ть *pf* (де́ньги) (**in** в+*acc*).

investigate /ɪnˈvestɪˌgeɪt/ *vt* иссле́довать *impf* & *pf*; (*law*) рассле́довать *impf* & *pf*. **investigation** /-ˈgeɪʃ(ə)n/ *n* иссле́дование; рассле́дование.

investment /ɪnˈvestmənt/ *n* инвести́ция, вклад. **investor** /-ˈvestə(r)/ *n* вкла́дчик.

inveterate /ɪnˈvetərət/ *adj* закорене́лый.

invidious /ɪnˈvɪdɪəs/ *adj* оскорби́тельный.

invigorate /ɪnˈvɪɡəˌreɪt/ *vt* оживля́ть *impf*, оживи́ть *pf*.

invincible /ɪnˈvɪnsɪb(ə)l/ *adj* непобеди́мый.

inviolable /ɪnˈvaɪələb(ə)l/ *adj* неруши́мый.

invisible /ɪnˈvɪzɪb(ə)l/ *adj* неви́димый.

invitation /ˌɪnvɪˈteɪʃ(ə)n/ *n* приглаше́ние. **invite** /ɪnˈvaɪt/ *vt* приглаша́ть *impf*, пригласи́ть *pf*. **inviting** /ɪnˈvaɪtɪŋ/ *adj* при-

влека́тельный.

invoice /'ɪnvɔɪs/ n факту́ра.

invoke /ɪn'vəʊk/ vt обраща́ться impf, обрати́ться pf к+dat.

involuntary /ɪn'vɒləntərɪ/ adj нево́льный.

involve /ɪn'vɒlv/ vt (entangle) вовлека́ть impf, вовле́чь pf; (entail) влечь impf за собо́й. **involved** /-'vɒlvd/ adj сло́жный.

invulnerable /ɪn'vʌlnərəb(ə)l/ adj неуязви́мый.

inward /'ɪnwəd/ adj вну́тренний. **inwardly** /-lɪ/ adv внутри́. **inwards** /'ɪnwədz/ adv внутрь.

iodine /'aɪədiːn/ n иод.

iota /aɪ'əʊtə/ n: **not an** ~ ни на йо́ту.

IOU /ˌaɪəʊ'juː/ n долгова́я распи́ска.

Iran /ɪ'rɑːn/ n Ира́н. **Iranian** /-'reɪnɪən/ n ира́нец, -нка; adj ира́нский.

Iraq /ɪ'rɑːk/ n Ира́к. **Iraqi** /-kɪ/ n ира́кец; жи́тель m, ~ ница Ира́ка; adj ира́кский.

irascible /ɪ'ræsɪb(ə)l/ adj раздражи́тельный.

irate /aɪ'reɪt/ adj гне́вный.

Ireland /'aɪələnd/ n Ирла́ндия.

iris /'aɪərɪs/ n (anat) ра́дужная оболо́чка; (bot) каса́тик.

Irish /'aɪərɪʃ/ adj ирла́ндский. **Irishman** /-mən/ n ирла́ндец. **Irishwoman** n ирла́ндка.

irk /ɜːk/ vt раздража́ть impf, раздражи́ть pf +dat. **irksome** /-səm/ adj раздражи́тельный.

iron /'aɪən/ n желе́зо; (for clothes) утю́г; adj желе́зный; vt гла́дить impf, вы́~ pf.

ironic(al) /aɪ'rɒnɪk(ə)l/ adj ирони́ческий. **irony** /'aɪrənɪ/ n иро́ния.

irradiate /ɪ'reɪdɪˌeɪt/ vt (subject to radiation) облуча́ть impf, облу-

чи́ть pf. **irradiation** /-'eɪʃ(ə)n/ n облуче́ние.

irrational /ɪ'ræʃən(ə)l/ adj неразу́мный.

irreconcilable /ɪˌrekən'saɪləb(ə)l/ adj непримири́мый.

irrefutable /ˌɪrɪ'fjuːtəb(ə)l/ adj неопроверж́имый.

irregular /ɪ'regjʊlə(r)/ adj нерегуля́рный; (gram) непра́вильный; (not even) неро́вный.

irrelevant /ɪ'relɪv(ə)nt/ adj неуме́стный.

irreparable /ɪ'repərəb(ə)l/ adj непоправи́мый.

irreplaceable /ˌɪrɪ'pleɪsəb(ə)l/ adj незамени́мый.

irrepressible /ˌɪrɪ'presɪb(ə)l/ adj неудержи́мый.

irreproachable /ˌɪrɪ'prəʊtʃəb(ə)l/ adj безупре́чный.

irresistible /ˌɪrɪ'zɪstɪb(ə)l/ adj неотрази́мый.

irresolute /ɪ'rezəˌluːt/ adj нереши́тельный.

irrespective /ˌɪrɪ'spektɪv/ adj: ~ **of** несмотря́ на+acc.

irresponsible /ˌɪrɪ'spɒnsɪb(ə)l/ adj безотве́тственный.

irretrievable /ˌɪrɪ'triːvəb(ə)l/ adj непоправи́мый.

irreverent /ɪ'revərənt/ adj непочти́тельный.

irreversible /ˌɪrɪ'vɜːsɪb(ə)l/ adj необрати́мый.

irrevocable /ɪ'revəkəb(ə)l/ adj неотменя́емый.

irrigate /'ɪrɪˌgeɪt/ vt ороша́ть impf, ороси́ть pf. **irrigation** /-'geɪʃ(ə)n/ n ороше́ние.

irritable /'ɪrɪtəb(ə)l/ adj раздражи́тельный. **irritate** /'ɪrɪˌteɪt/ vt раздража́ть impf, раздражи́ть pf. **irritation** /-'teɪʃ(ə)n/ n раздраже́ние.

Islam /'ɪzlɑːm/ n исла́м. **Islamic** /-'læmɪk/ adj мусульма́нский.

J

island, isle /'aɪlənd, aɪl/ *n* о́стров. **islander** /'aɪləndə(r)/ *n* островитя́нин, -я́нка.

isolate /'aɪsəˌleɪt/ *vt* изоли́ровать *impf* & *pf*. **isolation** /-'leɪʃ(ə)n/ *n* изоля́ция.

Israel /'ɪzreɪl/ *n* Изра́иль *m*. **Israeli** /-'reɪlɪ/ *n* израильтя́нин, -я́нка; *adj* изра́ильский.

issue /'ɪʃuː/ *n* (*question*) (спо́рный) вопро́с; (*of bonds etc.*) вы́пуск; (*of magazine*) но́мер; *vt* выпуска́ть *impf*, вы́пустить *pf*; (*give out*) выдава́ть *impf*, вы́дать *pf*.

isthmus /'ɪsməs/ *n* переше́ек.

IT *abbr* (*of* **information technology**) информа́тика.

it /ɪt/ *pron* он, она́, оно́; *demonstrative* э́то.

Italian /ɪ'tæljən/ *n* италья́нец, -нка; *adj* италья́нский.

italics /ɪ'tælɪks/ *n pl* курси́в; **in ~** курси́вом.

Italy /'ɪtəlɪ/ *n* Ита́лия.

itch /ɪtʃ/ *n* зуд; *vi* чеса́ться *impf*.

item /'aɪtəm/ *n* (*on list*) предме́т; (*in account*) статья́; (*on agenda*) пункт; (*in programme*) но́мер. **itemize** /-ˌmaɪz/ *vt* перечисля́ть *impf*, перечи́слить *pf*.

itinerant /aɪ'tɪnərənt/ *adj* стра́нствующий. **itinerary** /aɪ'tɪnərərɪ/ *n* маршру́т.

its /ɪts/ *poss pron* его́, её; свой.

itself /ɪt'self/ *pron* (*emph*) (он(о́)) сам(о́), (она́) сама́; (*refl*) себя́; **-ся** (*suffixed to vt*).

IVF *abbr* (*of* **in vitro fertilization**) экстракорпора́льное оплодотворе́ние.

ivory /'aɪvərɪ/ *n* слоно́вая кость.

ivy /'aɪvɪ/ *n* плющ.

jab /dʒæb/ *n* толчо́к; (*injection*) уко́л; *vt* ты́кать *impf*, ткнуть *pf*.

jabber /'dʒæbə(r)/ *vi* тарато́рить *impf*.

jack /dʒæk/ *n* (*cards*) вале́т; (*lifting device*) домкра́т; *vt* (**~ up**) поднима́ть *impf*, подня́ть *pf* домкра́том.

jackdaw /'dʒækdɔː/ *n* га́лка.

jacket /'dʒækɪt/ *n* (*tailored*) пиджа́к; (*anorak*) ку́ртка; (*on book*) (су́пер)обло́жка.

jackpot /'dʒækpɒt/ *n* банк.

jade /dʒeɪd/ *n* (*mineral*) нефри́т.

jaded /'dʒeɪdɪd/ *adj* утомлённый.

jagged /'dʒægɪd/ *adj* зазу́бренный.

jaguar /'dʒægjʊə(r)/ *n* ягуа́р.

jail /dʒeɪl/ *see* **gaol**

jam¹ /dʒæm/ *n* (*crush*) да́вка; (*in traffic*) про́бка; *vt* (*thrust*) впи́хивать *impf*, впихну́ть *pf* (*into* в+*acc*); (*wedge open*; *block*) закли́нивать *impf*, закли́нить *pf*; (*radio*) заглуша́ть *impf*, заглуши́ть *pf*; *vi* (*machine*) закли́нивать *impf*, закли́нить *pf impers*+*acc*.

jam² /dʒæm/ *n* (*conserve*) варе́нье, джем.

jangle /'dʒæŋg(ə)l/ *vi* (& *t*) звя́кать (+*instr*).

janitor /'dʒænɪtə(r)/ *n* привра́тник.

January /'dʒænjʊərɪ/ *n* янва́рь; *adj* янва́рский.

Japan /dʒə'pæn/ *n* Япо́ния. **Japanese** /dʒæpə'niːz/ *n* япо́нец, -нка; *adj* япо́нский.

jar¹ /dʒɑː(r)/ *n* (*container*) ба́нка.

jar² /dʒɑː(r)/ *vi* (*irritate*) раздража́ть *impf*, раздражи́ть *pf*

(**upon** +*acc*).

jargon /'dʒɑːɡən/ *n* жаргóн.

jasmin(e) /'dʒæzmɪn/ *n* жасмѝн.

jaundice /'dʒɔːndɪs/ *n* желтýха. **jaundiced** /-dɪst/ *adj* (*fig*) цинѝчный.

jaunt /dʒɔːnt/ *n* прогýлка.

jaunty /'dʒɔːntɪ/ *adj* бóдрый.

javelin /'dʒævəlɪn/ *n* копьё.

jaw /dʒɔː/ *n* чéлюсть; *pl* пасть, рот.

jay /dʒeɪ/ *n* сóйка.

jazz /dʒæz/ *n* джаз; *adj* джáзовый.

jealous /'dʒeləs/ *adj* ревнѝвый; (*envious*) завѝстливый; **be ~ of** (*person*) ревновáть *impf*; (*thing*) завѝдовать *impf*, по~ *pf* +*dat*; (*rights*) ревнѝво оберегáть *impf*, оберéчь *pf*. **jealousy** /-sɪ/ *n* рéвность; зáвисть.

jeans /dʒiːnz/ *n pl* джѝнсы (-сов) *pl*.

jeer /dʒɪə(r)/ *n* насмéшка; *vt & i* насмехáться *impf* (**at** над+*instr*).

jelly /'dʒelɪ/ *n* (*sweet*) желé *neut indecl*; (*aspic*) студéнь *m*. **jellyfish** *n* медýза.

jeopardize /'dʒepədaɪz/ *vt* подвергáть *impf*, подвéргнуть *pf* опáсности. **jeopardy** /-dɪ/ *n* опáсность.

jerk /dʒɜːk/ *n* рывóк; *vt* дёргать *impf* +*instr*, *vi* (*twitch*) дёргаться *impf*, дёрнуться *pf*. **jerky** /-kɪ/ *adj* нерóвный.

jersey /'dʒɜːzɪ/ *n* (*garment*) джéмпер; (*fabric*) джéрси *neut indecl*.

jest /dʒest/ *n* шýтка; **in ~** в шýтку; *vi* шутѝть *impf*, по~ *pf*. **jester** /-stə(r)/ *n* шут.

jet¹ /dʒet/ *n* (*stream*) струя́; (*nozzle*) соплó; **~ engine** реактѝвный двѝгатель *m*; **~ plane** реактѝвный самолёт.

jet² /dʒet/ *n* (*mineralogy*) гагáт; **~-black** чёрный как смоль.

jettison /'dʒetɪs(ə)n/ *vt* выбрáсывать *impf*, вýбросить *pf* за борт.

jetty /'dʒetɪ/ *n* прѝстань.

Jew /dʒuː/ *n* еврéй, еврéйка. **Jewish** /-ɪʃ/ *adj* еврéйский.

jewel /'dʒuːəl/ *n* драгоцéнность, драгоцéнный кáмень *m*. **jeweller** /-lə(r)/ *n* ювелѝр. **jewellery** /-lərɪ/ *n* драгоцéнности *f pl*.

jib /dʒɪb/ *n* (*naut*) клѝвер; *vi*: **~ at** уклонáться *impf* от+*gen*.

jigsaw /'dʒɪɡsɔː/ *n* (*puzzle*) мозáика.

jingle /'dʒɪŋɡ(ə)l/ *n* звя́канье; (*vt & i*) звя́кать *impf*, звя́кнуть *pf* (+*instr*).

job /dʒɒb/ *n* (*work*) рабóта; (*task*) задáние; (*position*) мéсто. **jobless** /-lɪs/ *adj* безрабóтный.

jockey /'dʒɒkɪ/ *n* жокéй; *vi* оттирáть *impf* друг дрýга.

jocular /'dʒɒkjʊlə(r)/ *adj* шутлѝвый.

jog /dʒɒɡ/ *n* (*push*) толчóк; *vt* подтáлкивать *impf*, подтолкнýть *pf*; *vi* бéгать *impf* трусцóй. **jogger** /-ɡə(r)/ *n* занимáющийся оздоровѝтельным бéгом. **jogging** /-ɡɪŋ/ *n* оздоровѝтельный бег.

join /dʒɔɪn/ *vt & i* соединя́ть(ся) *impf*, соединѝть(ся) *pf*; *vt* (*a group of people*) присоединя́ться *impf*, присоединѝться *pf* к+*dat*; (*as member*) вступáть *impf*, вступѝть *pf* в+*acc*; *vi*: **~ in** принимáть *impf*, приня́ть *pf* учáстие (в+*prep*); **~ up** вступáть *impf*, вступѝть *pf* в áрмию.

joiner /'dʒɔɪnə(r)/ *n* столя́р.

joint /dʒɔɪnt/ *n* соединéние; (*anat*) сустáв; (*meat*) кусóк;

adj совме́стный; (*common*) о́бщий.

joist /dʒɔɪst/ *n* перекла́дина.

joke /dʒəʊk/ *n* шу́тка; *vi* шути́ть *impf*, по~ *pf*. **joker** /-kə(r)/ *n* шутни́к; (*cards*) джо́кер.

jollity /'dʒɒlɪtɪ/ *n* весе́лье. **jolly** /-lɪ/ *adj* весёлый; *adv* о́чень.

jolt /dʒəʊlt/ *n* толчо́к; *vt & i* тряст́и(сь) *impf*.

jostle /'dʒɒs(ə)l/ *vt & i* толка́ть(ся) *impf*, толкну́ть(ся) *pf*.

jot /dʒɒt/ *n* йо́та; not a ~ ни на йо́ту; ~ (*down*) запи́сывать *impf*, записа́ть *pf*.

journal /'dʒɜːn(ə)l/ *n* журна́л; (*diary*) дневни́к. **journalese** /-'liːz/ *n* газе́тный язы́к. **journalism** /-lɪz(ə)m/ *n* журнали́стика. **journalist** /-lɪst/ *n* журнали́ст.

journey /'dʒɜːnɪ/ *n* путеше́ствие; *vi* путеше́ствовать *impf*.

jovial /'dʒəʊvɪəl/ *adj* весёлый.

joy /dʒɔɪ/ *n* ра́дость. **joyful**, **joyous** /-fʊl, -əs/ *adj* ра́достный. **joyless** /-lɪs/ *adj* безра́достный. **joystick** /n рыча́г управле́ния; (*comput*) джо́йстик.

jubilant /'dʒuːbɪlənt/ *adj* лику́ющий; be ~ ликова́ть *impf*. **jubilation** /-'leɪʃ(ə)n/ *n* ликова́ние.

jubilee /'dʒuːbɪˌliː/ *n* юбиле́й.

Judaism /'dʒuːdeɪˌɪz(ə)m/ *n* юдаи́зм.

judge /dʒʌdʒ/ *n* судья́ *m*; (*connoisseur*) цени́тель *m*; *vt & i* суди́ть *impf*. **judgement** /-mənt/ *n* (*legal decision*) реше́ние; (*opinion*) мне́ние; (*discernment*) рассуди́тельность.

judicial /dʒuːˈdɪʃ(ə)l/ *adj* суде́бный. **judiciary** /-ˈdɪʃɪərɪ/ *n* судьи́ *m pl*. **judicious** /-ˈdɪʃəs/ *adj* здравомы́слящий.

judo /'dʒuːdəʊ/ *n* дзюдо́ *neut in-*

jug /dʒʌɡ/ *n* кувши́н.

juggernaut /'dʒʌɡəˌnɔːt/ *n* (*lorry*) многото́нный грузови́к; (*fig*) неумоли́мая си́ла.

juggle /'dʒʌɡ(ə)l/ *vi* жонгли́ровать *impf*. **juggler** /'dʒʌɡlə(r)/ *n* жонглёр.

jugular /'dʒʌɡjʊlə(r)/ *n* яре́мная ве́на.

juice /dʒuːs/ *n* сок. **juicy** /-sɪ/ *adj* со́чный.

July /dʒuːˈlaɪ/ *n* ию́ль *m*; *adj* ию́льский.

jumble /'dʒʌmb(ə)l/ *n* (*disorder*) беспоря́док; (*articles*) барахло́; *vt* переп́утать pf, перепу́тать *pf*.

jump /dʒʌmp/ *n* прыжо́к, скачо́к; *vi* пры́гать *impf*, пры́гнуть *pf*, скака́ть *impf*; (*from shock*) вздра́гивать *impf*, вздро́гнуть *pf*; *vt* (~ *over*) перепры́гивать *impf*, перепры́гнуть *pf*; ~ at (*offer*) хвата́ться *impf*, хвати́ться *pf* за+*acc*; ~ up вска́кивать *impf*, вскочи́ть *pf*. **jumper** /'dʒʌmpə(r)/ *n* дже́мпер. **jumpy** /'dʒʌmpɪ/ *adj* не́рвный.

junction /'dʒʌŋkʃ(ə)n/ *n* (*rly*) у́зел; (*roads*) перекрёсток.

juncture /'dʒʌŋktʃ(ə)r/ *n*: at this ~ в э́тот моме́нт.

June /dʒuːn/ *n* ию́нь *m*; *adj* ию́ньский.

jungle /'dʒʌŋɡ(ə)l/ *n* джу́нгли (-лей) *pl*.

junior /'dʒuːnɪə(r)/ *adj* мла́дший; ~ school нача́льная шко́ла.

juniper /'dʒuːnɪpə(r)/ *n* можже́вельник.

junk /dʒʌŋk/ *n* (*rubbish*) барахло́.

jurisdiction /ˌdʒʊərɪsˈdɪkʃ(ə)n/ *n* юрисди́кция.

jurisprudence /ˌdʒʊərɪsˈpruːd(ə)ns/ *n* юриспруде́нция.

juror /'dʒʊərə(r)/ *n* прися́жный *sb*. **jury** /'dʒʊərɪ/ *n* прися́жные *sb*; (*in competition*) жюри́ *neut indecl*.

just /dʒʌst/ *adj* (*fair*) справедли́вый; (*deserved*) заслу́женный; *adv* (*exactly*) как раз, и́менно; (*simply*) про́сто; (*barely*) едва́; (*very recently*) то́лько что; ~ **in case** на вся́кий слу́чай.

justice /'dʒʌstɪs/ *n* (*proceedings*) правосу́дие; (*fairness*) справедли́вость; **do** ~ **to** отдава́ть *impf*, отда́ть *pf* до́лжное +*dat*.

justify /'dʒʌstɪfaɪ/ *vt* опра́вдывать *impf*, оправда́ть *pf*. **justification** /-fɪ'keɪʃ(ə)n/ *n* оправда́ние.

jut /dʒʌt/ *vi* (~ *out*) выдава́ться *impf*; выступа́ть *impf*.

juvenile /'dʒuːvənaɪl/ *n & adj* несовершенноле́тний *sb & adj*.

juxtapose /,dʒʌkstə'pəʊz/ *vt* помеща́ть, помести́ть *pf* ря́дом; (*for comparison*) сопоставля́ть *impf*, сопоста́вить *pf* (**with** *c*+*instr*).

K

kaleidoscope /kə'laɪdəskəʊp/ *n* калейдоско́п.

kangaroo /,kæŋgə'ruː/ *n* кенгуру́ *m indecl*.

Kazakhstan /,kæzæk'stɑːn/ *n* Казахста́н.

keel /kiːl/ *n* киль *m*; *vi*: ~ **over** опроки́дываться *impf*, опроки́нуться *pf*.

keen /kiːn/ *adj* (*enthusiastic*) по́лный энтузиа́зма; (*sharp*) о́стрый; (*strong*) си́льный; **be** ~ **on** увлека́ться *impf*, увле́чься *pf* +*instr*; (*want to do*) о́чень хоте́ть *impf* +*inf*.

keep[1] /kiːp/ *n* (*tower*) гла́вная ба́шня; (*maintenance*) содержа́ние.

keep[2] /kiːp/ *vt* (*possess, maintain*) держа́ть *impf*; храни́ть *impf*; (*observe*) соблюда́ть *impf*, соблюсти́ *pf* (*the law*); сде́рживать *impf*, сдержа́ть *pf* (*one's word*); (*family*) содержа́ть *impf*; (*diary*) вести́ *impf*; (*retain*) заде́рживать *impf*, задержа́ть *pf*; (*retain, reserve*) сохраня́ть *impf*, сохрани́ть *pf*; *vi* (*remain*) остава́ться *impf*; (*of food*) не по́ртиться *impf*; ~ **back** (*vt*) (*hold back*) уде́рживать *impf*, удержа́ть *pf*; (*vi*) держа́ться *impf* сза́ди; ~ **doing sth** всё +*verb*: **she** ~**s giggling** она́ всё хихи́кает; ~ **from** уде́рживаться *impf*, удержа́ться *pf* от+*gen*; **on** продолжа́ть *impf*, продо́лжить *pf* (+*inf*); ~ **up** (*with*) (*vi*) не отстава́ть *impf* (от+*gen*).

keepsake /'kiːpseɪk/ *n* пода́рок на па́мять.

keg /keg/ *n* бочо́нок.

kennel /'ken(ə)l/ *n* конура́.

kerb /kɜːb/ *n* край тротуа́ра.

kernel /'kɜːn(ə)l/ *n* (*nut*) ядро́; (*grain*) зерно́; (*fig*) суть.

kerosene /'kerəsiːn/ *n* кероси́н.

kettle /'ket(ə)l/ *n* ча́йник.

key /kiː/ *n* ключ; (*piano, typewriter*) кла́виш(а); (*mus*) тона́льность; *attrib* веду́щий, ключево́й; **keyboard** *n* клавиату́ра. **keyhole** *n* замо́чная сква́жина.

KGB *abbr* КГБ.

khaki /'kɑːkɪ/ *n & adj* ха́ки *neut, adj indecl*.

kick /kɪk/ *n* уда́р ного́й, пино́к; *vt* ударя́ть *impf*, уда́рить *pf* ного́й; пина́ть *impf*, пнуть *pf*; *vi* (*of horse etc.*) ляга́ться

kick-off /'kɪkɔːf/ n нача́ло (игры́).

kid¹ /kɪd/ n (goat) козлёнок; (child) малы́ш.

kid² /kɪd/ vt (deceive) обма́нывать impf, обману́ть pf; (joke) шути́ть impf, по~ pf.

kidnap /'kɪdnæp/ vt похища́ть impf, похи́тить pf.

kidney /'kɪdnɪ/ n по́чка.

kill /kɪl/ vt убива́ть impf, уби́ть pf. **killer** /-lə(r)/ n уби́йца m & f. **killing** /-lɪŋ/ n уби́йство; adj (murderous, fig) уби́йственный; (amusing) умори́тельный.

kiln /kɪln/ n о́бжиговая печь.

kilo /'kiːləʊ/ n кило́ neut indecl. **kilohertz** /'kɪlə,hɜːts/ n килоге́рц. **kilogram(me)** /'kɪlə,græm/ n килогра́мм. **kilometre** /'kɪlə,miːtə(r)/ n киломе́тр. **kilowatt** /'kɪlə,wɒt/ n килова́тт.

kilt /kɪlt/ n шотла́ндская ю́бка.

kimono /kɪ'məʊnəʊ/ n кимоно́ neut indecl.

kin /kɪn/ n (family) семья́; (collect, relatives) родня́.

kind¹ /kaɪnd/ n сорт, род; a ~ of что́-то вро́де+gen; this ~ of тако́й; **what** ~ **of** что (э́то, он, etc.) за +nom; ~ **of** (adv) как бу́дто, ка́к-то.

kind² /kaɪnd/ adj до́брый.

kindergarten /'kɪndə,gɑːt(ə)n/ n де́тский сад.

kindle /'kɪnd(ə)l/ vt зажига́ть impf, заже́чь pf; **kindling** /-dlɪŋ/ n расто́пка.

kindly /'kaɪndlɪ/ adj до́брый; adv любе́зно; (with imper) (request) бу́дьте добры́, +imper. **kindness** /'kaɪndnɪs/ n доброта́.

kindred /'kɪndrɪd/ adj: ~ **spirit** родна́я душа́.

kinetic /kɪ'netɪk/ adj кинети́ческий.

king /kɪŋ/ n коро́ль m (also chess, cards, fig); (draughts)

да́мка. **kingdom** /'kɪŋdəm/ n короле́вство; (fig) ца́рство. **kingfisher** /'kɪŋfɪʃə(r)/ n зиморо́док.

kink /kɪŋk/ n переги́б.

kinship /'kɪnʃɪp/ n родство́; (similarity) схо́дство. **kinsman, -woman** n ро́дственник, -ица.

kiosk /'kiːɒsk/ n кио́ск; (telephone) бу́дка.

kip /kɪp/ n сон; vi дры́хнуть impf.

kipper /'kɪpə(r)/ n копчёная селёдка.

Kirghizia /kɜː'gɪzɪə/ n Кирги́зия.

kiss /kɪs/ n поцелу́й; vt & i целова́ть(ся) impf, по~ pf.

kit /kɪt/ n (clothing) снаряже́ние; (tools) набо́р, компле́кт; vt: ~ **out** снаряжа́ть impf, снаряди́ть pf. **kitbag** n вещево́й мешо́к.

kitchen /'kɪtʃɪn/ n ку́хня; attrib ку́хонный; **garden** огоро́д.

kite /kaɪt/ n (toy) змей.

kitsch /kɪtʃ/ n китч.

kitten /'kɪt(ə)n/ n котёнок.

knack /næk/ n сноро́вка.

knapsack /'næpsæk/ n рюкза́к.

knead /niːd/ vt меси́ть impf, с~ pf.

knee /niː/ n коле́но. **kneecap** n коле́нная ча́шка.

kneel /niːl/ vi стоя́ть impf на коле́нях; (~ **down**) станови́ться impf, стать pf на коле́ни.

knickers /'nɪkəz/ n pl тру́сики (-ов) pl.

knick-knack /'nɪknæk/ n безделу́шка.

knife /naɪf/ n нож; vt коло́ть impf, за~ pf ножо́м.

knight /naɪt/ n (hist) ры́царь m; (holder of order) кавале́р; (chess) конь m. **knighthood** /-hʊd/ n ры́царское зва́ние.

knit /nɪt/ vt (garment) вяза́ть

impf, с~ *pf*; *vi* (*bones*) сра-
ста́ться *impf*, срасти́сь *pf*; ~
one's brows хму́рить *impf*, на-
~ *pf* бро́ви. **knitting** /-tɪŋ/ *n* (*action*) вяза́ние; (*object*) вяза́нье;
~-needle спи́ца. **knitwear** *n*
трикота́ж.

knob /nɒb/ *n* ши́шка, кно́пка;
(*door handle*) ру́чка. **knobb(l)y**
/'nɒb(l)ɪ/ *adj* ши́шкова́тый.

knock /nɒk/ *n* (*noise*) стук;
(*blow*) уда́р; vt & i (*strike*) уда-
ря́ть *impf*, уда́рить *pf* (*strike
door etc.*) стуча́ть *impf*, по~ *pf*
(at в+*acc*); ~ about (*treat
roughly*) колоти́ть *impf*, по~
pf; (*wander*) шата́ться *impf*; ~
down (*person*) сбива́ть *impf*,
сбить *pf* с ног; (*building*) сно-
си́ть *impf*, снести́ *pf*; ~ off сби-
ва́ть *impf*, сбить *pf*; (*stop work*)
шаба́шить *impf* (рабо́ту); (*deduct*) сба́влять *impf*, сба́вить
pf; ~ out выбива́ть *impf*, вы́-
бить *pf*; (*sport*) нокаути́ровать
impf & *pf*; ~-out нока́ут; ~ over
опроки́дывать *impf*, опроки́-
нуть *impf* нока́ут; ~ over
дверно́й молото́к. **knocker** /'nɒkə(r)/ *n*

knoll /nəʊl/ *n* буго́р.

knot /nɒt/ *n* у́зел; vt завя́зывать
impf, завяза́ть *pf* узло́м. **knotty**
/-tɪ/ *adj* (*fig*) запу́танный.

know /nəʊ/ *vt* знать *impf*; (~
how to) уме́ть *impf*, с~ *pf* +*inf*;
~-how уме́ние. **knowing**
/'nəʊɪŋ/ *adj* многозначи́тель-
ный. **knowingly** /'nəʊɪŋlɪ/ *adv*
созна́тельно. **knowledge**
/'nɒlɪdʒ/ *n* зна́ние; to my ~ на-
ско́лько мне изве́стно.

knuckle /'nʌk(ə)l/ *n* суста́в
па́льца; vi: ~ down to впря-
га́ться *impf*, впря́чься *pf*
в+*acc*; ~ under уступа́ть *impf*,
уступи́ть *pf* (to +*dat*).

Korea /kə'riːə/ *n* Коре́я.

ko(w)tow /kaʊ'taʊ/ *vi* (*fig*) ра-
боле́пствовать *impf* (to пе́ред
+*instr*).

Kremlin /'kremlɪn/ *n* Кремль *m*.

kudos /'kjuːdɒs/ *n* сла́ва.

L

label /'leɪb(ə)l/ *n* этике́тка,
ярлы́к; vt прикле́ивать *impf*,
прикле́ить *pf* ярлы́к к+*dat*.

laboratory /lə'bɒrətərɪ/ *n* лабо-
рато́рия.

laborious /lə'bɔːrɪəs/ *adj* кро-
потли́вый.

labour /'leɪbə(r)/ *n* труд; (*med*)
ро́ды (-дов) *pl*; *attrib* трудо-
во́й; ~ force рабо́чая си́ла;
~-intensive трудоёмкий; ~
Party лейбори́стская па́ртия;
vi труди́ться *impf*; *vt*: ~ a point
входи́ть *impf*, войти́ *pf* в
изли́шние подро́бности.

laboured /-bəd/ *adj*
затруднённый; (*style*) вы́му-
ченный. **labourer** /-bərə(r)/ *n*
черноробо́чий *sb*. **labourite**
/-bə,raɪt/ *n* лейбори́ст.

labyrinth /'læbərɪnθ/ *n* лаби-
ри́нт.

lace /leɪs/ *n* (*fabric*) кру́жево;
(*cord*) шнуро́к; vt (~ up) шну-
рова́ть *impf*, за~ *pf*.

lacerate /'læsə,reɪt/ *vt* (*also fig*)
терза́ть *impf*, ис~ *pf*. **lacer-
ation** /-'reɪʃ(ə)n/ *n* (*wound*) рва́-
ная ра́на.

lack /læk/ *n* недоста́ток (+*gen*,
в+*prep*), отсу́тствие; vt & i не
хвата́ть *impf*, хвати́ть *pf
impers* +*dat* (*person*), +*gen* (*object*).

lackadaisical /,lækə'deɪzɪk(ə)l/
adj то́мный.

laconic /lə'kɒnɪk/ *adj* лако-

ни́чный.

lacquer /ˈlækə(r)/ *n* лак; *vt* лакирова́ть *impf*, от~ *pf.*

lad /læd/ *n* па́рень *m.*

ladder /ˈlædə(r)/ *n* ле́стница.

laden /ˈleɪd(ə)n/ *adj* нагру́женный.

ladle /ˈleɪd(ə)l/ *n* (*spoon*) полови́к; *vt* че́рпать *impf*, черпну́ть *pf.*

lady /ˈleɪdɪ/ *n* да́ма, ле́ди *f indecl.* **ladybird** *n* бо́жья коро́вка.

lag¹ /læg/ *vi*: ~ **behind** отстава́ть *impf*, отста́ть *pf* (**от**+*gen*).

lag² /læg/ *vt* (*insulate*) изоли́ровать *impf & pf.*

lagoon /ləˈguːn/ *n* лагу́на.

lair /leə(r)/ *n* ло́говище.

laity /ˈleɪtɪ/ *n* (*in religion*) миря́не (-н) *pl.*

lake /leɪk/ *n* о́зеро.

lamb /læm/ *n* ягнёнок; (*meat*) бара́нина.

lame /leɪm/ *adj* хромо́й; **be** ~ хрома́ть *impf*; **go** ~ хроме́ть *impf*, о~ *pf*; *vt* кале́чить *impf*, о~ *pf.*

lament /ləˈment/ *n* плач; *vt* сожале́ть *impf* о+*prep.* **lamentable** /ˈlæməntəb(ə)l/ *adj* приско́рбный.

laminated /ˈlæmɪˌneɪtɪd/ *adj* сло́истый.

lamp /læmp/ *n* ла́мпа; (*in street*) фона́рь *m.* **lamp-post** *n* фона́рный столб. **lampshade** *n* абажу́р.

lance /lɑːns/ *n* пи́ка; *vt* (*med*) вскрыва́ть *impf*, вскрыть *pf* (ланце́том).

land /lænd/ *n* земля́; (*dry* ~) су́ша; (*country*) страна́; *vi* (*naut*) прича́ливать *impf*, прича́лить *pf*; *vt & i* (*aeron*) приземля́ть(ся) *impf*, приземли́ть(ся) *pf*; (*find o.s.*)

landing /-dɪŋ/ *n* (*aeron*) поса́дка; (*on stairs*) площа́дка. **~stage** при́стань. **landlady** *n* хозя́йка. **landlord** *n* хозя́ин. **landmark** *n* (*conspicuous object*) ориенти́р; (*fig*) ве́ха. **landowner** *n* землевладе́лец. **landscape** /ˈlændskeɪp/ *n* ландша́фт; (*also picture*) пейза́ж. **landslide** *n* о́ползень *m.*

lane /leɪn/ *n* (*in country*) доро́жка; (*street*) переу́лок; (*passage*) прохо́д; (*on road*) ряд; (*in race*) доро́жка.

language /ˈlæŋɡwɪdʒ/ *n* язы́к; (*style, speech*) речь.

languid /ˈlæŋɡwɪd/ *adj* то́мный.

languish /ˈlæŋɡwɪʃ/ *vi* томи́ться *impf.*

languor /ˈlæŋɡə(r)/ *n* то́мность.

lank /læŋk/ *adj* (*hair*) гла́дкий. **lanky** /-kɪ/ *adj* долговя́зый.

lantern /ˈlænt(ə)n/ *n* фона́рь *m.*

lap¹ /læp/ *n* (*of person*) коле́ни (-ней) *pl*; (*sport*) круг.

lap² /læp/ *vt* (*drink*) лака́ть *impf*, вы́~ *pf*; *vi* (*water*) плеска́ться *impf.*

lapel /ləˈpel/ *n* отворо́т.

lapse /læps/ *n* (*mistake*) оши́бка; (*interval*) промежу́ток; (*expiry*) истече́ние; *vi* впада́ть *impf*, впасть *pf* (**into** в+*acc*); (*expire*) истека́ть *impf*, исте́чь *pf.*

laptop /ˈlæptɒp/ *n* портати́вный компью́тер.

lapwing /ˈlæpwɪŋ/ *n* чи́бис.

larch /lɑːtʃ/ *n* ли́ственница.

lard /lɑːd/ *n* свино́е са́ло.

larder /ˈlɑːdə(r)/ *n* кладова́я *sb.*

large /lɑːdʒ/ *adj* большо́й; **at** ~ (*free*) на свобо́де; **by and** ~ вообще́ говоря́. **largely** /-lɪ/ *adv* в значи́тельной сте́пени.

largesse /lɑːˈʒes/ *n* ще́дрость.

lark¹ /lɑːk/ *n* (*bird*) жа́воронок.

lark² /lɑːk/ n прока́за; vi (~ about) резви́ться impf.

larva /ˈlɑːvə/ n личи́нка.

laryngitis /ˌlærɪnˈdʒaɪtɪs/ n ларинги́т. **larynx** /ˈlærɪŋks/ n горта́нь.

lascivious /ləˈsɪvɪəs/ adj похотли́вый.

laser /ˈleɪzə(r)/ n ла́зер.

lash /læʃ/ n (blow) уда́р пле́тью; (eyelash) ресни́ца; vt (beat) хлеста́ть impf, хлестну́ть pf; (tie) привя́зывать impf, привяза́ть pf (**to** к+dat).

last¹ /lɑːst/ adj (final) после́дний; (most recent) про́шлый; **the year** (etc.) ~ про́шлый год (и т.д.); ~ **but one** предпосле́дний; ~ **night** вчера́ ве́чером; **at** ~ наконе́ц; adv (after all others) по́сле всех; (on the last occasion) в после́дний раз; (lastly) наконе́ц.

last² /lɑːst/ vi (go on) продолжа́ться impf, продо́лжиться pf; дли́ться impf, про~ pf; (be served) сохраня́ться impf, сохрани́ться pf; (suffice) хвата́ть impf, хвати́ть pf. **lasting** /-tɪŋ/ adj (permanent) постоя́нный; (durable) про́чный.

lastly /ˈlɑːstlɪ/ adv в заключе́ние; наконе́ц.

latch /lætʃ/ n щеко́лда.

late /leɪt/ adj (tardy, recent) по́здний; (dead) поко́йный; **be** ~ **for** опа́здывать impf, опозда́ть pf на+acc; adv по́здно. **lately** /-lɪ/ adv в после́днее вре́мя. **later** /-tə(r)/ adj (of two) по́зже; **a year** ~ год спустя́; **see you** ~! пока́!

latent /ˈleɪt(ə)nt/ adj скры́тый.

lateral /ˈlætər(ə)l/ adj боково́й.

lath /lɑːθ/ n ре́йка.

lathe /leɪð/ n тока́рный стано́к.

lather /ˈlɑːðə(r)/ n (мы́льная

пе́на; vt & i мы́лить(ся) impf, на~ pf.

Latin /ˈlætɪn/ adj лати́нский; n лати́нский язы́к; ~-**American** латиноамерика́нский.

latitude /ˈlætɪˌtjuːd/ n свобо́да; (geog) широта́.

latter /ˈlætə(r)/ adj после́дний; ~-**day** совреме́нный. **latterly** /-lɪ/ adv в после́днее вре́мя.

lattice /ˈlætɪs/ n решётка.

Latvia /ˈlætvɪə/ n Ла́твия. **Latvian** /-ən/ n латви́ец, -и́йка; латы́ш, ~ка; adj латви́йский; латы́шский.

laud /lɔːd/ vt хвали́ть impf, по~ pf. **laudable** /-dəb(ə)l/ adj похва́льный.

laugh /lɑːf/ n смех; vi смея́ться impf (**at** над+instr); ~ **it off** отшу́чиваться impf, отшути́ться pf; ~-**ing-stock** посме́шище. **laughable** /-fəb(ə)l/ adj смешно́й. **laughter** /-tə(r)/ n смех.

launch¹ /lɔːntʃ/ vt (ship) спуска́ть impf, спусти́ть pf на́ воду; (rocket) запуска́ть impf, запусти́ть pf; (undertake) начина́ть impf, нача́ть pf; n спуск на́ воду; за́пуск. **launcher** /-tʃə(r)/ n (for rocket) пусково́е устано́вка. **launching pad** /ˈlɔːntʃɪŋ ˌpæd/ n пускова́я площа́дка.

launch² /lɔːntʃ/ n (naut) ка́тер.

launder /ˈlɔːndə(r)/ vt стира́ть impf, вы́~ pf. **laund(e)rette** /-ˈdret/ n пра́чечная sb самообслу́живания. **laundry** /-drɪ/ n (place) пра́чечная sb; (articles) бельё.

laurel /ˈlɒr(ə)l/ n ла́вр(овое де́рево).

lava /ˈlɑːvə/ n ла́ва.

lavatory /ˈlævətərɪ/ n убо́рная sb.

lavender /ˈlævɪndə(r)/ n лава́нда.

lavish /ˈlævɪʃ/ adj щедрый; (abundant) обильный; vt расточать impf (upon +dat).

law /lɔ:/ n закон; (system) право; (order) правопорядок. **law-court** n суд. **lawful** /-fʊl/ adj законный. **lawless** /-lɪs/ adj беззаконный.

lawn /lɔ:n/ n газон; ~-mower газонокосилка.

lawsuit /ˈlɔ:su:t/ n процесс.

lawyer /ˈlɔɪə(r)/ n адвокат, юрист.

lax /læks/ adj слабый. **laxative** /-sətɪv/ n слабительное sb. **laxity** /-sɪtɪ/ n слабость.

lay¹ /leɪ/ adj (non-clerical) светский.

lay² /leɪ/ vt (place) класть impf, положить pf; (cable, pipes) прокладывать impf, проложить pf; (carpet) стлать impf, по~ pf; (trap etc.) устраивать impf, устроить pf; (eggs) класть impf, положить pf; v abs (lay eggs) нестись impf, c~ pf; ~ aside откладывать impf, отложить pf; ~ bare раскрывать impf, раскрыть pf; ~ a bet держать impf пари (on на+acc); ~ down (relinquish) отказываться impf, отказаться pf от+gen; (rule etc.) устанавливать impf, установить pf; ~ off (workmen) увольнять impf, уволить pf; ~ out (spread) выкладывать impf, выложить pf; (garden) разбивать impf, разбить pf; ~ the table накрывать impf, накрыть pf стол (for (meal) к+dat); ~ up запасать impf, запасти pf +acc, +gen; be laid up быть прикованным к постели. **layabout** n бездельник.

layer /ˈleɪə(r)/ n слой, пласт.

layman /ˈleɪmən/ n мирянин; (non-expert) неспециалист.

laze /leɪz/ vi бездельничать impf. **laziness** /-zɪnɪs/ n лень. **lazy** /-zɪ/ adj ленивый; ~-bones лентяй, ~ка.

lead¹ /li:d/ n (example) пример; (leadership) руководство; (position) первое место; (theat) главная роль; (electr) провод; (dog's) поводок; vt ведущий indet, вести det; (be in charge of) руководить impf +instr; (induce) побуждать impf, побудить pf vt & i (cards) ходить impf (c+gen); (sport) занимать impf, занять pf первое место; ~ away уводить impf, увести pf; ~ to (result in) приводить impf, привести pf к+dat.

lead² /led/ n (metal) свинец. **leaden** /ˈled(ə)n/ adj свинцовый.

leader /ˈli:də(r)/ n руководитель m, ~ница, лидер; (mus) первая скрипка; (editorial) передовая статья. **leadership** n руководство.

leading /ˈli:dɪŋ/ adj ведущий, выдающийся; ~ article передовая статья.

leaf /li:f/ n лист; (of table) откидная доска; vi: ~ through перелистывать impf, перелистать pf. **leaflet** /ˈli:flɪt/ n листовка.

league /li:g/ n лига; in ~ with в союзе с +instr.

leak /li:k/ n течь, утечка; vi (escape) течь impf; (allow water to) ~ пропускать impf воду; ~ out просачиваться impf, просочиться pf.

lean¹ /li:n/ adj (thin) худой; (meat) постный.

lean² /li:n/ vt & i прислонять(ся) impf, прислонить(ся) pf (against к+dat); (be inclined)

быть скло́нным (to(wards)
к+dat); ~ **back** отки́дываться
impf, отки́нуться pf; ~ **out of**
высо́вываться impf, вы́суну-
ться pf в+acc. **leaning** /-nɪŋ/
n скло́нность.

leap /liːp/ n прыжо́к, скачо́к; vi
пры́гать impf, пры́гнуть pf;
скака́ть impf, ~ **year** високо́с-
ный год.

learn /lɜːn/ vt (a subject) учи́ть
impf, вы́~ pf; (to do sth) учи́ть-
ся impf, на~ pf +inf; (find
out) узнава́ть impf, узна́ть pf.
learned /-nɪd/ adj учёный.
learner /-nə(r)/ n учени́к, -и́ца.
learning /-nɪŋ/ n (studies) уче́-
ние; (erudition) учёность.

lease /liːs/ n аре́нда; vt (of
owner) сдава́ть impf, сдать pf в
аре́нду; (of tenant) брать impf,
взять pf в аре́нду. **leaseholder**
/-ˌhəʊldə(r)/ n аренда́тор.

leash /liːʃ/ n привя́зь.

least /liːst/ adj наиме́ньший,
мале́йший; adv ме́нее всего́; **at**
~ по кра́йней ме́ре; **not in the**
~ ничу́ть.

leather /ˈleðə(r)/ n ко́жа; attrib
ко́жаный.

leave[1] /liːv/ n (permission) раз-
реше́ние; (holiday) о́тпуск; **on**
~ в о́тпуске; **take (one's)** ~ про-
ща́ться impf, прости́ться pf (**of**
c+instr).

leave[2] /liːv/ vt & i оставля́ть
impf, оста́вить pf; (abandon)
покида́ть impf, поки́нуть pf;
(go away) уходи́ть impf, уйти́
pf (**from** от+gen); уезжа́ть impf,
уе́хать pf (**from** от+gen); (go
out of) выходи́ть impf, вы́йти
pf из+gen; (entrust) предостав-
ля́ть impf, предоста́вить pf
(**to** +dat); ~ **out** пропуска́ть
impf, пропусти́ть pf.

lecherous /ˈletʃərəs/ adj раз-

вра́тный.

lectern /ˈlektɜːn/ n аналойй; (in
lecture room) пюпи́тр.

lecture /ˈlektʃə(r)/ n (discourse)
ле́кция; (reproof) нота́ция; (
deliver ~s) чита́ть impf,
про~ pf ле́кцию (-ии) (on
по+dat); vt (admonish) чита́ть
impf, про~ pf нота́цию+dat; ~
room аудито́рия. **lecturer**
/-tʃərə(r)/ n ле́ктор; (univ) пре-
подава́тель m, ~ница.

ledge /ledʒ/ n вы́ступ; (shelf)
по́лочка.

ledger /ˈledʒə(r)/ n гла́вная
кни́га.

lee /liː/ n защи́та; adj подве́т-
ренный.

leech /liːtʃ/ n (worm) пия́вка.

leek /liːk/ n лук-поре́й.

leer /lɪə(r)/ vi криви́ться impf,
с~ pf.

leeward /ˈliːwəd/ n подве́трен-
ная сторона́; adj подве́т-
ренный.

leeway /ˈliːweɪ/ n (fig) свобо́да
де́йствий.

left /left/ n ле́вая сторона́; (the
~; polit) ле́вые sb pl; adj
ле́вый; adv нале́во, сле́ва (of
от+gen). **~hander** левша́ m &
f; **~wing** ле́вый.

left-luggage office /left ˈlʌɡɪdʒ
ˈɒfɪs/ n ка́мера хране́ния.

leftovers /ˈleftˌəʊvəz/ n pl оста́т-
ки m pl; (food) объе́дки
(-ков) pl.

leg /leg/ n нога́; (of furniture
etc.) но́жка; (of journey etc.)
эта́п.

legacy /ˈleɡəsɪ/ n насле́дство.

legal /ˈliːɡ(ə)l/ adj (of the law)
правово́й; (lawful) лега́льный.
legality /lɪˈɡælɪtɪ/ n лега́ль-
ность. **legalize** /ˈliːɡəlaɪz/ vt ле-
гализова́ть impf & pf.

legend /ˈledʒ(ə)nd/ n леге́нда.

legendary /-dʒəndərɪ/ adj легендáрный.

leggings /'legɪnz/ n pl вя́заные рейтýзы (-з) pl.

legible /'ledʒɪb(ə)l/ adj разбóрчивый.

legion /'liːdʒ(ə)n/ n легио́н.

legislate /'ledʒɪs,leɪt/ vi издавáть impf, издáть pf закóны. **legislation** /ˌledʒɪs'leɪʃ(ə)n/ n законодáтельство. **legislative** /'ledʒɪslətɪv/ adj законодáтельный. **legislator** /'ledʒɪs,leɪtə(r)/ n законодáтель m. **legislature** /'ledʒɪs,lətʃə(r)/ n законодáтельные учреждéния neut pl.

legitimacy /lɪ'dʒɪtɪməsɪ/ n законность; (of child) законнорождённость. **legitimate** /-mət/ adj закóнный; (child) законнорождённый. **legitimize** /-ˌmaɪz/ vt узакóнивать impf, узакóнить pf.

leisure /'leʒə(r)/ n свобóдное врéмя, досýг; **at ~** на досýге. **leisurely** /-lɪ/ adj неторопли́вый.

lemon /'lemən/ n лимóн. **lemonade** /ˌlemə'neɪd/ n лимонáд.

lend /lend/ vt давáть impf, дать pf взаймы́ (**to** +dat); одáлживать impf, одолжи́ть pf (**to** +dat).

length /leŋθ/ n длина́; (of time) продолжи́тельность; (of cloth) отрéз; **at ~** подрóбно. **lengthen** /'leŋθ(ə)n/ vt & i удлиня́ть(ся) impf, удлини́ть(ся) pf. **lengthways** adv в длину́, вдоль. **lengthy** /-θɪ/ adj дли́нный.

leniency /'liːnɪənsɪ/ n снисходи́тельность. **lenient** /-ənt/ adj снисходи́тельный.

lens /lenz/ n ли́нза; (phot) объекти́в; (anat) хруста́лик.

Lent /lent/ n вели́кий пост.

lentil /'lentɪl/ n чечеви́ца.

legendary — **legendary**

Leo /'liːəʊ/ n Лев.

leopard /'lepəd/ n леопáрд.

leotard /'liːə,tɑːd/ n трико́ neut indecl.

leper /'lepə(r)/ n прокажённый sb. **leprosy** /'leprəsɪ/ n прокáза.

lesbian /'lezbɪən/ n лесбия́нка; adj лесби́йский.

lesion /'liːʒ(ə)n/ n поврежде́ние.

less /les/ adj ме́ньший; adv ме́ньше, ме́нее; prep за вы́четом +gen.

lessee /le'siː/ n арендáтор.

lessen /'les(ə)n/ vt & i уменьшáть(ся) impf, уме́ньшить(ся) pf.

lesser /'lesə(r)/ adj ме́ньший.

lesson /'les(ə)n/ n урóк.

lest /lest/ conj (in order that not) чтóбы не; (that) как бы не.

let /let/ n (lease) сдáча в наём; vt (allow) позволя́ть impf, позвóлить pf +dat; разрешáть impf, разреши́ть pf +dat; (rent out) сдавáть impf, сдать pf внаём (**to** +dat); v aux (imperative) (1st person) давáй(те); (3rd person) пусть; **~ alone** не говоря́ уже́ о+prep; **~ down** (lower) опускáть impf, опусти́ть pf; (fail) подводи́ть impf, подвести́ pf; (disappoint) разочарóвывать impf, разочарова́ть pf; **~ go** выпускáть impf, вы́пустить pf; **~'s go** пойдёмте!; пошли́!; поéхали!; **~ in(to)** (admit) впускáть impf, впусти́ть pf в+acc; (into secret) посвящáть impf, посвяти́ть pf в+acc; **~ know** давáть impf, дать pf знать +dat; **~ off** (gun) вы́стрелить pf из+gen; (not punish) отпускáть impf, отпусти́ть pf без наказа́ния; **~ out** (release, loosen) выпускáть impf, вы́пустить pf; **~ through** пропускáть impf, пропусти́ть pf; **~ up** за-

тиха́ть *impf*, зати́хнуть *pf*.

lethal /'li:θ(ə)l/ *adj* (*fatal*) смерте́льный; (*weapon*) смертоно́сный.

lethargic /lı'θɑ:dʒık/ *adj* летарги́ческий. **lethargy** /'leθədʒı/ *n* летарги́я.

letter /'letə(r)/ *n* письмо́; (*symbol*) бу́ква; (*printing*) ли́тера; **~-box** почто́вый я́щик. **lettering** /-rıŋ/ *n* шрифт.

lettuce /'letıs/ *n* сала́т.

leukaemia /lu:'ki:mıə/ *n* лейке́мия.

level /'lev(ə)l/ *n* у́ровень; *adj* ро́вный; **~ crossing** (железнодоро́жный) перее́зд; **~-headed** уравнове́шенный; *vt* (*make ~*) выра́внивать *impf*, вы́ровнять *pf*; (*sport*) сра́внивать *impf*, сравня́ть *pf*; (*gun*) наводи́ть *impf*, навести́ *pf* (**at** в, на, +*acc*); (*criticism*) направля́ть *impf*, напра́вить *pf* (**at** про́тив+*gen*).

lever /'li:və(r)/ *n* рыча́г. **leverage** /-rıdʒ/ *n* де́йствие рычага́; (*influence*) влия́ние.

levity /'levıtı/ *n* легкомы́слие.

levy /'levı/ *n* (*tax*) сбор; *vt* (*tax*) взима́ть *impf* (**from** c+*gen*).

lewd /lju:d/ *adj* (*lascivious*) похотли́вый; (*indecent*) са́льный.

lexicon /'leksıkən/ *n* словарь *m*.

liability /laıə'bılıtı/ *n* (*responsibility*) отве́тственность (**for** за+*acc*); (*burden*) обу́за. **liable** /'laıəb(ə)l/ *adj* отве́тственный (**for** за+*acc*); (*susceptible*) подве́рженный (**to** +*dat*).

liaise /lı'eız/ *vi* подде́рживать *impf* связь (**c**+*instr*). **liaison** /-'eızɒn/ *n* связь; (*affair*) любо́вная связь.

liar /'laıə(r)/ *n* лгун, ~ья.

libel /'laıb(ə)l/ *n* клевета́; *vt* клевета́ть *impf*, на~ *pf* на+*acc*.

libellous /-bələs/ *adj* клеветни́ческий.

liberal /'lıbər(ə)l/ *n* либера́л; *adj* либера́льный; (*generous*) ще́дрый.

liberate /'lıbə,reıt/ *vt* освобожда́ть *impf*, освободи́ть *pf*. **liberation** /-'reıʃ(ə)n/ *n* освобожде́ние. **liberator** /'lıbə,reıtə(r)/ *n* освободи́тель *m*.

libertine /'lıbə,ti:n/ *n* распу́тник.

liberty /'lıbətı/ *n* свобо́да; **at ~** на свобо́де.

Libra /'li:brə/ *n* Весы́ (-со́в) *pl*.

librarian /laı'breərıən/ *n* библиоте́карь *m*. **library** /'laıbrərı/ *n* библиоте́ка.

libretto /lı'bretəʊ/ *n* либре́тто *neut indecl*.

licence[1] /'laıs(ə)ns/ *n* (*permission, permit*) разреше́ние, лице́нзия; (*liberty*) (изли́шняя) во́льность. **license, -ce**[2] /'laıs(ə)ns/ *vt* (*allow*) разреша́ть *impf*, разреши́ть *pf* +*dat*; дава́ть *impf*, дать *pf* пра́во +*dat*.

licentious /laı'senʃəs/ *adj* распу́щенный.

lichen /'laıkən/ *n* лиша́йник.

lick /lık/ *n* лиза́ние; *vt* лиза́ть *impf*, лизну́ть *pf*.

lid /lıd/ *n* кры́шка; (*eyelid*) ве́ко.

lie[1] /laı/ *n* (*untruth*) ложь; *vi* лгать *impf*, со~ *pf*.

lie[2] /laı/ *n*: **~ of the land** (*fig*) положе́ние веще́й; *vi* лежа́ть *impf*; (*be situated*) находи́ться *impf*; **~ down** ложи́ться *impf*, лечь *pf*; **~ in** остава́ться *impf* в посте́ли.

lieu /lju:/ *n*: **in ~ of** вме́сто+*gen*.

lieutenant /lef'tenənt/ *n* лейтена́нт.

life /laıf/ *n* жизнь; (*way of ~*) о́браз жи́зни; (*energy*) жи-

вость. **lifebelt** *n* спаса́тельный по́яс. **lifeboat** *n* спаса́тельная ло́дка. **lifebuoy** *n* спаса́тельный круг. **lifeguard** *n* спаса́тель *m*, -ница. **life-jacket** *n* спаса́тельный жиле́т. **lifeless** /-lɪs/ *adj* безжи́зненный. **lifelike** /-laɪk/ *adj* реалисти́чный. **lifeline** *n* спаса́тельный коне́ц. **lifelong** *adj* пожи́зненный. **life-size(d)** /-saɪz(d)/ *adj* в натура́льную величину́. **lifetime** *n* жизнь.

lift /lɪft/ *n* (*machine*) лифт, подъёмник; (*force*) подъёмная си́ла; **give s.o. a ~** подвози́ть *impf*, подвезти́ *pf*; *vt & i* поднима́ть(ся) *impf*, подня́ть(ся) *impf*.

ligament /'lɪɡəmənt/ *n* свя́зка.

light¹ /laɪt/ *n* свет, освеще́ние; (*source of ~*) ого́нь *m*, ла́мпа, фона́рь *m*; *pl* (*traffic ~s*) светофо́р; **can I have a ~?** мо́жно прикури́ть?; **~bulb** ла́мпочка; *adj* (*bright*) све́тлый; (*pale*) бле́дный; *vt & i* (*ignite*) зажига́ть(ся) *impf*, заже́чь(ся) *pf*; (*illuminate*) освеща́ть *impf*, освети́ть *pf*; **~ up** освеща́ть(ся) *impf*, освети́ть(ся) *pf*; (*begin to smoke*) закури́ть *pf*.

light² /laɪt/ *adj* (*not heavy*) лёгкий; **~-hearted** беззабо́тный.

lighten¹ /'laɪt(ə)n/ *vt* (*make lighter*) облегча́ть *impf*, облегчи́ть *pf*; (*mitigate*) смягча́ть *impf*, смягчи́ть *pf*.

lighten² /'laɪt(ə)n/ *vt* (*illuminate*) освеща́ть *impf*, освети́ть *pf*; *vi* (*grow bright*) светле́ть *impf*, по~ *pf*.

lighter /'laɪtə(r)/ *n* зажига́лка.

lighthouse /'laɪthaʊs/ *n* мая́к.

lighting /'laɪtɪŋ/ *n* освеще́ние.

lightning /'laɪtnɪŋ/ *n* мо́лния.

lightweight /'laɪtweɪt/ *n* (*sport*)

легкове́с; *adj* легкове́сный.

like¹ /laɪk/ *adj* (*similar*) похо́жий (на+*acc*); **what is he ~?** что он за челове́к?

like² /laɪk/ *vt* нра́виться *impf*, по~ *pf impers+dat*: **I ~ him** он мне нра́вится; люби́ть *impf*; *vi* (*wish*) хоте́ть *impf*; **if you ~** е́сли хоти́те; **I should ~** я хоте́л бы; мне хоте́лось бы. **likeable** /'laɪkəb(ə)l/ *adj* симпати́чный.

likelihood /'laɪklɪˌhʊd/ *n* вероя́тность. **likely** /'laɪklɪ/ *adj* (*probable*) вероя́тный; (*suitable*) подходя́щий.

liken /'laɪkən/ *vt* уподобля́ть *impf*, уподо́бить *pf* (**to** +*dat*).

likeness /'laɪknɪs/ *n* (*resemblance*) схо́дство; (*portrait*) портре́т.

likewise /'laɪkwaɪz/ *adv* (*similarly*) подо́бно; (*also*) то́же, та́кже.

liking /'laɪkɪŋ/ *n* вкус (**for** к+*dat*).

lilac /'laɪlək/ *n* сире́нь; *adj* сире́невый.

lily /'lɪlɪ/ *n* ли́лия; **~ of the valley** ла́ндыш.

limb /lɪm/ *n* член.

limber /'lɪmbə(r)/ *vi*: **~ up** размина́ться *impf*, размя́ться *pf*.

limbo /'lɪmbəʊ/ *n* (*fig*) состоя́ние неопределённости.

lime¹ /laɪm/ *n* (*mineralogy*) и́звесть. **limelight** *n*: **in the ~** (*fig*) в це́нтре внима́ния. **limestone** *n* известня́к.

lime² /laɪm/ *n* (*fruit*) лайм.

lime³ /laɪm/ *n* (**~-tree**) ли́па.

limit /'lɪmɪt/ *n* грани́ца, преде́л; *vt* ограни́чивать *impf*, ограни́чить *pf*. **limitation** /-'lɪmɪteɪʃ(ə)n/ *n* ограниче́ние. **limitless** /'lɪmɪtlɪs/ *adj* безграни́чный.

limousine /'lɪməˌziːn/ *n* лимузи́н.

limp[1] /lɪmp/ n хромота́; vi хрома́ть impf.

limp[2] /lɪmp/ adj мя́гкий; (fig) вя́лый.

limpid /ˈlɪmpɪd/ adj прозра́чный.

linchpin /ˈlɪntʃpɪn/ n чека́.

line[1] /laɪn/ n (long mark) ли́ния, черта́; (transport, tel) ли́ния; (cord) верёвка; (wrinkle) морщи́на; (limit) грани́ца; (row) ряд; (of words) строка́; (of verse) стих; vt (paper) линова́ть impf, раз∼ pf; vt & i (∼ up) выстра́ивать impf, выстроить(ся) pf в ряд.

line[2] /laɪn/ vt (clothes) класть impf, положи́ть pf на подкла́дку.

lineage /ˈlɪnɪɪdʒ/ n происхожде́ние.

linear /ˈlɪnɪə(r)/ adj лине́йный.

lined[1] /laɪnd/ adj (paper) лино́ванный; (face) морщи́нистый.

lined[2] /laɪnd/ adj (garment) на подкла́дке.

linen /ˈlɪnɪn/ n полотно́; collect бельё.

liner /ˈlaɪnə(r)/ n ла́йнер.

linesman /ˈlaɪnzmən/ n боково́й судья́ m.

linger /ˈlɪŋɡə(r)/ vi заде́рживаться impf, задержа́ться pf.

lingerie /ˈlæʒəriː/ n да́мское бельё.

lingering /ˈlɪŋɡərɪŋ/ adj (illness) затяжно́й.

lingo /ˈlɪŋɡəʊ/ n жарго́н.

linguist /ˈlɪŋɡwɪst/ n лингви́ст.

linguistic /lɪŋˈɡwɪstɪk/ adj лингвисти́ческий. **linguistics** /-ˈɡwɪstɪks/ n лингви́стика.

lining /ˈlaɪnɪŋ/ n (clothing etc.) подкла́дка; (tech) облицо́вка.

link /lɪŋk/ n (of chain) звено́; (connection) связь; vt соеди-

ня́ть impf, соедини́ть pf; свя́зывать impf, связа́ть pf.

lino(leum) /lɪˈnəʊlɪəm/ n лино́леум.

lintel /ˈlɪnt(ə)l/ n перемы́чка.

lion /ˈlaɪən/ n лев. **lioness** /-nɪs/ n льви́ца.

lip /lɪp/ n губа́; (of vessel) край. **lipstick** n губна́я пома́да.

liquefy /ˈlɪkwɪˌfaɪ/ vt & i превраща́ть(ся) impf, преврати́ть(ся) pf в жи́дкое состоя́ние.

liqueur /lɪˈkjʊə(r)/ n ликёр.

liquid /ˈlɪkwɪd/ n жи́дкость; adj жи́дкий.

liquidate /ˈlɪkwɪˌdeɪt/ vt ликвиди́ровать impf & pf. **liquidation** /-ˈdeɪʃ(ə)n/ n ликвида́ция; go into ∼ ликвиди́роваться impf & pf.

liquor /ˈlɪkə(r)/ n (спиртно́й) напи́ток.

liquorice /ˈlɪkərɪs/ n лакри́ца.

list[1] /lɪst/ n спи́сок; vt составля́ть impf, соста́вить pf спи́сок +gen; (enumerate) перечисля́ть impf, перечи́слить pf.

list[2] /lɪst/ vi (naut) накреня́ться impf, крени́ться impf, накрени́ться pf.

listen /ˈlɪs(ə)n/ vi слу́шать impf, по∼ pf (to +acc). **listener** /-nə(r)/ n слу́шатель.

listless /ˈlɪstlɪs/ adj апати́чный.

litany /ˈlɪtənɪ/ n лита́ния.

literacy /ˈlɪtərəsɪ/ n гра́мотность.

literal /ˈlɪtər(ə)l/ adj буква́льный.

literary /ˈlɪtərərɪ/ adj литерату́рный.

literate /ˈlɪtərət/ adj гра́мотный.

literature /ˈlɪtrətʃə(r)/ n литерату́ра.

lithe /laɪð/ adj ги́бкий.

lithograph /ˈlɪθəˌɡrɑːf/ n лито-

графия.

Lithuania /ˌlɪθjʊˈeɪnɪə/ n Литва́.
Lithuanian /-nɪən/ n лито́вец, -вка; adj лито́вский.
litigation /ˌlɪtɪˈɡeɪʃ(ə)n/ n тя́жба.
litre /ˈliːtə(r)/ n литр.
litter /ˈlɪtə(r)/ n (rubbish) со́р; (brood) помёт; vt (make untidy) сори́ть impf, на~ pf (with +instr).
little /ˈlɪt(ə)l/ adj немно́гое; ~ by ~ ма́ло-пома́лу; a ~ немно́го +gen; adj ма́ленький, небольшо́й; (in height) небольшо́го ро́ста; (in distance, time) коро́ткий; adv ма́ло, немно́го.
liturgy /ˈlɪtədʒɪ/ n литурги́я.
live¹ /laɪv/ adj живо́й; (coals) горя́щий; (mil) боево́й; (electr) под напряже́нием; (broadcast) прямо́й.
live² /lɪv/ vi жить impf; ~ down загла́живать impf, загла́дить pf; ~ on (feed on) пита́ться impf +instr; ~ through пережива́ть impf, пережи́ть pf; ~ until, to see дожива́ть impf, дожи́ть pf до+gen; ~ up to жить impf согла́сно +dat.
livelihood /ˈlaɪvlɪˌhʊd/ n сре́дства neut pl к жи́зни.
lively /ˈlaɪvlɪ/ adj живо́й.
liven (up) /ˈlaɪv(ə)n (ʌp)/ vt & i оживля́ть(ся) impf, оживи́ть(ся) pf.
liver /ˈlɪvə(r)/ n пе́чень; (cul) печёнка.
livery /ˈlɪvərɪ/ n ливре́я.
livestock /ˈlaɪvstɒk/ n скот.
livid /ˈlɪvɪd/ adj (angry) взбешённый.
living /ˈlɪvɪŋ/ n сре́дства neut pl к жи́зни; earn a ~ зараба́тывать impf, зарабо́тать pf на жизнь; adj живо́й; ~-room гости́ная sb.
lizard /ˈlɪzəd/ n я́щерица.

load /ləʊd/ n груз; (also fig) бре́мя neut; (electr) нагру́зка; pl (lots) ку́ча; vt (goods) грузи́ть impf, по~ pf; (vehicle) грузи́ть impf, на~ pf; (fig) обременя́ть impf, обремени́ть pf; (gun, camera) заряжа́ть impf, заряди́ть pf.
loaf¹ /ləʊf/ n буха́нка.
loaf² /ləʊf/ vi безде́льничать impf. **loafer** /ˈləʊfə(r)/ n безде́льник.
loan /ləʊn/ n заём; vt дава́ть impf, дать pf взаймы́.
loath, loth /ləʊθ/ predic: be ~ to не хоте́ть impf +inf.
loathe /ləʊð/ vt ненави́деть impf. **loathing** /ˈləʊðɪŋ/ n отвраще́ние. **loathsome** adj отврати́тельный.
lob /lɒb/ vt высоко́ подбра́сывать impf, подбро́сить pf.
lobby /ˈlɒbɪ/ n вестибю́ль m; (parl) кулуа́ры (-ров) pl.
lobe /ləʊb/ n (of ear) мо́чка.
lobster /ˈlɒbstə(r)/ n ома́р.
local /ˈləʊk(ə)l/ adj ме́стный.
locality /ləʊˈkælɪtɪ/ n ме́стность.
localized /ˈləʊkəˌlaɪzd/ adj локализо́ванный.
locate /ləʊˈkeɪt/ vt (place) помеща́ть impf, помести́ть pf; (find) находи́ть impf, найти́ pf; be ~d находи́ться impf.
location /ləʊˈkeɪʃ(ə)n/ n (position) местонахожде́ние; on ~ (cin) на нату́ре.
locative /ˈlɒkətɪv/ adj (n) ме́стный (паде́ж).
lock¹ /lɒk/ n (of hair) ло́кон; pl во́лосы (-о́с, -оса́м) pl.
lock² /lɒk/ n замо́к; (canal) шлюз; vt & i запира́ть(ся) impf, запере́ть(ся) pf; ~ out не впуска́ть impf; ~ up (imprison) сажа́ть impf, посади́ть pf;

(*close*) закрыва́ть(ся) *impf*, закры́ть(ся) *pf*.

locker /'lɒkə(r)/ *n* шка́фчик.

locket /'lɒkɪt/ *n* медальо́н.

locksmith /'lɒksmɪθ/ *n* сле́сарь *m*.

locomotion /ˌləʊkə'məʊʃ(ə)n/ *n* передвиже́ние. **locomotive** /-'məʊtɪv/ *n* локомоти́в.

lodge /lɒdʒ/ *n* (*hunting*) (охо́тничий) до́мик; (*porter's*) сторо́жка; (*Masonic*) ло́жа; *vt* (*complaint*) подава́ть *impf*, пода́ть *pf*; (*reside*) жить *impf* (*with* y+*gen*); (*stick*) заса́живать *impf*, засе́сть *pf*. **lodger** /-dʒə(r)/ *n* жиле́ц, жили́ца. **lodging** /-dʒɪŋ/ *n* (*also pl*) кварти́ра, (снима́емая) ко́мната.

loft /lɒft/ *n* (*attic*) черда́к.

lofty /'lɒftɪ/ *adj* о́чень высо́кий; (*elevated*) возвы́шенный.

log /lɒg/ *n* бревно́; (*for fire*) поле́но; ~**book** (*naut*) ва́хтенный журна́л; *vi*: ~ **off** (*comput*) выходи́ть *impf*, вы́йти *pf* из систе́мы; ~ **on** (*comput*) входи́ть *impf*, войти́ *pf* в систе́му.

logarithm /'lɒgərɪð(ə)m/ *n* логари́фм.

loggerhead /'lɒgəhed/ *n*: be at ~s быть в ссо́ре.

logic /'lɒdʒɪk/ *n* ло́гика. **logical** /-k(ə)l/ *adj* (*of logic*) логи́ческий; (*consistent*) логи́чный.

logistics /lə'dʒɪstɪks/ *n pl* организа́ция; (*mil*) материа́льно-техни́ческое обеспе́чение.

logo /'ləʊgəʊ/ *n* эмбле́ма.

loin /lɔɪn/ *n* (*pl*) поясни́ца; (*cul*) филе́йная часть.

loiter /'lɔɪtə(r)/ *vi* слоня́ться *impf*.

lone, lonely /ləʊn, 'ləʊnlɪ/ *adj* одино́кий. **loneliness** /'ləʊnlɪnɪs/ *n* одино́чество.

long[1] /lɒŋ/ *vi* (*want*) стра́стно

жела́ть *impf*, по~ *pf* (*for* +*gen*); (*miss*) тоскова́ть *impf* (*for* по+*dat*).

long[2] /lɒŋ/ *adj* (*space*) дли́нный; (*time*) до́лгий; (*in measurements*) длино́й в+*acc*; **in the ~ run** в коне́чном счёте; ~**-sighted** дальнозо́ркий; ~**-suffering** долготерпели́вый; ~**-term** долгосро́чный; ~**-winded** многоречи́вый; *adv* до́лго; **~ ago** (*уже́*) давно́; **as ~ as** пока́; **~ before** задо́лго до+*gen*.

longevity /lɒn'dʒevɪtɪ/ *n* долгове́чность.

longing /'lɒŋɪŋ/ *n* стра́стное жела́ние (*for* +*gen*); тоска́ (*for* по+*dat*); *adj* тоску́ющий.

longitude /'lɒŋgɪtjuːd/ *n* долгота́.

longways /'lɒŋweɪz/ *adv* в длину́.

look /lʊk/ *n* (*glance*) взгляд; (*appearance*) вид; (*expression*) выраже́ние; *vi* смотре́ть *impf*, по~ *pf* (at на, в, +*acc*); (*appear*) вы́глядеть *impf* +*instr*; (*face*) выходи́ть *impf* (*towards, on* на+*acc*); ~ **about** осма́триваться *impf*, осмотре́ться *pf*; ~ **after** (*attend to*) присма́тривать *impf*, присмотре́ть *pf* за+*instr*; ~ **down** on презира́ть *impf*; ~ **for** иска́ть *impf* +*acc*, +*gen*; ~ **forward to** предвкуша́ть *impf*, предвкуси́ть *pf*; ~ **in on** загля́дывать *impf*, загляну́ть *pf* к+*dat*; ~ **into** (*investigate*) рассма́тривать *impf*, рассмотре́ть *pf*; ~ **like** быть похо́жим на+*acc*; **it ~s like rain** похо́же на то, что бу́дет дождь; ~ **on** (*regard*) счита́ть *impf*, счесть *pf* (*as* +*instr*, за+*instr*); ~ **out** выгля́дывать *impf*, вы́глянуть *pf* (в окно́); быть насторо́же;

imper осторожно!; ~ **over, through** просматривать *impf*, просмотреть *pf*; ~ **round** (*inspect*) осматривать *impf*, осмотреть *pf*; ~ **up** (*raise eyes*) поднимать *impf*, поднять *pf* глаза; (*in dictionary etc.*) искать *impf*; (*improve*) улучшаться *impf*, улучшиться *pf*; ~ **up to** уважать *impf*.

loom¹ /luːm/ *n* ткацкий станок.

loom² /luːm/ *vi* вырисовываться *impf*, вырисоваться *pf*; (*fig*) надвигаться *impf*.

loop /luːp/ *n* петля; *vi* образовывать *impf*, образовать *pf* петлю; (*fasten with loop*) закреплять *impf*, закрепить *pf* петлёй; (*wind*) обматывать *impf*, обмотать *pf* (**around** вокруг+*gen*).

loophole /'luːphəʊl/ *n* бойница; (*fig*) лазейка.

loose /luːs/ *adj* (*free; not tight*) свободный; (*not fixed*) неприкреплённый; (*connection, screw*) слабый; (*lax*) распущенный; **at a** ~ **end** без дела.

loosen /-s(ə)n/ *vt & i* ослаблять(ся) *impf*, ослабить(ся) *pf*.

loot /luːt/ *n* добыча; *vt* грабить *impf*, o~ *pf*.

lop /lɒp/ *vt* (*tree*) подрезать *impf*, подрезать *pf*; (~ *off*) отрубать *impf*, отрубить *pf*.

lope /ləʊp/ *vi* бегать *indet*, бежать *det* вприпрыжку.

lopsided /lɒp'saɪdɪd/ *adj* кривобокий.

loquacious /lə'kweɪʃəs/ *adj* болтливый.

lord /lɔːd/ *n* (*master*) господин; (*eccl*) Господь; (*peer; title*) лорд; *vt*: **it over** помыкать *impf* +*instr*. **lordship** *n* (*title*) светлость.

lore /lɔː(r)/ *n* знания *neut pl*.

lorry /'lɒrɪ/ *n* грузовик.

lose /luːz/ *vt* терять *impf*, по~ *pf*; *vt & i* (*game etc.*) проигрывать *impf*, проиграть *pf*; (*clock*) отставать *impf*, отстать *pf*. **loss** /lɒs/ *n* потеря; (*monetary*) убыток; (*in game*) проигрыш.

lot /lɒt/ *n* жребий; (*destiny*) участь; (*of goods*) партия; **a** ~, ~**s** много; **the** ~ всё, все *pl*.

loth /ləʊθ/ *see* **loath**

lotion /'ləʊʃ(ə)n/ *n* лосьон.

lottery /'lɒtərɪ/ *n* лотерея.

loud /laʊd/ *adj* (*sound*) громкий; (*noisy*) шумный; (*colour*) кричащий; **out** ~ вслух. **loudspeaker** *n* громкоговоритель *m*.

lounge /laʊndʒ/ *n* гостиная *sb*; *vi* сидеть *impf* развалясь; (*idle*) бездельничать *impf*.

louse /laʊs/ *n* вошь. **lousy** /'laʊzɪ/ *adj* (*coll*) паршивый.

lout /laʊt/ *n* балбес, увалень *m*.

lovable /'lʌvəb(ə)l/ *adj* милый.

love /lʌv/ *n* любовь (**of, for** к+*dat*); **in** ~ **with** влюблённый в+*acc*; *vt* любить *impf*. **lovely** /'lʌvlɪ/ *adj* прекрасный; (*delightful*) прелестный. **lover** /'lʌvə(r)/ *n* любовник, -ица.

low /ləʊ/ *adj* низкий, невысокий; (*quiet*) тихий.

lower¹ /'ləʊə(r)/ *vt* опускать *impf*, опустить *pf*; (*price, voice, standard*) понижать *impf*, понизить *pf*.

lower² /'laʊə(r)/ *adj* нижний.

lowland /'ləʊlənd/ *n* низменность.

lowly /'ləʊlɪ/ *adj* скромный.

loyal /'lɔɪəl/ *adj* верный. **loyalty** /-tɪ/ *n* верность.

LP *abbr* (**of long-playing record**) долгоиграющая пластинка.

Ltd. *abbr (of* **Limited**) с ограниченной ответственностью.

lubricant /'lu:brɪkənt/ *n* смазка.

lubricate /-keɪt/ *vt* смазывать *impf*, смазать *pf*. **lubrication** /-'keɪʃ(ə)n/ *n* смазка.

lucid /'lu:sɪd/ *adj* ясный. **lucidity** /ˌlu:'sɪdɪtɪ/ *n* ясность.

luck /lʌk/ *n* (chance) случай; (good ~) счастье, удача; (bad ~) неудача. **luckily** /-kɪlɪ/ *adv* к счастью. **lucky** /-kɪ/ *adj* счастливый; **be** ~ везти *imp*, по~ *pf impers* +*dat*: **I was** ~ мне повезло.

lucrative /'lu:krətɪv/ *adj* прибыльный.

ludicrous /'lu:dɪkrəs/ *adj* смехотворный.

lug /lʌg/ *vt* (drag) таскать *indet*, тащить *det*.

luggage /'lʌgɪdʒ/ *n* багаж.

lugubrious /lʊ'gu:brɪəs/ *adj* печальный.

lukewarm /lu:k'wɔ:m/ *adj* тепловатый; (fig) прохладный.

lull /lʌl/ *n* (in storm) затишье; (interval) перерыв; *vt* (to sleep) убаюкивать *impf*, убаюкать *pf*; (suspicions) усыплять *impf*, усыпить *pf*.

lullaby /'lʌləˌbaɪ/ *n* колыбельная песня.

lumbar /'lʌmbə(r)/ *adj* поясничный.

lumber¹ /'lʌmbə(r)/ *vi* (move) брести *impf*.

lumber² /'lʌmbə(r)/ *n* (domestic) рухлядь; *vt* обременять *impf*, обременить *pf*. **lumberjack** /'lʌmbədʒæk/ *n* лесоруб.

luminary /'lu:mɪnərɪ/ *n* светило.

luminous /'lu:mɪnəs/ *adj* светящийся.

lump /lʌmp/ *n* ком; (swelling) опухоль; *vt*: ~ **together** смешивать *impf*, смешать *pf* (в

одно).

lunacy /'lu:nəsɪ/ *n* безумие.

lunar /'lu:nə(r)/ *adj* лунный.

lunatic /'lu:nətɪk/ *adj (n)* сумасшедший (sb).

lunch /lʌntʃ/ *n* обед; ~**-hour**, ~**-time** обеденный перерыв; *vi* обедать *impf*, по~ *pf*.

lung /lʌŋ/ *n* лёгкое sb.

lunge /lʌndʒ/ *vi* делать *impf*, с~ *pf* выпад (at против+*gen*).

lurch¹ /lɜ:tʃ/ *n*: **leave in the** ~ покидать *impf*, покинуть *pf* в беде.

lurch² /lɜ:tʃ/ *vi* (stagger) ходить *indet*, идти *det* шатаясь.

lure /lʊə(r)/ *n* приманка; *vt* заманивать *impf*, заманить *pf*.

lurid /'lʊərɪd/ *adj* (gaudy) кричащий; (details) жуткий.

lurk /lɜ:k/ *vi* затаиваться *impf*, затаиться *pf*.

luscious /'lʌʃəs/ *adj* сочный.

lush /lʌʃ/ *adj* пышный, сочный.

lust /lʌst/ *n* похоть (of, for к+*dat*); *vi* страстно желать *impf*, по~ *pf* (for +*gen*). **lustful** /-fʊl/ *adj* похотливый.

lustre /'lʌstə(r)/ *n* глянец. **lustrous** /'lʌstrəs/ *adj* глянцевитый.

lusty /'lʌstɪ/ *adj* (healthy) здоровый; (lively) живой.

lute /lu:t/ *n* (mus) лютня.

luxuriant /lʌg'zjʊərɪənt/ *adj* пышный.

luxuriate /lʌg'zjʊərɪˌeɪt/ *vi* наслаждаться *impf*, насладиться *pf* (in +*instr*).

luxurious /lʌg'zjʊərɪəs/ *adj* роскошный. **luxury** /'lʌgʒərɪ/ *n* роскошь.

lymph /lɪmf/ *attrib* лимфатический.

lynch /lɪntʃ/ *vt* линчевать *impf* & *pf*.

lyric /'lɪrɪk/ *n* лирика; *pl* слова

neut pl пе́сни. **lyrical** /-k(ə)l/ *adj* лири́ческий.

M

MA *abbr (of Master of Arts)* маги́стр гуманита́рных нау́к.

macabre /məˈkɑːbr(ə)/ *adj* жу́ткий.

macaroni /ˌmækəˈrəʊnɪ/ *n* макаро́ны (-н) *pl*.

mace /meɪs/ *n (of office)* жезл.

machination /ˌmækɪˈneɪʃ(ə)n/ *n* махина́ция.

machine /məˈʃiːn/ *n* маши́на; *(state ~)* аппара́т; *attrib* маши́нный; **~-gun** пулемёт; **~-tool** стано́к; *vt* обраба́тывать *impf*, обрабо́тать *pf* на станке́; *(sew)* шить *impf*, с~ *pf* на маши́не). **machinery** /-nərɪ/ *n (machines)* маши́ны *f pl*; *(of state)* аппара́т. **machinist** /-nɪst/ *n* маши́нист; *(sewing)* швёйник, -и́ца, швея́.

mackerel /ˈmækr(ə)l/ *n* ску́мбрия, макре́ль.

mackintosh /ˈmækɪntɒʃ/ *n* плащ.

mad /mæd/ *adj* сумасше́дший. **madden** /ˈmæd(ə)n/ *vt* беси́ть *impf*, вз~ *pf*. **madhouse** *n* сумасше́дший дом. **madly** /-lɪ/ *adv* безу́мно. **madman** *n* су-масше́дший *sb*. **madness** /-nɪs/ *n* сумасше́ствие. **madwoman** *n* сумасше́дшая *sb*.

madrigal /ˈmædrɪɡ(ə)l/ *n* мадрига́л.

maestro /ˈmaɪstrəʊ/ *n* маэ́стро *m indecl*.

Mafia /ˈmæfɪə/ *n* ма́фия.

magazine /ˌmæɡəˈziːn/ *n* журна́л; *(of gun)* магази́н.

maggot /ˈmæɡət/ *n* личи́нка.

magic /ˈmædʒɪk/ *n* ма́гия, волшебство́; *adj (also* **magical**) волше́бный. **magician** /mə-ˈdʒɪʃ(ə)n/ *n* волше́бник; *(conjurer)* фо́кусник.

magisterial /ˌmædʒɪˈstɪərɪəl/ *adj* авторите́тный.

magistrate /ˈmædʒɪstrət/ *n* судья́ *m*.

magnanimity /ˌmæɡnəˈnɪmɪtɪ/ *n* великоду́шие. **magnanimous** /mæɡˈnænɪməs/ *adj* великоду́шный.

magnate /ˈmæɡneɪt/ *n* магна́т.

magnesium /mæɡˈniːzɪəm/ *n* ма́гний.

magnet /ˈmæɡnɪt/ *n* магни́т. **magnetic** /-ˈnetɪk/ *adj* магни́тный; *(attractive)* притяга́тельный. **magnetism** /ˈmæɡnɪ-ˌtɪz(ə)m/ *n* магнети́зм; притяга́-тельность. **magnetize** /ˈmæɡnɪ-ˌtaɪz/ *vt* намагни́чивать *impf*, намагни́тить *pf*.

magnification /ˌmæɡnɪfɪ-ˈkeɪʃ(ə)n/ *n* увеличе́ние.

magnificence /mæɡˈnɪfɪs(ə)ns/ *n* великоле́пие. **magnificent** /-s(ə)nt/ *adj* великоле́пный.

magnify /ˈmæɡnɪˌfaɪ/ *vt* увели́-чивать *impf*, увели́чить *pf*; *(exaggerate)* преувели́чивать *impf*, преувели́чить *pf*. **magnifying glass** /-ˌfaɪɪŋ ɡlɑːs/ *n* увеличи́-тельное стекло́.

magnitude /ˈmæɡnɪˌtjuːd/ *n* вели-чина́; *(importance)* ва́жность.

magpie /ˈmæɡpaɪ/ *n* соро́ка.

mahogany /məˈhɒɡənɪ/ *n* кра́сное де́рево.

maid /meɪd/ *n* прислу́га. **maiden** /ˈmeɪd(ə)n/ *n adj (aunt etc)* неза-му́жняя; *(first)* пе́рвый; ~ **name** де́вичья фами́лия.

mail /meɪl/ *n (letters)* по́чта; ~ **order** почто́вый зака́з; *vt* по-

сыла́ть *impf*, посла́ть *pf* по по́чте.

maim /meɪm/ *vt* кале́чить *impf*, ис~ *pf*.

main /meɪn/ *n* (*gas*; *pl*) магистра́ль; **in the ~** в основно́м; *adj* основно́й, гла́вный; (*road*) магистра́льный. **mainland** *n* матери́к. **mainly** /-lɪ/ *adv* в основно́м. **mainstay** *n* (*fig*) гла́вная опо́ра.

maintain /meɪn'teɪn/ *vt* (*keep up*) подде́рживать *impf*, поддержа́ть *pf*; (*family*) содержа́ть *impf*; (*machine*) обслу́живать *impf*, обслужи́ть *pf*; (*assert*) утвержда́ть *impf*. **maintenance** /'meɪntənəns/ *n* подде́ржка; содержа́ние; обслу́живание.

maize /meɪz/ *n* кукуру́за.

majestic /mə'dʒestɪk/ *adj* вели́чественный. **majesty** /'mædʒɪstɪ/ *n* вели́чественность; (*title*) вели́чество.

major[1] /'meɪdʒə(r)/ *n* (*mil*) майо́р.

major[2] /'meɪdʒə(r)/ *adj* (*greater*) бо́льший; (*more important*) бо́лее ва́жный; (*main*) гла́вный; (*mus*) мажо́рный; *n* (*mus*) мажо́р. **majority** /mə'dʒɒrɪtɪ/ *n* большинство́; (*full age*) совершенноле́тие.

make /meɪk/ *vt* де́лать *impf*, с~ *pf*; (*produce*) производи́ть *impf*, произвести́ *pf*; (*prepare*) гото́вить *impf*, при~ *pf*; (*amount to*) равня́ться *impf* +*dat*; (*earn*) зараба́тывать *impf*, зарабо́тать *pf*; (*compel*) заставля́ть *impf*, заста́вить *pf*; (*reach*) добира́ться *impf*, добра́ться *pf* до+*gen*; (*be in time for*) успева́ть *impf*, успе́ть *pf* на+*acc*; **be made of** состоя́ть *impf* из+*gen*; **~ as if, though** де́лать *impf*, с~ *pf* вид, что; **~ a**

bed стели́ть *impf*, по~ *pf* посте́ль; **~ believe** притворя́ться *impf*, притвори́ться *pf*; **~believe** притво́рство; **~ do with** дово́льствоваться *impf*, у~ *pf* +*instr*; **~ off** удира́ть *impf*, удра́ть *pf*; **~ out** (*cheque*) выпи́сывать *impf*, вы́писать *pf*; (*assert*) утвержда́ть *impf*, утверди́ть *pf*; (*understand*) разбира́ть *impf*, разобра́ть *pf*; **~ over** передава́ть *impf*, переда́ть *pf*; **~ up** (*form, compose, complete*) составля́ть *impf*, соста́вить *pf*; (*invent*) выду́мывать *impf*, вы́думать *pf*; (*theat*) гримирова́ть(ся) *impf*, за~ *pf*; **~up** (*theat*) грим; (*cosmetics*) космети́ка; (*composition*) соста́в; **~ it up** мири́ться *impf*, по~ *pf* (**with** с+*instr*); **~ up for** возмеща́ть *impf*, возмести́ть *pf*; **~ up one's mind** реша́ться *impf*, реши́ться *pf* на что. **make** *pf*. **make** *n* ма́рка. **makeshift** *adj* вре́менный.

malady /'mælədɪ/ *n* боле́знь.

malaise /mə'leɪz/ *n* (*fig*) беспоко́йство.

malaria /mə'leərɪə/ *n* маляри́я.

male /meɪl/ *n* (*animal*) саме́ц; (*person*) мужчи́на *m*; *adj* мужско́й.

malevolence /mə'levələns/ *n* недоброжела́тельность. **malevolent** /-lənt/ *adj* недоброжела́тельный.

malice /'mælɪs/ *n* зло́ба. **malicious** /mə'lɪʃ(ə)s/ *adj* злобный.

malign /mə'laɪn/ *vt* клевета́ть *impf*, на~ *pf* +*acc*. **malignant** /-'lɪgnənt/ *adj* (*harmful*) зловре́дный; (*malicious*) злобный; (*med*) злока́чественный.

malinger /mə'lɪŋgə(r)/ *vi* притворя́ться *impf*, притвори́ться *pf* больны́м. **malingerer** /-rə(r)/

n симуля́нт.

mallard /'mælɑːd/ *n* кря́ква.

malleable /'mælɪəb(ə)l/ *adj* ко́вкий; (*fig*) пода́тливый.

mallet /'mælɪt/ *n* (деревя́нный) молото́к.

malnutrition /ˌmælnjuː'trɪʃ(ə)n/ *n* недоеда́ние.

malpractice /mæl'præktɪs/ *n* престу́пная небре́жность.

malt /mɔːlt/ *n* со́лод.

maltreat /mæl'triːt/ *vt* пло́хо обраща́ться *impf* c+*instr*.

mammal /'mæm(ə)l/ *n* млекопита́ющее *sb*.

mammoth /'mæməθ/ *adj* грома́дный.

man /mæn/ *n* (*human, person*) челове́к; (*human race*) челове́чество; (*male*) мужчи́на *m*; (*labourer*) рабо́чий *sb*; *pl* (*soldiers*) солда́ты *m pl*; *vt* (*furnish with men*) укомплекто́вывать *impf*, укомплектова́ть *pf* ли́чным соста́вом; ста́вить *impf*, по~ *pf* люде́й к+*dat*; (*stall etc.*) обслу́живать *impf*, обслужи́ть *pf*; (*gate, checkpoint*) стоя́ть *impf* на+*prep*.

manacle /'mænək(ə)l/ *n* нару́чник; *vt* надева́ть *impf*, наде́ть *pf* нару́чники на+*acc*.

manage /'mænɪdʒ/ *vt* (*control*) управля́ть *impf* +*instr*, *vi*(& *t*) (*cope*) справля́ться *impf*, спра́виться *pf* (c+*instr*); (*succeed*) суме́ть *pf*. **management** /-mənt/ *n* управле́ние (**of** +*instr*; (*the* ~) администра́ция. **manager** /-dʒə(r)/ *n* управля́ющий *sb* (**of** +*instr*); ме́неджер. **managerial** /-dʒɪərɪəl/ *adj* администрати́вный. **managing director** /'mænɪdʒɪŋ daɪ'rektə(r)/ *n* дире́ктор-распоряди́тель *m*.

mandarin /'mændərɪn/ *n* манда-ри́н.

mandate /'mændeɪt/ *n* манда́т. **mandated** /-tɪd/ *adj* подманда́тный. **mandatory** /-dətərɪ/ *adj* обяза́тельный.

mane /meɪn/ *n* гри́ва.

manful /'mænfʊl/ *adj* му́жественный.

manganese /'mæŋɡəˌniːz/ *n* ма́рганец.

manger /'meɪndʒə(r)/ *n* я́сли (-лей) *pl*; **dog in the** ~ соба́ка на се́не.

mangle /'mæŋɡ(ə)l/ *vt* (*mutilate*) кале́чить *impf*, ис~ *pf*.

mango /'mæŋɡəʊ/ *n* ма́нго *neut indecl*.

manhandle /'mænˌhænd(ə)l/ *vt* гру́бо обраща́ться *impf* c+*instr*.

manhole /'mænhəʊl/ *n* смотрово́й коло́дец.

manhood /'mænhʊd/ *n* возмужа́лость.

mania /'meɪnɪə/ *n* ма́ния. **maniac** /'meɪnɪæk/ *n* манья́к, -я́чка. **manic** /'mænɪk/ *adj* маниака́льный.

manicure /'mænɪˌkjʊə(r)/ *n* маникю́р; *vt* де́лать *impf*, с~ *pf* маникю́р +*dat*. **manicurist** /-ˌkjʊərɪst/ *n* маникю́рша.

manifest /'mænɪˌfest/ *adj* очеви́дный; *vt* (*display*) проявля́ть *impf*, прояви́ть *pf*; *n* манифе́ст. **manifestation** /-'teɪʃ(ə)n/ *n* проявле́ние. **manifesto** /-'festəʊ/ *n* манифе́ст.

manifold /'mænɪˌfəʊld/ *adj* разнообра́зный.

manipulate /mə'nɪpjʊˌleɪt/ *vt* манипули́ровать *impf* +*instr*. **manipulation** /-'leɪʃ(ə)n/ *n* манипуля́ция.

manly /'mænlɪ/ *adj* му́жественный.

mankind /mæn'kaɪnd/ *n* челове́чество.

manner /'mænə(r)/ *n* (*way*) о́браз; (*behaviour*) мане́ра; *pl* мане́ры *f pl.* **mannerism** /'mænərɪz(ə)m/ *n* мане́ра.

mannish /'mænɪʃ/ *adj* мужеподо́бный.

manoeuvrable /məˈnuːvrəb(ə)l/ *adj* манёвренный. **manoeuvre** /-'nuːvə(r)/ *n* манёвр; *vt & i* маневри́ровать *impf.*

manor /'mænə(r)/ *n* поме́стье; (*house*) поме́щичий дом.

manpower /'mæn,pauə(r)/ *n* челове́ческие ресу́рсы *m pl.*

manservant /'mæn,sɜːv(ə)nt/ *n* слуга́ *m.*

mansion /'mænʃ(ə)n/ *n* особня́к.

manslaughter /'mæn,slɔːtə(r)/ *n* непредумы́шленное уби́йство.

mantelpiece /'mænt(ə)l,piːs/ *n* ками́нная доска́.

manual /'mænjuəl/ *adj* ручно́й; *n* руково́дство. **manually** /-lɪ/ *adv* вручну́ю.

manufacture /,mænjʊˈfæktʃə(r)/ *n* произво́дство; *vt* производи́ть *impf*, произвести́ *pf.* **manufacturer** /-ˈfæktʃərə(r)/ *n* фабрика́нт.

manure /məˈnjʊə(r)/ *n* наво́з.

manuscript /'mænjʊskrɪpt/ *n* ру́копись.

many /'menɪ/ *adj & n* мно́го +*gen*, мно́гие *pl*; **how** ~ ско́лько +*gen.*

map /mæp/ *n* ка́рта; (*of town*) план; *vt*: ~ **out** намеча́ть *impf*, наме́тить *pf.*

maple /'meɪp(ə)l/ *n* клён.

mar /mɑː(r)/ *vt* по́ртить *impf*, ис~ *pf.*

marathon /'mærəθ(ə)n/ *n* марафо́н.

marauder /məˈrɔːdə(r)/ *n* мародёр. **marauding** /-dɪŋ/ *adj* мародёрский.

marble /'mɑːb(ə)l/ *n* мра́мор; (*toy*) ша́рик; *attrib* мра́морный.

March /mɑːtʃ/ *n* март; *adj* ма́ртовский.

march /mɑːtʃ/ *n* марш; *impf* маршировать *impf*, про~ *pf*; *n* марш.

mare /meə(r)/ *n* кобы́ла.

margarine /,mɑːdʒəˈriːn/ *n* маргари́н.

margin /'mɑːdʒɪn/ *n* (*on page*) по́ле; (*edge*) край; **profit** ~ при́быль; **safety** ~ запа́с про́чности.

marigold /'mærɪ,gəʊld/ *n* ного́тки (-ко́в) *pl.*

marijuana /,mærɪˈwɑːnə/ *n* марихуа́на.

marina /məˈriːnə/ *n* мари́на.

marinade /,mærɪˈneɪd/ *n* марина́д; *vt* маринова́ть *impf*, за~ *pf.*

marine /məˈriːn/ *adj* морско́й; (*soldier*) солда́т морско́й пехо́ты; *pl* морска́я пехо́та. **mariner** /'mærɪnə(r)/ *n* моря́к.

marital /'mærɪt(ə)l/ *adj* супру́жеский, бра́чный.

maritime /'mærɪ,taɪm/ *adj* морско́й; (*near sea*) примо́рский.

mark[1] /mɑːk/ *n* (*coin*) ма́рка.

mark[2] /mɑːk/ *n* (*for distinguishing*) ме́тка; (*sign*) знак; (*school*) отме́тка; (*trace*) след; **on your** ~**s** на старт! *vt* (*indicate*; *celebrate*) отмеча́ть *impf*, отме́тить *pf* (*school etc.*) проверя́ть *impf*, прове́рить *pf*; (*stain*) па́чкать *impf*, за~ *pf*; (*sport*) закрыва́ть *impf*, закры́ть *pf*; ~ **my words** помни́(те) мои́ слова́!; *vt* размеча́ть *impf*, разме́тить *pf.* **marker** /-kə(r)/ *n* знак; (*in book*) закла́дка.

market /'mɑːkɪt/ *n* ры́нок; ~ **garden** огоро́д; ~**-place** база́рная

marksman /'mɑːksmən/ n
стрело́к.

marmalade /'mɑːməˌleɪd/ n
апельси́новый джем.

maroon[1] /mə'ruːn/ adj (n)
(colour) тёмно-бордо́вый
(цвет).

maroon[2] /mə'ruːn/ vt (put
ashore) выса́живать impf, вы-
садить pf (на необита́емый
о́стров); (cut off) отреза́ть
impf, отре́зать pf.

marquee /mɑː'kiː/ n тэнт.

marquis /'mɑːkwɪs/ n марки́з.

marriage /'mærɪdʒ/ n брак;
(wedding) сва́дьба; attrib брач-
ный. **marriageable** /-dʒəb(ə)l/
adj: ~ age бра́чный во́зраст.
married /'mærɪd/ adj (man) же-
на́тый; (woman) заму́жняя, за́-
мужем; (to each other) жена́ты;
(of ~ persons) супру́жеский.

marrow /'mærəʊ/ n ко́стный
мозг; (vegetable) кабачо́к.

marry /'mærɪ/ vt (of man) же-
ни́ться impf & pf на +prep; (of
woman) выходи́ть impf, вы́йти
pf за́муж за +acc; vi (of couple)
пожени́ться pf.

marsh /mɑːʃ/ n боло́то. **marshy**
/-ʃɪ/ adj боло́тистый.

marshal /'mɑːʃ(ə)l/ n ма́ршал; vt
выстра́ивать impf, вы́строить
pf; (fig) собира́ть impf, со-
бра́ть pf.

marsupial /mɑː'suːpɪəl/ n су́мча-
тое живо́тное sb.

martial /'mɑːʃ(ə)l/ adj вое́нный;
~ law вое́нное положе́ние.

martyr /'mɑːtə(r)/ n му́ченик,
-ица; vt му́чить impf, за~ pf.
martyrdom /-dəm/ n му́чениче-
ство.

marvel /'mɑːv(ə)l/ n чу́до; vi изу-

мля́ться impf, изуми́ться pf.
marvellous /-ləs/ adj чу-
де́сный.

Marxist /'mɑːksɪst/ n маркси́ст;
adj маркси́стский. **Marxism**
/-sɪz(ə)m/ n маркси́зм.

marzipan /'mɑːzɪˌpæn/ n мар-
ципа́н.

mascara /mæ'skɑːrə/ n тушь.

mascot /'mæskɒt/ n талисма́н.

masculine /'mæskjʊlɪn/ adj
мужско́й; (gram) мужско́го
ро́да; (of woman) мужепо-
до́бный.

mash /mæʃ/ n карто́фельное
пюре́ neut indecl; vt размина́ть
impf, размя́ть pf.

mask /mɑːsk/ n ма́ска; vt маски-
рова́ть impf, за~ pf.

masochism /'mæsəˌkɪz(ə)m/ n
мазохи́зм. **masochist** /-kɪst/ n
мазохи́ст. **masochistic**
/-'kɪstɪk/ adj мазохи́стский.

mason /'meɪs(ə)n/ n ка́менщик;
(M~) масо́н. **Masonic** /mə
'sɒnɪk/ adj масо́нский. **masonry** /'meɪsənrɪ/ n ка́менная
кла́дка.

masquerade /ˌmæskə'reɪd/ n ма-
скара́д; vi: ~ as выдава́ть impf,
вы́дать pf себя́ за+acc.

Mass /mæs/ n (eccl) ме́сса.

mass /mæs/ n ма́сса; (majority)
большинство́; attrib ма́ссо-
вый; ~ **media** сре́дства neut pl
ма́ссовой информа́ции;
~-**produced** ма́ссового произ-
во́дства; ~ **production** ма́ссо-
вое произво́дство; vt
масси́ровать impf & pf.

massacre /'mæsəkə(r)/ n резня́;
vt выреза́ть impf, вы́резать pf.

massage /'mæsɑːʒ/ n масса́ж;
vt масси́ровать impf & pf. **mas-
seur, -euse** /mæ'sɜː(r), -'sɜːz/ n
массажи́ст, ~ка.

massive /'mæsɪv/ *adj* масси́вный; (*huge*) огро́мный.

mast /mɑːst/ *n* ма́чта.

master /'mɑːstə(r)/ *n* (*owner*) хозя́ин; (*of ship*) капита́н; (*teacher*) учи́тель *m*; (**M~**, *univ*) маги́стр; (*workman; artist*) ма́стер; (*original*) по́длинник, оригина́л; **be ~ of** владе́ть *impf* +*instr*; **~key** отмы́чка; *vt* (*overcome*) преодолева́ть *impf*, преодоле́ть *pf*; справля́ться *impf*, спра́виться *pf* с+*instr*; (*a subject*) овладева́ть *impf*, овладе́ть *pf* +*instr*. **masterful** /-fol/ *adj* вла́стный. **masterly** *adj* мастерско́й. **masterpiece** *n* шеде́вр. **mastery** /-rɪ/ *n* (*of a subject*) владе́ние *f* (*of* +*instr*).

masturbate /'mæstə,beɪt/ *vi* мастурби́ровать *impf*.

mat /mæt/ *n* ко́врик, (*at door*) полови́к; (*on table*) подста́вка.

match[1] /mætʃ/ *n* спи́чка. **matchbox** *n* спи́чечная коро́бка.

match[2] /mætʃ/ *n* (*equal*) ро́вня *m & f*; (*contest*) матч, состяза́ние; (*marriage*) па́ртия; *vi & t* (*go well* (*with*)) гармони́ровать *impf* (с+*instr*); подходи́ть *impf*, подойти́ *pf* (к+*dat*).

mate[1] /meɪt/ *n* (*chess*) мат.

mate[2] /meɪt/ *n* (*one of pair*) саме́ц, са́мка; (*fellow worker*) това́рищ; (*naut*) помо́щник капита́на; *vi* (*of animals*) спа́риваться *impf*, спа́риться *pf*.

material /mə'tɪərɪəl/ *n* материа́л; (*cloth*) мате́рия; *pl* (*necessary articles*) принадле́жности *f pl*. **materialism** /-'tɪərɪə,lɪz(ə)m/ *n* материали́зм. **materialistic** /-,tɪərɪə'lɪstɪk/ *adj* материалисти́ческий. **materialize** /-'tɪərɪə,laɪz/ *vi* осуществля́ться *impf*, осуществи́ться *pf*.

maternal /mə'tɜːn(ə)l/ *adj* мате-

ри́нский; **~ grandfather** де́душка с матери́нской стороны́. **maternity** /-'tɜːnɪtɪ/ *n* матери́нство; **~ leave** декре́тный о́тпуск; **~ ward** роди́льное отделе́ние.

mathematical /,mæθɪ'mætɪk(ə)l/ *adj* математи́ческий. **mathematician** /,mæθɪmə'tɪʃ(ə)n/ *n* матема́тик. **mathematics**, **maths** /mæθ'mætɪks, mæθs/ *n* матема́тика.

matinée /'mætɪ,neɪ/ *n* дневно́й спекта́кль *m*.

matriarchal /,meɪtrɪ'ɑːk(ə)l/ *adj* матриарха́льный. **matriarchy** /'meɪtrɪ,ɑːkɪ/ *n* матриарха́т.

matriculate /mə'trɪkjʊ,leɪt/ *vi* быть при́нятым в вуз. **matriculation** /-'leɪʃ(ə)n/ *n* зачисле́ние в вуз.

matrimonial /,mætrɪ'məʊnɪəl/ *adj* супру́жеский. **matrimony** /'mætrɪmənɪ/ *n* брак.

matrix /'meɪtrɪks/ *n* ма́трица.

matron /'meɪtrən/ *n* ста́ршая сестра́.

matt /mæt/ *adj* ма́товый.

matted /'mætɪd/ *adj* спу́танный.

matter /'mætə(r)/ *n* (*affair*) де́ло; (*question*) вопро́с; (*substance*) вещество́; (*philos; med*) мате́рия; (*printed*) материа́л; **a ~ of life and death** вопро́с жи́зни и сме́рти; **a ~ of opinion** спо́рное де́ло; **a ~ of taste** де́ло вку́са; **as a ~ of fact** факти́чески; **what's the ~?** в чём де́ло?; **what's the ~ with him?** что с ним?; **~-of-fact** *adj* проза́йчный; *vi* име́ть *impf* значе́ние; **it doesn't ~** э́то не име́ет значе́ния; **it ~s a lot to me** для меня́ э́то о́чень ва́жно.

matting /'mætɪŋ/ *n* рого́жа.

mattress /'mætrɪs/ *n* матра́с.

mature /mə'tjʊə(r)/ *adj* зре́лый;

vi зреть *impf,* co~ *pf.* **maturity** /-rɪtɪ/ *n* зрелость.

maul /mɔːl/ *vt* терзать *impf.*

mausoleum /ˌmɔːsəˈliːəm/ *n* мавзолей.

mauve /məʊv/ *adj* (*n*) розовато-лиловый (цвет).

maxim /ˈmæksɪm/ *n* сентенция.

maximum /ˈmæksɪməm/ *n* максимум; *adj* максимальный.

may /meɪ/ *v aux* (*possibility, permission*) мочь *impf,* c~ *pf;* (*possibility*) возможно, что +*indicative;* (*wish*) пусть +*indicative.*

May /meɪ/ *n* (*month*) май; *adj* майский. ~ **Day** Первое *sb* мая.

maybe /ˈmeɪbiː/ *adv* может быть.

mayonnaise /ˌmeɪəˈneɪz/ *n* майонез.

mayor /meə(r)/ *n* мэр. **mayoress** /ˈmeərɪs/ *n* жена мэра; женщина-мэр.

maze /meɪz/ *n* лабиринт.

meadow /ˈmedəʊ/ *n* луг.

meagre /ˈmiːgə(r)/ *adj* скудный.

meal[1] /miːl/ *n* еда; at ~times во время еды.

meal[2] /miːl/ *n* (*grain*) мука.

mealy /ˈmiːlɪ/ *adj:* ~-mouthed сладкоречивый.

mean[1] /miːn/ *adj* (*average*) средний; *n* (*middle point*) середина; *pl* (*method*) средство, способ; *pl* (*resources*) средства *neut pl;* by all ~s конечно, пожалуйста; by ~s of с помощью +*gen,* посредством +*gen;* by no ~s совсем не; ~s test проверка нуждаемости.

mean[2] /miːn/ *adj* (*ignoble*) подлый; (*miserly*) скупой; (*poor*) убогий.

mean[3] /miːn/ *vt* (*have in mind*) иметь *impf* в виду; (*intend*) на-

мереваться *impf* +*inf;* (*signify*) значить *impf.*

meander /mɪˈændə(r)/ *vi* (*stream*) извиваться *impf;* (*person*) бродить *impf.* **meandering** /-rɪŋ/ *adj* извилистый.

meaning /ˈmiːnɪŋ/ *n* значение. **meaningful** /-fʊl/ *adj* (много)значительный. **meaningless** /-lɪs/ *adj* бессмысленный.

meantime, meanwhile /ˈmiːntaɪm, ˈmiːnwaɪl/ *adv* между тем.

measles /ˈmiːz(ə)lz/ *n* корь. **measly** /-zlɪ/ *adj* ничтожный.

measurable /ˈmeʒərəb(ə)l/ *adj* измеримый. **measure** /ˈmeʒə(r)/ *n* мера; made to ~ сшитый по мерке; сделанный на заказ; *vt* измерять *impf,* измерить *pf;* (*for clothes*) снимать *impf,* снять *pf* мерку c+*gen; vi* иметь *impf* +*acc:* the room ~s 30 feet in length комната имеет тридцать футов в длину; ~ off, out отмерять *impf,* отмерить *pf;* ~ up to соответствовать *impf* +*dat.* **measured** /ˈmeʒəd/ *adj* (*rhythmical*) мерный. **measurement** /ˈmeʒəmənt/ *n* (*action*) измерение; *pl* (*dimensions*) размеры *m pl.*

meat /miːt/ *n* мясо. **meatball** *n* котлета. **meaty** /-tɪ/ *adj* мясистый; (*fig*) содержательный.

mechanic /mɪˈkænɪk/ *n* механик. **mechanical** /-k(ə)l/ *adj* механический; (*fig: automatic*) машинальный; ~ engineer инженер-механик; ~ engineering машиностроение. **mechanics** /-nɪks/ *n* механика. **mechanism** /ˈmekəˌnɪz(ə)m/ *n* механизм. **mechanization** /ˌmekənaɪˈzeɪʃ(ə)n/ *n* механизация. **mechanize** /ˈmekəˌnaɪz/ *vt* механизи-

ровать *impf & pf.*
medal /'med(ə)l/ *n* меда́ль. **medallion** /mɪ'dæljən/ *n* медальо́н. **medallist** /'medəlɪst/ *n* меда́лист.
meddle /'med(ə)l/ *vi* вме́шиваться *impf*, вмеша́ться *pf* (in, with в+*acc*).
media /'miːdɪə/ *pl of* medium
mediate /'miːdɪˌeɪt/ *vi* посре́дничать *impf*. **mediation** /-'eɪʃ(ə)n/ *n* посре́дничество. **mediator** /-ˌeɪtə(r)/ *n* посре́дник.
medical /'medɪk(ə)l/ *adj* медици́нский; ~ **student** ме́дик, -и́чка. **medicated** /'medɪˌkeɪtɪd/ *adj* (*impregnated*) пропи́танный лека́рством. **medicinal** /mɪ'dɪsɪn(ə)l/ *adj* (*of medicine*) лека́рственный; (*healing*) целе́бный. **medicine** /'medsɪn/ *n* медици́на; (*substance*) лека́рство.
medieval /ˌmedɪ'iːv(ə)l/ *adj* средневеко́вый.
mediocre /ˌmiːdɪ'əʊkə(r)/ *adj* посре́дственный. **mediocrity** /-'ɒkrɪtɪ/ *n* посре́дственность.
meditate /'medɪˌteɪt/ *vi* размышля́ть *impf*. **meditation** /-'teɪʃ(ə)n/ *n* размышле́ние. **meditative** /'medɪtətɪv/ *adj* заду́мчивый.
Mediterranean /ˌmedɪtə'reɪnɪən/ *adj* средиземномо́рский; ~ **Sea** Средизе́мное мо́ре.
medium /'miːdɪəm/ *n* (*means*) сре́дство; (*phys*) среда́; (*person*) ме́диум; *pl* (*mass media*) сре́дства *neut pl* ма́ссовой информа́ции; *adj* сре́дний; **happy** ~ золота́я середи́на.
medley /'medlɪ/ *n* смесь; (*mus*) попурри́ *neut indecl.*
meek /miːk/ *adj* кро́ткий.
meet /miːt/ *vt & i* встреча́ть(ся) *impf*, встре́тить(ся) *pf*; *vt*

(*make acquaintance*) знако́миться *impf*, по~ *pf* с+*instr*; (*assemble*) собира́ться *impf*, собра́ться *pf*. **meeting** /-ɪŋ/ *n* встре́ча; (*of committee*) заседа́ние, ми́тинг.
megalomania /ˌmegələ'meɪnɪə/ *vi* мегалома́ния.
megaphone /'megəˌfəʊn/ *n* мегафо́н.
melancholic /ˌmelən'kɒlɪk/ *adj* меланхоли́ческий. **melancholy** /'melənkəlɪ/ *n* грусть; *adj* уны́лый, гру́стный.
mellow /'meləʊ/ *adj* (*colour, sound*) со́чный; (*person*) доброду́шный; *vi* смягча́ться *impf*, смягчи́ться *pf.*
melodic /mɪ'lɒdɪk/ *adj* мелоди́ческий. **melodious** /-'ləʊdɪəs/ *adj* мелоди́чный. **melody** /'melədɪ/ *n* мело́дия.
melodrama /'meləˌdrɑːmə/ *n* мелодра́ма. **melodramatic** /ˌmelədrə'mætɪk/ *adj* мелодрамати́ческий.
melon /'melən/ *n* ды́ня; (*water-~*) арбу́з.
melt /melt/ *vt & i* раста́пливать(ся) *impf*, растопи́ть(ся) *pf*; (*smelt*) пла́вить(ся) *impf*, рас~ *pf*; (*dissolve*) растворя́ть(ся) *impf*, раствори́ть(ся) *pf*; *vi* (*thaw*) та́ять *impf*, рас~ *pf*; **~ing point** то́чка плавле́ния.
member /'membə(r)/ *n* член. **membership** /-ʃɪp/ *n* чле́нство; (*number of* ~) коли́чество чле́нов; *attrib* чле́нский.
membrane /'membreɪn/ *n* перепо́нка.
memento /mɪ'mentəʊ/ *n* сувени́р. **memoir** /'memwɑː(r)/ *n pl* мемуа́ры (-ров) *pl*; воспомина́ния *neut pl.* **memorable** /'memərəb(ə)l/ *adj* достопа́мят-

ный. **memorandum** /ˌmeməˈrændəm/ n записка. **memorial** /mɪˈmɔːrɪəl/ adj мемориальный; n памятник. **memorize** /ˈmeməˌraɪz/ vt запоминать impf, запомнить pf. **memory** /ˈmeməri/ n память; (recollection) воспоминание.

menace /ˈmenɪs/ n угроза; vt угрожать impf +dat. **menacing** /-sɪŋ/ adj угрожающий.

menagerie /mɪˈnædʒəri/ n зверинец.

mend /mend/ vt чинить impf, по~ pf; (clothes) штопать impf, за~ pf; ~ one's ways исправляться impf, исправиться pf.

menial /ˈmiːnɪəl/ adj низкий, чёрный.

meningitis /ˌmenɪnˈdʒaɪtɪs/ n менингит.

menopause /ˈmenəˌpɔːz/ n климакс.

menstrual /ˈmenstrʊəl/ adj менструальный. **menstruation** /-strʊˈeɪʃ(ə)n/ n менструация.

mental /ˈment(ə)l/ adj умственный; (of ~ illness) психический; ~ arithmetic счёт в уме. **mentality** /menˈtælɪti/ n ум; (character) склад ума.

mention /ˈmenʃ(ə)n/ n упоминать impf, упомянуть pf; don't ~ it не за что!; not to ~ не говоря уже o+prep.

menu /ˈmenjuː/ n меню neut indecl.

mercantile /ˈmɜːkənˌtaɪl/ adj торговый.

mercenary /ˈmɜːsɪnəri/ adj корыстный; (hired) наёмный; n наёмник.

merchandise /ˈmɜːtʃənˌdaɪz/ n товары m pl. **merchant** /ˈmɜːtʃənt/ n купец; торговец; ~ navy торговый флот.

merciful /ˈmɜːsɪfʊl/ adj милосердный. **mercifully** /-lɪ/ adv к счастью. **merciless** /ˈmɜːsɪlɪs/ adj беспощадный.

mercurial /mɜːˈkjʊərɪəl/ adj (person) изменчивый. **mercury** /ˈmɜːkjʊri/ n ртуть.

mercy /ˈmɜːsi/ n милосердие; at the ~ of во власти +gen.

mere /mɪə(r)/ adj простой; a ~ £40 всего лишь сорок фунтов. **merely** /ˈmɪəli/ adv только, просто.

merge /mɜːdʒ/ vt & i сливать(ся) impf, слить(ся) pf. **merger** /-dʒə(r)/ n объединение.

meridian /məˈrɪdɪən/ n меридиан.

meringue /məˈræŋ/ n меренга.

merit /ˈmerɪt/ n заслуга, достоинство; vt заслуживать impf, заслужить pf +gen.

mermaid /ˈmɜːmeɪd/ n русалка.

merrily /ˈmerɪli/ adv весело. **merriment** /ˈmerɪmənt/ n веселье. **merry** /ˈmeri/ adj весёлый; ~-go-round карусель; ~making веселье.

mesh /meʃ/ n сеть; vi сцепляться impf, сцепиться pf.

mesmerize /ˈmezməˌraɪz/ vt гипнотизировать impf, за~ pf.

mess /mes/ n (disorder) беспорядок; (trouble) беда; (eating-place) столовая sb; vi: ~ about возиться impf; ~ up портить impf, ис~ pf.

message /ˈmesɪdʒ/ n сообщение. **messenger** /ˈmesɪndʒə(r)/ n курьер.

Messiah /mɪˈsaɪə/ n мессия m. **Messianic** /ˌmesɪˈænɪk/ adj мессианский.

Messrs /ˈmesəz/ abbr господа (gen -д) m pl.

messy /ˈmesi/ adj (untidy) беспорядочный; (dirty) грязный.

metabolism /mɪ'tæbəlɪz(ə)m/ *n* обмен веществ.

metal /'met(ə)l/ *n* металл; *adj* металлический. **metallic** /mɪ'tælɪk/ *adj* металлический. **metallurgy** /mɪ'tælədʒɪ/ *n* металлургия.

metamorphosis /ˌmetə'mɔːfəsɪs/ *n* метаморфоза.

metaphor /'metəfə(r)/ *n* метафора. **metaphorical** /ˌmetə'fɒrɪk(ə)l/ *adj* метафорический.

metaphysical /ˌmetə'fɪzɪk(ə)l/ *adj* метафизический. **metaphysics** /-'fɪzɪks/ *n* метафизика.

meteor /'miːtɪə(r)/ *n* метеор. **meteoric** /ˌmiːtɪ'ɒrɪk/ *adj* метеорический. **meteorite** /'miːtɪəraɪt/ *n* метеорит. **meteorological** /ˌmiːtɪərə'lɒdʒɪk(ə)l/ *adj* метеорологический. **meteorology** /ˌmiːtɪə'rɒlədʒɪ/ *n* метеорология.

meter /'miːtə(r)/ *n* счётчик; *vt* измерять *impf*, измерить *pf*.

methane /'miːθeɪn/ *n* метан.

method /'meθəd/ *n* метод. **methodical** /mɪ'θɒdɪk(ə)l/ *adj* методичный.

Methodist /'meθədɪst/ *n* методист; *adj* методистский.

methodology /ˌmeθə'dɒlədʒɪ/ *n* методология.

methylated /'meθɪleɪtɪd/ *adj*: ~ **spirit(s)** денатурат.

meticulous /mə'tɪkjʊləs/ *adj* тщательный.

metre /'miːtə(r)/ *n* метр. **metric(al)** /'metrɪk((ə)l)/ *adj* метрический.

metronome /'metrənəʊm/ *n* метроном.

metropolis /mɪ'trɒpəlɪs/ *n* столица. **metropolitan** /ˌmetrə'pɒlɪt(ə)n/ *adj* столичный; *n* (*eccl*) митрополит.

mettle /'met(ə)l/ *n* характер.

Mexican /'meksɪkən/ *adj* мексиканский; *n* мексиканец, -анка. **Mexico** /'meksɪˌkəʊ/ *n* Мексика.

mezzanine /'metsəniːn/ *n* антресоли *f pl*.

miaow /miː'aʊ/ *int* мяу; *n* мяуканье; *vi* мяукать *impf*, мяукнуть *pf*.

mica /'maɪkə/ *n* слюда.

microbe /'maɪkrəʊb/ *n* микроб. **microchip** /'maɪkrəʊˌtʃɪp/ *n* чип, микросхема. **microcomputer** /'maɪkrəʊkəmˌpjuːtə(r)/ *n* микрокомпьютер. **microcosm** /'maɪkrəˌkɒz(ə)m/ *n* микрокосм. **microfilm** /'maɪkrəʊˌfɪlm/ *n* микрофильм. **micro-organism** /ˌmaɪkrəʊ'ɔːɡəˌnɪz(ə)m/ *n* микроорганизм. **microphone** /'maɪkrəˌfəʊn/ *n* микрофон. **microscope** *n* /'maɪkrəˌskəʊp/ микроскоп. **microscopic** /ˌmaɪkrə'skɒpɪk/ *adj* микроскопический. **microwave** /'maɪkrəʊˌweɪv/n микроволна; ~ **oven** микроволновая печь.

mid /mɪd/ *adj*: ~ **May** середина мая. **midday** /'mɪddeɪ/ *n* полдень *m*; *attrib* полуденный. **middle** /'mɪd(ə)l/ *n* середина; *adj* средний; ~**aged** средних лет; **M~ Ages** средние века *n pl*; ~**class** буржуазный; ~**man** посредник; ~**sized** среднего размера. **middleweight** *n* средний вес.

midge /mɪdʒ/ *n* мошка.

midget /'mɪdʒɪt/ *n* карлик, -ица.

midnight /'mɪdnaɪt/ *n* полночь; *attrib* полуночный. **midriff** /'mɪdrɪf/ *n* диафрагма. **midst** /mɪdst/ *n* середина. **midsummer** *n* середина лета. **midway** *adv* на полпути. **mid-week** *n* середина недели. **midwinter** *n* середина зимы.

midwife /ˈmɪdwaɪf/ n акушёрка.
midwifery /ˌmɪdˈwɪfərɪ/ n акушёрство.

might /maɪt/ n мощь; with all one's ~ изо всех сил. **mighty** /ˈmaɪtɪ/ adj мощный.

migraine /ˈmiːɡreɪn/ n мигрень.

migrant /ˈmaɪɡrənt/ adj кочующий; (bird) перелётный; n (person) переселёнец; (bird) перелётная птица. **migrate** /maɪˈɡreɪt/ vi мигрировать impf & pf. **migration** /-ˈɡreɪʃ(ə)n/ n миграция. **migratory** /-ˈɡreɪtərɪ/ adj кочующий; (bird) перелётный.

mike /maɪk/ n микрофон.

mild /maɪld/ adj мягкий.

mildew /ˈmɪldjuː/ n плесень.

mile /maɪl/ n мйля. **mileage** /-ldʒ/ n расстояние в мйлях; (of car) пробег. **milestone** n верстовой столб; (fig) веха.

militancy /ˈmɪlɪt(ə)nsɪ/ n войнственность. **militant** /-t(ə)nt/ adj войнствующий; n активист. **military** /-tərɪ/ adj военный; n военные sb pl. **militate** /-teɪt/ vi: ~ against говорить impf против+gen. **militia** /mɪˈlɪʃə/ n милиция. **militiaman** n милиционер.

milk /mɪlk/ n молоко; attrib молочный; vt доить impf, по~ pf. **milkman** n продавец молока. **milky** /-kɪ/ adj молочный; M~ Way Млечный Путь m.

mill /mɪl/ n мельница; (factory) фабрика; vt (grain etc.) молоть impf, с~ pf; (metal) фрезеровать impf, от~ pf; (coin) гуртить impf; vi: ~ around толпиться impf. **miller** /ˈmɪlə(r)/ n мельник.

millennium /mɪˈlenɪəm/ n тысячелетие.

millet /ˈmɪlɪt/ n (plant) просо;

(grain) пшено.

milligram(me) /ˈmɪlɪˌɡræm/ n миллиграмм. **millimetre** /-ˌmiːtə(r)/ n миллиметр.

million /ˈmɪljən/ n миллион. **millionaire** /-ˈneə(r)/ n миллионер. **millionth** /-jənθ/ adj миллионный.

millstone /ˈmɪlstəʊn/ n жёрнов; (fig) камень m на шее.

mime /maɪm/ n мим; (dumb-show) пантомима; vt изображать impf, изобразить pf мимически. **mimic** /ˈmɪmɪk/ n мимист; vt передразнивать impf, передразнить pf. **mimicry** /ˈmɪmɪkrɪ/ n имитация.

minaret /ˌmɪnəˈret/ n минарет.

mince /mɪns/ n (meat) фарш; vt рубить impf; (in machine) пропускать impf, пропустить pf через мясорубку; vi (walk) семенить impf; not ~ matters говорить impf без обиняков. **mincemeat** n начинка из изюма, миндаля и т.п. **mincer** n мясорубка.

mind /maɪnd/ n ум; bear in ~ иметь impf в виду; change one's ~ передумывать impf, передумать pf; make up one's ~ решаться impf, решиться pf; you're out of your ~ вы с ума сошли; vt (give heed to) обращать impf, обратить pf внимание на+acc; (look after) присматривать impf, присмотреть pf за+instr; I don't ~ я ничего не имею против; don't ~ me не обращай(те) внимания на меня!; ~ you don't forget смотри не забудь!; ~ your own business не вмешивайтесь в чужие дела!; never ~! ничего! **mindful** /-fʊl/ adj помнящий. **mindless** /-lɪs/ adj бессмысленный.

mine¹ /maɪn/ poss pron мой;

свой².

mine² /main/ n шáхта, руднйк; (fig) истóчник; (mil) мйна; vt (obtain from ~) добывáть impf, добы́ть pf; (mil) минйровать impf & pf. **minefield** n мйнное пóле. **miner** /'mainə(r)/ n шахтёр.

mineral /'minər(ə)l/ n минерáл; adj минерáльный; ~ **water** минерáльная водá. **mineralogy** /-'rælədʒɪ/ n минералóгия.

mingle /'mɪŋg(ə)l/ vt & i смéшивать(ся) impf, смешáть(ся) pf.

miniature /'mɪnɪtʃə(r)/ n миниатю́ра; adj миниатю́рный.

minibus /'mɪnɪˌbʌs/ n микроавтóбус.

minim /'mɪnɪm/ n (mus) половйнная нóта. **minimal** /-məl/ adj минимáльный. **minimize** /-ˌmaɪz/ vt (reduce) доводйть impf, довестй pf до мúнимума. **minimum** /-məm/ n мúнимум; adj минимáльный.

mining /'maɪnɪŋ/ n гóрное дéло.

minister /'mɪnɪstə(r)/ n минúстр; (eccl) свящéнник. **ministerial** /-'stɪərɪəl/ adj министéрский. **ministration** /-'streɪʃ(ə)n/ n пóмощь. **ministry** /'mɪnɪstrɪ/ n (polit) министéрство; (eccl) духовéнство.

mink /mɪŋk/ n нóрка; attrib нóрковый.

minor /'maɪnə(r)/ adj (unimportant) незначúтельный; (less important) второстепéнный; (mus) минóрный; (n person under age) несовершеннолéтний n; (mus) минóр. **minority** /-'nɒrɪtɪ/ n меньшинствó; (age) несовершеннолéтие.

minstrel /'mɪnstr(ə)l/ n менестрéль m.

mint¹ /mɪnt/ n (plant) мя́та;

(peppermint) пéречная мя́та.

mint² /mɪnt/ n (econ) монéтный двор; **in ~ condition** нóвенький; vt чекáнить impf, от~, вы́~ pf.

minuet /ˌmɪnjʊ'et/ n менуэ́т.

minus /'maɪnəs/ prep мúнус +acc; без+gen; n мúнус.

minuscule /'mɪnəˌskjuːl/ adj малю́сенький.

minute¹ /'mɪnɪt/ n минýта; pl протокóл.

minute² /maɪ'njuːt/ adj мéлкий. **minutiae** /-'njuːʃɪˌaɪ/ n pl мéлочи (-чéй) f pl.

miracle /'mɪrək(ə)l/ n чýдо. **miraculous** /-'rækjʊləs/ adj чудéсный.

mirage /'mɪrɑːʒ/ n мирáж.

mire /maɪə(r)/ n (mud) грязь; (swamp) болóто.

mirror /'mɪrə(r)/ n зéркало; vt отражáть impf, отразúть pf.

mirth /mɜːθ/ n весéлье.

misadventure /ˌmɪsəd'ventʃə(r)/ n несчáстный слýчай.

misapprehension /ˌmɪsæprɪ'henʃ(ə)n/ n недопонимáние.

misappropriate /ˌmɪsə'prəʊprɪˌeɪt/ vt незакóнно присвáивать impf, присвóить pf. **misbehave** /ˌmɪsbɪ'heɪv/ vi дýрно вестú impf себя́. **misbehaviour** /ˌmɪsbɪ'heɪvjə/ n дурнóе поведéние.

miscalculate /ˌmɪs'kælkjʊˌleɪt/ vt непрáвильно рассчúтывать impf, рассчитáть pf; (fig, abs) просчúтываться impf, просчитáться pf. **miscalculation** /-'leɪʃ(ə)n/ n просчёт. **miscarriage** /ˌmɪs'kærɪdʒ/ n (med) вы́кидыш; ~ **of justice** судéбная ошúбка. **miscarry** /mɪs'kærɪ/ vi (med) имéть impf вы́кидыш.

miscellaneous /ˌmɪsə'leɪnɪəs/ adj рáзный, разнообрáзный. **miscellany** /mɪ'selənɪ/ n смесь.

mischief /'mɪstʃɪf/ n (harm) вред; (naughtiness) озорство.
mischievous /'mɪstʃɪvəs/ adj озорной.
misconception /ˌmɪskən'sepʃ(ə)n/ n неправильное представление. **misconduct** /ˌmɪs'kɒndʌkt/ n дурное поведение.
misconstrue /ˌmɪskən'struː/ vt неправильно истолковывать impf, истолковать pf.
misdeed, misdemeanour /mɪs'diːd, ˌmɪsdɪ'miːnə(r)/ n проступок. **misdirect** /ˌmɪsdə'rekt/ vt неправильно направлять impf, направить pf; (letter) неправильно адресовать impf & pf.
miser /'maɪzə(r)/ n скупец. **miserable** /'mɪzərəb(ə)l/ adj (unhappy, wretched) несчастный, жалкий; (weather) скверный. **miserly** /'maɪzəlɪ/ adj скупой. **misery** /'mɪzərɪ/ n страдание.
misfire /mɪs'faɪə(r)/ vi давать impf, дать pf осечку. **misfit** /'mɪsfɪt/ n (person) неудачник. **misfortune** /mɪs'fɔːtjuːn/ n несчастье. **misgiving** /mɪs'ɡɪvɪŋ/ n опасение. **misguided** /mɪs'ɡaɪdɪd/ adj обманутый.
mishap /'mɪshæp/ n неприятность. **misinform** /ˌmɪsɪn'fɔːm/ vt неправильно информировать impf & pf. **misinterpret** /ˌmɪsɪn'tɜːprɪt/ vt неверно истолковывать impf, истолковать pf. **misjudge** /mɪs'dʒʌdʒ/ vt неверно оценивать impf, оценить pf. **misjudgement** /mɪs'dʒʌdʒmənt/ n неверная оценка.
mislay /mɪs'leɪ/ vt затерять pf. **mislead** /mɪs'liːd/ vt вводить impf, ввести pf в заблуждение.
mismanage /mɪs'mænɪdʒ/ vt плохо управлять impf + instr. **mismanagement** /mɪs'mænɪdʒmənt/ n плохое управ-

ление. **misnomer** /mɪs'nəʊmə(r)/ n неправильное название.
misogynist /mɪ'sɒdʒɪnɪst/ n женоненавистник. **misogyny** /-nɪ/ n женоненавистничество.
misplaced /mɪs'pleɪst/ adj неуместный. **misprint** /'mɪsprɪnt/ n опечатка. **misquote** /mɪs'kwəʊt/ vt неправильно цитировать impf, про~ pf. **misread** /mɪs'riːd/ vt (fig) неправильно истолковывать impf, истолковать pf. **misrepresent** /ˌmɪsreprɪ'zent/ vt искажать impf, исказить pf. **misrepresentation** /ˌmɪsˌreprɪzen'teɪʃ(ə)n/ n искажение.
Miss /mɪs/ n (title) мисс.
miss /mɪs/ n (in)промах; vi промахиваться impf, промахнуться pf; vt (fail to hit, see, hear) пропускать impf, пропустить pf; (train) опаздывать impf, опоздать pf на+acc; (regret absence of) скучать impf по+dat; ~ out пропускать impf, пропустить pf; ~ the point не понимать impf, понять pf сути.
misshapen /mɪs'ʃeɪpən/ adj уродливый.
missile /'mɪsaɪl/ n снаряд, ракета.
missing /'mɪsɪŋ/ adj отсутствующий, недостающий; (person) пропавший без вести.
mission /'mɪʃ(ə)n/ n миссия; командировка. **missionary** /'mɪʃənərɪ/ n миссионер. **missive** /'mɪsɪv/ n послание.
misspell /mɪs'spel/ vt неправильно писать impf, на~ pf. **misspelling** /-lɪŋ/ n неправильное написание.
mist /mɪst/ n туман; vt & i затуманивать(ся) impf, затуманить(ся) pf.

mistake /mɪˈsteɪk/ vt непра́вильно понима́ть impf, поня́ть pf; ~ **for** принима́ть impf, приня́ть pf за+acc; n оши́бка; **make a** ~ ошиба́ться impf, ошиби́ться pf. **mistaken** /-kən/ adj оши́бочный; **be** ~ ошиба́ться impf, ошиби́ться pf.

mister /ˈmɪstə(r)/ n ми́стер, госпо́дин.

mistletoe /ˈmɪs(ə)l.təʊ/ n оме́ла.

mistress /ˈmɪstrɪs/ n хозя́йка; (teacher) учи́тельница; (lover) любо́вница.

mistrust /mɪsˈtrʌst/ vt не доверя́ть impf +dat; n недове́рие. **mistrustful** /-fʊl/ adj недове́рчивый.

misty /ˈmɪsti/ adj тума́нный.

misunderstand /ˌmɪsʌndə 'stænd/ vt непра́вильно понима́ть impf, поня́ть pf. **misunderstanding** /-dɪŋ/ n недоразуме́ние.

misuse vt /mɪsˈjuːz/ непра́вильно употребля́ть impf, употреби́ть pf; (ill treat) ду́рно обраща́ться impf c+instr; n /-ˈjuːs/ непра́вильное употребле́ние.

mite /maɪt/ n (insect) клещ.

mitigate /ˈmɪtɪˌgeɪt/ vt смягча́ть impf, смягчи́ть pf. **mitigation** /-ˈgeɪʃ(ə)n/ n смягче́ние.

mitre /ˈmaɪtə(r)/ n ми́тра.

mitten /ˈmɪt(ə)n/ n рукави́ца.

mix /mɪks/ vt меша́ть impf, с~ pf; vi сме́шиваться impf, сме́шаться pf; (associate) обща́ться impf; ~ **up** (confuse) пу́тать impf, с~ pf; **get** ~**ed up in** замеша́ться impf, заме́шаться pf в+acc; n смесь. **mixer** /ˈmɪksə(r)/ n смеси́тель m; (cul) ми́ксер. **mixture** /ˈmɪkstʃə(r)/ n смесь; (medicine) миксту́ра.

moan /məʊn/ n стон; vi стона́ть impf, про~ pf.

moat /məʊt/ n (крепостно́й) ров.

mob /mɒb/ n толпа́; vt (attack) напада́ть impf, напа́сть pf толпо́й на+acc. **mobster** /-stə(r)/ n банди́т.

mobile /ˈməʊbaɪl/ adj подви́жной, передвижно́й; ~ **phone** портати́вный телефо́н. **mobility** /məˈbɪlɪti/ n подви́жность.

mobilize /ˈməʊbɪˌlaɪz/ vt & i мобилизова́ть(ся) impf & pf.

moccasin /ˈmɒkəsɪn/ n мокаси́н (gen pl -н).

mock /mɒk/ vt & i издева́ться impf над+instr; adj (sham) подде́льный; (pretended) мни́мый; ~**up** n маке́т. **mockery** /ˈmɒkərɪ/ n издева́тельство; (travesty) паро́дия.

mode /məʊd/ n (manner) о́браз; (method) ме́тод.

model /ˈmɒd(ə)l/ n (representation) моде́ль; (pattern, ideal) образе́ц; (artist's) нату́рщик, -ица; (fashion) манеке́нщик, -ица; (make) моде́ль; adj образцо́вый; vt лепи́ть impf, вы́~ pf; (clothes) демонстри́ровать impf & pf; vi (act as a ~) быть нату́рщиком, -ицей; быть манеке́нщиком, -ицей; ~ **after**, **on** создава́ть impf, созда́ть pf по образцу́ +gen.

modem /ˈməʊdem/ n моде́м.

moderate adj /ˈmɒdərət/ (various senses; polit) уме́ренный; (medium) сре́дний; vt /ˈmɒdəˌreɪt/ умеря́ть impf, уме́рить pf; vi (of storm) стиха́ть impf, сти́хнуть pf. **moderation** /ˌmɒdəˈreɪʃ(ə)n/ n уме́ренность; **in** ~ уме́ренно.

modern /ˈmɒd(ə)n/ adj совреме́нный; (language, history)

но́вый. **modernization** /ˌmɒdənaɪˈzeɪʃ(ə)n/ n модерниза́ция. **modernize** /ˈmɒdənaɪz/ vt модернизи́ровать impf & pf.

modest /ˈmɒdɪst/ adj скро́мный. **modesty** /-stɪ/ n скро́мность.

modification /ˌmɒdɪfɪˈkeɪʃ(ə)n/ n модифика́ция. **modify** /ˈmɒdɪˌfaɪ/ vt модифици́ровать impf & pf.

modish /ˈməʊdɪʃ/ adj мо́дный.

modular /ˈmɒdjʊlə(r)/ adj мо́дульный. **modulate** /-ˌleɪt/ vt модули́ровать impf. **modulation** /-ˈleɪʃ(ə)n/ n модуля́ция. **module** /ˈmɒdjuːl/ n мо́дуль m.

mohair /ˈməʊheə(r)/ n мохе́р.

moist /mɔɪst/ adj вла́жный. **moisten** /ˈmɔɪs(ə)n/ vt & i увлажня́ть(ся) impf, увлажни́ть(ся) pf. **moisture** /ˈmɔɪstʃə(r)/ n вла́га.

molar /ˈməʊlə(r)/ n (tooth) коренно́й зуб.

mole[1] /məʊl/ n (on skin) ро́динка.

mole[2] /məʊl/ n (animal; agent) крот.

molecular /məˈlekjʊlə(r)/ adj молекуля́рный. **molecule** /ˈmɒlɪˌkjuːl/ n моле́кула.

molest /məˈlest/ vt пристава́ть impf, приста́ть pf к+dat.

mollify /ˈmɒlɪˌfaɪ/ vt смягча́ть impf, смягчи́ть pf.

mollusc /ˈmɒləsk/ n моллю́ск.

molten /ˈməʊlt(ə)n/ adj распла́вленный.

moment /ˈməʊmənt/ n моме́нт, миг; at the ~ сейча́с; at the last ~ в после́днюю мину́ту; just a ~ сейча́с! **momentarily** /-ˈterɪlɪ/ adv на мгнове́ние. **momentary** /ˈməʊməntərɪ/ adj мгнове́нный. **momentous** /məˈmentəs/ adj ва́жный. **momentum** /məˈ-

'mentəm/ n коли́чество движе́ния; (impetus) движу́щая си́ла; gather ~ набира́ть impf, набра́ть pf ско́рость.

monarch /ˈmɒnək/ n мона́рх. **monarchy** /-kɪ/ n мона́рхия. **monastery** /ˈmɒnəstərɪ/ n монасты́рь m. **monastic** /məˈnæstɪk/ adj мона́шеский.

Monday /ˈmʌndeɪ/ n понеде́льник.

monetary /ˈmʌnɪtərɪ/ adj де́нежный. **money** /ˈmʌnɪ/ n де́ньги (-нег, -ньга́м) pl; **~-lender** ростовщи́к.

mongrel /ˈmʌŋɡr(ə)l/ n дворня́жка.

monitor /ˈmɒnɪtə(r)/ n (naut; TV) монито́р; vt проверя́ть impf, прове́рить pf.

monk /mʌŋk/ n мона́х.

monkey /ˈmʌŋkɪ/ n обезья́на.

mono /ˈmɒnəʊ/ n мо́но neut indecl. **monochrome** adj одноцве́тный. **monogamous** /məˈnɒɡəməs/ adj единобра́чный. **monogamy** /məˈnɒɡəmɪ/ n единобра́чие. **monogram** /ˈmɒnəˌɡræm/ n моногра́мма. **monograph** /ˈmɒnəɡrɑːf/ n моногра́фия. **monolith** /ˈmɒnəlɪθ/ n моноли́т. **monolithic** /ˌmɒnəˈlɪθɪk/ adj моноли́тный. **monologue** /ˈmɒnəˌlɒɡ/ n моноло́г. **monopolize** /məˈnɒpəˌlaɪz/ vt монополизи́ровать impf & pf. **monopoly** /məˈnɒpəlɪ/ n монопо́лия. **monosyllabic** /ˌmɒnəsɪˈlæbɪk/ adj односло́жный. **monosyllable** /ˈmɒnəˌsɪləb(ə)l/ n односло́жное сло́во. **monotone** /ˈmɒnəˌtəʊn/ n моното́нность; in a ~ моното́нно. **monotonous** /məˈnɒtən(ə)s/ adj моното́нный. **monotony** /məˈnɒtənɪ/ n моното́нность.

monsoon /mɒnˈsuːn/ n (wind) муссо́н; (rainy season) дождли́-

вый сезо́н.

monster /'mɒnstə(r)/ n чудо́вище. **monstrosity** /mɒn'strɒsɪtɪ/ n чудо́вище. **monstrous** /'mɒnstrəs/ adj чудо́вищный; (huge) грома́дный.

montage /mɒn'tɑːʒ/ n монта́ж.

month /mʌnθ/ n ме́сяц. **monthly** /-lɪ/ adj ме́сячный; n ежеме́сячник; adv ежеме́сячно.

monument /'mɒnjʊmənt/ n па́мятник. **monumental** /-'ment(ə)l/ adj монумента́льный.

moo /muː/ vi мыча́ть impf.

mood¹ /muːd/ n (gram) наклоне́ние.

mood² /muːd/ n настрое́ние. **moody** /-dɪ/ adj капри́зный.

moon /muːn/ n луна́. **moonlight** n лу́нный свет; vi халту́рить impf. **moonlit** /-lɪt/ adj лу́нный.

moor¹ /mʊə(r)/ n ме́стность, поро́сшая ве́реском n ве́ресковая пу́стошь.

moor² /mʊə(r)/ vt & i шварто́ва́ть(ся) impf, при~ pf. **mooring** /-rɪŋ/ n (place) прича́л; pl (cables) шварто́вы f n pl.

Moorish /'mʊərɪʃ/ adj маврита́нский.

moose /muːs/ n америка́нский лось m.

moot /muːt/ adj спо́рный.

mop /mɒp/ n шва́бра; vt протира́ть impf, протере́ть pf (шва́брой); ~ one's brow вытира́ть impf, вы́тереть pf лоб; ~ up вытира́ть impf, вы́тереть pf.

mope /məʊp/ vi хандри́ть impf.

moped /'məʊped/ n мопе́д.

moraine /mə'reɪn/ n море́на.

moral /'mɒr(ə)l/ adj мора́льный; n мора́ль f; pl нра́вы m pl. **morale** /mə'rɑːl/ n мора́льное состоя́ние. **morality** /mə'rælɪtɪ/ n нра́вственность, мора́ль.

moralize /'mɒrəˌlaɪz/ vi морализи́ровать impf.

morass /mə'ræs/ n боло́то.

moratorium /ˌmɒrə'tɔːrɪəm/ n морато́рий.

morbid /'mɔːbɪd/ adj боле́зненный.

more /mɔː(r)/ adj (greater quantity) бо́льше +gen; (additional) ещё; adv бо́льше; (forming comp) бо́лее; and what is ~ и бо́льше того́; ~ or less бо́лее и́ли ме́нее; once ~ ещё раз. **moreover** /mɔː'rəʊvə(r)/ adv сверх того́; кро́ме того́.

morgue /mɔːg/ n морг.

moribund /'mɒrɪˌbʌnd/ adj умира́ющий.

morning /'mɔːnɪŋ/ n у́тро; in the ~ у́тром; in the ~s по утра́м; attrib у́тренний.

moron /'mɔːrɒn/ n слабоу́мный sb.

morose /mə'rəʊs/ adj угрю́мый.

morphine /'mɔːfiːn/ n мо́рфий.

Morse (code) /mɔːs (kəʊd)/ n а́збука Мо́рзе.

morsel /'mɔːs(ə)l/ n кусо́чек.

mortal /'mɔːt(ə)l/ adj сме́ртный; (fatal) смерте́льный; n сме́ртный sb. **mortality** /-'tælɪtɪ/ n сме́ртность.

mortar /'mɔːtə(r)/ n (vessel) сту́п(к)а; (cannon) миномёт; (cement) известко́вый раство́р.

mortgage /'mɔːgɪdʒ/ n ссу́да на поку́пку до́ма; vt закла́дывать impf, заложи́ть pf.

mortify /'mɔːtɪˌfaɪ/ vt унижа́ть impf, уни́зить pf.

mortuary /'mɔːtjʊərɪ/ n морг.

mosaic /mə'zeɪk/ n моза́ика; adj моза́ичный.

mosque /mɒsk/ n мече́ть.

mosquito /mə'skiːtəʊ/ n комра́.

moss /mɒs/ *n* мох. **mossy** /-sɪ/ *adj* мши́стый.

most /məʊst/ *adj* наибо́льший; *n* наибо́льшее коли́чество; *adj* & *n* (majority) больши́нство +gen; бо́льшая часть +gen; *adv* бо́льше всего́, наибо́лее; (forming superl) са́мый. **mostly** /-lɪ/ *adv* гла́вным о́бразом.

MOT (test) *n* техосмо́тр.

motel /məʊˈtel/ *n* моте́ль *m*.

moth /mɒθ/ *n* мотылёк; (clothes-~) моль.

mother /ˈmʌðə(r)/ *n* мать; *vt* относи́ться *impf* по-матери́нски к +dat; **~-in-law** (wife's ~) тёща; (husband's ~) свекро́вь; **~-of-pearl** перламу́тр; *adj* перламу́тровый; **~ tongue** родно́й язы́к. **motherhood** *n* матери́нство. **motherland** *n* ро́дина. **motherly** /-lɪ/ *adj* матери́нский.

motif /məʊˈtiːf/ *n* моти́в.

motion /ˈməʊʃ(ə)n/ *n* движе́ние; (gesture) жест; (proposal) предложе́ние; *vt* показывать *impf*, показа́ть *pf* +dat жестом, чтобы +past. **motionless** /-lɪs/ *adj* неподви́жный. **motivate** /ˈməʊtɪveɪt/ *vt* побужда́ть *impf*, побуди́ть *pf*. **motivation** /ˌməʊtɪˈveɪʃ(ə)n/ *n* побужде́ние. **motive** /ˈməʊtɪv/ *n* моти́в; *adj* дви́жущий.

motley /ˈmɒtlɪ/ *adj* пёстрый.

motor /ˈməʊtə(r)/ *n* дви́гатель *m*, мото́р; **~ bike** мотоци́кл; **~ boat** мото́рная ло́дка; **~ car** автомоби́ль *m*; **~ cycle** мотоци́кл; **~-cyclist** мотоцикли́ст; **~ racing** автомоби́льные го́нки *f pl*; **~ scooter** мотороллер; **~ vehicle** автомаши́на. **motoring** /-rɪŋ/ *n* автомобили́зм. **motorist** /-rɪst/ *n* автомоби́лист, **~ка**. **motorize** /-ˌraɪz/

vt моторизова́ть *impf* & *pf*. **motorway** *n* автостра́да.

mottled /ˈmɒtəld/ *adj* кра́пчатый.

motto /ˈmɒtəʊ/ *n* деви́з.

mould¹ /məʊld/ *n* (shape) фо́рма, фо́рмочка; *vt* формова́ть *impf*, **c~** *pf*. **moulding** /-dɪŋ/ *n* (archit) лепно́е украше́ние.

mould² /məʊld/ *n* (fungi) пле́сень. **mouldy** /-dɪ/ *adj* запле́сневе́лый.

moulder /ˈməʊldə(r)/ *vi* разлага́ться *impf*, разложи́ться *pf*.

moult /məʊlt/ *vi* линя́ть *impf*, **вы~** *pf*.

mound /maʊnd/ *n* холм; (heap) на́сыпь.

Mount /maʊnt/ *n* (in names) гора́.

mount /maʊnt/ *vt* (ascend) поднима́ться *impf*, подня́ться *pf* на+acc; (~ a horse etc.) сади́ться *impf*, сесть *pf* на+acc; (picture) накле́ивать *impf*, накле́ить *pf* на карто́н; (gun) устана́вливать *impf*, установи́ть *pf*; **~ up** (accumulate) нака́пливаться *impf*, накопи́ться *pf*; *n* (for picture) карто́н; (horse) верхова́я ло́шадь.

mountain /ˈmaʊntɪn/ *n* гора́; *attrib* го́рный. **mountaineer** /-ˈnɪə(r)/ *n* альпини́ст, **~ка**. **mountaineering** /-ˈnɪərɪŋ/ *n* альпини́зм. **mountainous** /ˈmaʊntɪnəs/ *adj* гори́стый.

mourn /mɔːn/ *vt* опла́кивать *impf*, опла́кать *pf*; *vi* скорбе́ть *impf* (over о+prep). **mournful** /-fʊl/ *adj* ско́рбный. **mourning** /-nɪŋ/ *n* тра́ур.

mouse /maʊs/ *n* мышь.

mousse /muːs/ *n* мусс.

moustache /məˈstɑːʃ/ *n* усы́ (усо́в) *pl*.

mousy /'maʊsɪ/ *adj* мыши́ный; (*timid*) ро́бкий.

mouth *n* /maʊθ/ рот; (*poetical*) уста́ (-т) *pl*; (*entrance*) вход; (*of river*) у́стье; *vt* /maʊð/ говори́ть *impf*, сказа́ть *pf* одни́ми губа́ми. **mouthful** *n* глото́к. **mouth-organ** *n* губна́я гармо́ника. **mouthpiece** *n* мундшту́к; (*person*) ру́пор.

movable /'muːvəb(ə)l/ *adj* подвижно́й.

move /muːv/ *n* (*in game*) ход; (*change of residence*) перее́зд; (*movement*) движе́ние; (*step*) шаг; *vt & i* дви́гать(ся) *impf*, дви́нуть(ся) *pf*; *vt* (*affect*) тро́гать *impf*, тро́нуть *pf*; (*propose*) вноси́ть *impf*, внести́ *pf*; *vi* (*develop*) развива́ться *impf*, разви́ться *pf*; (~ *house*) переезжа́ть *impf*, перее́хать *pf*; ~ **away** (*vt & i*) удаля́ть(ся) *impf*, удали́ть(ся) *pf*; (*vi*) уезжа́ть *impf*, уе́хать *pf*; ~ **in** въезжа́ть *impf*, въе́хать *pf*; ~ **on** идти́ *impf*, пойти́ *pf* да́льше; ~ **out** съезжа́ть *impf*, съе́хать *pf* (**of** c+*gen*). **movement** /-mənt/ *n* движе́ние; (*mus*) часть *f*. **moving** /-vɪŋ/ *adj* дви́жущийся; (*touching*) тро́гательный.

mow /məʊ/ *vt* (*also* ~ **down**) коси́ть *impf*, c~ *pf*. **mower** /'məʊə(r)/ *n* коси́лка.

MP *abbr* (*of* **Member of Parliament**) член парла́мента.

Mr /'mɪstə(r)/ *abbr* ми́стер, господи́н. **Mrs** /'mɪsɪz/ *abbr* ми́ссис *f indecl*, госпожа́.

Ms /mɪz/ *n* миз, госпожа́.

much /mʌtʃ/ *adj & n* мно́го +*gen*; мно́гое *sb*; *adv* о́чень; (*with comp adj*) гора́здо.

muck /mʌk/ *n* (*dung*) наво́з; (*dirt*) грязь; ~ **about** вози́ться *impf*; ~ **out** чи́стить *impf*, вы-

pf; ~ **up** изга́живать *impf*, изга́дить *pf*.

mucous /'mjuːkəs/ *adj* сли́зистый. **mucus** /'mjuːkəs/ *n* слизь.

mud /mʌd/ *n* грязь. **mudguard** *n* крыло́.

muddle /'mʌd(ə)l/ *vt* пу́тать *impf*, c~ *pf*; *vi*: ~ **through** ко́е-ка́к справля́ться *impf*, спра́виться *pf* в беспоря́дке.

muddy /'mʌdɪ/ *adj* гря́зный; *vt* обры́згивать *impf*, обры́згать *pf* гря́зью.

muff /mʌf/ *n* му́фта.

muffle /'mʌf(ə)l/ *vt* (*for warmth*) заку́тывать *impf*, заку́тать *pf*; (*sound*) глуши́ть *impf*, за~ *pf*.

mug /mʌg/ *n* (*vessel*) кру́жка; (*face*) мо́рда.

muggy /'mʌgɪ/ *adj* сыро́й и тёплый.

mulch /mʌltʃ/ *n* му́льча; *vt* мульчи́ровать *impf & pf*.

mule /mjuːl/ *n* мул.

mull /mʌl/ *vt*: ~ **over** обду́мывать *impf*, обду́мать *pf*. **mulled** /mʌld/ *adj*: ~ **wine** глинтве́йн.

mullet /'mʌlɪt/ *n* (*grey* ~) кефа́ль; (*red* ~) бараву́лька.

multicoloured /'mʌltɪ,kʌləd/ *adj* многокра́сочный. **multifarious** /,mʌltɪ'feərɪəs/ *adj* разнообра́зный. **multilateral** /,mʌltɪ'lætər(ə)l/ *adj* многосторо́нний. **multimillionaire** /,mʌltɪ,mɪljə'neə(r)/ *n* мультимиллионе́р. **multinational** /,mʌltɪ'næʃ(ə)n(ə)l/ *adj* многонациона́льный.

multiple /'mʌltɪp(ə)l/ *adj* составно́й; (*numerous*) многочи́сленный; ~ **sclerosis** рассе́янный склеро́з; *n* кра́тное число́; **least common** ~ о́бщее наиме́ньшее кра́тное *sb*. **multiplication** /,mʌltɪplɪ'keɪʃ(ə)n/ *n* умноже́ние. **multiplicity** /,mʌltɪ'plɪsɪtɪ/ *n*

многочи́сленность. **multiply**
/'mʌltɪ,plaɪ/ vt (math) умножа́ть
impf, умно́жить pf; vi размно-
жа́ться impf, размно-
житься pf.

multi-storey /,mʌltɪ'stɔːrɪ/ adj
многоэта́жный.

multitude /'mʌltɪ,tjuːd/ n мно́же-
ство; (crowd) толпа́.

mum[1] /mʌm/ adj: keep ~ мол-
ча́ть impf.

mum[2] /mʌm/ n (mother) ма́ма.

mumble /'mʌmb(ə)l/ vt & i бор-
мота́ть impf, про~ pf.

mummy[1] /'mʌmɪ/ n (archaeol)
му́мия.

mummy[2] /'mʌmɪ/ n (mother)
ма́ма, ма́мочка.

mumps /mʌmps/ n сви́нка.

munch /mʌntʃ/ vt жева́ть impf.

mundane /mʌn'deɪn/ adj
земно́й.

municipal /mjuː'nɪsɪp(ə)l/ adj му-
ниципа́льный. **municipality**
/-'pælɪtɪ/ n муниципалите́т.

munitions /mjuː'nɪʃ(ə)ns/ n pl
вое́нное иму́щество.

mural /'mjʊər(ə)l/ n стенна́я ро́-
спись.

murder /'mɜːdə(r)/ n уби́йство;
vt убива́ть impf, уби́ть pf; (language) кове́ркать impf, ис~
pf. **murderer**, **murderess**
/'mɜːdərə(r), 'mɜːdərɪs/ n уби́йца
m & f. **murderous** /'mɜːdərəs/
adj уби́йственный.

murky /'mɜːkɪ/ adj тёмный,
мра́чный.

murmur /'mɜːmə(r)/ n шёпот; vt
& i шепта́ть impf, шепну́ть pf.

muscle /'mʌs(ə)l/ n му́скул.
muscular /'mʌskjʊlə(r)/ adj мы́-
шечный; (person) му́скули-
стый.

Muscovite /'mʌskə,vaɪt/ n моск-
ви́ч, ~ка.

muse /mjuːz/ vi размышля́ть

impf.

museum /mjuː'zɪəm/ n музе́й.

mush /mʌʃ/ n ка́ша.

mushroom /'mʌʃrʊm/ n гриб.

music /'mjuːzɪk/ n му́зыка;
(sheet ~) но́ты f pl; ~-hall мю́-
зик-хо́лл; ~ stand пюпи́тр.
musical /-k(ə)l/ adj музыка́ль-
ный; n опере́тта. **musician**
/mjuː'zɪʃ(ə)n/ n музыка́нт.

musk /mʌsk/ n му́скус.

musket /'mʌskɪt/ n мушке́т.

Muslim /'mʊzlɪm/ n мусульма́-
нин, -а́нка; adj мусульма́н-
ский.

muslin /'mʌzlɪn/ n мусли́н.

mussel /'mʌs(ə)l/ n ми́дия.

must /mʌst/ v aux (obligation)
до́лжен (-жна́) predic+inf; надо
impers+dat & inf; (necessity)
ну́жно impers+dat & inf; ~ not
(prohibition) нельзя́ impers+dat
& inf.

mustard /'mʌstəd/ n горчи́ца.

muster /'mʌstə(r)/ vt собира́ть
impf, собра́ть pf; (courage etc.)
собира́ться impf, собра́ться pf
c+instr.

musty /'mʌstɪ/ adj за́тхлый.

mutation /mjuː'teɪʃ(ə)n/ n му-
та́ция.

mute /mjuːt/ adj немо́й; n немо́й
sb; (mus) сурди́нка. **muted**
/-tɪd/ adj приглушённый.

mutilate /'mjuːtɪ,leɪt/ vt уве́чить
impf, из~ pf. **mutilation**
/-'leɪʃ(ə)n/ n уве́чье.

mutineer /,mjuːtɪ'nɪə(r)/ n мя-
те́жник. **mutinous** /'mjuːtɪnəs/
adj мяте́жный. **mutiny**
/'mjuːtɪnɪ/ n мяте́ж; vi бунто-
ва́ть impf, взбунтова́ться pf.

mutter /'mʌtə(r)/ vi бормота́ть
impf, n бормота́ние.

mutton /'mʌt(ə)n/ n бара́нина.

mutual /'mjuːtʃʊəl/ adj взаи́м-
ный; (common) о́бщий.

muzzle /'mʌz(ə)l/ n (animal's) мо́рда; (on animal) намо́рдник; (of gun) ду́ло; vt надева́ть impf, наде́ть pf намо́рдник на+acc; (fig) заставля́ть impf, заста́вить pf молча́ть.

my /maɪ/ poss pron мой; мой.

myopia /maɪ'əʊpɪə/ n близору́кость. **myopic** /-'ɒpɪk/ adj близору́кий.

myriad /'mɪrɪəd/ n мириа́ды pl; adj бесчи́сленный.

myrtle /'mɜːt(ə)l/ n мирт; attrib ми́ртовый.

myself /maɪ'self/ pron (emph) (я) сам, сама́; (refl) себя́; -ся (suffixed to vt).

mysterious /mɪ'stɪərɪəs/ adj таи́нственный. **mystery** /'mɪstərɪ/ n та́йна.

mystic(al) /'mɪstɪk(ə)l/ adj мисти́ческий; n ми́стик. **mysticism** /'mɪstɪˌsɪz(ə)m/ n мистици́зм. **mystification** /ˌmɪstɪfɪ'keɪʃ(ə)n/ n озада́ченность. **mystify** /'mɪstɪˌfaɪ/ vt озада́чивать impf, озада́чить pf.

myth /mɪθ/ n миф. **mythical** /'mɪθɪk(ə)l/ adj мифи́ческий. **mythological** /ˌmɪθə'lɒdʒɪk(ə)l/ adj мифологи́ческий. **mythology** /mɪ'θɒlədʒɪ/ n мифоло́гия.

N

nag¹ /næg/ n (horse) ло́шадь.

nag² /næg/ vt (also ~ at) пили́ть impf +acc; vi (of pain) ныть impf.

nail /neɪl/ n (finger-, toe-~) но́готь m; (metal spike) гвоздь m; ~ varnish лак для ногте́й; vt прибива́ть impf, приби́ть pf (гвоздя́ми).

naive /naɪ'iːv/ adj наи́вный. **naivety** /-tɪ/ n наи́вность.

naked /'neɪkɪd/ adj го́лый; ~ eye невооружённый глаз. **nakedness** /-nɪs/ n нагота́.

name /neɪm/ n назва́ние; (forename) и́мя neut; (surname) фами́лия; (reputation) репута́ция; what is his ~? как его́ зову́т?; ~plate доще́чка с фами́лией; ~sake тёзка m & f; vt называ́ть impf, назва́ть pf; (appoint) назнача́ть impf, назна́чить pf. **nameless** /-lɪs/ adj безымя́нный. **namely** /-lɪ/ adv (a) и́менно; то есть.

nanny /'nænɪ/ n ня́ня.

nap /næp/ n коро́ткий сон; vi вздремну́ть pf.

nape /neɪp/ n заги́вок.

napkin /'næpkɪn/ n салфе́тка.

nappy /'næpɪ/ n пелёнка.

narcissus /nɑː'sɪsəs/ n нарци́сс.

narcotic /nɑː'kɒtɪk/ adj наркоти́ческий; n нарко́тик.

narrate /nə'reɪt/ vt расска́зывать impf, рассказа́ть pf. **narration** /-'reɪʃ(ə)n/ n расска́з. **narrative** /'nærətɪv/ n расска́з; adj повествова́тельный. **narrator** /nə'reɪtə(r)/ n расска́зчик.

narrow /'nærəʊ/ adj у́зкий; vt & i су́живать(ся) impf, су́зить(ся) pf. **narrowly** /-lɪ/ adv (hardly) чуть, е́ле-е́ле; he ~ escaped drowning он чуть не утону́л. **narrow-minded** /ˌnærəʊ'maɪndɪd/ adj ограни́ченный. **narrowness** /'nærəʊnɪs/ n у́зость.

nasal /'neɪz(ə)l/ adj носово́й; (voice) гнуса́вый.

nasturtium /nə'stɜːʃəm/ n насту́рция.

nasty /'nɑːstɪ/ adj неприя́тный, проти́вный; (person) злой.

nation /'neɪʃ(ə)n/ n (people) наро́д; (country) страна́. **national** /'næʃ(ə)n(ə)l/ adj национа́льный, наро́дный; (of the state) госуда́рственный; ~ подданный sb. **nationalism** /'næʃənə,lɪz(ə)m/ n национали́зм. **nationalist** /'næʃənəlɪst/ n национали́ст, ~ка. **nationalistic** /,næʃənə'lɪstɪk/ adj националисти́ческий. **nationality** /,næʃə'nælɪtɪ/ n национа́льность; (citizenship) гражда́нство, по́дданство. **nationalization** /,næʃənəlaɪ'zeɪʃ(ə)n/ n национализа́ция. **nationalize** /'næʃənə,laɪz/ vt национализи́ровать impf & pf. **native** /'neɪtɪv/ n (~ of) уроже́нец, -нка (+gen); (aborigine) тузе́мец, -мка; (innate) приро́дный; (of one's birth) родно́й; (indigenous) тузе́мный; ~ land ро́дина; ~ language родно́й язы́к; ~ speaker носи́тель m языка́. **nativity** /nə'tɪvɪtɪ/ n Рождество́ (Христо́во). **natter** /'nætə(r)/ vi болта́ть impf.

natural /'nætʃər(ə)l/ adj есте́ственный, приро́дный; ~ resources приро́дные бога́тства neut pl; ~ selection есте́ственный отбо́р; n (mus) бека́р. **naturalism** /-,lɪz(ə)m/ n натурали́зм. **naturalist** /-lɪst/ n натурали́ст. **naturalistic** /,nætʃərə'lɪstɪk/ adj натуралисти́ческий. **naturalization** /,nætʃərəlaɪ'zeɪʃ(ə)n/ n натурализа́ция. **naturalize** /'nætʃərə,laɪz/ vt натурализи́ровать impf & pf. **naturally** /'nætʃərəlɪ/ adv есте́ственно. **nature** /'neɪtʃə(r)/ n приро́да; (character) хара́ктер; **by** ~ по приро́де.

naught /nɔːt/ n: come to ~ своди́ться impf, свести́сь pf к нулю́. **naughty** /'nɔːtɪ/ adj шаловли́вый. **nausea** /'nɔːzɪə/ n тошнота́. **nauseate** /-zɪ,eɪt/ vt тошни́ть impf impers от +gen. **nauseating** /-zɪ,eɪtɪŋ/ adj тошнотво́рный. **nauseous** /-zɪəs/ adj: I feel ~ меня́ тошни́т. **nautical** /'nɔːtɪk(ə)l/ n морско́й. **naval** /'neɪv(ə)l/ adj (вое́нно-)морско́й. **nave** /neɪv/ n неф. **navel** /'neɪv(ə)l/ n пупо́к. **navigable** /'nævɪgəb(ə)l/ adj судохо́дный. **navigate** /-,geɪt/ vt (ship) вести́ impf; (sea) пла́вать impf по+dat. **navigation** /,nævɪ'geɪʃ(ə)n/ n навига́ция. **navigator** /'nævɪ,geɪtə(r)/ n шту́рман. **navvy** /'nævɪ/ n землеко́п. **navy** /'neɪvɪ/ n вое́нно-морско́й флот; ~ blue тёмно-си́ний. **Nazi** /'nɑːtsɪ/ n наци́ст, ~ка; adj наци́стский. **Nazism** /'nɑːtsɪz(ə)m/ n наци́зм. **NB** abbr нотабе́не.

near /nɪə(r)/ adv бли́зко; ~ at hand под руко́й; ~ by ря́дом; prep во́зле+gen, о́коло+gen, у+gen; ~sighted близору́кий; vt & i приближа́ться impf, прибли́зиться pf к+dat. **nearly** /-lɪ/ adv почти́. **neat** /niːt/ adj (tidy) опря́тный, аккура́тный; (clear) чёткий; (undiluted) неразба́вленный. **nebulous** /'nebjʊləs/ adj не́ясный. **necessarily** /'nesəsərɪlɪ/ adv обяза́тельно. **necessary** /'nesəsərɪ/ adj необходи́мый; (inevitable) неизбе́жный. **necessitate** /nɪ'sesɪ,teɪt/ vt де́лать impf, с~ pf необходи́мым. **necessity**

/-'sesɪtɪ/ n необходимость; неизбежность; (object) предмет первой необходимости.

neck /nek/ n шея; (of garment) вырез; ~ **and** ~ голова в голову. **necklace** /'neklɪs/ n ожерелье. **neckline** n вырез.

nectar /'nektə(r)/ n нектар.

née /neɪ/ adj урождённая.

need /niːd/ n нужда; vt нуждаться impl в+prep; **I** (etc.) ~ мне (dat) нужен (-жна, -жно, -жны) +nom; **I** ~ **five roubles** мне нужно пять рублей.

needle /'niːd(ə)l/ n игла, иголка; (knitting) спица; (pointer) стрелка; vt придираться impl, придраться pf к+dat.

needless /'niːdlɪs/ adj ненужный; ~ **to say** разумеется. **needy** /'niːdɪ/ adj нуждающийся.

negation /nɪ'geɪʃ(ə)n/ n отрицание. **negative** /'negətɪv/ adj отрицательный; n отрицание; (phot) негатив.

neglect /nɪ'glekt/ vt пренебрегать impl, пренебречь pf +instr; не заботиться impl о+prep; n пренебрежение; (condition) заброшенность. **neglectful** /-fʊl/ adj небрежный, невнимательный (of к+dat). **negligence** /'neglɪdʒ(ə)ns/ n небрежность. **negligent** /-dʒ(ə)nt/ adj небрежный. **negligible** /-dʒɪb(ə)l/ adj незначительный.

negotiate /nɪ'gəʊʃɪ,eɪt/ vi вести impl переговоры; vt (arrange) заключать impl, заключить pf; (overcome) преодолевать impl, преодолеть pf. **negotiation** /nɪ,gəʊʃɪ'eɪʃ(ə)n/ n (discussion) переговоры m pl.

Negro /'niːgrəʊ/ n негр; adj негритянский.

neigh /neɪ/ n ржание; vi ржать impl.

neighbour /'neɪbə(r)/ n сосед ~ка. **neighbourhood** /-hʊd/ n местность; **in the** ~ **of** около +gen. **neighbouring** /-rɪŋ/ adj соседний. **neighbourly** /-lɪ/ adj добрососедский.

neither /'naɪðə(r)/ adv также не; тоже не; pron ни тот, ни другой; ~ ... **nor** ни... ни.

neon /'niːɒn/ n неон; attrib неоновый.

nephew /'nevjuː/ n племянник.

nepotism /'nepə,tɪz(ə)m/ n кумовство.

nerve /nɜːv/ n нерв; (courage) смелость; (impudence) наглость; **get on the** ~**s of** действовать impl, по~ pf +dat на нервы. **nervous** /'nɜːvəs/ adj нервный; ~ **breakdown** нервное расстройство. **nervy** /'nɜːvɪ/ adj нервозный.

nest /nest/ n гнездо; ~ **egg** сбережения neut pl; vi гнездиться impl. **nestle** /'nes(ə)l/ vi льнуть impl, при~ pf.

net¹ /net/ n сеть, сетка; vt (catch) ловить impl, поймать pf сетями.

net², **nett** /net/ adj чистый; vt получать impl, получить pf ... чистого дохода.

Netherlands /'neðələndz/ n Нидерланды (-ов) pl.

nettle /'net(ə)l/ n крапива.

network /'netwɜːk/ n сеть.

neurologist /njʊə'rɒlədʒɪst/ n невролог. **neurology** /-dʒɪ/ n неврология. **neurosis** /'rəʊsɪs/ n невроз. **neurotic** /-'rɒtɪk/ adj невротический.

neuter /'njuːtə(r)/ adj средний среднего рода; n средний род; vt кастрировать impl & pf. **neutral** /-tr(ə)l/ adj нейтраль

ный; *n* (*gear*) нейтра́льная ско́рость; **neutrality** /nju:'trælɪtɪ/ *n* нейтралите́т. **neutralize** /'nju:trəlaɪz/ *vt* нейтрализова́ть *impf & pf*. **neutron** /'nju:trɒn/ *n* нейтро́н.

never /'nevə(r)/ *adv* никогда́; ~ **again** никогда́ бо́льше; ~ **mind** ничего́!; всё равно́!; ~ **once** ни ра́зу. **nevertheless** /ˌnevəðə'les/ *conj, adv* тем не ме́нее.

new /nju:/ *adj* но́вый; (*moon, potatoes*) молодо́й. **new-born** новорождённый. **newcomer** /'nju:kʌmə(r)/ *n* пришле́ц. **newfangled** /'nju:fæŋɡ(ə)ld/ *adj* новомо́дный. **newly** /'nju:lɪ/ *adv* то́лько что, неда́вно. **newness** /'nju:nɪs/ *n* новизна́. **news** /nju:z/ *n* но́вость, -ти *pl*, изве́стие, -ия *pl*. **newsagent** *n* продаве́ц газе́т. **newsletter** *n* информацио́нный бюллете́нь *m*. **newspaper** *n* газе́та. **newsprint** *n* газе́тная бума́га. **newsreel** *n* кинохро́ника.

newt /nju:t/ *n* трито́н.

New Zealand /nju: 'zi:lənd/ *n* Но́вая Зела́ндия; *adj* новозела́ндский.

next /nekst/ *adj* сле́дующий, бу́дущий; *adv* (~ *time*) в сле́дующий раз; (*then*) пото́м, зате́м; ~ **door** (*house*) в сосе́днем до́ме; (*flat*) в сосе́дней кварти́ре; ~ **of kin** ближа́йший ро́дственник; ~ **to** ря́дом с+*instr*; (*fig*) почти́. **next-door** *adj* сосе́дний; ~ **neighbour** ближа́йший сосе́д.

nib /nɪb/ *n* перо́.

nibble /'nɪb(ə)l/ *vt & i* грызть *impf*; *vt* обгрыза́ть *impf*, обгрызть *pf*; (*grass*) щипа́ть *impf*; (*fish*) клева́ть *impf*.

nice /naɪs/ *adj* (*pleasant*) прия́тный, хоро́ший; (*person*)

ми́лый. **nicety** /'naɪsɪtɪ/ *n* то́нкость.

niche /ni:ʃ/ *n* ни́ша; (*fig*) своё ме́сто.

nick /nɪk/ *n* (*scratch*) цара́пина; (*notch*) зару́бка; **in the** ~ **of time** в са́мый после́дний моме́нт; *vt* (*scratch*) цара́пать *impf*, о~ *pf*; (*steal*) стибри́ть *pf*.

nickel /'nɪk(ə)l/ *n* ни́кель *m*.

nickname /'nɪkneɪm/ *n* про́звище; *vt* прозыва́ть *impf*, прозва́ть *pf*.

nicotine /'nɪkə,ti:n/ *n* никоти́н.

niece /ni:s/ *n* племя́нница.

niggardly /'nɪɡədlɪ/ *adj* скупо́й.

niggling /'nɪɡlɪŋ/ *adj* ме́лочный.

night /naɪt/ *n* ночь; (*evening*) ве́чер; **at** ~ но́чью; **last** ~ вчера́ ве́чером; *attrib* ночно́й; ~**club** ночно́й клуб. **nightcap** *n* ночно́й колпа́к; (*drink*) стака́нчик спиртно́го на́ ночь. **nightdress** *n* ночна́я руба́шка. **nightfall** *n* наступле́ние но́чи. **nightingale** /'naɪtɪŋˌɡeɪl/ *n* солове́й. **nightly** /'naɪtlɪ/ *adj* ежено́щный; *adv* ежено́щно. **nightmare** /'naɪtmeə(r)/ *n* кошма́р. **nightmarish** /'naɪtmeərɪʃ/ *adj* кошма́рный.

nil /nɪl/ *n* нуль *m*.

nimble /'nɪmb(ə)l/ *adj* прово́рный.

nine /naɪn/ *adj & n* де́вять; (*number* 9) девя́тка. **nineteen** /naɪn'ti:n/ *adj & n* девятна́дцать. **nineteenth** /naɪn'ti:nθ/ *adj & n* девятна́дцатый. **ninetieth** /'naɪntɪəθ/ *adj & n* девяно́стый. **ninety** /'naɪntɪ/ *adj & n* девяно́сто; (*decade*) девяно́стые го́ды (-до́в) *pl*. **ninth** /naɪnθ/ *adj & n* девя́тый.

nip /nɪp/ *n* (*pinch*) щипа́ть *impf*; щипну́ть *pf*; (*bite*) куса́ть *impf*,

укуси́ть pf; ~ **in the bud** пресека́ть impf, пресе́чь pf в заро́дыше; n щипо́к; уку́с; **there's a** ~ **in the air** во́здух па́хнет моро́зцем.

nipple /'nɪp(ə)l/ n сосо́к.

nirvana /nɪə'vɑːnə/ n нирва́на.

nit /nɪt/ n гни́да.

nitrate /'naɪtreɪt/ n нитра́т. **nitrogen** /'naɪtrədʒ(ə)n/ n азо́т.

no /nəʊ/ adj (not any) никако́й, не оди́н; (not a (fool etc.)) (совсе́м) не; adv нет; (nisколько) не+comp; n отрица́ние, отка́з; (in vote) го́лос «про́тив»; ~ **doubt** коне́чно, несомне́нно; ~ **longer** уже́ не, бо́льше не; **no one** никто́; ~ **wonder** не удиви́тельно.

Noah's ark /'nəʊəz 'ɑːk/ n Но́ев ковче́г.

nobility /nəʊ'bɪlɪtɪ/ n (class) дворя́нство; (quality) благоро́дство. **noble** /'nəʊb(ə)l/ adj дворя́нский; благоро́дный. **nobleman** n дворяни́н.

nobody /'nəʊbədɪ/ pron никто́; n ничто́жество.

nocturnal /nɒk'tɜːn(ə)l/ adj ночно́й.

nod /nɒd/ vi кива́ть impf, кивну́ть pf голово́й; n киво́к.

nodule /'nɒdjuːl/ n узело́к.

noise /nɔɪz/ n шум. **noiseless** /-lɪs/ adj бесшу́мный. **noisy** /'nɔɪzɪ/ adj шу́мный.

nomad /'nəʊmæd/ n коче́вник. **nomadic** /-'mædɪk/ adj коче́вий.

nomenclature /nəʊ'menklətʃə(r)/ n номенклату́ра.

nominal /'nɒmɪn(ə)l/ adj номина́льный. **nominate** /'nɒmɪ,neɪt/ vt (propose) выдвига́ть impf, вы́двинуть pf; (appoint) назнача́ть impf, назна́чить pf. **nomination** /,nɒmɪ'neɪʃ(ə)n/ n

выдвиже́ние; назначе́ние.

nominative /'nɒmɪnətɪv/ adj (n) имени́тельный (паде́ж). **nominee** /,nɒmɪ'niː/ n кандида́т.

non-alcoholic /,nɒnælkə'hɒlɪk/ adj безалкого́льный. **non-aligned** /,nɒnə'laɪnd/ adj неприсоедини́вшийся.

nonchalance /,nɒnʃələns/ n безза́ботность. **nonchalant** /-lənt/ n беззабо́тный.

non-commissioned /,nɒnkə'mɪʃ(ə)nd/ adj: ~ **officer** у́нтер-офице́р. **non-committal** /-'mɪt(ə)l/ adj укло́нчивый.

non-conformist /,nɒnkən'fɔːmɪst/ n нонконформи́ст; adj нонконформи́стский.

nondescript /'nɒndɪskrɪpt/ adj неопределённый.

none /nʌn/ pron (no one) никто́; (nothing) ничто́; (not one) ни оди́н; adv ниско́лько не; ~ **the less** тем не ме́нее.

nonentity /nɒ'nentɪtɪ/ n ничто́жество.

non-existent /,nɒnɪg'zɪst(ə)nt/ adj несуществу́ющий. **non-fiction** /nɒn'fɪkʃ(ə)n/ adj докумена́льный. **non-intervention** /,nɒnɪntə'venʃ(ə)n/ n невмеша́тельство. **non-party** adj беспарти́йный. **non-payment** /nɒn'peɪmənt/ n непла́тёж.

nonplus /nɒn'plʌs/ vt ста́вить impf, по~ pf в тупи́к.

non-productive /,nɒnprə'dʌktɪv/ adj непроизводи́тельный. **non-resident** /nɒn'rezɪd(ə)nt/ adj не прожива́ющий (где́-нибудь).

nonsense /'nɒns(ə)ns/ n ерунда́. **nonsensical** /nɒn'sensɪk(ə)l/ adj бессмы́сленный.

non-smoker /nɒn'sməʊkə(r)/ n (person) некуря́щий sb; (compartment) купе́ neut indecl, для некуря́щих. **non-stop**

noodles

'stop/ *adj* безостано́вочный; *(flight)* беспоса́дочный; без остано́вок; без поса́док.

non-violent /nɒn'vaɪələnt/ *adj* ненаси́льственный.

noodles /'nuːd(ə)lz/ *n pl* лапша́.

nook /nʊk/ *n* уголо́к.

noon /nuːn/ *n* по́лдень *m*.

no one /'nəʊwʌn/ *see* **no**

noose /nuːs/ *n* пе́тля.

nor /nɔː(r)/ *conj* и не; то́же; ни́ ... ни ... ни ...; ни́ ...

norm /nɔːm/ *n* но́рма. **normal** /'nɔːm(ə)l/ *adj* норма́льный. **normality** /nɔː'mælɪtɪ/ *n* норма́льность. **normalize** /'nɔːməlaɪz/ *vt* нормализова́ть *impf* & *pf*.

north /nɔːθ/ *n* се́вер; *(naut)* норд; *adj* се́верный; *adv* к се́веру, на се́вер. **~-east** се́веро-восто́к; **~-easterly**, **~-eastern** се́веро-восто́чный; **~-west** се́веро-за́пад; **~-westerly**, **-western** се́веро-за́падный. **northerly** /'nɔːðəlɪ/ *adj* се́верный. **northern** /'nɔːð(ə)n/ *adj* се́верный. **northerner** /'nɔːðənə(r)/ *n* северя́нин, -я́нка. **northward(s)** /'nɔːθwəd(z)/ *adv* на се́вер, к се́веру.

Norway /'nɔːweɪ/ *n* Норве́гия. **Norwegian** /nɔː'wiːdʒ(ə)n/ *adj* норве́жский; *n* норве́жец, -жка.

nose /nəʊz/ *n* нос; *vt:* **~ about, out** разню́хивать *impf*, разню́хать *pf*. **nosebleed** *n* кровоте́чение из но́су. **nosedive** *n* пике́ *neut indecl*.

nostalgia /nɒ'stældʒə/ *n* ностальги́я. **nostalgic** /-dʒɪk/ *adj* ностальги́ческий.

nostril /'nɒstrɪl/ *n* ноздря́.

not /nɒt/ *adv* не; нет; ни; **~ at all** ниско́лько, ничу́ть; *(reply to*

thanks) не сто́ит (благода́рности); **~ once** ни ра́зу; **~ that** не то, что́бы; **~ too** дово́льно +*neg*; **~ to say** что́бы не сказа́ть; **~ to speak of** не говоря́ уже́ о+*prep*.

notable /'nəʊtəb(ə)l/ *adj* заме́тный; *(remarkable)* замеча́тельный. **notably** /-blɪ/ *adv (especially)* осо́бенно; *(perceptibly)* заме́тно.

notary (public) /'nəʊtəri ('pʌblɪk)/ *n* нота́риус.

notation /nəʊ'teɪʃ(ə)n/ *n* нота́ция; *(mus)* но́тное письмо́.

notch /nɒtʃ/ *n* зару́бка; *vt:* **~ up** выи́грывать *impf*, вы́играть *pf*.

note /nəʊt/ *n (record)* заме́тка, за́пись; *(annotation)* примеча́ние; *(letter)* запи́ска; *(banknote)* банкно́т; *(mus)* но́та; *(tone)* тон; *(attention)* внима́ние; *vt* отмеча́ть *impf*, отме́тить *pf*; **~ down** запи́сывать *impf*, записа́ть *pf*. **notebook** *n* записна́я кни́жка. **noted** /'nəʊtɪd/ *adj* знамени́тый; изве́стный *(for* +*instr)*. **notepaper** *n* почто́вая бума́га. **noteworthy** /'nəʊtwɜːðɪ/ *adj* досто́йный внима́ния.

nothing /'nʌθɪŋ/ *n* ничто́, ничего́; **~ but** ничего́ кро́ме+*gen*, то́лько; **~ of the kind** ничего́ подо́бного; **come to ~** конча́ться *impf*, ко́нчиться *pf* ниче́м; **for ~** *(free)* да́ром; *(in vain)* зря, напра́сно; **have ~ to do with** не име́ть *impf* никако́го отноше́ния к+*dat*; **there is (was) ~ for it (but) to** ничего́ друго́го не остаётся (остава́лось) (как); **to say ~ of** не говоря́ уже́ о+*prep*.

notice /'nəʊtɪs/ *n (sign)* объявле́ние; *(warning)* предупрежде́-

ние; (*attention*) внима́ние; (*review*) о́тзыв; **give (in) one's ~** подава́ть *impf*, пода́ть *pf* заявле́ние об ухо́де с рабо́ты; **give s.o. ~** предупрежда́ть *impf*, предупреди́ть *pf* об увольне́нии; **take ~ of** обраща́ть *impf*, обрати́ть *pf* внима́ние на+*acc*; **~-board** доска́ для объявле́ний; *vt* замеча́ть *impf*, заме́тить *pf*. **noticeable** /-'nəʊtɪs(ə)l/ *adj* заме́тный. **notification** /ˌnəʊtɪfɪ'keɪʃ(ə)n/ *n* извеще́ние. **notify** /'nəʊtɪˌfaɪ/ *vt* извеща́ть *impf*, извести́ть *pf* (**of** *o*+*prep*).

notion /'nəʊʃ(ə)n/ *n* поня́тие. **notoriety** /ˌnəʊtə'raɪətɪ/ *n* дурна́я сла́ва. **notorious** /nəʊ'tɔːrɪəs/ *adj* пресловꙋ́тый.

notwithstanding /ˌnɒtwɪθ'stændɪŋ/ *prep* несмотря́ на+*acc*; *adv* тем не ме́нее.

nought /nɔːt/ *n* (*nothing*) *see* **naught**; (*zero*) нуль *m*; (*figure 0*) ноль *m*.

noun /naʊn/ *n* (и́мя *neut*) существи́тельное *sb*.

nourish /'nʌrɪʃ/ *vt* пита́ть *impf*, на~ *pf*. **nourishing** /-ʃɪŋ/ *adj* пита́тельный. **nourishment** /-mənt/ *n* пита́ние.

novel /'nɒv(ə)l/ *adj* но́вый; (*unusual*) необыкнове́нный; *n* рома́н. **novelist** /-lɪst/ *n* романи́ст. **novelty** /-tɪ/ *n* (*newness*) новизна́; (*new thing*) нови́нка.

November /nə'vembə(r)/ *n* ноя́брь *m*; *adj* ноя́брьский.

novice /'nɒvɪs/ *n* (*eccl*) послꙋ́шник, -ица; (*beginner*) новичо́к.

now /naʊ/ *adv* тепе́рь, сейча́с; (*immediately*) то́тчас же; (*next*) тогда́; *conj*: **~ (that)** раз, когда́; (*every*) **~ and again**, then вре́мя от вре́мени; **by ~** уже́; **from ~ on** впредь. **nowadays** /'naʊə-

ˌdeɪz/ *adv* в на́ше вре́мя.

nowhere /'nəʊweə(r)/ *adv* (*place*) нигде́; (*direction*) никꙋда́; *pron*: **I have ~ to go** мне не́куда пойти́.

noxious /'nɒkʃəs/ *adj* вре́дный.

nozzle /'nɒz(ə)l/ *n* со́пло.

nuance /'njuːɑːns/ *n* нюа́нс.

nuclear /'njuːklɪə(r)/ *adj* я́дерный. **nucleus** /-klɪəs/ *n* ядро́.

nude /njuːd/ *adj* обнажённый, наго́й; *n* обнажённая фигꙋ́ра.

nudge /nʌdʒ/ *vt* подта́лкивать *impf*, подтолкнꙋ́ть *pf* ло́ктем; *n* толчо́к ло́ктем.

nudity /'njuːdɪtɪ/ *n* нагота́.

nugget /'nʌgɪt/ *n* саморо́док.

nuisance /'njuːs(ə)ns/ *n* доса́да; (*person*) раздража́ющий челове́к.

null /nʌl/ *adj*: **~ and void** недействи́тельный. **nullify** /'nʌlɪˌfaɪ/ *vt* аннули́ровать *impf* & *pf*. **nullity** /'nʌlɪtɪ/ *n* недействи́тельность.

numb /nʌm/ *adj* онеме́лый; (*from cold*) окочене́лый; **go ~** онеме́ть *pf*; (*from cold*) окочене́ть *pf*.

number /'nʌmbə(r)/ *n* (*total*) коли́чество; (*total*; *symbol*; *math*; *gram*) число́; (*identifying numeral*; *item*) но́мер; **~-plate** номерна́я доще́чка; *vt* (*assign to*) нумерова́ть *impf*, за~, про~ *pf*; (*contain*) насчи́тывать *impf*; **~ among** причисля́ть *impf*, причи́слить *pf* к+*dat*; **his days are ~ed** его́ дни сочтены́.

numeral /'njuːmər(ə)l/ *n* ци́фра; (*gram*) (и́мя *neut*) числи́тельное *sb*. **numerical** /njuː-'merɪk(ə)l/ *adj* числово́й. **numerous** /'njuːmərəs/ *adj* многочи́сленный; (*many*) мно́го +*gen pl*.

nun /nʌn/ n мона́хиня. **nunnery** /'nʌnərɪ/ n (же́нский) монасты́рь m.

nuptial /'nʌpʃ(ə)l/ adj сва́дебный; n: pl сва́дьба.

nurse /nɜːs/ n (child's) ня́ня; (medical) медсестра́; vt (suckle) корми́ть impf, на~, по~ pf; (tend sick) уха́живать impf за +instr; **nursing home** санато́рий; дом престаре́лых. **nursery** /'nɜːsərɪ/ n (room) де́тская sb; (day ~) я́сли (-лей) pl; (for plants) пито́мник; ~ **rhyme** де́тские прибау́тки f pl; ~ **school** де́тский сад.

nut /nʌt/ n оре́х; (for bolt etc.) га́йка. **nutshell** n: **in a ~** в двух слова́х.

nutmeg /'nʌtmeg/ n муска́тный оре́х.

nutrient /'njuːtrɪənt/ n пита́тельное вещество́. **nutrition** /nju'trɪʃ(ə)n/ n пита́ние. **nutritious** /-'trɪʃəs/ adj пита́тельный.

nylon /'naɪlɒn/ n нейло́н; pl нейло́новые чулки́ (-ло́к) pl.

nymph /nɪmf/ n ни́мфа.

O

O /əʊ/ int о!; ах!

oaf /əʊf/ n неуклю́жий челове́к.

oak /əʊk/ n дуб; attrib дубо́вый.

oar /ɔː(r)/ n весло́. **oarsman** /'ɔːzmən/ n гребе́ц.

oasis /əʊ'eɪsɪs/ n оа́зис.

oath /əʊθ/ n прися́га; (expletive) руга́тельство.

oatmeal /'əʊtmiːl/ n овся́нка. **oats** /əʊts/ n pl овёс (овса́) collect.

obdurate /'ɒbdjʊərət/ adj упря́мый.

obedience /əʊ'biːdɪəns/ n послуша́ние. **obedient** /-ənt/ adj послу́шный.

obese /əʊ'biːs/ n ту́чный. **obesity** /-sɪtɪ/ n ту́чность.

obey /əʊ'beɪ/ vt слу́шаться impf, по~ pf +gen; (law, order) подчиня́ться impf, подчини́ться pf +dat.

obituary /ə'bɪtjʊərɪ/ n некроло́г.

object /'ɒbdʒɪkt/ (thing) предме́т; (aim) цель; (gram) дополне́ние; vi /əb'dʒekt/ возража́ть impf, возрази́ть pf (**to** про́тив +gen); **I don't ~** я не про́тив. **objection** /əb'dʒekʃ(ə)n/ n возраже́ние; **I have no ~** я не возража́ю. **objectionable** /əb'dʒekʃənəb(ə)l/ adj неприя́тный. **objective** /əb'dʒektɪv/ adj объекти́вный; n цель. **objectivity** /ˌɒbdʒek'tɪvɪtɪ/ n объекти́вность. **objector** /əb'dʒektə(r)/ n возража́ющий sb.

obligation /ˌɒblɪ'geɪʃ(ə)n/ n обяза́тельство; **I am under an ~** я обя́зан(а). **obligatory** /ə'blɪgətərɪ/ adj обяза́тельный. **oblige** /ə'blaɪdʒ/ vt обя́зывать impf, обяза́ть pf; **be ~d to** (grateful) быть обя́занным+dat. **obliging** /ə'blaɪdʒɪŋ/ adj услу́жливый.

oblique /ə'bliːk/ adj косо́й; (fig; gram) ко́свенный.

obliterate /ə'blɪtəreɪt/ vt (efface) стира́ть impf, стере́ть pf; (destroy) уничтожа́ть impf, уничто́жить pf. **obliteration** /-'reɪʃ(ə)n/ n стира́ние; уничтоже́ние.

oblivion /ə'blɪvɪən/ n забве́ние. **oblivious** /-vɪəs/ adj (forgetful) забы́вчивый; **to be ~ of** не замеча́ть impf +gen.

oblong /'ɒblɒŋ/ adj продолго-

ва́тый.

obnoxious /əb'nɒkʃəs/ adj проти́вный.

oboe /'əubəu/ n гобо́й.

obscene /əb'si:n/ adj непристо́йный. **obscenity** /-'senɪtɪ/ n непристо́йность.

obscure /əb'skjuə(r)/ adj (unclear) нея́сный; (little known) малоизве́стный; vt затемня́ть impf, затемни́ть pf; де́лать impf, ⁓ pf нея́сным. **obscurity** /-rɪtɪ/ n нея́сность; неизве́стность.

obsequious /əb'si:kwɪəs/ adj подобостра́стный.

observance /əb'zɜ:v(ə)ns/ n соблюде́ние; (rite) обря́д. **observant** /-v(ə)nt/ adj наблюда́тельный. **observation** /ˌɒbzə'veɪʃ(ə)n/ n наблюде́ние; (remark) замеча́ние. **observatory** /əb'zɜ:vətərɪ/ n обсервато́рия. **observe** /əb'zɜ:v/ vt (law etc.) соблюда́ть impf, соблюсти́ pf; (watch) наблюда́ть impf; (remark) замеча́ть impf, заме́тить pf. **observer** /əb'zɜ:və(r)/ n наблюда́тель m.

obsess /əb'ses/ vt пресле́довать impf; **obsessed by** одержи́мый +instr. **obsession** /-'seʃ(ə)n/ n одержи́мость; (idea) навя́зчивая иде́я. **obsessive** /-'sesɪv/ adj навя́зчивый.

obsolete /'ɒbsəli:t/ adj устаре́лый, вы́шедший из употребле́ния.

obstacle /'ɒbstək(ə)l/ n препя́тствие.

obstetrician /ˌɒbstə'trɪʃ(ə)n/ n акуше́р. **obstetrics** /əb'stetrɪks/ n акуше́рство.

obstinacy /'ɒbstɪnəsɪ/ n упря́мство. **obstinate** /'ɒbstɪnət/ adj упря́мый.

obstreperous /əb'strepərəs/ adj

бу́йный.

obstruct /əb'strʌkt/ vt загражда́ть impf, загради́ть pf; (hinder) препя́тствовать impf вос⁓ pf +dat. **obstruction** /-'strʌkʃ(ə)n/ n загражде́ние (obstacle) препя́тствие. **obstructive** /-'strʌktɪv/ adj загражда́ющий; препя́тствующий.

obtain /əb'teɪn/ vt получа́ть impf, получи́ть pf; достава́ть impf, доста́ть pf.

obtrusive /əb'tru:sɪv/ adj навя́зчивый; (thing) броса́ющийся в глаза́.

obtuse /əb'tju:s/ adj тупо́й.

obviate /'ɒbvɪˌeɪt/ vt устраня́ть impf, устрани́ть pf.

obvious /'ɒbvɪəs/ adj очеви́дный.

occasion /ə'keɪʒ(ə)n/ n слу́чай; (cause) по́вод; (occurrence) собы́тие; vt причиня́ть impf, причини́ть pf. **occasional** /-nəl/ adj ре́дкий. **occasionally** /-nəlɪ/ adv иногда́, вре́мя от вре́мени.

occult /ɒ'kʌlt/ adj окку́льтный n: the ⁓ окку́льт.

occupancy /'ɒkjʊpənsɪ/ n заня́тие. **occupant** /-pənt/ n жи́тель m, -ница. **occupation** /ˌɒkjʊ'peɪʃ(ə)n/ n заня́тие; (military ⁓) оккупа́ция; (profession) профе́ссия. **occupational** /-'peɪʃ(ə)nəl/ adj профессиона́льный; ⁓ therapy трудотерапи́я. **occupy** /'ɒkjʊˌpaɪ/ vt занима́ть impf, заня́ть pf; (mil) оккупи́ровать impf & pf.

occur /ə'kɜ:(r)/ vi (happen) случа́ться impf, случи́ться pf; (be found) встреча́ться impf; ⁓ to приходи́ть impf, прийти́ pf в го́лову+dat. **occurrence** /-'kʌrəns/ n слу́чай, происше́ствие.

ocean /'əuʃ(ə)n/ n океа́н.

oceanic /ˌəʊʃɪˈænɪk/ *adj* океанический.

o'clock /əˈklɒk/ *adv*: (at) six ~ (в) шесть часов.

octagonal /ɒkˈtæɡən(ə)l/ *adj* восьмиугольный.

octave /ˈɒktɪv/ *n* (*mus*) октава.

October /ɒkˈtəʊbə(r)/ *n* октябрь *m*; *adj* октябрьский.

octopus /ˈɒktəpəs/ *n* осьминог.

odd /ɒd/ *adj* (*strange*) странный; (*not in a set*) разрозненный; (*number*) нечётный; (*not paired*) непарный; (*casual*) случайный; **five hundred ~** пятьсот с лишним; **~ job** случайная работа. **oddity** /ˈɒdɪtɪ/ *n* странность; (*person*) чудак, -ачка. **oddly** /ˈɒdlɪ/ *adv* странно; **~ enough** как это ни странно. **oddment** /ˈɒdmənt/ *n* остаток. **odds** /ɒdz/ *n pl* шансы *m pl*; **be at ~ with** (*person*) не ладить с+*instr*; (*things*) не соответствовать *impf* +*dat*; (*short*) ~ неравные (почти равные) шансы *m pl*; **the ~ are that** вероятнее всего, что; ~ **and ends** обрывки *m pl*.

ode /əʊd/ *n* ода.

odious /ˈəʊdɪəs/ *adj* ненавистный.

odour /ˈəʊdə(r)/ *n* запах.

oesophagus /iːˈsɒfəɡəs/ *n* пищевод.

of /ɒv/ *prep expressing* 1. *origin*: из+*gen*: **he comes ~ a working-class family** он из рабочей семьи; 2. *cause*: от+*gen*: **he died ~ hunger** он умер от голода; 3. *authorship*: *gen*: **the works ~ Pushkin** сочинения Пушкина; 4. *material*: из +*gen*: **made ~ wood** сделанный из дерева; 5. *reference*: о+*prep*: **he talked ~ Lenin** он говорил о Ленине; 6. *partition*:

gen (*often in* -ы́(-ю)): **a glass ~ milk, tea** стакан молока, чаю; из+*gen*: **one ~ them** один из них; 7. *belonging*: *gen*: **the capital ~ England** столица Англии.

off /ɒf/ *adv*: *in phrasal vv, see v, e.g.* **clear ~** убираться; *prep* (*from surface of*) с+*gen*; (*away from*) от+*gen*; **~ and on** время от времени; **~-white** он не совсем белый.

offal /ˈɒf(ə)l/ *n* требуха.

offence /əˈfens/ *n* (*insult*) обида; (*against law*) проступок, преступление; **take ~** обижаться *impf*, обидеться *pf* (**at** на+*acc*). **offend** /əˈfend/ *vt* обижать *impf*, обидеть *pf*; **~ against** нарушать *impf*, нарушить *pf*. **offender** /əˈfendə(r)/ *n* правонарушитель *m*, -ница. **offensive** /əˈfensɪv/ *adj* (*attacking*) наступательный; (*insulting*) оскорбительный; (*repulsive*) противный; *n* нападение.

offer /ˈɒfə(r)/ *vt* предлагать *impf*, предложить *pf*; *n* предложение; **on ~** в продаже.

offhand /ɒfˈhænd/ *adj* бесцеремонный.

office /ˈɒfɪs/ *n* (*position*) должность; (*place, room etc.*) бюро *neut indecl*, контора, канцелярия. **officer** /ˈɒfɪsə(r)/ *n* должностное лицо; (*mil*) офицер. **official** /əˈfɪʃ(ə)l/ *adj* служебный; (*authorized*) официальный; *n* должностное лицо. **officiate** /əˈfɪʃɪˌeɪt/ *vi* (*eccl*) совершать *impf*, совершить *pf* богослужение. **officious** /əˈfɪʃəs/ *adj* (*intrusive*) навязчивый.

offing /ˈɒfɪŋ/ *n*: **be in the ~** предстоять *impf*.

off-licence /'ɒflaɪs(ə)ns/ n ви́нный магази́н. **off-load** vt разгружа́ть impf, разгрузи́ть pf. **off-putting** /'ɒfpʊtɪŋ/ adj отта́лкивающий. **offset** vt возмеща́ть impf, возмести́ть pf. **offshoot** n о́тпрыск. **offshore** adj прибре́жный. **offside** adv вне игры́. **offspring** n пото́мок; (collect) пото́мки m pl.

often /'ɒf(ə)n/ adv ча́сто.

ogle /'əʊg(ə)l/ vt & i смотре́ть impf с вожделе́нием на+acc.

ogre /'əʊgə(r)/ n велика́н-людое́д.

oh /əʊ/ int о!; ах!

ohm /əʊm/ n ом.

oil /ɔɪl/ n ма́сло; (petroleum) нефть; (paint) ма́сло, ма́сляные кра́ски f pl; vt сма́зывать impf, сма́зать pf. **~-painting** карти́на, напи́санная ма́сляными кра́сками; **~ rig** нефтяна́я вы́шка; **~-tanker** та́нкер; **~-well** нефтяна́я сква́жина. **oilfield** n месторожде́ние не́фти. **oilskin** n клеёнка; pl непромока́емый костю́м. **oily** /'ɔɪlɪ/ adj масляни́стый.

ointment /'ɔɪntmənt/ n мазь.

OK /əʊ'keɪ/ adv & adj хорошо́, норма́льно; int ла́дно!; vt одобря́ть impf, одобрить pf.

old /əʊld/ adj ста́рый; (ancient; of long standing) стари́нный; (former) бы́вший; **how ~ are you?** ско́лько тебе́, вам, (dat) лет?; **~ age** ста́рость; **~-age pension** пе́нсия по ста́рости; **old-fashioned** старомо́дный; **~ maid** ста́рая де́ва; **~ man** (also father, husband) стари́к; **~-man** стари́нный; **~ woman** стару́ха; (coll) стару́шка.

olive /'ɒlɪv/ n (fruit) оли́вка; (colour) оли́вковый цвет; adj оли́вковый. **~ oil** оли́вковое

ма́сло.

Olympic /ə'lɪmpɪk/ adj олимпи́йский; **~ games** Олимпи́йские и́гры f pl.

omelette /'ɒmlɪt/ n омле́т.

omen /'əʊmən/ n предзнаменова́ние. **ominous** /'ɒmɪnəs/ adj злове́щий.

omission /ə'mɪʃ(ə)n/ n про́пуск; (neglect) упуще́ние. **omit** /ə'mɪt/ vt (leave out) пропуска́ть impf, пропусти́ть pf; (neglect) упуска́ть impf, упусти́ть pf.

omnibus /'ɒmnɪbəs/ n (bus) авто́бус; (collection) колле́кция. **omnipotence** /ɒm'nɪpət(ə)ns/ n всемогу́щество. **omnipotent** /-t(ə)nt/ adj всемогу́щий. **omnipresent** /ˌɒmnɪ'prez(ə)nt/ adj вездесу́щий. **omniscient** /ɒm'nɪsɪənt/ adj всеве́дущий.

on /ɒn/ prep (position) на+prep; (direction) на+acc; (time) в+acc; **the next day** на сле́дующий день; **~ Mondays** (repeated action) по понеде́льникам (dat pl); **the first of June** пе́рвого ию́ня (gen); (concerning) по+prep, о+prep, на+acc; (time) вперёд; in phrasal vv, see vv, e.g. **move ~** идти́ да́льше; and so on и так да́лее, и т.д.; **be ~** (film etc.) идти́ impf; **further ~** да́льше; **later ~** по́зже.

once /wʌns/ adv (оди́н) раз; (on past occasion) одна́жды; (formerly) не́когда; **all at ~** неожи́данно; **at ~** сра́зу, неме́дленно; (if, when) как то́лько; **~ again, more** ещё раз; **~ and for all** раз и навсегда́; **~ or twice** не́сколько раз; **~ upon a time there lived** ... жил-бы́л... .

oncoming /'ɒn,kʌmɪŋ/ adj: **~ traffic** встре́чное движе́ние.

one /wʌn/ adj оди́н (одна́, -но́;

(*only, single*) еди́нственный; *n* один; *pron*: not usu translated; *v* translated in 2nd pers *sg* or by impers construction: ~ never knows никогда́ не зна́ешь; where can ~ buy this book? где мо́жно купи́ть э́ту кни́гу? ~ after another оди́н за други́м; ~ and all все до одного́; все как оди́н; ~ and only еди́нственный; ~ and the same оди́н и тот же; ~ another друг дру́га (*dat* -гу, *etc.*); ~ fine day в оди́н прекра́сный день; ~ o'clock час; ~-parent family семья́ с одни́м роди́телем; ~-sided, -track, -way односторо́нний; ~-time бы́вший; ~-way street у́лица односторо́ннего движе́ния.

onerous /ˈəʊnərəs/ *adj* тя́гостный.

oneself /wʌnˈself/ *pron* себя́; -ся (*suffixed to vt*).

onion /ˈʌnjən/ *n* (*plant; pl collect*) лук; (*single* ~) лу́ковица.

onlooker /ˈɒnˌlʊkə(r)/ *n* наблюда́тель *m*.

only /ˈəʊnlɪ/ *adj* еди́нственный; *adv* то́лько; if ~ е́сли бы то́лько; ~ just то́лько что; *conj* но.

onset /ˈɒnset/ *n* нача́ло.

onslaught /ˈɒnslɔːt/ *n* на́тиск.

onus /ˈəʊnəs/ *n* отве́тственность.

onward(s) /ˈɒnwəd(z)/ *adv* вперёд.

ooze /uːz/ *vt & i* сочи́ться *impf*.

opal /ˈəʊp(ə)l/ *n* опа́л.

opaque /əʊˈpeɪk/ *adj* непрозра́чный.

open /ˈəʊp(ə)n/ *adj* откры́тый; (*frank*) открове́нный; in the ~ air на откры́том во́здухе; ~-minded *adj* непредубеждённый; *vt & i* открыва́ть(ся) *impf*, откры́ть(ся) *pf*;

vi (*begin*) начина́ться *impf*, нача́ться *pf*; (*flowers*) распуска́ться *impf*, распусти́ться *pf*.

opening /-ɪŋ/ *n* откры́тие; (*aperture*) отве́рстие; (*beginning*) нача́ло; *adj* нача́льный, пе́рвый; (*introductory*) вступи́тельный.

opera /ˈɒprə/ *n* о́пера; *attrib* о́перный; ~-house о́перный теа́тр.

operate /ˈɒpəˌreɪt/ *vi* де́йствовать *impf* (**upon** на+*acc*); (*med*) опери́ровать *impf & pf* (**on** +*acc*); *vt* управля́ть *impf* +*instr*.

operatic /ˌɒpəˈrætɪk/ *adj* о́перный.

operating-theatre /ˈɒpəreɪtɪŋˌθɪətə/ *n* операцио́нная *sb*.

operation /ˌɒpəˈreɪʃ(ə)n/ *n* де́йствие; (*med; mil*) опера́ция.

operational /ˌɒpəˈreɪʃ(ə)l/ *adj* (*in use*) де́йствующий; (*mil*) операти́вный.

operative /ˈɒpərətɪv/ *adj* де́йствующий. **operator** /ˈɒpəˌreɪtə(r)/ *n* опера́тор; (*telephone*~) телефони́ст, ~ка.

operetta /ˌɒpəˈretə/ *n* опере́тта.

ophthalmic /ɒfˈθælmɪk/ *adj* глазно́й.

opinion /əˈpɪnjən/ *n* мне́ние; in my ~ по-мо́ему; ~ poll опро́с обще́ственного мне́ния. **opinionated** /-ˌneɪtɪd/ *adj* догмати́чный.

opium /ˈəʊpɪəm/ *n* о́пиум.

opponent /əˈpəʊnənt/ *n* проти́вник.

opportune /ˈɒpəˌtjuːn/ *adj* своевре́менный. **opportunism** /-ˈtjuːnɪz(ə)m/ *n* оппортуни́зм. **opportunist** /-ˈtjuːnɪst/ *n* оппортуни́ст. **opportunistic** /-ˈnɪstɪk/ *n* оппортуни́сти́ческий. **opportunity** /-ˈtjuːnɪtɪ/ *n* слу́чай, возмо́жность.

oppose /ə'pəʊz/ vt (resist) противиться +dat, воспр pf +dat; (speak etc. against) выступать impf, выступить pf против +gen. **opposed** /-'pəʊzd/ adj против (to +gen); **as ~ to** в противоположность +dat. **opposing** /-'pəʊzɪŋ/ adj противный; (opposite) противоположный. **opposite** /'ɒpəzɪt/ adj противоположный; (reverse) обратный; n противоположность; **just the ~** как раз наоборот; adv напротив; prep (на)против +gen. **opposition** /ˌɒpə'zɪʃ(ə)n/ n (resistance) сопротивление; (polit) оппозиция.

oppress /ə'pres/ vt угнетать impf. **oppression** /-'preʃ(ə)n/ n угнетение. **oppressive** /-'presɪv/ adj угнетающий. **oppressor** /-'presə(r)/ n угнетатель m.

opt /ɒpt/ vi выбирать impf, выбрать pf (for +acc); **~ out** не принимать impf участия (of в +prep).

optic /'ɒptɪk/ adj зрительный. **optical** /'ɒptɪk(ə)l/ adj оптический. **optician** /ɒp'tɪʃ(ə)n/ n оптик. **optics** /'ɒptɪks/ n оптика.

optimism /'ɒptɪˌmɪz(ə)m/ n оптимизм. **optimist** /-mɪst/ n оптимист. **optimistic** /-'mɪstɪk/ adj оптимистический. **optimum** /'ɒptɪməm/ adj оптимальный.

option /'ɒpʃ(ə)n/ n выбор. **optional** /-nəl/ adj необязательный.

opulence /'ɒpjʊləns/ n богатство. **opulent** /-lənt/ adj богатый.

opus /'əʊpəs/ n опус.

or /ɔː(r)/ conj или; **~ else** иначе; **~ so** приблизительно.

oracle /'ɒrək(ə)l/ n оракул.

oral /'ɔːr(ə)l/ adj устный; n устный экзамен.

orange /'ɒrɪndʒ/ n (fruit) апельсин; (colour) оранжевый цвет; attrib апельсиновый; adj оранжевый.

oration /ɔː'reɪʃ(ə)n/ n речь. **orator** /'ɒrətə(r)/ n оратор.

oratorio /ˌɒrə'tɔːrɪəʊ/ n оратория.

oratory /'ɒrətərɪ/ n (speech) красноречие.

orbit /'ɔːbɪt/ n орбита; vt вращаться impf по орбите вокруг +gen. **orbital** /-təl/ adj орбитальный.

orchard /'ɔːtʃəd/ n фруктовый сад.

orchestra /'ɔːkɪstrə/ n оркестр. **orchestral** /-'kestr(ə)l/ adj оркестровый. **orchestrate** /-ˌkɪstreɪt/ vt оркестровать impf & pf. **orchestration** /-ˌɔːkɪ'streɪʃ(ə)n/ n оркестровка.

orchid /'ɔːkɪd/ n орхидея.

ordain /ɔː'deɪn/ vt предписывать impf, предписать pf; (eccl) посвящать impf, посвятить pf (в духовный сан).

ordeal /ɔː'diːl/ n тяжёлое испытание.

order /'ɔːdə(r)/ n порядок; (command) приказ; (for goods) заказ; (insignia, medal; fraternity) орден; (archit) ордер; pl (holy ~) духовный сан; **in ~ to** (для того) чтобы +inf; vt (command) приказывать impf, приказать pf +dat; (goods etc.) заказывать impf, заказать pf.

orderly /-lɪ/ adj аккуратный; (quiet) тихий; n (med) санитар; (mil) ординарец.

ordinance /'ɔːdɪnəns/ n декрет.

ordinary /'ɔːdɪnərɪ/ adj обыкновенный, обычный.

ordination /ɔːdɪ'neɪʃ(ə)n/ n пос-

вяще́ние.

ore /ɔː(r)/ *n* руда́.

organ /'ɔːgən/ *n* о́рган; (*mus*) орга́н. **organic** /-'gænik/ *adj* органи́ческий. **organism** /-'nɪz(ə)m/ *n* органи́зм. **organist** /-nɪst/ *n* органи́ст. **organization** /,ɔːgənaɪ'zeɪʃ(ə)n/ *n* организа́ция. **organize** /'ɔːgənaɪz/ *vt* организо́вывать *impf* (*pres not used*), организова́ть *impf* (*in pres*) & *pf*; устра́ивать *impf*, устро́ить *pf*. **organizer** /-,naɪzə(r)/ *n* организа́тор.

orgy /'ɔːdʒɪ/ *n* о́ргия.

Orient /'ɔːrɪənt/ *n* Восто́к. **oriental** /,ɔːrɪ'ent(ə)l/ *adj* восто́чный. **orient, orientate** /'ɔːrɪənt, 'ɔːrɪənteɪt/ *vt* ориенти́ровать *impf* & *pf* (**o.s.** **-ся**). **orientation** /,ɔːrɪən'teɪʃ(ə)n/ *n* ориента́ция.

orifice /'ɒrɪfɪs/ *n* отве́рстие.

origin /'ɒrɪdʒɪn/ *n* происхожде́ние, нача́ло. **original** /ə'rɪdʒɪn(ə)l/ *adj* оригина́льный; (*initial*) первонача́льный; (*genuine*) по́длинный; *n* оригина́л. **originality** /ə,rɪdʒɪ'nælɪtɪ/ *n* оригина́льность. **originate** /ə'rɪdʒɪneɪt/ *vt* порожда́ть *impf*, породи́ть *pf*; *vi* брать *impf*, взять *pf* нача́ло (**from, in** в+*prep*, от+*gen*); (*arise*) возника́ть *impf*, возни́кнуть *pf*. **originator** /-'rɪdʒɪneɪtə(r)/ *n* а́втор, инициа́тор.

ornament *n* /'ɔːnəmənt/ украше́ние; *vt* /'ɔːnəment/ украша́ть *impf*, укра́сить *pf*. **ornamental** /-'ment(ə)l/ *adj* декорати́вный.

ornate /ɔː'neɪt/ *adj* витиева́тый.

ornithologist /,ɔːnɪ'θɒlədʒɪst/ *n* орнито́лог. **ornithology** /-dʒɪ/ *n* орнитоло́гия.

orphan /'ɔːf(ə)n/ *n* сирота́ *m & f*; *vt*: **be ~ed** сироте́ть *impf*, о~ *pf*. **orphanage** /-nɪdʒ/ *n* сирот-

ский дом. **orphaned** /'ɔːf(ə)nd/ *adj* осироте́лый.

orthodox /'ɔːθədɒks/ *adj* ортодокса́льный; (*eccl*,) правосла́вный. **orthodoxy** /-,dɒksɪ/ *n* ортодо́ксия; (**O~**) правосла́вие.

orthopaedic /,ɔːθə'piːdɪk/ *adj* ортопеди́ческий.

oscillate /'ɒsɪ,leɪt/ *vi* колеба́ться *impf*, no~ *pf*. **oscillation** /-'leɪʃ(ə)n/ *n* колеба́ние.

osmosis /ɒz'məʊsɪs/ *n* о́смос.

ostensible /ɒ'stensɪb(ə)l/ *adj* мни́мый. **ostensibly** /-blɪ/ *adv* я́кобы.

ostentation /,ɒsten'teɪʃ(ə)n/ *n* выставле́ние напока́з. **ostentatious** /-ʃəs/ *adj* показно́й.

osteopath /'ɒstɪə,pæθ/ *n* остеопа́т. **osteopathy** /,ɒstɪ'ɒpəθɪ/ *n* остеопа́тия.

ostracize /'ɒstrə,saɪz/ *vt* подверга́ть *impf*, подве́ргнуть *pf* остраки́зму.

ostrich /'ɒstrɪtʃ/ *n* стра́ус.

other /'ʌðə(r)/ *adj* друго́й, ино́й; тот; **every ~** ка́ждый второ́й; **every ~ day** че́рез день; **on the ~ hand** с друго́й стороны́; **on the ~ side** на той стороне́, по ту сто́рону; **one or the ~** тот и́ли ино́й; **the ~ day** на дня́х, неда́вно; **the ~ way round** наоборо́т; **the ~s** остальны́е *sb pl.* **otherwise** *adv* & *conj* и́наче, а то.

otter /'ɒtə(r)/ *n* вы́дра.

ouch /aʊtʃ/ *int* ой!, ай!

ought /ɔːt/ *v aux* до́лжен (-жна́) (бы) +*inf*.

ounce /aʊns/ *n* у́нция.

our, ours /aʊə(r), 'aʊəz/ *poss pron* наш; *abs* наш. **ourselves** /aʊə'selvz/ *pron* (*emph*) (мы) са́ми; (*refl*) себя́; **-ся** (*suffixed to vt*).

oust /aʊst/ *vt* вытесня́ть,

вы́теснить *pf.*

out /aʊt/ *adv* **1.** *in phrasal vv often rendered by pref* вы-; **2.:** *to be* ~ *in various senses:* he is ~ (*not at home*) его́ нет до́ма; (*not in office etc.*) вы́шел; (*of fashion*) вы́шел из мо́ды; (*be published*) вы́йти *pf* из печа́ти; (*of candle etc.*) поту́хнуть *pf*; (*of flower*) распусти́ться *pf*; (*be unconscious*) потеря́ть *pf* созна́ние; **3.:** ~-**and**— отъя́вленный; **4.:** ~ *of* из+*gen*, вне+*gen*; ~ *of date* устаре́лый, старомо́дный; ~ *of doors* на откры́том во́здухе; ~ *of work* безрабо́тный.

outbid /aʊtˈbɪd/ *vt* предлага́ть *impf*, предложи́ть *pf* бо́лее высо́кую це́ну, чем+*nom*. **outboard** *adj:* ~ *motor* подвесно́й мото́р *m.* **outbreak** *n* (*of anger, disease*) вспы́шка; (*of war*) нача́ло. **outbuilding** *n* надво́рная постро́йка. **outburst** *n* взрыв. **outcast** *n* изгна́нник. **outcome** *n* результа́т. **outcry** *n* (шу́мные) проте́сты *m pl.* **outdated** /aʊtˈdeɪtɪd/ *adj* устаре́лый. **outdo** *vt* превосходи́ть *impf*, превзойти́ *pf*.

outdoor /ˈaʊtdɔ:(r)/ *adj*, **outdoors** /-ˈdɔ:z/ *adv* на откры́том во́здухе, на у́лице.

outer /ˈaʊtə(r)/ *adj* (*external*) вне́шний, нару́жный; (*far from centre*) да́льний. **outermost** *adj* са́мый да́льний.

outfit /ˈaʊtfɪt/ *n* (*equipment*) снаряже́ние; (*set of things*) набо́р; (*clothes*) наря́д. **outgoing** *adj* уходя́щий; (*sociable*) общи́тельный. **outgoings** *n pl* изде́ржки *f pl.* **outgrow** *vt* выраста́ть *impf*, вы́расти *pf* из+*gen*. **outhouse** *n* надво́рная

постро́йка.

outing /ˈaʊtɪŋ/ *n* прогу́лка, экску́рсия.

outlandish /aʊtˈlændɪʃ/ *adj* дико́винный. **outlaw** *n* лицо́ вне зако́на; банди́т; *vt* объявля́ть *impf*, объяви́ть *pf* вне зако́на. **outlay** *n* изде́ржки *f pl.* **outlet** /ˈaʊtlɪt/ *n* выходно́е отве́рстие; (*fig*) вы́ход; (*market*) ры́нок; (*shop*) торго́вая то́чка. **outline** *n* очерта́ние, ко́нтур; (*sketch, summary*) набро́сок; *vt* очерти́ть *impf*, очерти́ть *pf*; (*plans etc.*) набра́сывать *impf*, наброса́ть *pf.* **outlive** *vt* пережи́ть *pf.* **outlook** *n* перспекти́вы *f pl*; (*attitude*) кругозо́р. **outlying** /ˈaʊtˌlaɪɪŋ/ *adj* перифери́йный. **outmoded** /aʊtˈməʊdɪd/ *adj* старомо́дный. **outnumber** *vt* чи́сленно превосходи́ть *impf*, превзойти́ *pf.* **out-patient** *n* амбулато́рный больно́й *sb.* **outpost** *n* форпо́ст. **output** *n* вы́пуск, проду́кция.

outrage /ˈaʊtreɪdʒ/ *n* безобра́зие; (*indignation*) возмуще́ние; *vt* оскорбля́ть *impf*, оскорби́ть *pf.* **outrageous** /-ˈreɪdʒəs/ *adj* возмути́тельный.

outright /ˈaʊtraɪt/ *adv* (*entirely*) вполне́; (*once for all*) раз (и) навсегда́; (*openly*) откры́то; *adj* прямо́й. **outset** *n* нача́ло; *at the* ~ внача́ле; *from the* ~ с са́мого нача́ла.

outside /aʊtˈsaɪd/ *n* нару́жная сторона́; *at the* ~ са́мое бо́льшее; *from the* ~ извне́; *on the* ~ снару́жи; *adj* нару́жный, вне́шний; *(extra)* кра́йний; *adv* (*on the* ~) снару́жи; (*to the* ~) нару́жу; (*out of doors*) на откры́том во́здухе, на у́лице; *prep* вне+*gen*; за преде́лами +*gen.* **outsider** /-də(r)/ *n* посто-

ро́нний sb; (sport) аутса́йдер.
outsize /'autsaiz/ adj бо́льше
станда́ртного разме́ра. **outskirts** n pl окра́ина. **outspoken**
/aut'spəukən/ adj прямо́й. **outstanding** /aut'stændɪŋ/ adj
(remarkable) выдаю́щийся;
(unpaid) неупла́ченный. **outstay** vt: ~ one's welcome заси́-
живаться impf, засиде́ться pf.
outstretched /'autstretʃt/ adj
распростёртый. **outstrip** vt об-
гоня́ть impf, обогна́ть pf.
outward /'autwəd/ adj (external)
вне́шний, нару́жный. **outwardly** /-lɪ/ adv вне́шне, на вид.
outwards /-wədz/ adv нару́жу.
outweigh /aut'weɪ/ vt переве́-
шивать impf, переве́сить pf.
outwit vt перехитри́ть pf.
oval /'əuv(ə)l/ adj ова́льный; n
ова́л.
ovary /'əuvərɪ/ n яи́чник.
ovation /əu'veɪʃ(ə)n/ n ова́ция.
oven /'ʌv(ə)n/ n (industrial) печь;
(domestic) духо́вка.
over /'əuvə(r)/ adv & prep with vv:
see vv; prep (above) над+instr;
(through, covering) по+dat;
(concerning) о+prep; (across)
че́рез+acc; (on the other side of)
по ту сто́рону+gen; (more than)
свы́ше+gen; бо́лее+gen; (with
age) за+acc; all ~ (finished) всё
ко́нчено; (everywhere) по-
всю́ду; all ~ the country по всей
стране́; ~ again ещё раз; ~
against по сравне́нию с+instr;
~ and above не говоря́ уже́
о+prep; ~ the telephone по те-
лефо́ну; ~ there вон там.
overall /'əuvərɔ:l/ n хала́т; pl
комбинезо́н; adj о́бщий. **overawe** vt внуша́ть impf, внуши́ть
pf благогове́йный страх+dat.
overbalance vi теря́ть impf,
по~ pf равнове́сие. **overbear-**

ing /əuvə'beərɪŋ/ adj вла́стный.
overboard adv (motion) за́
борт; (position) за́ бортом.
overcast adj о́блачный. **overcoat** n пальто́ neut indecl. **overcome** vt преодолева́ть impf,
преодоле́ть pf; adj охва́чен-
ный. **overcrowded** /,əuvə-
'kraudɪd/ adj перепо́лненный.
overcrowding /,əuvə'kraudɪŋ/ n
переполне́ние. **overdo** vt (cook)
пережа́ривать impf, пережа́-
рить pf; ~ it, things (work too
hard) переутомля́ться impf,
переутоми́ться pf; (go too far)
переба́рщивать impf, пере-
борщи́ть pf. **overdose** /'əuvədəus/ n чрез-
ме́рная до́за. **overdraft** n пре-
выше́ние креди́та; (amount)
долг ба́нку. **overdraw** vi превы-
ша́ть impf, превы́сить pf кре-
ди́т (в ба́нке). **overdue** adj
просро́ченный; be ~ (late) за-
па́здывать impf, запозда́ть pf.
overestimate vt переоце́нивать
impf, переоцени́ть pf. **overflow**
vi перелива́ться impf, пере-
ли́ться pf; (river etc.) разли-
ва́ться impf, разли́ться pf;
(outlet) перели́в. **overgrown**
/,əuvə'grəun/ adj заро́сший.
overhang vt & i выступа́ть impf
над+instr; n свес, вы́ступ.
overhaul /'əuvəhɔ:l/ vt ремонт-
и́ровать impf & pf; n ремо́нт.
overhead adv наверху́, над го-
лово́й; adj возду́шный, под-
весно́й; n: pl накладны́е
расхо́ды m pl. **overhear** vt не-
ча́янно слы́шать impf, у~ pf.
overheat vt перегрева́ть(ся)
impf, перегре́ть(ся) pf. **overjoyed** /əuvə'dʒɔɪd/ adj в вос-
то́рге (at от+gen). **overland** adj
сухопу́тный; adv по су́ше.
overlap vt части́чно покры-

вáть *impf*, покры́ть *pf*; *vi* частúчно совпадáть *impf*, совпáсть *pf*.

overleaf /ˌəʊvəˈliːf/ *adv* на оборóте. **overload** *vt* перегружáть *impf*, перегрузúть *pf*. **overlook** *vt* (*look down on*) смотрéть *impf* свéрху на+*acc*; (*of window*) выходúть *impf* на, в, +*acc*; (*not notice*) не замечáть *impf*, замéтить *pf* +*gen*; (~ *offence etc.*) прощáть *impf*, простúть *pf*.

overly /ˈəʊvəli/ *adv* слúшком.

overnight /ˌəʊvəˈnaɪt/ *adv* (*during the night*) зá ночь; (*suddenly*) неожúданно; **stay** ~ ночевáть *impf*, пере~ *pf*; *adj* ночнóй. **overpay** *vt* переплáчивать *impf*, переплатúть *pf*.

over-populated /ˌəʊvəˈpɒpjʊˌleɪtɪd/ *adj* перенаселённый. **over-population** *n* перенаселённость. **overpower** *vt* одолевáть *impf*, одолéть *pf*. **overpriced** /ˌəʊvəˈpraɪst/ *adj* завы́шенный в ценé. **over-production** *n* перепроизвóдство. **overrate** /ˌəʊvəˈreɪt/ *vt* переоцéнивать *impf*, переоценúть *pf*. **override** *vt* (*fig*) отвергáть *impf*, отвéргнуть *pf*. **overriding** /ˌəʊvəˈraɪdɪŋ/ *adj* глáвный, решáющий. **overrule** *vt* отвергáть *impf*, отвéргнуть *pf*. **overrun** *vt* (*conquer*) завоёвывать *impf*, завоевáть *pf*; **be** ~ **with** кишéть *impf* +*instr*.

overseas /ˌəʊvəˈsiːz/ *adv* за мóрем, чéрез мóре; *adj* замóрский. **oversee** /ˌəʊvəˈsiː/ *vt* надзирáть *impf* за+*instr*. **overseer** /ˈəʊvəˌsɪə(r)/ *n* надзирáтель *m*, ~ница. **overshadow** *vt* затмевáть *impf*, затмúть *pf*. **overshoot** *vi* переходúть *impf*, перейтú *pf* границу. **oversight** *n* случáйный недосмóтр. **over**

sleep *vi* просыпáть *impf*, проспáть *pf*. **overspend** *vi* трáтить *impf* слúшком мнóго. **overstate** *vt* преувелúчивать *impf*, преувелúчить *pf*. **overstep** *vt* переступáть *impf*, переступúть *pf* +*acc*, чéрез+*acc*.

overt /əʊˈvɜːt/ *adj* явный, откры́тый.

overtake /ˌəʊvəˈteɪk/ *vt* обгонять *impf*, обогнáть *pf*. **overthrow** *vt* свергáть *impf*, свéргнуть *pf*. **overtime** *n* (*work*) сверхурóчная рабóта; (*payment*) сверхурóчное *sb*; *adv* сверхурóчно.

overtone /ˈəʊvəˌtəʊn/ *n* скры́тый намёк.

overture /ˈəʊvəˌtjʊə(r)/ *n* предложéние; (*mus*) увертюра.

overturn *vt* & *i* опрокúдывать(ся) *impf*, опрокúнуть(ся) *pf*. **overwhelm** /ˌəʊvəˈwelm/ *vt* подавлять *impf*, подавúть *pf*. **overwhelming** /ˌəʊvəˈwelmɪŋ/ *adj* подавляющий. **overwork** *vt* & *i* переутомлять(ся) *impf*, переутомúть(ся) *pf*; *n* переутомлéние.

owe /əʊ/ *vt* (~ *money*) быть дóлжным +*acc* & *dat*; (*be indebted*) быть обязанным +*instr* & *dat*; **he, she,** ~**s three roubles** он дóлжен, онá должнá, мне три рубля; **she** ~**s him her life** онá обязана емý жúзнью. **owing** /ˈəʊɪŋ/ *adj* **be** ~ причитáться *impf* (**to** +*dat*); ~ **to** из-за+*gen*, по причúне+*gen*.

owl /aʊl/ *n* совá.

own /əʊn/ *adj* свой; (*свой*) сóбственный; **on one's** ~ самостоятельно; (*alone*) одúн; ~ (*possess*) владéть *impf* +*instr*; (*admit*) признавáть *impf*, признáть *pf*; ~ **up** признавáться

impf, призна́ться *pf*. **owner** /'əʊnə(r)/ *n* владе́лец. **ownership** /'əʊnəʃɪp/ *n* владе́ние (of +*instr*), со́бственность.

ox /ɒks/ *n* вол.

oxidation /ˌɒksɪ'deɪʃ(ə)n/ *n* окисле́ние. **oxide** /'ɒksaɪd/ *n* о́кись. **oxidize** /'ɒksɪdaɪz/ *vt* & *i* окисля́ть(ся) *impf*, окисли́ть(ся) *pf*. **oxygen** /'ɒksɪdʒ(ə)n/ *n* кислоро́д.

oyster /'ɔɪstə(r)/ *n* у́стрица.

ozone /'əʊzəʊn/ *n* озо́н.

P

pace /peɪs/ *n* шаг; (*fig*) темп; **keep ~ with** идти́ *impf* в но́гу c+*instr*; **set the ~** зада́вать *impf*, зада́ть *pf* темп; *vi*: **~ up and down** ходи́ть *indet* взад и вперёд. **pacemaker** *n* (*med*) электро́нный стимуля́тор.

pacifism /'pæsɪˌfɪz(ə)m/ *n* пацифи́зм. **pacifist** /-fɪst/ *n* пацифи́ст. **pacify** /-ˌfaɪ/ *vt* усмиря́ть *impf*, усмири́ть *pf*.

pack /pæk/ *n* у́зел, вьюк; (*soldier's*) ра́нец; (*hounds*) сво́ра; (*wolves*) ста́я; (*cards*) коло́да; *vt* (& *i*) упако́вывать(ся) *impf*, упакова́ть(ся) *pf*; (*cram*) наби-ва́ть(ся) *impf*, наби́ть *pf*. **package** /'pækɪdʒ/ *n* посы́лка, паке́т; **~ holiday** организо́ванная туристи́ческая пое́здка. **packaging** /-dʒɪŋ/ *n* упако́вка. **packet** /'pækɪt/ *n* паке́т; па́чка; (*large sum of money*) ку́ча де́нег. **packing-case** /'pækɪŋ keɪs/ *n* я́щик.

pact /pækt/ *n* пакт.

pad /pæd/ *n* (*cushion*) поду́-шечка; (*shin ~ etc.*) щито́к; (*of paper*) блокно́т; *vt* подбива́ть

impf, подби́ть *pf*. **padding** /'pædɪŋ/ *n* наби́вка.

paddle[1] /'pæd(ə)l/ *n* (*oar*) весло́; *vi* (*row*) грести́ *impf*.

paddle[2] /'pæd(ə)l/ *vi* (*wade*) ходи́ть *indet*, идти́ *det*, пойти́ *pf* босико́м по воде́.

paddock /'pædək/ *n* вы́гон.

padlock /'pædlɒk/ *n* вися́чий замо́к; *vt* запира́ть *impf*, запере́ть *pf* на вися́чий замо́к.

paediatric /ˌpiːdɪ'ætrɪk/ *adj* педиатри́ческий. **paediatrician** /ˌpiːdɪə'trɪʃ(ə)n/ *n* педиа́тр.

pagan /'peɪɡən/ *n* язы́чник, -ица; *adj* язы́ческий. **paganism** /-ˌnɪz(ə)m/ *n* язы́чество.

page[1] /peɪdʒ/ *n* (**~-boy**) паж; *vt* (*summon*) вызыва́ть *impf*, вы́звать *pf*.

page[2] /peɪdʒ/ *n* (*of book*) страни́ца.

pageant /'pædʒ(ə)nt/ *n* пы́шная проце́ссия. **pageantry** /-trɪ/ *n* пы́шность.

pail /peɪl/ *n* ведро́.

pain /peɪn/ *n* боль; *pl* (*efforts*) уси́лия; **~-killer** *neut pl*; **~-killer** обезбо́ливающее сре́дство; *vt* (*fig*) огорча́ть *impf*, огорчи́ть *pf*. **painful** /-fʊl/ *adj* боле́зненный; **be ~** (*part of body*) боле́ть *impf*. **painless** /-lɪs/ *adj* безбо-ле́зненный. **painstaking** /'peɪnz ˌteɪkɪŋ/ *adj* стара́тельный.

paint /peɪnt/ *n* кра́ска; *vt* кра́сить *impf*, по~ *pf*; (*portray*) писа́ть *impf*, на~ *pf* кра́сками. **paintbrush** *n* кисть. **painter** /-tə(r)/ *n* (*artist*) худо́жник, -ица; (*decorator*) маля́р. **painting** /-tɪŋ/ *n* (*art*) жи́вопись; (*picture*) карти́на.

pair /peə(r)/ *n* па́ра; *often not translated with n denoting a single object, e.g.* **a ~ of scissors** но́жницы -(ц) *pl*; **a ~ of trousers**

пáра брюк; vt спáривать *impf*, спáрить *pf*; ~ off разделяться *impf*, разделиться *pf* по пáрам.

Pakistan /ˌpɑːkɪˈstɑːn/ n Пакистáн. **Pakistani** /-nɪ/ n пакистáнец, -áнка; adj пакистáнский.

pal /pæl/ n приятель m, ~ница.

palace /ˈpælɪs/ n дворéц.

palatable /ˈpælətəb(ə)l/ adj вкýсный; (fig) приятный. **palate** /ˈpælət/ n нёбо; (fig) вкус.

palatial /pəˈleɪʃ(ə)l/ adj великолéпный.

palaver /pəˈlɑːvə(r)/ n (trouble) беспокóйство; (nonsense) чепухá.

pale¹ /peɪl/ n (stake) кол; **beyond the ~** невообразимый.

pale² /peɪl/ adj блéдный; vi блéднеть *impf*, по~ *pf*.

palette /ˈpælɪt/ n палитра.

pall¹ /pɔːl/ n покрóв.

pall² /pɔːl/ vi: ~ on надоедáть *impf*, надоéсть *pf* +dat.

palliative /ˈpælɪətɪv/ adj паллиативный; n паллиатив.

pallid /ˈpælɪd/ adj блéдный. **pallor** /ˈpælə(r)/ n блéдность.

palm¹ /pɑːm/ n (tree) пáльма; **P~ Sunday** Вéрбное воскресéнье.

palm² /pɑːm/ n (of hand) ладóнь; vt: ~ off всучивать *impf*, всучить *pf* (on +dat).

palpable /ˈpælpəb(ə)l/ adj осязáемый.

palpitations /ˌpælpɪˈteɪʃ(ə)nz/ n pl сердцебиéние.

paltry /ˈpɔːltrɪ/ adj ничтóжный.

pamper /ˈpæmpə(r)/ vt баловáть *impf*, из~ *pf*.

pamphlet /ˈpæmflɪt/ n брошюра.

pan¹ /pæn/ n (saucepan) кастрюля; (frying-~) сковородá; (of scales) чáшка; vt: ~ out про-

мывáть *impf*, промыть *pf*; (fig) выходить *impf*, выйти *pf*.

pan² /pæn/ vi (cin) панорамировать *impf* & *pf*.

panacea /ˌpænəˈsiːə/ n панацéя.

panache /pəˈnæʃ/ n рисóвка.

pancake /ˈpænkeɪk/ n блин.

pancreas /ˈpæŋkrɪəs/ n поджелýдочная железá.

panda /ˈpændə/ n пáнда.

pandemonium /ˌpændɪˈməʊnɪəm/ n гвалт.

pander /ˈpændə(r)/ vi: ~ to потвóрствовать *impf*, выйти *pf* +dat.

pane /peɪn/ n окóнное стеклó.

panel /ˈpæn(ə)l/ n панéль; (control-~) щит управлéния; (of experts) группа специалистов; (of judges) жюри neut indecl.

panelling /-lɪŋ/ n панéльная обшивка.

pang /pæŋ/ n pl мýки (-к) pl.

panic /ˈpænɪk/ n паника; ~-stricken охвáченный пáникой; vi впадáть *impf*, впасть *pf* в пáнику. **panicky** /-kɪ/ adj панический.

pannier /ˈpænɪə(r)/ n корзинка.

panorama /ˌpænəˈrɑːmə/ n панорáма. **panoramic** /-ˈræmɪk/ adj панорáмный.

pansy /ˈpænzɪ/ n анютины глáзки (-зок) pl.

pant /pænt/ vi дышáть *impf* с одышкой.

panther /ˈpænθə(r)/ n пантéра.

panties /ˈpæntɪz/ n pl трýсики (-ков) pl.

pantomime /ˈpæntəˌmaɪm/ n рождéственское представлéние. (dumb show) пантомима.

pantry /ˈpæntrɪ/ n кладовáя sb.

pants /pænts/ n pl трусы (-сóв) pl; (trousers) брюки (-к) pl.

papal /ˈpeɪp(ə)l/ adj пáпский.

paper /ˈpeɪpə(r)/ n бумáга; pl докумéнты m pl; (newspaper) га-

зе́та; (*wallpaper*) обо́и (-о́ев) *pl*; (*treatise*) докла́д; *adj* обо́йный; *vt* окле́ивать *impf*, окле́ить *pf* обо́ями. **paperback** *n* кни́га в бума́жной обло́жке. **paperclip** *n* скре́пка. **paperwork** *n* канцеля́рская рабо́та.

par /pɑː(r)/ *n*: feel below ∼ чу́вствовать *impf* себя́ неважно; **on a** ∼ **with** наравне́ с+*instr*.

parable /ˈpærəb(ə)l/ *n* при́тча.

parabola /pəˈræbələ/ *n* пара́бола.

parachute /ˈpærəˌʃuːt/ *n* парашю́т; *vi* спуска́ться *impf*, спусти́ться *pf* с парашю́том. **parachutist** /-tɪst/ *n* парашюти́ст.

parade /pəˈreɪd/ *n* пара́д; *vi* шество́вать *impf*; *vt* (*show off*) выставля́ть *impf*, вы́ставить *pf* напока́з.

paradise /ˈpærəˌdaɪs/ *n* рай.

paradox /ˈpærəˌdɒks/ *n* парадо́кс. **paradoxical** /ˌpærəˈdɒksɪk(ə)l/ *adj* парадокса́льный.

paraffin /ˈpærəfɪn/ *n* (∼ *oil*) кероси́н.

paragon /ˈpærəgən/ *n* образе́ц.

paragraph /ˈpærəˌɡrɑːf/ *n* абза́ц.

parallel /ˈpærəˌlel/ *adj* паралле́льный; *n* паралле́ль. **paralyse** /ˈpærəˌlaɪz/ *vt* парализова́ть *impf & pf*. **paralysis** /pəˈrælɪsɪs/ *n* парали́ч.

paramedic /ˌpærəˈmedɪk/ *n* медрабо́тник (без вы́сшего образова́ния).

parameter /pəˈræmɪtə(r)/ *n* пара́метр.

paramilitary /ˌpærəˈmɪlɪtərɪ/ *adj* полувое́нный.

paramount /ˈpærəˌmaʊnt/ *adj* первостепе́нный.

paranoia /ˌpærəˈnɔɪə/ *n* пара-

но́йя. **paranoid** /ˈpærəˌnɔɪd/ *adj*: **he is** ∼ он парано́ик.

parapet /ˈpærəpɪt/ *n* (*mil*) бру́ствер.

paraphernalia /ˌpærəfəˈneɪlɪə/ *n* принадле́жности *f pl*.

paraphrase /ˈpærəˌfreɪz/ *n* переска́з; *vt* переска́зывать *impf*, пересказа́ть *pf*.

parasite /ˈpærəˌsaɪt/ *n* парази́т. **parasitic** /ˌpærəˈsɪtɪk/ *adj* парази́тический.

parasol /ˈpærəˌsɒl/ *n* зо́нтик.

paratrooper /ˈpærəˌtruːpə(r)/ *n* парашюти́ст-деса́нтник.

parcel /ˈpɑːs(ə)l/ *n* паке́т, посы́лка.

parch /pɑːtʃ/ *vt* иссуша́ть *impf*, иссуши́ть *pf*; **become** ∼**ed** пересыха́ть *impf*, пересо́хнуть *pf*.

parchment /ˈpɑːtʃmənt/ *n* перга́мент.

pardon /ˈpɑːd(ə)n/ *n* проще́ние; (*law*) поми́лование; *vt* проща́ть *impf*, прости́ть *pf*; (*law*) поми́ловать *pf*.

pare /peə(r)/ *vt* (*fruit*) чи́стить *impf*, о∼ *pf*; ∼ **away, down** уре́зывать *impf*, уре́зать *pf*.

parent /ˈpeərənt/ *n* роди́тель *m*, ∼ница. **parentage** /-tɪdʒ/ *n* происхожде́ние. **parental** /pəˈrent(ə)l/ *adj* роди́тельский.

parentheses /pəˈrenθəˌsiːz/ *n pl* (*brackets*) ско́бки *f pl*.

parish /ˈpærɪʃ/ *n* прихо́д. **parishioner** /pəˈrɪʃənə(r)/ *n* прихожа́нин, -а́нка.

parity /ˈperɪtɪ/ *n* ра́венство.

park /pɑːk/ *n* парк; (*for cars etc.*) стоя́нка; *vt & abs* ста́вить *impf*, по∼ *pf* (маши́ну). **parking** /-kɪŋ/ *n* стоя́нка.

parliament /ˈpɑːləmənt/ *n* парла́мент. **parliamentarian** /ˌpɑːləmenˈteərɪən/ *n* парламен-

та́рий. **parliamentary**
/-'mentəri/ adj парла́ментский.

parlour /'pɑːlə(r)/ n гости́-
ная sb.

parochial /pə'rəʊkɪəl/ adj прихо́дский; (fig) ограни́ченный.
parochialism /-,lɪz(ə)m/ n ограни́ченность.

parody /'pærədɪ/ n паро́дия; vt пароди́ровать impf & pf.

parole /pə'rəʊl/ n че́стное сло́во; **on** ~ освобождённый под че́стное сло́во.

paroxysm /'pærək,sɪz(ə)m/ n пароксизм.

parquet /'pɑːkeɪ/ n парке́т; attrib парке́тный.

parrot /'pærət/ n попуга́й.

parry /'pærɪ/ vt пари́ровать impf & pf, от~ pf.

parsimonious /,pɑːsɪ'məʊnɪəs/ adj скупо́й.

parsley /'pɑːslɪ/ n петру́шка.

parsnip /'pɑːsnɪp/ n пастерна́к.

parson /'pɑːs(ə)n/ n свяще́нник.

part /pɑːt/ n часть; (in play) роль; (mus) па́ртия; **for the most** ~ бо́льшей ча́стью; **for my** ~ что каса́ется меня́; **take** ~ in уча́ствовать impf в+prep; ~**-time** (за́нятый) непо́лный рабо́чий день; vt & i (divide) разделя́ть impf, раздели́ть(ся) pf; vi (leave) расстава́ться impf, расста́ться pf (from, with c+instr); ~ **one's hair** де́лать impf, c~ pf себе́ пробо́р.

partake /pɑː'teɪk/ vi принима́ть impf, приня́ть pf уча́стие (in, of в+prep); (eat) есть impf, съ~ pf (of +acc).

partial /'pɑːʃ(ə)l/ adj части́чный; (biased) пристра́стный; ~ **to** неравноду́шный к+dat. **partiality** /,pɑːʃɪ'ælɪtɪ/ n (bias) пристра́стность. **partially** /'pɑːʃəlɪ/

adv части́чно.

participant /pɑː'tɪsɪpənt/ n уча́стник, -ица (in +gen). **participate** /-,peɪt/ vi уча́ствовать impf (in в+prep). **participation** /-'peɪʃ(ə)n/ n уча́стие.

participle /'pɑːtɪ,sɪp(ə)l/ n прича́стие.

particle /'pɑːtɪk(ə)l/ n части́ца.

particular /pə'tɪkjʊlə(r)/ adj осо́бый, осо́бенный; (fussy) разбо́рчивый; in ~ в ча́стности.

parting /'pɑːtɪŋ/ n (leave-taking) проща́ние; (of hair) пробо́р.

partisan /,pɑːtɪ'zæn/ n (adherent) сторо́нник; (mil) партиза́н; attrib (biased) пристра́стный; партиза́нский.

partition /pɑː'tɪʃ(ə)n/ n (wall) перегоро́дка; (polit) разде́л; vt разделя́ть impf, раздели́ть pf; ~ **off** отгора́живать impf, отгороди́ть pf.

partly /'pɑːtlɪ/ adv части́чно.

partner /'pɑːtnə(r)/ n (in business) компаньо́н; (in dance, game) партнёр, ~ша. **partnership** n това́рищество.

partridge /'pɑːtrɪdʒ/ n куропа́тка.

party /'pɑːtɪ/ n (polit) па́ртия; (group) гру́ппа; (social gathering) вечери́нка; (law) сторона́; **be a** ~ **to** принима́ть impf, приня́ть pf уча́стие в+prep; attrib парти́йный; ~ **line** ли́ния па́ртии; (telephone) о́бщий телефо́нный про́вод; ~ **wall** о́бщая стена́.

pass /pɑːs/ vt & i (go past; of time) проходи́ть impf, пройти́ pf (by ми́мо+gen); (travel past) проезжа́ть impf, прое́хать pf (by ми́мо+gen); (examination) сдать pf (экза́мен); vt (sport) пасова́ть impf, пасну́ть

pf; (*overtake*) обгоня́ть *impf*, обогна́ть *pf*; (*time*) проводи́ть *impf*, провести́ *pf*; (*hand on*) передава́ть *impf*, переда́ть *pf*; (*law, resolution*) утвержда́ть *impf*, утверди́ть *pf*; (*sentence*) выноси́ть *impf*, вы́нести *pf* (*upon* +*dat*); ~ **as, for** слыть *impf*, про~ *pf* +*instr*, за+*acc*; ~ **away** (*die*) сконча́ться *pf*; ~ **o.s. off as** выдава́ть *impf*, вы́дать *pf* себя́ за+*acc*; ~ **out** теря́ть *impf*, по~ *pf* созна́ние; ~ **over** (*in silence*) обходи́ть *impf*, обойти́ *pf* молча́нием; ~ **round** передава́ть *impf*, переда́ть *pf*; ~ **up** подава́ть *impf*, пода́ть *pf*; (*miss*) пропуска́ть *impf*, пропусти́ть *pf*; *n* (*permit*) пропуск; (*sport*) пас; (*geog*) перева́л; **come to ~** случа́ться *impf*, случи́ться *pf*; **make a ~ at** пристава́ть *impf*, приста́ть *pf* к+*dat*.

passable /ˈpɑːsəb(ə)l/ *adj* проходи́мый, прое́зжий; (*not bad*) неплохо́й.

passage /ˈpæsɪdʒ/ *n* прохо́д; (*of time*) тече́ние; (*sea trip*) рейс; (*in house*) коридо́р; (*in book*) отры́вок; (*mus*) пасса́ж.

passenger /ˈpæsɪndʒə(r)/ *n* пассажи́р.

passer-by /ˌpɑːsəˈbaɪ/ *n* прохо́жий *sb*.

passing /ˈpɑːsɪŋ/ *adj* (*transient*) мимолётный; *n*: **in ~** мимохо́дом.

passion /ˈpæʃ(ə)n/ *n* страсть (**for** к+*dat*). **passionate** /-nət/ *adj* стра́стный.

passive /ˈpæsɪv/ *adj* пасси́вный; (*gram*) страда́тельный; *n* страда́тельный зало́г. **passivity** /-ˈsɪvɪtɪ/ *n* пасси́вность.

Passover /ˈpɑːsəʊvə(r)/ *n* евре́йская Па́сха.

passport /ˈpɑːspɔːt/ *n* па́спорт.

password /ˈpɑːswɜːd/ *n* паро́ль *m*.

past /pɑːst/ *adj* про́шлый; (*gram*) проше́дший; *n* про́шлое *sb*; (*gram*) проше́дшее вре́мя *neut*; *prep* ми́мо+*gen*; (*beyond*) за+*instr*.

pasta /ˈpæstə/ *n* макаро́нные изде́лия *neut pl*.

paste /peɪst/ *n* (*of flour*) те́сто; (*creamy mixture*) па́ста; (*glue*) клей; (*jewellery*) страз; *vt* накле́ивать *impf*, накле́ить *pf*.

pastel /ˈpæst(ə)l/ *n* (*crayon*) пасте́ль; (*drawing*) рису́нок пасте́лью; *attrib* пасте́льный.

pasteurize /ˈpɑːstjəˌraɪz/ *vt* пастеризова́ть *impf* & *pf*.

pastime /ˈpɑːstaɪm/ *n* времяпрепровожде́ние.

pastor /ˈpɑːstə(r)/ *n* па́стор. **pastoral** /-r(ə)l/ *adj* (*bucolic*) пастора́льный; (*of pastor*) па́сторский.

pastry /ˈpeɪstrɪ/ *n* (*dough*) те́сто; (*cake*) пиро́жное *sb*.

pasture /ˈpɑːstjə(r)/ *n* (*land*) па́стбище.

pasty[1] /ˈpæstɪ/ *n* пирожо́к.

pasty[2] /ˈpeɪstɪ/ *adj* (~-**faced**) бле́дный.

pat /pæt/ *n* шлепо́к; (*of butter etc.*) кусо́к; *vt* хло́пать *impf*, по~ *pf*.

patch /pætʃ/ *n* запла́тка; (*over eye*) повя́зка (на глазу́); (*spot*) пятно́; (*of land*) уча́сток земли́; *vt* ста́вить *impf*, по~ *pf* запла́ту на+*acc*; ~ **up** (*fig*) ула́живать *impf*, ула́дить *pf*. **patchwork** *n* лоску́тная рабо́та; *attrib* лоску́тный. **patchy** /ˈpætʃɪ/ *adj* неро́вный.

pâté /ˈpæteɪ/ *n* паште́т.

patent /ˈpeɪt(ə)nt/ *adj* я́вный; ~ **leather** лакиро́ванная ко́жа; *n* пате́нт; *vt* патентова́ть *impf*,

за~ pf.

paternal /pə'tɜːn(ə)l/ adj отцóвский. **paternity** /-'tɜːnɪtɪ/ n отцóвство.

path /pɑːθ/ n тропúнка, тропá; (way) путь m.

pathetic /pə'θetɪk/ adj жáлкий.

pathological /ˌpæθə'lɒdʒɪk(ə)l/ adj патологúческий. **pathologist** /pə'θɒlədʒɪst/ n патóлог.

pathos /'peɪθɒs/ n пáфос.

pathway /'pɑːθweɪ/ n тропúнка, тропá.

patience /'peɪʃ(ə)ns/ n терпéние; (cards) пасьянс. **patient** /-ʃ(ə)nt/ adj терпелúвый; n больнóй sb, пациéнт, ~ка.

patio /'pætɪəʊ/ n террáса.

patriarch /'peɪtrɪ,ɑːk/ n патриáрх. **patriarchal** /-'ɑːk(ə)l/ adj патриархáльный.

patriot /'pætrɪət/ n патриóт, ~ка. **patriotic** /-trɪ'ɒtɪk/ adj патриотúческий. **patriotism** /'pætrɪə,tɪz(ə)m/ n патриотúзм.

patrol /pə'trəʊl/ n патрýль m; on ~ на дозóре; vt & i патрулúровать impf.

patron /'peɪtrən/ n покровúтель m; (of shop) клиéнт. **patronage** /'pætrənɪdʒ/ n покровúтельство. **patroness** /'peɪtrənɪs/ n покровúтельница. **patronize** /'pætrə,naɪz/ vt (treat condescendingly) снисходúтельно относúться impf, к+dat. **patronizing** /'pætrə,naɪzɪŋ/ adj покровúтельственный.

patronymic /ˌpætrə'nɪmɪk/ n óтчество.

patter /'pætə(r)/ vi (sound) барабáнить impf; n постýкивание.

pattern /'pæt(ə)n/ n (design) узóр; (model) образéц; (sewing) выкройка.

paunch /pɔːntʃ/ n брюшкó.

pauper /'pɔːpə(r)/ n беднáк

pause /pɔːz/ n пáуза, перерыв; (mus) фермáта; vi останáвливаться impf, останóвиться pf.

pave /peɪv/ vt мостúть impf, вы~ pf; ~ the way подготовлять impf, подготóвить pf пóчву (for для+gen). **pavement** /-mənt/ n тротуáр.

pavilion /pə'vɪljən/ n павильóн.

paw /pɔː/ n лáпа; vt трóгать impf лáпой; (horse) бить impf копытом.

pawn[1] /pɔːn/ n (chess) пéшка.

pawn[2] /pɔːn/ vt заклáдывать impf, заложúть pf. **pawnbroker** /-,brəʊkə(r)/ n ростовщúк. **pawnshop** n ломбáрд.

pay /peɪ/ vt платúть impf, за~, y~ pf (for за+acc); (bill etc.) оплáчивать impf, оплатúть pf; vi (be profitable) окупáться impf, окупúться pf; vt жáлованье, зарплáту; ~ packet получка; ~-roll платёжная вéдомость. **payable** /'peɪəb(ə)l/ adj подлежáщий уплáте. **payee** /peɪ'iː/ n получáтель m. **payment** /'peɪmənt/ n уплáта, платёж.

PC abbr (of personal computer) ПК (персонáльный компьютер); (of politically correct) политúчески коррéктный.

pea /piː/ n (also pl, collect) горóх.

peace /piːs/ n мир; in ~ в покóе; ~ and quiet мир и тишинá. **peaceable, peaceful** /'piːsəb(ə)l, 'piːsfʊl/ adj мúрный.

peach /piːtʃ/ n пéрсик.

peacock /'piːkɒk/ n павлúн.

peak /piːk/ n (of cap) козырёк; (summit, fig) вершúна; ~ hour часы m pl пик.

peal /piːl/ n (sound) звон, трезвóн; (of laughter) взрыв.

peanut /'piːnʌt/ n арáхис.

pear /peə(r)/ *n* гру́ша.

pearl /pɜːl/ *n* (*also fig*) жемчу́жина; *pl* (*collect*) же́мчуг.

peasant /ˈpezənt/ *n* крестья́нин, -я́нка; *attrib* крестья́нский.

peat /piːt/ *n* торф.

pebble /ˈpebəl/ *n* га́лька.

peck /pek/ *vt* & *vi* клева́ть *impf*, клю́нуть *pf* в клеве́к.

pectoral /ˈpektər(ə)l/ *adj* грудно́й.

peculiar /pɪˈkjuːlɪə(r)/ *adj* (*distinctive*) своеобра́зный; (*strange*) стра́нный; ~ **to** сво́йственный +*dat*. **peculiarity** /-ˈærɪtɪ/ *n* осо́бенность; стра́нность.

pecuniary /pɪˈkjuːnɪərɪ/ *adj* де́нежный.

pedagogical /ˌpedəˈgɒgɪk(ə)l/ *adj* педагоги́ческий.

pedal /ˈped(ə)l/ *n* педа́ль; *vi* нажима́ть *impf*, нажа́ть *pf* педа́ль; (*ride bicycle*) е́хать *impf*, по~ *pf* на велосипе́де.

pedant /ˈped(ə)nt/ *n* педа́нт. **pedantic** /pɪˈdæntɪk/ *adj* педанти́чный.

peddle /ˈped(ə)l/ *vt* торгова́ть *impf* вразно́с+*instr*.

pedestal /ˈpedɪst(ə)l/ *n* пьедеста́л.

pedestrian /pɪˈdestrɪən/ *adj* пешехо́дный; (*prosaic*) прозаи́ческий; *n* пешехо́д; ~ **crossing** перехо́д.

pedigree /ˈpedɪˌgriː/ *n* родосло́вная *sb*; *adj* поро́дистый.

pedlar /ˈpedlə(r)/ *n* разно́счик.

pee /piː/ *vi* пи-пи́ *neut indecl*; vi мочи́ться *impf*, по~ *pf*.

peek /piːk/ *vi* (~ **in**) загля́дывать *impf*, загляну́ть *pf*; (~ **out**) выгля́дывать *impf*, вы́глянуть *pf*.

peel /piːl/ *n* кожура́; *vt* очища́ть *impf*, очи́стить *pf*; *vi* (*skin*) шелуши́ться *impf*; (*paint*, ~ *off*) сходи́ть *impf*, сойти́ *pf* peel-ings /-lɪŋz/ *n pl* очи́стки (-ков) *pl*.

peep /piːp/ *vi* (~ **in**) загля́дывать *impf*, загляну́ть *pf*; (~ **out**) выгля́дывать *impf*, вы́глянуть *pf*; (*glance*) бы́стрый взгляд; ~**hole** глазо́к.

peer[1] /pɪə(r)/ *vi* всма́триваться *impf*, всмотре́ться *pf* (**at** в+*acc*).

peer[2] /pɪə(r)/ *n* (*noble*) пэр; (*person one's age*) све́рстник.

peeved /piːvd/ *adj* раздражённый. **peevish** /ˈpiːvɪʃ/ *adj* раздражи́тельный.

peg /peg/ *n* ко́лышек; (*clothes* ~) крючо́к; (*for hat etc.*) ве́шалка; **off the** ~ готовый; *vt* прикрепля́ть *impf*, прикрепи́ть *pf* ко́лышком, -ками.

pejorative /pɪˈdʒɒrətɪv/ *adj* уничижи́тельный.

pelican /ˈpelɪkən/ *n* пелика́н.

pellet /ˈpelɪt/ *n* ша́рик; (*shot*) дроби́на.

pelt[1] /pelt/ *n* (*skin*) шку́ра.

pelt[2] /pelt/ *vt* забра́сывать *impf*, заброса́ть *pf*; *vi* (*rain*) бараба́нить *impf*.

pelvis /ˈpelvɪs/ *n* таз.

pen[1] /pen/ *n* (*for writing*) ру́чка; ~**friend** друг по перепи́ске.

pen[2] /pen/ *n* (*enclosure*) заго́н.

penal /ˈpiːn(ə)l/ *adj* уголо́вный. **penalize** /-ˌlaɪz/ *vt* штрафова́ть *impf*, о~ *pf*. **penalty** /ˈpenltɪ/ *n* наказа́ние; (*sport*) штраф; ~ **area** штрафна́я площа́дка; ~ **kick** штрафно́й уда́р. **penance** /ˈpenəns/ *n* епитимья́.

penchant /ˈpɑ̃ʃɑ̃/ *n* скло́нность (**for** к+*dat*).

pencil /ˈpensɪl/ *n* каранда́ш; ~**sharpener** точи́лка.

pendant /'pend(ə)nt/ n подвеска.

pending /'pendıŋ/ adj (awaiting decision) ожидающий решения; prep (until) в ожидании +gen, до+gen.

pendulum /'pendjʊləm/ n маятник.

penetrate /'penı,treıt/ vt проникать impf, проникнуть pf в+acc. **penetrating** /-,treıtıŋ/ adj (sound) пронзительный. **penetration** /,penı'treıʃ(ə)n/ n проникновение; (insight) проницательность.

penguin /'peŋgwın/ n пингвин.

penicillin /,penı'sılın/ n пенициллин.

peninsula /pı'nınsjʊlə/ n полуостров.

penis /'pi:nıs/ n пенис.

penitence /'penıt(ə)ns/ n раскаяние. **penitent** /-t(ə)nt/ adj раскаивающийся; n кающийся грешник.

penknife /'pennaıf/ n перочинный нож.

pennant /'penənt/ n вымпел.

penniless /'penılıs/ adj без гроша.

penny /'penı/ n пенни neut indecl, пенс.

pension /'penʃ(ə)n/ n пенсия; vt: ~ off увольнять impf, уволить pf на пенсию. **pensionable** /-nəb(ə)l/ adj (age) пенсионный. **pensioner** /-nə(r)/ n пенсионер, ~ка.

pensive /'pensıv/ adj задумчивый.

pentagon /'pentəgən/ n пятиугольник; the P~ Пентагон. **Pentecost** /'pentı,kɒst/ n Пятидесятница.

penthouse /'penthaʊs/ n шикарная квартира на верхнем этаже.

pent-up /'pentʌp/ adj (anger etc.) сдерживаемый.

penultimate /pı'nʌltımət/ adj предпоследний.

penury /'penjərı/ n нужда.

peony /'pi:ənı/ n пион.

people /'pi:p(ə)l/ n pl (persons) люди pl; sg (nation) народ; vt населять impf, населить pf.

pepper /'pepə(r)/ n перец; vt перчить impf, на-, по~ pf. **peppercorn** n перчинка. **peppermint** /'pepə,mınt/ n перечная мята; (sweet) мятная конфета.

per /pɜ:(r)/ prep (for each) (person) на+acc; as ~ согласно+dat; ~ annum в год; ~ capita на человека; ~ hour в час; ~ se сам по себе.

perceive /pə'si:v/ vt воспринимать impf, воспринять pf.

per cent /pə 'sent/ adv & n процент. **percentage** /pə'sentıdʒ/ n процент; (part) часть.

perceptible /pə'septıb(ə)l/ adj заметный. **perception** /-'sepʃ(ə)n/ n восприятие; (quality) понимание. **perceptive** /-'septıv/ adj тонкий.

perch¹ /pɜ:tʃ/ n (fish) окунь m.

perch² /pɜ:tʃ/ n (roost) насест; vi садиться impf, сесть pf на+prep. **perched** /-d/ adj высоко сидящий, расположенный.

percussion /pə'kʌʃ(ə)n/ n (~ instruments) ударные инструменты m pl.

peremptory /pə'remptərı/ adj повелительный.

perennial /pə'renıəl/ adj (enduring) вечный; n (bot) многолетнее растение.

perestroika /,perı'strɔıkə/ n перестройка.

perfect adj /'pɜ:fıkt/ совершенный; (gram) перфектный;

перфе́кт; *vt* /pə'fekt/ соверше́нствовать *impf*, y~ *pf*. **perfection** /-'fekʃ(ə)n/ *n* соверше́нство. **perfective** /-'fektɪv/ *adj* (*n*) соверше́нный (вид).

perforate /'pɜːfəˌreɪt/ *vt* перфори́ровать *impf & pf*. **perforation** /-'reɪʃ(ə)n/ *n* перфора́ция.

perform /pə'fɔːm/ *vt* (*carry out*) исполня́ть *impf*, испо́лнить *pf*; (*theat, mus*) игра́ть *impf*, сыгра́ть *pf*; *vi* выступа́ть *impf*, вы́ступить *pf*; (*function*) рабо́тать *impf*. **performance** /-məns/ *n* исполне́ние; (*of person, device*) де́йствие; (*of play etc.*) представле́ние, спекта́кль *m*; (*of engine etc.*) эксплуатацио́нные ка́чества *neut pl*. **performer** /-mə(r)/ *n* исполни́тель *m*.

perfume /'pɜːfjuːm/ *n* духи́ (-хо́в) *pl*; (*smell*) арома́т.

perfunctory /pə'fʌŋktərɪ/ *adj* пове́рхностный.

perhaps /pə'hæps/ *adv* мо́жет быть.

peril /'perɪl/ *n* опа́сность, риск. **perilous** /-ləs/ *adj* опа́сный, риско́ванный.

perimeter /pə'rɪmɪtə(r)/ *n* вне́шняя грани́ца; (*geom*) пери́метр.

period /'pɪərɪəd/ *n* пери́од; (*epoch*) эпо́ха; (*menstrual*) ме́сячные *sb pl*. **periodic** /ˌpɪərɪ'ɒdɪk/ *adj* периоди́ческий. **periodical** /-'ɒdɪk(ə)l/ *adj* периоди́ческий; *n* периоди́ческое изда́ние.

peripheral /pə'rɪfər(ə)l/ *adj* перифери́йный. **periphery** /-'rɪfərɪ/ *n* перифери́я.

periscope /'perɪˌskəʊp/ *n* периско́п.

perish /'perɪʃ/ *vi* погиба́ть *impf*,

поги́бнуть *pf*; (*spoil*) по́ртиться *impf*, ис~ *pf*. **perishable** /-'ʃəb(ə)l/ *adj* скоропо́ртящийся.

perjure /'pɜːdʒə(r)/ *vt*: ~ o.s. наруша́ть *impf*, нару́шить *pf* кля́тву. **perjury** /-dʒərɪ/ *n* лжесвиде́тельство.

perk[1] /pɜːk/ *n* льго́та.

perk[2] /pɜːk/ *vi*: ~ up оживля́ться *impf*, ожи́виться *pf*. **perky** /-kɪ/ *adj* бо́йкий.

perm /pɜːm/ *n* пермане́нт. **permanence** /'pɜːmənəns/ *n* постоя́нство. **permanent** /-nənt/ *adj* постоя́нный.

permeable /'pɜːmɪəb(ə)l/ *adj* проница́емый. **permeate** /'pɜːmɪˌeɪt/ *vt* проника́ть *impf*, прони́кнуть *pf* в+*acc*.

permissible /pə'mɪsɪb(ə)l/ *adj* допусти́мый. **permission** /-'mɪʃ(ə)n/ *n* разреше́ние. **permissive** /-'mɪsɪv/ *adj* (сли́шком) либера́льный; ~ society о́бщество вседозво́ленности. **permissiveness** /-'mɪsɪvnɪs/ *n* вседозво́ленность. **permit** *vt* /pə'mɪt/ разреша́ть *impf*, разреши́ть *pf* +*dat*; *n* про́пуск.

permutation /ˌpɜːmjʊ'teɪʃ(ə)n/ *n* перестано́вка.

pernicious /pə'nɪʃəs/ *adj* па́губный.

perpendicular /ˌpɜːpən'dɪkjʊlə(r)/ *adj* перпендикуля́рный; *n* перпендикуля́р.

perpetrate /'pɜːpɪˌtreɪt/ *vt* соверша́ть *impf*, соверши́ть *pf*. **perpetrator** /-ˌtreɪtə(r)/ *n* вино́вник.

perpetual /pə'petjʊəl/ *adj* ве́чный. **perpetuate** /-tjʊˌeɪt/ *vt* увекове́чивать *impf*, увекове́чить *pf*. **perpetuity** /ˌpɜːpɪ'tjuːɪtɪ/ *n* ве́чность; in ~ навсегда́, на-

вечно.

perplex /pə'pleks/ vt озада́чивать impf, озада́чить pf. **perplexity** /-'pleksɪtɪ/ n озада́ченность.

persecute /'pɜːsɪˌkjuːt/ vt пресле́довать impf. **persecution** /-ˌkjuːʃ(ə)n/ n пресле́дование.

perseverance /ˌpɜːsɪ'vɪərəns/ n насто́йчивость. **persevere** /ˌpɜːsɪ'vɪə(r)/ vi насто́йчиво, продолжа́ть impf (**in, at** etc. +acc, inf).

Persian /'pɜːʃ(ə)n/ n перс, ∼ия́нка; adj перси́дский.

persist /pə'sɪst/ vi упо́рствовать impf (**in** в+prep); насто́йчиво продолжа́ть impf (**in** +acc, inf). **persistence** /-t(ə)ns/ n упо́рство. **persistent** /-t(ə)nt/ adj упо́рный.

person /'pɜːs(ə)n/ n челове́к; (in play; gram) лицо́; **in** ∼ ли́чно. **personable** /-nəb(ə)l/ adj привлека́тельный. **personage** /-nɪdʒ/ n ли́чность. **personal** /-n(ə)l/ adj ли́чный. **personality** /ˌpɜːsə'nælɪtɪ/ n ли́чность. **personally** /-nəlɪ/ adv ли́чно. **personification** /pəˌsɒnɪfɪ'keɪʃ(ə)n/ n олицетворе́ние. **personify** /-'sɒnɪˌfaɪ/ vt олицетворя́ть impf, олицетвори́ть pf.

personnel /ˌpɜːsə'nel/ n ка́дры (-ров) pl, персона́л; ∼ **department** отде́л ка́дров.

perspective /pə'spektɪv/ n перспекти́ва.

perspiration /ˌpɜːspɪ'reɪʃ(ə)n/ n пот. **perspire** /pə'spaɪə(r)/ vi поте́ть impf, вс∼ pf.

persuade /pə'sweɪd/ vt (convince) убежда́ть impf, убеди́ть pf (**of** в+prep); (induce) угова́ривать impf, уговори́ть pf. **persuasion** /-'sweɪʒ(ə)n/ n убежде́ние. **persuasive** /-'sweɪsɪv/

adj убеди́тельный.

pertain /pə'teɪn/ vi: ∼ **to** отно́сится impf отнести́сь pf к+dat.

pertinent /'pɜːtɪnənt/ adj уме́стный.

perturb /pə'tɜːb/ vt трево́жить impf, вс∼ pf.

peruse /pə'ruːz/ vt (read) внима́тельно чита́ть impf, про∼ pf; (fig) рассма́тривать impf, рассмотре́ть pf.

pervade /pə'veɪd/ vt наполня́ть impf. **pervasive** /-'veɪsɪv/ adj распространённый.

perverse /pə'vɜːs/ adj капри́зный. **perversion** /-'vɜːʃ(ə)n/ n извраще́ние. **pervert** /pə'vɜːt/ vt извраща́ть impf, изврати́ть pf; n /'pɜːvɜːt/ извращённый челове́к.

pessimism /'pesɪˌmɪz(ə)m/ n пессими́зм. **pessimist** /-mɪst/ n пессими́ст. **pessimistic** /-'mɪstɪk/ adj пессимисти́ческий.

pest /pest/ n вреди́тель m; (fig) зану́да. **pester** /'pestə(r)/ vt приста́вать impf, приста́ть pf к+dat. **pesticide** /'pestɪˌsaɪd/ n пестици́д.

pet /pet/ n (animal) дома́шнее живо́тное sb; (favourite) люби́мец, -мица; ∼ **shop** зоомагази́н; vt ласка́ть impf.

petal /'pet(ə)l/ n лепесто́к.

peter /'piːtə(r)/ vi: ∼ **out** (road) исчеза́ть impf, исче́знуть pf; (stream; enthusiasm) иссяка́ть impf, исся́кнуть pf.

petite /pə'tiːt/ adj ма́ленькая.

petition /pɪ'tɪʃ(ə)n/ n пети́ция; vt подава́ть impf, пода́ть pf проше́ние +dat. **petitioner** /-nə(r)/ n проси́тель m.

petrified /'petrɪˌfaɪd/ adj окамене́лый; **be** ∼ (fig) оцепене́ть pf

(with от+*gen*).

petrol /'petr(ə)l/ *n* бензи́н; ~ **pump** бензоколо́нка; ~ **station** бензозапра́вочная ста́нция; ~ **tank** бензоба́к. **petroleum** /pɪ'trəʊlɪəm/ *n* нефть.

petticoat /'petɪˌkəʊt/ *n* ни́жняя ю́бка.

petty /'petɪ/ *adj* ме́лкий; ~ **cash** де́ньги (де́нег, -ньга́м) *pl* на ме́лкие расхо́ды.

petulant /'petjʊlənt/ *adj* раздражи́тельный.

pew /pjuː/ *n* (церко́вная) скамья́.

phallic /'fælɪk/ *adj* фалли́ческий. **phallus** /'fæləs/ *n* фа́ллос.

phantom /'fæntəm/ *n* фанто́м.

pharmaceutical /ˌfɑːməˈsjuːtɪk(ə)l/ *adj* фармацевти́ческий. **pharmacist** /'fɑːməsɪst/ *n* фармаце́вт. **pharmacy** /-məsɪ/ *n* фармаци́я; (*shop*) апте́ка.

phase /feɪz/ *n* фа́за; *vt*: ~ **in, out** постепе́нно вводи́ть *impf*, упраздня́ть *impf*.

Ph.D. *abbr* (*of* Doctor *of* Philosophy) кандида́т нау́к.

pheasant /'fez(ə)nt/ *n* фаза́н.

phenomenal /fɪ'nɒmɪn(ə)l/ *adj* феномена́льный. **phenomenon** /fɪ'nɒmɪnən/ *n* феноме́н.

phial /faɪəl/ *n* пузырёк.

philanderer /fɪ'lændərə(r)/ *n* волоки́та *m*.

philanthropic /ˌfɪlən'θrɒpɪk/ *adj* филантропи́ческий. **philanthropist** /fɪ'lænθrəpɪst/ *n* филантро́п. **philanthropy** /-'lænθrəpɪ/ *n* филантро́пия.

philately /fɪ'lætəlɪ/ *n* филате́лия.

philharmonic /ˌfɪlhɑː'mɒnɪk/ *adj* филармони́ческий.

Philistine /'fɪlɪˌstaɪn/ *n* (*fig*) фили́стер.

philosopher /fɪ'lɒsəfə(r)/ *n* фило́соф. **philosophical** /ˌfɪləˈsɒfɪk(ə)l/ *adj* филосо́фский. **philosophize** /fɪ'lɒsəfaɪz/ *vi* филосо́фствовать *impf*. **philosophy** /fɪ'lɒsəfɪ/ *n* филосо́фия.

phlegm /flem/ *n* мокрота́. **phlegmatic** /fleg'mætɪk/ *adj* флегмати́ческий.

phobia /'fəʊbɪə/ *n* фо́бия.

phone /fəʊn/ *n* телефо́н; *vt* & *i* звони́ть *impf*, по~ *pf* +*dat*. See *also* telephone

phonetic /fə'netɪk/ *adj* фонети́ческий. **phonetics** /-tɪks/ *n* фоне́тика.

phoney /'fəʊnɪ/ *n* подде́льный.

phosphorus /'fɒsfərəs/ *n* фо́сфор.

photo /'fəʊtəʊ/ *n* фо́то *neut indecl*. **photocopier** /'fəʊtəˌkɒpɪə(r)/ *n* копирова́льная маши́на. **photocopy** /-ˌkɒpɪ/ *n* фотоко́пия; *vt* де́лать *impf*, с~ *pf* фотоко́пию +*gen*. **photogenic** /ˌfəʊtəʊ'dʒenɪk/ *adj* фотогени́чный. **photograph** /'fəʊtəˌɡrɑːf/ *n* фотогра́фия; *vt* фотографи́ровать *impf*, с~ *pf*. **photographer** /fə'tɒɡrəfə(r)/ *n* фото́граф. **photographic** /ˌfəʊtə'ɡræfɪk/ *adj* фотографи́ческий. **photography** /fə'tɒɡrəfɪ/ *n* фотогра́фия.

phrase /freɪz/ *n* фра́за; *vt* формули́ровать *impf*, с~ *pf*.

physical /'fɪzɪk(ə)l/ *adj* физи́ческий; ~ **education** физкульту́ра; ~ **exercises** заря́дка. **physician** /fɪ'zɪʃ(ə)n/ *n* врач. **physicist** /'fɪzɪsɪst/ *n* фи́зик. **physics** /'fɪzɪks/ *n* фи́зика.

physiological /ˌfɪzɪə'lɒdʒɪk(ə)l/ *adj* физиологи́ческий. **physiologist** /ˌfɪzɪ'ɒlədʒɪst/ *n* физио́лог. **physiology** /ˌfɪzɪ'ɒlədʒɪ/ *n* физиоло́гия. **physiotherapist** /ˌfɪzɪəʊ'θerəpɪst/ *n* физиотера-

пе́вт. **physiotherapy** /ˌfɪzɪəʊ-
'θerəpɪ/ n физиотерапия.

physique /fɪ'ziːk/ n телосло-
жение.

pianist /'pɪənɪst/ n пиани́ст, ~ка.

piano /pɪ'ænəʊ/ n фортепья́но
neut indecl; (grand) роя́ль m;
(upright) пиани́но neut indecl.

pick¹ /pɪk/ vt (flower) срыва́ть
impf, сорва́ть pf; (gather) соби-
ра́ть impf, собра́ть pf; (select)
выбира́ть impf, вы́брать pf; ~
one's nose, teeth ковыря́ть
impf, ковырну́ть pf в носу́, в
зуба́х; ~ a quarrel иска́ть impf
ссо́ры (with c+instr); ~ one's
way выбира́ть impf, вы́брать
pf доро́гу; ~ on (nag) придира́ться impf к+dat; ~ out отби-
ра́ть impf, отобра́ть pf; ~ up
(lift) поднима́ть impf, подня́ть
pf; (acquire) приобрета́ть impf,
приобрести́ pf; (fetch) (on foot)
заходи́ть impf, зайти́ pf за
+instr; (in vehicle) заезжа́ть
impf, зае́хать pf за+instr; (a
cold; a girl) подцепля́ть impf,
подцепи́ть pf; ~ up поднима́ться impf, подня́ться pf;
~-up (truck) пика́п; (electron)
звукоснима́тель m.

pick² /pɪk/ n вы́бор; (best part)
лу́чшая часть; take your ~ вы-
бира́й(те)!

pick³ /pɪk/, **pickaxe** /'pɪkæks/ n
кирка́.

picket /'pɪkɪt/ n (person) пике́т-
чик, -ища; (collect) пике́т; vt пи-
кети́ровать impf.

pickle /'pɪk(ə)l/ n соле́нье; vt со-
ли́ть impf, по~ pf. **pickled**
/-k(ə)ld/ adj солёный.

pickpocket /'pɪkpɒkɪt/ n кар-
ма́нник.

picnic /'pɪknɪk/ n пикни́к.

pictorial /pɪk'tɔːrɪəl/ adj изобра-
зи́тельный; (illustrated) иллю-

стри́рованный. **picture**
/'pɪktʃə(r)/ n карти́на; (of health
etc.) воплоще́ние; (film)
фильм; the ~s кино́ neut indecl;
vt (to o.s.) представля́ть impf,
предста́вить pf себе́. **picturesque** /ˌpɪktʃə'resk/ adj живо-
пи́сный.

pie /paɪ/ n пиро́г.

piece /piːs/ n кусо́к, часть; (one
of set) шту́ка; (of paper) ли-
сто́к; (mus, literature) произве-
де́ние; (chess) фигу́ра; (coin)
моне́та; break to ~s разбира́ть
impf, разобра́ть pf (на ча́сти);
~ of advice сове́т; ~ of information све́дение; ~ of news но́-
вость; ~-work сде́льщина;
~-worker сде́льщик; vt: ~
together воссоздава́ть impf,
воссозда́ть pf карти́ну +gen.
piecemeal adv по частя́м.

pier /pɪə(r)/ n (mole) мол; (pro-
jecting into sea) пирс; (of
bridge) бык; (between windows
etc.) просте́нок.

pierce /pɪəs/ vt пронза́ть impf,
пронзи́ть pf; (ears) прока́лы-
вать impf, проколо́ть pf. **piercing** /-sɪŋ/ adj пронзи́тельный.

piety /'paɪətɪ/ n набо́жность.

pig /pɪɡ/ n свинья́. **pigheaded**
/pɪɡ'hedɪd/ adj упря́мый. **piglet**
/'pɪɡlɪt/ n поросёнок. **pigsty**
/'pɪɡstaɪ/ n свина́рник. **pigtail**
/'pɪɡteɪl/ n

pigeon /'pɪdʒɪn/ n го́лубь;
~-hole отделе́ние для бума́г.

pigment /'pɪɡmənt/ n пигме́нт.
pigmentation /-'teɪʃ(ə)n/ n пиг-
мента́ция.

pike /paɪk/ n (fish) щу́ка.

pilchard /'pɪltʃəd/ n сарди́н(к)а.

pile¹ /paɪl/ n (heap) ку́ча, ки́па;
vt: ~ up сва́ливать impf, сва-
ли́ть pf в ку́чу; (load) нагру-
жа́ть impf, нагрузи́ть pf (with

+*instr*); *vi*: ~ **in(to)**, **on** забира́ться *impf*, забра́ться *pf* в+*acc*; ~ **up** накопля́ться, на-ка́пливаться *impf*, накопи́ться *pf*.

pile² /paɪl/ *n* (*on cloth etc.*) ворс.

piles /paɪlz/ *n pl* геморро́й collect.

pilfer /'pɪlfə(r)/ *vt* ворова́ть *impf*.

pilgrim /'pɪlgrɪm/ *n* пилигри́м. **pilgrimage** /-mɪdʒ/ *n* пало́мничество.

pill /pɪl/ *n* пилю́ля; **the** ~ противозача́точная пилю́ля.

pillage /'pɪlɪdʒ/ *vt* гра́бить *impf*, о~ *pf*; *v abs* мародёрствовать *impf*.

pillar /'pɪlə(r)/ *n* столб; ~**box** стоячий почто́вый я́щик.

pillion /'pɪljən/ *n* за́днее сиде́нье (мотоци́кла).

pillory /'pɪlərɪ/ *n* позо́рный столб; *vt* (*fig*) пригвожда́ть *impf*, пригвозди́ть *pf* к позо́рному столбу́.

pillow /'pɪləʊ/ *n* поду́шка. **pillowcase** *n* на́волочка.

pilot /'paɪlət/ *n* (*naut*) ло́цман; (*aeron*) пило́т; *adj* о́пытный, про́бный; *vt* пилоти́ровать *impf*.

pimp /pɪmp/ *n* сво́дник.

pimple /'pɪmp(ə)l/ *n* прыщ.

pin /pɪn/ *n* була́вка; (*peg*) па́лец; ~**point** то́чно определя́ть *impf*, определи́ть *pf*; ~**stripe** то́нкая поло́ска; *vt* прика́лывать *impf*, приколо́ть *pf*; (*press*) прижима́ть *impf*, прижа́ть *pf* (**against** к+*dat*).

pinafore /'pɪnəfɔ:(r)/ *n* пере́дник.

pincers /'pɪnsəz/ *n pl* (*tool*) кле́щи (-ще́й) *pl*, пинце́т; (*claw*) клешни́ *f pl*.

pinch /pɪntʃ/ *vt* щипа́ть *impf*,

(у)щипну́ть *pf*; (*finger in door etc.*) прищемля́ть *impf*, прищеми́ть *pf*; (*of shoe*) жать *impf*; (*steal*) стяну́ть *pf*; *n* щипо́к; (*of salt*) щепо́тка; **at** а ~ в кра́йнем слу́чае.

pine¹ /paɪn/ *vi* томи́ться *impf*; ~ **for** тоскова́ть *impf* по+*dat*, *prep*.

pine² /paɪn/ *n* (*tree*) сосна́.

pineapple /'paɪnæp(ə)l/ *n* анана́с.

ping-pong /'pɪŋpɒŋ/ *n* пинг-по́нг.

pink /pɪŋk/ *n* (*colour*) ро́зовый цвет; *adj* ро́зовый.

pinnacle /'pɪnək(ə)l/ *n* верши́на.

pint /paɪnt/ *n* пи́нта.

pioneer /ˌpaɪə'nɪə(r)/ *n* пионе́р, ~ка; *vt* прокла́дывать *impf*, проложи́ть *pf* путь к+*dat*.

pious /'paɪəs/ *adj* набо́жный.

pip¹ /pɪp/ *n* (*seed*) зёрнышко.

pip² /pɪp/ *n* (*sound*) бип.

pipe /paɪp/ *n* труба́; (*mus*) ду́дка; (*for smoking*) тру́бка; ~**dream** пуста́я мечта́; *vt* пуска́ть *impf*, пусти́ть *pf* по трубам; *vi* ~ **down** затиха́ть *impf*, зати́хнуть *pf*. **pipeline** *n* трубопрово́д; (*oil* ~) нефтепрово́д. **piper** /'paɪpə(r)/ *n* волы́нщик. **piping** /'paɪpɪŋ/ *adj*: ~ **hot** с пы́лу.

piquant /'pi:kənt/ *adj* пика́нтный.

pique /pi:k/ *n*: **in a fit of** ~ в поры́ве раздраже́ния.

pirate /'paɪərət/ *n* пира́т.

pirouette /ˌpɪru'et/ *n* пируэ́т; *vi* де́лать *impf*, с~ *pf* пируэ́т(ы).

Pisces /'paɪsɪz/ *n* Ры́бы *f pl*.

pistol /'pɪst(ə)l/ *n* пистоле́т.

piston /'pɪst(ə)n/ *n* по́ршень *m*.

pit /pɪt/ *n* я́ма; (*mine*) ша́хта; (*orchestra* ~) орке́стр; (*motor-*

racing) запра́вочно-ремо́нтный пункт; *vt*: ~ **against** выставля́ть *impf*, вы́ставить *pf* про́тив+*gen*.

pitch[1] /pɪtʃ/ *n* (*resin*) смола́; **~-black** чёрный как смоль; **~-dark** о́чень тёмный.

pitch[2] /pɪtʃ/ *vt* (*camp, tent*) разбива́ть *impf*, разби́ть *pf*; (*throw*) броса́ть *impf*, бро́сить *pf*; *vi* (*fall*) (у)па́сть *pf*; (*ship*) кача́ть *impf*, *n* (*football* ~ *etc.*) по́ле; (*degree*) у́ровень *m*; (*mus*) высота́; (*slope*) укло́н.

pitcher /ˈpɪtʃə(r)/ *n* (*vessel*) кувши́н.

pitchfork /ˈpɪtʃfɔːk/ *n* ви́лы (-л) *pl*.

piteous /ˈpɪtɪəs/ *adj* жа́лкий.

pitfall /ˈpɪtfɔːl/ *n* западня́.

pith /pɪθ/ *n* сердцеви́на; (*essence*) суть; **pithy** /ˈpɪθɪ/ *adj* (*fig*) содержа́тельный.

pitiful /ˈpɪtɪfʊl/ *adj* жа́лкий. **pitiless** /ˈpɪtɪlɪs/ *adj* безжа́лостный.

pittance /ˈpɪt(ə)ns/ *n* жа́лкие гроши́ (-ше́й) *pl*.

pity /ˈpɪtɪ/ *n* жа́лость; **it's a** ~ жа́лко, жаль; **take** ~ **on** сжа́литься *pf* над+*instr*; **what a** ~ как жа́лко!; *vt* жале́ть *impf*, по~ *pf*; **I** ~ **you** мне жаль тебя́.

pivot /ˈpɪvət/ *n* сте́ржень *m*; (*fig*) центр; *vi* враща́ться *impf*.

pixie /ˈpɪksɪ/ *n* эльф.

pizza /ˈpiːtsə/ *n* пи́цца.

placard /ˈplækɑːd/ *n* афи́ша, плака́т.

placate /pləˈkeɪt/ *vt* умиротворя́ть *impf*, умиротвори́ть *pf*.

place /pleɪs/ *n* ме́сто; **in** ~ **of** вме́сто+*gen*; **in the first, second,** ~ во-пе́рвых, во-вторы́х; **out of** ~ не на ме́сте; (*unsuitable*) неуме́стный; **take** ~ случа́ться *impf*, случи́ться *pf*; (*pre-arranged event*) состоя́ться *pf*; **take the** ~ **of** заменя́ть *impf*, замени́ть *pf*; *vt* (*stand*) ста́вить *impf*, по~ *pf*; (*lay*) класть *impf*, положи́ть *pf*; (*an order etc.*) помеща́ть *impf*, помести́ть *pf*.

placenta /pləˈsentə/ *n* плаце́нта.

placid /ˈplæsɪd/ *adj* споко́йный.

plagiarism /ˈpleɪdʒəˌrɪz(ə)m/ *n* плагиа́т. **plagiarize** /-ˌraɪz/ *vt* заи́мствовать *impf* & *pf*.

plague /pleɪɡ/ *n* чума́; *vt* му́чить *impf*, за~, из~ *pf*.

plaice /pleɪs/ *n* ка́мбала.

plain /pleɪn/ *n* равни́на; *adj* (*clear*) я́сный; (*simple*) просто́й; (*ugly*) некраси́вый; **~-clothes policeman** переоде́тый полице́йский *sb*.

plaintiff /ˈpleɪntɪf/ *n* исте́ц, исти́ца.

plaintive /ˈpleɪntɪv/ *adj* жа́лобный.

plait /plæt/ *n* коса́; *vt* плести́ *impf*, с~ *pf*.

plan /plæn/ *n* план; *vt* плани́ровать *impf*, за~, с~ *pf*; (*intend*) намерева́ться *impf* +*inf*.

plane[1] /pleɪn/ *n* (*tree*) плата́н.

plane[2] /pleɪn/ *n* (*tool*) руба́нок; *vt* строга́ть *impf*, вы́~ *pf*.

plane[3] /pleɪn/ *n* (*surface*) пло́скость; (*level*) у́ровень *m*; (*aeroplane*) самолёт.

planet /ˈplænɪt/ *n* плане́та.

plank /plæŋk/ *n* доска́.

plant /plɑːnt/ *n* расте́ние; (*factory*) заво́д; *vt* сажа́ть *impf*, посади́ть *pf*; (*fix firmly*) про́чно ста́вить *impf*, по~ *pf*; (*garden etc.*) заса́живать *impf*, засади́ть *pf* (*with* +*instr*).

plantation /plɑːnˈteɪʃ(ə)n/ *n* (*of trees*) (лесо)насажде́ние; (*of cotton etc.*) планта́ция.

plaque /plæk/ *n* дощечка.

plasma /'plæzmə/ *n* плазма.

plaster /'plɑːstə(r)/ *n* пластырь *m*; (*for walls etc*) штукатурка; (*of Paris*) гипс; *vt* штукатурить *impf*, от~, о~ *pf*; (*cover*) облеплять *impf*, облепить *pf*. **plasterboard** *n* сухая штукатурка. **plasterer** /-rə(r)/ *n* штукатур.

plastic /'plæstɪk/ *n* пластмасса; *adj* (*malleable*) пластичный; (*made of* ~) пластмассовый; ~ **surgery** пластическая хирургия.

plate /pleɪt/ *n* тарелка; (*metal sheet*) лист, (*in book*) вкладная) иллюстрация; (*name etc*.) дощечка.

plateau /'plætəʊ/ *n* плато *neut indecl*.

platform /'plætfɔːm/ *n* платформа; (*rly*) перрон.

platinum /'plætɪnəm/ *n* платина.

platitude /'plætɪˌtjuːd/ *n* банальность.

platoon /plə'tuːn/ *n* взвод.

plausible /'plɔːzɪb(ə)l/ *adj* правдоподобный.

play /pleɪ/ *vt & i* играть *impf*, сыграть *pf* (*game*) в+*acc*, (*instrument*) на+*prep*, (*record*) ставить *impf*, по~ *pf*; ~ **down** преуменьшать *impf*, преуменьшить *pf*; ~ **a joke, trick, on** подшучивать *impf*, подшутить *pf* над+*instr*; ~ **off** играть *impf*, сыграть *pf* решающую партию; ~**off** решающая встреча; ~ **safe** действовать *impf* наверняка; *n* игра; (*theat*) пьеса. **player** /'pleɪə(r)/ *n* игрок; (*actor*) актёр, актриса; (*musician*) музыкант. **playful** /'pleɪfʊl/ *adj* игривый. **playground** *n* площадка для игр.

playgroup, playschool *n* детский сад. **playing** /'pleɪɪŋ/: ~-**card** игральная карта; ~-**field** игровая площадка. **playmate** *n* друг детства. **plaything** *n* игрушка. **playwright** /'pleɪraɪt/ *n* драматург.

plea /pliː/ *n* (*entreaty*) мольба; (*law*) заявление. **plead** /pliːd/ *vi* умолять *impf* (**with** +*acc*; **for** o+*prep*); *vt* (*offer as excuse*) ссылаться *impf*, сослаться *pf* на+*acc*; ~ (**not**) **guilty** (не) признавать *impf*, признать *pf* себя виновным.

pleasant /'plez(ə)nt/ *adj* приятный. **pleasantry** /-trɪ/ *n* любезность. **please** /pliːz/ *vt* нравиться *impf*, по~ *pf* +*dat*; *imper* пожалуйста; будьте добры. **pleased** /pliːzd/ *adj* довольный; *predic* рад. **pleasing** /'pliːzɪŋ/, **pleasurable** /'pleʒərəb(ə)l/ *adj* приятный. **pleasure** /'pleʒə(r)/ *n* удовольствие.

pleat /pliːt/ *n* складка; *vt* плиссировать *impf*.

plebiscite /'plebɪsɪt/ *n* плебисцит.

plectrum /'plektrəm/ *n* плектр.

pledge /pledʒ/ *n* (*security*) залог; (*promise*) зарок, обещание; *vt* отдавать *impf*, отдать *pf* в залог; ~ **o.s.** обязываться *impf*, обязаться *pf*; ~ **one's word** давать *impf*, дать *pf* слово.

plentiful /'plentɪfʊl/ *adj* обильный. **plenty** /'plentɪ/ *n* изобилие; ~ **of** много+*gen*.

plethora /'pleθərə/ *n* (*fig*) изобилие.

pleurisy /'plʊərɪsɪ/ *n* плеврит.

pliable /'plaɪəb(ə)l/ *adj* гибкий.

pliers /'plaɪəz/ *n* плоскогубцы (-цев) *pl*.

plight /plaɪt/ n незави́дное положе́ние.

plimsolls /ˈplɪms(ə)lz/ n pl спорти́вные та́почки f pl.

plinth /plɪnθ/ n пли́нтус.

plod /plɒd/ vi тащи́ться impf.

plonk /plɒŋk/ vt плю́хнуть pf.

plot /plɒt/ n (of land) уча́сток; (of book etc.) фа́була; (conspiracy) за́говор; vt (on graph, map, etc.) наноси́ть impf, нанести́ pf на гра́фик, на ка́рту; v abs (conspire) составля́ть impf, соста́вить pf за́говор.

plough /plaʊ/ n плуг; vt паха́ть impf, вс∼ pf; vi: ∼ through проби́ва́ться impf, проби́ться pf сквозь+acc.

ploy /plɔɪ/ n уло́вка.

pluck /plʌk/ n (courage) сме́лость; vt (chicken) щипа́ть impf, об∼ pf; (mus) щипа́ть impf; (flower) срыва́ть impf, сорва́ть pf; ∼ up courage собра́ться impf, собра́ться pf с ду́хом; vi: ∼ at дёргать impf, дёрнуть pf. **plucky** /ˈplʌkɪ/ adj сме́лый.

plug /plʌg/ n (stopper) про́бка; (electr) ви́лка; (electr socket) розе́тка; vt (∼ up) затыка́ть impf, заткну́ть pf; ∼ in включа́ть impf, включи́ть pf.

plum /plʌm/ n сли́ва.

plumage /ˈpluːmɪdʒ/ n опере́ние.

plumb /plʌm/ n лот; adv вертика́льно; (fig) то́чно; vt измеря́ть impf, изме́рить pf глубину́+gen; (fig) проника́ть impf, прони́кнуть pf в+acc; ∼ in подключа́ть impf, подключи́ть pf.

plumber /ˈplʌmə(r)/ n водопрово́дчик. **plumbing** /-mɪŋ/ n водопрово́д.

plume /pluːm/ n (feather) перо́;

(on hat etc.) султа́н.

plummet /ˈplʌmɪt/ vi па́дать impf, (у)па́сть pf.

plump[1] /plʌmp/ adj пу́хлый.

plump[2] /plʌmp/ vi: ∼ for выбира́ть impf, вы́брать pf.

plunder /ˈplʌndə(r)/ vt гра́бить impf, о∼ pf n добы́ча.

plunge /plʌndʒ/ vt & i (immerse) погружа́ть impf, погрузи́ть(-ся) pf (into в+acc); vi (dive) ныря́ть impf, нырну́ть pf; (rush) броса́ться impf, бро́ситься pf. **plunger** /ˈplʌndʒə(r)/ n плу́нжер.

pluperfect /pluːˈpɜːfɪkt/ n давнопроше́дшее вре́мя neut.

plural /ˈplʊər(ə)l/ n мно́жественное число́. **pluralism** /-ˌlɪz(ə)m/ n плюрали́зм. **pluralistic** /-ˈlɪstɪk/ adj плюралисти́ческий.

plus /plʌs/ prep плюс+acc; n (знак) плюс.

plushy /ˈplʌʃɪ/ adj шика́рный.

plutonium /pluːˈtəʊnɪəm/ n плуто́ний.

ply /plaɪ/ vt (tool) рабо́тать impf +instr; (task) занима́ться impf +instr; (keep supplied) по́тчевать impf (with +instr); ∼ with questions засыпа́ть impf, засы́пать pf вопро́сами.

plywood /ˈplaɪwʊd/ n фане́ра.

p.m. adv по́сле полу́дня.

pneumatic /njuːˈmætɪk/ adj пневмати́ческий; ∼ drill отбо́йный молото́к.

pneumonia /njuːˈməʊnɪə/ n воспале́ние лёгких.

poach[1] /pəʊtʃ/ vt (cook) вари́ть impf; ∼ed egg яйцо́-пашо́т.

poach[2] /pəʊtʃ/ vi браконье́рствовать impf. **poacher** /-tʃə(r)/ n браконье́р.

pocket /ˈpɒkɪt/ n карма́н; out of ∼ в убы́тке; ∼ money карма́н-

ные де́ньги (-нег, -ньга́м) pl; vt
класть impf, положи́ть pf. в
карма́н.

pock-marked /'pɒkmɑːkt/ adj ря-
бо́й.

pod /pɒd/ n стручо́к.

podgy /'pɒdʒɪ/ adj то́л-
стенький.

podium /'pəʊdɪəm/ n трибу́на;
(conductor's) пульт.

poem /'pəʊɪm/ n стихотворе́-
ние; (longer) поэ́ма. **poet**
/'pəʊɪt/ n поэ́т. **poetess**
/'pəʊɪtɪs/ n поэте́сса. **poetic(al)**
/pəʊ'etɪk/ adj поэти́ческий.
poetry /'pəʊɪtrɪ/ n поэ́зия,
стихи́ m pl.

pogrom /'pɒgrəm/ n погро́м.

poignancy /'pɔɪnjənsɪ/ n ос-
трота́. **poignant** /'pɔɪnjənt/ adj
о́стрый.

point[1] /pɔɪnt/ n то́чка; (place;
in list) пункт; (in score) очко́; (in
time) моме́нт; (in space) ме́сто;
(essence) суть; (sense) смысл;
(sharp ~) остриё; (tip) ко́нчик;
(power ~) штéпсель m; pl (rly)
стре́лка; **be on the ~ of** (doing)
собира́ться impf, собра́ться pf
+inf; **beside, off the ~** некста́ти;
that is the ~ в э́том и де́ло; the
~ is that де́ло в том, что; **there
is no ~** (in doing) не име́ет
смы́сла (+inf); **to the ~** кста́ти;
~-blank прямо́й; **~ of view**
то́чка зре́ния.

point[2] /pɔɪnt/ vt (wall) расши́-
ва́ть impf, расши́ть pf швы
+gen; (gun etc.) наводи́ть impf,
навести́ pf (at на+acc); vi по-,
у-, ка́зывать impf, по-, у-, за-
за́ть pf (at, to на+acc). **pointed**
/'pɔɪntɪd/ adj (sharp) о́стрый.
pointer /'pɔɪntə(r)/ n указа́тель
m, стре́лка. **pointless** /'pɔɪntlɪs/
adj бессмы́сленный.

poise /pɔɪz/ n уравнове́шен-

ность. **poised** /pɔɪzd/ adj (composed) уравнове́шенный;
(ready) гото́вый (to к+dat).

poison /'pɔɪz(ə)n/ n яд; vt отрав-
ля́ть impf, отрави́ть pf. **poisonous** /'pɔɪzənəs/ adj
ядови́тый.

poke /pəʊk/ vt (prod) ты́кать
impf, ткнуть pf; **~ at** под-
шу́чивать impf, подшути́ть pf
над+instr; (thrust) сова́ть impf,
су́нуть pf; **~ the fire** меша́ть
impf, по~ pf у́гли в ками́не; n
тычо́к. **poker**[1] /'pəʊkə(r)/ n
(rod) кочерга́.

poker[2] /'pəʊkə(r)/ n (cards)
по́кер.

poky /'pəʊkɪ/ adj те́сный.

Poland /'pəʊlənd/ n По́льша.

polar /'pəʊlə(r)/ adj поля́рный;
~ bear бе́лый медве́дь m. **po-
larity** /pə'lærɪtɪ/ n поля́рность.
polarize /'pəʊlə,raɪz/ vt поляри-
зова́ть impf & pf. **pole**[1] /pəʊl/ n
(geog; phys) по́люс; **~-star** По-
ля́рная звезда́.

pole[2] /pəʊl/ n (rod) столб, шест;
~-vaulting прыжо́к с шесто́м.

Pole /pəʊl/ n поля́к, по́лька.

polecat /'pəʊlkæt/ n хорёк.

polemic /pə'lemɪk/ adj полеми́-
ческий; n поле́мика.

police /pə'liːs/ n поли́ция; (as pl)
полице́йские sb; (in Russia) ми-
ли́ция; **~ station** полице́йский
уча́сток. **policeman** n полице́й-
ский sb, полисме́н; (in Russia)
милиционе́р. **policewoman**
n же́нщина-полице́йский sb;
(in Russia) же́нщина-милици-
оне́р.

policy[1] /'pɒlɪsɪ/ n поли́тика.

policy[2] /'pɒlɪsɪ/ n (insurance)
по́лис.

polio /'pəʊlɪəʊ/ n полиомиели́т.

Polish /'pəʊlɪʃ/ adj по́льский.

polish /'pɒlɪʃ/ n (gloss, process)

полиро́вка; (*substance*) политу́ра; (*fig*) лоск; *vt* полирова́ть *impf*, от~ *pf*; ~ **off** расправля́ться *impf*, распра́виться *pf* c+*instr*. **polished** /-lıʃt/ *adj* отто́ченный.

polite /pə'laıt/ *adj* ве́жливый. **politeness** /-nıs/ *n* ве́жливость.

politic /'pɒlıtık/ *adj* полити́чный. **political** /pə'lıtıkəl/ *adj* полити́ческий; ~ **economy** политэконо́мика; ~ **prisoner** политзаключённый. **politician** /ˌpɒlı'tıʃ(ə)n/ *n* поли́тик. **politics** /'pɒlıtıks/ *n* поли́тика.

poll /pəʊl/ *n* (*voting*) голосова́ние; (*opinion* ~) опро́с; **go to the** ~**s** голосова́ть *impf*, про~ *pf*; *vt* получа́ть *impf*, получи́ть *pf*.

pollen /'pɒlən/ *n* пыльца́. **pollinate** /'pɒlıˌneıt/ *vt* опыля́ть *impf*, опыли́ть *pf*.

polling /'pəʊlıŋ/ *attrib*: ~ **booth** каби́на для голосова́ния; ~ **station** избира́тельный уча́сток.

pollutant /pə'lu:tənt/ *n* загрязни́тель *m*. **pollute** /-'lu:t/ *vt* загрязня́ть *impf*, загрязни́ть *pf*. **pollution** /-'lu:ʃ(ə)n/ *n* загрязне́ние.

polo /'pəʊləʊ/ *n* по́ло *neut indecl*; ~**-neck sweater** водола́зка.

polyester /ˌpɒlı'estə(r)/ *n* полиэфи́р. **polyethylene** /ˌpɒlı'eθılin/ *n* полиэтиле́н. **polyglot** /'pɒlıˌglɒt/ *n* полигло́т; *adj* многоязы́чный. **polygon** /'pɒlıgɒn/ *n* многоуго́льник. **polymer** /'pɒlımə(r)/ *n* полиме́р. **polystyrene** /ˌpɒlı'staıəˌri:n/ *n* полистиро́л. **polytechnic** /ˌpɒlı'teknık/ *n* техни́ческий вуз. **polythene** /'pɒlıθi:n/ *n* полиэтиле́н. **polyunsaturated**

/ˌpɒlıʌn'sætʃəˌreıtıd/ *adj*: ~ **fats** полиненасы́щенные жиры́ *m pl*. **polyurethane** /ˌpɒlı'jʊərəˌθeın/ *n* полиурета́н.

pomp /pɒmp/ *n* пы́шность. **pomposity** /pɒm'pɒsıtı/ *n* напы́щенность. **pompous** /'pɒmpəs/ *adj* напы́щенный.

pond /pɒnd/ *n* пруд.

ponder /'pɒndə(r)/ *vt* обду́мывать *impf*, обду́мать *pf*; *vi* размышля́ть *impf*, размы́слить *pf*. **ponderous** /'pɒndərəs/ *adj* тяжелове́сный.

pony /'pəʊnı/ *n* по́ни *m indecl*. **poodle** /'pu:d(ə)l/ *n* пу́дель *m*.

pool[1] /pu:l/ *n* (*of water*) прудо́к; (*puddle*) лу́жа; (*swimming* ~) бассе́йн.

pool[2] /pu:l/ *n* (*collective stakes*) совоку́пность ста́вок; (*common fund*) о́бщий фонд; *vt* объединя́ть *impf*, объедини́ть *pf*.

poor /pʊə(r)/ *adj* бе́дный; (*bad*) плохо́й; *n*: **the** ~ бедняки́ *m pl*. **poorly** /'pʊəlı/ *predic* нездоро́в.

pop[1] /pɒp/ *vt* & *vi* хло́пать *impf*, хло́пнуть *pf*; *vt* (*put*) бы́стро всу́нуть *pf* (**into** в+*acc*); *vi* забега́ть *impf*, забежа́ть *pf* к+*dat*; *n* хлопо́к.

pop[2] /pɒp/ *adj* поп-; ~ **concert** поп-конце́рт; ~ **music** поп-му́зыка.

pope /pəʊp/ *n* Па́па *m*.

poplar /'pɒplə(r)/ *n* то́поль *m*.

poppy /'pɒpı/ *n* мак.

populace /'pɒpjʊləs/ *n* просто́й наро́д. **popular** /-lə(r)/ *adj* наро́дный; (*liked*) популя́рный. **popularity** /ˌpɒpjʊ'lærıtı/ *n* популя́рность. **popularize** /'pɒpjʊləˌraız/ *vt* популяризи́ровать *impf* & *pf*. **populate** /'pɒpjʊˌleıt/ *vt* населя́ть *impf*, насели́ть *pf*. **population** /-'leıʃ(ə)n/ *n* населе́-

ние. **populous** /'pɒpjʊləs/ adj (много)лю́дный.

porcelain /'pɔːsəlɪn/ n фарфо́р.

porch /pɔːtʃ/ n крыльцо́.

porcupine /'pɔːkjʊˌpaɪn/ n дикобра́з.

pore¹ /pɔː(r)/ n по́ра.

pore² /pɔː(r)/ vi: ~ over погружа́ться impf, погрузи́ться pf в+acc.

pork /pɔːk/ n свини́на.

pornographic /ˌpɔːnə'græfɪk/ adj порнографи́ческий. **pornography** /pɔː'nɒɡrəfɪ/ n порногра́фия.

porous /'pɔːrəs/ adj по́ристый.

porpoise /'pɔːpəs/ n морска́я свинья́.

porridge /'pɒrɪdʒ/ n овся́ная ка́ша.

port¹ /pɔːt/ n (harbour) порт; (town) порто́вый го́род.

port² /pɔːt/ n (naut) ле́вый борт.

port³ /pɔːt/ n (wine) портве́йн.

portable /'pɔːtəb(ə)l/ adj порта́тивный.

portend /pɔː'tend/ vt предвеща́ть impf. **portent** /'pɔːtent/ n предзнаменова́ние. **portentous** /-'tentəs/ adj злове́щий.

porter¹ /'pɔːtə(r)/ n (at door) швейца́р.

porter² /'pɔːtə(r)/ n (carrier) носи́льщик.

portfolio /pɔːt'fəʊlɪəʊ/ n портфе́ль m; (artist's) па́пка.

porthole /'pɔːthəʊl/ n иллюмина́тор.

portion /'pɔːʃ(ə)n/ n часть, до́ля; (of food) по́рция.

portly /'pɔːtlɪ/ adj доро́дный.

portrait /'pɔːtrɪt/ n портре́т. **portray** /pɔː'treɪ/ vt изобража́ть impf, изобрази́ть pf. **portrayal** /-'treɪəl/ n изображе́ние.

Portugal /'pɔːtjʊɡ(ə)l/ n Португа́лия. **Portuguese** /ˌpɔːtjʊ'ɡiːz/

n португа́лец, -лка; adj португа́льский.

pose /pəʊz/ n по́за; vt (question) ста́вить impf, по~ pf; (a problem) представля́ть impf, предста́вить pf; vi пози́ровать impf; ~ as выдава́ть impf, вы́дать pf себя́ за+acc.

posh /pɒʃ/ adj шика́рный.

posit /'pɒzɪt/ vt постули́ровать impf & pf.

position /pə'zɪʃ(ə)n/ n положе́ние, пози́ция; in a ~ to в состоя́нии +inf; vt ста́вить impf, по~ pf.

positive /'pɒzɪtɪv/ adj положи́тельный; (convinced) уве́ренный; (proof) несомне́нный; n (phot) позити́в.

possess /pə'zes/ vt облада́ть impf +instr; владе́ть impf +instr; (of feeling etc.) овладева́ть impf, овладе́ть pf +instr. **possessed** /-'zest/ adj одержи́мый. **possession** /-'zeʃ(ə)n/ n владе́ние (of +instr); pl со́бственность. **possessive** /-'zesɪv/ adj собстве́ннический. **possessor** /-'zesə(r)/ n облада́тель m.

possibility /ˌpɒsɪ'bɪlɪtɪ/ n возмо́жность. **possible** /'pɒsɪb(ə)l/ adj возмо́жный; as much as ~ ско́лько возмо́жно; as soon as ~ как мо́жно скоре́е. **possibly** /'pɒsɪblɪ/ adv возмо́жно, мо́жет (быть).

post¹ /pəʊst/ n (pole) столб; vt (~ up) выве́шивать impf, вы́весить pf.

post² /pəʊst/ n (station) пост; (job) до́лжность; vt (station) расставля́ть impf, расста́вить pf; (appoint) назнача́ть impf, назна́чить pf.

post³ /pəʊst/ n (letters, ~ office) по́чта; by ~ по́чтой; attrib по-

что́вый; **~-box** почто́вый я́щик; **~-code** почто́вый и́ндекс; ~ **office** по́чта; *vt (send by ~)* отправля́ть *impf*, отпра́вить *pf* по по́чте; *(put in ~-box)* опуска́ть *impf*, опусти́ть *pf* в почто́вый я́щик.

postage /'pəustɪdʒ/ *n* почто́вый сбор, почто́вые расхо́ды *m pl*; ~ **stamp** почто́вая ма́рка.

postal /'pəust(ə)l/ *adj* почто́вый; **~-order** почто́вый перево́д. **postcard** *n* откры́тка.

poster /'pəustə(r)/ *n* афи́ша, плака́т.

poste restante /,pəust re'stɑ̃t/ *n* до востре́бования.

posterior /pɒ'stɪərɪə(r)/ *adj* за́дний; *n* зад.

posterity /pɒ'sterɪtɪ/ *n* пото́мство.

post-graduate /pəust'grædʒʊət/ *n* аспира́нт.

posthumous /'pɒstjʊməs/ *adj* посме́ртный.

postman /'pəustmən/ *n* почтальо́н. **postmark** *n* почто́вый ште́мпель *m*.

post-mortem /pəust'mɔːtəm/ *n* вскры́тие тру́па.

postpone /pəust'pəun/ *vt* отсро́чивать *impf*, отсро́чить *pf*. **postponement** /-mənt/ *n* отсро́чка.

postscript /'pəustskrɪpt/ *n* постскри́птум.

postulate /'pɒstjʊˌleɪt/ *vt* постули́ровать *impf & pf*.

posture /'pɒstʃə(r)/ *n* по́за, положе́ние.

post-war /pəust'wɔː(r)/ *adj* послевое́нный.

posy /'pəuzɪ/ *n* буке́тик.

pot /pɒt/ *n* горшо́к; *(cooking ~)* кастрю́ля; **~-shot** вы́стрел наугад; *vt (food)* консерви́ровать *impf*, за~ *pf*; *(plant)*

сажа́ть *impf*, посади́ть *pf* в горшо́к; *(billiards)* загоня́ть *impf*, загна́ть *pf* в лу́зу.

potash /'pɒtæʃ/ *n* пота́ш.

potassium /pə'tæsɪəm/ *n* ка́лий.

potato /pə'teɪtəu/ *n (also collect)* карто́шка *(no pl)*; *(plant; also collect)* карто́фель *m (no pl)*.

potency /'pəut(ə)nsɪ/ *n* си́ла. **potent** /'pəut(ə)nt/ *adj* си́льный. **potential** /pə'tenʃ(ə)l/ *adj* потенциа́льный; *n* потенциа́л. **potentiality** /pə,tenʃɪ'ælɪtɪ/ *n* потенциа́льность.

pot-hole /'pɒthəul/ *n (in road)* вы́боина.

potion /'pəuʃ(ə)n/ *n* зе́лье.

potter[1] /'pɒtə(r)/ *vi*: ~ **about** вози́ться *impf*.

potter[2] /'pɒtə(r)/ *n* гонча́р. **pottery** /'pɒtərɪ/ *n (goods)* гонча́рные изде́лия *neut pl*; *(place)* гонча́рня *sb*.

potty[1] /'pɒtɪ/ *adj (crazy)* поме́шанный *(about* на+*prep)*.

potty[2] /'pɒtɪ/ *n* ночно́й горшо́к.

pouch /pautʃ/ *n* су́мка.

poultry /'pəultrɪ/ *n* дома́шняя пти́ца.

pounce /pauns/ *vi*: ~ *(up)on* набра́сываться *impf*, набро́ситься *pf* на+*acc*.

pound[1] /paund/ *n (measure)* фунт, ~ **sterling** фунт сте́рлингов.

pound[2] /paund/ *vt (strike)* колоти́ть *impf*, по~ *pf* по+*dat*; в+*acc*; *vi (heart)* колоти́ться *impf*; ~ **along** *(run)* мча́ться *impf* с гро́хотом.

pour /pɔː(r)/ *vt* лить *impf*; ~ **out** налива́ть *impf*, нали́ть *pf*; *vi* ли́ться *impf*; **it is** ~**ing** *(with rain)* дождь льёт как из ведра́.

pout /paut/ *vi* ду́ть(ся) *impf*, на~ *pf*.

poverty /'pɒvətɪ/ *n* бе́дность;

~-stricken убо́гий.

POW *abbr* военнопле́нный *sb.*

powder /'paʊdə(r)/ *n* порошо́к; (*cosmetic*) пу́дра; *vt* пу́дрить *impf,* на~ *pf.* **powdery** /-rɪ/ *adj* порошкообра́зный.

power /'paʊə(r)/ *n* (*vigour*) си́ла; (*might*) могу́щество; (*ability*) спосо́бность; (*control*) власть; (*authorization*) полномо́чие; (*State*) держа́ва; **~ cut** переры́в электропита́ния; **~ point** розе́тка; **~ station** электроста́нция. **powerful** /-fʊl/ *adj* си́льный. **powerless** /-lɪs/ *adj* бесси́льный.

practicable /'præktɪkəb(ə)l/ *adj* осуществи́мый. **practical** /-tɪk(ə)l/ *adj* (*help, activities*) практи́ческий; (*person, object*) практи́чный. **practically** /-klɪ/ *adv* практи́чески. **practice** /'præktɪs/ *n* пра́ктика; (*custom*) обы́чай; (*mus*) заня́тия *neut pl*; **in ~** на пра́ктике; **put into ~** осуществля́ть *impf,* осуществи́ть *pf.* **practise** /'præktɪs/ *vt* (*also abs of doctor etc.*) практикова́ть *impf*; упражня́ться *impf* в+*prep*; (*mus*) занима́ться *impf,* заня́ться *pf* на+*prep*. **practised** /'præktɪst/ *adj* о́пытный. **practitioner** /præk'tɪʃənə(r)/ *n* (*doctor*) практику́ющий врач; **general ~** врач о́бщей пра́ктики.

pragmatic /præg'mætɪk/ *adj* прагмати́ческий. **pragmatism** /'prægmətɪz(ə)m/ *n* прагмати́зм. **pragmatist** /'prægmətɪst/ *n* прагма́тик.

prairie /'preərɪ/ *n* пре́рия.

praise /preɪz/ *vt* хвали́ть *impf,* по~ *pf*; *n* похвала́. **praiseworthy** /'preɪz,wɜːðɪ/ *adj* похва́льный.

pram /præm/ *n* де́тская коля́ска.

prance /prɑːns/ *vi* гарцева́ть *impf.*

prank /præŋk/ *n* вы́ходка.

prattle /'præt(ə)l/ *vi* лепета́ть; *n* ле́пет.

prawn /prɔːn/ *n* креве́тка.

pray /preɪ/ *vi* моли́ться *impf,* по~ *pf* (**to** +*dat*; **for** o+*prep*). **prayer** /'preə(r)/ *n* моли́тва.

preach /priːtʃ/ *vt & i* пропове́дывать *impf.* **preacher** /'priːtʃə(r)/ *n* пропове́дник.

preamble /priː'æmb(ə)l/ *n* преа́мбула.

pre-arrange /,priːə'reɪndʒ/ *vt* зара́нее организо́вывать *impf,* организова́ть *pf.*

precarious /prɪ'keərɪəs/ *adj* опа́сный.

precaution /prɪ'kɔːʃ(ə)n/ *n* предосторо́жность. **precautionary** /-ʃənərɪ/ *adj*: **~ measures** ме́ры предосторо́жности.

precede /prɪ'siːd/ *vt* предше́ствовать *impf* +*dat*. **precedence** /'presɪd(ə)ns/ *n* предпочте́ние. **precedent** /'presɪd(ə)nt/ *n* прецеде́нт. **preceding** /prɪ'siːdɪŋ/ *adj* предыду́щий.

precept /'priːsept/ *n* наставле́ние.

precinct /'priːsɪŋkt/ *n* двор; *pl* окре́стности *f pl.* **pedestrian ~** уча́сток для пешехо́дов; **shopping ~** торго́вый пасса́ж.

precious /'preʃəs/ *adj* драгоце́нный; (*style*) мане́рный; *adv* о́чень.

precipice /'presɪpɪs/ *n* обры́в.

precipitate *adj* /prɪ'sɪpɪtət/ (*person*) опроме́тчивый; *vt* /prɪ'sɪpɪ,teɪt/ (*throw down*) низверга́ть *impf,* низве́ргнуть *pf*; (*hurry*) ускоря́ть *impf,* ускори́ть *pf.* **precipitation** /prɪ,sɪpɪ'teɪʃ(ə)n/ *n*

(*meteorol*) осáдки *m pl.* **precipitous** /prɪˈsɪpɪtəs/ *adj* обры́вистый.

précis /ˈpreɪsiː/ *n* конспéкт.

precise /prɪˈsaɪs/ *adj* тóчный. **precisely** /-ˈsaɪslɪ/ *adv* тóчно; (*in answer*) и́менно. **precision** /-ˈsɪʒ(ə)n/ *n* тóчность.

preclude /prɪˈkluːd/ *vt* предотвращáть *impf*, предотврати́ть *pf*.

precocious /prɪˈkəʊʃəs/ *adj* рáно разви́вшийся.

preconceived /ˌpriːkənˈsiːvd/ *adj* предвзя́тый. **preconception** /ˌpriːkənˈsepʃ(ə)n/ *n* предвзя́тое мнéние.

pre-condition /ˌpriːkənˈdɪʃ(ə)n/ *n* предпосы́лка.

precursor /prɪˈkɜːsə(r)/ *n* предшéственник.

predator /ˈpredətə(r)/ *n* хи́щник. **predatory** /-tərɪ/ *adj* хи́щный.

predecessor /ˈpriːdɪˌsesə(r)/ *n* предшéственник.

predestination /priːˌdestɪˈneɪʃ(ə)n/ *n* предопределéние.

predetermine /ˌpriːdɪˈtɜːmɪn/ *vt* предрешáть *impf*, предрешить *pf*.

predicament /prɪˈdɪkəmənt/ *n* затрудни́тельное положéние.

predicate /ˈpredɪkət/ *n* (*gram*) сказýемое *sb.* **predicative** /prɪˈdɪkətɪv/ *adj* предикати́вный.

predict /prɪˈdɪkt/ *vt* предскáзывать *impf*, предскáзать *pf*. **predictable** /-ˈdɪktəb(ə)l/ *adj* предскáзуемый. **prediction** /-ˈdɪkʃ(ə)n/ *n* предскáзание.

predilection /ˌpriːdɪˈlekʃ(ə)n/ *n* пристрáстие (**for** к+*dat*).

predispose /ˌpriːdɪˈspəʊz/ *vt* предраспологáть *impf*, предрасположи́ть *pf* (**to** к+*dat*). **predisposition** /ˌpriːdɪspəˈzɪʃ(ə)n/ *n* предрасположéние

(**to** к+*dat*). **predominance** /prɪˈdɒmɪnəns/ *n* преоблáдание. **predominant** /-nənt/ *adj* преоблáдающий. **predominate** /-neɪt/ *vi* преоблáдать *impf*.

pre-eminence /priːˈemɪnəns/ *n* превосхóдство. **pre-eminent** /-nənt/ *adj* выдаю́щийся.

pre-empt /priːˈempt/ *vt* (*fig*) завладевáть *impf*, завладéть *pf* +*instr* прéжде други́х. **pre-emptive** /-tɪv/ *adj* (*mil*) упреждáющий.

preen /priːn/ *vt* (*of bird*) чи́стить *impf*, по~ *pf* клю́вом; ~ **o.s.** (*be proud*) горди́ться *impf* собóй.

pre-fab /ˈpriːfæb/ *n* сбóрный дом. **pre-fabricated** /priːˈfæbrɪˌkeɪtɪd/ *adj* сбóрный.

preface /ˈprefəs/ *n* предислóвие.

prefect /ˈpriːfekt/ *n* префéкт; (*school*) стáроста *m.*

prefer /prɪˈfɜː(r)/ *vt* предпочитáть *impf*, предпочéсть *pf*. **preferable** /ˈprefərəb(ə)l/ *adj* предпочти́тельный. **preference** /ˈprefərəns/ *n* предпочтéние. **preferential** /ˌprefəˈrenʃ(ə)l/ *adj* предпочти́тельный.

prefix /ˈpriːfɪks/ *n* пристáвка.

pregnancy /ˈpregnənsɪ/ *n* берéменность. **pregnant** /ˈpregnənt/ *adj* берéменная.

prehistoric /ˌpriːhɪˈstɒrɪk/ *adj* доистори́ческий.

prejudice /ˈpredʒʊdɪs/ *n* предубеждéние; (*detriment*) ущéрб; *vt* наноси́ть *impf*, нанести́ *pf* ущéрб+*dat*; ~ **against** предубеждáть *impf*, предуби́ть *pf* прóтив+*gen*; **be** ~**d against** имéть *impf* предубеждéние прóтив +*gen.*

preliminary /prɪˈlɪmɪnərɪ/ *adj*

предвари́тельный.
prelude /'prelju:d/ *n* прелю́дия.
premarital /,pri:'mærɪt(ə)l/ *adj* добра́чный.
premature /,premə'tjʊə(r)/ *adj* преждевре́менный.
premeditated /,pri:'medɪˌteɪtɪd/ *adj* преднаме́ренный.
premier /'premɪə(r)/ *adj* пе́рвый; *n* премье́р-мини́стр. **première** /'premɪˌeə(r)/ *n* премье́ра.
premise, premiss /'premɪs/ *n* (*logic*) (пред)посы́лка. **premises** /'premɪsɪz/ *n pl* помеще́ние.
premium /'pri:mɪəm/ *n* пре́мия.
premonition /,premə'nɪʃ(ə)n/ *n* предчу́вствие.
preoccupation /pri:ˌɒkjʊ'peɪʃ(ə)n/ *n* озабо́ченность; (*absorbing subject*) забо́та. **preoccupied** /-'ɒkjʊˌpaɪd/ *adj* озабо́ченный. **preoccupy** /-'ɒkjʊˌpaɪ/ *vt* поглоща́ть *impf*, поглоти́ть *pf*.
preparation /,prepə'reɪʃ(ə)n/ *n* приготовле́ние; *pl* подгото́вка (**for** к+*dat*); (*substance*) препара́т. **preparatory** /prɪ'pærətərɪ/ *adj* подготови́тельный. **prepare** /prɪ'peə(r)/ *vt & i* при-, под-, гото́вля́ть(ся) *impf*, при-, под-, гото́вить(ся) *pf* (**for** к+*dat*). **prepared** /prɪ'peəd/ *adj* гото́вый.
preponderance /prɪ'pɒndərəns/ *n* переве́с.
preposition /,prepə'zɪʃ(ə)n/ *n* предло́г.
prepossessing /,pri:pə'zesɪŋ/ *adj* привлека́тельный.
preposterous /prɪ'pɒstərəs/ *adj* неле́пый.
prerequisite /pri:'rekwɪzɪt/ *n* предпосы́лка.
prerogative /prɪ'rɒɡətɪv/ *n* прерога́тива.

presage /'presɪdʒ/ *vt* предвеща́ть *impf*.
Presbyterian /,prezbɪ'tɪərɪən/ *n* пресвитериа́нин, -а́нка; *adj* пресвитериа́нский.
prescribe /prɪ'skraɪb/ *vt* предпи́сывать *impf*, предписа́ть *pf*; (*med*) прописа́ть *impf*, прописа́ть *pf*. **prescription** /prɪ'skrɪpʃ(ə)n/ *n* (*med*) реце́пт.
presence /'prez(ə)ns/ *n* прису́тствие; ~ **of mind** прису́тствие ду́ха. **present** /'prez(ə)nt/ *adj* прису́тствующий; (*being dealt with*) да́нный; (*existing now*) ны́нешний; (*also gram*) настоя́щий; *predic* налицо́; **be** ~ прису́тствовать *impf* (**at** на+*prep*); ~**-day** ны́нешний; *n*: **the** ~ настоя́щее *sb*; (*gram*) настоя́щее вре́мя *neut*; (*gift*) пода́рок; **at** ~ в настоя́щее вре́мя *neut*; **for the** ~ пока́; *vt* (*introduce*) представля́ть *impf*, предста́вить *pf* (**to** +*dat*); (*award*) вруча́ть *impf*, вручи́ть *pf*; (*a play*) ста́вить *impf*, по~ *pf*; (*a gift*) преподноси́ть *impf*, преподнести́ *pf* (**with** +*acc*); ~ **o.s.** явля́ться *impf*, яви́ться *pf*. **presentable** /prɪ'zentəb(ə)l/ *adj* прили́чный.
presentation /,prezən'teɪʃ(ə)n/ *n* (*introducing*) представле́ние; (*awarding*) подноше́ние.
presentiment /prɪ'zentɪmənt/ *n* предчу́вствие.
presently /'prezntlɪ/ *adv* вско́ре.
preservation /,prezə'veɪʃ(ə)n/ *n* сохране́ние. **preservative** /prɪ'zɜ:vətɪv/ *n* консерва́нт. **preserve** /prɪ'zɜ:v/ *vt* (*keep safe*) сохраня́ть *impf*, сохрани́ть *pf*; (*maintain*) храни́ть *impf*; (*food*) консерви́ровать *impf*, за~ *pf*; *n* (*for game etc*) запове́дник; (*jam*) варе́нье.

preside /prɪ'zaɪd/ vi председа́тельствовать impf (at +prep). **presidency** /'prezɪdənsɪ/ n президе́нтство. **president** /'prezɪd(ə)nt/ n президе́нт. **presidential** /ˌprezɪ'denʃ(ə)l/ adj президе́нтский. **presidium** /prɪ'sɪdɪəm/ n прези́диум.

press /pres/ n (machine) пресс; (printing firm) типогра́фия; (publishing house) изда́тельство; (the ∼) пре́сса, печа́ть; ∼ **conference** пресс-конфере́нция; vt (button etc) нажима́ть impf, нажа́ть pf; (clasp) прижима́ть impf, прижа́ть pf; (iron) гла́дить impf, вы́- pf; (insist on) наста́ивать impf, настоя́ть pf на+prep; (urge) угова́ривать impf; ∼ on (make haste) потора́пливаться impf.

pressing /'presɪŋ/ adj неотло́жный. **pressure** /'preʃə(r)/ n давле́ние; ∼-**cooker** скорова́рка; ∼ **group** инициати́вная гру́ппа. **pressurize** /'preʃəˌraɪz/ vt (fig) ока́зывать impf, оказа́ть pf давле́ние на+acc. **pressurized** /'preʃəˌraɪzd/ adj гермети́ческий.

prestige /pre'stiːʒ/ n прести́ж. **prestigious** /pre'stɪdʒəs/ adj прести́жный.

presumably /prɪ'zjuːməblɪ/ adv предположи́тельно. **presume** /prɪ'zjuːm/ vt полага́ть impf; (venture) позволя́ть impf, позво́лить pf себе́. **presumption** /prɪ'zʌmpʃ(ə)n/ n предположе́ние; (arrogance) самонаде́янность. **presumptuous** /prɪ'zʌmptjuəs/ adj самонаде́янный.

presuppose /ˌpriːsə'pəʊz/ vt предполага́ть impf.

pretence /prɪ'tens/ n притво́рство. **pretend** /prɪ'tend/ vt притворя́ться impf, притвори́ться pf (to be +instr); де́лать impf, c∼ pf вид (что); vi: ∼ **to** претендова́ть impf на+acc. **pretender** /-'tendə(r)/ n претенде́нт. **pretension** /-'tenʃ(ə)n/ n прете́нзия. **pretentious** /-'tenʃəs/ adj претенцио́зный.

pretext /'priːtekst/ n предло́г.

prettiness /'prɪtɪnɪs/ n милови́дность. **pretty** /'prɪtɪ/ adj хоро́шенький; adv дово́льно.

prevail /prɪ'veɪl/ vi (predominate) преоблада́ть impf; ∼ **(up)on** угова́ривать impf, уговори́ть pf. **prevalence** /'prevələns/ n распростране́ние. **prevalent** /'prevələnt/ adj распространённый.

prevaricate /prɪ'værɪˌkeɪt/ vi уви́ливать impf увильну́ть pf.

prevent /prɪ'vent/ vt (stop from happening) предупрежда́ть impf, предупреди́ть pf; (stop from doing) меша́ть impf, по∼ pf +dat. **prevention** /-'venʃ(ə)n/ n предупрежде́ние. **preventive** /-'ventɪv/ adj предупреди́тельный.

preview /'priːvjuː/ n предвари́тельный просмо́тр.

previous /'priːvɪəs/ adj предыду́щий; adv: ∼ **to** до+gen; пре́жде чем +inf. **previously** /-lɪ/ adv ра́ньше.

pre-war /priː'wɔː(r)/ adj дово́енный.

prey /preɪ/ n (animal) добы́ча; (victim) же́ртва (to +gen); bird of ∼ хи́щная пти́ца; vi: ∼ **(up)on** (emotion etc.) му́чить impf.

price /praɪs/ n цена́; ∼-**list** прейскура́нт; vt назнача́ть impf, назна́чить pf це́ну +gen. **priceless** /-lɪs/ adj бесце́нный.

prick /prɪk/ vt колоть impf, у~ pf; (conscience) мучить impf; ~ up one's ears навострить pf уши; n укол. **prickle** /'prɪk(ə)l/ n (thorn) колючка; (spine) игла. **prickly** /-klɪ/ adj колючий.

pride /praɪd/ n гордость; ~ o.s. on гордиться impf +instr.

priest /priːst/ n священник; (non-Christian) жрец.

prig /prɪg/ n педант.

prim /prɪm/ adj чопорный.

primarily /'praɪmərɪlɪ/ adv первоначально; (above all) прежде всего. **primary** /'praɪmərɪ/ adj основной; ~ **school** начальная школа. **prime** /praɪm/ n: in one's ~ в расцвете сил; adj (chief) главный; n ~ **minister** премьер-министр; vt (engine) заправлять impf, заправить pf; (bomb) активизировать impf & pf; (with facts) напичкать impf & pf; (with paint etc.) грунтовать impf, за~ pf. **primer** /'praɪmə(r)/ n грунт. **prim(a)eval** /praɪ 'miːv(ə)l/ adj первобытный. **primitive** /'prɪmɪtɪv/ adj первобытный; (crude) примитивный. **primordial** /praɪ'mɔːdɪəl/ adj исконный.

primrose /'prɪmrəʊz/ n первоцвет; (colour) бледно-жёлтый цвет.

prince /prɪns/ n принц; (in Russia) князь. **princely** /'prɪnslɪ/ adj княжеский; (sum) огромный. **princess** /prɪnses/ n принцесса; (wife) княгиня; (daughter) княжна.

principal /'prɪnsɪp(ə)l/ n главный; n директор. **principality** /ˌprɪnsɪ'pælɪtɪ/ n княжество. **principally** /'prɪnsɪpəlɪ/ adv главным образом.

principle /'prɪnsɪp(ə)l/ n прин-

цип; in ~ в принципе; on ~ принципиально. **principled** /-p(ə)ld/ adj принципиальный.

print /prɪnt/ n (mark) след; (also phot) отпечаток; (printing) печать; (picture) оттиск; in ~ в продаже; out of ~ распроданный; vt (impress) запечатлевать impf, запечатлеть pf; (book etc.) печатать impf, на~ pf; (write) писать impf, на~ pf печатными буквами; (phot; ~ out, off) отпечатывать impf, отпечатать pf; ~ **out** of (computer etc.) распечатывать impf, распечатать pf; ~**out** распечатка. **printer** /-tə(r)/ n (person) печатник, типограф; (of computer) принтер. **printing** /-tɪŋ/ n печатание; ~**press** печатный станок.

prior /'praɪə(r)/ adj прежний; adv: ~ **to** до+gen. **priority** /praɪ 'ɒrɪtɪ/ n приоритет. **priory** /'praɪərɪ/ n монастырь m.

prise /praɪz/ vt: ~ **open** взламывать impf, взломать pf.

prism /'prɪz(ə)m/ n призма.

prison /'prɪz(ə)n/ n тюрьма; attrib тюремный; ~ **camp** лагерь m. **prisoner** /-nə(r)/ n заключённый sb; (~ **of war**) (военно)пленный sb.

pristine /'prɪstiːn/ adj нетронутый.

privacy /'prɪvəsɪ/ n уединение; (private life) частная жизнь. **private** /'praɪvət/ adj (personal) частный, личный; (confidential) конфиденциальный; in ~ наедине; в частной жизни; n рядовой sb.

privation /praɪ'veɪʃ(ə)n/ n лишение.

privilege /'prɪvɪlɪdʒ/ n привилегия. **privileged** /-lɪdʒd/ adj привилегированный.

privy /'prɪvɪ/ *adj*: ~ **to** посвящённый в+*acc*.

prize /praɪz/ *n* пре́мия, приз; ~**-winner** призёр; *vt* высоко́ цени́ть *impf*.

pro¹ /prəʊ/ *n*: ~**s and cons** до́воды *m pl* за и про́тив.

pro² /prəʊ/ *n* (*professional*) профессиона́л.

probability /ˌprɒbə'bɪlɪtɪ/ *n* вероя́тность. **probable** /'prɒbəb(ə)l/ *adj* вероя́тный. **probably** /-blɪ/ *adv* вероя́тно.

probate /'prəʊbeɪt/ *n* утвержде́ние завеща́ния.

probation /prə'beɪʃ(ə)n/ *n* испыта́тельный срок; (*law*) усло́вный пригово́р; **got two years** ~ получи́л два го́да усло́вно. **probationary** /-nərɪ/ *adj* испыта́тельный.

probe /prəʊb/ *n* (*med*) зонд; (*fig*) рассле́дование; *vt* зонди́ровать *impf*, (*fig*) рассле́довать *impf & pf*.

probity /'prəʊbɪtɪ/ *n* че́стность.

problem /'prɒbləm/ *n* пробле́ма, вопро́с; (*math*) зада́ча. **problematic** /-'mætɪk/ *adj* проблемати́чный.

procedural /prə'siːdjərəl/ *adj* процеду́рный. **procedure** /-'siːdjə(r)/ *n* процеду́ра. **proceed** /prə'siːd/ *vi* (*go further*) идти́ *impf*, пойти́ *pf* да́льше; (*act*) поступа́ть *impf*, поступи́ть *pf*; (*abs*, ~ **to say**; *continue*) продолжа́ть *impf*, продо́лжить *pf*; (*of action*) продолжа́ться *impf*, продо́лжиться *pf*; ~ **from** исходи́ть *impf* из, от+*gen*; (*begin to*) принима́ться *impf* +*inf*. **proceedings** /-'siːdɪŋz/ *n pl* (*activity*) де́ятельность *f*; (*legal* ~) судопроизво́дство; (*published report*) труды́ *m pl*, запи́ски *f pl*.

proceeds /'prəʊsiːdz/ *n pl* вы́ручка. **process** /'prəʊses/ *n* проце́сс; *vt* обраба́тывать *impf*, обрабо́тать *pf*. **procession** /prə'seʃ(ə)n/ *n* проце́ссия, ше́ствие.

proclaim /prə'kleɪm/ *vt* провозглаша́ть *impf*, провозгласи́ть *pf*. **proclamation** /ˌprɒklə'meɪʃ(ə)n/ *n* провозглаше́ние.

procure /prə'kjʊə(r)/ *vt* доставля́ть *impf*, доста́ть *pf*.

prod /prɒd/ *vt* ты́кать *impf*, ткнуть *pf*; *n* тычо́к.

prodigal /'prɒdɪg(ə)l/ *adj* расточи́тельный.

prodigious /prə'dɪdʒəs/ *adj* огро́мный. **prodigy** /'prɒdɪdʒɪ/ *n*: **child** ~ вундерки́нд.

produce /prə'djuːs/ (*evidence etc.*) представля́ть *impf*, предста́вить *pf*; (*ticket etc.*) предъявля́ть *impf*, предъяви́ть *pf*; (*play etc.*) ста́вить *impf*, по-~ *pf*; (*manufacture*; *cause*) производи́ть *impf*, произвести́ *pf*; *n* /'prɒdjuːs/ (*collect*) проду́кты *m pl*. **producer** /prə'djuːsə(r)/ *n* (*of play etc.*) режиссёр. **product** /'prɒdʌkt/ *n* проду́кт; (*result*) результа́т. **production** /prə'dʌkʃ(ə)n/ *n* произво́дство; (*of play etc.*) постано́вка. **productive** /prə'dʌktɪv/ *adj* продукти́вный; (*fruitful*) плодотво́рный. **productivity** /ˌprɒdʌk'tɪvɪtɪ/ *n* производи́тельность.

profane /prə'feɪn/ *adj* све́тский; (*blasphemous*) богоху́льный. **profanity** /-'fænɪtɪ/ *n* богоху́льство.

profess /prə'fes/ *vt* (*pretend*) притворя́ться *impf*, притвори́ться *pf* (**to be** +*instr*); (*declare*) заявля́ть *impf*, заяви́ть *pf*; (*faith*) испове́довать *impf*.

profession /prə'feʃ(ə)n/ n (job) профе́ссия. **professional** /prə'feʃ(ə)nəl/ adj профессиона́льный; n профессиона́л. **professor** /-'fesə(r)/ n профе́ссор.

proffer /'profə(r)/ vt предлага́ть impf, предложи́ть pf.

proficiency /prə'fiʃ(ə)nsɪ/ n уме́ние. **proficient** /-ʃ(ə)nt/ adj уме́лый.

profile /'prəʊfaɪl/ n про́филь m.

profit /'profɪt/ n (benefit) по́льза; (monetary) при́быль; vt приноси́ть impf, принести́ pf по́льзу +dat; vi: ~ from по́льзоваться impf, вос~ pf +instr; (financially) получа́ть impf, получи́ть pf при́быль на +prep. **profitable** /'profɪtəb(ə)l/ adj (lucrative) при́быльный; (beneficial) поле́зный. **profiteering** /-'tɪərɪŋ/ n спекуля́ция.

profligate /'profligət/ adj распу́тный.

profound /prə'faʊnd/ adj глубо́кий.

profuse /prə'fju:s/ adj оби́льный. **profusion** /-'fju:ʒ(ə)n/ n изоби́лие.

progeny /'prodʒɪnɪ/ n пото́мство.

prognosis /prog'nəʊsɪs/ n прогно́з.

program(me) /'prəʊgræm/ n програ́мма; vt программи́ровать impf, за~ pf. **programmer** /-mə(r)/ n программи́ст.

progress n /'prəʊgres/ прогре́сс; (success) успе́хи m pl; make ~ де́лать успе́хи, c~ pf успе́хи; vi /prə'gres/ продвига́ться impf, продви́нуться pf вперёд. **progression** /prə'greʃ(ə)n/ n продвиже́ние. **progressive** /prə'gresɪv/ adj прогресси́вный.

prohibit /prə'hɪbɪt/ vt запреща́ть impf, запрети́ть pf. **prohibition** /,prəʊhɪ'bɪʃ(ə)n/ n запреще́ние; (on alcohol) сухо́й зако́н. **prohibitive** /prə'hɪbɪtɪv/ adj запрети́тельный; (price) недосту́пный.

project vt /prə'dʒekt/ (plan) проекти́ровать impf, c~ pf; (a film) демонстри́ровать impf, про~ pf; vi (jut out) выступа́ть impf; n /'prodʒekt/ прое́кт. **projectile** /prə'dʒektaɪl/ n снаря́д. **projection** /prə'dʒekʃ(ə)n/ n (cin) прое́кция; (protrusion) вы́ступ; (forecast) прогно́з. **projector** /prə'dʒektə(r)/ n прое́ктор.

proletarian /,prəʊlɪ'teərɪən/ adj пролета́рский. **proletariat** /-rɪət/ n пролетариа́т.

proliferate /prə'lɪfəreɪt/ vi распространя́ть impf, распространи́ться pf. **proliferation** /-'reɪʃ(ə)n/ n распростране́ние.

prolific /prə'lɪfɪk/ adj плодови́тый.

prologue /'prəʊlɒg/ n проло́г.

prolong /prə'lɒŋ/ vt продлева́ть impf, продли́ть pf.

promenade /,promə'nɑ:d/ n ме́сто для гуля́нья; (at seaside) на́бережная sb; vi прогу́ливаться impf, прогуля́ться pf.

prominence /'promɪnəns/ n изве́стность. **prominent** /'promɪnənt/ adj выступа́ющий; (distinguished) выдаю́щийся.

promiscuity /,promɪ'skju:ɪtɪ/ n лёгкое поведе́ние. **promiscuous** /prə'mɪskjʊəs/ adj лёгкого поведе́ния.

promise /'promɪs/ n обеща́ние; vt обеща́ть impf & pf. **promising** /-sɪŋ/ adj многообеща́ющий.

promontory /'proməntərɪ/ n мыс.

promote /prə'məʊt/ vt (in rank) продвига́ть impf, продви́нуть

pf; (*assist*) способствовать *impf & pf +dat;* (*publicize*) рекламировать *impf.* promoter /-'məʊtə(r)/ *n* агент. promotion /-'məʊʃ(ə)n/ *n* (*in rank*) продвижение; (*comm*) реклама.

prompt /prɒmpt/ *adj* быстрый, немедленный; *adv* ровно; *vt* (*incite*) побуждать *impf,* побудить *pf* (to k+dat; +inf); (*speaker, also fig*) подсказывать *impf,* подсказать *pf +dat;* (*theat*) суфлировать *impf +dat;* *n* подсказка. prompter /-tə(r)/ *n* суфлёр.

prone /prəʊn/ *adj* (*лежащий*) ничком; *predic:* ~ to склонен (-онна, -онно) k+dat.

prong /prɒŋ/ *n* зубец.

pronoun /'prəʊnaʊn/ *n* местоимение.

pronounce /prə'naʊns/ *vt* (*declare*) объявлять *impf,* объявить *pf;* (*articulate*) произносить *impf,* произнести *pf.* pronounced /-'naʊnst/ *adj* явный; заметный. pronouncement /-'naʊnsmənt/ *n* заявление. pronunciation /prə,nʌnsɪ'eɪʃ(ə)n/ *n* произношение.

proof /pruːf/ *n* доказательство; (*printing*) корректура. ~-reader корректор; *adj* (*impenetrable*) непроницаемый (against для+gen); (*not yielding*) неподдающийся (against +dat).

prop¹ /prɒp/ *n* (*support*) подпорка; (*fig*) опора; *vt* (~ open, up) подпирать *impf,* подпереть *pf;* (*fig*) поддерживать *impf,* поддержать *pf.*

prop² /prɒp/ *n* (*theat*) see props

propaganda /,prɒpə'gændə/ *n* пропаганда.

propagate /'prɒpəgeɪt/ *vt & i*

размножать(ся) *impf,* размножить(ся) *pf;* (*disseminate*) распространять(ся) *impf,* распространить(ся) *pf.* propagation /-'geɪʃ(ə)n/ *n* размножение; распространение.

propel /prə'pel/ *vt* приводить *impf,* привести *pf* в движение. propeller /-'pelə(r)/ *n* винт.

propensity /prə'pensɪtɪ/ *n* наклонность (to k+dat; +inf).

proper /'prɒpə(r)/ *adj* (*correct*) правильный; (*suitable*) подходящий; (*decent*) пристойный; ~ noun имя собственное. properly /'prɒpəlɪ/ *adv* как следует.

property /'prɒpətɪ/ *n* (*possessions*) собственность, имущество; (*attribute*) свойство; (*theat*) реквизит.

prophecy /'prɒfɪsɪ/ *n* пророчество. prophesy /'prɒfɪ,saɪ/ *vt* пророчить *impf,* на~ *pf.* prophet /'prɒfɪt/ *n* пророк. prophetic /prə'fetɪk/ *adj* пророческий.

propitious /prə'pɪʃəs/ *adj* благоприятный.

proponent /prə'pəʊnənt/ *n* сторонник.

proportion /prə'pɔːʃ(ə)n/ *n* пропорция; (*due relation*) соразмерность; *pl* размеры *pl* pl пропорциональный. proportional /-n(ə)l/ *adj* пропорциональный. proportionate /-'pɔːʃən(ə)t/ *adj* соразмерный (to +dat; c+instr).

proposal /prə'pəʊz(ə)l/ *n* предложение. propose /prə'pəʊz/ *vt* предлагать *impf,* предложить *pf;* (*intend*) предполагать *impf;* *vi* (~ marriage) делать *impf,* c~ *pf* предложение (to +dat). proposition /,prɒpə'zɪʃ(ə)n/ *n* предложение.

propound /prə'paʊnd/ vt предлага́ть impf, предложи́ть pf на обсужде́ние.

proprietor /prə'praɪətə(r)/ n со́бственник, хозя́ин.

propriety /prə'praɪtɪ/ n прили́чие.

props /prɒps/ n pl (theat) реквизи́т.

propulsion /prə'pʌlʃ(ə)n/ n движе́ние вперёд.

prosaic /prə'zeɪɪk/ adj прозаи́ческий.

proscribe /prə'skraɪb/ vt (forbid) запреща́ть impf, запрети́ть pf.

prose /prəʊz/ n про́за.

prosecute /'prɒsɪkju:t/ vt пресле́довать impf. **prosecution** /-'kju:ʃ(ə)n/ n судебное пресле́дование; (prosecuting party) обвине́ние. **prosecutor** /'prɒsɪˌkju:tə(r)/ n обвини́тель m.

prospect n /'prɒspekt/ вид; (fig) перспекти́ва; vi /prə'spekt/ ~ **for** иска́ть impf. **prospective** /prə'spektɪv/ adj бу́дущий. **prospector** /prə'spektə(r)/ n разве́дчик. **prospectus** /prə'spektəs/ n проспе́кт.

prosper /'prɒspə(r)/ vi процвета́ть impf. **prosperity** /prɒ'sperɪtɪ/ n процвета́ние. **prosperous** /'prɒspərəs/ adj процвета́ющий; (wealthy) зажи́точный.

prostate (gland) /'prɒsteɪt (glænd)/ n проста́та.

prostitute /'prɒstɪˌtju:t/ n проститу́тка. **prostitution** /-'tju:ʃ(ə)n/ n проститу́ция.

prostrate /'prɒstreɪt/ adj распростёртый, (лежа́щий ничко́м; (exhausted) обесси́ленный; (with grief) уби́тый (with +instr).

protagonist /prə'tægənɪst/ n гла́вный геро́й; (in contest) протагони́ст.

protect /prə'tekt/ vt защища́ть impf, защити́ть pf. **protection** /-'tekʃ(ə)n/ n защи́та. **protective** /-'tektɪv/ adj защи́тный. **protector** /-'tektə(r)/ n защи́тник.

protégé(e) /'prɒtɪˌʒeɪ/ n протеже́ m & f indecl.

protein /'prəʊti:n/ n бело́к.

protest n /'prəʊtest/ проте́ст; vi /prə'test/ протестова́ть impf; vt (affirm) утвержда́ть impf.

Protestant /'prɒtɪst(ə)nt/ n протеста́нт, ~ка; adj протеста́нтский.

protestation /ˌprɒtɪ'steɪʃ(ə)n/ n (торже́ственное) заявле́ние (o+prep; что); (protest) проте́ст.

protocol /ˌprəʊtəˈkɒl/ n прото́кол.

proton /'prəʊtɒn/ n прото́н.

prototype /'prəʊtəˌtaɪp/ n прототи́п.

protract /prə'trækt/ vt тяну́ть impf. **protracted** /-'træktɪd/ adj дли́тельный.

protrude /prə'tru:d/ vi выдава́ться impf, вы́даться pf.

proud /praʊd/ adj го́рдый; be ~ **of** горди́ться impf +instr.

prove /pru:v/ vt дока́зывать impf, доказа́ть pf; vi ока́зываться impf, оказа́ться pf (to be +instr). **proven** /'pru:v(ə)n/ adj дока́занный.

provenance /'prɒvɪnəns/ n происхожде́ние.

proverb /'prɒvɜ:b/ n посло́вица. **proverbial** /prə'vɜ:bɪəl/ adj воше́дший в погово́рку; (well-known) общеизве́стный.

provide /prə'vaɪd/ vt (supply person) снабжа́ть impf, снабди́ть pf (with +instr); (supply thing)

предоставля́ть *impf*, предоста́вить *pf* (**to, for** +*dat*); дава́ть *impf*, дать *pf* (**to, for** +*dat*); *vi*: ~ **for** предусма́тривать *impf*, предусмотре́ть *pf* +*acc*; (~ **for family** *etc.*) содержа́ть *impf* +*acc*. **provided (that)** /-'vaidid/ *conj* при усло́вии, что; е́сли то́лько. **providence** /'prɒvid(ə)ns/ *n* провиде́ние; (*foresight*) предусмотри́тельность. **provident** /'prɒvid(ə)nt/ *adj* предусмотри́тельный. **providential** /-'denʃ(ə)l/ *adj* счастли́вый. **providing** /prə'vaidiŋ/ *see* **provided (that)**

province /'prɒvins/ *n* о́бласть; *pl* (*the* ~) прови́нция. **provincial** /prə'vinʃ(ə)l/ *adj* провинциа́льный.

provision /prə'viʒ(ə)n/ *n* снабже́ние; *pl* (*food*) прови́зия; (*in agreement* *etc.*) положе́ние; **make** ~ **against** принима́ть *impf*, приня́ть *pf* ме́ры про́тив+*gen*. **provisional** /-'viʒən(ə)l/ *adj* вре́менный. **proviso** /prə'vaizəʊ/ *n* усло́вие.

provocation /prɒvə'keiʃ(ə)n/ *n* провока́ция. **provocative** /prə'vɒkətiv/ *adj* провокацио́нный. **provoke** /prə'vəʊk/ *vt* провоци́ровать *impf*, c~ *pf*; (*call forth, cause*) вызыва́ть *impf*, вы́звать *pf*.

prow /praʊ/ *n* нос.

prowess /'praʊis/ *n* уме́ние.

prowl /praʊl/ *vi* ры́скать *impf*.

proximity /prɒk'simiti/ *n* бли́зость.

proxy /'prɒksi/ *n* полномо́чие; (*person*) уполномо́ченный *sb*, замести́тель *m*; **by** ~ по дове́ренности; **stand** ~ **for** быть *impf* замести́телем +*gen*.

prudence /'pru:d(ə)ns/ *n* благоразу́мие. **prudent** /-d(ə)nt/ *adj*

благоразу́мный.

prudery /'pru:dəri/ *n* притво́рная стыдли́вость. **prudish** /-diʃ/ *adj* ни в ме́ру стыдли́вый.

prune¹ /pru:n/ *n* (*plum*) черносли́в.

prune² /pru:n/ *vt* (*trim*) об-, под-, реза́ть *impf*, об-, под-, ре́зать *pf*.

pry /prai/ *vi* сова́ть *impf* нос (**into** в+*acc*).

PS *abbr* (*of* **postscript**) постскри́птум.

psalm /sɑ:m/ *n* псало́м.

pseudonym /'sju:dənim/ *n* псевдони́м.

psyche /'saiki/ *n* пси́хика. **psychiatric** /saiki'ætrik/ *adj* психиатри́ческий. **psychiatrist** /sai'kaiətrist/ *n* психиа́тр. **psychiatry** /sai'kaiətri/ *n* психиатри́я. **psychic** /'saikik/ *adj* яснови́дящий. **psychoanalysis** /saikəʊə'nælisis/ *n* психоана́лиз. **psychoanalyst** /saikəʊ'ænəlist/ *n* психоанали́тик. **psychoanalytic(al)** /saikəʊænə'litik(ə)l/ *adj* психоаналити́ческий. **psychological** /saikə'lɒdʒik(ə)l/ *adj* психологи́ческий. **psychologist** /sai'kɒlədʒist/ *n* психо́лог. **psychology** /sai'kɒlədʒi/ *n* психоло́гия. **psychopath** /'saikəpæθ/ *n* психопа́т. **psychopathic** /saikə'pæθik/ *adj* психопати́ческий. **psychosis** /sai'kəʊsis/ *n* психо́з. **psychotherapy** /saikəʊ'θerəpi/ *n* психотерапи́я.

PTO *abbr* (*of* **please turn over**) см. на об., смотри́ на оборо́те.

pub /pʌb/ *n* пивна́я *sb*.

puberty /'pju:bəti/ *n* полова́я зре́лость.

public /'pʌblik/ *adj* обще́ственный; (*open*) публи́чный, от-

кры́тый; ~ **school** ча́стная сре́дняя шко́ла; *n* пу́блика, обще́ственность; **in** ~ откры́то, публи́чно. **publication** /-ˈkeɪʃ(ə)n/ *n* изда́ние. **publicity** /-ˈlɪsɪtɪ/ *n* рекла́ма. **publicize** /ˈpʌblɪˌsaɪz/ *vt* реклами́ровать *impf* & *pf*. **publicly** /ˈpʌblɪklɪ/ *adv* публи́чно, откры́то. **publish** /ˈpʌblɪʃ/ *vt* публикова́ть *impf*, о~ *pf*; (*book*) издава́ть *impf*, изда́ть *pf*. **publisher** /ˈpʌblɪʃə(r)/ *n* изда́тель *m*. **publishing** /ˈpʌblɪʃɪŋ/ *n* (*business*) изда́тельское де́ло; ~ **house** изда́тельство.

pucker /ˈpʌkə(r)/ *vt & i* мо́рщить(ся) *impf*, с~ *pf*.

pudding /ˈpʊdɪŋ/ *n* пу́динг, *n* пека́нка. (*dessert*) сла́дкое *sb*.

puddle /ˈpʌd(ə)l/ *n* лу́жа.

puff /pʌf/ *n* (*of wind*) поры́в; (*of smoke*) дымо́к; ~ **pastry** слоёное те́сто; *vi* пыхте́ть *impf*; ~ **at** (*pipe etc.*) попы́хивать *impf* +*instr*, *vt*; ~ **up**, **out** (*inflate*) надува́ть *impf*, наду́ть *pf*.

pugnacious /pʌgˈneɪʃəs/ *adj* драчли́вый.

puke /pjuːk/ *vi* рвать *impf*, вы́~ *pf impers*+*acc*.

pull /pʊl/ *n* тя́га; *vt* тяну́ть *impf*, по~ *pf*; таска́ть *indet*, тащи́ть *det*, по~ *pf*; (*a muscle*) растя́гивать *impf*, растяну́ть *pf*; *vt & i* дёргать *impf*, дёрнуть *pf* (**at** (за)+*acc*); ~ **s.o.'s leg** разы́грывать *impf*, разыгра́ть *pf*; ~ **the trigger** спуска́ть *impf*, спусти́ть *pf* куро́к; ~ **apart**, **to pieces** разрыва́ть *impf*, разорва́ть *pf*; (*fig*) раскритикова́ть *pf*; ~ **down** (*demolish*) сноси́ть *impf*, снести́ *pf*; ~ **in** (*of train*) прибыва́ть *impf*, прибы́ть *pf*; (*of vehicle*) подъезжа́ть *impf*, подъ-

е́хать *pf* к обо́чине (доро́ги); ~ **off** (*garment*) стя́гивать *impf*, стяну́ть *pf*; (*achieve*) успе́шно заверша́ть *impf*, заверши́ть *pf*; ~ **on** (*garment*) натя́гивать *impf*, натяну́ть *pf*; ~ **out** (*vt*) (*remove*) выта́скивать *impf*, вы́тащить *pf*; (*vi*) (*withdraw*) отка́зываться *impf*, отказа́ться *pf* от уча́стия (**of** в+*prep*); (*of vehicle*) отъезжа́ть *impf*, отъе́хать *pf* от обо́чины (доро́ги); (*of train*) отходи́ть *impf*, отойти́ *pf* (от ста́нции); ~ **through** выжива́ть *impf*, вы́жить *pf*; ~ **o.s. together** брать *impf*, взять *pf* себя́ в ру́ки; ~ **up** (*vt*) подтя́гивать *impf*, подтяну́ть *pf*; (*vt & i*) (*stop*) остана́вливать(ся) *impf*, останови́ть(ся) *pf*; *n* тя́га; (*fig*) блат.

pulley /ˈpʊlɪ/ *n* блок.

pullover /ˈpʊləʊvə(r)/ *n* пуло́вер.

pulp /pʌlp/ *n* пу́льпа.

pulpit /ˈpʊlpɪt/ *n* ка́федра.

pulsate /pʌlˈseɪt/ *vi* пульси́ровать *impf*. **pulse** /pʌls/ *n* пульс.

pulses /ˈpʌlsɪz/ *n pl* (*food*) бобо́вые *sb*.

pulverize /ˈpʌlvəˌraɪz/ *vt* размельча́ть *impf*, размельчи́ть *pf*.

pummel /ˈpʌm(ə)l/ *vt* колоти́ть *impf*, по~ *pf*.

pump /pʌmp/ *n* насо́с; *vt* кача́ть *impf*; ~ **in(to)** вка́чивать *impf*, вкача́ть *pf*; ~ **out** выка́чивать *impf*, вы́качать *pf*; ~ **up** нака́чивать *impf*, накача́ть *pf*.

pumpkin /ˈpʌmpkɪn/ *n* ты́ква.

pun /pʌn/ *n* каламбу́р.

punch¹ /pʌntʃ/ *vt* (*with fist*) ударя́ть *impf*, уда́рить *pf* кулако́м; (*hole*) пробива́ть *impf*,

пробить *pf*; (*a ticket*) компости́ровать *impf*, про~ *pf*; ~**up** дра́ка; *n* (*blow*) уда́р кулако́м; (*for tickets*) компо́стер; (*for piercing*) перфора́тор.

punch² /pʌntʃ/ *n* (*drink*) пунш.

punctilious /pʌŋkˈtɪlɪəs/ *adj* щепети́льный.

punctual /ˈpʌŋktjʊəl/ *adj* пунктуа́льный. **punctuality** /ˌpʌŋktjʊˈælɪtɪ/ *n* пунктуа́льность.

punctuate /ˈpʌŋktjʊˌeɪt/ *vt* ста́вить *impf*, по~ *pf* зна́ки препина́ния в+*acc*; (*fig*) прерыва́ть *impf*, прерва́ть *pf*. **punctuation** /-ˈeɪʃ(ə)n/ *n* пунктуа́ция; ~ **marks** зна́ки *m pl* препина́ния.

puncture /ˈpʌŋktʃə(r)/ *n* проко́л; *vt* прока́лывать *impf*, проколо́ть *pf*.

pundit /ˈpʌndɪt/ *n* (*fig*) знато́к.

pungent /ˈpʌndʒ(ə)nt/ *adj* е́дкий.

punish /ˈpʌnɪʃ/ *vt* нака́зывать *impf*, наказа́ть *pf*. **punishable** /-ʃəb(ə)l/ *adj* наказу́емый. **punishment** /-mənt/ *n* наказа́ние. **punitive** /ˈpjuːnɪtɪv/ *adj* кара́тельный.

punter /ˈpʌntə(r)/ *n* (*gambler*) игро́к; (*client*) клие́нт.

puny /ˈpjuːnɪ/ *adj* хи́лый.

pupil /ˈpjuːpɪl/ *n* учени́к, -и́ца; (*of eye*) зрачо́к.

puppet /ˈpʌpɪt/ *n* марионе́тка, ку́кла.

puppy /ˈpʌpɪ/ *n* щено́к.

purchase /ˈpɜːtʃɪs/ *n* поку́пка; (*leverage*) то́чка опо́ры; *vt* покупа́ть *impf*, купи́ть *pf*. **purchaser** /-sə(r)/ *n* покупа́тель *m*.

pure /pjʊə(r)/ *adj* чи́стый.

purée /ˈpjʊəreɪ/ *n* пюре́ *neut indecl*.

purely /ˈpjʊəlɪ/ *adv* чи́сто.

purgatory /ˈpɜːgətərɪ/ *n* чисти́лище; (*fig*) му́ка. **purge** /pɜːdʒ/ *vt* очища́ть *impf*, очи́стить *pf*; *n* очище́ние; (*polit*) чи́стка.

purification /ˌpjʊərɪfɪˈkeɪʃ(ə)n/ *n* очи́стка. **purify** /ˈpjʊərɪˌfaɪ/ *vt* очища́ть *impf*, очи́стить *pf*.

purist /ˈpjʊərɪst/ *n* пури́ст.

puritan, P, /ˈpjʊərɪt(ə)n/ *n* пурита́нин, -а́нка. **puritanical** /-ˈtænɪk(ə)l/ *adj* пурита́нский.

purity /ˈpjʊərɪtɪ/ *n* чистота́.

purple /ˈpɜːp(ə)l/ *adj* (*n*) пу́рпурный, фиоле́товый (цвет).

purport /pəˈpɔːt/ *vt* претендова́ть *impf*.

purpose /ˈpɜːpəs/ *n* цель, наме́рение; **on** ~ наро́чно; **to no** ~ напра́сно. **purposeful** /-fʊl/ *adj* целеустремлённый. **purposeless** /-lɪs/ *adj* бесце́льный. **purposely** /-lɪ/ *adv* наро́чно.

purr /pɜː(r)/ *vi* мурлы́кать *impf*.

purse /pɜːs/ *n* кошелёк; *vt* поджима́ть *impf*, поджа́ть *pf*.

pursue /pəˈsjuː/ *vt* пресле́довать *impf*. **pursuit** /-ˈsjuːt/ *n* пресле́дование; (*pastime*) заня́тие.

purveyor /pəˈveɪə(r)/ *n* поста́вщик.

pus /pʌs/ *n* гной.

push /pʊʃ/ *vt* толка́ть *impf*, толкну́ть *pf*; (*press*) нажима́ть *impf*, нажа́ть *pf*; (*urge*) подта́лкивать *impf*, подтолкну́ть *pf*; *vi* толка́ться *impf*; **be** ~**ed for** име́ть *impf* ма́ло+*gen*; **he is** ~**ing fifty** ему́ ско́ро сту́кнет пятьдеся́т; ~ **one's way** прота́лкиваться *impf*, протолкну́ться *pf*; ~ **around** (*person*) помыка́ть *impf* +*instr*; ~ **aside** (*also fig*) отстраня́ть *impf*, отстрани́ть *pf*; ~ **away** отта́лкивать *impf*, оттолкну́ть *pf*; ~ **off** (*vi*) (*in boat*) отта́лкиваться *impf*, оттолкну́ться *pf* (от бе-

рега); (*go away*) убира́ться *impf*, убра́ться *pf*; ~ **on** (*vi*) продолжа́ть *impf* путь; *n* толчо́к; (*energy*) эне́ргия. **push-chair** *n* коля́ска. **pusher** /-ʃə(r)/ *n* (*drugs*) продаве́ц нарко́тиков. **pushy** /-ʃɪ/ *adj* напо́ристый.

puss, pussy(-cat) /pʊs, 'pʊsɪ(kæt)/ *n* ки́ска.

put /pʊt/ *vt* класть *impf*, положи́ть *pf*; (*upright*) ста́вить *impf*, по~ *pf*; (*into specified state*) приводи́ть *impf*, привести́ *pf*; (*express*) выража́ть *impf*, вы́разить *pf*; (*a question*) задава́ть *impf*, зада́ть *pf*; ~ **an end, a stop, to** класть *impf*, положи́ть *pf* коне́ц +*dat*; ~ **o.s. in another's place** ста́вить *impf*, по~ *pf* себя́ на ме́сто +*gen*; ~ **about** (*rumour etc.*) распространя́ть *impf*, распространи́ть *pf*; ~ **away** (*tidy*) убира́ть *impf*, убра́ть *pf*; (*save*) откла́дывать *impf*, отложи́ть *pf*; ~ **back** (*in place*) ста́вить *impf*, по~ *pf* на ме́сто; (*clock*) переводи́ть *impf*, перевести́ *pf* наза́д; ~ **by** (*money*) откла́дывать *impf*, отложи́ть *pf*; ~ **down** класть *impf*, положи́ть *pf*; (*suppress*) подавля́ть *impf*, подави́ть *pf*; (*write down*) запи́сывать *impf*, записа́ть *pf*; (*passengers*) выса́живать *impf*, вы́садить *pf*; (*attribute*) припи́сывать *impf*, приписа́ть *pf* (**to** +*dat*); ~ **forward** (*proposal*) предлага́ть *impf*, предложи́ть *pf*; (*clock*) переводи́ть *impf*, перевести́ *pf* вперёд; ~ **in** (*install*) устана́вливать *impf*, установи́ть *pf*; (*a claim*) предъявля́ть *impf*, предъяви́ть *pf*; (*interpose*) вставля́ть *impf*, вста́вить *pf*; ~ **in an appearance** появля́ться *impf*, появи́ться *pf*; ~ **off** (*postpone*) откла́дывать *impf*, отложи́ть *pf*; (*repel*) отта́лкивать *impf*, оттолкну́ть *pf*; (*dissuade*) отгова́ривать *impf*, отговори́ть *pf* от+*gen*, +*inf*; ~ **on** (*clothes*) надева́ть *impf*, наде́ть *pf*; (*kettle, a record, a play*) ста́вить *impf*, по~ *pf*; (*turn on*) включа́ть *impf*, включи́ть *pf*; (*add to*) прибавля́ть *impf*, приба́вить *pf*; ~ **on airs** ва́жничать *impf*; ~ **on weight** толсте́ть *impf*, по~ *pf*; ~ **out** (*vex*) обижа́ть *impf*, оби́деть *pf*; (*inconvenience*) затрудня́ть *impf*, затрудни́ть *pf*; (*a fire etc.*) туши́ть *impf*, по~ *pf*; ~ **through** (*tel*) соединя́ть *impf*, соедини́ть *pf* по телефо́ну; ~ **up** (*building*) стро́ить *impf*, по~ *pf*; (*hang up*) ве́шать *impf*, пове́сить *pf*; (*price*) повыша́ть *impf*, повы́сить *pf*; (*a guest*) дава́ть *impf*, дать *pf* ночле́г +*dat*; (*as guest*) ночева́ть *impf*, пере~ *pf*; ~ **up to** (*instigate*) подбива́ть *impf*, подби́ть *pf* на+*acc*; ~ **up with** терпе́ть *impf*.

putative /'pjuːtətɪv/ *adj* предполага́емый.

putrefy /'pjuːtrɪˌfaɪ/ *vi* гнить *impf*, с~ *pf*. **putrid** /'pjuːtrɪd/ *adj* гнило́й.

putty /'pʌtɪ/ *n* зама́зка.

puzzle /'pʌz(ə)l/ *n* (*enigma*) зага́дка; (*toy etc.*) головоло́мка; (*jigsaw*) моза́йка; *vt* озада́чивать *impf*, озада́чить *pf*; ~ **out** разга́дывать *impf*, разгада́ть *pf*; *vi*: ~ **over** лома́ть *impf* го́лову над+*instr*.

pygmy /'pɪɡmɪ/ *n* пигме́й.

pyjamas /pɪ'dʒɑːməz/ *n pl* пижа́ма.

pylon /'paɪlən/ *n* пило́н.

pyramid /'pɪrəmɪd/ *n* пирами́да.

pyre /'paɪə(r)/ n погреба́льный костёр.

python /'paɪθ(ə)n/ n питóн.

Q

quack¹ /kwæk/ n (sound) кря́канье; vi кря́кать impf, кря́кнуть pf.

quack² /kwæk/ n шарлата́н.

quad /kwɒd/ n (court) четырёхуго́льный двор; pl (quadruplets) четверо близнецо́в. **quadrangle** /'kwɒd,ræŋg(ə)l/ n (figure) четырёхуго́льник; (court) четырёхуго́льный двор. **quadrant** /'kwɒdrənt/ n квадра́нт. **quadruped** /'kwɒdrʊ,ped/ n четвероно́гое живо́тное sb. **quadruple** /'kwɒdrup(ə)l/ adj четверно́й; vt & i учетверя́ть(ся) impf, учетвери́ть(ся) pf. **quadruplets** /'kwɒdruplɪts/ n pl че́тверо близнецо́в.

quagmire /'kwɒg,maɪə(r)/ n боло́то.

quail /kweɪl/ n (bird) пе́репел.

quaint /kweɪnt/ adj причу́дливый.

quake /kweɪk/ vi дрожа́ть impf (with от+gen).

Quaker /'kweɪkə(r)/ n ква́кер, ~ка.

qualification /,kwɒlɪfɪ'keɪʃ(ə)n/ n (for post etc.) квалифика́ция; (reservation) огово́рка. **qualified** /'kwɒlɪ,faɪd/ adj компете́нтный; (limited) ограни́ченный. **qualify** /'kwɒlɪ,faɪ/ vt & i (prepare for post) гото́вить(ся) impf (for к+dat; +inf); vt (render fit) де́лать impf, с~ pf пригодным; (entitle) дава́ть impf, дать pf пра́во +dat (to на+acc); (limit): ~ what one says сде́лать

pf огово́рку; vi получа́ть impf, получи́ть pf дипло́м; ~ for (be entitled to) име́ть impf пра́во на+acc.

qualitative /'kwɒlɪtətɪv/ adj ка́чественный. **quality** /'kwɒlɪtɪ/ n ка́чество.

qualm /kwɑːm/ n сомне́ние; (of conscience) угрызе́ние со́вести.

quandary /'kwɒndərɪ/ n затрудни́тельное положе́ние.

quantify /'kwɒntɪ,faɪ/ vt определя́ть impf, определи́ть pf коли́чество +gen. **quantitative** /'kwɒntɪtətɪv/ adj коли́чественный. **quantity** /'kwɒntɪtɪ/ n коли́чество.

quarantine /'kwɒrən,tiːn/ n каранти́н.

quarrel /'kwɒr(ə)l/ n ссо́ра; vi ссо́риться impf, по~ pf (with с+instr; about, for из-за+gen). **quarrelsome** /-səm/ adj вздо́рный.

quarry¹ /'kwɒrɪ/ n (for stone etc.) каменоло́мня; vt добыва́ть impf, добы́ть pf.

quarry² /'kwɒrɪ/ n (prey) добы́ча.

quart /kwɔːt/ n ква́рта. **quarter** /'kwɔːtə(r)/ n че́тверть; (of year; of town) кварта́л; pl кварти́ра f pl; a ~ to one без че́тверти час; ~final четверть-фина́л; vt (divide) дели́ть impf, раз~ pf на четы́ре ча́сти; (lodge) расквартиро́вывать impf, расквартирова́ть pf. **quarterly** /'kwɔːtəlɪ/ adj кварта́льный; adv раз в кварта́л. **quartet** /kwɔː'tet/ n кварте́т.

quartz /kwɔːts/ n кварц.

quash /kwɒʃ/ vt (annul) аннули́ровать impf & pf; (crush) подавля́ть impf, подави́ть pf.

quasi- /'kweɪzaɪ/ in comb

квази-.

quaver /'kweɪvə(r)/ vi дрожа́ть impf; n (mus) восьма́я sb но́ты.

quay /kiː/ n на́бережная sb.

queasy /'kwiːzɪ/ adj: **I feel** ~ меня́ тошни́т.

queen /kwiːn/ n короле́ва; (cards) да́ма; (chess) ферзь m.

queer /kwɪə(r)/ adj стра́нный.

quell /kwel/ vt подавля́ть impf, подави́ть pf.

quench /kwentʃ/ vt (thirst) утоля́ть impf, утоли́ть pf; (fire, desire) туши́ть impf, по~ pf.

query /'kwɪərɪ/ n вопро́с; vi (express doubt) выража́ть impf вы́разить pf сомне́ние в+prep.

quest /kwest/ n по́иски m pl; ~ of в по́исках+gen. **question** /'kwestʃ(ə)n/ n вопро́с; beyond ~ вне сомне́ния; it is a ~ of э́то вопро́с+gen; it is out of the ~ об э́том не мо́жет быть и ре́чи; the person in ~ челове́к, о кото́ром идёт речь; the ~ is this де́ло в э́том; ~ mark вопроси́тельный знак; vt расспра́шивать impf, распроси́ть pf; (interrogate) допра́шивать impf допроси́ть pf; (doubt) сомнева́ться impf в+prep. **questionable** /'kwestʃənəb(ə)l/ adj сомни́тельный. **questionnaire** /ˌkwestʃə'neə(r)/ n вопро́сник.

queue /kjuː/ n о́чередь f; vi стоя́ть impf в о́череди.

quibble /'kwɪb(ə)l/ n софи́зм; (minor criticism) прида́рка; vi придира́ться impf, (argue) спо́рить impf.

quick /kwɪk/ adj ско́рый, бы́стрый; ~-tempered вспы́льчивый; ~-witted находчивый; to the ~ за живо́е; adv ско́ро, бы́стро; as imper скоре́е! **quicken** /'kwɪkən/ vt & i уско-

ря́ть(ся) impf, уско́рить(ся) pf.
quickness /'kwɪknɪs/ n бы-стро́та. **quicksand** n зыбу́чий песо́к. **quicksilver** n ртуть.

quid /kwɪd/ n фунт.

quiet /'kwaɪət/ n (silence) тишина́; (calm) споко́йствие; adj ти́хий; споко́йный; int ти́ше!; vt & i успока́ивать(ся) impf, успоко́ить(ся) pf.

quill /kwɪl/ n перо́; (spine) игла́.

quilt /kwɪlt/ n (стёганое) одея́ло; vt стега́ть impf, вы́~ pf. **quilted** /'kwɪltɪd/ adj стёганый.

quintessential /ˌkwɪntɪ'sensʃ(ə)l/ adj наибо́лее суще́ственный.

quintet /kwɪn'tet/ n квинте́т. **quins**, **quintuplets** /kwɪnz, 'kwɪntjʊplɪts/ n pl пять близне́цов.

quip /kwɪp/ n острота́; vi остри́ть impf, с~ pf.

quirk /kwɜːk/ n причу́да. **quirky** /-kɪ/ adj с причу́дами.

quit /kwɪt/ vt (leave) покида́ть impf, поки́нуть pf; (stop) переставáть impf, переста́ть pf; (give up) броса́ть impf, бро́сить pf; (resign) уходи́ть impf, уйти́ pf с+gen.

quite /kwaɪt/ adv (wholly) совсе́м; (rather) дово́льно; ~ a few дово́льно мно́го.

quits /kwɪts/ predic: we are ~ мы с тобо́й кви́ты; I am ~ with him я раскви́та́лся (past) с ним.

quiver /'kwɪvə(r)/ vi (tremble) трепета́ть impf; n тре́пет.

quiz /kwɪz/ n викторина. **quizzical** /'kwɪzɪk(ə)l/ adj насме́шливый.

quorum /'kwɔːrəm/ n кво́рум.

quota /'kwəʊtə/ n но́рма.

quotation /kwəʊ'teɪʃ(ə)n/ n цита́та; (of price) цена́; ~ marks кавы́чки (-чек) pl. **quote**

/kwəʊt/ *vt* цити́ровать *impf*, про~ *pf*; ссыла́ться *impf*, сосла́ться *pf* на+*acc*; (*price*) назнача́ть *impf*, назна́чить *pf*.

R

rabbi /'ræbaɪ/ *n* равви́н.
rabbit /'ræbɪt/ *n* кро́лик.
rabble /'ræb(ə)l/ *n* сброд.
rabid /'ræbɪd/ *adj* бе́шеный. **rabies** /'reɪbiːz/ *n* бе́шенство.
race¹ /reɪs/ *n* (*ethnic* ~) ра́са; род.
race² /reɪs/ *n* (*contest*) (*on foot*) бег; (*of cars etc.*; *fig*) го́нка, го́нки *f pl*; (*of horses*) ска́чки *pl*; ~**track** трек; (*for horse* ~) скакова́я доро́жка; *vi* (*compete*) состяза́ться *impf* в ско́рости; (*rush*) мча́ться *impf*; *vt* бежа́ть *impf* наперегонки́ с+*instr*. **racecourse** *n* ипподро́м. **racehorse** *n* скакова́я ло́шадь.
racial /'reɪʃ(ə)l/ *adj* ра́совый.
rac(ial)ism /'reɪʃəˌlɪz(ə)m, 'reɪsɪz(ə)m/ *n* раси́зм. **rac(ial)ist** /'reɪʃəlɪst, 'reɪsɪst/ *n* раси́ст, ~ка; *adj* раси́стский.
racing /'reɪsɪŋ/ *n* (*horses*) ска́чки *f pl*; (*cars*) го́нки *f pl*; ~ **car** го́ночный автомоби́ль *m*; ~ **driver** го́нщик.
rack /ræk/ *n* (*for hats etc.*) ве́шалка; (*for plates etc.*) стелла́ж; (*in train etc.*) се́тка; *vt*: ~ **one's brains** лома́ть *impf* себе́ го́лову.
racket¹ /'rækɪt/ *n* (*bat*) раке́тка.
racket² /'rækɪt/ *n* (*uproar*) шум; (*illegal activity*) рэ́кет. **racketeer** /ˌrækɪ'tɪə(r)/ *n* рэкети́р.
racy /'reɪsɪ/ *adj* колори́тный.
radar /'reɪdɑː(r)/ *n* (*system*) радиолока́ция; (*apparatus*) диолока́тор, рада́р; *attrib* рада́рный.
radiance /'reɪdɪəns/ *n* сия́ние. **radiant** /-dɪənt/ *adj* сия́ющий. **radiate** /-dɪˌeɪt/ *vt* & *i* излуча́ть(ся) *impf*, излучи́ться *pf*. **radiation** /-dɪ'eɪʃ(ə)n/ *n* излуче́ние. **radiator** /'reɪdɪˌeɪtə(r)/ *n* батаре́я; (*in car*) радиа́тор.
radical /'rædɪk(ə)l/ *adj* радика́льный; *n* радика́л.
radio /'reɪdɪəʊ/ *n* ра́дио *neut indecl*; (*set*) радиоприёмник; *vt* ради́ровать *impf* & *pf* +*dat*.
radioactive /ˌreɪdɪəʊ'æktɪv/ *adj* радиоакти́вный. **radioactivity** /-æk'tɪvɪtɪ/ *n* радиоакти́вность.
radiologist /ˌreɪdɪ'ɒlədʒɪst/ *n* радио́лог; рентгено́лог. **radiotherapy** /ˌreɪdɪəʊ'θerəpɪ/ *n* радиотерапи́я.
radish /'rædɪʃ/ *n* реди́ска.
radius /'reɪdɪəs/ *n* ра́диус.
raffle /'ræf(ə)l/ *n* лотере́я; *vt* разы́грывать *impf*, разыгра́ть *pf* в лотере́е.
raft /rɑːft/ *n* плот.
rafter /'rɑːftə(r)/ *n* (*beam*) стропи́ло.
rag /ræg/ *n* тря́пка; *pl* (*clothes*) лохмо́тья (-ьев) *pl*.
rage /reɪdʒ/ *n* я́рость; **all the** ~ после́дний крик мо́ды; *vi* беси́ться *impf*; (*storm etc.*) бушева́ть *impf*.
ragged /'rægɪd/ *adj* (*jagged*) зазу́бренный; (*of clothes*) рва́ный.
raid /reɪd/ *n* налёт; (*by police*) обла́ва; *vt* де́лать *impf*, с~ *pf* налёт на+*acc*.
rail /reɪl/ *n* пери́ла (-л) *pl*; (*rly*) рельс; **by** ~ по́ездом. **railing** /'reɪlɪŋ/ *n* пери́ла (-л) *pl*.
railway /'reɪlweɪ/ *n* желе́зная доро́га; *attrib* железнодоро́жный. **railwayman**

железнодоро́жник.

rain /rein/ n дождь m; v impers: **it is (was)** ~**ing** идёт (шёл) дождь; vt оси́пать impf, оси́пать pf +instr (**upon** +acc); vi оси́паться impf, оси́паться pf. **rainbow** n ра́дуга. **raincoat** n плащ. **raindrop** n дождева́я ка́пля. **rainfall** n (amount of rain) коли́чество оса́дков. **rainy** /'reini/ adj дождли́вый; ~**day** чёрный день m.

raise /reiz/ vt (lift) поднима́ть impf, подня́ть pf; (heighten) повы́шать impf, повы́сить pf; (provoke) вызыва́ть impf, вы́звать pf; (money) собира́ть impf, собра́ть pf; (children) расти́ть impf.

raisin /'reiz(ə)n/ n изю́минка n (collect) изю́м.

rake /reik/ n (tool) гра́бли (-бель & -блей) pl; vt греба́ть impf, (~ together, up) сгреба́ть impf, сгрести́ pf.

rally /'ræli/ vt & i спла́чивать(ся) impf, сплоти́ть(ся) pf; vi (after illness etc.) оправля́ться impf, опра́виться pf; n (meeting) слёт; (motoring ~) (а́вто)ра́лли neut indecl; (tennis) обме́н уда́рами.

ram /ræm/ n (sheep) бара́н; vt (beat down) трамбова́ть impf, y~ pf; (drive in) вбива́ть impf, вбить pf.

ramble /'ræmb(ə)l/ vi (walk) гуля́ться impf, прогуля́ться pf; (speak) бубни́ть impf; n прогу́лка. **rambling** /'ræmbliŋ/ adj (incoherent) бессвя́зный.

ramification /ˌræmɪfɪ'keɪʃ(ə)n/ n (fig) после́дствие.

ramp /ræmp/ n скат.

rampage /'ræmpeidʒ/ vi бу́йствовать impf.

rampant /'ræmpənt/ adj (plant)

бу́йный; (unchecked) безуде́ржный.

rampart /'ræmpɑːt/ n вал.

ramshackle /'ræmˌʃæk(ə)l/ adj ве́тхий.

ranch /rɑːntʃ/ n ра́нчо neut indecl.

rancid /'rænsɪd/ adj прого́рклый.

rancour /'ræŋkə(r)/ n зло́ба.

random /'rændəm/ adj случа́йный; **at** ~ науда́чу.

range /reɪndʒ/ n (of mountains) цепь; (artillery ~) полиго́н; (of voice) диапазо́н; (scope) круг, преде́лы m pl; (operating distance) да́льность; vi (vary) колеба́ться impf, impf; (wander) броди́ть impf; ~ **over** (include) охва́тывать impf, охвати́ть pf.

rank¹ /ræŋk/ n (row) ряд; (taxi ~) стоя́нка такси́; (grade) зва́ние, чин, ранг; vt (classify) классифици́ровать impf & pf; (consider) счита́ть impf (**as** +instr); vi: ~ **with** быть в числе́+gen.

rank² /ræŋk/ adj (luxuriant) бу́йный; (in smell) злово́нный; (gross) я́вный.

rankle /'ræŋk(ə)l/ vi боле́ть impf.

ransack /'rænsæk/ vt (search) обы́скивать impf, обша́рить pf; (plunder) гра́бить impf, o~ pf.

ransom /'rænsəm/ n вы́куп; vt выкупа́ть impf, вы́купить pf.

rant /rænt/ vi вопи́ть impf.

rap /ræp/ n стук; vt (rёзко) ударя́ть impf, уда́рить pf; vi стуча́ть impf, impf.

rape¹ /reɪp/ vt наси́ловать impf, из~ pf; n изнаси́лование.

rape² /reɪp/ n (plant) рапс.

rapid /'ræpɪd/ adj бы́стрый; n: поро́г, быстрина́. **rapidity**

/rə'pɪdɪtɪ/ n быстротá.

rapt /ræpt/ adj восхищённый; (absorbed) поглощённый. **rapture** /'ræptʃə(r)/ n востóрг. **rapturous** /'ræptʃərəs/ adj востóрженный.

rare[1] /reə(r)/ adj (of meat) недожáренный.

rare[2] /reə(r)/ adj рéдкий. **rarity** /'reərɪtɪ/ n рéдкость.

rascal /'rɑ:sk(ə)l/ n плут.

rash[1] /ræʃ/ n сыпь.

rash[2] /ræʃ/ adj опромéтчивый.

rasher /'ræʃə(r)/ n лóмтик (бекóна).

rasp /rɑ:sp/ n (file) рáшпиль m; (sound) скрéжет; vt: ~ **out** гáркнуть pf.

raspberry /'rɑ:zbərɪ/ n малина (no pl; usu collect).

rasping /'rɑ:spɪŋ/ adj (sound) скрипýчий.

rat /ræt/ n крыса; ~ **race** гóнка за успéхом.

ratchet /'rætʃɪt/ n храповик.

rate /reɪt/ n нóрма, стáвка; (speed) скóрость; pl мéстные налóги m pl; **at any** ~ во всяком слýчае; vt оцéнивать impf, оценить pf; (consider) считáть impf; vi считáться impf (**as** +instr).

rather /'rɑ:ðə(r)/ adv скорée; (somewhat) довóльно; **he (she) had (would)** ~ он (онá) предпочёл (-члá) бы+inf.

ratification /,rætɪfɪ'keɪʃ(ə)n/ n ратификáция. **ratify** /'rætɪfaɪ/ vt ратифицировать impf & pf.

rating /'reɪtɪŋ/ n оцéнка.

ratio /'reɪʃɪəʊ/ n пропóрция.

ration /'ræʃ(ə)n/ n паёк, рациóн; vt нормировать impf & pf; ~**ed** выдавáться impf, выдаться pf по кáрточкам.

rational /'ræʃ(ə)n(ə)l/ adj разýмный. **rationalism** /-,lɪz(ə)m/ n

рационализм. **rationality** /,ræʃə'nælɪtɪ/ n разýмность. **rationalize** /'ræʃənə,laɪz/ vt обосновывать impf, обосновать pf; (industry etc.) рационализировать impf & pf.

rattle /'ræt(ə)l/ vi & t (sound) гремéть impf (+instr); ~ **along** (move) грохотáть impf; ~ **off** (utter) отбарабáнить pf; n (sound) треск, грóхот; (toy) погремýшка. **rattlesnake** n гремýчая змея.

raucous /'rɔ:kəs/ adj рéзкий.

ravage /'rævɪdʒ/ vt опустошáть impf, опустошить pf; pl pl разрушительное дéйствие.

rave /reɪv/ vi брéдить impf; ~ **about** быть в востóрге от+gen.

raven /'reɪv(ə)n/ n вóрон.

ravenous /'rævənəs/ adj голóдный как волк.

ravine /rə'vi:n/ n ущéлье.

ravishing /'rævɪʃɪŋ/ adj восхитительный.

raw /rɔ:/ adj сырóй; (inexperienced) нéопытный; ~ **material(s)** сырьё (no pl).

ray /reɪ/ n луч.

raze /reɪz/ vt: ~ **to the ground** ровнять impf, c~ pf с землёй.

razor /'reɪzə(r)/ n бритва; ~**blade** лéзвие.

reach /ri:tʃ/ vt (attain, extend to, arrive at) достигáть impf, достичь & достигнуть pf +gen, до+gen; доходить impf, дойти pf до+gen; (with hand) дотягиваться impf, дотянýться pf до+gen; vi (extend) простирáться impf, n досягáемость; (pl, of river) течéние.

react /rɪ'ækt/ vi реагировать impf, от~, про~ pf (**to** на+acc). **reaction** /-'ækʃ(ə)n/ n реáкция. **reactionary**

/-'æk∫ənəri/ *adj* реакцио́нный; *n* реакционе́р. **reactor** /-'æktə(r)/ *n* реа́ктор.

read /ri:d/ *vt* чита́ть *impf*, прочесть *pf*; (*mus*) разбира́ть *impf*, разобра́ть *pf*; (~ a letter etc.) снима́ть, снять *pf* показа́ния +*gen*; (*univ*) изуча́ть *impf*; (*interpret*) толкова́ть *impf*. **readable** /'ri:dəb(ə)l/ *adj* интере́сный. **reader** /'ri:də(r)/ *n* чита́тель *m*, ~ница; (*book*) хрестома́тия.

readily /'redɪlɪ/ *adv* (*willingly*) охо́тно; (*easily*) легко́. **readiness** /'redɪnɪs/ *n* гото́вность.

reading /'ri:dɪŋ/ *n* чте́ние; (*on meter*) показа́ние.

ready /'redɪ/ *adj* гото́вый (**for** к+*dat*, **на**+*acc*); **get** ~ гото́виться *impf*; ~**-made** гото́вый; ~ **money** нали́чные де́ньги (-нег, -ньга́м) *pl*.

real /rɪəl/ *adj* настоя́щий, реа́льный; ~ **estate** недви́жимость. **realism** /-,lɪz(ə)m/ *n* реали́зм. **realist** /'rɪəlɪst/ *n* реали́ст. **realistic** /,rɪə'lɪstɪk/ *adj* реалисти́чный, -и́ческий. **reality** /rɪ'ælɪtɪ/ *n* действи́тельность; **in** ~ в действи́тельности. **realization** /,rɪəlaɪ'zeɪ∫(ə)n/ *n* (*of plan etc.*) реализа́ция; (*understanding*) осозна́ние. **realize** /'rɪəlaɪz/ *vt* (*plan etc.*) осуществля́ть *impf*, осуществи́ть *pf*; (*assets*) реализова́ть *impf* & *pf*; (*apprehend*) осознава́ть *impf*, осозна́ть *pf*. **really** /'rɪəlɪ/ *adv* действи́тельно, в са́мом де́ле.

realm /relm/ *n* (*kingdom*) короле́вство; (*sphere*) о́бласть.

reap /ri:p/ *vt* жать *impf*, сжать *pf*; (*fig*) пожина́ть *impf*, пожа́ть *pf*.

rear¹ /rɪə(r)/ *vt* поднима́ть

impf, подня́ть *pf*; (*children*) воспи́тывать *impf*, воспита́ть *pf*; *vi* (*of horse*) станови́ться *impf*, стать *pf* на дыбы́.

rear² /rɪə(r)/ *n* за́дняя часть; (*mil*) тыл; **bring up the** ~ замыка́ть *impf*, замкну́ть *pf* ше́ствие; *adj* за́дний; (*also mil*) тыльный. **rearguard** *n* арьерга́рд; ~ **action** арьерга́рдный бой.

rearmament /ri:'ɑ:məmənt/ *n* перевооруже́ние.

rearrange /,ri:ə'reɪndʒ/ *vt* меня́ть *impf*.

reason /'ri:z(ə)n/ *n* (*cause*) причи́на, основа́ние; (*intellect*) ра́зум, рассу́док; *vi* рассужда́ть *impf*; ~ **with** (*person*) угова́ривать *impf* +*acc*. **reasonable** /-nəb(ə)l/ *adj* разу́мный; (*inexpensive*) недорого́й.

reassurance /,ri:ə'∫ʊərəns/ *n* успока́ивание. **reassure** /-'∫ʊə(r)/ *vt* успока́ивать *impf*, успоко́ить *pf*.

rebate /ri:beɪt/ *n* ски́дка.

rebel *n* /'reb(ə)l/ повста́нец; *vi* /rɪ'bel/ восстава́ть *impf*, восста́ть *pf*. **rebellion** /rɪ'beljən/ *n* восста́ние. **rebellious** /rɪ'beljəs/ *adj* мяте́жный.

rebound *vi* /rɪ'baʊnd/ отска́кивать *impf*, отскочи́ть *pf*; *n* /'ri:baʊnd/ рикоше́т.

rebuff /rɪ'bʌf/ *n* отпо́р; *vt* дава́ть *impf*, дать *pf* отпо́р.

rebuild /ri:'bɪld/ *vt* перестра́ивать *impf*, перестро́ить *pf*.

rebuke /rɪ'bju:k/ *vt* упрека́ть *impf*, упрекну́ть *pf*; *n* упрёк.

rebuttal /rɪ'bʌt(ə)l/ *n* опроверже́ние.

recalcitrant /rɪ'kælsɪtrənt/ *adj* непоко́рный.

recall *vt* /rɪ'kɔ:l/ (*an official*) отзыва́ть *impf*, отозва́ть *pf*; (*re-*

member) вспоминать *impf*, вспомнить *pf*; *n* /'ri:kɔːl/ отзыв; (*memory*) память.

recant /rɪ'kænt/ *vi* отрекаться *impf*, отречься *pf*.

recapitulate /ˌri:kə'pɪtjʊˌleɪt/ *vt* резюмировать *impf & pf*.

recast /ri:'kɑːst/ *vt* переделывать *impf*, переделать *pf*.

recede /rɪ'si:d/ *vi* отходить *impf*, отойти *pf*.

receipt /rɪ'si:t/ *n* (*receiving*) получение; *pl* (*amount*) выручка; (*written ~*) квитанция; (*from till*) чек. **receive** /-'si:v/ *vt* (*admit, entertain*) принимать *impf*, принять *pf*; (*get, be given*) получать *impf*, получить *pf*. **receiver** /-'si:və(r)/ *n* (*radio, television*) приёмник; (*tel*) трубка.

recent /'ri:s(ə)nt/ *adj* недавний; (*new*) новый. **recently** /-lɪ/ *adv* недавно.

receptacle /rɪ'septək(ə)l/ *n* вместилище. **reception** /-'sepʃ(ə)n/ *n* приём; *~* **room** приёмная *sb*. **receptionist** /-'sepʃənɪst/ *n* секретарь *m*, -рша, в приёмной. **receptive** /-'septɪv/ *adj* восприимчивый.

recess /rɪ'ses/ *n* (*parl*) каникулы (-л) *pl*; (*niche*) ниша. **recession** /-'seʃ(ə)n/ *n* спад.

recipe /'resɪpɪ/ *n* рецепт.

recipient /rɪ'sɪpɪənt/ *n* получатель *m*.

reciprocal /rɪ'sɪprək(ə)l/ *adj* взаимный. **reciprocate** /-ˌkeɪt/ *v* отвечать *impf* (взаимностью) на+*acc*.

recital /rɪ'saɪt(ə)l/ *n* (*solnyj*) концерт. **recitation** /ˌresɪ'teɪʃ(ə)n/ *n* публичное чтение. **recite** /rɪ'saɪt/ *vt* декламировать *impf*, про~ *pf*; (*list*) перечислять *impf*, перечислить *pf*.

reckless /'reklɪs/ *adj* (*rash*) опрометчивый; (*careless*) неосторожный.

reckon /'rekən/ *vt* подсчитывать *impf*, подсчитать *pf*; (*also regard as*) считать *impf*, счесть *pf* (**to be** +*instr*); *vi*: *~* **on** рассчитывать *impf*, рассчитать *pf* на+*acc*; *~* **with** считаться *impf* с+*instr*. **reckoning** /'rekənɪŋ/ *n* счёт; **day of** *~* час расплаты.

reclaim /rɪ'kleɪm/ *vt* требовать *impf*, по~ *pf* обратно; (*land*) осваивать *impf*, освоить *pf*.

recline /rɪ'klaɪn/ *vi* полулежать *impf*.

recluse /rɪ'klu:s/ *n* затворник.

recognition /ˌrekəg'nɪʃ(ə)n/ *n* узнавание; (*acknowledgement*) признание. **recognize** /'rekəgˌnaɪz/ *vt* узнавать *impf*, узнать *pf*; (*acknowledge*) признавать *impf*, признать *pf*.

recoil /rɪ'kɔɪl/ *vi* отпрядывать *impf*, отпрянуть *pf*.

recollect /ˌrekə'lekt/ *vt* вспоминать *impf*, вспомнить *pf*. **recollection** /-'lekʃ(ə)n/ *n* воспоминание.

recommend /ˌrekə'mend/ *vt* рекомендовать *impf & pf*. **recommendation** /ˌrekəmen'deɪʃ(ə)n/ *n* рекомендация.

recompense /'rekəmˌpens/ *n* вознаграждение; *vt* вознаграждать *impf*, вознаградить *pf*.

reconcile /'rekənˌsaɪl/ *vt* примирять *impf*, примирить *pf*; *~* **o.s.** примиряться *impf*, примириться *pf* (**to** с+*instr*). **reconciliation** /ˌrekən‚sɪlɪ'eɪʃ(ə)n/ *n* примирение.

reconnaissance /rɪ'kɒnɪs(ə)ns/ *n* разведка. **reconnoitre** /ˌrekə'nɔɪtə(r)/ *vt* разведывать *impf*, разведать *pf*.

reconstruct /ˌri:kən'strʌkt/ *vt* перестраивать *impf*, пере-

стро́ить *pf.* **reconstruction** /-'strʌkʃən/ *n* перестро́йка.

record *vt* /rɪ'kɔːd/ запи́сывать *impf*, записа́ть *pf*; *n* /'rekɔːd/ за́пись; (*minutes*) протоко́л; (*gramophone* ~) грампласти́нка; (*sport etc.*) реко́рд; **off the** ~ неофициа́льно; *adj* реко́рдный; ~**breaker, -holder** рекордсме́н, ~ка; ~**player** прои́грыватель *m*. **recorder** /rɪ'kɔːdə(r)/ *n* (*mus*) блок-флéйта. **recording** /-dɪŋ/ *n* за́пись.

recount¹ /rɪ'kaʊnt/ *vt* (*narrate*) переска́зывать *impf*, пересказа́ть *pf*.

re-count² /ˌriː'kaʊnt/ *vt* (*count again*) пересчи́тывать *impf*, пересчита́ть *pf*; *n* пересчёт.

recoup /rɪ'kuːp/ *vt* возвраща́ть *impf*, верну́ть *pf* (**losses** поте́рянное).

recourse /rɪ'kɔːs/ *n*: **have** ~ **to** прибега́ть *impf*, прибе́гнуть *pf* к+*dat*.

recover /rɪ'kʌvə(r)/ *vt* (*regain possession*) получа́ть *impf*, получи́ть *pf* обра́тно; возвраща́ть *impf*, верну́ть *pf*; (*health*) поправля́ться *impf*, попра́виться *pf* (**from** по́сле +*gen*). **recovery** /-rɪ/ *n* возвраще́ние; выздоровле́ние.

recreate /ˌriːkrɪ'eɪt/ *vt* воссоздава́ть *impf*, воссозда́ть *pf*.

recreation /ˌrekrɪ'eɪʃ(ə)n/ *n* развлече́ние, о́тдых.

recrimination /rɪˌkrɪmɪ'neɪʃ(ə)n/ *n* взаи́мное обвине́ние.

recruit /rɪ'kruːt/ *n* новобра́нец; *vt* вербова́ть *impf*, за~ *pf*. **recruitment** /-mənt/ *n* вербо́вка.

rectangle /'rektæŋɡ(ə)l/ *n* прямоуго́льник. **rectangular** /rek'tæŋɡjʊlə(r)/ *adj* прямоуго́льный.

rectify /'rektɪˌfaɪ/ *vt* исправля́ть *impf*, испра́вить *pf*.

rector /'rektə(r)/ *n* (*priest*) прихо́дский свяще́нник; (*univ*) ре́ктор. **rectory** /-rɪ/ *n* дом прихо́дского свяще́нника.

rectum /'rektəm/ *n* прямáя кишкá.

recuperate /rɪ'kuːpəˌreɪt/ *vi* поправля́ться *impf*, попра́виться *pf*. **recuperation** /-ˌkuːpə'reɪʃ(ə)n/ *n* выздоровле́ние.

recur /rɪ'kɜː(r)/ *vi* повторя́ться *impf*, повтори́ться *pf*. **recurrence** /-'kʌrəns/ *n* повторе́ние. **recurrent** /-'kʌrənt/ *adj* повторя́ющийся.

recycle /riː'saɪk(ə)l/ *vt* перераба́тывать *impf*, перерабо́тать *pf*.

red /red/ *adj* кра́сный; (*of hair*) ры́жий; *n* кра́сный цвет; (*polit*) кра́сный *sb*; **in the** ~ в долгу́; ~**handed** с поли́чным; ~ **herring** ло́жный след; ~**hot** раскалённый докраснá; **R~ Indian** индéец, индиáнка; ~ **tape** волоки́та. **redcurrant** *n* крáсная сморóдина (*no pl*; *usu collect*). **redden** /'red(ə)n/ *vt* окра́шивать *impf*, окра́сить *pf* в кра́сный цвет; *vi* красне́ть *impf*, по~ *pf*. **reddish** /'redɪʃ/ *adj* краснова́тый; (*hair*) рыжева́тый.

redecorate /riː'dekəˌreɪt/ *vt* отде́лывать *impf*, отде́лать *pf*.

redeem /rɪ'diːm/ *vt* (*buy back*) выкупа́ть *impf*, вы́купить *pf*; (*from sin*) искупа́ть *impf*, искупи́ть *pf*. **redeemer** /-'diːmə(r)/ *n* искупи́тель *m*. **redemption** /-'dempʃ(ə)n/ *n* вы́куп; искупле́ние.

redeploy /ˌriːdɪ'plɔɪ/ *vt* передислоци́ровать *impf* & *pf*.

redo /riː'duː/ *vt* переде́лывать *impf*, переде́лать *pf*.

redouble /riːˈdʌb(ə)l/ vt удваивать impf, удвоить pf.

redress /rɪˈdres/ vt исправлять impf, исправить pf; ~ the balance восстанавливать impf, восстановить pf равновесие; n возмещение.

reduce /rɪˈdjuːs/ vt (decrease) уменьшать impf, уменьшить pf; (lower) снижать impf, снизить pf; (shorten) сокращать impf, сократить pf; (bring to) доводить impf, довести pf (to в+acc). **reduction** /-ˈdʌkʃ(ə)n/ n уменьшение, снижение, сокращение; (discount) скидка.

redundancy /rɪˈdʌnd(ə)nsɪ/ n (dismissal) увольнение. **redundant** /-d(ə)nt/ adj излишний; **make** ~ увольнять impf, уволить pf.

reed /riːd/ n (plant) тростник; (in oboe etc.) язычок.

reef /riːf/ n риф.

reek /riːk/ n вонь; vi: ~ (of) вонять impf (+instr).

reel[1] /riːl/ n катушка; vt: ~ off (story etc.) отбарабанить pf.

reel[2] /riːl/ vi (stagger) пошатываться impf, пошатнуться pf.

refectory /rɪˈfekt(ə)rɪ/ n (in monastery) трапезная sb; (univ) столовая sb.

refer /rɪˈfɜː(r)/ vt (direct) отсылать impf, отослать pf (to к+dat); vi: ~ to (cite) ссылаться impf, сослаться pf на+acc; (mention) упоминать impf, упомянуть pf +acc. **referee** /refəˈriː/ n судья m; vt судить impf. **reference** /ˈref(ə)rəns/ n (to book etc.) ссылка; (mention) упоминание; (testimonial) характеристика; ~ book справочник. **referendum** /refəˈrendəm/ n референдум.

refine /rɪˈfaɪn/ vt очищать impf, очистить pf. **refined** /-d/ adj (in style etc.) утончённый; (in manners) культурный. **refinement** /-mənt/ n утончённость. **refinery** /-nərɪ/ n (oil ~) нефтеочистительный завод.

refit /riːˈfɪt/ vt переоборудовать impf & pf.

reflect /rɪˈflekt/ vt отражать impf, отразить pf; vi размышлять impf, размыслить pf (on о+prep). **reflection** /-ˈflekʃ(ə)n/ n отражение; размышление; **on** ~ подумав. **reflective** /-ˈflektɪv/ adj (thoughtful) серьёзный. **reflector** /-ˈflektə(r)/ n рефлектор.

reflex /ˈriːfleks/ n рефлекс; adj рефлекторный. **reflexive** /rɪˈfleksɪv/ adj (gram) возвратный.

reform /rɪˈfɔːm/ vt реформировать impf & pf; vt & i (of people) исправлять(ся) impf, исправить(ся) pf; n реформа; исправление. **Reformation** /refəˈmeɪʃ(ə)n/ n Реформация.

refract /rɪˈfrækt/ vt преломлять impf, преломить pf.

refrain[1] /rɪˈfreɪn/ n припев.

refrain[2] /rɪˈfreɪn/ vi воздерживаться impf, воздержаться pf (from от+gen).

refresh /rɪˈfreʃ/ vi освежать impf, освежить pf. **refreshments** /-mənts/ n pl напитки m pl.

refrigerate /rɪˈfrɪdʒəˌreɪt/ vt охлаждать impf, охладить pf. **refrigeration** /rɪˈfrɪdʒəˈreɪʃ(ə)n/ n охлаждение. **refrigerator** /rɪˈfrɪdʒəˌreɪtə(r)/ n холодильник.

refuge /ˈrefjuːdʒ/ n убежище; **take** ~ находить impf, найти pf убежище. **refugee** /refjuˈdʒiː/ n беженец, -нка.

refund vt /rɪˈfʌnd/ возвращать

impf, возврати́ть *pf*; (*expenses*) возмеща́ть *impf*, возмести́ть *pf*; *n* /'riːfʌnd/ возвраще́ние (де́нег); возмеще́ние.

refusal /rɪ'fjuːz(ə)l/ *n* отка́з. **refuse**[1] /rɪ'fjuːz/ *vt* (*decline to accept*) отка́зываться *impf*, отказа́ться *pf* от+*gen*; (*decline to do sth*) отка́зываться *impf*, отказа́ться *pf* +*inf*; (*deny s.o. sth*) отка́зывать *impf*, отказа́ть *pf* +*dat*+в+*prep*.

refuse[2] /'refjuːs/ *n* му́сор.

refute /rɪ'fjuːt/ *vt* опроверга́ть *impf*, опрове́ргнуть *pf*.

regain /rɪ'geɪn/ *vt* возвраща́ть *impf*, верну́ть *pf*.

regal /'riːg(ə)l/ *adj* короле́вский.

regalia /rɪ'geɪlɪə/ *n pl* рега́лии *f pl*.

regard /rɪ'gɑːd/ *vt* смотре́ть *impf*, по~ *pf* на+*acc*; (*take into account*) счита́ться *impf* с+*instr*; **as** ~s счита́ть *impf* +*instr*, за+*instr*; **as** ~s что каса́ется+*gen*; (*esteem*) уваже́ние; *pl* приве́т. **regarding** /-dɪŋ/ *prep* относи́тельно +*gen*. **regardless** /-lɪs/ *adv* не обраща́я внима́ния; ~ **of** не счита́ясь с+*instr*.

regatta /rɪ'gætə/ *n* рега́та.

regenerate /rɪ'dʒenə,reɪt/ *vt* перерожда́ть *impf*, перероди́ть *pf*.

regent /'riːdʒ(ə)nt/ *n* ре́гент.

régime /reɪ'ʒiːm/ *n* режи́м.

regiment /'redʒɪmənt/ *n* полк. **regimental** /-'ment(ə)l/ *adj* полково́й. **regimentation** /,redʒɪmən'teɪʃ(ə)n/ *n* регламента́ция.

region /'riːdʒ(ə)n/ *n* регио́н. **regional** /-nəl/ *adj* региона́льный.

register /'redʒɪstə(r)/ *n* рее́стр; (*also mus*) реги́стр; *vt* реги-

стри́ровать *impf*, за~ *pf*; (*a letter*) отправля́ть *impf*, отпра́вить *pf* заказны́м. **registered** /-təd/ *adj* (*letter*) заказно́й. **registrar** /,redʒɪ'strɑː(r)/ *n* регистра́тор. **registration** /,redʒɪ'streɪʃ(ə)n/ *n* регистра́ция; ~ **number** но́мер маши́ны. **registry** /'redʒɪstrɪ/ *n* регистрату́ра; ~ **office** загс.

regret /rɪ'gret/ *vt* сожале́ть *impf* о+*prep*; *n* сожале́ние. **regretful** /-fol/ *adj* по́лный сожале́ния. **regrettable** /-'gretəb(ə)l/ *adj* приско́рбный. **regrettably** /-'gretəblɪ/ *adv* к сожале́нию.

regular /'regjolə(r)/ *adj* регуля́рный; (*also gram*) пра́вильный; *n* (*coll*) завсегда́тай. **regularity** /,regjo'lærɪtɪ/ *n* регуля́рность. **regulate** /'regjo,leɪt/ *vt* регули́ровать *impf*, у~ *pf*. **regulation** /,regjo'leɪʃ(ə)n/ *n* регули́рование; *pl* пра́вила *neut pl*.

rehabilitate /,riːhə'bɪlɪ,teɪt/ *vt* реабилити́ровать *impf* & *pf*. **rehabilitation** /-,bɪlɪ'teɪʃ(ə)n/ *n* реабилита́ция.

rehearsal /rɪ'hɜːs(ə)l/ *n* репети́ция. **rehearse** /-'hɜːs/ *vt* репети́ровать *impf*, от~ *pf*.

reign /reɪn/ *n* ца́рствование; *vi* ца́рствовать *impf*; (*fig*) цари́ть *impf*.

reimburse /,riːɪm'bɜːs/ *vt* возмеща́ть *impf*, возмести́ть *pf* (+*dat of person*). **reimbursement** /-mənt/ *n* возмеще́ние.

rein /reɪn/ *n* по́вод.

reincarnation /,riːɪnkɑː'neɪʃ(ə)n/ *n* перевоплоще́ние.

reindeer /'reɪndɪə(r)/ *n* се́верный оле́нь *m*.

reinforce /,riːɪn'fɔːs/ *vt* подкрепля́ть *impf*, подкрепи́ть *pf*. **reinforcement** /-mənt/ *n* (*also pl*) подкрепле́ние.

reinstate /ˌriːɪnˈsteɪt/ vt восстанавливать impf, восстановить pf. **reinstatement** /-mənt/ n восстановление.

reiterate /riːˈɪtəˌreɪt/ vt повторять impf, повторить pf.

reject /rɪˈdʒekt/ vt отвергать impf, отвергнуть pf; (as defective) браковать impf, за~ pf; n /ˈriːdʒekt/ брак. **rejection** /-ˈdʒekʃ(ə)n/ n отказ (of от+gen).

rejoice /rɪˈdʒɔɪs/ vi радоваться impf, об~ pf (in, at +dat). **rejoicing** /-sɪŋ/ n радость.

rejoin /riːˈdʒɔɪn/ vt (вновь) присоединяться impf, присоединиться pf к+dat.

rejuvenate /rɪˈdʒuːvɪˌneɪt/ vt омолаживать impf, омолодить pf.

relapse /rɪˈlæps/ n рецидив; vi снова впадать impf, впасть pf (into в+acc); (into illness) снова заболевать impf, заболеть pf.

relate /rɪˈleɪt/ vt (tell) рассказывать impf, рассказать impf, связать pf; vi относиться impf к+dat. **related** /-tɪd/ adj родственный. **relation** /-ˈleɪʃ(ə)n/ n отношение; (person) родственник, -ица. **relationship** n связь; (kinship) родство. **relative** /ˈrelətɪv/ adj относительный; n родственник, -ица. **relativity** /ˌreləˈtɪvɪtɪ/ n относительность.

relax /rɪˈlæks/ vt ослаблять impf, ослабить pf; vi (rest) расслабляться impf, расслабиться pf. **relaxation** /ˌriːlækˈseɪʃ(ə)n/ n ослабление; (rest) отдых.

relay /ˈriːleɪ/ n (shift) смена; (sport) эстафета; (electr) реле neut indecl; vt передавать impf,

передать pf.

release /rɪˈliːs/ vt (set free) освобождать impf, освободить pf; (unfasten, let go) отпускать impf, отпустить pf; (film etc.) выпускать impf, выпустить pf; n освобождение; выпуск.

relegate /ˈrelɪˌgeɪt/ vt переводить impf, перевести pf (в низшую группу). **relegation** /-ˈgeɪʃ(ə)n/ n перевод (в низшую группу).

relent /rɪˈlent/ vi смягчаться impf, смягчиться pf. **relentless** /-lɪs/ adj непрестанный.

relevance /ˈrelɪv(ə)ns/ n уместность. **relevant** /-(ə)nt/ adj относящийся к делу; уместный.

reliability /rɪˌlaɪəˈbɪlɪtɪ/ n надёжность. **reliable** /-ˈlaɪəb(ə)l/ adj надёжный. **reliance** /-ˈlaɪəns/ n доверие. **reliant** /-ˈlaɪənt/ adj: be ~ upon зависеть impf от+gen.

relic /ˈrelɪk/ n остаток, реликвия.

relief¹ /rɪˈliːf/ n (art, geol) рельеф.

relief² /rɪˈliːf/ n (alleviation) облегчение; (assistance) помощь; (in duty) смена. **relieve** /-ˈliːv/ vt (alleviate) облегчать impf, облегчить pf; (replace) сменять impf, сменить pf; (unburden) освобождать impf, освободить pf (of от+gen).

religion /rɪˈlɪdʒ(ə)n/ n религия. **religious** /-ˈlɪdʒəs/ adj религиозный.

relinquish /rɪˈlɪŋkwɪʃ/ vt оставлять impf, оставить pf; (right etc.) отказываться impf, отказаться pf от+gen.

relish /ˈrelɪʃ/ n (enjoyment) смак; (cul) приправа; vt смаковать impf.

relocate /ˌriːləʊˈkeɪt/ vt & i пере-

меща́ть(ся) *impf*, перемести́ть(ся) *pf*.

reluctance /rɪ'lʌkt(ə)ns/ *n* неохо́та. **reluctant** /-t(ə)nt/ *adj* неохо́тный; **be ~ to** не жела́ть *impf* +*inf*.

rely /rɪ'laɪ/ *vi* полага́ться *impf*, положи́ться *pf* (**on** на+*acc*).

remain /rɪ'meɪn/ *vi* остава́ться *impf*, оста́ться *pf*. **remainder** /-'meɪndə(r)/ *n* оста́ток. **remains** /-'meɪnz/ *n* pl оста́тки *m* pl; (*human ~*) оста́нки (-ков) pl.

remand /rɪ'mɑːnd/ *vt* содержа́ть *impf* под стра́жей; **be on ~** содержа́ться *impf* под стра́жей.

remark /rɪ'mɑːk/ *vt* замеча́ть *impf*, заме́тить *pf*; *n* замеча́ние. **remarkable** /-'mɑːkəb(ə)l/ *adj* замеча́тельный.

remarry /rɪ:'mærɪ/ *vi* вступа́ть *impf*, вступи́ть *pf* в но́вый брак.

remedial /rɪ'miːdɪəl/ *adj* лече́бный. **remedy** /'remɪdɪ/ *n* сре́дство (**for** от, про́тив+*gen*); *vt* исправля́ть *impf*, испра́вить *pf*.

remember /rɪ'membə(r)/ *vt* по́мнить *impf*, вспомина́ть *impf*, вспо́мнить *pf*; (*greet*) передава́ть *impf*, переда́ть *pf* приве́т от+*gen* (**to** +*dat*). **remembrance** /-'membrəns/ *n* па́мять.

remind /rɪ'maɪnd/ *vt* напомина́ть *impf*, напо́мнить *pf* +*dat* (**of** +*acc*, о+*prep*). **reminder** /-də(r)/ *n* напомина́ние.

reminiscence /,remɪ'nɪs(ə)ns/ *n* воспомина́ние. **reminiscent** /-'nɪs(ə)nt/ *adj* напомина́ющий.

remiss /rɪ'mɪs/ *predic adj* небре́жный. **remission** /rɪ'mɪʃ(ə)n/ *n* (*pardon*) отпуще́ние; (*med*) реми́ссия. **remit** /rɪ'mɪt/ *vt* пересыла́ть *impf*, пересла́ть *pf*. **remittance** /rɪ'mɪt(ə)ns/ *n* пере-

во́д де́нег; (*money*) де́нежный перево́д.

remnant /'remnənt/ *n* оста́ток.

remonstrate /'remən,streɪt/ *vi*: **~ with** с увеща́вя *impf* +*acc*.

remorse /rɪ'mɔːs/ *n* угрызе́ния *neut pl* со́вести. **remorseful** /-fʊl/ *adj* по́лный раска́яния. **remorseless** /-lɪs/ *adj* безжа́лостный.

remote /rɪ'məʊt/ *adj* отдалённый; **~ control** дистанцио́нное управле́ние.

removal /rɪ'muːv(ə)l/ *n* (*taking away*) удале́ние; (*of obstacles*) устране́ние. **remove** /-'muːv/ *vt* (*take away*) убира́ть *impf*, убра́ть *pf*; (*get rid of*) устраня́ть *impf*, устрани́ть *pf*.

remuneration /rɪ,mjuːnə'reɪʃ(ə)n/ *n* вознагражде́ние. **remunerative** /-'mjuːnərətɪv/ *adj* вы́годный.

renaissance /rɪ'neɪs(ə)ns/ *n* возрожде́ние; **the R~** Возрожде́ние.

render /'rendə(r)/ *vt* воздава́ть *impf*, возда́ть *pf*; (*help etc.*) ока́зывать *impf*, оказа́ть *pf*; (*role etc.*) исполня́ть *impf*, испо́лнить *pf*; (*stone*) штукату́рить *impf*, о~, от~ *pf*. **rendering** /-rɪŋ/ *n* исполне́ние.

rendezvous /'rɒndɪ,vuː/ *n* (*meeting*) свида́ние.

renegade /'renɪ,geɪd/ *n* ренега́т, ~ка.

renew /rɪ'njuː/ *vt* (*extend; continue*) возобновля́ть *impf*, возобнови́ть *pf*; (*replace*) обновля́ть *impf*, обнови́ть *pf*. **renewal** /-'njuːəl/ *n* (возобновле́ние.

renounce /rɪ'naʊns/ *vt* отверга́ть *impf*, отве́ргнуть *pf*; (*claim*) отка́зываться *impf*, отказа́ться *pf* от+*gen*.

renovate /ˈrenəˌveɪt/ vt ремонти́ровать impf, от~ pf. **renovation** /-ˈveɪʃ(ə)n/ n ремо́нт.

renown /rɪˈnaʊn/ n сла́ва. **renowned** /-ˈnaʊnd/ adj изве́стный; be ~ for сла́виться impf +instr.

rent /rent/ n (for home) кварти́рная пла́та; (for premises) (аре́ндная пла́та, vt (of tenant) арендова́ть impf & pf; (of owner) сдава́ть impf & pf. **renunciation** /rɪˌnʌnsɪˈeɪʃ(ə)n/ n (repudiation) отрица́ние; (of claim) отка́з.

rep /rep/ n (comm) аге́нт.

repair /rɪˈpeə(r)/ vt ремонти́ровать impf, от~ pf; n (also pl) ремо́нт (only sg); почи́нка; in good/bad ~ в хоро́шем/плохо́м состоя́нии.

reparations /ˌrepəˈreɪʃ(ə)nz/ n pl репара́ции f pl.

repatriate /riːˈpætrɪˌeɪt/ vt репатрии́ровать impf & pf. **repatriation** /-ˌpætrɪˈeɪʃ(ə)n/ n репатриа́ция.

repay /rɪˈpeɪ/ vt отпла́чивать impf, отплати́ть pf (person +dat). **repayment** /-mənt/ n отпла́та.

repeal /rɪˈpiːl/ vt отменя́ть impf, отмени́ть pf; n отме́на.

repeat /rɪˈpiːt/ vt & i повторя́ть(ся) impf, повтори́ть(ся) pf; n повторе́ние. **repeatedly** /-tɪdlɪ/ adv неоднокра́тно.

repel /rɪˈpel/ vt отта́лкивать impf, оттолкну́ть pf; (enemy) отража́ть impf, отрази́ть pf.

repent /rɪˈpent/ vi раска́иваться impf, раска́яться pf. **repentance** /-ˈpent(ə)ns/ n раска́яние. **repentant** /-ˈpent(ə)nt/ adj раска́ивающийся.

repercussion /ˌriːpəˈkʌʃ(ə)n/ n после́дствие.

repertoire /ˈrepəˌtwɑː(r)/ n репертуа́р. **repertory** /ˈrepətərɪ/ n (store) запа́с; (repertoire) репертуа́р; ~ **company** постоя́нная тру́ппа.

repetition /ˌrepɪˈtɪʃ(ə)n/ n повторе́ние. **repetitious, repetitive** /ˌrepɪˈtɪʃəs, rɪˈpetɪtɪv/ adj повторя́ющийся.

replace /rɪˈpleɪs/ vt (put back) класть impf, положи́ть pf обра́тно; (substitute) заменя́ть impf, замени́ть pf (by +instr). **replacement** /-mənt/ n заме́на.

replay /ˈriːpleɪ/ n переигро́вка.

replenish /rɪˈplenɪʃ/ vt пополня́ть impf, попо́лнить pf.

replete /rɪˈpliːt/ adj насы́щенный; (sated) сы́тый.

replica /ˈreplɪkə/ n ко́пия.

reply /rɪˈplaɪ/ vt & i отвеча́ть impf, отве́тить pf (to на+acc); n отве́т.

report /rɪˈpɔːt/ vt сообща́ть impf, сообщи́ть pf; vi докла́дывать impf, доложи́ть pf; (present o.s.) явля́ться impf, яви́ться pf; n сообще́ние; докла́д; (school) та́бель m; (sound) звук взры́ва, вы́стрела. **reporter** /-tə(r)/ n корреспонде́нт.

repose /rɪˈpəʊz/ n (rest) о́тдых; (peace) поко́й.

repository /rɪˈpɒzɪtərɪ/ n храни́лище.

repossess /ˌriːpəˈzes/ vt изыма́ть impf, изъя́ть pf за непла́тёж.

reprehensible /ˌreprɪˈhensɪb(ə)l/ adj предосуди́тельный.

represent /ˌreprɪˈzent/ vt представля́ть impf; (portray) изобража́ть impf, изобрази́ть pf. **representation** /-zenˈteɪʃ(ə)n/ n (being represented) представи́тельство; (statement of case) представле́ние; (portrayal) из-

ображе́ние. **representative** /'zentətɪv/ adj изображающий (of +acc); (typical) типичный; n представитель m.

repress /rɪ'pres/ vt подавля́ть impf, подави́ть pf. **repression** /-'preʃ(ə)n/ n подавле́ние, репре́ссия. **repressive** /-'presɪv/ adj репресси́вный.

reprieve /rɪ'priːv/ vt отсро́чивать impf, отсро́чить pf +dat приведе́ние в исполне́ние (сме́ртного) пригово́ра; n отсро́чка приведе́ния в исполне́ние (сме́ртного) пригово́ра; (fig) переды́шка.

reprimand /'reprimɑːnd/ n вы́говор; vt де́лать impf, с~ pf вы́говор +dat.

reprint /ˌriː'prɪnt/ переизда́вать impf, переизда́ть pf; n /'riːprɪnt/ переизда́ние.

reprisal /rɪ'praɪz(ə)l/ n отве́тная ме́ра.

reproach /rɪ'prəʊtʃ/ vt упрека́ть impf, упрекну́ть pf (with в+prep). **reproachful** /-fʊl/ adj укори́зненный.

reproduce /ˌriːprə'djuːs/ vt воспроизводи́ть impf, воспроизвести́ pf; vi размножа́ться impf, размно́житься pf. **reproduction** /-'dʌkʃ(ə)n/ n (action) воспроизведе́ние; (object) репроду́кция; (of offspring) размноже́ние. **reproductive** /-'dʌktɪv/ adj воспроизводи́тельный.

reproof /rɪ'pruːf/ n вы́говор. **reprove** /rɪ'pruːv/ vt де́лать impf с~ pf вы́говор +dat.

reptile /'reptaɪl/ n пресмыка́ющееся sb.

republic /rɪ'pʌblɪk/ n респу́блика. **republican** /-kən/ adj республика́нский; n республика́нец, -нка.

repudiate /rɪ'pjuːdɪˌeɪt/ vt (renounce) отка́зываться impf, отказа́ться pf от+gen; (reject) отверга́ть impf, отве́ргнуть pf. **repudiation** /-ˌpjuːdɪ'eɪʃ(ə)n/ n отка́з от+gen.

repugnance /rɪ'pʌgnəns/ n отвраще́ние. **repugnant** /-nənt/ adj проти́вный.

repulse /rɪ'pʌls/ vt отража́ть impf, отрази́ть pf n отвраще́ние. **repulsion** /-'pʌlʃ(ə)n/ n отвраще́ние. **repulsive** /-'pʌlsɪv/ adj отврати́тельный.

reputable /'repjʊtəb(ə)l/ adj по́льзующийся хоро́шей репута́цией. **reputation, repute** /ˌrepjʊ'teɪʃ(ə)n, rɪ'pjuːt/ n репута́ция. **reputed** /-'pjuːtɪd/ adj предполага́емый. **reputedly** /-'pjuːtɪdlɪ/ adv по о́бщему мне́нию.

request /rɪ'kwest/ n про́сьба; by, on, ~ по про́сьбе; vt проси́ть impf, по~ pf +acc, +gen (person +acc).

requiem /'rekwɪˌem/ n ре́квием.

require /rɪ'kwaɪə(r)/ vt (demand; need) тре́бовать impf, по~ pf +gen; (need) нужда́ться impf в+prep. **requirement** /-mənt/ n тре́бование; (necessity) потре́бность. **requisite** /'rekwɪzɪt/ adj необходи́мый; n необходи́мая вещь. **requisition** /ˌrekwɪ'zɪʃ(ə)n/ n реквизи́ция; vt реквизи́ровать impf & pf.

resale /ˌriː'seɪl/ n перепрода́жа.

rescind /rɪ'sɪnd/ vt отменя́ть impf, отмени́ть pf.

rescue /'reskjuː/ vt спаса́ть impf, спасти́ pf n спасе́ние. **rescuer** /'reskjuːə(r)/ n спаси́тель m.

research /rɪ'sɜːtʃ/ n иссле́дование (+gen); (occupation) иссле́довательская рабо́та; vi: ~ into иссле́довать impf & pf

+*acc.* **researcher** /-ˈtʃə(r)/ *n* исследователь *m.*

resemblance /rɪˈzembləns/ *n* сходство. **resemble** /-ˈzemb(ə)l/ *vt* походить *impf* на+*acc.*

resent /rɪˈzent/ *vt* возмущаться *impf*, возмутиться *pf* от+*gen.* **resentful** /-fʊl/ *adj* возмущённый. **resentment** /-mənt/ *n* возмущение.

reservation /ˌrezəˈveɪʃ(ə)n/ *n* (*doubt*) оговорка; (*booking*) предварительный заказ; (*land*) резервация. **reserve** /rɪˈzɜːv/ *vt* (*keep*) резервировать *impf* & *pf*; (*book*) заказывать *impf*, заказать *pf*; *n* (*stock*; *mil*) запас, резерв; (*sport*) запасной игрок; (*nature* ~ *etc.*) заповедник; (*proviso*) оговорка; (*self-restraint*) сдержанность; *attrib* запасной. **reserved** /-ˈzɜːvd/ *adj* (*person*) сдержанный. **reservist** /-ˈzɜːvɪst/ *n* резервист. **reservoir** /ˈrezəˌvwɑː(r)/ *n* (*for water*) водохранилище; (*for other fluids*) резервуар.

resettle /riːˈset(ə)l/ *vt* переселять *impf*, переселить *pf.* **resettlement** /-mənt/ *n* переселение.

reshape /riːˈʃeɪp/ *vt* видоизменять *impf*, видоизменить *pf.*

reshuffle /riːˈʃʌf(ə)l/ *n* перестановка.

reside /rɪˈzaɪd/ *vi* проживать *impf.* **residence** /ˈrezɪd(ə)ns/ *n* (*residing*) проживание; (*abode*) местожительство; (*official* ~ *etc.*) резиденция. **resident** /ˈrezɪd(ə)nt/ *n* (постоянный) житель *m*, ~ница *f*; *adj* проживающий; (*population*) постоянный. **residential** /ˌrezɪˈden(ə)l/ *adj* жилой.

residual /rɪˈzɪdjʊəl/ *adj* остаточный. **residue** /ˈrezɪˌdjuː/ *n* остаток.

resign /rɪˈzaɪn/ *vt* отказываться *impf*, отказаться *pf* от+*gen.*; *vi* уходить *impf*, уйти *pf* в отставку; ~ **o.s. to** покоряться *impf*, покориться *pf* +*dat.* **resignation** /ˌrezɪɡˈneɪʃ(ə)n/ *n* отставка, заявление об отставке; (*being resigned*) покорность. **resigned** /rɪˈzaɪnd/ *adj* покорный.

resilient /rɪˈzɪlɪənt/ *adj* выносливый.

resin /ˈrezɪn/ *n* смола.

resist /rɪˈzɪst/ *vt* сопротивляться *impf* +*dat.*; (*temptation*) устоять *pf* перед+*instr.* **resistance** /-ˈzɪst(ə)ns/ *n* сопротивление. **resistant** /-ˈzɪst(ə)nt/ *adj* стойкий.

resolute /ˈrezəˌluːt/ *adj* решительный. **resolution** /ˌrezəˈluːʃ(ə)n/ *n* (*character*) решительность; (*vow*) зарок; (*at meeting etc.*) резолюция; (*of problem*) разрешение. **resolve** /rɪˈzɒlv/ *vt* (*decide*) решать *impf*, решить *pf*; (*settle*) разрешать *impf*, разрешить *pf*; *n* решительность; (*decision*) решение.

resonance /ˈrezənəns/ *n* резонанс. **resonant** /ˈrezənənt/ *adj* звучный.

resort /rɪˈzɔːt/ *vi*: ~ **to** прибегать *impf*, прибегнуть *pf* к+*dat.*; (*place*) курорт; **in the last** ~ в крайнем случае.

resound /rɪˈzaʊnd/ *vi* (*of sound etc.*) раздаваться *impf*, раздаться *pf*; (*of place*) оглашаться *impf*, огласиться *pf* (**with** +*instr*).

resource /rɪˈzɔːs/ *n* (*usu pl*) ресурс. **resourceful** /-fʊl/ *adj* находчивый.

respect /rɪˈspekt/ *n* (*relation*) от-

ноше́ние; (*esteem*) уваже́ние; with ~ to что каса́ется+*gen*; vt уважа́ть *impf*. **respectable** /-'spektəb(ə)l/ *adj* прили́чный. **respectable** /-'spektə'bılıtı/ n респекта́бельность. **respectably** /-'spektəbl/ *adj* прили́чный. **respectful** /-'spektful/ *adj* почти́тельный. **respective** /-'spektıv/ *adj* свой. **respectively** /-'spektıvlı/ *adv* соотве́тственно.

respiration /,respı'reıʃ(ə)n/ n дыха́ние. **respirator** /'respı,reıtə(r)/ n респира́тор. **respiratory** /гı 'spırətərı/ *adj* дыха́тельный.

respite /'respaıt/ n переды́шка.

resplendent /rı'splendənt/ *adj* блиста́тельный.

respond /rı'spɒnd/ vi: ~ отвеча́ть *impf*, отве́тить *pf* на+*acc*; (*react*) реаги́ровать *impf*, про~, от~ *pf* на+*acc*. **response** /-'spɒns/ n отве́т; (*reaction*) о́тклик. **responsibility** /-,spɒnsı'bılıtı/ n отве́тственность; (*duty*) обя́занность. **responsible** /-'spɒnsıb(ə)l/ *adj* отве́тственный (**to** пе́ред +*instr*, **for** за+*acc*); (*reliable*) надёжный. **responsive** /-'spɒnsıv/ *adj* отзы́вчивый.

est[1] /rest/ vi отдыха́ть *impf*, отдохну́ть *pf*; vt (*place*) класть *impf*, положи́ть *pf*; (*allow to* ~) дава́ть *impf*, дать *pf* о́тдых+*dat*; (*in repose*) поко́й; (*peace*) поко́й; (*mus*) па́уза; (*support*) опо́ра.

est[2] /rest/ n (*remainder*) оста́ток; (*the others*) остальны́е *sb pl*.

restaurant /'restə,rɒnt/ n рестора́н.

restful /'restful/ *adj* успока́ивающий.

restitution /,restı'tjuːʃ(ə)n/ n возвраще́ние.

restive /'restıv/ *adj* беспоко́йный.

restless /'restlıs/ *adj* беспоко́йный.

restoration /,restə'reıʃ(ə)n/ n реставра́ция; (*return*) восстановле́ние. **restore** /rı'stɔː(r)/ vt реставри́ровать *impf* & *pf*; (*return*) восстана́вливать *impf*, восстанови́ть *pf*.

restrain /rı'streın/ vt уде́рживать *impf*, удержа́ть *pf* (**from** от+*gen*). **restraint** /-'streınt/ n сде́ржанность.

restrict /rı'strıkt/ vt ограни́чивать *impf*, ограни́чить *pf*. **restriction** /-'strıkʃ(ə)n/ n ограниче́ние. **restrictive** /-'strıktıv/ *adj* ограничи́тельный.

result /rı'zʌlt/ vi сле́довать *impf*, происходи́ть *impf* (**from** из+*gen*); ~ **in** конча́ться *impf*, ко́нчиться *pf* +*instr*, n результа́т; **as a** ~ в результа́те (**of** +*gen*).

resume /rı'zjuːm/ vt & *i* возобновля́ть(ся) *impf*, возобнови́ть(ся) *pf*. **résumé** /'rezjʊ,meı/ n резюме́ neut indecl. **resumption** /rı'zʌmpʃ(ə)n/ n возобновле́ние.

resurrect /,rezə'rekt/ vt (*fig*) воскреша́ть *impf*, воскреси́ть *pf*. **resurrection** /-'rekʃ(ə)n/ n (*of the dead*) воскресе́ние; (*fig*) воскреше́ние.

resuscitate /rı'sʌsı,teıt/ vt приводи́ть *impf*, привести́ *pf* в созна́ние.

retail /'riːteıl/ n ро́зничная прода́жа; *attrib* ро́зничный; *adv* в ро́зницу; vt продава́ть *impf*, прода́ть *pf* в ро́зницу; vi продава́ться *impf* в ро́зницу. **retailer** /-lə(r)/ n ро́зничный торго́вец.

retain /rɪ'teɪn/ vt уде́рживать *impf*, удержа́ть *pf*.

retaliate /rɪ'tælɪˌeɪt/ vi отпла́чивать *impf*, отплати́ть *pf* тем же. **retaliation** /-ˌtælɪ'eɪʃ(ə)n/ n отпла́та, возме́здие.

retard /rɪ'tɑːd/ vt замедля́ть *impf*, заме́длить *pf*. **retarded** /-dɪd/ adj отста́лый.

retention /rɪ'tenʃ(ə)n/ n удержа́ние. **retentive** /-'tentɪv/ adj (*memory*) хоро́ший.

reticence /'retɪs(ə)ns/ n сде́ржанность. **reticent** /-s(ə)nt/ adj сде́ржанный.

retina /'retɪnə/ n сетча́тка.

retinue /'retɪˌnjuː/ n сви́та.

retire /rɪ'taɪə(r)/ vi (*withdraw*) удаля́ться *impf*, удали́ться *pf*; (*from office etc.*) уходи́ть *impf*, уйти́ *pf* в отста́вку. **retired** /-'taɪəd/ adj в отста́вке. **retirement** /-'taɪəmənt/ n отста́вка. **retiring** /-'taɪrɪŋ/ adj скро́мный.

retort[1] /rɪ'tɔːt/ vt отвеча́ть *impf*, отве́тить *pf* ре́зко; n возраже́ние.

retort[2] /rɪ'tɔːt/ n (*vessel*) рето́рта.

retrace /rɪ'treɪs/ vt: ~ one's steps возвраща́ться *impf*, возврати́ться *pf*.

retract /rɪ'trækt/ vt (*draw in*) втя́гивать *impf*, втяну́ть *pf*; (*take back*) брать *impf*, взять *pf* наза́д.

retreat /rɪ'triːt/ vi отступа́ть *impf*, отступи́ть *pf*; n отступле́ние; (*withdrawal*) уедине́ние; (*place*) убе́жище.

retrenchment /rɪ'trentʃmənt/ n сокраще́ние расхо́дов.

retrial /'riːtraɪəl/ n повто́рное слу́шание де́ла.

retribution /ˌretrɪ'bjuːʃ(ə)n/ n возме́здие.

retrieval /rɪ'triːv(ə)l/ n возвра-

ще́ние; (*comput*) по́иск (ин форма́ции); vt брать *impf*, взять *pf* обра́тно.

retrograde /'retrəˌgreɪd/ adj (*fig*) реакцио́нный. **retrospec** /'retrəˌspekt/ n: in ~ ретроспе́к ти́вно. **retrospective** /-'spektɪv adj (*law*) име́ющий обра́тну́ си́лу.

return /rɪ'tɜːn/ vt & i (*give back come back*) возвраща́ть(ся *impf*, возврати́ть(ся *impf*, вер ну́ть(ся *pf*; vt (*elect*) избира́т *impf*, избра́ть *pf*; n возвраще́ ние; возвра́т; (*profit*) при быль; by ~ обра́тной по́чтой in ~ возвра́т (for +*gen*); man happy ~s! с днём рожде́ния ~ match отве́тный матч; ~ ticket обра́тный биле́т.

reunion /riː'juːnjən/ n встре́ч (друзе́й и т. п.); **family** ~ сбо всей семьёй. **reunite** /ˌriːjuː'naɪ vt воссоединя́ть *impf*, воссо́е дини́ть *pf*.

reuse /riː'juːz/ vt сно́ва испо́ль зовать *impf* & *pf*.

rev /rev/ n оборо́т; vt & i: ~ u рва́ть(ся) *pf*.

reveal /rɪ'viːl/ vt обнару́живат *impf*, обнару́жить *pf*. **revealin** /-lɪŋ/ adj показа́тельный.

revel /'rev(ə)l/ vi пирова́ть *imp* ~ in наслажда́ться *imp* +*instr*.

revelation /ˌrevə'leɪʃ(ə)n/ n от кровéние.

revenge /rɪ'vendʒ/ vt: ~ o.s мстить *impf*, ото~ *pf* (fo за+*acc*; on +*dat*); n месть.

revenue /'revəˌnjuː/ n дохо́д.

reverberate /rɪ'vɜːbəˌreɪt/ vi o ража́ться *impf*. **reverberatio** /-'reɪʃ(ə)n/ n отраже́ние; (fig о́тзвук.

revere /rɪ'vɪə(r)/ vt почита́т *impf*. **reverence** /'revərəns/ n п

чтéние. **Reverend** /'revərənd/ *adj* (*in title*) (егó) преподóбие.
reverent(ial) /'revərənt/, /,revə'ren∫(ə)l/ *adj* почти́тельный.
reverie /'revərɪ/ *n* мечтáние.
reversal /rɪ'vɜːs(ə)l/ *n* (*change*) изменéние; (*of decision*) отмéна. **reverse** /rɪ'vɜːs/ *adj* обрáтный; ~ **gear** зáдний ход; *vt* (*change*) изменя́ть *impf*, измени́ть *pf*; (*decision*) отменя́ть *impf*, отмени́ть *pf*; *vi* давáть *impf*, дать *pf* зáдний ход; *n* (*the* ~) обрáтное *sb*, противополóжное *sb*; (~ *gear*) зáдний ход; (~ *side*) обрáтная сторонá. **reversible** /-'vɜːsɪb(ə)l/ *adj* обрáтимый; (*cloth*) двусторóнний. **reversion** /-'vɜːʃ(ə)n/ *n* возвращéние. **revert** /-'vɜːt/ *vi* возвращáться *impf* (**to** в+*acc*, к+*dat*); (*law*) переходи́ть *impf*, перейти́ *pf* (**to** к+*dat*).

review /rɪ'vjuː/ *n* (*re-examination*) пересмóтр; (*mil*) парáд; (*survey*) обзóр; (*criticism*) рецéнзия; *vt* (*re-examine*) пересмáтривать *impf*, пересмотрéть *pf*; (*survey*) обозревáть *impf*, обозрéть *pf*; (*troops etc.*) принимáть *impf*, приня́ть *pf* парáд+*gen*; (*books etc.*) рецензи́ровать *impf*, про~ *pf*. **reviewer** /-'vjuːə(r)/ *n* рецензéнт.

revise /rɪ'vaɪz/ *vt* пересмáтривать *impf*, пересмотрéть *impf*, исправля́ть *impf*, испрáвить *pf*; *vi* (*for exam*) готóвиться *impf* (**for** к+*dat*). **revision** /-'vɪʒ(ə)n/ *n* пересмóтр, исправлéние.

revival /rɪ'vaɪv(ə)l/ *n* возрождéние; (*to life etc.*) оживлéние. **revive** /-'vaɪv/ *vt* возрождáть *impf*, возроди́ть *pf*; (*resuscitate*) оживля́ть *impf*, оживи́ть

pf; *vi* оживáть *impf*, ожи́ть *pf*.
revoke /rɪ'vəʊk/ *vt* отменя́ть *impf*, отмени́ть *pf*.
revolt /rɪ'vəʊlt/ *n* бунт; *vt* вызывáть *impf*, вызвать *pf* отвращéние у+*gen*; *vi* бунтовáть *impf*, взбунтовáться *pf*. **revolting** /-'vəʊltɪŋ/ *adj* отврати́тельный.
revolution /,revə'luːʃ(ə)n/ *n* (*single turn*) оборóт; (*polit*) револю́ция. **revolutionary** /-'luːʃənərɪ/ *adj* революциóнный; *n* революционéр. **revolutionize** /-'luːʃə,naɪz/ *vt* революционизи́ровать *impf* & *pf*. **revolve** /rɪ'vɒlv/ *vt* & *i* вращáть(ся) *impf*. **revolver** /rɪ'vɒlvə(r)/ *n* револьвéр.
revue /rɪ'vjuː/ *n* ревю́ *neut indecl*.
revulsion /rɪ'vʌlʃ(ə)n/ *n* отвращéние.
reward /rɪ'wɔːd/ *n* вознаграждéние; *vt* (воз)награждáть *impf*, (воз)награди́ть *pf*.
rewrite /riː'raɪt/ *vt* перепи́сывать *impf*, переписáть *pf*; (*recast*) передéлывать *impf*, передéлать *pf*.
rhapsody /'ræpsədɪ/ *n* рапсóдия.
rhetoric /'retərɪk/ *n* рито́рика. **rhetorical** /rɪ'tɒrɪk(ə)l/ *adj* ритори́ческий.
rheumatic /ruː'mætɪk/ *adj* ревмати́ческий. **rheumatism** /'ruːmə,tɪz(ə)m/ *n* ревмати́зм.
rhinoceros /raɪ'nɒsərəs/ *n* носорóг.
rhododendron /,rəʊdə'dendrən/ *n* рододéндрон.
rhubarb /'ruːbɑːb/ *n* ревéнь *m*.
rhyme /raɪm/ *n* ри́фма; *pl* (*verse*) стихи́ *m pl*; *vt* & *i* рифмовáть(ся) *impf*.
rhythm /'rɪð(ə)m/ *n* ритм. **rhyth-**

mic(al) /'rɪðmɪk(ə)l/ *adj* ритми́ческий, -чный.

rib /rɪb/ *n* ребро́.

ribald /'rɪb(ə)ld/ *adj* непристо́йный.

ribbon /'rɪbən/ *n* ле́нта.

rice /raɪs/ *n* рис.

rich /rɪtʃ/ *adj* бога́тый; (*soil*) ту́чный; (*food*) жи́рный. **riches** /'rɪtʃɪz/ *n pl* бога́тство. **richly** /'rɪtʃlɪ/ *adv* (*fully*) вполне́.

rickety /'rɪkɪtɪ/ *adj* (*shaky*) расша́танный.

ricochet /'rɪkəʃeɪ/ *vi* рикошети́ровать *impf* & *pf*.

rid /rɪd/ *vt* освобожда́ть *impf*, освободи́ть *pf* (of от+*gen*); get ~ of избавля́ться *impf*, изба́виться *pf* от+*gen*. **riddance** /'rɪd(ə)ns/ *n*: good ~! скатертью доро́га!

riddle /'rɪd(ə)l/ *n* (*enigma*) зага́дка.

riddled /'rɪd(ə)ld/ *adj*: ~ with изрешечённый; (*fig*) прони́занный.

ride /raɪd/ *vi* е́здить *indet*, е́хать *det*, по~ *pf* (on horseback верхо́м); *vt* е́здить *indet*, е́хать *det*, по~ *pf* в, на+*prep*; *n* пое́здка, езда́. **rider** /-də(r)/ *n* вса́дник, -ица; (*clause*) дополне́ние.

ridge /rɪdʒ/ *n* хребе́т; (on cloth) ру́бчик; (of roof) конёк.

ridicule /'rɪdɪ,kjuːl/ *n* насме́шка; *vt* осме́ивать *impf*, осме́ять *pf*. **ridiculous** /rɪ'dɪkjʊləs/ *adj* смешно́й.

riding /'raɪdɪŋ/ *n* (horse-~) (верхова́я) езда́.

rife /raɪf/ *predic* распространённый.

riff-raff /'rɪfræf/ *n* подо́нки (-ков) *pl.*

rifle /'raɪf(ə)l/ *n* винто́вка; *vt* (*search*) обы́скивать *impf*, обы-

ска́ть *pf*.

rift /rɪft/ *n* тре́щина (also *fig*).

rig /rɪg/ *vt* оснаща́ть *impf*, оснасти́ть *pf*; ~ out наряжа́ть *impf*, наряди́ть *pf*; ~ up ска́лачивать *impf*, сколоти́ть *pf*; *n* бурова́я устано́вка. **rigging** /-gɪŋ/ *n* такела́ж.

right /raɪt/ *adj* (*position*; justified; polit) пра́вый; (*correct*) пра́вильный; (the one wanted) тот; (*suitable*) подходя́щий; *vt* **angle** прямо́й у́гол; *vt* исправля́ть *impf*, испра́вить *pf*; *n* пра́во; (what is just) справедли́вость; (~ side) пра́вая сторона́; (the R~; polit) пра́вые *sl pl*; be in the ~ быть пра́вым; by ~s по пра́ву; ~ of way пра́во прохо́да, прое́зда; *adv* (*straight*) пря́мо; (*exactly*) то́чно, как раз; (to the full) соверше́нно; (*correctly*) пра́вильно; как сле́дует; (on the ~ спра́во (of от+*gen*); (to the ~ напра́во; ~ **away** сейча́с.

righteous /'raɪtʃəs/ *adj* (person) пра́ведный; (action) справедли́вый.

rightful /'raɪtfʊl/ *adj* зако́нный.

rigid /'rɪdʒɪd/ *adj* жёсткий; (*strict*) стро́гий. **rigidity** /rɪ'dʒɪdɪtɪ/ *n* жёсткость; стро́гость.

rigmarole /'rɪgmə,rəʊl/ *n* каните́ль.

rigorous /'rɪgərəs/ *adj* стро́гий. **rigour** /'rɪgə(r)/ *n* стро́гость.

rim /rɪm/ *n* (of wheel) о́бод; (spectacles) опра́ва. **rimless** /-lɪs/ *adj* без опра́вы.

rind /raɪnd/ *n* кожура́.

ring[1] /rɪŋ/ *n* кольцо́; (circle) круг; (boxing) ринг; (circus) (цирково́я) аре́на; ~ **road** кольцева́я доро́га; *vt* (*encircle*) окружа́ть *impf*, окружи́ть *pf*.

ing² /rɪŋ/ vi (sound) звони́ть impf, по~ pf; (ring out, of shot etc.) раздава́ться impf, разда́ться pf; (of place) огласи́ться impf, огласи́ться pf (with +instr); ~ up звони́ть impf, по~ pf в+acc; ~ back перезва́нивать impf, перезвони́ть pf; ~ off пове́сить pf тру́бку; ~ up звони́ть impf, по~ pf +dat; n звон, звоно́к.

ingleader n глава́рь m.

ingtone n мело́дия звонка́, рингто́н (в моби́льном телефо́не).

ink /rɪŋk/ n като́к.

inse /rɪns/ vt полоска́ть impf, вы́~ pf; n полоска́ние.

iot /raɪət/ n бунт; vi бу́йствовать impf; (of plants) бу́йно разраста́ться impf, разрасти́сь pf; vi бунтова́ть impf, взбунтова́ться pf. **riotous** /ˈraɪətəs/ adj бу́йный.

ip /rɪp/ vt & i рва́ть(ся) impf; разо~ pf; ~ up разрыва́ть impf, разорва́ть pf; n про́реха, разре́з.

ipe /raɪp/ adj зре́лый, спе́лый. **ripen** /ˈraɪpən/ vt де́лать impf, с~ pf зре́лым; vi созрева́ть impf, созре́ть pf. **ripeness** /-nɪs/ n зре́лость.

ipple /ˈrɪp(ə)l/ n рябь; vt & i покрыва́ть(ся) impf, покры́ть(ся) pf ря́бью.

ise /raɪz/ vi поднима́ться impf, подня́ться pf; повыша́ться impf, повы́ситься pf; (get up) встава́ть impf, встать pf; (rebel) восстава́ть impf, восста́ть pf; (sun etc.) в(о)сходи́ть impf, взойти́; n подъём, возвыше́ние; (in pay) приба́вка; (sun etc.) восхо́д. **riser** /-zə(r)/ n: **he is an early ~** он ра́но встаёт.

isk /rɪsk/ n риск; vt рискова́ть

impf, рискну́ть pf +instr. **risky** /-kɪ/ adj риско́ванный.

risqué /ˈrɪskeɪ/ adj непристо́йный.

rite /raɪt/ n обря́д. **ritual** /ˈrɪtjʊəl/ n ритуа́л; adj ритуа́льный.

rival /ˈraɪv(ə)l/ n сопе́рник, -ица; adj сопе́рничающий; vt сопе́рничать impf c+instr. **rivalry** /-rɪ/ n сопе́рничество.

river /ˈrɪvə(r)/ n река́. **riverside** attrib прибре́жный.

rivet /ˈrɪvɪt/ n заклёпка; vt заклёпывать impf, заклепа́ть pf; (fig) прико́вывать impf, прикова́ть pf (on к+dat).

road /rəʊd/ n доро́га; (street) у́лица; **~block** загражде́ние на доро́ге; **~-map** (доро́жная) ка́рта; **~ sign** доро́жный знак. **roadside** n обо́чина; attrib придоро́жный. **roadway** n мостова́я sb.

roam /rəʊm/ vt & i броди́ть impf (по+dat).

roar /rɔː(r)/ n (animal's) рёв; vi реве́ть impf.

roast /rəʊst/ vt & i жа́рить(ся) impf, за~, из~ pf; adj жа́реный; **~ beef** ро́стбиф; n жарко́е sb.

rob /rɒb/ vt гра́бить impf, о~ pf; красть impf, у~ pf y+gen (of +acc); (deprive) лиша́ть impf, лиши́ть pf (of +gen). **robber** /ˈrɒbə(r)/ n граби́тель m. **robbery** /ˈrɒbərɪ/ n грабёж.

robe /rəʊb/ n (also pl) ма́нтия.

robin /ˈrɒbɪn/ n мали́новка.

robot /ˈrəʊbɒt/ n ро́бот.

robust /rəʊˈbʌst/ adj кре́пкий.

rock¹ /rɒk/ n (geol) (го́рная) поро́да; (cliff etc.) скала́; (large stone) большо́й ка́мень m; **on the ~s** (in difficulty) на мели́; (drink) со льдом.

rock² /rɒk/ vt & i кача́ть(ся) pf; vi (mus)

рок; **~ing-chair** кача́лка; **~ and roll** рок-н-ро́лл.

rockery /ˈrɒkərɪ/ n альпина́рий.

rocket /ˈrɒkɪt/ n раке́та; vi подска́кивать impf, подскочи́ть pf.

rocky /ˈrɒkɪ/ adj скали́стый; (shaky) ша́ткий.

rod /rɒd/ n (stick) прут; (bar) сте́ржень m; (fishing-~) у́дочка.

rodent /ˈrəʊd(ə)nt/ n грызу́н.

roe[1] /rəʊ/ n икра́; (soft) моло́ки (-о́к) pl.

roe[2] /rəʊ/ (-deer) n косу́ля.

rogue /rəʊg/ n плут.

role /rəʊl/ n роль.

roll[1] /rəʊl/ n (cylinder) руло́н; (register) рее́стр; (bread) бу́лочка; **~-call** переклича́.

roll[2] /rəʊl/ vt & i катáть(ся) indet, кати́ть(ся) det, по~ pf; (~ up) свёртывать(ся) impf, сверну́ть(ся) pf; vt (~ out) (dough) раска́тывать impf, раскатáть pf; vi (sound) греме́ть impf; **~ over** перевора́чиваться impf, переверну́ться pf; (of drums) бараба́нная дробь; (of thunder) раска́т.

roller /ˈrəʊlə(r)/ n (small) ро́лик; (large) като́к; (for hair) бигуди́ neut indecl; **~-skates** коньки́ m pl на ро́ликах.

rolling /ˈrəʊlɪŋ/ adj (of land) холми́стый; **~-pin** ска́лка. **~-stock** подвижно́й соста́в.

Roman /ˈrəʊmən/ n ри́млянин, -я́нка; adj ри́мский; **~ Catholic** (n) като́лик, -и́чка; (adj) ри́мско-католи́ческий.

romance /rəʊˈmæns/ n (tale; love affair) рома́н; (quality) рома́нтика.

Romanesque /ˌrəʊməˈnesk/ adj рома́нский.

Romania /rəʊˈmeɪnɪə/ n Румы́ния. **Romanian** /-nɪən/ n румы́н, ~ка; adj румы́нский.

romantic /rəʊˈmæntɪk/ adj романти́чный, -ческий. **romanticism** /-tɪˌsɪz(ə)m/ n романти́зм.

romp /rɒmp/ vi вози́ться impf.

roof /ruːf/ n кры́ша; **~ of the mouth** нёбо; vt крыть impf, по~ крыть pf.

rook[1] /rʊk/ n (chess) ладья́.

rook[2] /rʊk/ n (bird) грач.

room /ruːm/ n (in house; hotel) ко́мната; (space) ме́сто. **roomy** /ˈruːmɪ/ adj просто́рный.

roost /ruːst/ n насе́ст.

root[1] /ruːt/ n ко́рень m; **take ~** укореня́ться impf, укорени́ться pf; vi пуска́ть impf, пусти́ть pf ко́рни; **~ out** вырыва́ть impf, вы́рвать pf с ко́рнем; **rooted to the spot** прико́ванный к ме́сту.

root[2] /ruːt/ vi (rummage) ры́ться impf; **~ for** боле́ть impf за +acc.

rope /rəʊp/ n верёвка; **~-ladder** верёвочная ле́стница; vt: **~** (enlist) втяга́ть impf, втяну́ть pf; **~ off** o(т)гора́живать impf, о(т)городи́ть pf верёвкой.

rosary /ˈrəʊzərɪ/ n чётки (-ток) pl.

rose /rəʊz/ n ро́за; (nozzle) се́тка.

rosemary /ˈrəʊzmərɪ/ n розмари́н.

rosette /rəʊˈzet/ n розе́тка.

rosewood /ˈrəʊzwʊd/ n ро́зовое де́рево.

roster /ˈrɒstə(r)/ n расписа́ние дежу́рств.

rostrum /ˈrɒstrəm/ n трибу́на.

rosy /ˈrəʊzɪ/ adj ро́зовый; (cheeks) румя́ный.

rot /rɒt/ n гниль; (*nonsense*) вздор; vi гнить impf, c~ pf, vt гноить impf, c~ pf.

rota /'rəʊtə/ n расписание дежурств. **rotary** /'rəʊtərɪ/ adj вращательный, ротационный. **rotate** /rəʊ'teɪt/ vt & i вращать(ся) impf. **rotation** /-'teɪʃ(ə)n/ n вращение; in ~ по очереди.

rote /rəʊt/ n: by ~ наизусть.

rotten /'rɒt(ə)n/ adj гнилой; (*fig*) отвратительный.

rotund /rəʊ'tʌnd/ adj (*round*) круглый; (*plump*) полный.

rouble /'ruːb(ə)l/ n рубль m.

rough /rʌf/ adj (*uneven*) неровный; (*coarse*) грубый; (*sea*) бурный; (*approximate*) приблизительный; ~ copy черновик; n: the ~ трудности f pl; vt: ~ it жить impf без удобств. **roughage** /'rʌfɪdʒ/ n грубая пища. **roughly** /'rʌflɪ/ adv грубо; (*approximately*) приблизительно.

roulette /ruː'let/ n рулетка.

round /raʊnd/ adj круглый; ~-shouldered сутулый; n (*object*) круг; (*circuit*; *also pl*) обход; (*sport*) тур, раунд; (*series*) ряд; (*ammunition*) взрыв; (*of applause*) взрыв; adv вокруг; (*in a circle*) по кругу; all ~ кругом; all the year ~ круглый год; prep вокруг+gen; кругом +gen; по+dat; ~ the corner за угол, (*position*) за углом; vt (*go*) ~ огибать impf, обогнуть pf; ~ off (*complete*) завершать impf, завершить pf; ~ up сгонять impf, согнать pf; ~-up загон; (*raid*) облава. **roundabout** n (*merry-go-round*) карусель; (*road junction*) кольцевая транспортная развязка; adj окольный.

rouse /raʊz/ vt будить impf, раз~ pf; (*to action etc.*) побуждать impf, побудить pf (to к+dat); **rousing** /'raʊzɪŋ/ adj восторженный.

rout /raʊt/ n (*defeat*) разгром.

route /ruːt/ n маршрут, путь m.

routine /ruː'tiːn/ n заведённый порядок, режим; adj установленный; очередной.

rove /rəʊv/ vi скитаться impf.

row¹ /rəʊ/ n (*line*) ряд.

row² /rəʊ/ vi (*in boat*) грести impf.

row³ /raʊ/ n (*dispute*) ссора; (*noise*) шум; vi ссориться impf, по~ pf.

rowdy /'raʊdɪ/ adj буйный.

royal /'rɔɪəl/ adj королевский; (*majestic*) великолепный. **royalist** /-lɪst/ n роялист; adj роялистский. **royalty** /-tɪ/ n член, члены pl, королевской семьи; (*fee*) авторский гонорар.

rub /rʌb/ vt & i тереть(ся) impf; (*polish*; *chafe*) натирать impf, натереть pf; (~ dry) вытирать impf, вытереть pf; ~ in, on втирать impf, втереть pf; ~ out стирать impf, стереть pf; it in растравлять impf, растравить pf рану.

rubber /'rʌbə(r)/ n резина; (*eraser*; *also* ~ band) резинка; attrib резиновый; ~-stamp (*fig*) штамповать impf.

rubbish /'rʌbɪʃ/ n мусор; (*nonsense*) чепуха.

rubble /'rʌb(ə)l/ n щебень m.

rubella /ruː'belə/ n краснуха.

ruby /'ruːbɪ/ n рубин.

ruck /rʌk/ n (~ up) мять impf, из~, c~ pf.

rucksack /'rʌksæk/ n рюкзак.

rudder /'rʌdə(r)/ n руль m.

ruddy /'rʌdɪ/ adj (*face*) румяный; (*damned*) проклятый.

rude /ru:d/ adj грубый. **rudeness** /-nis/ n грубость.

rudimentary /ˌru:dɪˈment(ə)rɪ/ adj рудиментарный. **rudiments** /ˈru:dɪmənts/ n pl основы f pl.

rueful /ˈru:fʊl/ adj печальный.

ruff /rʌf/ n (frill) брыжи (-жей) pl; (of feathers, hair) кольцо (перьев, шерсти) вокруг шеи.

ruffian /ˈrʌfɪən/ n хулиган.

ruffle /ˈrʌf(ə)l/ n оборка; vt (hair) ерошить impf, взъ~ pf; (water) рябить impf, идти det; (person) смущать impf, смутить pf.

rug /rʌg/ n (mat) ковёр; (wrap) плед.

rugby /ˈrʌgbɪ/ n регби neut indecl.

rugged /ˈrʌgɪd/ adj (rocky) скалистый.

ruin /ˈru:ɪn/ n (downfall) гибель; (building, ruins) развалины f pl, руины f pl; vt губить impf, по~ pf. **ruinous** /-nəs/ adj губительный.

rule /ru:l/ n правило; (for measuring) линейка; (government) правление; **as a** ~ как правило; vt & i править impf (+instr); (decree) постановлять impf, постановить pf; ~ **out** исключать impf, исключить pf. **ruled** /ru:ld/ adj линованный. **ruler** /ˈru:lə(r)/ n (person) правитель m, ~ница; (object) линейка. **ruling** /ˈru:lɪŋ/ n (of court etc.) постановление.

rum /rʌm/ n (drink) ром.

Rumania(n) /rəˈmeɪnɪə(n)/ see Romania(n)

rumble /ˈrʌmb(ə)l/ vi грохотать impf; n грохотание.

ruminant /ˈru:mɪnənt/ n жва́чное (животное) sb. **ruminate** /-ˌneɪt/ vi (fig) размышлять impf (**over**, **on** +prep).

rummage /ˈrʌmɪdʒ/ vi рыться

impf.

rumour /ˈru:mə(r)/ n слух; vt: **it is** ~ed **that** ходят слухи (pl), что.

rump /rʌmp/ n крестец; ~ **steak** ромштекс.

rumple /ˈrʌmp(ə)l/ vt мять impf, из~, с~ pf; (hair) ерошить impf, взъ~ pf.

run /rʌn/ n бег; vi бегать indet, бежать det, по~ pf; (work, of machines) работать impf; (ply, of bus etc.) ходить indet, идти det; (seek election) выставлять impf, выставить pf свою кандидатуру (of play etc.) идти impf; (of ink, dye) расплываться impf, расплыться pf; (flow) течь impf (of document) гласить impf; (manage; operate) управлять impf +instr; (a business etc. вести impf; ~ **dry, low** иссякать impf, иссякнуть pf; ~ **risks** рисковать impf; ~ **across, into** (meet) встречаться impf встретиться pf c+instr; ~ **away** (flee) убегать impf, убежать pf ~ **down** (knock down) задавить pf; (disparage) принижать impf принизить pf; **be** ~ **down** (of person) переутомиться pf (in past tense); ~**down** (decayed) запущенный; ~ **in** (engine) обкатывать impf, обкатать pf; ~ **into** see ~ **across;** ~ **out** кончаться impf, кончиться pf; ~ **out of** истощать impf, истощить pf свой запас +gen; ~ **over** (glance over) бегло просматривать impf, просмотреть pf; (injure) задавить pf; ~ **through** (pierce) прокалывать impf, проколоть pf; (money) прома́тывать impf, промота́ть pf; (review) повторять impf, повторить pf; ~ **to** (reach) (of money) хватать impf, хватить

pf impers+gen на+*acc*; **the money won't ~ to a car** э́тих де́нег не хва́тит на маши́ну; **~ up against** ната́лкиваться *impf*, натолкну́ться *pf* на+*acc*; *n* бег; (*sport*) перебе́жка; (*journey*) пое́здка; (*period*) полоса́; **at a ~ бего́м; on the ~** в бега́х; **~ on** большо́й спрос на+*acc*; **in the long ~** в конце́ концо́в.

rung /rʌŋ/ *n* ступе́нька.

runner /'rʌnə/ *n* (*also tech*) бегу́н; (*of sledge*) по́лоз; (*bot*) побе́г; **~ bean** фасо́ль; **~-up** уча́стник, заня́вший второ́е ме́сто. **running** /'rʌnɪŋ/ *n* бег; (*management*) управле́ние (*of* +*instr*); **be in the ~** име́ть *impf* ша́нсы; (*of* бегу́щий; (*of* ~) берегово́й; (*after pl n, in succession*) подря́д; **~ commentary** репорта́ж; **~ water** водопрово́д. **runway** *n* взлётно-поса́дочная полоса́.

rupee /ruːˈpiː/ *n* ру́пия.

rupture /ˈrʌptʃə(r)/ *n* разры́в; *vt & i* прорыва́ть(ся) *impf*, прорва́ть(ся) *pf*.

rural /ˈrʊər(ə)l/ *adj* се́льский.

ruse /ruːz/ *n* уло́вка.

rush¹ /rʌʃ/ *n* (*bot*) тростни́к.

rush² /rʌʃ/ *vt & i* (*hurry*) торопи́ть(ся) *impf*, по~ *pf*; *vi* (*dash*) броса́ться *impf*, бро́ситься *pf*; (*of water*) нести́сь *impf*; по~ *pf*; *vt* (*to hospital etc.*) умча́ть *pf*; *n* (*of blood etc.*) прили́в; (*hurry*) спе́шка; **be in a ~** торопи́ться *impf*; **~-hour(s)** часы́ *m pl* пик.

Russia /ˈrʌʃə/ *n* Росси́я. **Russian** /-ʃ(ə)n/ *n* ру́сский *sb*; *adj* (*of ~ nationality, culture*) ру́сский; (*of ~ State*) росси́йский.

rust /rʌst/ *n* ржа́вчина; *vi* ржаве́ть *impf*, за~, по~ *pf*.

rustic /ˈrʌstɪk/ *adj* дереве́нский.

rustle /ˈrʌs(ə)l/ *n* ше́лест, шо́рох, шурша́ние; *vi & t* шелесте́ть *impf* (+*instr*); **~ up** раздобыва́ть *impf*; раздобы́ть *pf*.

rusty /ˈrʌstɪ/ *adj* ржа́вый.

rut /rʌt/ *n* коле́я.

ruthless /ˈruːθlɪs/ *adj* безжа́лостный.

rye /raɪ/ *n* рожь; *attrib* ржано́й.

S

Sabbath /ˈsæbəθ/ *n* (*Jewish*) суббо́та; (*Christian*) воскресе́нье.

sabbatical /səˈbætɪk(ə)l/ *n* годи́чный о́тпуск.

sable /ˈseɪb(ə)l/ *n* со́боль.

sabotage /ˈsæbətɑːʒ/ *n* диве́рсия; *vt* саботи́ровать *impf & pf*. **saboteur** /ˌsæbəˈtɜː(r)/ *n* диверса́нт.

sabre /ˈseɪbə(r)/ *n* са́бля.

sachet /ˈsæʃeɪ/ *n* упако́вка.

sack¹ /sæk/ *vt* (*plunder*) разгра́бить *pf*.

sack² /sæk/ *n* мешо́к; (*dismissal*): **get the ~** быть уво́ленным; *vt* увольня́ть *impf*, уво́лить *pf*. **sacking** /-kɪŋ/ *n* (*hessian*) мешкови́на.

sacrament /ˈsækrəmənt/ *n* та́инство; (*Eucharist*) прича́стие. **sacred** /ˈseɪkrɪd/ *adj* свяще́нный, свято́й. **sacrifice** /ˈsækrɪfaɪs/ *n* же́ртва; *vt* же́ртвовать *impf*, по~ *pf* +*instr*. **sacrilege** /ˈsækrɪlɪdʒ/ *n* святота́тство. **sacrosanct** /ˈsækrəʊˌsæŋkt/ *adj* свяще́нный.

sad /sæd/ *adj* печа́льный, гру́стный. **sadden** /-d(ə)n/ *vt* печа́лить *impf*, о~ *pf*.

saddle /ˈsæd(ə)l/ *n* седло́; *vt* седла́ть *impf*, о~ *pf*; (*burden*) об-

ремня́ть *impf*, обремени́ть *pf* (with +*instr*).

sadism /'seɪdɪz(ə)m/ *n* сади́зм. **sadist** /-dɪst/ *n* сади́ст. **sadistic** /sə'dɪstɪk/ *adj* сади́стский.

sadness /'sædnɪs/ *n* печа́ль, грусть.

safe /seɪf/ *n* сейф; *adj* (*unharmed*) невреди́мый; (*out of danger*) в безопа́сности; (*secure*) безопа́сный; (*reliable*) надёжный; ~ **and sound** цел и невреди́м. **safeguard** *n* предохрани́тельная ме́ра; *vt* предохраня́ть *impf*, предохрани́ть *pf*. **safety** /-tɪ/ *n* безопа́сность; ~**belt** реме́нь *m* безопа́сности; ~ **pin** англи́йская була́вка; ~**valve** предохрани́тельный кла́пан.

sag /sæg/ *vi* (*of rope, curtain*) провиса́ть *impf*, прови́снуть *pf*; (*of ceiling*) прогиба́ться *impf*, прогну́ться *pf*.

saga /'sɑːgə/ *n* са́га.

sage[1] /seɪdʒ/ *n* (*herb*) шалфе́й.

sage[2] /seɪdʒ/ *n* (*person*) мудре́ц; *adj* му́дрый.

Sagittarius /ˌsædʒɪ'teərɪəs/ *n* Стреле́ц.

sail /seɪl/ *n* па́рус; *vt* (*a ship*) управля́ть *impf* +*instr*; *vi* пла́вать *indet*, плыть *det*; (*depart*) отплыва́ть *impf*, отплы́ть *pf*. **sailing** /-lɪŋ/ *n* (*sport*) па́русный спорт; ~**ship** па́русное су́дно. **sailor** /-lə(r)/ *n* матро́с, моря́к.

saint /seɪnt/ *n* свято́й *sb*. **saintly** /-lɪ/ *adj* свято́й.

sake /seɪk/ *n*: **for the ~ of** ра́ди+*gen*.

salad /'sæləd/ *n* сала́т; ~**dressing** припра́ва к сала́ту.

salami /sə'lɑːmɪ/ *n* саля́ми *f indecl*.

salary /'sælərɪ/ *n* жа́лованье.

sale /seɪl/ *n* прода́жа; (*also*

amount sold) сбыт (*no pl*); (*with reduced prices*) распрода́жа; **be for ~** продава́ться *impf*. **saleable** /-ləb(ə)l/ *adj* хо́дкий. **salesman** /'seɪlzmən/ *n* продаве́ц. **saleswoman** /'seɪlzˌwʊmən/ *n* продавщи́ца.

salient /'seɪlɪənt/ *adj* основно́й.

saliva /sə'laɪvə/ *n* слюна́.

sallow /'sæləʊ/ *adj* желтова́тый.

salmon /'sæmən/ *n* ло́сось *m*.

salon /'sælɒn/ *n* сало́н. **saloon** /sə'luːn/ *n* (*on ship*) сало́н; (*car*) седа́н; (*bar*) бар.

salt /sɔːlt/ *n* соль; ~ **water** морска́я вода́; ~**water** морско́й; *adj* солёный; ~ **vt** соли́ть *impf*, по~ *pf*. **salty** /-tɪ/ *adj* солёный.

salutary /'sæljʊtərɪ/ *adj* благотво́рный. **salute** /sə'luːt/ *n* отда́ние че́сти; (*with guns*) салю́т; *vt* & *i* отдава́ть *impf*, отда́ть *pf* честь (+*dat*).

salvage /'sælvɪdʒ/ *n* спасе́ние; *vt* спаса́ть *impf*, спасти́ *pf*.

salvation /sæl'veɪʃ(ə)n/ *n* спасе́ние; **S~ Army** А́рмия спасе́ния.

salve /sælv/ *n* мазь; *vt*: ~ **one's conscience** успока́ивать *impf* со́весть.

salvo /'sælvəʊ/ *n* залп.

same /seɪm/ *adj*: **the ~** тот же (са́мый); (*applying to both or all*) оди́н; (*identical*) одина́ковый; *pron*: **the ~** одно́ и то́ же; то же са́мое; *adv*: **the ~** таки́м же о́бразом, так же; **all the ~** всё-таки, тем не ме́нее. **sameness** /-nɪs/ *n* однообра́зие.

samovar /'sæməvɑː(r)/ *n* самова́р.

sample /'sɑːmp(ə)l/ *n* образе́ц; *vt* про́бовать *impf*, по~ *pf*.

sanatorium /ˌsænə'tɔːrɪəm/ *n* санато́рий.

sanctify /ˈsæŋktɪˌfaɪ/ vt освящать impf, освятить pf. **sanctimonious** /ˌsæŋktɪˈməʊnɪəs/ adj ханжеский. **sanction** /ˈsæŋkʃ(ə)n/ n санкция; vt санкционировать impf & pf. **sanctity** /ˈsæŋktɪtɪ/ n (holiness) святость; (sacredness) священность. **sanctuary** /ˈsæŋktjʊərɪ/ n святилище; (refuge) убежище; (for wild life) заповедник.

sand /sænd/ n песок; vt (~ down) шкурить impf, по~ pf; ~dune дюна.

sandal /ˈsænd(ə)l/ n сандалия.

sandalwood /ˈsænd(ə)lwʊd/ n сандаловое дерево.

sandbank /ˈsændbæŋk/ n отмель.

sandpaper /ˈsændˌpeɪpə(r)/ n шкурка; vt шлифовать impf, от~ pf шкуркой.

sandstone /ˈsændstəʊn/ n песчаник.

sandwich /ˈsænwɪdʒ/ n бутерброд; vt: ~ between втискивать impf, втиснуть pf между +instr.

sandy /ˈsændɪ/ adj (of sand) песчаный; (like sand) песочный; (hair) рыжеватый.

sane /seɪn/ adj нормальный; (sensible) разумный.

sang-froid /sɑ̃ˈfrwɑː/ n самообладание.

sanguine /ˈsæŋgwɪn/ adj оптимистический.

sanitary /ˈsænɪtərɪ/ adj санитарный; гигиенический; ~ towel гигиеническая подушка. **sanitation** /ˌsænɪˈteɪʃ(ə)n/ n (conditions) санитарные условия neut pl; (system) водопровод и канализация. **sanity** /ˈsænɪtɪ/ n психическое здоровье; (good sense) здравый смысл.

sap /sæp/ n (bot) сок; vt (exhaust) истощать impf, истощить pf.

sapling /ˈsæplɪŋ/ n саженец.

sapphire /ˈsæfaɪə(r)/ n сапфир.

sarcasm /ˈsɑːkæz(ə)m/ n сарказм. **sarcastic** /sɑːˈkæstɪk/ adj саркастический.

sardine /sɑːˈdiːn/ n сардина.

sardonic /sɑːˈdɒnɪk/ adj сардонический.

sash[1] /sæʃ/ n (scarf) кушак.

sash[2] /sæʃ/ n (frame) скользящая рама; ~-window подъёмное окно.

satanic /səˈtænɪk/ adj сатанинский.

satchel /ˈsætʃ(ə)l/ n ранец, сумка.

satellite /ˈsætəˌlaɪt/ n спутник, сателлит (also fig); ~ dish параболическая антенна; тарелка (coll); ~ TV спутниковое телевидение.

satiate /ˈseɪʃɪˌeɪt/ vt насыщать impf, насытить pf.

satin /ˈsætɪn/ n атлас.

satire /ˈsætaɪə(r)/ n сатира. **satirical** /səˈtɪrɪk(ə)l/ adj сатирический. **satirist** /ˈsætɪrɪst/ n сатирик. **satirize** /-ˌraɪz/ vt высмеивать impf, высмеять pf.

satisfaction /ˌsætɪsˈfækʃ(ə)n/ n удовлетворение. **satisfactory** /-ˈfækt(ə)rɪ/ adj удовлетворительный. **satisfy** /ˈsætɪsˌfaɪ/ vt удовлетворять impf, удовлетворить pf; (hunger, curiosity) утолять impf, утолить pf.

saturate /ˈsætʃəˌreɪt/ vt насыщать impf, насытить pf; I got ~d (by rain) я промок до нитки. **saturation** /ˌsætʃəˈreɪʃ(ə)n/ n насыщение.

Saturday /ˈsætəˌdeɪ/ n суббота.

sauce /sɔːs/ n соус; (cheek) наглость. **saucepan** /n кастрюля. **saucer** /ˈsɔːsə(r)/ n блюдце.

saucy /'sɔːsɪ/ *adj* на́глый.

Saudi /'saʊdɪ/ *n* сау́довец, -вка; *adj* сау́довский. **Saudi Arabia** /,saʊdɪ əˈreɪbɪə/ *n* Сау́довская Ара́вия.

sauna /'sɔːnə/ *n* фи́нская ба́ня.

saunter /'sɔːntə(r)/ *vi* прогу́ливаться *impf*.

sausage /'sɒsɪdʒ/ *n* соси́ска; (*salami-type*) колбаса́.

savage /'sævɪdʒ/ *adj* ди́кий; (*fierce*) свире́пый; (*cruel*) жесто́кий; *n* дика́рь *m*; *vt* искуса́ть *pf*. **savagery** /-rɪ/ *n* ди́кость; жесто́кость.

save /seɪv/ *vt* (*rescue*) спаса́ть *impf*, спасти́ *pf*; (*money*) копи́ть *impf*, на~ *pf*; (*put aside, keep*) бере́чь *impf*; (*avoid using*) эконо́мить *impf*, с~ *pf*; *vi*: ~ up копи́ть *impf*, на~ *pf* де́ньги.

savings /-vɪŋz/ *n pl* сбереже́ния *neut pl*; ~ **bank** сберега́тельная ка́сса. **saviour** /-vjə(r)/ *n* спаси́тель *m*.

savour /'seɪvə(r)/ *vt* смакова́ть *impf*.

savoury /'seɪvərɪ/ *adj* пика́нтный; (*fig*) поря́дочный.

saw /sɔː/ *n* пила́; *vt* пили́ть *impf*; ~ **up** распи́ливать *impf*, распили́ть *pf*. **sawdust** *n* опи́лки (-лок) *pl*.

saxophone /'sæksəfəʊn/ *n* саксофо́н.

say /seɪ/ *vt* говори́ть *impf*, сказа́ть *pf*; **to** ~ **nothing of** не говоря́ уже́ о+*prep*; **that is to** ~ то есть; (*let us*) ска́жем; **it is said** (**that**) говоря́т (что); (*in opinion*) мне́ние, (*influence*) влия́ние; **have one's** ~ вы́сказаться *pf*. **saying** /'seɪŋ/ *n* погово́рка.

scab /skæb/ *n* (*on wound*) струп; (*polit*) штрейкбре́хер.

scabbard /'skæbəd/ *n* но́жны (*gen* -жен) *pl*.

scaffold /'skæfəʊld/ *n* эшафо́т. **scaffolding** /-dɪŋ/ *n* леса́ (-со́в) *pl*.

scald /skɔːld/ *vt* обва́ривать *impf*, обвари́ть *pf*.

scale /skeɪl/ *n* (*ratio*) масшта́б; (*grading*) шкала́; (*mus*) га́мма; *vt* (*climb*) взбира́ться *impf*, взобра́ться *pf* на+*acc*; ~ **down** понижа́ть *impf*, пони́зить *pf*.

scales¹ /skeɪlz/ *n pl* (*of fish*) чешуя́ (*collect*).

scales² /skeɪlz/ *n pl* весы́ (-со́в) *pl*.

scallop /'skɒləp/ *n* гребешо́к; (*decoration*) фесто́н.

scalp /skælp/ *n* ко́жа головы́.

scalpel /'skælp(ə)l/ *n* ска́льпель *m*.

scaly /'skeɪlɪ/ *adj* чешу́йчатый; (*of boiler etc.*) покры́тый на́кипью.

scamper /'skæmpə(r)/ *vi* бы́стро бе́гать *impf*; (*frolic*) резви́ться *impf*.

scan /skæn/ *vt* (*intently*) рассма́тривать *impf*, (*quickly*) просма́тривать *impf*, просмотре́ть *impf*; (*med*) просве́чивать *impf*, просвети́ть *pf*; *n* просве́чивание.

scandal /'skænd(ə)l/ *n* сканда́л; (*gossip*) спле́тни (-тен) *pl*. **scandalize** /-,laɪz/ *vt* шоки́ровать *impf* & *pf*. **scandalous** /-ləs/ *adj* сканда́льный.

Scandinavia /,skændɪˈneɪvɪə/ *n* Скандина́вия. **Scandinavian** /-vɪən/ *adj* скандина́вский.

scanner /'skænə(r)/ *n* (*comput, med*) ска́нер.

scanty /'skæntɪ/ *adj* ску́дный.

scapegoat /'skeɪpɡəʊt/ *n* козёл отпуще́ния.

scar /skɑː(r)/ *n* шрам; *vt* оставля́ть *impf*, оста́вить *pf* шрам на+*prep*.

scarce /skeəs/ *adj* дефици́тный;

scare *(rare)* ре́дкий. **scarcely** /-lɪ/ *adv* едва́. **scarcity** /-sɪtɪ/ *n* дефици́т; ре́дкость.

scare /skeə(r)/ *vt* пуга́ть *impf*, ис~, на~ *pf*; ~ **away**, **off** отпу́гивать *impf*, отпугну́ть *pf*; *n* па́ника. **scarecrow** *n* пу́гало.

scarf /skɑːf/ *n* шарф.

scarlet /ˈskɑːlɪt/ *adj* (*n*) а́лый (цвет).

scathing /ˈskeɪðɪŋ/ *adj* уничтожа́ющий.

scatter /ˈskætə(r)/ *vt* & *i* рассыпа́ть(ся) *impf*, рассы́пать(ся) *pf*; *(disperse)* рассе́ивать(ся) *impf*, рассе́ять(ся) *pf*; ~**-brained** ве́треный. **scattered** /-təd/ *adj* разбро́санный; *(sporadic)* отде́льный.

scavenge /ˈskævɪndʒ/ *vi* ры́ться *impf* в отбро́сах. **scavenger** /-dʒə(r)/ *n* (*person*) мусо́рщик; (*animal*) живо́тное *sb*, пита́ющееся па́далью.

scenario /sɪˈnɑːrɪəʊ/ *n* сцена́рий. **scene** /siːn/ *n* (*place of disaster etc.*) ме́сто; (*place of action*) ме́сто де́йствия; (*view*) вид, пейза́ж; (*picture*) карти́на; (*theat*) сце́на, явле́ние; (*incident*) сце́на; **behind the** ~**s** за кули́сами; **make a** ~ устра́ивать *impf*, устро́ить *pf* сце́ну. **scenery** /ˈsiːnərɪ/ *n* (*theat*) декора́ция; (*landscape*) пейза́ж. **scenic** /ˈsiːnɪk/ *adj* живопи́сный.

scent /sent/ *n* (*smell*) арома́т; (*perfume*) духи́ (-хо́в) *pl*; (*trail*) след. **scented** /-tɪd/ *adj* души́стый.

sceptic /ˈskeptɪk/ *n* ске́птик. **sceptical** /-k(ə)l/ *adj* скепти́ческий. **scepticism** /-tɪˌsɪz(ə)m/ *n* скептици́зм.

schedule /ˈʃedjuːl/ *n* (*timetable*) расписа́ние; *vt* составля́ть *impf*, соста́вить *pf* расписа́ние +*gen*.

schematic /skɪˈmætɪk/ *adj* схемати́ческий. **scheme** /skiːm/ *n* (*plan*) прое́кт; (*intrigue*) махина́ция; *vi* интригова́ть *impf*.

schism /ˈskɪz(ə)m/ *n* раско́л.

schizophrenia /ˌskɪtsəˈfriːnɪə/ *n* шизофрени́я. **schizophrenic** /-ˈfrenɪk/ *adj* шизофрени́ческий; *n* шизофре́ник.

scholar /ˈskɒlə(r)/ *n* учёный *sb*; **scholarly** /-lɪ/ *adj* учёный. **scholarship** *n* учёность; (*payment*) стипе́ндия.

school /skuːl/ *n* шко́ла; *attrib* шко́льный; *vt* (*train*) приуча́ть *impf*, приучи́ть *pf* (**to** к+*dat*, +*inf*). **school-book** *n* уче́бник. **schoolboy** *n* шко́льник. **schoolgirl** *n* шко́льница. **schooling** /-lɪŋ/ *n* обуче́ние. **school-leaver** /-ˌliːvə(r)/ *n* вы́пускник, -ища́. **school teacher** *n* учи́тель *m*, ~ница.

schooner /ˈskuːnə(r)/ *n* шху́на.

sciatica /saɪˈætɪkə/ *n* и́шиас.

science /ˈsaɪəns/ *n* нау́ка; ~ **fiction** нау́чная фанта́стика. **scientific** /ˌsaɪənˈtɪfɪk/ *adj* нау́чный. **scientist** /ˈsaɪəntɪst/ *n* учёный *sb*.

scintillating /ˈsɪntɪˌleɪtɪŋ/ *adj* блиста́тельный.

scissors /ˈsɪzəz/ *n pl* но́жницы (-ц) *pl*.

scoff /skɒf/ *vi* (*mock*) смея́ться *impf* (**at** над+*instr*).

scold /skəʊld/ *vt* брани́ть *impf*, вы́~ *pf*.

scoop /skuːp/ *n* (*large*) черпа́к; (*ice-cream* ~) ло́жка для моро́женого; *vt* (~ *out*, *up*) вычёрпывать *impf*, вы́черпать *pf*.

scooter /ˈskuːtə(r)/ *n* (*motor* ~) мотороллер.

scope /skəʊp/ *n* (*range*) преде́лы

m pl; (chance) возмо́жность.

scorch /skɔːtʃ/ vt (fingers) обжига́ть impf, обжёчь pf; (clothes) сжига́ть impf, сжечь pf.

score /skɔː(r)/ n (of points etc.) счёт; (mus) партиту́ра; pl (great numbers) мно́жество; vt (notch) де́лать impf, c~ pf зару́бки на+prep; (points etc.) получа́ть impf, получи́ть pf; (mus) оркестрова́ть impf & pf; vi (keep ~) вести́ impf, c~ pf счёт. **scorer** /-rə(r)/ n счётчик.

scorn /skɔːn/ n презре́ние; vt презира́ть impf презре́ть pf. **scornful** /-fʊl/ adj презри́тельный.

Scorpio /'skɔːpɪəʊ/ n Скорпио́н.

scorpion /'skɔːpɪən/ n скорпио́н.

Scot /skɒt/ n шотла́ндец, -дка. **Scotch** /skɒtʃ/ n (whisky) шотла́ндское ви́ски neut indecl. **Scotland** n Шотла́ндия. **Scots**, **Scottish** /skɒts, 'skɒtɪʃ/ adj шотла́ндский.

scoundrel /'skaʊndrəl/ n подле́ц.

scour[1] /'skaʊə(r)/ vt (cleanse) отчища́ть impf, отчи́стить pf.

scour[2] /'skaʊə(r)/ vt & i (rove) рыска́ть impf (по+dat).

scourge /skɜːdʒ/ n бич.

scout /skaʊt/ n разве́дчик; (S~) бойска́ут; vi: ~ about разы́скивать (for +acc).

scowl /skaʊl/ vi хму́риться impf, на~ pf; n хму́рый взгляд.

scrabble /'skræb(ə)l/ vi: ~ about ры́ться impf.

scramble /'skræmb(ə)l/ vi кара́бкаться impf, вс~ pf; (struggle) дра́ться impf (for за+acc); ~d eggs яи́чница-болту́нья.

scrap[1] /skræp/ n (fragment etc.) кусо́чек; pl оста́тки m pl; pl (of food) объе́дки -ков pl; ~ metá металло́лом; vt сдава́ть impf сдать pf в утиль.

scrap[2] /skræp/ n (fight) дра́ка; v дра́ться impf.

scrape /skreɪp/ vt скрести́ impf (graze) цара́пать impf, o~ pf ~ off отскреба́ть impf, отскре сти́ pf; ~ through (exam) с тру до́м выде́рживать impf выдержать pf; ~ together на скреба́ть impf, наскрести́ pf.

scratch /skrætʃ/ vt цара́пат impf, o~ pf; vt & i (when itching чеса́ть(ся) impf, по~ pf; n ца ра́пина.

scrawl /skrɔːl/ n кара́кул f pl; v писа́ть impf, на~ pf кара́ кулями.

scrawny /'skrɔːnɪ/ adj сухо па́рый.

scream /skriːm/ n крик; vi кри ча́ть impf, кри́кнуть pf.

screech /skriːtʃ/ n визг; vi виз жа́ть impf.

screen /skriːn/ n ши́рма; (cin TV) экра́н; ~**play** сцена́рий; v (protect) защища́ть impf, за щити́ть pf; (hide) укрыва́т impf, укры́ть pf; (show film etc. демонстри́ровать impf & pf (check on) проверя́ть impf прове́рить pf; ~ off отгора́жи вать impf, отгороди́ть pf ши́рмой.

screw /skruː/ n винт; vt (~ on привинчивать impf, привин ти́ть pf; (~ up) зави́нчивать impf, завинти́ть pf; (crumple ко́мкать impf, c~ pf; ~ up one's eyes щу́риться impf, co~ pf **screwdriver** n отвёртка.

scribble /'skrɪb(ə)l/ vt строчи́т impf, на~ pf; n кара́кули f pl.

script /skrɪpt/ n (of film etc.) сце-

на́рий; (*of speech etc.*) текст; (*writing system*) письмо́; ~**writer** сценари́ст.

Scripture /'skrɪptʃə(r)/ *n* свяще́нное писа́ние.

scroll /skrəʊl/ *n* сви́ток; (*design*) завито́к; *vi* (*comput*) прокру́чивать *impf*, прокрути́ть *pf*.

scrounge /skraʊndʒ/ *vt* (*cadge*) стре́льнуть *impf*, стрельну́ть *pf*; *vi* попроша́йничать *impf*.

scrub¹ /skrʌb/ *n* (*brushwood*) куста́рник; (*area*) за́росли *f pl*.

scrub² /skrʌb/ *vt* мыть *impf*, вы́~ *pf* щёткой.

scruff /skrʌf/ *n*: by the ~ of the neck за ши́ворот.

scruffy /'skrʌfɪ/ *adj* обо́рванный.

scrum /skrʌm/ *n* схва́тка вокру́г мяча́.

scruple /'skruːp(ə)l/ *n* (*also pl*) колеба́ния *neut pl*; угрызе́ния *neut pl* со́вести. **scrupulous** /-pjʊləs/ *adj* скрупулёзный.

scrutinize /'skruːtɪˌnaɪz/ *vt* рассма́тривать *impf*. **scrutiny** /'skruːtɪnɪ/ *n* рассмотре́ние.

scuffed /skʌft/ *adj* поцара́панный.

scuffle /'skʌf(ə)l/ *n* пота́совка.

sculpt /skʌlpt/ *vt* вая́ть *impf*, из~ *pf*. **sculptor** /-tə(r)/ *n* ску́льптор. **sculpture** /-tʃə(r)/ *n* скульпту́ра.

scum /skʌm/ *n* на́кипь.

scurrilous /'skʌrɪləs/ *adj* непристо́йный.

scurry /'skʌrɪ/ *vi* поспе́шно бе́гать *indet*, бежа́ть *det*.

scuttle /'skʌt(ə)l/ *vi* (*run away*) удира́ть *impf*, удра́ть *pf*.

scythe /saɪð/ *n* коса́.

sea /siː/ *n* мо́ре; *attrib* морско́й; ~ **front** на́бережная *sb*; ~**gull** ча́йка; ~**level** у́ровень *m* мо́ря; ~**lion** морско́й лев;

~**shore** побере́жье. **seaboard** *n* побере́жье. **seafood** *n* проду́кты *m pl* мо́ря.

seal¹ /siːl/ *n* (*on document etc.*) печа́ть; *vt* скрепля́ть *impf*, скрепи́ть *pf* печа́тью; (*close*) запеча́тывать *impf*, запеча́тать *pf*; ~ **up** заде́лывать *impf*, заде́лать *pf*.

seal² /siːl/ *n* (*zool*) тюле́нь *m*; (*fur*~) ко́тик.

seam /siːm/ *n* шов; (*geol*) пласт.

seaman /'siːm(ə)n/ *n* моря́к, матро́с.

seamless /'siːmlɪs/ *adj* без шва.

seamstress /'semstrɪs/ *n* швея́.

seance /'seɪɑːs/ *n* спирити́ческий сеа́нс.

seaplane /'siːpleɪn/ *n* гидросамолёт.

searing /'sɪərɪŋ/ *adj* паля́щий.

search /sɜːtʃ/ *vt* обы́скивать *impf*, обыска́ть *pf*; *vi* иска́ть *impf* (**for** +*acc*); *n* по́иски *m pl*; о́быск; ~**party** по́исковая гру́ппа. **searching** /-tʃɪŋ/ *adj* (*look*) испыту́ющий. **searchlight** *n* проже́ктор.

seasick /'siːsɪk/ *adj*: **I was** ~ меня́ укача́ло. **seaside** *n* бе́рег мо́ря.

season /'siːz(ə)n/ *n* сезо́н; (*one of four*) вре́мя *neut* го́да; ~ **ticket** сезо́нный биле́т; *vt* (*flavour*) приправля́ть *impf*, приправля́ть *pf*. **seasonable** /-nəb(ə)l/ *adj* по сезо́ну; (*timely*) своевре́менный. **seasonal** /-n(ə)l/ *adj* сезо́нный. **seasoning** /-nɪŋ/ *n* припра́ва.

seat /siːt/ *n* (*place*) ме́сто; (*of chair*) сиде́нье; (*chair*) стул; (*bench*) скамья́; (*of trousers*) зад; ~ **belt** привязно́й реме́нь *m*; *vt* сажа́ть *impf*, посади́ть *pf*;

(of room etc.) вмеща́ть impf, вмести́ть pf; be ~ed сади́ться impf, сесть pf. **seaweed** /'siːwiːd/ n морска́я во́доросль.

secateurs /ˌsekəˈtɜːz/ n pl сека́тор.

secede /sɪˈsiːd/ vi отка́лываться impf, отколо́ться pf. **secession** /-ˈseʃ(ə)n/ n отко́л.

secluded /sɪˈkluːdɪd/ adj укро́мный. **seclusion** /-ˈkluːʒ(ə)n/ n укро́мность.

second[1] /'sekənd/ adj второ́й; ~-class второкла́ссный; ~-hand подёржанный; (of information) из вторы́х рук; ~-rate второразря́дный; on ~ sight яснови́дение; on ~ thoughts взве́сив всё ещё раз; have ~ thoughts переду́мывать impf, переду́мать pf (about +acc); n второ́й sb; (date) второ́е (число́) sb; (time) секу́нда sb; (comm) това́р второ́го со́рта; ~ hand (of clock) секу́ндная стре́лка; vt (support) подде́рживать impf, поддержа́ть pf; (transfer) откомандиро́вывать impf откомандирова́ть pf. **secondary** /-dərɪ/ adj втори́чный, второстепе́нный; (education) сре́дний. **secondly** /-lɪ/ adv во-вторы́х.

secrecy /'siːkrɪsɪ/ n секре́тность. **secret** /'siːkrɪt/ n та́йна, секре́т; adj та́йный, секре́тный; (hidden) потайно́й.

secretarial /ˌsekrɪˈteərɪəl/ adj секрета́рский. **secretariat** /-'teərɪət/ n секретариа́т. **secretary** /'sekrɪtərɪ/ n секрета́рь m, -рша; (minister) мини́стр.

secrete /sɪˈkriːt/ vt (conceal) укрыва́ть impf, укры́ть pf; (med) выделя́ть impf, выде-

лить pf. **secretion** /-ˈkriːʃ(ə)n/ n укрыва́ние; (med) выделе́ние.

secretive /'siːkrɪtɪv/ adj скры́тный.

sect /sekt/ n се́кта. **sectarian** /sekˈteərɪən/ adj секта́нтский.

section /'sekʃ(ə)n/ n се́кция; (of book) разде́л; (geom) сече́ние. **sector** /'sektə(r)/ n се́ктор.

secular /'sekjʊlə(r)/ adj све́тский. **secularization** /ˌsekjʊləraɪ-'zeɪʃ(ə)n/ n секуляриза́ция.

secure /sɪˈkjʊə(r)/ adj (safe) безопа́сный; (firm) надёжный; (emotionally) уве́ренный; vt (fasten) закрепля́ть impf, закрепи́ть pf; (guarantee) обеспе́-чивать impf, обеспе́чить pf; (obtain) достава́ть impf, доста́ть pf. **security** /-ˈkjʊərɪtɪ/ n безопа́сность; (guarantee) зало́г; pl це́нные бума́ги f pl.

sedate /sɪˈdeɪt/ adj степе́нный. **sedation** /sɪˈdeɪʃ(ə)n/ n успокое́-ние. **sedative** /'sedətɪv/ n успока́ивающее сре́дство.

sedentary /'sedəntərɪ/ adj сидя́чий.

sediment /'sedɪmənt/ n оса́док.

seduce /sɪˈdjuːs/ vt соблазня́ть impf, соблазни́ть pf. **seduction** /-ˈdʌkʃ(ə)n/ n обольще́ние. **seductive** /-ˈdʌktɪv/ adj соблазни́тельный.

see /siː/ vt & i ви́деть impf, у~ pf; vt (watch, look) смотре́ть impf, по~ pf; (find out) узнава́ть impf, узна́ть pf; (understand) понима́ть impf, поня́ть pf; (meet) ви́деться impf, у~ pf c+instr; (imagine) представля́ть impf, предста́вить себе́; (escort, ~ off) провожа́ть impf, проводи́ть pf; ~ about (attend to) забо́титься impf, по~ pf o+prep; ~ through (fig) по~ pf ви́деть impf, наскво́зь+acc.

seed /siːd/ *n* се́мя *neut*. **seedling**
/-lɪŋ/ *n* сея́нец; *pl* расса́да.
seedy /-dɪ/ *adj* (*shabby*)
потрёпанный.

seeing (that) /'siːɪŋ (ðæt)/ *conj*
ввиду́ того́, что.

seek /siːk/ *vt* иска́ть *impf* +*acc,*
gen.

seem /siːm/ *vi* каза́ться *impf,*
по~ *pf* (+*instr*). **seemingly**
/-mɪŋlɪ/ *adv* по-ви́димому.

seemly /'siːmlɪ/ *adj* прили́чный.

seep /siːp/ *vi* проса́чиваться
impf, просочи́ться *pf.*

seethe /siːð/ *vi* кипе́ть *impf,*
вс~ *pf.*

segment /'segmənt/ *n* отре́зок;
(*of orange etc.*) до́лька; (*geom*)
сегме́нт.

segregate /'segrɪ,geɪt/ *vt* отде-
ля́ть *impf,* отдели́ть *pf.* **segre-
gation** /,segrɪ'geɪʃ(ə)n/ *n*
сегрега́ция.

seismic /'saɪzmɪk/ *adj* сейсми́-
ческий.

seize /siːz/ *vt* хвата́ть *impf,*
схвати́ть *pf; vi:* ~ **up** заеда́ть
impf, зае́сть *pf impers*+*acc;* ~
upon ухва́тываться *impf,* ухва-
ти́ться *pf* за+*acc.* **seizure**
/'siːʒə(r)/ *n* захва́т; (*med*) при-
па́док.

seldom /'seldəm/ *adv* ре́дко.

select /sɪ'lekt/ *adj* и́збранный;
vt отбира́ть *impf,* отобра́ть *pf.*
selection /-'lekʃ(ə)n/ *n* (*choice*)
вы́бор. **selective** /-'lektɪv/ *adj*
разбо́рчивый.

self /self/ *n* со́бственное «я»
neut indecl.

self- /self/ *in comb* само-; ~-
absorbed эгоцентри́чный; ~-
assured самоуве́ренный; ~-
catering (accommodation)
жильё с ку́хней; ~-**centred** эго-
центри́чный; ~-**confessed** от-
крове́нный; ~-**confidence**

самоуве́ренность; ~-**confident**
самоуве́ренный; ~-**conscious**
засте́нчивый; ~-**contained**
(*person*) незави́симый; (*flat
etc.*) отде́льный; ~-**control**
самооблада́ние; ~-**defence**
самозащи́та; ~-**denial** само-
отрече́ние; ~-**determination**
самоопределе́ние; ~-**effacing**
скро́мный; ~-**employed
person** незави́симый пред-
принима́тель *m;* ~-**esteem**
самоуваже́ние; ~-**evident**
очеви́дный; ~-**governing** само-
управля́ющий; ~-**help** само-
по́мощь; ~-**importance**
самомне́ние; ~-**imposed**
доброво́льный; ~-**indulgent**
избало́ванный; ~-**interest**
со́бственный интере́с; ~-**pity**
жа́лость к себе́; ~-**portrait** ав-
топортре́т; ~-**preservation**
самосохране́ние; ~-**reliance**
самостоя́тельность; ~-**respect**
самоуваже́ние; ~-**righteous** *adj*
ха́нжеский; ~-**sacrifice** само-
поже́ртвование; ~-**satisfied**
самодово́льный; ~-**service**
самообслу́живание (*attrib: in
gen after it*); ~-**styled** самозва́н-
ный; ~-**sufficient** самостоя́-
тельный.

selfish /'selfɪʃ/ *adj* эгоисти́чный.
selfless /'selflɪs/ *adj* самоот-
ве́рженный.

sell /sel/ *vt* & *i* продава́ть(ся)
impf, прода́ть(ся) *pf; vt* (*deal in*)
торгова́ть *impf* +*instr;* ~ **out of**
распродава́ть *impf,* распро-
да́ть *pf.* **seller** /-lə(r)/ *n* прода-
ве́ц. **selling** /-lɪŋ/ *n* прода́жа.
sell-out /-aʊt/ *n:* the play was a
~ пье́са прошла́ с аншла́гом.

Sellotape /'selə,teɪp/ *n* (*propr*)
ли́пкая ле́нта.

semantic /sɪ'mæntɪk/ *adj* семан-
ти́ческий. **semantics** /-tɪks/ *n*

семáнтика.

semblance /'sembləns/ n вúдимость.

semen /'si:mən/ n сéмя neut.

semi- /'semɪ/ in comb полу-; ~detached house дом, разделённый óбщей стенóй.

semibreve /-ˌbri:v/ n цéлая нóта.

semicircle n полукрýг.

semicircular /-'sɜ:kjʊlə(r)/ adj полукрýглый. **semicolon** /-'kəʊlən/ n тóчка с запятóй.

semiconductor /-kən,dʌktə(r)/ n полупроводнúк. **semifinal** /-'faɪnəl/ n полуфинáл.

seminar /'semɪnɑ:(r)/ n семинáр. **seminary** /-nərɪ/ n семинáрия.

semiquaver /'semɪ,kweɪvə(r)/ n шестнáдцатая нóта.

semitone /'semɪ,təʊn/ n полутóн.

senate /'senɪt/ n сенáт; (univ) совéт. **senator** /'senətə(r)/ n сенáтор.

send /send/ vt посылáть impf, послáть pf (for за+instr); ~ off отправлять impf, отправить pf; ~off прóводы (-дов) pl. **sender** /-də(r)/ n отправúтель m.

senile /'si:naɪl/ adj стáрческий. **senility** /sɪ'nɪlɪtɪ/ n стáрческое слабоýмие.

senior /'si:nɪə(r)/ adj (n) стáрший (sb); ~ citizen старúк, старýха. **seniority** /,si:nɪ'ɒrɪtɪ/ n старшинствó.

sensation /sen'seɪʃ(ə)n/ n сенсáция; (feeling) ощущéние. **sensational** /-'seɪʃən(ə)l/ adj сенсациóнный.

sense /sens/ n чýвство; (good ~) здрáвый смысл; (meaning) смысл; pl (sanity) ум; vt чýвствовать impf. **senseless** /-lɪs/ adj бессмýсленный.

sensibility /,sensɪ'bɪlɪtɪ/ n чýвствúтельность; pl самолюбúе.

sensible /'sensɪb(ə)l/ adj благоразýмный. **sensitive** /'sensɪtɪv/ adj чувствúтельный; (touchy) обúдчивый. **sensitivity** /,sensɪ'tɪvɪtɪ/ n чувствúтельность.

sensory /'sensərɪ/ adj чувствúтельный.

sensual /'sensjʊəl/, **sensuous** /'sensjʊəs/ adj чýвственный.

sentence /'sent(ə)ns/ n (gram) предложéние; (law) приговóр; vt приговáривать impf, приговорúть pf (to к+dat).

sentiment /'sentɪmənt/ n (feeling) чýвство; (opinion) мнéние. **sentimental** /,sentɪ'ment(ə)l/ adj сентиментáльный. **sentimentality** /,sentɪmen'tælɪtɪ/ n сентиментáльность.

sentry /'sentrɪ/ n часовóй sb.

separable /'sepərəb(ə)l/ adj отделúмый. **separate** /'sepərət/ adj отдéльный; vt & i отделять(ся) impf, отделúть(ся) pf. **separation** /,sepə'reɪʃ(ə)n/ n отделéние. **separatism** /'sepər,ɪtɪz(ə)m/ n сепаратúзм. **separatist** /'sepərətɪst/ n сепаратúст.

September /sep'tembə(r)/ n сентябрь m; adj сентябрьский.

septic /'septɪk/ adj септúческий.

sepulchre /'sepəlkə(r)/ n могúла.

sequel /'si:kw(ə)l/ n (result) послéдствие; (continuation) продолжéние. **sequence** /-kwəns/ n послéдовательность; ~ of events ход событий.

sequester /sɪ'kwestə(r)/ vt секвестровáть impf & pf.

sequin /'si:kwɪn/ n блёстка.

Serb(ian) /'sɜ:b(ɪən)/ adj сéрбский; n серб, ~ка. **Serbia** /'sɜ:bɪə/ n Сéрбия. **Serbo-**

Croat(ian) /ˌsɜ:bəʊˈkrəʊæt, ˌsɜ:bəʊkrəʊˈeɪʃ(ə)n/ *adj* сербско-хорва́тский.

serenade /ˌserəˈneɪd/ *n* серена́да.

serene /sɪˈriːn/ *adj* споко́йный. **serenity** /-ˈrenɪtɪ/ *n* споко́йствие.

serf /sɜːf/ *n* крепостно́й *sb*. **serfdom** /-dəm/ *n* крепостно́е пра́во.

sergeant /ˈsɑːdʒ(ə)nt/ *n* сержа́нт.

serial /ˈsɪərɪəl/ *adj*: ~ **number** серийный но́мер; *n* (*story*) рома́н с продолже́нием; (*broadcast*) серийная постано́вка. **serialize** /-ˌlaɪz/ *vt* ста́вить *impf*, по~ *pf* в не́сколько приёмов. **series** /ˈsɪərɪz/ *n* (*succession*) ряд; (*broadcast*) се́рия переда́ч.

serious /ˈsɪərɪəs/ *adj* серьёзный. **seriousness** /-nɪs/ *n* серьёзность.

sermon /ˈsɜːmən/ *n* про́поведь.

serpent /ˈsɜːpənt/ *n* змея́.

serrated /seˈreɪtɪd/ *adj* зазу́бренный.

serum /ˈsɪərəm/ *n* сы́воротка.

servant /ˈsɜːv(ə)nt/ *n* слуга́ *m*, служа́нка. **serve** /sɜːv/ *vt* служи́ть *impf*, по~ *pf* +*dat* (**as**, **for** +*instr*); (*attend to*) обслу́живать *impf*, обслужи́ть *pf*; (*food*; *ball*) подава́ть *impf*, пода́ть *pf*; (*sentence*) отбыва́ть *impf*, отбы́ть *pf*; (*writ* etc.) вруча́ть *impf*, вручи́ть *pf* (**on** +*dat*); *vi* (*be suitable*) годи́ться (**for** на +*acc*, для+*gen*); (*sport*) подава́ть *impf*, пода́ть *pf* мяч; **it ~s him right** поде́лом ему́ (*dat*). **server** /ˈsɜːvə(r)/ *n* (*comput*) се́рвер. **service** /ˈsɜːvɪs/ *n* (*act of serving*; *branch of public work*; *eccl*) слу́жба; (*quality of*

~) обслу́живание; (*of car* etc.) техобслу́живание; (*set of dishes*) серви́з; (*sport*) пода́ча; (*transport*) сообще́ние; **at your** ~ к ва́шим услу́гам; *vt* (*car*) проводи́ть *impf*, провести́ *pf* техобслу́живание +*gen*; ~ **charge** пла́та за обслу́живание; ~ **station** ста́нция обслу́живания. **serviceable** /-səb(ə)l/ *n* (*useful*) поле́зный; (*durable*) про́чный. **serviceman** *n* военнослу́жащий *sb*.

serviette /ˌsɜːvɪˈet/ *n* салфе́тка.

servile /ˈsɜːvaɪl/ *adj* рабо́ле́пный.

session /ˈseʃ(ə)n/ *n* заседа́ние, се́ссия.

set¹ /set/ *vt* (*put*; ~ **clock**, **trap**) ста́вить *impf*, по~ *pf*; (*table*) накрыва́ть *impf*, накры́ть *pf*; (*bone*) вправля́ть *impf*, впра́вить *pf*; (*hair*) укла́дывать *impf*, уложи́ть *pf*; (*bring into state*) приводи́ть *impf*, привести́ *pf* (**in**, **to** в+*acc*); (*example*) подава́ть *impf*, пода́ть *pf*; (*task*) задава́ть *impf*, зада́ть *pf*; *vi* (*solidify*) тверде́ть *impf*, за~ *pf*; застыва́ть *impf*, засты́(нуть) *pf*; (*sun* etc.) заходи́ть *impf*, зайти́ *pf*; сади́ться *impf*, сесть *pf*; ~ **about** (*begin*) начина́ть *impf*, нача́ть *pf*; (*attack*) напада́ть *impf*, напа́сть *pf* на+*acc*; ~ **back** (*impede*) препя́тствовать *impf*, вос~ *pf* +*dat*; ~**back** неуда́ча; ~ **in** наступа́ть *impf*, наступи́ть *pf*; ~ **off** (*on journey*) отправля́ться *impf*, отпра́виться *pf*; (*enhance*) оттеня́ть *impf*, оттени́ть *pf*; ~ **out** (*state*) излага́ть *impf*, изложи́ть *pf*; (*on journey*) see ~ **off**; ~ **up** (*business*) осно́вывать *impf*, основа́ть *pf*

set² /set/ *n* набо́р, компле́кт; (*of*

dishes) серви́з; (*radio*) приёмник; (*television*) телеви́зор; (*tennis*) сет; (*theat*) декора́ция; (*cin*) съёмочная площа́дка.

set³ /set/ *adj* (*established*) устано́вленный.

settee /se'tiː/ *n* дива́н.

setting /'setɪŋ/ *n* (*frame*) опра́ва; (*surroundings*) обстано́вка; (*of mechanism etc.*) устано́вка; (*of sun etc.*) захо́д.

settle /'set(ə)l/ *vt* (*decide*) реши́ть *impf*, реши́ть *pf*; (*reconcile*) ула́живать *impf*, ула́дить *pf*; (*a bill etc.*) опла́чивать *impf*, оплати́ть *pf*; (*calm*) успока́ивать *impf*, успоко́ить *pf*; *vi* поселя́ться *impf*, посели́ться *pf*; (*subside*) оседа́ть *impf*, осе́сть *pf*; ~ **down** уса́живаться *impf*, усе́сться *pf* (**to** за+*acc*). **settlement** /-mənt/ *n* поселе́ние; (*agreement*) соглаше́ние; (*payment*) упла́та. **settler** /'setlə(r)/ *n* поселе́нец.

seven /'sev(ə)n/ *adj & n* семь; (*number 7*) семёрка. **seventeen** /ˌsev(ə)n'tiːn/ *adj & n* семна́дцать. **seventeenth** /ˌsev(ə)n'tiːnθ/ *adj & n* семна́дцатый. **seventh** /'sev(ə)nθ/ *adj & n* седьмо́й; (*fraction*) седьма́я *sb*. **seventieth** /'sev(ə)ntɪθ/ *adj & n* семидеся́тый. **seventy** /'sev(ə)ntɪ/ *adj & n* се́мьдесят; *pl* (*decade*) семидеся́тые го́ды (-до́в) *m pl*.

sever /'sevə(r)/ *vt* (*cut off*) отреза́ть *impf*, отре́зать *pf*; (*relations*) разрыва́ть *impf*, разорва́ть *pf*.

several /'sevr(ə)l/ *pron* (*adj*) не́сколько (+*gen*).

severance /'sevərəns/ *n* разры́в; ~ **pay** выходно́е посо́бие.

severe /sɪ'vɪə(r)/ *adj* стро́гий, су-

ро́вый; (*pain, frost*) си́льный; (*illness*) тяжёлый. **severity** /-'verɪtɪ/ *n* стро́гость, суро́вость.

sew /səʊ/ *vt* шить *impf*, с~ *pf*; ~ **on** пришива́ть *impf*, приши́ть *pf*; ~ **up** зашива́ть *impf*, заши́ть *pf*.

sewage /'suːɪdʒ/ *n* сто́чные во́ды *f pl*; ~**-farm** поля́ *neut pl* ороше́ния. **sewer** /'suːə(r)/ *n* сто́чная труба́. **sewerage** /-rɪdʒ/ *n* канализа́ция.

sewing /'səʊɪŋ/ *n* шитьё; ~ **machine** швейная маши́на.

sex /seks/ *n* (*gender*) пол; (*sexual activity*) секс; **have** ~ име́ть *impf* сноше́ние. **sexual** /'seksjʊəl/ *adj* полово́й, сексуа́льный; ~ **intercourse** полово́е сноше́ние. **sexuality** /ˌseksjʊ'ælɪtɪ/ *n* сексуа́льность. **sexy** /'seksɪ/ *adj* эроти́ческий.

sh /ʃ/ *int* ти́ше!; тсс!

shabby /'ʃæbɪ/ *adj* ве́тхий.

shack /ʃæk/ *n* лачу́га.

shackles /'ʃæk(ə)lz/ *n pl* око́вы (-в) *pl*.

shade /ʃeɪd/ *n* тень; (*of colour, meaning*) отте́нок; (*lamp-~*) абажу́р; **a** ~ чуть-чу́ть; *vt* затеня́ть *impf*, затени́ть *pf*; (*eyes etc.*) заслоня́ть *impf* заслони́ть *pf*; (*drawing*) тушева́ть *impf*, за~ *pf*. **shadow** /'ʃædəʊ/ *n* тень; *vt* (*follow*) та́йно следи́ть *impf* за+*instr*. **shadowy** /'ʃædəʊɪ/ *adj* тёмный. **shady** /'ʃeɪdɪ/ *adj* тени́стый; (*suspicious*) подозри́тельный.

shaft /ʃɑːft/ *n* (*of spear*) дре́вко; (*arrow*) стрела́; (*of light*) луч; (*of cart*) огло́бля; (*axle*) вал; (*mine, lift*) ша́хта.

shaggy /'ʃægɪ/ *adj* лохма́тый.

shake /ʃeɪk(ə)n/ *vt & i* трясти́(сь) *impf*; *vi* (*tremble*) дро-

жа́ть *impf*; *vt* (*weaken*) колеба́ть *impf*, по~ *pf*; (*shock*) потряса́ть *impf* потрясти́ *pf*; ~ hands пожима́ть *impf*, пожа́ть *pf* ру́ку (with +*dat*); ~ one's head пока́чивать *impf*, покача́ть *pf* голово́й; ~ off стря́хивать *impf*, стряхну́ть *pf*; (*fig*) избавля́ться *impf*, изба́виться *pf* от+*gen*.

shaky /ˈʃeɪkɪ/ *adj* ша́ткий.

shallow /ˈʃæləʊ/ *adj* ме́лкий; (*fig*) пове́рхностный.

sham /ʃæm/ *n* & *vt* & *i* притворя́ться *impf*, притвори́ться *pf* +*instr*; *n* притво́рство; (*person*) притво́рщик, -ица; *adj* притво́рный.

shambles /ˈʃæmb(ə)lz/ *n* хао́с.

shame /ʃeɪm/ *n* (*guilt*) стыд; (*disgrace*) позо́р; **what a ~!** как жаль!; *vt* стыди́ть *impf*, при~ *pf*. **shameful** /-fʊl/ *adj* позо́рный. **shameless** /-lɪs/ *adj* бессты́дный.

shampoo /ʃæmˈpuː/ *n* шампу́нь *m*.

shanty¹ /ˈʃæntɪ/ *n* (*hut*) хиба́рка; **~ town** трущо́ба.

shanty² /ˈʃæntɪ/ *n* (*song*) матро́сская пе́сня.

shape /ʃeɪp/ *n* фо́рма; *vt* придава́ть *impf*, прида́ть *pf* фо́рму+*dat*; *vi*: **~ up** скла́дываться *impf*, сложи́ться *pf*. **shapeless** /-lɪs/ *adj* бесфо́рменный. **shapely** /-lɪ/ *adj* стро́йный.

share /ʃeə(r)/ *n* до́ля; (*econ*) а́кция; *vt* дели́ть *impf*, по~ *pf*; (*opinion etc.*; ~ out) разделя́ть *impf*, раздели́ть *pf*. **shareholder** /-ˌhəʊldə(r)/ *n* акционе́р.

shark /ʃɑːk/ *n* аку́ла.

sharp /ʃɑːp/ *adj* о́стрый; (*steep*) круто́й; (*sudden, harsh*) ре́зкий; *n* (*mus*) дие́з; *adv* (*with time*) ро́вно; (*of angle*) кру́то. **sharpen** /-pən/ *vt* точи́ть *impf*,

на~ *pf*.

shatter /ˈʃætə(r)/ *vt* & *i* разбива́ть(ся) *impf*, разби́ть(ся) *pf* вдре́безги; *vt* (*hopes etc.*) разруша́ть *impf*, разру́шить *pf*.

shave /ʃeɪv/ *vt* & *i* брить(ся) *impf*, по~ *pf* бри́тве. **shaver** /-və(r)/ *n* электри́ческая бри́тва.

shawl /ʃɔːl/ *n* шаль.

she /ʃiː/ *pron* она́.

sheaf /ʃiːf/ *n* сноп; (*of papers*) свя́зка.

shear /ʃɪə(r)/ *vt* стричь *impf*, о~ *pf*. **shears** /ʃɪəz/ *n pl* но́жницы (-ц) *pl*.

sheath /ʃiːθ/ *n* но́жны (*gen* -жен) *pl*.

shed¹ /ʃed/ *n* сара́й.

shed² /ʃed/ *vt* (*tears, blood, light*) пролива́ть *impf*, проли́ть *pf*; (*skin, clothes*) сбра́сывать *impf*, сбро́сить *pf*.

sheen /ʃiːn/ *n* блеск.

sheep /ʃiːp/ *n* овца́. **sheepish** /-pɪʃ/ *adj* сконфу́женный. **sheepskin** *n* овчи́на; **~ coat** дублёнка.

sheer /ʃɪə(r)/ *adj* (*utter*) су́щий; (*textile*) прозра́чный; (*rock etc.*) отве́сный.

sheet /ʃiːt/ *n* (*on bed*) простыня́; (*of glass, paper, etc.*) лист.

sheikh /ʃeɪk/ *n* шейх.

shelf /ʃelf/ *n* по́лка.

shell /ʃel/ *n* (*of mollusc*) ра́ковина; (*seashell*) раку́шка; (*of tortoise*) щит; (*of egg, nut*) скорлупа́; (*of building*) о́стов; (*explosive ~*) снаря́д; *vt* (*peas etc.*) лущи́ть *impf*, об~ *pf*; (*bombard*) обстре́ливать *impf*, обстреля́ть *pf*. **shellfish** /ˈʃelfɪʃ/ *n* (*mollusc*) моллю́ск; (*crustacean*) ракообра́зное *sb*.

shelter /ˈʃeltə(r)/ *n* убе́жище; *vt*

(*provide with refuge*) приюти́ть pf; vt & i укрыва́ть(ся) impf, укры́ть(ся) pf.

shelve[1] /ʃelv/ vt (*defer*) откла́дывать impf, отложи́ть pf.

shelve[2] /ʃelv/ vi (*slope*) отло́го спуска́ться impf.

shelving /ʃelvɪŋ/ n (*shelves*) стелла́ж.

shepherd /ʃepəd/ n пасту́х; vt проводи́ть impf, провести́ pf.

sherry /ʃerɪ/ n хе́рес.

shield /ʃiːld/ n щит; vt защища́ть impf, защити́ть pf.

shift /ʃɪft/ vt & i (*change position*) перемеща́ть(ся) impf, перемести́ть(ся) pf; (*change*) меня́ть(ся) impf; n перемеще́ние; переме́на; (*of workers*) сме́на; ~ **work** сме́нная рабо́та. **shifty** /-tɪ/ adj скользкий.

shimmer /ʃɪmə(r)/ vi мерца́ть impf; n мерца́ние.

shin /ʃɪn/ n го́лень.

shine /ʃaɪn/ vi свети́ть(ся) impf; (*glitter*) блесте́ть impf; (*excel*) блиста́ть impf; (*sun, eyes*) сия́ть impf; vt (*a light*) освеща́ть impf, освети́ть pf фонарём (on +acc); n гля́нец.

shingle /ʃɪŋ(ə)l/ n (*pebbles*) га́лька.

shingles /ʃɪŋ(ə)lz/ n опоя́сывающий лиша́й.

shiny /ʃaɪnɪ/ adj блестя́щий.

ship /ʃɪp/ n кора́бль m; су́дно; vt (*transport*) перевози́ть impf, перевезти́ pf; (*dispatch*) отправля́ть impf, отпра́вить pf. **ship-building** n судострое́ние. **shipment** /-mənt/ n (*dispatch*) отпра́вка; (*goods*) па́ртия. **shipping** /-pɪŋ/ n суда́ (-до́в) pl. **shipshape** adv в по́лном поря́дке. **shipwreck** n кораблекруше́ние; **be ~ed** терпе́ть impf, по~ pf кораблекруше-

ние. **shipyard** n верфь.

shirk /ʃɜːk/ vt уви́ливать impf, увильну́ть pf от+gen.

shirt /ʃɜːt/ n руба́шка.

shit /ʃɪt/ n (*vulg*) говно́; vi срать impf, по~ pf.

shiver /ʃɪvə(r)/ vi (*tremble*) дрожа́ть impf; n дрожь.

shoal /ʃəʊl/ n (*of fish*) ста́я.

shock /ʃɒk/ n (*emotional*) потрясе́ние; (*impact*) уда́р, толчо́к; (*electr*) уда́р то́ком; (*med*) шок; vt шоки́ровать impf. **shocking** /-kɪŋ/ adj (*outrageous*) сканда́льный; (*awful*) ужа́сный.

shoddy /ʃɒdɪ/ adj халту́рный.

shoe /ʃuː/ n ту́фля; vt подко́вывать impf, подкова́ть pf. **shoelace** n шнуро́к. **shoemaker** /-ˌmeɪkə(r)/ n сапо́жник. **shoestring** n: **on a ~** с небольши́ми сре́дствами.

shoo /ʃuː/ int кш!; vt прогоня́ть impf, прогна́ть pf.

shoot /ʃuːt/ vt & i стреля́ть impf, вы́стрелить pf (a gun в +gen; at в+acc); (*arrow*) пуска́ть impf, пусти́ть pf; (*kill*) застрели́ть pf; (*execute*) расстре́ливать impf, расстреля́ть pf; (*hunt*) охо́титься impf, на+acc; (*football*) бить impf (по воро́там); (*cin*) снима́ть impf, снять pf (фильм); (*fly swiftly*) проноси́ться impf, пронести́сь pf; ~ **down** (*aircraft*) сбива́ть impf, сбить pf; ~ **up** (*grow*) бы́стро расти́ impf, по~ pf; (*prices*) подска́кивать impf, подскочи́ть pf; n (*branch*) росто́к, побе́г; (*hunt*) охо́та. **shooting** /-tɪŋ/ n стрельба́; (*hunting*) охо́та; ~**gallery** тир.

shop /ʃɒp/ n магази́н; (*workshop*) мастерска́я sb, adj; ~ **assistant** продаве́ц, -вщи́ца

~-lifter магази́нный вор; ~-lifting воровство́ в магази́нах; ~ steward цехово́й ста́роста m; ~-window витри́на; vi де́лать impf, c~ pf поку́пки (f pl).
shopkeeper /-,ki:pə(r)/ n ла́вочник. shopper /'ʃɒpə(r)/ n покупа́тель m, ~ница. shopping /'ʃɒpɪŋ/ n поку́пки f pl; go, do one's ~ де́лать impf, c~ pf поку́пки; ~ centre торго́вый центр.
shore¹ /ʃɔ:(r)/ n бе́рег.
shore² /ʃɔ:(r)/ vt: ~ up подпира́ть impf, подпере́ть pf.
short /ʃɔ:t/ adj коро́ткий; (not tall) ни́зкого ро́ста; (deficient) недоста́точный; be ~ of испы́тывать impf, испыта́ть pf недоста́ток в+prep; (curt) ре́зкий; in ~ одни́м сло́вом; ~-change обсчи́тывать impf, обсчита́ть pf; ~ circuit коро́ткое замыка́ние; ~ cut коро́ткий путь m; ~ list оконча́тельный спи́сок; ~-list включа́ть impf, включи́ть pf в оконча́тельный спи́сок; ~-lived недолгове́чный; ~-sighted близору́кий; (fig) недальнови́дный; ~ story расска́з; in ~ supply дефици́тный; ~-tempered вспы́льчивый; ~-term краткосро́чный; ~-wave коротково́лновый. shortage /-tɪdʒ/ n недоста́ток. shortcoming /-,kʌmɪŋ/ n недоста́ток. shorten /-t(ə)n/ vt & i укора́чивать(ся) impf, укороти́ть(ся) pf. shortfall n дефици́т. shorthand n стеногра́фия; ~ typist машини́стка-стенографи́стка. shortly /-lɪ/ adv: ~ after вско́ре (по́сле+gen); ~ before незадо́лго (до+gen).
shorts /ʃɔ:ts/ n pl шо́рты (-т) pl.

should /ʃʊd/ v aux (ought) до́лжен (бы) +inf: you ~ know that вы должны́ э́то знать; he ~ be here soon он до́лжен бы быть тут ско́ро; (conditional) бы +past: I ~ say я бы сказа́л(а); I ~ like я бы хоте́л(а).
shoulder /'ʃəʊldə(r)/ n плечо́; ~-blade лопа́тка; ~-strap брете́лька; взва́ливать impf, взвали́ть pf на пле́чи; (fig) брать impf, взять pf на себя́.
shout /ʃaʊt/ n крик; vi крича́ть impf, кри́кнуть pf; ~ down перекри́кивать impf, перекрича́ть pf.
shove /ʃʌv/ n толчо́к; vt & i толка́ть(ся) impf, толкну́ть pf; ~ off (coll) убира́ться impf, убра́ться pf.
shovel /'ʃʌv(ə)l/ n лопа́та; vt (~ up) сгреба́ть impf, сгрести́ pf.
show /ʃəʊ/ vt пока́зывать impf, показа́ть pf; (exhibit) выставля́ть impf, вы́ставить pf (film etc.) демонстри́ровать impf, про~ pf; vi (also ~ up) быть ви́дным, заме́тным; ~ off (vi) привлека́ть impf; привлёчь pf к себе́ внима́ние; ~ up see vi; (appear) появля́ться impf; яви́ться pf impf; n (exhibition) вы́ставка; (theat) спекта́кль m, шоу neut indecl; (effect) ви́димость; ~ of hands голосова́ние подня́тием руки́; ~ business шоу-би́знес; ~-case витри́на; ~-jumping соревнова́ние по скачка́м; ~-room сало́н. show-down n развязка.

shower /'ʃaʊə(r)/ n (rain) дождик; (hail; fig) град; (~-bath) душ; vt осыпа́ть impf, осы́пать pf +instr (on +acc); vi принима́ть impf, приня́ть pf душ.

showery /-rɪ/ adj дождли́вый.

showpiece /'ʃəʊpiːs/ n образе́ц.

showy /'ʃəʊɪ/ adj показно́й.

shrapnel /'ʃræpn(ə)l/ n шрапне́ль.

shred /ʃred/ n клочо́к; not a ~ ни ка́пли; vt мельчи́ть impf, из~ pf.

shrewd /ʃruːd/ adj проница́тельный.

shriek /ʃriːk/ vi визжа́ть impf; взви́гнуть pf.

shrill /ʃrɪl/ adj пронзи́тельный.

shrimp /ʃrɪmp/ n креве́тка.

shrine /ʃraɪn/ n святы́ня.

shrink /ʃrɪŋk/ vi сади́ться impf, сесть pf; (recoil) отпря́нуть pf; vt вызыва́ть impf, вы́звать pf уса́дку y+gen; ~ **from** избега́ть impf +gen. **shrinkage** /-kɪdʒ/ n уса́дка.

shrivel /'ʃrɪv(ə)l/ vi смо́рщиваться impf, смо́рщиться pf.

shroud /ʃraʊd/ n са́ван; vt (fig) оку́тывать impf, оку́тать pf (in +instr).

Shrove Tuesday /ʃrəʊv/ n вто́рник на ма́сленой неде́ле.

shrub /ʃrʌb/ n куст. **shrubbery** /-bərɪ/ n куста́рник.

shrug /ʃrʌg/ vt & i пожима́ть impf, пожа́ть pf (плеча́ми).

shudder /'ʃʌdə(r)/ n содрога́ние; vi содрога́ться impf, содрогну́ться pf.

shuffle /'ʃʌf(ə)l/ vt & i (one's feet) ша́ркать impf (нога́ми); (cards) тасова́ть impf, с~ pf.

shun /ʃʌn/ vt избега́ть impf +gen.

shunt /ʃʌnt/ vi (rly) маневри́ровать impf, с~ pf; vt (rly) переводи́ть impf, перевести́ pf на запасно́й путь.

shut /ʃʌt/ vt & i (also ~ down) закрыва́ть(ся) impf, закры́ть(ся) pf; ~ **out** (exclude) исключа́ть impf, исключи́ть pf; (fence off) загора́живать impf, загороди́ть pf; (keep out) не пуска́ть impf, пусти́ть pf; ~ **up** (vi) замолча́ть pf; (imper) за́ткни́сь!

shutter /'ʃʌtə(r)/ n ста́вень m; (phot) затво́р.

shuttle /'ʃʌt(ə)l/ n челно́к.

shy¹ /ʃaɪ/ adj засте́нчивый.

shy² /ʃaɪ/ vi (in alarm) отпря́дывать impf, отпря́нуть pf.

Siberia /saɪ'bɪərɪə/ n Сиби́рь. **Siberian** /-rɪən/ adj сиби́рский; n сибиря́к, -я́чка.

sick /sɪk/ adj больно́й; be ~ (vomit) рвать impf, вы́~ pf impers +acc: he was ~ его́ вы́рвало; feel ~ тошни́ть impf impers +acc; be ~ of надоеда́ть impf, надое́сть pf +nom (object) & dat (subject): I'm ~ of her она́ мне надое́ла; ~-leave о́тпуск по боле́зни. **sicken** /-kən/ vt вызыва́ть impf, вы́звать pf тошноту́, (disgust) отвраще́ние, y+gen; vi заболева́ть impf, заболе́ть pf. **sickening** /-kənɪŋ/ adj отврати́тельный.

sickle /'sɪk(ə)l/ n серп.

sickly /'sɪklɪ/ adj боле́зненный; (nauseating) тошнотво́рный. **sickness** /'sɪknɪs/ n боле́знь; (vomiting) тошнота́.

side /saɪd/ n сторона́; (of body) бок; ~ **by** ~ ря́дом (with c+instr); on the ~ на стороне́; vi: ~ **with** встава́ть impf, встать pf на сто́рону+gen; ~-**effect** побо́чное де́йствие; ~-**step** (fig) уклоня́ться impf, уклони́ться pf от+gen; ~-**track** (distract) отвлека́ть impf, отвле́чь

pf. **sideboard** *n* буфе́т; *pl* ба́ки (-к) *pl.* **sidelight** *n* боково́й фона́рь *m.* **sideline** *n* (*work*) побо́чная рабо́та.

sidelong /ˈsaɪdlɒŋ/ *adj* (*glance*) косо́й.

sideways /ˈsaɪdweɪz/ *adv* бо́ком.

siding /ˈsaɪdɪŋ/ *n* запасно́й путь *m.*

sidle /ˈsaɪd(ə)l/ *vi*: ~ **up to** подходи́ть *impf*, подойти́ *pf* к (*+dat*) бочко́м.

siege /siːdʒ/ *n* оса́да; **lay** ~ **to** осажда́ть *impf*, осади́ть *pf*; **raise the** ~ **of** снима́ть *impf*, снять *pf* оса́ду с+*gen*.

sieve /sɪv/ *n* си́то; *vt* просе́ивать *impf*, просе́ять *pf.*

sift /sɪft/ *vt* просе́ивать *impf*, просе́ять *pf*; (*fig*) тща́тельно рассма́тривать *impf*, рассмотре́ть *pf.*

sigh /saɪ/ *vi* вздыха́ть *impf*, вздохну́ть *pf*; *n* вздох.

sight /saɪt/ *n* (*faculty*) зре́ние; (*view*) вид; (*spectacle*) зре́лище; *pl* достопримеча́тельности *pl*; (*on gun*) прице́л; **at first** ~ с пе́рвого взгля́да; **catch** or **know by sight** знать *impf* в лицо́; **lose** ~ **of** теря́ть *impf*, по~ *pf* из ви́ду; (*fig*) упуска́ть *impf*, упусти́ть *pf* из ви́ду.

sign /saɪn/ *n* знак; (*indication*) при́знак; (~**board**) вы́веска; *vt* & *abs* подпи́сывать(ся) *impf*, подписа́ть(ся) *pf*; *vi* (*give* ~) подава́ть *impf*, пода́ть *pf* знак; ~ **on** (*as unemployed*) запи́сываться *impf*, записа́ться *pf* в спи́ски безрабо́тных; (~ **up**) нанима́ться *impf*, наня́ться *pf.*

signal /ˈsɪɡn(ə)l/ *n* сигна́л; *vt* & *i* сигнализи́ровать *impf* & *pf.*

signal-box *n* сигна́льная бу́дка.

signatory /ˈsɪɡnətərɪ/ *n* подписа́вший *sb*; (*of treaty*) сторона́, подписа́вшая до́говор.

signature /ˈsɪɡnətʃə(r)/ *n* по́дпись.

significance /sɪɡˈnɪfɪkəns/ *n* значе́ние. **significant** /-kənt/ *adj* значи́тельный. **signify** /ˈsɪɡnɪˌfaɪ/ *vt* означа́ть *impf.*

signpost /ˈsaɪnpəʊst/ *n* указа́тельный столб.

silage /ˈsaɪlɪdʒ/ *n* си́лос.

silence /ˈsaɪləns/ *n* молча́ние, тишина́; *vt* заста́вить *pf* замолча́ть. **silencer** /-sə(r)/ *n* глуши́тель *m.* **silent** /ˈsaɪlənt/ *adj* (*not speaking*) безмо́лвный; (*of film*) немо́й; (*without noise*) ти́хий; **be** ~ молча́ть *impf.*

silhouette /ˌsɪluːˈet/ *n* силуэ́т; *vt*: **be** ~**d** вырисо́вываться *impf*, вы́рисоваться *pf* (**against** на фо́не+*gen*).

silicon /ˈsɪlɪkən/ *n* кре́мний. **silicone** /-ˌkəʊn/ *n* сили-ко́н.

silk /sɪlk/ *n* шёлк; *attrib* шёлко-вый. **silky** /-kɪ/ *adj* шелкови́-стый.

sill /sɪl/ *n* подоко́нник.

silly /ˈsɪlɪ/ *adj* глу́пый.

silo /ˈsaɪləʊ/ *n* си́лос.

silt /sɪlt/ *n* ил.

silver /ˈsɪlvə(r)/ *n* серебро́; (*cutlery*) столо́вое серебро́; *adj* (*of* ~) сере́бряный; (*silvery*) серебри́стый; ~-**plated** посеребрённый; **silversmith** *n* серебряны́х дел ма́стер. **silverware** /ˈsɪlvəˌweə(r)/ *n* столо́вое серебро́. **silvery** /ˈsɪlvərɪ/ *adj* серебри́стый.

SIM (card) /sɪm/ *n* сим-ка́рта.

similar /ˈsɪmɪlə(r)/ *adj* подо́бный (**to** +*dat*). **similarity** /ˌsɪmɪˈlærɪtɪ/ *n* схо́дство. **similarly** /ˈsɪmɪləlɪ/ *adv* подо́бным о́бразом.

simile /'sımılı/ n сравне́ние.

simmer /'sımə(r)/ vt кипяти́ть *impf* на ме́дленном огне́; vi кипе́ть *impf* на ме́дленном огне́; ~ **down** успока́иваться *impf*, успоко́иться *pf*.

simper /'sımpə(r)/ vi жема́нно улыба́ться *impf*, улыбну́ться *pf*.

simple /'sımp(ə)l/ adj просто́й; ~**-minded** тупова́тый. **simplicity** /sım'plısıtı/ n простота́. **simplify** /'sımplıfaı/ vt упроща́ть *impf*, упрости́ть *pf*. **simply** /'sımplı/ adv про́сто.

simulate /'sımjʊleıt/ vt притворя́ться *impf*, притвори́ться *pf* +*instr*; (*conditions etc.*) модели́ровать *impf* & *pf*. **simulated** /-leıtıd/ adj (*pearls etc.*) иску́сственный.

simultaneous /sıməl'teınıəs/ adj одновреме́нный.

sin /sın/ n грех; vi греши́ть *impf*, со~ *pf*.

since /sıns/ adv с тех пор; prep с+*gen*; conj с тех пор как; (*reason*) так как.

sincere /sın'sıə(r)/ adj и́скренний. **sincerely** /-'sıəlı/ adv и́скренне; yours ~ и́скренне Ваш. **sincerity** /-'serıtı/ n и́скренность.

sinew /'sınju:/ n сухожи́лие.

sinful /'sınfʊl/ adj грехо́вный.

sing /sıŋ/ vt & i петь *impf*, про~, с~ *pf*.

singe /sındʒ/ vt пали́ть *impf*, о~ *pf*.

singer /'sıŋə(r)/ n певе́ц, -ви́ца.

single /'sıŋg(ə)l/ adj оди́н; (*unmarried*) (*of man*) нежена́тый; (*of woman*) незаму́жняя; (*bed*) односпа́льный; ~**-handed** без посторо́нней по́мощи; ~**-minded** целеустремлённый; ~ **parent** мать/оте́ц-одино́чка;

~ **room** ко́мната на одного́; n (*ticket*) биле́т в оди́н коне́ц; (*tennis etc.*) одино́чная игра́; ~ **out** выделя́ть *impf*, вы́делить *pf*. **singly** /'sıŋglı/ adv по-одному́.

singular /'sıŋgjʊlə(r)/ n еди́нственное число́; adj еди́нственный; (*unusual*) необыча́йный. **singularly** /-ləlı/ adv необыча́йно.

sinister /'sınıstə(r)/ adj злове́щий.

sink /sıŋk/ vi (*descend slowly*) опуска́ться *impf*, опусти́ться *pf*; (*in mud etc.*) погружа́ться *impf*, погрузи́ться *pf*; (*in water*) тону́ть *impf*, по~ *pf*; vt (*ship*) топи́ть *impf*, по~ *pf*; (*pipe post*) вка́пывать *impf*, вкопа́ть *pf*; n ра́ковина.

sinner /'sınə(r)/ n гре́шник -и́ца.

sinus /'saınəs/ n па́зуха.

sip /sıp/ vt пить *impf*, ма́ленькими глотка́ми; n ма́ленький глото́к.

siphon /'saıf(ə)n/ n сифо́н; ~ (*also fig*) перека́чивать *impf* перекача́ть *pf*.

sir /sɜ:(r)/ n сэр.

siren /'saıərən/ n сире́на.

sister /'sıstə(r)/ n сестра́; ~**-in-law** (*husband's sister*) золо́вка (*wife's sister*) своя́ченица (*brother's wife*) неве́стка.

sit /sıt/ vi (*be sitting*) сиде́ть *impf*; (~ **down**) сади́ться *impf*, сесть *pf*; (*parl, law*) заседа́ть *impf*; vt уса́живать *impf*, уса-ди́ть *pf*; (*exam*) сдава́ть *impf* ~ **back** отки́дываться *impf*, отки́нуться *pf*; ~ **down** сади́ться *impf*, сесть *pf*; ~ **up** приподни-ма́ться *impf*, приподня́ться *pf* (*not go to bed*) не ложи́ться *impf* спать.

site /saɪt/ n (where a thing takes place) ме́сто; (where a thing is) местоположе́ние.

sitting /ˈsɪtɪŋ/ n (parl etc.) заседа́ние; (for meal) сме́на; **~-room** гости́ная sb.

situated /ˈsɪtjoˌeɪtɪd/ adj: be ~ находи́ться impf.

situation /ˌsɪtjʊˈeɪʃ(ə)n/ n местоположе́ние; (circumstances) положе́ние; (job) ме́сто.

six /sɪks/ adj & n шесть; (number 6) шестёрка. **sixteen** /ˌsɪksˈtiːn/ adj & n шестна́дцать. **sixteenth** /-ˈtiːnθ/ adj & n шестна́дцатый. **sixth** /sɪksθ/ adj & n шесто́й; (fraction) шеста́я sb. **sixtieth** /ˈsɪkstɪəθ/ adj & n шестидеся́тый. **sixty** /ˈsɪkstɪ/ adj & n шестьдеся́т; pl (decade) шестидеся́тые го́ды (-до́в) m pl.

size /saɪz/ n разме́р; vt: ~ **up** оце́нивать impf, оцени́ть pf. **sizeable** /ˈsaɪzəb(ə)l/ adj значи́тельный.

sizzle /ˈsɪz(ə)l/ vi шипе́ть impf.

skate[1] /skeɪt/ n (fish) скат.

skate[2] /skeɪt/ n (ice-~) конёк; (roller-~) конёк на ро́ликах; vi ката́ться impf на конька́х; **skating-rink** като́к.

skeleton /ˈskelɪt(ə)n/ n скеле́т.

sketch /sketʃ/ n зарисо́вка; (theat) скетч; vt & i зарисо́вывать impf, зарисова́ть pf. **sketchy** /-tʃɪ/ adj схемати́ческий; (superficial) пове́рхностный.

skew /skjuː/ adj косо́й; **on the ~** ко́со.

skewer /ˈskjuːə(r)/ n ве́ртел.

ski /skiː/ n лы́жа; **~-jump** трампли́н; vi ходи́ть impf на лы́жах.

skid /skɪd/ n зано́с; vi заноси́ть impf, занести́ pf impers+acc.

skier /ˈskiːə(r)/ n лы́жник. **skiing** /ˈskiːɪŋ/ n лы́жный спорт.

skilful /ˈskɪlfʊl/ adj иску́сный. **skill** /skɪl/ n мастерство́; (countable) поле́зный на́вык. **skilled** /skɪld/ adj иску́сный; (trained) квалифици́рованный.

skim /skɪm/ vt снима́ть impf, снять pf (cream сли́вки pl, scum наки́пь); vi скользи́ть impf (over, along по+dat); ~ **through** бе́гло просма́тривать impf, просмотре́ть pf; adj: ~ **milk** снято́е молоко́.

skimp /skɪmp/ vt & i скупи́ться impf (на+acc). **skimpy** /-pɪ/ adj ску́дный.

skin /skɪn/ n ко́жа; (hide) шку́ра; (of fruit etc.) кожура́; (on milk) пе́нка; vt сдира́ть impf, содра́ть pf ко́жу, шку́ру, c+gen; (fruit) снима́ть impf, снять pf кожуру́ c+gen. **skinny** /-nɪ/ adj то́щий.

skip[1] /skɪp/ vi скака́ть impf; (with rope) пры́гать impf че́рез скака́лку; vt (omit) пропуска́ть impf, пропусти́ть pf.

skip[2] /skɪp/ n (container) скип.

skipper /ˈskɪpə(r)/ n (naut) шки́пер.

skirmish /ˈskɜːmɪʃ/ n схва́тка.

skirt /skɜːt/ n ю́бка; vt обходи́ть impf, обойти́ pf стороно́й; **~ing-board** пли́нтус.

skittle /ˈskɪt(ə)l/ n ке́гля; pl ке́гли f pl.

skulk /skʌlk/ vi (hide) скрыва́ться impf; (creep) кра́сться impf.

skull /skʌl/ n че́реп.

skunk /skʌŋk/ n скунс.

sky /skaɪ/ n не́бо. **skylark** n жа́воронок. **skylight** n окно́ в кры́ше. **skyline** n горизо́нт. **skyscraper** /-ˌskreɪpə(r)/ n небоскрёб.

slab /slæb/ *n* плита́; (*of cake etc.*) кусо́к.

slack /slæk/ *adj* (*loose*) сла́бый; (*sluggish*) вя́лый; (*negligent*) небре́жный *n* (*of rope*) сла́бина; *pl* брю́ки (-к) *pl*. **slacken** /-kən/ *vt* ослабля́ть *impf*, осла́бить *pf*; *vt & i* (*slow down*) замедля́ть(ся) *impf*, заме́длить(ся) *pf*; *vi* ослабева́ть *impf*, ослабе́ть *pf*.

slag /slæg/ *n* шлак.

slam /slæm/ *vt & i* захло́пывать(ся) *impf*, захло́пнуть(ся) *pf*.

slander /ˈslɑːndə(r)/ *n* клевета́; *vt* клевета́ть *impf*, на~ *pf* на+*acc*. **slanderous** /-rəs/ *adj* клеветни́ческий.

slang /slæŋ/ *n* жарго́н. **slangy** /slæŋɪ/ *adj* жарго́нный.

slant /slɑːnt/ *vt & i* наклоня́ть(ся) *impf*, наклони́ть(ся) *pf*; *n* укло́н. **slanting** /-tɪŋ/ *adj* косо́й.

slap /slæp/ *vt* шлёпать *impf*, шлёпнуть *pf*; *n* шлепо́к; *adv* пря́мо. **slapdash** *adj* небре́жный. **slapstick** *n* фарс.

slash /slæʃ/ *n* (*cut*) поро́ть *impf*, рас~ *pf*; (*fig*) уре́зывать *impf*, уре́зать *pf*; *n* разре́з; (*sign*) дробь.

slat /slæt/ *n* пла́нка.

slate[1] /sleɪt/ *n* сла́нец; (*for roofing*) (кро́вельная) пли́тка.

slate[2] /sleɪt/ *vt* (*criticize*) разноси́ть *impf*, разнести́ *pf*.

slaughter /ˈslɔːtə(r)/ *n* (*of animals*) убо́й; (*massacre*) резня́; *vt* (*animals*) ре́зать *impf*, за~ *pf*; (*people*) убива́ть *impf*, уби́ть *pf*. **slaughterhouse** *n* бо́йня.

Slav /slɑːv/ *n* славяни́н, -я́нка; *adj* славя́нский.

slave /sleɪv/ *n* раб, рабы́ня; *vi*

рабо́тать *impf* как раб. **slavery** /-vərɪ/ *n* ра́бство.

Slavic /ˈslɑːvɪk/ *adj* славя́нский.

slavish /ˈsleɪvɪʃ/ *adj* ра́бский.

Slavonic /sləˈvɒnɪk/ *adj* славя́нский.

slay /sleɪ/ *vt* убива́ть *impf*, уби́ть *pf*.

sleazy /ˈsliːzɪ/ *adj* убо́гий.

sledge /sledʒ/ *n* са́ни (-не́й) *pl*.

sledge-hammer /ˈsledʒˌhæmə(r)/ *n* кува́лда.

sleek /sliːk/ *adj* гла́дкий.

sleep /sliːp/ *n* сон; **go to ~** засыпа́ть *impf*, засну́ть *pf*; *vi* спать *impf*; (*spend the night*) ночева́ть *impf*, пере~ *pf*. **sleeper** /-pə(r)/ *n* спя́щий *sb*; (*on track*) шпа́ла; (*sleeping-car*) спа́льный ваго́н.

sleeping /-pɪŋ/ *adj* спя́щий; **~-bag** спа́льный мешо́к; **~-car** спа́льный ваго́н; **~-pill** снотво́рная табле́тка. **sleepless** /-lɪs/ *adj* бессо́нный. **sleepy** /-pɪ/ *adj* со́нный.

sleet /sliːt/ *n* мо́крый снег.

sleeve /sliːv/ *n* рука́в; (*of record*) конве́рт.

sleigh /sleɪ/ *n* са́ни (-не́й) *pl*.

sleight-of-hand /ˌslaɪtəvˈhænd/ *n* ло́вкость рук.

slender /ˈslendə(r)/ *adj* (*slim*) то́нкий; (*meagre*) ску́дный; (*of hope etc.*) сла́бый.

sleuth /sluːθ/ *n* сы́щик.

slice /slaɪs/ *n* кусо́к; *vt* (~ *up*) наре́зать *impf*, нареза́ть *pf*.

slick /slɪk/ *adj* (*dextrous*) ло́вкий; (*crafty*) хи́трый; *n* нефтяна́я плёнка.

slide /slaɪd/ *vi* скользи́ть *impf*; *vt* (*drawer etc.*) задвига́ть *impf*, задви́нуть *pf*; *n* (*children's ~*) го́рка; (*microscope ~*) предме́тное стекло́; (*phot*) диапозити́в, слайд; (*for hair*) зако́лка. **sliding** /-dɪŋ/ *adj*

(door) задвижно́й.

slight[1] /slaɪt/ adj (slender) то́нкий; (inconsiderable) небольшо́й; (light) лёгкий; **not the ~est** ни мале́йший, -шей (gen); **not in the ~est** ничу́ть.

slight[2] /slaɪt/ vt пренебрега́ть impf, пренебре́чь pf +instr; n оби́да.

slightly /'slaɪtlɪ/ adv слегка́, немно́го.

slim /slɪm/ adj то́нкий; (chance etc.) сла́бый; vi худе́ть impf, по-~ pf.

slime /slaɪm/ n слизь. **slimy** /-mɪ/ adj сли́зистый; (person) ско́льзкий.

sling /slɪŋ/ vt (throw) швыря́ть impf, швырну́ть pf; (suspend) подве́шивать impf, подве́сить pf; n (med) пе́ревязь.

slink /slɪŋk/ vi кра́сться impf.

slip /slɪp/ n (mistake) оши́бка; (garment) комбина́ция; (pillowcase) на́волочка; (paper) листо́чек; ~ **of the tongue** обмо́лвка; **give the ~** ускользну́ть pf от+gen; vi скользи́ть impf, скользну́ть pf; (fall over) поскользну́ться pf; (from hands etc.) выска́льзывать impf, вы́скользнуть pf; vt (insert) сова́ть impf, су́нуть pf; ~ **off** (depart) ускольза́ть impf, ускользну́ть pf; ~ **up** (make mistake) ошиба́ться impf, ошиби́ться pf. **slipper** /-pə(r)/ n та́пок, та́пка. **slippery** /-pərɪ/ adj ско́льзкий.

slit /slɪt/ vt разреза́ть impf, разре́зать pf; (throat) перереза́ть pf; n щель; (cut) разре́з.

slither /'slɪðə(r)/ vi скользи́ть impf.

sliver /'slɪvə(r)/ n ще́пка.

slob /slɒb/ n неря́ха m & f.

slobber /'slɒbə(r)/ vi пуска́ть

impf, пусти́ть pf слю́ни.

slog /slɒg/ vt (hit) си́льно ударя́ть impf, уда́рить pf; (work) упо́рно рабо́тать impf.

slogan /'sləʊgən/ n ло́зунг.

slop /slɒp/ n: pl помо́и (-о́ев) pl; vt & i выпле́скивать(ся) impf, вы́плескать(ся) pf.

slope /sləʊp/ n (artificial) накло́н; (geog) склон; vi име́ть impf накло́н. **sloping** /-pɪŋ/ adj накло́нный.

sloppy /'slɒpɪ/ adj (work) неря́шливый; (sentimental) сентимента́льный.

slot /slɒt/ n отве́рстие; ~-**machine** автома́т; vt: ~ **in** вставля́ть impf, вста́вить pf.

sloth /sləʊθ/ n лень.

slouch /slaʊtʃ/ vi (stoop) суту́литься impf.

slovenly /'slʌvənlɪ/ adj неря́шливый.

slow /sləʊ/ adj ме́дленный; (tardy) медли́тельный; (stupid) тупо́й; (business) вя́лый; **be ~** (clock) отстава́ть impf, отста́ть pf; adv ме́дленно; vt & i (~ **down, up**) замедля́ть(ся) impf, заме́длить(ся) pf.

sludge /slʌdʒ/ n (mud) грязь; (sediment) отсто́й.

slug /slʌg/ n (zool) слизня́к.

sluggish /'slʌgɪʃ/ adj вя́лый.

sluice /sluːs/ n шлюз.

slum /slʌm/ n трущо́ба.

slumber /'slʌmbə(r)/ n сон; vi спать impf.

slump /slʌmp/ n спад; vi ре́зко па́дать impf, (у)па́сть pf; (of person) сва́ливаться impf, свали́ться pf.

slur /slɜː(r)/ vt говори́ть impf невня́тно; n (stigma) пятно́.

slush /slʌʃ/ n сля́коть.

slut /slʌt/ n (sloven) неря́ха; (trollop) потаску́ха.

sly /slaɪ/ adj хи́трый; on the ~ тайко́м.

smack¹ /smæk/ vi: ~ of па́хнуть impf +instr.

smack² /smæk/ n (slap) шлепо́к; vt шлёпать impf, шлёпнуть pf.

small /smɔːl/ adj ма́ленький, небольшо́й, ма́лый; (of agent, particles; petty) ме́лкий; ~ change ме́лочь; ~scale мелкомасшта́бный; ~ talk све́тская бесе́да.

smart¹ /smɑːt/ vi са́днить impf impers.

smart² /smɑːt/ adj элега́нтный; (brisk) бы́стрый; (cunning) ло́вкий; (sharp) смека́листый (coll).

smash /smæʃ/ vt & i разбива́ть(ся) impf, разби́ть(ся) pf; vi: ~ into вреза́ться impf, вре́заться pf в+acc; n (crash) гро́хот; (collision) столкнове́ние; (blow) си́льный уда́р.

smattering /ˈsmætərɪŋ/ n пове́рхностное зна́ние.

smear /smɪə(r)/ vt сма́зывать impf, сма́зать pf; (dirty) па́чкать impf, за~, ис~ pf; (discredit) поро́чить impf, о~ pf; (spot) пятно́; (slander) клевета́; (med) мазо́к.

smell /smel/ n (sense) обоня́ние; (odour) за́пах; vt чу́вствовать impf за́пах+gen; (sniff) ню́хать impf, по~ pf; vi: ~ of па́хнуть impf +instr. **smelly** /-lɪ/ adj воню́чий.

smelt /smelt/ vt (ore) пла́вить impf; (metal) выплавля́ть impf, вы́плавить pf.

smile /smaɪl/ vi улыба́ться impf, улыбну́ться pf; n улы́бка.

smirk /smɜːk/ vi ухмыля́ться impf, ухмыльну́ться pf; n ухмы́лка.

smith /smɪθ/ n кузне́ц.

smithereens /ˌsmɪðəˈriːnz/ n (in)to ~ вдре́безги.

smithy /ˈsmɪðɪ/ n ку́зница.

smock /smɒk/ n блу́за.

smog /smɒg/ n тума́н (дымом).

smoke /sməʊk/ n дым; ~screen дымова́я заве́са; vt & i (cigarette etc.) кури́ть impf, по~ pf; vt (cure; colour) копти́ть impf за~ pf; vi (abnormally) дыми́ть impf; (of fire) дыми́ться impf. **smoker** /-kə(r)/ n кури́льщик -ица, куря́щий sb. **smoky** /-kɪ/ adj ды́мный.

smooth /smuːð/ adj (surface etc. гла́дкий; (movement etc.) ро́вный; vt пр

snap /snæp/ *vi* (*of dog or person*) огрыза́ться *impf*, огрызну́ться *pf* (**at** на+*acc*); *vt* & *i* (*break*) обрыва́ть(ся) *impf*, оборва́ть(ся) *pf*; *vt* (*make sound*) щёлкать *impf*, щёлкнуть *pf* +*instr*; ~ **up** (*buy*) расхва́тывать *impf*, расхвата́ть *pf*; *n* (*sound*) щёлк; (*photo*) сни́мок; *adj* (*decision*) скоропали́тельный. **snappy** /-pɪ/ *adj* (*brisk*) живо́й; (*stylish*) шика́рный. **snapshot** /'snæpʃɒt/ *n* сни́мок.

snare /sneə(r)/ *n* лову́шка.

snarl /snɑːl/ *vi* рыча́ть *impf*, за~ *pf*; *n* рыча́ние.

snatch /snætʃ/ *vt* хвата́ть *impf*, (с)хвати́ть *pf*; *vi*: ~ **at** хвата́ться *impf*, (с)хвати́ться *pf* за+*acc*; *n* (*fragment*) обры́вок.

sneak /sniːk/ *vi* (*slink*) кра́сться *impf*; *vi* (*steal*) ста́щить *pf*; *n* я́бедник, -ица (*coll*). **sneaking** /-kɪŋ/ *adj* та́йный. **sneaky** /-kɪ/ *adj* лука́вый.

sneer /snɪə(r)/ *vi* насмеха́ться *impf* (**at** над+*instr*).

sneeze /sniːz/ *vi* чиха́ть *impf*, чихну́ть *pf*; *n* чиха́нье.

snide /snaɪd/ *adj* ехи́дный.

sniff /snɪf/ *vi* шмы́гать *impf*, шмыгну́ть *pf* но́сом; *vt* ню́хать *impf*, по~ *pf*.

snigger /'snɪɡə(r)/ *vi* хихи́кать *impf*, хихикну́ть *pf*; *n* хихи́канье.

snip /snɪp/ *vt* ре́зать *impf* (но́жницами); ~ **off** среза́ть *impf*, сре́зать *pf*.

snipe /snaɪp/ *vi* стреля́ть *impf* из укры́тия (**at** в+*acc*); (*fig*) напада́ть *impf*, напа́сть *pf* на+*acc*. **sniper** /-pə(r)/ *n* сна́йпер.

snippet /'snɪpɪt/ *n* отре́зок; *pl* (*of news etc.*) обры́вки *m pl*.

snivel /'snɪv(ə)l/ *vi* (*run at nose*) распуска́ть *impf*, распусти́ть *pf* со́пли; (*whimper*) хны́кать *impf*.

snob /snɒb/ *n* сноб. **snobbery** /-bərɪ/ *n* сноби́зм. **snobbish** /-bɪʃ/ *adj* сноби́стский.

snoop /snuːp/ *vi* шпио́нить *impf*; ~ **about** разню́хивать *impf*, разню́хать *pf*.

snooty /'snuːtɪ/ *adj* чва́нный.

snooze /snuːz/ *vi* вздремну́ть *pf*; *n* коро́ткий сон.

snore /snɔː(r)/ *vi* храпе́ть *impf*.

snorkel /'snɔːk(ə)l/ *n* шно́ркель *m*.

snort /snɔːt/ *vi* фы́ркать *impf*, фы́ркнуть *pf*.

snot /snɒt/ *n* со́пли (-ле́й) *pl*.

snout /snaʊt/ *n* ры́ло, мо́рда.

snow /snəʊ/ *n* снег; ~**-white** белосне́жный; *vi*: **it is** ~**ing**, **it snows** идёт снег; ~**ed under** зава́ленный рабо́той; **we were** ~**ed up**, **in** нас занесло́ сне́гом. **snowball** *n* снежо́к. **snowdrop** *n* подсне́жник. **snowflake** *n* снежи́нка. **snowman** *n* сне́жная ба́ба. **snowstorm** *n* мете́ль. **snowy** /-ɪ/ *adj* сне́жный; (*snow-white*) белосне́жный.

snub /snʌb/ *vt* игнори́ровать *impf* & *pf*.

snuff[1] /snʌf/ *n* (*tobacco*) ню́хательный таба́к.

snuff[2] /snʌf/ *vt*: ~ **out** туши́ть *impf*, по~ *pf*.

snuffle /'snʌf(ə)l/ *vi* сопе́ть *impf*.

snug /snʌɡ/ *adj* ую́тный.

snuggle /'snʌɡ(ə)l/ *vi*: ~ **up to** прижима́ться *impf*, прижа́ться *pf* к+*dat*.

so /səʊ/ *adv* так; (*in this way*) так; (*thus, at beginning of sentence*) ита́к; (*also*) та́кже, то́же; *conj* (*therefore*) так что, поэ́тому; **and** ~ **on** и так да́лее; **if**

~ в тако́м слу́чае; ~ ... as так(о́й)... как; ~ as to с тем что́бы; ~called так называ́емый; (in) ~ far as насто́лько; ~ long! пока́!; ~ long as поско́льку; ~ much насто́лько; ~ much до тако́й сте́пени; ~ much the better тем лу́чше; ~ that что́бы; ~ ... that так... что; ~ to say, speak так сказа́ть; ~ what? ну и что?

soak /səʊk/ vt мочи́ть impf, на~ pf; (drench) прома́чивать impf, промочи́ть pf; ~ up впи́тывать impf, впита́ть pf; vi: ~ through проса́чиваться impf, просочи́ться pf; get ~ed промока́ть impf, промо́кнуть pf.

soap /səʊp/ n мы́ло; vt мы́лить impf, на~ pf; ~ opera многосери́йная переда́ча; ~ powder стира́льный порошо́к. **soapy** /-pɪ/ adj мы́льный.

soar /sɔː(r)/ vi пари́ть impf; (prices) подска́кивать impf, подскочи́ть pf.

sob /sɒb/ vi рыда́ть impf; n рыда́ние.

sober /ˈsəʊbə(r)/ adj тре́звый; vt & i: ~ up отрезвля́ть(ся) impf, отрезви́ть(ся) pf. **sobriety** /səˈbraɪɪtɪ/ n тре́звость.

soccer /ˈsɒkə(r)/ n футбо́л.

sociable /ˈsəʊʃəb(ə)l/ adj общи́тельный. **social** /ˈsəʊʃ(ə)l/ adj обще́ственный, социа́льный; S~ Democrat социа́л-демокра́т; ~ sciences обще́ственные нау́ки f pl; ~ security социа́льное обеспе́чение. **socialism** /-lɪz(ə)m/ n социали́зм. **socialist** /-lɪst/ n социали́ст; adj социалисти́ческий. **socialize** /-laɪz/ vt обща́ться impf. **society** /sə'saɪətɪ/ n о́бщество. **sociological** /ˌsəʊsɪə'lɒdʒɪk(ə)l/ adj социологи́ческий. **sociolo**

gist /ˌsəʊsɪ'ɒlɪdʒɪst/ n социо́лог. **sociology** /ˌsəʊsɪ'ɒlədʒɪ/ n социоло́гия.

sock /sɒk/ n носо́к.

socket /ˈsɒkɪt/ n (eye) впа́дина (electr) штепсель m; (for bulb) патро́н.

soda /ˈsəʊdə/ n со́да; ~-water содова́я вода́.

sodden /ˈsɒd(ə)n/ adj промо́кший.

sodium /ˈsəʊdɪəm/ n на́трий.

sodomy /ˈsɒdəmɪ/ n педера́стия.

sofa /ˈsəʊfə/ n дива́н.

soft /sɒft/ adj мя́гкий; (sound) ти́хий; (colour) нея́ркий; (malleable) нея́ркий; (tender) нежный; ~ drink безалкого́льный напи́ток. **soften** /ˈsɒf(ə)n/ vt & i смягча́ть(ся) impf, смягчи́ть(ся) pf. **softness** /ˈsɒftnɪs/ n мя́гкость. **software** /-weə(r)/ n програ́ммное обеспе́чение.

soggy /ˈsɒgɪ/ adj сыро́й.

soil[1] /sɔɪl/ n по́чва.

soil[2] /sɔɪl/ vt па́чкать impf, за~ pf.

solace /ˈsɒləs/ n утеше́ние.

solar /ˈsəʊlə(r)/ adj со́лнечный.

solder /ˈsəʊldə(r)/ n припо́й; vt паять impf; (~ together) спа́ивать impf, спая́ть pf. **soldering iron** /-rɪŋ 'aɪən/ n пая́льник.

soldier /ˈsəʊldʒə(r)/ n солда́т.

sole[1] /səʊl/ n (of foot, shoe) подо́шва.

sole[2] /səʊl/ n (fish) морско́й язы́к.

sole[3] /səʊl/ adj еди́нственный.

solemn /ˈsɒləm/ adj торже́ственный. **solemnity** /səˈlemnɪtɪ/ n торже́ственность.

solicit /sə'lɪsɪt/ vt проси́ть impf, по~ pf +acc, gen, o+prep; (of prostitute) пристава́ть impf к мужчи́нам. **solicitor** /-'lɪsɪtə(r)/

n адвока́т. **solicitous** /-'lısıtəs/ *adj* забо́тливый.

solid /'sɒlıd/ *adj* (*not liquid*) твёрдый; (*not hollow; continuous*) сплошно́й; (*firm*) про́чный; (*pure*) чи́стый; *n* твёрдое те́ло; *pl* твёрдая пи́ща. **solidarity** /ˌsɒlı'dærıtı/ *n* солида́рность. **solidify** /sə'lıdı ˌfaı/ *vi* затверде́вать *impf*, затверде́ть *pf*. **solidity** /-'lıdıtı/ *n* твёрдость; про́чность.

soliloquy /sə'lıləkwı/ *n* моноло́г.

solitary /'sɒlıtərı/ *adj* одино́кий, уединённый; ~ **confinement** одино́чное заключе́ние. **solitude** /ˈsɒlıˌtjuːd/ *n* одино́чество, уедине́ние.

solo /'səʊləʊ/ *n* со́ло *neut indecl*; *adj* со́льный; *adv* со́ло. **soloist** /-ıst/ *n* соли́ст *m*, ~ка.

solstice /'sɒlstıs/ *n* солнцестоя́ние.

soluble /'sɒljʊb(ə)l/ *adj* раствори́мый. **solution** /sə'luː ʃ(ə)n/ *n* раство́р; (*of puzzle etc.*) реше́ние. **solve** /sɒlv/ *vt* реша́ть *impf*, реши́ть *pf*. **solvent** /'sɒlv(ə)nt/ *adj* растворя́ющий; (*financially*) платёжеспосо́бный; *n* раствори́тель *m*.

sombre /'sɒmbə(r)/ *adj* мра́чный.

some /sʌm/ *adj & pron* (*any*) како́й-нибудь; (*a certain*) како́й-то; (*a certain amount or number of*) не́который, a often expressed by noun in (*partitive*) *gen*; (*several*) не́сколько+*gen*; (~ *people, things*) не́которые *pl*; ~ **day** когда́-нибудь; ~ **more** ещё; ~ ... **others** одни́ ... други́е. **somebody**, **someone** /'sʌmbədı, 'sʌmwʌn/ *n, pron* (*def*) кто́-то; (*indef*) кто́-нибудь. **somehow** /'sʌmhaʊ/ *adv* ка́к-

то; ка́к-нибудь; (*for some reason*) почему́-то; ~ **or other** так и́ли ина́че.

somersault /'sʌməˌsɒlt/ *n* са́льто *neut indecl*; *vi* кувырка́ться *impf*, кувыр(к)ну́ться *pf*.

something /'sʌmθıŋ/ *n & pron* (*def*) что́-то; (*indef*) что́-нибудь; ~ **like** (*approximately*) приблизи́тельно; (*a thing like*) что́-то вро́де+*gen*. **sometime** /'sʌmtaım/ *adv* когда́-то; *adj* бы́вший. **sometimes** /-taımz/ *adv* иногда́. **somewhat** /'sʌmwɒt/ *adv* не́сколько, дово́льно. **somewhere** /'sʌmweə(r)/ *adv* (*position*) (*def*) где́-то; (*indef*) где́-нибудь; (*motion*) куда́-то; куда́-нибудь.

son /sʌn/ *n* сын; ~-**in-law** зять *m*.

sonata /sə'nɑːtə/ *n* сона́та.

song /sɒŋ/ *n* пе́сня.

sonic /'sɒnık/ *adj* звуково́й.

sonnet /'sɒnıt/ *n* соне́т.

soon /suːn/ *adv* ско́ро; (*early*) ра́но; as ~ as то́лько; as ~ as possible как мо́жно скоре́е; ~er or later ра́но и́ли по́здно; the ~er the better чем ра́ньше, тем лу́чше.

soot /sʊt/ *n* са́жа, ко́поть.

soothe /suːð/ *vt* успока́ивать *impf*, успоко́ить *pf*; (*pain*) облегча́ть *impf*, облегчи́ть *pf*.

sophisticated /sə'fıstıˌkeıtıd/ *adj* (*person*) иску́шенный; (*equipment*) сло́жный.

soporific /ˌsɒpə'rıfık/ *adj* снотво́рный.

soprano /sə'prɑːnəʊ/ *n* сопра́но (*voice*) *neut & (person) f indecl*.

sorcerer /'sɔːsərə(r)/ *n* колду́н. **sorcery** /'sɔːsərı/ *n* колдовство́.

sordid /'sɔːdıd/ *adj* гря́зный.

sore /sɔː(r)/ *n* боля́чка; *adj* боль-

ной; my throat is ~ у меня́ боли́т го́рло.

sorrow /'sɒrəʊ/ n печа́ль. **sorrowful** /-fʊl/ adj печа́льный.

sorry /'sɒrɪ/ adj жа́лкий; predic: be ~ жале́ть impf (about o+prep); жаль impers+dat (for +gen); ~! извини́(те)!

sort /sɔːt/ n род, вид, сорт; vt (also ~ out) сортирова́ть impf, рас~ pf; (also fig) разбира́ть impf, разобра́ть pf.

sortie /'sɔːtiː/ n вы́лазка.

SOS n (ра́дио)сигна́л бе́дствия.

soul /səʊl/ n душа́.

sound[1] /saʊnd/ adj (healthy, thorough) здоро́вый; (in good condition) испра́вный; (logical) здра́вый, разу́мный; (of sleep) кре́пкий.

sound[2] /saʊnd/ n (noise) звук, шум; attrib звуково́й; ~ effects звуковы́е эффе́кты m pl; vi звуча́ть impf, про~ pf.

sound[3] /saʊnd/ n (naut) измеря́ть impf, изме́рить pf глубину́ +gen; ~ out (fig) зонди́ровать impf, по~ pf; n зонд.

sound[4] /saʊnd/ n (strait) проли́в.

soup /suːp/ n суп; vt: ~ed up форси́рованный.

sour /'saʊə(r)/ adj ки́слый; ~ cream смета́на; vt & i (fig) озлобля́ть(ся) impf, озло́бить(ся) pf.

source /sɔːs/ n исто́чник; (of river) исто́к.

south /saʊθ/ n юг; (naut) зюйд; adj ю́жный; adv к ю́гу, на юг; ~-east n ю́го-восто́к; ~-west n ю́го-за́пад. **southerly** /'sʌðəlɪ/ adj ю́жный. **southern** /'sʌðən/ adj ю́жный. **southerner** /'sʌðənə(r)/ n южа́нин, -а́нка.

southward(s) /'saʊθwədz/ adv на юг, к ю́гу.

souvenir /ˌsuːvəˈnɪə(r)/ n сувени́р.

sovereign /'sɒvrɪn/ adj сувере́нный; n мона́рх. **sovereignty** /-tɪ/ n суверените́т.

soviet /'səʊvɪət/ n сове́т; S~ Union Сове́тский Сою́з; adj (S~) сове́тский.

sow[1] /saʊ/ n свинья́.

sow[2] /səʊ/ vt (seed) се́ять impf, по~ pf; (field) засева́ть impf, засе́ять pf.

soya /'sɔɪə/ n: ~ bean со́евый боб.

spa /spaː/ n куро́рт.

space /speɪs/ n (place, room) ме́сто; (expanse) простра́нство; (interval) промежу́ток (outer ~) ко́смос; attrib косми́ческий; vt расставля́ть impf, расста́вить pf с промежу́тками. **spacecraft, -ship** n косми́ческий кора́бль.

spacious /'speɪʃəs/ adj просто́рный.

spade /speɪd/ n (tool) лопа́та; pl (cards) пи́ки (пик) pl.

spaghetti /spəˈgetɪ/ n спаге́тти neut indecl.

Spain /speɪn/ n Испа́ния.

span /spæn/ n (of bridge) пролёт; (aeron) разма́х; vt (of bridge) соединя́ть impf, соедини́ть pf сто́роны +gen; (river) берега́ +gen; (fig) охва́тывать impf, охвати́ть pf.

Spaniard /'spænjəd/ n испа́нец, -нка. **Spanish** /'spænɪʃ/ adj испа́нский.

spank /spæŋk/ vt шлёпать impf, шлёпнуть pf.

spanner /'spænə(r)/ n га́ечный ключ.

spar[1] /spaː(r)/ n (aeron) лонжеро́н.

spar² /spɑː(r)/ vi боксировать impf; (fig) препираться impf.

spare /speə(r)/ adj запасной; (extra, to ~) лишний; (of seat, time) свободный; ~ **parts** запасные части f pl; ~ **room** комната для гостей; n: pl запчасти f pl; vt (grudge) жалеть impf, по~ pf +acc, gen; he ~d **no pains** он не жалел трудов; (do without) обходиться impf, обойтись pf без+gen; (time) уделять impf, уделить pf; (show mercy towards) щадить impf, по~ pf; (save from) избавлять impf, избавить pf от+gen: ~ **me the details** избавьте меня от подробностей.

spark /spɑːk/ n искра; ~**plug** запальная свеча; vt (~ off) вызывать impf, вызвать pf.

sparkle /ˈspɑːk(ə)l/ vi сверкать impf.

sparrow /ˈspærəʊ/ n воробей.

sparse /spɑːs/ adj редкий.

Spartan /ˈspɑːt(ə)n/ adj спартанский.

spasm /ˈspæz(ə)m/ n спазм.

spasmodic /spæzˈmɒdɪk/ adj спазмодический.

spastic /ˈspæstɪk/ n паралитик.

spate /speɪt/ n разлив; (fig) поток.

spatial /ˈspeɪʃ(ə)l/ adj пространственный.

spatter, splatter /ˈspætə(r), ˈsplætə(r)/ vt (liquid) брызгать impf +instr; (person etc.) забрызгивать impf, забрызгать pf (with +instr); vi плескать(ся) impf, плеснуть pf.

spatula /ˈspætjʊlə/ n шпатель m.

spawn /spɔːn/ vt & i метать impf (икру); vt (fig) порождать impf, породить pf.

speak /spiːk/ vt & i говорить impf, сказать pf; vi (make speech) выступать impf, выступить pf (с речью); (~ **out**) высказываться impf, высказаться pf (for за+acc; against против+gen). **speaker** /-kə(r)/ n говорящий sb; (giving speech) выступающий sb; (orator) оратор; (S~, parl) спикер; (loud-~) громкоговоритель m.

spear /spɪə(r)/ n копьё; vt пронзать impf, пронзить pf копьём. **spearhead** vt возглавлять impf, возглавить pf.

special /ˈspeʃ(ə)l/ adj особый, специальный. **specialist** /ˈspeʃəlɪst/ n специалист, ~ка. **speciality** /ˌspeʃɪˈælɪtɪ/ n (dish) фирменное блюдо; (subject) специальность. **specialization** /ˌspeʃəlaɪˈzeɪʃ(ə)n/ n специализация. **specialize** /ˈspeʃəlaɪz/ vt & i специализировать(ся) impf & pf. **specially** /ˈspeʃəlɪ/ adv особенно.

species /ˈspiːʃiːz/ n вид.

specific /sprˈsɪfɪk/ adj особенный. **specification(s)** /ˌspesɪfɪˈkeɪʃ(ə)nz/ n спецификация. **specify** /ˈspesɪfaɪ/ vt уточнять impf, уточнить pf.

specimen /ˈspesɪmən/ n образец, экземпляр.

speck /spek/ n крапинка, пятнышко. **speckled** /-k(ə)ld/ adj крапчатый.

spectacle /ˈspektək(ə)l/ n зрелище; pl очки (-ков) pl.

spectacular /spekˈtækjʊlə(r)/ adj эффектный; (amazing) потрясающий.

spectator /spekˈteɪtə(r)/ n зритель m.

spectre /ˈspektə(r)/ n призрак.

spectrum /ˈspektrəm/ n спектр.

speculate /'spekjʊˌleɪt/ vi (*meditate*) размышля́ть *impf*, размы́слить *pf* (**on** о+*prep*); (*conjecture*) гада́ть *impf*; (*comm*) спекули́ровать *impf*. **speculation** /ˌspekjʊ'leɪʃ(ə)n/ n (*conjecture*) дога́дка; (*comm*) спекуля́ция. **speculative** /'spekjʊlətɪv/ adj гипотети́ческий; спекуляти́вный. **speculator** /'spekjʊˌleɪtə(r)/ n спекуля́нт.

speech /spiːtʃ/ n речь. **speechless** /-lɪs/ adj онеме́вший.

speed /spiːd/ n ско́рость; vi мча́ться *impf*, про~ *pf*; (*illegally*) превыша́ть *impf*, превы́сить *pf* ско́рость; ~ **up** ускоря́ть(ся) *impf*, уско́рить(ся) *pf*. **speedboat** n быстрохо́дный ка́тер. **speedometer** /spiː'dɒmɪtə(r)/ n спидо́метр. **speedy** /'spiːdɪ/ adj бы́стрый.

spell[1] /spel/ n (*charm*) загово́р.

spell[2] /spel/ vt (*say*) произноси́ть *impf*, произнести́ *pf* по бу́квам; (*write*) пра́вильно писа́ть *impf*, на~ *pf*; **how do you ~ that word?** как пи́шется э́то сло́во?

spell[3] /spel/ n (*period*) пери́од.

spellbound /'spelbaʊnd/ adj заача́рованный.

spelling /'spelɪŋ/ n правописа́ние.

spend /spend/ vt (*money*; *effort*) тра́тить *impf*, ис~, по~ *pf*; (*time*) проводи́ть *impf*, провести́ *pf*.

sperm /spɜːm/ n спе́рма.

sphere /sfɪə(r)/ n сфе́ра; (*ball*) шар. **spherical** /'sferɪk(ə)l/ adj сфери́ческий.

spice /spaɪs/ n пря́ность; vt направля́ть *impf*, припра́вить *pf*. **spicy** /-sɪ/ adj пря́ный; (*fig*) пика́нтный.

spider /'spaɪdə(r)/ n пау́к.

spike /spaɪk/ n (*point*) остриё; (*on fence*) зубе́ц; (*on shoes*) шип.

spill /spɪl/ vt & i (*liquid*) пролива́ть(ся) *impf*, проли́ть(ся) *pf*; (*dry substance*) рассыпа́ть(ся) *impf*, рассы́пать(ся) *pf*.

spin /spɪn/ vt (*thread etc.*) прясти́ *impf*, с~ *pf*; (*coin*) подбра́сывать *impf*, подбро́сить *pf*; vt & i (*turn*) кружи́ть(ся) *impf*; ~ **ou** (*prolong*) затя́гивать *impf*, затяну́ть *pf*.

spinach /'spɪnɪdʒ/ n шпина́т.

spinal /'spaɪn(ə)l/ adj спинно́й. ~ **column** спинно́й хребе́т; ~ **cord** спинно́й мозг.

spindle /'spɪnd(ə)l/ n ось m. **spindly** /-dlɪ/ adj дли́нный и то́нкий.

spine /spaɪn/ n (*anat*) позвоно́чник, хребе́т; (*prickle*) игла́; (*of book*) корешо́к. **spineless** /-lɪs/ adj (*fig*) бесхара́ктерный.

spinning /'spɪnɪŋ/ n пряде́ние; ~**wheel** пря́лка.

spinster /'spɪnstə(r)/ n незаму́жняя же́нщина.

spiral /'spaɪər(ə)l/ adj спира́льный; (*staircase*) винтово́й; n спира́ль; vi (*rise sharply*) ре́зко возраста́ть *impf*, возрасти́ *pf*.

spire /spaɪə(r)/ n шпиль m.

spirit /'spɪrɪt/ n дух, душа́; pl (*mood*) настрое́ние; pl (*drinks*) спиртно́е sb; ~**-level** ватерпа́с; vt: ~ **away** та́йно уноси́ть *impf*, унести́ *pf* (*turn*). **spirited** /-tɪd/ adj живо́й. **spiritual** /-tjʊəl/ adj духо́вный. **spiritualism** /-tjʊəˌlɪz(ə)m/ n спиритизм. **spiritualist** /-tjʊəlɪst/ n спири́ст.

spit[1] /spɪt/ n (*skewer*) ве́ртел.

spit[2] /spɪt/ vi плева́ть *impf*, плю́нуть *pf*; (*of rain*) мороси́ть *impf*; (*of fire*) разбры́згивать

impf, разбры́згать *pf* и́скры; (*sizzle*) шипе́ть *impf*; *vt*: ~ **out** выплёвывать *impf*, вы́плюнуть *pf*; ~**ing image** то́чная ко́пия; *n* слюна́.

spite /spaɪt/ *n* зло́ба; **in** ~ **of** несмотря́ на+*acc*. **spiteful** /-fəl/ *adj* зло́бный.

spittle /'spɪt(ə)l/ *n* слюна́.

splash /splæʃ/ *vt* (*person*) забры́згивать *impf*, забры́згать *pf* (**with** +*instr*); (*liquid*) бры́згать *impf* +*instr*; *vi* плеска́ть(ся) *impf*, плесну́ть *pf*; (*move*) шлёпать *impf*, шлёпнуть *pf* (**through** по+*dat*); *n* (*act*, *sound*) плеск; (*mark made*) пятно́.

splatter /'splætə(r)/ *see* **spatter**

spleen /spliːn/ *n* селезёнка.

splendid /'splendɪd/ *adj* великоле́пный. **splendour** /-ə(r)/ *n* великоле́пие.

splice /splaɪs/ *vt* (*ropes etc.*) сра́щивать *impf*, срасти́ть *pf*; (*film*, *tape*) скле́ивать *impf*, скле́ить *pf* концы́+*gen*.

splint /splɪnt/ *n* ши́на.

splinter /'splɪntə(r)/ *n* оско́лок; (*in skin*) зано́за; *vt* & *i* расщепля́ть(ся) *impf*, расщепи́ть(ся) *pf*.

split /splɪt/ *n* расще́лина, расще́п; (*schism*) раско́л; *pl* шпага́т; *vt* & *i* расщепля́ть(ся) *impf*, расщепи́ть(ся) *pf*; раска́лывать(ся) *impf*, расколо́ть(ся) *pf*; *vt* (*divide*) дели́ть *impf*, раз~ *pf*; ~ **second** мгнове́ние о́ка; ~ **up** (*part company*) расходи́ться *impf*, разойти́сь *pf*.

splutter /'splʌtə(r)/ *vi* бры́згать *impf* слюно́й; *vt* (*utter*) говори́ть *impf* захлёбываясь.

spoil /spɔɪl/ *n* (*booty*) добы́ча; *vt* & *i* (*damage*; *decay*) по-

ртить(ся) *impf*, ис~ *pf*; *vt* (*indulge*) балова́ть *impf*, из~ *pf*.

spoke /spəʊk/ *n* спи́ца.

spokesman /'spəʊksmən/, **-woman** /-ˌwʊmən/ *n* представи́тель *m*, ~ница.

sponge /spʌndʒ/ *n* гу́бка; ~ **cake** бискви́т; *vt* (*wash*) мыть *impf*, вы́~, по~ гу́бкой; *vi*: ~ **on** жить *impf* на счёт+*gen*. **sponger** /-dʒə(r)/ *n* прижива́льщик. **spongy** /-dʒɪ/ *adj* гу́бчатый.

sponsor /'spɒnsə(r)/ *n* спо́нсор; *vt* финанси́ровать *impf* & *pf*.

spontaneity /ˌspɒntə'niːɪtɪ/ *n* спонта́нность. **spontaneous** /spɒn'teɪnɪəs/ *adj* спонта́нный.

spoof /spuːf/ *n* паро́дия.

spooky /'spuːkɪ/ *adj* жу́ткий.

spool /spuːl/ *n* кату́шка.

spoon /spuːn/ *n* ло́жка; *vt* че́рпать *impf*, черпну́ть *pf* ло́жкой. **spoonful** /-fʊl/ *n* ло́жка.

sporadic /spə'rædɪk/ *adj* спорад

и́ческий.

sport /spɔːt/ *n* спорт; ~**s car** спорти́вный автомоби́ль *m*; *vt* щеголя́ть *impf*, щегольну́ть *pf* +*instr*. **sportsman** *n* спортсме́н. **sporty** /-tɪ/ *adj* спорти́вный.

spot /spɒt/ *n* (*place*) ме́сто; (*mark*) пятно́; (*pimple*) пры́щик; **on the** ~ на ме́сте; (*at once*) сра́зу; ~ **check** вы́борочная прове́рка; *vt* (*notice*) замеча́ть *impf*, заме́тить *pf*. **spotless** /-lɪs/ *adj* абсолю́тно чи́стый. **spotlight** *n* прожектор; быть внима́ние. **spotty** /-tɪ/ *adj* прыщева́тый.

spouse /spaʊz/ *n* супру́г, ~а.

spout /spaʊt/ *vi* бить *impf* струёй; хлы́нуть *pf*; (*pontificate*) ора́торствовать *impf*; *vt* изверга́ть *impf*, изве́ргнуть *pf*; (*verses etc.*) деклами́ровать

impf, про~ *pf*; *n* (*tube*) но́сик; (*jet*) струя́.

sprain /sprein/ *vt* растя́гивать *impf*, растяну́ть *pf*; *n* растяже́ние.

sprawl /sprɔːl/ *vi* (*of person*) разва́ливаться *impf*, развали́ться *pf*; (*of town*) раски́дываться *impf*, раски́нуться *pf*.

spray¹ /sprei/ *n* (*flowers*) ве́т(о)чка.

spray² /sprei/ *n* бры́зги (-г) *pl*; (*atomizer*) пульвериза́тор; *vt* опры́скивать *impf*, опры́скать *pf* (*with* +*instr*); (*cause to scatter*) распыля́ть *impf*, распыли́ть *pf*.

spread /spred/ *vt & i* (*news, disease, etc.*) распространя́ть(ся) *impf*, распространи́ть(ся) *pf*; *vt* (~ *out*) расстила́ть *impf*, разостла́ть *pf*; (*unfurl, unroll*) развёртывать *impf*, разверну́ть *pf*; (*bread etc.* +*acc*; *butter etc.* +*instr*) нама́зывать *impf*, нама́зать *pf*; *n* (*expansion*) распростране́ние; (*span*) разма́х; (*feast*) пир; (*paste*) па́ста.

spree /spriː/ *n* кутёж; **go on a ~** кути́ть *impf*, кутну́ть *pf*.

sprig /sprig/ *n* ве́точка.

sprightly /'spraitli/ *adj* бо́дрый.

spring /spriŋ/ *vi* (*jump*) пры́гать *impf*; *vt* (*tell unexpectedly*) неожи́данно сообща́ть *impf*, сообщи́ть *pf* (*on* +*dat*); **~ a leak** дава́ть *impf*, дать *pf* течь; **~ from** (*originate*) происходи́ть *impf*, произойти́ *pf* +*gen*; *n* (*jump*) прыж(о́)к; (*season*) весна́, *attrib* весе́нний; (*water*) исто́чник; (*elasticity*) упру́гость; (*coil*) пружи́на; **~-clean** генера́льная убо́рка.

springboard *n* трампли́н.

sprinkle /'spriŋk(ə)l/ *vt* (*with liquid*) опры́скивать *impf*, опры-

скать *pf* (**with** +*instr*); (*with solid*) посыпа́ть *impf*, посы́пать *pf* (**with** +*instr*). **sprinkler** /-klə(r)/ *n* разбрызгива́тель *m*.

sprint /sprint/ *vi* бежа́ть *impf* на коро́ткую диста́нцию; (*rush*) рвану́ться *pf*; *n* спринт. **sprinter** /-tə(r)/ *n* спри́нтер.

sprout /spraut/ *vi* пуска́ть *impf*, пусти́ть *pf* ростки́; *n* росто́к *pl* брюссе́льская капу́ста.

spruce¹ /spruːs/ *adj* наря́дный элега́нтный; *vt*: **~ o.s. up** приводи́ть *impf*, привести́ *pf* себя́ в поря́док.

spruce² /spruːs/ *n* ель.

spur /spɜː(r)/ *n* шпо́ра; (*fig*) сти́мул; **on the ~ of the moment** под влия́нием мину́ты; *vt*: **~ on** подхлёстывать *impf*, подхлестну́ть *pf*.

spurious /'spjʊəriəs/ *adj* подде́льный.

spurn /spɜːn/ *vt* отверга́ть *impf*, отве́ргнуть *pf*.

spurt /spɜːt/ *n* (*jet*) струя́; (*effort*) рыво́к; *vi* бить *impf* струёй; (*make an effort*) де́лать *impf*, с~ *pf* рыво́к.

spy /spai/ *n* шпио́н; *vi* шпио́нить *impf* (**on** за+*instr*). **spying** /-iŋ/ *n* шпиона́ж.

squabble /'skwɒb(ə)l/ *n* перебра́нка; *vi* вздо́рить *impf*, по~ *pf*.

squad /skwɒd/ *n* кома́нда, гру́ппа.

squadron /'skwɒdrən/ *n* (*mil*) эскадро́н; (*naut*) эска́дра; (*aeron*) эскадри́лья.

squalid /'skwɒlid/ *adj* убо́гий.

squall /skwɔːl/ *n* шквал.

squalor /'skwɒlə(r)/ *n* убо́жество.

squander /'skwɒndə(r)/ *vt* растра́чивать *impf*, растра-

тить *pf.*

square /skweə(r)/ *n* (*shape*) квадра́т; (*in town*) пло́щадь; (*on paper, material*) кле́тка; (*instrument*) наго́льник; *adj* квадра́тный; (*meal*) пло́тный; ~ **root** квадра́тный ко́рень *m*; *vt* (*accounts*) своди́ть *impf*, свести́ *pf*; (*math*) возводи́ть *impf*, возвести́ *pf* в квадра́т; *vi* (*correspond*) соотве́тствовать *impf* (**with** +*dat*).

squash /skwɒʃ/ *n* (*crowd*) толку́чка; (*drink*) сок; *vt* разда́вливать *impf*, раздави́ть *pf*; (*suppress*) подавля́ть *impf*, подави́ть *pf*; *vi* вти́скиваться *impf*, вти́снуться *pf.*

squat /skwɒt/ *adj* призе́мистый; *vi* сиде́ть *impf* на ко́рточках; ~ **down** сади́ться *impf*, сесть *pf* на ко́рточки.

squatter /'skwɒtə(r)/ *n* незако́нный жиле́ц.

squawk /skwɔːk/ *n* клёкот; *vi* клекота́ть *impf.*

squeak /skwiːk/ *n* писк; (*of object*) скрип; *vi* пища́ть *impf*, пи́скнуть *pf*; (*of object*) скрипе́ть *impf*, скри́пнуть *pf.*
squeaky /-kɪ/ *adj* пискли́вый, скрипу́чий.

squeal /skwiːl/ *n* визг; *vi* визжа́ть *impf*, ви́згнуть *pf.*

squeamish /'skwiːmɪʃ/ *adj* брезгли́вый.

squeeze /skwiːz/ *n* (*crush*) да́вка; (*pressure*) сжа́тие; (*hand*) пожа́тие; *vt* дави́ть *impf*, сжима́ть *impf*, сжать *pf*; ~ **in** впи́хивать(ся), впи́хнуть(ся) *pf*; вти́скивать(ся) *impf*, вти́снуть(ся) *pf*; ~ **out** выжима́ть *impf*, вы́жать *pf*; ~ **through** проти́скивать(ся) *impf*, проти́снуть(ся) *pf.*

squelch /skweltʃ/ *vi* хлю́пать

impf, хлю́пнуть *pf.*

squid /skwɪd/ *n* кальма́р.

squint /skwɪnt/ *n* косогла́зие; *vi* коси́ть *impf*; (*screw up eyes*) щу́риться *impf.*

squire /'skwaɪə(r)/ *n* сквайр, поме́щик.

squirm /skwɜːm/ *vi* (*wriggle*) извива́ться *impf*, изви́ться *pf.*

squirrel /'skwɪr(ə)l/ *n* бе́лка.

squirt /skwɜːt/ *n* струя́; *vi* бить *impf* струёй; *vt* пуска́ть *impf*, пусти́ть *pf* струю́ (*substance* +*gen*; **at** на+*acc*).

St. *abbr* (*of Street*) ул., у́лица; (*of Saint*) св., Свято́й, -а́я.

stab /stæb/ *n* уда́р (ножо́м *etc.*); (*pain*) внеза́пная о́страя боль; *vt* наноси́ть *impf*, нанести́ *pf* уда́р (ножо́м *etc.*) (*person* +*dat*).

stability /stə'bɪlɪtɪ/ *n* усто́йчивость, стаби́льность. **stabilize** /'steɪbɪˌlaɪz/ *vt* стабилизи́ровать *impf & pf.*

stable /'steɪb(ə)l/ *adj* усто́йчивый, стаби́льный; (*psych*) уравнове́шенный; *n* коню́шня.

staccato /stə'kɑːtəʊ/ *n* стакка́то *neut indecl*; *adv* стакка́то; *adj* отры́вистый.

stack /stæk/ *n* ку́ча; *vt* скла́дывать *impf*, сложи́ть *pf* в ку́чу.

stadium /'steɪdɪəm/ *n* стадио́н.

staff /stɑːf/ *n* (*personnel*) штат, сотру́дники *m pl*; (*stick*) по́сох, жезл; *adj* шта́тный; (*mil*) штабно́й.

stag /stæg/ *n* саме́ц-оле́нь *m.*

stage /steɪdʒ/ *n* (*theat*) сце́на; (*period*) ста́дия; *vt* (*theat*) ста́вить *impf*, по~ *pf*; (*organize*) организо́вать *impf & pf*; ~**-manager** *n* режиссёр.

stagger /'stægə(r)/ *vi* шата́ться *impf*, шатну́ться *pf*; *vt* (*hours of*

work etc.) распределя́ть *impf*, распредели́ть *pf*. **be staggered** /-gəd/ *vi* поража́ться *impf*, порази́ться *pf*. **staggering** /-gərɪŋ/ *adj* потряса́ющий.

stagnant /'stægnənt/ *adj* (water) стоя́чий; (fig) засто́йный.

stagnate /stæg'neɪt/ *vi* застаива́ться *impf*, застоя́ться *pf*; (fig) косне́ть *impf*, за~ *pf*.

staid /steɪd/ *adj* степе́нный.

stain /steɪn/ *n* пятно́; (dye) кра́ска; *vt* па́чкать *impf*, за~, ис~ *pf*; (dye) окра́шивать *impf*, окра́сить *pf*. **~ed glass** цветно́е стекло́. **stainless** /-lɪs/ *adj*: **~ steel** нержаве́ющая сталь.

stair /steə(r)/ *n* ступе́нька. **staircase**, **stairs** /'steəkeɪs, steəz/ *n pl* ле́стница.

stake /steɪk/ *n* (stick) кол; (comm) до́ля; **be at ~** быть поста́вленным на ка́рту; *vt* (mark out) огора́живать *impf*, огороди́ть *pf* ко́льями; (support) укрепля́ть *impf*, укрепи́ть *pf* колом; (risk) ста́вить *impf*, по~ *pf* на ка́рту.

stale /steɪl/ *adj* несве́жий; (musty, damp) за́тхлый; (hackneyed) изби́тый.

stalemate /'steɪlmeɪt/ *n* пат; (fig) тупи́к.

stalk /stɔːk/ *n* сте́бель *m*; *vt* высле́живать *impf*; *vi* (& *t*) (stride) ше́ствовать *impf* (по+*dat*).

stall /stɔːl/ *n* сто́йло; ларёк; *pl* (theat) партёр; *vi* (of engine) гло́хнуть *impf*, за~ *pf*; (play for time) отти́гивать *impf*, оттяну́ть *pf* вре́мя; *vt* (engine) неча́янно заглуша́ть *impf*, заглуши́ть *pf*.

stallion /'stæljən/ *n* жеребе́ц.

stalwart /'stɔːlwət/ *adj* сто́йкий; *n* сто́йкий приве́рженец.

stamina /'stæmɪnə/ *n* выносли-

вость.

stammer /'stæmə(r)/ *vi* заика́ться *impf*; *n* заика́ние.

stamp /stæmp/ *n* печа́ть; (postage) (почто́вая) ма́рка; (печа́ть) штампова́ть *impf*; *vi* то́пать *impf*, то́пнуть *pf* (нога́ми); **~ out** побороть *pf*.

stampede /stæm'piːd/ *n* пани́ческое бе́гство; *vi* обраща́ться *impf* в пани́ческое бе́гство.

stance /stɑːns/ *n* пози́ция.

stand /stænd/ *n* (hat, coat) ве́шалка; (music) пюпи́тр; (umbrella, support) подста́вка; (booth) ларёк; (taxi) стоя́нка; (at stadium) трибу́на; (position) пози́ция; (resistance) сопротивле́ние; *vi* стоя́ть *impf*; *vt*, *vi* встава́ть *impf*, встать *pf*; (remain in force) остава́ться *impf* оста́ться в си́ле; *vt* (put) ста́вить *impf*, по~ *pf*; (endure) терпе́ть *impf*, по~ *pf*; **~ back** отходи́ть *impf*, отойти́ *pf* (from от+gen); (not go forward) стоя́ть *impf* позади́; **~ by** (*vi*) (not interfere) не вме́шиваться *impf*, вмеша́ться *pf*; (be ready) быть *impf* на гото́ве; (*vt*) (support) подде́рживать *impf*, поддержа́ть *pf*; (stick to) приде́рживаться *impf* +gen; **~ down** (resign) уходи́ть *impf*, уйти́ *pf* с поста́ (as +gen); **~ for** (signify) означа́ть *impf* (tolerate): **I shall not ~ for it** я не потерплю́; **~ in** замести́тель *m*; **~ in** (for) замеща́ть *impf*, замести́ть *pf*; **~ out** выделя́ться *impf*, вы́делиться *pf*; **~ up** встава́ть *impf*, встать *pf*; **~ up for** (defend) отста́ивать *impf*, отстоя́ть *pf*; **~ up to** (endure) выде́рживать *impf*, вы́держать *pf*; (not give in to) противостоя́ть *impf* +dat.

standard /'stændəd/ n (norm) станда́рт, норм; (flag) зна́мя neut; ~ **of living** жи́зненный у́ровень m; adj норма́льный, станда́ртный. **standardization** /ˌstændədaɪ'zeɪʃ(ə)n/ n нормализа́ция, стандартиза́ция. **standardize** /'stændədaɪz/ vt стандартизи́ровать impf & pf; нормализова́ть impf & pf.

standing /'stændɪŋ/ n положе́ние; adj (upright) стоя́чий; (permanent) постоя́нный.

standpoint /'stændpɔɪnt/ n то́чка зре́ния.

standstill /'stændstɪl/ n остано́вка, засто́й, па́уза; **be at a ~** стоя́ть impf на мёртвой то́чке; **bring (come) to a ~** остана́вливать(ся) impf, останови́ть(ся) pf.

stanza /'stænzə/ n строфа́.

staple¹ /'steɪp(ə)l/ n (metal bar) скоба́; (for paper) скре́пка; vt скрепля́ть impf, скрепи́ть pf.

staple² /'steɪp(ə)l/ n (product) гла́вный проду́кт; adj осно́вной.

star /stɑː(r)/ n звезда́; (asterisk) звёздочка; vi игра́ть impf, сыгра́ть pf гла́вную роль. **starfish** n морска́я звезда́.

starboard /'stɑːbəd/ n пра́вый борт.

starch /stɑːtʃ/ n крахма́л; vt крахма́лить impf, на~ pf. **starchy** /-tʃɪ/ adj крахма́листый; (prim) чо́порный.

stare /steə(r)/ n при́стальный взгляд; vi при́стально смотре́ть impf (at на+acc).

stark /stɑːk/ adj (bare) го́лый; (desolate) пусты́нный; (sharp) ре́зкий; adv соверше́нно.

starling /'stɑːlɪŋ/ n скворе́ц.

starry /'stɑːrɪ/ adj звёздный.

start /stɑːt/ n нача́ло; (sport)

старт; vi начина́ться impf, нача́ться pf; (engine) заводи́ться impf, завести́сь pf; (set out) отправля́ться impf, отпра́виться pf; (shudder) вздра́гивать impf, вздро́гнуть pf; (sport) старто́ва́ть impf & pf; vt начина́ть impf, нача́ть pf (gerund, inf, +inf; by, +gerund с того́, что…; **with** +instr, c+gen); (car, engine) заводи́ть impf, завести́ pf; (fire, rumour) пуска́ть impf, пусти́ть pf; (found) осно́вывать impf, основа́ть pf. **starter** /-tə(r)/ n (tech) ста́ртер; (cul) заку́ска. **starting-point** /-tɪŋ pɔɪnt/ n отправно́й пункт.

startle /'stɑːt(ə)l/ vt испуга́ть pf.

starvation /stɑː'veɪʃ(ə)n/ n го́лод. **starve** /stɑːv/ vi голода́ть impf; (to death) умира́ть impf, умере́ть pf с го́лоду; vt мори́ть impf, по~, у~ pf го́лодом. **starving** /stɑːvɪŋ/ adj голода́ющий; (hungry) о́чень голо́дный.

state /steɪt/ n (condition) состоя́ние; (polit) госуда́рство, штат; adj (ceremonial) торже́ственный, пара́дный; (polit) госуда́рственный; vt (announce) заявля́ть impf, заяви́ть pf; (expound) излага́ть impf, изложи́ть pf. **stateless** /-lɪs/ adj не име́ющий гражда́нства. **stately** /-lɪ/ adj вели́чественный. **statement** /-mənt/ n заявле́ние; (comm) отчёт. **statesman** n госуда́рственный де́ятель m.

static /'stætɪk/ adj неподви́жный.

station /'steɪʃ(ə)n/ n (rly) вокза́л, ста́нция; (social) обще́ственное положе́ние; (meteorological, hydro-electric power, radio etc.) ста́нция; (post) пост,

vt размеща́ть *impf*, размести́ть *pf*.

stationary /'steɪʃənərɪ/ *adj* неподви́жный.

stationery /'steɪʃənərɪ/ *n* канцеля́рские принадле́жности *f pl*; (*writing-paper*) почто́вая бума́га; ~ **shop** канцеля́рский магази́н.

statistic /stə'tɪstɪk/ *n* статисти́ческое да́нное. **statistical** /-'tɪstɪk(ə)l/ *adj* статисти́ческий. **statistician** /ˌstætɪ'stɪʃ(ə)n/ *n* стати́стик. **statistics** /stə'tɪstɪks/ *n* стати́стика.

statue /'stætjuː/ *n* ста́туя. **statuette** /ˌstætjʊ'et/ *n* статуэ́тка.

stature /'stætʃə(r)/ *n* рост; (*merit*) кали́бр.

status /'steɪtəs/ *n* ста́тус. **status quo** /ˌsteɪtəs 'kwəʊ/ *n* ста́тус-кво́ *neut indecl*.

statute /'stætjuːt/ *n* стату́т. **statutory** /-tərɪ/ *adj* устано́вленный зако́ном.

staunch /stɔːntʃ/ *adj* ве́рный.

stave /steɪv/ *vt*: ~ **off** предотвраща́ть *impf*, предотврати́ть *pf*.

stay /steɪ/ *n* (*time spent*) пребыва́ние; *vi* (*remain*) остава́ться *impf*, оста́ться *pf* (**to dinner** обе́дать); (*put up*) остана́вливаться *impf*, останови́ться *pf* (**at** (*place*) в+*prep*; **at** (*friends* *etc*) у+*gen*); (*live*) жить; ~ **behind** остава́ться *impf*, оста́ться *pf*; ~ **in** остава́ться *impf*, оста́ться *pf* до́ма; ~ **up** не ложи́ться *impf* спать; (*trousers*) держа́ться *impf*. **staying-power** /'steɪŋ ˌpaʊə/ *n* выно́сливость.

stead /sted/ *n*: **stand s.o. in good** ~ оказа́ться *impf*, оказа́ться *pf* поле́зным кому́-л.

steadfast /'stedfɑːst/ *adj* сто́йкий, непоколеби́мый.

steady /'stedɪ/ *adj* (*firm*) усто́йчивый; (*continuous*) непреры́вный; (*wind, temperature*) ро́вный; (*speed*) постоя́нный; (*unshakeable*) непоколеби́мый *vt* (*boat etc.*) приводи́ть *impf*, привести́ *pf* в равнове́сие.

steak /steɪk/ *n* бифште́кс.

steal /stiːl/ *vt & abs* ворова́ть *impf*, с~ *pf*; красть *impf*, у~ *pf* *vi* (*creep*) кра́сться *impf*; подкра́дываться *impf*, подкра́сться *pf*. **stealth** /stelθ/ *n*: **by** ~ укра́дкой. **stealthy** /-θɪ/ *adj* ворова́тый, та́йный, скры́тый.

steam /stiːm/ *n* пар; **at full** ~ на всех пара́х; **let off** ~ (*fig*) дава́ть *impf*, дать *pf* вы́ход свои́м чу́вствам; *vt* па́рить *impf*; *vi* па́риться *impf*, по~ *pf*; (*vessel*) ходи́ть *indet*, идти́ *det* на пара́х; ~ **up** (*mist over*) запотева́ть *impf*, запоте́ть *pf*; поте́ть *impf*, за~, от~ *pf*; ~ **engine** парова́я маши́на. **steamer, steamship** /-mə(r), -ʃɪp/ *n* парохо́д. **steamy** /-mɪ/ *adj* напо́лненный па́ром; (*passionate*) горя́чий.

steed /stiːd/ *n* конь *m*.

steel /stiːl/ *n* сталь; *adj* стально́й; *vt*: ~ **o.s.** ожесточа́ть *impf*, ожесточи́ть *pf*; ~ **works** сталелите́йный заво́д. **steely** /-lɪ/ *adj* стально́й.

steep¹ /stiːp/ *adj* круто́й; (*excessive*) чрезме́рный.

steep² /stiːp/ *vt* (*immerse*) погружа́ть *impf*, погрузи́ть *pf* (**in** в+*acc*); (*saturate*) пропи́тывать *impf*, пропита́ть *pf* (**in** +*instr*).

steeple /'stiːp(ə)l/ *n* шпиль *m*. **steeplechase** *n* ска́чки *f pl* с препя́тствиями.

steer /stɪə(r)/ vt управля́ть impf, пра́вить impf +instr; vi abs рули́ть impf; ~ clear of избега́ть impf, избежа́ть pf +gen. **steering-wheel** /'stɪərɪŋ,wiːl/ n руль m.

stem[1] /stem/ n сте́бель m; (of wine-glass) но́жка; (ling) осно́ва; vi: ~ from происходи́ть impf, произойти́ pf от+gen.

stem[2] /stem/ vt (stop) остана́вливать impf, останови́ть pf.

stench /stentʃ/ n злово́ние.

stencil /'stensɪl/ n трафаре́т; (tech) шабло́н; vt наноси́ть impf, нанести́ pf по трафаре́ту. **stencilled** /-sɪld/ adj трафаре́тный.

step /step/ n (pace, action) шаг; (dance) па neut indecl; (of stairs, ladder) ступе́нь; ~ **by** ~ шаг за ша́гом; **in** ~ в но́гу; **out of** ~ не в но́гу; **take** ~**s** принима́ть impf, приня́ть pf ме́ры vi шага́ть impf, шагну́ть pf; ступа́ть impf, ступи́ть pf; ~ **aside** сторони́ться impf, по~ pf; ~ **back** отступа́ть impf, отступи́ть pf; ~ **down** (resign) уходи́ть impf, уйти́ pf в отста́вку; ~ **forward** выступа́ть impf, вы́ступить pf; ~ **in** (intervene) вме́шиваться impf, вмеша́ться pf; ~ **on** наступа́ть impf, наступи́ть pf (**s.o.'s foot** кому́-л. на но́гу); ~ **over** переша́гивать impf, перешагну́ть pf +acc, че́рез+acc; ~ **up** (increase) повыша́ть impf, повы́сить pf. **step-ladder** n стремя́нка. **stepping-stone** /'stepɪŋ,stəʊn/ n ка́мень m для перехо́да; (fig) сре́дство. **steps** /steps/ n pl ле́стница.

stepbrother /'step,brʌðə(r)/ n сво́дный брат. **stepdaughter** /'step,dɔːtə(r)/ n па́дчерица.

stepfather /'step,fɑːðə(r)/ n о́тчим. **stepmother** /'step,mʌðə(r)/ n ма́чеха. **stepsister** /'step,sɪstə(r)/ n сво́дная сестра́. **stepson** /'stepsʌn/ n па́сынок.

steppe /step/ n степь.

stereo /'sterɪəʊ/ n (system) стереофони́ческая систе́ма; (stereophony) стереофо́ния; adj (recorded in ~) сте́рео indecl.

stereophonic /-'fɒnɪk/ adj стереофони́ческий. **stereotype** /-,taɪp/ n стереоти́п. **stereotyped** /-,taɪpt/ adj стереоти́пный.

sterile /'steraɪl/ adj стери́льный. **sterility** /stə'rɪlɪtɪ/ n стери́льность. **sterilization** /,sterɪlaɪ'zeɪʃ(ə)n/ n стерилиза́ция. **sterilize** /'sterɪ,laɪz/ vt стерилизова́ть impf & pf.

sterling /'stɜːlɪŋ/ n сте́рлинг; **pound** ~ фунт сте́рлингов; adj сте́рлинговый.

stern[1] /stɜːn/ n корма́.

stern[2] /stɜːn/ adj суро́вый, стро́гий.

stethoscope /'steθə,skəʊp/ n стетоско́п.

stew /stjuː/ n (cul) мя́со тушёное вме́сте с овоща́ми; vt & i (cul) туши́ть(ся) impf, с~ pf; (fig) томи́ть(ся) impf.

steward /'stjuːəd/ n бортпроводни́к **stewardess** /-dɪs/ n стюарде́сса.

stick[1] /stɪk/ n па́лка; (of chalk etc.) па́лочка; (hockey) клю́шка.

stick[2] /stɪk/ vt (spear) зака́лывать impf, заколо́ть pf; (make adhere) прикле́ивать impf, прикле́ить pf (**to** к+dat); (coll) (put) ста́вить impf, по~ pf; (lay) класть impf, положи́ть pf; (endure) терпе́ть impf, вы́~ pf; vi (adhere) ли́пнуть impf (**to**

k+dat); прилипа́ть impf, прили́пнуть pf (**to** к+dat); ~ **in** (thrust in) втыка́ть impf, воткну́ть pf; (into opening) всо́вывать impf, всу́нуть pf; ~ **on** (glue on) накле́ивать impf, накле́ить pf; ~ **out** (thrust out) высо́вывать impf, вы́сунуть pf; (from из+gen); (project) торча́ть impf; ~ **to** (keep to) приде́рживаться impf, придержа́ться pf +gen; (remain at) не отвлека́ться impf от+gen; ~ **together** держа́ться impf вме́сте; ~ **up for** заступа́ться impf, заступи́ться pf; **be, get, stuck** застрева́ть impf, застря́ть pf. **sticker** /-kǝ(r)/ n накле́йка.

sticky /'stɪkɪ/ adj ли́пкий.

stiff /stɪf/ adj жёсткий, неги́бкий; (prim) чо́порный; (difficult) тру́дный; (penalty) суро́вый; **be** ~ (ache) боле́ть impf. **stiffen** /-f(ǝ)n/ vt де́лать impf, c~ pf жёстким; vi станови́ться impf, стать pf жёстким. **stiffness** /-nɪs/ n жёсткость; (primness) чо́порность.

stifle /'staɪf(ǝ)l/ vt души́ть impf, за~ pf; (suppress) подавля́ть impf, подави́ть pf; (sound) заглуша́ть impf, заглуши́ть pf; vi задыха́ться impf, задохну́ться pf. **stifling** /-lɪŋ/ adj удуша́ющий.

stigma /'stɪgmǝ/ n клеймо́.

stile /staɪl/ n перела́з (coll).

stilettos /strɪˈletǝʊz/ n pl ту́фли f pl на шпи́льках.

still /stɪl/ adv (всё) ещё; (nevertheless) тем не ме́нее; (motionless) неподви́жно; **stand** ~ не дви́гаться impf, дви́нуться pf; n (quiet) тишина́; adj ти́хий; (immobile) неподви́жный. **stillborn** adj мертворождённый.

still life n натюрмо́рт. **stillness** /-nɪs/ n тишина́.

stilted /'stɪltɪd/ adj ходу́льный.

stimulant /'stɪmjʊlǝnt/ n возбужда́ющее сре́дство. **stimulate** /-,leɪt/ vt возбужда́ть impf, воз-буди́ть pf. **stimulating** /-,leɪtɪŋ/ adj возбуди́тельный. **stimulation** /-'leɪʃ(ǝ)n/ n возбужде́ние. **stimulus** /'stɪmjʊlǝs/ n сти́мул.

sting /stɪŋ/ n (wound) уку́с; (stinger, fig) жа́ло; vt жа́лить impf, у~ pf; vi (burn) жечь impf. **stinging** /'stɪŋɪŋ/ adj (caustic) язви́тельный.

stingy /'stɪndʒɪ/ adj скупо́й.

stink /stɪŋk/ n вонь; vi воня́ть impf (**of** +instr). **stinking** /-kɪŋ/ adj воню́чий.

stint /stɪnt/ n срок; vi: ~**on** скупи́ться impf, по~ pf на+acc.

stipend /'staɪpend/ n (salary) жа́лование; (grant) стипе́ндия.

stipulate /'stɪpjʊ,leɪt/ vt обусло́вливать impf, обусло́вить pf. **stipulation** /-'leɪʃ(ǝ)n/ n усло́вие.

stir /stɜː(r)/ n (commotion) шум; vt (mix) меша́ть impf, по~ pf; (excite) волнова́ть impf, вз~ pf; vi (move) шевели́ться impf, шевельну́ться pf; ~ **up** возбужда́ть impf, возбуди́ть pf. **stirring** /-rɪŋ/ adj волну́ющий.

stirrup /'stɪrǝp/ n стре́мя neut.

stitch /stɪtʃ/ n стежо́к; (knitting) пе́тля; (med) шов; (pain) ко́лики f pl; vt (embroider, make line of ~es) строчи́ть impf, про~ pf; (join by sewing, make, suture) сшива́ть impf, сшить pf; ~ **up** зашива́ть impf, заши́ть pf. **stitching** /-tʃɪŋ/ n (stitches) стро́чка.

stoat /stǝʊt/ n горноста́й.

stock /stɒk/ n (store) запа́с; (of shop) ассортиме́нт; (live-

скот; (cul) бульо́н; (lineage) семья́; (fin) а́кции f pl; in ~ в нали́чии; out of ~ распро́дан; take ~ of крити́чески оце́нивать impf, оцени́ть pf; adj станда́ртный; vt име́ть в нали́чии; ~ up запаса́ться impf, запасти́сь pf (with +instr).

stockbroker n биржево́й ма́клер. **stock-exchange** n би́ржа. **stockpile** n запа́с; vt нака́пливать impf, накопи́ть pf. **stock-taking** n переучёт.

stocking /'stɒkɪŋ/ n чуло́к.

stocky /'stɒkɪ/ adj призе́мистый.

stodgy /'stɒdʒɪ/ adj тяжёлый.

stoic(al) /'stəʊɪk((ə)l)/ adj сто́йческий. **stoicism** /'stəʊɪsɪz(ə)m/ n стоици́зм.

stoke /stəʊk/ vt топи́ть impf.

stolid /'stɒlɪd/ adj флегмати́чный.

stomach /'stʌmək/ n желу́док, (also surface of body) живо́т; vt терпе́ть impf, по~ pf. **stomach ache** /'stʌmək eɪk/ n боль в животе́.

stone /stəʊn/ n ка́мень m; (of fruit) ко́сточка; adj ка́менный; vt побива́ть impf, поби́ть pf камня́ми; (fruit) вынима́ть impf, вы́нуть pf ко́сточки из+gen. **Stone Age** n ка́менный век **stone-deaf** adj соверше́нно глухо́й. **stone-mason** n ка́менщик. **stonily** /-nɪlɪ/ adv с ка́менным выраже́нием, хо́лодно. **stony** /-nɪ/ adj ка́менистый; (fig) ка́менный.

stool /stuːl/ n табуре́т, табуре́тка.

stoop /stuːp/ n суту́лость; vt & i сутулить(ся) impf, с~ pf; (bend down) наклоня́ть(ся) impf, наклони́ть(ся) pf; ~ to (abase o.s.) унижа́ться impf, уни-

зи́ться pf до+gen; (condescend) снисходи́ть impf, снизойти́ pf до+gen. **stooped, stooping** /stuːpt, 'stuːpɪŋ/ adj суту́лый.

stop /stɒp/ n остано́вка; put a ~ to положи́ть pf коне́ц +dat; vt остана́вливать impf, останови́ть pf; (discontinue) прекраща́ть impf, прекрати́ть pf; (restrain) уде́рживать impf, удержа́ть pf (from от+gen); vi остана́вливаться impf, останови́ться pf; (discontinue) прекраща́ться impf, прекрати́ться pf; (cease) перестава́ть impf, переста́ть pf (+inf); ~ up vt затыка́ть impf, заткну́ть pf. **stop-page** /-pɪdʒ/ n остано́вка; (strike) забасто́вка. **stopper** /-pə(r)/ n про́бка. **stop-press** n экстренное сообще́ние в газе́те. **stop-watch** n секундоме́р.

storage /'stɔːrɪdʒ/ n хране́ние.

store /stɔː(r)/ n запа́с; (storehouse) склад; (shop) магази́н; set ~ by цени́ть impf; what is in ~ for me? что ждёт меня́ впереди́?; vt запаса́ть impf, запасти́ pf; (put into storage) сдава́ть impf, сдать pf на хране́ние. **storehouse** n склад. **store-room** кладова́я sb.

storey /'stɔːrɪ/ n эта́ж.

stork /stɔːk/ n а́ист.

storm /stɔːm/ n бу́ря, (thunder ~) гроза́; vt (mil) штурмова́ть impf; vi бушева́ть impf. **stormy** /-mɪ/ adj бу́рный.

story /'stɔːrɪ/ n расска́з, по́весть; (anecdote) анекдо́т; (plot) фа́була; ~-teller расска́зчик.

stout /staʊt/ adj (strong) кре́пкий; (staunch) сто́йкий; (portly) доро́дный.

stove /stəʊv/ n (with fire inside)

печь; (*cooker*) плита́.

stow /stəʊ/ *vt* укла́дывать *impf*, уложи́ть *pf*. **stowaway** /'stəʊ‚weɪ/ *n* безбиле́тный пассажи́р.

straddle /'stræd(ə)l/ *vt* (*sit astride*) сиде́ть *impf* верхо́м на+*prep*; (*stand astride*) стоя́ть *impf*, расста́вив но́ги над +*instr*.

straggle /'stræg(ə)l/ *vi* отстава́ть *impf*, отста́ть *pf*. **straggler** /-glə(r)/ *n* отста́вший *sb*. **straggling** /-glɪŋ/ *adj* разбро́санный. **straggly** /-glɪ/ *adj* растрёпанный.

straight /streɪt/ *adj* прямо́й; (*undiluted*) неразба́вленный; *predic* (*in order*) в поря́дке; *adv* пря́мо; ~ **away** сра́зу. **straighten** /'streɪt(ə)n/ *vt* & *i* выпрямля́ть(ся) *impf*, вы́прямить(ся) *pf*; *vt* (*put in order*) поправля́ть *impf*, попра́вить *pf*. **straightforward** *adj* прямо́й; (*simple*) просто́й.

strain¹ /streɪn/ *n* (*tension*) натяже́ние; (*sprain*) растяже́ние; (*effort, exertion*) напряже́ние; (*tendency*) скло́нность; (*sound*) звук; *vt* (*stretch*) натя́гивать *impf*, натяну́ть *pf*; (*sprain*) растя́гивать *impf*, растяну́ть *pf*; (*exert*) напряга́ть *impf*, напря́чь *pf*; (*filter*) проце́живать *impf*, процеди́ть *pf*; *vi* (*also exert o.s.*) напряга́ться *impf*, напря́чься *pf*. **strained** *adj* натя́нутый. **strainer** /streɪnd/ *n* (*tea* ~) си́течко; (*sieve*) си́то.

strain² /streɪn/ *n* (*breed*) поро́да.

strait(s) /streɪt(s)/ *n* (*geog*) проли́в. **strait-jacket** *n* смири́тельная руба́шка. **straits** *n pl* (*difficulties*) затрудни́тельное положе́ние.

strand¹ /strænd/ *n* (*hair, rope*) прядь; (*thread, also fig*) нить.

strand² /strænd/ *vt* сажа́ть *impf*, посади́ть *pf* на мель. **stranded** /-dɪd/ *adj* на мели́.

strange /streɪndʒ/ *adj* стра́нный; (*unfamiliar*) незнако́мый; (*alien*) чужо́й. **strangely** /-lɪ/ *adv* стра́нно. **strangeness** /-nɪs/ *n* стра́нность. **stranger** /'streɪndʒə(r)/ *n* незнако́мец.

strangle /'stræŋg(ə)l/ *vt* души́ть *impf*, за~ *pf*. **stranglehold** *n* мёртвая хва́тка. **strangulation** /‚stræŋgjʊ'leɪʃ(ə)n/ *n* удуше́ние.

strap /stræp/ *n* реме́нь *m*; *vt* (*tie up*) стя́гивать *impf*, стяну́ть *pf* ремнём. **strapping** /-pɪŋ/ *adj* ро́слый.

stratagem /'strætədʒəm/ *n* хи́трость. **strategic** /strə'tiːdʒɪk/ *adj* стратеги́ческий. **strategist** /'strætɪdʒɪst/ *n* страте́г. **strategy** /'strætɪdʒɪ/ *n* страте́гия.

stratum /'strɑːtəm/ *n* слой.

straw /strɔː/ *n* соло́ма; (*drinking* ~) соло́минка; **the last** ~ после́дняя ка́пля; *adj* соло́менный.

strawberry /'strɔːbərɪ/ *n* клубни́ка (*no pl*; *usu collect*); (*wild* ~) земляни́ка (*no pl*; *usu collect*).

stray /streɪ/ *vi* сбива́ться *impf*, сби́ться *pf*; (*digress*) отклоня́ться *impf*, отклони́ться *pf*; *adj* (*lost*) заблуди́вшийся; (*homeless*) бездо́мный; *n* (*from flock*) отби́вшееся от ста́да живо́тное *sb*; ~ **bullet** шальна́я пу́ля.

streak /striːk/ *n* полоса́ (*of luck* везе́ния); (*tendency*) жи́лка; *vi* (*rush*) проноси́ться *impf*, пронести́сь *pf*. **streaked** /-kt/ *adj* с полоса́ми (**with** +*gen*). **streaky** /-kɪ/ *adj* полоса́тый; (*meat*) с просло́йками жи́ра.

stream /stri:m/ n (*brook, tears*) ручёй; (*brook, flood, tears, people etc.*) поток; (*current*) течёние; up/down ~ вверх/вниз по течёнию; vi течь impf; (*rush*) проноситься impf, пронестись pf; (*blow*) развеваться impf **streamer** /-mə(r)/ n вымпел. **stream-lined** adj обтекáемый; (*fig*) хорошо налáженный.

street /stri:t/ n ýлица; adj ýличный; ~ lamp ýличный фонáрь m.

strength /streŋθ/ n сила; (*numbers*) чи́сленность; on the ~ of в си́лу+gen. **strengthen** /-θ(ə)n/ vt уси́ливать impf, уси́лить pf.

strenuous /'strenjʊəs/ adj (*work*) трýдный; (*effort*) напряжённый.

stress /stres/ n напряжéние; (*mental*) стресс; (*emphasis*) ударéние; vt (*accent*) стáвить impf, по~ pf ударéние на+acc; (*emphasize*) подчёркивать impf, подчеркнýть pf. **stressful** /-fʊl/ adj стрéссовый.

stretch /stretʃ/ n (*expanse*) отрéзок; at a ~ (*in succession*) подрáд; vt & i (*widen, spread out*) растя́гивать impf, растянýть(ся) pf; (*in length*, ~ *limbs*) вытя́гивать impf, вытянуть(ся) pf; (*tauten*) натя́гивать impf, натянýть(ся) pf; (*extend, e.g. rope*), ~ forth *limbs*) протя́гивать impf, протянýть pf; vi (*material, land*) тянýться impf; ~ one's legs (*coll*) размина́ть impf, размя́ть pf но́ги. **stretcher** /-tʃə(r)/ n носи́лки (-лок) pl. **strew** /stru:/ vt разбрáсывать impf, разбросáть pf; ~ with посыпáть impf, посы́пать pf +instr.

stricken /'strɪkən/ adj поражённый.

strict /strɪkt/ adj стрóгий. **stricture(s)** /'strɪktʃəz/ n (стрóгая) крити́ка.

stride /straɪd/ n (большóй) шаг; pl (*fig*) успéхи m pl; to take sth in one's ~ преодолевáть impf, преодолéть pf что-л. без уси́лий; vi шагáть impf.

strident /'straɪd(ə)nt/ adj рéзкий.

strife /straɪf/ n раздóр.

strike /straɪk/ n (*refusal to work*) забастóвка; (*mil*) удáр; vi (*be on* ~) бастовáть impf; (*go on* ~) забастовáть impf; (*attack*) ударя́ть impf, удáрить pf; (*the hour*) бить impf, про~ pf; vt (*hit*) ударя́ть impf, удáрить pf; (*impress*) поражáть impf, порази́ть pf; (*discover*) открывáть impf, откры́ть pf; (*match*) зажигáть impf, зажéчь pf; (*the hour*) бить impf, про~ pf; (*occur to*) приходи́ть impf, прийти́ pf в гóлову+dat; ~ off вычёркивать impf, вы́черкнуть pf; ~ up начинáть impf, начáть pf. **striker** /-kə(r)/ n забастóвщик. **striking** /-kɪŋ/ adj порази́тельный.

string /strɪŋ/ n бечёвка; (*mus*) струнá; (*series*) ряд; pl (*mus*) стрýнные инструмéнты m pl; ~ bag, ~ vest сéтка; vt (*thread*) низáть impf, на~ pf; ~ along (*coll*) води́ть impf за нос; ~ out (*prolong*) растя́гивать impf, растянýть pf; ~ strung up (*tense*) напряжённый. **stringed** /strɪŋd/ adj стрýнный. **stringy** /'strɪŋɪ/ adj (*fibrous*) волокни́стый; (*meat*) жи́листый.

stringent /'strɪndʒ(ə)nt/ adj стрóгий.

strip¹ /strɪp/ n полосá, полóска.

strip² /strɪp/ vt (undress) раздева́ть impf, разде́ть pf; (deprive) лиша́ть impf, лиши́ть pf (of +gen); ~ off (tear off) сдира́ть impf, содра́ть pf; (undress) раздева́ться impf, разде́ться pf. **strip-tease** n стрипти́з.

stripe /straɪp/ n полоса́к. **striped** /straɪpt/ adj полоса́тый.

strive /straɪv(ə)n/ vi (endeavour) стреми́ться impf (for к+dat); (struggle) боро́ться impf (for за+acc; against про́тив+gen).

stroke /strəʊk/ n (blow, med) уда́р; (of oar) взмах; (swimming) стиль m; (of pen etc.) штрих; (piston) ход; vt гла́дить impf, по~ pf.

stroll /strəʊl/ n прогу́лка; vi прогу́ливаться impf, прогуля́ться pf.

strong /strɒŋ/ adj си́льный; (stout; of drinks) кре́пкий; (healthy) здоро́вый; (opinion etc.) твёрдый. **stronghold** n кре́пость. **strong-minded, strong-willed** /-'maɪndɪd, -'wɪld/ adj реши́тельный.

structural /'strʌktʃər(ə)l/ adj структу́рный. **structure** /'strʌktʃə(r)/ n структу́ра; (building) сооруже́ние; vt организова́ть impf & pf.

struggle /'strʌg(ə)l/ n борьба́; vi боро́ться impf (for за+acc; against про́тив+gen); (writhe, with (fig)) би́ться (with над +instr).

strum /strʌm/ vi бренча́ть impf (on на+prep).

strut¹ /strʌt/ n (vertical) сто́йка; (horizontal) распо́рка.

strut² /strʌt/ vi ходи́ть indet, идти́ det го́голем.

stub /stʌb/ n огры́зок; (cigarette) оку́рок; (counterfoil) корешо́к; vt: ~ one's toe ударя́ться

impf, уда́риться pf ного́й (on на+acc); ~ out гаси́ть impf по~ pf.

stubble /'stʌb(ə)l/ n жнивьё; (hair) щети́на.

stubborn /'stʌbən/ adj упря́мый. **stubbornness** /-nɪs/ n упря́мство.

stucco /'stʌkəʊ/ n штукату́рка.

stud¹ /stʌd/ n (collar, cuff) за́понка; (nail) гвоздь m с большо́й шля́пкой; vt (bestrew) усе́ивать impf, усе́ять pf (with +instr).

stud² /stʌd/ n (horses) ко́нный заво́д.

student /'stjuːd(ə)nt/ n студе́нт, ~ка.

studied /'stʌdɪd/ adj напускно́й.

studio /'stjuːdɪəʊ/ n сту́дия.

studious /'stjuːdɪəs/ adj лю́бящий нау́ку; (diligent) стара́тельный.

study /'stʌdɪ/ n изуче́ние; pl заня́тия neut pl; (investigation) иссле́дование; (art, mus) этю́д; (room) кабине́т; vt изуча́ть impf, изучи́ть pf; учи́ться impf, об~ pf+dat; (scrutinize) рассма́тривать impf, рассмотре́ть pf; vi (take lessons) учи́ться impf, об~ pf; (do one's studies) занима́ться impf.

stuff /stʌf/ n (material) материа́л; (things) ве́щи f pl; vt наби́вать impf, наби́ть pf; (cul) начиня́ть impf, начини́ть pf; (cram into) запи́хивать impf, запиха́ть pf (into в+acc); (shove into) сова́ть impf, су́нуть pf (into в+acc); vi (overeat) объеда́ться impf, объе́сться pf. **stuffiness** /-fɪnɪs/ n духота́. **stuffing** /-fɪŋ/ n наби́вка; (cul) начи́нка. **stuffy** /-fɪ/ adj ду́шный.

stumble /'stʌmb(ə)l/ vi (also fig)

stump спотыкáться *impf*, споткнýться *pf* (over o+*acc*); ~ upon натыкáться *impf*, наткнýться *pf* на+*acc*. **stumbling-block** *n* кáмень *m* преткновéния.

stump /stʌmp/ *n* (tree) пень *m*; (pencil) огрызок; (limb) культя́; *vt* (perplex) стáвить *impf*, по~ *pf* в тупи́к.

stun /stʌn/ *vt* (also fig) оглушáть *impf*, оглуши́ть *pf*. **stunning** /-nɪŋ/ *adj* потрясáющий.

stunt[1] /stʌnt/ *n* трюк.

stunt[2] /stʌnt/ *vt* задéрживать *impf*, задержáть *pf* рост+*gen*. **stunted** /-tɪd/ *adj* низкорóслый.

stupefy /ˈstjuːpɪˌfaɪ/ *vt* оглушáть *impf*, оглуши́ть *pf*. **stupendous** /stjuːˈpendəs/ *adj* колоссáльный. **stupid** /ˈstjuːpɪd/ *adj* глýпый. **stupidity** /stjuːˈpɪdɪtɪ/ *n* глýпость *f*. **stupor** /ˈstjuːpə(r)/ *n* оцепенéние.

sturdy /ˈstɜːdɪ/ *adj* крéпкий.

stutter /ˈstʌtə(r)/ *n* заикáние; *vi* заикáться *impf*.

sty[1] /staɪ/ *n* (pig~) свинáрник.

sty[2] /staɪ/ *n* (on eye) ячмéнь *m*.

style /staɪl/ *n* стиль *m*; (taste) вкус; (fashion) мóда; (sort) род; (of hair) причёска. **stylish** /-lɪʃ/ *adj* мóдный. **stylist** /-lɪst/ *n* (of hair) парикмáхер. **stylistic** /-ˈlɪstɪk/ *adj* стилисти́ческий. **stylize** /-laɪz/ *vt* стилизовáть *impf* & *pf*. **stylus** /ˈstaɪləs/ *n* иглá звукоснимáтеля.

suave /swɑːv/ *adj* обходи́тельный.

subconscious /sʌbˈkɒnʃəs/ *adj* подсознáтельный; *n* подсознáние. **subcontract** *vt* давáть *impf*, дать *pf* подря́дчику. **subcontractor** *n* подря́дчик. **sub-**

divide *vt* подразделя́ть *impf*, подраздели́ть *pf*. **subdivision** *n* подразделéние. **subdue** /səbˈdjuː/ *vt* покоря́ть *impf*, покори́ть *pf*. **subdued** /səbˈdjuːd/ *adj* (suppressed, dispirited) подáвленный; (soft) мя́гкий; (indistinct) приглушённый.

sub-editor *n* помóщник редáктора.

subject *n* /ˈsʌbdʒɪkt/ (theme) тéма; (discipline, theme) предмéт; (question) вопрóс; (thing on to which action is directed) объéкт; (gram) подлежáщее *sb*; (national) пóдданный *sb*; *adj*: ~ to (susceptible to) подвéрженный+*dat*; (on condition that) при услóвии, что; éсли; be ~ to (change etc.) подлежáть *impf* +*dat*; *vt* /səbˈdʒekt/ ~ to подверга́ть *impf*, подвéргнуть *pf* +*dat*. **subjection** /səbˈdʒekʃ(ə)n/ *n* подчинéние. **subjective** /səbˈdʒektɪv/ *adj* субъекти́вный. **subjectivity** /ˌsʌbdʒekˈtɪvɪtɪ/ *n* субъекти́вность *f*. **subject-matter** *n* (of book, lecture) содержáние, тéма; (of discussion) предмéт.

subjugate /ˈsʌbdʒʊˌgeɪt/ *vt* покоря́ть *impf*, покори́ть *pf*. **subjugation** /ˌsʌbdʒʊˈgeɪʃ(ə)n/ *n* покорéние.

subjunctive (mood) /səbˈdʒʌŋktɪv (muːd)/ *n* сослагáтельное наклонéние.

sublet /sʌbˈlet/ *vt* передавáть *impf*, передáть *pf* в субарéнду.

sublimate /ˈsʌblɪˌmeɪt/ *vt* сублими́ровать *impf* & *pf*. **sublimation** /ˌsʌblɪˈmeɪʃ(ə)n/ *n* сублимáция. **sublime** /səˈblaɪm/ *adj* возвы́шенный.

subliminal /səbˈlɪmɪn(ə)l/ *adj* подсознáтельный. **sub-machine-gun** /ˌsʌbməˈʃiːnˌgʌn/ *n*

автома́т. **submarine** /ˌsʌbmə'riːn/ n подво́дная ло́дка. **submerge** /səb'mɜːdʒ/ vt погрузи́ть impf, погрузи́ть pf. **submission** /-'mɪʃ(ə)n/ n подчине́ние; (for inspection) представле́ние. **submissive** /-'mɪsɪv/ adj поко́рный. **submit** /-'mɪt/ vi подчиня́ться impf, подчини́ться pf (to +dat); vt представля́ть impf, предста́вить pf. **subordinate** /sə'bɔːdɪnət/ n подчинённый sb; adj подчинённый; (secondary) второстепе́нный; (gram) прида́точный; vt /sə'bɔːdɪˌneɪt/ подчиня́ть impf, подчини́ть pf. **subscribe** /səb'skraɪb/ vi подпи́сываться impf, подписа́ться pf (to на+acc); ~ to (opinion) присоединя́ться impf, присоедини́ться pf к+dat. **subscriber** /-'skraɪbə(r)/ n подпи́счик; абоне́нт. **subscription** /-'skrɪpʃ(ə)n/ n подпи́ска, абонеме́нт; (fee) взнос. **subsection** /ˈsʌbˌsekʃ(ə)n/ n подразде́л. **subsequent** /'sʌbsɪkwənt/ adj после́дующий. **subsequently** /'sʌbsɪkwəntlɪ/ adv впосле́дствии. **subservient** /səb'sɜːvɪənt/ adj раболе́пный. **subside** /səb'saɪd/ vi утиха́ть impf, уты́ть pf; (soil) оседа́ть impf, осе́сть pf. **subsidence** /səb'saɪd(ə)ns/ n (soil) оседа́ние. **subsidiary** /səb'sɪdɪərɪ/ adj вспомога́тельный; (secondary) второстепе́нный; n филиа́л. **subsidize** /'sʌbsɪˌdaɪz/ vt субсиди́ровать impf & pf. **subsidy** /'sʌbsɪdɪ/ n субси́дия. **subsist** /səb'sɪst/ vi (live) жить impf (on +instr). **substance** /'sʌbst(ə)ns/ n вещество́; (essence) су́щность, суть; (content) содержа́ние. **substantial** /səb'stænʃ(ə)l/

adj (durable) про́чный; (considerable) значи́тельный; (food) пло́тный. **substantially** /səb'stænʃəlɪ/ adv (basically) в основно́м; (considerably) значи́тельно. **substantiate** /səb'stænʃɪˌeɪt/ vt обосно́вывать impf, обоснова́ть pf. **substitute** /'sʌbstɪˌtjuːt/ n (person) замести́тель m; (thing) заме́на; vt заменя́ть impf, замени́ть pf +instr (for +acc); I ~ water for milk заменя́ю молоко́ во́дой. **substitution** /ˌsʌbstɪ'tjuːʃ(ə)n/ n заме́на. **subsume** /səb'sjuːm/ vt относи́ть impf, отнести́ pf к какой-л. катего́рии. **subterfuge** /'sʌbtəˌfjuːdʒ/ n уве́ртка. **subterranean** /ˌsʌbtə'reɪnɪən/ adj подзе́мный. **subtitle** /'sʌbˌtaɪt(ə)l/ n подзаголо́вок; (cin) субти́тр.

subtle /'sʌt(ə)l/ adj то́нкий. **subtlety** /'sʌtltɪ/ n то́нкость. **subtract** /səb'trækt/ vt вычита́ть impf, вы́честь pf. **subtraction** /-'trækʃ(ə)n/ n вычита́ние. **suburb** /'sʌbɜːb/ n при́город. **suburban** /sə'bɜːbən/ adj при́городный. **subversion** /səb'vɜːʃ(ə)n/ n подрывна́я де́ятельность. **subversive** /səb'vɜːsɪv/ adj подрывно́й. **subway** /'sʌbweɪ/ n подзе́мный перехо́д.

/sək'siːd/ vi удава́ться impf, уда́ться pf; the plan will ~ план уда́стся; he ~ed in buying the book ему́ удало́сь купи́ть кни́гу; (be successful) преуспева́ть impf, преуспе́ть pf (in в+prep); (follow) сменя́ть impf, смени́ть pf; (be heir) насле́довать impf & pf (to +dat). **succeeding** /-dɪŋ/ adj после́дующий. **success** /sək'ses/ n успе́х. **successful** /sək-

'sesful/ adj успéшный. **succession** /sək'seʃ(ə)n/ n (series) ряд;
(to throne) престолонаслéдие;
right of ~ пра́во наслéдования;
in ~ подря́д, оди́н за други́м.
successive /sək'sesɪv/ adj (consecutive) послéдовательный.
successor /sək'sesə(r)/ n преéмник.

succinct /sək'sɪŋkt/ adj сжáтый.
succulent /'sʌkjʊlənt/ adj сóч-
ный.
succumb /sə'kʌm/ vi (to pressure) уступáть impf, уступи́ть
pf (+dat); (to temptation)
поддавáться impf, поддáться
pf (to +dat).
such /sʌtʃ/ adj такóй; ~ **people**
такие лю́ди; ~ **as** (for example)
так например; (of a kind as)
такóй как; ~ **beauty as yours**
такáя красотá как вáша; (that
which) тот, котóрый; **I shall read**
~ **books as I like** я бу́ду читáть
те кни́ги, котóрые мне нрáв-
ятся; ~ **as** такóй, чтóбы; **his
illness was not** ~ **as to cause anxiety** его болéзнь былá не такáя
(серьёзная), чтóбы вы́звать
беспокóйство; ~ **and** ~ такóй-
то; pron такóв; ~ **was his character** такóв был егó харáктер;
as ~ сам по себé; ~ **is not the
case** это не так. **suchlike** pron
(inanimate) томý подóбное;
(people) такие лю́ди и д.

suck /sʌk/ vt сосáть impf; ~ **in**
всáсывать impf, всосáть pf;
(engulf) засáсывать impf, засо-
сáть pf; ~ **out** высáсывать
impf, высосать pf; ~ **up to** (coll)
подли́зываться impf, подли-
зáться pf +dat. **sucker** /-kə(r)/
n (biol, rubber device) присóска;
(bot) корневóй побéг. **suckle**
/'sʌk(ə)l/ vt корми́ть impf, на~ pf
грýдью. **suction** /'sʌkʃ(ə)n/ n

всáсывание.

sudden /'sʌd(ə)n/ adj внезáп-
ный. **suddenly** /-lɪ/ adv вдруг.
suddenness /-nɪs/ n внезáп-
ность.
sue /suː/ vt & i подавáть impf,
подáть pf в суд (на+acc); ~ **s.o.
for damages** предъявля́ть impf,
предъяви́ть pf (к) комý-л. иск
о возмещéнии ущéрба.
suede /sweɪd/ n зáмша; adj зá-
мшевый.
suet /'suːɪt/ n нýтряно́е сáло.
suffer /'sʌfə(r)/ vt страдáть impf,
по~ pf +instr, от+gen; (loss, defeat) терпéть impf, по~ pf; (tolerate) терпéть impf; vi
страдáть impf, по~ pf (from
+instr, от+gen). **sufferance**
/-rəns/ n: **he is here on** ~ егó
здесь тéрпят. **suffering** /-rɪŋ/ n
страдáние.
suffice /sə'faɪs/ vi & t быть до-
стáточным (для+gen); хватáть
impf, хвати́ть pf impers+gen
(+dat). **sufficient** /-fiʃ(ə)nt/ adj
достáточный.
suffix /'sʌfɪks/ n сýффикс.
suffocate /'sʌfəkeɪt/ vt удушáть
impf, удуши́ть pf; vi задыхáться impf, задохнýться pf.
suffocating /-tɪŋ/ adj удушли-
вый. **suffocation** /ˌsʌfə'keɪʃ(ə)n/
n удушéние.
suffrage /'sʌfrɪdʒ/ n избирá-
тельное пра́во.
suffuse /sə'fjuːz/ vt заливáть
impf, зали́ть pf (with +instr).
sugar /'ʃʊɡə(r)/ n сáхар; adj сáхарный; vt подслáщивать
impf, подсласти́ть pf; ~ **basin**
сáхарница; ~ **beet** сáхарная
свёкла; ~ **cane** сáхарный
тростни́к. **sugary** /-rɪ/ adj сáхарный; (fig) слащáвый.
suggest /sə'dʒest/ vt предлагáть
impf, предложи́ть pf; (evoke)

напоминáть *impf*, напóмнить *pf*; (*imply*) намекáть *impf*, намекнýть *pf* на+*acc*; (*indicate*) говорить *impf* o+*prep*. **suggestion** /-'dʒestʃ(ə)n/ *n* предложéние; (*psych*) внушéние.

suggestive /-'dʒestɪv/ *adj* вызывáющий мысли (*of* o+*prep*); (*indecent*) соблазнительный.

suicidal /ˌsuːɪ'saɪd(ə)l/ *adj* самоубийственный; (*fig*) губительный. **suicide** /'suːɪˌsaɪd/ *n* самоубийство; **commit** ~ совершить *impf*, совершить *pf* самоубийство.

suit /suːt/ *n* (*clothing*) костюм; (*law*) иск; (*cards*) масть; follow ~ (*fig*) следовать *impf*, по~ *pf* примéру; *vt* (*be convenient for*) устрáивать *impf*, устрóить *pf*; (*adapt*) приспосáбливать *impf*, приспособить *pf* (*be~able for*, *match*) подходить *impf*, подойти *pf* (+*dat*); (*look attractive on*) идти *impf* +*dat*. **suitability** /ˌsuːtə'bɪlɪtɪ/ *n* пригóдность. **suitable** /'suːtəb(ə)l/ *adj* (*fitting*) подходящий; (*convenient*) удóбный. **suitably** /'suːtəblɪ/ *adv* соотвéтственно. **suitcase** *n* чемодáн.

suite /swiːt/ *n* (*retinue*) свита; (*furniture*) гарнитýр; (*rooms*) апартáменты *m pl*; (*mus*) сюита.

suitor /'suːtə(r)/ *n* поклóнник.

sulk /sʌlk/ *vi* дýться *impf*. **sulky** /-kɪ/ *adj* надýтый.

sullen /'sʌlən/ *adj* угрюмый.

sully /'sʌlɪ/ *vt* пятнáть *impf*, за~ *pf*.

sulphur /'sʌlfə(r)/ *n* сéра. **sulphuric** /sʌl'fjʊərɪk/ *adj*: ~ **acid** сéрная кислотá.

sultana /sʌl'tɑːnə/ *n* (*raisin*) изюмина; *pl* кишмиш (*collect*).

sultry /'sʌltrɪ/ *adj* знóйный.

sum /sʌm/ *n* сýмма; (*arithmetical problem*) арифмéтическая задáча; *pl* арифмéтика; ~ **up** *vi* & *t* (*summarize*) подводить *impf*, подвести *pf* итóг (+*gen*); *vt* (*appraise*) оцéнивать *impf*, оценить *pf*.

summarize /'sʌməˌraɪz/ *vt* суммировать *impf* & *pf*. **summary** /'sʌmərɪ/ *n* резюмé *neut indecl*, свóдка; *adj* суммáрный; (*dismissal*) бесцеремóнный.

summer /'sʌmə(r)/ *n* лéто; *attrib* лéтний. **summer-house** *n* бесéдка.

summit /'sʌmɪt/ *n* вершина; ~ **meeting** встрéча на верхáх.

summon /'sʌmən/ *vt* вызывáть *impf*, вызвать *pf*; ~ **up** one's **courage** собирáться *impf*, собрáться *pf* с дýхом. **summons** /-mənz/ *n* вызов; (*law*) повéстка в суд; *vt* вызывáть *impf*, вызвать *pf* в суд.

sumptuous /'sʌmptjʊəs/ *adj* роскóшный.

sun /sʌn/ *n* сóлнце; **in the** ~ на сóлнце. **sunbathe** *vi* загорáть *impf*. **sunbeam** *n* сóлнечный луч. **sunburn** *n* загáр; (*inflammation*) сóлнечный ожóг. **sunburnt** /-bɜːnt/ *adj* загорéлый; **become** ~ загорáть *impf*, загорéть *pf*.

Sunday /'sʌndeɪ/ *n* воскресéнье.

sundry /'sʌndrɪ/ *adj* рáзный; **all and** ~ всé и вся.

sunflower /'sʌnflaʊə(r)/ *n* подсóлнечник. **sun-glasses** *n pl* очки (-кóв) *pl* от сóлнца.

sunken /'sʌŋkən/ *adj* (*cheeks, eyes*) впáлый; (*submerged*) погружённый; (*ship*) затóпленный; **below certain level**) ниже (какóго-л. ýровня).

sunlight /'sʌnlaɪt/ *n* сóлнечный

свет. **sunny** /'sʌnɪ/ *adj* со́лнеч-
ный. **sunrise** *n* восхо́д со́лнца.
sunset *n* зака́т. **sunshade** *n*
(*parasol*) зо́нтик; (*awning*)
наве́с. **sunshine** *n* со́лнечный
свет. **sunstroke** *n* со́лнечный
уда́р. **suntan** *n* зага́р. **sun-
tanned** /'sʌntænd/ *adj* заго-
ре́лый.

super /'su:pə(r)/ *adj* замеча́тель-
ный. **superb** /su:'pз:b/ *adj* пре-
восхо́дный. **supercilious**
/,su:pə'sɪlɪəs/ *adj* высокоме́р-
ный. **superficial** /-'fɪʃ(ə)l/ *adj*
пове́рхностный. **superficiality**
/-,fɪʃɪ'ælɪtɪ/ *n* пове́рхностность.
superfluous /su:'pз:flʊəs/ *adj*
ли́шний. **superhuman** /,su:pə-
'hju:mən/ *adj* сверхчелове́-
ский. **superintendent** /,su:pərɪn-
'tendənt/ *n* заве́дующий *sb* (*of*
+*instr*); (*police*) ста́рший поли-
це́йский офице́р. **superior** /su:-
'pɪərɪə(r)/ *n* ста́рший *sb*; *adj*
(*better*) превосхо́дный; (*in*
rank) ста́рший; (*haughty*) вы-
сокоме́рный. **superiority** /su:-
,pɪərɪ'ɒrɪtɪ/ *n* превосхо́дство.
superlative /su:'pз:lətɪv/ *adj*
превосхо́дный; *n* (*gram*) пре-
восхо́дная сте́пень. **superman** *n*
сверхчелове́к. **supermarket** *n*
универса́м. **supernatural** *adj*
сверхъесте́ственный. **super-
power** *n* сверхдержа́ва. **super-
sede** /,su:pə'si:d/ *vt* заменя́ть
impf, замени́ть *pf*. **supersonic**
/,su:pə'sɒnɪk/ *adj* сверхзвуково́й. **superstition** /,su:pə'stɪʃ(ə)n/ *n* суеве́рие.
superstitious /,su:pə'stɪʃ(ə)s/ *adj*
суеве́рный. **superstructure** *n*
надстро́йка. **supervise** /'su:pə-
,vaɪz/ *vt* наблюда́ть *impf* за
+*instr*. **supervision** /,su:pə-
'vɪʒ(ə)n/ *n* надзо́р. **supervisor**
/'su:pə,vaɪzə(r)/ *n* нача́льник; (*of*
studies) руководи́тель *m*.

supper /'sʌpə(r)/ *n* у́жин; **have ~**
у́жинать *impf*, по~ *pf*.

supple /'sʌp(ə)l/ *adj* ги́бкий.
suppleness /-nɪs/ *n* ги́бкость.

supplement /'sʌplɪmənt/ (*to*
book) дополне́ние; (*to periodical*) приложе́ние; *vt* /'sʌplɪ
,ment/ дополня́ть *impf*, допо́л-
нить *pf*. **supplementary** /,sʌplɪ
'mentərɪ/ *adj* дополни́тельный.

supplier /sə'plaɪə(r)/ *n* поста́в-
щи́к. **supply** /sə'plaɪ/ *n* (*stock*)
запа́с; (*econ*) предложе́ние; *pl*
(*mil*) припа́сы (-ов) *pl*, *vt* снаб-
жа́ть *impf*, снабди́ть *pf* (**with**
+*instr*).

support /sə'pɔ:t/ *n* подде́ржка;
vt подде́рживать *impf*, поддер-
жа́ть *pf*; (*family*) содержа́ть
impf. **supporter** /-tə(r)/ *n* сто-
ро́нник; (*sport*) боле́льщик.
supportive /-tɪv/ *adj* уча́ст-
ливый.

suppose /sə'pəʊz/ *vt* (*think*) по-
лага́ть *impf*; (*presuppose*) пред-
полага́ть *impf*, предположи́ть
pf; (*assume*) допуска́ть *impf*,
допусти́ть *pf*. **supposed**
/-'pəʊzd/ *adj* (*assumed*) предпо-
лага́емый. **supposition** /,sʌpə
'zɪʃ(ə)n/ *n* предположе́ние.

suppress /sə'pres/ *vt* подавля́ть
impf, подави́ть *pf*. **suppression**
/-'preʃ(ə)n/ *n* подавле́ние.

supremacy /su:'preməsɪ/ *n* гос-
по́дство. **supreme** /-'pri:m/ *adj*
верхо́вный.

surcharge /'sз:tʃɑːdʒ/ *n* на-
це́нка.

sure /ʃʊə(r)/ *adj* уве́ренный (**of**
в+*prep*; **that** что); (*reliable*) ве́р-
ный; **~ enough** действи́тельно;
he is ~ to come он обяза́тельно
придёт; **make ~ of** (*convince
o.s.*) убежда́ться *impf*, убе-
ди́ться *pf* в+*prep*; **make ~ that**
(*check up*) проверя́ть *impf*,

проверить *pf* что. **surely**
/'ʃʊəlɪ/ *adv* наверняка. **surety**
/'ʃʊərɪtɪ/ *n* порука; **stand ~ for**
ручаться *impf*, поручиться *pf*
за+*acc*.

surf /sɜːf/ *n* прибой; *vi* заниматься *impf*, заняться *pf* сёрфингом.

surface /'sɜːfɪs/ *n* поверхность; *(exterior)* внешность; **on the ~** *(fig)* внешне; **under the ~** *(fig)* по существу; *adj* поверхностный; *vi* всплывать *impf*, всплыть *pf*.

surfeit /'sɜːfɪt/ *n* *(surplus)* излишек

surge /sɜːdʒ/ *n* волна; *vi* *(rise, heave)* вздыматься *impf*; *(emotions)* нахлынуть *pf*; **~ forward** ринуться *pf* вперёд.

surgeon /'sɜːdʒ(ə)n/ *n* хирург.
surgery /'sɜːdʒərɪ/ *n* *(treatment)* хирургия; *(place)* кабинет; *(hours)* приёмные часы *m pl* (врача). **surgical** /'sɜːdʒɪk(ə)l/ *adj* хирургический.

surly /'sɜːlɪ/ *adj* *(morose)* угрюмый; *(rude)* грубый.

surmise /sə'maɪz/ *vt & i* предполагать *impf*, предположить *pf*.

surmount /sə'maʊnt/ *vt* преодолевать *impf*, преодолеть *pf*.

surname /'sɜːneɪm/ *n* фамилия.

surpass /sə'pɑːs/ *vt* превосходить *impf*, превзойти *pf*.

surplus /'sɜːpləs/ *n* излишек; *adj* излишний.

surprise /sə'praɪz/ *n* *(astonishment)* удивление; *(surprising thing)* сюрприз; *vt* удивлять *impf*, удивить *pf*; *(come upon suddenly)* заставать *impf*, застать *pf* врасплох; **be ~d** *(at)* удивляться *impf*, удивиться *pf* (+*dat*). **surprising** /-zɪŋ/ *adj* удивительный.

surreal /sə'rɪəl/ *adj* сюр-

реалистический. **surrealisn**
/-ɪz(ə)m/ *n* сюрреализм. **sur**
realist /-lɪst/ *n* сюрреалист; *ad*
сюрреалистический.

surrender /sə'rendə(r)/ *n* сдача
(renunciation) отказ; *vt* сдавать
impf, сдать *pf*; *(give up)* отказываться *impf*, отказаться *p*
от+*gen*; *vi* сдаваться *impf*
сдаться *pf*; **~ o.s. to** предаваться *impf*, предаться *pf*.
+*dat*.

surreptitious /ˌsʌrəp'tɪʃəs/ *adj*
тайный.

surrogate /'sʌrəgət/ *n* заменитель *m*.

surround /sə'raʊnd/ *vt* окружать *impf*, окружить *pf* (**with**
+*instr*). **surrounding** /-dɪŋ/ *adj*
окружающий. **surroundings**
/-dɪŋz/ *n* *(environs)* окрестности *f pl*; *(milieu)* среда.

surveillance /sɜː'veɪləns/ *n*
надзор.

survey /'sɜːveɪ/ *n* *(review)* обзор;
(inspection) инспекция; *(poll)*
опрос; *vt* /sə'veɪ/ *(review)* обозревать *impf*, обозреть *pf*; *(inspect)* инспектировать *impf*,
про~ *pf*; *(poll)* опрашивать
impf, опросить *pf*. **surveyor** /sə
'veɪə(r)/ *n* инспектор.

survival /sə'vaɪv(ə)l/ *n* *(surviving)*
выживание; *(relic)* пережиток.
survive /-'vaɪv/ *vt* переживать
impf, пережить *pf*; *vi* выживать
impf, выжить *pf*. **survivor**
/-'vaɪvə(r)/ *n* уцелевший *sb*;
(fig) борец.

susceptible /sə'septɪb(ə)l/ *adj*
подверженный (**to** влиянию
+*gen*); *(sensitive)* чувствительный (**to** к+*dat*); *(impressionable)*
впечатлительный.

suspect *n* /'sʌspekt/ подозреваемый *sb*; *adj* подозрительный;
vt /sə'spekt/ подозревать *impf*

(of в+*prep*); (*assume*) полага́ть *impf*.

suspend /sə'spend/ *vt* (*hang*) подве́шивать *impf*, подве́сить *pf*; (*delay*) приостана́вливать *impf*, приостанови́ть *pf*; (*debar temporarily*) вре́менно отстраня́ть *impf*, отстрани́ть *pf*; ~ed sentence усло́вный пригово́р. **suspender** /-'spendə(r)/ *n* (*stocking*) подвя́зка. **suspense** /-'spens/ *n* неизве́стность. **suspension** /-'spenʃ(ə)n/ *n* (*halt*) приостано́вка; (*of car*) рессо́ры *f pl*; ~ **bridge** вися́чий мост.

suspicion /sə'spiʃ(ə)n/ *n* подозре́ние; **on** ~ по подозре́нию (**of** в+*loc*); (*trace*) отте́нок. **suspicious** /-'spiʃəs/ *adj* подозри́тельный.

sustain /sə'stein/ *vt* (*support*) подде́рживать *impf*, поддержа́ть *pf*; (*suffer*) потерпе́ть *pf*. **sustained** /-'steind/ *adj* непреры́вный. **sustenance** /'sʌstinəns/ *n* пи́ща.

swab /swɒb/ *n* (*mop*) шва́бра; (*specimen*) (*med*) тампо́н; (*specimen*) мазо́к.

swagger /'swægə(r)/ *vi* расха́живать *impf* с ва́жным ви́дом.

swallow[1] /'swɒləʊ/ *n* глото́к; *vt* прогла́тывать *impf*, проглоти́ть *pf*; ~ **up** поглоща́ть *impf*, поглоти́ть *pf*.

swallow[2] /'swɒləʊ/ *n* (*bird*) ла́сточка.

swamp /swɒmp/ *n* боло́то; *vt* зали́вать *impf*, зали́ть *pf*; (*fig*) зава́ливать *impf*, завали́ть *pf* (**with** +*instr*). **swampy** /-pɪ/ *adj* боло́тистый.

swan /swɒn/ *n* ле́бедь *m*.

swap /swɒp/ *n* обме́н; *vt* (*for different thing*) меня́ть *impf*, об~, по~ *pf* (**for** на+*acc*); (*for*

similar thing) обме́ниваться *impf*, обменя́ться *pf* +*instr*.

swarm /swɔːm/ *n* рой; (*crowd*) толпа́; *vi* рои́ться *impf*; толпи́ться *impf*; (*teem*) кише́ть *impf* (**with** +*instr*).

swarthy /'swɔːðɪ/ *adj* сму́глый.

swastika /'swɒstɪkə/ *n* сва́стика.

swat /swɒt/ *vt* прихло́пывать *impf*, прихло́пнуть *pf*.

swathe /sweɪð/ *n* (*expanse*) простра́нство; *vt* (*wrap*) заку́тывать *impf*, заку́тать *pf*.

sway /sweɪ/ *n* (*influence*) влия́ние; (*power*) власть *vt* & *i* кача́ть(ся) *impf*, качну́ть(ся) *pf*; *vt* (*influence*) име́ть *impf* влия́ние на+*acc*.

swear /sweə(r)/ *vi* (*vow*) кля́сться *impf*, по~ *pf*; (*curse*) руга́ться *impf*, ругну́ться *pf*; ~**word** руга́тельство.

sweat /swet/ *n* пот; *vi* поте́ть *impf*, вс~ *pf*. **sweater** /-tə(r)/ *n* сви́тер. **sweatshirt** *n* тёплая футбо́лка с дли́нными рука́вами. **sweaty** /-tɪ/ *adj* по́тный.

swede /swiːd/ *n* брю́ква.

Swede /swiːd/ *n* швед, ~дка.

Sweden /-d(ə)n/ *n* Шве́ция.

Swedish /-dɪʃ/ *adj* шве́дский.

sweep /swiːp/ *n* (*span*) разма́х; (*chimney*~) трубочи́ст; *vt* подмета́ть *impf*, подмести́ *pf*; *vi* (*go majestically*) ходи́ть *indet*, идти́ *det*, пойти́ *pf* велича́во; (*move swiftly*) мча́ться *impf*; ~ **away** смета́ть *impf*, смести́ *pf*. **sweeping** /-pɪŋ/ *adj* (*changes*) радика́льный; (*statement*) огу́льный.

sweet /swiːt/ *n* (*sweetmeat*) конфе́та; (*dessert*) сла́дкое *sb*; *adj* сла́дкий; (*fragrant*) души́стый; (*dear*) ми́лый. **sweeten** /-t(ə)n/ *vt* подсла́щивать *impf*, подсласти́ть *pf*. **sweetheart** *n*

возлю́бленный, -нная *sb.*

sweetness /-nɪs/ *n* сла́дость.

swell /swel/ *vi* (*up*) опуха́ть *impf*, опу́хнуть *pf*; *vt & i* (*a sail*) надува́ть(ся) *impf*, наду́ть(ся) *pf*; *vt* (*increase*) увели́чивать *impf*, увели́чить *pf*; *n* (*of sea*) зыбь. **swelling** /-lɪŋ/ *n* о́пухоль.

swelter /'sweltə(r)/ *vi* изнемога́ть *impf* от жары́. **sweltering** /-rɪŋ/ *adj* зно́йный.

swerve /swɜːv/ *vi* ре́зко свёртывать, свора́чивать *impf*, сверну́ть *pf*.

swift /swɪft/ *adj* бы́стрый.

swig /swɪg/ *n* глото́к; *vt* хлеба́ть *impf.*

swill /swɪl/ *n* пойло; *vt* (*rinse*) полоска́ть *impf*, вы́~ *pf.*

swim /swɪm/ *vi* пла́вать *indet*, плыть *det impf*; *vt* (*across*) перепплыва́ть *impf*, переплы́ть *pf* +*acc*, че́рез+*acc.* **swimmer** /-mə(r)/ *n* пловец, -вчи́ха. **swimming** /-mɪŋ/ *n* пла́вание. **swimming-pool** *n* бассе́йн для пла́вания. **swim-suit** *n* купа́льный костю́м.

swindle /'swɪnd(ə)l/ *vt* обма́нывать *impf*, обману́ть *pf*; *n* обма́н. **swindler** /-dlə(r)/ *n* моше́нник.

swine /swaɪn/ *n* свинья́.

swing /swɪŋ/ *vi* кача́ться *impf*, качну́ться *pf*; *vt* кача́ть *impf*, качну́ть *pf* +*acc*, *instr*, (*arms*) разма́хивать *impf* +*instr* в кача́ние; (*shift*) крен; (*seat*) каче́ли (-лей) *pl*; **in full ~** в по́лном разга́ре.

swingeing /'swɪndʒɪŋ/ *adj* (*huge*) грома́дный;   (*forcible*) си́льный.

swipe /swaɪp/ *n* си́льный уда́р; *vt* с си́лой ударя́ть *impf*, уда́рить *pf.*

swirl /swɜːl/ *vi* крути́ться *impf*

(*of snow*) вихрь *m.*

swish /swɪʃ/ *vi* (*cut the air*) рассека́ть *impf*, рассе́чь *pf* во́здух со сви́стом; (*rustle*) шелесте́т *impf*; *vt* (*tail*) взма́хивать взмахну́ть *pf* +*instr*; (*brandish*) разма́хивать *impf* +*instr*; *n* (о whip) свист; (*rustle*) ше́лест.

Swiss /swɪs/ *n* швейца́рец -ца́рка; *adj* швейца́рский.

switch /swɪtʃ/ *n* (*electr*) выключа́тель *m*; (*change*) измене́ние *vt & i* (*also ~ over*) переключа́ть(ся) *impf*, переключи́ть(ся) *pf*; (*swap*) меня́ться *impf*, об~, по~ *pf* +*instr*; **~ off** выключа́ть *impf*, вы́ключить *pf*; **~ on** включа́ть *impf*, включи́ть *pf.* **switchboard** *n* коммута́тор.

Switzerland /'swɪtsələnd/ *n* Швейца́рия.

swivel /'swɪv(ə)l/ *vt & i* враща́ть(ся) *impf.*

swollen /'swəʊlən/ *adj* взду́тый.

swoon /swuːn/ *n* о́бморок; *vi* па́дать *impf*, упа́сть *pf* в о́бморок.

swoop /swuːp/ *vi*: **~ down** налета́ть *impf*, налете́ть *pf* (**on** на+*acc*); *n* налёт; **at one fell ~** одни́м уда́ром.

sword /sɔːd/ *n* меч.

sycophantic /ˌsɪkəˈfæntɪk/ *adj* льсти́вый.

syllable /'sɪləb(ə)l/ *n* слог.

syllabus /'sɪləbəs/ *n* програ́мма.

symbol /'sɪmb(ə)l/ *n* си́мвол. **symbolic(al)** /sɪm'bɒlɪk(ə)l/ *adj* символи́ческий. **symbolism** /'sɪmbəˌlɪz(ə)m/ *n* символи́зм. **symbolize** /'sɪmbəˌlaɪz/ *vt* символизи́ровать *impf.*

symmetrical /sɪ'metrɪk(ə)l/ *adj* симметри́ческий. **symmetry** /'sɪmɪtrɪ/ *n* симметри́я.

T

sympathetic /ˌsɪmpə'θetɪk/ *adj* сочу́вственный. **sympathize** /'sɪmpəˌθaɪz/ *vi* сочу́вствовать *impf* (**with** +*dat*). **sympathizer** /'sɪmpəˌθaɪzə(r)/ *n* сторо́нник. **sympathy** /'sɪmpəθɪ/ *n* сочу́вствие.

symphony /'sɪmfənɪ/ *n* симфо́ния.

symposium /sɪm'pəʊzɪəm/ *n* симпо́зиум.

symptom /'sɪmptəm/ *n* симпто́м. **symptomatic** /ˌsɪmptə'mætɪk/ *adj* симтомати́чный.

synagogue /'sɪnəˌgɒg/ *n* синаго́га.

synchronization /ˌsɪŋkrənaɪ'zeɪʃ(ə)n/ *n* синхрониза́ция. **synchronize** /'sɪŋkrəˌnaɪz/ *vt* синхронизи́ровать *impf* & *pf*.

syndicate /'sɪndɪkət/ *n* синдика́т.

syndrome /'sɪndrəʊm/ *n* синдро́м.

synonym /'sɪnənɪm/ *n* сино́ним. **synonymous** /sɪ'nɒnɪməs/ *adj* синоними́ческий.

synopsis /sɪ'nɒpsɪs/ *n* конспе́кт.

syntax /'sɪntæks/ *n* си́нтаксис.

synthesis /'sɪnθɪsɪs/ *n* си́нтез. **synthetic** /sɪn'θetɪk/ *adj* синтети́ческий.

syphilis /'sɪfɪlɪs/ *n* си́филис.

Syria /'sɪrɪə/ *n* Си́рия. **Syrian** /-rɪən/ *n* сири́ец, сири́йка; *adj* сири́йский.

syringe /sɪ'rɪndʒ/ *n* шприц; *vt* спринцева́ть *impf*.

syrup /'sɪrəp/ *n* сиро́п; (*treacle*) па́тока.

system /'sɪstəm/ *n* систе́ма; (*network*) сеть; (*organism*) органи́зм. **systematic** /ˌsɪstə'mætɪk/ *adj* систематический. **systematize** /'sɪstəmaˌtaɪz/ *vt* систематизи́ровать *impf* & *pf*.

tab /tæb/ *n* (*loop*) пе́телька; (*on uniform*) петли́ца; (*of boot*) ушко́; **keep ~s on** следи́ть *impf* за+*instr*.

table /'teɪb(ə)l/ *n* стол; (*chart*) табли́ца; **~cloth** ска́терть; **~spoon** столо́вая ло́жка; **~ tennis** насто́льный те́ннис; *vt* (*for discussion*) предлага́ть *impf*, предложи́ть *pf* на обсужде́ние.

tableau /'tæbləʊ/ *n* жива́я карти́на.

tablet /'tæblɪt/ *n* (*pill*) табле́тка; (*of stone*) плита́; (*memorial ~*) мемориа́льная доска́; (*name plate*) доще́чка.

tabloid /'tæblɔɪd/ *n* (*newspaper*) малоформа́тная газе́та; (*derog*) бульва́рная газе́та.

taboo /tə'buː/ *n* табу́ *neut indecl*; *adj* запрещённый.

tacit /'tæsɪt/ *adj* молчали́вый. **taciturn** /'tæsɪˌtɜːn/ *adj* неразгово́рчивый.

tack[1] /tæk/ *n* (*nail*) гвоздик; (*stitch*) намётка; (*naut*) галс; (*fig*) курс; *vt* (*fasten*) прикрепля́ть *impf*, прикрепи́ть *pf* гво́здиками; (*stitch*) смётывать *impf*, смета́ть *pf* на живу́ю ни́тку; (*fig*) добавля́ть *impf*, доба́вить *pf* ((**on**)**to** +*dat*); *vi* (*naut*) лави́ровать *impf*.

tack[2] /tæk/ *n* (*riding*) сбру́я (*collect*).

tackle /'tæk(ə)l/ *n* (*requisites*) снасть (*collect*); (*sport*) блоки́ровка; *vt* (*problem*) бра́ться *impf*, взя́ться *pf* за+*acc*; (*sport*) блоки́ровать *impf* & *pf*.

tacky /'tækɪ/ *adj* ли́пкий.

tact /tækt/ *n* такт(и́чность). **tactful** /-fʊl/ *adj* такти́чный.

tactical /'tæktɪk(ə)l/ *adj* такти́ческий. **tactics** /'tæktɪks/ *n pl* та́ктика.

tactless /'tæktlɪs/ *adj* беста́ктный.

tadpole /'tædpəʊl/ *n* голова́стик.

Tadzhikistan /ˌtædʒɪkɪ'stɑːn/ *n* Таджикиста́н.

tag /tæg/ *n* (*label*) ярлы́к; (*of lace*) наконе́чник; *vt* (*label*) прикрепля́ть *impf*, прикрепи́ть *pf* ярлы́к на+*acc*; *vi*: ~ **along** (*follow*) тащи́ться *impf* сза́ди; **may I** ~ **along?** мо́жно с ва́ми?

tail /teɪl/ *n* хвост; (*of shirt*) ни́жний коне́ц; (*of coat*) фа́лда; (*of coin*) обра́тная сторона́ моне́ты; **heads or** ~**s?** орёл и́ли ре́шка? *pl* (*coat*) фрак; *vt* (*shadow*) выслеживать *impf*; *vi*: ~ **away, off** постепе́нно уменьша́ться *impf*; (*grow silent, abate*) затиха́ть *impf*, зати́хнуть *pf*. **tailcoat** *n* фрак.

tailor /'teɪlə(r)/ *n* портно́й *sb*; ~**-made** сши́тый на зака́з; (*fig*) сде́ланный индивидуа́льно.

taint /teɪnt/ *vt* по́ртить *impf*, ис~ *pf*.

Taiwan /taɪ'wɑːn/ *n* Тайва́нь *m*.

take /teɪk/ *vt* (*various senses*) брать *impf*, взять *pf*; (*also seize, capture*) захва́тывать *impf*, захвати́ть *pf*; (*receive, accept,* ~ *breakfast;* ~ *medicine;* ~ *steps*) принима́ть *impf*, приня́ть *pf*; (*convey, escort*) провожа́ть *impf*, проводи́ть *pf*; (*public transport*) е́здить *indet*, е́хать *det*, по~ *pf* +*instr*, на+*prep*; (*photograph*) снима́ть *impf*, снять *pf*; (*occupy;* ~ *time*) занима́ть *impf*, заня́ть *pf*; (*impers*) **how long does it** ~ ско́лько вре́мени ну́жно?; (*size in clothing*) носи́ть *impf*; (*exam*) сда-

ва́ть *impf*; *vi* (*be successful*) име́ть *impf* успе́х (*of injection*) прива́ться *impf*, приви́ться *pf*; ~ **after** походи́ть *impf* на+*acc*; ~ **away** (*remove*) убира́ть *impf*, убра́ть *pf*; (*subtract*) вычита́ть *impf*, вы́честь *pf* ~**-away** магази́н, где продаю́т на вы́нос; ~ **back** (*return*) возвраща́ть *impf*, возврати́ть *pf*; (*retrieve, retract*) брать *impf* взять *pf* наза́д; ~ **down** (*in writing*) запи́сывать *impf*, записа́ть *pf*; (*remove*) снима́ть *impf*, снять *pf*; ~ **s.o., sth for, to be** приня́ть *impf*, приня́ть *pf* за+*acc*; ~ **from** отнима́ть *impf*, отня́ть *pf* y, от+*gen*; ~ **in** (*carry in*) вноси́ть *impf*, внести́ *pf*; (*lodgers; work*) брать *impf*, взять *pf*; (*clothing*) ушива́ть *impf*, уши́ть *pf*; (*understand*) понима́ть *impf*, поня́ть *pf*; (*deceive*) обма́нывать *impf*, обману́ть *pf*; ~ **off** (*clothing*) снима́ть *impf*, снять *pf*; (*mimic*) передра́знивать *impf*, передразни́ть *pf*; (*aeroplane*) взлета́ть *impf*, взлете́ть *pf*; ~ **off** (*imitation*) подража́ние; (*aeron*) взлёт; ~ **on** (*undertake; hire*) брать *impf*, взять *pf* на себя́; (*acquire*) приобрета́ть *impf*, приобрести́ *pf*; (*at game*) сража́ться *impf*, срази́ться *pf* c+*instr* (**at** в+*acc*); ~ **out** вынима́ть *impf*, вы́нуть *pf*; (*dog*) выводи́ть *impf*, вы́вести *pf* (**for a walk** на прогу́лку); (*to theatre, restaurant etc.*) приглаша́ть *impf*, пригласи́ть *pf* (**to** в+*acc*); **we took them out every night** мы приглаша́ли их куда́-нибудь ка́ждый ве́чер; ~ **it out on** срыва́ть *impf*, сорва́ть *pf* всё на +*prep*; ~ **over** принима́ть *impf*, приня́ть *pf* руково́дство

+instr; ~ **to** (thing) пристраститься pf к+dat; (person) привязываться impf, привязаться pf к+dat; (begin) становиться impf, стать pf +inf; ~ **up** (interest oneself in) заниматься impf, заняться pf; (with an official etc.) обращаться impf, обратиться pf c+instr, к+dat; (challenge) принимать impf, принять pf; (time, space) занимать impf, занять pf; ~ **up with** (person) связываться impf, связаться pf c+instr; n (cin) дубль m.

taking /'teɪkɪŋ/ adj привлекательный.

takings /'teɪkɪnz/ n pl сбор.

talcum powder /'tælkəm 'paʊdə(r)/ n тальк.

tale /teɪl/ n рассказ.

talent /'tælənt/ n талант. **talented** –tɪd/ adj талантливый.

talk /tɔːk/ vi разговаривать impf (**to, with** c+instr); (gossip) сплетничать impf, на~ pf; vt & i говорить impf, по~ pf; ~ **down to** говорить impf свысока c+instr; ~ **into** уговаривать impf, уговорить pf +inf; ~ **out of** отговаривать impf, отговорить pf +inf, от~+gen; ~ **over** (discuss) обсуждать impf, обсудить pf; ~ **round** (persuade) переубеждать impf, переубедить pf; (lecture) беседа; pl переговоры (-ров) pl. **talkative** /'tɔːkətɪv/ adj разговорчивый. **talker** /'tɔːkə(r)/ n говорящий sb; (chatterer) болтун (coll); (orator) оратор. **talking-to** n (coll) выговор.

tall /tɔːl/ adj высокий; (in measurements) ростом в+acc.

tally /'tælɪ/ n (score) счёт; vi соответствовать (**with** +dat).

talon /'tælən/ n коготь m.

tambourine /ˌtæmbə'riːn/ n бубен.

tame /teɪm/ adj ручной; (insipid) пресный; vt приручать impf, приручить pf. **tamer** /'teɪmə(r)/ n укротитель m.

tamper /'tæmpə(r)/ vi: ~ **with** (meddle) трогать impf, тронуть pf; (forge) подделывать impf, подделать pf.

tampon /'tæmpɒn/ n тампон.

tan /tæn/ n (sun) загар; adj желтовато-коричневый; vt (hide) дубить impf, вы~ pf; (beat) (coll) дубасить impf, от~ pf; vi загорать impf, загореть pf; (of sun) tanned загорелый.

tang /tæŋ/ n (taste) резкий привкус; (smell) острый запах.

tangent /'tændʒ(ə)nt/ n (math) касательная sb; (trigonometry) тангенс; **go off at a** ~ отклоняться impf, отклониться pf от темы.

tangerine /ˌtændʒə'riːn/ n мандарин.

tangible /'tændʒɪb(ə)l/ adj осязаемый.

tangle /'tæŋg(ə)l/ vt & i запутывать(ся) impf, запутаться pf; n путаница.

tango /'tæŋgəʊ/ n танго neut indecl.

tangy /'tæŋɪ/ adj острый; резкий.

tank /tæŋk/ n бак; (mil) танк.

tankard /'tæŋkəd/ n кружка.

tanker /'tæŋkə(r)/ n (sea) танкер; (road) автоцистерна.

tantalize /'tæntəlaɪz/ vt дразнить impf.

tantamount /'tæntəˌmaʊnt/ predic равносилен (-льна) pf (+dat).

tantrum /'tæntrəm/ n приступ

раздраже́ния.

tap¹ /tæp/ n кран; vt (resources) испо́льзовать impf & pf; (telephone conversation) подслу́шивать impf.

tap² /tæp/ n (knock) стук; vt стуча́ть impf, по~ pf в+acc, по+dat; ~-dance (vi) отбива́ть impf, отби́ть pf чечётку; (n) чечётка; ~-dancer чечёточник, -ица.

tape /teɪp/ n (cotton strip) тесьма́; (adhesive, magnetic, measuring, etc.) ле́нта; ~-measure руле́тка; ~-recorder магнитофо́н; ~ recording за́пись; vt (seal) заклеи́вать impf, закле́ить pf; (record) запи́сывать impf, записа́ть pf на ле́нту.

taper /ˈteɪpə(r)/ vt & i су́живать(ся) impf, су́зить(ся) pf.

tapestry /ˈtæpɪstrɪ/ n гобеле́н.

tar /tɑː(r)/ n дёготь m.

tardy /ˈtɑːdɪ/ adj (slow) ме́дли-тельный; (late) запозда́лый.

target /ˈtɑːgɪt/ n мише́нь, цель.

tariff /ˈtærɪf/ n тари́ф.

tarmac /ˈtɑːmæk/ n (material) гудро́н; (road) гудрони́рованное шоссе́ neut indecl; (runway) бетони́рованная площа́дка; vt гудрони́ровать impf & pf.

tarnish /ˈtɑːnɪʃ/ vt де́лать impf, с~ pf ту́склым; (fig) пятна́ть impf, за~ pf; vi тускне́ть impf, по~ pf.

tarpaulin /tɑːˈpɔːlɪn/ n брезе́нт.

tarragon /ˈtærəgən/ n эстраго́н.

tart¹ /tɑːt/ n (pie) сла́дкий пиро́г.

tart² /tɑːt/ adj (taste) ки́слый; (fig) ко́лкий.

tart³ /tɑːt/ n (prostitute) шлю́ха.

tartan /ˈtɑːt(ə)n/ n шотла́ндка.

tartar /ˈtɑːtə(r)/ n ви́нный ка́мень m.

task /tɑːsk/ n зада́ча; take to ~

де́лать impf, с~ pf вы́говор+dat; ~ force операти́вная гру́ппа.

Tass /tæs/ abbr ТАСС, Телегра́фное аге́нтство Сове́тского Сою́за.

tassel /ˈtæs(ə)l/ n ки́сточка.

taste /teɪst/ n (also fig) вкус; take a ~ of про́бовать impf, по~ pf vt чу́вствовать вкус impf, по~ pf; ~ вкус+gen; (sample) про́бовать impf, по~ pf; (fig) вкуша́ть impf, вкуси́ть pf; (wine etc.) дегусти́ровать impf & pf; vi иметь impf вкус, привкус (of +gen). **tasteful** /-fʊl/ adj (сде́ланный) со вкусом. **tasteless** /-lɪs/ adj безвку́сный. **tasting** /-tɪŋ/ n дегуста́ция. **tasty** /-tɪ/ adj вку́сный.

tatter /ˈtætə(r)/ n pl лохмо́тья (-ьев) pl. **tattered** /-d/ adj изо́рванный.

tattoo /təˈtuː/ n (design) татуиро́вка; vt татуи́ровать impf & pf.

taunt /tɔːnt/ n насме́шка; vt насмеха́ться impf над+instr.

Taurus /ˈtɔːrəs/ n Теле́ц.

taut /tɔːt/ adj ту́го натя́нутый; туго́й.

tavern /ˈtæv(ə)n/ n таве́рна.

tawdry /ˈtɔːdrɪ/ adj мишу́рный.

tawny /ˈtɔːnɪ/ adj рыжева́то-кори́чневый.

tax /tæks/ n нало́г; ~-free освобождённый от нало́га; vt облага́ть impf, обложи́ть pf нало́гом; (strain) напряга́ть impf, напря́чь pf; (patience) испы́тывать impf, испыта́ть pf. **taxable** /ˈtæksəb(ə)l/ adj подлежа́щий обложе́нию нало́гом. **taxation** /tækˈseɪʃ(ə)n/ n обложе́ние нало́гом. **taxing** /ˈtæksɪŋ/ adj утоми́тельный. **taxpayer** n налогопла-

тельщик.

axi /'tæksɪ/ *n* такси́ *neut indecl*; ~**-driver** води́тель *m* такси́; ~**rank** стоя́нка такси́; *vi* (*aeron*) рули́ть *impf*.

ea /tiː/ *n* чай; ~ **bag** паке́тик с сухи́м ча́ем; ~ **cloth**, ~ **towel** полоте́нце для посу́ды; ~ **cosy** чехо́льчик (для ча́йника); ~**cup** ча́йная ча́шка; ~**leaf** ча́йный лист; ~**pot** ча́йник; ~**spoon** ча́йная ло́жка; ~**strainer** ча́йное си́течко.

each /tiːtʃ/ *vt* учи́ть *impf*, на~ *pf* (*person +acc; subject +dat, inf*); преподава́ть *impf* (*subject +acc*); (*coll*) проу́чивать *impf*, проучи́ть *pf*. **teacher** /'tiːtʃə(r)/ *n* учи́тель *m*, ~ница; преподава́тель *m*, ~ница; ~**training college** педагоги́ческий институ́т. **teaching** /'tiːtʃɪŋ/ *n* (*instruction*) обуче́ние; (*doctrine*) уче́ние.

teak /tiːk/ *n* тик; *attrib* ти́ковый.

team /tiːm/ *n* (*sport*) кома́нда; (*of people*) брига́да; (*of horses etc.*) упря́жка; ~**-mate** член той же кома́нды; ~**work** сотру́дничество; *vi* (~ *up*) объединя́ться *impf*, объедини́ться *pf*.

tear¹ /teə(r)/ *n* (*rent*) проре́ха; *vt* (*also* ~ *up*) рвать *impf*; (*also* ~ *up*) разрыва́ть *impf*, разорва́ть *pf*; *vi* рва́ться *impf*; (*rush*) мча́ться *impf*; ~ **down, off** срыва́ть *impf*, сорва́ть *pf*; ~ **out** вырыва́ть *impf*, вы́рвать *pf*.

tear² /tɪə(r)/ *n* (~*drop*) слеза́; ~**gas** слезоточи́вый газ. **tearful** /-fʊl/ *adj* слезли́вый.

tease /tiːz/ *vt* дразни́ть *impf*.

teat /tiːt/ *n* сосо́к.

technical /'teknɪk(ə)l/ *adj* техни́ческий; ~ **college** техни́ческое учи́лище. **technicality** /ˌteknɪ'kælɪtɪ/ *n* форма́льность. **technically** /'teknɪklɪ/ *adv* (*strictly*) форма́льно. **technician** /tek'nɪʃ(ə)n/ *n* те́хник. **technique** /-'niːk/ *n* те́хника; (*method*) ме́тод. **technology** /-'nɒlədʒɪ/ *n* техноло́гия, те́хника. **technological** /ˌteknə'lɒdʒɪk(ə)l/ *adj* технологи́ческий. **technologist** /tek'nɒlədʒɪst/ *n* техно́лог.

teddy-bear /'tedɪˌbeə(r)/ *n* медве́жонок.

tedious /'tiːdɪəs/ *adj* ску́чный. **tedium** /'tiːdɪəm/ *n* ску́ка.

teem¹ /tiːm/ *vi* (*swarm*) кише́ть *impf* (*with +instr*).

teem² /tiːm/ *vi*: it is ~**ing** (*with rain*) дождь льёт как из ведра́.

teenage /'tiːneɪdʒ/ *adj* ю́ношеский. **teenager** /-dʒə(r)/ *n* подро́сток. **teens** /tiːnz/ *n pl* во́зраст от трина́дцати до девятна́дцати лет.

teeter /'tiːtə(r)/ *vi* кача́ться *impf*, качну́ться *pf*.

teethe /tiːð/ *vi*: the child is teething у ребёнка проре́зываются зу́бы; **teething troubles** (*fig*) нача́льные пробле́мы *f pl*.

teetotal /tiː'təʊt(ə)l/ *adj* тре́звый. **teetotaller** /-lə(r)/ *n* тре́звенник.

telecommunication(s) /ˌtelɪkəˌmjuːnɪ'keɪʃ(ə)nz/ *n* да́льняя связь. **telegram** /'telɪˌgræm/ *n* телегра́мма. **telegraph** /'telɪˌgrɑːf/ *n* телегра́ф; ~ **pole** телегра́фный столб. **telepathic** /ˌtelɪ'pæθɪk/ *adj* телепати́ческий. **telepathy** /tɪ'lepəθɪ/ *n* телепа́тия. **telephone** /'telɪˌfəʊn/ *n* телефо́н; *vt* (*message*) телефони́ровать *impf & pf +acc*, o+*prep*; (*person*) звони́ть *impf*, по~ *pf* (*по телефо́ну*) +*dat*; ~ **box** телефо́нная бу́дка; ~ **directory** телефо́нная кни́га; ~

exchange телефо́нная ста́нция; ~ number но́мер телефо́на. **telephonist** /tɪˈlefənɪst/ n телефони́ст, ~ка. **telephoto lens** /ˈtelɪ ˌfəʊtəʊ lenz/ n телеобъекти́в.

telescope /ˈtelɪˌskəʊp/ n телеско́п. **telescopic** /ˌtelɪˈskɒpɪk/ adj телескопи́ческий. **televise** /ˈtelɪˌvaɪz/ vt пока́зывать impf, показа́ть pf по телеви́дению. **television** /ˈtelɪˌvɪʒ(ə)n/ n телеви́дение; (set) телеви́зор; attrib телевизио́нный. **telex** /ˈteleks/ n те́лекс.

tell /tel/ vt & i (relate) расска́зывать impf, рассказа́ть pf (thing told +acc, о+prep; person told +dat); (utter, inform) говори́ть impf, сказа́ть pf (thing uttered +acc; thing informed about о+prep; person informed +dat); (order) веле́ть impf & pf +dat; ~ **one thing from another** отлича́ть impf, отличи́ть pf +acc от+gen; vi (have an effect) ска́зываться impf, сказа́ться pf (on на+prep); ~ **off** отчи́тывать impf, отчита́ть pf; ~ **on,** ~ **tales about** я́бедничать impf, на~ pf на+acc+dat. **teller** /ˈtelə(r)/ n (of story) расска́зчик; (of votes) счётчик; (in bank) касси́р. **telling** /ˈtelɪŋ/ adj (effective) эффекти́вный; (significant) многозначи́тельный. **telltale** n спле́тник; adj преда́тельский. **temerity** /tɪˈmerɪtɪ/ n дёрзость.

temp /temp/ n рабо́тающий sb вре́менно; vi рабо́тать impf вре́менно. **temper** /ˈtempə(r)/ n (character) нрав; (mood) настрое́ние; (anger) гнев; **lose one's** ~ выходи́ть impf, вы́йти pf из себя́; vt (fig) смягча́ть impf, смягчи́ть pf. **temperament** /ˈtemprəmənt/ n

темпера́мент. **temperamental** /ˌtemprəˈment(ə)l/ adj темпера́ментный. **temperance** /ˈtempərəns/ n (moderation) уме́ренность; (sobriety) трёзвенность. **temperate** /ˈtempərət/ adj уме́ренный. **temperature** /ˈtemprɪtʃə(r)/ n температу́ра; (high ~) повы́шенная температу́ра; **take s.o.'s** ~ измеря́ть impf, изме́рить pf температу́ру +dat. **tempest** /ˈtempɪst/ n бу́ря. **tempestuous** /temˈpestjʊəs/ adj бу́рный.

template /ˈtemplɪt/ n шабло́н. **temple**[1] /ˈtemp(ə)l/ n (religion) храм. **temple**[2] /ˈtemp(ə)l/ n (anat) висо́к.

tempo /ˈtempəʊ/ n темп. **temporal** /ˈtempər(ə)l/ adj (of time) временно́й; (secular) мирско́й. **temporary** /ˈtempərərɪ/ adj вре́менный. **tempt** /tempt/ vt соблазня́ть impf, соблазни́ть pf; ~ **fate** испы́тывать impf, испыта́ть pf судьбу́. **temptation** /tempˈteɪʃ(ə)n/ n собла́зн. **tempting** /ˈtemptɪŋ/ adj соблазни́тельный.

ten /ten/ adj & n де́сять; (number 10) деся́тка. **tenth** /tenθ/ adj & n деся́тый.

tenable /ˈtenəb(ə)l/ adj (logical) разу́мный.

tenacious /tɪˈneɪʃəs/ adj це́пкий. **tenacity** /-ˈnæsɪtɪ/ n це́пкость.

tenancy /ˈtenənsɪ/ n (renting) наём помеще́ния; (period) срок аре́нды. **tenant** /ˈtenənt/ n аренда́тор.

tend[1] /tend/ vi (be apt) име́ть скло́нность (**to** к+dat, +inf).

end² /tend/ vt (look after) уха́живать impf за+instr.

tendency /'tendənsı/ n тенде́нция. **tendentious** /ten'denʃəs/ adj тенденцио́зный.

tender¹ /'tendə(r)/ vt (offer) предлага́ть impf, предложи́ть pf; vi (make ~ for) подава́ть impf, пода́ть pf заявку (на торга́х) в предложе́ние; legal ~ зако́нное платёжное сре́дство.

tender² /'tendə(r)/ adj (delicate, affectionate) не́жный. **tenderness** /-nıs/ n не́жность.

tendon /'tendən/ n сухожи́лие.

tendril /'tendrıl/ n у́сик.

tenement /'tenımənt/ n (dwelling-house) жилой дом; ~house многоквартирный дом.

tenet /'tenıt/ n до́гмат, при́нцип.

tennis /'tenıs/ n те́ннис.

tenor /'tenə(r)/ n (direction) направле́ние; (purport) смысл; (mus) те́нор.

tense¹ /tens/ n вре́мя neut.

tense² /tens/ vt напряга́ть impf, напря́чь pf; adj напряжённый. **tension** /'tenʃ(ə)n/ n напряже́ние.

tent /tent/ n пала́тка.

tentacle /'tentək(ə)l/ n щу́пальце.

tentative /'tentətıv/ adj (experimental) про́бный; (preliminary) предвари́тельный.

tenterhooks /'tentə,huks/ n pl: be on ~ сиде́ть impf как на иго́лках.

tenth /tenθ/ see ten

tenuous /'tenjuəs/ adj (fig) неубеди́тельный.

tenure /'tenjə(r)/ n (of property) владе́ние; (of office) пребыва́ние в до́лжности; (period) срок; (guaranteed employment) несменя́емость.

tepid /'tepıd/ adj теплова́тый.

term /tɜːm/ n (period) срок; (univ) семе́стр; (school) че́тверть; (technical word) те́рмин; (expression) выраже́ние; pl (conditions) усло́вия neut pl; (relations) отноше́ния neut pl; on good ~s в хоро́ших отноше́ниях; come to ~s with (resign o.s. to) покоря́ться impf, покори́ться pf к+dat; vt называ́ть impf, назва́ть pf.

terminal /'tɜːmın(ə)l/ adj коне́чный; (med) смерте́льный; n (electr) зажи́м; (computer, aeron) термина́л; (terminus) коне́чная остано́вка.

terminate /'tɜːmı,neıt/ vt & i конча́ть(ся) impf, ко́нчить(ся) pf (in +instr.). **termination** /-'neıʃ(ə)n/ n прекраще́ние.

terminology /,tɜːmı'nɒlədʒı/ n терминоло́гия.

terminus /'tɜːmınəs/ n коне́чная остано́вка.

termite /'tɜːmaıt/ n терми́т.

terrace /'terəs/ n терра́са; (houses) ряд домо́в.

terracotta /,terə'kɒtə/ n терракота.

terrain /te'reın/ n ме́стность.

terrestrial /tə'restrıəl/ adj земно́й.

terrible /'terıb(ə)l/ adj ужа́сный. **terribly** /-blı/ adv ужа́сно.

terrier /'terıə(r)/ n терье́р.

terrific /tə'rıfık/ adj (huge) огро́мный; (splendid) потряса́ющий. **terrify** /'terı,faı/ vt ужаса́ть impf, ужасну́ть pf.

territorial /,terı'tɔːrıəl/ adj территориа́льный. **territory** /'terıtərı/ n террито́рия.

terror /'terə(r)/ n у́жас; (person, polit) терро́р. **terrorism** /'terə,rız(ə)m/ n террори́зм. **terrorist**

/'terərɪst/ *n* террори́ст, ~ка. **terrorize** /'terə,raɪz/ *vt* терроризи́ровать *impf* & *pf*.

terse /tɜːs/ *adj* кра́ткий.

tertiary /'tɜːʃərɪ/ *adj* трети́чный; (*education*) вы́сший.

test /test/ *n* испыта́ние, про́ба; (*exam*) экза́мен; контро́льная рабо́та; (*analysis*) ана́лиз; ~**tube** проби́рка; *vt* (*try out*) испы́тывать *impf*, испыта́ть *pf*; (*check up on*) проверя́ть *impf*, прове́рить *pf*; (*give exam to*) экзаменова́ть *impf*, про~ *pf*.

testament /'testəmənt/ *n* завеща́ние; Old, New T~ Ве́тхий, Но́вый заве́т.

testicle /'testɪk(ə)l/ *n* яи́чко.

testify /'testɪ,faɪ/ *vi* свиде́тельствовать *impf* (в по́льзу +*gen*; **against** про́тив+*gen*); (*declare*) заявля́ть *impf*, заяви́ть *pf*; (*be evidence of*) свиде́тельствовать о+*prep*.

testimonial /,testɪ'məʊnɪəl/ *n* рекоменда́ция. **testimony** /'testɪmənɪ/ *n* свиде́тельство.

tetanus /'tetənəs/ *n* столбня́к.

tetchy /'tetʃɪ/ *adj* раздражи́тельный.

tête-à-tête /,teɪtɑː'teɪt/ *n* & *adv* тет-а-те́т.

tether /'teðə(r)/ *n*: **be at, come to the end of one's** ~ дойти́ *pf* до то́чки; *vt* привя́зывать *impf*, привяза́ть *pf*.

text /tekst/ *n* текст; ~ **message** SMS/CMC-сообще́ние; *vt* посыла́ть *impf*, посла́ть *pf* SMS (+*dat*). **textbook** *n* уче́бник.

textile /'tekstaɪl/ *adj* тексти́льный; *n* ткань; *pl* тексти́ль *m* (*collect*).

textual /'tekstjʊəl/ *adj* тексто́вой.

texture /'tekstʃə(r)/ *n* тексту́ра.

than /ðæn/ *conj* (*comparison*) чем; **other** ~ (*except*) кро́ме+*gen*.

thank /θæŋk/ *vt* благодари́ть *impf*, по~ *pf* (**for** за+*acc*); ~ **God** сла́ва Бо́гу; ~ **you** спаси́бо; благодарю́ вас; *n pl* благода́рность; **~s to** (*good result*) благодаря́ +*dat*; (*bad result*) из-за+*gen*. **thankful** /-fʊl/ *adj* благода́рный. **thankless** /-lɪs/ *adj* неблагода́рный. **thanksgiving** /'θæŋks,gɪvɪŋ/ *n* благодаре́ние.

that /ðæt/ *demonstrative adj* & *pron* тот; ~ **which** тот кото́рый; *rel pron* кото́рый; что; (*purpose*) что́бы; *adv* так, до тако́й сте́пени.

thatched /θætʃt/ *adj* соло́менный.

thaw /θɔː/ *vt* раста́пливать *impf*, растопи́ть *pf*; *vi* та́ять *impf*, рас~ *pf*; *n* о́ттепель.

the /ðə, ðiː/ *def article, not translated*; *adv* **the ... the ...** чем ...тем; ~ **more** ~ **better** чем бо́льше, тем лу́чше.

theatre /'θɪətə(r)/ *n* теа́тр; (*lecture* ~) аудито́рия; (*operating* ~) операцио́нная *sb*; **~-goer** театра́л. **theatrical** /θɪ'ætrɪk(ə)l/ *adj* театра́льный.

theft /θeft/ *n* кра́жа.

their, theirs /ðeə(r), ðeəz/ *poss pron* их; свой.

theme /θiːm/ *n* те́ма.

themselves /ðəm'selvz/ *pron* (*emph*) (они́) са́ми; (*refl*) себя́; -ся (*suffixed to vt*).

then /ðen/ *adv* (*at that time*) тогда́; (*after that*) пото́м; **now and** ~ вре́мя от вре́мени; *conj* в тако́м слу́чае, тогда́; *adj* тогда́шний; **by** ~ к тому́ вре́мени; **since** ~ с тех пор.

thence /ðens/ *adv* отту́да. **thenceforth, -forward** /ðens'fɔːθ, -'fɔːwəd/ *adv* с того́/э́того

зре́мени.

theologian /θɪə'ləʊdʒ(ə)n/ n тео-лог. **theological** /-'lɒdʒɪk(ə)l/ adj теологи́ческий. **theology** /θɪ'ɒlədʒɪ/ n теоло́гия.

theorem /'θɪərəm/ n теоре́ма. **theoretical** /ˌθɪə'retɪk(ə)l/ adj теорети́ческий. **theorize** /'θɪəraɪz/ vi теоретизи́ровать impf. **theory** /'θɪərɪ/ n тео́рия.

therapeutic /ˌθerə'pjuːtɪk/ adj терапевти́ческий. **therapist** /'θerəpɪst/ n (psychotherapist) психотерапе́вт. **therapy** /'θerəpɪ/ n терапи́я.

there /ðeə(r)/ adv (place) там; (direction) туда́; int вот!; ну!; ~ s, are есть, име́ется (-ются); ~ you are (on giving sth) пожа́-луйста. **thereabouts** /'ðeərə baʊts/ adv (near) побли́зости; (approximately) приблизи́-тельно. **thereafter** adv по́сле э́того. **thereby** adv таки́м о́б-разом. **therefore** adv поэ́тому. **therein** adv в э́том. **thereupon** adv затем.

thermal /'θɜːm(ə)l/ adj тепло-во́й, терми́ческий; (underwear) тёплый. **thermometer** /θə'mɒmɪtə(r)/ n термо́метр, гра́дусник. **thermos** /'θɜːmɒs/ n те́рмос. **thermostat** /'θɜːməˌstæt/ n термоста́т.

thesis /'θiːsɪs/ n (proposition) те́зис; (dissertation) диссер-та́ция.

they /ðeɪ/ pron они́.

thick /θɪk/ adj то́лстый, (in measurements) толщино́й в+acc; (dense) густо́й; (stupid) глу́пый; ~-skinned толстоко́-жий. **thicken** /'θɪkən/ vt & i (máke thicker) утол-ща́ть(ся) impf, утол-сти́ть(ся) pf; (make, become denser) сгуща́ть(ся) impf, сгу-

сти́ть(ся) pf; vi (become more intricate) усложня́ться impf, усложни́ться pf. **thicket** /'θɪkɪt/ n ча́ща. **thickness** /'θɪknɪs/ n (also dimension) толщина́; (density) густота́; (layer) слой. **thickset** adj корена́стый.

thief /θiːf/ n вор. **thieve** /θiːv/ vi ворова́ть impf. **thievery** /'θiːvərɪ/ n воровство́.

thigh /θaɪ/ n бедро́.

thimble /'θɪmb(ə)l/ n напёрсток.

thin /θɪn/ adj (slender; not thick) то́нкий; (lean) худо́й; (too liquid) жи́дкий; (sparse) ре́дкий; vt & i де́лать(ся) impf, с~ pf то́нким, жи́дким, etc; vi (also ~ out) реде́ть impf, по~ pf; vt: ~ out прореживать impf, проре-ди́ть pf.

thing /θɪŋ/ n вещь; (object) предме́т; (matter) де́ло.

think /θɪŋk/ vt & i (about, of o+prep); (consider) счита́ть impf, счесть pf (to be +instr, за+acc; that что); vi (reflect, reason) мы́слить impf; (intend) намерева́ться impf (of doing +inf); ~ out проду́мывать impf, проду́мать pf; ~ over обду́мывать impf, обду́-мать pf; ~ up, of приду́мывать impf, приду́мать pf. **thinker** /'θɪŋkə(r)/ n мысли́тель m. **thinking** /'θɪŋkɪŋ/ adj мы́сля-щий; n (reflection) размышле́-ние; to my way of ~ по моему́ мне́нию.

third /θɜːd/ adj & n тре́тий; (fraction) треть; T~ World страны́ f pl тре́тьего ми́ра.

thirst /θɜːst/ n жа́жда (for +gen (fig)); vi (fig) жа́ждать impf (for +gen). **thirsty** /'θɜːstɪ/ adj: be ~ хоте́ть impf пить.

thirteen /θɜː'tiːn/ adj & n три-на́дцать. **thirteenth** /-'tiːnθ/

adj & *n* тридца́тый.

thirtieth /'θɜːtɪɪθ/ *adj* & *n* тридца́тый. **thirty** /'θɜːtɪ/ *adj* & *n* три́дцать; *pl* (*decade*) тридца́тые го́ды (-дов) *m pl*.

this /ðɪs/ *demonstrative adj* & *pron* э́тот; not так; ~ **morning** сего́дня у́тром.

thistle /'θɪs(ə)l/ *n* чертополо́х.

thither /'ðɪðə(r)/ *adv* туда́.

thorn /θɔːn/ *n* шип. **thorny** /'θɔːnɪ/ *adj* колю́чий; (*fig*) терни́стый.

thorough /'θʌrə/ *adj* основа́тельный; (*complete*) соверше́нный. **thoroughbred** /-,bred/ *adj* чистокро́вный. **thoroughfare** /-,feə(r)/ *n* прое́зд; (*walking*) прохо́д. **thoroughgoing** /-,gəʊ̃ɪŋ/ *adj* радика́льный. **thoroughly** /-lɪ/ *adv* (*completely*) соверше́нно. **thoroughness** /-nɪs/ *n* основа́тельность.

though /ðəʊ/ *conj* хотя́; несмотря́ на то, что; **as** ~ как бу́дто; *adv* одна́ко.

thought /θɔːt/ *n* мысль; (*meditation*) размышле́ние; (*intention*) наме́рение; *pl* (*opinion*) мне́ние. **thoughtful** /-fʊl/ *adj* заду́мчивый; (*considerate*) внима́тельный. **thoughtless** /-lɪs/ *adj* необду́манный; (*inconsiderate*) невнима́тельный.

thousand /'θaʊz(ə)nd/ *adj* & *n* ты́сяча. **thousandth** /'θaʊz(ə)nθ/ *adj* & *n* ты́сячный.

thrash /θræʃ/ *vt* бить *impf*, по~ *pf*; ~ **out** (*discuss*) обстоя́тельно обсужда́ть *impf*, обсуди́ть *pf*; *vi*: ~ **about** мета́ться *impf*. **thrashing** /-ʃɪŋ/ *n* (*beating*) взбу́чка (*coll*).

thread /θred/ *n* ни́тка, нить (*also fig*); (*of screw etc.*) резьба́;

vt (*needle*) продева́ть *impf*, проде́ть *pf* ни́тку в+*acc* (*beads*) нани́зывать *impf*, низа́ть *pf*; ~ **one's way** пробира́ться *impf*, пробра́ться *pf* (**through** че́рез+*acc*). **threadbare** /-beə/ *adj* потёртый.

threat /θret/ *n* угро́за. **threaten** /-t(ə)n/ *vt* угрожа́ть *impf*, грози́ть *impf*, при~ *pf* (*person* +*dat*; **with** +*instr*; **to do** +*inf*).

three /θriː/ *adj* & *n* три; (*numb 3*) тро́йка. ~**dimensional** трёхме́рный; ~**quarters** три че́тверти. **threefold** *adj* тройно́й; *adv* втро́йне. **threesome** /-səm/ *n* тро́йка.

thresh /θreʃ/ *vt* молоти́ть *impf*. **threshold** /'θreʃəʊld/ *n* поро́г.

thrice /θraɪs/ *adv* три́жды.

thrift /θrɪft/ *n* бережли́вость. **thrifty** /-tɪ/ *adj* бережли́вый.

thrill /θrɪl/ *n* тре́пет; *vt* восхища́ть *impf*, восхити́ть *pf*; **thrilled** быть в восто́рге **thriller** /-lə(r)/ *n* приключе́нческий, детекти́вный (*nove* рома́н, (*film*) фильм. **thrilling** /-lɪŋ/ *adj* захва́тывающий.

thrive /θraɪv/ *vi* процвета́ть *impf*.

throat /θrəʊt/ *n* го́рло.

throb /θrɒb/ *vi* (*heart*) си́льно би́ться *impf*; пульси́ровать *impf*; *n* бие́ние; пульса́ция.

throes /θrəʊz/ *n pl*: **in the** ~ в м чи́тельных попы́тках.

thrombosis /θrɒm'bəʊsɪs/ тромбо́з.

throne /θrəʊn/ *n* трон, престо́л **come to the** ~ вступа́ть *impf* вступи́ть *pf* на престо́л.

throng /θrɒŋ/ *n* толпа́; *vi* то пи́ться *impf*; *vt* заполня́ть *impf* заполня́ть *pf*.

throttle /'θrɒt(ə)l/ *n* (*tech*) дро сель *m*; *vt* (*strangle*) души́

impf, за~ *pf*; *(tech)* дроссели́-
ровать *impf* & *pf*; ~ **down** сба́в-
ля́ть *impf*, сба́вить *pf* газ.

hrough /θruː/ *prep (across, via, ~ opening)* сквозь+*acc*; *(esp thick of)* сквозь+*acc*; *(air, streets etc.)* по+*dat*; *(agency)* посре́дством+*gen*; *(reason)* из-
-за+*gen*; *adv* наскво́зь; *(from beginning to end)* до конца́; **be ~ with** *(sth)* ока́нчивать *impf*, око́нчить *pf*; *(s.o.)* порыва́ть *impf*, порва́ть *pf* c+*instr*; **put ~** *(on telephone)* соединя́ть *impf*, соедини́ть *pf*; **~ and ~** соверше́нно; *adj (train)* прямо́й; *(traffic)* сквозно́й. **throughout** *adv* повсю́ду, во всех отноше́-
ниях; *prep* по всему́ (всей, всему́); по всем)+*dat*; *(from beginning to end)* с нача́ла до конца́+*gen*.

hrow /θrəʊ/ *n* бросо́к; *vt* бро-
са́ть *impf*, бро́сить *pf*; *(confuse)* смуща́ть *impf*, смути́ть *pf*; *(rider)* сбра́сывать *impf*, сбро́-
сить *pf*; *(party)* устра́ивать *impf*, устро́ить *pf*; ~ **o.s. into** броса́ться *impf*, бро́ситься *pf* в+*acc*; ~ **away, out** выбра́сы-
вать *impf*, вы́бросить *pf*; ~ **down** сбра́сывать *impf*, сбро́-
сить *pf*; ~ **in** *(add)* добавля́ть *impf*, доба́вить *pf*; *(sport)* вбра́-
сывать *impf*, вбро́сить *pf*; ~**in** вбра́сывание мяча́; ~ **off** сбра́-
сывать *impf*, сбро́сить *pf*; ~
open распа́хивать *impf*, рас-
пахну́ть *pf*; ~ **out** *(see also ~ away)* *(expel)* выгоня́ть *impf*, вы́гнать *pf*; *(reject)* отверга́ть *impf*, отве́ргнуть *pf*; ~ **over, ~ up** *(abandon)* броса́ть *impf*, бро́сить *pf*; ~ **up** подбра́сы-
вать *impf*, подбро́сить *pf*; *(vomit)* рвать *impf*, вы́~ *pf* *imp-*
ers; **he threw up** его́ вы́рвало.

thrush /θrʌʃ/ *n (bird)* дрозд.

thrust /θrʌst/ *n (shove)* толчо́к; *(tech)* тя́га; *vt (shove)* толка́ть *impf*, толкну́ть *pf*; *(~ into, out of; give sharply, carelessly)* со-
ва́ть *impf*, су́нуть *pf*.

thud /θʌd/ *n* глухо́й звук; *vi* па́-
дать *impf*, *pf* с глухи́м сту́ком.

thug /θʌg/ *n* головоре́з *(coll)*.

thumb /θʌm/ *n* большо́й па́лец; **under the ~ of** под башмако́м у+*gen*; *vt*: ~ **through** перели́-
стывать *impf*, перелиста́ть *pf*; ~ **a lift** голосова́ть *impf*, про~ *pf*.

thump /θʌmp/ *n (blow)* тяжёлый уда́р; *(thud)* глухо́й звук, стук; *vt* колоти́ть *impf*, по~ *pf* в+*acc*, по+*dat*; *vi* колоти́ться *impf*.

thunder /'θʌndə(r)/ *n* гром; *vi* греме́ть *impf*; **it thunders** гром греми́т. **thunderbolt** *n* уда́р мо́лнии. **thunderous** /-rəs/ *adj* громово́й. **thunderstorm** *n* гроза́. **thundery** /-rɪ/ *adj* гро-
зово́й.

Thursday /'θɜːzdeɪ/ *n* четве́рг.

thus /ðʌs/ *adv* так, таки́м о́б-
разом.

thwart /θwɔːt/ *vt* меша́ть *impf*, по~ *pf*+*dat*; *(plans)* расстра́и-
вать *impf*, расстро́ить *pf*.

thyme /taɪm/ *n* тимья́н.

thyroid /'θaɪrɔɪd/ *n* (~ **gland**) щитови́дная железа́.

tiara /tɪ'ɑːrə/ *n* тиа́ра.

tick /tɪk/ *n (noise)* ти́канье; *(mark)* пти́чка; *vi* ти́кать *impf*, ти́кнуть *pf*; *vt* отмеча́ть *impf*, отме́тить *pf* пти́чкой; ~ **off** *(scold)* отде́лывать *impf*, отде́-
лать *pf*.

ticket /'tɪkɪt/ *n* биле́т; *(label)* ярлы́к; *(season ~)* ка́рточка; *(cloakroom ~)* номеро́к; *(receipt)* квита́нция; ~ **collector**

контролёр; ~ **office** (билéтная) кácca.

tickle /'tɪk(ə)l/ *n* щекóтка; *vt* щекотáть *impf*, по~ *pf*; (*amuse*) весели́ть *impf*, раз~ *pf*; *vi* щекотáть *impf*, по~ *pf impers*: **my throat** ~**s** у меня́ щекóчет в гóрле. **ticklish** /'tɪklɪʃ/ *adj* (*fig*) щекотли́вый; **to be** ~ боя́ться *impf* щекóтки.

tidal /'taɪd(ə)l/ *adj* прили́во-отли́вный; ~ **wave** прили́вная волнá.

tide /taɪd/ *n* прили́в и отли́в; **high** ~ прили́в; **low** ~ отли́в; (*current, tendency*) течéние; **the** ~ **turns** (*fig*) собы́тия принимáют другóй оборóт; *vt*: ~ **over** помогáть *impf*, помóчь *pf* +*dat of person* спрáвиться (*difficulty* с+*instr*); **will this money** ~ **you over?** вы протя́нете с э́тими деньгáми?

tidiness /'taɪdɪnɪs/ *n* аккурáтность. **tidy** /-dɪ/ *adj* аккурáтный; (*considerable*) порядочный; *vt* убирáть *impf*, убрáть *pf*; приводи́ть *impf*, привести́ *pf* в поря́док.

tie /taɪ/ *n* (*garment*) гáлстук; (*cord*) связь; (*link; tech*) связь; (*equal points etc.*) рáвный счёт; **end in a** ~ закáнчиваться *impf*, закóнчиться *pf* вничью́; (*burden*) обу́за; *pl* (*bonds*) у́зы (уз) *pl*; *vt* связывать *impf*, связáть *pf* (*also fig*); (~ **up**) завя́зывать, завязáть; (*restrict*) ограни́чивать *impf*, ограни́чить *pf*; ~ **down** (*fasten*) привя́зывать *impf*, привязáть *pf*; ~ **up** (*tether*) привя́зывать *impf*, привязáть *pf*; (*parcel*) перевя́зывать *impf*, перевязáть *pf*; *vi* (*be* ~*d*) завя́зываться *impf*, завязáться *pf*; (*sport*) сыгрáть

pf вничью́; ~ **in, up, with** совпадáть *impf*, совпáсть *pf* с+*instr*.

tier /tɪə(r)/ *n* ряд, я́рус.

tiger /'taɪɡə(r)/ *n* тигр.

tight /taɪt/ *adj* (*cramped*) тéсный; у́зкий; (*strict*) стрóгий; (*taut*) тугóй; ~ **corner** *fig* трудное положéние. **tighten** /-t(ə)n/ *vt* & *i* натя́гивать *impf*, натяну́ться *pf*; (*clench, contract*) сжимáть(ся) *impf*, сжáться *pf*; ~ **one's belt** потуже затя́гивать *impf*, затяну́ть пояс (*also fig*); ~ **up** (*discipline etc.*) подтя́гивать *impf*, подтяну́ть *pf* (*coll*). **tightly** /-lɪ/ *adv* (*strongly*) прóчно; (*closely, cramped*) тéсно. **tightrope** *n* натя́нутый канáт. **tights** /taɪts/ *pl* колгóтки (-ток) *pl*.

tile /taɪl/ *n* (*roof*) черепи́ца (*also collect*); (*decorative*) кáфель *m* (*also collect*); *vt* крыть *impf*, по~ *pf* черепи́цей, кáфелем. **tiled** /-d/ *adj* (*roof*) черепи́чный; (*floor*) кáфельный.

till[1] /tɪl/ *prep* до+*gen*; **not** ~ тóлько (**Friday** в пя́тницу; **the next day** на сле́дующий день); *conj* покá не; **not** ~ тóлько когдá.

till[2] /tɪl/ *n* кácca.

till[3] /tɪl/ *vt* возде́лывать *impf*, возде́лать *pf*.

tiller /'tɪlə(r)/ *n* (*naut*) ру́мпель *m*.

tilt /tɪlt/ *n* наклóн; **at full** ~ пóлным хóдом; *vt* & *i* наклоня́ть(ся) *impf*, наклони́ть(ся) *pf*; (*heel* (*over*)) крени́ться *impf*, на~ *pf*.

timber /'tɪmbə(r)/ *n* лесоматериáл.

time /taɪm/ *n* врéмя *neut*; (*occasion*) раз; (*mus*) такт; (*sport*) тайм; *pl* (*period*) временá *pl*

in comparison) раз; **five ~s as big** в пять раз бо́льше; (*multiplication*) **four ~s four** четы́режды четы́ре; **~ and ~ again, ~ after ~** не раз, ты́сячу раз; **at a ~** ра́зом, одновреме́нно; **at the same ~** в то же вре́мя; **at ~s** времена́ми; **at the same ~** в то же вре́мя; **before my ~** до меня́; **for a long ~** до́лго; (*up to now*) **давно́; for the ~ being** пока́; **from ~ to ~** вре́мя от вре́мени; (*early enough*) во́-время; **~ with ~**) со вре́менем; **in good ~** заблаговре́менно; **in ~ with** в такт +*dat*; **in no ~** момента́льно; **on ~** во́-время; **one at a ~** по одному́; **be in ~** успева́ть *impf*, успе́ть *pf* (**for** к+*dat*, на+*acc*); **have ~ to** (*manage*) успева́ть *impf*, успе́ть *pf* +*inf*; **have a good ~** хорошо́ проводи́ть *impf*, провести́ *pf* вре́мя; **~ is ~** пора́ (**to** +*inf*); **what is the ~?** кото́рый час?; **~ bomb** бо́мба заме́дленного де́йствия; **~-consuming** отнима́ющий мно́го вре́мени; **~ difference** ра́зница во вре́мени; **~-lag** отстава́ние во вре́мени; **~ zone** часово́й по́яс; *vt* (*choose ~*) выбира́ть *impf*, вы́брать *pf* +*gen*; (*ascertain ~ of*) измеря́ть *impf*, изме́рить *pf* вре́мя +*gen*. **timeless** /-lɪs/ *adj* ве́чный. **timely** /-lɪ/ *adj* своевре́менный. **timetable** *n* расписа́ние; гра́фик.

mid /'tɪmɪd/ *adj* ро́бкий.

n /'tɪn/ *n* (*metal*) о́лово; (*container*) ба́нка; (*cake-~*) фо́рма; (*baking ~*) про́тивень *m*; **~ foil** (*оловя́нная фольга́); **~-opener** консе́рвный нож; **~ned food** консе́рвы (-вов) *pl*.

nge /tɪndʒ/ *n* отте́нок; *vt* (*also ~*) слегка́ окра́шивать *impf*,

окра́сить *pf*.

tingle /'tɪŋlɪŋ/ *vi* (*sting*) коло́ть *impf impers*; **my fingers ~** у меня́ ко́лет па́льцы; **his nose ~d** with the cold моро́з пощи́пывал ему́ нос; (*burn*) горе́ть *impf*.

tinker /'tɪŋkə(r)/ *vi*: **~ with** вози́ться *impf* с+*instr*.

tinkle /'tɪŋk(ə)l/ *n* звон, звя́канье; *vi* (& *t*) звене́ть *impf* (+*instr*).

tinsel /'tɪns(ə)l/ *n* мишура́.

tint /tɪnt/ *n* отте́нок; *vt* подкра́шивать *impf*, подкра́сить *pf*.

tiny /'taɪnɪ/ *adj* кро́шечный.

tip[1] /tɪp/ *n* (*end*) ко́нчик.

tip[2] /tɪp/ *n* (*money*) чаевы́е (-ы́х) *pl*; (*advice*) сове́т; (*dump*) сва́лка; *vt* & *i* (*tilt*) наклоня́ть(ся) *impf*, наклони́ть(ся) *pf*; (*give*) дава́ть *impf*, дать *pf* (*person* +*dat*; *money* де́ньги на чай, *information* ча́стную информа́цию); **~ out** выва́ливать *impf*, вы́валить *pf*; **~ over, up** (*vt* & *i*) опроки́дывать(ся) *impf*, опроки́нуть(ся) *pf*.

Tippex /'tɪpeks/ *n* (*propr*) бели́ла.

tipple /'tɪp(ə)l/ *n* напи́ток.

tipsy /'tɪpsɪ/ *adj* подвы́пивший.

tiptoe /'tɪptəʊ/ *n*: **on ~** на цы́почках.

tip-top /'tɪptɒp/ *adj* превосхо́дный.

tirade /taɪ'reɪd/ *n* тира́да.

tire /'taɪə(r)/ *vt* (*weary*) утомля́ть *impf*, утоми́ть *pf*; *vi* утомля́ться *impf*, утоми́ться *pf*. **tired** /'taɪəd/ *adj* уста́лый; **be ~ of: I am ~ of him** он мне надое́л; **I am ~ of playing** мне надое́ло игра́ть; **~ out** изму́ченный. **tiredness** /'taɪədnɪs/ *n* уста́лость. **tireless** /'taɪəlɪs/ *adj* неутоми́мый. **tiresome** /'taɪəsəm/

adj надоéдливый. **tiring** /'taɪərɪŋ/ *adj* утомительный.

tissue /'tɪʃu:/ *n* ткань; (*handkerchief*) бумáжная салфéтка. **tissue-paper** *n* папирóсная бумáга.

tit¹ /tɪt/ *n* (*bird*) синица.

tit² /tɪt/ *n:* ~ **for tat** зуб за зуб.

titbit /'tɪtbɪt/ *n* лáкомый кусóк; (*news*) пикáнтная нóвость.

titillate /'tɪtɪ,leɪt/ *vt* щекотáть *impf*, по~ *pf*.

title /'taɪt(ə)l/ *n* (*of book etc.*) заглáвие; (*rank*) звáние; (*sport*) звáние чемпиóна; ~**-holder** чемпиóн; ~**-page** титульный лист; ~ **role** заглáвная роль. **titled** /'taɪt(ə)ld/ *adj* титулóванный.

titter /'tɪtə(r)/ *n* хихиканье; *vi* хихикать *impf*, хихикнуть *pf*.

to /tu:/ *prep* (*town, a country, theatre, school, etc.*) в+*acc*; (*the sea, the moon, the ground, postoffice, meeting, concert, north, etc.*) на+*acc*; (*the doctor; towards, up* ~; ~ *one's surprise etc.*) к+*dat*; (*with accompaniment of*) под+*acc*; (*in toast*) за+*acc*; (*time*): **ten minutes** ~ **three** без десяти три; (*compared with*) в сравнéнии с+*instr*; **it is ten** ~ **one** that дéвять из десяти за то, что; ~ **the left (right)** налéво (напрáво); (*in order to*) чтóбы +*inf*; *adv:* **shut the door** ~ закрыть дверь; **come** ~ приходить *impf*, прийти *pf* в сознáние; ~ **and fro** взад и вперёд.

toad /təʊd/ *n* жáба. **toadstool** *n* погáнка.

toast /təʊst/ *n* (*bread*) поджáренный хлеб; (*drink*) тост; *vt* (*bread*) поджáривать *impf*, поджáрить *pf*; (*drink*) пить *impf*, вы~ *pf* за здорóвье +*gen*.

toaster /'təʊstə(r)/ *n* тóстер.

tobacco /tə'bækəʊ/ *n* табáк. **tobacconist's** /-kənɪsts/ *n* (*sho*... табáчный магазин.

toboggan /tə'bɒgən/ *n* сáн(-ней) *pl; vi* катáться *impf* с саня́х.

today /tə'deɪ/ *adv* сегóдня; (*now adays*) в нáши дни; *n* сегó́дняшний день *m*; ~**'s newspap** сегóдняшняя газéта.

toddler /'tɒdlə/r/ *n* малы́ш.

toe /təʊ/ *n* пáлец ноги; (*of so etc.*) носóк; *vt:* ~ **the line** (*fi* ходи́ть *indet* по стрýнке.

toffee /'tɒfɪ/ *n* (*substance*) ири́ (*a single* ~) ири́ска.

together /tə'geðə(r)/ *adv* вмéст (*simultaneously*) одновремéнно.

toil /tɔɪl/ *n* тяжёлый труд; трудиться *impf*.

toilet /'tɔɪlɪt/ *n* туалéт; ~ **pap** туалéтная бумáга. **toiletrie** /-trɪz/ *n pl* туалéтные принадлéжности *f pl*.

token /'təʊkən/ *n* (*sign*) знá (*coin substitute*) жетóн; **as a** of в знак ~дат симвó лический.

tolerable /'tɒlərəb(ə)l/ *adj* терпи́ мый; (*satisfactory*) удовлетвори́тельный. **tolerance** /'tɒlərəns/ *n* терпи́мость. **tole ant** /-rənt/ *adj* терпи́мый. **tole ate** /-,reɪt/ *vt* терпéть *impf*, по *pf*; (*allow*) допускáть *impf*, до пусти́ть *pf*. **toleration** /,tɒlə 'reɪ/ə/n/ *n* терпи́мость.

toll¹ /təʊl/ *n* (*duty*) пóшлин **take its** ~ скáзываться *imp* сказáться *pf* (**on** на+*prep*).

toll² /təʊl/ *vi* звони́ть *impf*, по~ *pf*.

tom(-cat) /'tɒm(kæt)/ *n* кот.

tomato /tə'mɑːtəʊ/ *n* помидóр *attrib* томáтный.

◑mb /tuːm/ n моги́ла. **tomb-
stone** /'təʊm-/ n надгро́бный ка́-
мень m.
◑mboy /'tɒmbɔɪ/ n сорване́ц.
◑me /təʊm/ n том.
◑morrow /tə'mɒrəʊ/ adv за́в-
тра; n за́втрашний день m; ~
morning за́втра у́тром; **the day
after** ~ послеза́втра; **see you** ~
до за́втра.
◑n /tʌn/ n то́нна; (pl, lots)
ма́сса.
◑ne /təʊn/ n тон; vt: ~ **down**
смягча́ть impf, смягчи́ть pf; ~
up тонизи́ровать impf & pf.
◑ngs /tɒŋz/ n щипцы́ (-цо́в) pl.
◑ngue /tʌŋ/ n язы́к; ~**-in-cheek**
с насме́шкой, ирони́чески;
~**-tied** косноязы́чный;
~**-twister** скорогово́рка.
◑nic /'tɒnɪk/ n (med) тонизи́-
рующее сре́дство; (mus) то́-
ника; (drink) напи́ток «то́ник».
◑night /tə'naɪt/ adv сего́дня ве́-
чером.
◑nnage /'tʌnɪdʒ/ n тонна́ж.
◑nsil /'tɒns(ə)l/ n минда́лина.
◑nsillitis /ˌtɒnsɪ'laɪtɪs/ n тон-
зилли́т.
◑o /tuː/ adv сли́шком; (also)
та́кже, то́же; (very) о́чень;
(moreover) к тому́ же; **none** ~
не сли́шком.
◑ol /tuːl/ n инструме́нт; (fig)
ору́дие.
◑ot /tuːt/ n гудо́к; vi гуде́ть
impf.
◑oth /tuːθ/ n зуб; (tech) зубе́ц;
attrib зубно́й; ~**brush** зубна́я
щётка. **toothache** n зубна́я
боль. **toothless** /-lɪs/ adj беззу́-
бый. **toothpaste** n зубна́я
па́ста. **toothpick** n зубочи́стка.
◑oothy /-θɪ/ adj зуба́стый
(coll).
◑p¹ /tɒp/ n (toy) волчо́к.
◑p² /tɒp/ n (of object; fig) верх;

(of hill etc.) верши́на; (of tree)
верху́шка; (of head) маку́шка;
(lid) кры́шка; (upper part)
ве́рхняя часть; ~ **hat** цили́ндр;
~**-heavy** переве́шивающий в
свое́й ве́рхней ча́сти; ~**-secret**
соверше́нно секре́тный; **on** ~
of (position) на+prep, сверх
+gen; (on to) на+acc; **on** ~ **of
everything** сверх всего́; **from** ~
to bottom све́рху до́низу; **at the**
~ **of one's voice** во весь го́лос;
at ~ **speed** во весь опо́р; adj
ве́рхний, вы́сший, са́мый вы-
со́кий; (foremost) пе́рвый; vt
(cover) покрыва́ть impf, по-
кры́ть pf; (exceed) превосхо-
ди́ть impf, превзойти́ pf; (cut
off) обреза́ть impf, обре́зать
pf ве́рхушку +gen; ~ **up** (with
liquid) долива́ть impf, до-
ли́ть pf.
topic /'tɒpɪk/ n те́ма, предме́т.
topical /'tɒpɪk(ə)l/ adj ак-
туа́льный.
topless /'tɒplɪs/ adj с об-
нажённой гру́дью.
topmost /'tɒpməʊst/ adj са́мый
ве́рхний; са́мый ва́жный.
topographical /ˌtɒpə'ɡræfɪk(ə)l/
adj топографи́ческий. **topography** /tə'pɒɡrəfɪ/ n топо-
гра́фия.
topple /'tɒp(ə)l/ vt & i опроки́-
дывать(ся) impf, опроки́-
нуть(ся) pf.
topsy-turvy /ˌtɒpsɪ'tɜːvɪ/ adj
поверну́тый вверх дном; (disorderly) беспоря́дочный; adv
вверх дном.
torch /tɔːtʃ/ n электри́ческий
фона́рь m; (flaming) фа́кел.
torment /'tɔːment/ n муче́ние,
му́ка; vt му́чить impf, за-,
из- pf.
tornado /tɔː'neɪdəʊ/ n торна́до
neut indecl.

torpedo /tɔː'piːdəʊ/ n торпе́да; vt торпеди́ровать impf & pf.

torrent /'tɒrənt/ n пото́к **torrential** /tə'renʃ(ə)l/ adj (rain) проли́вный.

torso /'tɔːsəʊ/ n ту́ловище; (art) торс.

tortoise /'tɔːtəs/ n черепа́ха. **tortoise-shell** n черепа́ха.

tortuous /'tɔːtjʊəs/ adj изви́листый.

torture /'tɔːtʃə(r)/ n пы́тка; (fig) му́ка; vt пыта́ть impf; (torment) му́чить impf, за∼, из∼.

toss /tɒs/ n бросо́к; **win (lose) the ∼** (не) выпада́ть impf, вы́пасть pf жре́бий impers (**I won the ∼** мне вы́пал жре́бий); vt броса́ть impf, бро́сить pf; (coin) подбра́сывать impf, подбро́сить pf; (head) вски́дывать impf, вски́нуть pf; (salad) переме́шивать impf, перемеша́ть pf; vi (in bed) мета́ться impf; ∼ **aside, away** отбра́сывать impf, отбро́сить pf; ∼ **up** броса́ть impf, бро́сить pf жре́бий.

tot[1] /tɒt/ n (child) малы́ш; (of liquor) глото́к.

tot[2] /tɒt/ vt & i : ∼ **up** (vt) скла́дывать impf, сложи́ть pf; (vi) равня́ться impf (**to** +dat).

total /'təʊt(ə)l/ n ито́г, су́мма; adj о́бщий; (complete) по́лный; **in ∼** в це́лом, вме́сте; vt подсчи́тывать impf, подсчита́ть pf; vi равня́ться impf +dat. **totalitarian** /ˌtəʊtælɪ'teərɪən/ adj тоталита́рный. **totality** /təʊ'tælɪtɪ/ n вся су́мма це́ликом; **the ∼ of** весь. **totally** /'təʊtəlɪ/ adv соверше́нно.

totter /'tɒtə(r)/ vi шата́ться impf.

touch /tʌtʃ/ n прикоснове́ние; (sense) осяза́ние; (shade) отте́нок; (taste) при́вкус; (small

amount) чу́точка; (of illnes▌ лёгкий при́ступ; **get in** ∼ wi▌ свя́зываться impf, связа́ться c+instr; **keep in (lose)** ∼ wi▌ подде́рживать impf, подде жа́ть (теря́ть impf, по∼ p▌ связь, конта́кт c+instr; **put th▌ finishing** ∼**es to** отде́лыва impf, отде́лать pf; vt (light▌ прикаса́ться impf, прикос▌ ну́ться pf к+dat; каса́ться imp коснýться pf +gen; (also dr turb; affect) тро́гать impf, тр▌ нуть pf; (be comparable wit▌ идти́ impf в сравне́ние c+instr▌ vi (be contiguous; come into co▌ tact) соприкаса́ться impf, c▌ прикоснýться pf; ∼ **dow** приземля́ться impf, приземли́ться pf (aeron) соверша́ть impf, соверши́ть pf поса́дку; ∼ **(up)on** (fig) каса́ться impf, ко▌ нýться pf +gen; ∼ **up** попра▌ вля́ть impf, попра́вить p▌ **touched** /tʌtʃt/ adj тро́нуты▌ **touchiness** /'tʌtʃɪnɪs/ n оби́дчи▌ вость. **touching** /'tʌtʃɪŋ/ adj тро́гательный. **touchstone** /'tʌtʃstəʊn/ n про́бный ка́мень m. **touch▌ /'tʌtʃɪ/ adj оби́дчивый.

tough /tʌf/ adj жёсткий; (du▌ able) про́чный; (difficult) тру́д ный; (hardy) выно́сливы▌ **toughen** /'tʌf(ə)n/ vt & i д▌ лать(ся) impf, c∼ pf жёстки▌

tour /tʊə(r)/ n (journey) путеше́ ствие, пое́здка; (excursion) э▌ ску́рсия; (of artistes) гастро́л f pl; (of duty) объе́зд; vi &▌ путеше́ствовать impf (п▌ +dat); (theat) гастроли́ровать impf. **tourism** /'tʊərɪz(ə)m/ n т▌ ри́зм. **tourist** /'tʊərɪst/ n тури́с ∼ка.

tournament /'tʊənəmənt/ n турни́р.

tousle /'tʊz(ə)l/ vt взъеро́шивать impf, взъеро́шить

(coll).

out /taʊt/ n зазыва́ла m; (ticket ~) жучо́к

ow /təʊ/ vt букси́ровать impf; n: on ~ на букси́ре.

owards /tə'wɔːdz/ prep к+dat.

owel /'taʊəl/ n полоте́нце.

ower /'taʊə(r)/ n ба́шня; vi вы́-ситься impf, возвыша́ться impf (above над+instr).

own /taʊn/ n го́род; attrib городско́й; ~ hall ра́туша. **townsman** /'taʊnzmən/ n горожа́нин.

oxic /'tɒksɪk/ adj токси́ческий.

oy /tɔɪ/ n игру́шка; vi: ~ with (sth in hands) верте́ть impf in рука́х; (trifle with) игра́ть impf (c)+instr.

race /treɪs/ n след; vt (track (down)) высле́живать impf, вы́следить pf; (copy) кальки́ровать impf, c~ pf; ~ out (plan) набра́сывать impf, наброса́ть pf; (map, diagram) черти́ть impf, на~ pf.

tracing-paper /'treɪsɪŋ,peɪpə(r)/ n ка́лька.

track /træk/ n (path) доро́жка; (mark) след; (rly) путь m, (sport, on tape) доро́жка; (on record) за́пись; ~ suit трениро́вочный костю́м; off the beaten ~ в глуши́; go off the ~ (fig) отклоня́ться impf, отклони́ться pf от те́мы; keep ~ of следи́ть impf за+instr; lose ~ of теря́ть impf, по~ pf след+gen; vt просле́живать impf, проследи́ть pf; ~ down высле́живать impf, вы́следить pf.

tract¹ /trækt/ n (land) простра́нство.

tract² /trækt/ n (pamphlet) брошю́ра.

tractor /'træktə(r)/ n тра́ктор.

trade /treɪd/ n торго́вля; (occupation) профе́ссия, ремесло́; ~

mark фабри́чная ма́рка; ~ **union** профсою́з; ~**unionist** член профсою́за; vi торгова́ть impf (in +instr); vt (swap like things) обме́ниваться impf, обменя́ться pf +instr; (~ for sth different) обме́нивать impf, обменя́ть pf (for на+acc); ~ in сдава́ть impf, сдать pf в счёт поку́пки но́вого. **trader**, **tradesman** /-də(r), -dzmən/ n торго́вец. **trading** /-dɪŋ/ n торго́вля.

tradition /trə'dɪʃ(ə)n/ n тради́ция. **traditional** /-n(ə)l/ adj традицио́нный. **traditionally** /-nəlɪ/ adv по тради́ции.

traffic /'træfɪk/ n движе́ние; (trade) торго́вля; ~ jam про́бка; vi торгова́ть impf (in +instr). **trafficker** /-kə(r)/ n торго́вец (in +instr). **traffic-lights** pl светофо́р.

tragedy /'trædʒɪdɪ/ n траге́дия. **tragic** /'trædʒɪk/ adj траги́ческий.

trail /treɪl/ n (trace, track) след; (path) тропи́нка; vt (track) высле́живать impf, вы́следить pf; vt & i (drag) таска́ть(ся) indet, тащи́ть(ся) det. **trailer** /-lə(r)/ n (on vehicle) прице́п; (cin) (ки-но)ро́лик.

train /treɪn/ n по́езд; (of dress) шлейф; vt (instruct) обуча́ть impf, обучи́ть pf (in +dat); (prepare) гото́вить impf (for к+dat); (sport) трениро́вать impf, на~ pf; (animals) дрессирова́ть impf, вы́~ pf; (aim) наводи́ть impf, навести́ pf; (plant) направля́ть impf, напра́вить pf рост+gen; vi приготовля́ться impf, пригото́виться pf (for к+dat); (sport) трениро́ваться impf, на~ pf. **trainee** /-'niː/ n стажёр,

практика́нт. **trainer** /-nə(r)/ n (sport) тре́нер; (of animals) дрессиро́вщик; (shoe) кроссо́вка. **training** /-nɪŋ/ n обуче́ние; (sport) трениро́вка; (of animals) дрессиро́вка; ~**college** (teachers') педагоги́ческий институ́т.

traipse /treɪps/ vi таска́ться indet, тащи́ться det.

trait /treɪ/ n черта́.

traitor /ˈtreɪtə(r)/ n преда́тель m, ~ница.

trajectory /trəˈdʒektərɪ/ n траекто́рия.

tram /træm/ n трамва́й.

tramp /træmp/ n (vagrant) бродя́га m; vi (walk heavily) то́пать impf. **trample** /-p(ə)l/ vt топта́ть impf, по~, ис~ pf; ~ down вы́таптывать impf, вы́топтать pf; ~ **on** (fig) попира́ть impf, попра́ть pf.

trampoline /ˌtræmpəˈliːn/ n бату́т.

trance /trɑːns/ n транс.

tranquil /ˈtræŋkwɪl/ adj споко́йный. **tranquillity** /-ˈkwɪlɪtɪ/ n споко́йствие. **tranquillize** /ˈtræŋkwɪˌlaɪz/ vt успока́ивать impf, успоко́ить pf. **tranquillizer** /-ˌlaɪzə(r)/ n транквилиза́тор.

transact /trænˈzækt/ vt (business) вести́ impf; (a deal) заключа́ть impf, заключи́ть pf. **transaction** /-ˈzækʃ(ə)n/ n де́ло, сде́лка; pl (publications) труды́ m pl.

transatlantic /ˌtrænzətˈlæntɪk/ adj трансатланти́ческий.

transcend /trænˈsend/ vt превосходи́ть impf, превзойти́ pf. **transcendental** /ˌtrænsenˈdent(ə)l/ adj (philos.) трансценде́нтальный.

transcribe /trænˈskraɪb/ vt (copy out) перепи́сывать impf,

переписа́ть pf. **transcript** /ˈtrænskrɪpt/ n ко́пия. **transcription** /trænˈskrɪpʃ(ə)n/ n (copy) ко́пия.

transfer n /ˈtrænsfɜː(r)/ n (of objects) перено́с, перемеще́ние; (of money; of people) перево́д; (of property) переда́ча; (design) переводна́я карти́нка; vt /træn'fɜː(r)/ (objects) переноси́ть impf, перенести́ pf; переме-ща́ть impf, перемести́ть pf (money; people; design) переводи́ть impf, перевести́ pf; (property) передава́ть impf, переда́ть pf; vi (to different job) переходи́ть impf, перейти́ pf (change trains etc.) переса́живаться impf, пересе́сть pf. **transferable** /ˈtrænsˌfɜːrəb(ə)l/ adj допуска́ющий переда́чу.

transfix /trænsˈfɪks/ vt (fig) прико́вывать impf, прикова́ть pf к ме́сту.

transform /trænsˈfɔːm/ vt & (i) преобразо́вывать(ся) impf преобразова́ть(ся) pf; ~ **into** (i) превраща́ть(ся) impf, превра́тить(ся) pf в+acc. **transformation** /ˌtrænsfəˈmeɪʃ(ə)n/ n преобразова́ние; превраще́ние. **transformer** /trænsˈfɔːmə(r)/ n трансформа́тор.

transfusion /trænsˈfjuːʒ(ə)n/ n перелива́ние (кро́ви).

transgress /trænzˈgres/ vt нару-ша́ть impf, нару́шить pf; (sin) греши́ть impf, за~ pf. **transgression** /-ˈgreʃ(ə)n/ n нару-ше́ние; (sin) грех.

transience /ˈtrænzɪəns/ n мимолётность. **transient** /ˈtrænzɪənt/ adj мимолётный.

transistor /trænˈzɪstə(r)/ n транзи́стор; ~ **radio** транзи́стор-ный приёмник.

transit /ˈtrænzɪt/ n транзи́т; **in** ~

(*goods*) при перево́зке; (*person*) по пути́; ~ **camp** транзи́тный ла́герь *m*. **transition** /-'zɪʃ(ə)n/ *n* перехо́д. **transitional** /-'zɪʃənəl/ *adj* перехо́дный. **transitive** /'trænsɪtɪv/ *adj* перехо́дный. **transitory** /'trænsɪtərɪ/ *adj* мимолётный.

ranslate /træn'sleɪt/ *vt* переводи́ть *impf*, перевести́ *pf*. **translation** /-'leɪʃən/ *n* перево́д. **translator** /-'leɪtə(r)/ *n* перево́дчик.

ranslucent /trænz'lu:s(ə)nt/ *adj* полупрозра́чный.

ransmission /trænz'mɪʃ(ə)n/ *n* переда́ча. **transmit** /-'mɪt/ *vt* передава́ть *impf*, переда́ть *pf*. **transmitter** /-'mɪtə(r)/ *n* (ра́дио)переда́тчик.

ransparency /træns'pærənsɪ/ *n* (*phot*) диапозити́в. **transparent** /-rənt/ *adj* прозра́чный.

ranspire /træn'spaɪə(r)/ *vi* (*become known*) обнару́живаться *impf*, обнару́житься *pf*; (*occur*) случа́ться *impf*, случи́ться *pf*.

ransplant *vt* /træns'plɑ:nt/ переса́живать *impf*, пересади́ть *pf*; (*med*) де́лать *impf*, с~ *pf* переса́дку+*gen*; *n* /'trænsplɑ:nt/ (*med*) переса́дка.

ransport *n* /'trænspɔ:t/ (*various senses*) тра́нспорт; (*conveyance*) перево́зка; *attrib* тра́нспортный; *vt* /træns'pɔ:t/ перевози́ть *impf*, перевезти́ *pf*. **transportation** /ˌtrænspɔ:-'teɪʃ(ə)n/ *n* тра́нспорт, перево́зка.

ranspose /træns'pəʊz/ *vt* переставля́ть *impf*, переста́вить *pf*; (*mus*) транспони́ровать *impf* & *pf*. **transposition** /ˌtrænspə-'zɪʃ(ə)n/ *n* перестано́вка (*mus*) транспони́ровка.

ransverse /'trænzvɜːs/ *adj* по-

перечный.

transvestite /trænz'vestaɪt/ *n* трансвести́т.

trap /træp/ *n* лову́шка (*also fig*), западня́; *vt* (*catch*) лови́ть *impf*, пойма́ть *pf* (в лову́шку); (*jam*) защемля́ть *impf*, защеми́ть *pf*. **trapdoor** *n* люк.

trapeze /trə'pi:z/ *n* трапе́ция.

trapper /'træpə(r)/ *n* звероло́в.

trappings /'træpɪŋz/ *n pl* (*fig*) (*exterior attributes*) вне́шние атрибу́ты *m pl*; (*adornments*) украше́ния *neut pl*.

trash /træʃ/ *n* дрянь (*coll*). **trashy** /-ʃɪ/ *adj* дрянно́й.

trauma /'trɔ:mə/ *n* тра́вма. **traumatic** /-'mætɪk/ *adj* травмати́ческий.

travel /'træv(ə)l/ *n* путеше́ствие; ~ **agency** бюро́ *neut indecl* путеше́ствий; ~ **sick: be** ~**-sick** ука́чивать *impf*; укача́ть *pf impers* +*acc*; **I am** ~**-sick in cars** меня́ в маши́не ука́чивает; *vi* путеше́ствовать *impf*; *vt* объезжа́ть *impf*, объе́хать *pf*. **traveller** /-lə(r)/ *n* путеше́ственник; (*salesman*) коммивояжёр; ~'**s cheque** тури́стский чек.

traverse /'trævəs/ *vt* пересека́ть *impf*, пересе́чь *pf*.

travesty /'trævɪstɪ/ *n* паро́дия.

trawler /'trɔːlə(r)/ *n* тра́улер.

tray /treɪ/ *n* подно́с; **in-** (**out-**)~ корзи́нка для входя́щих (исходя́щих) бума́г.

treacherous /'tretʃərəs/ *adj* преда́тельский; (*unsafe*) надёжный. **treachery** /'tretʃərɪ/ *n* преда́тельство.

treacle /'tri:k(ə)l/ *n* па́тока.

tread /tred/ *n* похо́дка; (*stair*) ступе́нька; (*of tyre*) протекто́р; *vi* ступа́ть *impf*, ступи́ть *pf*; ~ **on** наступа́ть *impf*, наступи́ть *pf* на+*acc*; *vt* топта́ть *impf*.

treason /'tri:z(ə)n/ n изме́на.

treasure /'treʒə(r)/ n сокро́вище; vt высоко́ цени́ть impf.

treasurer /'treʒərə(r)/ n казначе́й. **treasury** /'treʒəri/ n (also fig) сокро́вищница; **the T~** госуда́рственное казначе́йство.

treat /tri:t/ n (pleasure) удово́льствие; (entertainment) угоще́ние; vt (have as guest) угоща́ть impf, угости́ть pf (to +instr); (med) лечи́ть impf (for +gen; with +instr); (behave towards) обраща́ться impf c+instr; (process) обраба́тывать impf, обрабо́тать pf (with +instr); (discuss) тракто́вать impf o+prep; (regard) относи́ться impf, отнести́сь pf к+dat (as как к+dat). **treatise** /-tis/ n тракта́т. **treatment** /-mənt/ n (behaviour) обраще́ние; (med) лече́ние; (processing) обрабо́тка; (discussion) тракто́вка. **treaty** /-ti/ n догово́р.

treble /'treb(ə)l/ adj тройно́й; (trebled) утро́енный; adv втро́е; n (mus) дискант; vt & i утра́ивать(ся) impf, утро́ить(ся) pf.

tree /tri:/ n де́рево.

trek /trek/ n (migration) пересе́ление; (journey) путеше́ствие; vi (migrate) переселя́ться impf, пересели́ться pf; (journey) путеше́ствовать impf.

trellis /'trelis/ n шпале́ра; (for creepers) решётка.

tremble /'tremb(ə)l/ vi дрожа́ть impf (with от+gen). **trembling** /-blɪŋ/ n дрожь; **in fear and ~** трепеща́.

tremendous /trɪ'mendəs/ adj (huge) огро́мный; (excellent) потряса́ющий.

tremor /'tremə(r)/ n дрожь; (earthquake) толчо́к. **tremulous**

/-mjuləs/ adj дрожа́щий.

trench /trentʃ/ n кана́ва, ров; (mil) око́п.

trend /trend/ n направле́ние, тенде́нция. **trendy** /-dɪ/ adj мо́дный.

trepidation /,trepɪ'deɪʃ(ə)n/ n тре́пет.

trespass /'trespəs/ n (on property) наруше́ние грани́ц; vi наруша́ть impf, нару́шить pf грани́цу (on +gen); (fig) вторга́ться impf, вто́ргнуться pf (on в+acc). **trespasser** /-sə(r)/ n наруши́тель.

trestle /'tres(ə)l/ n ко́злы (-зел, -злам) pl; **~ table** стол на ко́злах.

trial /traɪəl/ n (test) испыта́ние (also ordeal), про́ба; (law) проце́сс, суд; (sport) попы́тка; **on ~** (probation) на испыта́нии; (of objects) взя́тый на про́бу; (law) под судо́м; **~ and error** ме́тод проб и оши́бок.

triangle /'traɪæŋg(ə)l/ n треуго́льник. **triangular** /-'æŋgjʊlə(r)/ adj треуго́льный.

tribal /'traɪb(ə)l/ adj племенно́й. **tribe** /traɪb/ n пле́мя neut.

tribulation /,trɪbjʊ'leɪʃ(ə)n/ n го́ре, несча́стье.

tribunal /traɪ'bjuːn(ə)l/ n трибуна́л.

tributary /'trɪbjʊtəri/ n прито́к. **tribute** /'trɪbjuːt/ n дань; **pay ~** (fig) отдава́ть impf, отда́ть pf дань (уваже́ния) (to +dat).

trice /traɪs/ n: **in a ~** мгнове́нно.

trick /trɪk/ n (ruse) хи́трость; (deception) обма́н; (conjuring ~) фо́кус; (stunt trick) (joke) шу́тка; (habit) привы́чка; (cards) взя́тка; **play a ~ on** сыгра́ть impf, сыгра́ть pf шу́тку c+instr; vt обма́нывать impf,

обману́ть *pf.* **trickery** /-kərɪ/ *n* обма́н.

ickle /'trɪk(ə)l/ *vi* сочи́ться *impf.*

ickster /'trɪkstə(r)/ *n* обма́н-щик. **tricky** /-kɪ/ *adj* сло́жный.

icycle /'traɪsɪk(ə)l/ *n* трёх-колёсный велосипе́д.

rifle /'traɪf(ə)l/ *n* пустя́к; **a** ~ (*adv*) немно́го +*gen*; *vi* шути́ть *impf.*, по~ *pf* (**with** c+*instr*). **trifling** /-flɪŋ/ *adj* пустяко́вый.

rigger /'trɪgə(r)/ *n* (*of gun*) куро́к; *vt*: ~ **off** вызыва́ть *impf.*, вы́звать *pf.*

rill /trɪl/ *n* трель.

rilogy /'trɪlədʒɪ/ *n* трило́гия.

rim /trɪm/ *n* поря́док, гото́в-ность; **in fighting** ~ в боево́й гото́вности; **in good** ~ (*sport*) в хоро́шей фо́рме; (*haircut*) под-стри́жка; *adj* опря́тный; *vt* (*cut, clip, cut off*) подреза́ть *impf.*, подре́зать *pf*; (*hair*) под-стрига́ть *impf.*, подстри́чь *pf* (*a dress etc.*) отде́лывать *impf.*, от-де́лать *pf.* **trimming** /-mɪŋ/ *n* (*on dress*) отде́лка; (*to food*) гарни́р.

rinity /'trɪnɪtɪ/ *n* Тро́ица.

rinket /'trɪŋkɪt/ *n* безделу́шка.

rio /'triːəʊ/ *n* три́о *neut indecl*; (*of people*) тро́йка.

rip /trɪp/ *n* пое́здка, путеше́-ствие, экску́рсия; (*business* ~) командиро́вка; *vi* (*stumble* ~ **up**) спотыка́ться *impf.*, спот-кну́ться *pf* (**over** o+*acc*); *vt* (*also* ~ **up**) подставля́ть *impf.*, под-ста́вить *pf* но́жку +*dat* (*also fig*); (*confuse*) запу́тывать *impf.*, запу́тать *pf.*

riple /'trɪp(ə)l/ *adj* тройно́й; (*tripled*) утро́енный; *vt & i* утра́ивать(ся) *impf.*, утро́ить-(ся) *pf.* **triplet** /'trɪplɪt/ *n* (*mus*) трио́ль; (*one of* ~s) близне́ц

(из тро́йни); *pl* тро́йня.

tripod /'traɪpɒd/ *n* трено́жник.

trite /traɪt/ *adj* бана́льный.

triumph /'traɪəmf/ *n* торжество́, побе́да; *vi* торжествова́ть *impf*, вос~ *pf* (**over** над+*instr*). **triumphal** /traɪ'ʌmf(ə)l/ *adj* триумфа́льный. **triumphant** /traɪ'ʌmf(ə)nt/ *adj* (*exultant*) торжеству́ющий; (*victorious*) победоно́сный.

trivia /'trɪvɪə/ *n pl* ме́лочи (-че́й) *pl*. **trivial** /-vɪəl/ *adj* незначи́-тельный. **triviality** /ˌtrɪvɪ'ælɪtɪ/ *n* тривиа́льность. **trivialize** /'trɪvɪəˌlaɪz/ *vt* опошля́ть *impf*, опо́шлить *pf.*

trolley /'trɒlɪ/ *n* теле́жка; (*table on wheels*) сто́лик на колёси-ках. **trolley-bus** *n* тролле́йбус.

trombone /trɒm'bəʊn/ *n* тромбо́н.

troop /truːp/ *n* гру́ппа, отря́д; *pl* (*mil*) войска́ *neut pl*; *vi* идти́ *impf*, по~ *pf* стро́ем.

trophy /'trəʊfɪ/ *n* трофе́й; (*prize*) приз.

tropic /'trɒpɪk/ *n* тро́пик. **trop-ical** /-k(ə)l/ *adj* тропи́ческий.

trot /trɒt/ *n* рысь; *vi* рыси́ть *impf*; (*rider*) е́здить *indet*, е́хать *det*, по~ *pf* ры́сью; (*horse*) ходи́ть *indet*, идти́ *det*, пойти́ *pf* ры́сью.

trouble /'trʌb(ə)l/ *n* (*worry*) бес-поко́йство, трево́га; (*misfor-tune*) беда́; (*unpleasantness*) неприя́тности *f pl*; (*effort, pains*) труд; (*care*) забо́та; (*dis-repair*) неиспра́вность (**with** в+*prep*); (*illness*) боле́знь; **heart** ~ больно́е се́рдце; ~**maker** нарушитель *m*, ~**ница** споко́йствия; **ask for** ~ напра́шиваться *impf*, напро-си́ться *pf* на неприя́тности; **be**

in ~ име́ть *impf* неприя́тности; get into ~ попа́сть *pf* в беду́; take ~ стара́ться *impf*, по~ *pf*; take the ~ труди́ться *impf*, по~ *pf* (+*inf*); the ~ is (that) беда́ в том, что; *vt* (*make anxious, disturb, give pain*) беспоко́ить *impf*; may I ~ you for ...? мо́жно попроси́ть у вас +*acc*?; *vi* (*take the* ~) труди́ться *impf*. **troubled** /'trʌb(ə)ld/ *adj* беспоко́йный. **troublesome** *adj* (*restless, fidgety*) беспоко́йный; (*capricious*) капри́зный; (*difficult*) тру́дный.

trough /trof/ *n* (*for food*) корму́шка.

trounce /traʊns/ *vt* (*beat*) поро́ть *impf*, вы́~ *pf*; (*defeat*) разбива́ть *impf*, разби́ть *pf*.

troupe /truːp/ *n* тру́ппа.

trouser-leg /'traʊzə,leg/ *n* штани́на (*coll*). **trousers** /'traʊzəz/ *n pl* брю́ки (-к) *pl*, штаны́ (-но́в) *pl*.

trout /traʊt/ *n* форе́ль.

trowel /'traʊəl/ *n* (*for building*) мастеро́к; (*garden* ~) садо́вый сово́к.

truancy /'truːənsɪ/ *n* прогу́л. **truant** /'truːənt/ *n* прогу́льщик; play ~ прогу́ливать *impf*, прогуля́ть *pf*.

truce /truːs/ *n* переми́рие.

truck[1] /trʌk/ *n*: have no ~ with не име́ть никаки́х дел с+*instr*.

truck[2] /trʌk/ *n* (*lorry*) грузови́к; (*rly*) ваго́н-платфо́рма.

truculent /'trʌkjʊlənt/ *adj* свире́пый.

trudge /trʌdʒ/ *vi* уста́ло тащи́ться *impf*.

true /truː/ *adj* (*faithful, correct*) ве́рный; (*correct*) пра́вильный; (*story*) правди́вый; (*real*) настоя́щий; come ~ сбыва́ться

impf, сбы́ться *pf*.

truism /'truːɪz(ə)m/ *n* трюи́зм.

truly /'truːlɪ/ *adv* (*sincerely*) и́скренне; (*really, indeed*) действи́тельно; yours ~ пре́данный Вам.

trump /trʌmp/ *n* ко́зырь *m*; бить *impf*, по~ *pf* ко́зырем; ~ up фабрикова́ть *impf*, с~ *pf*.

trumpet /'trʌmpɪt/ *n* труба́; (*proclaim*) труби́ть *impf* о+*prep*. **trumpeter** /-tə(r)/ *n* труба́ч.

truncate /trʌŋ'keɪt/ *vt* усека́ть *impf*, усе́чь *pf*.

truncheon /'trʌntʃ(ə)n/ *n* дуби́нка.

trundle /'trʌnd(ə)l/ *vt & i* ката́ть(ся) *indet*, кати́ть(ся) *det*, по~ *pf*.

trunk /trʌŋk/ *n* (*stem*) ствол; (*anat*) ту́ловище; (*elephant's*) хо́бот; (*box*) сунду́к; *pl* (*swimming*) пла́вки (-вок) *pl*; (*boxing etc.*) трусы́ (-со́в) *pl*; ~ саll вы́зов по междугоро́дному телефо́ну; ~ road магистра́льная доро́га.

truss /trʌs/ *n* (*girder*) фе́рма; (*med*) грыжево́й банда́ж; (*tie up, bird*) свя́зывать *impf*, связа́ть *pf*; (*reinforce*) укрепля́ть *impf*, укрепи́ть *pf*.

trust /trʌst/ *n* дове́рие; (*body of trustees*) опе́ка; (*property held in* ~) дове́рительная со́бственность; (*econ*) трест; take on ~ принима́ть *impf*, приня́ть *pf* на ве́ру; *vt* доверя́ть *impf*, дове́рить *pf* +*dat* (with +*acc*; to +*inf*); *vi* (*hope*) наде́яться *impf*, по~ *pf*. **trustee** /trʌs'tiː/ *n* опеку́н. **trustful, trusting** /-fʊl, -ɪŋ/ *adj* дове́рчивый. **trustworthy** /-,wɜːðɪ, -tɪ/ *adj* надёжный. **trusty** /-,wɜːðɪ, -tɪ/ *adj* надёжный.

truth /truːθ/ *n* пра́вда; tell the

говори́ть *impf*, сказа́ть *pf*
пра́вду; **to tell you the** ~ по
пра́вде говоря́. **truthful** /-fʊl/
adj правди́вый.

y /traɪ/ *n* (*attempt*) попы́тка;
(*test, trial*) испыта́ние, про́ба;
vt (*taste; sample*) про́бовать
impf, по~ *pf*; (*patience*) испы́-
тывать *impf*, испыта́ть *pf*;
(*law*) суди́ть *impf* (**for** за+*acc*);
vi (*endeavour*) стара́ться *impf*,
по~ *pf*; ~ **on** (*clothes*) приме-
ря́ть *impf*, приме́рить *pf*. **try-
ing** /'traɪɪŋ/ *adj* тру́дный.

sar /zɑː(r)/ *n* царь *m*. **tsarina**
/zɑː'riːnə/ *n* цари́ца.

-shirt /'tiːʃɜːt/ *n* футбо́лка.

ιb /tʌb/ *n* ка́дка; (*bath*) ва́нна;
(*of margarine etc.*) упако́вка.

ιbby /'tʌbɪ/ *adj* то́лстенький.

ιbe /tjuːb/ *n* тру́бка, труба́;
(*toothpaste etc.*) тю́бик; (*underground*) метро́ *neut indecl*.

ιber /'tjuːbə(r)/ *n* клу́бень *m*.

tuberculosis /tjʊˌbɜːkjʊ'ləʊsɪs/ *n*
туберкулёз.

ιbing /'tjuːbɪŋ/ *n* тру́бы *m pl*.
tubular /'tjuːbjʊlə(r)/ *adj* тру́б-
чатый.

ιck /tʌk/ *n* (*in garment*)
скла́дка; *vt* (*thrust into, away*)
засо́вывать *impf*, засу́нуть *pf*;
(*hide away*) пря́тать *impf*, с~
pf; ~ **in** (*shirt etc.*) заправля́ть
impf, запра́вить *pf*; ~ **in, up**
(*blanket, skirt*) подтыка́ть *impf*,
подоткну́ть *pf*; ~ **up** (*sleeves*)
засу́чивать *impf*, засучи́ть *pf*;
(*in bed*) укрыва́ть *impf*,
укры́ть *pf*.

uesday /'tjuːzdeɪ/ *n* вто́рник.

uft /tʌft/ *n* пучо́к.

ug /tʌg/ *vt, vi* тяну́ть *impf*, по~ *pf*;
vi (*sharply*) дёргать *impf*,
дёрнуть *pf* (**at** за+*acc*); *n*
рыво́к; (*tugboat*) букси́р.

uition /tjuː'ɪʃ(ə)n/ *n* обуче́ние (**in**

+*dat*).

tulip /'tjuːlɪp/ *n* тюльпа́н.

tumble /'tʌmb(ə)l/ *vi* (*fall*) па́-
дать *impf*, (у)па́сть *pf*; *n* паде́-
ние. **tumbledown** *adj*
полуразру́шенный. **tumbler**
/-blə(r)/ *n* стака́н.

tumour /'tjuːmə(r)/ *n* о́пухоль.

tumult /'tjuːmʌlt/ *n* (*uproar*)
сумато́ха; (*agitation*) волне́-
ние. **tumultuous** /tjʊ-
'mʌltjʊəs/ *adj* шу́мный.

tuna /'tjuːnə/ *n* туне́ц.

tundra /'tʌndrə/ *n* ту́ндра.

tune /tjuːn/ *n* мело́дия; **in** ~ в
тон, (*of instrument*) настро́ен-
ный; **out of** ~ не в тон, фаль-
ши́вый, (*of instrument*)
расстро́енный; **change one's** ~
(пере)меня́ть *pf* тон; *vt* (*instrument*,
radio) настра́ивать *impf*, на-
стро́ить *pf*; (*engine etc.*) регу-
ли́ровать *impf*, от~ *pf*; **in**
настра́ивать *impf*, настро́ить
(*radio*) ра́дио (**to** на+*acc*); *vi*: ~
up настра́ивать *impf*, на-
стро́ить *pf* инструме́нт(ы).
tuneful /-fʊl/ *adj* мелоди́чный.

tuner /'tjuːnə(r)/ *n* (*mus*)
настро́йщик; (*receiver*)
приёмник.

tunic /'tjuːnɪk/ *n* туни́ка; (*of uniform*) ки́тель *m*.

tuning /'tjuːnɪŋ/ *n* настро́йка;
(*of engine*) регулиро́вка; ~**-fork**
камерто́н.

tunnel /'tʌn(ə)l/ *n* тунне́ль *m*; *vi*
прокла́дывать *impf*, проло-
жи́ть *pf* тунне́ль в.

turban /'tɜːbən/ *n* тюрба́н.

turbine /'tɜːbaɪn/ *n* турби́на.

turbulence /'tɜːbjʊləns/ *n* бу́р-
ность; (*aeron*) турбуле́нт-
ность. **turbulent** /-lənt/ *adj*
бу́рный.

tureen /tjʊ'riːn/ *n* су́пник.

turf /tɜːf/ *n* дёрн.
turgid /ˈtɜːdʒɪd/ *adj* (*pompous*) напы́щенный.
Turk /tɜːk/ *n* ту́рок, турча́нка. **Turkey** /ˈtɜːkɪ/ *n* Ту́рция.
turkey /ˈtɜːkɪ/ *n* индю́к, *f* инде́йка; (*dish*) индю́шка.
Turkish /ˈtɜːkɪʃ/ *adj* туре́цкий. **Turkmenistan** /tɜːkˌmenɪˈstɑːn/ *n* Туркмениста́н.
turmoil /ˈtɜːmɔɪl/ *n* (*disorder*) беспоря́док; (*uproar*) сумато́ха.
turn /tɜːn/ *n* (*change of direction*) поворо́т; (*revolution*) оборо́т; (*service*) услу́га; (*change*) измене́ние; (*one's* ~ *to do sth*) о́чередь; (*theat*) но́мер; ~ **of phrase** оборо́т ре́чи; **at every** ~ на ка́ждом шагу́; **by, in turn(s)** по о́череди; *vt* (*handle, key, car around, etc.*) повора́чивать *impf*, поверну́ть *pf*; (*revolve, rotate*) враща́ть *impf*; (*page*; *on its face*) перевёртывать *impf*, переверну́ть *pf*; (*direct*) направля́ть *impf*, напра́вить *pf*; (*cause to become*) де́лать *impf*, с~ *pf* +*instr*; (*on lathe*) точи́ть *impf*; *vi* (*change direction*) повора́чивать *impf*, поверну́ть *pf*; (*rotate*) враща́ться *impf*; (~ *round*) повора́чиваться *impf*, поверну́ться *pf*; (*become*) станови́ться *impf*, стать *pf* +*instr*; ~ **against** ополча́ться *impf*, ополчи́ться *pf* на+*acc*, про́тив+*gen*; ~ **around** *see* ~ **round**; ~ **away** (*vt & i*) отвора́чивать(ся) *impf*, отверну́ть(ся) *pf*; (*refuse admittance*) прогоня́ть *impf*, прогна́ть *pf*; ~ **back** (*vi*) повора́чивать *impf*, поверну́ть *pf* наза́д; (*vt*) (*bend back*) отгиба́ть *impf*, отогну́ть *pf*; ~ **down** (*refuse*) отклоня́ть *impf*, отклони́ть *pf*; (*collar*) отгиба́ть *impf*, отогну́ть *pf*; (*ma*[...] *quieter*) де́лать *impf*, с~ [...] ти́ше; ~ **grey** (*vi*) седе́ть *im*[...] по~ *pf*; ~ **in** (*so as to face i*[...] *wards*) повора́чивать *impf*, п[...] верну́ть *pf* вовну́трь; ~ **insi**[...] **out** вывора́чивать *impf*, выве[...] нуть *pf* наизна́нку; ~ **in**[...] (*change into*) (*vt & i*) превр[...] ща́ть(ся) *impf*, преврати́ть(с[...] *pf* в+*acc*; (*street*) свора́чиват[...] *impf*, сверну́ть *pf* на+*acc*; ~ **o**[...] (*light, radio etc.*) выключа́т[...] *impf*, вы́ключить *pf*; (*tap*) з[...] крыва́ть *impf*, закры́ть *pf*; (*v*[...] (*branch off*) свора́чивать *imp*[...] сверну́ть *pf*; ~ **on** (*light, rad*[...] *etc.*) включа́ть *impf*, включи́т[...] *pf*; (*tap*) открыва́ть *impf*, о[...] кры́ть *pf*; (*attack*) напада́т[...] *impf*, напа́сть *pf* на+*acc*; ~ **o**[...] (*light etc.*): *see* ~ **off**; (*prove t*[...] *be*) ока́зываться *impf*, ока[...] за́ться *pf* (**to be** +*instr*); (*driv*[...] *out*) выгоня́ть *impf*, вы́гнат[...] *pf*; (*pockets*) вывёртыват[...] *impf*, вы́вернуть *pf*; (*be presen*[...] приходи́ть *impf*, прийти *p*[...] (*product*) выпуска́ть *impf*, вы́[...] пустить *pf*; ~ **over** (*page, on i*[...] *face, roll over*) (*vt & i*) пере[...] вёртывать(ся) *impf*, пере[...] верну́ть(ся) *pf*; (*hand over*[...] передава́ть *impf*, переда́ть *p*[...] (*think about*) обду́мывать *imp*[...] обду́мать *pf*; (*overturn*) (*vt & i*[...] опроки́дывать(ся) *impf*, опро[...] ки́нуть(ся) *pf*; ~ **pale** бледне́т[...] *impf*, по~ *pf*; ~ **red** красне́т[...] *impf*, по~ *pf*; ~ **round** (*vi*) (*ro*[...] *tate*; ~ *one's back*; ~ *to face sth*[...] повёртываться *impf*, повер[...] ну́ться *pf*; (~ *to face*) обора́чи[...] ваться *impf*, оберну́ться *pf*; (*vt*[...] повёртывать *impf*, поверну́т[...] *pf*; ~ **sour** скиса́ть *impf*, ски́с[...] нуть *pf*; ~ **to** обраща́ться *imp*[...]

обрати́ться *pf* к+*dat* (for за +*instr*); ~ **up** (*appear*) появля́ться *impf*, появи́ться *pf*; (*be found*) находи́ться *impf*, найти́сь *pf*; (*shorten garment*) подши́ва́ть *impf*, подши́ть *pf*; (*crop up*) подвёртываться *impf*, подверну́ться *pf*; (*bend up; stick up*) (*vt & i*) загиба́ть(ся) *impf*, загну́ть(ся) *pf*; (*make louder*) де́лать *impf*, с~ *pf* гро́мче; ~ **up one's nose** вороти́ть *impf* нос (**at** от+*gen*) (*coll*); ~ **upside down** перевора́чивать *impf*, переверну́ть *pf* вверх дном.
turn-out *n* коли́чество приходя́щих. **turn-up** *n* (*on trousers*) обшла́г.

urner /'tɜːnə/ *n* то́карь *m*.
urning /'tɜːnɪŋ/ *n* (*road*) поворо́т. **turning-point** *n* поворо́тный пункт.
urnip /'tɜːnɪp/ *n* ре́па.
urnover /'tɜːnəʊvə(r)/ *n* (*econ*) оборо́т; (*of staff*) теку́честь рабо́чей си́лы.
urnpike /'tɜːnpaɪk/ *n* доро́жная заста́ва.
urnstile /'tɜːnstaɪl/ *n* турнике́т.
urntable /'tɜːnteɪb(ə)l/ *n* (*rly*) поворо́тный круг; (*gramophone*) диск.
urpentine /'tɜːpəntaɪn/ *n* скипида́р.
urquoise /'tɜːkwɔɪz/ *n* (*material, stone*) бирюза́; *adj* бирюзо́вый.
urret /'tʌrɪt/ *n* ба́шенка.
urtle /'tɜːt(ə)l/ *n* черепа́ха.
turtle-dove /'tɜːt(ə)l‚dʌv/ *n* го́рлица.
usk /tʌsk/ *n* би́вень *m*, клык.
tussle /'tʌs(ə)l/ *n* дра́ка; *vi* дра́ться *impf* (for за+*acc*).
tutor /'tjuːtə(r)/ *n* (*private teacher*) ча́стный дома́шний учи́тель *m*, ~ница; (*univ*) пре-

подава́тель *m*, ~ница; (*primer*) уче́бник; *vt* (*instruct*) обуча́ть *impf*, обучи́ть *pf* (**in** +*dat*); (*give lessons to*) дава́ть *impf*, дать *pf* уро́ки+*dat*; (*guide*) руководи́ть *impf* +*instr*.
tutorial /juː'tɔːrɪəl/ *n* консульта́ция.
tutu /'tuːtuː/ *n* (*ballet*) па́чка.
TV *abbr* (*of* television) ТВ, телеви́дение; (*set*) телеви́зор.
twang /twæŋ/ *n* (*of string*) ре́зкий звук (натя́нутой струны́); (*voice*) гнуса́вый го́лос.
tweak /twiːk/ *n* щипо́к; *vt* щипа́ть *impf*, (у)щипну́ть *pf*.
tweed /twiːd/ *n* твид.
tweezers /'twiːzəz/ *n pl* пинце́т.
twelfth /twelfθ/ *adj & n* двена́дцатый. **twelve** /twelv/ *adj & n* двена́дцать.
twentieth /'twentɪθ/ *adj & n* двадца́тый. **twenty** /'twentɪ/ *adj & n* два́дцать; *pl* (*decade*) двадца́тые го́ды (-до́в) *m pl.*
twice /twaɪs/ *adv* два́жды; ~ **as** вдво́е, в два ра́за +*comp*.
twiddle /'twɪd(ə)l/ *vt* (*turn*) верте́ть *impf* +*acc, instr*; (*toy with*) игра́ть *impf* +*instr*; ~ **one's thumbs** (*fig*) безде́льничать *impf.*
twig /twɪg/ *n* ве́точка, прут.
twilight /'twaɪlaɪt/ *n* су́мерки (-рек) *pl.*
twin /twɪn/ *n* близне́ц; *pl* (*Gemini*) Близнецы́ *m pl*; ~ **beds** па́ра однспа́льных крова́тей; ~ **brother** брат-близне́ц; ~ **town** го́род-побрати́м.
twine /twaɪn/ *n* бечёвка, шпага́т; *vt* (*twist, weave*) вить *impf*, с~ *pf*; *vt & i* (~ **round**) обвива́ть(ся) *impf*, обви́ть(ся) *pf.*
twinge /twɪndʒ/ *n* при́ступ (бо́ли); (*of conscience*) угрызе́ние.

twinkle /'twɪŋk(ə)l/ *n* мерца́ние; (*of eyes*) огонёк; *vi* мерца́ть *impf*, сверкну́ть *impf*. **twinkling** /-klɪŋ/ *n* мерца́ние; **in the ~ of an eye** в мгнове́ние о́ка.

twirl /twɜːl/ *vt & i* (*twist, turn*) верте́ть(ся) *impf*; (*whirl, spin*) кружи́ть(ся) *impf*.

twist /twɪst/ *n* (*bend*) изги́б, поворо́т; (~ing) круче́ние; (*in story*) поворо́т фа́булы; *vt* скру́чивать *impf*, крути́ть *impf*, с~ *pf*; (*distort*) искажа́ть *impf*, искази́ть *pf*; (*sprain*) подвёртывать *impf*, подверну́ть *pf*; *vi* (*climb, meander, twine*) ви́ться *impf*. **twisted** /-tɪd/ *adj* искривлённый (*also fig*).

twit /twɪt/ *n* дура́к.

twitch /twɪtʃ/ *n* подёргивание; *vt & i* дёргать(ся) *impf*, дёрнуть(ся) *pf* (**at** за+*acc*).

twitter /'twɪtə(r)/ *n* щёбет; *vi* щебета́ть *impf*, чири́кать *impf*.

two /tuː/ *adj & n* два, две (*f*); (*collect; 2 pairs*) дво́е; (*number 2*) дво́йка; **in ~** (*in half*) на́двое, попола́м; **~seater** двухме́стный (автомоби́ль); **~way** двусторо́нний. **twofold** *adj* двойно́й; *adv* вдво́йне. **twosome** *n* па́ра.

tycoon /taɪ'kuːn/ *n* магна́т.

type /taɪp/ *n* тип, род; (*printing*) шрифт; *vt* писа́ть *impf*, на~ *pf* на маши́нке. **typescript** *n* маши́нопись. **typewriter** *n* пи́шущая маши́нка. **typewritten** /'taɪp,rɪt(ə)n/ *adj* маши́нопи́сный.

typhoid /'taɪfɔɪd/ *n* брюшно́й тиф.

typical /'tɪpɪk(ə)l/ *adj* типи́чный.

typify /'tɪpɪ,faɪ/ *vt* служи́ть *impf*, по~ *pf* типи́чным приме́ром +*gen*.

typist /'taɪpɪst/ *n* машини́стка.

typography /taɪ'pɒɡrəfɪ/ *n* кни́гопеча́тание; (*style*) офор мле́ние.

tyrannical /tɪ'rænɪk(ə)l/ *adj* ти рани́ческий. **tyrant** /'taɪrənt/ тира́н.

tyre /'taɪə(r)/ *n* ши́на.

U

ubiquitous /juː'bɪkwɪtəs/ *ad* вездесу́щий.

udder /'ʌdə(r)/ *n* вы́мя *neut*.

UFO *abbr* (*of* **unidentified flying object**) НЛО, неопо́знанный летя́ющий объе́кт.

ugh /əx/ *int* тьфу!

ugliness /'ʌɡlɪnɪs/ *n* уро́дство **ugly** /-lɪ/ *adj* некраси́вый уро́дливый; (*unpleasant*) не прия́тный.

UK *abbr* (*of* **United Kingdom**) Со еди́нённое Короле́вство.

Ukraine /juː'kreɪn/ *n* Украи́на **Ukrainian** /-nɪən/ *n* украи́нец -нка; *adj* украи́нский.

ulcer /'ʌlsə(r)/ *n* я́зва.

ulterior /ʌl'tɪərɪə(r)/ *ad* скры́тый.

ultimate /'ʌltɪmət/ *adj* (*final*) по сле́дний, оконча́тельный (*purpose*) коне́чный. **ultimately** /-lɪ/ *adv* в коне́чном счёте, в конце́ концо́в. **ultimatum** /,ʌlt 'meɪtəm/ *n* ультима́тум.

ultrasound /'ʌltrə,saʊnd/ *n* ультразву́к. **ultra-violet** /,ʌltrə'vaɪələt/ *adj* ультрафиоле́товый.

umbilical /ʌm'bɪlɪk(ə)l/ *adj*: **~ cord** пупови́на.

umbrella /ʌm'brelə/ *n* зо́нтик зонт.

umpire /'ʌmpaɪə(r)/ *n* судья́ *m*; *vt & i* суди́ть *impf*.

mpteenth /ˌʌmpˈtiːnθ/ adj: for the ~ time в который раз.

nabashed /ˌʌnəˈbæʃt/ adj без всякого смущения. **unabated** /ˌʌnəˈbeɪtɪd/ adj неослабленный. **unable** /ʌnˈeɪbl/ adj: be ~ to не мочь impf, c~ pf; быть не в состоянии; (not know how to) не уметь impf, c~ pf. **unabridged** /ˌʌnəˈbrɪdʒd/ adj некращённый. **unaccompanied** /ˌʌnəˈkʌmpənɪd/ adj без сопровождения; (mus) без аккомпанемента. **unaccountable** /ˌʌnəˈkaʊntəb(ə)l/ adj необъяснимый. **unaccustomed** /ˌʌnəˈkʌstəmd/ adj (not accustomed) непривыкший (to к+dat); (unusual) непривычный. **unadulterated** /ˌʌnəˈdʌltəreɪtɪd/ adj настоящий; (utter) чистейший. **unaffected** /ˌʌnəˈfektɪd/ adj непринуждённый. **unaided** /ʌnˈeɪdɪd/ adj без помощи, самостоятельный. **unambiguous** /ˌʌnæmˈbɪɡjʊəs/ adj недвусмысленный. **unanimity** /ˌjuːnəˈnɪmɪtɪ/ n единодушие. **unanimous** /juːˈnænɪməs/ adj единодушный. **unanswerable** /ʌnˈɑːnsərəb(ə)l/ adj (irrefutable) неопровержимый. **unarmed** /ʌnˈɑːmd/ adj невооружённый. **unashamed** /ˌʌnəˈʃeɪmd/ adj бессовестный. **unassailable** /ˌʌnəˈseɪləb(ə)l/ adj неприступный; (irrefutable) неопровержимый. **unassuming** /ˌʌnəˈsjuːmɪŋ/ adj скромный. **unattainable** /ˌʌnəˈteɪnəb(ə)l/ adj недосягаемый. **unattended** /ˌʌnəˈtendɪd/ adj без присмотра. **unattractive** /ˌʌnəˈtræktɪv/ adj непривлекательный. **unauthorized** /ʌnˈɔːθəraɪzd/ adj неразрешённый. **unavailable** /ˌʌnəˈveɪləb(ə)l/ adj

имеющийся в наличии, недоступный. **unavoidable** /ˌʌnəˈvɔɪdəb(ə)l/ adj неизбежный. **unaware** /ˌʌnəˈweə(r)/ predic: be ~ of не сознавать impf +acc; не знать impf o+prep. **unawares** /ˌʌnəˈweəz/ adv врасплох.

unbalanced /ʌnˈbælənst/ adj (psych) неуравновешенный. **unbearable** /ʌnˈbeərəb(ə)l/ adj невыносимый. **unbeatable** /ʌnˈbiːtəb(ə)l/ adj (unsurpassable) не могущий быть превзойдённым; (invincible) непобедимый. **unbeaten** /ʌnˈbiːtən/ adj (undefeated) непокорённый; (unsurpassed) непревзойдённый. **unbelief** /ˌʌnbɪˈliːf/ n неверие. **unbelievable** /ˌʌnbɪˈliːvəb(ə)l/ adj невероятный. **unbeliever** /ˌʌnbɪˈliːvə(r)/ n неверующий sb. **unbiased** /ʌnˈbaɪəst/ adj беспристрастный. **unblemished** /ʌnˈblemɪʃt/ adj незапятнанный. **unblock** /ʌnˈblɒk/ vt прочищать impf, прочистить pf. **unbolt** /ʌnˈbəʊlt/ vt отпирать impf, отпереть pf. **unborn** /ʌnˈbɔːn/ adj ещё не рождённый. **unbounded** /ʌnˈbaʊndɪd/ adj неограниченный. **unbreakable** /ʌnˈbreɪkəb(ə)l/ adj небьющийся. **unbridled** /ʌnˈbraɪd(ə)ld/ adj разнузданный. **unbroken** /ʌnˈbrəʊkən/ adj (intact) неразбитый, целый; (continuous) непрерывный; (unsurpassed) непобитый; (horse) необъезженный. **unbuckle** /ʌnˈbʌk(ə)l/ vt расстёгивать impf, расстегнуть pf. **unburden** /ʌnˈbɜːd(ə)n/ vt: ~ o.s. отводить impf, отвести pf душу. **unbutton** /ʌnˈbʌt(ə)n/ vt расстёгивать impf, расстег-

нуть *pf.*

uncalled-for /ʌnˈkɔːldfɔː(r)/ *adj* неуме́стный. **uncanny** /ʌn-ˈkænɪ/ *adj* жу́ткий, сверхъесте́ственный. **unceasing** /ʌnˈsiːsɪŋ/ *adj* непреры́вный. **uncere-monious** /ˌʌnserɪˈməʊnɪəs/ *adj* бесцеремо́нный. **uncertain** /ʌn-ˈsɜːt(ə)n/ *adj (not sure, hesitating)* неуве́ренный; *(indeterminate)* неопределённый, нея́сный; **be ~** *(not know for certain)* не знать *impf;* **in no ~ terms** недвусмы́сленно. **uncertainty** /ʌnˈsɜːt(ə)ntɪ/ *n* неизве́стность; неопределённость. **unchal-lenged** /ʌnˈtʃælɪndʒd/ *adj* не вызыва́ющий возраже́ний. **unchanged** /ʌnˈtʃeɪndʒd/ *adj* неизмени́вшийся. **unchanging** /ʌnˈtʃeɪndʒɪŋ/ *adj* неизменя́ющийся. **uncharacteristic** /ˌʌnkærəktəˈrɪstɪk/ *adj* нетипи́чный. **uncharitable** /ʌn-ˈtʃærɪtəb(ə)l/ *adj* немилосе́рдный, жесто́кий. **uncharted** /ʌn-ˈtʃɑːtɪd/ *adj* неиссле́дованный. **unchecked** /ʌnˈtʃekt/ *adj (unre-strained)* необу́зданный. **un-civilized** /ʌnˈsɪvɪˌlaɪzd/ *adj* нецивилизо́ванный. **un-claimed** /ʌnˈkleɪmd/ *adj* невостре́бованный.

uncle /ˈʌŋk(ə)l/ *n* дя́дя *m.*

unclean /ʌnˈkliːn/ *adj* нечи́стый. **unclear** /ʌnˈklɪə(r)/ *adj* нея́сный. **uncomfortable** /ʌnˈkʌmftəb(ə)l/ *adj* неудо́бный. **uncommon** /ʌn-ˈkɒmən/ *adj* необыкнове́нный; *(rare)* ре́дкий. **uncommunica-tive** /ˌʌnkəˈmjuːnɪkətɪv/ *adj* неразгово́рчивый, сде́ржанный. **uncomplaining** /ˌʌnkəmˈpleɪnɪŋ/ *adj* безро́потный. **uncompli-cated** /ʌnˈkɒmplɪˌkeɪtɪd/ *adj* несло́жный. **uncompromising** /ʌnˈkɒmprəˌmaɪzɪŋ/ *adj* бескомпро-

ми́ссный. **unconceale** /ˌʌnkənˈsiːld/ *adj* нескрыва́емый. **unconcerned** /ˌʌnkən-ˈsɜːnd/ *adj (unworried)* безза-бо́тный; *(indifferent)* равно-ду́шный. **unconditional** /ˌʌnkən-ˈdɪʃən(ə)l/ *adj* безогово́рочный безусло́вный. **unconfirmed** /ˌʌnkənˈfɜːmd/ *adj* неподтверждённый. **unconnected** /ˌʌnkəˈnektɪd/ *adj* ~ **with** н связанный c+*instr.* **uncon-scious** /ʌnˈkɒnʃəs/ *adj (also un-intentional)* бессозна́тельный *(predic)* без созна́ния; **be ~** не сознава́ть *impf* +*gen;* п подсозна́тельное *sb.* **uncon-sciousness** /ʌnˈkɒnʃəsnɪs/ *n* бессозна́тельное состоя́ние. **unconstitutional** /ˌʌnkɒnstɪ-ˈtjuːʃən(ə)l/ *adj* неконституци́онный. **uncontrollable** /ˌʌnkənˈtrəʊləb(ə)l/ *adj* неудержи́мый. **uncontrolled** /ˌʌnkən-ˈtrəʊld/ *adj* бесконтро́льный. **unconventional** /ˌʌnkən-ˈvenʃən(ə)l/ *adj* необы́чный, ориги́нальный. **unconvincing** /ˌʌnkənˈvɪnsɪŋ/ *adj* неубеди́тельный. **uncooked** /ʌnˈkʊkt/ *adj* сыро́й. **uncooperative** /ˌʌnkəʊ-ˈɒpərətɪv/ *adj* неотзы́вчивый. **uncouth** /ʌnˈkuːθ/ *adj* гру́бый. **uncover** /ʌnˈkʌvə(r)/ *vt* раскрыва́ть *impf,* раскры́ть *pf.* **un-critical** /ʌnˈkrɪtɪk(ə)l/ *adj* некрити́чный.

unctuous /ˈʌŋktjʊəs/ *adj* еле́йный.

uncut /ʌnˈkʌt/ *adj* неразре́зан-ный; *(unabridged)* несо-кращённый. **undamaged** /ʌnˈdæmɪdʒd/ *adj* неповреждённый. **undaunted** /ʌnˈdɔːntɪd/ *adj* бесстра́шный. **undecided** /ˌʌndɪˈsaɪdɪd/ *adj (not settled)* нерешённый; *(irreso-*

/ute/ нерешительный. **undefeated** /ˌʌndɪˈfiːtɪd/ adj
непокорённый. **undemanding**
/ˌʌndɪˈmɑːndɪŋ/ adj нетребовательный. **undemocratic** /ˌʌndeməˈkrætɪk/ adj недемократический. **undeniable** /ˌʌndɪˈnaɪəb(ə)l/ adj неоспоримый.

nder /ˈʌndə(r)/ prep (position) под+instr; (direction) под+acc; (fig) под +instr; (less than) меньше+gen; (in view of, in the reign, time of) при+prep; ~-**age** несовершеннолетний; ~ **way** на ходу; adv (position) внизу; (direction) вниз; (less) меньше. **ndercarriage** /ˈʌndəkærɪdʒ/ n шасси neut indecl. **underclothes** /ˈʌndəkləʊðz/ n pl нижнее бельё. **undercoat** /ˈʌndə-
kəʊt/ n (of paint) грунтовка. **undercover** /ˈʌndəˌkʌvə(r)/ adj тайный. **undercurrent** /ˈʌndə-
kʌrənt/ n подводное течение; (fig) скрытая тенденция. **undercut** /ˌʌndəˈkʌt/ vt (price) назначать impf, назначить pf более низкую цену чем+nom. **underdeveloped** /ˌʌndədɪˈveləpt/ adj слаборазвитый. **underdog** /ˈʌndəˌdɒg/ n неудачник. **underdone** /ˌʌndəˈdʌn/ adj недожаренный. **underemployment** /ˈʌndəɪmˈplɔɪmənt/ n неполная занятость. **underestimate** vt /ˌʌndərˈestɪmeɪt/ недооценивать impf, недооценить pf; n /ˌʌndərˈestɪmət/недооценка. **underfoot** /ˌʌndəˈfʊt/ adv под ногами. **undergo** /ˌʌndəˈgəʊ/ vt подвергаться impf, подвергнуться pf +dat; (endure) переносить impf, перенести pf. **under-
graduate** /ˌʌndəˈgrædjʊət/ n студент, ~ка. **underground** /ˈʌndə-
graʊnd/ n (rly) метро neut in-

decl; (fig) подполье; adj подземный, (fig) подпольный; adv под землёй; (fig) подпольно. **undergrowth** /ˈʌndəgrəʊθ/ n подлесок. **underhand** /ˈʌndə-
hænd/ adj закулисный. **under-
lie** /ˌʌndəˈlaɪ/ vt (fig) лежать impf в основе +gen. **underline** /ˌʌndəˈlaɪn/ vt подчёркивать impf, подчеркнуть pf. **underlying** /ˌʌndəˈlaɪɪŋ/ adj лежащий в основе. **underling** /ˈʌndəlɪŋ/ n подчинённый sb.
undermine /ˌʌndəˈmaɪn/ vt (authority) подрывать impf, подорвать pf; (health) разрушать impf, разрушить pf.
underneath /ˌʌndəˈniːθ/ adv (position) внизу; (direction) вниз; prep (position) под+instr; (direction) под+acc; n нижняя часть; adj нижний.
undernourished /ˌʌndəˈnʌrɪʃt/ adj исхудалый; be ~ недоедать impf.
underpaid /ˌʌndəˈpeɪd/ adj низкооплачиваемый. **underpants** /ˈʌndəpænts/ n pl трусы (-сов) pl. **underpass** /ˈʌndəpɑːs/ n проезд под полотном дороги; тоннель m. **underpin** /ˌʌndə-
ˈpɪn/ vt подводить impf, подвести pf фундамент под+acc; (fig) поддерживать impf, поддержать pf. **underprivileged** /ˌʌndəˈprɪvɪlɪdʒd/ adj обделённый; (poor) бедный. **underrate** /ˌʌndəˈreɪt/ vt недооценивать impf, недооценить pf.
underscore /ˌʌndəˈskɔː(r)/ vt подчёркивать impf, подчеркнуть pf. **under-secretary** /ˌʌndəˈsekrətərɪ/ n заместитель m министра. **underside** /ˈʌndə-
saɪd/ n нижняя сторона, низ. **undersized** /ˈʌndəˌsaɪzd/ adj ма-

лоро́слый. **understaffed** /ˌʌndə'stɑːft/ adj неукомплекто́ванный.

understand /ˌʌndə'stænd/ vt понима́ть impf, поня́ть pf; (have heard say) слы́шать impf.

understandable /ˌʌndə'stændəb(ə)l/ adj поня́тный.

understanding /ˌʌndə'stændɪŋ/ n понима́ние; (agreement) соглаше́ние; adj (sympathetic) отзы́вчивый.

understate /ˌʌndə'steɪt/ vt преуменьша́ть impf, преуме́ньшить pf. **understatement** /ˌʌndə'steɪtmənt/ n преуменьше́ние.

understudy /'ʌndəˌstʌdɪ/ n дублёр.

undertake /ˌʌndə'teɪk/ vt (enter upon) предпринима́ть impf, предприня́ть pf; (responsibility) брать impf, взять pf на себя́; (+inf) обязываться impf, обяза́ться pf. **undertaker** /ˌteɪkə(r)/ n гробовщи́к. **undertaking** /ˌʌndə'teɪkɪŋ/ n предприя́тие; (pledge) гара́нтия.

undertone /ˌʌndəˌtəʊn/ n (fig) подте́кст; in an ~ вполго́лоса.

underwater /ˌʌndə'wɔːtə(r)/ adj подво́дный. **underwear** /ˌʌndə-ˌweə(r)/ n ни́жнее бельё. **underweight** /ˌʌndə'weɪt/ adj исхуда́лый. **underworld** /ˌʌndəˌwɜːld/ n (mythology) преиспо́дняя sb; (criminals) престу́пный мир. **underwrite** /ˌʌndə'raɪt/ vt (guarantee) гаранти́ровать impf & pf. **underwriter** /ˌʌndəˌraɪtə(r)/ n страхо́вщик.

undeserved /ˌʌndɪ'zɜːvd/ adj незаслу́женный. **undesirable** /ˌʌndɪ'zaɪərəb(ə)l/ adj нежела́тельный; n нежела́тельное лицо́. **undeveloped** /ˌʌndɪ-'veləpt/ adj неразви́тый; (land) незастро́енный. **undignified**

/ʌn'dɪgnɪˌfaɪd/ adj недосто́йный. **undiluted** /ˌʌndaɪ'ljuːtɪd/ adj неразба́вленный. **undisciplined** /ʌn'dɪsɪplɪnd/ adj недисциплини́рованный. **undiscovered** /ˌʌndɪ'skʌvəd/ adj неоткры́тый. **undisguise** /ˌʌndɪs'gaɪzd/ adj я́вный. **undisputed** /ˌʌndɪ'spjuːtɪd/ adj бесспо́рный. **undistinguishe** /ˌʌndɪ'stɪŋgwɪʃt/ adj заура́дный. **undisturbed** /ˌʌndɪ'stɜːbd/ adj (untouched) нетро́нутый; (peaceful) споко́йный. **undivided** /ˌʌndɪ'vaɪdɪd/ adj: ~ attention по́лное внима́ние. **undo** /ʌn'duː/ vt (open) открыва́ть impf, откры́ть pf; (untie) развя́зывать impf, развяза́ть pf; (unbutton, unhook, unbuckle расстёгивать impf, расстегну́ть pf; (destroy, cancel) уничтожа́ть impf, уничто́жить pf. **undoubted** /ʌn'daʊtɪd/ adj несомне́нный. **undoubtedly** /ʌn'daʊtɪdlɪ/ adv несомне́нно. **undress** /ʌn'dres/ vt & i разде-ва́ть(ся) impf, разде́ть(ся) pf. **undue** /ʌn'djuː/ adj чрезме́рный. **unduly** /ʌn'djuːlɪ/ adv чрезме́рно.

undulating /'ʌndjʊˌleɪtɪŋ/ adj волни́стый; (landscape) холми́стый.

undying /ʌn'daɪɪŋ/ adj (eternal) ве́чный.

unearth /ʌn'ɜːθ/ vt (dig up) выка́пывать impf, вы́копать pf из земли́; (fig) раска́пывать impf раскопа́ть pf. **uneasiness** /ʌn'iːzɪnɪs/ n (anxiety) беспоко́йство; (awkwardness) нело́вкость. **uneasy** /ʌn'iːzɪ/ adj беспоко́йный; нело́вкий. **economic** /ˌiːnɪkə'nɒmɪk/ adj нерента́бельный. **uneconomical** /ˌiːnɪkə'nɒmɪk(ə)l/ adj

etc.) неэкономи́чный; (*person*) неэконо́мный. **uneducated** /ʌn'edjuˌkeɪtɪd/ *adj* необразо́ванный. **unemployed** /ˌʌnɪm'plɔɪd/ *adj* безрабо́тный. **unemployment** /ˌʌnɪm'plɔɪmənt/ *n* безрабо́тица. ~ **benefit** посо́бие по безрабо́тице. **unending** /ʌn'endɪŋ/ *adj* бесконе́чный. **unenviable** /ʌn'envɪəb(ə)l/ *adj* незави́дный. **unequal** /ʌn'iːkw(ə)l/ *adj* нера́вный. **unequalled** /ʌn'iːkw(ə)ld/ *adj* непревзойдённый. **unequivocal** /ˌʌnɪ'kwɪvək(ə)l/ *adj* недвусмы́сленный. **unerring** /ʌn'ɜːrɪŋ/ *adj* безоши́бочный.

uneven /ʌn'iːv(ə)n/ *adj* нерóвный. **uneventful** /ˌʌnɪ'ventful/ *adj* непримеча́тельный. **unexceptional** /ˌʌnɪk'sepʃən(ə)l/ *adj* обы́чный. **unexpected** /ˌʌnɪk'spektɪd/ *adj* неожи́данный. **unexplored** /ˌʌnɪk'splɔːd/ *adj* неиссле́дованный.

unfailing /ʌn'feɪlɪŋ/ *adj* неизме́нный; (*inexhaustible*) неисчерпа́емый. **unfair** /ʌn'feə(r)/ *adj* несправедли́вый. **unfaithful** /ʌn'feɪθful/ *adj* неве́рный. **unfamiliar** /ˌʌnfə'mɪljə(r)/ *adj* незнако́мый; (*unknown*) неве́домый. **unfashionable** /ʌn'fæʃənəb(ə)l/ *adj* немо́дный. **unfasten** /ʌn'fɑːs(ə)n/ *vt* (*detach, untie*) открепля́ть *impf*, открепи́ть *pf*; (*undo, unbutton, unhook*) расстёгивать *impf*, расстегну́ть *pf*; (*open*) открыва́ть *impf*, откры́ть *pf*. **unfavourable** /ʌn'feɪvərəb(ə)l/ *adj* неблагоприя́тный. **unfeeling** /ʌn'fiːlɪŋ/ *adj* бесчу́вственный. **unfinished** /ʌn'fɪnɪʃt/ *adj* незако́нченный. **unfit** /ʌn'fɪt/ *adj* него́дный; (*unhealthy*) нездоро́вый. **unflagging** /ʌn-

'flægɪŋ/ *adj* неослабева́ющий. **unflattering** /ʌn'flætərɪŋ/ *adj* нелéстный. **unflinching** /ʌn'flɪntʃɪŋ/ *adj* непоколеби́мый. **unfold** /ʌn'fəʊld/ *vt* & *i* развёртывать(ся) *impf*, разверну́ть(ся) *pf*, *vi* (*fig*) раскрыва́ться *impf*, раскры́ться *pf*. **unforeseen** /ˌʌnfɔː'siːn/ *adj* непредви́денный. **unforgettable** /ˌʌnfə'getəb(ə)l/ *adj* незабыва́емый. **unforgivable** /ˌʌnfə'gɪvəb(ə)l/ *adj* непрости́тельный. **unforgiving** /ˌʌnfə'gɪvɪŋ/ *adj* непроща́ющий. **unfortunate** /ʌn'fɔːtʃənət/ *adj* несча́стный; (*regrettable*) неуда́чный; *n* неуда́чник. **unfortunately** /ʌn'fɔːtʃənətlɪ/ *adv* к сожале́нию. **unfounded** /ʌn'faʊndɪd/ *adj* необосно́ванный. **unfriendly** /ʌn'frendlɪ/ *adj* недружелю́бный. **unfulfilled** /ˌʌnfʊl'fɪld/ *adj* (*hopes etc.*) неосуществлённый; (*person*) неудовлетворённый. **unfurl** /ʌn'fɜːl/ *vt* & *i* развёртывать(ся) *impf*, разверну́ть(ся) *pf*. **unfurnished** /ʌn'fɜːnɪʃt/ *adj* немебли́рованный.

ungainly /ʌn'geɪnlɪ/ *adj* неуклю́жий. **ungovernable** /ʌn'gʌvənəb(ə)l/ *adj* неуправля́емый. **ungracious** /ʌn'greɪʃəs/ *adj* нелюбе́зный. **ungrateful** /ʌn'greɪtful/ *adj* неблагода́рный. **unguarded** /ʌn'gɑːdɪd/ *adj* (*incautious*) неосторо́жный.

unhappiness /ʌn'hæpɪnəs/ *n* несча́стье. **unhappy** /ʌn'hæpɪ/ *adj* несчастли́вый. **unharmed** /ʌn'hɑːmd/ *adj* невреди́мый. **unhealthy** /ʌn'helθɪ/ *adj* нездоро́вый; (*harmful*) вре́дный. **unheard-of** /ʌn'hɜːdɒv/ *adj* неслы́ханный. **unheeded** /ʌn'hiːdɪd/ *adj* незаме́ченный. **un-**

heeding /ʌnˈhiːdɪŋ/ adj невнима́тельный. **unhelpful** /ʌnˈhelpfʊl/ adj бесполе́зный; (person) неотзы́вчивый. **unhesitating** /ʌnˈhezɪteɪtɪŋ/ adj реши́тельный. **unhesitatingly** /ʌnˈhezɪteɪtɪŋlɪ/ adv без колеба́ния. **unhindered** /ʌnˈhɪndəd/ adj беспрепя́тственный. **unhinge** /ʌnˈhɪndʒ/ vt (fig) расстра́ивать impf, расстро́ить pf. **unholy** /ʌnˈhəʊlɪ/ adj (impious) нечести́вый; (awful) ужа́сный. **unhook** /ʌnˈhʊk/ vt (undo hooks of) расстёгивать impf, расстегну́ть pf; (uncouple) расцепля́ть impf, расцепи́ть pf. **unhurt** /ʌnˈhɜːt/ adj невреди́мый.

unicorn /ˈjuːnɪkɔːn/ n единоро́г.

unification /ˌjuːnɪfɪˈkeɪʃ(ə)n/ n объедине́ние.

uniform /ˈjuːnɪfɔːm/ n фо́рма; adj единообра́зный; (unchanging) постоя́нный. **uniformity** /ˌjuːnɪˈfɔːmɪtɪ/ n единообра́зие.

unify /ˈjuːnɪfaɪ/ vt объединя́ть impf, объедини́ть pf.

unilateral /ˌjuːnɪˈlætər(ə)l/ adj односторо́нний.

unimaginable /ˌʌnɪˈmædʒɪnəb(ə)l/ adj невообрази́мый. **unimaginative** /ˌʌnɪˈmædʒɪnətɪv/ adj лишённый воображе́ния, прозаи́чный. **unimportant** /ˌʌnɪmˈpɔːt(ə)nt/ adj нева́жный. **uninformed** /ˌʌnɪnˈfɔːmd/ adj (ignorant) несве́дущий (about в+prep); (ill-informed) неосведомлённый. **uninhabited** /ˌʌnɪnˈhæbɪtɪd/ adj необита́емый. **uninhibited** /ˌʌnɪnˈhɪbɪtɪd/ adj нестеснённый. **uninspired** /ˌʌnɪnˈspaɪəd/ adj бана́льный. **unintelligible** /ˌʌnɪnˈtelɪdʒɪb(ə)l/ adj непоня́тный. **unintentional** /ˌʌnɪnˈtenʃən(ə)l/ adj неча́янный

unintentionally /ˌʌnɪnˈtenʃənəlɪ/ adv неча́янно. **uninterested** /ʌnˈɪntrəstɪd/ adj безразли́чный. **uninteresting** /ʌnˈɪntrəstɪŋ/ adj неинтере́сный. **uninterrupted** /ˌʌnɪntəˈrʌptɪd/ adj непреры́вный.

union /ˈjuːnjən/ n (alliance) сою́з; (joining together, alliance) объедине́ние; (trade ~) профсою́з. **unionist** /ˈjuːnjənɪst/ n член профсою́за; (poli) унионист.

unique /juˈniːk/ adj уника́льный.

unison /ˈjuːnɪs(ə)n/ n: in ~ (mu) в унисо́н; (fig) в согла́сии.

unit /ˈjuːnɪt/ n едини́ца; (mil) часть.

unite /juˈnaɪt/ vt & i соединя́ть(ся) impf, соедини́ть(ся) pf; объединя́ть(ся) impf, объедини́ть(ся) pf. **united** /juˈnaɪtɪd/ adj соединённый, объединённый; U~ Kingdom Соединённое Короле́вство; U~ Nations Организа́ция Объединённых На́ций; U~ States Соединённые Шта́ты Аме́рики. **unity** /ˈjuːnɪtɪ/ n еди́нство.

universal /ˌjuːnɪˈvɜːs(ə)l/ adj всео́бщий; (many-sided) универса́льный. **universe** /ˈjuːnɪvɜːs/ n вселе́нная sb; (world) мир.

university /ˌjuːnɪˈvɜːsɪtɪ/ n университе́т; attrib университе́тский.

unjust /ʌnˈdʒʌst/ adj несправедли́вый. **unjustifiable** /ʌnˈdʒʌstɪˌfaɪəb(ə)l/ adj непрости́тельный. **unjustified** /ʌnˈdʒʌstɪfaɪd/ adj неоправданный.

unkempt /ʌnˈkempt/ adj неча́санный. **unkind** /ʌnˈkaɪnd/ adj недо́брый, злой. **unknown** /ʌnˈnəʊn/ adj неизве́стный.

unlawful /ʌnˈlɔːfʊl/ adj незаконный. **unleaded** /ʌnˈledɪd/ adj неэтилированный. **unleash** /ʌnˈliːʃ/ vt (also fig) развязывать impf, развязать pf.

unless /ənˈles/ conj если... не.

unlike /ʌnˈlaɪk/ adj непохожий (на+acc); (in contradistinction to) в отличие от+gen. **unlikely** /ʌnˈlaɪklɪ/ adj маловероятный; **it is ~ that** вряд ли. **unlimited** /ʌnˈlɪmɪtɪd/ adj неограниченный. **unlit** /ʌnˈlɪt/ adj неосвещённый. **unload** /ʌnˈləʊd/ vt (vehicle etc.) разгружать impf, разгрузить pf; (goods etc.) выгружать impf, выгрузить pf. **unlock** /ʌnˈlɒk/ vt отпирать impf, отпереть pf; открывать impf, открыть pf. **unlucky** /ʌnˈlʌkɪ/ adj (number etc.) несчастливый; (unsuccessful) неудачный.

unmanageable /ʌnˈmænɪdʒəb(ə)l/ adj трудный, непокорный. **unmanned** /ʌnˈmænd/ adj автоматический. **unmarried** /ʌnˈmærɪd/ adj холостой; (of man) неженатый; (of woman) незамужняя. **unmask** /ʌnˈmɑːsk/ vt (fig) разоблачать impf, разоблачить pf. **unmentionable** /ʌnˈmenʃənəb(ə)l/ adj неупоминаемый. **unmistakable** /ʌnmɪˈsteɪkəb(ə)l/ adj несомненный, ясный. **unmitigated** /ʌnˈmɪtɪɡeɪtɪd/ adj (thorough) отъявленный. **unmoved** /ʌnˈmuːvd/ adj: **be ~** оставаться impf, остаться pf равнодушен, -шна.

unnatural /ʌnˈnætʃər(ə)l/ adj неестественный. **unnecessary** /ʌnˈnesəsərɪ/ adj ненужный. **unnerve** /ʌnˈnɜːv/ vt лишать impf, лишить pf мужества; (upset) расстраивать impf, рас-

строить pf. **unnoticed** /ʌnˈnəʊtɪst/ adj незамеченный.

unobserved /ʌnəbˈzɜːvd/ adj незамеченный. **unobtainable** /ʌnəbˈteɪnəb(ə)l/ adj недоступный. **unobtrusive** /ʌnəbˈtruːsɪv/ adj скромный, ненавязчивый. **unoccupied** /ʌnˈɒkjʊpaɪd/ adj незанятый, свободный; (house) пустой. **unofficial** /ʌnəˈfɪʃ(ə)l/ adj неофициальный. **unopposed** /ʌnəˈpəʊzd/ adj не встретивший сопротивления. **unorthodox** /ʌnˈɔːθədɒks/ adj неортодоксальный.

unpack /ʌnˈpæk/ vt распаковывать impf, распаковать pf. **unpaid** /ʌnˈpeɪd/ adj (bill) неуплаченный; (person) не получающий платы; (work) бесплатный. **unpalatable** /ʌnˈpælətəb(ə)l/ adj невкусный; (unpleasant) неприятный. **unparalleled** /ʌnˈpærəleld/ adj несравнимый. **unpleasant** /ʌnˈplez(ə)nt/ adj неприятный. **unpleasantness** /ʌnˈplez(ə)ntnɪs/ n неприятность. **unpopular** /ʌnˈpɒpjʊlə(r)/ adj непопулярный. **unprecedented** /ʌnˈpresɪdentɪd/ adj беспрецедентный. **unpredictable** /ʌnprɪˈdɪktəb(ə)l/ adj непредсказуемый. **unprejudiced** /ʌnˈpredʒʊdɪst/ adj беспристрастный. **unprepared** /ʌnprɪˈpeəd/ adj неподготовленный, неготовый. **unpossessing** /ʌnprɪˈpəˈzesɪŋ/ adj непривлекательный. **unpretentious** /ʌnprɪˈtenʃəs/ adj простой, без претензий. **unprincipled** /ʌnˈprɪnsɪp(ə)ld/ adj беспринципный. **unproductive** /ʌnprəˈdʌktɪv/ adj непродуктивный. **unprofitable** /ʌnˈprɒfɪtəb(ə)l/ adj невыгодный. **unpromising** /ʌnˈprɒmɪsɪŋ/ adj

малообеща́ющий. **unprotected** /ˌʌnprə'tektɪd/ adj незащищённый. **unproven** /ʌn'pruːvən/ adj недока́занный. **unprovoked** /ˌʌnprə'vəʊkt/ adj непровоци́рованный. **unpublished** /ʌn'pʌblɪʃt/ adj неопублико́ванный, неи́зданный. **unpunished** /ʌn'pʌnɪʃt/ adj безнака́занный.

unqualified /ʌn'kwɒlɪˌfaɪd/ adj неквалифици́рованный; (unconditional) безогово́рочный. **unquestionable** /ʌn'kwestʃənəb(ə)l/ adj несомне́нный, неоспори́мый. **unquestionably** /ʌn'kwestʃənəbli/ adv несомне́нно, бесспо́рно.

unravel /ʌn'ræv(ə)l/ vt & i распу́тывать(ся) impf, распу́тать(ся) pf; (solve) разга́дывать impf, разгада́ть pf. **unread** /ʌn'red/ adj (book etc.) непрочи́танный. **unreadable** /ʌn'riːdəb(ə)l/ adj (illegible) неразбо́рчивый; (boring) неудобочита́емый. **unreal** /ʌn'rɪəl/ adj нереа́льный. **unrealistic** /ˌʌnrɪə'lɪstɪk/ adj не реа́льный. **unreasonable** /ʌn'riːznəb(ə)l/ adj (person) неразу́мный; (behaviour, demand, price) необосно́ванный. **unrecognizable** /ʌn'rekəɡˌnaɪzəb(ə)l/ adj неузнава́емый. **unrecognized** /ʌn'rekəɡˌnaɪzd/ adj непри́знанный. **unrefined** /ˌʌnrɪ'faɪnd/ adj неочи́щенный; (manners etc.) гру́бый. **unrelated** /ˌʌnrɪ'leɪtəd/ adj не име́ющий отноше́ния (to к+dat); (person) не свя́занный (to c+instr); we are ~ мы не ро́дственники. **unrelenting** /ˌʌnrɪ'lentɪŋ/ adj (ruthless) безжа́лостный; (unremitting) неосла́бный. **unreliable** /ˌʌnrɪ'laɪəb(ə)l/ adj ненадёжный. **unremarkable** /ˌʌn-

unremitting /ˌʌnrɪ'mɪtɪŋ/ adj (incessant) беспреста́нный. **unrepentant** /ˌʌnrɪ'pent(ə)nt/ adj нераска́явшийся. **unrepresentative** /ˌʌnreprɪ'zentətɪv/ adj нетипи́чный. **unrequited** /ˌʌnrɪ'kwaɪtɪd/ adj: ~ love неразделённая любо́вь. **unreserved** /ˌʌnrɪ'zɜːvd/ adj (full) по́лный; (open) откове́нный; (unconditional) безогово́рочный; (seat) незаброни́рованный. **unresolved** /ˌʌnrɪ'zɒlvd/ adj нереше́нный в беспоко́йстве; (polit) волне́ния neut pl. **unrestrained** /ˌʌnrɪ'streɪnd/ adj несде́ржанный. **unrestricted** /ˌʌnrɪ'strɪktɪd/ adj неограни́ченный. **unripe** /ʌn'raɪp/ adj незре́лый. **unrivalled** /ʌn'raɪv(ə)ld/ adj бесподо́бный. **unroll** /ʌn'rəʊl/ vt & i развёртывать(ся) impf, разверну́ть(ся) pf. **unruffled** /ʌn'rʌf(ə)ld/ adj (smooth) гла́дкий; (calm) споко́йный. **unruly** /ʌn'ruːlɪ/ adj непоко́рный.

unsafe /ʌn'seɪf/ adj опа́сный; (insecure) ненадёжный. **unsaid** /ʌn'sed/ adj: leave ~ молча́ть impf о+prep. **unsaleable** /ʌn'seɪləb(ə)l/ adj нехо́дкий. **unsalted** /ʌn'sɔːltɪd/ adj не солёный. **unsatisfactory** /ˌʌnsætɪs'fæktərɪ/ adj неудовлетвори́тельный. **unsatisfied** /ʌn'sætɪsfaɪd/ adj неудовлетворённый. **unsavoury** /ʌn'seɪvərɪ/ adj (unpleasant) неприя́тный; (disreputable) сомни́тельный. **unscathed** /ʌn'skeɪðd/ adj (predic) цел и невреди́м. **unscheduled** /ʌn'ʃedjuːld/ adj (transport) внеочередно́й.

(*event*) незапланированный.
unscientific /ˌʌnsaɪən'tɪfɪk/ *adj*
ненаучный. **unscrew** /ʌn'skruː/
vt & *i* отвинчивать(ся) *impf*,
отвинтить(ся) *pf*. **unscrupu-
lous** /ʌn'skruːpjʊləs/ *adj* беспринципный. **unseat** /ʌn'siːt/ *vt* (*of
horse*) сбрасывать *impf*, сбросить *pf* с седла; (*parl*) лишать
impf, лишить *pf* парламентского мандата.

unseemly /ʌn'siːmlɪ/ *adj* непо-
добающий. **unseen** /ʌn'siːn/
adj невидимый. **unselfcon-
scious** /ˌʌnself'kɒnʃəs/ *adj* непосредственный. **unselfish** /ʌn
'selfɪʃ/ *adj* бескорыстный. **un-
settle** /ʌn'set(ə)l/ *vt* выбивать
impf, выбить *pf* из колеи; (*upset*)
расстраивать *impf*, рас-
строить *pf*. **unsettled** /ʌn
'set(ə)ld/ *adj* (*weather*) неустойчивый; (*unresolved*) не-
решённый. **unsettling** /-'setlɪŋ/
adj волнующий. **unshakeable**
/ʌn'ʃeɪkəb(ə)l/ *adj* непоколебимый. **unshaven** /ʌn'ʃeɪv(ə)n/ *adj*
небритый. **unsightly** /ʌn'saɪtlɪ/
adj неприглядный, уродливый. **unsigned** /ʌn'saɪnd/ *adj*
неподписанный. **unskilful** /ʌn
'skɪlfʊl/ *adj* неумелый. **unskilled** /ʌn'skɪld/ *adj* неквали-
фицированный. **unsociable**
/ʌn'səʊʃəb(ə)l/ *adj* необщитель-
ный. **unsold** /ʌn'səʊld/ *adj* не-
проданный. **unsolicited** /ˌʌnsə
'lɪsɪtɪd/ *adj* непрошеный. **unsolved** /ʌn'sɒlvd/ *adj* нерешённый. **unsophisticated**
/ˌʌnsə'fɪstɪˌkeɪtɪd/ *adj* простой.
unsound /ʌn'saʊnd/ *adj* (*unhealthy, unwholesome*) нездоро-
вый; (*not solid*) непрочный;
(*unfounded*) необоснованный;
of ~ mind душевнобольной.
unspeakable /ʌn'spiːkəb(ə)l/ *adj*

(*inexpressible*) невыразимый;
(*very bad*) отвратительный.
unspecified /ʌn'spesɪˌfaɪd/ *adj*
точно не указанный, неопределённый. **unspoilt** /ʌn'spɔɪlt/
adj неиспорченный. **unspoken**
/ʌn'spəʊkən/ *adj* невысказан-
ный. **unstable** /ʌn'steɪb(ə)l/ *adj*
неустойчивый; (*mentally*) неуравновешенный. **unsteady**
/ʌn'stedɪ/ *adj* неустойчивый.
unstuck /ʌn'stʌk/ *adj*: come ~
отклеиваться *impf*, от-
клеиться *pf*; (*fig*) проваливаться *impf*, провалиться *pf*.
unsuccessful /ˌʌnsək'sesfʊl/ *adj*
неудачный, безуспешный. **unsuitable** /ʌn'suːtəb(ə)l/ *adj* неподходящий. **unsuited** /ʌn
'suːtɪd/ *adj* непригодный. **un-
sung** /ʌn'sʌŋ/ *adj* невоспетый.
unsupported /ˌʌnsə'pɔːtɪd/ *adj*
неподдержанный. **unsure** /ʌn
'ʃʊə(r)/ *adj* неуверенный (of o.s.
в себе). **unsurpassed** /ˌʌnsə
'pɑːst/ *adj* непревзойдённый.
unsurprising /ˌʌnsə'praɪzɪŋ/ *adj*
неудивительный. **unsus-
pected** /ˌʌnsə'spektɪd/ *adj* (*unforeseen*) непредвиденный.
unsuspecting /ˌʌnsə'spektɪŋ/ *adj*
неподозревающий. **unsweet-
ened** /ʌn'swiːt(ə)nd/ *adj* непод-
слащённый. **unswerving** /ʌn
'swɜːvɪŋ/ *adj* непоколебимый.
unsympathetic /ˌʌnsɪmpə'θetɪk/
adj несочувствующий. **unsys-
tematic** /ˌʌnsɪstə'mætɪk/ *adj* не-
систематичный.

untainted /ʌn'teɪntɪd/ *adj* неиспорченный. **untangle** /ʌn
'tæŋɡ(ə)l/ *vt* распутывать *impf*,
распутать *pf*. **untapped** /ʌn
'tæpt/ *adj*: ~ resources неис-
пользованные ресурсы *m pl*.
untenable /ʌn'tenəb(ə)l/ *adj* не-
состоятельный. **untested** /ʌn

'testid/ *adj* неиспы́танный. **un-thinkable** /ʌnˈθɪŋkəb(ə)l/ *adj* невообрази́мый. **unthinking** /ʌnˈθɪŋkɪŋ/ *adj* безду́мный. **untidi-ness** /ʌnˈtaɪdɪnɪs/ *n* неопря́тность; (*disorder*) беспоря́док. **untidy** /ʌnˈtaɪdɪ/ *adj* неопря́тный; (*in disorder*) в беспоря́дке. **untie** /ʌnˈtaɪ/ *vt* развя́зывать *impf*, развяза́ть *pf*; (*set free*) освобожда́ть *impf*, освободи́ть *pf*.

until /ənˈtɪl/ *prep* до+*gen*; not ~ не ра́ньше+*gen*; ~ then до тех пор; *conj* пока́, пока́... не; not ~ то́лько когда́.

untimely /ʌnˈtaɪmlɪ/ *adj* (*premature*) безвре́менный; (*inappropriate*) неуме́стный. **untiring** /ʌnˈtaɪərɪŋ/ *adj* неутоми́мый. **untold** /ʌnˈtəʊld/ *adj* (*incalculable*) бессчётный, несме́тный; (*inexpressible*) невырази́мый. **untouched** /ʌnˈtʌtʃt/ *adj* нетро́нутый; (*indifferent*) равноду́шный. **untoward** /ˌʌntəˈwɔːd/ *adj* неблагоприя́тный. **untrained** /ʌnˈtreɪnd/ *adj* необу́ченный. **untried** /ʌnˈtraɪd/ *adj* неиспы́танный. **untroubled** /ʌnˈtrʌb(ə)ld/ *adj* споко́йный. **untrue** /ʌnˈtruː/ *adj* неве́рный. **untrustworthy** /ʌnˈtrʌstˌwɜːðɪ/ *adj* ненадёжный. **untruth** /ʌnˈtruːθ/ *n* непра́вда, ложь. **untruthful** /ʌnˈtruːθfʊl/ *adj* лжи́вый.

unusable /ʌnˈjuːzəb(ə)l/ *adj* непригодный. **unused** /ʌnˈjuːzd/ *adj* неиспо́льзованный; (*unaccustomed*) /ʌnˈjuːst/ непривы́кший (to к+*dat*); I am ~ to this я к э́тому не привы́к. **unusual** /ʌnˈjuːʒʊəl/ *adj* необыкнове́нный, необы́чный. **unusually** /ʌnˈjuːʒʊəlɪ/ *adv* необыкнове́нно. **unutterable** /ʌnˈʌtərəb(ə)l/ *adj* невырази́мый.

unveil /ʌnˈveɪl/ *vt* (*statue*) торже́ственно открыва́ть *impf*, открыть *pf*; (*disclose*) обнаро́довать *impf & pf*.

unwanted /ʌnˈwɒntɪd/ *adj* нежеланный. **unwarranted** /ʌnˈwɒrəntɪd/ *adj* неоправданный. **unwary** /ʌnˈweərɪ/ *adj* неосторо́жный. **unwavering** /ʌnˈweɪvərɪŋ/ *adj* неколеби́мый. **unwelcome** /ʌnˈwelkəm/ *adj* нежела́тельный; (*unpleasant*) неприя́тный. **unwell** /ʌnˈwel/ *adj* нездоро́вый. **unwieldy** /ʌnˈwiːldɪ/ *adj* громо́здкий. **unwilling** /ʌnˈwɪlɪŋ/ *adj* несклонный; be ~ не хоте́ть *impf*, за~ *pf* (to +*inf*). **unwillingly** /ʌnˈwɪlɪŋlɪ/ *adv* неохо́тно. **unwillingness** /ʌnˈwɪlɪŋnɪs/ *n* неохо́та. **unwind** /ʌnˈwaɪnd/ *vt & i* разма́тывать(ся) *impf*, размота́ть(ся) *pf*; (*rest*) отдыха́ть *impf*, отдохну́ть *pf*. **unwise** /ʌnˈwaɪz/ *adj* не(благо)разу́мный. **unwitting** /ʌnˈwɪtɪŋ/ *adj* нево́льный. **unwittingly** /ʌnˈwɪtɪŋlɪ/ *adv* нево́льно. **unworkable** /ʌnˈwɜːkəb(ə)l/ *adj* неприменимый. **unworldly** /ʌnˈwɜːldlɪ/ *adj* не от ми́ра сего́. **unworthy** /ʌnˈwɜːðɪ/ *adj* недосто́йный. **unwrap** /ʌnˈræp/ *vt* развёртывать *impf*, разверну́ть *pf*. **unwritten** /ʌnˈrɪt(ə)n/ *adj*: ~ law непи́саный зако́н.

unyielding /ʌnˈjiːldɪŋ/ *adj* упо́рный, неподатли́вый.

unzip /ʌnˈzɪp/ *vt* расстёгивать *impf*, расстегну́ть *pf* (мо́лнию+*gen*).

up /ʌp/ *adv* (*motion*) наве́рх, вверх; (*position*) наверху́, вверху́; ~ and down вверх и вниз; (*back and forth*) взад и вперёд; ~ to (*towards*) к+*dat*; (*as far as, until*) до+*gen*; ~

now до сих пор; be ~ against иметь *impf* дело c+*instr*; it is ~ to you+*inf*, это вам+*inf*, вы должны+*inf*; what's ~? что случилось?; в чём дело?; your time is ~ ваше время истекло; ~ and about he isn't; he isn't ~ yet он ещё не встал; he isn't ~ to this job он не годится для этой работы; *prep* (along) (вдоль) по+*dat*; (along) (вдоль) по+*dat*; *vt* (hoist) повышать *impf*, повысить *pf*; *vi* (leap up) взять *pf*; ~-to-date современный; *adj* (fashionable) модный; ~-and-coming многообещающий; *n*: ~s and downs (fig) превратности *f pl* судьбы.

pbringing /ˈʌpˌbrɪŋɪŋ/ *n* воспитание.

pdate /ʌpˈdeɪt/ *vt* модернизировать *impf & pf*; (a book etc.) дополнять *impf*, дополнить *pf*.

pgrade /ʌpˈgreɪd/ *vt* повышать *impf*, повысить *pf* (по службе).

pheaval /ʌpˈhiːv(ə)l/ *n* потрясение.

phill /ˈʌpˌhɪl/ *adj* (fig) тяжёлый; *adv* в гору.

phold /ʌpˈhəʊld/ *vt* поддерживать *impf*, поддержать *pf*.

pholster /ʌpˈhəʊlstə(r)/ *vt* обивать *impf*, обить *pf*. **upholsterer** /-rə(r)/ *n* обойщик. **upholstery** /-rɪ/ *n* обивка.

pkeep /ˈʌpkiːp/ *n* содержание.

pland /ˈʌplənd/ *n* гористая часть страны; *adj* нагорный.

plift /ʌpˈlɪft/ *vt* поднимать *impf*, поднять *pf*.

p-market /ʌpˈmɑːkɪt/ *adj* дорогой.

pon /əˈpɒn/ *prep* (position) на +*prep*, (motion) на+*acc*; see on

pper /ˈʌpə(r)/ *adj* верхний; (so-

cially, in rank) высший; gain the ~ hand одерживать *impf*, одержать *pf* верх (over над+*instr*); *n* передок. **uppermost** *adj* самый верхний, высший; be ~ in person's mind больше всего занимать *impf*, занять *pf* мысли кого-л.

upright /ˈʌpraɪt/ *n* стойка; *adj* вертикальный; (honest) честный; ~ piano пианино *neut indecl*.

uprising /ˈʌpˌraɪzɪŋ/ *n* восстание.

uproar /ˈʌprɔː(r)/ *n* шум, гам.

uproot /ʌpˈruːt/ *vt* вырывать *impf*, вырвать *pf* с корнем; (people) выселять *impf*, выселить *pf*.

upset *n* /ˈʌpset/ расстройство; *vt* /ʌpˈset/ расстраивать *impf*, расстроить *pf*; (overturn) опрокидывать *impf*, опрокинуть *pf*; *adj* (miserable) расстроенный; ~ stomach расстройство желудка.

upshot /ˈʌpʃɒt/ *n* развязка, результат.

upside-down /ˌʌpsaɪdˈdaʊn/ *adj* перевёрнутый вверх дном; *adv* вверх дном; (in disorder) в беспорядке.

upstairs /ʌpˈsteəz/ *adv* (position) наверху; (motion) наверх; *n* верхний этаж; *adj* находящийся в верхнем этаже.

upstart /ˈʌpstɑːt/ *n* выскочка *m & f*.

upstream /ˈʌpstriːm/ *adv* против течения; (situation) вверх по течению.

upsurge /ˈʌpsɜːdʒ/ *n* подъём, волна.

uptake /ˈʌpteɪk/ *n*: be quick on the ~ быстро соображать *impf*, сообразить *pf*.

upturn /ˈʌptɜːn/ *n* (fig) улучше-

ние. **upturned** /-tɜ:nd/ *adj* (*face etc.*) поднятый кверху; (*inverted*) перевёрнутый.

upward /ˈʌpwəd/ *adj* направленный вверх. **upwards** /-wədz/ *adv* вверх; ~ **of** свыше+*gen*.

uranium /juˈreɪnɪəm/ *n* уран.

urban /ˈɜːbən/ *adj* городской.

urbane /ɜːˈbeɪn/ *adj* вежливый.

urchin /ˈɜːtʃɪn/ *n* мальчишка *m*.

urge /ɜːdʒ/ *n* (*incitement*) побуждение; (*desire*) желание; *vt* (*impel*, ~ *on*) подгонять *impf*, подогнать *pf*; (*warn*) предупреждать *impf*, предупредить *pf*; (*try to persuade*) убеждать *impf*.

urgency /ˈɜːdʒ(ə)nsɪ/ *n* срочность, важность; **a matter of great** ~ срочное дело. **urgent** /ˈɜːdʒ(ə)nt/ *adj* срочный; (*insistent*) настоятельный. **urgently** /ˈɜːdʒ(ə)ntlɪ/ *adv* срочно.

urinate /ˈjʊərɪneɪt/ *vi* мочиться *impf*, по~ *pf*. **urine** /ˈjʊərɪn/ *n* моча.

urn /ɜːn/ *n* урна.

US(A) *abbr* (*of* United States of America) США, Соединённые Штаты Америки.

usable /ˈjuːzəb(ə)l/ *adj* годный к употреблению. **usage** /ˈjuːsɪdʒ/ *n* употребление; (*treatment*) обращение; (*utilization*) употребление, пользование; (*benefit*) польза; (*application*) применение; **it is no** ~ **(-ing)** бесполезно (+*inf*); **make** ~ **of** использовать *impf* & *pf*; пользоваться *impf* +*instr*; *vt* /juːz/ употреблять *impf*, употребить *pf*; пользоваться *impf* +*instr*, (*apply*) применять *impf*, применить *pf*; (*treat*) обращаться *impf* c+*instr*; **I** ~**d to see him** оне я часто его встречал; **be, get** ~**d to** привыкать *impf*, привыкнуть *pf* (**to**

к+*dat*); ~ **up** расходовать *impf* из~ *pf*. **used** /juːzd/ *adj* (*second hand*) старый. **useful** /ˈjuːs-/ *adj* полезный; **come in** ~, **prov** ~ пригодиться *pf* (**to** +*dat* **useless** /ˈjuːslɪs/ *adj* бесполе ный. **user** /ˈjuːzə(r)/ *n* потреби тель *m*.

usher /ˈʌʃə(r)/ *n* (*theat*) билетё *vt* (*lead in*) вводить *impf*, вве сти *pf*; (*proclaim*, ~ **in**) возве щать *impf*, возвестить *pf* **usherette** /ˌʌʃəˈret/ *n* б летёрша.

USSR *abbr* (*of* Union of Sovi Socialist Republics) СССР Союз Советских Социалист ческих Республик.

usual /ˈjuːʒʊəl/ *adj* обыкнове ный, обычный; **as** ~ как об чно. **usually** /-lɪ/ *ad* обыкновенно, обычно.

usurp /juːˈzɜːp/ *vt* узурпироват *impf* & *pf*. **usurper** /-ˈzɜːpə(r)/ *n* узурпатор.

usury /ˈjuːʒərɪ/ *n* ростовщич ство.

utensil /juːˈtens(ə)l/ *n* инстру мент; *pl* утварь, посуда.

uterus /ˈjuːtərəs/ *n* матка.

utilitarian /ˌjuːtɪlɪˈteərɪən/ *adj* ут литарный. **utilitarianis** /-ˌnɪz(ə)m/ *n* утилитаризм. **uti ity** /juːˈtɪlɪtɪ/ *n* полезность; *p* **public utilities** коммунальн услуги *f pl*. **utilize** /ˈjuːtɪlaɪz/ *v* использовать *impf* & *pf*.

utmost /ˈʌtməʊst/ *adj* (*extrem* крайний; **this is of the** ~ **impor ance to me** это для меня крайне важно; *n*: **do one's** ~ д лать *impf*, с~ *pf* всё возмо жное.

Utopia /juːˈtəʊpɪə/ *n* утопи **utopian** /-pɪən/ *adj* утопи ский.

utter /ˈʌtə(r)/ *attrib* полный, аб

солю́тный; (*out-and-out*) отъя́вленный (*coll*); vt произноси́ть *impf*, произнести́ *pf*; (*let out*) издава́ть *impf*, изда́ть *pf*. **utterance** /ˈʌtərəns/ n (*uttering*) произнесе́ние; (*pronouncement*) выска́зывание. **utterly** /ˈʌtəli/ adv соверше́нно.

Uzbek /ˈʌzbek/ n узбе́к, -е́чка. **Uzbekistan** /ˌʌzbekɪˈstɑːn/ n Узбекиста́н.

V

vacancy /ˈveɪkənsɪ/ n (*for job*) вака́нсия, свобо́дное ме́сто; (*at hotel*) свобо́дный но́мер. **vacant** /-kənt/ adj (*post*) вака́нтный; (*post; not engaged, free*) свобо́дный; (*empty*) пусто́й; (*look*) отсу́тствующий. **vacate** /vəˈkeɪt/ vt освобожда́ть *impf*, освободи́ть *pf*. **vacation** /vəˈkeɪʃ(ə)n/ n кани́кулы (-л) *pl*; (*leave*) о́тпуск.

vaccinate /ˈvæksɪˌneɪt/ vt вакцини́ровать *impf* & *pf*. **vaccination** /-ˈneɪʃ(ə)n/ n приви́вка (*against*, от, про́тив +*gen*). **vaccine** /ˈvæksiːn/ n вакци́на.

vacillate /ˈvæsɪˌleɪt/ vi колеба́ться *impf*. **vacillation** /-ˈleɪʃ(ə)n/ n колеба́ние.

vacuous /ˈvækjʊəs/ adj пусто́й. **vacuum** /ˈvækjʊəm/ n ва́куум; (*fig*) пустота́; vt пылесо́сить *impf*, про~ *pf*; ~ **cleaner** пылесо́с; ~ **flask** те́рмос.

vagabond /ˈvægəˌbɒnd/ n бродя́га *m*. **vagary** /ˈveɪgərɪ/ n капри́з. **vagina** /vəˈdʒaɪnə/ n влага́лище. **vagrant** /ˈveɪgrənt/ n бродя́га *m*. **vague** /veɪg/ adj (*indeterminate,*

uncertain) неопределённый; (*unclear*) нея́сный; (*dim*) сму́тный; (*absent-minded*) рассе́янный. **vagueness** /-nɪs/ n неопределённость, нея́сность; (*absent-mindedness*) рассе́янность.

vain /veɪn/ adj (*futile*) тще́тный, напра́сный; (*empty*) пусто́й; (*conceited*) тщесла́вный; **in** ~ напра́сно.

vale /veɪl/ n дол, доли́на.

valentine /ˈvælənˌtaɪn/ n (*card*) поздрави́тельная ка́рточка с днём свято́го Валенти́на.

valet /ˈvælɪt/ n камерди́нер.

valiant /ˈvæljənt/ adj хра́брый.

valid /ˈvælɪd/ adj действи́тельный; (*weighty*) ве́ский. **validate** /-ˌdeɪt/ vt (*ratify*) утвержда́ть *impf*, утверди́ть *pf*. **validity** /vəˈlɪdɪtɪ/ n действи́тельность; (*weightiness*) ве́скость.

valley /ˈvælɪ/ n доли́на.

valour /ˈvælə(r)/ n до́блесть.

valuable /ˈvæljʊəb(ə)l/ adj це́нный; n pl це́нности f pl. **valuation** /ˌvæljʊˈeɪʃ(ə)n/ n оце́нка. **value** /ˈvæljuː/ n це́нность; (*math*) величина́; pl це́нности f pl; ~**-added tax** нало́г на доба́вленную сто́имость; ~ **judgement** субъекти́вная оце́нка; vt (*estimate*) оце́нивать *impf*, оцени́ть *pf*; (*hold dear*) цени́ть *impf*.

valve /vælv/ n (*tech, med, mus*) кла́пан; (*tech*) ве́нтиль m; (*radio*) электро́нная ла́мпа.

vampire /ˈvæmpaɪə(r)/ n вампи́р.

van /væn/ n фурго́н.

vandal /ˈvænd(ə)l/ n ванда́л. **vandalism** /-də,lɪz(ə)m/ n вандали́зм. **vandalize** /-də,laɪz/ vt разруша́ть *impf*, разру́шить *pf*.

vanguard /ˈvængɑːd/ n аванга́рд.

vanilla /vəˈnɪlə/ n вани́ль.

vanish /ˈvænɪʃ/ vi исчеза́ть impf, исче́знуть pf.

vanity /ˈvænɪtɪ/ n (futility) тщета́; (conceit) тщесла́вие.

vanquish /ˈvæŋkwɪʃ/ vt побежда́ть impf, победи́ть pf.

vantage-point /ˈvɑːntɪdʒpɔɪnt/ n (mil) наблюда́тельный пункт; (fig) вы́годная пози́ция.

vapour /ˈveɪpə(r)/ n пар.

variable /ˈveərɪəb(ə)l/ adj изме́нчивый; (weather) неусто́йчивый, переме́нный; n (math) переме́нная (величина́). **variance** /ˈveərɪəns/ n: be at ~ with (contradict) противоре́чить impf +dat; (disagree) расходи́ться impf, разойти́сь pf во мне́ниях с+instr. **variant** /-rɪənt/ n вариа́нт. **variation** /-rɪˈeɪʃ(ə)n/ n (varying) измене́ние; (variant) вариа́нт; (variety) разнови́дность; (mus) вариа́ция.

varicose /ˈværɪˌkəʊs/ adj: ~ veins расшире́ние вен.

varied /ˈveərɪd/ adj разнообра́зный. **variegated** /ˈveərɪˌgeɪtɪd/ adj разноцве́тный. **variety** /vəˈraɪətɪ/ n разнообра́зие; (sort) разнови́дность; (a number) ряд; ~ show варьете́ neut indecl. **various** /ˈveərɪəs/ adj ра́зный.

varnish /ˈvɑːnɪʃ/ n лак; vt лакирова́ть impf, от~ pf.

vary /ˈveərɪ/ vt разнообра́зить impf, меня́ть impf; vi (change) меня́ться impf; (differ) разни́ться impf.

vase /vɑːz/ n ва́за.

Vaseline /ˈvæsɪˌliːn/ n (propr) вазели́н.

vast /vɑːst/ adj грома́дный. **vastly** /-lɪ/ adv значи́тельно.

VAT abbr (of value-added tax) нало́г на доба́вленную сто́имость.

vat /væt/ n чан, бак.

vaudeville /ˈvɔːdəvɪl/ n водеви́ль m.

vault¹ /vɔːlt/ n (leap) прыжо́к; перепры́гивать impf, перепры́гнуть pf; vi прыга́ть impf.

vault² /vɔːlt/ n (arch, covering) свод; (cellar) по́греб; (tomb) склеп. **vaulted** /-tɪd/ adj сво́дчатый.

VDU abbr (of visual display unit) монито́р.

veal /viːl/ n теля́тина.

vector /ˈvektə(r)/ n (math) ве́ктор.

veer /vɪə(r)/ vi (change direction) изменя́ть impf, измени́ть pf направле́ние; (turn) повора́чивать impf, повороти́ть pf.

vegetable /ˈvedʒɪtəb(ə)l/ n о́вощ; adj овощно́й. **vegetarian** /ˌvedʒɪˈteərɪən/ n вегетариа́нец, -нка; attrib вегетариа́нский. **vegetate** /ˈvedʒɪˌteɪt/ vi (fig) прозяба́ть impf. **vegetation** /ˌvedʒɪˈteɪʃ(ə)n/ n расти́тельность.

vehemence /ˈviːməns/ n (force) си́ла; (passion) стра́стность. **vehement** /-mənt/ adj (forceful) си́льный; (passionate) стра́стный.

vehicle /ˈviːɪk(ə)l/ n тра́нспортное сре́дство; (motor ~) автомоби́ль m; (medium) сре́дство.

veil /veɪl/ n вуа́ль; (fig) заве́са. **veiled** /veɪld/ adj скры́тый.

vein /veɪn/ n ве́на; (of leaf, streak) жи́лка; in the same ~ в том же ду́хе.

velocity /vɪˈlɒsɪtɪ/ n ско́рость.

velvet /ˈvelvɪt/ n ба́рхат; adj ба́рхатный. **velvety** /-tɪ/ adj ба́рхатистый.

ending-machine /'vendɪŋ/ n торго́вый автома́т. **vendor** /-də(r)/ n прода́вец.

vendetta /ven'detə/ n венде́тта.

veneer /vɪ'nɪə(r)/ n фане́ра, (fig) лоск.

venerable /'venərəb(ə)l/ adj почте́нный. **venerate** /-,reɪt/ vt благогове́ть impf пе́ред+instr. **veneration** /,venə'reɪʃ(ə)n/ n благогове́ние.

venereal /vɪ'nɪərɪəl/ adj венери́ческий.

venetian blind /vɪ'ni:ʃ(ə)n blaɪnd/ n жалюзи́ neut indecl.

vengeance /'vendʒ(ə)ns/ n месть; **with a** ~ вовсю́. **vengeful** /'vendʒful/ adj мсти́тельный.

venison /'venɪs(ə)n/ n оле́нина.

venom /'venəm/ n яд. **venomous** /-məs/ adj ядови́тый.

vent[1] /vent/ n (opening) вы́ход (also fig), отве́рстие; vt (feelings) дава́ть impf, дать pf вы́ход+dat; излива́ть impf, изли́ть pf (on на+acc).

vent[2] /vent/ n (slit) разре́з.

ventilate /'ventɪ,leɪt/ vt прове́тривать impf, прове́трить pf. **ventilation** /-'leɪʃ(ə)n/ n вентиля́ция. **ventilator** /'ventɪ,leɪtə(r)/ n вентиля́тор.

ventriloquist /ven'trɪlə,kwɪst/ n чревовеща́тель m.

venture /'ventʃə(r)/ n предприя́тие; vi (dare) осме́ливаться impf, осме́литься pf; vt (risk) рискова́ть impf+instr.

venue /'venju:/ n ме́сто.

veranda /və'rændə/ n вера́нда.

verb /vɜ:b/ n глаго́л. **verbal** /'vɜ:b(ə)l/ adj (oral) у́стный; (relating to words) слове́сный; (gram) отглаго́льный. **verbatim** /vɜ:'beɪtɪm/ adj досло́вный;

adv досло́вно. **verbose** /vɜ:'bəʊs/ adj многосло́вный.

verdict /'vɜ:dɪkt/ n пригово́р.

verge /vɜ:dʒ/ n (also fig) край; (of road) обо́чина; (fig) грань; **on the** ~ **of** на гра́ни+gen; **he was on the** ~ **of telling all** он чуть не рассказа́л всё; vi: ~ **on** грани́чить impf c+instr.

verification /,verɪfɪ'keɪʃ(ə)n/ n прове́рка; (confirmation) подтвержде́ние. **verify** /'verɪ,faɪ/ vt (check) проверя́ть impf, прове́рить pf; (confirm) подтвержда́ть impf, подтверди́ть pf.

vermin /'vɜ:mɪn/ n вреди́тели m pl.

vernacular /və'nækjʊlə(r)/ n родно́й язы́к; ме́стный диале́кт; (homely language) разгово́рный язы́к.

versatile /'vɜ:sə,taɪl/ adj многосторо́нний.

verse /vɜ:s/ n (also bibl) стих; (stanza) строфа́; (poetry) стихи́ m pl. **versed** /vɜ:st/ adj о́пытный, све́дущий (in в+prep).

version /'vɜ:ʃ(ə)n/ n (variant) вариа́нт; (interpretation) ве́рсия; (text) текст.

versus /'vɜ:səs/ prep про́тив+gen.

vertebra /'vɜ:tɪbrə/ n позвоно́к, pl позвоно́чки. **vertebrate** /-brət/ n позвоно́чное живо́тное sb.

vertical /'vɜ:tɪk(ə)l/ adj вертика́льный; n вертика́ль.

vertigo /'vɜ:tɪ,gəʊ/ n головокруже́ние.

verve /vɜ:v/ n жи́вость, энтузиа́зм.

very /'verɪ/ adj (that ~ same) тот са́мый; (this ~ same) э́тот са́мый; **at that** ~ **moment** в тот са́мый моме́нт; (precisely) как раз; **you are the** ~ **person I was**

looking for как раз вас я иска́л; **the ~** (even the) да́же, оди́н; **the ~ thought frightens me** одна́, да́же, мысль об э́том меня́ пуга́ет; (the extreme) са́мый; **at the ~ end** в са́мом конце́; adv о́чень; **~ much** о́чень; **~ much +comp** гора́здо +comp; **~ +superl, superl;** **~ first** са́мый пе́рвый; **~ well** (agreement) хорошо́, ла́дно; **not ~ +neg.**

vessel /'ves(ə)l/ n сосу́д; (ship) су́дно.

vest[1] /vest/ n ма́йка; (waistcoat) жиле́т.

vest[2] /vest/ vt (with power) облека́ть impf, обле́чь pf (with +instr). **vested** /-tɪd/ adj: **~ interest** ли́чная заинтересо́ванность; **~ interests** (entrepreneurs) кру́пные предпринима́тели m pl.

vestibule /'vestɪ,bju:l/ n вестибю́ль m.

vestige /'vestɪdʒ/ n (trace) след; (sign) при́знак.

vestments /'vestmənts/ n pl (eccl) облаче́ние. **vestry** /'vestrɪ/ n ри́зница.

vet /vet/ n ветерина́р; vt (fig) проверя́ть impf, прове́рить pf.

veteran /'vetərən/ n ветера́н; adj ста́рый.

veterinary /'vetə,rɪnərɪ/ adj ветерина́рный; n ветерина́р.

veto /'vi:təʊ/ n ве́то neut indecl; vt налага́ть impf, наложи́ть pf ве́то на+acc.

vex /veks/ vt досажда́ть impf, досади́ть pf +dat. **vexation** /vek'seɪʃ(ə)n/ n доса́да. **vexed** /vekst/ adj (annoyed) серди́тый; (question) спо́рный. **vexatious** /vek'seɪʃəs/, **vexing** /'veksɪŋ/ adj доса́дный.

via /'vaɪə/ prep че́рез+acc.

viable /'vaɪəb(ə)l/ adj (able to survive) жизнеспосо́бный; (feasible) осуществи́мый.

viaduct /'vaɪə,dʌkt/ n виаду́к.

vibrant /'vaɪbrənt/ adj (lively) живо́й. **vibrate** /vaɪ'breɪt/ vi вибри́ровать impf; vt (make ~) заставля́ть impf, заста́вить pf вибри́ровать. **vibration** /vaɪ'breɪʃ(ə)n/ n вибра́ция. **vibrate** /vɪ'breɪtə(r)/ n вибра́то neut in decl.

vicar /'vɪkə(r)/ n приходски́й свяще́нник. **vicarage** /-rɪdʒ/ n дом свяще́нника.

vicarious /vɪ'keərɪəs/ adj чужо́й.

vice[1] /vaɪs/ n (evil) поро́к.

vice[2] /vaɪs/ n (tech) тиски́ (-ко́в) pl.

vice- in comb ви́це-, замести́тель m; **~-chairman** замести́тель m председа́теля. **~-chancellor** (univ) проре́ктор. **~-president** ви́це-президе́нт. **viceroy** /'vaɪsrɔɪ/ n ви́це-коро́ль m.

vice versa /,vaɪsɪ 'vɜ:sə/ adv наоборо́т.

vicinity /vɪ'sɪnɪtɪ/ n окре́стность; **in the ~** побли́зости (of +gen).

vicious /'vɪʃəs/ adj зло́бный; **~ circle** поро́чный круг.

vicissitude /vɪ'sɪsɪ,tju:d/ n превра́тность.

victim /'vɪktɪm/ n же́ртва; (of accident) пострада́вший sb. **victimization** /,vɪktɪmaɪ'zeɪʃ(ə)n/ n пресле́дование. **victimize** /'vɪktɪ,maɪz/ vt пресле́довать impf.

victor /'vɪktə(r)/ n победи́тель m, -ница. **Victorian** /vɪk'tɔ:rɪən/ adj викториа́нский. **victorious** /vɪk'tɔ:rɪəs/ adj победоно́сный. **victory** /'vɪktərɪ/ n

побе́да.

ideo /'vɪdɪəʊ/ *n* (~ recorder, ~ cassette, ~ film) ви́део *neut indecl*; ~ **camera** видеока́мера; ~ **cassette** видеокассе́та; ~ (cassette) **recorder** видеомагнитофо́н; ~ **game** видеоигра́; ~ *vt* запи́сывать *impf*, записа́ть *pf* на ви́део.

ie /vaɪ/ *vi* сопе́рничать *impf* (with c+*instr*; for в+*prep*).

Vietnam /ˌvjet'næm/ *n* Вьетна́м.

Vietnamese /ˌvjetnə'miːz/ *n* вьетна́мец, -мка; *adj* вьетна́мский.

iew /vju:/ *n* (prospect, picture) вид; (opinion) взгляд; (viewing) просмо́тр; (inspection) осмо́тр; **in ~ of** ввиду́+*gen*; **on ~** вы́ставленный для обозре́ния; **with a ~ to** с це́лью+*gen*, +*inf*; *vt* (pictures etc.) рассма́тривать *impf*; (inspect) осма́тривать *impf*, осмотре́ть *pf*; (mentally) смотре́ть *impf* на+*acc*. **viewer** /'vjuːə(r)/ *n* зри́тель *m*, ~ница. **viewfinder** /'vju:ˌfaɪndə(r)/ *n* видоиска́тель *m*. **viewpoint** *n* то́чка зре́ния.

vigil /'vɪdʒɪl/ *n* бде́ние; **keep ~** дежу́рить *impf*. **vigilance** /-ləns/ *n* бди́тельность. **vigilant** /-lənt/ *adj* бди́тельный. **vigilante** /ˌvɪdʒɪ'lænti/ *n* дру́жинник.

vigorous /'vɪɡərəs/ *adj* си́льный, энерги́чный. **vigour** /'vɪɡə(r)/ *n* си́ла, эне́ргия.

vile /vaɪl/ *adj* гну́сный. **vilify** /'vɪlɪˌfaɪ/ *vt* черни́ть *impf*, о~ *pf*.

villa /'vɪlə/ *n* ви́лла.

village /'vɪlɪdʒ/ *n* дере́вня; *attrib* дереве́нский. **villager** /-dʒə(r)/ *n* жи́тель *m* дере́вни.

villain /'vɪlən/ *n* злоде́й.

vinaigrette /ˌvɪnɪ'ɡret/ *n* припра́ва из у́ксуса и оли́вкового

ма́сла.

vindicate /'vɪndɪˌkeɪt/ *vt* опра́вдывать *impf*, оправда́ть *pf*. **vindication** /-'keɪʃ(ə)n/ *n* оправда́ние.

vindictive /vɪn'dɪktɪv/ *adj* мсти́тельный.

vine /vaɪn/ *n* виногра́дная лоза́.

vinegar /'vɪnɪɡə(r)/ *n* у́ксус.

vineyard /'vɪnjəd/ *n* виногра́дник.

vintage /'vɪntɪdʒ/ *n* (year) год; (fig) вы́пуск; *attrib* (wine) ма́рочный; (car) архаи́ческий.

viola /vɪ'əʊlə/ *n* (mus) альт.

violate /'vaɪəˌleɪt/ *vt* (treaty, privacy) наруша́ть *impf*, нару́шить *pf*; (grave) оскверня́ть *impf*, оскверни́ть *pf*. **violation** /-'leɪʃ(ə)n/ *n* наруше́ние; оскверне́ние.

violence /'vaɪələns/ *n* (physical coercion, force) наси́лие; (strength, force) си́ла. **violent** /-lənt/ *adj* (person, storm, argument) свире́пый; (pain) си́льный; (death) наси́льственный. **violently** /-ləntli/ *adv* си́льно, о́чень.

violet /'vaɪələt/ *n* (bot) фиа́лка; (colour) фиоле́товый цвет; *adj* фиоле́товый.

violin /ˌvaɪə'lɪn/ *n* скри́пка. **violinist** /-nɪst/ *n* скрипа́ч, ~ка.

VIP *abbr* (of very important person) о́чень ва́жное лицо́.

viper /'vaɪpə(r)/ *n* гадю́ка.

virgin /'vɜːdʒɪn/ *n* де́вственница, (male) де́вственник; **V~ Mary** де́ва Мари́я. **virginal** /-ɪn(ə)l/ *adj* де́вственный. **virginity** /və'dʒɪnɪti/ *n* де́вственность. **Virgo** /'vɜːɡəʊ/ *n* Де́ва.

virile /'vɪraɪl/ *adj* мужественный. **virility** /-'rɪlɪti/ *n* му́жество.

virtual /'vɜːtjʊəl/ *adj* факти́ческий; (*comput*) виртуа́льный. **virtually** /-lɪ/ *adv* факти́чески.

virtue /'vɜːtjuː/ *n* (*excellence*) доброде́тель; (*merit*) досто́инство; **by ~ of** на основа́нии+*gen*. **virtuosity** /,vɜːtjʊ'ɒsɪtɪ/ *n* виртуо́зность. **virtuoso** /,vɜːtjʊ'əʊsəʊ/ *n* виртуо́з. **virtuous** /'vɜːtjʊəs/ *adj* доброде́тельный.

virulent /'vɪrʊlənt/ *adj* (*med*) вируле́нтный; (*fig*) зло́бный.

virus /'vaɪərəs/ *n* ви́рус.

visa /'viːzə/ *n* ви́за.

vis-à-vis /,viːzɑː'viː/ *prep* (*with regard to*) по отноше́нию к+*dat*.

viscount /'vaɪkaʊnt/ *n* вико́нт. **viscountess** /-tɪs/ *n* виконте́сса.

viscous /'vɪskəs/ *adj* вя́зкий.

visibility /,vɪzɪ'bɪlɪtɪ/ *n* ви́димость. **visible** /'vɪzɪb(ə)l/ *adj* ви́димый. **visibly** /'vɪzɪblɪ/ *adv* я́вно, заме́тно.

vision /'vɪʒ(ə)n/ *n* (*sense*) зре́ние; (*apparition*) виде́ние; (*dream*) мечта́; (*insight*) проница́тельность. **visionary** /'vɪʒənərɪ/ *adj* (*unreal*) призра́чный; (*impracticable*) неосуществи́мый; (*insightful*) проница́тельный; *n* (*dreamer*) мечта́тель *m*.

visit /'vɪzɪt/ *n* посеще́ние, визи́т; *vt* посеща́ть *impf*, посети́ть *pf*; (*call on*) заходи́ть *impf*, зайти́ *pf* к+*dat*. **visitation** /,vɪzɪ'teɪʃ(ə)n/ *n* официа́льное посеще́ние. **visitor** /'vɪzɪtə(r)/ *n* гость *m*, посети́тель *m*.

visor /'vaɪzə(r)/ *n* (*of cap*) козырёк; (*in car*) солнцезащи́тный щито́к; (*of helmet*) забра́ло.

vista /'vɪstə/ *n* перспекти́ва, вид.

visual /'vɪzjʊəl/ *adj* (*of vision*) зри́тельный; (*graphic*) нагля́дный; **~ aids** нагля́дные посо́бия *neut pl*. **visualize** /-,laɪ... *vt* представля́ть *impf*, предста́вить *pf* себе́.

vital /'vaɪt(ə)l/ *adj* абсолю́тно необходи́мый (**to, for** для+*gen* (*essential to life*) жи́зненный; **~ importance** первостепе́нно ва́жности. **vitality** /vaɪ'tælɪtɪ/ *n* (*liveliness*) эне́ргия. **vitall** /'vaɪtəlɪ/ *adv* жи́зненно.

vitamin /'vɪtəmɪn/ *n* витами́н.

vitreous /'vɪtrɪəs/ *adj* стекля́нный.

vitriolic /,vɪtrɪ'ɒlɪk/ *adj* (*fig* е́дкий.

vivacious /vɪ'veɪʃəs/ *adj* живо́й **vivacity** /vɪ'væsɪtɪ/ *n* жи́вость.

viva (voce) /'vaɪvə ('vəʊtʃɪ у́стный экза́мен.

vivid /'vɪvɪd/ *adj* (*bright*) я́ркий (*lively*) живо́й. **vividness** /- *n* я́ркость; жи́вость.

vivisection /,vɪvɪ'sekʃ(ə)n/ *n* виви се́кция.

vixen /'vɪks(ə)n/ *n* лиси́ца са́мка.

viz. /vɪz/ *adv* то есть, а и́менно

vocabulary /və'kæbjʊlərɪ/ *n* (*range, list, of words*) словáр *m*; (*range of words*) запа́с слов (*of a language*) слова́рный со ста́в.

vocal /'vəʊk(ə)l/ *adj* голосово́й (*mus*) вока́льный; (*noisy*) шу́м ный; **~ chord** голосова́я свя́зка. **vocalist** /-lɪst/ *n* певе́ц -ви́ца.

vocation /və'keɪʃ(ə)n/ *n* призва́ ние. **vocational** /-n(ə)l/ *adj* профессиона́льный.

vociferous /və'sɪfərəs/ *ad* шу́мный.

vodka /'vɒdkə/ *n* во́дка.

vogue /vəʊg/ *n* мо́да; в

мо́де.

oice /vɔɪs/ n го́лос; ~ mail го́лосовая по́чта; vt выража́ть impf, вы́разить pf.

oid /vɔɪd/ n пустота́; adj (empty) пусто́й; (invalid) недействи́тельный; ~ of лишённый +gen.

olatile /ˈvɒlətaɪl/ adj (chem) лету́чий; (person) непостоя́нный, неусто́йчивый.

olcanic /vɒlˈkænɪk/ adj вулкани́ческий. **volcano** /-ˈkeɪnəʊ/ n вулка́н.

ole /vəʊl/ n (zool) полёвка.

olition /vəˈlɪʃ(ə)n/ n во́ля; by one's own ~ по свое́й во́ле.

olley /ˈvɒlɪ/ n (missiles) залп; (fig) град; (sport) уда́р с лёта; vt (sport) уда́рить impf, ударя́ть pf с лёта. **volleyball** n волейбо́л.

olt /vəʊlt/ n вольт. **voltage** /ˈvəʊltɪdʒ/ n напряже́ние.

oluble /ˈvɒljʊb(ə)l/ adj говорли́вый.

olume /ˈvɒljuːm/ n (book) том; (capacity, size) объём; (loudness) гро́мкость. **voluminous** /vəˈljuːmɪnəs/ adj обши́рный.

oluntary /ˈvɒləntərɪ/ adj доброво́льный. **volunteer** /vɒlənˈtɪə(r)/ n доброво́лец; vt предлага́ть impf, предложи́ть pf; vi (offer) вызыва́ться impf, вы́зваться pf (inf, +inf; for в+acc); (mil) идти́ impf, пойти́ pf доброво́льцем.

oluptuous /vəˈlʌptjʊəs/ adj сластолюби́вый.

omit /ˈvɒmɪt/ n рво́та; vt (& i) рвать impf, вы́рвать pf impers (+instr); he was ~ing blood его́ рва́ло кро́вью.

oracious /vəˈreɪʃəs/ adj прожо́рливый; (fig) нена́сытный.

ortex /ˈvɔːteks/ n (also fig) водово́рот, вихрь m.

vote /vəʊt/ n (poll) голосова́ние; (individual ~) го́лос; (the ~) (suffrage) пра́во го́лоса; (resolution) во́тум no pl; ~ of no confidence во́тум недове́рия (in +dat); ~ of thanks выраже́ние благода́рности; vi голосова́ть impf, про~ pf (for за+acc; against про́тив+gen); vt (allocate by ~) ассигнова́ть impf & pf; (deem) признава́ть impf, призна́ть pf; the film was ~d a failure фильм был при́знан неуда́чным; ~ in избира́ть impf, избра́ть pf голосова́нием. **voter** /-tə(r)/ n избира́тель m.

vouch /vaʊtʃ/ vi: ~ for руча́ться impf, поручи́ться pf за та+acc. **voucher** /-tʃə(r)/ n тало́н.

vow /vaʊ/ n обе́т; v: кля́сться impf, по~ pf в+prep.

vowel /ˈvaʊəl/ n гла́сный sb.

voyage /ˈvɔɪɪdʒ/ n путеше́ствие.

vulgar /ˈvʌlɡə(r)/ adj вульга́рный, гру́бый, по́шлый. **vulgarity** /-ˈɡærɪtɪ/ n вульга́рность, по́шлость.

vulnerable /ˈvʌlnərəb(ə)l/ adj уязви́мый.

vulture /ˈvʌltʃə(r)/ n гриф; (fig) хи́щник.

W

wad /wɒd/ n комо́к; (bundle) па́чка. **wadding** /-dɪŋ/ n ва́та; (padding) наби́вка.

waddle /ˈwɒd(ə)l/ vi ходи́ть indet, идти́ det, пойти́ pf вперева́лку (coll).

wade /weɪd/ vt & i (river) переходи́ть impf, перейти́ pf вброд; vi: ~ through (mud etc.) проби́ра́ться impf, пробра́ться pf по+dat; (sth boring etc.) одоле-

вать *impf*, одолеть *pf*.

wafer /'weɪfə(r)/ *n* вафля.

waffle¹ /'wɒf(ə)l/ *n* (*dish*) вафля.

waffle² /'wɒf(ə)l/ *vi* трепаться *impf*.

waft /wɒft/ *vt & i* нести(сь) *impf*, по~ *pf*.

wag /wæɡ/ *vt & i* (*tail*) вилять *impf*, вильнуть *pf* (+*instr*); *vt* (*finger*) грозить *impf*, по~ *pf* +*instr*.

wage¹ /weɪdʒ/ *n* (*pay*) see wages

wage² /weɪdʒ/ *vt*: ~ war вести *impf*, про~ *pf* войну.

wager /'weɪdʒə(r)/ *n* пари *neut indecl*; *vi* держать *impf* пари (that что); *vt* ставить *impf*, по~ *pf*.

wages /'weɪdʒɪz/ *n pl* заработная плата.

waggle /'wæɡ(ə)l/ *vt & i* помахивать *impf*, помахать *pf* (+*instr*).

wag(g)on /'wæɡən/ *n* (*carriage*) повозка; (*cart*) телега; (*rly*) вагон-платформа.

wail /weɪl/ *n* вопль *m*; *vi* вопить *impf*.

waist /weɪst/ *n* талия; (*level of* ~) пояс; ~-deep, high (*adv*) по пояс. **waistband** *n* пояс. **waistcoat** *n* жилет. **waistline** *n* талия.

wait /weɪt/ *n* ожидание; lie in ~ (for) подстерегать *impf*; подстеречь *pf*; *vi* (*& t*) (*also* ~ for) ждать *impf* (+*gen*); *vi* (*be a waiter, waitress*) быть официантом, -кой; ~ on обслуживать *impf*, обслужить *pf*. **waiter** /-tə(r)/ *n* официант. **waiting** /-tɪŋ/ *n*: ~-list список *impf*; ~-room приёмная *sb*; (*rly*) зал ожидания. **waitress** /-trɪs/ *n* официантка.

waive /weɪv/ *vt* отказываться *impf*, отказаться *pf* от+*gen*.

wake¹ /weɪk/ *n* (*at funeral*) поминки (-нок) *pl*.

wake² /weɪk/ *n* (*naut*) кильватер; in the ~ of по следу +*gen*, +*instr*.

wake³ /weɪk/ *vt* (*also* ~ up) будить *impf*, раз~ *pf*; *vi* (*also* ~ up) просыпаться *impf*, проснуться *pf*.

Wales /weɪlz/ *n* Уэльс.

walk /wɔːk/ *n* (*walking*) ходьба; (*gait*) походка; (*stroll*) прогулка; (*path*) тропа; ~-out (*strike*) забастовка; (*as protest*) демонстративный уход; ~-over лёгкая победа; ten minutes' ~ from here десять минут ходьбы отсюда; go for a ~ идти *impf*, пойти *pf* гулять; from all ~s of life всех слоёв общества; *vi* ходить *indet*, идти *det*, пойти *pf*; гулять *impf*, по~ *pf*; ~ away, off уходить *impf*, уйти *pf*; ~ in входить *impf*, войти *pf*; ~ out выходить *impf*, выйти *pf*; ~ out on бросать *impf*, бросить *pf*; (*traverse*) обходить *impf*, обойти *pf*; (*take for* ~) выводить *impf*, вывести *pf* гулять. **walker** /'wɔːkə(r)/ *n* ходок. **walkie-talkie** /ˌwɔːkiˈtɔːki/ *n* рация. **walking** /'wɔːkɪŋ/ *n* ходьба; ~-stick трость.

Walkman /'wɔːkmən/ *n* (*propr*) вокмен.

wall /wɔːl/ *n* стена; *vt* обносить *impf*, обнести *pf* стеной; ~ up (*door, window*) заделывать *impf*, заделать *pf*; (*brick up* ~) замуровывать *impf*, замуровать *pf*.

wallet /'wɒlɪt/ *n* бумажник.

wallflower /'wɔːlˌflaʊə(r)/ *n* желтофиоль.

wallop /'wɒləp/ *n* сильный удар; *vt* сильно ударять *impf*, уда-

allow /'wɒləʊ/ vi валя́ться impf; ~ **in** (give o.s. up to) погружа́ться impf, погрузи́ться pf в+acc.

allpaper /'wɔːl,peɪpə(r)/ n обо́и (обо́ев) pl.

alnut /'wɔːlnʌt/ n гре́цкий оре́х; (wood, tree) оре́ховое де́рево, оре́х.

alrus /'wɔːlrəs/ n морж.

altz /wɔːls/ n вальс; vi вальси́ровать impf.

van /væn/ adj бле́дный.

vand /wɒnd/ n па́лочка.

vander /'wɒndə(r)/ vi броди́ть impf; (also of thoughts etc.) блужда́ть impf; ~ **from the point** отклоня́ться impf, отклони́ться pf от те́мы. **wanderer** /-rə(r)/ n стра́нник.

vane /weɪn/ n: **be on the ~** убыва́ть impf v убыва́ть impf, убы́ть pf; (weaken) ослабева́ть impf, ослабе́ть pf.

vangle /'wæŋg(ə)l/ vt заполуча́ть impf, заполучи́ть pf.

vant /wɒnt/ n (lack) недоста́ток; (requirement) потре́бность; (desire) жела́ние; **for ~ of** за недоста́тком +gen; vt хоте́ть impf, за~ pf +gen, acc; (need) нужда́ться impf в+prep; **I ~ you to come at six** я хочу́, что́бы ты пришёл в шесть.

wanting /-tɪŋ/ adj: **be ~** недоста́вать impf (impers+gen); **experience is ~** недоста́ёт о́пыта.

wanton /'wɒnt(ə)n/ adj (licentious) распу́тный; (senseless) бессмы́сленный.

war /wɔː(r)/ n война́; (attrib) вое́нный; **at ~** в состоя́нии войны́; **~ memorial** па́мятник па́вшим в войне́.

(child etc.) подопе́чный sb; (distrct) райо́н; vt: **~ off** отража́ть impf, отрази́ть pf.

warden /'wɔːd(ə)n/ n (prison) нача́льник; (college) ре́ктор; (hostel) коменда́нт.

warder /'wɔːdə(r)/ n тюре́мщик.

wardrobe /'wɔːdrəʊb/ n платяно́й шкаф.

warehouse /'weəhaʊs/ n склад.

wares /weəz/ n pl изде́лия neut pl, това́ры m pl.

warfare /'wɔːfeə(r)/ n война́.

warhead /'wɔːhed/ n боева́я голо́вка.

warily /'weərɪlɪ/ adv осторо́жно.

warlike /'wɔːlaɪk/ adj вои́нственный.

warm /wɔːm/ n тепло́; adj (also fig) тёплый; **~-hearted** серде́чный; vt & i (heat)(ся) impf; согрева́ть(ся) impf, согре́ть(ся) pf; ~ **up** (food etc.) подогрева́ть impf, подогре́ть pf; (liven up) оживля́ть(ся) impf, оживи́ть(ся) pf; (sport) размина́ться impf, размя́ться pf; (mus) разы́грываться impf, разыгра́ться pf. **warmth** /wɔːmθ/ n тепло́; (cordiality) серде́чность.

warn /wɔːn/ vt предупрежда́ть impf, предупреди́ть pf (about о+prep). **warning** /-nɪŋ/ n предупрежде́ние.

warp /wɔːp/ vt & i (wood) коро́бить(ся) impf, по~, с~ pf; vt (pervert) извраща́ть impf, изврати́ть pf.

warrant /'wɒrənt/ n (for arrest etc.) о́рдер; vt (justify) опра́вдывать impf, оправда́ть pf; (guarantee) гаранти́ровать impf & pf. **warranty** /-tɪ/ n гара́нтия.

warrior /'wɒrɪə(r)/ n во́ин.

warship /'wɔːʃɪp/ n вое́нный ко-

рабль *m*.

wart /wɔːt/ *n* борода́вка.

wartime /ˈwɔːtaɪm/ *n*: in ~ во вре́мя войны́.

wary /ˈweərɪ/ *adj* осторо́жный.

wash /wɒʃ/ *n* мытьё; (*thin layer*) то́нкий слой; (*lotion*) примо́чка; (*surf*) прибо́й; (*back-wash*) попу́тная волна́; **at the** ~ в сти́рке; **have a** ~ мы́ться *impf*, по~ *pf*; **~-basin** умыва́льник; **~-out** (*fiasco*) прова́л; **~-room** умыва́льная *sb*; *vt & i* мы́ть(ся) *impf*, вы́~, по~ *pf*; *vt* (*clothes*) стира́ть *impf*, вы́~ *pf*; (*of sea*) омыва́ть *impf*; ~ **away**, **off**, **out** смыва́ть(ся) *impf*, смы́ть(ся) *pf*; (*carry away*) сноси́ть *impf*, снести́ *pf*; ~ **out** (*rinse*) спола́скивать *impf*, сполосну́ть *pf*; ~ **up** (*dishes*) мы́ть *impf*, вы́~, по~ *pf* (посу́ду); ~ **one's hands of it** умыва́ть *impf*, умы́ть *pf* ру́ки.

washed-out /wɒʃtˈaʊt/ *adj* (*exhausted*) утомлённый. **washer** /ˈwɒʃə(r)/ *n* (*tech*) ша́йба. **washing** /ˈwɒʃɪŋ/ *n* (*of clothes*) сти́рка; (*clothes*) бельё; **~-machine** стира́льная маши́на; **~-powder** стира́льный порошо́к; **~-up** (*action*) мытьё посу́ды; (*dishes*) гря́зная посу́да; **~-up liquid** жи́дкое мы́ло для мытья́ посу́ды.

wasp /wɒsp/ *n* оса́.

wastage /ˈweɪstɪdʒ/ *n* уте́чка. **waste** /weɪst/ *n* (*desert*) пусты́ня; (*refuse*) отбро́сы *m pl*; (*of time, money, etc.*) тра́та; **go to** ~ пропада́ть *impf*, пропа́сть *pf* да́ром; *adj* (*desert*) пусты́нный; (*superfluous*) нену́жный; (*uncultivated*) невозде́ланный; **lay** ~ опустоша́ть *impf*, опусто́шить *pf*; **~land** пусты́рь *m*; ~ **paper** нену́жные бума́ги *f pl*;

(*for recycling*) макулату́ра; ~ **products** отхо́ды (-дов) *pl*; **~-paper basket** корзи́на для бума́ги; *vt* тра́тить *impf*, ис~ *pf*; (*time*) теря́ть *impf*, по~ *pf*; *vi*: ~ **away** ча́хнуть *impf*, за~ *pf*. **wasteful** /-fʊl/ *adj* расточи́тельный.

watch /wɒtʃ/ *n* (*timepiece*) часы́ (-со́в) *pl*; (*duty*) дежу́рство; (*naut*) ва́хта; **keep** ~ **over** наблюда́ть *impf* за+*instr*, ~ **dog** сторожево́й пёс; **~-tower** сторожева́я ба́шня; *vt* (*observe*) наблюда́ть *impf* (*keep an eye on*) следи́ть *impf* за+*instr*; (*look after*) смотре́ть *impf*, по~ *pf* за+*instr*; ~ **television**, **film** смотре́ть *impf*, по~ *pf* телеви́зор, фильм; *vi* смотре́ть *impf*; ~ **out** (*be careful*) бере́чься *impf* (for+*gen*); ~ **out** for+*gen*; ~ **out**! осторо́жно! **watchful** /-fʊl/ *adj* бди́тельный. **watchman** (ночно́й) сто́рож. **watchword** ло́зунг.

water /ˈwɔːtə(r)/ *n* вода́; **~-colour** акваре́ль; **~-heater** кипяти́льник; **~-main** водопрово́дная магистра́ль; ~ **melon** арбу́з; **~-pipe** водопрово́дная труба́; **~-ski** (*n*) во́дная лы́жа; ~ **ski** водолы́жный спорт; **~-supply** водоснабже́ние; **~-way** во́дный путь *m*; *vt* (*flowers etc.*) полива́ть *impf*, поли́ть *pf*; (*animals*) пои́ть *impf*, на~ *pf*; (*irrigate*) ороша́ть *impf*, ороси́ть *pf*; *vi* (*eyes*) слези́ться *impf*; (*mouth*): **my mouth** ~**s** у меня́ слю́нки теку́т; ~ **down** разбавля́ть *impf*, разба́вить *pf*. **watercourse** *n* ру́сло. **watercress** /-kres/ *n* кресс водяно́й. **waterfall** *n* водопа́д. **waterfront** *n* часть го́рода примыка́ющая

к бе́регу. **watering-can** /ˈwɔːtərɪŋˌkæn/ n ле́йка. **waterlogged** /ˈwɔːtəˌlɒgd/ adj заболо́ченный. **watermark** n водяно́й знак. **waterproof** adj непромока́емый; n непромока́емый плащ. **watershed** n водоразде́л. **waterside** n бе́рег. **watertight** adj водонепроница́емый; (fig) неопровержи́мый. **waterworks** n pl водопрово́дные сооруже́ния neut pl. **watery** /ˈwɔːtəri/ adj водяни́стый.

watt /wɒt/ n ватт.

wave /weɪv/ vt (hand etc.) маха́ть impf, махну́ть pf +instr; (flag) размахивать impf +instr; vi (∼ hand) маха́ть, по∼ pf (at +dat); (flutter) развева́ться impf; ∼ aside отма́хиваться impf, отмахну́ться pf от+gen; ∼ down остана́вливать impf, останови́ть pf; n (in various senses) волна́; (of hand) взмах; (in hair) зави́вка. **wavelength** n длина́ волны́. **waver** /ˈweɪvə(r)/ vi колеба́ться impf. **wavy** /ˈweɪvi/ adj волни́стый.

wax /wæks/ n воск; (in ear) се́ра; vt вощи́ть impf, на∼ pf. **waxwork** n восковая фигу́ра; pl музе́й восковых фигу́р.

way /weɪ/ n (road, path, route; fig) доро́га, путь m; (direction) сторона́; (manner) о́браз; (method) спо́соб; (respect) отноше́ние; (habit) привы́чка; by the ∼ (fig) кста́ти, ме́жду про́чим; on the ∼ по доро́ге, по пути́; this ∼ (direction) сюда́; (in this ∼) таки́м о́бразом; the other ∼ round наоборо́т; under ∼ на ходу́; be in the ∼ меша́ть impf; get out of the ∼ уходи́ть impf, уйти́ pf с доро́ги; give ∼ (yield) поддава́ться impf, подда́ться pf (to +dat); (collapse)

обру́шиваться impf, обру́шиться pf; go out of one's ∼ стара́ться impf, по∼ pf изо всех сил +inf; get, have, one's own ∼ добива́ться impf, доби́ться pf своего́; make ∼ уступа́ть impf, уступи́ть pf доро́гу (for +dat). **waylay** vt (lie in wait for) подстерега́ть impf, подстере́чь pf; (stop) перехва́тывать impf, перехвати́ть pf по пути́. **wayside** adj придоро́жный; n; fall by the ∼ выбыва́ть impf, вы́быть pf из стро́я.

wayward /ˈweɪwəd/ adj своенра́вный.

WC abbr (of water-closet) убо́рная sb.

we /wiː/ pron мы.

weak /wiːk/ adj сла́бый. **weaken** /-kən/ vt ослабля́ть impf, осла́бить pf; vi ослабева́ть impf, о∼ pf. **weakling** /-lɪŋ/ n (person) сла́бый челове́к; (plant) сла́бое расте́ние. **weakness** /-nɪs/ n сла́бость.

weal /wiːl/ n (mark) рубе́ц.

wealth /welθ/ n бога́тство; (abundance) изоби́лие. **wealthy** /-θɪ/ adj бога́тый.

wean /wiːn/ vt отнима́ть impf, отня́ть pf от груди́; (fig) отуча́ть impf, отучи́ть pf (of, from от+gen).

weapon /ˈwepən/ n ору́жие. **weaponry** /-rɪ/ n вооруже́ние.

wear /weə(r)/ vt (wearing) носи́ть; (clothing) оде́жда; (∼ and tear) изно́с; vt носи́ть impf (also be+prep); **what shall I** ∼? что мне наде́ть? vi носи́ться impf; ∼ off (pain, novelty) проходи́ть impf, пройти́ pf; (cease to have effect) перестава́ть impf, переста́ть pf де́йствовать; ∼ out (clothes) изна́шивать(ся) impf, износи́ть(ся) pf; (exhaust)

му́чивать *impf*, изму́чить *pf*.

weariness /'wɪərɪnɪs/ *n* уста́лость. **wearing**, **wearisome** /'weərɪŋ, 'wɪərɪsəm/ *adj* утоми́тельный. **weary** /'wɪərɪ/ *adj* уста́лый; *vt & i* утомля́ть(ся) *impf*, утоми́ть(ся) *pf*.

weasel /'wiːz(ə)l/ *n* ла́ска.

weather /'weðə(r)/ *n* пого́да; **be under the** ~ нева́жно себя́ чу́вствовать *impf*; ~-**beaten** обве́тренный; ~ **forecast** прогно́з пого́ды; *vt* (*storm etc.*) выде́рживать *impf*, вы́держать *pf*; (*wood*) подверга́ть *impf*, подве́ргнуть *pf* атмосфе́рным влия́ниям. **weather-cock**, **weathervane** /'weðəkɒk, 'weðəveɪn/ *n* флю́гер. **weatherman** *n* метеоро́лог.

weave[1] /wiːv/ *vt & i* (*fabric*) ткать *impf*, со~ *pf*; *vt* (*fig; also wreath etc.*) плести́ *impf*, с~ *pf*. **weaver** /-və(r)/ *n* ткач, ~и́ха.

weave[2] /wiːv/ *vi* (*wind*) виться *impf*.

web /web/ *n* (*cobweb; fig*) паути́на; (*fig*) сплете́ние; (**the** Web) (*comput*) Всеми́рная паути́на; ~ **page** веб-страни́ца, страни́ца в Интерне́те. **webbed** /webd/ *adj* перепо́нчатый. **weblog** *n* сетево́й журна́л, блог. **weblogger** *n* бл́оггер. **website** *n* сайт, веб-сайт.

wedded /-dɪd/ *adj* супру́жеский; ~ **to** (*fig*) пре́данный +*dat*. **wedding** /-dɪŋ/ *n* сва́дьба, бракосочета́ние; ~-**cake** сва́дебный торт; ~-**day** день *m* сва́дьбы; ~-**dress** подвене́чное пла́тье; ~-**ring** обруча́льное кольцо́.

wedge /wedʒ/ *n* клин; *vt* (~ *open*) закли́нивать *impf*, закли́нить *pf*; *vt & i*: ~ **(in)to** вкли́ни-

вать(ся) *impf*, вкли́нить(ся) *pf* (в+*acc*).

wedlock /'wedlɒk/ *n* брак; **born out of** ~ рождённый вне бра́ка, внебра́чный.

Wednesday /'wenzdeɪ/ *n* среда́.

weed /wiːd/ *n* сорня́к; ~-**killer** гербици́д; *vt* поло́ть *impf*, вы́~ *pf*; ~ **out** удаля́ть *impf*, удали́ть *pf*. **weedy** /'wiːdɪ/ *adj* (*person*) то́щий.

week /wiːk/ *n* неде́ля; ~-**end** суббо́та и воскресе́нье, выходны́е *sb pl*. **weekday** *n* бу́дний день *m*. **weekly** /'wiːklɪ/ *adj* еженеде́льный; (*wage*) неде́льный; *adv* еженеде́льно; *n* еженеде́льник.

weep /wiːp/ *vi* пла́кать *impf*. **weeping willow** /'wiːpɪŋ 'wɪləʊ/ *n* плаку́чая и́ва.

weigh /weɪ/ *vt* (*also fig*) взве́шивать *impf*, взве́сить *pf*; (*consider*) обду́мывать *impf*, обду́мать *pf*; *vt & i* (*so much*) ве́сить *impf*; ~ **down** отягоща́ть *impf*, отяготи́ть *pf*; ~ **on** тяготи́ть *impf*; ~ **out** отве́шивать *impf*, отве́сить *pf*; ~ **up** (*appraise*) оце́нивать *impf*, оцени́ть *pf*. **weight** /weɪt/ *n* (*also authority*) вес; (*load, also fig*) тя́жесть; (*sport*) шта́нга; (*influence*) влия́ние; **lose** ~ худе́ть *impf*, по~ *pf*; **put on** ~ толсте́ть *impf*, по~ *pf*; ~-**lifter** штанги́ст; ~-**lifting** подня́тие тяжеле́й; *vt* (*make heavier*) утяжеля́ть *impf*, утяжели́ть *pf*. **weightless** /'weɪtlɪs/ *adj* невесо́мый. **weighty** /'weɪtɪ/ *adj* ве́ский.

weir /wɪə(r)/ *n* плоти́на.

weird /wɪəd/ *adj* (*strange*) стра́нный.

welcome /'welkəm/ *n* приём, *adj* жела́нный; (*pleasant*) прия́тный; **you are** ~ (*don't mention it*)

пожа́луйста; **you are ~ to use my bicycle** мой велосипе́д к ва́шим услу́гам; **you are ~ to stay the night** вы мо́жете переночева́ть у меня́/нас; *vt* до́бро пожа́ловать! (& *pf in past tense*); *int* до́бро пожа́ловать!

veld /weld/ *vt* сва́ривать *impf*, свари́ть *pf.* **welder** /-də(r)/ *n* сва́рщик.

welfare /'welfeə(r)/ *n* благосостоя́ние; **W~ State** госуда́рство всео́бщего благосостоя́ния.

well¹ /wel/ *n* коло́дец; (*for stairs*) ле́стничная кле́тка.

well² /wel/ *vi*: **~ up** (*anger etc.*) вскипа́ть *impf*, вскипе́ть *pf*; **tears ~ed up** глаза́ напо́лнились слеза́ми.

well³ /wel/ *adj* (*healthy*) здоро́вый; **feel ~** чу́вствовать *impf*, по~ *pf* себя́ хорошо́, здоро́вым; **get ~** поправля́ться *impf*, попра́виться *pf*; **look ~** хорошо́ вы́глядеть *impf*; **all is ~** всё в поря́дке; *int* ну(!); *adv* хорошо́; (*very much*) о́чень; **as ~** то́же; **as ~ as** (*in addition to*) кро́ме+*gen*; **it may ~ be true** вполне́ возмо́жно, что э́то так; **very ~!** хорошо́!; ~ **done!** молоде́ц! ~**-balanced** уравнове́шенный; ~**-behaved** (благо)воспи́танный; ~**-being** благополу́чие; ~**-bred** благовоспи́танный; ~**-built** кре́пкий; ~**-defined** чёткий; ~**-disposed** благоскло́нный; ~ **done** (*cooked*) прожа́ренный; ~**-fed** отко́рмленный; ~**-founded** обосно́ванный; ~**-groomed** (*person*) хо́леный; ~**-heeled** состоя́тельный; ~**-informed** (хорошо́) осведомлённый (**about** в+*prep*); ~**-known** изве́стный; ~**-mean-**

ing де́йствующий из лу́чших побужде́ний; ~**-nigh** почти́; ~**-off** состоя́тельный; ~**-paid** хорошо́ опла́чиваемый; ~**-preserved** хорошо́ сохрани́вшийся; ~**-to-do** состоя́тельный; ~**-wisher** доброжела́тель *m*.

wellington (boot) /'welɪŋt(ə)n (buːt)/ *n* рези́новый сапо́г.

Welsh /welʃ/ *adj* уэ́льский. **Welshman** *n* валли́ец. **Welshwoman** *n* валли́йка.

welter /'weltə(r)/ *n* пу́таница.

wend /wend/ *vt*: ~ **one's way** держа́ть *impf* путь.

west /west/ *n* за́пад; (*naut*) вест; *adj* за́падный; *adv* на за́пад, к за́паду. **westerly** /'westəlɪ/ *adj* за́падный. **western** /'west(ə)n/ *adj* за́падный; *n* (*film*) ве́стерн. **westward(s)** /'westwəd(z)/ *adv* на за́пад, к за́паду.

wet /wet/ *adj* мо́крый; (*paint*) непросо́хший; (*rainy*) дождли́вый; ~ **through** промо́кший до ни́тки *n* (*dampness*) вла́жность; (*rain*) дождь *m*; *vt* мочи́ть *impf*, на~ *pf*.

whack /wæk/ *n* (*blow*) уда́р; *vt* колоти́ть *impf*, по~ *pf*. **whacked** /wækt/ *adj* разби́тый.

whale /weɪl/ *n* кит.

wharf /wɔːf/ *n* при́стань.

what /wɒt/ *pron* (*interrog, int*) что; (*how much*) ско́лько; (*rel*) (то), что; ~ **(...) for** заче́м; ~ **if** а что е́сли; ~ **is your name** как вас зову́т?; ~ (*interrog, int*) како́й; ~ **kind of** како́й. **whatever, whatsoever** /wɒt'evə(r), ˌwɒtsəu'evə(r)/ *pron* что бы ни+*past* (**you think** что бы вы ни ду́мали); всё, что (**take ~ you want** возьми́те всё, что хоти́те); *adj* како́й бы ни+*past* (**books he read(s)** каки́е бы

книги он ни прочитал); (at all): there is no chance ~ нет никакой возможности; is there any chance ~? есть ли хоть какая-нибудь возможность?

wheat /wiːt/ n пшеница.

wheedle /ˈwiːd(ə)l/ vt (coax into doing) уговаривать impf, уговорить pf с помощью лести; ~ out of вымаивать impf, выманить pf y+gen.

wheel /wiːl/ n колесо; (steering ~, helm) руль m; (potter's) гончарный круг; vt (push) катать indet, катить det, по~ pf; vt & i (turn) повёртывать(ся) impf, повернуть(ся) pf; vi (circle) кружиться impf. **wheelbarrow** n тачка. **wheelchair** n инвалидное кресло.

wheeze /wiːz/ vi сопеть impf.

when /wen/ adv когда; conj когда, в то время как; (whereas) тогда как; (if) если; (although) хотя. **whence** /wens/ adv откуда. **whenever** /wenˈevə(r)/ adv когда же; conj (every time) всякий раз когда; (at any time) когда; (no matter when) когда бы ни+past; we shall have dinner ~ you arrive во сколько бы вы ни приехали, мы пообедаем.

where /weə(r)/ adv & conj (place) где; (whither) куда; from ~ откуда. **whereabouts** /ˈweərəˌbaʊts/ adv где; n местонахождение. **whereas** /weərˈæz/ conj тогда как; хотя. **whereby** /weəˈbaɪ/ adv & conj посредством чего. **wherein** /weərˈɪn/ adv & conj в чём. **wherever** /weərˈevə(r)/ adv & conj (place) где бы ни+past; (whither) куда бы ни+past; ~ he goes куда бы он ни пошёл; ~ you like где/куда хотите. **wherewithal** /ˈweərwɪ-

ˌðɔːl/ n средства neut pl.

whet /wet/ vt точить impf, на~ pf; (fig) возбуждать impf, возбудить pf.

whether /ˈweðə(r)/ conj ли; don't know ~ he will come я не знаю, придёт ли он; ~ he comes or not придёт (ли) он или нет.

which /wɪtʃ/ adj (interrog, rel) какой; pron (interrog) какой; (person) кто; (rel) который (person) (rel to whole statement) что; ~ i ~? (persons) кто из них кто?; (things) что-что? **whichever** /wɪtʃˈevə(r)/ adj & pron какой бы ни+past (~ book you choose какую бы книгу ты ни брал); любой (take ~ book you want возьми/take любую книгу).

whiff /wɪf/ n запах.

while /waɪl/ n время neut; a little ~ недолго; a long ~ долго; for a long ~ (up to now) давно; for a ~ на время; in a little ~ скоро; it is worth ~ стоит это сделать; vt: ~ away проводить impf, провести pf; conj пока; в то время как; (although) хотя (contrast) a; we went to the cinema ~ they went to the theatre мы ходили в кино, а они в театр. **whilst** /waɪlst/ see while

whim /wɪm/ n прихоть, каприз. **whimper** /ˈwɪmpə(r)/ vi хныкать impf; (dog) скулить impf.

whimsical /ˈwɪmzɪk(ə)l/ adj капризный; (odd) причудливый.

whine /waɪn/ n (wail) вой; (whimper) хныканье; vi (dog) скулить impf; (wail) выть impf; (whimper) хныкать impf.

whinny /ˈwɪnɪ/ vi тихо ржать impf.

whip /wɪp/ n кнут, хлыст; vt (lash) хлестать impf, хлестнуть pf; (cream) сбивать impf

:бить pf; ~ off скидывать impf, скинуть pf; ~ out выхватывать impf, выхватить pf; ~round быстро повёртываться impf, повернуться pf; ~round сбор денег; ~ up (stir up) разжигать impf, разжечь pf

whirl /wз:l/ n (of dust, fig) вихрь m; (turmoil) суматоха; vt & i кружить(ся) impf, за~ pf. **whirlpool** n водоворот. **whirlwind** n вихрь m.

whirr /wз:(r)/ vi жужжать impf.

whisk /wɪsk/ n (of twigs etc.) веничек; (utensil) мутовка; (movement) помахивание; vt (cream etc.) сбивать impf, сбить pf; ~ away, off (brush off) смахивать impf, смахнуть pf; (take away) быстро уносить impf, унести pf.

whisker /'wɪskə(r)/ n (human) волос на лице; (animal) ус; pl (human) бакенбарды f pl.

whisky /'wɪskɪ/ n виски neut indecl.

whisper /'wɪspə(r)/ n шёпот; vt & i шептать impf, шепнуть pf.

whistle /'wɪs(ə)l/ n (sound) свист; (instrument) свисток; vi свистеть impf, свистнуть pf; vt насвистывать impf.

white /waɪt/ adj белый; (hair) седой; (pale) бледный; (with milk) с молоком; paint ~ красить impf, по~ pf в белый свет; ~-collar worker служащий sb; ~ lie невинная ложь; ~ (colour) белый цвет; (egg, eye) белок; (~ person) белый sb. **whiten** /-t(ə)n/ vt белить impf, на~, по~, вы́~ pf; vi белеть impf, по~ pf. **whiteness** /-nɪs/ n белизна. **whitewash** n побелка; vt белить impf, по~ pf; (fig) обелять impf, обелить pf.

whither /'wɪðə(r)/ adv & conj куда.

Whitsun /'wɪts(ə)n/ n Троица.

whittle /'wɪt(ə)l/ vt: ~ down уменьшать impf, уменьшить pf.

whiz(z) /wɪz/ vi: ~ past просвистеть pf.

who /hu:/ pron (interrog) кто; (rel) который.

whoever /hu:'evə(r)/ pron кто бы ни~past; (he who) тот, кто.

whole /həʊl/ adj (entire) весь, целый; (intact, of number) целый; n (thing complete) целое sb; (all there is) весь; (sum) сумма; on the ~ в общем. **wholehearted** /-'ha:tɪd/ adj беззаветный. **whole-heartedly** /-'ha:tɪdlɪ/ adv от всего сердца. **wholemeal** adj из непросеянной муки. **wholesale** adj оптовый; (fig) массовый; adv оптом. **wholesaler** n оптовый торговец. **wholesome** adj здоровый. **wholly** /'həʊllɪ/ adv полностью.

whom /hu:m/ pron (interrog) кого etc.; (rel) которого etc.

whoop /hu:p/ n крик; vi кричать impf, крикнуть pf; ~ it up бурно веселиться impf; ~ing cough коклюш.

whore /hɔ:(r)/ n проститутка.

whose /hu:z/ pron (interrog, rel) чей; (rel) которого.

why /waɪ/ adv почему; int да ведь!

wick /wɪk/ n фитиль m.

wicked /'wɪkɪd/ adj дикий. **wickedness** /-nɪs/ n дикость.

wicker /'wɪkə(r)/ attrib плетёный.

wicket /'wɪkɪt/ n (cricket) воротца.

wide /waɪd/ adj широкий; (extensive) обширный; (in measurements) в+acc шириной;

awake по́лный внима́ния; ~
open широко́ откры́тый; adv
(off target) ми́мо це́ли. **widely**
/'waɪdlɪ/ adv широко́. **widen**
/-d(ə)n/ vt & i расширя́ть(ся)
impf, расши́рить(ся) pf.
widespread adj распространённый.

widow /'wɪdəʊ/ n вдова́.
widowed /'wɪdəʊd/ adj овдове́в-
ший. **widower** /'wɪdəʊə(r)/ n
вдове́ц.

width /wɪtθ/ n ширина́; (fig)
широта́; (of cloth) полотни́ще.

wield /wiːld/ vt (brandish) раз-
ма́хивать impf +instr; (power)
по́льзоваться impf +instr.

wife /waɪf/ n жена́.

wig /wɪg/ n пари́к.

wiggle /'wɪg(ə)l/ vt & i (move)
шевели́ть(ся) impf, по~, ше-
вельну́ть(ся) pf (+instr).

wigwam /'wɪgwæm/ n вигва́м.

wild /waɪld/ adj ди́кий; (flower)
полево́й; (uncultivated) невоз-
де́ланный; (tempestuous) бу́й-
ный; (furious) нейсто́вый;
(ill-considered) необду́манный;
be ~ about быть без ума́
от+gen; ~-goose chase сумас-
бро́дная зате́я; n: pl де́бри
(-рей) pl. **wildcat** adj (unofficial)
неофициа́льный. **wilderness**
/'wɪldənɪs/ n пусты́ня. **wildfire**:
spread like ~ распростра-
ня́ться impf, распростра-
ни́ться pf с молниено́сной
быстрото́й. **wildlife** n жива́я
приро́да. **wildness** /'waɪldnɪs/ n
ди́кость.

wile /waɪl/ n хи́трость.

wilful /'wɪlfʊl/ adj (obstinate)
упря́мый; (deliberate) пред-
наме́ренный.

will /wɪl/ n во́ля; (~power) си́ла
во́ли; (at death) завеща́ние;
against one's ~ про́тив во́ли; of

one's own free ~ доброво́льно;
with a ~ с энтузиа́змом; good
~ до́брая во́ля; make one's ~
писа́ть impf, на~ pf завеща́-
ние; v aux хоте́ть impf, за~ pf
+gen, acc; v aux: he ~ be
president он бу́дет президе́н-
том; he ~ return tomorrow ~
вернётся за́втра; ~ you open
the window? откро́йте окно́,
пожа́луйста. **willing** /'wɪlɪŋ/ adj
гото́вый; (eager) ста́ра́тель-
ный. **willingly** /'wɪlɪŋlɪ/ adv
охо́тно. **willingness** /'wɪlɪŋnɪs/ n
гото́вность.

willow /'wɪləʊ/ n и́ва.

willy-nilly /ˌwɪlɪ'nɪlɪ/ adv во́лей-
нево́лей.

wilt /wɪlt/ vi поника́ть impf, по-
ни́кнуть pf.

wily /'waɪlɪ/ adj хи́трый.

win /wɪn/ n вы́игрыш; vt & i вы-
и́грывать impf, вы́играть pf; vi
(obtain) добива́ться impf, до-
би́ться pf +gen; ~ over угова́-
ривать impf, уговори́ть pf;
(charm) располага́ть impf, рас-
положи́ть pf к себе́.

wince /wɪns/ vi вздра́гивать
impf, вздро́гнуть pf.

winch /wɪntʃ/ n лебёдка; подни-
ма́ть impf, подня́ть pf с по́-
мощью лебёдки.

wind¹ /wɪnd/ n (air) ве́тер;
(breath) дыха́ние; (flatulence)
ве́тры m pl; ~ instrument духо-
во́й инструме́нт; ~-swept от-
кры́тый ве́трам; get ~ of
проню́хивать impf, проню́-
хать pf; vt (make gasp) заста-
вля́ть impf, заста́вить pf
задохну́ться.

wind² /waɪnd/ vi (meander)
ви́ться impf; извива́ться impf;
vt (coil) нама́тывать impf, на-
мота́ть pf; (watch) заводи́ть
impf, завести́ pf; (wrap) уку́ты-

зать *impf*, укýтать *pf*; ~ **up** (*vt reel*) смáтывать *impf*, смотáть *pf*; (*watch*) *see* wind²; (*vt & i end*) кончáть(ся) *impf*, кóнчить(ся) *pf*. **winding** *adj* (*meandering*) извилистый; ~ **staircase** винтовáя.

indfall /'wmdfɔːl/ *n* пáдалица; (*fig*) золотóй дождь.

windmill /'wmdmɪl/ *n* ветряна́я мéльница.

indow /'wmdəʊ/ *n* окнó; (*of shop*) витрина; ~**box** нарýжный я́щик для цветóв; ~**cleaner** мóйщик óкон; ~**dressing** оформлéние витрин; (*fig*) показýха; ~**frame** окóнная páма; ~**ledge** подокóнник; ~**pane** окóнное стеклó; ~**shopping** рассмáтривание витрин; ~**sill** подокóнник.

windpipe /'wmdpaɪp/ *n* дыхáтельное гóрло. **windscreen** *n* ветровóе стеклó; ~ **wiper** дворник. **windsurfer** /'wmd,sɜːfə(r)/ *n* виндсёрфинги́ст. **windsurfing** /'wmd,sɜːfɪŋ/ *n* виндсёрфинг. **windward** /'wmdwəd/ *adj* наве́тренный. **windy** /'wmdɪ/ *adj* вéтреный.

wine /wam/ *n* винó; ~ **bar** ви́нный погребóк; ~ **bottle** ви́нная бутылка; ~ **list** кáрта вин; ~**tasting** дегустáция вин. **wineglass** /'wamɡlɑːs/ *n* рю́мка. **winery** /'wamərɪ/ *n* ви́нный завóд. **winy** /'wamɪ/ *adj* ви́нный.

wing /wɪŋ/ *n* (*also polit*) крылó; (*archit*) флигель *m*; (*sport*) фланг; *pl* (*theat*) кули́сы *f pl*. **winged** /wɪŋd/ *adj* крылáтый.

wink /wɪŋk/ *n* (*blink*) моргáние; (*as sign*) подми́гивание; *vi* мигáть *impf*, мигнýть *pf*; ~ **at** подми́гивать *impf*, подми́гнуть *pf* +*dat*; (*fig*) смотрéть

impf, по~ *pf* сквозь пáльцы на+*acc*.

winkle /'wɪŋk(ə)l/ *vt*: ~ **out** выко́вы́ривать *impf*, вы́ковы́рять *pf*.

winner /'wmə(r)/ *n* победи́тель *m*, ~ница. **winning** /'wmɪŋ/ *adj* (*victorious*) вы́игравший; (*shot etc.*) решáющий; (*charming*) обая́тельный; *n*: *pl* вы́игрыш; ~**post** фи́нишный столб.

winter /'wmtə(r)/ *n* зимá; *attrib* зи́мний. **wintry** /'wmtrɪ/ *adj* зи́мний; (*cold*) холóдный.

wipe /waɪp/ *vt* (*also* ~ *out inside of*) вытирáть *impf*, вы́тереть *pf*; ~ **away, off** стирáть *impf*, стерéть *pf*; ~ **out** (*exterminate*) уничтожáть *impf*, уничтóжить *pf*; (*cancel*) смывáть *impf*, смыть *pf*.

wire /'waɪə(r)/ *n* прóволока; (*carrying current*) провóд; ~ **netting** прóволочная сéтка. **wireless** /-lɪs/ *n* рáдио *neut indecl*. **wiring** /-rɪŋ/ *n* электропровóдка. **wiry** /-rɪ/ *adj* жи́листый.

wisdom /'wɪzdəm/ *n* мýдрость; ~ **tooth** зуб мýдрости. **wise** /waɪz/ *adj* мýдрый; (*prudent*) благоразýмный.

wish /wɪʃ/ *n* желáние; **with best ~es** всего́ хоро́шего, с наилýчшими пожелáниями; *vt* хотéть *impf*, за~ *pf* (**I ~ I could see him** как мне хотéлось бы его́ ви́деть; **I ~ to go** я хочу́ пойти́; **I ~ you to come early** я хочу́, чтобы вы рáно пришли́; **I ~ the day were over** хорошо́ бы день уже́ ко́нчился); желáть *impf* +*gen* (**~ you luck** желáю вам удáчи); (*congratulate on*) поздравля́ть *impf*, поздрáвить *pf* (**I ~ you a happy birthday** поздравля́ю тебя́ с днём рожде-

ния); *vi:* ~ **for** жела́ть *impf* +gen; мечта́ть *impf* o+*prep.*

wishful /-fʊl/ *adj:* ~ **thinking** самообольще́ние; приня́тие жела́емого за действи́тельное.

wisp /wɪsp/ *n (of straw)* пучо́к; *(hair)* клочо́к; *(smoke)* стру́йка.

wisteria /wɪˈstɪərɪə/ *n* глици́ния.

wistful /ˈwɪstfʊl/ *adj* тоскли́вый.

wit /wɪt/ *n (mind)* ум; *(wittiness)* остроу́мие; *(person)* остря́к; **be at one's ~'s end** не знать *impf* что де́лать.

witch /wɪtʃ/ *n* ве́дьма; ~-**hunt** охо́та за ве́дьмами. **witchcraft** *n* колдовство́.

with /wɪð/ *prep (in company of, together* ~) (вме́сте) с+*instr;* *(as a result of)* от+*gen;* *(at house of, in keeping of)* у+*gen;* *(by means of)* +*instr;* *(in spite of)* несмотря́ на+*acc;* *(including)* включа́я+*acc;* ~ **each another** друг с дру́гом.

withdraw /wɪðˈdrɔː/ *vt (retract)* брать *impf,* взять *pf* наза́д; *(hand)* отдёргивать *impf,* отдёрнуть *pf;* *(cancel)* снима́ть *impf,* снять *pf;* *(mil)* выводи́ть *impf,* вы́вести *pf;* *(money from circulation)* изыма́ть *impf,* изъя́ть *pf* из обраще́ния; *(diplomat etc.)* отзыва́ть *impf,* отозва́ть *pf;* *(from bank)* брать *impf,* взять *pf;* *vi* удаля́ться *impf,* удали́ться *pf;* *(drop out)* выбыва́ть *impf,* вы́быть *pf;* *(mil)* отходи́ть *impf,* отойти́ *pf.* **withdrawal** /-ˈdrɔːəl/ *n (retraction)* взя́тие наза́д; *(cancellation)* сня́тие; *(mil)* отхо́д; *(money from circulation)* изъя́тие; *(departure)* ухо́д. **withdrawn** /-ˈdrɔːn/ *adj* за́мкнутый.

wither /ˈwɪðə(r)/ *vi* вя́нуть *impf,*

за~ *pf.* **withering** /-rɪŋ/ *adj (fig)* уничтожа́ющий.

withhold /wɪðˈhəʊld/ *vt (refuse grant)* не дава́ть *impf,* дать *pf* +gen; *(payment)* уде́рживать *impf,* удержа́ть *pf; (information)* ута́ивать *impf,* утаи́ть *pf.*

within /wɪˈðɪn/ *prep (inside)* внутри́+*gen,* в+*prep;* (~ the limits of) в преде́лах +*gen; (time)* в тече́ние +*gen; adv* внутри́; **from** ~ изнутри́.

without /wɪˈðaʊt/ *prep* без+*gen;* ~ **saying good-bye** не проща́ясь; **do** ~ обходи́ться *impf,* обойти́сь *pf* без+*gen.*

withstand /wɪðˈstænd/ *vt* выде́рживать *impf,* вы́держать *pf.*

witness /ˈwɪtnɪs/ *n (person)* свиде́тель *m;* *(eye—)* очеви́дец *m;* *(to signature etc.)* завери́тель *m;* **bear** ~ **to** свиде́тельствовать *impf,* за~ *pf;* ~-**box** ме́сто для свиде́тельских показа́ний; *vt* быть свиде́телем+*gen; (document etc.)* заверя́ть *impf,* заве́рить *pf.*

witticism /ˈwɪtɪsɪz(ə)m/ *n* остро́та. **witty** /ˈwɪtɪ/ *adj* остроу́мный.

wizard /ˈwɪzəd/ *n* волше́бник, колду́н.

wizened /ˈwɪz(ə)nd/ *adj* морщи́нистый.

wobble /ˈwɒb(ə)l/ *vt & i* шата́ть(ся) *impf,* шатну́ть(ся) *pf; vi (voice)* дрожа́ть *impf.* **wobbly** /ˈwɒblɪ/ *adj* ша́ткий.

woe /wəʊ/ *n* го́ре; ~ **is me!** го́ре мне! **woeful** /-fʊl/ *adj* жа́лкий.

wolf /wʊlf/ *n* волк; *vt* пожира́ть *impf,* пожра́ть *pf.*

woman /ˈwʊmən/ *n* же́нщина. **womanizer** /-ˌnaɪzə(r)/ *n* волоки́та. **womanly** /ˈwʊmənlɪ/ *adj* же́нственный.

womb /wuːm/ *n* ма́тка.

wonder /'wʌndə(r)/ n чу́до; (*amazement*) изумле́ние; **it's no** ~ неудиви́тельно; vt интересова́ться impf (I ~ **who will come** интере́сно, кто придёт); vi: **I shouldn't** ~ **if** неудиви́тельно бу́дет, е́сли; **I ~ if you could help me** не могли́ бы вы мне помо́чь?; ~ **at** удивля́ться impf, удиви́ться pf +dat. **wonderful, wondrous** /'wʌndəful, 'wʌndrəs/ adj замеча́тельный.

wont /wəʊnt/ n: **as is his** ~ по своему́ обыкнове́нию; **predic: be** ~ **to** име́ть привы́чку+inf.

woo /wuː/ vt уха́живать impf за +instr.

wood /wʊd/ n (*forest*) лес; (*material*) де́рево; (*firewood*) дрова́ pl. **woodcut** n гравю́ра на де́реве. **wooded** /'wʊdɪd/ adj леси́стый. **wooden** /'wʊd(ə)n/ adj (*also fig*) деревя́нный. **woodland** n леси́стая ме́стность; *attrib* лесно́й. **woodpecker** /'wʊd,pekə(r)/ n дя́тел. **woodwind** n деревя́нные духовы́е инструме́нты m pl. **woodwork** n столя́рная рабо́та; (*wooden parts*) деревя́нные ча́сти (-те́й) pl. **woodworm** n жучо́к. **woody** /'wʊdɪ/ adj (*plant etc.*) деревяни́стый; (*wooded*) леси́стый.

wool /wʊl/ n шерсть. **woollen** /'wʊlən/ adj шерстяно́й. **woolly** /'wʊlɪ/ adj шерсти́стый; (*indistinct*) нея́сный.

word /wɜːd/ n сло́во; (*news*) изве́стие; **by** ~ **of mouth** у́стно; **have a** ~ **with** поговори́ть pf c+instr; **in a** ~ одни́м сло́вом; **in other** ~**s** други́ми слова́ми; ~ **for** ~ сло́во в сло́во; ~ **processor** компью́тер+(изда́тель) m; vt выража́ть impf, вы́разить pf; формули́ровать impf,

c~ *pf.* **wording** /'wɜːdɪŋ/ n формулиро́вка.

work /wɜːk/ n рабо́та; (*labour, toil; scholarly* ~) труд; (*occupation*) заня́тие; (*studies*) заня́тия neut pl; (*of art*) произведе́ние; (*book*) сочине́ние; pl (*factory*) заво́д; (*mechanism*) механи́зм; **at** ~ (*doing*) за рабо́той; (*at place of* ~) на рабо́те; **out of** ~ безрабо́тный; ~**force** рабо́чая си́ла; ~**load** нагру́зка; vi (*also function*) рабо́тать impf (**at, on** над+instr); (*study*) занима́ться impf, заня́ться pf; (*also toil, labour*) труди́ться impf; (*have effect, function*) де́йствовать impf; (*succeed*) удава́ться impf, уда́ться pf; vt (*operate*) управля́ть impf +instr; (*bring about*) обраща́ться impf c+instr; (*wonders*) твори́ть impf, **co**~ pf; (*soil*) обраба́тывать impf, обрабо́тать pf; (*compel to* ~) заставля́ть impf, заста́вить pf рабо́тать; ~ **in** вставля́ть impf, вста́вить pf; ~ **off** (*debt*) отраба́тывать impf, отрабо́тать pf; (*weight*) сгоня́ть impf, согна́ть pf; (*energy*) дава́ть impf, дать pf вы́ход +dat; ~ **out** (*solve*) находи́ть impf, найти́ pf реше́ние +gen; (*plans etc.*) разраба́тывать impf, разрабо́тать pf; (*sport*) тренирова́ться impf; **everything** ~**ed out well** всё ко́нчилось хорошо́; ~ **out at** (*amount to*) составля́ть impf, соста́вить pf; ~ **up** (*perfect*) выраба́тывать impf, вы́работать pf; (*excite*) возбужда́ть impf, возбуди́ть pf; (*appetite*) нагу́ливать impf, нагуля́ть pf. **workable** /'wɜːkəb(ə)l/ adj осуществи́мый, реа́льный. **workaday** /'wɜːkə,deɪ/ adj бу́дничный. **workaholic** /,wɜːkə'hɒlɪk/ n тру-

женик. **worker** /'wɜːkə(r)/ *n* рабо́тник; (*manual*) рабо́чий *sb.*

working /'wɜːkɪŋ/ *adj*: ~ **class** рабо́чий класс; ~ **hours** рабо́чее вре́мя *neut*; ~ **party** коми́ссия. **workman** *n* рабо́тник. **workmanlike** /'wɜːkmən,laɪk/ *adj* иску́сный. **workmanship** *n* иску́сство, мастерство́. **workshop** *n* мастерска́я *sb.*

world /wɜːld/ *n* мир, свет; *attrib* мирово́й; ~**-famous** всеми́рно изве́стный; ~ **war** мирова́я война́; ~**-wide** всеми́рный. **worldly** /'wɜːldlɪ/ *adj* мирско́й; (*person*) о́пытный.

worm /wɜːm/ *n* червь *m*; (*intestinal*) глист; *vt*: ~ **o.s. into** вкра́дываться *impf*, вкра́сться *pf* в+*acc*; ~ **out** выведывать *impf*, вы́ведать *pf* (**of** y+*gen*); ~**'s way** пробира́ться *impf*, пробра́ться *pf.*

worry /'wʌrɪ/ *n* (*anxiety*) беспоко́йство; (*care*) забо́та; *vt* беспоко́ить *impf*, о~ *pf*; *vi* беспоко́иться *impf*, о~ *pf* (**about** o+*prep*).

worse /wɜːs/ *adj* ху́дший; *adv* ху́же; *n*: **from bad to** ~ всё ху́же и ху́же. **worsen** /'wɜːs(ə)n/ *vt & i* ухудша́ть(ся) *impf*, уху́дшить(ся) *pf.*

worship /'wɜːʃɪp/ *n* поклоне́ние (**of** +*dat*); (*service*) богослуже́ние; *vt* поклоня́ться *impf* +*dat*; (*adore*) обожа́ть *impf*. **worshipper** /-pə(r)/ *n* поклони́тель, -ица.

worst /wɜːst/ *adj* наиху́дший, са́мый плохо́й; *adv* ху́же всего́; *n* са́мое плохо́е.

worth /wɜːθ/ *n* (*value*) цена́, це́нность; (*merit*) досто́инство; **give me a pound's** ~ **of petrol** да́йте мне бензи́на на фунт; *adj*: **be** ~ (*of equal value to*) сто́ить *impf* (**what is it** ~?

ско́лько э́то сто́ит?); (*deserve* сто́ить *impf* +*gen* (**is this film** ~ **seeing?** сто́ит посмотре́ть э́тот фильм?). **worthles** /'wɜːθlɪs/ *adj* ничего́ не сто́я щий; (*useless*) бесполе́зный. **worthwhile** *adj* сто́ящий. **worthy** /'wɜːðɪ/ *adj* досто́йный.

would /wʊd/ *v aux* (*conditional*) **he** ~ **be angry if he found out** он бы рассерди́лся, е́сли бы узна́л; (*expressing wish*) **she** ~ **like to know** она́ бы хоте́ла знать; **I** ~ **rather** я бы пред почёл; (*expressing indirec speech*) **he said he** ~ **be late** он сказа́л, что придёт по́здно.

would-be /'wʊdbiː/ *adj*: ~ **acto** челове́к мечта́ющий стат актёром.

wound /wuːnd/ *n* ра́на; *vt* ра́нить *impf & pf.* **wounded** /-dɪd/ *adj* ра́неный.

wrangle /'ræŋɡ(ə)l/ *n* пререка́ние; *vi* пререка́ться *impf.*

wrap /ræp/ *n* (*shawl*) шаль; *vt* (*also* ~ **up**) завёртывать *impf*, заверну́ть *pf*; ~ **up** (**in wraps**) заку́тывать(ся) *impf*, заку́тать(ся) *pf*; ~**ped up in** (*fig*) поглощённый +*instr.* **wrapper** /-pə(r)/ *n* обёртка. **wrapping** /-pɪŋ/ *n* обёртка; ~ **paper** обёрточная бума́га.

wrath /rɒθ/ *n* гнев.

wreak /riːk/ *vt*: ~ **havoc on** разоря́ть *impf*, разори́ть *pf.*

wreath /riːθ/ *n* вено́к.

wreck /rek/ *n* (*ship*) оста́нки (-ов) корабля́ *m*; (*vehicle, person, building, etc.*) разва́лина; *vt* (*destroy, also fig*) разруша́ть *impf*, разру́шить *pf*; **be** ~**ed** терпе́ть *impf*, по~ *pf* круше́ние; (*of plans etc.*) ру́хнуть *pf.* **wreckage** /'rekɪdʒ/ *n* обло́мки *m pl* круше́ния.

wren /ren/ *n* крапи́вник.

wrench /rentʃ/ *n* (*jerk*) дёрганье; (*tech*) га́ечный ключ; (*fig*) боль; *vt* (*snatch, pull out*) вырыва́ть *impf*, ~ **open** взла́мывать *impf*, взлома́ть *pf*.

wrest /rest/ *vt* (*wrench*) вырыва́ть *impf*, вы́рвать *pf* (**from** у+*gen*).

wrestle /'res(ə)l/ *vi* боро́ться *impf*. **wrestler** /'reslə(r)/ *n* боре́ц. **wrestling** /'reslŋ/ *n* борьба́.

wretch /retʃ/ *n* несча́стный *sb*; (*scoundrel*) него́дяй. **wretched** /'retʃɪd/ *adj* жа́лкий; (*unpleasant*) скве́рный.

wriggle /'rɪg(ə)l/ *vi* извива́ться *impf*, изви́ться *pf*; (*fidget*) ёрзать *impf*; ~ **out of** увили́вать *impf*, увильну́ть от+*gen*.

wring /rɪŋ/ *vt* (*also* ~ **out**) выжима́ть *impf*, вы́жать *pf*; (*extort*) исторга́ть *impf*, исто́ргнуть *pf* (**from** у+*gen*); (*neck*) свёртывать *impf*, сверну́ть *pf* (**of** +*dat*); ~ **one's hands** лома́ть *impf*, с~ *pf* ру́ки.

wrinkle /'rɪŋk(ə)l/ *n* морщи́на; *vt* & *i* мо́рщить *impf*, с~ & на~ *pf*.

wrist /rɪst/ *n* запя́стье; ~-**watch** нару́чные часы́ (-со́в) *pl*.

writ /rɪt/ *n* пове́стка.

write /raɪt/ *vt* & *i* писа́ть *impf*, на~ *pf*; ~ **down** запи́сывать *impf*, записа́ть *pf*; ~ **off** (*cancel*) спи́сывать *impf*, списа́ть *pf*; **the car was a ~-off** маши́на была́ соверше́нно испо́рчена; ~ **out** выпи́сывать *impf*, вы́писать *pf* (**in full** по́лностью); ~ **up** (*account of*) подро́бно опи́сывать *impf*, описа́ть *pf*; (*notes*) перепи́сывать *impf*, переписа́ть *pf*; ~-**up** (*report*) отчёт. **writer** /'raɪtə(r)/ *n* писа́тель *m*,

~ница.

writhe /raɪð/ *vi* ко́рчиться *impf*, с~ *pf*.

writing /'raɪtŋ/ *n* (*handwriting*) по́черк; (*work*) произведе́ние; **in** ~ в пи́сьменной фо́рме; ~-**paper** почто́вая бума́га.

wrong /rɒŋ/ *adj* (*incorrect*) непра́вильный, неве́рный; (*the wrong* ...) не тот (**I have bought the** ~ **book** я купи́л не ту кни́гу; **you've got the** ~ **number** (*tel*) вы не туда́ попа́ли); (*mistaken*) непра́вый (**you are** ~ ты непра́в); (*unjust*) несправедли́вый; (*sinful*) дурно́й; (*out of order*) нела́дный; (*side of cloth*) ле́вый; ~ **side out** наизна́нку; ~ **way round** наоборо́т; *n* зло; (*injustice*) несправедли́вость; **be in the** ~ быть непра́вым; **do** ~ греши́ть *impf*, со~ *pf*; *adv* непра́вильно, неве́рно; **go** ~ не получа́ться *impf*, получи́ться *pf*; *vt* обижа́ть *impf*, оби́деть *pf*; (**be unjust to**) быть несправедли́вым к+*dat*. **wrongdoer** /'rɒŋˌduːə(r)/ *n* престу́пник, гре́шник, -ица. **wrongful** /-fol/ *adj* несправедли́вый. **wrongly** /-lɪ/ *adv* непра́вильно; (*unjustly*) несправедли́во.

wrought /rɔːt/ *adj*: ~ **iron** сва́рочное желе́зо.

wry /raɪ/ *adj* (*smile*) криво́й; (*humour*) сухо́й, ирони́ческий.

X

xenophobia /ˌzenəˈfəʊbɪə/ *n* ксенофо́бия.

X-ray /'eksreɪ/ *n* (*picture*) рентге́н(овский сни́мок); *pl* (*radiation*) рентге́новы лучи́ *m pl*; (*photograph*) де́лать *impf*, с~

pf рентге́н +*gen.*

Y

yacht /jɒt/ *n* я́хта. **yachting**
/'jɒtɪŋ/ *n* па́русный спорт.
yachtsman *n* яхтсме́н.

yank /'jæŋk/ *vt* рвану́ть *pf.*

yap /jæp/ *vi* тя́вкать *impf*, тя́в-
кнуть *pf.*

yard[1] /jɑːd/ *n* (*piece of ground*)
двор.

yard[2] /jɑːd/ *n* (*measure*) ярд.
yardstick *n* (*fig*) мери́ло.

yarn /jɑːn/ *n* пря́жа; (*story*) рас-
ска́з.

yawn /jɔːn/ *n* зево́к; *vi* зева́ть
impf, зевну́ть *pf*; (*chasm etc.*)
зия́ть *impf.*

year /jɪə(r)/ *n* год; ~ **in,** ~ **out** из
го́да в год. **yearbook** *n* ежего́д-
ник. **yearly** /'jɪəlɪ/ *adj* ежего́д-
ный, годово́й; *adv* ежего́дно.

yearn /jɜːn/ *vi* тоскова́ть *impf*
(for по+*dat*). **yearning** /-nɪŋ/ *n*
тоска́ (for по+*dat*).

yeast /jiːst/ *n* дро́жжи (-же́й) *pl.*

yell /jel/ *n* крик; *vi* крича́ть *impf*,
кри́кнуть *pf.*

yellow /'jeləʊ/ *adj* жёлтый; *n*
жёлтый цвет. **yellowish** /-ɪʃ/
adj желтова́тый.

yelp /jelp/ *n* визг; *vi* визжа́ть
impf, взви́згнуть *pf.*

yes /jes/ *adv*, *n* да; *n* утвержде́ние,
согла́сие; (*in vote*) го́лос "за".

yesterday /'jestədeɪ/ *adv* вчера́;
n вчера́шний день *m*; ~ **morning**
вчера́ у́тром; **the day before**
~ позавчера́; ~**'s newspaper**
вчера́шняя газе́та.

yet /jet/ *adv* (*still*) ещё; (*so far*)
до сих пор; (*in questions*) уже́;
(*nevertheless*) тем не ме́нее; ~
пока́, до сих пор; **not** ~ ещё

не; *conj* одна́ко, но.

yew /juː/ *n* тис.

Yiddish /'jɪdɪʃ/ *n* и́диш.

yield /jiːld/ *n* (*harvest*) урожа́й;
(*econ*) дохо́д; *vt* (*fruit, revenue
etc.*) приноси́ть *impf*, принести́
pf; дава́ть *impf*, дать *pf*; (*give
up*) сдава́ть *impf*, сдать *pf*; (*give
in*) (*to enemy etc.*) усту-
па́ть *impf*, уступи́ть *pf* (*to*
+*dat*); (*give way*) поддава́ть-
ся *impf*, подда́ться *pf* (*to* +*dat*).

yoga /'jəʊgə/ *n* йо́га.

yoghurt /'jɒgət/ *n* кефи́р.

yoke /jəʊk/ *n* (*also fig*) ярмо́;
(*fig*) иго; (*of dress*) коке́тка; *vt*
впряга́ть *impf*, впрячь *pf* в
ярмо́.

yolk /jəʊk/ *n* желто́к.

yonder /'jɒndə(r)/ *adv* вон там;
adj вон тот.

you /juː/ *pron* (*familiar sg*) ты;
(*familiar pl, polite sg & pl*) вы;
(*one*) *not usu translated*; *v translated in 2nd pers sg or by imper
construction*: ~ **never know** ни-
когда́ не зна́ешь.

young /jʌŋ/ *adj* молодо́й;
the ~ молодёжь; *n* (*collect-*
ively) детёныши *m pl.* **youngster**
/'jʌŋstə(r)/ *n* ма́льчик, де́вочка.

your(s) /jɔː(z)/ *poss pron* (*famil-*
iar sg; also in letter) твой; (*fa-*
miliar pl, polite sg & pl; *also in
letter*) ваш; свой. **yourself** /jɔː-
'self/ *pron* (*emph*) (*familiar sg*)
(ты) сам (*m*), сама́ (*f*); (*famil-*
iar pl, polite sg & pl) вы сами;
(*refl*) себя́, -ся (*suffixed to vt*);
by ~ (*independently*) самостоя́-
тельно, сам; (*alone*) оди́н.

youth /juːθ/ *n* (*age*) мо́лодость;
(*young man*) ю́ноша *m*; (*col-*
lect, as pl) молодёжь; ~ **club**
молодёжный клуб; ~ **hostel**
молодёжная турба́за. **youthful**
/-fʊl/ *adj* ю́ношеский.

Yugoslavia /ˈjuːɡəˈslɑːvɪə/ n
Югосла́вия.

Z

zany /ˈzeɪnɪ/ adj смешно́й.

zeal /ziːl/ n рве́ние, усе́рдие.

zealot /ˈzelət/ n фана́тик. **zealous** /ˈzeləs/ adj ре́вностный,
усе́рдный.

zebra /ˈzebrə/ n зе́бра.

zenith /ˈzenɪθ/ n зени́т.

zero /ˈzɪərəʊ/ n нуль m, ноль m.

zest /zest/ n (piquancy) пика́нт-
ность; (ardour) энтузиа́зм; ~
for life жизнера́достность.

zigzag /ˈzɪɡzæɡ/ n зигза́г; adj
зигзагообра́зный; vi де́лать
impf, с~ pf зигза́ги; идти́ det
зигза́гами.

zinc /zɪŋk/ n цинк.

Zionism /ˈzaɪəˌnɪz(ə)m/ n сио-
ни́зм. **Zionist** /ˈzaɪənɪst/ n сио-
ни́ст.

zip /zɪp/ n (~ fastener)
(застёжка-) мо́лния; vt & i: ~
up застёгивать(ся) impf, за-
стегну́ть(ся) pf на мо́лнию.

zodiac /ˈzəʊdɪˌæk/ n зодиа́к; sign
of the ~ знак зодиа́ка.

zombie /ˈzɒmbɪ/ n челове́к спя-
щий на ходу́.

zone /zəʊn/ n зо́на; (geog) по́яс.

zoo /zuː/ n зоопа́рк. **zoological**
/ˌzəʊəˈlɒdʒɪk(ə)l/ adj зоологи́че-
ский; ~ garden(s) зоологи́че-
ский сад. **zoologist** /zəʊ-
ˈɒlədʒɪst/ n зоо́лог. **zoology** /zəʊ-
ˈɒlədʒɪ/ n зооло́гия.

zoom /zuːm/ vi (rush) мча́ться
impf; ~ in (phot) де́лать impf,
с~ pf наплы́в; ~ lens объекти́в
с переме́нным фо́кусным рас-
стоя́нием.

Zulu /ˈzuːluː/ adj зулу́сский; n
зулу́с, ~ка.

pendix I Spelling Rules

assumed that the user is acquainted with the following
lling rules which affect Russian declension and
jugation.

ы, ю, and **я** do not follow **г, к, х, ж, ч, ш,** and **щ;**
:ead, **и, у,** and **а** are used, e.g. **ма́льчик**и, **кричу́;**
жа́т, ноча́ми, similarly, **ю** and **я** do not follow **ц;**
:ead, **у** or **а** are used.

Unstressed **о** does not follow **ж, ц, ч, ш,** or **щ;**
:ead, **е** is used, e.g. **му́ж**ем, **ме́сяц**ев, **хоро́ш**ее.

pendix II Declension of Russian Adjectives

e following patterns are regarded as regular and are not
•wn in the dictionary entries.

gular	nom	acc	gen	dat	instr	prep
:sculine	тёпл|**ый**	~ый	~ого	~ому	~ым	~ом
:minine	тёпл|**ая**	~ую	~ой	~ой	~ой	~ой
:uter	тёпл|**ое**	~ое	~ого	~ому	~ым	~ом

.ral	nom	acc	gen	dat	instr	prep
:sculine	тёпл|**ые**	~ые	~ых	~ым	~ыми	~ых
:minine	тёпл|**ые**	~ые	~ых	~ым	~ыми	~ых
:uter	тёпл|**ые**	~ые	~ых	~ым	~ыми	~ых

The following patterns are regarded as regular and are ne
shown in the dictionary entries. Forms marked * should
particularly noted.

1 *Masculine*

Singular	nom	acc	gen	dat	instr	prep
	обéд	~	~а	~у	~ом	~е
	слýча|й	~й	~я	~ю	~ем	~е
	марш	~	~а	~у	~ем	~е
	карандáш	~	~á	~ý	~óм*	~é
	сценáри|й	~й	~я	~ю	~ем	~и*
	портфéл|ь	~ь	~я	~ю	~ем	~е

Singular	nom	acc	gen	dat	instr	prep
	обéд|ы	~ы	~ов	~ам	~ами	~ах
	слýча|и	~и	~ев	~ям	~ями	~ях
	мáрш|и	~и	~ей*	~ам	~ами	~ах
	карандаш|и	~и	~éй*	~áм	~áми	~áх
	сценáри|и	~и	~ев*	~ям	~ями	~ях
	портфéл|и	~и	~ей*	~ям	~ями	~ях

2 *Feminine*

Singular	nom	acc	gen	dat	instr	prep
	газéт|а	~у	~ы	~е	~ой	~е
	бáн|я	~ю	~и	~е	~ей	~е
	лúни|я	~ю	~и	~и*	~ей	~и*
	стáту|я	~ю	~и	~е*	~ей	~е*
	бол|ь	~ь	~и	~и*	~ью*	~и*

ral	nom	acc	gen	dat	instr	prep
	газе́т|ы	~ы	~	~ам	~ами	~ах
	ба́н|и	~и	~ь*	~ям	~ями	~ях
	ли́ни|и	~и	~й*	~ям	~ями	~ях
	ста́ту|и	~и	~й*	~ям	~ями	~ях
	бо́л|и	~и	~ей*	~ям	~ями	~ях

Neuter

gular	nom	acc	gen	dat	instr	prep
	чу́вств|о	~о	~а	~у	~ом	~е
	учи́лищ|е	~е	~а	~у	~ем	~е
	зда́ни|е	~е	~я	~ю	~ем	~и*
	уще́л|ье	~ье	~ья	~ью	~ьем	~ье

ral	nom	acc	gen	dat	instr	prep
	чу́вств|а	~а	~	~ам	~ами	~ах
	учи́лищ|а	~а	~	~ам	~ами	~ах
	зда́ни|я	~я	~й*	~ям	~ями	~ях
	уще́л|ья	~ья	~ий*	~ьям	~ьями	~ьях

Appendix IV Conjugation of Russian Verbs

The following patterns are regarded as regular and are not
shown in the dictionary entries.

1. **-e-** conjugation

(a) **чита́|ть**	~ю	~ешь	~ет	~ем	~ете	~ют
(b) **сия́|ть**	~ю	~ешь	~ет	~ем	~ете	~ют
(c) **про́б|овать**	~ую	~уешь	~ует	~уем	~уете	~уют
(d) **рис|ова́ть**	~ую	~у́ешь	~у́ет	~у́ем	~у́ете	~у́ют

2. **-и-** conjugation

(a) **говор|и́ть**	~ю	~и́шь	~и́т	~и́м	~и́те	~я́т
(b) **стро́|ить**	~ю	~ишь	~ит	~им	~ите	~ят

Notes

1. Also belonging to the **-e-** conjugation are:

i) most other verbs in **-ать** (but see Note 2(v) below)
e.g. **жа́ждать** (жа́жду, -ждешь); **пря́тать** (пря́чу, -чешь);
колеба́ть (колéблю, -блешь).

ii) verbs in **-еть** for which the 1st pers sing **-ею** is
given, e.g. **жалéть**.

iii) verbs in **-нуть** for which the 1st pers sing **-ну** is
given (e.g. **вя́нуть**), **ю** becoming **у** in the 1st pers sing and
3rd pers pl.

iv) verbs in **-ять** which drop the **я** in conjugation, e.g.
ла́ять (ла́ю, ла́ешь); **сéять** (сéю, сéешь).

Also belonging to the **-и-** conjugation are:

i) verbs in consonant + **-ить** which change the ~~con~~sonant in the first person singular, e.g. **досади́ть** (~~-жу́~~, -ади́шь), or insert an **-л-**, e.g. **доба́вить** (доба́влю, ~~-и~~шь).

ii) other verbs in vowel + **-ить**, e.g. **затаи́ть**, ~~кл~~**е́ить** (as 2b above).

iii) verbs in **-еть** for which the 1st pers sing is given as ~~con~~sonant + **ю** or **у**, e.g. **звене́ть** (-ню́, -ни́шь), **ви́деть** (~~ви́~~жу, ви́дишь).

iv) two verbs in **-ять** (**стоя́ть, боя́ться**).

v) verbs in **-ать** whose stem ends in **ч, ж, щ**, or **ш**, ~~no~~t changing between the infinitive and conjugation, ~~e.g~~. **крича́ть** (-чу́, -чи́шь). Cf. Note 1(i).

Английские неправильные глаголы

Инфинитив	Простое прошедшее	Причастие прошедшего времени	Инфинитив	Простое прошедшее	Причастие прошедшего времени
be	was	been	**drink**	drank	drunk
bear	bore	borne	**drive**	drove	driven
beat	beat	beaten	**eat**	ate	eaten
become	became	become	**fall**	fell	fallen
begin	began	begun	**feed**	fed	fed
bend	bent	bent	**feel**	felt	felt
bet	bet,	bet,	**fight**	fought	fought
	betted	betted	**find**	found	found
bid	bade, bid	bidden, bid	**flee**	fled	fled
bind	bound	bound	**fly**	flew	flown
bite	bit	bitten	**freeze**	froze	frozen
bleed	bled	bled	**get**	got	got
blow	blew	blown			gotten
break	broke	broken	**give**	gave	given
breed	bred	bred	**go**	went	gone
bring	brought	brought	**grow**	grew	grown
build	built	built	**hang**	hung,	hung,
burn	burnt,	burnt,		hanged (*vt*)	hanged
	burned	burned	**have**	had	had
burst	burst	burst	**hear**	heard	heard
buy	bought	bought	**hide**	hid	hidden
catch	caught	caught	**hit**	hit	hit
choose	chose	chosen	**hold**	held	held
cling	clung	clung	**hurt**	hurt	hurt
come	came	come	**keep**	kept	kept
cost	cost,	cost,	**kneel**	knelt	knelt
	costed (*vt*)	costed	**know**	knew	known
cut	cut	cut	**lay**	laid	laid
deal	dealt	dealt	**lead**	led	led
dig	dug	dug	**lean**	leaned,	leaned,
do	did	done		leant	leant
draw	drew	drawn	**learn**	learnt,	learnt,
dream	dreamt,	dreamt,		learned	learned
	dreamed	dreamed	**leave**	left	left

Инфинитив	Простое прошедшее	Причастие прошедшего времени	Инфинитив	Простое прошедшее	Причастие прошедшего времени
d	lent	lent	**speak**	spoke	spoken
	let	let	**spell**	spelled, spelt	spelled, spelt
e	lay	lain			
	lost	lost	**spend**	spent	spent
ke	made	made	**spit**	spat	spat
an	meant	meant	**spoilt**	spoilt, spoiled	spoilt, spoiled
et	met	met			
y	paid	paid	**spread**	spread	spread
	put	put	**spring**	sprang	sprung
d	read	read	**stand**	stood	stood
e	rode	ridden	**steal**	stole	stolen
g	rang	rung	**stick**	stuck	stuck
e	rose	risen	**sting**	stung	stung
n	ran	run	**stride**	strode	stridden
y	said	said	**strike**	struck	struck
e	saw	seen	**swear**	swore	sworn
ek	sought	sought	**sweep**	swept	swept
l	sold	sold	**swell**	swelled	swollen, swelled
nd	sent	sent			
t	set	set	**swim**	swam	swum
w	sewed	sewn, sewed	**swing**	swung	swung
			take	took	taken
ake	shook	shaken	**teach**	taught	taught
ine	shone	shone	**tear**	tore	torn
oe	shod	shod	**tell**	told	told
oot	shot	shot	**think**	thought	thought
ow	showed	shown	**throw**	threw	thrown
ut	shut	shut	**thrust**	thrust	thrust
ng	sang	sung	**tread**	trod	trodden
nk	sank	sunk	**understand**	understood	understood
t	sat	sat			
eep	slept	slept	**wake**	woke	woken
ing	slung	slung	**wear**	wore	worn
nell	smelt, smelled	smelt, smelled	**win**	won	won
			write	wrote	written

The Russian Alphabet

Capital Letters	Lower-case Letters	Letter names		Capital Letters	Lower-case Letters	Letter names
А	а	а		С	с	эс
Б	б	бэ		Т	т	тэ
В	в	вэ		У	у	у
Г	г	гэ		Ф	ф	эф
Д	д	дэ		Х	х	ха
Е	е	е		Ц	ц	цэ
Ё	ё	ё		Ч	ч	че
Ж	ж	жэ		Ш	ш	ша
З	з	зэ		Щ	щ	ща
И	и	и		Ъ	ъ	твёрдый знак
Й	й	и кра́ткое		Ы	ы	ы
К	к	ка		Ь	ь	мя́гкий знак
Л	л	эль				
М	м	эм		Э	э	э
Н	н	эн		Ю	ю	ю
О	о	о		Я	я	я
П	п	пэ				
Р	р	эр				

глийский алфавит

авные буквы	Строчные буквы	Названия букв	Заглавные буквы	Строчные буквы	Названия букв
	a	/eɪ/	N	n	/en/
	b	/biː/	O	o	/əʊ/
	c	/siː/	P	p	/piː/
	d	/diː/	Q	q	/kjuː/
	e	/iː/	R	r	/ɑː(r)/
	f	/ef/	S	s	/es/
	g	/dʒiː/	T	t	/tiː/
	h	/eɪtʃ/	U	u	/juː/
	i	/aɪ/	V	v	/viː/
	j	/dʒeɪ/	W	w	/ˈdʌb(ə)ljuː/
	k	/keɪ/	X	x	/eks/
	l	/el/	Y	y	/waɪ/
	m	/em/	Z	z	/zed/

Other titles in the
Oxford Russian range

Oxford Russian Dictionary
ISBN 0-18-860160-3
180,000 words and phrases, and 290,000 translations – the most comprehensive Russian and English dictionary available

Concise Oxford Russian Dictionary
ISBN 0-19-860152-2
120,000 words and phrases, and 190,000 translations

Pocket Oxford Russian Dictionary
ISBN 0-19-861006-8
90,000 words and phrases, and 120,000 translations

Oxford Beginner's Russian Dictionary
ISBN 0-19-860032-1
Designed for English speakers just starting to learn Russian

Oxford Russian Grammar and Verbs
ISBN 0-19-860380-0
Comprehensive coverage of all the key points of Russian grammar

Abbreviations/Условные сокращени

abbr	abbreviation	сокращение	cul	culinary	кулинария
abs	absolute	абсолютный	dat	dative (case)	дательный
acc	accusative (case)	винительный падеж			падеж
			def	definite	определённый
adj, adjs	adjective(s)	имя прилагательное, имена прилагательные	derog	derogatory	пренебрежительное
			det	determinate	определённый
			dim	diminutive	уменьшительное
adv, adv	adverb(s)	наречие, наречия	eccl	ecclesiastical	церковный термин
aeron	aeronautics	авиация	econ	economics	экономика
agric	agriculture	сельское хозяйство	electr	electricity	электротехник
			electron	electronics	электроника
anat	anatomy	анатомия	emph	emphatic	усилительное
approx	approximate(ly)	приблизительный, -о	esp	especially	особенно
			etc.	etcetera	и так далее
archaeol	archaeology	археология	f	feminine	женский род
archit	architecture	архитектура	fig	figurative	в переносном смысле
astron	astronomy	астрономия			
attrib	attributive	определительное, атрибутивное	fut	future (tense)	будущее врем
			g	genitive (case)	родительный падеж
aux	auxiliary	вспомогательный глагол	geog	geography	география
			geol	geology	геология
bibl	biblical	библейский термин	geom	geometry	геометрия
			gram	grammar	грамматика
biol	biology	биология	hist	historical	история
bot	botany	ботаника	imper	imperative	повелительное наклонение
chem	chemistry	химия			
cin	cinema(tography)	кинематография	impers	impersonal	безличное
			impf	imperfective	несовершенный вид
coll	colloquial	разговорное			
collect	collective	собирательное (существительное)	indecl	indeclinable	несклоняемое
			indef	indefinite	неопределённый
comb	combination	сочетание	indet	indeterminate	неопределённый
comm	commerce	коммерческий термин			
			inf	infinitive	инфинитив
comp	comparative	сравнительная степень	instr	instrumental (case)	творительный падеж
comput	computing	вычислительная техника	int	interjection	междометие
			interrog	interrogative	вопросительный
conj, conjs	conjunction(s)	союз, -ы			
			ling	linguistics	лингвистика